ᐯᐦᐃᔭᐁᐧᐃᐣ ᐃᑗᐃᐧᓇ

nēhiýawēwin: itwēwina

Cree: Words

Dr. S. Fritz Forkel

د. سليمان فريتس فوركل

ד״ר שלמה פריץ פורקל

Skén:nen Rón:nis

ᓀᐦᐃᔭᐍᐏᐣ ᐃᑘᐏᓇ

nēhiýawēwin: itwēwina

Cree: Words

compiled by
Arok Wolvengrey
ē-kī-māwasakōnahk ōma

edited by
members of the Cree Editing Council

Freda Ahenakew
Judy Bear
Elizabeth Lachance
Doreen Oakes
Solomon Ratt
Velma Baptiste-Willet
Edie Hyggen
Rita Lowenberg
Jean Okimāsis
Dolores Sand

ōk ōki nēhiýawēwin kā-māmawi-oýastācik
kā-kī-oýastācik ōma

asici / with

Mary Bighead
Leon Night
Mary Louise Rockthunder
Douglas Martin
Darren Okemaysim
Jim Whitefish

ēkwa / and
Elessar Wolvengrey

Canadian Plains Research Center
University of Regina
Regina, Saskatchewan
2001

National Library of Canada Cataloguing in Publication Data

Wolvengrey, Arok, 1965–
  nēhiýawēwin

(Canadian plains reference works, 1205-3341 ; 3)
ISBN 0-88977-127-8

1. Cree language — Dictionaries — English. 2. English language —
Dictionaries — Cree. I. University of Regina. Canadian Plains Research
Center. II. Title.

PM988.W658 2001   497'   C2001-911148-7

Cover Design: Donna Achtzehner (CPRC), Arok Wolvengrey

Printed and bound in Canada by:
Houghton Boston, Saskatoon

ᑭᑲᐧ ᑲ ᒪᓯᓇᐦᐃᑲᑌᑭ ᐆᒐ
kīkwaya kā-masinahikātēki ōta
Contents

1

ᓀᐦᐃᔭᐤᐁᐧᐃᐣ ᐋᑲᔮᓯᒧᐃᐧᐣ
nēhiýawēwin-ākaýāsīmowin
Cree-English

List of Abbreviations vi

Acknowledgements vii

Foreword ix

Cree: Pronunciation and Orthography

   1. The Cree Language xiii

   2. The Sounds of Cree xiii

Cree-English

   3. An Introduction to the Cree-English Entries xxxi

The Cree-English Entries 1

Common Terms 252

2

ᐋᑲᔮᓯᒧᐃᐧᐣ ᓀᐦᐃᔭᐤᐁᐧᐃᐣ
ākaýāsīmowin-nēhiýawēwin
English-Cree

List of Abbreviations lxxii

English-Cree

   4. An Introduction to the English-Cree Entries lxxiii

The English-Cree Entries 257

Common Terms 618

List of Abbreviations

adj.	English adjective
adv.	English adverb
also	introduces alternate spellings or forms
anim	animate
cf.	compare with (another closely related form, which is also listed separately)
dem	demonstrative
dim	diminutive
e.g.	for example
-ed	English past tense verb form
-en	English past participle or passive verb form
excl	exclusive
hab	habitual
i.e.	in other words
imp	imperative
inan	inanimate
incl	inclusive
-ing	English progressive verb form
INM	indeclinable nominal
intrj.	English interjection
IPC	indeclinable particle
IPH	indeclinable particle phrase
IPN	indeclinable prenominal particle
IPP	indeclinable pre-particle
IPV	indeclinable preverb
lit	literal translation
loc	locative
n.	English noun
NA	animate noun
NDA	dependent animate noun
NDI	dependent inanimate noun
NI	inanimate noun
npC	northern Plains Cree
obv	obviative
pC	Plains Cree - Y dialect
pl	plural or English plural noun form
pl-'s	English plural possessive form
poss	possessive form
PR	pronoun
pr.	English pronoun
prep.	English preposition
prox	proximate
rdpl	reduplicated

-s	English third person present tense verb form
-'s	English possessive noun form
sC	Swampy Cree - N dialect
see also	introduces synonyms or alternate forms (also listed separately)
sg	singular
s/he	animate subject (either "she" or "he" or "it" (if animate but non-human))
v.	English verb
VAI	animate intransitive verb
VAIt	"animate intransitive verb which is syntactically transitive
VII	inanimate intransitive verb
VTA	transitive animate verb
VTI	transitive inanimate verb
voc	vocative
wC	Woods Cree - TH dialect
~	replaces the heading word in a multi-word expression
~~	replaces a phrasal subheading in a longer expression
[ ]	square brackets enclose additional grammatical information

Acknowledgements

This volume would not have been possible without the past contributions of elders and scholars in the field of Cree language studies. We wish also to acknowledge the contributions of time and effort of the Cree Language Retention Committee (CLRC), both in editing and in fundraising. The institutions, including tribal councils, school boards, and schools, who loaned the time and expertise of these professionals to take part in this project are gratefully acknowledged, with particular thanks going to the Saskatchewan Indian Federated College.

In the preparation of the manuscript, special thanks go to Colin Carter, Solomon Ratt and Arok Wolvengrey for the design of the syllabic font, to Jean Okimāsis and Solomon Ratt for additional SRO proofreading, to Solomon Ratt and Arok Wolvengrey for proofreading all Syllabics entries, and to Elessar Wolvengrey, Leon Night and Jean Okimāsis for proofreading the English-Cree entries at various stages in development.

Gratitude is also due to all those who supported the publication fund through donations to the CLRC and support of the language festivals which the CLRC sponsors. The publication was also funded in part by a grant to the CLRC from the Saskatchewan Aboriginal Languages Initiative (SALI), money made available for work on aboriginal languages by Heritage Canada through the Assembly of First Nations. Lastly, we would like to express our gratitude to those who contributed substantial personal donations to the final publication.

mistahi kinanāskomitinān

ᓂᐣᑕᐨ ᒪᓯᓇᐦᐃᐤᐃᐧ
nistam masinahikēwin
Foreword

No dictionary is ever complete and this is certainly true of the current volume. Languages change continually, so as soon as a dictionary or descriptive grammar is ready for publication, no matter how comprehensive it may be, it begins to fall out of date. New words are continually being added to a language, while old vocabulary is lost through disuse, and ultimately forgotten. Sounds, word formation, sentence patterns and meanings all change over time. The differences that arise in these ways are not always obvious to speakers of a language, but become quite evident when that language is spoken in different areas leading to distinct dialects. Attempts to capture every vocabulary item and every difference of dialect for a language before the final publication of a dictionary would result in a futile wait through eternity. Not wanting to wait quite that long, we offer this volume as the first edition of an ongoing project which will evolve and be updated with continued research and observation.

As a starting point, this volume contains in excess of 15,000 Cree entries. Given the extensive word formation rules of the Cree language, many of these entries must be translated by entire sentences in English. As a result, the English-Cree glossary often lists a single Cree word under a number of different English keywords, resulting in well over 35,000 English entries. Despite this size, there are limits on the contents of this dictionary. This book is most certainly not an attempt to translate English into Cree. First and foremost, the purpose of this book is to document the Cree language (as defined subsequently), provide a guide to its spoken form for non-speakers and a guide to its written forms for speakers and non-speakers alike. The goal has thus been to collect the vocabulary of Cree as it is spoken by fluent speakers in much of western Canada, whether elders (*kēhtē-ayak*) or young people *(osk-āyak)*. The words recorded herein have been gathered from diverse sources, including elicitation, recorded conversations and narrative, and publications of many kinds. The bibliography of materials consulted, given following this introduction, demonstrates just how diverse the written sources are. Included are words and expressions found in children's stories, language teaching texts, grammars and reference books of all levels, and in stories from the sacred to the profane; from the legends of *wīsahkēcāhk* to historical accounts by those who lived the history; from lectures on proper behaviour to humorous accounts of the opposite.

In addition to the written sources, this volume has benefitted from the knowledge of a number of Cree language professionals and Elders who acted as editors and consultants in the final preparation of this dictionary. In particular, gratitude is extended to the members of the Cree Language Retention Committee's Cree Editing Council, a group of Cree Elders and professionals in the field of education, including curriculum designers and language instructors from Kindergarten to University level. These individuals, listed altogether on the title page, include Jean Okimāsis, Solomon Ratt, and especially Freda Ahenakew, whose written works have contributed greatly to the contents of this volume.

Given such diverse sources, the words in this book cover many areas of daily life, but some topic areas will have been covered better than others and gaps will certainly remain. Doubtless some common vocabulary has been missed this time around and, as with any living language, new words are constantly being added. Some of the newer ones may not have been recorded yet, or even achieved common usage, and no attempt has been made here to dictate one new form over another possible one, especially where many regional variants may exist. With the aid of the Cree speaking community, as well as through further research and publication, attempts to fill such gaps will be made in future editions of this work. Comments on and constructive criticism of the current edition are welcome and may be sent to the Cree Editing Council at the following address:

nēhiȳawēwin āsōnamātowin saskāciwanihk /
    Saskatchewan Cree Language Retention Inc.
c/o The Department of Indian Languages,
    Literatures, and Linguistics
SIFC - Regina Campus
Room 118, College West
University of Regina
Regina, SK S4S 0A2

or in care of the publisher:

Canadian Plains Research Center
University of Regina
Regina, SK S4S 0A2

It is hoped that this and future editions will help promote and stimulate literacy in the Cree speaking community, as well as facilitate the attempts of many non-speakers to learn this vital First Nations language.

ēkosi.
Arok Wolvengrey
ohpahowi-pīsim, 2001

Written Sources

Ahenakew, Freda. 1987. *Cree Language Structures: A Cree Approach.* Winnipeg: Pemmican Publications, Inc.

Ahenakew, Freda, ed. 1986. *kiskinahamawākan-ācimowinisa / Student Stories.* Winnipeg: Algonquian and Iroquoian Linguistics.

———. 1987. *A Preliminary Check-list of Plains Cree Medical Terms.* Saskatoon: Saskatchewan Indian Languages Institute, Federation of Saskatchewan Indian Nations.

Ahenakew, Freda and H.C. Wolfart, eds. 1987. *wāskahikaniwiyiniw-ācimowina / Stories of the House People.* Edited and translated by Freda Ahenakew. Winnipeg: The University of Manitoba Press.

———. 1993. *kinēhiȳāwiwininaw-nēhiȳawēwin / The Cree Language is Our Identity: The La Ronge Lectures of Sarah Whitecalf.* Edited and translated by H.C. Wolfart and Freda Ahenakew. Winnipeg: The University of Manitoba Press.

———. 1997. *kwayask ē-kī-pē-kiskinowāpahtihicik / Their Example Showed Me the Way.* Edited and translated by Freda Ahenakew and H.C. Wolfart. Edmonton: The University of Alberta Press.

———. 1998. *kōhkominawak otācimowiniwāwa / Our Grandmothers' Lives as Told in Their Own Words.* Regina: Canadian Plains Research Center.

Anonymous. 1984. *Nēhiȳawētān: Kindergarten and Grade One (teacher's manual: Cree).* Saskatoon: Saskatchewan Indian Languages Institute, Federation of Saskatchewan Indian Nations.

———. 1984. *Nēhiyawētān: Grade Two (teacher's manual and workbook: Cree)*. Saskatoon: Saskatchewan Indian Languages Institute, Federation of Saskatchewan Indian Nations.

———. 1984. *Nēhiyawētān: Grade Three (teacher's manual and workbook: Cree)*. Saskatoon: Saskatchewan Indian Languages Institute, Federation of Saskatchewan Indian Nations.

Edwards, Mary. 1961. *Cree: An Intensive Language Course*. 2nd Edition, revised by Ida McLeod. Saskatoon: Saskatchewan Indian Cultural College, Federation of Saskatchewan Indians.

Hunter, Emily and Betty Karpinski. 1990. *Cree 101 (workbooks and textbooks)*. Edmonton: University of Alberta.

Okimāsis, Jean L. and Solomon Ratt. 1999. *Cree, Language of the Plains (text, workbook and tape set)*. Regina: Canadian Plains Research Center.

Wolfart, H. Christoph. 1973. *Plains Cree: A Grammatical Study*. Transactions of the American Philosophical Society, n.s. vol. 63, pt. 5. Philadelphia.

Additional Reference Works

Ahenakew, Freda and H.C. Wolfart, eds. 1998. *ana kā-pimwēwēhahk okakēskihkēmowina / The Counselling Speeches of Jim Kā-Nīpitēhtēw*. Winnipeg: The University of Manitoba Press.

Anderson, Anne. 1975. *Plains Cree Dictionary in the "Y" Dialect*. Edmonton.

Bloomfield, Leonard. "Plains Cree Lexicon" (ms).

LeClaire, Nancy and George Cardinal. 1998. *Alberta Elders' Cree Dictionary / alperta ohci kehtehayak nehiyaw otwestamākewasinahikan*. Edited by Earl Waugh. Edmonton: The University of Alberta Press and Duval House Publishing.

Mandelbaum, David G. 1979. *The Plains Cree: An Ethnographic, Historical, and Comparative Study*. Regina: Canadian Plains Research Center.

Watkins, E.A., Rev. 1938. *A Dictionary of the Cree Language*. Edited by Ven. R. Faries. Toronto: Anglican Book Centre.

Wolfart, H.C., and Freda Ahenakew. 1998. *The Student's Dictionary of Literary Plains Cree*. Winnipeg: Algonquian and Iroquoian Linguistics.

ᓀᐦᐃᔮᐍᐏᐣ

ᑖᓂᓯ ᐁ ᐃᓯ ᐲᑭᐢᑵᕽ ᐁᑿ ᑖᓂᓯ ᐁ ᐃᓯ ᒪᓯᓇᐦᐃᑳᑌᐠ

nēhiýawēwin:

tānisi ē-isi-pīkiskwēhk ēkwa tānisi ē-isi-masinahikātēk

Cree:

Pronunciation and Orthography

1. The Cree Language

The Cree language is spoken in a number of dialects over a very large geographical area in Canada. East Cree and the closely related Montagnais and Naskapi are spoken on the eastern shores of James Bay and through Labrador respectively. Attikamek Cree (or the "R" dialect) is also spoken in Quebec. The Moose Cree (or "L") dialect is found in Ontario along James Bay and Hudson's Bay, and Eastern Swampy Cree is also found in this area and through much of Northwestern Ontario. The Swampy Cree dialect as a whole is known as the "N" dialect, but differences between eastern and western regions can be quite great and the differences between eastern Swampy Cree in Ontario and western Swampy Cree in Manitoba are considerable. Woods Cree (or the "TH" dialect) is also spoken in Manitoba (where it is sometimes known as Rock Cree) and in north central Saskatchewan. Plains Cree (or the "Y" dialect) is spoken in southern and central Saskatchewan and through central Alberta. The Cree language is also spoken in communities in northeastern British Columbia, the NorthWest Territories, and at Rocky Boy, Montana.

Dialect differences in general, especially in vocabulary, make it difficult, if not impossible, to include all dialects in a single reference work, such as a grammar or a dictionary. The words in this book, too, focus only on Cree speech as found in a portion of the total Cree-speaking area. The main sources of the data in this book come from the various regions through Saskatchewan and Alberta where the "Y" dialect or Plains Cree is spoken. Even this area does not constitute a homogeneous speech community, and variation in vocabulary and, to a lesser extent, pronunciation, can still be found. Where available, some of this variation is noted in individual entries and cross-referenced. Additionally, attempts have been made to make the "Y" dialect data in the entries more accessible to both the Woods or "TH" dialect speakers of Saskatchewan and speakers of western Swampy Cree or the "N" dialect at Cumberland House, Saskatchewan, as well as to communities of both Woods and Swampy Cree in Manitoba. As discussed subsequently in the section on the Cree sound and spelling systems, this is accomplished by marking the most important of the sound changes between these various dialects. While the result is not a complete reference work for either Woods or western Swampy Cree, it does provide valuable information for both of these dialects, especially in comparison with Plains Cree. Certainly, the western dialects as a whole do share many features which are captured in the dictionary entries and in the discussion of Cree pronunciation and orthography which follows.

2. The Sounds of Cree

Just as no dictionary is ever complete, no writing system can ever represent all the fine differences of sound that speakers of all languages use in everyday speech. However, each and every language has its own unique system of sound patterns — its **phonemic** system — which can be accurately represented. Many of the sounds found in Cree may also be heard in other languages, such as English, French, or Ojibwa, but each language's sound system is unique, and each requires a specific writing system tailor-made to represent the individual language. The phonemic system of the Cree language requires a writing system or **orthography** designed specifically to meet the needs of a system not found in any other language.[1]

In actual fact, two unique and equally appropriate orthographies are available for use in writing Cree: the standard roman orthography (SRO) and Syllabics. Both of these systems are utilized in the Cree-English section of this book and specific aspects and conventions of each of these orthographies will be discussed below. This will highlight the important characteristics of these two very different writing systems. The most important difference is that the SRO is an **alphabet**, while the Syllabic system, as suggested by the name, is primarily a **syllabary**.

Most Canadians are more familiar with alphabetic writing systems, which consist of distinct symbols (or unique combinations of symbols) for each and every sound, whether consonant or vowel. For an alphabet to fully reflect the phonemic system of a language, a unique symbol should be used for each distinct sound or **phoneme**.[2] Modifications of the Roman alphabet are now used for writing many languages, English and French included, and one specific version, the International Phonetic Alphabet (IPA) is used by linguists when describing phonemic systems in general. In describing and representing the phonemic system of Cree, alphabetic systems are most appropriate, and the SRO will be used to illustrate this.

In contrast, a syllabary consists of a number of symbols which represent the possible syllables of a language. The syllable is a notoriously difficult concept to define, but one which most speakers of any language have little trouble in identifying. Syllables consist of a single beat or pulse and it is a relatively simple matter to count the beats in any word or utterance. For instance, most if not all speakers of Canadian English would agree that words like "see" and "do" have only one syllable, "believe" and "achieve" each have two, "recognize" and "understand" have three, and so on. Similarly, Cree speakers will agree that words like *mwāc* and *nās* have only one syllable (a rarity in Cree), *sisīp* and *maskwa* have two, *mahkēsīs* and *mahihkan* have three, and so on. The general ease with which speakers of all languages can identify syllables has lead to the use of a number of distinct syllabaries as writing systems throughout the world.

In general, each symbol in a syllabary represents a minimal syllable in a language, usually a single vowel or a combination of a single consonant (C) and vowel (V). For a syllabary to be phonemically consistent with a language, there should be a distinct symbol for each possible syllable. This can be complicated by the complexity of the phonemic system of a language. Generally, only those languages with a reasonably small number of distinct sounds and a relatively small number of possible consonant clusters (i.e. combinations of two or more consonants) are suited to syllabic writing systems. It is possible to represent more complex combinations, such as CCVC combinations, but this often renders a syllabic system too unwieldy. The more distinct sounds and the more complex syllables that must be represented, the more symbols that are necessary and this can fast defeat the purpose of using a syllabary as a simple, natural orthography for a language. Shortcuts can also be taken, such as the introduction of specific symbols to represent consonants when they are not followed by any vowel. As we will see, this is a convention found in the Cree Syllabary, and hence, Cree Syllabics really consist of a mixture of syllabic and alphabetic symbols.

Before we see how the SRO and Syllabic orthographies work to represent Cree, we must look at the distinct sounds or phonemes which are important for the Cree language.[3]

2.1 The Cree Sound System and the Standard Roman Orthography

The Cree phonemic system consists of a relatively small number of distinct sounds. In Plains Cree, there are ten consonants and seven vowels for a total of 17 phonemes. The exact qualities of these sounds differ slightly across Cree dialects, so the Plains Cree phonemes will be described first, with notes on sound variation for Woods and Swampy Cree where appropriate.

2.1.1 Consonants

The ten consonants of Plains Cree, as represented in the SRO are: **p, t, k, c, m, n, s, h, w,** and **y**. Many of these are quite similar to their English counterparts, but there are still some very important differences from the English sound-letter correspondences. The first three consonants, **p, t,** and **k,** are always "unaspirated" (i.e. are not followed by a puff of air when spoken). They may therefore sound somewhat closer to "b", "d" and "g" to some English listeners:

p as in English s**p**ill, (not as in **p**ill where the "p" sound is followed by a puff of air).

t as in English s**t**ill, (not as in **t**ill where the "t" sound is followed by a puff of air).

k as in English s**k**ill, (not as in **k**ill where the "k" sound is followed by a puff of air).

c represents a range of sound from "ts", as at the end of English ca**ts**, to "ch", as in English **ch**ur**ch** or ca**tch**. The "c" symbol usually represents a "ts" sound for Plains Cree, while other dialects more commonly have a "ch" sound. These two sounds (i.e. "ts" and "ch") never contrast with one another in Cree - they are one and the same phoneme with only minor sound variation across dialects - so only a single symbol is needed to represent this single phoneme. The exact pronunciation of the **c** in any given speech community can be determined merely by listening to spoken Cree. Additionally, this sound is always unaspirated (i.e. not followed by a puff of air; as with **p, t, k**).

When these four consonants, **p, t, k,** and **c,** occur between vowels within words, there is a tendency in some (primarily eastern) dialects to pronounce them a bit closer to English "b", "d", "g", and "j" respectively. This voicing phenomenon is not commonly found in either Plains or Woods Cree. Only in Swampy Cree (as spoken at Cumberland House, SK, for instance) is there a tendency to use the more voiced consonants. Even here, it is most apparent with the pronunciation of **k** occasionally sounding more like English "g" in "gall". In English, however, the alternation of these two sounds, as in "kill" and "gill", is very important and can signal a difference in meaning. In contrast, there are no such pairs of words in any dialect of Cree which differ by the alternation of [k] and [g] sounds. It is simply not an important difference in Cree. Thus, only one symbol, **k,** is needed to represent this sound and only **k** is used in the SRO. Where **k** may sound more like an English [g], this is a predictable fact of the pronunciation of the particular dialect. Using the symbol "g" to represent this would be imposing a feature of the English sound system (i.e. the contrast of /k/ and /g/) on a language which does not share that feature. A monolingual speaker of Swampy Cree, with no knowledge of English pronunciation, would never pay any attention to the difference between [k] and [g] since it is not important for Cree.

The remaining consonants are:

m as in English **m**o**m**.

n as in English **n**u**n**.

s as in English **s**i**s**. This can occasionally sound more like the "sh" sound in **sh**ell, but again, these are not two distinct sounds in the western Cree dialects. Though the difference between "s" and "sh" sounds is important for English and the eastern Cree dialects, it will never indicate a difference in meaning in any of the Cree dialects of Saskatchewan or westward. Thus, only **s** is required for these dialects. In eastern Cree dialects, where the "sh" sound is important, the symbol **š** is used. In a very few words in this glossary where the "sh" sound is commonly heard, this may be included as a variant pronunciation (e.g. nimosōm, "my grandfather"; *also* nimošōm).

h as in English **h**eat. This sound rarely occurs at the beginning of Cree words, but unlike the English sound, it frequently occurs immediately before consonants in Cree. This breath of air, or "aspiration", is very important and can signal the difference in meaning between two words (e.g. ni**h**tiy "tea" vs. nitiy "my bum").

w   as in English **wo<u>w</u>**.

y   as in English **<u>y</u>a<u>y</u>**.

These final three consonants, **h**, **w** and **y**, have a considerable effect on the pronunciation of vowels, but this will be discussed below in section 2.1.2.

The descriptions thus far are based primarily on the Plains Cree dialect, though much of it holds true for all three dialects of Cree spoken in Saskatchewan and westward. There are, however, some small differences in the sounds of each dialect, of which the most important must be noted. In addition to these ten consonants present in Plains and Swampy Cree, Woods Cree has one additional consonant:

th   This sequence of letters is the only strict holdover from English spelling convention, and it represents the louder or "voiced-th" sound in English **th**en, not the whispered or "voice-less-th" sound in **th**in. In Linguistics, the symbol used for this sound would be [ð], but English convention has, in this case, won out and virtually all Woods Cree material uses the English spelling combination of "th".

This sound only occurs in Woods Cree. Where Woods Cree words contain this sound, Plains Cree has **y** and Swampy Cree has **n**. For this reason Plains Cree is often referred to as the "Y" dialect, Swampy Cree as the "N" dialect, and Woods Cree as the "TH" dialect. Two of the most common examples demonstrating this difference are given in the following chart:

	Plains Cree	Swampy Cree	Woods Cree
"I; me"	ni*y*a	ni*n*a	ni*th*a
"Cree"	nēhi*y*aw	nēhi*n*aw	nihi*th*aw

These examples will be repeated and further elaborated upon below in conjunction with the discussion of vowels.

The additional alphabetic symbols familiar to English speakers that do not occur in the preceding description are absent because there are no equivalent sounds required for them in the sound system of western Cree dialects. Eastern dialects do include š ("sh"), as noted above, while Moose Cree has **l** and Attikamek has **r**. However, none of these are present in the western dialects represented in this book.

2.1.2 Vowels

There are seven distinct vowels in most dialects of Cree. The most outstanding feature of the Cree vowel system is the distinction between the short (**a, i, o**) and long (**ā, ē, ī, ō**) vowels, which differ chiefly in the duration for which each is held. Simply put, long vowels are pronounced for a longer period of time (about twice as long as the short vowels). This important difference is recognized in the SRO by marking all long vowels with an overposed macron ($^-$; e.g. ā, ī) or circumflex ($^\wedge$; e.g. â, î).[4] The use of either of these markers of vowel length are acceptable and both are commonly used. The macron is certainly simpler for handwriting, but even in today's age of the computer, it has often proven difficult to find fonts which include macron-vowels. Thus, the use of the circumflex has become a standard variant for published Cree material. In this publication, however, the macron has been chosen.

In addition to vowel length or quantity, there is also a slight difference in vowel quality between long and short vowels. The symbols and approximate equivalents for the Cree vowels are as follows:

a   as in English b<u>u</u>t.

ā   as in the syllable f<u>a</u> in the song scale, "do, re, mi, **fa**, so …" Most English dialects really do not have a sound very close to Cree **ā**. English f<u>a</u>ther is often cited as an example, but only when it is spoken with an Irish accent is a close approximation heard; this sound is also pronounced for a longer duration than for the shorter **a**.

ē   as in English b<u>ay</u>, though without gliding the tongue towards the roof of the mouth at the end of the English sound. The sound in German z<u>eh</u>n ("ten") is actually closer, for it is a true long vowel as in Cree.

i   as in English b<u>i</u>t.

ī   as in English b<u>ea</u>t, again without the upward glide of the tongue. The sound in German s<u>ie</u>ben ("seven") is more accurate, corresponding closely to the true long vowel of Cree.

o   as in English b<u>oo</u>k, though with a large amount of variation in actual pronunciation. Regional and even personal differences can result in a sound closer to the vowel of b<u>oa</u>t, though not sustained like a long vowel (see **ō** immediately below).

ō   as in English b<u>oa</u>t, again without the upward glide of the tongue. The sound in German B<u>oo</u>t ("boat") is more accurate, corresponding closely to the true long vowel of Cree. As with short **o**, this vowel can also exhibit a great deal of variation in pronunciation, and can seem closer to the vowel sound in English b<u>oo</u>t. This accounts for the common representation of this sound with the English "oo" or French "ou" spellings. Hence, the first syllable of Moosomin, for English speakers, is the same as in the English pronunciation of "moose". However, both derive ultimately from Cree *mōswa*, and the first syllable of this word in Plains Cree usually has a sound closer to that in the name M<u>o</u>ses, not m<u>oo</u>se.

It cannot be emphasized enough that the English and German examples mentioned here are mere approximations of the sounds in Cree. The only true way to hear and become used to the exact quality of these vowels is to listen to actual Cree speech.

One complication of the Cree vowel system is the effect that certain consonant sounds have in altering the basic pronunciations given above. Thus, when followed by **h**, **w**, or **y**, many of the vowels may seem to have slightly different sounds. The basic sound of these consonants is not markedly different from its sound in English, but the effect on preceding vowels is important and will be noted below:

h   The effect of an "h-consonant" cluster (**hC** or "pre-aspirated" consonants, where "C" stands for any consonant, e.g. **hp**, **ht**, **hc**, **hk**) on the preceding vowel is very important because, in most cases, the distinction between long and short vowels is neutralized. In other words, it is usually very difficult, if not impossible, to tell the difference between long and short vowels before a combination of **h** and another consonant. Before **hC**, long and short vowels seem to merge into a single vowel which is short in duration, but closer to the quality of the long vowel. Hence in:

ahC and **āhC**   both vowels sound as in f<u>a</u> (like **ā**), but short in duration (like **a**).

ihC and **īhC**   both vowels sound as in English b<u>ea</u>t, without the upward glide of the tongue (like **ī**), but short in duration (like **i**).

ohC and **ōhC**   both vowels sound as in English b<u>oa</u>t, without the upward glide of the tongue (like **ō**), but short in duration (like **o**).

This description of the effect of **h** on vowels holds for Plains and some areas of Woods Cree. In other areas of Woods Cree and many areas of Swampy Cree speech, however, a different sound change is occurring. Instead of causing long and short vowels to neutralize (as essentially short vowels), it is more common in these varieties for the **h** to disappear between a vowel and consonant, and for the vowel to become long. In essence, Plains and some Woods Cree dialects are neutralizing vowel-h-consonant (VhC) sequences to short vowel-hC sequences, while some Woods and Swampy Cree dialects are neutralizing VhC sequences to long vowel-C. In this book, the Plains Cree forms are given with VhC spellings. In order to convert these for Swampy Cree, it is often possible to simply lengthen the vowel and remove the **h** (e.g. pC: *askihk* "pail, kettle"; sC: *askik*. Thus: ihC → īC). This must be done with care, however, since not all Swampy Cree areas are subject to this change and it is necessary to determine the exact status of VhC sequences in any given region.

w   When following a vowel, **w** often sounds something like the short **o** or long **ō** vowels. It is very similar to these vowels for they all include "rounding" of the lips in their pronunciation. **w** has the following effects:

aw as in Canadian English ab<u>ou</u>t.

āw as in English n<u>ow</u>.

ēw like a combination of English "ay-oo", and hence the common attempt to spell Cree words like *nāpēw* ("man") as "Napayo" in English.

iw this combination varies in pronunciation from a sound similar to that in English n<u>ew</u>, to the sounds of Cree short **o**, or long **ō**. The **w** effectively "rounds" the vowel.

īw like a combination of English "ee-oo".

ow this combination sounds very much as in English kn<u>ow</u>, and it is difficult to tell the difference between short **o** and long **ō** — before **w**, both vowels sound long. By spelling convention, when no dialect-internal means are available for determining the length of the vowel before **w**, the vowel is spelled as short **o** (e.g. *pC: manitow* "spirit"). Such examples are generally found only in nouns, since additional clues can be used to determine the length of the vowel in verbs (e.g. *mīciso* "eat", *pasikō* "get up").

ōw this combination sounds very much as in English kn<u>ow</u>, and it is difficult to tell the difference between short **o** and long **ō** - before **w** for both vowels sound long.

y   This sound, when following a vowel, often has a quality much like the short **i** or long **ī** vowels, since these vowels and **y** are very similar in the place and manner in which they are produced in the mouth. In nouns and names, **y** usually only follows short vowels, and it has the following effects:

ay as in Canadian English b<u>i</u>te.

iy this combination sounds very much like the long **ī**, and it is not possible to tell the difference between short **i** and long **ī** before **y**. Before **y**, both vowels sound long. By spelling convention, where no dialect-internal means are available for determining the length of the vowel before **y**, the vowel will always be spelled as a short **i**. Such examples are generally only found in nouns (and, as a side-effect, the "iy" spelling at the end of words can be used to signal the occurrence of a noun in opposition to any other part of speech).

oy this combination is similar to the sound in English b<u>oy</u>, or b<u>uoy</u>.

Long vowels may also precede **y** when a suffix beginning with **y** (e.g. *-yān*) is added to a verb stem ending in a long vowel. In such cases, **y** has less effect on the preceding vowel, though again short **i** and long **ī** tend to neutralize before **y**. In verbs, however, it is always possible to determine the length of the vowel by listening to forms of the verb in which **y** does not follow:

| ē-apiyān | "as I'm sitting" | nitapin | "I sit" | apik! | "sit!" |
| ē-tapasīyān | "as I'm fleeing" | nitapasīn | "I flee" | tapasīk! | "flee!" |

Though the exact length of the vowel before **y** may be difficult to determine in the first examples of each set, it becomes obvious in the second and third examples. Thus, the verb *api* "sit" is always spelled with a short vowel **i** and *tapasi* "flee" is always spelled with a long vowel **ī**.

The same principle can be used to determine the quality of certain vowels before a **w**:

apiw	"s/he sits"	nitapin	"I sit"	apik!	"sit!"
nikamow	"s/he sings"	ninikamon	"I sing"	nikamok!	"sing!"
pasikōw	"s/he stands up"	nipasikōn	"I stand up"	pasikōk!	"stand up!"

Though the vowel may sound like an **o** or an **ō** in all three of the initial examples, due to the following **w**, the second and third examples of each set again disambiguate the actual quality of the vowel. Thus, *api* "sit" is always spelled with a final short vowel **i**, *nikamo* "sing" is always spelled with a final short vowel **o**, and *pasikō* "stand up" is always spelled with a final long vowel **ō**.

Finally, we return to some examples of dialect variation to illustrate three more important points of the SRO in use in this book:

	Plains Cree	Swampy Cree	Woods Cree
"I; me"	niya	nina	nitha
"Cree"	nēhiyaw	nēhinaw	nīhithaw

As noted above, the sequence of **iy** always sounds long, so that even where the other dialects make a distinction between **i** (as in *nēhinaw*) and **ī** (as in *nīna*), this difference is neutralized in Plains Cree and always spelled with the short **i**.

Secondly, Woods Cree is also the only western dialect in which an additional distinct sound (**th**) occurs. In Plains Cree, this sound occurs as **y** and cannot be differentiated from the other **y**-sound which occurs in all dialects. Similarly Woods **th** is **n** in Swampy, which cannot be differentiated from the other **n**-sound common to all dialects. Only from Woods Cree can we tell which Plains **y** or Swampy **n** actually corresponds to **th**. The following chart gives additional examples of **y** and **n** sounds which do not change across the dialects:

	Plains Cree	Swampy Cree	Woods Cree
"one"	pēyak	pēyak	piyak
"two"	niso	niso	niso

Thus, not all Plains Cree **y**-sounds or Swampy Cree **n**-sounds alternate with Woods Cree **th**, and only someone familiar with Woods Cree can tell which is which and which will switch! In this dictionary, however, an attempt has been made to mark the Plains Cree **y**-sounds which alternate with Swampy **n** and Woods **th**. Towards this purpose, the symbol **ý** (or **y** with an overposed acute accent ´) occurs in Plains Cree words to indicate a corresponding Woods **th** or Swampy **n**. Similarly, for those few Swampy words cited specifically, the symbol **ñ** (or **n** with an overposed tilde ~) is used where Plains will have **y** and Woods **th**. Thus, the words given in the last two example sets will appear as follows:

	Plains Cree	Swampy Cree	Woods Cree
"I; me"	*niẏa*	*nin̄a*	*nītha*
"Cree"	*nēhiẏaw*	*nēhin̄aw*	*nihithaw*
"one"	*pēyak*	*pēyak*	*piyak*
"two"	*n̲iso*	*n̲iso*	*n̲iso*

When writing Plains Cree, it is not necessary to use the "accented-y" (ẏ) symbol, unless the material is intended for use beyond Plains Cree. Similarly, adding the tilde to "n" (ñ) is not necessary when writing Swampy Cree, except for cross-dialectal purposes. Thus, these are not symbols that will normally be encountered in written Cree texts and, though you will find them in the dictionary entries, they can be ignored by speakers of Plains and Swampy Cree respectively. They are used merely as an aid to speakers of the dialects other than that in which each specific word is found.

The third point concerns a difference between Woods Cree (as well as northern Plains Cree) and the other dialects of Cree and is illustrated in the form of the words for "Cree (person)" and "one". Where Plains and Swampy have the vowel ē, as described above, Woods Cree has a long ī-sound instead (though spelled i before y). Thus, Woods Cree has one less vowel sound than the other dialects, with Woods ī corresponding to both ī and ē in Plains and Swampy:

	Plains Cree	Swampy Cree	Woods Cree
"play!"	*mētawē*	*mētawē*	*mītawī*
"turn around!"	*kwēskī*	*kwēskī*	*kwīskī*

Not all Woods Cree long ī sounds correspond with Plains or Swampy long ē, and only someone familiar with Plains or Swampy Cree can tell which is which! Since Plains Cree is the dialect primarily utilized in this book, the distinction between ē and ī is maintained and speakers of Woods (and northern Plains) Cree will be able to adjust by replacing ē with ī as appropriate.

From this discussion, it may appear that the differences between Plains, Woods and Swampy Cree are relatively few and minor. Besides the major difference between **y, th** and **n**, however, other minor sound changes are evident, such as the tendency in Swampy for the sequence of **wa** to sound more like **o** when following consonants, or for the consonants **p, t, c**, and especially **k** to be closer to English "b", "d", "j" and "g" respectively when they occur between vowels. In addition to these differences, which the orthography does not indicate, vocabulary variation also introduces many differences between the western Cree dialects. Though some of this variation is indicated, much remains as yet unrecorded and, as such, cannot yet be found in the dictionary entries.

2.2 The Cree Sound System and Cree Syllabics

The alternative to the alphabetic SRO are the Cree Syllabics or *cahkipēhikana*, also known by the common, first-learned symbol sequence ∨∧>< or *pēpipopa*. This system is primarily a syllabary in which a single symbol represents a syllable or sequence of consonant plus vowel (e.g. ∨ = pē, ∧ = pi, etc.). The full system as used for writing the western Cree dialects is given on page xxi.

A unique aspect to this syllabary is that a consistent symbol is used for each consonant, differing only in orientation (or direction) based on vowel quality. As such, the symbols can be introduced with respect to the Cree phonemic system, beginning with the vowels.

ᒋᑉᐯᐦᐃᑲᓇ

cahkipēhikana / Syllabics

	ē	i	o	a	ī	ō	ā	finals
	▽	△	▷	◁	△̇	▷̇	◁̇	
w	▽•	△•	▷•	◁•	△̇•	▷̇•	◁̇•	°
p	∨	∧	>	<	∧̇	>̇	<̇	'
t	∪	∩	⊃	⊂	∩̇	⊃̇	⊂̇	´
k	٩	ρ	ᑯ	ᑲ	ρ̇	ᑯ̇	ᑲ̇	`
c	ᒉ	ᒋ	ᒍ	ᒐ	ᒋ̇	ᒍ̇	ᒐ̇	‒
m	ᒣ	ᒥ	ᒧ	ᒪ	ᒥ̇	ᒧ̇	ᒪ̇	ᒼ
n	ᓀ	ᓂ	ᓄ	ᓇ	ᓂ̇	ᓄ̇	ᓇ̇	ᐤ
s	ᓭ	ᓯ	ᓱ	ᓴ	ᓯ̇	ᓱ̇	ᓴ̇	ᐢ
š	ᔅ	ᔆ	ᔇ	ᔈ	ᔆ̇	ᔇ̇	ᔈ̇	ǂ
y	ᔦ	ᔨ	ᔪ	ᔭ	ᔨ̇	ᔪ̇	ᔭ̇	+
th	ᕉ	ᕊ	ᕋ	ᕌ	ᕊ̇	ᕋ̇	ᕌ̇	ǂ

| l ᣂ | | r ᣭ | | h " | | hk ˣ | |

Corrigenda

š ᒐ | ᒉ | ᔆ | ᣭ | ᔇ | ᔆ̇ | ᔆ̇ | ᐤ

2.2.1 Vowels

Words in Cree can begin with vowels alone, not preceded by any consonant. Thus, a syllable can consist of a vowel alone and syllabic symbols are needed for each vowel. The basic syllabic vowel symbol is a triangle (e.g. ▼), altering its orientation to correspond with the four basic vowel qualities, represented by the sequence ē, i, o, a, or ▼ ▲ ▷ ◁. Just as vowel length or quantity is marked (by a macron or circumflex) in the SRO, an overposed dot can be added to indicate a long vowel in syllabics (e.g. ī, ō, ā are ▲̇ ▷̇ ◁̇ respectively). Note, however, that ē, as the only long vowel without a short vowel counterpart, is always unmarked in syllabics.[5] In fact, many fluent speakers tend not to bother marking vowel length at all, leaving only the four basic orientations of the vowel triangle to represent the seven vowels of Cree. The syllabic chart shows the four basic symbols first, with the three additional long-vowel symbols following. In this book, vowel length is always indicated. These seven vowel symbols will only occur at the beginning of words, where no consonant precedes, or following special symbols for [h], [l] and [r] sounds (ᐦ, ᐠ and ᐟ respectively), since there are no syllabic symbols specific to these consonants in combination with vowels in use for writing the western dialects.[6] Additionally, the triangle symbol can also be used when a vowel is preceded by a [w] (but no other consonant). The preceding [w] is indicated by placing a dot after the vowel triangle (e.g. ▼• = wē, ▲• = wi, ▷• = wo, ◁• = wa).[7] All other instances of vowels will be in combination with a single consonant (C) or consonant-[w] (Cw) sequence, in which case other symbols will be used based on the quality of the consonant.

2.2.2 Consonants

Most of the Cree consonants have two different types of representation in the western Syllabics. The most common type corresponds to the vowel triangle, in which a specific symbol represents each consonant and its orientation indicates the quality of a following vowel. Thus, the following syllabic symbols have these Plains Cree CV correspondences (giving the **Cē** symbol as basic):

$$\mathbf{V} = \text{pē}; \ \mathbf{U} = \text{tē}; \ \mathbf{ᕈ} = \text{kē}; \ \mathbf{ᐱ} = \text{cē}; \ \mathbf{ᒷ} = \text{mē}; \ \mathbf{ᐁ} = \text{nē}; \ \mathbf{ᔦ} = \text{sē}; \ \mathbf{ᐟ} = \text{yē}$$

The remaining two Plains Cree consonants have already been mentioned above. There is no separate symbol specific to [w]. Instead, a dot is placed following the appropriate symbol when [w] precedes a vowel. Furthermore, the [w] dot need not follow only the vowel triangle. In a consonant-[w]-vowel sequence (**CwV**), the basic CV symbol is used with the [w] dot following:

$$\mathbf{V•} = \text{pwē}; \ \mathbf{U•} = \text{twē}; \ \mathbf{ᕈ•} = \text{kwē, etc.}$$

There is also no symbol for [h] in combination with vowels, In fact, fluent speakers very often omit marking [h] altogether. However, a traditional symbol does exist for it and, in this book, [h] is consistently represented by the small raised symbol or "final" ᐦ. This is an example of the second (and more alphabetic) type of consonant symbol found in the western Syllabics. Finals are small raised symbols which represent consonants alone, not followed immediately by a vowel. This is most common at the ends of words, where each consonant may occur. Thus, the finals and their corresponding consonants are:

$$\mathbf{'} = \text{p}; \ \mathbf{´} = \text{t}; \ \mathbf{`} = \text{k}; \ \mathbf{¯} = \text{c}; \ \mathbf{�c} = \text{m}; \ \mathbf{ᵓ} = \text{n}; \ \mathbf{ᵃ} = \text{s}; \ \mathbf{+} = \text{y}; \ \mathbf{°} = \text{w}; \ \mathbf{ᐦ} = \text{h}$$

There is an additional final for the extremely common combination [hk]: ×. This symbol can only be used at the ends of words, for though the [hk] cluster can occur word internally in SRO spellings, the [k] will always be part of the following syllable and, hence, × cannot be used in such a position:

SRO	Syllabics	translation
askihk	◁ᐣᖅˣ	"kettle; pail"
mahihkan	ᒪ"ᐊ"ᖇᐤ	"wolf"
pihkohk	ᐱ"ᗧˣ	"in the ashes"

In contrast, it is possible for certain other finals to occur word internally, particularly ˄ [s] and " [h], as demonstrated in the preceding examples.[8] The symbols for [l] and [r] (ᐸ and ᐳ respectively) can even occur initially, but are primarily used for names of non-Cree origin.

Two further sets of symbols have not yet been introduced, for these are not used for writing Plains Cree. Just as Woods Cree requires the "th" spelling for the [ð] sound, so also does it require both a special syllabic symbol and a final. Both of the symbols used in this book and becoming common in the west are modifications of the **y** syllabic symbols, recognizing the alternation of Woods Cree [ð] with Plains Cree [y]:

$$\text{◄} = y\bar{e} ; \quad \text{◄} = th\bar{i} ; \quad \text{+} = \text{final y} ; \quad \text{*} = \text{final th}$$

These examples illustrate not only the **th** syllabic symbols, but also another modification that is made when using Syllabics to write Woods Cree. Given the merger of Plains Cree ē and ī as Woods Cree ī, there is no need for syllabic symbols in Woods Cree for syllables containing ē. Thus, the Plains Cree ē syllabics are used for Woods Cree ī syllabics, while the short i syllabics (e.g. ▲) are never marked as long in Woods Cree. In some cases, this means that the same spelling can be used for both Woods and Plains Cree words, even though the pronunciation differs:

Syllabics	Plains Cree SRO	Woods Cree SRO	translation
ᑎᑕᐅ·	*mētawē*	*mītawī*	"play!"

However, other words may sound identical in the two dialects, but receive different syllabic spellings:

Syllabics	Plains Cree SRO	Woods Cree SRO	translation
ᑕᐸᕁ	*tapasī*	——	"flee!"
ᑕᐸᔅ	——	*tapasī*	"flee!"

In this book, only the Plains Cree spelling is given, even where the SRO indicates that a Plains **y** alternates with Woods **th** or Swampy **n** (i.e. ý). In order to convert the Plains Cree y syllabic spellings to Woods Cree, simply substitute the appropriate **th** syllabic (and adjust any ī syllabic to the corresponding ē syllabic).

Finally, the entire row in the syllabics chart (p xxi) beginning with the symbol š is superfluous for all western dialects of Cree. However, the [š] sound is found in eastern dialects of Cree, as well as in Saulteaux and all other Ojibwa dialects. As such, the š syllabic symbols are not uncommon, and have been included in the chart for reference, even though they will not be found elsewhere in this book. As mentioned above, [š] is not a distinct sound in the western dialects and even when it does occur it is merely a variant of [s]. Thus, only the s syllabic symbols are required for writing the western Cree dialects.

2.3 Other Considerations of Sound and Conventions of Spelling

A very important aspect of any language, and one rarely if ever represented in spelling, is the stress or intonation pattern. The Cree stress pattern differs considerably from that of

English and can present many problems for the non-speaker, especially since stress is not generally marked in either Cree spelling system (see further discussion below). Although the best way to learn where to place stress in Cree words and utterances is to listen to a fluent speaker of Cree, the following simplified rules may help.[9] In the examples that follow, the syllable with primary stress in the Cree word will be boldfaced, while in the rough English pronunciations given in curled brackets, primary stress is indicated by capital letters.

In two syllable words, the final (or ultimate) syllable is typically given the main stress:

Cree	rough English pronunciation	translation
wa**cask**	{wuh TSUSK}	"muskrat"
a**tim**	{uh TIM}	"dog"

In words of three or more syllables, the third last (or anti-penultimate) syllable receives the main stress, while the final syllable also receives some stress:

Cree	rough English pronunciation	translation
maskisin	{MUSS kiss sin}	"moccasin; shoe"
mas**kis**ina	{muss KISS sin nuh}	"moccasins; shoes"

This is not a common pattern in English, but it does occasionally occur as in the following examples:

English	rough English pronunciation
medicine	{MED dis sin}
me**dic**inal	{med DIS sin nul}

However, this pattern won't hold for English if the second last (or penultimate) syllable is heavy or long (i.e. contains a tense or complex vowel or a vowel plus at least one consonant in that same syllable):

English	rough English pronunciation		
a**moe**ba	{uh MEE buh}	(not	{UM mee buh})
um**brel**la	{um BREL luh}	(not	{UM brel luh})

In contrast, anti-penultimate stress does hold in Cree regardless of the length of the vowel of the penultimate:

Cree	rough English pronunciation	translation
awāsis	{UH waa sis}	"child"
piyēsis	{PEE yay cease}	"bird"

This pattern can be particularly difficult for English speakers to adjust to since the long (or tense) vowel in English speech tends to attract stress. However, it is very important when speaking Cree to keep vowel length and stress separate. Pronouncing *piyēsis* as {pee YAY cease} is just as incorrect in Cree as pronouncing "syllable" as {sil LAB bull} in English.

In Cree words of more than four syllables, the anti-penultimate retains the primary stress, but there are also secondary stresses which generally occur every second syllable to the left or right (with secondary stresses in small caps):[10]

Cree	rough pronunciation	translation
sēwēpicikan	{SAY way PIT tsig GUN}	"phone"
ātayōhkēwina	{aa TIE yoh KAY win NUH}	"legends"
kiskinwahamātowikamik	{KISS kin WUH hum MAA toe WICK kum MICK}	"school"

The placement of stress can have several effects on the pronunciation of syllables and words. Perhaps the most common effect in Cree is the complete loss or deletion of unstressed short vowels and, thus, the syllable to which they belong. This is also a process which should be quite familiar to speakers and spellers of English. For instance, the word "laboratory", despite being spelled as if it had five syllables (as it originally did), is commonly pronounced with only four (e.g. {LAB bret TOR ree} in North America, or {lub BOR ret TREE} in Britain). In this case, one consistent spelling helps unite the word for all English dialects despite pronunciation differences. Some SRO spellings accomplish this same purpose by ignoring certain features of surface pronunciation. In Cree, vowel or syllable loss occurs most commonly when the unstressed vowel is a short [i], but this vowel is retained in spelling, even when it is rarely, if ever, pronounced:

Cree SRO	rough pronunciation	translation
tānisi	{TAAN si}	"how; hello, how are you?"
tānitē	{TAAN tay}	"where"

The SRO spelling of these examples often strikes fluent speakers as odd because of the presence of the "silent-i" after the "n". However, there are some very sound reasons for including the "i" vowel in the spelling. For instance, we can find evidence for the presence of the vowel in the way the words in question have been formed. These particular examples, *tānisi* and *tānitē*, are made up of an initial question or interrogative particle /tān-/ (which never occurs alone) plus the particles *isi* (indicating manner, i.e. "so, thus") and *itē* (indicating location, i.e. "there; where"). These latter two particles can occur alone, but never without the initial vowel [i]. Thus, the derivations of these two words are as follows:

tān- "?" + *isi* "so, thus, in such a manner" = *tānisi* "in what manner; how"
tān- "?" + *itē* "there, in such a place" = *tānitē* "in what place; where"

Hence, we have evidence based on the word structure for the inclusion of the "silent-i". More importantly for our discussion here, though, is the stress pattern indicated in these examples. In the rough pronunciation, there appear to be only two syllables, but the stress does not fall on the final syllable, as predicted by our earlier rule. This suggests the stressed syllable is really the anti-penultimate (or third last), at least in origin, and that the unstressed syllable has simply been deleted. Thus, the SRO spelling helps to indicate the origin of these words as three-syllable words, both explaining and indicating the proper stress pattern. If, in contrast, these words were really just two syllable words, spelled without the "silent-i", we might expect the following stress patterns and pronunciations:

modified Cree	rough pronunciation	translation
tānsi	{taan SI}	"??"
tāntē	{taan TAY}	"??"

Pronouncing these words in this way is simply incorrect and, thus, no sensible translation can be given. Taken together, the evidence from both **phonology** (the sound system; in this case:

stress) and **morphology** (word formation) argue very strongly for the SRO spelling, despite the predictable feature of vowel loss in the spoken language.

Another instance of stress pattern and syllable loss affecting pronunciation can be found in the process known as "sandhi" (cf. Wolfart 1973, 1996). In Cree, this involves the collapse of two separate vowels to a single vowel at a word or **morpheme** boundary, occurring when two morphemes (meaningful elements of a language) or words are joined together in building larger words. One common source for this occurs when a particle ending in a vowel is added to a vowel-initial noun or verb. In such cases, two alternate pronunciations are often possible:

particle	verb		resulting word	pronunciation
māci	*pīkiskwēw*		*māci-pīkiskwēw*	{MAA tsi PEE kiss KWAYO}
"begin"	"s/he speaks"		"s/he starts speaking"	
māci	*atoskēw*		*māci-atoskēw*	{MAA tsi YUT tose KAYO}
"begin"	"s/he works"		"s/he starts working"	
		or	*māc-ātoskēw*	{MAA TSAA tose KAYO}
			"s/he starts working"	

The first example simply shows the basic process of combining a preverb with a verb with a hyphen indicating the boundary in the SRO. The second example can be said in two ways. In the first, slower and more deliberate pronunciation, the two vowels are kept distinct[11] and all five syllables are pronounced with the predictable stress pattern. In casual, rapid or everyday speech, however, it is more common for the two vowels at the boundary (indicated by the hyphen) to collapse to a single long vowel, which can share features of both original vowels. In this case, the word is reduced to four syllables when the resulting vowel retains anti-penultimate stress and becomes the long **ā**. In this example, the hyphen remains in the SRO spelling in order to indicate that such a collapse has occurred. This can be contrasted with the following word:

mātatoskēw {maa TUT tose KAYO}   "s/he begins work"
/māt-/ + *atoskēw*

Here, rather than combining the particle *māci* with the verb, another root morpheme has been combined with the verb and the initial vowel of the verb has not been affected (i.e. no lengthening has occurred). Thus, the use of the hyphen becomes a very important tool in SRO spelling for distinguishing different types of boundaries and word formation processes.

The hyphen can even become another SRO signal of the stress pattern within words, although this is generally limited to instances in which the element following the hyphen consists of only two syllables. Examples include the following:

Cree SRO	rough pronunciation	translation
osk-āya	{ose SKY ya}	"young one; new things"
osk-āyis	{ose SKY yis}	"youngster"
miyw-āyāw	{mee WHY yow}	"s/he is well"
miywāsin	{MEE waa sin}	"it is good"
pīhc-āyihk	{peeh TSIE yeehk}	"inside"
pīhcāyihk	{PEEH tsie yeehk}	"inside"

nīhc-āyihk	{neeh TSIE yeehk}	"down, below"
nīhcāyihk	{NEEH tsie yeehk}	"down, below"

The first examples, *osk-āya* and *osk-āyis*, are both formed by adding the particle *oski* "new, young" to the root /*ay*-/ "one; person, creature" (itself found in many other words, such as *kēhtē-aya* "elder"). In *osk-āya*, the final vowel is a marker for number (either the archaic animate singular or the inanimate plural) which is required in order to meet the minimum word requirement of two syllables. In *osk-āyis*, the second syllable following the hyphen is provided by the diminutive suffix /-*is*/. In both cases, sandhi has occurred collapsing the last syllable of *oski* with the initial vowel of /*ay*-/. Similarly, in both examples, the hyphen marks this boundary as well as indicating the stress pattern. Without the hyphen, we might predict the following incorrect pronunciations:[12]

Cree SRO	rough pronunciation	translation
oskāya	{OSE sky ya}	"??"
oskāyis	{OSE sky yis}	"??"

In this case, the rough pronunciations are incorrect. Instead, the hyphen must be included and serves the very important function in the Cree SRO of indicating the correct stress pattern.

The next set of examples illustrates the importance of the hyphen in terms of a contrast between very similar forms.

Cree SRO	rough pronunciation	translation
miyw-āyāw	{mee WHY yow}	"s/he is well"
miywāsin	{MEE waa sin}	"it is good"

Both *miyw-āyāw* and *miywāsin* contain the root /*miyw*-/ "good, well". In *miywāsin*, the verb root is modified by the two verbal suffixes /-*ā*/ "VII classifier" and /-*sin*/ "diminutive" in the creation of a three-syllable stem. As such, it has normal anti-penultimate stress. In contrast, *miyw-āyāw* consists of the verb stem *ayā*- "to be" compounded with the particle *miyo*, with sandhi accounting for the collapse of the two vowels and subsequent shift of stress from the original [o] to the new lengthened vowel **ā**. If this were merely a normal three-syllable word, as with *miywāsin*, we would expect a quite different stress pattern:

miywāyāw	{MEE why yow}	"??"

However, this is incorrect. The hyphen, indicating sandhi, again gives valuable information about the stress pattern.

The final two sets of examples illustrate how variation can occur across the dialects or even among speakers of a single community. The variant spellings given for the next two words indicate variant stress patterns. Where stress appears to be on the second last syllable, the hyphen provides us with this information. Where stress appears on the third last, no hyphen is necessary.[13]

pīhc-āyihk	{peeh TSIE yeehk}	"inside"
pīhcāyihk	{PEEH tsie yeehk}	"inside"
nīhc-āyihk	{neeh TSIE yeehk}	"down, below"
nīhcāyihk	{NEEH tsie yeehk}	"down, below"

This is where the two Cree orthographies diverge somewhat. As exemplified, the SRO allows for some hint of the stress pattern in the way the collapsed syllable is displayed, but the Syllabics do not allow for such a marker of sandhi:[14]

Cree SRO	Cree Syllabics	translation
osk-āya	ᐅᐢᑳᔭ	"young one; new things"
osk-āyis	ᐅᐢᑳᔨᐢ	"youngster"
miyw-āyāw	ᒥᔻᔮᐤ	"s/he is well"
miywāsin	ᒥᔻᓯᐣ	"it is good"
pīhc-āyihk	ᐲᐦᒑᔨᕽ	"inside"
pīhcāyihk	ᐲᐦᒑᔨᕽ	"inside"
nīhc-āyihk	ᓃᐦᒑᔨᕽ	"down, below"
nīhcāyihk	ᓃᐦᒑᔨᕽ	"down, below"

The difference is due to the nature of these two distinct orthographies. Whereas the SRO is alphabetic, and each sound can be displayed, the Syllabics are primarily a syllabary and, as such, individual syllables take precedence over the constituent consonants and vowels. The alphabetic SRO permits the representation of word formation boundaries and of stress phenomena through the use of hyphens between letters, but these hyphens often fall inside a syllable, as in our first examples, repeated here:

Cree SRO	syllable divisions	Cree Syllabics
osk-āya	os . k-ā . ya	ᐅᐢᑳᔭ
osk-āyis	os . k-ā . yis	ᐅᐢᑳᔨᐢ

The division of syllables in this way is not possible in Syllabics. While the SRO can give both *oski-ayis* and *osk-āyis* as alternatives, Syllabics provide ᐅᐢᑭ ᐊᔨᐢ or ᐊᐢᑳᔨᐢ. The first of each pair is rather artificial and largely rejected by speakers (especially in the case of the Syllabics example). The latter examples are much preferred, but the SRO example gives extensive phonological and morphological information about the word through the use of hyphenation, while the Syllabics example represents only the basic sounds and syllables of the word, without specific information about stress pattern or word formation. This is not a failure of the Syllabics, but merely an indication of the difference between these two valid writing systems. Much, if not all, of the additional information found in the SRO is superfluous to fluent speakers in any case.

In instances of sandhi, it is becoming standard practice to allow both possible SRO spellings, much as we can alternate "do not" with "don't" in English. Very often it is the reduced or collapsed form which is preferable to fluent speakers, but both versions can be found within the dictionary listings. When both are deemed equally acceptable, they are both listed and cross-referenced (i.e. cf. …). If one is clearly preferred, the other may only be listed as a variant spelling (i.e. also …). In contrast, the Syllabics spelling that accompanies each entry will reflect the preferred, collapsed form, not necessarily mirroring the cited SRO standard. In other words, expanded or "full" SRO spellings and collapsed or reduced SRO spellings alike will be accompanied by the preferred Syllabics spelling.

Notes

[1]Attempts to spell one language with the spelling system of another are ill-advised at best. Certainly, attempts to spell any language with a modified English system fail to recognize a couple of important points. First, the spelling of the English language has long since ceased to reflect the actual pronunciation of English. After centuries of sound change,

during which English spelling has not been greatly modified, the conventions of English writing now function more to unify many diverse dialects than to represent the actual pronunciation of English. Very few symbols in the "English" alphabet have specific sounds consistently and uniquely associated with them. For instance, if you wish to use the symbol "g" because a sound in the target language "sounds" like an English "g," does that mean "g" as in "gall" (i.e. [g]), or "g" as in "gel" (i.e. [j])? Do we choose the letter "e" to represent the so-called English "E" sound (i.e. [i]) because English uses "e" for some instances of this sound (but also represents it with "ee," "ea," "ei," "eo," "ey," "ae," "ie," "oe," "i" and "y" as well)? Clearly, the English system works only for English due to long historical English convention. Attempts to use this (lack of a) system for another language are inappropriate. Most importantly, however, is the fact that any such attempt is a diminishment of, if not a complete insult to, the unique phonemic system of any other language. Each and every language has its own unique system and its own unique history. For any writing system to be appropriate for a language, it must reflect the unique character of that language. Anything less is disrespectful.

[2]Thus, the "English" alphabet is clearly not phonemic. In the variety of Canadian English spoken in western Canada, for instance, there are 38 distinct phonemes but, of course, only 26 different symbols in the spelling system. Additional sounds are represented by combinations of sounds (e.g. "th" for [θ] in "thin" and [ð] in "then," "sh" for [š] in "ship," "ng" for [ŋ] in "king," etc.).

[3]Much of the following discussion of the pronunciation and SRO spelling of Cree is adapted from Wolvengrey 1998.

[4]In some locations, such as throughout much of Alberta, the long vowel ē is simply written as "**e**" without a marker for vowel length. This is apparently done since it is the only long vowel which does not have a short vowel counterpart, and it is therefore felt by some that it is not absolutely necessary to distinguish it from any other similar vowel (cf. **a** vs. **ā**). In the SRO, as followed in this book, the fact that this vowel is indeed long is recognized by the consistent use of the macron to mark all long vowels including ē. See also footnote 5.

[5]Corresponding to this lack of vowel length marking in Syllabics is the Alberta practice of leaving the long vowel ē unmarked as "**e**." See footnote 4.

[6]Syllabic symbols do exist for writing **lV** and **rV** sequences, but these do not occur in the western dialects and, therefore, are not included here. No current version of the syllabics includes a symbol specific to **hV** sequences.

[7]In writing the eastern dialects, the [w] dot is commonly placed preceding the vowel syllabic, rather than following as in the system utilized here.

[8]Other finals are also rare, if not non-existent, word internally in formal written Syllabics. This is due to phonotactic constraints on consonant clusters in Cree such that no consonants other than [h] and [s] (and [š] in eastern dialects) occur as the initial consonant in a CC or CCw cluster. In less formal writing, recognizing the collapse of syllables in rapid speech, certain other finals can occur internally: For instance, the verb *pimipahtā* ∧ᒉ<"Ċ "run!" can be pronounced with the loss of the second "i," and this can lead to a non-standard syllabic spelling of ∧ᶜ<"Ċ. The fuller, uncollapsed (or expanded) standard spelling is followed in this book.

[9]These are only simplified rules, and certain exceptions will not be dealt with here. A full description of Cree word stress and utterance intonation patterns is still required. For additional discussion along the lines of that given here, cf. Okimāsis and Ratt, 1999; Wolfart 1996.

[10]Again, this is a simplification of the actual situation. Syllable weight (or vowel length) does have some effect on secondary stress to the left (or preceding) the primarily stressed anti-penultimate syllable, but the discussion is too complex for the current volume and the best way to learn remains listening closely to a fluent Cree speaker. See also footnote 9.

[11]Often a glide such as [y], [w] or [h] is inserted to keep the vowels separate, and the exact glide depends on the quality of the vowels being kept separate.

[12]On the other hand, if any dialect exists in which the stress pattern has shifted in order to provide these "incorrect" forms, then it would be entirely appropriate to drop the hyphen and treat these words as normal three syllable words with anti-penultimate stress. Correctness is in the speech of the speakers.

[13]For speakers with anti-penultimate stress, the stress has simply shifted with the reanalysis of words which were compounds in origin, but which are no longer treated as such.

[14]Strictly speaking, the SRO spellings for *miyw-āyāw* and *miywāsin* also convey the presence of the constituent root /*miyw-*/ which is often ignored when writing Syllabics. As such, the Syllabics forms given above are still somewhat modified to more closely match the SRO. Alternate forms would be ᒥᐊᐧᐩᐤ and ᒥᐊᐧᕁ respectively.

ᗫᐦᐃᕀᐯᐧᐃᐤ ᐋᑲᕀᐢᒧᐃᐤ

nēhiýawēwin - ākaýāsīmowin
Cree-English

3. An Introduction to the Cree-English Entries

There is an important difference between the way Cree entries are cited in the Cree-English section (volume 1) as compared to the English-Cree section (volume 2). In the Cree-English section, all Cree entries (with the exception of certain particles (e.g. *IPV*s and *IPN*s)) are given in a form which can occur in isolation as a word. This means that some words, particularly verbs, are inflected (see discussion below). In contrast, the Cree entries in the English-Cree section are given in uninflected stem form, which allows for the prediction of various word forms, but which may not always match any actual Cree word. Speakers of the Cree language often prefer inflected forms which match actual words over the more abstract stem forms. For people just learning Cree, the stem forms are often helpful in predicting various word forms beyond just the single form cited. As such, the Cree-English section is designed for Cree speakers, while the English-Cree section is geared more towards students and learners of the Cree language. Both sections (and both volumes) can and should be used together. The discussion in this section will introduce the format of the Cree-English entries and act as a guide to the use of the Cree entries of volume 1. Throughout, various abbreviations will be introduced and explained, but the reader may also find it useful to refer to the full list of abbreviations on page vi.

3.1 Alphabetization

The entries in the Cree-English section are alphabetized according to the familiar sequence of the English alphabet as far as it is applicable to Cree, with the placement of short vowels before long vowels. Thus the sequence of the Cree SRO letters is as follows:

1) **a, ā, c, ē, h, i, ī, k, m, n, o, ō, p, s, t, w, y**

For example, *akask* will be alphabetized before *akām*, *ahpin* before *ahpīhcihēw*, and *āsoyāhtik* before *āsōnam*, etc. Additionally, some entries consist of complex words including hyphenation (e.g. *kēhtē-aya* "elder", *sīsīp-wāwi* "duck egg") or even entire phrases of two or more words (e.g. *āhci piko* "nevertheless", *ēkwa mīna* "and also"). In such cases, the order of presentation will be the following:

    a) the single word first;
    b) all entries in which the single word occurs in a phrase;
    c) all words in which a sequence of sounds occurs in a complex word joined to following elements by a hyphen;
    d) all forms in which the combination of letters happens to begin a word.

This sequence is illustrated by the following examples from the actual dictionary entries:

2) a)   **ahpō** ᐊᕈᑰ
          IPC even, possibly; or, or else
    b)   **ahpō cī** ᐊᕈᑰ ᒉ
          IPH or else
        ahpō ētikwē ᐊᕈᑰ ᐁᑎᑰ
          IPH maybe, perhaps [*also* ahpwētikwē]

ahpō piko ▷"⟩ ∧ᗡ
IPH even if; and yet

d) **ahpōnāni** ◁"⟩ᇫσ
IPC if only it were so; of course not, not any, not even

The preceding example illustrates the occurrence of single words (a) before phrases containing that same single word (b), and these phrases before words which happen to start with the same sequence as the single word alone (d). It also illustrates the continued alphabetization of phrases by the letters of the second (or subsequent) word, where the first word remains constant.

The next example illustrates the occurrence of single words (a) before hyphenated forms containing the single word (c), and of hyphenated forms before words which happen to start with the same sequence as the single (pre-hyphen) word alone (d):

3) a) **sīsīp** ᒡᒥ
NA duck

c) **sīsīp-sākahikanihk** ᒡᒥ ᒡᑊ∧ᑕσˣ
INM Duck Lake, SK [*loc*]

sīsīp-wāwi ᒡᒥ ◁·∆·
NI duck egg [*pl*: sīsīp-wāwa]

d) **sīsīpaskihk** ᒡᒡ<ᑊ₽ˣ
NA teapot, tea kettle, kettle with spout [*pl*: -wak]

sīsīpasiniy ᒡᒡ<ᒉσᐩ
NI duck shot [*pl generally*]

Note, in particular, that the element following the hyphen will dictate subsequent alphabetization (e.g. -*sākahikanihk* before -*wāwi*), but all such forms come before longer words which happen to include the same sequence of sounds regardless of what the next (non-hyphenated) sound will be (e.g. …*p-wāwi* before …*paskihk*). In the Cree-English entries, then, hyphens are treated as outranking or coming before all the letters of the alphabet, but the space at the end of a word outranks even hyphens.

Though each Cree entry includes the Syllabic representation of the Cree word, the sequence of entries does not reflect any preferred sequence of the Syllabic symbols. Nevertheless, in the consonant sections (i.e. c, k, m, n, p, s, t, w, y) which have Syllabic symbols for each different initial syllable (e.g. < = pa, ⟨ = pā, V = pē, etc.), subheadings are given for each change of initial Syllabic symbol.

3.2 Main Entries

The first line of each entry consists of the Cree entry represented in both the SRO and Syllabics, with the SRO in boldface:

4) **mahihkan** Ľ"∆"ᑲᐟ

On occasion the Cree entry is too long to fit both versions on the same line. When this occurs, the Syllabic version follows on the next line, indented two spaces as follows:

5) **kihci-kiskinwahamātowikamik**
  ᑭ"ᒋ ᑭᐣᑭᒐ·"◁ᒡᑐ∆·ᑲᒥˋ

On the next line following the heading itself, each entry is identified by a Cree part-of-speech code, immediately followed by the English translation(s). Additional grammatical notes (as discussed below) will occur in square brackets ([ ]) at the end of each entry:

6) **kihci-kiskinwahamātowikamik**
   ᑭᐦᒋ ᑭᐢᑭᓇᐧᐦᐊᒫᑐᐃᐧᑲᒥᐠ
   NI university [*pl*: -wa]

The part-of-speech code, which is indented four spaces and italicized, is very important because the word class also gives valuable information about the specific form of the entry itself. In the following sections, each word class and its respective subdivisions are illustrated through examples from the dictionary's entries.

3.2.1 Particles

One major word class in Cree is the generic class of particles. Unlike nouns and verbs, described below, particles are typically invariant in form (i.e. are never marked in distinct inflectional forms) and are therefore referred to as "indeclinable" particles, identified by the code *IP*. Several different subtypes of particles occur, classified by their distribution in words, phrases and sentences. The most common are the independent particles (*IPC*), many of which have adverbial function (e.g. specifying time, place, manner, etc.):

7) **otākosīhk ᐅᑖᑯᓰᕽ**
   IPC yesterday

   pimic-āyihk ᐱᒥᒑᔨᕽ
   IPC beside, alongside [also pimicāyihk]

   nisihkāc ᓂᓯᐦᑳᐨ
   IPC slowly, carefully [cf. nasihkāc]

When more than one acceptable version of a word occurs, the variant form(s) will be listed separately, but also cross-referenced by a grammatical note that indicates to the reader that the current entry can be compared (*cf.*) with another form. More restricted or doubtful variant forms (often simply variant spellings) are not listed as separate entries in the dictionary, but are indicated by the grammatical note [*also*].

Occasionally, two or more particles form a set particle phrase (*IPH*) and such a phrase will be given a separate entry:

8) **māka mīna ᒫᑲ ᒦᓇ**
   IPH as usual

Another common particle type is the preverb (*IPV*). Preverbs come before (or are **prefixed** to) verbs. Because they cannot occur alone (i.e. are **bound** forms), they are always listed in the Cree-English entries with a following hyphen (in the SRO; hyphens are not used in Syllabics):

9) **kakwē- ᑲᑵ**
   IPV try to, attempt to
   [*see also* koci- *IPV*]

Preverbs serve a number of functions, including the marking of various verbal categories like tense (e.g. past and future), aspect (e.g. beginning, ending, ongoing, repeating, etc.), and manner adverbials.

Less common, but following the same pattern, are "prenouns" (*IPN*), which come before nouns. Again, these are listed with hyphens to indicate their bound status:

  10) **nōsē-** ᓄᐢ

      IPN female

Prenouns often have functions similar to English adjectives, as they modify nouns. Some particles can be used as both *IPV*s and *IPN*s. These are given separate entries for each particle type:

  11) **miẏo-** ᒥᔪ

      IPN good, nice

    miẏo- ᒥᔪ

      IPV good, well, beautiful, valuable

A final, quite uncommon, particle type is the pre-particle (*IPP*). This refers to an element which can be added to other parts of speech in the formation of particles:

  12) **kapē-** ᑲᐯ

      IPP all, entire, always; throughout,
           for the full duration of

  13) **kapē-ayi** ᑲᐯ ᐊᕀ

      IPC all the time, for the entire
           period, throughout   [*cf.* ayi *IPC*]

    kapē-kīsik ᑲᐯ ᑭᓯᐠ

      IPC all day, all day long   [*cf.* kīsik *NI*; kīsikāw *VII*]

    kapē-nīpin ᑲᐯ ᓂᐱᐣ

      IPC all summer, all summer long   [*cf.* nīpin *VII*]

These examples show the pre-particle *kapē-* attached to another particle, or noun, or verb in the derivation of additional particles. Other free particles can serve this same function, but only those which do not occur alone will be classified as *IPP*.

In contrast to particles, the other two main word classes in Cree, nouns and verbs, can occur in a number of distinct word forms (i.e. **inflected** forms), and these will be discussed each in turn below.

3.2.2 Nouns

All nouns are identified by the code *N*, but are subdivided by the distinction between animate (*NA*) and inanimate (*NI*) nouns. This system of noun classification (or **grammatical gender**) is exceptionally important to Cree grammar and the gender or class of a noun will affect the form of virtually all other words (e.g. verbs, pronouns, etc.) which interact with the noun. For the most part, animate nouns are those which refer to living beings, such as humans, animals, and most trees. However, there are also many other nouns (such as special or spiritually important items) which are classed as animate, and these must simply be learned by non-speakers. All nouns not classed as animate are inanimate.

Most nouns appear in the dictionary entries in their singular forms, usually without specification of appropriate plural forms.[1] However, different plural markers are used for animate and inanimate nouns respectively. Since it is not possible to tell the gender or noun class from the appearance of a singular noun, the part-of-speech code is important in allowing the user of this dictionary to predict the form of the plural. The regular plural marker for animate nouns is <u>-ak</u>, while the regular plural ending for inanimate nouns is <u>-a</u>. Thus, the plural forms of all regular nouns can be predicted simply by knowing the gender of the noun:

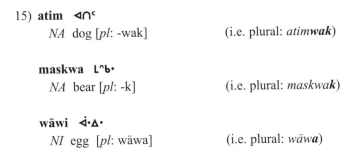

14) **ēmihkwān** ᐁᒥᐦᒁᐣ
NA spoon (therefore, the plural is *ēmihkwān**ak***)

astotin ᐊᐢᑐᑎᐣ
NI hat (i.e. plural: *astotin**a***)

Some nouns, however, do not take the regular plural endings. When this is the case, the irregular plural ending, or the entire irregular plural form, will be given as a grammatical note in square brackets at the end of the entry:

15) **atim** ᐊᑎᒼ
NA dog [*pl*: -wak] (i.e. plural: *atim**wak***)

maskwa ᒪᐢᑿ
NA bear [*pl*: -k] (i.e. plural: *maskwa**k***)

wāwi ᐚᐏ
NI egg [*pl*: wāwa] (i.e. plural: *wāw**a***)

Occasionally, a noun will not have a plural form, such as with mass nouns, and this will be indicated by the note [*sg only*], which means that only the singular form occurs:

16) **ýēkaw** ᖧᑲᐤ
NI sand [*sg only*]

In contrast, some nouns will be cited in the plural form, and when this occurs, the grammatical note will simply indicate that the form is plural:

17) **acikāsipakwa** ᐊᒋᑳᓯᐸᑿ
NI bearberry leaves [*pl*]

If the noun can only appear in the plural, the note will state [*pl only*].

The indication of irregular plural forms can also help predict locative and diminutive forms built from nouns. **Locatives** (which indicate place or location) are formed by adding the locative ending <u>*-ihk*</u> (or <u>*-ināhk*</u>) to the singular form of nouns.[2] However, if a noun has an irregular plural which includes a [w] (i.e. *NA* <u>*-wak*</u> or *NI* <u>*-wa*</u>), the locative ending will be <u>*-ohk*</u> (or <u>*-onāhk*</u>):

18) **askihk** ◁ᣂᑭˣ

    NA pail; kettle [*pl*: -wak]   (i.e. locative: *askihk**ohk*** "in the pail")

19) **mostos** ᒍᣂᑐᣂ

    NA cow; buffalo [*pl*: -wak]   (i.e. locative: *mostos**onāhk*** "in buffalo country")

Where predictable, basic locative forms are not usually listed separately. However, locatives are occasionally given separate entries if the meaning is not readily predictable. Such locative forms are generally treated as particles (i.e. *IPC*, see section 3.5.3 below) and the abbreviation *loc* is given to indicate that it is a locative formation, sometimes accompanied by the non-locative nominal form:

20) **mēnikanihk** ᒷᣂᑲᣂˣ

    IPC in the corral; on the fence
    [*loc*; *cf.* mēnikan]

This same basic pattern can be found in the treatment of diminutive nouns. **Diminutives** (or forms which indicate something is smaller than the norm) are generally formed by adding the ending *-is* (or *-isis*) to the singular form of regular nouns.[3] However, if a noun has an irregular plural which includes a [w] (i.e. *NA* *-wak* or *NI* *-wa*), the diminutive ending will be *-os* (or *-osis*):

21) **askihk** ◁ᣂᑭˣ

    NA pail; kettle [*pl*: -wak]   (i.e. diminutive: *askihk**os***)

Additionally, any instance of [t] in a noun will generally change to [c] in the diminutive:

22) **atim** ◁ᑎᣂ

    NA dog [*pl*: -wak]   (i.e. diminutive: *acimosis* "puppy")

Because of this sound change, recognized in the spelling system, regular and diminutive forms of a noun may be found in widely separated places in the dictionary (e.g. *acimosis* and *atim*; *cēhcapiwinis* "small chair; highchair" and *tēhtapiwin* "chair"). For further discussion and examples of noun pluralization, diminutive and locative patterns, consult such teaching texts as those by Ahenakew (1987) or Okimāsis and Ratt (1999).

All examples discussed thus far have been free (or **independent**) nouns, but another important subdivision among Cree nouns is that between independent nouns and **dependent** nouns. Dependent nouns are those which cannot stand alone as words but must be marked in some way for a possessive relationship. Most dependent nouns in Cree represent kinship terms and body parts, although some other special possessions also occur in dependent form. Dependent nouns can be either animate (e.g. kinship terms) or inanimate (e.g. most body parts), such that two further subclasses of nouns marked in the entries are animate dependent nouns (*NDA*) and inanimate dependent nouns (*NDI*).

Since dependent nouns must have some element prefixed to them to occur as full Cree words, they will be found only in certain places in the Cree-English section. All dependent nouns are cited, at the very least, in their first person singular possessive (1*poss*) form, which is marked by one of three variants of the 1*poss* prefix: *n-*, *ni-*, or *nit-*. Thus, virtually all dependent nouns will be found in the **n** section:

23) **nohkom** ᓄᐦᑯᒼ
NDA my grandmother [*also* nōhkom]

24) **nisit** ᓂᓯᐟ
NDI my foot

Many dependent nouns, excluding those marking kinship, can also take an unspecified possessor prefix, with the varying forms: *m-*, *mi-*, or *mit-*. Dependent nouns of this subtype will thus also occur in the **m** section:

25) **misit** ᒥᓯᐟ
NDI foot

Kinship terminology cannot take this unspecified possessor prefix. Instead, a complex construction built on a third person verbal form is used as an independent noun form. Such words then include a variant of the third person singular prefix: *w-*, *o-*, or *ot-*, and these forms will thus be found in the **o** and **w** sections:

26) **ohkomimāw** ᐅᐦᑯᒥᒫᐤ
NA grandmother

In addition, some kinship terms occur in special forms of address known as **vocatives** (*voc*). These are usually related to the 1*poss* forms:

27) **nohkō** ᓄᐦᑰ
NDA Grandmother! [*voc*]

Finally, the common form of some dependent nouns has shifted from the unspecified possessor to the third person possessive (3*poss*) form, thus also including one of the 3*poss* variant prefixes: *w-*, *o-*, or *ot-*.

28) **oskan** ᐅᐢᑲᐣ
NI bone [*cf.* miskan]

29) **wiyaw** ᐃᐧᔭᐤ
NDI his/her body; body [*cf.* miyaw "corpse"]

However, neither regular third person forms nor second person forms (including the 2*poss* prefix variants *k-*, *ki-*, or *kit-*) are given separate entries. Hence, dependent nouns will be found exclusively in the **m**, **n**, **o**, and **w** sections of the Cree-English entries.

In summation, the subtypes of nouns listed in the Cree entries are these:

NA	animate noun
NDA	animate dependent noun
NDI	inanimate dependent noun
NI	inanimate noun

There is one additional code, *INM*, which also refers to a nominal (noun-like) part-of-speech. The abbreviation indicates an "indeclinable nominal", or one that does not take the usual nominal markings (such as plural marking, locative endings, etc.). These are typically verbal constructions which are used as the names of things as if they were nouns:

30) **kā-nikamōmakahk** ᑲ ᓂᑲᒧᒪᑲᕽ

> *INM* record player [*lit*: "that which sings";
> *cf. VII* nikamōmakan]

kā-nīmihitocik ᑲ ᓃᒥᐦᐃᑐᒋᐠ

> *INM* Northern Lights, aurora borealis [*lit*:
> "(they) who are dancing";
> *cf. VAI* nīmihitow; *wC*: wāwāhtīw *VII*]

Such forms are typically built from *VII* or *VAI* stems with conjunct mode inflections (often introduced by the relativizer /kā-/). Both singular and plural forms are possible, but this is marked by verbal rather than nominal pluralizers. For further information, see the discussion of verbs below (in section 3.2.3) and in more detailed grammatical materials (such as those listed under Written Sources).

Related to the class of nouns are the pronouns (*PR*), which can also be divided by gender. Though this is not indicated in the word-class abbreviation, specific pronouns (either independent, demonstrative or interrogative) are identified as animate or inanimate in the bracketed grammatical notes:

31) **awa** ᐊᐊᐧ

> *PR* this [*anim prox sg*]

Grammatical categories (and abbreviations) commonly associated with the class of pronouns include the following: animate (*anim*), inanimate (*inan*), proximate (*prox*), obviative (*obv*), singular (*sg*), plural (*pl*, or simply *p* when co-occuring with person markers), first person (1), second person (2), animate third person (3), inanimate third person (0), inclusive (*incl* and/or 21), exclusive (*excl* and/or 1p), and demonstrative (*dem*). Again, for further information on these categories consult appropriate Cree grammars and/or language teaching materials (e.g. see lists of Written Sources and Additional Reference Works following the foreward).

3.2.3 Verbs

All verbs are identified by the code *V*, but as with nouns there are several very important subdivisions to the class of verbs in Cree grammar. Traditionally, Cree verbs are divided into four main classes based on two intersecting criteria. Again, the notion of gender is very important, but equally important for verbs is the notion of transitivity. In the simplest terms, verbs can be divided into two types, transitive and intransitive. **Transitive** verbs are those which represent an action or event which involves two or more distinct participants. This most commonly involves a transfer of action from one participant (the agent, actor, or subject) to another (the patient, goal, or object). In other words, transitive verbs take an object, as in the following English examples:

32) They   elected   a new chief.
    subject   transitive verb object

The wolves	chased	a moose.
subject	transitive verb	object

Many transitive verbs, as in the above examples, cannot occur without their objects. The following sentences are not acceptable in English (as indicated by a preceding asterisk (*)) because the necessary object has been omitted:

33) *They elected.

   *The wolves chased.

In contrast, many other verbs only involve a single participant, without any action transfered to an object. When a verb does not take an object, it is called **intransitive**, as in the following examples:

34) The magician	disappeared.
subject	intransitive verb

A book	fell.
subject	intransitive verb

Such intransitive verbs cannot take an object and examples in which an object is included are unacceptable in English:

35) *The magician disappeared her assistant.

   *A book fell the table.

Occasionally, English verbs can occur with or without an object. As such, they can be both transitive or intransitive.

36) The wolves	ate	a moose.
subject	transitive verb	object

The wolves	ate.
subject	intransitive verb

In Cree, however, there is generally a clear distinction between transitive and intransitive verbs and the same verb form cannot be used for both:

37) *ōki mahihkanak*	*kī-**mōwēwak***	*mōswa.*
these wolves	ate	a moose
subject	transitive verb	object

38) *ōki mahihkanak*	*kī-**mīcisowak.***
these wolves	ate
subject	intransitive verb

In addition to this clear distinction, transitive and intransitive verbs are both divided into two subclasses in Cree, based on the gender of one of the participants. The division of intransitive verbs, which have only one participant, is based on the gender of that lone participant or subject. This results in two types of intransitive verbs: **Inanimate Intransitive Verbs** (*VII*) and **Animate Intransitive Verbs** (*VAI*). In contrast, the division of Cree transitive verbs is based on the gender of the object or goal. The two resulting types are: **Transitive Inanimate Verbs** (*VTI*) and Transitive Animate Verbs (*VTA*). Each of these classes of Cree verbs will be discussed individually below.

3.2.3.1 VII

Inanimate Intransitive Verbs (*VII*) are those which have a single, inanimate participant, which therefore acts as subject of the verb. Most *VII*s attribute states to their inanimate participant or specify natural states such as weather terminology. They cannot be used in the Imperative (or command forms), since one cannot insist on rain falling, or command an inanimate object to do anything, etc. In actual use, *VII*s can occur in a limited number of forms based on grammatical mode (Independent or Conjunct) and the person and number of the subject. The full range of possibilities can be found in teaching texts and grammars (e.g. Ahenakew 1987, Okimāsis and Ratt 1999). In the Cree-English entries, *VII*s are generally listed in the third person singular (0) Independent mode form, which means they agree with a singular inanimate subject. For many *VII*s, this will mean that the citation form of the verb ends in a *-w* which, as the marker of the third person inanimate singular, is generally translated in English as "it":

39) **mihkwāw** ᴦ"ᑫ·°
    VII it is red [*wC*: miskwāw, mithkwāw]

This example illustrates that the format of verbal entries is the same as for nouns (as discussed above). The SRO and Syllabic versions of the verb are given first, followed on the next line by the verb code and the translation(s). Any additional grammatical notes (such as the indication of dialect differences) will occur in square brackets at the end of the entry.

From the citation form, it can be observed that a Cree verb can stand alone as an entire sentence. Of course, it is also possible for additional elements (e.g. nouns, pronouns, etc.) to occur with the verb to give more information about the subject:

40) *mihkwāw*   *anima*   *maskisin.*
    (it) is red   that   shoe
    That shoe is red.

Thus, the third person singular *-w* inflection can stand as the sole marker of the subject or agree with other elements in a sentence.

In contrast to this inflected form, the uninflected stem, as listed in the English-Cree glossary (volume 2), can be found by removing the *-w* inflection, as with *mihkwā-*. However, the stem form will never occur on its own as a word. For this reason, it seems incomplete to Cree speakers and is not listed as an uninflected stem in the Cree-English section. In order to use a *VII* with a subject other than third person singular Independent (e.g. third person singular (0) Conjunct, third person plural (0p) Independent or Conjunct, etc.), the *-w* inflection must be replaced by the appropriate ending (i.e. the appropriate ending must be added to the uninflected stem form). In this way, the third person singular Independent form (of the Cree-English section, volume 1) or the stem form (of the English-Cree glossary, volume 2) can be used as models to create additional forms of each Cree verb.

There are also a large set of *VII*s which do not take the _-w_ inflection in the third person singular Independent. *VII*s of this type always end in an [n], as in the following example:

41) **pahkihtin** <"ᑭ"ᑎᑉ
     VII it falls, it falls down

With such *VII*s, the citation form is the same as the stem form (e.g. _pahkihtin-_) and the [n] is not generally deleted before the addition of other *VII* inflections (with the exception of certain conjunct forms; cf. Ahenakew 1987, Okimāsis and Ratt 1999).

Occasionally, *VII*s can occur with or without an [n]. When this occurs, both forms may be given separate entries or, at the least, the more restricted form will be cross-referenced as a grammatical note to the main entry:

42) **pīkopaýin** ᐱᑯ<ᔾᐱᑉ
     VII it is broken, it breaks down [*cf.* pīkopaýiw VII]

43) **pīkopaýiw** ᐱᑯ<ᔾᐱ°
     VII it is broken [*cf.* pīkopaýin]

If there is a possible ambiguity with some other citation form, the Cree part of speech will also be added. This occurs with the cross-reference to *pīkopayiw* in the above examples, because this verb form may be either *VII* or *VAI* (i.e. "it is broken; s/he is broke").

Occasionally, *VII*s will be listed in third person plural (0p) Independent form, where the verb is generally or always used in the plural. When this occurs, it will be indicated by both the translation (i.e. "they") and a grammatical note:

44) **māmawaskitēwa** ᒫᒪ◁•ᐣᑭᑌ◁•
     VII they stand in a cluster (e.g. plants) [*pl*]

     asamonwa ◁ᓱᒧᓇ•
     VII they are in a cluster, they are clustered together [*always pl*]

In such cases, the stem form can be found by removing the *VII* third person plural (0p) Independent inflection _-wa_, and this will be true whether or not the stem ends in [n]. For additional information on Inanimate Intransitive Verbs, please consult appropriate grammatical descriptions.

3.2.3.2 VAI

Animate Intransitive Verbs (*VAI*) are those which have an animate participant, which therefore acts as subject of the verb. Since the subject is animate, the range of person agreement is much greater for *VAI*s than for *VII*s. *VAI*s can refer to first person (singular (1), plural exclusive (1p) and plural inclusive (21)), second person (singular (2), plural (2p)) and animate third person (singular (3), plural (3p) and obviative (3')). The range of meanings for *VAI*s is also greater than for *VII*s since *VAI*s can include not only states and events, but also actions accomplished by volitional (animate) agents. Additionally, *VAI*s can occur in the Independent, Conjunct and Imperative modes. For most *VAI*s, the second person singular Imperative (or command form) will be identical to the stem form.[4] However, in order to remain consistent with the listing of *VII*s, the citation form for *VAI*s (and all other verbs) is the third person singular Independent form. For most *VAI* stems (all those which end in a vowel), this again means that a third person singular inflection _-w_ is included in the citation form:

45) **mihkonākosiw ᒥᐦᑯᓈᑯᓯᐤ**

VAI s/he looks reddish

The entry layout is identical to that for *VII*s. Since the subject is animate, however, the translation is now given as "s/he". This abbreviation is meant to indicate that there is no distinction of natural gender (i.e. masculine versus feminine) indicated in third person forms in Cree. Thus "s/he" is a shorthand way of giving the translation as "she or he", since the verb could be referring to either. In many cases, however, the animate participant being indicated by the -*w* inflection need not be human at all. Therefore, "s/he" can also be read as "it":

46) *mihkonākosiw* *ana* *asikan.*
(s/he) looks reddish that sock
That sock looks reddish.

mihkonākosiw.
It looks reddish.

Some verbs will necessarily take an animate noun which will always or almost always refer to a human referent and thus "s/he" will be limited to either "she" or "he":

47) **masinahikēw ᒪᓯᓇᐦᐃᑫᐤ**
VAI s/he writes, s/he is literate

Still other verbs may be less likely to refer to humans at all, so that "s/he" can sometimes be read merely as "it":

48) **akosīw ᐊᑯᓰᐤ**
VAI s/he perches aloft

Thus, the meaning of each individual verb will determine how "s/he" must be interpreted. When it is obvious the verb absolutely cannot refer to human referents, "it" will be used in place of "s/he":

49) **kinwāýowēw ᑭᓈᐧᔪᐁᐧᐤ**
VAI it is long-tailed [*also* kinoýowēw]

Similarly, some verbs might be specific to female or male referents and, in such cases, the appropriate pronoun ("she" or "he") is used:

50) **pwāwīw ᐚᐑᐤ**
VAI she is pregnant

As with *VII*s, some *VAI*s require plural subjects and these will be cited in the plural with "they" as translation and a corresponding grammatical note:

51) **māmawōpaýiwak ᒫᒪᐞᐸᔨᐘᐠ**
VAI they get together, they assemble [*pl*]

The animate third person plural (3p) Independent marker is _-wak_ and this can be removed to reveal the stem form or (if appropriate) the second person singular Imperative. The addition of other person markers (to the stem or in place of _-w_ or _-wak_) will yield other inflected forms of each verb (see appropriate grammatical materials for more detail).

As with _VII_ stems, some _VAI_s do not take the animate third person singular Independent _-w_ suffix, but instead end with an [n] which is part of the stem:

52) **pahkisin** ᐸᐦᑭᓯᐣ
     VAI s/he falls, s/he falls down

If pluralized, the regular 3p Independent suffix _-wak_ is added.

53) **asisinwak** ᐊᓯᓯᓇᐧᐠ
     VAI they lie together (as pigs in a pen) [_pl_]

Such verbs have their own rules for inflection and details can be sought in the appropriate sources.

3.2.3.2.1 VAIt

There is a very important subset of verbs which are often classified as _VAI_s (_cf._ Wolfart 1973, 1996; Ahenakew 1987) because they take the same inflectional endings as other _VAI_s. However, unlike other _VAI_s, this extensive set of verbs does take objects and are, therefore, clearly transitive rather than intransitive. For this reason, others have treated them as a subclass of Transitive Inanimate Verbs (_VTI_s; _cf._ Okimāsis and Ratt 1999). Neither of these two analyses is incorrect; they have simply come about due to the use of two distinct criteria of classification. When referred to as _VAI_s, the criterion being cited as most important is the morphological (i.e. word-structure) criterion of the inflectional endings. When referred to as _VTI_s (class 2, for example), the criterion being cited as most important is the syntactic (i.e. sentence-structure) criterion of transitivity. Both of these are valid bases for classification, but unfortunately these morphological and syntactic criteria do not coincide in all cases in the Cree language. Hence, some verbs appear to be treated morphologically as if they were intransitive when they are, in fact, syntactically transitive. In order to recognize this important subclass, the intermediate abbreviation of _VAIt_ has been utilized in this dictionary.

54) **osīhtāw** ᐅᓰᐦᑖᐤ
     VAIt s/he makes s.t., s/he prepares s.t.,
     s/he builds s.t.

VAIt will mark a verb as being one of those which is treated morphologically as if it were an animate intransitive verb (_VAI_). In the above example, for instance, the _VAI_ third person singular inflection _-w_ can be removed to yield the stem form _osīhtā-_ ("make s.t.") or the second person singular Imperative _osīhtā_ ("make it! prepare it!"), just as with all regular _VAI_s. As can be seen in this same example, however, _VAIt_ also marks this verb as one which is transitive despite the fact that it is not treated morphologically like a transitive inanimate verb (_VTI_). Thus, the abbreviation "s.t." ("something" or "something inanimate") is included in the translation, indicating that the verb takes an inanimate object (see _VTI_s below). _VAIt_ therefore corresponds to the classification of _VAI_ in many works, such as those of Ahenakew (1987), Wolfart (1973, 1996), and Ahenakew and Wolfart (e.g. 1997)[5], but also corresponds to _VTI_ class 2 and 3 in works produced, for instance, at the Saskatchewan Indian Federated College (cf. Okimāsis and Ratt 1999). All of the notes pertaining to _VAI_s given above will also apply to _VAIt_s.

3.2.3.3 VTI

Transitive Inanimate Verbs (*VTIs*) are those which take both an animate subject and an inanimate object. The range of animate subject participants is the same as for *VAIs*, including all first, second and third persons. Now, however, the action of the verb is directed toward a distinct inanimate participant, which can be singular or plural. This distinction of number is never specified on the verb so that the same form of a verb can refer to either a singular or plural object. Again, as with *VIIs* and *VAIs*, the citation form will be the Independent mode, third person singular subject (acting on an inanimate object), as in the following example:

55) **wāpahtam** ᐁᐧᐸᐦᑕᒼ

    VTI s/he sees s.t.

The third person singular subject is again abbreviated as "s/he" indicating only that the subject is animate and may be male, female, or even a non-human (but animate) participant depending on the meaning of the verb. The object is abbreviated "s.t." for "something" or "something inanimate", and can in fact refer to a singular inanimate object ("it") or a plural inanimate object ("them"):[6]

56) *wāpahtam*   *anima*   *masinahikan.*
    s/he sees (it)   that   book
    S/he sees that book.

    wāpahtam   *anihi*   *masinahikana.*
    s/he sees (them) those   books
    S/he sees those books.

    wāpahtam.
    S/he sees it. (or) S/he sees them.

In the preceding examples, the verb does not change despite the change in the number of the object from singular to plural. *VTIs* only change to agree with the number and person of the animate subject:

57) *niwāpahtēn.*
    I see it/them.

    kiwāpahtēnāwāw.
    You (pl) see it/them.

As already mentioned, the citation form of *VTIs* in the Cree-English glossary is the third person singular subject form. In order to find the stem form of VTIs, the ending *-am* must be removed. The result (e.g. *wāpaht-*) will be the form of each *VTI* as listed in the English-Cree glossary (of volume 2), which allows for the addition of all other person marking affixes (cf. Ahenakew 1987; Okimāsis and Ratt 1999). However, as with *VIIs*, the stem form does not constitute a complete word on its own and is not recognized as such by fluent speakers. Instead, a more acceptable and more commonly cited form is the second person singular (2) Imperative, which has an *-a* added to the stem form. Another way to determine the 2 Imperative is to remove the *-m* from the third person singular Independent citation form:

58) **nitonam** σ⊃ᑫᶜ

> *VTI* s/he seeks s.t., s/he looks for s.t.
> [*cf.* natonam]

> *nitona*!
> Look for it! (or) Look for them!

Many of the notes given above for *VAI*s can apply equally well to *VTI*s and few need be repeated here. It should be noted, however, that some *VTI*s will ordinarily or obligatorily occur with plural subjects. These will be cited in third person plural Independent form with the subject translated as "they":

59) **pēyako-itēýihtamwak** ᐺᕐᐃ ᐃᐁᕈᐦᑕᒪᐧ

> *VTI* they think as one, they are unanimous [*pl*]

Here the pluralizer *-wak* has been added to indicate the third person subject is plural. Thus, *-amwak* must be removed from such a form to determine the base stem.

As discussed above, the subclass of *VAIt*s behave syntactically just as if they were transitive inanimate verbs (i.e. they take an inanimate object). Because of this, they have at times been treated as a subtype of *VTI*s. Okimāsis and Ratt (1999), for instance, refer to the *VTI*s discussed so far as *VTI* class 1, and use the terms *VTI* class 2 and 3 to cover what are here called *VAIt*s. The distinction of two subclasses of the VAIts is again based on morphological criteria. *VTI* class 2 is identified by the fact that they usually end in the sequence *-htā-*, or at least the long vowel [ā], as in the following examples:

60) **ayamihtāw** ᐊᕌᒥᐦᒑᐤ

> *VAIt* s/he reads s.t.

> **pimohtatāw** ᐱᒍᐦᒣᒑᐤ

> *VAIt* s/he carries s.t., s/he takes s.t. along

> **nitotamāw** σ⊃ᑕᒣᐤ

> *VAIt* s/he requests s.t., s/he asks for s.t.

VTI class 3 consists of the leftovers whose stem forms follow no particular pattern, but which are nevertheless transitive despite being inflected just like *VAI*s:

61) **mīciw** ᒌᒋᐤ

> *VAIt* s/he eats s.t.

In this dictionary, however, all such stems are merely identified as *VAIt*s.

In contrast to the *VAIt*s, there is also a class of verbs which seems to be intransitive in actual use, but are nevertheless marked morphologically as if they are *VTI*s. These are not numerous and are not marked in this dictionary. In some cases these correspond with English verbs which can be used both transitively or intransitively:

62) She understands.
> intransitive

He understands Cree.
   transitive   object

nisitohtam ᓂᓯᑐᐦᑕᒼ

   VTI s/he understands; s/he understand s.t.

In other cases, there does not usually appear to be any object possible, but the verb is still inflected like other *VTI*s (i.e. the same *-am* ending can be removed to reveal the stem form):

63) **māham** ᒫᐦᐊᒼ

   VTI s/he canoes downriver,

   s/he paddles downstream

Ultimately, it may prove desirable to isolate this subtype of verb as well (perhaps with an abbreviation like *VTIi*), but as this remains a very small class of verbs in comparison to the very common *VAI*ts, this has not be done in the present volume.

3.2.3.4 VTA

Transitive Animate Verbs (*VTA*s) are those which take two distinct animate participants as subject and object respectively. Now that both the main participants in a verb can be animate, the interaction of persons becomes much more complicated. For *VTA*s, the full range of person and number distinctions can be specified for both the subject and the object and this makes for some very complex inflectional forms. In the Cree-English section, however, the citation form will consistently be the Independent form in which a third person singular "proximate" (3) subject is acting on a third person "obviative" object. The distinction between proximate and obviative is very important in Cree grammar, serving to distinguish between two third persons in the same clause or sentence. In any clause, only one third person participant can be proximate, while all others must be obviative. For our purposes here, the *VTA* subject will be treated as the proximate participant, while the object is obviative.[7] The citation form will thus consist of a verb stem plus the Independent mode inflection indicating a singular third person proximate acting on a third person obviative (i.e. *-ēw*):

64) **wāpamēw** ᐚᐸᒣᐤ

   VTA s/he sees s.o.

Again, the third person singular (proximate) subject is represented by the non-gender specific abbreviation, "s/he", while the obviative object is represented by "s.o." which can be read as "someone" or "something animate". The obviative object will be grammatically animate, but that does not necessarily mean the referent will be one that can be referred to as "him" or "her" in English:

65) *wāpamēw*   *mēriwa.*

   s/he sees (s.o.)   Mary

   S/he sees Mary.

   wāpamēw   *cāniwa.*

   s/he sees (s.o.)   Johnny

   S/he sees Johnny.

wāpamēw   *pahkwēsikana.*
s/he sees (s.o.)   bannock
S/he sees bannock.

wāpamēw.
S/he sees him/her/it.

Thus, in practice, the abbreviation "s.o." can stand for "him", "her" or "it".

From the cited *VTA* forms, the linguistic stems can be found by removing the _-ēw_ inflection. In some cases this will leave a stem form which is identical to the second person singular Imperative acting on a third person singular object:

66) **wīcihēw**   ⏃·ᒋᐦᐁᐤ
     VTA   s/he helps s.o.

     wīcih!
     Help him/her!

     wīcihik!
     Help them!

67) **nitonawēw**   ᓂᑐᐊᐁᐧᐤ
     VTA   s/he seeks s.o., s/he looks for s.o.
     [*cf.* natonawēw]

     nitonaw!
     Look for him/her/it!

     nitonawik!
     Look for them!

Sometimes, as with _wīcih-_ "help s.o.", the stem form will be perfectly regular, while others will undergo some irregular inflection in various *VTA* forms. For instance, stems like _nitonaw-_ "look for s.o.", which end in a sequence of [aw], are examples of one type of irregularity found elsewhere in the *VTA* paradigms (*cf.* Ahenakew 1987; Okimāsis and Ratt 1999)[8]. However, these irregularities are not evident in the citation forms found in this dictionary.

In other cases, the removal of the _-ēw_ inflection yields a form which cannot stand alone as a word in Cree, but must be modified in one of a number of ways before it can be properly inflected in other forms. A number of *VTA* stems end in a sequence of a consonant followed by a [w] (or [Cw] forms). Sequences of [hw] and [sw] are most common, but [mw] and [pw] are also found. When one of these [Cw] sequences occurs before the _-ēw_ inflection, it is fully pronounced. However, this stem final sequence will be realized in different ways depending on other inflections that are added. If nothing is added, as in basic imperative forms (i.e. second person singular acting on third person singular), then the [w] is neither pronounced nor written. If, on the other hand, certain [i]-initial suffixes are added, the [wi] sequence is actually pronounced and written as [o]:

68) **kīwētisahwēw** Ʞᐁ·ᐣᔆᐳᐠᐁ·ᵒ

    VTA s/he drives s.o. back home,
    s/he sends s.o. back home

    kīwētisah!
    Send him/her home!

    kīwētisahok!
    Send them home!

69) **kitamwēw** ᑭᑕᒼᐁ·ᵒ

    VTA s/he eats s.o. up, s/he eats all of s.o.;
    s/he smokes s.o. done

    kitam!
    Eat it all up!

    kitamok!
    Eat them all up!

In these examples, the stems _kīwētisahw-_ "send s.o. home" and _kitamw-_ "eat up all of s.o." must drop the final [w] when no suffix follows, but have [o] rather than [w] in certain forms where [i] is found with regular *VTA* stems (*cf. wīcihik* "help them!").

    Another irregularity occurs when a *VTA* stem ends in a [t]. *VTA*s with a [t] before the _-ēw_ ending sometimes change this [t] to [s]:

70) **nātēw** ᐊᒪᐁ·ᵒ

    VTA s/he fetches s.o., s/he goes for s.o.,
    s/he goes to get s.o.

    nās!
    Fetch him/her/it!

    nāsik!
    Fetch them!

71) **nakatēw** ᐊᑲᑕᐁ·ᵒ

    VTA s/he leaves s.o., s/he abandons s.o.,
    s/he leaves s.o. behind

    nakas!
    Leave him/her/it!

    nakasik!
    Leave them!

Thus, the stems _nāt-_ "fetch s.o." and _nakat-_ "leave s.o." must occur as [nās-] and [nakas-] in certain forms. For further details on all of these irregularities and their full paradigms, see Ahenakew (1987) and Okimāsis and Ratt (1999).

3.3 The Derivation of Additional Stems

Verbs, nouns, and particles are the three main word classes of Cree, with subdivisions among each class, as discussed above. However, there are also many recognizable patterns or subtypes among these classes and subclasses which deserve special notice. These patterns reflect productive means used by Cree speakers to create or **derive** new words, converting from one class to another (e.g. *VAI NI*). This is particularly prevalent with regard to verbs and many patterns of **derivation** involve changes between the subclasses of verbs (e.g. *VTI→VAI*; *VAI→VTA*, etc.). Such derivations are generally accomplished through the addition of particular endings (or **suffixes**) and the glossary contains many examples of basic stems modified by various suffixes to increase the number of distinct words. Some of these derivational processes are very common and can be used to create additional vocabulary beyond that listed in the current edition. As such, a description of some of these forms will give the user of this dictionary the means to expand on the entries actually found herein. This is not meant as an exhaustive list of the complex derivational possibilities of the Cree language and is merely an attempt to illustrate some of the more common forms.

3.3.1 VII /-makan-/

By definition, *VAI*s are verbs which take a single animate participant, and many of the states, events or actions represented by *VAI*s would normally be restricted to an animate participant or agent. For this reason, such *VAI*s would not normally have a corresponding *VII* stem, since an inanimate participant would not normally be considered capable of the same range of activities as animate participants. Nevertheless, context may sometimes require reference to actions by grammatically inanimate participants. When this is the case, *VAI* stems can be converted to *VII* stems by the addition of the suffix /-makan-/. Such a verb indicates that the action is being attributed to an inanimate noun, rather than the usual animate participant:

72) **pimohtēw** ᐱᒧᐦᑌᐤ

    VAI s/he walks, s/he walks along;

    s/he goes along

    VAI stem: *pimohtē-* "walk (along)" + -makan-
                      → VII stem: *pimohtēmakan-* "go along"

    pimohtēmakan ᐱᒧᐦᑌᒪᑲᐣ

    VII it goes on its own, it functions

It is important to note three things about this derivation. First, in common with derivations in general, the suffix is added to the stem form, not the third person singular citation form. Thus, before adding this suffix to a *VAI* verb found in the Cree-English glossary, the third person singular Independent inflection -*w* must be removed. Second, the derivation itself may not drastically alter the meaning of the verb, but simply allow for a larger range of referents (i.e. inanimate nouns) to serve as the subject of the verb. Third, when this suffix is added to a *VAI* which ends in a short vowel, the vowel is typically lengthened before /-makan-/:

73) **nikamow** ᓂᑲᒧᐤ

    VAI s/he sings [cf. nakamow]

    VAI stem: *nikamo-* "sing" + *-makan-* → *VII* stem: *nikamōmakan-* "sing"

nikamōmakan σ∙ᒋᒥᏞᑉ

    VII it sings

This derivation can be used quite productively, but would not normally be added to a *VAI* stem if a corresponding *VII* stem already occurs:

74) **pimātisiw** ᐱᒧᑎᓯᐤ

    VAI s/he lives, s/he is alive

and

    pimātan ᐱᒧᑕᐣ

    VII it has life, it lives

so **pimātisimakan* is not a necessary derivation (though not impossible).

As with all derivations, the best judge of their acceptability will be a fluent native speaker of the Cree language.

3.3.2 VII /-ikātē-/

Additional *VII* stems can be created by modifying stems of the *VTI* class through the addition of the suffix /-ikātē-/. This verb ending changes a transitive *VTI* into an intransitive *VII* by removing the reference to the animate subject of the more basic *VTI*. When this occurs, the only participant remaining is the inanimate object of the original *VTI*. The inanimate participant is then the only one to which the new, derived verb can refer, and a verb which only refers to a lone inanimate participant is by definition an inanimate intransitive verb (*VII*; see 3.2.2.1 above). The following examples show how *VTIs* can be converted to *VIIs* by the addition of /-ikātē-/:

75) **miskam** ᒥᔅᑲᐨ

    VTI s/he finds s.t.

    VTI stem *misk-* "find s.t." + *-ikātē-* → VII stem *miskikātē-* "be found"

    miskikātēw ᒥᔅᑭᑲᑌᐤ

    VII it is found

76) **nitonam** σᑐᓇᐨ

    VTI s/he seeks s.t., s/he looks
    for s.t.

    VTI stem *niton-* "seek s.t." + *-ikātē-* → VII stem *nitonikātē-* "be looked for"

    nitonikātēw σᑐσᑲᑌᐤ

    VII it is looked for

Note again that this process involves the addition of the suffix /-ikātē-/ to the stem form of the *VTI*, not to the third person singular animate subject citation form. Thus, to use this derivational process and convert a *VTI* found in the Cree-English glossary into a corresponding *VII*, the third person singular *VTI* ending *-am* must first be removed from the *VTI* citation form before the addition of /-ikātē-/.[9] It is also important to note that *VTI* stems which end in a [t] will commonly have the [t] changed to a [c] when /-ikāte-/ is added:

77) **wāpahtam** ᐙᐸᵸᐦᑕᒼ
    VTI s/he sees s.t.

VTI stem *wāpaht-* "see s.t." + *-ikātē-*   VII stem *wāpahcikātē-* "be seen"

wāpahcikātēw ᐙᐸᵸᐦᒋᑲᑌᐤ
    VII it is seen

It is also possible for some *VAIt* stems to undergo this type of derivation. Remember that *VAIt*s are also transitive and, therefore, can also have an animate subject removed leaving only a lone inanimate participant. When /-ikātē-/ is added to a *VAIt*, the *VAIt* stem must be treated as if it were a *VTI* stem (i.e. by removal of the stem-final [ā]):

78) **osīhtāw** ᐅᓰᐦᑖᐤ
    VAIt s/he makes s.t., s/he prepares s.t.,
    s/he builds s.t.

VAIt stem *osīhtā-* "make s.t." → "VTI" stem *osīht-*

"VTI" stem *osīht-* + *-ikātē-* → VII stem *osīhcikātē-* "be made"

osīhcikātēw ᐅᓰᐦᒋᑲᑌᐤ
    VII it is built, it is made, it is prepared

Care should be taken, however, when applying this process to *VAIt*s, since not all *VAIt*s appear to permit this derivation.[10] The best judgment on the acceptability or rejection of a form created in this way will be that of a fluent native speaker of Cree.

3.3.3 VAI /-ikē-/

Whereas /-ikātē-/ signals the removal of the animate subject of a *VTI*, the suffix /-ikē-/ downplays the importance of the *VTI* inanimate object. When added to *VTI* stems, /-ikē-/ represents a general object (which is often translated as "things") or removes the object entirely, and leaves only a lone animate participant marked on the verb. By definition, a verb which refers only to an animate participant is an animate intransitive verb (*VAI*; see 3.2.2.2 above). Thus, the addition of /-ikē-/ derives a *VAI* stem from an original *VTI*, as in the following examples:

79) **nitonam** ᓂᑐᓇᒼ
    VTI s/he seeks s.t., s/he looks for s.t.

VTI stem *niton-* "seek s.t." + *-ikē-* → VII stem *nitonikē-* "seek things"

nitonikēw ᓂᑐᓂᑫᐤ
    VAI s/he takes a look, s/he seeks things,
    s/he looks for things

80) **pimotam** ᐱᒍᑦᶜ

> *VTI* s/he shoots an arrow at s.t.,
> s/he shoots s.t. with an arrow

> VTI stem *pimot-* "shoot an arrow at s.t." + *-ikē-*
> → VII stem *pimocikē-* "shoot arrows"

pimocikēw ᐱᒍᣋᖊᑅ

> *VAI* s/he shoots arrows

The second example, *pimocikēw*, shows that a stem-final [t] again changes to [c] when the suffix /-ikē-/ is added.

This suffix can also be added to some *VAIt*s, as in the following example:

81) **osīhtāw** ᐅᣋᵘᒼᑕᑅ

> *VAIt* s/he makes s.t., s/he prepares s.t.,
> s/he builds s.t.

> VAIt stem *osīhtā-* "make s.t." → "VTI" stem *osīht-*

> "VTI" stem *osīht-* + *-ikē-* → VAI stem *osīhcikē-* "make things"

osīhcikēw ᐅᣋᵘᖊᑅ

> *VAI* s/he manufactures things;
> s/he makes things

In order to accomplish this, the *VAIt* stem must first be treated as a *VTI* stem by removal of the stem final [ā], just as was shown for the addition of /-ikātē-/.

3.3.4 VAI /-iwē/

A similar process occurs with the addition of the suffix /-iwē-/, which is frequently employed to derive *VAI*s from *VTA* stems. It has the same effect as /-ikē-/ in that it downplays or removes all reference to the object. In this case, the animate object of a *VTA* is reduced to an understood but unspecified object (often translated as "people" or "others"). When this occurs, the verb is converted to a *VAI* with overt reference only to an animate subject:

82) **kakwātakihēw** ᑲᑲᐧᑕᑭᐦᐁᑅ

> *VTA* s/he distresses s.o., s/he torments s.o.,
> s/he tortures s.o.; s/he mistreats s.o.

> VTA stem *kakwātakih-* "torment s.o." + *-iwē-*
> → VAI stem *kakwātakihiwē-* "torment people"

kakwātakihiwēw ᑲᑲᐧᑕᑭᐦᐃᐁᐧᑅ

> *VAI* s/he torments people, s/he antagonizes people

Most of the examples including this suffix to be found in the dictionary are formed, as in the preceding example, by addition to regular *VTA* stems. The few examples of this suffix added to irregular stems do suggest that the same irregularities occur as those discussed earlier for *VTA* stems in general. For instance, if a *VTA* stem ends in [t], this stem-final [t] will change to [s] before /-iwē-/:

83) **kitotēw** ᑭᐅᐤ°

    VTA s/he addresses s.o., s/he talks to s.o.,

    s/he speaks to s.o.

    VTA stem *kitot-* "talk to s.o." + *-iwē-* → VAI stem *kitosiwē-* "talk to people"

    kitosiwēw ᑭᐅᕒᐁᐧ°

    VAI s/he talks to people

84) **nakatēw** ᖬᑲᐤ°

    VTA s/he leaves s.o., s/he abandons s.o.

    s/he leaves s.o. behind

    VTA stem *nakat-* "leave s.o." + *-iwē-*

                            → VAI stem *nakasiwē-* "leave others behind"

    nakasiwēw ᖬᑲᕒᐁᐧ°

    VAI s/he is ahead, s/he outdistances people,

    s/he outruns everyone

Stems ending in consonant-[w] ([Cw]) sequences merge the [w] and the suffix-initial [i] to an [o]:

85) **otahwēw** ᐅᒉᐧᐁᐧ°

    VTA s/he catches s.o. (e.g. fish) in a net;

    s/he beats s.o. in a game or contest

    VTA stem *otahw-* "beat s.o." + *-iwē-* → VAI stem *otahowē-* "win"

    otahowēw ᐅᒉᐅᐁᐧ°

    VAI s/he wins, s/he wins in gambling

86) **paskoswēw** ᐸᐢᑯᕐᐧ°

    VTA s/he cuts s.o.'s hair

    VTA stem *paskosw-* "cut s.o.'s hair" + *-iwē-* → VAI stem *paskosowē-* "cut hair"

    paskosowēw ᐸᐢᑯᓱᐁᐧ°

    VAI s/he cuts hair, s/he is a barber

The final class of irregular *VTA* stems, those ending in an [aw] sequence, do not appear to occur with the /-iwē-/ suffix. Instead, [aw] stems take the /-ikē-/ suffix. Thus, the /-ikē-/ suffix can also be used to derive *VAI*s from *VTA* stems. When this occurs, the sequence of [aw+i] collapses to a long [ā]:

87) **pistiskawēw ᐱᐢᑎᐢᑲᐍᐤ**
VTA s/he steps on s.o. accidentally,
s/he bumps or knocks into s.o. by mistake

VTA stem *pistiskaw-* "step on s.o. by accident" + *-ikē-*
→ VAI stem *pistiskāke-* "step on people by accident"

pistiskākēw ᐱᐢᑎᐢᑳᑫᐤ
VAI s/he steps on people by accident

This is merely a simplified treatment of the complexities of this derivational pattern. However, it does demonstrate that even the "irregular" stems display a certain amount of predictability.

3.3.5 VAI /-iso-/ and /-ito-/

Two other suffixes are commonly used to derive *VAI* stems from *VTA*s. These are the reflexive /-iso-/ and the reciprocal /-ito-/. The reflexive /-iso-/ suffix indicates that the animate subject and animate object of a *VTA* refer to the same participant. In English, this is accomplished by the use of reflexive pronouns (e.g. "myself", "yourselves", etc.) in object position:

88)	She	helps	herself.
	subject	transitive	object

In Cree, however, since only one distinct participant is involved, reflexive forms are treated as intransitive verbs with a lone animate participant. Thus, the addition of the reflexive /-iso-/ to *VTA* stems derives *VAI* stems:

89) **wīcihēw ᐑᒋᐦᐁᐤ**
VTA s/he helps s.o.

VTA stem *wīcih-* "help s.o." + *-iso-* → VAI stem *wīcihiso-* "help oneself"

wīcihisow ᐑᒋᐦᐃᓱᐤ
VAI s/he helps him/herself

As the example shows, the third person reflexive forms found in citation are translated by "him/herself", again representing the fact that the distinction between masculine and feminine is unmarked in Cree. The actual form in translation will depend on context, but the citation forms are given outside of any particular context, so the somewhat awkward "him/herself" is used instead. Due to the nature of the animate gender, the appropriate reflexive could, given the proper context, even be best translated as "itself".

The addition of the reflexive suffix to a regular *VTA* stem, as in the preceding example, is straightforward. However, as noted in the earlier discussion of *VTA* stems (section 3.2.3.4), some stems are irregular and some of these irregularities are evident in the derivation of reflexive *VAI*s. One irregularity not encountered here is that of the [t]-final *VTA* stems, which in this case do not change to [s]:

90) **nakwātēw** ᐊᑊᐧᐁᐧ°

    VTA s/he snares s.o.

    VTA stem *nakwāt-* "snare s.o." + *-iso-*
                           → VAI stem *nakwātiso-* "snare oneself"

    nakwātisow ᐊᑊᐧᐣᓱ°

    VAI s/he snares him/herself, s/he
    catches him/herself in a snare

However, both [Cw] and [aw] stems undergo the familiar changes. The [w] of [Cw] sequences merges with the initial [i] of the reflexive to yield [o]:

91) **paskiswēw** ᐸᔅᑭᐢᐧᐁᐧ°

    VTA s/he cuts through s.o. (e.g. yarn)

    VTA stem *paskisw-* "cut through s.o." + *-iso-*
                        → VAI stem *paskisoso-* "cut oneself free"

    paskisosow ᐸᔅᑭᓱᓱ°

    VAI s/he cuts him/herself free

While in stems ending in [aw], this sequence collapses with the initial [i] of the reflexive to yield a long [ā]:

92) **pēhtawēw** ᐯᐦᑕᐧᓱ°

    VTA s/he hears s.o.

    VTA stem *pēhtaw-* "hear s.o." + *-iso-* → VAI stem *pēhtāso-* "hear oneself"

    pēhtāsow ᐯᐦᑕᐧᐁᐧ°

    VAI s/he hears him/herself

Finally, there still exist in spoken Cree some older reflexive forms (also called "middle reflexives") which appear to be formed with the suffix /-o-/:

93) **mamihcimēw** ᒪᒥᐦᒋᐤ°

    VTA s/he praises s.o., s/he boasts about s.o.

    VTA stem: *mamihcim-* "praise s.o." + *-o-*
                        → VAI stem: *mamihcimo-* "brag (about oneself)"

    mamihcimow ᒪᒥᐦᒋᒧ°

    VAI s/he boasts, s/he brags about
    him/herself, s/he is boastful [*cf.* mamihcimisow;
    see also kakihcimow]

In many instances, reflexives of both types, /-o-/, and /-iso-/ are in use:

94) **wāpamow** ᐧᐊᐸᒍᵒ

    VAI s/he looks at him/herself in a mirror

    wāpamisow ᐧᐊᐸᒋᕁᵒ

    VAI s/he sees him/herself

While these two reflexive forms sometimes appear to be interchangeable, with (nearly) identical meanings, the older (middle) reflexives are often more specialized in meaning and are certainly more restricted in occurrence. The newer reflexive suffix /-iso-/ is extremely productive and can be added to most VTA stems, provided the meaning of the verb itself lends itself to such a derivation.

Reciprocal /-ito-/ is employed in the exact same way as reflexive /-iso-/. Reciprocal forms are used when two participants are performing the same action on "one another". In one sense, then, the animate subject and animate object again do not appear to be distinct and reciprocal verb forms are thus treated similarly to reflexives: both are coded as animate intransitive verbs (*VAI*s). Since reciprocals will, however, involve two participants acting upon one another, the citation forms are typically plural:

95) **wīcihēw** ᐃᐧᒋᐦᐁᵒ

    VTA s/he helps s.o.

    VTA stem *wīcih-* "help s.o." + *-ito-* → VAI stem *wīcihito-* "help one another"

    wīcihitowak ᐃᐧᒋᐦᐃᑐᐊᐧᐠ

    VAI they help one another

Irregular *VTA* stems require the same modifications when adding /-ito-/ as for the reflexive. [Cw]-final stems will always result in [o] in place of the expected [wi] sequence:

96) **patahwēw** ᐸᑕᐦᐍᐁᵒ

    VTA s/he misses s.o. (by tool or shot)

    VTA stem: *patahw-* "miss s.o." + *-ito-*

                       → VAI stem *patahoto-* "miss one another"

    patahotowak ᐸᑕᐦᐅᑐᐊᐧᐠ

    VAI they miss one another (by tool or shot)

The combination of [aw] plus the initial [i] of the reciprocal collapses to a long [ā]:

97) **nakiskawēw** ᓇᑭᐢᑲᐁᐧᐁᵒ

    VTA s/he meets s.o., s/he encounters s.o.

    VTA stem: *nakiskaw-* "meet s.o." + *-ito-*

                       → VAI stem: *nakiskāto-* "meet one another"

nakiskātowak ⌐ᑭᐣᖬᗡᐊᐧ

VAI they meet one another

Furthermore, another irregularity may or may not reappear. Whereas the reflexive does not generally cause [t] stems to change to [s], the reciprocal may trigger the change of [t] to [s], and sometimes both forms (with and without change) have been recorded:

98) **nakatēw** ⌐ᕒᑌ°

    VTA s/he leaves s.o., s/he abandons s.o.

    s/he leaves s.o. behind

    VTA stem *nakat-* "leave s.o." + *-ito-*

                 → VAI stem *nakasito-* "leave one another behind"

    nakasitowak ⌐ᕒᒥᗡᐊᐧ

    VAI they leave one another behind,

    each in turn; they race one another

or

    VTA stem *nakat-* "leave s.o." + *-ito-*

                 → VAI stem *nakatito-* "leave one another behind"

    nakatitowak ⌐ᕒᑎᗡᐊᐧ

    VAI they race one another

As with reflexives, there is an older reciprocal derivation still in evidence in some words. This involves the use of a suffix /-to-/, rather than /-ito-/, and its addition often causes a change in the basic *VTA* stem form:

99) **wīkimēw** ᐅᐧᑭᐟ°

    VTA s/he marries s.o.; s/he lives with s.o.

    VTA stem: *wīkim-* "live with s.o." + *-to-*

               VAI stem: *wīkihto-* "be married (to one another)"

    wīkihtow ᐅᐧᑭᐦᗡ°

    VAI s/he gets married, s/he is married;

    [*pl*:] they are married to one another,

    they live together

Again, there are examples of stems which occur with both the older and newer reciprocal forms:

100) **wāpahtowak** ᐁᐧᐸᐦᗡᐊᐧ

    VAI they see one another [*cf.* wāpamitowak]

wāpamitowak ᐄ·ᐊᑊᑐᐊ·ᐣ

    VAI they see one another [*cf.* wāpahtowak]

In some cases, the meanings are (nearly) identical, but with other stems, the older reciprocal forms have specialized meanings. Again, the newer suffix is far more productive in modern spoken Cree.

3.3.6 VTA /-amaw-/

    Most of the derivational processes seen thus far have the effect of removing one or another of the participants from a transitive verb, thus detransitivizing the stem and creating intransitive verbs. The reverse process is also possible and participants can be added to transitivize stems as well. A very common means of deriving new *VTA* stems is to add the complex suffix /-amaw-/ to *VTI* (and some *VAIt*) stems.[11] This has the effect of adding another animate participant, typically functioning as a "benefactive" or one who benefits or receives something through the action of the verb, and creating **ditransitive** verbs or verbs with two objects. The animate benefactive then serves as the primary object of the derived *VTA* while the secondary object may be animate or inanimate (and is then typically represented by the abbreviation (it/him)):

101) **saskaham** ᓴᐢᑲᑊᐊᒼ

    VTI s/he kindles s.t., s/he ignites s.t.
    (e.g. a lamp); s/he sets s.t on fire

    VTI stem *saskah-* "light s.t." + *-amaw-*
                     → VTA stem *saskahamaw-* "light (it) for s.o."

saskahamawēw ᓴᐢᑲᑊᐊᒪᐁᐧ·ᐤ

    VTA s/he sets fire to (it/him) for s.o.;
    s/he lights (it/him) for s.o.

Stems derived in this way are full *VTA* stems of the [aw]-final type, and can be secondarily derived in any of the appropriate patterns already discussed above with the corresponding irregularities applying. For instance, following the rule stated earlier (in 3.3.4) for *VTA* stems ending in the [aw] sequence, the suffix /-ikē-/, rather than /-iwē-/, is added to these derived ditransitives in order to create a general or unspecified benefactive (e.g. "for people; for others"):

102) **kiskinwahamawēw** ᑭᐢᑭᓇᐧ·ᐦᐊᒪᐁᐧ·ᐤ

    VTA s/he teaches s.o., s/he teaches (it) to s.o.

    VTA stem *kiskinwahamaw-* "teach (it to) s.o." + *-ikē-*
                   → VAI stem *kiskinwahamākē-* "teach; teach people"

kiskinwahamākēw ᑭᐢᑭᓇᐧ·ᐦᐊᒪᑫᐧᐤ

    VAI s/he teaches, s/he teaches (it)
    to people

3.3.7 NI /-win-/

    Derivations are by no means restricted to shifts between verb types. Verb stems can also be used to derive full nouns in Cree. One example involves the very common suffix /-win-/ added to *VAI* stems in the derivation of inanimate nouns (*NI*s). This suffix can be added productively to virtually all vowel-final *VAI* stems to create *NI*s which represent the action coded by the verb:

103) **kiskinwahamākēw** ᏢᐨᏕᐊᐧᐦᐋᑰᑯ°

    VAI s/he teaches, s/he teaches (it)
    to people

    VAI stem: *kiskinwahamākē-* "teach" + *-win-*
                  → NI stem: *kiskinwahamākēwin-* "teaching"

kiskinwahamākēwin ᏢᐨᏕᐊᐧᐦᐋᑰᐊᐧ·ᐣ

    NI teaching, education; lessons
    instructions [*also* kiskinohamākēwin]

In some cases, the meaning that results from the derivation is not so straightforward, but the noun is nevertheless related to the verbal meaning in some way:

104) **mētawēw** ᒣᑕᐁᐧ·°

    VAI s/he plays

    VAI stem *mētawē-* "play" + *-win-* → NI stem *mētawēwin-*

mētawēwin ᒣᑕᐁᐧ·ᐊᐧ·ᐣ

    NI game

105) **mīcisow** ᒦᒋᓱ°

    VAI s/he eats, s/he has a meal

    VAI stem *mīciso-* "eat" + *-win-* → NI stem *mīcisowin-*

mīcisowin ᒦᒋᓱᐊᐧ·ᐣ

    NI meal; eating, eating habits; food

106) **mīciw** ᒦᒋ°

    VAIt s/he eats s.t.

    VAIt stem *mīci-* "eat s.t." + *-win-* → NI stem *mīciwin-*

mīciwin ᒦᒋᐊᐧ·ᐣ
    NI food

The last example shows that certain *VAIt* stems can also undergo this derivation.[12]

3.3.8 NA /o- -w/ and VAI /o- -i/

    In English, nouns meaning "one who does X" (where X equals the meaning of a verb) can be freely derived from verbs by the addition of the suffix -er:

107) Verb stem: <u>sing</u> + <u>-er</u>   Noun stem: <u>singer</u>

In Cree, a very similar derivation is accomplished, creating animate nouns through the addition of the discontinuous combination of a prefix /o-/ and a suffix /-w/ to *VAI* stems:

108) **nikamow** ᓂᑲᒧᐤ

    VAI s/he sings

    <u>o-</u> + VAI stem: <u>*nikamo-*</u> "sing" + <u>*-w*</u> → NA stem: <u>*onikamow-*</u> "singer"

    onikamow ᐅᓂᑲᒧᐤ

    NA singer

If the original verb begins with a vowel, the prefix must take the shape /ot-/:

109) **atoskēw** ᐊᑐᐢᑮᐤ

    VAI s/he works

    <u>*ot-*</u> + VAI stem: <u>*atoskē-*</u> "work" + <u>*-w-*</u> → NA stem: <u>*otatoskēw-*</u> "worker"

    otatoskēw ᐅᑕᑐᐢᑮᐤ

    NA worker

Many such examples can be found in the **o** section of the Cree-English glossary.

A very similar derivational pattern works in the opposite direction, converting nouns (animate or inanimate) to *VAI* stems, and represents the meaning "have X" (where X stands for the meaning of the original noun, generally restricted to those which can be owned or to terms of human relationship). This derivation is accomplished by adding the discontinuous combination of a prefix /o-/ and a suffix /-i/ to nouns:[13]

110) **kitohcikan** ᑭᑐᐦᒋᑲᐣ

    NI musical instrument; radio

    <u>o-</u> + NI stem: <u>*kitohcikan-*</u> "musical instrument" + <u>*-i-*</u>

                            → VAI stem: <u>*okitohcikani-*</u> "have musical instruments"

    okitohcikaniw ᐅᑭᑐᐦᒋᑲᓂᐤ

    VAI s/he has musical instruments

Again, if the original noun stem begins with a vowel, the prefix must take the shape /ot-/:

111) **akohp** ᐊᑯᐦᑉ

    NI blanket

    <u>*ot-*</u> + NI stem: <u>*akohp-*</u> "blanket" + <u>*-i-*</u>

                            → VAI stem: <u>*otakohpi-*</u> "have a blanket"

otakohpiw ᐅᑕᑯᐦᐱᐤ
VAI s/he has a blanket

One complication to this pattern is introduced if the noun stem begins with an [o]. In such cases, this vowel is generally lengthened to [ō] when the [ot-] prefix is added:

112) **ospwākan** ᐅᐢᐹᑲᐣ
NA pipe

ot- + NA stem: ospwākan- "pipe" + -i-
→ VAI stem: otōspwākani- "have a pipe"

otōspwākaniw ᐅᑑᐢᐹᑲᓂᐤ
VAI s/he has a pipe

This particular derivational process can also include dependent noun stems, but the added complications posed by these forms will not be discussed here. For more information, consult more detailed grammatical materials on Cree.

3.4 Other Abbreviations

Throughout the Cree-English entries, there are numerous additional abbreviations and conventions of translation which reoccur. Though full grammatical descriptions of the processes indicated will not be given here, certain common forms cannot be ignored.

The abbreviation *rdpl* indicates that a form is "reduplicated". **Reduplication** is a process found in Cree whereby the initial consonant (and/or vowel) of a verb stem or preverb particle is copied and attached as a prefix (cf. Ahenakew and Wolfart 1983). Reduplicated forms have been included in the glossary in a couple of different ways. Sometimes, a reduplicated form of a stem is given as a grammatical note within the basic entry:

113) **nipahēw** ᓂᐸᐦᐁᐤ
VTA s/he kills s.o. [*rdpl*: na-nipahēw]

Reduplicated forms are also occasionally cited as full entries, but are not commonly cross-referenced with their unreduplicated counterparts, since the written form, with hyphenation, makes this obvious:

114) **nāh-nakīw** ᓈᐦ ᓇᑮᐤ
VAI s/he stops now and then [*rdpl*]

Only where a stem resulting from reduplication is written without the telltale hyphenation, is the basic stem cross-referenced:

115) **nānitawāpiw** ᓈᓂᑕᐚᐱᐤ
VAI s/he looks around [*rdpl*; *cf.* nitawāpiw]

Finally, some stems now occur almost exclusively in their reduplicated forms, such that the unreduplicated form is either not cited or a note indicates that the reduplicated form is more common:

116) **namipaýiw** ᐊᒥᐸᔫ°

    VAI s/he shakes, s/he shivers

    [*usually rdpl*: nanamipaýiw]

    nanamipaýiw ᐊᐊᒥᐸᔫ°

    VAI s/he shakes; s/he has his/her entire body shake

In contrast, however, the absence of a reduplicated form should definitely not be taken to suggest that a reduplicated form does not or cannot exist in spoken Cree. Reduplication is a very productive process and the inclusion of even just regularly reduplicated verb stems could nearly double the size of the current Cree-English glossary. Only a limited number of examples have therefore been included.

Another common abbreviation is *hab* indicating a **habitual** form. This generally refers to a derivation, commonly of *VAI* stems, in which the suffix /-ski-/ is added to characterize the verbal action as one that occurs "a lot", "habitually", "again and again", etc:

117) **nipāskiw** ᓂᐹᐢᑭ°

    VAI s/he sleeps all the time, s/he sleeps constantly,

    s/he likes to sleep [*hab*]

    cf. **nipāw** ᓂᐹ°

    VAI s/he sleeps, s/he is asleep

These habitual forms can be converted to nouns by simply omitting the final [i] and verbal inflections, as in the following example:[14]

118) **nipāsk** ᓂᐹᐢᐠ

    NA sleepyhead; sleeper [*hab*]

Thus, habitual nominals are very similar to diminutives, as discussed in 3.2.2 above. Similarly, the diminutive (*dim*) is also extremely common in verbal derivation, where the suffix /-si-/ is added to form diminutive verbs:

119) **nipāsiw** ᓂᐹᓯ°

    VAI s/he dozes, naps, sleeps a little [*dim*]

This is again most common with *VAI* stems, though the diminutive can be used with other verb stems as well. The highly productive nature of this derivation could again be used to greatly expand the number of actual entries given in the current glossary.

Occasionally, a Cree term is not a literal match for the English translation. In such cases, attempts have been made to give a literal translation of the Cree term as well. Literal translations are introduced by the abbreviation *lit*: meaning "literally":

120) **amisko-wīhkaskwa** ᐊᒥᐢᑯ ᐄᐱᐦᑲᐢᑲᐧ

    NI mint [*pl*; *lit*: "beaver-sweetgrass"]

Many entries are cross-listed with other related entries in the glossary, and there are several ways in which this cross-listing is accomplished. The abbreviation *cf.* directs the reader's attention to a related or alternative form which is listed as a separate entry:

121) **kakwāhýaki-** ᐤᑲᐤᐦᐟᔨᑭ
    IPV greatly, extremely, overwhelmingly;
    with startled surprise [*cf.* kakwāýaki-]

The phrase *see also* directs the reader's attention to additional entries which are not morphologically related but which may be synonymous (i.e. have similar or identical meanings):

122) **kaskatin** ᑲᐢᑲᑎᐣ
    VII it freezes, it freezes up [*see also* āhkwatin]

Alternative forms which are not listed as separate entries are indicated merely by the word *also*:

123) **kaskitēwākamiw** ᑲᐢᑭᑌᐤᐊᐧᑲᒥ°
    VII it is black liquid [*also* kaskitēwākamin]

    Finally, due to the diverse sources from which the Cree entries have been gathered, the language of translation, which has largely been left without unnecessary editorial tampering, can appear at times inconsistent. Certain authors might have used words or phrases in English which are no longer in common usage, or at least not in common use among speakers of English as a second language, while others have more carefully taken into account the dialect of the audience or are simply more recent. As an aid to "translate" the English into English, as it were, certain set phrases are listed below with some more common equivalencies:

124) "hither" = "coming here", "towards here", "to here" or simply "here"

    "thither" = "going there", "towards there", "to there" or simply "there"

    "thus" = "in such a manner" or "in a certain way"

    It is hoped that these notes will prove valuable to those using the dictionary, both in deciphering the entries themselves, and in allowing speakers and learners alike to expand their Cree vocabulary beyond that actually found in this edition.

Notes

    [1]This differs from the format of nouns as displayed in the English-Cree section, where the linguistic stem forms are given, even where these do not correspond with actual spoken words in Cree. This is further discussed in the introduction to the English-Cree section (see volume 2).

    [2]This is a very simplified description of locative formation. Certain nouns which take the regular plural suffix will, nevertheless, form irregular locative forms. If, for instance, the noun ends in a vowel-[y] (Vy) or vowel-[w] (Vw) sequence, diminutive forms will lengthen the vowel, drop the [y] or [w], and simply add *-hk*:

singular		locative	
mēskanaw	"road"	*mēskanāhk*	"on the road"
sīpiy	"river"	*sīpīhk*	"in the river"

[3]This is a very simplified description of diminutive formation. Certain nouns which take the regular plural suffix will, nevertheless, form irregular diminutive forms. If, for instance, the noun ends in a vowel-[y] (Vy) or vowel-[w] (Vw) sequence, diminutive forms will lengthen the vowel, drop the [y] or [w], and simply add *-s* (or *-sis*):

singular		diminutive	
mēskanaw	"road"	*mēskanās*	"path"
sīpiy	"river"	*sīpīsis*	"stream"

[4]The exceptions will be [n]-final stems which require the addition of *-i* to create second person singular Imperative forms.

[5]In the glossaries included in the publications of Ahenakew and Wolfart, this inanimate transitive object has come to be indicated by the inclusion of a bracketed (optional?) "it," as illustrated in the following example (Ahenakew and Wolfart 1997:168):

    e.g.   **manācihtā-** *VAI* treat (it) with respect

[6]This is a simplification. The object is actually obviative, though this is not explicitly marked on the noun in Plains Cree. In non-Plains dialects, such as the Woods Cree example here, the demonstrative pronoun and the noun indicate the obviative status of the object noun:

    e.g.   *wāpahtam*   *animīthiw*   *masinahikanithiw.*
                  s/he sees (it)   that (obv)   book
                  S/he sees that book.

[7]This is not always the case, and it is certainly possible for the subject to be obviative and the object to be proximate. However, such complex forms will not be cited in this dictionary. For detailed descriptions of the *VTA* paradigms, consult the appropriate teaching texts (e.g. Ahenakew 1987, Okimāsis and Ratt 1999).

[8]*VTA* stems can occur in vowel-[w] ([Vw]) sequences other than [aw] (e.g. [ēw], [iw]), but these are not common and show even more irregularities which will not be discussed here.

In subsequent examples of *VTA* stem irregularities, only [aw] stems will be considered.

[9]If not, the result will simply be incorrect and unrecognizable as a Cree word:

    e.g.   *miskam* + *-ikātē-* → *miskamikātē-* "??"
    cf.   *miskam* – *-am* → *misk-* + *-ikātē-* → *miskikātē-* "be found"

The first form is incorrect, while the second is a correct *VII* stem which only requires appropriate inflection to make it an acceptable Cree word:

    e.g.   *miskikātē-* + *-w* → *miskikātēw* "it is found"

[10]For instance, those *VAIts* which do not end in an [ā] (also referred to elsewhere as *VTI* class 3), cannot take the suffix /-ikātē-/. Additionally, many *VAIs* and *VAIts* can be inflected by unspecified (or "indefinite") actor forms which have the same function as the /-ikātē-/ suffix. Some *VAIts* may pattern more like *VAIs* in the use of *VAI* unspecified actor forms, rather than the *VTI* unspecified actor represented by the /-ikātē-/ suffix. For more information on the unspecified actor forms, see Ahenakew (1987) and Wolfart (1973) (where these forms are referred to as the "indefinite actor" paradigms).

[11]Alternatively, this derivation could be seen as one in which the suffix /-aw-/ is added to the third person singular citation form of *VTIs*. However, this explanation will not work for those *VAIts* which can similarly be derived by /-amaw-/.

[12]A similar, though slightly more complex derivation can be applied to some *VTI* stems to create *NIs*:

e.g.   **kiskēyihtam** Pⁿᑫᐳ"Cᶜ
VTI s/he knows; s/he knows s.t.

VTI stem: *kiskēýiht-* + *-amo-* + *-win*
        → NI stem: *kiskēýiht**amowin*-* "knowledge"

kiskēyihtamowin Pⁿᑫᐳ"Cᒐᐃᐩ
NI knowledge

Thus, an *NI* derived from a *VTI* appears to include an additional suffix *-amo-* or, conversely, to be derived from an extension of the third person inflected form *kiskēýihtam(w)-* plus the regular *-win* suffix.

[13]For many animate nouns to be derived in this way, an additional suffix /-im/ must first be attached to the noun stem:

e.g.   **pīsimohkān** ᐱᒉᒍ"�᾿ᐩ
NA clock, watch

o- + NA stem: *pīsimohkān-* "watch" + *-im* + *i-*
        → VAI stem: *opīsimohkān**imi*-* "have a watch"

opīsimohkānimiw ᐅᐱᒉᒍ"க�σᒥ°
VAI s/he has a watch

Examples of this type indicate the clear relationship of this derivation to possessive marking, where the /-im/ suffix also occurs. The complications posed by this pattern will not be discussed further here.

[14]Conversely, this could be characterized as a derivation which adds a nominal habitual suffix of the form /-sk-/.

References

Ahenakew, Freda. 1987. *Cree Language Structures: A Cree Approac*h. Winnipeg: Pemmican Publications Inc.

Ahenakew, Freda, and H.C. Wolfart. 1983. "Productive Reduplication in Plains Cree," pp. 369–77 in William Cowan (ed.), *Actes du Quatorzieme Congres des Algonquinistes.* Ottawa: Carleton University Press.

——, eds. 1997. *kwayask ē-kī-pē-kiskinowāpahtihicik / Their Example Showed Me the Way.* Edited and translated by Freda Ahenakew and H.C. Wolfart. Edmonton: The University of Alberta Press.

Okimāsis, Jean L. and Solomon Ratt. 1999. *Cree: Language of the Plains.* Textbook, workbook and tape set. Regina: Canadian Plains Research Center.

Wolfart, H.C. 1996. "Sketch of Cree, an Algonquian Language," pp. 390–439 in Ives Goddard (ed.), *Handbook of the North American Indian*, Vol. 17: *Languages.* Washington: Smithsonian Institute.

——. 1973. *Plains Cree: A Grammatical Study.* Transactions of the American Philosophical Society, new series, vol. 63, pt. 5. Philadelphia.

Wolvengrey, Arok. 1998. "On the Spelling and Pronunciation of First Nations Languages and Names in Saskatchewan." *Prairie Forum* 23, no. 1: 113–25.

a

ᐊ

acāhkos ᐊᒑᐦᑯᐢ
NA star [*dim*; *cf.* atāhk]

acāhkos kā-osōsit
ᐊᒑᐦᑯᐢ ᑳ ᐅᓲᓯᐟ
INM comet, tailed star [*dim*; *also* atāhk kā-osoyit]

acāhkosa kā-otakohpit
ᐊᒑᐦᑯᓴ ᑳ ᐅᑕᑯᐦᐱᐟ
INM Starblanket [*Cree chief*; *also* acāhkosa k-ōtakohpit; *lit*: "one who has stars as a blanket"; *cf.* STARBLANKET]

acāhkosiwiw ᐊᒑᐦᑯᓯᐃᐧᐤ
VAI it is a star; s/he is a star (*e.g.* movie, sports, etc.)

acāwēwikamikos ᐊᒑᐁᐧᐃᐧᑲᒥᑯᐢ
NI little store, shop [*dim*, *cf.* atāwēwikamik]

acici ᐊᒋᒋ
IPC head down; upside down [*see also* āpoci]

acici- ᐊᒋᒋ
IPV head down; upside down [*see also* āpoci-]

acici-wēpinam ᐊᒋᒋ ᐁᐧᐱᓇᒼ
VTI s/he throws s.t. top down, in bent position

acici-wēpinēw ᐊᒋᒋ ᐁᐧᐱᓀᐤ
VTA s/he throws s.o. head first, in bent position

acicikāpawiw ᐊᒋᒋᑳᐸᐃᐧᐤ
VAI s/he stands bent over

acicipayihow ᐊᒋᒋᐸᔨᐦᐅᐤ
VAI s/he throws him/herself head first, falling forward; s/he throws him/herself on all fours; s/he somersaults

acicipayiw ᐊᒋᒋᐸᔨᐤ
VAI s/he falls head first, s/he falls bent forward

acicisin ᐊᒋᒋᓯᐣ
VAI s/he lies with head down or facing away [*cf.* acitisin]

aciciwihēw ᐊᒋᒋᐃᐧᐦᐁᐤ
VTA s/he arrives ahead of s.o.

acihkos ᐊᒋᐦᑯᐢ
NA caribou calf, fawn [*dim*, *also* atihkos]

acihkosis ᐊᒋᐦᑯᓯᐢ
NA caribou calf, fawn [*dim*, *also* atihkosis]

acikāsimin ᐊᒋᑳᓯᒥᐣ
NI evergreen berry; kinnikinnick berry, ground cedar berry [*cf.* cikāsimin]

acikāsipakwa ᐊᒋᑳᓯᐸᑿ
NI bearberry leaves [*pl*; *Arctostaphylos uva-ursi*; "plant-like evergreen (mixed with tobacco)"; *cf.* cikāsipakwa]

acimomēyisimin ᐊᒋᒧᒣᔨᓯᒥᐣ
NI cactus berry, red berry from a cactus [*lit*: "little dog-feces berry"]

acimosis ᐊᒋᒧᓯᐢ
NA pup, puppy; small dog [*dim*, *cf.* atim]

acitakocin ᐊᒋᑕᑯᒋᐣ
VAI s/he hangs head downwards

acitakotāw ᐊᒋᑕᑯᑖᐤ
VAIt s/he hangs s.t. head down

acitakotēw ᐊᒋᑕᑯᑌᐤ
VTA s/he hangs s.o. head down

acitakotēw ᐊᒋᑕᑯᑌᐤ
VII it hangs head downwards

acitamow ᐊᒋᑕᒧᐤ
VAI s/he hangs with bottom up, it hangs with bottom up

acitaskihēw ᐊᒋᑕᐢᑭᐦᐁᐤ
VTA s/he sets s.o. upside down

acitaskisow ᐊᒋᑕᐢᑭᓱᐤ
VAI s/he stands (bent over) with head near ground (as when hoeing, etc.)

acitaskitāw ᐊᒋᑕᐢᑭᑖᐤ
VAIt s/he sets s.t. upside down (*e.g.* a post in the ground)

acitaskitēw ᐊᒋᑕᐢᑭᑌᐤ
VII it is set upside down (*e.g.* a post in the ground)

acitastāw ᐊᒋᑕᐢᑖᐤ
VAIt s/he puts s.t. upside down

acitastēw ᐊᒋᑕᐢᑌᐤ
VII it is upside down, it is set upside down

acitinam ᐊᒋᑎᓇᒼ
VTI s/he holds s.t. upside down

acitinēw ᐊᒋᑎᓀᐤ
VTA s/he holds s.o. with head down, s/he holds s.o. upside down

acitisin ᐊᒋᑎᓯᐣ
VAI s/he lies with head down or facing away [*cf.* acicisin]

aciẏaw ᐊᒋᔭᐤ
IPC for a short while, a short time, a little while

acos ᐊᒍᐢ
NA arrow, little arrow [*dim*; *cf.* acosis, atos]

acosis ᐊᒍᓯᐢ
NA arrow, little arrow [*dim*; *cf.* acos, atos]

acoskācasiw ᐊᒍᐢᑳᒐᓯᐤ
VAIt s/he works a little at s.t. [*dim*; *cf.* atoskātam]

acoskēsiw ᐊᒋᐢᑫᓯᐤ
VAI s/he works a little [*dim*; *cf.* atoskēw]

ahā ᐊᐦᐋ
IPC [*discourse particle signifying agreement*; *cf.* āha]

ahām ᐊᐦᐋᒼ
IPC okay then; okay already, hurry up [*cf.* hām]

ahāw ᐊᐦᐋᐤ
IPC okay; ready, let's go [*cf.* hāw]

ahcahk ᐊᐦᒐᕽ
NA soul, spirit [*pl*: -wak; *also* ahcāhk]

ahcahkowan ᐊᐦᒐᐦᑯᐊᐧᐣ
VII it is spiritual [*also* ahcāhkowan]

ahcahkowi- ᐊᐦᒐᐦᑯᐃᐧ
IPV spiritual [*also* ahcāhkowi]

ahcahkowin ᐊᐦᒐᐦᑯᐃᐧᐣ
NI spirituality [*also* ahcāhkowin]

ahcahkowiw ᐊᐦᒐᐦᑯᐃᐧᐤ
VAI it is a spirit [*also* ahcāhkowiw]

ahcāpahciy ᐊᐦᒑᐸᐦᒋᐩ
NI bowstring [*see also* pīminahkwānis]

ahcāpāhtik ᐊᐦᒑᐹᐦᑎᐠ
NI bow stick, stick previously used as a bow [*pl*: -wa]

ahcāpiy ᐊᐦᒑᐱᐩ
NI bow [*NA in wC*]

ahcāpīhkawēw ᐊᐦᒑᐲᐦᑲᐍᐤ
VTA s/he makes a bow for s.o. [*also* ahcāpīhkamawēw]
ahcāpīhkākēw ᐊᐦᒑᐲᐦᑳᑫᐤ
VAI s/he makes a bow from something
ahcāpīhkēw ᐊᐦᒑᐲᐦᑫᐤ
VAI s/he makes a bow
ahēw ᐊᐦᐁᐤ
VTA s/he puts s.o., s/he places s.o.; s/he sets s.o. down [*also* ahýēw, aýēw; *wC*: athīw; *sC*: añēw]
ahkāmasiniy ᐊᐦᑳᒪᓯᓂᕀ
NI round stone for breaking bones
ahkwēhtawapiwak ᐊᐦᑵᐦᑕᐘᐱᐘᐠ
VAI they sit in layers on top of one another
ahkwēhtawastāw ᐊᐦᑵᐦᑕᐘᐢᑖᐤ
VAIt s/he piles s.t. in layers on top of one another
ahkwēhtawastēwa ᐊᐦᑵᐦᑕᐘᐢᑌᐘ
VII they are piled in layers on top of one another
ahkwētawēskam ᐊᐦᑵᑕᐍᐢᑲᒼ
VTI s/he wears several layers of s.t.
ahkwētawēskawēw ᐊᐦᑵᑕᐍᐢᑲᐍᐤ
VTA s/he wears several layers of s.o. (*i.e.* animate clothing)
ahkwētawēskikēw ᐊᐦᑵᑕᐍᐢᑭᑫᐤ
VAI s/he wears several layers of clothing
ahpihc ᐊᐦᐱᐦᐨ
NA tobacco [*cf.* ahpiht]
ahpihcis ᐊᐦᐱᐦᒋᐢ
NA pouch, tobacco pouch [*dim*]
ahpiht ᐊᐦᐱᐦᐟ
NA pouch, tobacco pouch [*cf.* ahpihc]
ahpin ᐊᐦᐱᐣ
NI hide; parchment
ahpinēkino-was ᐊᐦᐱᓀᑭᓄᐘᐢ
NI parchment bag [*pl*: ahpinēkino-wata; *dim*: ahpinēkino-wacis]
ahpīhcihēw ᐊᐦᐲᐦᒋᐦᐁᐤ
VTA s/he bruises s.o., s/he makes s.o. black and blue; s/he wrongs s.o.
ahpīhcimēw ᐊᐦᐲᐦᒋᒣᐤ
VTA s/he verbally abuses s.o., s/he wrongs s.o. verbally, s/he slanders s.o., s/he badmouths s.o.
ahpīhcimow ᐊᐦᐲᐦᒋᒧᐤ
VAI s/he is verbally abused, s/he is wronged verbally, s/he is slandered, s/he is badmouthed
ahpīhcisiw ᐊᐦᐲᐦᒋᓯᐤ
VAI s/he has bruises; s/he is blue with bruises [*cf.* ahpīhtisiw]
ahpīhtahosow ᐊᐦᐲᐦᑕᐦᐅᓱᐤ
VAI s/he bruises him/herself
ahpīhtahwēw ᐊᐦᐲᐦᑕᐦᐍᐤ
VTA s/he bruises s.o. (by beating)
ahpīhtan ᐊᐦᐲᐦᑕᐣ
VII it is bruised; it is blue with bruises
ahpīhtāpiw ᐊᐦᐲᐦᑖᐱᐤ
VAI s/he has a black eye
ahpīhtinākosiw ᐊᐦᐲᐦᑎᓈᑯᓯᐤ
VAI s/he looks bruised, beaten up; s/he appears purple
ahpīhtinākwan ᐊᐦᐲᐦᑎᓈᑿᐣ
VII it looks bruised, beaten; it looks well used, worn out; it appears purple
ahpīhtipaýiw ᐊᐦᐲᐦᑎᐸᔨᐤ
VAI s/he becomes bruised; s/he turns purple, blue
ahpīhtipaýiwin ᐊᐦᐲᐦᑎᐸᔨ�札ᐣ
NI bruise
ahpīhtisiw ᐊᐦᐲᐦᑎᓯᐤ
VAI s/he has a bruise, s/he is bruised [*cf.* ahpīhcisiw]
ahpīhtīhkasow ᐊᐦᐲᐦᑏᐦᑲᓱᐤ
VAI s/he is burnt, s/he is scorched
ahpō ᐊᐦᐴ
IPC even, possibly; or, or else
ahpō cī ᐊᐦᐴ ᒌ
IPH or else
ahpō ētikwē ᐊᐦᐴ ᐁᑎᑵ
IPH maybe, perhaps [*also* ahpwētikwē]
ahpō piko ᐅᐦᐴ ᐱᑯ
IPH even if; and yet
ahpōnāni ᐊᐦᐴᓈᓂ
IPC if only it were so; of course not, not any, not even [*foregone conclusion that something is not the case*]
ahtay ᐊᐦᑕᕀ
NA pelt; fur, animal skin
akahkway ᐊᑲᐦᑿᕀ
NA bloodsucker [*wC*: akaskway, akathkway]
akahkwayimin ᐊᑲᐦᑿᔨᒥᐣ
NA spiral shell [*wC*: akathkwayimin]
akask ᐊᑲᐢᐠ
NA knobbed arrow, knob-shaped arrow head [*pl*: -wak; *cf.* akwask]
akām ᐊᑳᒼ
IPC across, at the far side
akāmaham ᐊᑳᒪᐦᐊᒼ
VTI s/he crosses s.t. (*e.g.* water) by paddling or rowing
akāmaskiy ᐊᑳᒪᐢᑭᕀ
NI the land across the water, overseas [*also* akam-āskiy]
akāmaskīhk ᐊᑳᒪᐢᑮᕽ
IPC overseas, across the ocean; in the land across the water [*also* akām-āskīhk]
akāmāyihk ᐊᑳᒫᔨᕽ
IPC at the other side of a place
akāmi- ᐊᑳᒥ
IPP across
akāmi-mēskanāhk ᐊᑳᒥ ᒣᐢᑲᓈᕽ
IPC across the road
akāmi-sākahikanihk ᐊᑳᒥ ᓵᑲᐦᐃᑲᓂᕽ
IPC across the lake [*cf.* akāmihk]
akāmi-sīpiy ᐊᑳᒥ ᓰᐱᕀ
NI the river across
akāmi-sīpīhk ᐊᑳᒥ ᓰᐲᕽ
IPC across the river
akāmi-tipahaskān ᐊᑳᒥ ᑎᐸᐦᐊᐢᑳᐣ
IPC across the border; United States [*cf.* awasi-tipahaskān; *see also* kihci-mōhkomāninähk]
akāmihk ᐊᑳᒥᕽ
IPC across, on the far side; across (water or land)
akāmiskotēhk ᐊᑳᒥᐢᑯᑌᕽ
IPC at the far side of the fire
akāmiskotēw ᐊᑳᒥᐢᑯᑌᐤ
NI the far side of the fire
akāmōtēnaw ᐊᑳᒨᑌᓇᐤ
NI town across the way
akāmōtēnāhk ᐊᑳᒨᑌᓈᕽ
IPC across town, across the settlement
akāwā ᐊᑳᐚ
IPC hardly, barely, with difficulty [*cf.* akāwāc]
akāwāc ᐊᑳᐚᐨ
IPC hardly, barely, with difficulty [*cf.* akāwā]
akāwāci- ᐊᑳᐚᒋ
IPV wishfully
akāwāci-māmitonēyihtam ᐊᑳᐚᒋ ᒫᒥᑐᓀᔨᐦᑕᒼ
VTI s/he thinks wishfully of s.t.
akāwātam ᐊᑳᐚᑕᒼ
VTI s/he desires s.t., s/he wishes for s.t.
akāwātamawēw ᐊᑳᐚᑕᒪᐍᐤ
VTA s/he desires (it/him) from s.o., s/he desires (it/him) for s.o.
akāwātamowin ᐊᑳᐚᑕᒧᐏᐣ
NI wishing, desire
akāwātēw ᐊᑳᐚᑌᐤ
VTA s/he desires s.o., s/he wishes for s.o., s/he lusts for s.o.
akāwātēyihtam ᐊᑳᐚᑌᔨᐦᑕᒼ
VTI s/he grieves for s.t., s/he longs for s.t.
akāwātēýimēw ᐊᑳᐚᑌᔨᒣᐤ
VTA s/he grieves for s.o., s/he longs for s.o.

akāwēyihtam ⊲ᑫᐁᐧᔭᐦᒉᐦᐨ
VTI s/he is disappointed in
s.t.; be shocked by s.t., be
bothered by s.t.

akāwēyihtamihikow
ᐊᑫᐧᔭᐦᒉᐦᒋᒪᐦᐃᑯᐤ
VTA s/he is bothered by a
promise s/he made to do s.t.
[*inanimate actor form of*
akāwēyihtamih-]

akihcikanāpisk ⊲ᑭᐦᒋᑲᓈᐱᐢᐠ
NI coin-sorter; calculator
[*pl*: -wa]

akihcikanāpiskos ⊲ᑭᐦᒋᑲᓈᐱᐢᑯᐢ
NI coin-sorter, coin bank
[*dim*]

akihcikēw ⊲ᑭᐦᒋᑫᐤ
VAI s/he counts

akihcikēwin ⊲ᑭᐦᒋᑫᐎᐣ
NI counting [*cf.*
akihtāsowin]

akihtam ⊲ᑭᐦᒉᐨ
VTI s/he counts s.t.; s/he
adds s.t. [*cf.* akihtāw]

akihtamawēw ⊲ᑭᐦᒉᒪᐁᐧᐤ
VTA s/he counts (them) for
s.o.

akihtāw ⊲ᑭᐦᒐᐤ
VAIt s/he counts s.t. [*cf.*
akihtam]

akihtāson ⊲ᑭᐦᒐᓱᐣ
NI number, numeral;
phone-number; [*pl*:] numbers
[*cf.* akihtāsowin]

akihtāsow ⊲ᑭᐦᒐᓱᐤ
VAI s/he counts

akihtāsowin ⊲ᑭᐦᒐᓱᐎᐣ
NI counting, the act of
counting; phone-number [*cf.*
akihcikēwin, akihtāson]

akihtēw ⊲ᑭᐦᑌᐤ
VII it is counted

akik ⊲ᑭᐠ
NA snot, rheum, discharge
from nostrils; discharge from
bloodsuckers [*cf.* mitakikom
NDA]

akikwamow ⊲ᑭᑲᐧᒧᐤ
VAI s/he is attached (to
something), s/he is stuck (to
something)

akimēw ⊲ᑭᒣᐤ
VTA s/he counts s.o.

akinē ⊲ᑭᓀ
IPC in succession, one after
the other; collectively

akinēnam ⊲ᑭᓀᓇᒼ
VTI s/he picks s.t. one after
another

akinēskam ⊲ᑭᓀᐢᑲᐨ
VTI s/he passes s.t. (*pl*)
successively

akinēskawēw ⊲ᑭᓀᐢᑲᐁᐧᐤ
VTA s/he passes s.o. (*pl*)
successively; she visits s.o.
(*pl*) one by one

akinēwēskam ⊲ᑭᓀᐁᐧᐢᑲᐨ
VTI s/he makes tracks in

snow, sand, mud; s/he passes
s.t. (*pl*) successively

akinēwēyihtam ⊲ᑭᓀᐁᐧᔭᐦᒉᐦᐨ
VTI s/he thinks of one thing
at a time, s/he thinks of s.t.
(*pl*) successively, one after
another

akinēwēyimēw ⊲ᑭᓀᐁᐧᔭᒣᐤ
VTA s/he thinks of s.o. (*pl*)
successively, s/he considers
s.o. one after another

akisow ⊲ᑭᓱᐤ
VAI s/he is counted, listed;
s/he is accountable, trusted

ako- ⊲ᑯ
IPV sticking on

ako-sakaham ⊲ᑯ ᓴᑲᐦᐊᐨ
VTI s/he nails s.t. on (to
something)

ako-sakahwēw ⊲ᑯ ᓴᑲᐦᐧᐁᐤ
VTA s/he nails s.o. on (to
something)

akoci- ⊲ᑯᒋ
IPV hanging

akoci-wanihikēw
⊲ᑯᒋ ᐊᐧᓂᐦᐃᑫᐤ
VAI s/he sets hanging traps

akoci-wēpinam ⊲ᑯᒋ ᐁᐧᐱᓇᐨ
VTI s/he throw s.t. onto (it)
so as to hang; throw s.t. over
top, onto (it)

akoci-wēpinēw ⊲ᑯᒋ ᐁᐧᐱᓀᐤ
VTA s/he throws s.o. onto
(it) so as to hang; s/he throws
s.o. over top (*e.g.* over
willow bushes)

akocihcēskawēw ⊲ᑯᒋᐦᒉᐢᑲᐁᐧᐤ
VTA s/he puts s.o.'s hand on
something

akocikan ⊲ᑯᒋᑲᐣ
NI cupboard, shelf; closet,
compartment

akocikanēyāpiy ⊲ᑯᒋᑲᓀᔮᐱᕀ
NI clothesline, cord for
hanging

akocikanihkānis ⊲ᑯᒋᑲᓂᐦᑳᓂᐢ
NI shelf [*dim*]

akocikanis ⊲ᑯᒋᑲᓂᐢ
NI hanger; small
compartment [*dim*]

akocikēw ⊲ᑯᒋᑫᐤ
VAI s/he hangs things (*e.g.*
clothes) up, s/he hangs
clothes on a clothesline

akocimow ⊲ᑯᒋᒧᐤ
VAI s/he hangs on (to
something)

akocin ⊲ᑯᒋᐣ
VAI s/he hangs, s/he is
hanging, s/he is suspended
[*rdpl*: ay-akocin]

akocipayiw ⊲ᑯᒋᐸᔨᐤ
VAI s/he is caught aloft; it
gets caught on something

akocipayiw ⊲ᑯᒋᐸᔨᐤ
VII it gets caught on
something

akocipāskisikanāhtik
⊲ᑯᒋᐹᐢᑭᓯᑲᓈᐦᒋᐠ
NI gun-rack

akocipāskisikanēw
⊲ᑯᒋᐹᐢᑭᓯᑲᓀᐤ
VAI s/he places a gun on a
gun-rack

akocīstam ⊲ᑯᒌᐢᑕᐨ
VTI s/he waits in an elevated
place for s.t.; s/he hangs near
s.t.

akocīstamawēw ⊲ᑯᒌᐢᑕᒪᐁᐧᐤ
VTI s/he goes and waits for
(it/him) for s.o.

akocīstawēw ⊲ᑯᒌᐢᑕᐁᐧᐤ
VTI s/he waits in an elevated
place for s.o.; s/he hangs
near s.o., s/he clings to s.o.

akocīw ⊲ᑯᒌᐤ
VAI s/he hangs on by his/her
hands

akohcimēw ⊲ᑯᐦᒋᒣᐤ
VTA s/he puts s.o. into
water, s/he soaks s.o. in
water, s/he immerses s.o. in
water

akohcin ⊲ᑯᐦᒋᐣ
VAI s/he is in water [*cf.*
akohtin]

akohp ⊲ᑯᐦᑊ
NI blanket [*also NA*]

akohpihkawēw ⊲ᑯᐦᐱᐦᑲᐁᐧᐤ
VTA s/he makes blankets for
s.o.

akohpihkēw ⊲ᑯᐦᐱᐦᑫᐤ
VAI s/he makes blankets

akohpis ⊲ᑯᐦᐱᐢ
NI small blanket;
wagon-robe [*dim*]

akohtatāw ⊲ᑯᐦᑕᑖᐤ
VAIt s/he puts s.t. in to soak

akohtēw ⊲ᑯᐦᑌᐤ
VII it is in water [*cf.*
akohtin]

akohtin ⊲ᑯᐦᑎᐣ
VII it soaks, it is in water
[*cf.* akohcin; akohtēw]

akohtitāw ⊲ᑯᐦᑎᑖᐤ
VAIt s/he soaks s.t. in water,
s/he puts s.t. into water

akokwaham ⊲ᑯᑲᐧᐦᐊᐨ
VTI s/he staples s.t. on

akokwahwēw ⊲ᑯᑲᐧᐦᐧᐁᐤ
VTA s/he staples s.t. on

akokwācikan ⊲ᑯᑲᐧᒋᑲᐣ
NI braid, trimming (*e.g.* on
clothing)

akokwācikanis ⊲ᑯᑲᐧᒋᑲᓂᐢ
NI small braids, small
ornament (*e.g.* sequin) used
for trimming (*i.e.* on
clothing) [*dim*]

akokwāsow ⊲ᑯᑲᐧᓱᐤ
VAI s/he sews trimming (*e.g.*
on a dress)

akokwātam ⊲ᑯᑲᐧᑕᐨ
VTI s/he sews s.t. on

akokwātēw ◁ᑫᐷ·ᑌᵒ
VTA s/he sews s.o. on

akonam ◁ᑫᐤᖅ
VTI s/he holds s.t. in place;
s/he puts, sticks, holds s.t. in
place against something else

akonamawēw ◁ᑫᐤᒷᑕᐸ·ᵒ
VTA s/he holds (it/him) on
for s.o. (as heat to the chest);
s/he holds (it/him) up against
s.o.

akonēw ◁ᑫᐤᵒ
VTA s/he holds s.o. in place;
s/he puts, sticks, holds s.o. in
place against something else

akopayȋw ◁ᑯᐸᐧᑊᵒ
VII it sticks, it holds in place
(e.g. as a magnet, from static
electricity, etc.)

akopison ◁ᑯᐱᔅᑊ
NI compress, poultice,
plaster [cf. akopisowin]

akopisow ◁ᑯᐱᔅᵒ
VAI s/he has a compress tied
on him/herself, s/he has a
poultice on

akopisowin ◁ᑯᐱᔅᐃᐧᐣ
NI compress; plaster [cf.
akopison]

akopitam ◁ᑯᐱᑕᒼ
VTI s/he applies a poultice
to s.t.

akopitamawēw ◁ᑯᐱᑕᒷᑕᐸ·ᵒ
VTA s/he applies a wet
poultice (to it/him) for s.o.

akopitamowin ◁ᑯᐱᑕᒧᐃᐧᐣ
NI wet poultice

akopitēw ◁ᑯᐱᑌᵒ
VTA s/he ties a compress on
s.o., s/he applies a poultice to
s.o.

akopitisow ◁ᑯᐱᑎᓱᵒ
VAI s/he applies a poultice
to him/herself

akosȋw ◁ᑯᔒᵒ
VAI s/he perches aloft, s/he
is perched up on s.t.

akosȋwin ◁ᑯᔒᐃᐧᐣ
NI a perch, a place to sit
aloft

akoskam ◁ᑯᐢᑲᒼ
VTI s/he steps on s.t. so as
to press it against something
else; s/he presses s.t. up
against something else with
his/her foot or body

akoskiwasam ◁ᑯᐢᑭᐊᐧᓴᒼ
VTI s/he seals s.t. with wax;
s/he makes an imprint with a
hot object

akoskiwasikan ◁ᑯᐢᑭᐊᐧᓯᑲᐣ
NI sealing wax; object used
to apply glue, paste, wax

akoskiwasikēw ◁ᑯᐢᑭᐊᐧᓯᑫᐤᵒ
VAI s/he seals things with
wax; s/he makes imprints
with a hot object

akostaham ◁ᑯᐢᑕᑕᒼᖅ
VTI s/he sews s.t. on (as
trimming)

akostahamawēw ◁ᑯᐢᑕᑕᒼᑕᐸ·ᵒ
VTA s/he sews (it/him) on
for s.o.

akostahow ◁ᑯᐢᑕᐦᐅᵒ
VAI it is sewn on

akostahwēw ◁ᑯᐢᑕᐦᐅᐸ·ᵒ
VTA s/he sews s.o. on (as
trimming)

akotamawēw ◁ᑯᑕᒷᑕᐸ·ᵒ
VTA s/he hangs (it/him) up
for s.o. [also akotawēw]

akotamāsow ◁ᑯᑕᒫᓱᵒ
VAI s/he hangs s.t. up for
him/herself

akotaskihkwān ◁ᑯᑕᐢᑭᐦᑿᐣ
NI stick for hanging a kettle
over the fire

akotāpān ◁ᑯᑖᐸᐣ
NI travois

akotāskocin ◁ᑯᑖᐢᑯᒋᐣ
VAI s/he hangs snagged on a
tree

akotāskwahwēw ◁ᑯᑖᐢᑿᐦᐅᐸ·ᵒ
VTA s/he hangs s.o. on a tree
(by tool)

akotāson ◁ᑯᑖᓱᐣ
NI flag

akotāw ◁ᑯᑖᵒ
VAIt s/he hangs s.t. up

akotēw ◁ᑯᑌᵒ
VII it hangs, it is hanging
[cf. akotin]

akotēw ◁ᑯᑌᵒ
VTA s/he hangs s.o. up [also
akoýēw; possibly: akohýēw]

akotin ◁ᑯᑎᐣ
VII it hangs, it is hanging
[cf. akotēw VII]

akotisow ◁ᑯᑎᓱᵒ
VAI s/he hangs him/herself
up

akwaham ◁ᐸᐦᒼᖅ
VTI s/he pastes s.t. on (the
wall) [also akoham]

akwahamawēw ◁ᐸᐦᒷᑕᐸ·ᵒ
VTA s/he pastes (it/him) on
for s.o. [also akwahamawēw]

akwahikēw ◁ᐸᐦᐃᑫᐤᵒ
VAI s/he pastes things up;
s/he hangs wallpaper

akwahonān ◁ᐸᐦᐅᓈᐣ
NI shawl; cover [cf.
akwanahon, akwanān]

akwahow ◁ᐸᐦᐅᵒ
VAI s/he covers him/herself

akwahpitam ◁ᐸᐦᐱᑕᒼ
VTI s/he ties s.t. on

akwahpitamawēw ◁ᐸᐦᐱᑕᒷᑕᐸ·ᵒ
VTA s/he ties (it/him) on for
s.o.

akwahpitēw ◁ᐸᐦᐱᑌᵒ
VTA s/he ties s.o. on

akwahwēw ◁ᐸᐦᐅᐸ·ᵒ
VTA s/he pastes s.o. on (the
wall) [also akohwēw]

akwamohēw ◁ᐸᒧᐦᐁᐧᵒ
VTA s/he makes s.o. stick (to
something); s/he glues s.o.
on

akwamohtāw ◁ᐸᒧᐦᑖᵒ
VAIt s/he sticks s.t. on; s/he
fastens s.t. by sticking,
glueing; s/he attaches s.t.

akwamon ◁ᐸᒧᐣ
VII it is attached, it sticks on
[wC: "it stays at one spot on
the water"]

akwamow ◁ᐸᒧᵒ
VAI s/he sticks on [wC:
"s/he stays at one spot on the
water"]

akwamowin ◁ᐸᒧᐃᐧᐣ
NI glue, paste

akwanaham ◁ᐸᐧᓇᐦᒼᖅ
VTI s/he covers s.t. up

akwanahamawēw ◁ᐸᐧᓇᐦᒷᑕᐸ·ᵒ
VTA s/he covers (it/him) up
for s.o.

akwanahikan ◁ᐸᐧᓇᐦᐃᑲᐣ
NI cover, lid; tarp, canvas
covering

akwanahon ◁ᐸᐧᓇᐦᐅᐣ
NI cover; blanket, shawl [cf.
akwahonān, akwanān]

akwanahosow ◁ᐸᐧᓇᐦᓱᵒ
VAI s/he covers him/herself
up

akwanahow ◁ᐸᐧᓇᐦᐅᵒ
VAI s/he wraps him/herself
in blanket, s/he covers
him/herself up, s/he is
covered

akwanahowin ◁ᐸᐧᓇᐦᐅᐃᐧᐣ
NI covering

akwanahwēw ◁ᐸᐧᓇᐦᐅᐸ·ᵒ
VTA s/he covers s.o. up

akwanāhkwēhtēw ◁ᐸᐧᓈᐦᑿᐦᑌᵒ
VAI s/he walks with his/her
face covered

akwanāhkwēnēw ◁ᐸᐧᓈᐦᑿᓀᐧᵒ
VTA s/he covers s.o.'s face,
s/he veils s.o.'s face (e.g. a
baby's)

akwanāhkwēsimēw
◁ᐸᐧᓈᐦᑿᓯᒣᵒ
VTA s/he lays s.o. down with
face covered; s/he puts s.o. to
bed with that one's face
covered

akwanāhkwēsin ◁ᐸᐧᓈᐦᑿᓯᐣ
VAI s/he has his/her own
face covered while sleeping;
s/he lies with his/her face
covered

akwanāhkwēw ◁ᐸᐧᓈᐦᑿᐧᵒ
VTA s/he has his/her own
face covered

akwanān ◁ᐸᐧᓈᐣ
NI shawl [cf. akwahonān,
akwanahon]

akwanāpowēham ◁ᐸᐧᓈᐳᐁᐧᐦᒼᖅ
VTI s/he puts the cover or
lid on s.t.

akwanāpowēhikan ᐊᑿᓈᐳᐍᐦᐃᑲᐣ
NI dish cover; lid (for a kettle or pail) [*also* akwanāpwēhikan]
akwanāpowēhikāsow ᐊᑿᓈᐳᐍᐦᐃᑳᓱᐤ
VAI it is covered (as a vessel capable of containing liquid), it has a lid
akwanāpowēhikēw ᐊᑿᓈᐳᐍᐦᐃᑫᐤ
VAI s/he covers things, s/he puts lids on things
akwask ᐊᑿᐢᐠ
NA knobbed arrow, knob-shaped arrow head [*pl*: -wak; *cf.* akask]
akwāhikanēkin ᐊᒀᐦᐃᑲᓀᑭᐣ
NI wagon cover of cloth or leather
akwāhonāhtik ᐊᒀᐦᐅᓈᐦᑎᐠ
NI stick used to pull objects from water [*pl*: -wa]
akwāhwēw ᐊᒀᐦᐍᐤ
VTA s/he takes s.o. from water or fire by tool
akwākohtin ᐊᒀᑯᐦᑎᐣ
VII it is mouldy; it is rusty [*also* ākwākohtin]
akwākomākosiw ᐊᒀᑯᒫᑯᓯᐤ
VAI it smells mouldy
akwākomākwan ᐊᒀᑯᒫᑿᐣ
VII it smells mouldy
akwākopiy ᐊᒀᑯᐱᐩ
NI green, slimy water [*also* ākwākopiy]
akwākopīwi-sākahikan ᐊᒀᑯᐲᐏ ᓵᑲᐦᐃᑲᐣ
NI Green Lake, SK [*loc generally*]
akwākosiw ᐊᒀᑯᓯᐤ
VAI it is mouldy; it is rusty [*also* ākwākosiw]
akwāminakasiy ᐊᒀᒥᓇᑲᓯᐩ
NA thorn, thorn-bush [*cf.* okāminakasiy; *also* akāminakasiy; *wC*: akāwininakasiy]
akwānam ᐊᒀᓇᒼ
VTI s/he takes s.t. from water or fire by hand; s/he lifts s.t. out of the water or off the stove
akwānēw ᐊᒀᓀᐤ
VTA s/he takes s.o. from water or fire by hand; s/he lifts s.o. out of the water or off the stove
akwāpicikēw ᐊᒀᐱᒋᑫᐤ
VAI s/he fishes with a seine net; s/he pulls things from the water
akwāpitam ᐊᒀᐱᑕᒼ
VTI s/he pulls s.t. from the water; s/he drags s.t. out of the water
akwāpitēw ᐊᒀᐱᑌᐤ
VTA s/he pulls s.o. from the water; s/he drags s.t. out of the water
akwāsiwēpaham ᐊᒀᓯᐍᐸᐦᐊᒼ
VTI s/he knocks s.t. out of the water or fire by tool
akwātaskinēw ᐊᒀᑕᐢᑭᓀᐤ
VII it is not full
akwāwān ᐊᒀᐚᐣ
NI drying rack
akwāwānihkēw ᐊᒀᐚᓂᐦᑫᐤ
VAI s/he makes a drying rack
akwāwēpahwēw ᐊᒀᐍᐸᐦᐍᐤ
VTA s/he knocks s.o. out of the water or fire by tool
akwāwēw ᐊᒀᐍᐤ
VAI s/he dries meat
akwāýāhokow ᐊᒀᔮᐦᐅᑯᐤ
VAI s/he drifts to the shore [*also* akwāýāhikow]
akwāýāstan ᐊᒀᔮᐢᑕᐣ
VII it drifts ashore
amisk ᐊᒥᐢᐠ
NA beaver [*pl*: -wak]
amisko-kipahikan ᐊᒥᐢᑯ ᑭᐸᐦᐃᑲᐣ
NI beaver dam
amisko-sākahikan ᐊᒥᐢᑯ ᓵᑲᐦᐃᑲᐣ
NI Amisk Lake, SK [*loc generally*; *lit*: "beaver lake"]; Beaver Lake, AB [*loc generally*]
amisko-sīpiy ᐊᒥᐢᑯ ᓰᐱᐩ
NI beaver river
amisko-wāti ᐊᒥᐢᑯ ᐚᑎ
NI beaver hole [*pl*: amisko-wāta]
amisko-wātihkān ᐊᒥᐢᑯ ᐚᑎᐦᑳᐣ
NI beaver hole
amisko-wīhkaskwa ᐊᒥᐢᑯ ᐑᐦᑲᐢᑿ
NI mint [*pl*; *lit*: "beaver-grass"]
amisko-wīsti ᐊᒥᐢᑯ ᐑᐢᑎ
NI beaver lodge [*pl*: amisko-wīsta]
amiskohōsiwayān ᐊᒥᐢᑯᐦᐆᓯᐘᔮᐣ
NA beaver pelt [*cf.* amiskwayān]
amiskomin ᐊᒥᐢᑯᒥᐣ
NA yellow blackberry
amiskominānāhtik ᐊᒥᐢᑯᒥᓈᓈᐦᑎᐠ
NI yellow blackberry tree [*pl*: -wa; *lit*: "beaver-berry bush"]
amiskosip ᐊᒥᐢᑯᓯᑊ
NA wood duck [*lit*: "beaver duck"]
amiskosīs ᐊᒥᐢᑯᓰᐢ
NA water insect
amiskosoy ᐊᒥᐢᑯᓱᐩ
NI beavertail
amiskowacīwiýiniwak ᐊᒥᐢᑯᐘᒌᐏᔨᓂᐘᐠ
NA Beaver Hills People [*pl*; *division of the Cree*; *see also* natimīwiyiniwak; nātakāmīwiýiniwak]
amiskowiw ᐊᒥᐢᑯᐏᐤ
VAI s/he is a beaver
amiskowiyās ᐊᒥᐢᑯᐏᔮᐢ
NI beaver meat
amiskowiýiniw ᐊᒥᐢᑯᐏᔨᓂᐤ
NA Beaver Indian man; fur-trader
amiskwaciy-wāskahikan ᐊᒥᐢᑿᒋᐩ ᐚᐢᑲᐦᐃᑲᐣ
NI Edmonton, AB [*lit*: "Beaver Hills House"; *also* amiskowaciy-wāskahikan]
amiskwayān ᐊᒥᐢᑿᔮᐣ
NA beaver-pelt [*dim*: amiskwayānis; *also* amiskowayān]
amiskwayānēscocinis ᐊᒥᐢᑿᔮᓀᐢᒍᒋᓂᐢ
NI small beaver-pelt hat [*dim*]
ana ᐊᓇ
PR that [*anim prox sg*]
anakway ᐊᓇᑿᐩ
NA sleeve [*also NDA* -anakway-, -nakway-; *cf.* 3: wanakwaya, onakwaya "his/her sleeve(s)"]
anāskason ᐊᓈᐢᑲᓱᐣ
NI mattress pad; cushion, potholder; an item placed under oneself or a hot pot,
anāskasow ᐊᓈᐢᑲᓱᐤ
VAI s/he places a mat for him/herself; s/he lies on s.t., s/he has s.t. under him/her
anāskasowin ᐊᓈᐢᑲᓱᐏᐣ
NI bedding
anāskāhtam ᐊᓈᐢᑳᐦᑕᐣ
VTI s/he puts a new floor down (on s.t.)
anāskāhtēw ᐊᓈᐢᑳᐦᑌᐤ
VAI s/he covers the floor, s/he spreads s.t. on the ground
anāskākēw ᐊᓈᐢᑳᑫᐤ
VAI s/he uses something as a floor covering
anāskān ᐊᓈᐢᑳᐣ
NI mat, matting; floor, floor covering, carpet; sheet; quilt
anāskānāhtik ᐊᓈᐢᑳᓈᐦᑎᐠ
NI floor board; [*pl*: -wa] flooring
anāskānis ᐊᓈᐢᑳᓂᐢ
NI baby blanket; small sheet, mat, matting, blanket [*dim*]
anāskāsimon ᐊᓈᐢᑳᓯᒧᒼ
NI mattress
anāskēstamawēw ᐊᓈᐢᑫᐢᑕᒪᐍᐤ
VTA s/he puts flooring (a mat, etc.) down for s.o.
anāskēw ᐊᓈᐢᑫᐤ
VAI s/he puts flooring down, s/he lays carpet, s/he puts down linoleum; s/he lays

mats, s/he spreads a blanket; s/he uses s.t. as a covering; s/he lays s.t. on the ground or floor

anāskēwin ᐊᓈᐢᑫᐃᐧᐣ
NI flooring, linoleum; something used as matting

ani ᐊᓂ
IPC indeed [*emphatic*; *emphasizes preceding word as actual*]

anihi ᐊᓂᐦᐃ
PR that, those [*anim obv / inan pl*]

aniki ᐊᓂᑭ
PR those [*anim prox pl*]

anikwacās ᐊᓂᑲᐧᒑᐢ
NA squirrel; gopher [*also* anikwacāsk(wak); *sC*: anikwacās, alikwacās]

anikwacāsi-mīciwin ᐊᓂᑲᐧᒑᓯ ᒦᒋᐃᐧᐣ
NI peanut butter [*see also* pakānipimiy]

anikwacāsi-pimiy ᐊᓂᑲᐧᒑᓯ ᐱᒥᕁ
NI gopher fat

anima ᐊᓂᒪ
IPC it is that; the fact that [*predicative, factive; cf.* anima *PR*]

anima ᐊᓂᒪ
PR that [*inan sg*]

animēýiw ᐊᓂᒣᔨᐤ
PR that [*inan obv; dialectal; archaic in pC*]

aniskamān ᐊᓂᐢᑲᒫᐣ
NA hitch, clasp; button [*see also* sakwāskohon]

anita ᐊᓂᑕ
IPC there, at that place

anohc ᐊᓄᐦᐨ
IPC now, today

anohc kā-ispaýik ᐊᓄᐦᐨ ᑳ ᐃᐢᐸᔨᐠ
IPH this week

anohc kā-kīsikāk ᐊᓄᐦᐨ ᑳ ᑮᓯᑳᐠ
IPH today

anohc-kaskāpiskahikana ᐊᓄᐦᐨ ᑲᐢᑳᐱᐢᑲᐦᐃᑲᓇ
NI today's canned goods [*always pl*]

anohcihkē ᐊᓄᐦᒋᐦᑫ
IPC but now, just recently, not long ago

anōmin ᐊᓅᒥᐣ
NA oatmeal [*cf.* ayōmināpoy; *also* ānōmin, manōmin; *see also* kīkisēpā-mīciwin]

apahkwācīs ᐊᐸᐦᑲᐧᒌᐢ
NA bat (flying mammal) [*dim*]

apahkwān ᐊᐸᐦᑲᐧᐣ
NI thatch; roof; shingle

apahkwānaskosiya ᐊᐸᐦᑲᐧᓇᐢᑯᓯᕀ
NI water-reeds [*pl*]

apahkwānis ᐊᐸᐦᑲᐧᓂᐢ
NI shingle [*dim*]

apahkwāson ᐊᐸᐦᑲᐧᓱᐣ
NI tent; canvas, tent canvas covering

apahkwātam ᐊᐸᐦᑲᐧᑕᒼ
VTI s/he roofs s.t.; s/he shingles the roof

apahkwātamawēw ᐊᐸᐦᑲᐧᑕᒪᐁᐧᐤ
VTA s/he roofs for s.o., s/he shingles the roof for s.o.

apahkwātēw ᐊᐸᐦᑲᐧᑌᐤ
VII it has a roof, it is roofed

apahkwāw ᐊᐸᐦᑲᐧᐤ
VAI s/he roofs, s/he engages in roofing; s/he shingles the roof

apahkwēw ᐊᐸᐦᑫᐧᐤ
VAI s/he thatches s.t.; s/he covers a dwelling

apasoy ᐊᐸᓱᕀ
NI tentpole; fence pole [*also NA*]

apasoyāhtik ᐊᐸᓱᔮᐦᑎᐠ
NI pole, stick for tentpole [*pl:* -wa; *also NA, pl:* -wak]

apihci- ᐊᐱᐦᒋ
IPN small [*cf.* apisci-, apisi-]

apihci- ᐊᐱᐦᒋ
IPV small [*cf.* apisci-]

apihēw ᐊᐱᐦᐁᐧᐤ
VTA s/he makes s.o. sit

apihkān ᐊᐱᐦᑳᐣ
NI braid

apihkātam ᐊᐱᐦᑳᑕᒼ
VTI s/he braids s.t.; s/he knits s.t.

apihkātēw ᐊᐱᐦᑳᑌᐤ
VII it is braided

apihkātēw ᐊᐱᐦᑳᑌᐤ
VTA s/he braids s.o.; s/he knits s.o.

apihkēpicikan ᐊᐱᐦᑫᐱᒋᑲᐣ
NI knitting machine; horse halter

apihkēs ᐊᐱᐦᑫᐢ
NA Chinese person; spider [*see also* aýapihkēsis, ocaýapīhkēsis]

apihkēsīs ᐊᐱᐦᑫᓰᐢ
NA spider [*cf.* aýapīhkēsis, ocaýapīhkēsis]

apihkēsīs-aýapiy ᐊᐱᐦᑫᓰᐢ ᐊᔭᐱᕀ
NA spider web

apihkēsīs-sakimēwaýān ᐊᐱᐦᑫᓰᐢ ᓴᑭᒣᐊᐧᔮᐣ
NA spider web [*cf.* sakimēwaýān]

apihkēstamawēw ᐊᐱᐦᑫᐢᑕᒪᐁᐧᐤ
VTA s/he braids (it/him) for s.o.; s/he knits (it/him) for s.o.

apihkēw ᐊᐱᐦᑫᐤ
VAI s/he braids, s/he braids hair; s/he weaves, s/he makes a net; s/he knits, s/he does knitting

apini-kēskēw ᐊᐱᓂ ᑫᐢᑫᐤ
VAI s/he turns while sitting, s/he turns in his/her seat; [*rdpl:*] s/he is hyperactive, s/he is unable to sit still [*cf.* ay-apini-kēskēw]

apisam ᐊᐱᓴᒼ
VTI s/he warms s.t.

apisāpēkan ᐊᐱᓵᐯᑲᐣ
VII it is small (*e.g.* thread, rope)

apisāpēkisiw ᐊᐱᓵᐯᑭᓯᐤ
VAI it is small (*e.g.* thread size) [*cannot be used to describe a human being*]

apisāsin ᐊᐱᓵᓯᐣ
NI small thing

apisāsin ᐊᐱᓵᓯᐣ
VII it is small

apisāskosiw ᐊᐱᓵᐢᑯᓯᐤ
VAI s/he is slender (as a tree)

apiscatim ᐊᐱᐢᒐᑎᒼ
NA small dog [*pl:* -wak]

apiscawāsis ᐊᐱᐢᒐᐋᐧᓯᐢ
NA small child; new born baby [*see also* oskawāsis]

apiscānakos ᐊᐱᐢᒑᓇᑯᐢ
NA small female dog, bitch

apiscāpakwanīs ᐊᐱᐢᒑᐸᑲᐧᓃᐢ
NI little flower [*dim; cf.* wāpakwaniy]

apiscāpānis ᐊᐱᐢᒑᐹᓂᐢ
NI buggy; small car [*dim*]

apiscāwāsisiwiw ᐊᐱᐢᒑᐋᐧᓯᓯᐃᐧᐤ
VAI s/he is a little child

apisci- ᐊᐱᐢᒋ
IPN small, little [*cf.* apihci-, apisi-]

apisci- ᐊᐱᐢᒋ
IPV small, little [*cf.* apihci-, apisi-]

apisci-kahkākīs ᐊᐱᐢᒋ ᑲᐦᑳᑮᐢ
NA magpie [*dim; cf.* kahkākiw]

apisci-kīskisis ᐊᐱᐢᒋ ᑮᐢᑭᓯᐢ
NA tomtit (bird) [*dim*]

apisci-niskis ᐊᐱᐢᒋ ᓂᐢᑭᐢ
NA laughing goose; small goose [*dim; cf.* niska]

apisci-pāskisikanis ᐊᐱᐢᒋ ᐹᐢᑭᓯᑲᓂᐢ
NI 22 rifle; small gun [*dim; cf.* pāskisikan]

apisci-pihēsis ᐊᐱᐢᒋ ᐱᐦᐁᓯᐢ
NA prairie hen; grouse [*dim; cf.* pihēw]

apisci-sīpīsis ᐊᐱᐢᒋ ᓰᐲᓯᐢ
NI Little Creek; Milk River [*dim; cf.* sīpiy]

apisci-wāskahikan ᐊᐱᐢᒋ ᐋᐧᐢᑲᐦᐃᑲᐣ
NI small house [*dim*]

apiscicāpānis ᐊᐱᐢᒋᒑᐹᓂᐢ
NI buggy, Democrat [*dim*]

apiscicāpiw ᐊᐱᐢᒋᒑᐱᐤ
VAI s/he has small eyes [*cf.* apiscicāpisiw]

apiscikātēw ◁ᐱᕐᑲᐁᑌᐤ
  VAI s/he has slender legs
apiscikwayawēw ◁ᐱᕐᑲᐣᐯᐁᐧᐤ
  VAI s/he has a slender neck
apiscisam ◁ᐱᕐᓴᒼ
  VTI s/he cuts s.t. into small pieces
apiscisasiw ◁ᐱᕐᓴᓯᐤ
  VAIt s/he cuts s.t. into very small pieces [*dim*]
apiscisipis ◁ᐱᕐᓯᐱᐢ
  NA teal (duck) [*dim*]
apiscisiskam ◁ᐱᕐᓯᐢᑲᒼ
  VTI s/he has small tracks, s/he makes small tracks
apisciyawēsiw ◁ᐱᕐᐸᐁᐧᓯᐤ
  VAI s/he has a small waist; s/he is slender [*dim*]
apisciyēkāsin ◁ᐱᕐᐁᑳᓯᐣ
  VII it is narrow (material)
apisciýinīs ◁ᐱᕐᐱᓂᐢ
  NA dwarf; short person [*dim*]
apisi- ◁ᐱᐢ
  IPN small, tiny [*cf.* apihci-, apisci-]
apisi- ◁ᐱᐢ
  IPV small, tiny [*cf.* apihci-, apisci-]
apisicāpisiw ◁ᐱᓴᐱᓯᐤ
  VAI s/he has small eyes [*dim; cf.* apiscicāpiw]
apisicihcānis ◁ᐱᓯᐦᒑᓂᐢ
  NI little finger [*dim*]
apisicihcēsiw ◁ᐱᓯᐦᒉᓯᐤ
  VAI s/he has small hands [*dim*]
apisiminakāsiw ◁ᐱᓯᒥᓇᑳᓯᐤ
  VII it has small berries [*dim*]
apisimōsos ◁ᐱᓯᒨᓱᐢ
  NA deer [*pl*: -wak (*sometimes* -ak)]
apisimōsoswayān ◁ᐱᓯᒨᓱᐢᐧᐊᔮᐣ
  NA deer-hide, deerskin [*also* apisimōswayān]
apisimōsowiyās ◁ᐱᓯᒨᓱᐃᔮᐢ
  NI venison, deer meat
apisisicānis ◁ᐱᓯᓯᒑᓂᐢ
  NI little toe [*dim*]
apisisihtāw ◁ᐱᓯᓯᐦᑖᐤ
  VAIt s/he makes s.t. small
apisīs ◁ᐱᓰᐢ
  IPC a little, a little bit
apisīsi- ◁ᐱᓰᐢ
  IPV small
apisīsisiw ◁ᐱᓰᓯᓯᐤ
  NA small person or animal
apisīsisiw ◁ᐱᓰᓯᓯᐤ
  VAI s/he is small
apiskway ◁ᐱᐢᒁᐤ
  NA osprey
apisow ◁ᐱᓱᐤ
  VAI s/he warms him/herself
apist- ◁ᐱᐢᐟ
  IPV small
apistacihkos ◁ᐱᐢᑕᒋᐦᑯᐢ
  NA antelope [*dim; cf.* atihk]
apistinaskwās ◁ᐱᐢᑎᓇᐢᒀᐢ
  NA grey squirrel

apiswēw ◁ᐱᐢᐁᐧᐤ
  VTA s/he warms s.o.
apiw ◁ᐱᐤ
  VAI s/he sits, s/he sits down, s/he is present; s/he is available; s/he is there, s/he is situated; s/he is at home, s/he stays at home [*in the latter sense, often rdpl*: ay-apiw]
apiwikamik ◁ᐱᐃᑲᒥᐠ
  NI living room, sitting room [*pl*: -wa; *also* apīwikamik]
apiwin ◁ᐱᐃᐣ
  NI seat; settee; seat (as in government) [*see also* kihcapiwin]
apiwinis ◁ᐱᐃᓂᐢ
  NI seat, chair [*dim; cf.* apiwin]
apīstam ◁ᐱᐢᑕᒼ
  VTI s/he sits near s.t.; s/he lives close to s.t.
apīstawēw ◁ᐱᐢᑕᐁᐧᐤ
  VTA s/he sits near s.o.; s/he lives close to s.o.
apoy ◁ᐳᐩ
  NA paddle; shovel, spade [*see also* mōnihikākan]
apoyahikākanis ◁ᐳᕀᐦᐊᑳᑲᓂᐢ
  NI hoe; shovel
apwān ◁ᐧᐋᐣ
  NI roast
apwānāsk ◁ᐧᐋᓈᐢᐠ
  NI roasting spit, spit (for cooking); fish cooked with split willow sticks [*pl*: -wa]
apwēpahtāw ◁ᐁᐧᐸᐦᑖᐤ
  VAI s/he sweats while running
apwēsiw ◁ᐁᐧᓯᐤ
  VAI he sweats, she perspires
apwēsiwin ◁ᐁᐧᓯᐃᐣ
  NI sweating; perspiration; labouring
apwēw ◁ᐁᐧᐤ
  VAI s/he makes a roast, s/he roasts over a fire (on a spit)
apwēyāw ◁ᐁᐧᔮᐤ
  VII it is warm enough to perspire
asaham ᐊᓴᐦᐊᒼ
  VTI s/he puts s.t. (*pl*) together in a heap
asahēw ᐊᓴᐦᐁᐧᐤ
  VTA s/he puts s.o. (*pl*) together in a heap
asahkēskiw ᐊᓴᐦᑫᐢᑭᐤ
  VAI s/he feeds people all the time, habitually; s/he is given to feeding people [*hab*]
asahkēw ᐊᓴᐦᑫᐤ
  VAI s/he gives food; s/he feeds people; s/he holds a feast, banquet
asahkēwikamik ᐊᓴᐦᑫᐃᑲᒥᐠ
  NI ration house [*pl*: -wa]
asahpitam ᐊᓴᐦᐱᑕᒼ
  VTI s/he ties s.t. together into a bunch, bundle

asahpitēw ᐊᓴᐦᐱᑌᐤ
  VTA s/he ties s.o. together into a bunch, bundle
asahtowak ᐊᓴᐦᑐᐊᐧᐠ
  VAI they feed one another
asahtowikamik ᐊᓴᐦᑐᐃᑲᒥᐠ
  NI band office [*pl*: -wa; "ration-house", *cf.* asahkēwikamik; *see also* askīhkān-atoskēwikamik]
asahtowin ᐊᓴᐦᑐᐃᐣ
  NI rations
asamastimwān ᐊᓴᒪᐢᑎᒳᐣ
  NI manger, oatbox; green-feed [*also NA in reference to* "oats"]
asamastimwēw ᐊᓴᒪᐢᑎᒣᐤ
  VAI s/he feeds his/her horses or dogs
asamēw ᐊᓴᒣᐤ
  VTA s/he feeds s.o., s/he gives s.o. food; s/he hands out rations to s.o.
asamisow ᐊᓴᒥᓱᐤ
  VAI s/he feeds him/herself, s/he prepares his/her own meals
asamokwāwa ᐊᓴᒧᒀᐊᐧ
  VII they are bunched
asamonam ᐊᓴᒧᓇᒼ
  VTI s/he clusters s.t.; s/he holds s.t. together
asamonwa ᐊᓴᒧᓇᐧ
  VII they are in a cluster, they are clustered together [*always pl*]
asamopitāw ᐊᓴᒧᐱᑖᐤ
  VAIt s/he closes s.t. (*e.g.* pouch) with a gathering string
asamopitēw ᐊᓴᒧᐱᑌᐤ
  VII it is closed with a gathering string
asamowak ᐊᓴᒧᐊᐧᐠ
  VAI they are in a cluster [*always pl*]
asapāp ᐊᓴᐹᐱ
  NA thread [*cf.* sēstak]
asapiwak ᐊᓴᐱᐊᐧᐠ
  VAI they are in a heap
asascikana ᐊᓴᐢᒋᑲᓇ
  NI things piled together [*pl*]
asaskisowak ᐊᓴᐢᑭᓱᐊᐧᐠ
  VAI they grow in a clump or mass
asaskitēwa ᐊᓴᐢᑭᑌᐊᐧ
  VII they grow in a clump or mass
asastān ᐊᓴᐢᑖᐣ
  NI pile of cordwood
asastāw ᐊᓴᐢᑖᐤ
  VAIt s/he piles s.t. up (as wood)
asastēwa ᐊᓴᐢᑌᐊᐧ
  VII they are piled up, they are heaped up [*cf.* oskana kā-asastēki "Pile of Bones (Regina, SK)"]

asawāpahtam ⊲ᗯᐧ⊲ᐧ<"Cᶜ
VTI s/he waits and watches
for s.t.; s/he looks out for s.t.

asawāpamēw ⊲ᗯᐧ⊲ᐧ<ᒼ°
VTA s/he looks out for s.o.,
s/he waits and watches for
s.o., s/he lies in watch for
s.o.

asawāpiw ⊲ᗯᐧ⊲ᐧᐱ°
VAI s/he looks around, s/he
looks out; s/he waits and
watches

asawāpiwikamik ⊲ᗯᐧ⊲ᐧᐱᐞᐁᐧᐟᐦ
NI watchtower; lighthouse
[*pl*: -wa]

asawāpiwin ⊲ᗯᐧ⊲ᐧᐱᐞᐧ
NI hunting-blind; a place to
watch from; look-out,
lighthouse, watchtower;
looking out

asayḗtiwak ⊲ᗯᔑᐣ⊲ᐧᐟ
VAI they are together (as a
bunch, herd) [*pl*]

asāhtin ⊲ᐦᐣᐳ
VII it is dull, it is blunt

asām ⊲ᐦᒼ
NA snowshoe

asāmāhtik ⊲ᐦᒪᐞᐣᐳ
NA stick for making a
snowshoe [*pl*: -wak]

asāmḗyāpiy ⊲ᐦᒼᔨᐱᐞ
NI strap of snowshoe

asāskonam ⊲ᐦᔑᐠᐊᐧᒼ
VTI s/he carries a pile (of
firewood) by hand

asāsow ⊲ᐦᔭᐅ°
VAI s/he is tattooed

asāsowēw ⊲ᐦᔭᐁᐧᐧᐦ
NA one who tattoos, tattoo
artist

asāwāc ⊲ᐦᐧ⊲ᐧᐦ
IPC in contrary direction,
perversely [*cf.* ayasāwāc]

ascascwās ⊲ᐣᒋᐧᒋᐧᐦ
NA curds, cottage cheese

ascāskwahikanis
  ⊲ᐣᒋᐧᐟᐦᐁᐧᐟᐦᐊᑲᐟᐦ
NI buckle; gate latch, door
latch [*dim*]

ascikēw ⊲ᐣᒋᕐᕐ°
VAI s/he places things there;
s/he bets

ascikēwikamik ⊲ᐣᒋᕐᕐᐁᐧ⊲ᐧᐟᐦ
NI storehouse, storage room,
storage building [*pl*: -wa;
wC: astāsowikamik]

ascipahkwānis ⊲ᐣᒋ<"ᐧᒼᐸᐟᐦ
NI tentpole pin [*dim*; *pl*: the
14 "pins" holding together
the tipi hide]

ascisis ⊲ᐣᒋᑎᐟ
NA small mitten [*dim*; *also*
astisis; *cf.* astis]

ascocinis ⊲ᐣᒍᒋᐟᐦ
NI bonnet; small cap [*dim*;
also astotinis; *cf.* astotin]

asē- ⊲ᐦ
IPV backwards, back,

---

motion going backwards
[*also* āsē-]

asē-wēpinam ⊲ᐦᐁᐧᐱᐊᐧᐟᐦ
VTI s/he flings s.t. back

asē-wēpinēw ⊲ᐦᐁᐧᐱᐊᐧᐤ°
VTA s/he flings s.o. back

asēciwan ⊲ᐦᒋᐧᐣ
VII it flows back as an eddy
at a falls

asēhāw ⊲ᐦᐦᐧᐊᐧ°
VAI s/he flies back, s/he flies
backwards

asēhtahāhtēw ⊲ᐦᐦᐟᐦᐧ⊲ᐧ"ᐁᐧ°
VTA s/he tracks s.o. back,
s/he follows s.o.'s track
backwards

asēhtahēw ⊲ᐦᐦᐟᐦᐁᐧᐁᐧ°
VTA s/he makes s.o. walk
backwards; s/he makes s.o.
backtrack; s/he takes s.o.
back

asēhtahwēw ⊲ᐦᐦᐟᐦᐧᐁᐧᐧ°
VTA s/he knocks s.o. back

asēhtēw ⊲ᐦᐦᐟᐁᐧ°
VAI s/he walks back, s/he
walks backwards

asēkāpawiw ⊲ᐦᐠ<ᐊᐧᐱᐧ°
VAI s/he steps backwards

asēkinam ⊲ᐦᐠᐁᐧᐟᐦ
VTI s/he lays or gathers s.t.
together as cloth

asēkocin ⊲ᐦᐠᐅᒋᐣ
VAI s/he flies back, s/he flies
backwards, s/he goes
backwards

asēmakan ⊲ᐦᒪᑲᐣ
VII it goes backwards, it
moves down

asēnam ⊲ᐦᐊᐧᐟᐦ
VTI s/he refuses s.t. [*also*
āsēnam]

asēnamawēw ⊲ᐦᐊᐧᒪᐧᐁᐧ°
VTA s/he returns (it/him) to
s.o.; s/he creates a hindrance
for s.o.

asēnēw ⊲ᐦᐊᐧᐤ°
VTA s/he rejects s.o., s/he
refuses s.o., s/he puts s.o.
back [*also* āsēnēw]

asēnikātēw ⊲ᐦᐊᐧᐠᐁᐧᐳ
VII it is refused, it is turned
down

asēpahtāw ⊲ᐦᐸᐧ"ᒋᐧ°
VAI s/he runs back; s/he runs
backwards

asēpaýiw ⊲ᐦ<ᔭᐳ°
VAI s/he drives backwards;
s/he moves back, s/he moves
back quickly (as a machine)

asēpaýihow ⊲ᐦ<ᔭᐦᐃᐧᐟ°
VAI s/he throws him/herself
backwards, s/he jumps
backwards; s/he backs down
(as from a challenge)

asēpitam ⊲ᐦᐱᐊᐧCᶜ
VTI s/he pulls s.t. back

asēpitēw ⊲ᐦᐱᐤᐅ°
VTA s/he pulls s.o. back

---

asēpiw ⊲ᐦᐱᐱ°
VAI s/he sits back

asēsin ⊲ᐦᐟᐟ
NI vamp, tongue of
moccasin [*pl*: -wa]

asēsin ⊲ᐦᐟᐟ
VAI s/he moves back while
sleeping or lying

asēskawēw ⊲ᐦᐣᒝᐅᐧᐧ°
VTA s/he forces s.o. back by
advancing

asētācimow ⊲ᐦᒋᒋᐃᐧᐳ°
VAI s/he crawls back, s/he
crawls backwards

asētisaham ⊲ᐦᐣᒋᐦ"⊲ᐧᐟᐦ
VTI s/he sends s.t. back, s/he
mails s.t. back

asētisahwēw ⊲ᐦᐣᒋᐦ"ᐧᐅᐧ°
VTA s/he sends s.o. back,
s/he mails s.o. back

asēya- ⊲ᐦᔭ
IPV in a group

asēyas ⊲ᐦᔭᐣ
IPC in a group

asicāpātam ⊲ᒋᒐ<ᒋᐧCᶜ
VTI s/he pulls s.t. along

asicāpātēw ⊲ᒋᒐ<ᒋᐧᐅ°
VTA s/he pulls s.o. along
(*e.g.* children in a toboggan)

asicāyi ⊲ᒋᒐᔨ
IPC up against; next to,
beside

asicāyihk ⊲ᒋᒐᔨᐞ
IPC beside; up against

asici ⊲ᒋᒋ
IPC with, together with,
along with, in a group,
accompanied by; against

asicimēw ⊲ᒋᒋᒼᐁᐧ°
VTA s/he links s.o.'s name
with another (*e.g.* an affair, a
partnership, etc.)

asicipitam ⊲ᒋᒋᐱᐊᐧCᶜ
VTI s/he pulls s.t. against
(something); s/he moves s.t.
next to (something)

asicipitēw ⊲ᒋᒋᐱᐤᐅ°
VTA s/he pulls s.o. against
(something); s/he moves s.o.
next to (something)

asikan ⊲ᒋ\ᑲᐟ
NA sock, stocking [*poss*:
(-im); *dim*: asikanis]

asikanēyāpiy ⊲ᒋ\ᑲᔨᐱᐞᐱ
NI yarn

asikanihkawēw ⊲ᒋ\ᑲᐧᐳ"ᑲᐧᐅᐧ°
VTA s/he makes socks for
s.o., s/he knits socks for s.o.

asikanihkākan ⊲ᒋ\ᑲᐧᐳ"ᑲᑲᐟ
NI knitting needle

asikanihkēw ⊲ᒋ\ᑲᐧᐳ"ᕐ°
VAI s/he makes socks, s/he
knits socks

asimākanisihkān-askiy
  ⊲ᒋᒪᑲᐧᐳᒻᐳ"ᐸᐞ ⊲ᐣᐱᐧ
NI Asimakaniseekan Askiy
[*lit*: "soldier/veteran land";
*urban Cree reserve in
Saskatoon, SK*]

asinam ᐊᓯᓇᒼ
VTI s/he holds s.t. (*pl*) together in a bunch

asināpiy ᐊᓯᓈᐱᐩ
NI sinker on fishline

asinēw ᐊᓯᓀᐤ
VTA s/he holds s.o. (*pl*) together in a bunch (*e.g.* money)

asiniy ᐊᓯᓂᐩ
NA rock, stone

asiniy ᐊᓯᓂᐩ
NI bullet [*see also* mōswasiniy]

asinīs ᐊᓯᓃᐢ
NA stone; peach pit [*dim*]

asinīsis ᐊᓯᓃᓯᐢ
NA pebble, little rock

asinīskāwi-sākahikan ᐊᓯᓃᐢᑳᐏ ᓵᑲᐦᐃᑲᐣ
NI Smoothstone Lake, SK

asinīskāwiýiniw ᐊᓯᓃᐢᑳᐏᔨᓂᐤ
NA Woods Cree, Woods Cree person; [*pl*:] the Woods Cree ["Rock People"; *cf.* sakāwiýiniw]

asinīwaciy ᐊᓯᓃᐘᒋᐩ
NI rock hill, rock cliff; the Rocky Mountains; Rocky Boy, Montana

asinīwacīsihk ᐊᓯᓃᐘᒌᓯᕽ
IPC Rocky Boy, Montana

asinīwacīwiw ᐊᓯᓃᐘᒌᐏᐤ
VII it is a rock hill, it is a rocky mountain

asinīwan ᐊᓯᓃᐘᐣ
VII it is rocky, there are many stones

asinīwat ᐊᓯᓃᐘᐟ
NI bag for shells, bullets

asinīwāskahikan ᐊᓯᓃᐚᐢᑲᐦᐃᑲᐣ
NI stone house

asinīwēw ᐊᓯᓃᐍᐤ
VAI s/he sounds like an Assiniboine, Nakota, Stoney person; s/he speaks Assiniboine, Nakota, Stoney

asinīwi-pāwistikohk ᐊᓯᓃᐏ ᐹᐏᐢᑎᑯᕽ
INM Stoney Rapids, SK [*loc*; *Dene community*]

asinīwipaýihcikan ᐊᓯᓃᐏᐸᔨᐦᒋᑲᐣ
NA cement; something made in cement; cement-making machine

asinīwipwāt ᐊᓯᓃᐏᐺᐟ
NA Nakota, Assiniboine (Stoney) [*also* asinīpwāt(is)]

asinīwipwātināhk ᐊᓯᓃᐏᐺᑎᓈᕽ
INM Nakota country, Assiniboine country

asinīwiw ᐊᓯᓃᐏᐤ
VAI s/he is stone, it is made of stone or cement

asinīwiýākan ᐊᓯᓃᐏᔮᑲᐣ
NI stone dish, graniteware cup

asinīwospwākan ᐊᓯᓃᐓᐢᐹᑲᐣ
NA stone-pipe

asisinwak ᐊᓯᓯᓌᐠ
VAI they lie together (as pigs in a pen)

asisiy ᐊᓯᓯᐩ
NI waterweed

asiskisin ᐊᓯᐢᑭᓯᐣ
VAI s/he has an open wound (from falling); s/he has a flesh wound

asiskisiw ᐊᓯᐢᑭᓯᐤ
VAI s/he has an open wound, s/he has a flesh wound

asiskiswēw ᐊᓯᐢᑭᓷᐤ
VTA s/he wounds s.o. (by scraping)

asiskitān ᐊᓯᐢᑭᑖᐣ
NI calf of the leg [*cf.* 1: nitasiskitān "the calf of my leg"]

asiskiy ᐊᓯᐢᑭᐩ
NI soil, dirt, earth; clay; mud

asiskīhkēw ᐊᓯᐢᑮᐦᑫᐤ
VAI s/he mixes mud, s/he mixes mortar; s/he mixes clay

asiskīhkwān ᐊᓯᐢᑮᐦᒀᐣ
NI fireplace

asiskīhkwānāpisk ᐊᓯᐢᑮᐦᒀᓈᐱᐢᐠ
NI brick; grate inside of stove [*pl*: -wa]; *NA* cast-iron pail [*pl*: -wak]

asiskīnam ᐊᓯᐢᑮᓇᒼ
VTI s/he plasters s.t. with clay

asiskīnamawēw ᐊᓯᐢᑮᓇᒪᐍᐤ
VTA s/he plasters (it/him) for s.o.

asiskīnēw ᐊᓯᐢᑮᓀᐤ
VTA s/he plasters s.o. with clay

asiskīwan ᐊᓯᐢᑮᐘᐣ
VII it is dusty, it is muddy

asiskīwi-kocawānāpiskos ᐊᓯᐢᑮᐏ ᑯᒐᐚᓈᐱᐢᑯᐢ
NA mud-stove [*dim*]

asiskīwihēw ᐊᓯᐢᑮᐏᐦᐁᐤ
VTA s/he muddies s.o., s/he makes s.o. dirty

asiskīwihkwēw ᐊᓯᐢᑮᐏᐦᑵᐤ
VAI s/he has soil on his/her face, s/he has dirt on his/her face

asiskīwihtāw ᐊᓯᐢᑮᐏᐦᑖᐤ
VAIt s/he muddies s.t., s/he makes s.t. dirty

asiskīwikamikos ᐊᓯᐢᑮᐏᑲᒥᑯᐢ
NI mud shack [*dim*]

asiskīwinisow ᐊᓯᐢᑮᐏᓂᓱᐤ
VAI s/he puts clay on him/herself

asiskīwiw ᐊᓯᐢᑮᐏᐤ
VAI s/he is muddy, it is dusty; s/he is covered with clay

asiskīwiýākan ᐊᓯᐢᑮᐏᔮᑲᐣ
NI earthenware dish

asiskīwiýākanihkamawēw ᐊᓯᐢᑮᐏᔮᑲᓂᐦᑲᒪᐍᐤ
VTA s/he makes pottery for s.o.

asiskīwiýākanihkēw ᐊᓯᐢᑮᐏᔮᑲᓂᐦᑫᐤ
VAI s/he makes pottery, s/he makes earthenware dishes

asiskīwospwākan ᐊᓯᐢᑮᐓᐢᐹᑲᐣ
NA clay pipe

asitahpisow ᐊᓯᑕᐦᐱᓱᐤ
VAI s/he is tied close to s.t.

asitahpitam ᐊᓯᑕᐦᐱᑕᒼ
VTI s/he ties s.t. fast to something

asitahpitēw ᐊᓯᑕᐦᐱᑌᐤ
VTA s/he ties s.o. fast to something

asitahpitisow ᐊᓯᑕᐦᐱᑎᓱᐤ
VAI s/he ties him/herself fast to s.t.

asitakimisow ᐊᓯᑕᑭᒥᓱᐤ
VAI s/he includes him/herself, s/he counts him/herself in [*also* asitakimow]

asitinēw ᐊᓯᑎᓀᐤ
VTA s/he places s.o. with something

asiwacikan ᐊᓯᐘᒋᑲᐣ
NI pouch, pocket; purse, suitcase; storage container, receptacle; can, jar, vessel

asiwacikanis ᐊᓯᐘᒋᑲᓂᐢ
NI pouch, pocket; envelope; small vessel [*dim*]

asiwacikēw ᐊᓯᐘᒋᑫᐤ
VAI s/he places things in, inside

asiwahēw ᐊᓯᐘᐦᐁᐤ
VTA s/he puts s.o. inside (a bag or box)

asiwasow ᐊᓯᐘᓱᐤ
VAI s/he is inside, s/he is closed in, s/he is contained within

asiwatan ᐊᓯᐘᑕᐣ
VII it is inside [*cf.* asiwatēw]

asiwatāw ᐊᓯᐘᑖᐤ
VAIt s/he puts s.t. inside (a bag or box)

asiwatēw ᐊᓯᐘᑌᐤ
VII it is inside, it is closed in

askamawēw ᐊᐢᑲᒪᐍᐤ
VTA s/he lies in wait watching for s.o.

askatāw ᐊᐢᑲᑖᐤ
VAI s/he lies in wait

askatihkway ᐊᐢᑲᑎᐦᑿᐩ
NI stone bound in leather (used as a weapon)

askāhtik ᐊᐢᑳᐦᑎᐠ
NI green wood (cut from green logs) [*pl*: -wa; *also* askihtak]

askāhtikwāhtik ᐊᐢᑳᐦᑎᑳᐧᐦᑎᐠ
NA green tree; freshly peeled tree [*pl*: -wak]; *NI* freshly peeled log, stick [*pl*: -wa; *cf.* askihtak]

askāpiw ᐊᐢᑳᐱᐤ
VAI s/he has red flesh showing around his/her eyes

askāwikanēw ᐊᐢᑳᐃᐧᑲᓀᐤ
VAI s/he has raw wounds on his/her back

askēkin ᐊᐢᑫᑭᐣ
NI fresh rawhide [*pl*: -wa]

askēkinowiw ᐊᐢᑫᑭᓄᐃᐧᐤ
VII it is fresh rawhide

aski ᐊᐢᑭ
IPN raw, fresh

aski-pahkwēsikan
ᐊᐢᑭ ᐸᐦᑫᐧᓯᑭᐣ
NA flour [*see also* pahkwēsikan, sikwāwakinikan]

askihk ᐊᐢᑭᕽ
NA pail; kettle [*pl*: -wak; *cf.* 1: nitaskihkom *NDA* “my kettle, my pail”; *wC slang*: “my vagina”]

askihkohkān ᐊᐢᑭᐦᑯᐦᑳᐣ
NA train engine, steam engine; engine, motor

askihkohkānis ᐊᐢᑭᐦᑯᐦᑳᓂᐢ
NA tractor; motor [*dim*]

askihkos ᐊᐢᑭᐦᑯᐢ
NA little pail; little kettle, pot; outboard motor [*dim*; *see also* askihkohkān, pakāhcikan-askihk]

askihtak ᐊᐢᑭᐦᑕᐠ
NI green wood (cut from green logs) [*pl*: -wa; *cf.* askāhtik]

askihtako- ᐊᐢᑭᐦᑕᑯ
IPN green (blue) [*see also* sīpihko-]

askihtako-kīsowahpison
ᐊᐢᑭᐦᑕᑯ ᑮᓱᐊᐧᐦᐱᓱᐣ
NA green scarf

askihtakonākosiw
ᐊᐢᑭᐦᑕᑯᓈᑯᓯᐤ
VAI s/he looks green (blue)

askihtakonākwan ᐊᐢᑭᐦᑕᑯᓈᑲᐧᐣ
VAI it looks green (blue)

askihtakosiw ᐊᐢᑭᐦᑕᑯᓯᐤ
VAI s/he is green (blue) [*see also* sīpihkosiw]

askihtakoskāw ᐊᐢᑭᐦᑕᑯᐢᑳᐤ
VII there is much green (*e.g.* grass, forest)

askihtakwan ᐊᐢᑭᐦᑕᑲᐧᐣ
VII it is green (*e.g.* coat or blanket) [*cf.* askihtakwāw]

askihtakwasikan ᐊᐢᑭᐦᑕᑲᐧᓯᑲᐣ
NA green sock

askihtakwāpakwaniy
ᐊᐢᑭᐦᑕᑳᐧᐸᑲᐧᓂᐩ
NI blue flower

askihtakwāpakwanīw
ᐊᐢᑭᐦᑕᑳᐧᐸᑲᐧᓃᐤ
VII it has blue flowers

askihtakwāpēkan ᐊᐢᑭᐦᑕᑳᐧᐯᑲᐣ
VII it is a green (blue) string

askihtakwāw ᐊᐢᑭᐦᑕᑳᐧᐤ
VII it be green (blue) [*see also* sīpihkwāw]

askimātam ᐊᐢᑭᒫᑕᒼ
VTI s/he laces s.t., s/he knots s.t., s/he loops s.t.

askimātēw ᐊᐢᑭᒫᑌᐤ
VTA s/he laces s.o. (*e.g.* snowshoe)

askipow ᐊᐢᑭᐳᐤ
VAI s/he eats s.t. raw, s/he eats raw meat

askipwāwi ᐊᐢᑭᐹᐧᐃᐧ
NI potato, wild potato [*pl*: askipwāwa; *cf.* napatāk]

askisiw ᐊᐢᑭᓯᐤ
VAI s/he is raw, it is raw

askitin ᐊᐢᑭᑎᐣ
VII it is raw

askitiw ᐊᐢᑭᑎᐤ
VAI it is raw, it is uncooked (*e.g.* flour)

askiy ᐊᐢᑭᐩ
NI land; country, earth, world

askiya ᐊᐢᑭᔭ
NI moss; powdered wood for swaddling bag [*always pl*]

askīhk ᐊᐢᑮᕽ
INM on the land; reserve [*loc*; *cf.* askīhkān; *see also* iskonikan]

askīhkān ᐊᐢᑮᐦᑳᐣ
NI reserve [*cf.* askīhk; *see also* iskonikan]

askīhkān-akihtāsowin
ᐊᐢᑮᐦᑳᐣ ᐊᑭᐦᑖᓱᐃᐧᐣ
NI treaty number

askīhkān-atoskēwikamik
ᐊᐢᑮᐦᑳᐣ ᐊᑐᐢᑭᐃᐧᑲᒥᐠ
NI band office [*pl*: -wa; *see also* asahtowikamik]

askīwakipow ᐊᐢᑮᐊᐧᑭᐳᐤ
VAI s/he eats raw meat

askīwan ᐊᐢᑮᐊᐧᐣ
VII it is one year, it is summer; it is earth, it is land [*cf.* askīwiw *VII*]

askīwan ᐊᐢᑮᐊᐧᐣ
VII it is mossy

askīwaskamikāw ᐊᐢᑮᐊᐧᐢᑲᒥᑳᐤ
VII it is boggy, it is mossy land

askīwi-pimiy ᐊᐢᑮᐃᐧ ᐱᒥᐩ
NI coal oil, petroleum

askīwi-sīwīhtākan
ᐊᐢᑮᐃᐧ ᓰᐄᐧᐦᑖᑭᐣ
NI pepper [*see also* papēskomin, pēskōmin, wīsakat]

askīwin ᐊᐢᑮᐃᐧᐣ
NI year

askīwiw ᐊᐢᑮᐃᐧᐤ
VAI s/he has land; s/he has a farm

askīwiw ᐊᐢᑮᐃᐧᐤ
VII it is one year, it is summer; it is land, it is earth [*cf.* askīwan]

askoc ᐊᐢᑯᐨ
IPC next to [*cf.* aýaskoc, iýaskoc]

askocistikwānēhpisow
ᐊᐢᑯᒋᐢᑎᑳᐧᓀᐦᐱᓱᐤ
VAI s/he ties his/her own head in a kerchief

askonān ᐊᐢᑯᓈᐣ
NI fish trap, weir

askonēw ᐊᐢᑯᓀᐤ
VAI s/he traps fish

askoskam ᐊᐢᑯᐢᑲᒼ
VTI s/he follows s.t.

askotāskopison ᐊᐢᑯᑖᐢᑯᐱᓱᐣ
NI cradleboard

askowēhēw ᐊᐢᑯᐁᐧᐦᐁᐤ
VTA s/he follows s.o.

askowēw ᐊᐢᑯᐁᐧᐤ
VTA s/he follows s.o.

askowiskawēw ᐊᐢᑯᐃᐧᐢᑲᐁᐧᐤ
VTA s/he comes next after s.o. (in age); s/he is next to s.o., s/he follows s.o. (in birth, age, height, or position); s/he is taller than s.o. [*also* askōskawēw]

askowiskotātowak
ᐊᐢᑯᐃᐧᐢᑯᑖᑐᐊᐧᐠ
VAI they come one after the other; they stand in descending order based on height

askōtawiskāw ᐊᐢᑰᑕᐃᐧᐢᑳᐤ
VAI s/he comes empty-handed, s/he did not make a kill

askōtowak ᐊᐢᑰᑐᐊᐧᐠ
VAI they follow one another

asohikan ᐊᓱᐦᐃᑲᐣ
NI goose blind; decoy (for wild birds)

asohikanihkēw ᐊᓱᐦᐃᑲᓂᐦᑫᐤ
VAI s/he makes a blind (for hunting)

asohikēw ᐊᓱᐦᐃᑫᐤ
VAI s/he watches from a blind

asotam ᐊᓱᑕᒼ
VTI s/he promises s.t. [*cf.* asototam]

asotamawēw ᐊᓱᑕᒪᐁᐧᐤ
VTA s/he promises (it/him) to s.o.

asotamākēwin ᐊᓱᑕᒫᑫᐃᐧᐣ
NI promise, vow (that one makes)

asotamākowin ᐊᓱᑕᒫᑫᐃᐧᐣ
NI promise, vow (that is made to one)

asototam ᐊᓱᑐᑕᒼ
VTI s/he promises s.t. [*cf.* asotam]

aspacihtin ᐊᐢᐸᒋᐦᑎᐣ
VII it is a hammering noise cushioned by a layer of something

aspaham ᐊᐢᐸᐦᐊᒼ
VTI s/he places s.t. on a flat surface

aspahakēmow ᐊᐢᐸᐦᐊᑫᒧᐤ
VAI s/he asks to have someone speak on his/her behalf

aspahakēmowin ᐊᐢᐸᐦᐊᑫᒧᐃᐧᐣ
NI object given when asking a favour

aspahcikan ᐊᐢᐸᐦᒋᑲᐣ
NI relish, especially fat, with food; spread for bread; jam; peanut butter [*cf.* aspascikan]

aspahcikēw ᐊᐢᐸᐦᒋᑫᐤ
VAI s/he eats a relish with his/her food [*cf.* aspascikēw]

aspahēw ᐊᐢᐸᐦᐁᐤ
VTA s/he places s.o. on a mat

aspahikan ᐊᐢᐸᐦᐃᑲᐣ
NI place mats; desk mats

aspahpison ᐊᐢᐸᐦᐱᓱᐣ
NI wrapper around a baby in a moss bag

aspapiw ᐊᐢᐸᐱᐤ
VAI s/he sits on something (*e.g.* blanket)

aspapiwin ᐊᐢᐸᐱᐃᐧᐣ
NI saddle; chair cushion

aspascākanis ᐊᐢᐸᐢᒑᑲᓂᐢ
NI apron; small apron (for a child) [*dim*; *cf.* aspastākan]

aspascikan ᐊᐢᐸᐢᒋᑲᐣ
NI relish, especially fat, with food; spread for bread; jam; peanut butter; tablecloth [*cf.* aspahcikan; aspascikanēkin]

aspascikanēkin ᐊᐢᐸᐢᒋᑲᓀᑭᐣ
NI tablecloth [*pl*: -wa]

aspaskosāwān ᐊᐢᐸᐢᑯᓵᐋᐧᐣ
NI leaves or bark mixed with tobacco

aspastākan ᐊᐢᐸᐢᑖᑲᐣ
NI apron

aspastākanihkamawēw ᐊᐢᐸᐢᑖᑲᓂᐦᑲᒪᐁᐧᐤ
VTA s/he makes an apron for s.o.

aspastākanihkākēw ᐊᐢᐸᐢᑖᑲᓂᐦᑳᑫᐤ
VAI s/he makes an apron from something

aspastākanihkēw ᐊᐢᐸᐢᑖᑲᓂᐦᑫᐤ
VAI s/he makes aprons

aspastāw ᐊᐢᐸᐢᑖᐤ
VAIt s/he puts a mat under s.t.

aspastēpiw ᐊᐢᐸᐢᑌᐱᐤ
VAI s/he rests his/her own feet on a stool

aspatahikan ᐊᐢᐸᑕᐦᐃᑲᐣ
NI chopping block

aspatāskopison ᐊᐢᐸᑖᐢᑯᐱᓱᐣ
NI leg-rest, made of sticks strung together

aspatāskopisow ᐊᐢᐸᑖᐢᑯᐱᓱᐤ
VAI s/he ties his/her own legs onto a leg rest

aspatisin ᐊᐢᐸᑎᓯᐣ
VAI s/he lies leaning on something

aspatotēw ᐊᐢᐸᑐᑌᐤ
VTA s/he accompanies his/her request of s.o. with a gift

aspāpowēw ᐊᐢᐹᐳᐁᐧᐤ
VAI s/he uses seasoning

aspāwikanēhikan ᐊᐢᐹᐃᐧᑲᓀᐦᐃᑲᐣ
NI saddle blanket

aspāwikanēskocikēw ᐊᐢᐹᐃᐧᑲᓀᐢᑯᒋᑫᐤ
VAI s/he prepares a saddle

aspēýimēw ᐊᐢᐯᔨᒣᐤ
VTA s/he relies on s.o.

aspēýimow ᐊᐢᐯᔨᒧᐤ
VAI s/he relies; s/he relies on s.t. for support; s/he trusts, s/he places confidence

aspēýimototawēw ᐊᐢᐯᔨᒧᑐᑕᐁᐧᐤ
VTA s/he relies on s.o.

aspēýimowin ᐊᐢᐯᔨᒧᐃᐧᐣ
NI reliance, trust

aspihēw ᐊᐢᐱᐦᐁᐤ
VTA s/he treats s.o. badly; s/he gives s.o. less than their share

aspin ᐊᐢᐱᐣ
IPC away, off; ago; the last I knew; gone for good, gone for the present; since; just

aspinam ᐊᐢᐱᓇᒼ
VTI s/he holds s.t. with a pot holder; s/he uses a pot holder

aspinikan ᐊᐢᐱᓂᑲᐣ
NI pot holder

aspinikātēw ᐊᐢᐱᓂᑳᑌᐤ
VII it is held with a pot holder

aspinoyē ᐊᐢᐱᓄᔦ
IPC Happy New Year (New Year's Greeting)

aspisimēw ᐊᐢᐱᓯᒣᐤ
VTA s/he lies on s.o. (s.t. animate)

aspisimon ᐊᐢᐱᓯᒧᐣ
NI mattress

aspisimow ᐊᐢᐱᓯᒧᐤ
VAI s/he lies on something

aspisin ᐊᐢᐱᓯᐣ
VAI s/he lies on something

aspisitēsimow ᐊᐢᐱᓯᑌᓯᒧᐤ
VAI s/he puts his/her own feet on a footstool

aspisitēsimowin ᐊᐢᐱᓯᑌᓯᒧᐃᐧᐣ
NI foot stool; door mat

aspiskocikēw ᐊᐢᐱᐢᑯᒋᑫᐤ
VAI s/he makes a saddle

aspiskwēsimow ᐊᐢᐱᐢᑫᐧᓯᒧᐤ
VAI s/he lies with his/her own head on something; s/he lays his/her own face on a pillow

aspiskwēsimon ᐊᐢᐱᐢᑫᐧᓯᒧᐣ
NI pillow; afterbirth, placenta

aspiskwēsimonihkawēw ᐊᐢᐱᐢᑫᐧᓯᒧᓂᐦᑲᐁᐧᐤ
VTA s/he makes pillows for s.o.

aspiskwēsimonis ᐊᐢᐱᐢᑫᐧᓯᒧᓂᐢ
NI cushion, small pillow [*dim*]

aspiýihkāsow ᐊᐢᐱᔨᐦᑳᓱᐤ
VAI s/he is so called as a last name, surname; s/he has the same last name (as s.o.)

aspiýihkāsowin ᐊᐢᐱᔨᐦᑳᓱᐃᐧᐣ
NI surname

aspiýihkātēw ᐊᐢᐱᔨᐦᑳᑌᐤ
VTA s/he names s.o. after (s.o.)

astahcikow ᐊᐢᑕᐦᒋᑯᐤ
VAI s/he leaves s.t. here (for later retrieval); s/he makes a cache

astahcikowin ᐊᐢᑕᐦᒋᑯᐃᐧᐣ
NI cache

astamawēw ᐊᐢᑕᒪᐁᐧᐤ
VTA s/he puts (it/him) on s.o.; s/he applies (it/him) to s.o.; s/he places (it/him) for s.o., s/he bets with s.o.

astamāsow ᐊᐢᑕᒫᓱᐤ
VAI s/he puts (it/him) on him/herself; s/he places (it/him) for him/herself

astāhamawēw ᐊᐢᑖᐦᐊᒪᐁᐧᐤ
VTA s/he fears s.o. will frighten game away before it can be procured

astāhēw ᐊᐢᑖᐦᐁᐤ
VTA s/he frightens s.o.

astākanask ᐊᐢᑖᑲᓇᐢᐠ
NI reed [*pl*: -wa]

astāsiw ᐊᐢᑖᓯᐤ
VAI s/he is afraid, s/he is suspicious; s/he lives in fear; s/he expects danger

astāsiwin ᐊᐢᑖᓯᐃᐧᐣ
NI fearful apprehension

astāskamikwa ᐊᐢᑖᐢᑲᒥᑲᐧ
NI moss; roots [*pl*]

astāw ᐊᐢᑖᐤ
VAIt s/he puts s.t. there, s/he places s.t. there

astāwātam ᐊᐢᑖᐋᐧᑕᒼ
VTI s/he puts feathers on s.t. (*e.g.* an arrow)

astāwēw ᐊᐢᑖᐁᐧᐤ
VAI s/he attaches feathers

astēw ᐊᐢᑌᐤ
VII it is there, it sits there; it is placed

astinwān ᐊᐢᑎᓈᐧᐣ
NI sinew

astipahkwān ᐊᐢᑎᐸᐦᑳᐧᐣ
NI top flap of tipi [*pl*: *the flaps which control the airflow into the tipi from the top*; *cf.* akwāpahkwān]
astis ᐊᐢᑎᐢ
NA mitt, mitten; glove [*dim*: ascisis]
astis ᐊᐢᑎᐢ
NI thread made from dried sinew [*cf.* astisiy]
astisēwakwa ᐊᐢᑎᓭᐊᐧᑲᐧ
NI lengthwise muscles on back [*pl*]
astisihkawēw ᐊᐢᑎᓯᐦᑲᐁᐧᐤ
VTA s/he makes mitts for s.o.
astisihkākēw ᐊᐢᑎᓯᐦᑳᑫᐤ
VAI s/he makes mitts from something
astisihkēw ᐊᐢᑎᓯᐦᑫᐤ
VAI s/he makes mitts; s/he makes sinew thread [*in latter sense, also* astisīhkēw]
astisiy ᐊᐢᑎᓯᐩ
NI thread made from sinew [*cf.* astis *NI*]
astostohtin ᐊᐢᑐᐢᑐᐦᑎᐣ
VII it curdles; it clots
astotin ᐊᐢᑐᑎᐣ
NI hat, cap, headgear [*poss*: (-im)]
astotinihkawēw ᐊᐢᑐᑎᓂᐦᑲᐁᐧᐤ
VTA s/he makes a hat for s.o.
astotinihkēw ᐊᐢᑐᑎᓂᐦᑫᐤ
VAI s/he makes hats
aswaham ᐊᓴᐧᐦᐊᒼ
VTI s/he waits eagerly for s.t., s/he lies in wait for s.t.; s/he catches s.t. as it drips
aswahikēw ᐊᓴᐧᐦᐃᑫᐤ
VAI s/he lies in wait with a weapon; s/he is on one's guard [*cf.* aswēhikēw]
aswahwēw ᐊᓴᐧᐦᐁᐧᐤ
VTA s/he waits eagerly for s.o., s/he lies in wait to ambush s.o.
aswēhikēw ᐊᓭᐧᐦᐃᑫᐤ
VAI s/he lies in wait (to shoot) [*also* asawēhikēw; *cf.* aswahikēw]
aswēýihtam ᐊᓭᐧᔨᐦᑕᒼ
VTI s/he is careful of s.t.; s/he guards against s.t.; s/he is on his/her guard against s.t. [*also* asawēýihtam]
aswēýimēw ᐊᓭᐧᔨᒣᐤ
VTA s/he guards against s.o.; s/he is on his/her guard against s.o. [*also* asawēýimēw]
atahamāsow ᐊᑕᐦᐊᒫᓱᐤ
VAI s/he pounds (it/him) out for him/herself
atamihēw ᐊᑕᒥᐦᐁᐤ
VTA s/he makes s.o. smile; s/he pleases s.o., s/he makes s.o. glad; s/he makes s.o. grateful, indebted; s/he treats s.o. well [*used to thank s.o.*: *e.g.* kitatamihin "you please me"]
atamihow ᐊᑕᒥᐦᐅᐤ
VAI s/he does well for him/herself
atamimēw ᐊᑕᒥᒣᐤ
VTA s/he makes s.o. thankful by speech
atamiskawēw ᐊᑕᒥᐢᑲᐁᐧᐤ
VTA s/he greets s.o., s/he sends greetings to s.o.; s/he says hello to s.o.; s/he shakes hands with s.o.; s/he hugs s.o. in greeting, s/he kisses s.o. in greeting; s/he bids s.o. farewell
atamiskay ᐊᑕᒥᐢᑲᐩ
NI gristle
atamiskākēwin ᐊᑕᒥᐢᑳᑫᐃᐧᐣ
NI greeting by handshake or kiss
atamiskātowak ᐊᑕᒥᐢᑳᑐᐊᐧᐠ
VAI they greet one another
atamiskātowin ᐊᑕᒥᐢᑳᑐᐃᐧᐣ
NI greetings
atamiskotātowak ᐊᑕᒥᐢᑯᑖᑐᐊᐧᐠ
VAI they greet one another
atāhk ᐊᑖᕽ
NA star [*pl*: -wak; *cf.* acāhkos]
atāhkakohp ᐊᑖᐦᑲᑯᐦᑊ
NA Starblanket; Ahtahkakoop Reserve [*male personal name, Cree chief; Reserve name*]
atāhkowiw ᐊᑖᐦᑯᐃᐧᐤ
VAI it is a star; s/he is a star [*cf.* acāhkosiwiw]
atāmēw ᐊᑖᒣᐤ
VTA s/he buys (it/him) from s.o., s/he buys for s.o.
atāmaskosīwak ᐊᑖᒪᐢᑯᓰᐊᐧᐠ
IPC under the grass
atāmayiwinis ᐊᑖᒪᔨᐃᐧᓂᐢ
NA underwear
atāmākan ᐊᑖᒫᑲᐣ
NA buyer of furs; salesperson
atāmākonak ᐊᑖᒫᑯᓇᐠ
IPC under the snow [*wC*: atāmikonik]
atāmākonēw ᐊᑖᒥᑯᓀᐤ
VAI s/he is under the snow [*also* atāmikonēw]
atāmēýihtam ᐊᑖᒣᔨᐦᑕᒼ
VTI s/he accuses s.t., s/he suspects s.t.
atāmēýihtākosiw ᐊᑖᒣᔨᐦᑖᑯᓯᐤ
VAI s/he is suspected
atāmēýimēw ᐊᑖᒣᔨᒣᐤ
VTA s/he blames s.o. in one's thoughts, s/he accuses s.o. in one's thoughts, s/he suspects s.o. [*rdpl*: ay-atāmēýimēw]
atāmēýimowin ᐊᑖᒣᔨᒧᐃᐧᐣ
NI suspicion
atāmicāsis ᐊᑖᒥᒑᓯᐢ
NA shorts; underwear [*dim*]
atāmihk ᐊᑖᒥᕽ
IPC beneath, under; deep down
atāmihtak ᐊᑖᒥᐦᑕᐠ
IPC under the boards
atāmimēw ᐊᑖᒥᒣᐤ
VTA s/he accuses s.o.
atāmipakonak ᐊᑖᒥᐸᑯᓇᐠ
IPC under the blanket
atāmipēk ᐊᑖᒥᐯᐠ
IPC underwater [*cf.* atāmipīhk]
atāmipēk ᐊᑖᒥᐯᐠ
NI deep water [*loc*: atāmipēkohk]
atāmipēkīw-mōswa ᐊᑖᒥᐯᑮᐤ ᒨᓴᐧ
NA water moose [*pl*: -k]
atāmipēkohk ᐊᑖᒥᐯᑯᕽ
IPC in deep water
atāmipīhk ᐊᑖᒥᐲᕽ
IPC underwater [*cf.* atāmipēk]
atāmiskamikohk ᐊᑖᒥᐢᑲᒥᑯᕽ
IPC deep down in the ground
atāmitowak ᐊᑖᒥᑐᐊᐧᐠ
VAI they trade (it/him) with one another, they barter (it/him) with one another; they buy (it/him) from one another
atāmiyawa ᐊᑖᒥᔭᐊᐧ
NI inside of the body, the insides; entrails, internal organs (of an animal) [*pl*]
atāmohtak ᐊᑖᒧᐦᑕᐠ
IPC under the canoe
atāwākan ᐊᑖᐋᐧᑲᐣ
NI fur, pelt; exchange
atāwākēw ᐊᑖᐋᐧᑫᐤ
VAI s/he sells (things)
atāwēkamik ᐊᑖᐁᐧᑲᒥᐠ
NI store, tradinghouse [*pl*: -wa]
atāwēsinahikan ᐊᑖᐁᐧᓯᓇᐦᐃᑲᐣ
NI account book
atāwēstamawēw ᐊᑖᐁᐧᐢᑕᒪᐁᐧᐤ
VTA s/he buys (it/him) for s.o.
atāwēstamākēw ᐊᑖᐁᐧᐢᑕᒫᑫᐤ
VAI s/he buys (it/him) for people, s/he is a middle-man
atāwēstamāsow ᐊᑖᐁᐧᐢᑕᒫᓱᐤ
VAI s/he buys (it/him) for him/herself
atāwēw ᐊᑖᐁᐧᐤ
VAI s/he buys, s/he trades; s/he buys s.t., s/he trades s.t.
atāwēwikamik ᐊᑖᐁᐧᐃᐧᑲᒥᐠ
NI store, trading-post [*pl*: -wa]
atāwēwikamikohkātam ᐊᑖᐁᐧᐃᐧᑲᒥᑯᐦᑳᑕᒼ
VTI s/he makes it to a store

atāwēwikamikohkēw ᐊᑖᐍᐏᑲᒥᑯᐦᑫᐤ
VAI s/he builds a store

atāwēwikamikowiýiniw ᐊᑖᐍᐏᑲᒥᑯᐏᔨᓂᐤ
NA storekeeper [*cf.* atāwēwiýiniw]

atāwēwin ᐊᑖᐍᐏᐣ
NI purchase; buying; [*pl*:] groceries; supplies

atāwēwiýiniw ᐊᑖᐍᐏᔨᓂᐤ
NA storekeeper [*cf.* atāwēwikamikowiýiniw]

ati ᐊᑎ
IPC progressively [*most common as a preverb*; *cf.* ati *IPV*]

ati- ᐊᑎ
IPV begin to, beginning; progressively, proceed to, going on, progressing; on the way [*cf.* ati *IPC*]

ati-itohtēw ᐊᑎ ᐃᑐᐦᑌᐤ
VAI s/he begins going along [*also* at-ītohtēw]

ati-mēstitēw ᐊᑎ ᒣᐢᑎᑌᐤ
VII it is boiling away, it is boiling low, it is starting to evaporate

ati-miyw-āyāw ᐊᑎ ᒥᔼᔮᐤ
VAI s/he improves (in health)

ati-nātam ᐊᑎ ᓈᑕᒼ
IPC before the hour [*cf.* nātam]

ati-otākosin ᐊᑎ ᐅᑖᑯᓯᐣ
VII it is early evening, it is approaching evening

atihk ᐊᑎᕽ
NA caribou; goat [*pl*: -wak; *see also* māyacihkos]

atihkamēk ᐊᑎᐦᑲᒣᐠ
NA whitefish [*pl*: -wak]

atihkamēkoskāw ᐊᑎᐦᑲᒣᑯᐢᑳᐤ
VII there are many whitefish, whitefish are numerous [*sg only*]

atihkowayān ᐊᑎᐦᑯᐘᔮᐣ
NA caribou hide

atihkowiyās ᐊᑎᐦᑯᐏᔮᐢ
NI caribou meat; venison

atihkwapēmak ᐊᑎᐦᑿᐯᒪᐠ
NA birch or deer willow [*pl*: -wa]

atihkwasiniy ᐊᑎᐦᑿᓯᓂᐩ
NA hockey stone; caribou testicle

atihtēminiskāw ᐊᑎᐦᑌᒥᓂᐢᑳᐤ
VII there are many ripe berries; it is the time when berries are ripe

atihtēw ᐊᑎᐦᑌᐤ
VII it is ripe, it is coloured; it runs (as in colour)

atim ᐊᑎᒼ
NA dog; horse; beast of burden

atimapiw ᐊᑎᒪᐱᐤ
VAI s/he sits with his/her back towards others; s/he sits facing away from speaker

atimāpamēw ᐊᑎᒫᐸᒣᐤ
VTA s/he sees s.o. going away

atimēw ᐊᑎᒣᐤ
VTA s/he catches up to s.o., s/he overtakes s.o.

atimi- ᐊᑎᒥ
IPV going away from speaker, towards addressee

atimihāw ᐊᑎᒥᐦᐋᐤ
VAI s/he flies away (in the direction of the addressee); s/he flies onward

atimikāpawiw ᐊᑎᒥᑳᐸᐏᐤ
VAI s/he stands facing away from speaker

atimipahtāw ᐊᑎᒥᐸᐦᑖᐤ
VAI s/he runs away; s/he runs in the addressee's direction; s/he runs on ahead away from speaker

atimipaýiw ᐊᑎᒥᐸᔨᐤ
VAI s/he runs on ahead, s/he drives on ahead

atimisin ᐊᑎᒥᓯᐣ
VAI s/he lies facing away from speaker; s/he lies with one's back towards others

atimiskanawēw ᐊᑎᒥᐢᑲᓇᐍᐤ
VAI s/he leaves tracks away

atimitiýēsin ᐊᑎᒥᑎᔦᓯᐣ
VAI s/he lies with his/her buttocks facing away from speaker (and towards addressee)

atimo-kisēýiniw ᐊᑎᒧ ᑭᓭᔨᓂᐤ
NA dog of an old man [*used as a curse*; *also voc*]

atimo-mīciwin ᐊᑎᒧ ᒦᒋᐏᐣ
NI dog food

atimohtēw ᐊᑎᒧᐦᑌᐤ
VAI s/he walks away, s/he walks away from speaker

atimosita ᐊᑎᒧᓯᑕ
NI cactus, prickly-pear cactus [*pl*; *lit*: "dog-feet"]

atimositēmina ᐊᑎᒧᓯᑌᒥᓇ
NI "dogfoot" berries; fruit of the prickly-pear cactus

atimospikay ᐊᑎᒧᐢᐱᑲᐩ
NA Dogrib (Athapaskan) Indian

atimotāpānāsk ᐊᑎᒧᑖᐹᓈᐢᐠ
NA dog-sled [*pl*: -wak]

atimotāpānēyāpiya ᐊᑎᒧᑖᐹᓀᔮᐱᔭ
NI dog harness [*pl*]

atimwastim ᐊᑎᒷᐢᑎᒼ
NA dog of a dog [*pl*: -wak]

atimwēwitam ᐊᑎᒵᐏᑕᒼ
VTI s/he noises s.t. going away from speaker (and in direction of addressee)

atisam ᐊᑎᓴᒼ
VTI s/he tans s.t., s/he dyes s.t.

atisikan ᐊᑎᓯᑲᐣ
NI dye, trade-dye

atisikēmakan ᐊᑎᓯᑫᒪᑲᐣ
VII it is a dying-agent, it yields a dye

atisikēw ᐊᑎᓯᑫᐤ
VAI s/he dyes things

atisonākosiw ᐊᑎᓱᓈᑯᓯᐤ
VAI s/he looks tan, s/he appears tan; s/he looks brown, s/he appears brown

atisonākwan ᐊᑎᓱᓈᑿᐣ
VII it looks tan, it appears tan; it looks brown, it appears brown

atisow ᐊᑎᓱᐤ
VAI s/he is tan, s/he is brown; s/he is dyed; s/he is ripe

atiswēw ᐊᑎᓷᐤ
VTA s/he tans s.o., s/he dyes s.o. (*e.g.* porcupine-quills)

atohow ᐊᑐᐦᐅᐤ
VAI s/he chokes, s/he chokes on food or liquid

atos ᐊᑐᐢ
NA arrow [*dim*: acos, acosis; *also* 2-3 *IMP VTA*: "ask him/her to do s.t.", *cf.* atotēw]

atoskahākan ᐊᑐᐢᑲᐦᐋᑲᐣ
NA employee, hired man

atoskahēw ᐊᑐᐢᑲᐦᐁᐤ
VTA s/he puts s.o. to work, s/he makes s.o. work; s/he employs s.o., s/he hires s.o.

atoskawēw ᐊᑐᐢᑲᐍᐤ
VTA s/he works for s.o., s/he is employed by s.o. [*rdpl*: ay-acoskawēw [*dim*]]

atoskākowin ᐊᑐᐢᑳᑯᐏᐣ
NI work done for one

atoskāsow ᐊᑐᐢᑳᓱᐤ
VAI s/he works for him/herself

atoskātam ᐊᑐᐢᑳᑕᒼ
VTI s/he works at or on s.t.

atoskātēw ᐊᑐᐢᑳᑌᐤ
VTA s/he works at or on s.o.

atoskēhākan ᐊᑐᐢᑫᐦᐋᑲᐣ
NA nursing aide, orderly [*cf.* atoskēýākan]

atoskēmakan ᐊᑐᐢᑫᒪᑲᐣ
VII it works, it functions

atoskēmow ᐊᑐᐢᑫᒧᐤ
VAI s/he employs people (*e.g.* for magic/medicine); s/he gets people to do things, s/he hires people; s/he asks to have s.t. repaired

atoskēstamawēw ᐊᑐᐢᑫᐢᑕᒪᐍᐤ
VTA s/he works for or in place of s.o.; s/he does s.o.'s work for him/her

atoskēstawēw ᐊᑐᐢᑫᐢᑕᐍᐤ
VTA s/he works in s.o.'s place; s/he works for s.o. (as part of a group)

atoskēstākēw ⊲⊃ˢ⁹ˢĊ⁹°
  VAI s/he gives personal help
atoskēw ⊲⊃ˢ⁹°
  VAI s/he works
atoskēwi-kīsikāw
  ⊲⊃ˢ⁹∆· ᐲᒼᑊᐤ
  VII it is Monday ["work-day"; *see also* pēyako-kīsikāw]
atoskēwin ⊲⊃ˢ⁹∆⁻ᐧ
  NI work, labour, employment
atoskēwinihkēw ⊲⊃ˢ⁹∆·ᓂᒻ⁹°
  VAI s/he makes work (for someone)
atoskēwitās ⊲⊃ˢ⁹∆·Ċˢ
  NA overalls; work pants
atoskēyākan ⊲⊃ˢ⁹ᑫᑊᑭ
  NA servant, workman [*cf.* atoskēhākan]
atoskēyākaniskwēw
  ⊲⊃ˢ⁹ᑫᑊᑭᓭˢ⁹·°
  NA female servant
atotēw ⊲⊃∪°
  VTA s/he makes a request of s.o., s/he asks s.o. to do something; s/he engages s.o. for something, s/he employs s.o.; s/he commands s.o.
atotiskawēw ⊲⊃ᑊᑭᐁ·°
  VTA s/he hinders s.o., s/he keeps s.o. back
atōspiy ⊲ᔆᐱᐧ
  NA older tree; orange-coloured willow
atōspow ⊲ᔆ⊃°
  VAI s/he eats off of something
atōspowinānāhtik
  ⊲ᔆᐳ∆·ᓯᓬᐦᐣ
  NI table [*pl*: -wa; *see also* mīcisowināhtik]
aw ⊲°
  IPC all right, fine, let's go [*cf.* haw, hāw]
aw māka ⊲° ᒣᑲ
  IPH all right, let's go [*cf.* hāw māka]
awa ⊲⊲·
  PR this [*anim prox sg*; *demonstrative*]
awacipitēw ⊲⊲ᑺᐱ∪°
  VTA s/he pulls s.o. away (with one)
awahē! ⊲⊲·ᐦᐁ
  IPC be careful! take care! [*sg*; *pl*: awahēk!]
awahkākan ⊲⊲·ᐦᑳᑲ
  NA slave [*cf.* awahkān]
awahkān ⊲⊲·ᐦᑳᐣ
  NA slave [*dim*: awahkānis; *cf.* awahkākan]
awahkēw ⊲⊲·ᐦ⁹°
  VAI s/he has a slave
awas ⊲⊲·ᐣ
  IPC go on; go away; get out of my way [*sg*; *pl*: awasitik]

awasāpisk ⊲⊲·ᓯᐱᐢ
  IPC beyond the rocks; beyond the Rocky Mountains; British Columbia
awasāyihk ⊲⊲·ᓯᐩ
  IPC beyond the place, beyond the bush
awascahēs ⊲⊲·ᑊᒡ
  IPC a little further
awasēwēkamik ⊲⊲·ᐦ∇·ᑲᒡ
  IPC at the other side of the house
awasēwēmakan ⊲⊲·ᐦ∇·ᒪᑲᐣ
  VII it goes round a bend; it goes behind an obstacle to vision, it goes out of sight
awasēwēpahtāw ⊲⊲·ᐦ∇·ᐸᐦᐟ°
  VAI s/he runs round behind an obstacle to vision, s/he runs out of sight
awasēwēpayihow
  ⊲⊲·ᐦᒡ·ᐸᔨᐦᐅ
  VAI s/he throws him/herself to the other side of an obstacle, out of sight
awasēwēskam ⊲⊲·ᐦᒡ·ᐢᑲᐨ
  VTI s/he goes around s.t. by canoe
awasēwēw ⊲⊲·ᐦᒡ·°
  VAI s/he goes behind an obstacle to vision, out of sight; the sun sets
awasi- ⊲⊲·ᐩ
  IPP before; beyond, after; off
awasi ispī ⊲⊲·ᐩ ∆ᐢᐱ
  IPH the time before [*also* awasīspī]
awasi-nīpinohk ⊲⊲·ᐩ ᓀᐱᓄᐠ
  IPC the summer before last
awasi-otākosīhk ⊲⊲·ᐩ ᐅᒐᑯᓯᐠ
  IPC day before yesterday [*cf.* awasitākosīhk]
awasi-piponohk ⊲⊲·ᐩ ᐱᐳᓄᐠ
  IPC the winter before last
awasi-tipahaskān
  ⊲⊲·ᐩ ᑎᐸᐦᐊᐢᑳᐣ
  IPC United States ["beyond the border"; *cf.* akāmi-tipahaskān; *see also* kihci-mōhkomānināhk]
awasi-tipiskāki ⊲⊲·ᐩ ᑎᐱᐢᑳᑭ
  IPC the night after next
awasi-tipiskohk ⊲⊲·ᐩ ᑎᐱᐢᑯᐠ
  IPC the night before last
awasi-wāpahki ⊲⊲·ᐩ ᐧᐋᐸᐦᑭ
  IPC the day after tomorrow
awasimē ⊲⊲·ᐩᒷ
  IPC further, beyond; more
awasita ⊲⊲·ᐩᑕ
  IPC go on; go away; on, to the further side (in time or space); further on, beyond, more
awasitākosīhk ⊲⊲·ᐩᒐᑯᓯᐟ
  IPC day before yesterday [*cf.* awasi-otākosīhk]

awasitē ⊲⊲·ᐩᐁ
  IPC go on; go away; on, to the further side (in time or space); beyond, further over there
awasitēw ⊲⊲·ᐩᐁ°
  VII it is beyond
awasow ⊲⊲·ᐩ°
  VAI s/he warms up, s/he warms him/herself
awasowi-kotawānāpisk
  ⊲⊲·ᐩ∆· ᐠᑕ⊲·ᓯᐱᐢ
  NA warming-stove, heater [*pl*: -wak; *also NI*, *pl*: -wa; *dim*: awasowi-kocawānāpiskos]
awasowin ⊲⊲·ᐩ∆ᐧ
  NI the act of warming oneself
awaswākan ⊲⊲·ᐩᑲᐧ
  NI heater [*perhaps also NA*]
awāsis ⊲⊲·ᐩ
  NA child [*cf.* nicawāsimis, nitawāsimis *NDA*]
awāsicāpānāskos
  ⊲⊲·ᐩᒑᓫᓭᐣᐟ
  NA baby stroller [*dim*]
awāsisihkāsow ⊲⊲·ᐩᔑᐦᑳᓲ°
  VAI s/he pretends to be a child; s/he is clinging like a child, s/he is needy like a child
awāsisisōniyās ⊲⊲·ᐩᔑᓲᓂᔮᐢ
  IPC family allowance [*lit*: "child-money"]
awāsisiwēw ⊲⊲·ᐩᔑᐁ·°
  VAI s/he speaks like a child
awāsisīhkān ⊲⊲·ᐩᔑᐦᑳᐣ
  NA doll [*dim*: awāsisīhkānis; *see also* aýisiýinīhkān]
awāsisiwiw ⊲⊲·ᐩᔑᐃ·°
  VAI s/he is a child
awāsisiwiwin ⊲⊲·ᐩᔑᐃ·∆·ᐧ
  NI being a child, childhood
awēkā ⊲ᐁ·ᑲ
  IPC or else, if you prefer
awēkā cī ⊲ᐁ·ᑲ ᒌ
  IPH or else [*also* awikācī]
awēna ⊲ᐁ·ᓇ
  PR who [*anim prox sg*; *sC*; *cf.* awina]
awēska ⊲ᐁ·ᐢᑲ
  IPC there, by surprise
awēýiwa ⊲ᐁ·ᔨᐧ
  IPC who [*anim obv*; *wC*: awīthiwa; *cf.* awiniwa]
awihēw ⊲∆·ᐦᐁ°
  VTA s/he lends (it/him) to s.o.; s/he rents (it/him) out to s.o., s/he loans (it/him) to s.o.
awihitowak ⊲∆·ᐦᐃᐟ⊲·ᐢ
  VAI they lend to one another
awihitowin ⊲∆·ᐦᐃᐟ∆·ᐧ
  NI lease
awihiwēw ⊲∆·ᐦᐃᐁ·°
  VAI s/he lends (it/him) to people; s/he rents (it/him) out to people

awihiwēwin ⊲⊃·ᐦᐃᐧ∇·ᐃ·ᐧᐤ
NI lending

awiya ⊲ᐃ·ᐧ
PR someone [anim obv; indefinite]

awiyak ⊲ᐃ·ᐧᔭᐠ
PR someone, somebody [anim prox sg and pl]; [in negative clause:] anyone, anybody [indefinite]

awiyā! ⊲ᐃ·ᐧ
IPC ouch! [exclamation]

awīna ⊲ᐃ·ᐡ
PR who, whose [anim prox sg; interrogative]

awīna ētikwē ⊲ᐃ·ᐡ ∇ᑎᖏ·
IPH I don't know who; I wonder who

awīnihi ⊲ᐃ·ᓂᐦᐃ
PR who, whose [anim obv / inan pl; cf. awiniwa]

awīniki ⊲ᐃ·ᓂᐠ
PR who, whose [anim prox pl]

awīnipan ⊲ᐃ·ᓂᐸᐣ
PR nobody; gone, be gone, someone not here any more; I wonder what's become of him/her

awīniwa ⊲ᐃ·ᓂᐧ·
PR who, whose [anim obv; cf. awinihi]

awīta ⊲ᐃ·ᐨ
IPC here it is, here s/he is [anim prox sg]

awītē ⊲ᐃ·ᐁ
IPC so here you are! here s/he is over here [anim prox sg]

ay ⊲ᐩ
IPC hey! [exclamation]

ay ⊲ᐩ
IPC thanks [exclamation]

ay-apini-kēskēw ⊲ᐩ ⊲ᐱᓂ ᖏᐢᖃᐤ
VAI s/he is hyperactive, s/he is unable to sit still [rdpl; cf. apini-kēskēw]

ay-apisāsin ⊲ᐩ ⊲ᐱᓵᓯᐣ
VII it is small [rdpl]

ay-apisīskīsikos ⊲ᐩ ⊲ᐱᓰᐢᑮᓯᑯᐢ
NA bear [dim; rdpl; lit: "little eyes"]

ay-apiw ⊲ᐩ ⊲ᐱᐤ
VAI s/he sits, s/he is seated; s/he is at home, s/he stays at home [rdpl; cf. apiw]

ay-ay ⊲ᐩ ⊲ᐩ
IPC thank you [cf. ay-hay, hay-hay]

ay-āhci ⊲ᐩ ⊲ᐦᐨ
IPC from one to another [rdpl]

ay-āpihtaw ⊲ᐩ ⊲ᐱᐦᐟᐊᐤ
IPC half-and-half [rdpl]

ay-āpihtawakām ⊲ᐩ ⊲ᐱᐦᐟᐊᐧᑳᐠ
IPC halfway across the water [rdpl]

ay-āskawi ⊲ᐩ ⊲ᐢᑲᐧ·
IPC from time to time, a few at a time [rdpl]

ay-hay ⊲ᐩ ᐦᐊᐩ
IPC thank you [cf. ay-ay, hay-hay]

ay-itāpiw ⊲ᐩ ⊲ᐧᑖᐱᐤ
VAI s/he looks around [rdpl]

ay-itēw ⊲ᐩ ⊲ᐅᐤ
VTA s/he says so to s.o, s/he says so of s.o. [rdpl; cf. itēw]

ay-itinamawēw ⊲ᐩ ⊲ᑎᓇᒪᐧ·ᐤ
VTA s/he makes signs to s.o.; s/he holds (it/him) in a certain way for s.o. [rdpl]

ay-itisinam ⊲ᐩ ⊲ᑎᓯᓇᒼ
VTI s/he holds s.t. thither or thus [rdpl]

ay-itiskēw ⊲ᐩ ⊲ᑎᐢᑫᐤ
VAI s/he steps thither or thus [rdpl]

ay-itwēw ⊲ᐩ ⊲ᐅᐧ·ᐤ
VAI s/he speaks so [rdpl]

aya ⊲ᐧ
IPC ah, well, hmm [hesitation; cf. ayahk, ayi IPC]

aya ⊲ᐧ
NA one, person [pl: ayak; generally only in compounds]

aya ⊲ᐧ
PR the one [anim prox sg / anim obv / inan pl; weak demonstrative, generally only in compounds]

ayaham ⊲ᐧᐦ⊲ᒼ
VTI s/he covers s.t. with earth; s/he hoes s.t., s/he hills s.t.

ayahcaskosiya ⊲ᐧᐦᐸᐢᑯᐢᔭ
NI other people's hay [pl]

ayahcisīhēw ⊲ᐧᐦᐸᓯᐦᐧ·ᐤ
VTA s/he alters s.o. (e.g. pants) [rdpl]

ayahcisīhtāw ⊲ᐧᐦᐸᓯᐦᑖᐤ
VAIt s/he alters s.t., s/he remodels s.t. [rdpl]

ayahciýiniw ⊲ᐧᐦᐸᔨᓂᐤ
NA Blackfoot; Slavey; enemy; stranger

ayahciýinimow ⊲ᐧᐦᐸᔨᓂᒧᐤ
VAI s/he speaks Blackfoot; s/he speaks a strange language

ayahciýinimowin ⊲ᐧᐦᐸᔨᓂᒧᒍᐃᐧᐣ
NI Blackfoot language; a strange language

ayahciýinīnāhk ⊲ᐧᐦᐸᔨᓃᓈᕽ
IPC in the Blackfoot country, in enemy territory

ayahciýiniwikimāw ⊲ᐧᐦᐸᔨᓂᒍᐃ·ᑭᒫᐤ
NA Blackfoot chief, enemy chief

ayahikākan ⊲ᐧᐦᐃᑳᑲᐣ
NI hoe, hiller, tool for covering potatoes with earth [cf. aýayihikan]

aýahikātēw ⊲ᐧᐦᐃᑳᑌᐤ
VII it is hilled, it is covered with earth; it is hoed (e.g. a garden)

aýahikēstamawēw ⊲ᐧᐦᐃᑫᐢᑕᒪᐧ·ᐤ
VTA s/he hoes (it/him) for s.o.

aýahikēw ⊲ᐧᐦᐃᑫᐤ
VAI s/he hoes things, s/he covers things with earth, s/he hill things

ayahk ⊲ᐧᐠ
IPC ah, well [hesitation; cf. aya IPC, ayi IPC]

ayahpipaýiw ⊲ᐧᐦᐱᐸᔩᐤ
VAI s/he staggers about

ayahtēýimēw ⊲ᐧᐦᐅᔨᒣᐤ
VTA s/he envies s.o.; s/he resents s.o.

ayahwēw ⊲ᐧᐦᐧ·ᐤ
VTA s/he hoes s.o.; s/he covers s.o. with earth

ayak ⊲ᐧᐠ
PR the ones [anim prox pl; weak demonstrative, generally only in compounds]

aýakaskāpiskāw ⊲ᐧᑲᐢᑳᐱᐢᑳᐤ
VII it is wide (metal)

aýakaskāpiskisiw ⊲ᐧᑲᐢᑳᐱᐢᑭᓯᐤ
VAI it is wide (metal)

aýakaskāw ⊲ᐧᑲᐢᑳᐤ
VII it is wide

aýakaskēkan ⊲ᐧᑲᐢᑫᑲᐣ
VII it is wide (cloth)

aýakaskēkin ⊲ᐧᑲᐢᑫᑭᐣ
NI wide material, wide cloth [pl: -wa]

aýakaskēyāpiy ⊲ᐧᑲᐢᑫᔮᐱᐩ
NI a wide strap

aýakaski-mēskanaw ⊲ᐧᑲᐢᑭ ᒣᐢᑲᓇᐤ
NI wide road, highway

aýakaskicihcān ⊲ᐧᑲᐢᑭᒋᐦᒑᐣ
NI palm of the hand

aýakaskicihcēw ⊲ᐧᑲᐢᑭᒋᐦᒐᐤ
VAI s/he has broad hands

aýakaskihkwēw ⊲ᐧᑲᐢᑭᐦᒁ·ᐤ
VAI s/he has a broad face; s/he has a wide pail

aýakaskihtāw ⊲ᐧᑲᐢᑭᐦᑖᐤ
VAIt s/he widens s.t.

aýakaskikotēw ⊲ᐧᑲᐢᑭᑯᑌᐤ
VAI s/he has a broad nose; it has a broad beak

aýakaskisitēw ⊲ᐧᑲᐢᑭᓯᑌᐤ
VAI s/he has broad feet

aýakaskisiw ⊲ᐧᑲᐢᑭᓯᐤ
VAI s/he is broad, s/he is wide

ayamākan ⊲ᐧᒫᑲᐣ
NI telephone, phone

ayamihāhkasow ⊲ᐧᒥᐦᐋᐦᑲᓱᐤ
VAI s/he pretends to pray

ayamihāhtahēw ⊲ᐧᒥᐦᐋᐦᑕᐦᐧ·ᐤ
VTA s/he makes s.o. go to church, s/he takes s.o. to mass

ayamihāw ᐊᔭᒥᐦᐋᐤ
VAI s/he prays; s/he hold a church service, s/he attends mass [*in latter sense, often in unspecified actor form*: ayamihāniwan "there is prayer, mass is held"]

ayamihāwi-kīsikāw ᐊᔭᒥᐦᐋᐏ ᑮᓯᑳᐤ
VII it is Sunday [*cf.* ayamihēwi-kīsikāw]

ayamihāwin ᐊᔭᒥᐦᐋᐏᐣ
NI prayer; praying, saying prayers; church service, religious observance; religion; the Roman Catholic church

ayamihcikēw ᐊᔭᒥᐦᒋᑫᐤ
VAI s/he reads

ayamihcikēwikamik ᐊᔭᒥᐦᒋᑫᐏᑲᒥᐠ
NI reading room; library [*pl*: -wa]

ayamihcikēwin ᐊᔭᒥᐦᒋᑫᐏᐣ
NI reading; [*Christian*:] bible verse

ayamihēmina ᐊᔭᒥᐦᐁᒥᓇ
NI rosary beads, rosaries

ayamihēstamawēw ᐊᔭᒥᐦᐁᐢᑕᒪᐌᐤ
VTA s/he prays for s.o., s/he says prayers for s.o.

ayamihēstamākēw ᐊᔭᒥᐦᐁᐢᑕᒫᑫᐤ
VAI s/he prays for all

ayamihēstamākēwin ᐊᔭᒥᐦᐁᐢᑕᒫᑫᐏᐣ
NI prayer offered by a group

ayamihēstawēw ᐊᔭᒥᐦᐁᐢᑕᐌᐤ
VTA s/he prays to s.o.

ayamihēw ᐊᔭᒥᐦᐁᐤ
VTA s/he talks to s.o. [*more commonly wC and sC; see also* pīkiskwātēw]

ayamihēwasinahikan ᐊᔭᒥᐦᐁᐘᓯᓇᐦᐃᑲᐣ
NI prayer book

ayamihēwāhtik ᐊᔭᒥᐦᐁᐚᐦᑎᐠ
NA cross; crucifix (of wood) [*pl*; -wak]

ayamihēwātisiw ᐊᔭᒥᐦᐁᐚᑎᓯᐤ
VAI s/he lives a Christian life, s/he is of religious disposition

ayamihēwātisiw ᐊᔭᒥᐦᐁᐚᑎᓯᐤ
NA Christian

ayamihēwi- ᐊᔭᒥᐦᐁᐏ
IPV of the Christian religion, of church

ayamihēwi-kīsikāw ᐊᔭᒥᐦᐁᐏ ᑮᓯᑳᐤ
NI Sunday

ayamihēwi-kīsikāw ᐊᔭᒥᐦᐁᐏ ᑮᓯᑳᐤ
VII it is Sunday [*cf.* ayamihāwi-kīsikāw]

ayamihēwi-nikamowin ᐊᔭᒥᐦᐁᐏ ᓂᑲᒧᐏᐣ
NI hymn

ayamihēwi-saskamon ᐊᔭᒥᐦᐁᐏ ᓴᐢᑲᒧᐣ
NI the host; Holy Communion

ayamihēwikamik ᐊᔭᒥᐦᐁᐏᑲᒥᐠ
NI church, church building [*pl*: -wa]

ayamihēwikimāw ᐊᔭᒥᐦᐁᐏᑭᒫᐤ
NA minister, preacher, priest, missionary [*see also* ayamihēwiýiniw]

ayamihēwisīhtwāwin ᐊᔭᒥᐦᐁᐏᓰᐦ� ᐀
NI Christian living

ayamihēwiskwēw ᐊᔭᒥᐦᐁᐏᐢᑵᐤ
NA nun

ayamihēwiýiniw ᐊᔭᒥᐦᐁᐏᔨᓂᐤ
NA priest, minister, preacher, missionary [*also* ayamihēwīnaw; *see also* ayamihēwikimāw]

ayamihitowak ᐊᔭᒥᐦᐃᑐᐘᐠ
VAI they speak to one another [*more commonly wC and sC; see also* pīkiskwātitowak]

ayamihkwāmiw ᐊᔭᒥᐦᒁᒥᐤ
VAI s/he talks in his/her sleep

ayamihtāw ᐊᔭᒥᐦᑖᐤ
VAIt s/he reads s.t.

ayamihtōtam ᐊᔭᒥᐦᑑᑕᒼ
VTI s/he argues about s.t.

ayamiw ᐊᔭᒥᐤ
VAI s/he talks [*more commonly wC and sC; see also* pīkiskwēw]

ayamiwin ᐊᔭᒥᐏᐣ
NI speech, word [*more commonly wC and sC; cf.* pīkiskwēwin, itwēwin]

aýapacāwahkāw ᐊᔭᐸᒑᐘᐦᑳᐤ
VII it is a hilly place

aýapacinās ᐊᔭᐸᒋᓈᐢ
NI small hill; rolling hill country [*dim*]

aýapihtakāw ᐊᔭᐱᐦᑕᑳᐤ
VII it is a net-like structure of boards [*also* ahýapihtakāw; *wC*: athapihtakāw]

aýapinam ᐊᔭᐱᓇᒼ
VTI s/he turns s.t. upside down

aýapinēw ᐊᔭᐱᓀᐤ
VTA s/he turns s.o. upside down

aýapinikēw ᐊᔭᐱᓂᑫᐤ
VAI s/he turns everything upside down; s/he is always disturbing things

aýapiy ᐊᔭᐱᐩ
NA net [*also* ahýapiy; *wC*: athapiy]

aýapīhkākēw ᐊᔭᐲᐦᑳᑫᐤ
VAI s/he makes a net out of s.t.

aýapīhkēw ᐊᔭᐲᐦᑫᐤ
VAI s/he makes nets

aýapīhkēsiw ᐊᔭᐲᐦᑫᓯᐤ
NA large spider

aýapīhkēsiw ᐊᔭᐲᐦᑫᓯᐤ
VAI s/he crochets, s/he knits a little [*dim*]

aýapīhkēsīs ᐊᔭᐲᐦᑫᓰᐢ
NA small spider [*dim; see also* apihkēs]

aýapīhkēsīskāw ᐊᔭᐲᐦᑫᓰᐢᑳᐤ
VII there are many spiders, spiders are numerous [*sg only*]

aýapīhkwēpicikan ᐊᔭᐲᐦᑵᐱᒋᑲᐣ
NI halter (for a horse)

aýapīs ᐊᔭᐲᐢ
NA small net [*dim; cf.* aýapiy]

aýapīwasapāp ᐊᔭᐲᐘᓴᐹᑊ
NA net twine

ayasāwāc ᐅᔭᓵᐚᐨ
IPC in contradiction, perversely [*cf.* asāwāc]

ayaskāpiw ᐊᔭᐢᑳᐱᐤ
VAI s/he have red flesh showing around one's eyes

ayaskīmow ᐊᔭᐢᑮᒧᐤ
NA Eskimo

aýaskoc ᐊᔭᐢᑯᐨ
IPC at the end; one after another [*cf.* askoc, iýaskoc]

aýayihikan ᐊᔭᔨᐦᐃᑲᐣ
NI hoe [*cf.* ayahikākan]

ayācihtāw ᐊᔮᒋᐦᑖᐤ
VAIt s/he alters s.t.

ayācimēsitēw ᐊᔮᒋᒣᓯᑌᐤ
VAI s/he has splay feet, s/he is splay-footed

aýāhkwacāwahkāsin ᐊᔮᐦᑲᒑᐘᐦᑳᓯᐣ
VII it is a small ravine [*dim*]

aýāhkwacāwahkāw ᐊᔮᐦᑲᒑᐘᐦᑳᐤ
VII it is a ravine

aýākonēw ᐊᔮᑯᓀᐤ
VAI s/he is drifted over (by snow)

aýākonēw ᐊᔮᑯᓀᐤ
VII it is drifted over (by snow)

aýākonēham ᐊᔮᑯᓀᐦᐊᒼ
VTI s/he covers s.t. with snow

aýākonēhwēw ᐊᔮᑯᓀᐦᐌᐤ
VTA s/he covers s.o. with snow

ayākwāmisiw ᐊᔮᒁᒥᓯᐤ
VAI s/he is careful [*cf.* yākwāmisiw]

ayānikamik ᐊᔮᓂᑲᒥᐠ
NI clothes closet [*pl*: -wa; *see also* ayiwinis-akocikan]

ayānisa ᐊᔮᓂᓴ
NI clothes; rags, pieces of cloth; [*pl*; *sg*: "article of clothing"; *dim, also* ayānisis]

ayāniwat ⊲ᐅᔪ⊲·ᐟ
NI rag bag

ayāniwiw ⊲ᐅᔪᐃ·ᐤ
VII it is a possession

ayāsahpitam ⊲ᐅᔅᣲᐱᑕᐨ
VTI s/he ties s.t. in a bundle

ayāsēkinam ⊲ᐅᖬᐅᑫᐊᐨ
VTI s/he gathers s.t. together as cloth

ayāsīhtam ⊲ᐅᓰᣲᐨᐨ
VTI s/he responds to s.t., s/he makes a statement, s/he writes a letter in response

ayāsō- ⊲ᐅᓲ
IPV a little here and there

ayāsōw ⊲ᐅᓲᐤ
IPC here and there

ayātamohtāw ⊲ᐅᑕᒧᐦᑖᐤ
VAIt s/he fastens s.t. firmly

ayātan ⊲ᐅᑕᐣ
VII it is set firmly

ayātaskitāw ⊲ᐅᑕᐢᑭᑖᐤ
VAIt s/he plants s.t. firmly

ayātaskitēw ⊲ᐅᑕᐢᑭᑌᐤ
VII it is planted firmly

ayātastāw ⊲ᐅᑕᐢᑖᐤ
VAIt s/he places s.t. in solid

ayātastēw ⊲ᐅᑕᐢᑌᐤ
VII it rests firmly in place

ayātinam ⊲ᐅᑎᓇᐨ
VTI s/he holds s.t. firmly

ayātinēw ⊲ᐅᑎᓀᐤ
VTA s/he holds s.o. firmly

ayāw ⊲ᐅ
VAI s/he is, s/he is there; s/he lives there, s/he stays there

ayāw ⊲ᐅᐤ
VAIt s/he has s.t., s/he owns s.t.

ayāw ⊲ᐅᐤ
VII it is, it is there

ayāwahkaham ⊲ᐅ⊲ᣲᐦᣲ⊲ᐨ
VTI s/he buries s.t. in the ground

ayāwahkahwēw ⊲ᐅ⊲ᣲᐦᣲᐤᐤ·ᐤ
VTA s/he buries s.o. in the ground

ayāwēw ⊲ᐅᐁ·ᐤ
VTA s/he has s.o., s/he owns s.o.

ayāwin ⊲ᐅᐃᐧ
NI place of residence; state of being

ayāwin ⊲ᐅᐃᐧ
NI possession, thing owned

ayēhkwēsis ⊲ᐊᣲᐧᐁᔨᐢ
NA young castrated bull; steer [*dim*]

ayēhkwēw ⊲ᐊᣲᐧᐁᐤ
NA castrated animal, bull; ox

ayēhkwēwatim ⊲ᐊᣲᐧᐁᐊᑎᐨ
NA castrated horse (gelding) or dog

ayēkomow ⊲ᐊᑯᒧᐤ
VAI s/he stays underwater

ayēnānēw ⊲ᐊᓈᐁᐤ
IPC eight [*cf.* ayinānēw]

ayēnānēw-tahtwāpisk ⊲ᐊᓈᐁᐤ ᑖᐦᐨ·ᐱᐢᐠ
IPC eight dollars [*cf.* ayinānēw-tahtwāpisk]

ayēnānēwāw ⊲ᐊᓈᐁ·⊲·ᐤ
IPC eight times [*also* ayēnānēwowāw; *cf.* ayinānēwāw]

ayēnānēwi-misit ⊲ᐊᓈᐁᐃᐧ· ᒥᐟ
IPC eight feet; eight-foot [*cf.* ayinānēwi-misit]

ayēnānēwimitanaw ⊲ᐊᓈᐁᐃᐧ·ᒥᑕᓇᐤ
IPC eighty [*also* ayēnānēmitanaw; *cf.* ayinānēwimitanaw]

ayēnānēwosāp ⊲ᐊᓈᐁᐅᐧᓵᑊ
IPC eighteen [*cf.* ayinānēwosāp]

ayēnānēwopiponēw ⊲ᐊᓈᐁᐅᐧᐱᐳᓀᐤ
VAI s/he is eight years old [*cf.* ayinānēwopiponēw]

ayēsihtin ⊲ᐊᓯᐦᐟ
VII it leaves its imprint, it leaves a print, it leaves a mark [*also* ēsihtin-]

ayēsisin ⊲ᐊᓯᓯᐣ
VAI s/he leaves his/her imprint or mark

ayēskomow ⊲ᐊᐢᑯᒧᐤ
VAI s/he is tired

ayēskosin ⊲ᐊᐢᑯᓯᐣ
VAI s/he is exhausted, s/he is tired [*cf.* ayēskosiw]

ayēskosiw ⊲ᐊᐢᑯᓯᐤ
VAI s/he is exhausted, s/he is tired [*cf.* ayēskosin]

ayēskotisahwēw ⊲ᐊᐢᑯᑎᓴᐦᐤᐁ·ᐤ
VTA s/he tires s.o. out

ayēskwapiw ⊲ᐊᐢᐧᑲᐱᐤ
VAI s/he is stiff from sitting

ayētiskam ⊲ᐊᑎᐢᑲᐨ
VTI s/he leaves tracks on s.t.; s/he tracks s.t. up (*e.g.* a carpet)

ayētiskawēw ⊲ᐊᑎᐢᑲᐁᐧ·ᐤ
VTA s/he leaves tracks on s.o.; s/he tracks s.o. up (*e.g.* snow)

ayētiskiw ⊲ᐊᑎᐢᑭᐤ
VAI s/he leaves tracks

ayi ⊲ᐱ
IPC ah, well, hm [*hesitation; cf.* aya *IPC*, ayi- *IPV*]

ayi- ⊲ᐱ
IPV ah, hm [*hesitation; cf.* aya *IPC*, ayi *IPC*]

ayi ⊲ᐱ
NI one, thing [*pl:* aya; *often compounded*]

ayi ⊲ᐱ
PR the one [*inan sg; often compounded*]

ayicīminak ⊲ᐱᒌᒥᓇᐠ
NA peas [*pl*]

ayihk ⊲ᐱᐠ
IPC ah [*hesitation; often locative*]

ayinānēw ⊲ᐱᓈᐁᐤ
IPC eight [*cf.* ayēnānēw]

ayinānēw-tahtwāpisk ⊲ᐱᓈᐁᐤ ᑖᐦᐨ·ᐱᐢᐠ
IPC eight dollars [*cf.* ayēnānēw-tahtwāpisk]

ayinānēwāw ⊲ᐱᓈᐁ·⊲·ᐤ
IPC eight times [*also* ayinānēwowāw; *cf.* ayēnānēwāw]

ayinānēwi-misit ⊲ᐱᓈᐁᐃᐧ· ᒥᐟ
IPC eight feet; eight-foot [*cf.* ayēnānēwi-misit]

ayinānēwomitanaw ⊲ᐱᓈᐅᐧᒥᑕᓇᐤ
IPC eighty [*also* ayinānēmitanaw; *cf.* ayēnānēwimitanaw]

ayinānēwosāp ⊲ᐱᓈᐅᐧᓵᑊ
IPC eighteen [*cf.* ayēnānēwosāp]

ayinānēwopiponēw ⊲ᐱᓈᐅᐧᐱᐳᓀᐤ
VAI s/he is eight years old [*cf.* ayēnānēwopiponēw]

ayinisow ⊲ᐱᓂᓲᐤ
VAI s/he flees

aýis ⊲ᐱᐢ
IPC for, because, so it is, cannot be changed [*causal conjunction; cf.* aýisk]

aýis ⊲ᐱᐢ
NA someone [*dim*]

aýisac ⊲ᐱᓴᐨ
IPC unwillingly

aýisipiy ⊲ᐱᓯᐱᐩ
NI plain water

aýisiýiniw ⊲ᐱᓯᔨᓂᐤ
NA person, human being; [*pl:*] people [*cf.* aýisiýinisis]

aýisiýinīhkān ⊲ᐱᓯᔨᓃᐦᑳᐣ
NA effigy, doll [*see also* awāsisīhkān]

aýisiýinināhk ⊲ᐱᓯᔨᓂᓈᐦᐠ
IPC in the land of mortal men

aýisiýiniwiw ⊲ᐱᓯᔨᓂᐃᐧ·ᐤ
VAI s/he is a person, s/he is a human being

aýisiýiniwiwin ⊲ᐱᓯᔨᓂᐃᐧ·ᐃ·ᐣ
NA human life

aýisiýinīsis ⊲ᐱᓯᔨᓃᓯᐢ
NA young person [*dim; cf.* aýisiýiniw]

aýisiýinīpan ⊲ᐱᓯᔨᓃᐸᐣ
NA deceased person

aýisk ⊲ᐱᐢᐠ
IPC for, because [*causal conjunction; cf.* aýis]

aýiwatēyāskwahosow ⊲ᐱᐊ·ᑌᔮᐢᐧᑲᐦᐅᓲᐤ
VAI s/he enlarges him/herself at the belly with sticks

aýiwāk ⊲ᐱ⊲·ᐢ
IPC more, more than, greater than, in excess; [*in numeral phrases:*] plus

aýiwāk ōma ᐊᔨᐛᐠ ᐆᒪ
IPH there is more here
aýiwākastāw ᐊᔨᐛᑲᐢᑖᐤ
VAIt s/he puts more of s.t. out, s/he places more of s.t. out
aýiwākēs ᐊᔨᐛᑫᐢ
IPC in excess, more [*dim*]
aýiwākēsīs ᐊᔨᐛᑫᓰᐢ
IPC in excess, a bit more [*dim*]
aýiwākēýihtam ᐊᔨᐛᑫᔨᐦᑕᒼ
VTI s/he thinks more of s.t., s/he prefers s.t.
aýiwākēýihtākosiw ᐊᔨᐛᑫᔨᐦᑖᑯᓯᐤ
VAI s/he is thought of most highly
aýiwākēýihtākwan ᐊᔨᐛᑫᔨᐦᑖᒀᐣ
VII it is thought of most highly
aýiwākēýimēw ᐊᔨᐛᑫᔨᒣᐤ
VTA s/he thinks more of s.o., s/he thinks more highly of s.o.; s/he regards s.o. more highly; s/he prefers s.o.
aýiwākihkin ᐊᔨᐛᑭᐦᑭᐣ
IPC goodness gracious [*exclamation*]
aýiwākipaýin ᐊᔨᐛᑭᐸᔨᐣ
VII it is in excess, there is some left over [*also* aýiwākipaýiw]
aýiwākipaýiw ᐊᔨᐛᑭᐸᔨᐤ
VAI s/he has more than enough, s/he has a surplus, s/he has plenty; it is left over, it is in excess
aýiwākipēw ᐊᔨᐛᑭᐯᐤ
VAI s/he is too deep in the water
aýiwākipēw ᐊᔨᐛᑭᐯᐤ
VII it is too deep in the water, the water is too deep
aýiwākiskawēw ᐊᔨᐛᑭᐢᑲᐍᐤ
VTA s/he outstatures s.o., s/he is greater in stature than s.o.
aýiwākitonāmēw ᐊᔨᐛᑭᑐᓈᒣᐤ
VTA s/he out-talks s.o.
ayiwihēw ᐊᔨᐐᐦᐁᐤ
VTA s/he outdoes s.o.
ayiwin ᐊᔨᐐᐣ
NI article of clothing; [*pl*:] clothing; apparel
ayiwinisa ᐊᔨᐐᓂᓴ
NI clothes; clothing, apparel [*dim*; *pl*; sg: ayiwinis "article of clothing"]
ayiwinisi-akocikan ᐊᔨᐐᓂᓯ ᐊᑯᒋᑲᐣ
NI clothes closet [*see also* ayānikamik]
ayiwinisis ᐊᔨᐐᓂᓯᐢ
NI small article of clothing; [*pl*:] clothes; clothing, apparel [*dim*]
ayiwiw ᐊᔨᐐᐤ
VAI s/he is such and such a creature [*generally prefixed by a descriptive IPV*]
ayiwiw ᐊᔨᐐᐤ
VII it is such and such a thing [*generally prefixed by a descriptive IPV*]
ayīhcihēw ᐊᔩᐦᒋᐦᐁᐤ
VTA s/he confirms s.o.
aýīk ᐊᔩᐠ
NA frog, toad
aýīki-nōnācikan ᐊᔩᑭ ᓅᓈᒋᑲᐣ
NI mushroom; a certain water plant
aýīki-pīsim ᐊᔩᑭ ᐲᓯᒼ
NA Frog Moon; April [*wC*: May]
aýīkis ᐊᔩᑭᐢ
NA frog, small frog [*dim*]
aýīkisis ᐊᔩᑭᓯᐢ
NA tadpole [*dim*]
aýīkisiwiw ᐊᔩᑭᓯᐐᐤ
VAI s/he is a frog
ayītaw ᐊᔩᑕᐤ
IPC at both ends, on both sides
ayītawakām ᐊᔩᑕᐙᑳᒼ
IPC on both banks, on both sides of the river
ayītawāpitakāw ᐊᔩᑕᐛᐱᑕᑳᐤ
VII it is two-edged; it is a saw with teeth on both sides
ayītawāyihk ᐊᔩᑕᐛᔨᕽ
IPC in between
ayītawihkwākan ᐊᔩᑕᐐᐦᒂᑲᐣ
NA Wihtikow with face on both sides
ayītawihkwākanēw ᐊᔩᑕᐐᐦᒂᑲᓀᐤ
VAI s/he has two faces, s/he has faces on both sides
ayītawinisk ᐊᔩᑕᐐᓂᐢᐠ
IPC at both arms
ayītawiskanaw ᐊᔩᑕᐐᐢᑲᓇᐤ
IPC at both sides of the road
ayītawiskīsik ᐊᔩᑕᐐᐢᑮᓯᐠ
NA two-faced Wihtikow, "eyes on both sides" [*pl*: -wak]
ayōminask ᐊᔫᒥᓇᐢᐠ
NA linseed meal [*pl*: -wak; *cf.* anōmin]
ayōmināpoy ᐊᔫᒥᓈᐳᐩ
NI oatmeal, porridge [*cf.* anōmin; *see also* kīkisēpā-mīciwin]
aýōskan ᐊᔫᐢᑲᐣ
NA raspberry
aýōskanāhtik ᐊᔫᐢᑲᓈᐦᑎᐠ
NA raspberry bush [*pl*: -wak; *also* aýōhkanāhtik]
aýōskanāhtikoskāw ᐊᔫᐢᑲᓈᐦᑎᑯᐢᑳᐤ
VII there are many raspberry bushes, be an abundance of raspberry bushes
aýwāstan ᐊᔮᐧᐢᑕᐣ
VII it is calm (*i.e.* the wind)
aýwāstin ᐊᔮᐧᐢᑎᐣ
VII it is calm
aýwēpihēw ᐊᔦᐧᐱᐦᐁᐤ
VTA s/he gives s.o. a rest
aýwēpiw ᐊᔦᐧᐱᐤ
VAI s/he rests, s/he takes a rest [*also* aýiwēpiw]
aýwēpiwi-kīsikāw ᐊᔦᐧᐱᐐ ᑮᓯᑳᐤ
VII it is a holiday
aýwēpiwin ᐊᔦᐧᐱᐐᐣ
NI rest; resting; resting place, campground [*cf. VAI unspecified actor*: aýwēpiwināniwan "holiday"; *see also* kapēsiwin]

ā
ᐋ

ā ᐋ
IPC ah, well, oh [*introductory*; *exclamation*]

ācikāstēpicikan ᐋᒋᑳᐢᑌᐱᒋᑲᐣ
NI movie, moving picture; picture, photograph [*cf.* cikāstēpicikan]

ācikēhwēw ᐋᒋᑫᐦᐍᐤ
VTA s/he trips s.o.

ācikēwēpahwēw ᐋᒋᑫᐍᐸᐦᐍᐤ
VTA s/he trips and throws s.o.

ācimēw ᐋᒋᒣᐤ
VTA s/he tells about s.o., s/he talks about s.o.; s/he narrates about s.o.

ācimikowisiw ᐋᒋᒥᑯᐏᓯᐤ
VAI s/he is told about by the powers

ācimikowisiwin ᐋᒋᒥᑯᐏᓯᐏᐣ
NI fame

ācimisow ᐋᒋᒥᓱᐤ
VAI s/he tells about him/herself, s/he talks about him/herself

ācimostamawēw ᐋᒋᒧᐢᑕᒪᐍᐤ
VTA s/he tells tales to s.o.

ācimostawēw ᐋᒋᒧᐢᑕᐍᐤ
VTA s/he tells a story to s.o., s/he tells news to s.o.; s/he tells s.o. about (it/him), s/he gives s.o. an account

ācimostāsow ᐋᒋᒧᐢᑖᓱᐤ
VAI s/he narrates to him/herself, s/he talks to him/herself

ācimostātowak ᐋᒋᒧᐢᑖᑐᐘᐠ
VAI they tell stories to one another, they narrate to one another, they tell one another about (it)

ācimostātowin ᐋᒋᒧᐢᑖᑐᐏᐣ
NI news told to one another

ācimow ᐋᒋᒧᐤ
VAI s/he tells, s/he tells a story; s/he tells news, s/he gives an account, s/he narrates; s/he tells his/her own story

ācimowasinahikan ᐋᒋᒧᐘᓯᓇᐦᐃᑲᐣ
NI newspaper

ācimowasinahikanis ᐋᒋᒧᐘᓯᓇᐦᐃᑲᓂᐢ
NI newsletter [*dim*]

ācimowin ᐋᒋᒧᐏᐣ
NI story, true story, account, report; news; what is being told

ācimowinis ᐋᒋᒧᐏᓂᐢ
NI story [*dim*]

ācimōhēw ᐋᒋᒨᐦᐁᐤ
VTA s/he makes s.o. tell about (it), s/he has s.o. tell a story

ācisin ᐋᒋᓯᐣ
VAI s/he is blocked

āciwikaham ᐋᒋᐏᑲᐦᐊᒼ
VTI s/he hews s.t. short, s/he chops s.t. short

āciwikahwēw ᐋᒋᐏᑲᐦᐍᐤ
VTA s/he hews s.o. short, s/he chops s.o. short

āciwinam ᐋᒋᐏᓇᒼ
VTI s/he makes s.t. less; s/he lessens s.t.

āciwinamawēw ᐋᒋᐏᓇᒪᐍᐤ
VTA s/he gives s.o. less (*e.g.* food)

āciwinēw ᐋᒋᐏᓀᐤ
VTA s/he gives s.o. less; s/he removes part of s.o.'s allotment, earnings

āciwipotāw ᐋᒋᐏᐳᑖᐤ
VAIt s/he saws s.t. short

āciwipotēw ᐋᒋᐏᐳᑌᐤ
VTA s/he saws s.o. short

āciwisam ᐊᒋᐏᓴᒼ
VTI s/he cuts s.t. short

āciwiswēw ᐊᒋᐏᓷᐤ
VTA s/he cuts s.o. short

ācītin ᐋᒌᑎᐣ
VII it catches in the corners so as to be blocked or stuck

āh ᐋᐦ
IPC ah, oh, och! [*denotes displeasure*]

āh ᐋᐦ
IPC eh? [*interrogative*; *i.e.* "what's that?"]

āh-ayinānēw ᐋᐦ ᐊᔨᓈᓀᐤ
IPC eight by eight; eight each

āh-ayītaw ᐋᐦ ᐊᔩᑕᐤ
IPC on both sides [*rdpl*; *cf.* ayītaw]

āha ᐋᐦᐊ
IPC yes; as I told you [*affirmative*; *cf.* ēha; *wC*: īhī, *sC*: ēhē]

āhāsis ᐋᐦᐋᓯᐢ
NA baby crow [*dim*]

āhāsiw ᐋᐦᐋᓯᐤ
NA crow

āhāsiwimina ᐋᐦᐋᓯᐏᒥᓇ
NI juniper berries [*pl*]

āhāsiwimināhtik ᐋᐦᐋᓯᐏᒥᓈᐦᑎᐠ
NI juniper berry bush [*pl*: -wa; *see also* kahkākīwāhtik]

āhāw ᐋᐦᐋᐤ
IPC yes, fine, all right, okay [*cf.* aw, hāw, ahāw]

āhcanicihcān ᐋᐦᒐᓂᒋᐦᒑᐣ
NI ring finger [*cf.* āhcanicihcīs]

āhcanicihcēw ᐋᐦᒐᓂᒋᐦᒉᐤ
VAI s/he has several rings

āhcanicihciy ᐋᐦᒐᓂᒋᐦᒋᐩ
NI ringed hand

āhcanicihcīs ᐋᐦᒐᓂᒋᐦᒌᐢ
NI ring finger [*cf.* āhcanicihcān; *also* āhcaniwicihcīs]

āhcanis ᐋᐦᒐᓂᐢ
NA ring [*also* ahcānis]

āhci ᐋᐦᒋ
IPC still, nevertheless, despite everything; more; in a different place

āhci- ᐋᐦᒋ
IPV to a different place

āhci piko ᐋᐦᒋ ᐱᑯ
IPH still, nevertheless; despite the odds; in spite of; all the more [*cf.* āhciko]

āhci-ayāw ᐋᐦᒋ ᐊᔮᐤ
VAI s/he moves his/her own abode, s/he moves from one place to another [*also* āhc-āyāw]

āhci-kapēsiw ᐋᐦᒋ ᑲᐯᓯᐤ
VAI s/he changes campsite

āhci-kipaham ᐋᐦᒋ ᑭᐸᐦᐊᒼ
VTI s/he recloses s.t., s/he closes s.t. again

āhci-kipahwēw ᐋᐦᒋ ᑭᐸᐦᐍᐤ
VTA s/he closes s.o. in another section

āhci-wīkiw ᐋᐦᒋ ᐑᑭᐤ
VAI s/he moves to another place of residence

āhcihisow ᐋᐦᒋᐦᐃᓱᐤ
VAI s/he moves him/herself

āhcikāpawiw ◁ᵁᖔᑊ<ᐁ·°
 VAI s/he stands further over; s/he takes a new stand

āhciko ◁ᵁᖇᑯ
 IPC nevertheless [*cf.* āhci piko]

āhcinākohēw ◁ᵁᖇᐧᑯᵁᐁ°
 VTA s/he changes s.o.'s appearance

āhcinākohisow ◁ᵁᖇᐧᑯᵁᐁ◁ᓱ
 VAI s/he changes his/her own appearance

āhcinākohtāw ◁ᵁᖇᐧᑯᵁᐨᐧ°
 VAIt s/he changes s.t.'s appearance

āhcinākosiw ◁ᵁᖇᐧᑯᓯ°
 VAI s/he appears different

āhcipayiw ◁ᵁᖇ<ᐱ°
 VII it moves

āhcipiciw ◁ᵁᖇᐱᖇ°
 VAI s/he moves camp, s/he moves to another place

āhcipitam ◁ᵁᖇᐱᐧᑕᐨ
 VTI s/he moves s.t. over by pulling; s/he pulls s.t. away

āhcipitēw ◁ᵁᖇᐱᐁᐤ°
 VTA s/he moves s.o. over by pulling

āhcisiýihkāsow ◁ᵁᖇᐧᔭᔥᑳᓱ
 VAI s/he is renamed

āhcisiýihkātēw ◁ᵁᖇᐧᔭᔥᑳᐁᑌ°
 VTA s/he renames s.o.

āhcisīhēw ◁ᵁᖇᔨᐤᐁᐤ°
 VTA s/he alters s.o. (*e.g.* pants)

āhcisīhow ◁ᵁᖇᔨᐤᐃ°
 VAI s/he changes his/her own clothes

āhcisīhtāw ◁ᵁᖇᔨᐨᐧᐃ°
 VAIt s/he alters s.t.

āhciwinam ◁ᵁᖇ△·ᐊᐨᐤ
 VTI s/he decreases s.t.

āhciwinēw ◁ᵁᖇ△·ᐢᐤ°
 VTA s/he lowers s.o.'s wages or earnings

āhciwipayiw ◁ᵁᖇ△·<ᐱ°
 VII it shrinks; it shrivels

āhcīw ◁ᵁᖇ°
 VAI s/he moves to a different location

āhkamēýihtam ◁ᵁ᛫ᖴᔭᐤᐢᐨ
 VTI s/he continues to think of future deeds or tasks

āhkamēýihtamowin ◁ᵁᖴᔭᐢᐤᒧᒍᐃ△ᐤ
 NI perseverence

āhkamēýimēw ◁ᵁᖴᔭᐤᒥᐤ°
 VTA s/he hopes s.o. perseveres

āhkamēýimow ◁ᵁᖴᔭᐤᒧ°
 VAI s/he is persistant, s/he persists in his/her will, s/he does his/her best, s/he tries hard; s/he perseveres; s/he is energetic

āhkamēýimowin ◁ᵁᖴᔭᐤᒧᒍ△ᐤ
 NI earnest effort

āhkami- ◁ᵁᖴᖆ
 IPV persistently, untiringly,

unfailingly, unceasingly, unwaveringly; keep on, persevere [*also* ahkami-]

āhkamihtāw ◁ᵁᖴᖇᐤᐨᐧᐤ°
 VAIt s/he keeps at s.t

āhki ◁ᵁᑊ
 IPC pretend, pretense; lightly [*see also* yāhki]

āhkik ◁ᵁᑊᐧ
 NA seal (animal) [*pl*: -wak]

āhkiko-pimiy ◁ᵁᑊᑯ ᐱᖆᑊ
 NA seal oil

āhkikos ◁ᵁᑊᑯᐢ
 NA baby seal [*dim*]

āhkikoskāw ◁ᵁᑊᑯᐢᑳᐤ°
 VII there are many seals, seals are abundant

āhkikoswayān ◁ᵁᑊᑯᐢᐧᐊᔮᐣ
 NI seal skin

āhkikowiyās ◁ᵁᑊᑯ△·ᔮᐢᐣ
 NI seal meat

āhkikowiýin ◁ᵁᑊᑯ△·ᔨᐣ
 NA seal fat

āhkisīhow ◁ᵁᑊᔨᐤᐃ°
 VAI s/he dresses lightly

āhkiskow ◁ᵁᑊᐢᑯᐤ
 NA chicken; pheasant

āhkiskōs ◁ᵁᑊᐢᑰᐢ
 NA partridge [*dim*]

āhkohēw ◁ᵁᑯᐧᐁᐤ°
 VTA s/he gives s.o. a sharp pain, s/he gives s.o. a great deal of pain; s/he hurts s.o.

āhkohisow ◁ᵁᑯᐤ△ᓱ
 VAI s/he hurts him/herself

āhkohtēwisiw ◁ᵁᑯᐨᐤ△ᓯ°
 VAI s/he is caustic (as lye)

āhkosiw ◁ᵁᑯᓯ°
 VAI s/he is sick, s/he is ill; s/he is in labour, s/he has labour pains [*rdpl*: ay-āhkosiw]

āhkosiwin ◁ᵁᑯᓯ△ᐤ
 NI illness, sickness

āhkosiwinis ◁ᵁᑯᓯ△·ᐢᐣ
 NI minor illness [*dim*]

āhkosīhēw ◁ᵁᑯᔨᐤᐧᐁ°
 VTA s/he makes s.o. sick

āhkosīhitowak ◁ᵁᑯᔨᐤ△ᑐᐊᐧ
 VAI they make one another sick

āhkosīskawēw ◁ᵁᑯᔨᐢᑲᐤᐁᐤ°
 VTA s/he makes s.o. sick [*commonly in inanimate actor VTA paradigm, e.g.* nitāhkosiskākon pihtwāwin "smoking sickens me"]

āhkosīwasinahikan ◁ᵁᑯᔨᐤᐧᐊ◁·ᓇᐤᐃᖭᐨᐢ
 NI hospitalization card

āhkosīwikamik ◁ᵁᑯᔨᐤ△·ᖅᑊ
 NI hospital [*pl*: -wa]

āhkosīwikamikos ◁ᵁᑯᔨᐤ△·ᖅᑯᐢ
 NI clinic; small hospital [*dim*]

āhkospakosiw ◁ᵁᑯᐢ<ᑯᓯ°
 VAI s/he has a strong, sharp, or bitter taste

āhkospakwan ◁ᵁᑯᐢ<ᐳᐤ
 VII it has a strong, sharp, or bitter taste

āhkoýawēsiw ◁ᵁᑯᔭᐤᐁᓯ°
 VAI s/he is so angry s/he cannot speak

āhkwaci-pimiy ◁ᵁᖄᖇ ᐱᖆᑊ
 NI hard grease; tallow [*congealing when cold; found in association with the internal organs*]

āhkwacihcikan ◁ᵁᖄᖇᐤᖅᐨ
 NI deep freeze, freezer

āhkwacihcikanis ◁ᵁᖄᖇᐤᖅᖃᐣ
 NI freezer [*dim*]

āhkwacihtāw ◁ᵁᖄᖇᐨᐧ°
 VAIt s/he freezes s.t.

āhkwacikan ◁ᵁᖄᖇᖅᐨ
 NI freezer

āhkwaciw ◁ᵁᖄᖇ°
 VAI s/he freezes, s/he is frozen

āhkwakihtēw ◁ᵁᖄᐤᖄᐤᐧᐱᐤ°
 VII it is expensive

āhkwakisow ◁ᵁᖄ·ᖅᐤᓱ°
 VAI it is expensive or costly

āhkwan ◁ᵁᖄᐤ
 VII it is painful; it is tart

āhkwatāwākēw ◁ᵁᖄ·ᐨᐧᐁᐧ·ᖴᐧᐁ°
 VAI s/he sells s.o. at a dear price; s/he sells s.o. at a high price

āhkwatāwēw ◁ᵁᖄ·ᐨᐧᐁᐧ·°
 VAI s/he buys s.o. at a dear price; s/he buys s.o. at a high price

āhkwatihcikan ◁ᵁᖄ·ᖇᐨᖅᐨ
 NI refrigerator, fridge; freezer [*see also* tahkascikan]

āhkwatihcikātēw ◁ᵁᖄ·ᖇᐨᖅᑳᐁᑌᐤ
 VII it is (purposefully) frozen

āhkwatihtāw ◁ᵁᖄ·ᖇᐨᐧᐤ°
 VAIt s/he freezes s.t.; s/he lets s.t. freeze

āhkwatimēw ◁ᵁᖄ·ᖇᐤᑎᐤ°
 VTA s/he freezes s.o.

āhkwatin ◁ᵁᖄ·ᖇᐣ
 VII it is freezing, it is frozen, it is frozen hard

āhkwatinam ◁ᵁᖄ·ᖇᓇᐨ
 VTI s/he freezes s.t.

āhkwatisimēw ◁ᵁᖄ·ᖇᓯᑎᐤ°
 VTA s/he freezes s.o.

āhkwākamin ◁ᵁᖄ·ᖴᐣ
 VII it is a strong, sharp, or bitter liquid

āhkwākamiw ◁ᵁᖄ·ᖴᐤ°
 VII it is bitter (*i.e.* liquid)

āhkwāpahtēw ◁ᵁᖄ·<ᐤᐧᐁᐤ°
 VII there are strong, acrid, acidic fumes, there is strong smoke; it is lye

āhkwāstēw ◁ᵁᖄ·ᐢᐧᐁ°
 VII it is fierce sunlight

āhkwātisiw ◁ᵁᖄ·ᖇᓯ°
 VAI s/he is stern, s/he is sharp, s/he is of severe

disposition, s/he is ferocious;
s/he is hot-tempered
āhkwātisiwin ᐋᐦᑳᐟᐃᓯᐃᐧᐣ
NI wickedness, viciousness
āhkwātonamow ᐋᐦᑳᐟᐅᓇᒧᐤ
VAI s/he speaks boldly
āhkwēhtawastēwa
ᐋᐦᑴᐦᑕᐊᐧᐢᑌᐊᐧ
VII they are piled up,
crosswise; they are laid on
top of one another
āhpin ᐋᐦᐱᐣ
NI rawhide
āhpin-ōsi ᐋᐦᐱᐣ ᐆᓯ
NI rawhide boat [*pl*: -ōsa]
āhpinihkēw ᐋᐦᐱᓂᐦᑫᐤ
VAI s/he tans rawhide
āhtahēw ᐋᐦᑕᐦᐁᐤ
VTA s/he puts s.o.
elsewhere, s/he places s.o.
elsewhere
āhtahow ᐋᐦᑕᐦᐅᐤ
VAI s/he flies to another
place
āhtapiw ᐋᐦᑕᐱᐤ
VAI s/he moves as s/he sits,
s/he moves elsewhere, s/he
moves to sit elsewhere
āhtascikan ᐋᐦᑕᐢᒋᑲᐣ
NI surveyor's pole; object
used to move things from
one place to another
āhtaskēw ᐋᐦᑕᐢᑫᐤ
VAI s/he moves from one
reserve to another, s/he
moves from one land to
another, s/he changes his/her
land; s/he emigrates
āhtaskicikan ᐋᐦᑕᐢᑭᒋᑲᐣ
NI transplant, transplanted
vegetable
āhtaskicikēw ᐋᐦᑕᐢᑭᒋᑫᐤ
VAI s/he transplants
vegetables
āhtaskihēw ᐋᐦᑕᐢᑭᐦᐁᐤ
VTA s/he transplants s.o.
āhtastāw ᐋᐦᑕᐢᑖᐤ
VAIt s/he moves s.t.'s place;
s/he puts s.t. elsewhere, s/he
places s.t. elsewhere
āhtisin ᐋᐦᑎᓯᐣ
VAI s/he moves as s/he lies;
s/he lies in a new place
āhtohtēw ᐋᐦᑑᐦᑌᐤ
VAI s/he walks to another
place or area
āhtokēw ᐋᐦᑑᑫᐤ
VAI s/he moves camp
āhtotatāw ᐋᐦᑑᑕᑖᐤ
VAIt s/he moves s.t. to
another place
ākawaskwēw ᐋᑲᐊᐧᐢᑫᐧᐤ
VAI s/he goes behind a cloud
(*e.g.* the sun or moon)
ākawastēham ᐋᑲᐊᐧᐢᑌᐦᐊᒼ
VTI s/he shades s.t. (*e.g.* a
window), s/he places s.t. in
shade; s/he shelters s.t.

ākawastēhk ᐋᑲᐊᐧᐢᑌᕽ
IPC in the shade [*also*
ākawāstēk]
ākawastēhon ᐋᑲᐊᐧᐢᑌᐦᐅᐣ
NI umbrella; wagon cover
ākawastēhow ᐋᑲᐊᐧᐢᑌᐦᐅᐤ
VAI s/he shades him/herself
ākawastēhwēw ᐋᑲᐊᐧᐢᑌᐦᐁᐧᐤ
VTA s/he shades s.o.; s/he
places s.o. in shade
ākawastēsimow ᐋᑲᐊᐧᐢᑌᓯᒧᐤ
VAI s/he sits in the shade,
s/he lies down in the shade
ākawastēsin ᐋᑲᐊᐧᐢᑌᓯᐣ
VAI s/he lies in the shade,
s/he sits in the shade
ākawastēskam ᐋᑲᐊᐧᐢᑌᐢᑲᒼ
VTI s/he shades s.t. with
his/her own shadow
ākawastēskawēw ᐋᑲᐊᐧᐢᑌᐢᑲᐁᐧᐤ
VTA s/he shades s.o. with
his/her own shadow
ākawastēw ᐋᑲᐊᐧᐢᑌᐤ
VII it is shady
ākawāyihk ᐋᑲᐋᔨᕽ
IPC behind the thing
ākawēwēmakan ᐋᑲᐁᐧᐁᐧᒪᑲᐣ
VII it goes behind an
obstacle to vision (*e.g.*
cloud), it goes out of sight
ākawēwēpahtāw ᐋᑲᐁᐧᐁᐧᐸᐦᑖᐤ
VAI s/he runs behind an
obstacle to vision, out of
sight
ākawēwēw ᐋᑲᐁᐧᐁᐧᐤ
VAI s/he goes behind an
obstacle to vision, out of
sight
ākayāsīmototawēw
ᐋᑲᔮᓰᒧᑐᑕᐁᐧᐤ
VTA s/he speaks English to
s.o.
ākayāsīmow ᐋᑲᔮᓰᒧᐤ
VAI s/he speaks English
ākayāsīmowin ᐋᑲᔮᓰᒧᐃᐧᐣ
NI the English language;
speaking English
ākayāsīw ᐋᑲᔮᓰᐤ
NA Englishman
ākayāsīwastāw ᐋᑲᔮᓰᐊᐧᐢᑖᐤ
VAIt s/he puts s.t. into
English, s/he translates s.t.
into English
ākayāsīwi-ayamihēwiýiniw
ᐋᑲᔮᓰᐃᐧ ᐊᔭᒥᐦᐁᐃᐧᔨᓂᐤ
NA Anglican minister
ākayāsīwiskwēw ᐋᑲᔮᓰᐃᐧᐢᑫᐧᐤ
NA English woman
ākayāsīwiýiniw ᐋᑲᔮᓰᐃᐧᔨᓂᐤ
NA English speaker
ākohkwēhon ᐋᑯᐦᑴᐦᐅᐣ
NI veil, shade for eyes;
blinders
ākohkwēnēw ᐋᑯᐦᑴᓀᐤ
VTA s/he covers s.o.'s face;
s/he shades s.o.'s face
ākohkwēpisow ᐋᑯᐦᑴᐱᓱᐤ
VAI s/he is blindfolded

ākohkwēpitēw ᐋᑯᐦᑴᐱᑌᐤ
VTA s/he blindfolds s.o.
ākohkwēpitisow ᐋᑯᐦᑴᐱᑎᓱᐤ
VAI s/he blindfolds
him/herself
ākohkwēw ᐋᑯᐦᑴᐤ
VAI s/he has a covered face
ākō- ᐋᑰ
IPV covered, shielded
ākō-wēpinam ᐋᑰ ᐁᐧᐱᓇᒼ
VTI s/he flings s.t. to shield
or out of sight
ākō-wēpinēw ᐋᑰ ᐁᐧᐱᓀᐤ
VTA s/he flings s.o. to shield
or out of sight
ākō-wiyipāw ᐋᑰ ᐃᐧᔨᐹᐤ
VII it is covered in dirt [*cf.*
wiyipāw, wipāw]
ākōham ᐋᑰᐦᐊᒼ
VTI s/he shields s.t.; s/he
covers s.t.
ākōhikākēw ᐋᑰᐦᐃᑳᑫᐤ
VAI s/he uses s.t. to obscure
light [*i.e. covering a window
with a blind, blanket, etc.*]
ākōhosow ᐋᑰᐦᐅᓱᐤ
VAI s/he covers him/herself
ākōhwēw ᐋᑰᐦᐁᐧᐤ
VTA s/he conceals s.o.; s/he
covers s.o.
ākōnam ᐋᑰᓇᒼ
VTI s/he puts s.t. on or over
(it)
ākōnēw ᐋᑰᓀᐤ
VTA s/he puts s.o. on or over
(it)
ākōpaýihow ᐋᑰᐸᔨᐦᐅᐤ
VAI s/he flings him/herself
into shelter, out of sight,
around the corner
ākōpitam ᐋᑰᐱᑕᒼ
VTI s/he draws the blinds to
obscure light; s/he pulls s.t.
so as to cover
ākōsimow ᐋᑰᓯᒧᐤ
VAI s/he shields him/herself;
s/he dances behind someone
or something
ākōsipēyāw ᐋᑰᓯᐯᔮᐤ
VII it is dewy, there is dew
on the grass
ākōstikwānēhēw ᐋᑰᐢᑎᑳᓀᐦᐁᐤ
VTA s/he covers s.o.'s head
(with a scarf)
ākōstikwānēhow ᐋᑰᐢᑎᑳᓀᐦᐅᐤ
VAI s/he wears his/her own
scarf; s/he is dressed with a
hat; s/he wears a head
covering
ākōstikwānēw ᐋᑰᐢᑎᑳᓀᐤ
VAI s/he covers his/her own
head
ākōyāpahpisow ᐋᑰᔮᐸᐦᐱᓱᐤ
VAI s/he has his/her own
eyes shielded or blindfolded
ākōyāpahpitēw ᐋᑰᔮᐸᐦᐱᑌᐤ
VTA s/he blindfolds s.o.'s
eyes

ākōyāpahpitisow ⊲ᒡᔆ<"ᐱᑎᓴᵒ
VAI s/he blindfolds
him/herself

ākwaham ⊲ᑊᐧᐦ⊲ᒡ
VTI s/he covers s.t. up

ākwahwēw ⊲ᑊᐦᐧᐁ·ᵒ
VTA s/he covers s.o. up

ākwask ⊲ᑊᐧᕁ
IPC heading off, in the way

ākwaskipahtāw ⊲ᑊᐦᑊ<"ᐨᵒ
VAI s/he runs and heads s.o.
off, s/he heads s.o. off
running

ākwaskipayīhow ⊲ᑊᐦᑊ<ᔭ"ᐳᵒ
VAI s/he moves quickly in
front of something

ākwaskiskawēw ⊲ᑊᐦᑊᐦᐳᐁ·ᵒ
VTA s/he heads s.o. off

ākwaskitinēw ⊲ᑊᐦᑊᑎᐧᵒ
VTA s/he puts his/her own
arm around s.o., s/he hugs
s.o.

ākwaskīw ⊲ᑊᐦᑊᵒ
VAI s/he goes ahead; s/he is
protective of a sibling

ākwaskohtēw ⊲ᑊᐦᒡ"ᑌᵒ
VAI s/he walks heading off

ākwā- ⊲ᑊ·
IPV quite a lot; well on its
way, in progress of time

ākwā-kīsikāw ⊲ᑊ· ᖊᕠᑯᵒ
VII it is high day

ākwāc ⊲ᑊ·
IPC quite a lot; well on its
way, a long ways, more than
halfway

ākwāhkatisow ⊲ᑊ·"ᑫᑎᓴᵒ
VAI s/he is very thin from
hunger; s/he is very hungry

ākwāhkatotēw ⊲ᑊ·"ᑫᒍᐤᵒ
VII it is very dry and hard

ākwāhonihtak ⊲ᑊ·"ᐳᓂ"ᐨᐧ
NI driftwood

ākwāskam ⊲ᑊᐦᐧᕝ
IPC really, rather;
overanxious; [in negative
clauses:] not really, not as
much

ākwāskam ⊲ᑊᐦᐧᕝ
VTI s/he heads s.t. off

ākwāskawēw ⊲ᑊᐦᐯᐁ·ᵒ
VTA s/he heads s.o. off

ākwātaskinēw ⊲ᑊ·ᑕᐦᑭ ᐁ·ᵒ
VAI s/he is quite full, it is
more than half-full (e.g. pail)

ākwāyāhokow ⊲ᑊ·ᔭ"ᐳᑯᵒ
VAI s/he drifts to shore, s/he
floats to shore (from the
wind)

ākwāyāhotēw ⊲ᑊ·ᔭ"ᐳᑌᵒ
VII it floats to shore

ākwāyāhtik ⊲ᑊ·ᔭ"ᑎᐧ
NI driftwood [pl: -wa]

ākwāyāsiw ⊲ᑊ·ᔭᓯᵒ
VAI s/he is blown ashore

ākwāyāsow ⊲ᑊ·ᔭᓱᵒ
VAI s/he is blown dry

ākwāyāstan ⊲ᑊ·ᔭᐦᑕᐧ
VII it is blown ashore

ākwāyāw ⊲ᑊ·ᔭᵒ
VII it is late

āmaciwēhtahēw ⊲ᒪᒋᐁ·"ᐨ"ᐁ·ᵒ
VTA s/he takes s.o. up, s/he
takes s.o. uphill or upstairs

āmaciwēhtatāw ⊲ᒪᒋᐁ·"ᐨᐨᵒ
VAIt s/he takes s.t. up; s/he
takes s.t. uphill or upstairs

āmaciwēpahēw ⊲ᒪᒋᐁ·<"ᐁ·ᵒ
VTA s/he takes s.o. uphill
(by vehicle), s/he takes s.o.
upstairs

āmaciwēpahtāw ⊲ᒪᒋᐁ·<"ᐨᵒ
VAI s/he runs up, s/he runs
uphill or upstairs

āmaciwēpayīw ⊲ᒪᒋᐁ·<ᔭᵒ
VAI s/he goes uphill, s/he
rides uphill (by horse or
vehicle)

āmaciwēpicikan ⊲ᒪᒋᐁ·ᐱᒋᐧᕁ
NI elevator; ski lift

āmaciwēpitam ⊲ᒪᒋᐁ·ᐱᐨᒡ
VTI s/he pulls s.t. up

āmaciwēpitēw ⊲ᒪᒋᐁ·ᐱᐅᵒ
VTA s/he pulls s.o. up

āmaciwētācimow ⊲ᒪᒋᐁ·ᐨᕑᒍᵒ
VAI s/he crawls uphill or
upstairs

āmaciwētāpāsow ⊲ᒪᒋᐁ·ᐨ<ᐧᓴᵒ
VAI s/he drives uphill

āmaciwētowahēw
⊲ᒪᒋᐁ·ᒍ⊲"ᐁ·ᵒ
VTA s/he carries s.o. uphill
or upstairs on his/her back

āmaciwētowatāw ⊲ᒪᒋᐁ·ᒍ⊲·ᐨᵒ
VAIt s/he carries s.t. uphill
or upstairs on his/her back

āmaciwētowatēw ⊲ᒪᒋᐁ·ᒍ⊲·ᐅᵒ
VAI s/he carries things uphill
or upstairs on his/her back

āmaciwēw ⊲ᒪᒋᐁ·ᵒ
VAI s/he climbs up, s/he
walks up, s/he goes uphill or
upstairs

āmaciwēyahkinam
⊲ᒪᒋᐁ·ᔭ"ᕽᓇᕝ
VTI s/he pushes s.t. uphill or
upstairs

āmaciwēyahkinēw
⊲ᒪᒋᐁ·ᔭ"ᕽᐧᵒ
VTA s/he pushes s.o. uphill
or upstairs

āmaciwēyāhtawīw
⊲ᒪᒋᐁ·ᔭ"ᐨᐊ·ᵒ
VAI s/he climbs up a tree,
s/he crawls up

āmaciwīspimowinihk
⊲ᒪᒋᐃ·ᐦᐱᒧᐃᐧ ᓂᐦᐠ
INM Stanley Mission, SK
[loc; wC community]

āmi- ⊲ᒥ
IPV almost

āmī ⊲ᒪ
IPC dear one [conveys
"tender love"]

āmī ⊲ᒪ
IPC exclamation of
sympathy

āmīw ⊲ᒪᵒ
VAI it goes upstream to
spawn (i.e. fish)

āmow ⊲ᒍᵒ
NA bee, honey-bee, wasp

āmow-mēyi ⊲ᒍᵒ ᑭᑋ
NI honey

āmow-piyēsis ⊲ᒍᵒ ᐱᔭ ᔆ
NA hummingbird

āmow-wacistwan ⊲ᒍᵒ ⊲ᐧᐨᐧᐧᐧ
NI bee's nest [cf. wacistwan;
also -waciston]

āmōs ⊲ᒍᐧ
NA bee [dim]

āmōsis ⊲ᒍᕑᐧ
NA little bee [dim]

āmōsīhcikan ⊲ᒍᕑᓴ"ᕑᕁᑊ
NI honey [lit: "what a bee
makes", cf. āmow-osīhcikan]

āmōsīsipāskwat ⊲ᒍᕑᕑᐧ<ᐧᕁ·
NI honey

āmōskāw ⊲ᒍᕑᕝᵒ
VII there are many bees,
bees are abundant

ānisīhcicikan ⊲ᓂᕑᒡ"ᕑᕑᕁᑊ
NI antidote

āniskē ⊲ᓂᕑᕯ
IPC successively, one
joining to the other

āniskētastāw ⊲ᓂᕑᕯᐨᕟᐨᵒ
VAIt s/he places s.t. so as to
join [also āniskēstastāw]

āniski- ⊲ᓂᕑᑭ
IPV succession, extension

āniski-ohtāwīmāw
⊲ᓂᕑᑭ ᐅ"ᐨᐊ·ᒥ·ᵒ
NA forefather; great
grandfather

āniskohikan ⊲ᓂᕑᒡ"ᐧᕝᐧᕁᑊ
NI a splice

āniskohpicikan ⊲ᓂᕑᒡ"ᐱᒋᐧᕁᑊ
NI knot [made from tying
two ropes]

āniskohtāw ⊲ᓂᕑᒡ"ᐨᵒ
VAIt s/he lengthens s.t.; s/he
joins s.t.

āniskoscikēw ⊲ᓂᕑᒡᕑᒋᕯᵒ
VAI s/he makes an extension

āniskotāpān ⊲ᓂᕑᒡᐨᐸ<ᐧ
NA great grandparent, great
grandchild [cf. -āniskotāpān-
NDA]

āniskotāpān ⊲ᓂᕑᒡᐨᐸ<ᐧ
NI thing next in order

āniskotāpēw ⊲ᓂᕑᒡᐨᐸᐯᵒ
VAI s/he has a great
grandchild [cf.
nitāniskotāpān]

āniskowaskāw ⊲ᓂᕑᒡ⊲·ᐧᕝᵒ
VII it is full of reeds

āniskowaskoskāw
⊲ᓂᕑᒡ⊲·ᐧᕁᐧᕝᵒ
VII there are many reeds

āniskowaskwa ⊲ᓂᕑᒡ⊲·ᐧᕽᵒ
NI reeds, bullrushes [pl]

āniskōhōcikan ⊲ᓂᕑᒡ"ᐳᕑᕁᑊ
NI string of beads tied end
to end

āniskōhpitam ᐋᓂᐢᑰᐦᐱᑕᒼ
VTI s/he ties s.t. end to end, s/he lengthens s.t. (*i.e.* by tying on an extra length)

āniskōhpitēw ᐋᓂᐢᑰᐦᐱᑌᐤ
VII it is tied end to end

āniskōhpitēw ᐋᓂᐢᑰᐦᐱᑌᐤ
VTA s/he ties s.o. end to end, s/he lengthens s.o. (*i.e.* by tying on an extra length)

āniskōkanān ᐋᓂᐢᑰᑲᓈᐣ
NI joint; [*pl*:] vertebrae

āniskōkwātam ᐋᓂᐢᑰᑹᑕᒼ
VTI s/he sews s.t. on as an extension

āniskōskitēw ᐋᓂᐢᑰᐢᑭᑌᐤ
VII it adjoins a larger thing

āniskōstēw ᐋᓂᐢᑰᐢᑌᐤ
VII it extends, it is extended

ānwēhcikātēw ᐋᓊᐦᒋᑳᑌᐤ
VII it is denied, it is disbelieved

ānwēhtam ᐋᓊᐦᑕᒼ
VTI s/he doubts s.t., s/he rejects s.t., s/he denies s.t., s/he disbelieves s.t.

ānwēhtamowin ᐋᓊᐦᑕᒧᐏᐣ
NI disbelief

ānwēhtaskiw ᐋᓊᐦᑕᐢᑭᐤ
VAI s/he is in the habit of disbelief; s/he is a cynic [*hab*]

ānwēhtawēw ᐋᓊᐦᑕᐍᐤ
VTA s/he rejects s.o., s/he denies s.o., s/he disbelieves s.o.

ānwēhtāsow ᐋᓊᐦᑖᓱᐤ
VAI s/he disbelieves him/herself

āpacihēw ᐋᐸᒋᐦᐁᐤ
VTA s/he uses s.o., s/he makes use of s.o. (*e.g.* porcupine-quills); s/he does s.o. service

āpacihcikan ᐋᐸᒋᐦᒋᑲᐣ
NI utensil, tool, implement; appliance; machine

āpacihcikanis ᐋᐸᒋᐦᒋᑲᓂᐢ
NI small tool, small appliance [*dim*]

āpacihitowin ᐋᐸᒋᐦᐃᑐᐏᐣ
NI helping one another, mutual benefit

āpacihiwēw ᐋᐸᒋᐦᐃᐍᐤ
VAI s/he serves people; s/he takes advantage of others

āpacihow ᐋᐸᒋᐦᐅᐤ
VAI s/he does him/herself service

āpacihtamōhēw ᐋᐸᒋᐦᑕᒨᐦᐁᐤ
VTA s/he makes s.o. use (it/him)

āpacihtāw ᐋᐸᒋᐦᑖᐤ
VAIt s/he uses s.t., s/he makes use of s.t.

āpacihtāwin ᐋᐸᒋᐦᑖᐏᐣ
NI (piece of) furniture

āpaham ᐋᐸᐦᐊᒼ
VTI s/he loosens s.t. by tool; s/he unties s.t., s/he unwraps s.t., s/he untangles s.t.

āpahamawēw ᐋᐸᐦᐊᒪᐍᐤ
VTA s/he unties (it/him) for s.o., s/he unwraps (it/him) for s.o., s/he untangles (it/him) for s.o.

āpahikan ᐋᐸᐦᐃᑲᐣ
NI wrench

āpahikanis ᐋᐸᐦᐃᑲᓂᐢ
NI small wrench [*dim*]

āpahikāsow ᐋᐸᐦᐃᑳᓱᐤ
VAI s/he is freed, s/he is untied

āpahikātēw ᐋᐸᐦᐃᑳᑌᐤ
VII it is loosened, it is unwound

āpahikēw ᐋᐸᐦᐃᑫᐤ
VAI s/he loosens (things) by tool

āpahkawihēw ᐋᐸᐦᑲᐏᐦᐁᐤ
VTA s/he brings s.o. to consciousness

āpahkawisiw ᐋᐸᐦᑲᐏᓯᐤ
VAI s/he returns to his/her senses

āpahkwēwikamik ᐋᐸᐦᑵᐏᑲᒥᐠ
NI big top; tent [*pl*: -wa]

āpahōnikan ᐋᐸᐦᐆᓂᑲᐣ
NI bolt

āpahōnikanis ᐋᐸᐦᐆᓂᑲᓂᐢ
NI bolt [*dim*]

āpahōpaýiw ᐋᐸᐦᐆᐸᔨᐤ
VII it unwinds (as a bolt)

āpahōstēham ᐋᐸᐦᐆᐢᑌᐦᐊᒼ
VTI s/he unscrews s.t., s/he unwinds s.t. (with a wrench)

āpahōstēhikan ᐋᐸᐦᐆᐢᑌᐦᐃᑲᐣ
NI monkey wrench

āpahōstēhwēw ᐋᐸᐦᐆᐢᑌᐦᐍᐤ
VTA s/he unwinds s.o. (with a wrench)

āpahwēw ᐋᐸᐦᐍᐤ
VTA s/he unharnesses s.o.; s/he untie s.o., s/he unbinds s.o.

āpakosīs ᐋᐸᑯᓰᐢ
NA mouse [*dim*; *cf.* wāpakosīs]

āpakosīsi-mīciwin
ᐋᐸᑯᓰᓯ ᒦᒋᐏᐣ
NI cheese [*see also* mākwahcikan]

āpakosīsi-nōtokēw
ᐋᐸᑯᓰᓯ ᓅᑐᑫᐤ
NA Old Mouse Woman [*legendary name*; *pl*: āpakosīsi-nōtokēwak]

āpakosīsi-pīway ᐋᐸᑯᓰᓯ ᐲᐘᕀ
NA mouse-coloured horse; *NI* mouse fur

āpakosīsiwiw ᐋᐸᑯᓰᓯᐏᐤ
VAI s/he is a mouse

āpasāpahtam ᐋᐸᓵᐸᐦᑕᒼ
VTI s/he looks back and sees s.t.; s/he looks back at s.t.

āpasāpamēw ᐋᐸᓵᐸᒣᐤ
VTA s/he looks back at s.o.

āpasāpiw ᐋᐸᓵᐱᐤ
VAI s/he looks back

āpatan ᐋᐸᑕᐣ
VII it is used, it is useful

āpatisiw ᐋᐸᑎᓯᐤ
VAI it is used, s/he is useful [*also dim*: āpacisiw]

āpatisiwin ᐋᐸᑎᓯᐏᐣ
NI work; usefulness

āpāpiskaham ᐋᐹᐱᐢᑲᐦᐊᒼ
VTI unlock s.t. [*see also* āpihkokaham, kipāpiskaham]

āpāpiskahikan ᐋᐹᐱᐢᑲᐦᐃᑲᐣ
NI key [*see also* āpihkokahikan, kipāpiskahikan]

āpēhow ᐋᐯᐦᐅᐤ
VAI s/he seeks revenge

āpēhowin ᐋᐯᐦᐅᐏᐣ
NI revenge

āpihci- ᐋᐱᐦᒋ
IPV halfway

āpihkohow ᐋᐱᐦᑯᐦᐅᐤ
VAI s/he unties him/herself, s/he gets loose, s/he becomes untied or unfettered; it is unleashed

āpihkohtāw ᐋᐱᐦᑯᐦᑖᐤ
VAIt s/he undoes s.t.

āpihkokaham ᐋᐱᐦᑯᑲᐦᐊᒼ
VTI s/he unlocks s.t. [*see also* āpāpiskaham, kipāpiskaham]

āpihkokahikan ᐋᐱᐦᑯᑲᐦᐃᑲᐣ
NI key [*see also* āpāpiskahikan, kipāpiskahikan]

āpihkonam ᐋᐱᐦᑯᓇᒼ
VTI s/he unties s.t., s/he undoes s.t.

āpihkonēw ᐋᐱᐦᑯᓀᐤ
VTA s/he unties s.o.

āpihkonisow ᐋᐱᐦᑯᓂᓱᐤ
VAI s/he unties him/herself

āpihkopaýiw ᐋᐱᐦᑯᐸᔨᐤ
VII it comes unfastened, it comes untied

āpihkopitam ᐋᐱᐦᑯᐱᑕᒼ
VTI s/he unties s.t.

āpihkopitēw ᐋᐱᐦᑯᐱᑌᐤ
VTA s/he unties s.o., s/he pulls s.o. untied

āpihkotēw ᐋᐱᐦᑯᑌᐤ
VAI s/he is in an untied state; it is unwound

āpihkwaham ᐋᐱᐦᑿᐦᐊᒼ
VTI s/he unlocks s.t.

āpihkwahikan ᐋᐱᐦᑿᐦᐃᑲᐣ
NI tool for unfastening; key; lock

āpihkwahikanis ᐋᐱᐦᑿᐦᐃᑲᓂᐢ
NI small lock; little key [*dim*]

āpihkwahtam ᐋᐱᐦᑿᐦᑕᒼ
VTI s/he bites s.t. so as to untie it

āpiht ᐋᐱᐦᐟ
NI flint for starting fire

āpihtaw ᐋᐱᐦᑕᐤ
IPC half

āpihtawanohk ᐋᐱᐦᑕᐗᓄᕽ
IPC halfway

āpihtawi- ᐋᐱᐦᑕᐗ·
IPV half

āpihtawikosisān ᐋᐱᐦᑕᐗᐠᐅᓯᓵᐣ
NA Métis, halfbreed [also āpihtākosisān]

āpihtawikosisāniskwēw
ᐋᐱᐦᑕᐗᐠᐅᓯᓵᓂᐢᑫᐤ
NA Métis woman, halfbreed woman [also āpihtākosisāniskwēw]

āpihtā- ᐋᐱᐦᑖ
IPV half

āpihtā-kīsikaniw
ᐋᐱᐦᑖ ᑮᓯᑲᓂᐤ
VAI s/he has lunch; s/he takes time off for lunch

āpihtā-kīsikani-mīcisowin
ᐋᐱᐦᑖ ᑮᓯᑲᓂ ᒥᒋᓱᐃᐣ
NI lunch, dinner

āpihtā-kīsikanohk
ᐋᐱᐦᑖ ᑮᓯᑲᓄᕽ
IPC south [lit: "at mid-day"; see also sāwanohk]

āpihtā-kīsikanōtāhk
ᐋᐱᐦᑖ ᑮᓯᑲᓄᑖᕽ
IPC south [lit: "toward noon"; see also sāwanohk]

āpihtā-kīsikāki ᐋᐱᐦᑖ ᑮᓯᑲᑭ
IPC at noon, when it's noon (12:00 p.m.)

āpihtā-kīsikāw ᐋᐱᐦᑖ ᑮᓯᑳᐤ
VII it be noon (12:00 p.m.)

āpihtā-kīsikāwi- ᐋᐱᐦᑖ ᑮᓯᑳᐤ·
IPV at noon

āpihtā-kīsikāwi-mīcisow
ᐋᐱᐦᑖ ᑮᓯᑳᐤ· ᒥᒋᓱ
VAI s/he eats at noon; s/he has lunch

āpihtā-kīsikāwi-mīcisowin
ᐋᐱᐦᑖ ᑮᓯᑳᐤ· ᒥᒋᓱᐃᐣ
NI noon meal, lunch

āpihtā-nīpin ᐋᐱᐦᑖ ᓃᐱᐣ
VII it is midsummer

āpihtā-pipon ᐋᐱᐦᑖ ᐱᐳᐣ
VII it is midwinter

āpihtā-piponi-pīsim
ᐋᐱᐦᑖ ᐱᐳᓂ ᐲᓯᐢ
NA Mid-Winter Moon; January [see also kisē-pīsim]

āpihtā-tipiskāw ᐋᐱᐦᑖ ᑎᐱᐢᑳᐤ
VII it is midnight (12:00 a.m.)

āpihtāw ᐋᐱᐦᑖᐤ
VII it is half

āpihtāwi-kīsikāw
ᐋᐱᐦᑖᐤ· ᑮᓯᑳᐤ
VII it is Wednesday [lit: "middle-day"; see also nisto-kīsikāw]

āpihtāwipayiw ᐋᐱᐦᑖᐤ·ᐸᔨᐤ
VII it is Wednesday, it is mid-week; it is at the half-way point [see also nisto-kīsikāw]

āpihtāwitākosiw ᐋᐱᐦᑖᐤ·ᑖᐠᐅᓯᐤ
VII it is halfway through afternoon

āpihtōsiyaw ᐋᐱᐦᑑᓯᔭᐤ
IPC on the body, to the waist; upper half of the body (in reference to a corpse in a coffin]

āpisisin ᐋᐱᓯᓯᐣ
VAI s/he revives; s/he rises from the dead

āpisīhkwasiw ᐋᐱᓰᐦᒁᓯᐤ
VAI s/he awakens from a nightmare

āpisīnikan ᐋᐱᓰᓂᑲᐣ
NA reviver; someone who rises from the dead

āpiyikāsow ᐋᐱᔨᑳᓱᐤ
VAI s/he is untied

āpiyikātēw ᐋᐱᔨᑳᑌᐤ
VII it is untied

āpocikwānipayiw ᐋᐳᒋᑾᓂᐸᔨᐤ
VAI s/he somersaults, s/he turns upside down

āpocikwānipitam ᐋᐳᒋᑾᓂᐱᑕᒼ
VTI s/he turns s.t. upside down

āpocikwānipitēw ᐋᐳᒋᑾᓂᐱᑌᐤ
VTA s/he turns s.o. upside down

āpocikwānīw ᐋᐳᒋᑾᓃᐤ
VAI s/he somersaults, s/he does a somersault

āpocipayiw ᐋᐳᒋᐸᔨᐤ
VAI s/he falls head over heels

āpocipayīmakan ᐋᐳᒋᐸᔩᒪᑲᐣ
VII it turns around

āpohtān ᐋᐳᐦᑖᐣ
NI edible innards of a moose, "hunter's treat"

āpohtēw ᐋᐳᐦᑌᐤ
VAI he returns with big game (from hunting); he gives the hunter's treat [cf. āpohtān]

āpotaham ᐋᐳᑕᐦᐊᒼ
VTI s/he turns s.t. upside down; s/he turns s.t. inside out

āpotinam ᐋᐳᑎᓇᒼ
VTI s/he turns s.t. inside out

āpotinēw ᐋᐳᑎᓀᐤ
VTA s/he turns s.o. inside out

āsaw ᐋᓴᐤ
IPC at the far side, beyond [cf. āsowa...]

āsawi- ᐋᓴᐤ·
IPV in passing something on [also āsō-]

āsawinamawēw ᐋᓴᐤᐃᓇᒪᐌᐤ
VTA s/he passes (it/him) on to s.o. [cf. āsōnamawēw]

āsay ᐋᓴᐩ
IPC already; without delay [cf. sāsay; also aspectual]

āsay cī ᐋᓴᐩ ᒌ
IPH already? are you ready?

āsay mīna ᐋᓴᐩ ᒦᓇ
IPH again, already again

āscamicahis ᐋᐢᒐᒥᒐᐦᐃᐢ
IPC on the hither side; closer to the speaker [dim]

āsē- ᐋᓭ
see asē

āsiskam ᐋᓯᐢᑲᒼ
VTI s/he arrives before s.t., s/he arrives before the proceedings

āsiskamātowak ᐋᓯᐢᑲᒫᑑᐗᐠ
VAI they outstrip one another; they arrive before another

āsiskawēw ᐋᓯᐢᑲᐌᐤ
VTA s/he arrives before s.o., s/he gets ahead of s.o.

āsiskākēw ᐋᓯᐢᑳᑫᐤ
VAI s/he arrives before people, s/he gets ahead of people

āsitē ᐋᓯᑌ
IPC opposite

āsitēyimēw ᐋᓯᑌᔨᒣᐤ
VTA s/he suspects s.o. jealously

āsiyān ᐋᓯᔮᐣ
NA loin-cloth, breech clout; diaper [cf. mitāsiyān]

āskaw ᐋᐢᑲᐤ
IPC once in a while, from time to time, sometimes

āskāskaw ᐋᐢᑳᐢᑲᐤ
IPC from time to time [cf. ay-āskaw]

āsohtatāw ᐋᓱᐦᑕᑖᐤ
VAIt s/he leans s.t. across something; s/he carries s.t. across something [also āsōhtatāw]

āsohtāw ᐋᓱᐦᑖᐤ
VAIt s/he leans s.t. up against something (e.g. a wall)

āsohtitāw ᐋᓱᐦᑎᑖᐤ
VAIt s/he lays s.t. to lean

āsokan ᐋᓱᑲᐣ
NI bridge; wharf, pier [also āsokwan]

āsokanāhtik ᐋᓱᑲᓈᐦᑎᐠ
NA a log placed across a stream [pl: -wak]

āsokanihkēw ᐋᓱᑲᓂᐦᑫᐤ
VAI s/he build bridges, s/he makes a ford [also āsokwanihkēw]

āsokāham ᐋᓱᑳᐦᐊᒼ
VTI s/he swims across [cf. āsōwakāham, āsōwaham]

āsokāmatin ᐋᓱᑳᒪᑎᐣ
VII it freezes across

āsokāmēham ᐋᓱᑳᒣᐦᐊᒼ
VTI s/he goes across by canoe

āsokāmēhtēw ᐋᓱᑳᒣᐦᑌᐤ
VAI s/he walks across (a river or bridge)

āsokāmēpaýiw ᐋᓱᑳᒣᐸᔨᐤ
VAI s/he goes across by boat or canoe
āsokāmēhtahēw ᐋᓱᑳᒣᐦᑕᐦᐁᐤ
VTA s/he takes s.o. across (the water)
āsokāmēýātakāw ᐋᓱᑳᒣᔮᑕᑳᐤ
VAI s/he wades across shallow water, s/he wades across
āsokāmohtēw ᐋᓱᑳᒧᐦᑌᐤ
VAI s/he walks across
āsokāmow ᐋᓱᑳᒧᐤ
VAI s/he flees across, s/he escapes across (to the other side)
āsowaham ᐋᓱᐘᐦᐊᒼ
VTI s/he crosses s.t. (*e.g.* a river), s/he crosses over; s/he crosses s.t. by canoe
āsowahasiw ᐋᓱᐘᐦᐊᓯᐤ
VAI s/he makes a short crossing, s/he crosses a short distance [*dim*]
āsowahēw ᐋᓱᐘᐦᐁᐤ
VTA s/he takes s.o. across
āsowahow ᐋᓱᐘᐦᐅᐤ
VAI s/he crosses by him/herself
āsowahonān ᐋᓱᐘᐦᐅᓈᐣ
NI a crossing
āsowahoýēw ᐋᓱᐘᐦᐅᔦᐤ
VTA s/he ferries s.o. across
āsowakāmē ᐋᓴᐘᑳᒣ
IPC across the stream, to the far bank
āsowakāmēw ᐋᓱᐘᑲᒣᐤ
VAI s/he crosses a body of water, s/he fords a stream, s/he crosses a river at a shallow ford; s/he crosses the ice by foot
āsowakāmēýāhtawīw
ᐋᓱᐘᑳᒣᔮᐦᑕᐑᐤ
VAI s/he crosses on a bridge
āsowakāmēýātakāw
ᐋᓱᐘᑳᒣᔮᑕᑳᐤ
VAI s/he wades across, s/he swims across
āsowē ᐋᓱᐍ
IPC one after the other
āsowi- ᐋᓱᐏ
IPV in turn, in succession
āsowīhtamawēw ᐋᓱᐑᐦᑕᒪᐍᐤ
VTA s/he passes a message to s.o.
āsoy ᐋᓱᐩ
NI ice chisel
āsoyāhtik ᐋᓱᔮᐦᑎᐠ
NI ice chisel handle [*pl*: -wa]
āsōnam ᐋᓲᓇᒼ
VTI s/he puts out his/her hand for an offering, s/he receives s.t. by hand
āsōnamawēw ᐋᓲᓇᒪᐍᐤ
VTA s/he passes (it/him) on to s.o. [*cf.* āsawinamawēw]
āsōnamātowin ᐋᓲᓇᒫᑐᐏᐣ
NI passing things on
āsōnē ᐋᓲᓀ
IPC especially, in particular; especially now
āsōpaýiw ᐋᓲᐸᔨᐤ
VII it goes from one to another; it is catching, it is contagious
āsōsimēw ᐋᓲᓯᒣᐤ
VTA s/he places s.o. leaning
āsōsimow ᐋᓲᓯᒧᐤ
VAI s/he leans against something (*e.g.* a wall)
āsōsin ᐋᓲᓯᐣ
VAI s/he leans on something
āsōskamawēw ᐋᓲᐢᑲᒪᐍᐤ
VTA s/he infects s.o.
āspataskopisowin
ᐋᐢᐸᑕᐢᑯᐱᓱᐏᐣ
NI back rest (for a chief)
āspīs ᐋᐢᐲᐢ
IPC seldom; here and there among the rest
āsponēsiw ᐋᐢᐳᓀᓯᐤ
VAI s/he is resentful; s/he is greedy
āsponēýihtam ᐋᐢᐳᓀᔨᐦᑕᒼ
VTI s/he thinks resentfully (of s.t.); s/he covets s.t.
āsponēýimēw ᐋᐢᐳᓀᔨᒣᐤ
VTA s/he resents s.o. (for taking more than giving)
āsponisiw ᐋᐢᐳᓂᓯᐤ
VAI s/he is greedy, s/he is stingy, s/he is covetous
āsponisiwin ᐋᐢᐳᓂᓯᐏᐣ
NI covetousness
āstam ᐋᐢᑕᒼ
IPC come here! [*pl*: āstamik, āstamitik]
āstamahcāw ᐋᐢᑕᒪᐦᒑᐤ
IPC the hill opposite; on this side of the hill
āstamēhk ᐋᐢᑕᒣᕽ
IPC less
āstamihk ᐋᐢᑕᒥᕽ
IPC on this side
āstamipaýiw ᐋᐢᑕᒥᐸᔨᐤ
VAI it becomes less, it runs low (*e.g.* money)
āstamispī ᐋᐢᑕᒥᐢᐲ
IPC lately, more recently; before
āstamispīhk ᐋᐢᑕᒥᐢᐲᕽ
IPC at a time closer to the present; more recently
āstamita ᐋᐢᑕᒥᑕ
IPC later; on this side, closer; on the hither side (in time or space); this way over
āstamitakām ᐋᐢᑕᒥᑕᑳᒼ
IPC this side of the water
āstamitē ᐋᐢᑕᒥᑌ
IPC later; on this side, closer; on the higher side (in time or space)
āstamitē isi ᐋᐢᑕᒥᑌ ᐃᓯ
IPH over this way
āstamitik ᐋᐢᑕᒥᑎᐠ
IPC all of you come here!
āstamiýikohk ᐋᐢᑕᒥᔨᑯᕽ
IPC too little; less than
āstamohtēw ᐋᐢᑕᒧᐦᑌᐤ
VAI s/he walks hither, s/he walks towards speaker
āstawēham ᐋᐢᑕᐍᐦᐊᒼ
VTI s/he extinguishes s.t., s/he puts out the fire
āstawēhamawēw ᐋᐢᑕᐍᐦᐊᒪᐍᐤ
VTA s/he puts the fire out for s.o.
āstawēhikēw ᐋᐢᑕᐍᐦᐃᑫᐤ
VAI s/he extinguishes the fire; s/he fights fire
āstawēnam ᐋᐢᑕᐍᓇᒼ
VTI s/he puts out a fire or turns off a light, lamp, or flashlight; s/he extinguishes s.t. by hand
āstawēnikēw ᐋᐢᑕᐍᓂᑫᐤ
VAI s/he extinguishes the light, s/he turns out the lights
āstawēpaýiw ᐋᐢᑕᐍᐸᔨᐤ
VII it goes out suddenly (as a flame) by itself
āstawēpicikēw ᐋᐢᑕᐍᐱᒋᑫᐤ
VAI s/he turns off the lights
āstawēskam ᐋᐢᑕᐍᐢᑲᒼ
VTI s/he extinguishes s.t. by foot
āstawēskawēw ᐋᐢᑕᐍᐢᑲᐍᐤ
VTA s/he extinguishes s.o. by foot
āstawēw ᐋᐢᑕᐍᐤ
VAI it goes out (*e.g.* pipe)
āstawēw ᐋᐢᑕᐍᐤ
VII it is out, it goes out (*e.g.* fire)
āstawēyāpocikan ᐋᐢᑕᐍᔮᐳᒋᑲᐣ
NI fire extinguisher
āstawēyāpowacikan
ᐋᐢᑕᐍᔮᐳᐘᒋᑲᐣ
NI fire extinguisher
āstawēyāpowatāw
ᐋᐢᑕᐍᔮᐳᐘᑖᐤ
VAIt s/he extinguishes s.t. (with water)
āstē- ᐋᐢᑌ
IPV ceasing; quit
āstē-ayāw ᐋᐢᑌ ᐊᔮᐤ
VAI s/he recovers from illness, s/he is gradually restored
āstē-kīsikāw ᐋᐢᑌ ᑮᓯᑳᐤ
VII it is a bright day, it is good weather
āstēkamāw ᐋᐢᑌᑲᒫᐤ
VII it is still water, the water is still
āstēkamin ᐋᐢᑌᑲᒥᐣ
VII it settles (as tea leaves);

it is still water, the water is still
āstēkamiw ᐋᐢᑌᑲᒥᐤ
VII the water has calmed; it is still water, it is calm water [*after having once been windswept*]
āstēpaýiw ᐋᐢᑌᐸᔨᐤ
VAI s/he feels better (in health)
āstēpaýiw ᐋᐢᑌᐸᔨᐤ
VII it ceases
āstēpēw ᐋᐢᑌᐯᐤ
VAI s/he sobers up
āstēpwēsiw ᐋᐢᑌᐻᓯᐤ
VAI s/he stops being hot, s/he stops sweating
āstēsin ᐋᐢᑌᓯᐣ
VAI s/he rests, s/he lies down to rest [*also* āstēsiniw]
āstētāhtam ᐋᐢᑌᑖᐦᑕᒼ
VTI s/he stops panting
āstētāmosin ᐋᐢᑌᑖᒧᓯᐣ
VAI s/he stops for a rest in flight
āstēyākamin ᐋᐢᑌᔮᑲᒥᐣ
VAI it settles (as tea)
āstwāhtowak ᐋᐢᑶᐦᑐᐘᐠ
VAI they bet, they bet one another, they place things for one another
āstwāhtowin ᐋᐢᑶᐦᑐᐏᐣ
NI wager, bet
āstwākēw ᐋᐢᑶᑫᐤ
VAI s/he stakes something, s/he wagers something
āstwākēwin ᐋᐢᑶᑫᐏᐣ
NI stake, wager
āstwāw ᐋᐢᑶᐤ
VAI s/he lays a bet, s/he lays down so much (money)
āswahcikēw ᐋᓵᐦᒋᑫᐤ
VAI s/he awaits food with an open mouth (*e.g.* baby, bird)
āswahēw ᐋᓵᐦᐁᐤ
VTA s/he places s.o. to lean against something
āswahtam ᐋᓵᐦᑕᒼ
VTI s/he awaits s.t. (as food) with an open mouth
āswamēw ᐋᓵᒣᐤ
VTA s/he awaits s.o. (as food) with an open mouth
āswastāw ᐋᓵᐢᑖᐤ
VAIt s/he places s.t. to lean against something
āswāskokāpawiw ᐋᔃᐢᑯᑳᐸᐏᐤ
VAI s/he stands leaning on something (of wood)
āta ᐋᑕ
IPC although, even though, in vain; on the other hand [*concessive conjunction*; *cf.* āta *IPV*]
āta- ᐋᑕ
IPV although, in vain [*cf.* āta *IPC*]
āta wiya ᐋᑕ ᐏᔭ
IPH though, although; nonetheless, anyway
ātakāmakisin ᐋᑕᑳᒪᑭᓯᐣ
VAI s/he is blocked by water
ātamiskwēýiw ᐋᑕᒥᐢᑵᔨᐤ
VAI s/he turns his/her own head away
ātawēýihtam ᐋᑕᐍᔨᐦᑕᒼ
VTI s/he rejects s.t., s/he refuses s.t.; s/he dislikes s.t.
ātawēýimēw ᐋᑕᐍᔨᒣᐤ
VAI s/he rejects s.o., s/he refuses s.o.; s/he dislikes s.o., s/he disdains s.o.
ātawināsow ᐋᑕᐏᓈᓱᐤ
VAI s/he disdains his/her own looks
ātaýōhkan ᐋᑕᔫᐦᑲᐣ
NA spirit being, spirit power, spirit guardian, spirit animal
ātaýōhkan ᐋᑕᔫᐦᑲᐣ
NI sacred story; legend [*cf.* ātayōhkēwin]
ātaýōhkawēw ᐋᑕᔫᐦᑲᐍᐤ
VTA s/he tells sacred stories or legends to s.o.
ātaýōhkātam ᐋᑕᔫᐦᑳᑕᒼ
VTI s/he tells a sacred story of s.t.
ātaýōhkātēw ᐋᑕᔫᐦᑳᑌᐤ
VTA s/he tells a sacred story of s.o.
ātaýōhkēw ᐋᑕᔫᐦᑫᐤ
VAI s/he tells a sacred story or legend
ātaýōhkēwin ᐋᑕᔫᐦᑫᐏᐣ
NI sacred story, legend [*cf.* ātayōhkan *NI*]
ātiht ᐋᑎᐦᐟ
IPC some
ātiman ᐋᑎᒪᐣ
NI lace of snowshoe
ātisin ᐋᑎᓯᐣ
VAI s/he is blocked
ātiskawēw ᐋᑎᐢᑲᐍᐤ
VTA s/he blocks s.o. with his/her body
ātocikātēw ᐋᑐᒋᑳᑌᐤ
VII it is told of, it is talked about
ātotam ᐋᑐᑕᒼ
VTI s/he tells about s.t., s/he gives an account of s.t. [*rdpl*: ay-ātotam]
ātotamawēw ᐋᑐᑕᒪᐍᐤ
VTA s/he tells about (it/him) for s.o.
ātotākosiw ᐋᑐᑖᑯᓯᐤ
VAI s/he is famed
ātotēw ᐋᑐᑌᐤ
VTA s/he tells about s.o
āw ᐋᐤ
IPC ah, oh [*exclamation*]
āwacikan ᐋᐘᒋᑲᐣ
NI wheel barrow; thing used for hauling
āwacikēw ᐋᐘᒋᑫᐤ
VAI s/he hauls things
āwacimihtēw ᐋᐘᒋᒥᐦᑌᐤ
VAI s/he hauls firewood [*wC*: āwacinihtēw]
āwacipitam ᐋᐘᒋᐱᑕᒼ
VTI s/he pulls s.t.; s/he pulls a load, s/he hauls s.t. by pulling
āwacipitēw ᐋᐘᒋᐱᑌᐤ
VTA s/he pulls s.o.; s/he hauls s.o. by pulling
āwacitāpēw ᐋᐘᒋᑖᐯᐤ
VAI s/he pulls s.t., s/he drags s.t. home (*e.g.* wood)
āwahēw ᐋᐚᐦᐁᐤ
VTA s/he hauls s.o.
āwatamawēw ᐋᐘᑕᒪᐍᐤ
VAI s/he hauls (it/him) for s.o.
āwatamāsow ᐋᐘᑕᒫᓱᐤ
VAI s/he hauls (it/him) for him/herself
āwataskosīwākan
ᐋᐘᑕᐢᑯᓰᐚᑲᐣ
NI hay-rack
āwataskosīwēw ᐋᐘᑕᐢᑯᓰᐍᐤ
VAI s/he hauls hay
āwatawāsiswākan
ᐋᐘᑕᐚᓯᔂᑲᐣ
NA school bus
āwatawiswākan ᐋᐘᑕᐏᔂᑲᐣ
NI railroad car; truck [*cf.* āwatāswākan]
āwatāw ᐋᐘᑖᐤ
VAIt s/he hauls s.t., s/he hauls s.t. by carrying; s/he carries s.t. off
āwatāhtikwēw ᐋᐘᑖᐦᑎᑵᐤ
VAI s/he takes part in a pole dance; s/he hauls poles
āwatāswākan ᐋᐘᑖᔂᑲᐣ
NA truck [*cf.* āwatawiswākan]
āwatēw ᐋᐘᑌᐤ
VTA s/he carries s.o. off
āwēpaýiw ᐋᐍᐸᔨᐤ
VAI s/he staggers
āýapāskwēýāw ᐋᔭᐹᐢᑵᔮᐤ
VII it is a land with clumps of trees
āýimakihtēw ᐋᔨᒪᑭᐦᑌᐤ
VII it is expensive, costly (spiritually)
āýimakisow ᐋᔨᒪᑭᓱᐤ
VAI it is expensive, costly (spiritually)
āýiman ᐋᔨᒪᐣ
NI difficult thing [*cf.* kā-āyimahk]
āýiman ᐋᔨᒪᐣ
VII it is difficult
āýimanohk ᐋᔨᒪᓄᕽ
IPC in a difficult place
āýimāc ᐋᔨᒫᐨ
IPC with difficulty, barely, scarcely

āýimāpisin ᐋᔦᒫᐱᓯᐣ
VAI s/he looks difficult to one
āýimēýihtam ᐋᔦᒣᔦᐦᑕᒼ
VTI s/he considers s.t. difficult, s/he thinks s.t. is difficult
āýimihēw ᐋᔦᒥᐦᐁᐤ
VTA s/he gives s.o. a difficult time, s/he troubles s.o.
āýimihtowak ᐋᔦᒥᐦᑐᐘᒃ
VAI they make it difficult for one another
āýimihtowin ᐋᔦᒥᐦᑐᐎᐣ
NI trouble
āýimimēw ᐋᔦᒥᒣᐤ
VTA s/he makes things difficult for s.o. by speech
āýimipaýiw ᐋᔦᒥᐸᔦᐤ
VII it gives trouble
āýimisiw ᐋᔦᒥᓯᐤ
VAI s/he has a difficult time; s/he is difficult, s/he is troublesome; s/he is demanding, s/he is constantly in need of attention from his/her parents; s/he is of difficult disposition
āýimisiwin ᐋᔦᒥᓯᐎᐣ
NI hardship
āýimisīwatim ᐋᔦᒥᓰᐘᏘᒼ
NA wild, difficult horse [*pl*: -wak]
āýimīw ᐋᔦᒦᐤ
VAI s/he has a difficult time, task or life
āýimōhtowin ᐋᔦᒨᐦᑐᐎᐣ
NI gossip; talking about one another [*cf.* āýimōmitowin]
āýimōmēw ᐋᔦᒨᒣᐤ
VTA s/he speaks of s.o. (causing trouble); s/he causes trouble by speaking of s.o.; s/he gossips about s.o.
āýimōmitowin ᐋᔦᒨᒥᑐᐎᐣ
NI gossip; talking about one another [*cf.* āýimōhtowin]
āýimōmiwēw ᐋᔦᒨᒥᐍᐤ
VAI s/he speaks against people habitually
āýimōtam ᐋᔦᒨᑕᒼ
VTI s/he speaks of s.t.
āýīci- ᐋᔩᒋ
IPV firmly, tightly
āýītinam ᐋᔩᑎᓇᒼ
VTI s/he holds s.t. tightly or firmly
āýītinēw ᐋᔩᑎᓀᐤ
VTA s/he holds s.o. tightly or firmly
āýwahpinēw ᐋᔫᐦᐱᓀᐤ
VAI s/he is helpless from disease; s/he is deteriorating, s/he is becoming worse

C

ᒐ

ca-cahkacahikēsiw
ᒐ ᒡᐦᒐᒡᐦᐊᐦᐃᑫᓯᐤ
VAI it gives little pecks with its beak [*rdpl*; *dim*; *cf.* cahkatahikēw]

ca-cahkaham ᒐ ᒡᐦᐊᐦᐋᒡ
VTI s/he pokes at s.t. with a stick [*rdpl*]

ca-cahkataham ᒐ ᒡᐦᐊᑕᐦᐋᒡ
VTI it pecks at s.t. (as a woodpecker) [*rdpl*; *also* cāh-cahkataham]

ca-cahkatahikēw ᒐ ᒡᐦᐊᑕᐦᐃᑫᐅᐧ
VAI it pecks, it pecks at things (as a woodpecker) [*rdpl*]

cacahkāskwāw ᒐᒐᒡᐦᐋᐢᒀᐤ
VII there are high waves, the waves are high [*see also* mamahkāhan]

cacahkimahcihow ᒐᒐᒡᐦᐃᒪᐦᒋᐦᐅᐤ
VAI s/he has a severe, stabbing pain in the chest

cacahkwanīyiw ᒐᒐᒡᐦᐊᐧᓂᔩᐤ
VAI s/he stands on his/her toes

cacāstapipayin ᒐᒑᐢᑕᐱᐸᔨᐣ
VII it is fast, it is quick [*rdpl*]

cacāstapiwēw ᒐᒑᐢᑕᐱᐅᐧᐤ
VAI s/he talks fast [*rdpl*; *dim*; *cf.* tatāstapiwēw]

cacēkahkwān ᒐᒉᑲᐦᒁᐣ
NI lance, dart

cacēmāpicēs ᒐᒉᒫᐱᒉᐢ
NA short-toothed person [*rdpl*; *dim*; *cf.* cimāpitēw *VAI*]

cacimāsin ᒐᒋᒫᓯᐣ
VII it is short [*rdpl*; *cf.* cimāsin]

caciwihēw ᒐᒋᐎᐦᐁᐤ
VTA s/he takes s.o. by surprise; s/he outdoes s.o.

cahcahkāyow ᒡᐦᒐᐦᑳᔔ
NA blackbird [*also* cahcāhkāyow]

cahcahkāyōsis ᒡᐦᒐᐦᑳᔫᓯᐢ
NA small blackbird, blackbird hatchling [*dim*; *cf.* cahcahkāyow]

cahcahkāyōskāw ᒡᐦᒐᐦᑳᔫᐢᑳᐤ
VII there are many blackbirds, blackbirds are abundant [*sg only*]

cahcahkiw ᒡᐦᒐᐦᑭᐤ
NA pelican; crane [*also* cahcāhkiw-]

cahcahkiw-sākahikanihk ᒡᐦᒐᐦᑭᐤ ᓵᑲᐦᐃᑲᓂᐦᐠ
INM Pelican Lake First Nation, SK [*also* Chitek Lake, SK]

cahcakipēwasinastēwēkin ᒡᐦᒐᑭᐯᐊᐧᓯᓇᐢᑌᐁᐧᑭᐣ
NI polka dot material [*pl*: -wa]

cahkahwēw ᒡᐦᐊᐦᐁᐧᐤ
VTA s/he pokes s.o. (with a stick)

cahkasinaham ᒡᐦᐊᓯᓇᐦᐊᒡ
VTI s/he writes s.t. in Cree syllabics; s/he puts on artwork

cahkasinahikan ᒡᐦᐊᓯᓇᐦᐃᑲᐣ
NI a letter written in Cree syllabics; artwork

cahkasinastēw ᒡᐦᐊᓯᓇᐢᑌᐤ
VII it is spotted, it is covered in polka dots

cahkastāw ᒡᐦᐊᐢᒖ
VAIt s/he puts s.t. in a high pile

cahkastēhwēw ᒡᐦᐊᐢᑌᐦᐁᐧᐤ
VTA s/he prods s.o. on

cahkastēw ᒡᐦᐊᐢᑌᐤ
VII it is in a high pile

cahkataham ᒡᐦᐊᑕᐦᐋᒡ
VTI s/he pokes at s.t. with beak of stick; s/he plays bingo

cahkatahikēw ᒡᐦᐊᑕᐦᐃᑫᐅᐧ
VAI s/he pokes at things with a stick or beak; s/he plays bingo

cahkatahwēw ᒡᐦᐊᑕᐦᐁᐧᐤ
VTA s/he pokes s.o. with a beak or stick

cahkatayēnēw ᒡᐦᐊᑕᔦᓀᐤ
VTA s/he pokes s.o.'s belly, s/he spurs s.o.'s belly

cahkatinaw ᒡᐦᐊᑎᓇᐤ
NI a steep, pointed hill

cahkatināw ᒡᐦᐊᑎᓈᐤ
VII it is a steep, pointed hill [*see also* mohkatināw]

cahkākonēham ᒡᐦᐋᑯᓀᐦᐊᒡ
VTI s/he jabs a hole into s.t. as snow

cahkāpahwēw ᒡᐦᐋᐸᐦᐁᐧᐤ
VTA s/he jabs s.o. in the eye with something

cahkāpēs ᒡᐦᐋᐯᐢ
NI spirit-being; Man-in-the-Moon [*dim*; *more common in Eastern dialects*]

cahkāpēw ᒡᐦᐋᐯᐤ
NI spirit-being; Man-in-the-Moon

cahkāpicin ᒡᐦᐋᐱᒋᐣ
VAI s/he has his/her eye punctured by a sliver, stick; s/he gets snagged in the eye

cahkāpiskāw ᒡᐦᐋᐱᐢᑳᐤ
VII it is a pointed rock

cahkās ᒡᐦᐋᐢ
NI ice-cream [*dim*; *cf.* tahkāw]

cahkāsikēw ᒡᐦᐋᓯᑫᐤ
VAI it shines [*e.g. sun, flashlight, torch*]

cahkāskwēyāw ᒡᐦᐋᐢᒁᐁᔮᐤ
NI pointed bush

cahkāskwēyiw ᒡᐦᐋᐢᒁᐁᔨᐤ
VAI s/he sticks his/her own head up

cahkihtitāw ᒡᐦᐱᐦᑎᒑ
VAIt s/he throws s.t. to stick up

cahkinam ᒡᐦᐱᓇᒡ
VTI s/he pokes s.t. with a finger, elbow, etc.

cahkinēw ᒡᐦᐱᓀᐤ
VTA s/he pokes s.o. with a finger, elbow, etc.

cahkipēham ᒡᐦᐱᐯᐦᐋᒡ
VTI s/he marks s.t. with diacritical symbols, s/he marks s.t. with syllabic symbols

cahkipēhikan ᒡᐦᐱᐯᐦᐃᑲᐣ
NA diacritical mark in syllabary; syllabic symbol [*also NI*]

cahkisēhikan ᒡᐦᐱᓭᐦᐃᑲᐣ
NI flint, detonating cap on cartridge, shell

cahkisimēw ᒡᐦᐱᓯᒣᐤ
VTA s/he stubs s.o. (e.g. cigarette)

cahkitōnēsin ᒡᐦᐱᑑᓀᓯᐣ
VAI s/he has a swollen (protruding) mouth (from falling)

cahkopicēsak ᒐᐦᑯᐱᒉᓴᐠ
NA sheaves [*pl*; *dim*; *cf.*
tahkopitēw]

cahkopisōsak ᒐᐦᑯᐱᓲᓴᐠ
NA sheaves [*pl*; *dim*; *cf.*
tahkopiswēw *VTA*]

canawīw ᒐᓇᐤᐁᐧᐤ
VAI s/he is busy

capahcāsin ᒐᐸᐦᒐᓯᐣ
VII it is low [*dim*]

capahciy̌inīs ᒐᐸᐦᒋᔨᓃᐢ
NA short person, dwarf
[*dim*]

capasīs ᒐᐸᓰᐢ
IPC below, further down,
lower down, down low;
bottom [*also* capasis]

cawāscēs ᒐᐚᐢᒉᐢ
NI small ravine, narrows;
street, side-street [*dim*]

cawāscēsihk ᒐᐚᐢᒉᓯᕽ
IPC in a small ravine, in a
narrows; on a side-street
[*loc*; *dim*]

cawāsihk ᒐᐚᓯᕽ
IPC in a small ravine, in a
narrows; on the street [*loc*;
dim]

ᒐ

cācikacēsip ᒐᒋᑲᒉᓯᑊ
NA water-hen

cāh ᒐᐦ
IPC [*exclamation of disgust*]

cāh-cahkasinahikāsow
ᒐᐦ ᒐᐦᑲᓯᓇᐦᐃᑳᓱᐤ
VAI s/he has marks on
his/her body [*rdpl*]

cāh-cahkatāmow ᒐᐦ ᒐᐦᑲᑖᒧᐤ
VAI s/he has sharp pains in
breathing, s/he suffers
shortness of breath [*rdpl*]

cāh-cahkipēkahwēw
ᒐᐦ ᒐᐦᑭᐯᑲᐦᐌᐧᐤ
VTA s/he paints dots on s.o.
[*rdpl*]

cāh-cahkiyēhēw ᒐᐦ ᒐᐦᑭᔦᐦᐁᐧᐤ
VAI s/he has sharp pains in
breathing, s/he suffers
shortness of breath [*rdpl*]

cāh-cimatāw ᒐᐦ ᒋᒪᑖᐤ
VAIt s/he erects s.t. upright
(everywhere) (e.g. fence
posts) [*rdpl*]

cāh-cīki ᒐᐦ ᒌᑭ
IPC close, nearby [*rdpl*]

cāh-cīpokocēsiw ᒐᐦ ᒌᐳᑯᒉᓯᐤ
VAI s/he has a sharp little
nose [*rdpl*; *dim*; *cf.*
cīpokotēw]

cāhcāmosikan ᒐᐦᒐᒧᓯᑲᐣ
NI snuff; pepper

cāhcāmosiw ᒐᐦᒐᒧᓯᐤ
VAI s/he sneezes [*dim*; *cf.*
cāhcāmow]

cāhcāmoskawēw ᒐᐦᒐᒧᐢᑲᐌᐧᐤ
VTA s/he makes s.o. sneeze

cāhcāmoskākēw ᒐᐦᒐᒧᐢᑳᑫᐧᐤ
VAI s/he uses something to
induce sneezing

cāhcāmoskākow ᒐᐦᒐᒧᐢᑳᑯᐤ
VTA s/he is made to sneeze
by s.t. [*inanimate actor form
of VTA* cāhcāmoskaw-]

cāhcāmow ᒐᐦᒐᒧᐤ
VAI s/he sneezes

cāhkāskisow ᒐᐦᑳᐢᑭᓱᐤ
VAI it burns completely, all
the way (as a tree)

cāhkāskitēw ᒐᐦᑳᐢᑭᑌᐧᐤ
VII it burns completely; it is
a flaming fire, shooting
upward

cāhkāyowēw ᒐᐦᑳᔪᐌᐧᐤ
VAI it cocks its tail (as a
horse)

cāhkipay̌iw ᒐᐦᑭᐸᔨᐤ
VII it comes suddenly to a
head (as in boiling), it comes
to a point

cāpān! ᒐᐹᐣ
NDA Great Grandparent!;
Great Grandchild [*voc*; *cf.*
nocāpān]

cāpihcicikan ᒐᐱᐦᒋᒋᑲᐣ
NI handle

cāpihcicikanis ᒐᐱᐦᒋᒋᑲᓂᐢ
NI spear, lance

cāstapīw ᒐᐢᑕᐱᐤ
VAI s/he hurries up [*dim*; *cf.*
tāstapīw]

ᑫ

cēcēmipahtāw ᒉᒉᒥᐸᐦᑖᐤ
VAI s/he trots

cēh ᒉᐦ
IPC [*exclamation of disgust*]

cēhcapisiw ᒉᐦᒐᐱᓯᐤ
VAI s/he rides a little [*dim*;
cf. tēhtapiw]

cēhcapiwinis ᒉᐦᒐᐱᐃᐧᓂᐢ
NI baby chair, highchair;
little chair [*dim*]

cēkahpīs ᒉᑲᐦᐲᐢ
NA jackfish [*English loan*;
see also iy̌inito-kinosēw]

cēskwa ᒉᐢᒁ
IPC wait, wait a minute;
presently, yet; soon; in the
future [*cf.* namóya cēskwa]

cēskwa pitamā ᒉᐢᒁ ᐱᒐᒫ
IPH wait a while, a little
while

cēsos ᒉᓱᐢ
NA Jésus [*adapted from
French*; *cf.* cīsas]

ᒋ

cihcicāpānāskos ᒋᐦᒋᒐᐹᓈᐢᑯᐢ
NA buggy, cart; small wagon
[*dim*]

cihcipayapiskikanis
ᒋᐦᒋᐸᔭᐱᐢᑭᑲᓂᐢ
NI bicycle [*dim*]

cihcipipay̌is ᒋᐦᒋᐱᐸᔨᐢ
NA wheel [*dim*; *also*
tihtipipayis]

cihcipistikwān-ātayōhkēwin
ᒋᐦᒋᐱᐢᑎᒁᐣ ᐋᑕᔫᐦᑫᐃᐧᐣ
NI sacred story of the rolling
head

cihcīkinam ᒋᐦᒌᑭᓇᒼ
VTI s/he scratches s.t.

cihcīkinēw ᒋᐦᒌᑭᓀᐤ
VTA s/he scratches s.o.

cihcīkipitam ᒋᐦᒌᑭᐱᑕᒼ
VTI s/he scratches s.t.

cihcīkipitēw ᒋᐦᒌᑭᐱᑌᐤ
VTA s/he scratches s.o.

cihcīkipititowak ᒋᐦᒌᑭᐱᑎᑐᐊᐧᐠ
VAI they scratch one another

cihcīkiw ᒋᐦᒌᑭᐤ
VAI s/he scratches, s/he
itches him/herself [*also*
cihcīkiw, cīhcīkiw]

cihcīkwahtam ᒋᐦᒌᑿᐦᑕᒼ
VTI s/he nibbles at s.t., s/he
nibbles meat off a bone

cihcīkwamēw ᒋᐦᒌᑿᒣᐤ
VTA s/he nibbles at s.o.

cihcīpāpiw ᒋᐦᒌᐹᐱᐤ
VAI s/he has a twitching eye,
s/he quivers at the eye or
eyelid

cihkē ᒋᐦᑫ
IPC recently [*cf.* anohcihkē]

cihkomisīs ᒋᐦᑯᒥᓰᐢ
NA wolverine

cikahkwān ᒋᑲᐦᑿᐣ
NA gambling toy shaped
like a knife-blade; stick in
woman's stick game

cikahkwān ᒋᑲᐦᑿᐣ
NI lance

cikahkwātam ᒋᑲᐦᑿᑕᒼ
VTI s/he throws a dart at s.t.

cikahkwātēw ᒋᑲᐦᑿᑌᐤ
VTA s/he throws a dart at
s.o.

cikahkwēw ᒋᑲᐦᑴᐤ
VAI s/he throws darts; s/he
plays four stick game

cikahkwēwēpahwēw
ᒋᑲᐦᑴᐌᐧᐸᐦᐌᐧᐤ
VTA s/he knocks s.o. down
with a shot

cikahkwēwin ᒋᑲᐦᑴᐃᐧᐣ
NI stick game

cikawāsis ᒋᑲᐚᓯᐢ
IPC few

cikawāsisinwa ᒋᑲᐚᓯᓯᓌ
VII they are few in number
[*also* cakawāsisinwa]

cikawāsisiwak ᒋᑲᐚᓯᓯᐊᐧᐠ
VAI they are few in number
[*also* cakawāsisiwak]

cikāhkwēpay̌iw ᒋᑳᐦᑴᐸᔨᐤ
VAI s/he becomes
unconscious

cikāscēpaẏīs ᒋᑳᐢᒉᐸᔩᐢ
NI film, movie [*dim*; *cf.* cikāstēpaẏiw, cikāstēpaẏihcikan]
cikāsimin ᒋᑳᓯᒥᐣ
NI partridge berry [*also* cakāsimin; *cf.* acikāsimin]
cikāsipakwa ᒋᑳᓯᐸᑿ
NI bearberry leaves, partridge berry plants [*pl*; *Arctostaphylos uva-ursi; used as tobacco*; *also NA*; *also* cakāsipakwa; *cf.* acikāsipakwa]
cikāstēhtin ᒋᑳᐢᑌᐦᑎᐣ
VII it makes a shadow
cikāstēpaẏiw ᒋᑳᐢᑌᐸᔨᐤ
VAI s/he casts a shadow
cikāstēpaẏiw ᒋᑳᐢᑌᐸᔨᐤ
VII it casts a shadow
cikāstēpaẏihcikan ᒋᑳᐢᑌᐸᔨᐦᒋᑲᐣ
NI television, t.v.
cikāstēpēkisin ᒋᑳᐢᑌᐯᑭᓯᐣ
VAI s/he is reflected in the water
cikāstēpicikan ᒋᑳᐢᑌᐱᒋᑲᐣ
NI movie camera; movie; picture frame [*cf.* ācikāstēpicikan]
cikāstēpison ᒋᑳᐢᑌᐱᓱᐣ
NI picture, photograph
cikāstēsimow ᒋᑳᐢᑌᓯᒧᐤ
VAI s/he makes a shadow
cikāstēsin ᒋᑳᐢᑌᓯᐣ
VAI s/he has his/her shadow seen
cikāstēsiw ᒋᑳᐢᑌᓯᐤ
VAI s/he is in shadow
cikāstēskawēw ᒋᑳᐢᑌᐢᑲᐍᐤ
VTA s/he shadows s.o.
cikēmā ᒋᑫᒫ
IPC of course, certainly, naturally, obviously, as might be expected, as a natural result, certain consequence; evidently; because [*confirming what could not reasonably be doubted*]
cikēmā anima ᒋᑫᒫ ᐊᓂᒪ
IPH sure, sure enough
cimacēs ᒋᒪᒉᐢ
NI fence-post, picket [*dim*; *cf.* cimatēw]
cimacikēw ᒋᒪᒋᑫᐤ
VAI s/he stooks, s/he ties sheaves into stooks
cimahēw ᒋᒪᐦᐁᐤ
VTA s/he places s.o. (e.g. tree) upright, plant s.o. upright; stand s.o. up
cimasow ᒋᒪᓱᐤ
VAI s/he stands upright; he has an erection, he has an erect penis
cimatahkwēw ᒋᒪᑕᐦᑵᐤ
VAI s/he throws darts to stand upright
cimatāw ᒋᒪᑖᐤ
VAIt s/he places s.t. upright, s/he plants s.t. upright; s/he stands s.t. up, s/he erects s.t.
cimatē-wēpinam ᒋᒪᑌ ᐍᐱᓇᒼ
VTI s/he throws s.t. so that it sticks upright
cimatēw ᒋᒪᑌᐤ
VII it stands upright, it stands erect; it is erected
cimāniskwēw ᒋᒫᓂᐢᑵᐤ
VAI s/he has short hair
cimāpēkan ᒋᒫᐯᑲᐣ
VII it is short (e.g. as string)
cimāpēkasin ᒋᒫᐯᑲᓯᐣ
VII it is rather short [*dim*]
cimāpitēw ᒋᒫᐱᑌᐤ
VAI s/he has short teeth
cimāsin ᒋᒫᓯᐣ
VII it is short
cimāsko-nāpēw ᒋᒫᐢᑯ ᓈᐯᐤ
NA short man
cimāskosiw ᒋᒫᐢᑯᓯᐤ
VAI s/he is short (as a tree)
cimāskwan ᒋᒫᐢᑿᐣ
VII it is short (as a board)
cimāwikanēw ᒋᒫᐏᑲᓀᐤ
VAI s/he has a short back
cimāyowēw ᒋᒫᔪᐍᐤ
VAI it has a short tail
cimēkaham ᒋᒣᑲᐦᐊᒼ
VTI s/he shortens s.t. [*also* cēmēkaham]
cimēkahwēw ᒋᒣᑲᐦᐍᐤ
VTA s/he shortens s.o. (e.g. pants) [*also* cēmēkahwēw]
cimēkasākēw ᒋᒣᑲᓵᑫᐤ
VAI she has a short dress [*also*: cēmēkasākēw]
cimicihcēw ᒋᒥᒋᐦᒉᐤ
VAI s/he has short hands
cimicihciy ᒋᒥᒋᐦᒋᐩ
NI a short hand
cimicihcīs ᒋᒥᒋᐦᒌᐢ
NI short finger
cimihtawakēw ᒋᒥᐦᑕᐘᑫᐤ
VAI s/he has short ears
cimikasēw ᒋᒥᑲᓭᐤ
VAI s/he has short nails, it has short claws
cimikātēw ᒋᒥᑳᑌᐤ
VAI s/he has short legs
cimikotēw ᒋᒥᑯᑌᐤ
VAI s/he has a short nose; it has a short beak
cimikwayawēw ᒋᒥᑿᔭᐍᐤ
VAI s/he has a short neck
cimipaẏiw ᒋᒥᐸᔨᐤ
VII it shrinks, it shortens suddenly
cimipitonēw ᒋᒥᐱᑐᓀᐤ
VAI s/he has short arms
cimisāwātam ᒋᒥᓵᐚᑕᒼ
VTI s/he cuts s.t. short
cimisihtāw ᒋᒥᓯᐦᑖᐤ
VAIt s/he shortens s.t.
cimisisiw ᒋᒥᓯᓯᐤ
VAI s/he is short of stature; s/he is very short
cimisitēw ᒋᒥᓯᑌᐤ
VAI s/he has short feet
cimitēskanēw ᒋᒥᑌᐢᑲᓀᐤ
VAI s/he has short horns
cimiyawēw ᒋᒥᔭᐍᐤ
VAI s/he has a short body
cipahikanis ᒋᐸᐦᐃᑲᓂᐢ
NI minute [*dim*; *cf.* tipahikan]
ciscēmās ᒋᐢᒉᒫᐢ
NA tobacco [*dim*]
cistāwēw ᒋᐢᑖᐍᐤ
VAI s/he makes echoing noises
cistēmāw ᒋᐢᑌᒫᐤ
NA tobacco
cistwāsiw ᒋᐢᑤᓯᐤ
VAI s/he makes a bet, s/he wagers [*see also* astwāsiw]
ciyawisisiw ᒋᔭᐏᓯᓯᐤ
VAI it holds little (e.g. pipe, kettle)
ciẏāhāw ᒋᔮᐦᐋᐤ
VAI s/he is late, s/he is not ready [*cf.* taciwihāw]
ciyēkwac ᒋᔦᑿᐨ
IPC opposite of expected, reversal of the norm; instead [*also* ciyakwāc]

ᒌ

cī ᒌ
IPC [*question marker, follows questioned element*; *cf. sC and most areas of wC*: nā *IPC*]
cīhcīkom ᒋᐦᒌᑯᒼ
NA wart [*cf.* micīhcīkom; *also* micihcīkom]
cīhcīkomiw ᒋᐦᒌᑯᒥᐤ
VAI s/he has a wart [*cf.* ocīhcīkomiw; *also* cihcīkomiw]
cīhcīkosam ᒌᐦᒌᑯᓴᒼ
VTI s/he cuts meat off s.t. (e.g. bone)
cīhcīkosikāsow ᒌᐦᒌᑯᓯᑳᓱᐤ
VAI s/he is shaven bare
cīhcīkoswēw ᒌᐦᒌᑯᔃᐤ
VTA s/he clips s.o. very short, s/he crops s.o.'s hair very short
cīhcīkwahtam ᒌᐦᒌᑿᐦᑕᒼ
VTI s/he gnaws the meat off of s.t.
cīhcīpicikēw ᒌᐦᒌᐱᒋᑫᐤ
VAI s/he rakes, s/he scratches
cīhcīpipaẏin ᒌᐦᒌᐱᐸᔨᐣ
VII it quivers
cīhcīpipaẏiw ᒌᐦᒌᐱᐸᔨᐤ
VAI s/he quivers
cīhkāpisin ᒌᐦᑳᐱᓯᐣ
VAI s/he is pleased at the sight

cīhkēýihtam ᒌᐦᑫᔨᐦᑕᒼ
VTI s/he likes s.t., approve of s.t.; s/he is eager for s.t.; s/he is proud of s.t.

cīhkēýihtākosiw ᒌᐦᑫᔨᐦᑖᑯᓯᐤ
VAI s/he is important; s/he is well-liked

cīhkēýimēw ᒌᐦᑫᔨᒣᐤ
VTA s/he likes s.o., s/he takes to s.o.

cīhkēýimow ᒌᐦᑫᔨᒧᐤ
VAI s/he is vain; s/he tries with pride and confidence

cīhkēýimowin ᒌᐦᑫᔨᒧᐏᐣ
NI vanity, pride, self esteem

cīhkīstam ᒌᐦᑮᐢᑕᒼ
VTI s/he enjoys s.t.; s/he is enthusiastic

cīkaham ᒌᑲᐦᐊᒼ
VTI s/he chops s.t.

cīkahikan ᒌᑲᐦᐃᑲᐣ
NI axe

cīkahikan-sākahikanihk
ᒌᑲᐦᐃᑲᐣ ᓵᑲᐦᐃᑲᓂᕽ
INM Wollaston, SK [*lit*: "at hatchet lake"]

cīkahikanāhtik ᒌᑲᐦᐃᑲᓈᐦᑎᐠ
NI axe-handle [*pl*: -wa]

cīkahikanis ᒌᑲᐦᐃᑲᓂᐢ
NI hatchet, tomahawk [*dim*]

cīkahikanispwākan
ᒌᑲᐦᐃᑲᓂᐢᐚᑲᐣ
NA ax-handled pipe

cīkahikākanis ᒌᑲᐦᐃᑳᑲᓂᐢ
NI small hatchet [*dim*]

cīkahikēw ᒌᑲᐦᐃᑫᐤ
VAI s/he chops, s/he cuts

cīkahiskiwākan ᒌᑲᐦᐃᐢᑭᐚᑲᐣ
NI pick (digging tool)

cīkahosow ᒌᑲᐦᐅᓱᐤ
VAI s/he chops him/herself

cīkahwēw ᒌᑲᐦᐍᐤ
VTA s/he chops s.o.

cīkakām ᒌᑲᑳᒼ
IPC close to the shore

cīkāhtaw ᒌᑳᐦᑕᐤ
IPC close, nearby; in the area, thereabouts

cīkāsk ᒌᑳᐢᐠ
IPC along the waterside; along the edge

cīkāskohtin ᒌᑳᐢᑯᐦᑎᐣ
VII it lies near the edge

cīkāskwahpitam ᒌᑳᐢᑿᐦᐱᑕᒼ
VTI s/he ties s.t. to wood

cīki ᒌᑭ
IPC close, close by, near, nearby, near to

cīkināhk ᒌᑭᓈᕽ
NA nit, louse [*pl*: -wak]

cīkiskanaw ᒌᑭᐢᑲᓇᐤ
IPC near to the road

cīkiskīsik ᒌᑭᐢᑮᓯᐠ
IPC close to the eye

cīkiskotēw ᒌᑭᐢᑯᑌᐤ
IPC by the fire

cīmān ᒌᒫᐣ
NI canoe [*poss*: (-im)]

cīpacikāpawiw ᒌᐸᒋᑳᐸᐏᐤ
VAI s/he stands very straight

cīpahcāw ᒌᐸᐦᒑᐤ
VII it is steep

cīpataham ᒌᐸᑕᐦᐊᒼ
VTI s/he drives s.t. into the ground; s/he puts s.t. on a spit

cīpatahāhkow ᒌᐸᑕᐦᐋᐦᑯᐤ
VAI s/he roasts on a spit

cīpatahikan ᒌᐸᑕᐦᐃᑲᐣ
NI spit (for roasting)

cīpatamow ᒌᐸᑕᒧᐤ
VAI it projects out

cīpatapiw ᒌᐸᑕᐱᐤ
VAI s/he sits erect, s/he sits up

cīpay ᒌᐸᕀ
NA ghost; dead person, corpse

cīpayāmatisow ᒌᐸᔮᒪᑎᓱᐤ
VAI s/he is visited by ghosts

cīpayāmatisōstawēw
ᒌᐸᔮᒪᑎᓲᐢᑕᐍᐤ
VTA s/he talks as a ghost with s.o.

cīpayēkin ᒌᐸᔦᑭᐣ
NI shroud (for the dead) [*pl*: -wa]

cīpēhcakowēs ᒌᐯᐦᒐᑯᐍᐢ
NA grey horse [*dim*; *also* cīpēhtakowēs]

cīpēhtako- ᒌᐯᐦᑕᑯ
IPV blue, greyish blue

cīpēhtakowēw ᒌᐯᐦᑕᑯᐍᐤ
VAI it is blue or grey

cīpēhtakwāpikwanīskāw
ᒌᐯᐦᑕᒁᐱᑿᓃᐢᑳᐤ
VII there are many blue or grey flowers

cīpēhtakwāpikwanīwiw
ᒌᐯᐦᑕᒁᐱᑿᓃᐏᐤ
VII it has blue or grey flowers

cīpēhtakwāw ᒌᐯᐦᑕᒁᐤ
VII it is blue or grey

cīpipaýiw ᒌᐱᐸᔨᐤ
VAI s/he moves with a jerk, s/he twitches

cīpipitāw ᒌᐱᐱᑖᐤ
VAIt s/he jerks s.t. pulling

cīpipitēw ᒌᐱᐱᑌᐤ
VTA s/he jerks s.o. pulling

cīpitonēw ᒌᐱᑐᓀᐤ
VAI s/he twitches at the mouth, s/he jerks at the mouth

cīpohkotam ᒌᐳᐦᑯᑕᒼ
VTI s/he whittles s.t. to a point

cīpohkotēw ᒌᐳᐦᑯᑌᐤ
VII it is whittled to a point

cīpohkotēw ᒌᐳᐦᑯᑌᐤ
VTA s/he whittles s.o. to a point

cīpokotēw ᒌᐳᑯᑌᐤ
VAI s/he has a pointed nose

cīpominakās ᒌᐳᒥᓇᑳᐢ
NI cartridge, shell

cīponam ᒌᐳᓇᒼ
VTI s/he sharpens s.t. (by hand), s/he makes s.t. sharp

cīponēw ᒌᐳᓀᐤ
VTA s/he sharpens s.o. (by hand), s/he makes s.o. sharp

cīpopēhikan ᒌᐳᐯᐦᐃᑲᐣ
NI diamond (card suit)

cīposam ᒌᐳᓴᒼ
VTI s/he sharpens s.t. by cutting, s/he cuts s.t. to a sharp point

cīposcowiýākanisīs
ᒌᐳᐢᒍᐏᔮᑲᓂᓰᐢ
NA shrew, mole

cīposiw ᒌᐳᓯᐤ
VAI it is pointed; it is a pear (i.e. fruit) [*cf.* kā-cīposicik "pears"]

cīposwēw ᒌᐳᓷᐤ
VTA s/he sharpens s.o. by cutting, s/he cuts s.o. to a sharp point

cīpotonēw ᒌᐳᑐᓀᐤ
VAI s/he has pointed lips; s/he has pursed lips

cīpotōn ᒌᐳᑑᐣ
NA one pointing with the lips;
NI pointed lips

cīpwaskisow ᒌᐺᐢᑭᓱᐤ
VAI it stands with a point

cīpwaskitēw ᒌᐺᐢᑭᑌᐤ
VII it is a pointed article standing up, it stands with a point

cīpwastotin ᒌᐺᐢᑐᑎᐣ
NI toque; pointed hat

cīpwāw ᒌᐻᐤ
VII it is pointed; it is sharp

cīpwēkascikēw ᒌᐰᑲᐢᒋᑫᐤ
VAI s/he makes a pointed pile

cīpwēyān ᒌᐰᔮᐣ
NA Dene, Chipewyan [*also* cīpowēyān; *cf.* wēcīpwayān, wēcīpwāyaniw]

cīpwēyāninahk ᒌᐰᔮᓂᓈᕽ
INM Dene country, Chipewyan country [*also* cīpowēyaninahk]

cīsa ᒌᓴ
NA Cisa [personal name of Trickster; cf. cīsihēw]

cīsas ᒌᓴᐢ
NA Jesus [*adapted from English*; *cf.* cēsos]

cīsāwānāpoy ᒌᓵᐚᓈᐳᕀ
NI soup of meat strips

cīsāwānis ᒌᓵᐚᓂᐢ
NI strip of meat

cīsāwātam ᒌᓵᐚᑕᒼ
VTI s/he chops s.t. into strips

cīscahikanis ᒌᐢᒐᐦᐃᑲᓂᐢ
NI fork; small awl [*dim*; *see also* cīstahāsēpon; oskācik]

cīscēkahikanis ᒌᐢᒉᑲᐦᐃᑲᓂᐢ
NI tent peg

cīscipitēw ᑭᐢᙆᐱᑌᐤ
VTA s/he scratches s.o. [also
cīscīscipitēw]

cīsihēw ᑭᕠᐦᐁᐤ
VTA s/he misleads s.o., s/he
deceives s.o., s/he fools s.o.

cīsihiwēskiw ᑭᕠᐦᐃᐁᐧᐢᑭᐤ
VAI s/he is a deceiver, s/he
habitually deceives people
[hab]

cīsihow ᑭᕠᐦᐅᐤ
VAI s/he has a
misconception; s/he is
mistaken

cīsimēw ᑭᕡᒣᐤ
VTA s/he misleads s.o. by
speech

cīsiskawēw ᑭᕡᐢᑲᐁᐧᐤ
VTA s/he flirts with s.o. by
slight body contact

cīskāpitēw ᑭᐢᑲᐱᑌᐤ
VAI s/he grinds his/her own
teeth

cīst ᑭᐢᐟ
IPC see here! [exclamation]

cīstaham ᑭᐢᑕᐦᐊᒼ
VTI s/he pierces s.t.; s/he
punctures s.t.

cīstahaskosīwākan
ᑭᐢᑕᐦᐊᐢᑯᓰ�wᐊᑲᐣ
NI hay fork

cīstahaskwasowākan
ᑭᐢᑕᐦᐊᐢᑿᓱ�wᐊᑲᐣ
NI pitchfork

cīstahāsēpon ᑭᐢᑕᐦᐊᓭᐳᐣ
NI table fork [also
cīstāsēpon, cīstāsēpwān]

cīstahāskwatēw ᑭᐢᑕᐦᐊᐢᑿᑌᐤ
VTA s/he crucifies s.o.; s/he
nails or pins s.o. down

cīstahāskwātam ᑭᐢᑕᐦᐊᐢᑿᑕᒼ
VTI s/he makes a target and
shoots; s/he chooses s.t. as a
target and shoots

cīstahāskwātēw ᑭᐢᑕᐦᐊᐢᑿᑌᐤ
VTA s/he chooses s.o. as a
target and shoots

cīstahēw ᑭᐢᑕᐦᐁᐤ
VTA s/he pierces s.o.; s/he
gives s.o. an injection,
needle; s/he pricks s.o. with
an awl or pin [cf. cīstahwēw]

cīstahikan ᑭᐢᑕᐦᐃᑲᐣ
NI hay fork; spear, lance;
tent peg; awl

cīstahikēw ᑭᐢᑕᐦᐃᑫᐤ
VAI s/he gives an injection

cīstahowin ᑭᐢᑕᐦᐅᐃᐧᐣ
NI vaccination

cīstahwēw ᑭᐢᑕᐦᐧᐁᐤ
VTA s/he pricks s.o., s/he
pierces s.o., s/he jabs s.o.,
s/he spears s.o. with a
pointed object; s/he give s.o.
an injection, s/he injects s.o.,
s/he vaccinates s.o. [cf.
cīstahēw]

cīstaskosīwākan ᑭᐢᑕᐢᑯᓰᐧᐊᑲᐣ
NI pitchfork

cīstaskosīwākēw ᑭᐢᑕᐢᑯᓰᐧᐊᑫᐤ
VAI s/he pitches hay

cīstatēyāpiy ᑭᐢᑕᑌᔮᐱᕀ
NI sinew

cīstāskosonākan ᑭᐢᒐᐢᑯᓱᓈᑲᐣ
NI pitchfork

cīstāskwan ᑭᐢᒐᐢᑴᐣ
NI nail [see also sakahikan]

cīstāwēsin ᑭᐢᒐᐧᐁᓯᐣ
VAI s/he makes an echo
[also cīstāwēsin]

cīstāwēyāw ᑭᐢᒐᐧᐁᔮᐤ
VII echoes are heard, there
are echoes [also cīstāwēyāw]

cīstēkahokan ᑭᐢᑌᑲᐦᐅᑲᐣ
NI tent peg

cīstēkahokanāhtik
ᑭᐢᑌᑲᐦᐅᑲᓈᐦᑎᐠ
NI tent peg [pl: -wa]

cīstikwēnēw ᑭᐢᑎᑴᓀᐤ
VTA s/he pinches s.o.'s neck;
s/he chokes s.o. [also:
cīscīstikwēnēw]

cīstikwēpitēw ᑭᐢᑎᑴᐱᑌᐤ
VTA s/he chokes s.o.; s/he
pinches s.o.'s neck (pulling)
[also cīscīstikwēpitēw]

cīstikwēyawēpitēw
ᑭᐢᑎᑴᔭᐧᐁᐱᑌᐤ
VTA s/he chokes s.o.; s/he
pinches s.o.'s neck (pulling)

cīstinam ᑭᐢᑎᓇᒼ
VTI s/he pinches s.t.

cīstinēw ᑭᐢᑎᓀᐤ
VTA s/he pinches s.o.

cīstinitowak ᑭᐢᑎᓂᑐᐊᐧᐠ
VAI they pinch one another

cīstipitam ᑭᐢᑎᐸᑕᒼ
VTI s/he scratches s.t.

cīstipitēw ᑭᐢᑎᐸᑌᐤ
VTA s/he scratches s.o.

cīstipititowak ᑭᐢᑎᐸᑎᑐᐊᐧᐠ
VAI they scratch one another

cīwēhtawakēw ᑭᐧᐁᐦᑕᐊᐧᑫᐤ
VAI s/he has ringing ears [cf.
cowēskihtēw]

cīwēw ᑭᐧᐁᐤ
VII it is calm, peaceful

cīwēyāw ᑭᐧᐁᔮᐤ
VII it is very calm

J

cohcōnamāsow ᒍᐦᒍᓇᒫᓱᐤ
VAI he masturbates

cohcōsimāpōs ᒍᐦᒍᓯᒫᐴᐢ
NI milk [dim; lit: "breast
liquid"; cf. tohtōsāpoy]

cowēhikanāpisīs ᒍᐧᐁᐦᐃᑲᓈᐱᓰᐢ
NA dragonfly [cf.
cōwēhkanāpisis; also
cwēhohikanāpisis]

cowēskihtēw ᒍᐧᐁᐢᑭᐦᑌᐤ
VAI s/he has ringing ears
[also cīwēskihtēw; cf.
cīwēhtawakēw]

J

cōcōs ᒍᒍᐢ
NI baby's soother, nipple of
a baby's bottle

cōhkāp ᒍᐦᑳᑊ
NA person with wide-open
eyes

cōhkāpisiw ᒍᐦᑳᐱᓯᐤ
VAI s/he opens his/her own
eyes a little [dim; cf.
tōhkāpiw]

cōwēhkanāpisīs ᒍᐧᐁᐦᑲᓈᐱᓰᐢ
NA dragonfly [cf.
cowēhikanāpisis]

cōwēhkasow ᒍᐧᐁᐦᑲᓱᐤ
VAI it hisses as it cooks; it
makes a sizzling sound while
cooking

ē
▽

ē- ▽
IPV [grammatical preverb: complementizer; defines a changed conjunct clause]

ēcika ▽ᒥᑲ
IPC what is this!; and so it appears that [exclamation; usually occurs with a demonstrative pronoun]

ēcika ana ▽ᒥᑲ ◁ᣞ
IPH what is that! so that's it [expression of surprise or discovery]

ēcika ani ▽ᒥᑲ ◁ᣔ
IPH so that's it; so it is [expression of surprise or discovery]

ēcika anima ▽ᒥᑲ ◁ᣔᒫ
IPH what is that! so that's it [expression of surprise or discovery]

ēcika ōma ▽ᒥᑲ ᐅᒫ
IPH what is this! and so it appears [expression of surprise or discovery]

ēcikwē ▽ᒥᖴ·
IPC I guess, probably [personal inference; cf. ētikwē, ētokwē]

ēha ▽ᐦ◁
IPC yes [often with glottal closure, i.e. ēha'; cf. āha, sC: ēhē, wC: īhī]

ēhē ▽ᐦ▽
IPC yes [sC; cf. pC: ēha, āha; wC: īhī]

ēhēy ▽ᐦ▽ᣔ
IPC [discourse particle]

ēkamā ▽ᑲᒲ
IPC there is not, it is not the case [cf. yēkamā]

ēkā ▽ᑲ
IPC no; not; don't [negator in certain conjunct clauses; cf. ēkāwiýa, ēkāy, ēkāýa, kāwiýa, kāya]

ēkā ēsa ▽ᑲ ▽ᓴ
IPH you shouldn't have ...; well, you should not have

ēkā kīkway ▽ᑲ ᑮᒁᣞ
IPH nothing, not, not at all, not any

ēkā nānitaw ▽ᑲ ᓈᓂᑕ°
IPH nowhere, nothing; don't do anything

ēkāwiýa ▽ᑲᐊᣞ
IPC no; not; don't you dare; don't [negator in conjunct and imperative clauses; cf. ēkā, ēkāy, ēkāýa, kāwiýa, kāya]

ēkāy ▽ᑲᣞ
IPC not; don't [negator in conjunct and imperative clauses; cf. ēkā, ēkāwiya, ēkāya, kāwiýa, kāya]

ēkāýa ▽ᑲᣔ
IPC not; don't [negator in conjunct and imperative clauses; cf. ēkā, ēkāwiýa, ēkāy, kāwiýa, kāýa]

ēko-tahto ▽ᑯ ᒼᐦᑐ
IPC so many, that many

ēkoni ▽ᑯᓂ
PR those, those are the ones; this, this is the one (previously mentioned) [inan pl / anim obv; cf. ēwakoni]

ēkonik ▽ᑯᓂᐠ
PR those, those are the ones (previously mentioned) [anim prox pl; cf. ēwakonik]

ēkosi ▽ᑯᓯ
IPC so, thus, in that way; right, alright; there, that's it, that is all; well; enough; good-bye

ēkosi ani ▽ᑯᓯ ◁ᓂ
IPH that's the way; that's it, that's right [also ēkos āni]

ēkosi ani kiyām ▽ᑯᓯ ◁ᓂ ᑭᣌᒼ
IPH nevermind; let it go as is [also ēkos āni kiyām]

ēkosi isi ▽ᑯᓯ ᐃᓯ
IPH just so, like that; thus, in that way; that is how it is [also ēkos īsi]

ēkosi māka ▽ᑯᓯ ᒫᑲ
IPH that's it; so long, good-bye; I'd better be going

ēkosi mīna ▽ᑯᓯ ᒦᓇ
IPC also

ēkosi nawac ▽ᑯᓯ ᓇᐘᐨ
IPH better, that's better

ēkosi pita ▽ᑯᓯ ᐱᑕ
IPH that's it for now

ēkosi pitamā ▽ᑯᓯ ᐱᑕᒫ
IPH that's it for now

ēkospī ▽ᑯᐢᐲ
IPC then; at that time [cf. ēkospīhk]

ēkospīhk ▽ᑯᐢᐲᐦᐠ
IPC then, at that time; since [cf. ēkospī]

ēkota ▽ᑯᑕ
IPC there, right there; at that very place [dim: ēkoca]

ēkota mwēhci ▽ᑯᑕ ᒧᐦᒋ
IPH at that exact place

ēkotē ▽ᑯᑌ
IPC over there; a place in that direction

ēkotowahk ▽ᑯᑐᐊᐦᐠ
IPC of that kind, like that [also: ēkotowa; cf. wC: ikwatowahk]

ēkotowihk ▽ᑯᑐᐃᐦᐠ
IPC in that place, a place like that, in such a place [also: ēkotowi]

ēkotowiw ▽ᑯᑐᐃ·°
VAI it is of that kind

ēkotowiwiw ▽ᑯᑐᐊ·ᐃ·°
VAI it is of that kind

ēkoýikohk ▽ᑯᣔᑯᐦᐠ
IPC that much, to that degree, to that extent; that's enough; only then [cf. ēkwaýikohk, ēwakoýikohk]

ēkōma ▽ᑯᒪ
IPC this is it [inan sg; cf. ēwako ōma]

ēkwa ▽ᑿ·
IPC and, also; then; now

ēkwa ani ▽ᑿ· ◁ᓂ
IPH it was then; well, that's it [conclusion; cf. ēkwāni]

ēkwa mīna ▽ᑿ· ᒦᓇ
IPH and now; also

ēkwa wiýa ▽ᑿ· ᐃ·ᣞ
IPH and then, it was then; then s/he ...

ēkwatik ▽ᑿ·ᓂᐠ
IPC let's go [also ēkotik]

ēkwaýāc ▽ᑿ·ᣓᐨ
IPC only now, for the first time, just then [cf. ēkwaýāk, ēkwēýāc, ēkwēýāk]

ēkwaýāk ▽ᑿ·ᣓᐠ
IPC only now, for the first time, just then [cf. ēkwaýāc, ēkwēýāc, ēkwēýāk]

ēkwaýikohk ▽ᑿ·ᣔᑯᐦᐠ
IPC that much, to that extent, up to that point; enough; not so, not as

[*negative comparative*; *cf.* ēkoýikohk, ēwakoýikohk]

ēkwāna ᐁᑳᓇ
PR that's him/her [*anim prox sg*; *cf.* ēwako ana; *also* ēwakw āna]

ēkwāni ᐁᑳᓂ
IPC that's the end, that's all [*cf.* ēkwa ani]

ēkwānihi ᐁᑳᓂᐦᐃ
PR that's them; and then there are those [*inan pl / anim obv*; *cf.* ēwako anihi; *also* ēwakw ānihi]

ēkwāniki ᐁᑳᓂᑭ
PR that's them; and then there are those [*anim prox pl*; *cf.* ēwako aniki; *also* ēwakw āniki]

ēkwānima ᐁᑳᓂᒪ
PR that's it [*inan sg*; *cf.* ēwako anima; *also*: ēwakw ānima]

ēkwāwa ᐁᑳᐘ
PR this is him/her [*anim prox sg*; *cf.* ēwako awa; *also* ēwakw āwa]

ēkwēýāc ᐁᑵᔮᐨ
IPC only now, for the first time; exactly then, not before that time [*cf.* ēkwaýāc, ēkwaýāk, ēkwēýāk]

ēkwēýāk ᐁᑵᔮᐠ
IPC exactly then, not before that time [*cf.* ēkwaýāc, ēkwaýāk, ēkwēýāc]

ēmihkwān ᐁᒥᐦᑳᐣ
NA spoon; ladle

ēmihkwānis ᐁᒥᐦᑳᓂᐢ
NA table spoon, teaspoon [*dim*]

ēsa ᐁᓴ
IPC I understand; apparently, reportedly, so it appears, evidently; this one; because of something [*information received from others*; *reference to time past*; *see also* ētikwē, pakahkam]

ēsa ᐁᓴ
NA clam shell, sea shell [*pl*: ēsak]

ēsa anima ᐁᓴ ᐊᓂᒪ
IPH apparently that

ēsa ōma ᐁᓴ ᐆᒪ
IPH apparently this

ēsahamānis ᐁᓴᐦᐊᒫᓂᐢ
NA spoon; clam used as a spoon [*dim*]

ēsawēhkwak ᐁᓴᐍᐦᑿᐠ
NA square needle for sewing leather [*pl*: -wak; *also* asawēhkwak; *cf.* isawēhkwak]

ēsawēhkwakos ᐁᓴᐍᐦᑿᑯᐢ
NA small square needle for sewing leather [*dim*; *also* asawēhkwakos; *cf.* isawēhkwakos]

ēsēhtin ᐁᓭᐦᑎᐣ
VII it leaves a print, it leaves a mark

ēsikāciminak ᐁᓯᑳᒋᒥᓇᐠ
NA cylindrical white beads [*pl*]

ēsis ᐁᓯᐢ
NA shell, seashell; small clam shell [*dim*]

ēsisis ᐁᓯᓯᐢ
NA small shell, small seashell [*dim*]

ēskan ᐁᐢᑲᐣ
NA horn, antler [*cf.* mitēskan *NDA*]

ēskanikan ᐁᐢᑲᓂᑲᐣ
NA part of a horn, antler

ēskēw ᐁᐢᑫᐤ
VAI s/he makes a hole in the ice to hunt beaver [*wC and npC*: iskīw]

ēskwa ᐁᐢᑿ
IPC while; wait [*also*: ēskwā; *cf.* cēskwa]

ētataw ᐁᑕᑕᐤ
IPC barely, barely enough; not hardly [*commenting on someone's inability to do something due to a hindrance of some kind*]

ētatawisiw ᐁᑕᑕᐏᓯᐤ
VAI it barely exists; s/he is almost dead, s/he is very ill and unable to move

ētikwē ᐁᑎᑵ
IPC apparently, I guess, I suppose, presumably; about (doubtful) [*dubitative*; *personal inference*; *see also* ēsa, pakahkam; *cf.* ēcikwē, ētokwē]

ētokē ᐁᑐᑫ
IPC I wonder, I don't know [*wC*: itokī; *cf.* ēcikwē, ētikwē, ētokwē]

ētokwē ᐁᑐᑵ
IPC maybe, I guess, presumably, perhaps; about (doubtful) [*personal inference*; *cf.* ēcikwē, ētikwē, ētokē]

ēwako ᐁᐘᑯ
PR this (previously mentioned), that one; the same one [*anim prox sg / inan sg*; *resumptive demonstrative*; *also* ēyako; *wC*: iyako]

ēwako ani ᐁᐘᑯ ᐊᓂ
IPH and so after that [*also* ēwakw āni; *cf.* ēkwāni]

ēwako ohci ᐁᐘᑯ ᐅᐦᒋ
IPC that's the reason, that's why

ēwako ōma ᐁᐘᑯ ᐆᒪ
PR this same one [*previously mentioned*; *inan sg*; *also* ēkōma, ēwak ōma]

ēwako ōma ohci ᐁᐘᑯ ᐆᒪ ᐅᐦᒋ
IPH about this; this is why, this is the reason for this [*also* ēwak ōm ōhci]

ēwakoni ᐁᐘᑯᓂ
PR those, those are the ones; this, this is the one [*previously mentioned*; *inan pl / anim obv*]

ēwakonik ᐁᐘᑯᓂᐠ
PR those, those are the ones [*previously mentioned*; *anim prox pl*]

ēwakoniwiw ᐁᐘᑯᓂᐏᐤ
VAI s/he is of a that kind [*previously mentioned*]

ēwakoýikohk ᐁᐘᑯᔨᑯᕽ
IPC that much, to that extent; that's enough [*cf.* ēkoýikohk, ēkwaýikohk]

ēwakoýiw ᐁᐘᑯᔨᐤ
PR this [*previously mentioned*; *inan obv*; *archaic in pC*]

ēwakwā ᐁᐘᑳ
PR there s/he is [*previously mentioned*; *anim prox sg*; *archaic*; *cf.* ēwakwāwa]

ēwakwāna ᐁᐘᑳᓇ
PR that same one [*previously mentioned*; *anim prox sg*; *also* ēwakw āna]

ēwakwānihi ᐁᐘᑳᓂᐦᐃ
PR those same ones, that same one [*previously mentioned*; *inan pl / anim obv*; *also* ēwakw ānihi]

ēwakwāniki ᐁᐘᑳᓂᑭ
PR those same ones [*previously mentioned*; *anim prox pl*; *also* ēwakw āniki]

ēwakwānima ᐁᐘᑳᓂᒪ
PR that same one [*previously mentioned*; *inan sg*; *also* ēwakw ānima]

ēwakwāwa ᐁᐘᑳᐘ
PR this same one [*previously mentioned*; *anim prox sg*; *also* ēwakw āwa]

ēwakwē ᐁᐘᑵ
PR there it is [*previously mentioned*; *inan sg*; *archaic*]

ēwakwēhā ᐁᐘᑵᐦᐋ
IPC there they are [*previously mentioned*; *inan pl*; *archaic*]

ēwakwēhkāk ᐁᐘᑵᐦᑳᐠ
IPC there they are [*previously mentioned*; *anim prox pl*; *archaic*]

ēy ᐁᕀ
IPC hey! [*discourse particle*: *introductory*; *exclamatory*]

ēyāpic ▽ᒪ∧ˉ
IPC further, in due course, again; still [*cf.* kēyāpic, kēyāpit]

ēyihkwēw ▽ᔑ"ᖑ·°
NA steer; castrated animal; transvestite, hermaphrodite

ēyihkwēwatim ▽ᔑ"ᖑ·◁·∩ᶜ
NA gelding [*pl*: -wak]

ēýik ▽ᔑˋ
NA ant [*pl*: -wak; *wC*: "ant, spider"]

ēýiko-wīsti ▽ᔑᗪ ᐏ·ᓀ∩
NI anthill

ēýikohk ▽ᔑᗪˣ
IPC so much; as far, as long; when; [*when in combination with* nawac:] than [*cf.* iýikohk]

ēýikohkwēyimow ▽ᔑᗪ"ᖑ·ᔑᒍ°
VAI s/he has courage to such an extent; s/he has confidence only so far

ēýikos ▽ᔑᗪˆ
NA ant, small ant [*dim, also* ēýikosis; *wC*: "ant; spider"]

ēýikosiwiw ▽ᔑᗪᒉᐧ·°
VAI it is an ant

ēýikoskāw ▽ᔑᗪˆᑊ°
VII there are numerous ants, ants are abundant

ēýiwē ▽ᔑ▽·
IPC better than nothing; anyway [*cf.* ēýiwēhk]

ēýiwēhk ▽ᔑ▽·ˣ
IPC anyway, nevertheless; to a fair extent, as well as may be, better than nothing; so-so; despite shortcomings [*cf.* ēýiwē]

ēyīnimiw ▽ᔑᓂᒥ°
VAI s/he has ringworm

h

ll

ha "◄
 IPC ha, so [*interjection; can be used when something happens to someone despite repeated warnings*]

haha "◄"◄
 IPC ha [*interjection*]

hay-hay "◄⁺ "◄⁺
 IPC thanks, thank you; denotes thanfulness [*cf.* ay-ay, ay-hay]

hā "◄
 IPC who? what? [*discourse particle*]

hā "◄
 IPC oh! [*expression of reluctant acknowledgement*]

hām "◄ᶜ
 IPC now then [*hortatory, indicating readiness or impatience*]

hām ēkwa "◄ᶜ ▽ь·
 IPH now then [*hortatory, indicating readiness or impatience*]

hāw "◄°
 IPC now then; ready, all right, let's go, come on; well [*hortatory, indicating readiness or impatience; sometimes with nasalized vowel, i.e.* "hānw"]

hāw māka "◄° ίь
 IPC come on then

hēy "▽⁺
 IPC hey [*exclamation*]

hēy hēy "▽⁺ "▽⁺
 IPC expression of deep concern; expression denoting pleasure at seeing someone [*discourse particle*]

i

icāpahkānis ᐃᒑᐸᐦᑳᓂᐢ
  NI small spy glass [*dim*, *cf.* itāpahkan]

ici ᐃᒋ
  IPC then, later, afterward [*wC*: nici]

icwahikanis ᐃᒡᐧᐊᐦᐃᑲᓂᐢ
  NI small sign or symbol (for directions) [*dim*; *cf.* itwahikan]

ihkastēw ᐃᐦᑲᐢᑌᐤ
  VII it dries up, it has dried up (i.e. something formerly containing water)

ihkatawahkāw ᐃᐦᑲᑕᐊᐧᐦᑳᐤ
  VII it is a marshy depression

ihkatawāw ᐃᐦᑲᑕᐞᐤ
  NI slough, marsh [*also* īhkatawāw]

ihkatawāw ᐃᐦᑲᑕᐞᐤ
  VII it is a marshy depression, it is a stagnant pond, it is a slough

ihkatawāwaskosiya
ᐃᐦᑲᑕᐞᐊᐢᑯᓯᕀ
  NI marsh grass, marsh plants

ihkatawāwipēyāw
ᐃᐦᑲᑕᐞᐃᐯᔮᐤ
  NI wet slough [*also* īhkatawāwipēyāw]

ihkēyihtam ᐃᐦᑫᔨᐦᑕᒼ
  VTI s/he is tired of s.t.

ihkēyimēw ᐃᐦᑫᔨᒣᐤ
  VTA s/he is tired of s.o.

ihkin ᐃᐦᑭᐣ
  VII it happens, it occurs, it takes place

ihkipayiw ᐃᐦᑭᐸᔨᐤ
  VII it recedes, there are receding waters, there is a lowering of water

ihkipayihēw ᐃᐦᑭᐸᔨᐦᐁᐤ
  VTA s/he drains s.o.

ihkipayíhtāw ᐃᐦᑭᐸᔨᐦᑖᐤ
  VTI s/he drains s.t.

ihkopiwi-pīsim ᐃᐦᑯᐱᐤᐃ· ᐲᓯᒼ
  NA Frost Moon, November [*cf.* iyikopiwi-pīsim, yiyihkopiwi-pīsim]

ihkwa ᐃᐦᑲ
  NA louse (insect) [*pl*:] ihkwak [*cf.* mitihkom *NDA*]

ihtakon ᐃᐦᑕᑯᐣ
  VII it exists, it is there [*also* ihtakwan]

ihtakow ᐃᐦᑕᑯᐤ
  VAI it exists, s/he is there

ihtasimēw ᐃᐦᑕᓯᒣᐤ
  VTA s/he perseveres in talking to s.o.

ihtasiwak ᐃᐦᑕᓯᐊᐧᐠ
  VAI they are so many, they are as many

ihtatēyihtam ᐃᐦᑕᑌᔨᐦᑕᒼ
  VTI s/he thinks s.t. is there, s/he expects s.t. to be there

ihtatēyimēw ᐃᐦᑕᑌᔨᒣᐤ
  VTA s/he thinks s.o. is there, s/he expects s.o. to be there

ihtatwēwitam ᐃᐦᑕᑐᐁᐧᐃᑕᒼ
  VTI s/he makes a lot of noise talking

ihtāw ᐃᐦᑖᐤ
  VAI s/he exists, s/he is there

ihtāwin ᐃᐦᑖᐃᐧᐣ
  NI abode, place of residence; existence

ihtiw ᐃᐦᑎᐤ
  VAI s/he does so, s/he fares so; s/he is doing s.t.

ihtiwin ᐃᐦᑎᐃᐧᐣ
  NI way of doing things, custom

isapiko ᐃᓴᐱᑯ
  IPC the fact is, in fact; really [*also* ēsapiko, sapiko]

isawēhkwak ᐃᓴᐁᐧᐦᑲᐧᐠ
  NA square needle for sewing leather [*pl*: -wak; *also* asawēhkwak; *cf.* ēsawēhkwak]

isawēhkwakos ᐃᓴᐁᐧᐦᑲᐧᑯᐢ
  NA small square needle for sewing leather [*dim*; *also* asawēhkwakos; *cf.* ēsawēhkwakos]

isawēsk ᐃᓴᐁᐧᐢᐠ
  NI sword [*pl*: -wa; *cf.* sawēsk]

isawēyāw ᐃᓴᐁᐧᔮᐤ
  VII it is square [*also* asawēyāw]

isi ᐃᓯ
  IPC so, thus, this way; there; to, towards [*used at the end of a locative phrase*; *cf.* isi *IPV*]

isi- ᐃᓯ
  IPV so, this way, thus, thither, such [*cf.* isi *IPC*]

isi-ayāw ᐃᓯ ᐊᔮᐤ
  VAI s/he is thus, s/he is thus in health, s/he is in such shape; s/he is unwell, s/he is in poor health [*also* is-āyāw]

isi-kitow ᐃᓯ ᑭᑐᐤ
  VAI s/he cries in such a way, s/he calls in such a way (as an animal's call)

isi-miyāhtam ᐃᓯ ᒥᔮᐦᑕᒼ
  VTI s/he smells s.t. thus

isi-pīkiskwēwin ᐃᓯ ᐲᑭᐢᒀᐃᐧᐣ
  NI speaking thus, such a language

isi-wēpaham ᐃᓯ ᐁᐧᐸᐦᐊᒼ
  VTI s/he knocks s.t. thither or thus; s/he forces s.t. away (by tool)

isi-wēpinam ᐃᓯ ᐁᐧᐱᓇᒼ
  VTI s/he tosses s.t. thither or thus, s/he throws s.t. there

isi-wēpinamawēw
ᐃᓯ ᐁᐧᐱᓇᒪᐌᐤ
  VTA s/he tosses (it/him) thither or thus to s.o.

isi-wēpinēw ᐃᓯ ᐁᐧᐱᓀᐤ
  VTA s/he tosses s.o. thither or thus, s/he throws s.o. there

isi-wēpinikēw ᐃᓯ ᐁᐧᐱᓂᑫᐤ
  VAI s/he throws things there; s/he manages things thus

isi-wēpiskam ᐃᓯ ᐁᐧᐱᐢᑲᒼ
  VTI s/he pushes s.t. thither or thus by foot

isi-wēpiskawēw ᐃᓯ ᐁᐧᐱᐢᑲᐌᐤ
  VTA s/he pushes s.o. thither or thus by foot

isicimēw ᐃᓯᒋᒣᐤ
  VAI s/he paddles thither; s/he goes there by water (e.g. in a boat)

isihtam ᐃᓯᐦᑕᒼ
  VTI s/he hears s.t. so

isihtawēw ᐃᓯᐦᑕᐌᐤ
  VTA s/he understands s.o., s/he hears s.o. so

isihtitāw ᐃᓯᐦᑎᑖᐤ
  VAIt s/he places s.t. so

isikamāw ᐃᓯᑲᒫᐤ
  VII it is shaped thus as a shoreline; the body of water has such a shape

isikamāw ᐃᓯᑲᒫᐤ
  VII it is thus shaped as water; the body of water is such a shape

isikāpawiw ᐃᕆᐸᐧᐊᐤ
VAI s/he stands so

isikātēsin ᐃᕆᐸᑕᐅᕈ
VAI s/he lies with legs that way

isikwātam ᐃᕆᐧᐊᑕᒡ
VTI s/he sews s.t. thus

isimākosiw ᐃᕆᒪᑯᕘ
VAI s/he smells so

isimākwan ᐃᕆᒪᐸᐧ
VII it smells so

isimēw ᐃᕆᒪᐧ
VTA s/he speaks so to s.o.

isimēw ᐃᕆᒪᐧ
VTA s/he places s.o. so (i.e. in a certain position)

isinam ᐃᕆᓇᒡ
VTI s/he sees s.t. thus; s/he thinks s/he sees s.t.

isinawēw ᐃᕆᓇᐧᐊᐤ
VTA s/he sees s.o. thus

isinākosiw ᐃᕆᒪᑯᕘ
VAI s/he looks thus, s/he gives such an appearance (e.g. colour, etc.), s/he appears so; s/he resembles

isinākosiwin ᐃᕆᒪᑯᕆᐧᐊ
NI appearance, resemblance

isinākwan ᐃᕆᒪᐸᐧ
VII it looks thus, it gives such an appearance (e.g. colour, etc.), it appears so

isiniskēpayihow ᐃᕆᓂᓱᓇᑫᐸᔭᐦᐤᐤ
VAI s/he throws his/her own arms thus

isiniskēstawēw ᐃᕆᓂᓱᓇᑫᓯᑕᐧᐊᐤ
VTA s/he makes hand signs to s.o., s/he gestures to s.o.

isiniskēw ᐃᕆᓂᓱᑫᐧ
VAI s/he has his/her own arm thither or thus

isiniskēyiw ᐃᕆᓂᓱᑫᔭᐤ
VAI s/he moves his/her own arms thus

isipitam ᐃᕆᐱᑕᒡ
VTI s/he pulls s.t. there

isipitēw ᐃᕆᐱᑌᐧ
VTA s/he pulls s.o. there

isisimēw ᐃᕆᕆᒪᐧ
VTA s/he lays s.o. so

isisin ᐃᕆᕆᕈ
VAI s/he lies down so, s/he falls so

isisitēw ᐃᕆᕆᑌᐧ
VAI s/he has such a foot

isistāw ᐃᕆᓇᐸᑕᐧ
VAI s/he performs a ceremony so

isistāwin ᐃᕆᓇᐸᑕᐧᐊ
NI traditional ceremony

isitācimow ᐃᕆᑕᒋᒧᐤ
VAI s/he crawls thither

isitāpahēw ᐃᕆᑕᐸᐦᐁᐧᐊᐤ
VTA s/he makes s.o. pull thither or thus

isitāpāsow ᐃᕆᑕᐸᓴᐤ
VAI s/he drives thither or thus

isitāpēw ᐃᕆᑕᐸᐧᐊᐤ
VAI s/he drags thither

isiwēpan ᐃᕆᐧᐁᐸᕈ
VII it is in such a state; it happens thus, it goes thither or thus; it is such weather

isiwēpisiw ᐃᕆᐧᐁᐱᓯᐤ
VAI s/he has such a disposition, s/he is of such a temperment

isiwēpisiwin ᐃᕆᐧᐁᐱᓯᐧᐊ
NI disposition, behaviour

isiyihkācikātēw ᐃᕆᓯᐦᑳᒋᑳᑌᐤ
VII it is named thus

isiyihkāsow ᐃᕆᓯᐦᑳᓱᐤ
VAI s/he is named thus, s/he has such a name

isiyihkāsowin ᐃᕆᓯᐦᑳᓱᐧᐊ
NI name, given name

isiyihkātam ᐃᕆᓯᐦᑳᑕᒡ
VTI s/he calls s.t. thus, s/he gives s.t. such a name; s/he uses such a name for s.t. [cf. isiyihkātāw]

isiyihkātāw ᐃᕆᓯᐦᑳᑖᐧ
VAIt s/he calls s.t. thus, s/he uses such a name for s.t. [cf. isiyihkātam]

isiyihkātēw ᐃᕆᓯᐦᑳᑌᐤ
VII it is called thus, it has such a name

isiyihkātēw ᐃᕆᓯᐦᑳᑌᐤ
VTA s/he calls s.o. thus, s/he gives s.o. such a name; s/he uses such a name for s.o.

isiyihkātisow ᐃᕆᓯᐦᑳᑎᓱᐤ
VAI s/he calls him/herself so, s/he names him/herself so

isīhcikan ᐃᓯᐦᒋᐸᐧ
NI deed

isīhcikātēw ᐃᓯᐦᒋᐸᑌᐤ
VII it is made so

isīhcikēw ᐃᓯᐦᒋᑫᐧ
VAI s/he does things thus, s/he makes things thus, s/he settles things thus, s/he proceeds thus; s/he performs a ceremony thus, s/he performs such a ritual

isīhcikēwin ᐃᓯᐦᒋᑫᐧᐊ
NI culture; the doing so, such rite; what is thus done, such activities; act

isīhēw ᐃᓯᐦᐁᐧ
VTA s/he dresses s.o. so; s/he makes s.o. thus, s/he prepares s.o. thus

isīhkam ᐃᓯᐦᐸᑕ
VTI s/he bothers with s.t. thus

isīhkawēw ᐃᓯᐦᐸᐧᐊᐤ
VTA s/he bothers s.o. thus

isīhow ᐃᓯᐦᐤ
VAI s/he is thus dressed, s/he is thus equipped; s/he dresses him/herself so

isīhtāw ᐃᓯᐦᑖᐧ
VAIt s/he makes s.t. thus,

s/he prepares s.t. thus [i.e. to his/her own liking]

isīhtwāwin ᐃᓯᐦᒼᒡᑖᐧᐊᐧ
NI way of doing things; such rite, worship, custom [also isīhtāwin]

iska ᐊᐦᐸ
IPC it seems (through dream or magic) [also ēska]

iskāniyē ᐊᐦᐳᓯᕙ
IPC it seems (through dream or magic)

iskēkāni ᐊᐦᑫᐸᓯ
IPC it seems (through dream or magic)

iskipēw ᐊᐦᐱᐸᐧ
VII it floods, it is a flood, it is flooded [also yiskipēw; wC: thiskipiw]

iskiskawēw ᐊᐦᐱᓴᐸᐧᐊᐤ
VTA s/he wears s.o. out by treading

isko ᐊᐦᐸ
IPC so far, to such an extent, to this point; as far as, up to, up until [cf. isko IPV, iskohk IPC]

isko- ᐊᐦᐸ
IPV so far, to such an extent [cf. isko IPC, iskohk]

iskocēhikanis ᐊᐦᐸᑐᓯᒼᐸᓱᕈ
NI a match, a fire-starter [dim]

iskocēs ᐊᐦᐸᑐᓯ
NI spark [dim]

iskohēw ᐊᐦᐸᒼᐧ
VTA s/he leaves s.o. over

iskohēw ᐊᐦᐸᒼᐧᐊᐤ
VTA s/he makes s.o. such a height

iskohk ᐊᐦᐸ˟
IPC so far, to such a point; as far as, up until; this far [cf. isko IPC]

iskohkasow ᐊᐦᐸᒼᐸᓱᐤ
VAI it is burnt done, it is burnt up to a certain point

iskohtāw ᐊᐦᐸᒼᑖᐧ
VAIt s/he leaves s.t. as a leftover

iskohtāw ᐊᐦᐸᒼᑖᐧ
VAIt s/he makes s.t. such a length

iskokāpawiw ᐊᐦᐸᑲᐸᐧᐊᐤ
VAI s/he stands to such a height

iskonam ᐊᐦᐸᓇᒡ
VTI s/he holds s.t. so far; s/he leaves a portion of s.t.; s/he takes a portion of s.t. and leaves the rest

iskonamawēw ᐊᐦᐸᓇᒪᐧᐊᐤ
VTA s/he puts (it/him) so far for s.o.; s/he leaves a portion of (it/him) for s.o.

iskonamāsow ᐊᐦᐸᓇᒪᓱᐤ
VAI s/he keeps s.t. back for him/herself

iskonēw ᐃᐢᑯᓀᐤ
VTA s/he leaves so much of s.o.; s/he leaves a portion of s.o.; s/he takes a portion of s.o. and leaves the rest

iskonikan ᐃᐢᑯᓂᑲᐣ
NI reserve, reservation; portion; leftover [*see also* askīhkān]

iskonikanīwasinahikan ᐃᐢᑯᓂᑲᓃᐊᐧᓯᓇᐦᐃᑲᐣ
NI Treaty card

iskonikowisiw ᐃᐢᑯᓂᑯᐃᐧᓯᐤ
VAI s/he is left over (e.g. to survive) by the powers

iskopahikan ᐃᐢᑯᐸᐦᐃᑲᐣ
NI hoist

iskopaýiw ᐃᐢᑯᐸᔨᐤ
VAI s/he has just so much left

iskopēkāw ᐃᐢᑯᐯᑳᐤ
VII it goes so far, it extends so far (as water)

iskopēw ᐃᐢᑯᐯᐤ
VAI s/he is so deep in water, in liquid; s/he stands just so high in water

iskopicikan ᐃᐢᑯᐱᒋᑲᐣ
NI leftover piece of cloth

iskopitam ᐃᐢᑯᐱᑕᐣ
VTI s/he pulls s.t. up

iskopitēw ᐃᐢᑯᐱᑌᐤ
VTA s/he pulls s.o. so far; s/he pulls s.o. up (e.g. socks)

iskosam ᐃᐢᑯᓴᑦ
VTI s/he cuts s.t. just so long

iskosāwācikan ᐃᐢᑯᓵᐋᐧᒋᑲᐣ
NI clipping, scrap cloth

iskosihēw ᐃᐢᑯᓯᐦᐁᐤ
VTA s/he makes s.o. so long

iskosiw ᐃᐢᑯᓯᐤ
VAI it extends so far, it is so long; s/he is so tall, s/he is of such height

iskoskiwēw ᐃᐢᑯᐢᑭᐁᐧᐤ
VAI s/he is so far in the mud

iskoswēw ᐃᐢᑯᓭᐧᐤ
VTA s/he cuts s.o. just so long

iskotēmākwan ᐃᐢᑯᑌᒫᑲᐧᐣ
VII it smells like fire [*cf.* iskotēwakan]

iskotēw ᐃᐢᑯᑌᐤ
NI fire

iskotēwakan ᐃᐢᑯᑌᐊᐧᑲᐣ
VII it smells like fire [*cf.* iskotēmākwan]

iskotēwan ᐃᐢᑯᑌᐊᐧᐣ
VII it has fire (within), it is fiery [*cf.* iskotēwiw]

iskotēwāpoy ᐃᐢᑯᑌᐋᐧᐳᐩ
NI whiskey, alcohol, liquor

iskotēwiw ᐃᐢᑯᑌᐃᐧᐤ
VII it is fiery, it has fire (within) [*cf.* iskotēwan]

iskotēwitāpān ᐃᐢᑯᑌᐃᐧᑖᐹᐣ
NA train [*see also* pīwāpiskotāpān]

iskotēwotāpānāsk ᐃᐢᑯᑌᐅᐧᑖᐹᓈᐢᐠ
NA train [*pl*: -wak; *see also* pīwāpiskotāpān]

iskotōskwanēw ᐃᐢᑯᑑᐢᑲᐧᓀᐤ
VAI s/he has an elbow so long

iskwa ᐃᐢᑲᐧ
IPC so far, to the end

iskwahtam ᐃᐢᑲᐧᐦᑕᑦ
VTI s/he leaves s.t. from eating, s/he eats only a portion of s.t. [*cf.* iskwastam]

iskwamēw ᐃᐢᑲᐧᒣᐤ
VTA s/he leaves s.o. from eating, s/he eats only a portion of s.o. (e.g. fish)

iskwapiw ᐃᐢᑲᐧᐱᐤ
VAI s/he has just so much left

iskwascikan ᐃᐢᑲᐧᐢᒋᑲᐣ
NI leavings of food, food scrap

iskwastam ᐃᐢᑲᐧᐢᑕᐣ
VTI s/he leaves s.t. from eating, s/he eats only a portion of s.t. [*cf.* iskwahtam]

iskwastamawēw ᐃᐢᑲᐧᐢᑕᒪᐁᐧᐤ
VTA s/he leaves (it/him) for s.o. from eating

iskwatahikan ᐃᐢᑲᐧᑕᐦᐃᑲᐣ
NA treestump

iskwāhcēmāpiskos ᐃᐢᑳᐧᐦᒉᒫᐱᐢᑯᐢ
NI doorknob [*dim*]

iskwāhcēmis ᐃᐢᑳᐧᐦᒉᒥᐢ
NI small door [*dim*]

iskwāhēw ᐃᐢᑳᐧᐦᐁᐤ
VTA s/he kills nearly all of s.o.

iskwāhitowak ᐃᐢᑳᐧᐦᐃᑐᐊᐧᐠ
VAI they nearly kill one another off

iskwāhtawātēw ᐃᐢᑳᐧᐦᑕᐋᐧᑌᐤ
VTA s/he climbs up after s.o.

iskwāhtawīhtahēw ᐃᐢᑳᐧᐦᑕᐄᐧᐦᑕᐦᐁᐤ
VTA s/he climbs up with s.o.; s/he takes s.o. up

iskwāhtawīpahtāw ᐃᐢᑳᐧᐦᑕᐄᐧᐸᐦᑖᐤ
VAI s/he climbs up at a run

iskwāhtawīw ᐃᐢᑳᐧᐦᑕᐄᐧᐤ
VAI s/he climbs up

iskwāhtāsow ᐃᐢᑳᐧᐦᑖᓱᐤ
VAI s/he kills (it/him) off for his/her own benefit; s/he nearly kills (it/him) off but leaves a few

iskwāhtēm ᐃᐢᑳᐧᐦᑌᑦ
NI door

iskwāhtēmahokan ᐃᐢᑳᐧᐦᑌᒪᐦᐅᑲᐣ
NI door stick, stick for closing a tipi

iskwāhtēmāhtik ᐃᐢᑳᐧᐦᑌᒫᐦᑎᐠ
NI door frame [*pl*: -wa]

iskwāhtēmiwiw ᐃᐢᑳᐧᐦᑌᒥᐃᐧᐤ
VII it is a door

iskwāpēkamon ᐃᐢᑳᐧᐯᑲᒧᐣ
VII it goes so far as the rope will go

iskwāpihkēpitēw ᐃᐢᑳᐧᐱᐦᑫᐱᑌᐤ
VTA s/he pulls s.o. so far on a rope

iskwāpisona ᐃᐢᑳᐧᐱᓱᓇ
NI suspenders

iskwāpiw ᐃᐢᑳᐧᐱᐤ
VAI s/he sees such a distance

iskwāskosiw ᐃᐢᑳᐧᐢᑯᓯᐤ
VAI it is such a length (e.g. a stick)

iskwāw ᐃᐢᑳᐧᐤ
VII it is such a length, it is such a height

iskwēcākan ᐃᐢᑫᐧᒑᑲᐣ
NA last child, youngest child

iskwēcihcānis ᐃᐢᑫᐧᒋᐦᒑᓂᐢ
NI last, little finger [*dim*]

iskwēcihcīs ᐃᐢᑫᐧᒋᐦᒌᐢ
NI little finger [*dim*]

iskwēhkāsow ᐃᐢᑫᐧᐦᑳᓱᐤ
VAI s/he pretends to be a woman, s/he acts like a woman [*often said of young girls trying to act older*]

iskwēs ᐃᐢᑫᐧᐢ
NA teenage girl, little girl [*dim*]

iskwēsis ᐃᐢᑫᐧᓯᐢ
NA girl, little girl [*dim*]

iskwēsisāpoy ᐃᐢᑫᐧᓯᓵᐳᐩ
NI beer [*cf.* iskwēsisihkānāpoy]

iskwēsisihkān ᐃᐢᑫᐧᓯᓯᐦᑳᐣ
NA barley; girl doll [*also NI*]

iskwēsisihkānāpoy ᐃᐢᑫᐧᓯᓯᐦᑳᓈᐳᐩ
NI beer [*cf.* iskwēsisāpoy]

iskwēsisiwiw ᐃᐢᑫᐧᓯᓯᐃᐧᐤ
VAI she is a little girl

iskwēsitānis ᐃᐢᑫᐧᓯᑖᓂᐢ
NI little toe [*dim*]

iskwēsiwiw ᐃᐢᑫᐧᓯᐃᐧᐤ
VAI she is a girl, she is like a girl child

iskwēw ᐃᐢᑫᐧᐤ
NA woman, female adult

iskwēw-atoskēw ᐃᐢᑫᐧᐤ ᐊᑐᐢᑫᐤ
VAI s/he does woman's work

iskwēw-atoskēwin ᐃᐢᑫᐧᐤ ᐊᑐᐢᑫᐃᐧᐣ
NI woman's work

iskwēw-atoskēyākan ᐃᐢᑫᐧᐤ ᐊᑐᐢᑫᔮᑲᐣ
NA maid, female servant; woman's servant

iskwēw-āya ᐃᐢᑫᐧᐤ ᐋᔭ
NA female being

iskwēw-āyi ᐃᐢᑫᐧᐤ ᐋᔨ
NI thing pertaining to a female

iskwēwasākay ᐃᐢᑫᐧᐊᐧᓵᑲᐩ
NI woman's coat, dress or skirt

iskwēwastotin ᐃᐢᑫᐧᐊᐧᐢᑐᑎᐣ
NI woman's hat

iskwēwiw ᐃᐢᑫᐧᐃᐧᐤ
VAI she is a woman, she reaches womanhood, she becomes a woman

iskwēwitās ᐃᐢᑫᐧᐃᐧᑖᐢ
NA woman's leggings, women's slacks, jeans or bloomers

iskwēyāc ᐃᐢᑫᐧᔮᐢ
IPC last, at last, finally; at the end of it all; the last one/time; youngest [*also* iskwāyāc]

iskwēyānihk ᐃᐢᑫᐧᔮᓂᕁ
IPC at the very end, at the last

ispacinās ᐃᐢᐸᒋᓈᐢ
NI small hill [*dim; also* ispatinās]

ispacināsin ᐃᐢᐸᒋᓈᓯᐣ
VII it is quite high; it is a small hill [*dim*]

ispacināsiw ᐃᐢᐸᒋᓈᓯᐤ
VII it is a small hill [*dim*]

ispahcāw ᐃᐢᐸᐦᒑᐤ
VII it is high ground, the ground is so high

ispahēw ᐃᐢᐸᐦᐁᐤ
VTA s/he drives s.o. there quickly

ispahtawiw ᐃᐢᐸᐦᑕᐃᐧᐤ
VAI s/he climbs up high; s/he climbs stairs, s/he goes upstairs; s/he climbs up a tree [*see also* āmaciwēw, iskwahtawiw]

ispahtāw ᐃᐢᐸᐦᑖᐤ
VAI s/he runs thus or there

ispakocin ᐃᐢᐸᑯᒋᐣ
VII it hangs high (e.g. the moon)

ispakosiw ᐃᐢᐸᑯᓯᐤ
VAI it tastes so, it has such a flavour

ispakwan ᐃᐢᐸᒁᐣ
VII it tastes so, it has such a flavour

ispapiw ᐃᐢᐸᐱᐤ
VAI s/he sits aloft, s/he sits on s.t.; s/he sits just so high

ispaskitēw ᐃᐢᐸᐢᑭᑌᐤ
VII it is such a height

ispastāw ᐃᐢᐸᐢᑖᐤ
VAIt s/he piles s.t. so high, s/he places s.t. so high

ispastēw ᐃᐢᐸᐢᑌᐤ
VII it is piled high

ispatinaw ᐃᐢᐸᑎᓇᐤ
NI hill; hilly region [*also* aspatinaw; *cf.* ispatināw]

ispatināw ᐃᐢᐸᑎᓈᐤ
VII it is a hill

ispayíhēw ᐃᐢᐸᔩᐦᐁᐤ
VTA s/he affects s.o. thus, it happens thus to s.o.; s/he takes s.o. there quickly

ispayíhow ᐃᐢᐸᔩᐦᐅᐤ
VAI s/he throws him/herself thither or thus; s/he moves toward there quickly

ispayíhtāw ᐃᐢᐸᔩᐦᑖᐤ
VAIt s/he takes s.t. there quickly

ispayin ᐃᐢᐸᔨᐣ
VII it is, it becomes; it goes there; it happens thus, it occurs thus [*used as a measurement of time*: kā-ispayík "one week"; *or follows time specification*: e.g. pēyak tipahikan ispayin "it's one o'clock", *lit*: "one hour is happening"; *cf.* ispayíyiw]

ispayiw ᐃᐢᐸᔨᐤ
VAI s/he goes, s/he rides, s/he drives, s/he travels thus or there; s/he moves along

ispayíw ᐃᐢᐸᔩᐤ
VAI s/he is thus affected; s/he is thus afflicted; s/he fares thus; s/he goes there, s/he drives there; s/he moves thus

ispayíw ᐃᐢᐸᔩᐤ
VII it takes place thus, it occurs thus; it has passed (e.g. days, years); it goes thither or thus [*cf.* ispayín]

ispāhkē-wēpinam
ᐃᐢᐹᐦᑫ ᐄᐧᐸᓇᒼ
VTI s/he flings s.t. upward

ispāhkē-wēpinēw
ᐃᐢᐹᐦᑫ ᐄᐧᐱᓀᐤ
VTA s/he flings s.t. upward

ispāhkēkocin ᐃᐢᐹᐦᑫᑯᒋᐣ
VAI s/he flies up into the air

ispāhkēnam ᐃᐢᐹᐦᑫᓇᒼ
VTI s/he lifts s.t.

ispāhkēnēw ᐃᐢᐹᐦᑫᓀᐤ
VTA s/he lifts s.o.

ispāhkēpayíw ᐃᐢᐹᐦᑫᐸᔩᐤ
VAI s/he goes up there

ispāhkēpayíhow ᐃᐢᐹᐦᑫᐸᔩᐦᐅᐤ
VAI s/he darts aloft

ispāhkēpitēw ᐃᐢᐹᐦᑫᐱᑌᐤ
VTA s/he hoists s.o. up

ispāhkēw ᐃᐢᐹᐦᑫᐤ
VAI s/he goes upward

ispākonakāw ᐃᐢᐹᑯᓇᑳᐤ
VII it is deep snow

ispākonēw ᐃᐢᐹᑯᓀᐤ
VII the snow is piled deeply, it is a deep pile of snow

ispāpiskāw ᐃᐢᐹᐱᐢᑳᐤ
VII it is a high rock or mountain

ispāskosiw ᐃᐢᐹᐢᑯᓯᐤ
VAI s/he is such a height (as a tree)

ispāskwēyāw ᐃᐢᐹᐢᑵᔮᐤ
VII it is a high, thick-wooded area

ispāw ᐃᐢᐹᐤ
VII it is high, it is so high, it is so tall

ispi- ᐃᐢᐱ
IPV then, when

ispic ᐃᐢᐱᐨ
IPC than

ispiciw ᐃᐢᐱᒋᐤ
VAI s/he moves there, s/he moves camp thither

ispiciwin ᐃᐢᐱᒋᐃᐧᐣ
NI journey

ispicīhēw ᐃᐢᐱᒌᐦᐁᐤ
VTA s/he moves s.o. there (belongings and all)

ispihāw ᐃᐢᐱᐦᐋᐤ
VAI s/he flies there

ispikāpawiw ᐃᐢᐱᑳᐸᐃᐧᐤ
VAI s/he is just so tall, s/he stands just so tall

ispimihk ᐃᐢᐱᒥᕁ
IPC up, up above; in the air, on high, high up; upstairs

ispisi ᐃᐢᐱᓯ
IPC on ahead, meanwhile

ispisipayíw ᐃᐢᐱᓯᐸᔩᐤ
VAI s/he goes on ahead [*cf.* ispihcipayíw]

ispisiskāw ᐃᐢᐱᓯᐢᑳᐤ
VAI s/he goes so fast

ispisiw ᐃᐢᐱᓯᐤ
VAI s/he is so tall, it goes so far; it is just so high up

ispisīhēw ᐃᐢᐱᓰᐦᐁᐤ
VTA s/he raises s.o. thus; s/he builds s.o. higher

ispisīhtāw ᐃᐢᐱᓰᐦᑖᐤ
VAIt s/he builds s.t. high

ispisīwin ᐃᐢᐱᓰᐃᐧᐣ
NI an attempt

ispiskwahcāw ᐃᐢᐱᐢᑿᐦᒑᐤ
NI hilly land

ispiskwēyíw ᐃᐢᐱᐢᑵᔨᐤ
VAI s/he raises his/her own head

ispisohtēw ᐃᐢᐱᓱᐦᑌᐤ
VAI s/he walks on ahead

ispisow ᐃᐢᐱᓱᐤ
VAI s/he travels there by vehicle

ispitam ᐃᐢᐱᑕᒼ
VTI s/he pulls s.t. thither or thus, s/he draws s.t. thither or thus, s/he brings s.t. hither [*rdpl*: ay-ispitam]

ispitamawēw ᐃᐢᐱᑕᒪᐁᐧᐤ
VTA s/he pulls (it/him) thither or thus for s.o.

ispitēw ᐃᐢᐱᑌᐤ
VTA s/he pulls s.o. thither or thus, s/he draws s.o. thither or thus

ispī ᐃᐢᐲ
IPC then, at such a time; when; until [*cf.* ispīhk]

ispīhcāw ᐃᐢᐲᐦᒑᐤ
VII it extends so far, it is of such size (e.g. country); it is so big, large or long

ispīhci ᐃᐢᐲᐦᒋ
IPC for now, in the meantime

ispīhci- ᐃᔅᐱᐦᒋ
IPV meanwhile, beforehand

ispīhci wiya ᐃᔅᐱᐦᒋ ᐃᔾ
IPH instead of

ispīhci-askīwiw ᐃᔅᐱᐦᒋ ᐊᔅᑮᐃᐧᐤ
VII it is a certain number of
years since, it has been years
[*also* ispihc-āskiwiw]

ispīhcikitiw ᐃᔅᐱᐦᒋᑭᑎᐤ
VAI s/he is of such a large
size [*cf.* ispihtikitiw]

ispīhcikonēwēw ᐃᔅᐱᐦᒋᑯᓀᐁᐧᐤ
VAI s/he has a mouth of
such a capacity

ispīhcipayiw ᐃᔅᐱᐦᒋᐸᔨᐤ
VAI s/he goes on ahead [*cf.*
ispisipayiw]

ispīhcipayiw ᐃᔅᐱᐦᒋᐸᔨᐤ
VII it goes ahead [*cf.*
ispisipayiw]

ispīhcisīw ᐃᔅᐱᐦᒋᓰᐤ
VAI s/he is of a such an age;
it extends such a distance, it
is of such a size [*cf.*
ispihtisīw]

ispīhk ᐃᔅᐱᕽ
IPC when [*cf.* ispī]

ispīhtakotēw ᐃᔅᐱᐦᑕᑯᑌᐤ
VII it flies so far

ispīhtan ᐃᔅᐱᐦᑕᐣ
VII it is such a time of the
year [*cf.* ispīhtāwan]

ispīhtayakaskāw ᐃᔅᐱᐦᑕᔭᑲᔅᑳᐤ
VII it is thus in width; it is a
certain width, it is so broad

ispīhtāskosiw ᐃᔅᐱᐦᑖᐢᑯᓯᐤ
VAI s/he is such a height, it
is such a thickness

ispīhtāskwan ᐃᔅᐱᐦᑖᐢᑲᐧᐣ
VII it is such a thickness

ispīhtāskwapihkēw
ᐃᔅᐱᐦᑖᐢᑲᐧᐱᐦᑫᐧᐤ
VAI s/he has braids of such
thickness; s/he braids hair to
such a thickness

ispīhtāwan ᐃᔅᐱᐦᑖᐊᐧᐣ
VII it is so far in the year
[*cf.* ispīhtan]

ispīhtēkan ᐃᔅᐱᐦᑌᑲᐣ
VII it is such a length or
width (e.g. paper)

ispīhtēkisiw ᐃᔅᐱᐦᑌᑭᓯᐤ
VAI s/he is such a length or
width; it is so big a cloth

ispīhtēyihtam ᐃᔅᐱᐦᑌᔨᐦᑕᒼ
VTI s/he regards s.t. so; s/he
holds s.t. in such regard

ispīhtēyihtākosiw
ᐃᔅᐱᐦᑌᔨᐦᑖᑯᓯᐤ
VAI s/he is considered so
much; s/he is worth so much

ispīhtēyihtākosiwin
ᐃᔅᐱᐦᑌᔨᐦᑖᑯᓯᐃᐧᐣ
NI worth, regard

ispīhtēyihtākwan
ᐃᔅᐱᐦᑌᔨᐦᑖᑲᐧᐣ
VII it is considered so much;
it is worth so much

ispīhtēyimēw ᐃᔅᐱᐦᑌᔨᒣᐧᐤ
VTA s/he regards s.o. so;
s/he holds s.o. in such regard

ispīhtikitiw ᐃᔅᐱᐦᑎᑭᑎᐤ
VAI s/he is just so big [*cf.*
ispīhcikitiw]

ispīhtinikwan ᐃᔅᐱᐦᑎᓂᑲᐧᐣ
VII it is just so heavy

ispīhtinikwatiw ᐃᔅᐱᐦᑎᓂᑲᐧᑎᐤ
VAI s/he is thus in weight;
s/he is a certain weight, s/he
is just so heavy

ispīhtisīw ᐃᔅᐱᐦᑎᓰᐤ
VAI s/he is such in age, s/he
is so many years old; s/he
extends thus [*cf.* ispīhcisīw]

ita ᐃᑕ
IPC where; there; there
where

itaham ᐃᑕᐦᐊᒼ
VTI s/he handles s.t. so by
tool

itahcāw ᐃᑕᐦᒑᐤ
VII it is such a shape (as a
geographic feature); it has
such characteristics (as a
landform)

itahcikēw ᐃᑕᐦᒋᑫᐤ
VAI s/he eats so

itahēw ᐃᑕᐦᐁᐧᐤ
VTA s/he places s.o. so

itahkamikan ᐃᑕᐦᑲᒥᑲᐣ
VII it is an event, a
happening; it is done thus; it
happens thus; it goes on that
way

itahkamikihtāw ᐃᑕᐦᑲᒥᑭᐦᑖᐤ
VAIt s/he makes s.t. go on
that way

itahkamikisiw ᐃᑕᐦᑲᒥᑭᓯᐤ
VAI s/he does things thus,
s/he busies him/herself thus,
s/he is thus occupied; s/he
goes on that way

itahpisow ᐃᑕᐦᐱᓱᐤ
VAI s/he is so tied, s/he is
harnessed thus

itahpitam ᐃᑕᐦᐱᑕᒼ
VTI s/he ties s.t. so

itahpitēw ᐃᑕᐦᐱᑌᐤ
VTA s/he ties s.o. so

itahtasiwak ᐃᑕᐦᑕᓯᐊᐧᐠ
VAI they are so many

itahtinwa ᐃᑕᐦᑎᓇᐧ
VII they are so many

itahto- ᐃᑕᐦᑐ
IPV in such number

itahtopiponēw ᐃᑕᐦᑐᐱᐳᓀᐤ
VAI s/he is so many years
(winters) old [*cf.*
itahtopiponwēw;
tahtopiponwēw]

itahtopiponwēw ᐃᑕᐦᑐᐱᐳᓇᐧᐤ
VAI s/he is so old, s/he is so
many winters [*cf.*
itahtopiponēw;
tahtopiponwēw]

itahtopiponwēwin
ᐃᑕᐦᑐᐱᐳᓇᐧᐃᐧᐣ
NI having so many years,
winters; the number of one's
years, one's age [*also*
itahtopiponēwin]

itakihkēw ᐃᑕᑭᐦᑫᐧᐤ
VAI s/he values things so;
s/he fixes a price; s/he counts
so

itakihtam ᐃᑕᑭᐦᑕᒼ
VTI s/he charges so much
for s.t., s/he values s.t. so,
s/he prices s.t. so; s/he counts
s.t. thus

itakihtamawēw ᐃᑕᑭᐦᑕᒪᐁᐧᐤ
VTA s/he values (it/him) so
for s.o., s/he prices (it/him)
so for s.o.; s/he gives s.o.
such a price on (it/him)

itakihtēw ᐃᑕᑭᐦᑌᐤ
VII it is counted thus, it
costs so much; it is held in
such esteem

itakimēw ᐃᑕᑭᒣᐤ
VTA s/he counts s.o. thus;
s/he value s.o. so, s/he prices
s.o. so

itakisow ᐃᑕᑭᓱᐤ
VAI s/he is counted thus; it
is held in such esteem, it has
such a function; it is worth
so much, it costs so much

itakocin ᐃᑕᑯᒋᐣ
VAI s/he hangs thus or there,
s/he is suspended thus or
there; s/he flies thus or there,
s/he travels (by motor)

itakotēw ᐃᑕᑯᑌᐤ
VII it hangs thither or thus;
it flies thither or thus

itam ᐃᑕᒼ
VTI s/he says thus to or
about s.t.; s/he calls s.t. thus

itamahcihow ᐃᑕᒪᐦᒋᐦᐅᐤ
VAI s/he feels thus, s/he is in
such health [*cf.* nānitaw
itamahcihow "s/he feels
unwell"]

itamahcihowin ᐃᑕᒪᐦᒋᐦᐅᐃᐧᐣ
NI health

itamohēw ᐃᑕᒧᐦᐁᐧᐤ
VTA s/he attaches s.o. thus

itamohtāw ᐃᑕᒧᐦᑖᐤ
VAIt s/he attaches s.t. thus

itamon ᐃᑕᒧᐣ
VII it hangs thus; it runs
thus (e.g. road); it goes in
such a direction

itamow ᐃᑕᒧᐤ
VAI it is thus attached; it
hangs thus, it hangs in such a
direction

itamow ᐃᑕᒧᐤ
VII it is thus attached

itapihkātam ᐃᑕᐱᐦᑳᑕᒼ
VTI s/he braids s.t. thus; s/he
knits s.t. thus

itapihkēw ᐃᑕᐱᐦᑫᐤ
VAI s/he braids thus; s/he knits thus
itapiw ᐃᑕᐱᐤ
VAI s/he sits thus or there, s/he is present thus or there; s/he is thus placed
itasinaham ᐃᑕᓯᓇᐦᐊᒼ
VTI s/he writes or draws s.t. thus
itasinahikātēw ᐃᑕᓯᓇᐦᐃᑳᑌᐤ
VII it is so marked or written
itasinahikēw ᐃᑕᓯᓇᐦᐃᑫᐤ
VAI s/he writes thus, s/he handwrites, s/he draw thus
itasinahikēwin ᐃᑕᓯᓇᐦᐃᑫᐏᐣ
NI handwriting; drawing
itasināsow ᐃᑕᓯᓈᓱᐤ
VAI s/he is so coloured, s/he is coloured; s/he is marked thus
itasināson ᐃᑕᓯᓈᓱᐣ
NI colour [*cf.* itasināsowin]
itasināsowin ᐃᑕᓯᓈᓱᐏᐣ
NI colour [*cf.* itasināson]
itasināstēw ᐃᑕᓯᓈᐢᑌᐤ
VII it is so coloured, it is coloured; it is marked thus
itasināstēham ᐃᑕᓯᓈᐢᑌᐦᐊᒼ
VTI s/he colours s.t. so
itasiwātam ᐃᑕᓯᐚᑕᒼ
VTI s/he judges s.t., s/he orders s.t.
itasiwātēw ᐃᑕᓯᐚᑌᐤ
VTA s/he gives s.o. such a command; s/he judges s.o.; s/he rules thus for s.o.
itasiwēw ᐃᑕᓯᐍᐤ
VAI s/he commands thus, s/he rules thus; s/he states an opinion
itasiwēwin ᐃᑕᓯᐍᐏᐣ
NI command; such ruling; consultation
itaskihēw ᐃᑕᐢᑭᐦᐁᐤ
VTA s/he places s.o. upright
itaskitēw ᐃᑕᐢᑭᑌᐤ
VII it stands thus (e.g. lodge)
itaskōtowak ᐃᑕᐢᑰᑐᐊᐧᐠ
VAI they thus follow one on the other
itastāw ᐃᑕᐢᑖᐤ
VAIt s/he places s.t. thus or there
itastēw ᐃᑕᐢᑌᐤ
VII it is placed thus or there, it is located thus or there; it is written thus
itatāmow ᐃᑕᑖᒧᐤ
VAI s/he sings thus; s/he thus commits a slip of the tongue
itatāmowin ᐃᑕᑖᒧᐏᐣ
NI sounds produced when singing or breathing
itatiswēw ᐃᑕᑎᐢᐍᐤ
VTA s/he dyes s.o. (e.g. porcupine-quills) thus or in such a colour
itatoskēw ᐃᑕᑐᐢᑫᐤ
VAI s/he works thus or there
itācihow ᐃᑖᒋᐦᐅᐤ
VAI s/he travels there or thus; s/he leads his/her life thus
itācihowin ᐃᑖᒋᐦᐅᐏᐣ
NI travelling thus; leading one's life thus
itācimēw ᐃᑖᒋᒣᐤ
VTA s/he tells thus about s.o., s/he narrates thus about s.o.
itācimikosiw ᐃᑖᒋᒥᑯᓯᐤ
VAI s/he is thus narrated of
itācimostawēw ᐃᑖᒋᒧᐢᑕᐍᐤ
VTA s/he tells s.o. thus about (it); s/he narrates thus to s.o., s/he tells s.o. such a story
itācimow ᐃᑖᒋᒧᐤ
VAI s/he tells thus, s/he narrates thus; s/he tells such a story, s/he tells news thus; s/he crawls there, s/he crawls to such a point
itācimowin ᐃᑖᒋᒧᐏᐣ
NI daily news
itāhkohtowak ᐃᑖᐦᑯᐦᑐᐊᐧᐠ
VAI they are thus related to one another
itāhkōmēw ᐃᑖᐦᑰᒣᐤ
VTA s/he is related thus to s.o.; s/he has s.o. as such a relative, s/he uses such a kin-term for s.o. [*also* itāhkomēw]
itāhkōmitowin ᐃᑖᐦᑰᒥᑐᐏᐣ
NI relationship
itāhkōmow ᐃᑖᐦᑰᒧᐤ
VAI s/he has kinship, s/he is thus related
itāhokow ᐃᑖᐦᐅᑯᐤ
VAI s/he is carried along by current
itāhoyēw ᐃᑖᐦᐅᔦᐤ
VTA s/he ferries s.o. along
itāhpiw ᐃᑖᐦᐱᐤ
VAI s/he laughs thus
itāhpihēw ᐃᑖᐦᐱᐦᐁᐤ
VTA s/he laughs at s.o. thus
itākamiw ᐃᑖᑲᒥᐤ
VII it is a liquid of such a colour
itāmow ᐃᑖᒧᐤ
VAI s/he flees there or thus
itāp ᐃᑖᑊ
IPC then (in the future); sometime later, afterwards [*wC*: nitāp]
itāpacihēw ᐃᑖᐸᒋᐦᐁᐤ
VTA s/he uses s.o. thus
itāpacihtāw ᐃᑖᐸᒋᐦᑖᐤ
VAIt s/he uses s.t. thus, s/he uses such (things)
itāpahkanahikan ᐃᑖᐸᐦᑲᓇᐦᐃᑲᐣ
NI binoculars
itāpahkanahikēw ᐃᑖᐸᐦᑲᓇᐦᐃᑫᐤ
VAI s/he looks through binoculars
itāpahkān ᐃᑖᐸᐦᑳᐣ
NI spy glass
itāpahtam ᐃᑖᐸᐦᑕᒼ
VTI s/he looks at s.t. thus
itāpamēw ᐃᑖᐸᒣᐤ
VTA s/he looks at s.o. thus
itāpatakēyihtam ᐃᑖᐸᑕᑫᔨᐦᑕᒼ
VTI s/he finds s.t. worthy
itāpatakēyimēw ᐃᑖᐸᑕᑫᔨᒣᐤ
VTA s/he finds s.o. worthy
itāpatakēyimow ᐃᑖᐸᑕᑫᔨᒧᐤ
VAI s/he uses his/her own mind thus, s/he makes such use of his/her own mental faculties
itāpatan ᐃᑖᐸᑕᐣ
VII it is thus used, it is of such use, it is useful
itāpatisiw ᐃᑖᐸᑎᓯᐤ
VAI s/he is useful
itāpatisiwin ᐃᑖᐸᑎᓯᐏᐣ
NI purpose, usefulness
itāpēkamohtāw ᐃᑖᐯᑲᒧᐦᑖᐤ
VAIt s/he attaches s.t. thither or thus by rope; s/he aligns a rope (line, etc.) in such a way
itāpēkinēw ᐃᑖᐯᑭᓀᐤ
VTA s/he leads s.o. (e.g. horse) thus or there; s/he holds s.o. thus on a rope (by hand); s/he aligns s.o. (e.g. porcupine-quills) thus (e.g. end-to-end)
itāpipaýihow ᐃᑖᐱᐸᔨᐦᐅᐤ
VAI s/he glances thus or there quickly
itāpisin ᐃᑖᐱᓯᐣ
VAI s/he views s.t. in a certain manner, s/he has such a reaction to a view of s.t.
itāpiw ᐃᑖᐱᐤ
VAI s/he looks thus or there [*rdpl*: ay-itāpiw]
itāsiw ᐃᑖᓯᐤ
VAI s/he is blown thither; s/he sails on
itāskaciw ᐃᑖᐢᑲᒋᐤ
VAI s/he is thus frozen
itāskisow ᐃᑖᐢᑭᓱᐤ
VAI s/he is burnt (e.g. a tree)
itāskitēw ᐃᑖᐢᑭᑌᐤ
VII it is burnt
itāskocimēw ᐃᑖᐢᑯᒋᒣᐤ
VTA s/he snags s.o. thus on a branch, wood, etc.
itāskocin ᐃᑖᐢᑯᒋᐣ
VAI s/he is snagged thus on a branch, wood, etc.
itāskonam ᐃᑖᐢᑯᓇᒼ
VTI s/he holds s.t. so

itāskonēw ᐃᑖᐢᑯᓀᐤ
VTA s/he holds s.o. so
itāskonikākēw ᐃᑖᐢᑯᓂᑳᑫᐤ
VAI s/he points the pipe or pipestem with something, s/he uses something to point the pipe or pipestem
itāskonikēw ᐃᑖᐢᑯᓂᑫᐤ
VAI s/he points the pipe or pipestem; s/he holds a pipe ceremony
itāskonikēwin ᐃᑖᐢᑯᓂᑫᐃᐧᐣ
NI pointing the pipe or pipestem; pipe ceremony
itāskosiw ᐃᑖᐢᑯᓯᐤ
VAI it is such a stick
itāskotin ᐃᑖᐢᑯᑎᐣ
VAI s/he is snagged thus on a branch, wood, etc.
itāspinatēw ᐃᑖᐢᐱᓇᑌᐤ
VTA s/he assails s.o. so, s/he injures s.o. so
itāspinēmēw ᐃᑖᐢᐱᓀᒣᐤ
VTA s/he calls s.o. such in anger, s/he angrily calls s.o. such a name, s/he thus scolds s.o. in anger, s/he reproves s.o. so
itāspinēw ᐃᑖᐢᐱᓀᐤ
VAI s/he has such a disease; s/he is ill for such a time, s/he is ill for the duration
itāspinēwin ᐃᑖᐢᐱᓀᐃᐧᐣ
NI epidemic; sickness
itāstan ᐃᑖᐢᑕᐣ
VII it is blown there
itātakāw ᐃᑖᑕᑳᐤ
VAI s/he swims or wades thither or thus
itātihkēw ᐃᑖᑎᐦᑫᐤ
VAI s/he digs thither or thus
itātisiw ᐃᑖᑎᓯᐤ
VAI s/he is of such character or disposition; s/he acts thus, s/he has such conduct, s/he behaves thus
itātisiwin ᐃᑖᑎᓯᐃᐧᐣ
NI conduct, behaviour
itātotam ᐃᑖᑐᑕᒼ
VTI s/he tells s.t. thus
itē ᐃᑌ
IPC there, over there, thither, wherever
itēham ᐃᑌᐦᐊᒼ
VTI s/he stirs s.t.
itēhkē ᐃᑌᐦᑫ
IPC in that direction [*wC*: itihkī]
itēhkē isi ᐃᑌᐦᑫ ᐃᓯ
IPH in that direction
itēhwēw ᐃᑌᐦᐁᐧᐤ
VTA s/he stirs s.o. [*also* itēhēw]
itēkinam ᐃᑌᑭᓇᒼ
VTI s/he folds s.t. thus
itēnam ᐃᑌᓇᒼ
VTI s/he shuffles s.t. (e.g. cards)
itēnikēw ᐃᑌᓂᑫᐤ
VAI s/he shuffles cards
itēw ᐃᑌᐤ
VTA s/he says thus to s.o., s/he says thus about s.o.; s/he calls s.o. thus [*rdpl*: itītēw]
itēwēpaham ᐃᑌᐁᐧᐸᐦᐊᒼ
VTI s/he stirs s.t. so by tool
itēyatiwak ᐃᑌᔭᑎᐊᐧᐠ
VAI they are such in number, they are that many
itēýihcikan ᐃᑌᔦᐦᒋᑲᐣ
NI such thought
itēýihtam ᐃᑌᔦᐦᑕᒼ
VTI s/he thinks thus of or about s.t. [*rdpl*: ay-itēýihtam]
itēýihtamopaýiw ᐃᑌᔦᐦᑕᒧᐸᔦᐤ
VAI s/he thinks of (it/him) suddenly
itēýihtamowin ᐃᑌᔦᐦᑕᒧᐃᐧᐣ
NI thought; intention
itēýihtākan ᐃᑌᔦᐦᑖᑲᐣ
NI such thought; idea
itēýihtākosiw ᐃᑌᔦᐦᑖᑯᓯᐤ
VAI s/he is thus thought of, s/he is thus considered
itēýihtākwan ᐃᑌᔦᐦᑖᑲᐧᐣ
VII it is thus thought of, it is thus considered
itēýimēw ᐃᑌᔦᒣᐤ
VTA s/he thinks thus of or about s.o.
itēýimikowisiw ᐃᑌᔦᒥᑯᐃᐧᓯᐤ
VAI s/he is thus thought of by the powers
itēýimisow ᐃᑌᔦᒥᓱᐤ
VAI s/he thinks thus about him/herself, s/he assesses him/herself so
itēýimisowin ᐃᑌᔦᒥᓱᐃᐧᐣ
NI self-estimation
itēýimow ᐃᑌᔦᒧᐤ
VAI s/he thinks thus of him/herself; s/he thinks of (it/him) for him/herself
itihkwāmiw ᐃᑎᐦᑳᐧᒥᐤ
VAI s/he sleeps so
itihtam ᐃᑎᐦᑕᒼ
VTI s/he hears s.t. thus
itihtawēw ᐃᑎᐦᑕᐁᐧᐤ
VTA s/he hears s.o. thus
itihtākosiw ᐃᑎᐦᑖᑯᓯᐤ
VAI s/he sounds thus, s/he has such a sound; s/he is heard thus
itihtākosīhkāsow ᐃᑎᐦᑖᑯᓰᐦᑳᓱᐤ
VAI s/he pretends to be heard making such a noise, s/he acts as if to make such a noise
itihtākwan ᐃᑎᐦᑖᑲᐧᐣ
VII it is heard thus; it sounds thus
itikitiw ᐃᑎᑭᑎᐤ
VAI s/he is so big
itikowisiw ᐃᑎᑯᐃᐧᓯᐤ
VAI s/he is told so by higher powers
itinam ᐃᑎᓇᒼ
VTI s/he moves s.t. thither or thus by hand; s/he holds s.t. thus
itinamawēw ᐃᑎᓇᒪᐁᐧᐤ
VTA s/he moves (it/him) so by hand for s.o.
itinēw ᐃᑎᓀᐤ
VTA s/he moves s.o. thither or thus by hand; s/he holds s.o. thus
itinikēw ᐃᑎᓂᑫᐤ
VAI s/he acts thus, s/he fares thus, s/he does things thus; s/he gets into such (e.g. deplorable) things
itipēw ᐃᑎᐯᐤ
VAI s/he is thus from drink
itisaham ᐃᑎᓴᐦᐊᒼ
VTI s/he sends s.t. there, s/he drives s.t. thither
itisahamawēw ᐃᑎᓴᐦᐊᒪᐁᐧᐤ
VTA s/he sends (it/him) to s.o. thus or there; s/he drives (it/him) thither to s.o.
itisahamātowak ᐃᑎᓴᐦᐊᒫᑐᐊᐧᐠ
VAI they send (it/him) to one another
itisahikan ᐃᑎᓴᐦᐃᑲᐣ
NI parcel
itisahikēw ᐃᑎᓴᐦᐃᑫᐤ
VAI s/he sends things thither, s/he drives things thither; s/he sends a parcel
itisahwākan ᐃᑎᓴᐦᐋᐧᑲᐣ
NA messenger; scout
itisahwēw ᐃᑎᓴᐦᐁᐧᐤ
VTA s/he sends s.o. thus or there; s/he drives s.o. thither
itisam ᐃᑎᓴᒼ
VTI s/he cuts s.t. thus
itisinam ᐃᑎᓯᓇᒼ
VTI s/he holds s.t. thither or thus
itisinamawēw ᐃᑎᓯᓇᒪᐁᐧᐤ
VTA s/he hands (it/him) to s.o.
itisinēw ᐃᑎᓯᓀᐤ
VTA s/he holds s.o. thither or thus
itiskanawēw ᐃᑎᐢᑲᓇᐁᐧᐤ
VAI s/he makes tracks thither or thus
itiskēw ᐃᑎᐢᑫᐤ
VAI s/he steps thither or thus [*also* isi-tahkoskēw]
itiskwāstawēstēw ᐃᑎᐢᑳᐧᐢᑕᐁᐧᐢᑌᐤ
VII the door is in such a location
itiskwēkotēw ᐃᑎᐢᑫᐧᑯᑌᐤ
VAI s/he hangs with head in such a position; it flies with its head that way
itiskwēpiw ᐃᑎᐢᑫᐧᐱᐤ
VAI s/he sits with head that way

itiskwēsin ᐃᑎᐢᑵᓯᐣ
VAI s/he lies with head that way

itiskwēstawēw ᐃᑎᐢᑵᐢᑕᐍᐤ
VTA s/he faces s.o.

itiskwēýiw ᐃᑎᐢᑵᖨᐤ
VAI s/he turns his/her own head thither or thus

itistahikēw ᐃᑎᐢᑕᐦᐃᑫᐤ
VAI s/he sews things on thus

itistahwēw ᐃᑎᐢᑕᐦᐍᐤ
VTA s/he sews s.o. (e.g. porcupine-quills) on thus

itiswēw ᐃᑎᓭᐤ
VTI s/he cuts s.o. thus

ititowak ᐃᑎᑐᐘᐠ
VAI they say thus to or about one another

itohtahēw ᐃᑐᐦᑕᐦᐁᐤ
VTA s/he takes s.o. thus or there, s/he leads s.o. thither

itohtahisow ᐃᑐᐦᑕᐦᐃᓱᐤ
VAI s/he gets him/herself there

itohtatam ᐃᑐᐦᑕᑕᑦ
VTI s/he takes s.t. thither [*cf.* itohtatāw]

itohtatamawēw ᐃᑐᐦᑕᑕᒪᐍᐤ
VTA s/he takes (it/him) there to or for s.o.

itohtatāw ᐃᑐᐦᑕᑖᐤ
VAIt s/he takes s.t. there [*cf.* itohtatam]

itohtēmakan ᐃᑐᐦᑌᒪᑲᐣ
VII it goes, it goes there or thus

itohtēw ᐃᑐᐦᑌᐤ
VAI s/he goes, s/he goes there or thus

itohtēwin ᐃᑐᐦᑌᐏᐣ
NI goal of journey, destination

itowahk ᐃᑐᐘᕽ
IPC this kind, a certain kind [*also* itowa]

itowatēw ᐃᑐᐘᑌᐤ
VAI s/he carries a load on his/her own back thither or thus

itowihk ᐃᑐᐏᕽ
IPC in such a place, in this place [*wC*: "that kind"]

itōtam ᐃᑑᑕᑦ
VTI s/he does s.t. thus, s/he does thus, s/he acts thus [*cf.* tōtam]

itōtamawēw ᐃᑑᑕᒪᐍᐤ
VTA s/he does thus to s.o. [*cf.* tōtamawēw]

itōtamāsow ᐃᑑᑕᒫᓱᐤ
VAI s/he does (it) so for him/herself [*cf.* tōtamāsow]

itōtamōhēw ᐃᑑᑕᒨᐦᐁᐤ
VTA s/he makes s.o. act thus, s/he makes s.o. do thus [*cf.* tōtamōhēw]

itōtawēw ᐃᑑᑕᐍᐤ
VTA s/he does thus to s.o. [*cf.* tōtawēw]

itwaham ᐃᑗᐦᐊᑦ
VTI s/he points s.t. out

itwahamawēw ᐃᑗᐦᐊᒪᐍᐤ
VTA s/he points (it/him) out to s.o.

itwahikan ᐃᑗᐦᐃᑲᐣ
NI sign (for directions)

itwahikanicihcān ᐃᑗᐦᐃᑲᓂᒋᐦᒑᐣ
NI index finger

itwahikanicihcīs ᐃᑗᐦᐃᑲᓂᒋᐦᒌᐢ
NI index finger, pointing finger [*dim*]

itwahikākēw ᐃᑗᐦᐃᑳᑫᐤ
VAI s/he points s.t. out; s/he uses something to point things out

itwahwēw ᐃᑗᐦᐍᐤ
VTA s/he points his/her finger at s.o., s/he points at s.o.; s/he points s.o. out

itwēmakan ᐃᑵᒪᑲᐣ
VII it says so (e.g. a book), it has such a meaning

itwēskiw ᐃᑵᐢᑭᐤ
VAI s/he says so all the time [*hab*]

itwēstamawātam ᐃᑵᐢᑕᒪᐚᑕᑦ
VTI s/he translates s.t.

itwēstamawēw ᐃᑵᐢᑕᒪᐍᐤ
VTA s/he says so for s.o.; s/he speaks for s.o.; s/he interprets for s.o.; s/he translates for s.o.; he speaks on behalf of s.o. (in making a date or betrothal)

itwēstamākēw ᐃᑵᐢᑕᒫᑫᐤ
VAI s/he interprets

itwēstamākēw ᐃᑵᐢᑕᒫᑫᐤ
NA interpreter

itwēstamākēwin ᐃᑵᐢᑕᒫᑫᐏᐣ
NI interpretation, translation

itwēstamāsow ᐃᑵᐢᑕᒫᓱᐤ
VAI s/he interprets for him/herself

itwēw ᐃᑵᐤ
VAI s/he says so, s/he says thus, s/he calls (it) so; it has such a meaning [*rdpl*: ay-itwēw, itītwēw]

itwēwēhkasow ᐃᑵᐍᐦᑲᓱᐤ
VAI it burns with such noise

itwēwēmēw ᐃᑵᐍᒣᐤ
VTA s/he speaks a lot to s.o.

itwēwēw ᐃᑵᐍᐤ
VAI s/he makes such noise

itwēwin ᐃᑵᐏᐣ
NI word; the saying so, such speech

itwēwitam ᐃᑵᐏᑕᑦ
VTI s/he noises s.t. so; [*rdpl*: ay-itwēwitam:] s/he makes continuous utterances

iýaskohc ᐃᖬᐢᑯᐦᐨ
IPC next in sequence

iyaw ᐃᔭᐤ
IPC well now; oops [*introductory*; *exclamation*]

iyawis ᐅᔭᐏᐢ
IPC entirely, whole

iyāpēsis ᐃᔮᐯᓯᐢ
NA young bull; young animal [*dim*]

iyāpēw ᐃᔮᐯᐤ
NA buck, bull moose; male [*cf.* yiyāpēw]

iyāyaw ᐃᔮᔭᐤ
IPC instead, by preference; first thing, preferably, rather; eagerly, with full intent [*cf.* yāyaw]

iyāyita ᐃᔮᔨᑕ
IPC where no-one knows

iýihtēw ᐃᖨᐦᑌᐤ
VII it thaws [*wC*: thihtīw; *see also* tihkitēw]

iýikohk ᐃᖨᑯᕽ
IPC so much, to such a degree, to such an extent; until, when time comes; more

iýikopiwi-pīsim ᐃᖨᑯᐱᐏ ᐲᓯᑦ
NA Frost Moon; November [*cf.* ihkopiwi-pīsim, ýiýīkopīwi-pīsim]

iyinamawēw ᐃᔨᓇᒪᐍᐤ
VTA s/he allows s.o. to do s.t.

iýinaskihk ᐃᖨᓇᐢᑭᕽ
NA kettle [*pl*: -wak]

iýināhtik ᐃᖨᓈᐦᑎᐠ
NA white spruce [*pl*: -wak]

iýini- ᐃᖨᓂ
IPN common, plain [*cf.* iýinito-]

iýini-kinosēw ᐃᖨᓂ ᑭᓄᓭᐤ
NA large fish, ordinary fish; pike, jackfish

iýinico-pimīs ᐃᖨᓂᒍ ᐱᒦᐢ
NI ordinary grease [*dim*; *cf.* iýinito-pimiy]

iýinihkēwin ᐃᖨᓂᐦᑫᐏᐣ
NI custom

iýinimin ᐃᖨᓂᒥᐣ
NI blueberry

iýiniminiskāw ᐃᖨᓂᒥᓂᐢᑳᐤ
VII there is an abundance of blueberries, blueberries are abundant

iýinisip ᐃᖨᓂᓯᑊ
NA mallard duck

iýinisipis ᐃᖨᓂᓯᐱᐢ
NA mallard duckling [*dim*]

iýinito- ᐃᖨᓂᑐ
IPN common, plain [*cf.* iýini-]

iýinito-kinosēw ᐃᖨᓂᑐ ᑭᓄᓭᐤ
NA ordinary fish; pike, jackfish

iýinito-pimiy ᐃᖨᓂᑐ ᐱᒥᐩ
NI ordinary grease [*less easily congealed, found especially in association with muscle tissue, and including bone-marrow or* "marrow-fat"; *cf.* iýinico-pimīs]

iẏinitōskātāsk ᐃᕆᓂᑑᐢᑳᕈᐢ
NA wild carrot [*pl*: -wak]

iẏiniw ᐃᕆᓂᐤ
NA First Nations person, Indian; person, man [*usually wC*: ithiniw; *but in some areas of wC* (*e.g. La Ronge*): itiniw]

iẏiniwacis ᐃᕆᓂᐊᕒᐣ
NA bean, green bean

iẏiniwihkāsow ᐃᕆᓂᐃᐧᐦᑳᓱ
VAI s/he has a traditional, native name; s/he has an Indian name

iẏiniwihkātam ᐃᕆᓂᐃᐧᐦᑳᑕᒼ
VTI s/he gives s.t. a traditional, native name; s/he gives s.t. an Indian name

iẏiniwihkātēw ᐃᕆᓂᐃᐧᐦᑳᑌᐤ
VTA s/he gives s.o. a traditional, native name; s/he gives s.o. an Indian name

iẏinīhkān ᐃᕆᓃᐦᑳᐣ
NA an image, likeness of man

iẏinīhkēw ᐃᕆᓃᐦᑫᐤ
VAI s/he makes an image

iẏinīnāhk ᐃᕆᓃᓈᕽ
IPC in the land of mortal men

iẏinīsiw ᐃᕆᓃᓯᐤ
VAI s/he is clever, s/he is smart, s/he is wise

iẏinīsiwin ᐃᕆᓃᓯᐃᐧᐣ
NI wisdom, intelligence; knowledge

iẏinīwistikwān ᐃᕆᓃᐃᐧᐢᑎᒁᐣ
NI human head

iẏipahtāw ᐃᕆᐸᐦᑖᐤ
VAI s/he trots

iẏipahtāwatim ᐃᕆᐸᐦᑖᐊᐧᑎᒼ
NA trotting horse [*pl*: -wak]

iyisāc ᐃᕆᓵᐨ
IPC half-heartedly, hesitantly, unwillingly, against one's will

iyisāhow ᐃᕆᓵᐦᐅᐤ
VAI s/he resists, s/he resists temptation, s/he exercises restraint

iyisāhowin ᐃᕆᓵᐦᐅᐃᐧᐣ
NI resistance, resisting temptation, restraint

iyiwanisiw ᐃᕆᐊᐧᓂᓯᐤ
VAI s/he is short of supplies

iyiwēskam ᐃᕆᐍᐢᑲᒼ
VTI s/he goes to s.t. against orders

iyīhkostēw ᐃᕆᐦᑯᐢᑌᐤ
VAI s/he has a hare-lip

iyīhkwatin ᐃᕆᐦᑿᑎᐣ
VII it is frosty, there is hoar frost

iyīhkwēw ᐃᕆᐦᒁᐤ
VAI s/he is unsexed, androgynous;
NA transvestite [*cf.* ēyīhkwēw]

iyīkatē ᐃᕆᑲᑌ
IPC aside, off to one side [*see* īkatē, yīkatē]

iyīpēhcāw ᐃᕆᐯᐦᒑᐤ
NI sloping ground

iyīpēnēw ᐃᕆᐯᓀᐤ
VTA s/he tilts s.o. by hand

iyīpēpaẏihow ᐃᕆᐯᐸᕆᐦᐅᐤ
VAI s/he throws him/herself so as to lean over

iyīpēpaẏiw ᐃᕆᐯᐸᕆᐤ
VII it slants to one side

iyīpēsin ᐃᕆᐯᓯᐣ
VAI s/he lies on his/her own side [*wC*: thithipīsin]

iyīpēyāw ᐃᕆᐯᔮᐤ
VII it slopes, it slants

iyōskisiw ᐃᔪᐢᑭᓯᐤ
VAI s/he is soft, s/he is tender [*cf.* yōskisiw]

ī Á

ī Á
IPC lo! look! behold!
[*exclamation*]

īh Á"
IPC lo! look! behold!
[*exclamation*]

īhī Á"Á
IPC enemy in sight!
[*exclamation*]; [*wC*:] yes

īhkēyíhtam Á"ᑫ"Cᶜ
VTI s/he is impatient over
s.t.; s/he is anxious about s.t.,
s/he feels anxiety over s.t.

īkatē ÁᏏU
IPC aside, off to one side
[*cf.* yīkatē; *also* iyīkatē]

īkatē- ÁᏏU
IPV aside, off to one side

īkatē-kwāskohtiw
ÁᏏU Ꮟ·ᐁ"∩ᐤ
VAI s/he jumps aside

īkatē-tihtipinam
ÁᏏU ∩"∩ᐯᐨᶜ
VTI s/he rolls s.t. aside

īkatē-tihtipinamawēw
ÁᏏU ∩"∩ᐯᐊᐯᐧ·°
VTA s/he rolls (it/him) aside
for s.o.

īkatē-tihtipinēw
ÁᏏU ∩"∩ᐯᐤ°
VTA s/he rolls s.o. aside

īkatē-wēpinam ÁᏏU ᐁ·ᐁᶜ
VTI s/he throws s.t. aside,
s/he tosses s.t. aside, s/he
flings s.t. aside

īkatē-wēpinamawēw
ÁᏏU ᐁ·ᐁᐊᐯ·°
VTA s/he throws (it/him)
aside for s.o.

īkatē-wēpinēw ÁᏏU ᐁ·ᐁ ᐤ°
VTA s/he throws s.o. aside,
s/he tosses s.o. aside, s/he
flings s.o. aside

īkatēhēw ÁᏏU"ᐁ°
VTA s/he puts s.o. aside

īkatēhtahēw ÁᏏU"C"ᐁ°
VTA s/he leads s.o. aside

īkatēhtatāw ÁᏏU"CĊ°
VAIt s/he takes s.t. aside

īkatēhtēw ÁᏏU"U°
VAI s/he walks off to one
side; s/he walks away [*cf.*
īkatēhtēw]

īkatēkāpawiw ÁᏏUᏏ<ᐊ·°
VAI s/he stands aside, s/he
steps aside

īkatēnam ÁᏏUᐊᶜ
VTI s/he takes s.t. aside; s/he
clears the way

īkatēnamawēw ÁᏏUᐊᐯ·°
VTA s/he take (it/him) aside
for s.o.; clear the way for s.o.

īkatēnamāsow ÁᏏUᐊᏏᒍ°
VAI s/he thrusts (it/him)
aside for him/herself

īkatēnēw ÁᏏUᐤ°
VTA s/he pushes s.o. aside,
s/he thrusts s.o. aside by
hand; s/he takes s.o. aside,
s/he takes s.o. off to the side

īkatēpahtāw ÁᏏU<"Ċ°
VAI s/he runs offside, s/he
runs aside

īkatēpayíhow ÁᏏU<ᐢ"ᐤ°
VAI s/he moves aside
quickly

īkatēpayín ÁᏏU<ᐢᐣ
VII it moves off to the side,
it moves sideways (e.g.
braided strips of rabbitskin)
[*cf.* īkatēpayin]

īkatēpiciw ÁᏏUᐱᎥ°
VAI s/he moves camp to one
side

īkatēpitam ÁᏏUᐱCᶜ
VTI s/he pulls s.t. aside

īkatēpitēw ÁᏏUᐱU°
VTA s/he pulls s.o. aside

īkatēstamawēw ÁᏏUᐣCᒪᐁ·°
VTA s/he thrusts (it/him)
aside for s.o.

īkatēstamāsow ÁᏏUᐣCᒪᒍ°
VAI s/he thrusts (it/him)
aside for him/herself

īkatēstawēw ÁᏏUᐣCᐁ·°
VTA s/he goes off to the side
from s.o., s/he goes away
from s.o. [*cf.* yīkatēstawēw]

īkatēstāw ÁᏏUᐣĊ°
VAIt s/he sets s.t. aside, s/he
lays s.t. down off to the side

īkatētācimow ÁᏏUĊᒋᒍ°
VAI s/he crawls off to one
side

īkatētāpēw ÁᏏUĊᐯ°
VAI s/he drags off to one
side

īkinikēw ÁᏐᑫᐟ°
VAI s/he milk (e.g. a cow)
by hand [*cf.* yīkinikēw]

īkinikēsiw ÁᏐᒐᐟᐟ°
VAI s/he milk a little by
hand [*dim*; *cf.* yīkinikēw]

īni- Áᒐ
IPN common, ordinary [*see*
iýini-, iýinito-]

ītawiyaw ÁCᎥᐧᐟ°
IPC at the sides [*cf.* ayītaw]

īwahikan Á◁ᐧ"ÁᏏᐢ
NA pounded meat [*pl
generally*; *cf.* -īwahikan-
NDA, yīwahikan]

īwahikanihkēw Á◁ᐧ"ÁᏏᒐ"ᑫ°
VAI s/he makes pemmican
[*cf.* yīwahikanihkēw]

k

ᑲ

ka ᑲ
IPC oh! yes [*discourse particle*; *accepting information*; *cf.* kah, kā]

ka- ᑲ
IPV [*grammatical preverb*: *future* "will, shall"; *infinitive*; *optative* "ought, should"; *cf.* kika-, kita-, ta-, tita-]

ka-kāsīyāpahwēw ᑲᑳᓰᔮᐸᐦᐍᐤ
VTA s/he wipes s.o.'s eyes [*rdpl*]

ka-kāsīyāpiw ᑲᑳᓰᔮᐱᐤ
VAI s/he wipes his/her own eyes [*rdpl*]

ka-kiýāskiskiw ᑲ ᑭᔮᐢᑭᐢᑭᐤ
VAI s/he tells lies [*rdpl*]

ka-kī- ᑲ ᑮ
IPV can, be able to; may; should, ought to [*cf.* kita-kī-, ta-kī-]

kahkahkīhkēsiw ᑲᐦᑲᐦᑮᐦᑫᓯᐤ
VAI it is square [*rdpl*]

kahkahkīhkēyāw ᑲᐦᑲᐦᑮᐦᑫᔮᐤ
VII it is square [*rdpl*]

kahkāpēwiw ᑲᐦᑳᐯᐏᐤ
VAI s/he is of whole body

kahkiýaw ᑲᐦᑭᔭᐤ
IPC all, every; the full amount

kahkiýaw awiyak ᑲᐦᑭᔭᐤ ᐊᐃᐧᔭᐠ
PR everyone

kahkiýaw kīkway ᑲᐦᑭᔭᐤ ᑮᑲᐧᕀ
PR everything

kahkiýawisiw ᑲᐦᑭᔭᐃᐧᓯᐤ
VAI it is entire, whole

kahkwēýihtam ᑲᐦᑫᐧᔦᐦᑕᒼ
VTI s/he is jealous, s/he is jealous of s.t.

kahkwēýimēw ᑲᐦᑫᐧᔨᒣᐤ
VTA s/he is jealous of s.o.

kakayēsihēw ᑲᑲᔦᓯᐦᐁᐤ
VTA s/he deceives s.o.; s/he uses evil magic on s.o. [*rdpl*; *also* kakayēyihēw]

kakayēsisiw ᑲᑲᔦᓯᓯᐤ
VAI s/he cheats, s/he is deceitful [*rdpl*; *also* kakayēyisiw]

kakayēsisiwin ᑲᑲᔦᓯᓯᐎᐣ
NI cheating [*rdpl*; *also* kakayēyisiwin]

kakayēsisiwiw ᑲᑲᔦᓯᓯᐏᐤ
VAI s/he is a cheat [*rdpl*; *also* kakayēyisiwiw]

kakayēsisīhēw ᑲᑲᔦᓯᓰᐦᐁᐤ
VTA s/he cheats s.o. [*rdpl*; *also* kakayēyisīhēw]

kakāspakicihciy ᑲᑳᐢᐸᑭᒋᐦᒋᕀ
NA bear [*lit*: "thick paw"; *rdpl*; *cf.* kispakāw]

kakāýawātisiw ᑲᑳᔭᐚᑎᓯᐤ
VAI s/he is diligent, s/he is hard-working, s/he is of industrious disposition; s/he is active, s/he is agile

kakāýawisīw ᑲᑳᔭᐏᓰᐤ
VAI s/he works hard, s/he is a hard-worker; s/he is hard-working, s/he is industrious, s/he is diligent

kakēhtawēýihtam ᑲᑫᐦᑕᐍᔨᐦᑕᒼ
VTI s/he is wise, s/he thinks wisely

kakēhtānam ᑲᑫᐦᑖᓇᒼ
VTI s/he immerses s.o. by hand

kakēhtānēw ᑲᑫᐦᑖᓀᐤ
VTA s/he immerses s.o. by hand

kakēkinam ᑲᑫᑭᓇᒼ
VTI s/he picks s.t. out

kakēkinamawēw ᑲᑫᑭᓇᒪᐍᐤ
VTA s/he picks (it/him) out for s.o.

kakēkinamākēw ᑲᑫᑭᓇᒫᑫᐤ
VAI s/he picks (it/him) out for people

kakēkinēw ᑲᑫᑭᓀᐤ
VTA s/he picks s.o. out

kakēkinikēw ᑲᑫᑭᓂᑫᐤ
VAI s/he picks things out

kakēpāci- ᑲᑫᐹᒋ
IPV stupidly

kakēpāci-tōtam ᑲᑫᐹᒋ ᑑᑕᒼ
VTI s/he does stupid things

kakēpātinikēw ᑲᑫᐹᑎᓂᑫᐤ
VAI s/he acts stupidly, s/he does foolish things

kakēpātinikēwin ᑲᑫᐹᑎᓂᑫᐎᐣ
NI stupid and awkward handling

kakēpātis ᑲᑫᐹᑎᐢ
NA fool, stupid person

kakēpātisiw ᑲᑫᐹᑎᓯᐤ
VAI s/he is foolish, s/he is stupid; s/he lives foolishly; s/he is stubborn [*dim*: kakēpācisiw]

kakēpātisiwin ᑲᑫᐹᑎᓯᐎᐣ
NI foolishness, stupidity

kakēpihcēs ᑲᑫᐱᐦᒉᐢ
NA deaf person

kakēpihtēw ᑲᑫᐱᐦᑌᐤ
VAI s/he is deaf; s/he fails to listen

kakēpihtēwin ᑲᑫᐱᐦᑌᐎᐣ
NI deafness

kakēpiskam ᑲᑫᐱᐢᑲᒼ
VTI s/he blocks s.t. [*cf.* kipiskam]

kakēpiskawēw ᑲᑫᐱᐢᑲᐍᐤ
VTA s/he crowds s.o., s/he blocks s.o. [*cf.* kipiskawēw]

kakēskihkēmow ᑲᑫᐢᑭᐦᑫᒧᐤ
VAI s/he lectures people, s/he counsels people, s/he preaches at people

kakēskihkēmowin ᑲᑫᐢᑭᐦᑫᒧᐎᐣ
NI lecture, counsel; lecturing, counselling

kakēskimāwasow ᑲᑫᐢᑭᒫᐘᓱᐤ
VAI s/he lectures (his/her own) children, s/he counsels (his/her own) children; s/he cautions (his/her own) children; s/he advises (his/her own) children

kakēskimāwasowin ᑲᑫᐢᑭᒫᐘᓱᐎᐣ
NI instructions and lectures (for children)

kakēskimēw ᑲᑫᐢᑭᒣᐤ
VTA s/he lectures s.o., s/he counsels s.o.; s/he preaches to s.o.

kakēskimisow ᑲᑫᐢᑭᒥᓱᐤ
VAI s/he counsels him/herself

kakēskimiwēw ᑲᑫᐢᑭᒥᐍᐤ
VAI s/he preaches, s/he counsels

kakēskimowin ᑲᑫᐢᑭᒧᐎᐣ
NI sermon

kakēskwēw ᑲᑫᐢᑵᐤ
VAI s/he preaches

kakihcimoskiw ᑲᑭᐦᒋᒧᐢᑭᐤ
VAI s/he is a braggart [*hab*; *see also* mamihcimoskiw]

kakihcimow ᑲᑭᐦᒋᒧᐤ
VAI s/he boasts, s/he brags [*see also* mamihcimow]

kakihcimowin ᑲᑭᐦᒋᒧᐎᐣ
NI boasting [*see also* mamihcimowin]

kakiýipīw ᑲᑭᔨᐲᐤ
VAI s/he hurries [*rdpl*]

kakīsahwāw ᑲᑮᓴᐦᐛᐤ
VAI it grows feathers, it is a fledgling

kakwayāhow ᑲᑿᔮᐦᐅᐤ
VAI s/he hurries, s/he hurries up [*cf.* kwayāhow]

kakwāhýahkamik ᑲᒁᐦᔭᐦᑲᒥᐠ
IPC goodness gracious [*also* kakwāhýakahkamik]

kakwāhýakēýatiwak ᑲᒁᐦᔭᑫᔭᑎᐙᐠ
VAI they are in vast numbers

kakwāhýakēýatinwa ᑲᒁᐦᔭᑫᔭᑎᓌ
VII they are in vast numbers

kakwāhýaki- ᑲᒁᐦᔭᑭ
IPV greatly, extremely, overwhelmingly; with startled surprise [*cf.* kakwāýaki-]

kakwāhýakihēw ᑲᒁᐦᔭᑭᐦᐁᐤ
VTA s/he does (s.t.) outrageous to s.o.

kakwāhýakinākosiw ᑲᒁᐦᔭᑭᓈᑯᓯᐤ
VAI s/he is of outrageous appearance

kakwāhýakinākwan ᑲᒁᐦᔭᑭᓈᑿᐣ
VII it is of outrageous appearance

kakwāhýakinikēw ᑲᒁᐦᔭᑭᓂᑫᐤ
VAI s/he runs at a great speed; s/he does outrageous things

kakwānwāw ᑲᒁᓎᐤ
VII it is a long object [*cf.* kinwāw]

kakwātakahkatisow ᑲᒁᑕᑲᐦᑲᑎᓱᐤ
VAI s/he is terribly hungry; s/he is terribly thin, s/he has a starved look about him/her

kakwātakatāmow ᑲᒁᑕᑲᑖᒧᐤ
VAI s/he wails; s/he has a difficult time breathing

kakwātakatāmowin ᑲᒁᑕᑲᑖᒧᐏᐣ
NI intense crying and wailing; difficult breathing

kakwātakatotēw ᑲᒁᑕᑲᑐᑌᐤ
VTA s/he is mean and orders s.o. around, s/he runs s.o. off that one's feet

kakwātakāhpiw ᑲᒁᑕᑳᐦᐱᐤ
VAI s/he laughs a lot, s/he laughs til it hurts; s/he laughs him/herself sick

kakwātakāpākwēhēw ᑲᒁᑕᑳᐹᑵᐦᐁᐤ
VTA s/he denies s.o. liquid causing mortification, s/he makes s.o. suffer thirst

kakwātakāpākwēhow ᑲᒁᑕᑳᐹᑵᐦᐅᐤ
VAI s/he suffers mortification by denying him/herself liquid, s/he makes him/herself suffer thirst

kakwātakāposwēw ᑲᒁᑕᑳᐳᓳᐤ
VTA s/he torments s.o. with smoke

kakwātakēýihtam ᑲᒁᑕᑫᔨᐦᑕᒼ
VTI s/he is tormented, s/he is tormented about s.t.

kakwātakēýimēw ᑲᒁᑕᑫᔨᒣᐤ
VTA s/he is distressed by s.o. (*i.e.* a loss); s/he feels deeply for s.o. in sickness

kakwātakēýimow ᑲᒁᑕᑫᔨᒧᐤ
VAI s/he feels distressed, helpless, miserable; s/he feels self-pity

kakwātakēýimowin ᑲᒁᑕᑫᔨᒧᐏᐣ
NI misery, agony; helplessness

kakwātakihēw ᑲᒁᑕᑭᐦᐁᐤ
VTA s/he distresses s.o., s/he torments s.o., s/he tortures s.o.; s/he mistreats s.o.

kakwātakihisow ᑲᒁᑕᑭᐦᐃᓱᐤ
VAI s/he makes him/herself miserable, s/he makes him/herself suffer, s/he torments him/herself

kakwātakihiwēw ᑲᒁᑕᑭᐦᐃᐍᐤ
VAI s/he torments people, s/he antagonizes people

kakwātakihow ᑲᒁᑕᑭᐦᐅᐤ
VAI s/he suffers, s/he makes him/herself suffer

kakwātakihtāw ᑲᒁᑕᑭᐦᑖᐤ
VAIt s/he suffers, s/he is distressed; s/he suffers because of s.t., s/he has difficulties because of s.t.

kakwātakihtāwin ᑲᒁᑕᑭᐦᑖᐏᐣ
NI suffering and misery

kakwātakimēw ᑲᒁᑕᑭᒣᐤ
VTA s/he speaks meanly to s.o., s/he nags s.o.

kakwātakiýēhēw ᑲᒁᑕᑭᔦᐦᐁᐤ
VAI s/he breathes with difficulty

kakwātakīw ᑲᒁᑕᑮᐤ
VAI s/he has difficulties, s/he has a handicap

kakwāýaki- ᑲᒁᔭᑭ
IPV greatly, extremely [*cf.* kakwāhýaki-]

kakwāýakinikēw ᑲᒁᔭᑭᓂᑫᐤ
VAI s/he acts with great speed, s/he acts abruptly; it bucks violently

kakwāýakiyawēhēw ᑲᒁᔭᑭᔭᐍᐦᐁᐤ
VTA s/he makes s.o. terribly angry

kakwē- ᑲᑵ
IPV try to, attempt to [*see also* koci- *IPV*]

kakwē-cīsimēw ᑲᑵ ᒌᓯᒣᐤ
VTA s/he tries to deceive s.o.

kakwē-paskiýākēw ᑲᑵ ᐸᐢᑭᔮᑫᐤ
VAI s/he competes, s/he tries to defeat by competition

kakwē-tōtam ᑲᑵ ᑑᑕᒼ
VTI s/he tries to do s.t.

kakwēci- ᑲᑵᒋ
IPV inquire [*cf. wC*: kakwīci-]

kakwēcihkēmow ᑲᑵᒋᐦᑫᒧᐤ
VAI s/he asks, s/he asks people; s/he asks for s.t., s/he asks a question of people

kakwēcihkēmowin ᑲᑵᒋᐦᑫᒧᐏᐣ
NI question

kakwēcihtam ᑲᑵᒋᐦᑕᒼ
VTI s/he questions s.t., s/he asks s.t. a question

kakwēcimēw ᑲᑵᒋᒣᐤ
VTA s/he asks s.o., s/he asks s.o. a question; s/he makes a request of s.o.; s/he asks s.o. about (it/them)

kakwēciýawēhitowak ᑲᑵᒋᔭᐍᐦᐃᑐᐙᐠ
VAI they try to outdo one another, they try to arrive first

kakwēciýāhow ᑲᑵᒋᔮᐦᐅᐤ
VAI s/he hurries, s/he tries to hurry

kakwēciýāhtowak ᑲᑵᒋᔮᐦᑐᐙᐠ
VAI they compete with time

kakwētawēýihtam ᑲᑵᑕᐍᔨᐦᑕᒼ
VTI s/he misses s.t., s/he longs for s.t.

kakwēyācihēw ᑲᑵᔮᒋᐦᐁᐤ
VTA s/he gets s.o. ready

kakwēyācihtāw ᑲᑵᔮᒋᐦᑖᐤ
VAIt s/he gets s.t. ready

kakwēyāhow ᑲᑵᔮᐦᐅᐤ
VAI s/he hurries

kamāciwaham ᑲᒫᒋᐙᐦᐊᒼ
VTI s/he dances the thank you dance, s/he dances the joy dance [*traditional dance following a give-away*; *archaic*: "s/he dances the scalp dance"]

kamāciwisimow ᑲᒫᒋᐏᓯᒧᐤ
VAI s/he dances the thank you dance, s/he dances the joy dance [*traditional dance following a give-away*; *archaic*: "s/he dances the scalp dance"]

kamāmak ᑲᒫᒪᐠ
NA butterfly [*pl*: -wak]

kamāmakos ᑲᒫᒪᑯᐢ
NA butterfly, small butterfly; moth [*dim*]

kamāmakoskāw ᑲᒫᒪᑯᐢᑳᐤ
VII it is infested by moths or butterflies; there are many butterflies

kanak ᑲᓇᐠ
IPC for a moment, for a short while

kanakē ᑲᓇᑫ
IPC at least; even if only; for a short while [*see also* aciyaw, nōmanakēs]

kanakēkā ᑲᓇᑫᑳ
IPC more especially

kanawāpahcikēw ᑲᓇᐚᐸᐦᒋᑫᐤ
VAI s/he looks things over, s/he observes [*cf.* kanawāpahkēw]

kanawāpahkān ᑲᓇᐚᐸᐦᑳᐣ
NI spyglass

kanawāpahkānēhikēw ᑲᓇᐚᐸᐦᑳᓀᐦᐃᑫᐤ
VAI s/he uses a spyglass

kanawāpahkēw ᑲᓇᐚᐸᐦᑫᐤ
VAI s/he observes [*cf.* kanawāpahcikēw]

kanawāpahtam ᑲᓇᐚᐸᐦᑕᒼ
VTI s/he looks at s.t.

kanawāpamēw ᑲᓇᐚᐸᒣᐤ
VTA s/he looks at s.o.; s/he looks after s.o.

kanawāpamikowisiw ᑲᓇᐚᐸᒥᑯᐏᓯᐤ
VAI s/he is cared for by higher powers

kanawāpamisow ᑲᓇᐚᐸᒥᓱᐤ
VAI s/he looks at him/herself

kanawāpamisowin ᑲᓇᐚᐸᒥᓱᐏᐣ
NI self-evaluation

kanawāpokēw ᑲᓇᐚᐳᑫᐤ
VAI s/he tends the house, s/he looks after a household, s/he keeps house; s/he house-sits

kanawēwitipiskwēw ᑲᓇᐍᐏᑎᐱᐢᑵᐤ
VAI s/he watches all night

kanawēýihcikāsow ᑲᓇᐍᔨᐦᒋᑳᓱᐤ
VAI s/he is kept, s/he is tended

kanawēýihcikātēw ᑲᓇᐍᔨᐦᒋᑳᑌᐤ
VII it is preserved, it is kept

kanawēýihēw ᑲᓇᐍᔨᐦᐁᐤ
VTA s/he tends s.o.; s/he keeps s.o.; s/he owns s.o.

kanawēýihtahikēw ᑲᓇᐍᔨᐦᑕᐦᐃᑫᐤ
NA one who tends things

kanawēýihtam ᑲᓇᐍᔨᐦᑕᒼ
VTI s/he keeps s.t., s/he preserves s.t., s/he looks after s.t., s/he takes care of s.t.

kanawēýihtamawēw ᑲᓇᐍᔨᐦᑕᒪᐍᐤ
VTA s/he keeps (it/him) for s.o.; s/he takes care of (it/him) for s.o.

kanawēýihtamohēw ᑲᓇᐍᔨᐦᑕᒧᐦᐁᐤ
VTA s/he asks s.o. to look after (it/him); s/he leaves (it/him) in s.o.'s care, s/he leaves (it/him) to be looked after by s.o.

kanawēýimāyatihkowēw ᑲᓇᐍᔨᒫᔭᑎᐦᑯᐍᐤ
VAI s/he tends sheep, s/he herds sheep, s/he is a shepherd

kanawēýimāwasow ᑲᓇᐍᔨᒫᐘᓱᐤ
VAI s/he babysits, s/he looks after (his/her own) children

kanawēýimēw ᑲᓇᐍᔨᒣᐤ
VTA s/he looks after s.o., s/he takes care of s.o., s/he tends s.o., s/he keeps s.o., s/he guards s.o. closely

kanawēýimiskwēwēskiw ᑲᓇᐍᔨᒥᐢᑵᐍᐢᑭᐤ
VAI he watches his own wife possessively [*hab*]

kanawēýimiskwēwēw ᑲᓇᐍᔨᒥᐢᑵᐍᐤ
VAI he guards his wife and/or daughters; he guards his female relatives; s/he guards a female's honour

kanawēýimiskwēwēwin ᑲᓇᐍᔨᒥᐢᑵᐍᐏᐣ
NI guarding women; possessive wife-watching

kanawēýimostosowēw ᑲᓇᐍᔨᒧᐢᑐᓱᐍᐤ
VAI s/he takes care of cattle, s/he herds cattle

kanawēýiskwāhtawēw ᑲᓇᐍᔨᐢᒁᐦᑕᐍᐤ
VAI s/he is a doorkeeper, s/he is a goalkeeper

kanawēýiskwāhtēmēw ᑲᓇᐍᔨᐢᒁᐦᑌᒣᐤ
VAI s/he is a doorkeeper, s/he is a goalkeeper

kanawi-tipiskēw ᑲᓇᐏ ᑎᐱᐢᑫᐤ
VAI s/he stays overnight

kanawi-tipiskwēw ᑲᓇᐏ ᑎᐱᐢᑵᐤ
VAI s/he watches all night

kanāci- ᑲᓈᒋ
IPV clean

kanāci-wāskahikan ᑲᓈᒋ ᐚᐢᑲᐦᐃᑲᐣ
NI a clean house

kanācihcikanēwāhtik ᑲᓈᒋᐦᒋᑲᓀᐚᐦᑎᐠ
NA ramrod (for a chimney) [*pl*: -wak]

kanācihcikēw ᑲᓈᒋᐦᒋᑫᐤ
VAI s/he cleans

kanācihēw ᑲᓈᒋᐦᐁᐤ
VTA s/he cleans s.o.

kanācihisow ᑲᓈᒋᐦᐃᓱᐤ
VAI s/he tidies him/herself

kanācihow ᑲᓈᒋᐦᐅᐤ
VAI s/he cleans him/herself, s/he keeps him/herself clean

kanācihtamawēw ᑲᓈᒋᐦᑕᒪᐍᐤ
VTA s/he cleans (it/him) for s.o.

kanācihtāw ᑲᓈᒋᐦᑖᐤ
VAIt s/he cleans, s/he cleans s.t.; s/he cleans s.t. out (*e.g.* intestine); s/he tidies up

kanācinākosiw ᑲᓈᒋᓈᑯᓯᐤ
VAI s/he looks clean, s/he gives a clean appearance, it looks spotless

kanācinākwan ᑲᓈᒋᓈᑿᐣ
VII it looks clean

kanātan ᑲᓈᑕᐣ
VII it is clean, is tidy

kanātapiw ᑲᓈᑕᐱᐤ
VAI s/he lives in a clean house

kanātastēw ᑲᓈᑕᐢᑌᐤ
VII it is clean

kanātāpāwahisow ᑲᓈᑖᐹᐘᐦᐃᓱᐤ
VAI s/he washes him/herself clean

kanātāpāwatāw ᑲᓈᑖᐹᐘᑖᐤ
VAIt s/he washes s.t. clean with water

kanātēýihtamowin ᑲᓈᑌᔨᐦᑕᒧᐏᐣ
NI clean thoughts

kanātēýimēw ᑲᓈᑌᔨᒣᐤ
VTA s/he has respect for s.o.

kanātisiw ᑲᓈᑎᓯᐤ
VAI it is clean, it is tidy [*third person objects only*; *not personal human cleanliness*]

kani ᑲᓂ
IPC oh yes, I just remembered, I had forgotten; of course, come to think, now that I remember [*introductory, indicating an interruption*; *sometimes post-modifiying*; *cf.* kanihk]

kanihk ᑲᓂᕽ
IPC oh yes, I just remembered, I had forgotten; of course [*cf.* kani]

kanika ᑲᓂᑲ
IPC actually

kanikā ᑲᓂᑳ
IPC desiredly

kanōhkawēw ᑲᓅᐦᑲᐍᐤ
VTA s/he pursues s.o. stubbornly, s/he dogs s.o.

kapatēham ᑲᐸᑌᐦᐊᒼ
VTI s/he dishes s.t. out, s/he scoops s.t. out

kapatēhoyēw ᑲᐸᑌᐦᐅᔦᐤ
VTA s/he brings s.o. to shore

kapatēhtahēw ᑲᐸᑌᐦᑕᐦᐁᐤ
VTA s/he takes s.o. to shore, s/he hits s.o. to shore

kapatēhtatāw ᑲᐸᑌᐦᑕᑖᐤ
VAIt s/he takes s.t. to shore; s/he hits s.t. to shore; s/he throws s.t. to shore

kapatēhwēw ᑲᐸᑌᐦᐍᐤ
VTA s/he dishes s.o. out, s/he scoops s.o. out

kapatēnam ᑲᐸᑌᓇᒼ
VTI s/he beaches s.t. (*e.g.* a

canoe); s/he takes s.t. from the water
kapatēnāsow ᑲᐸᑌᓈᓱᐤ
VAI s/he unloads (a boat), s/he puts things ashore
kapatēnēw ᑲᐸᑌᓀᐤ
VTA s/he frees s.o. from water; s/he removes s.o. from water (by hand)
kapatēnisow ᑲᐸᑌᓂᓱᐤ
VAI s/he gets him/herself out of the water
kapatēsipaýihow ᑲᐸᑌᓯᐸᔨᐦᐅᐤ
VAI s/he gets out of a canoe quickly
kapatēsiwēpiskawēw ᑲᐸᑌᓯᐍᐱᐢᑲᐍᐤ
VTA s/he kicks s.o. onto shore
kapatēskwēw ᑲᐸᑌᐢᑵᐤ
VAI s/he takes food from a kettle with a spoon or ladle
kapatēwēpaham ᑲᐸᑌᐍᐸᐦᐊᒼ
VTI s/he beaches s.t. (*e.g.* canoe) with a batting motion, s/he knocks s.t. out of the water
kapatēwēpinam ᑲᐸᑌᐍᐱᓇᒼ
VTI s/he throws s.t. on shore
kapatēwēpinēw ᑲᐸᑌᐍᐱᓀᐤ
VTA s/he throws s.o. on shore
kapatēwēpinikēw ᑲᐸᑌᐍᐱᓂᑫᐤ
VAI s/he throws things on shore
kapatēýāhokow ᑲᐸᑌᔮᐦᐅᑯᐤ
VAI s/he drifts to shore, s/he is washed to shore by the current, s/he is blown to shore by the wind [*cf.* kapāýāhokow]
kapatēýāsiw ᑲᐸᑌᔮᓯᐤ
VAI s/he is blown to shore
kapatēýāstan ᑲᐸᑌᔮᐢᑕᐣ
VII it is blown to shore by wind; the wind is blowing shoreward
kapānam ᑲᐹᓇᒼ
VTI s/he pulls s.t. to shore
kapāpahtāw ᑲᐹᐸᐦᑖᐤ
VAI s/he runs to land
kapātowin ᑲᐹᑐᐏᐣ
NI portage; a setting ashore
kapāw ᑲᐹᐤ
VAI s/he goes ashore, s/he lands, s/he comes ashore; s/he gets out of a canoe or boat
kapāwēpinam ᑲᐹᐍᐱᓇᒼ
VTA s/he tosses s.t. ashore
kapāwēpinēw ᑲᐹᐍᐱᓀᐤ
VTA s/he tosses s.o. ashore
kapāwin ᑲᐹᐏᐣ
NI dock; area for docking boats, landing area for boats
kapāwinihk ᑲᐹᐏᓂᕽ
INM Athabasca Landing [*loc*]

kapāýāhokow ᑲᐹᔮᐦᐅᑯᐤ
VAI s/he drifts to shore [*cf.* kapatēýāhokow]
kapē- ᑲᐯ
IPP all, entire, always; throughout, for the full duration of
kapē- ᑲᐯ
IPV for the full duration of; always
kapē-ayi ᑲᐯ ᐊᔨ
IPC all the time, for the entire period, throughout [*cf.* kapē-ayihk]
kapē-ayihk ᑲᐯ ᐊᔨᕽ
IPC all the time [*cf.* kapē-ayi]
kapē-kīsik ᑲᐯ ᑮᓯᐠ
IPC all day, all day long
kapē-nīpin ᑲᐯ ᓃᐱᐣ
IPC all summer, all summer long
kapē-pipon ᑲᐯ ᐱᐳᐣ
IPC all winter, all winter long
kapē-tipisk ᑲᐯ ᑎᐱᐢᐠ
IPC all night, all night long
kapēsihēw ᑲᐯᓯᐦᐁᐤ
VTA s/he makes s.o. stay overnight
kapēsimostawēw ᑲᐯᓯᒧᐢᑕᐍᐤ
VTA s/he camps overnight near s.o. [*cf.* kapēsīstawēw]
kapēsiw ᑲᐯᓯᐤ
VAI s/he camps, s/he stays overnight
kapēsiwikamik ᑲᐯᓯᐏᑲᒥᐠ
NI hotel, motel [*pl*: -wa]
kapēsiwin ᑲᐯᓯᐏᐣ
NI camp, campsite
kapēsīstawēw ᑲᐯᓰᐢᑕᐍᐤ
VTA s/he camps with s.o., s/he stays overnight with s.o. [*cf.* kapēsimostawēw]
kapēwin ᑲᐯᐏᐣ
NI campsite
kapiskam ᑲᐱᐢᑲᒼ
VTI s/he misses s.t. by coming late
kaskacipaýiw ᑲᐢᑲᒋᐸᔨᐤ
VII it breaks off (*e.g.* a tree limb)
kaskaciwēpaham ᑲᐢᑲᒋᐍᐸᐦᐊᒼ
VTI s/he breaks s.t. with a tool
kaskahpitam ᑲᐢᑲᐦᐱᑕᒼ
VTI s/he ties s.t. so it does not loosen
kaskahpitēw ᑲᐢᑲᐦᐱᑌᐤ
VTA s/he ties s.o. in a bundle (with a blanket)
kaskam ᑲᐢᑲᒼ
VTI s/he crosses (water) by a shorter way
kaskamācāyāw ᑲᐢᑲᒫᒑᔮᐤ
VII it is closed in; it is in need of air; it is stifling, it is heat enclosed

kaskamocāw ᑲᐢᑲᒧᒑᐤ
VII it is hot and stuffy
kaskamocēkasikan ᑲᐢᑲᒧᒉᑲᓯᑲᐣ
NI pressure cooker
kaskamohtihkasikan ᑲᐢᑲᒧᐦᑎᐦᑲᓯᑲᐣ
NI old fashioned plum pudding (steamed in a can)
kaskamohtihkasikēw ᑲᐢᑲᒧᐦᑎᐦᑲᓯᑫᐤ
VAI s/he makes pudding, s/he steams pudding in a can
kaskamohtihkasikēwin ᑲᐢᑲᒧᐦᑎᐦᑲᓯᑫᐏᐣ
NI pudding; the process of making pudding
kaskaskisiw ᑲᐢᑲᐢᑭᓯᐤ
NI ember
kaskaskisīhkan ᑲᐢᑲᐢᑭᓰᐦᑲᐣ
NI coal
kaskatahwēw ᑲᐢᑲᑕᐦᐍᐤ
VTA s/he breaks s.o.'s bone (*e.g.* by shot)
kaskatin ᑲᐢᑲᑎᐣ
VII it freezes, it freezes up [*see also* āhkwatin]
kaskatinowi-pīsim ᑲᐢᑲᑎᓄᐏ ᐲᓯᒼ
NA Freezing Moon; October [*see also* pimihamowi-pīsim; *also* kaskatino-pīsim]
kaskatisimēw ᑲᐢᑲᑎᓯᒣᐤ
VTA s/he throws s.o. so as to break his bone
kaskatisin ᑲᐢᑲᑎᓯᐣ
VAI s/he has a fracture (from falling), s/he breaks a bone (by falling)
kaskatiskawēw ᑲᐢᑲᑎᐢᑲᐍᐤ
VTA s/he kicks s.o. so as to break a bone
kaskatwānam ᑲᐢᑲᑵᓇᒼ
VTI s/he breaks s.t. off by hand
kaskatwāpitam ᑲᐢᑲᑵᐱᑕᒼ
VTI s/he yanks s.t. to break it
kaskatwātihkwanēnam ᑲᐢᑲᑵᑎᐦᑿᓀᓇᒼ
VTI s/he breaks off a branch of s.t.
kaskatwātihkwanēnēw ᑲᐢᑲᑵᑎᐦᑿᓀᓀᐤ
VTA s/he breaks off a branch of s.o.
kaskawahkamin ᑲᐢᑲᐘᐦᑲᒥᐣ
VII it is foggy [*see also* ýīkowan]
kaskawan ᑲᐢᑲᐘᐣ
VII it is foggy [*see also* ýīkowan]
kaskawanipēscāsin ᑲᐢᑲᐘᓂᐯᐢᒑᓯᐣ
VII it is drizzling [*dim*]
kaskawanipēstāw ᑲᐢᑲᐘᓂᐯᐢᑖᐤ
VII it is misty, there is a light drizzle, there is a light rain

kaskāciwahtēw ᐦᐦᒋᐊᐧᐦᑌᐤ
VAI it is boiled until tender

kaskāciwasam ᐦᐦᒋᐊᐧᓴᐧᒼ
VTI s/he boils s.t. until tender

kaskāpahtēw ᐦᐦᐸᐦᑌᐤ
NI smoke [*cf.* kaskāpahtēw *VII*]

kaskāpahtēw ᐦᐦᐸᐦᑌᐤ
VII it is smoky; it appears smokey; it is smoking, it emits smoke (*e.g.* a chimney); it is smoked

kaskāpasam ᐦᐦᐸᓴᐧᒼ
VTI s/he smokes s.t.; s/he treats s.t. (*e.g.* hide) with smoke

kaskāpasow ᐦᐦᐸᓱᐤ
VAI it is smoked; it gets smoked out

kaskāpaswēw ᐦᐦᐸᓱᐧᐤ
VTA s/he smokes s.o. (*e.g.* deerhide, salmon); s/he treats s.o. with smoke

kaskāpiskaham ᐦᐦᐱᐢᑲᐦᐊᐧᒼ
VTI s/he preserves s.t., s/he cans s.t.; s/he closes s.t. with metal.

kaskāpiskahikan ᐦᐦᐱᐢᑲᐦᐃᑲᐣ
NI canned goods; key; lock; chain for shackles [*see also* āpāpiskahikan, kipāpiskahikan]

kaskāpiskahikātēw ᐦᐦᐱᐢᑲᐦᐃᑳᑌᐤ
VII it is preserved, canned

kaskāpiskahwēw ᐦᐦᐱᐢᑲᐦᐧᐤ
VTA s/he preserves s.o., s/he cans s.o.; s/he closes s.o. with metal

kaskāpiskisikan ᐦᐦᐱᐢᑭᓯᑲᐣ
NI canned food; tin of canned food

kaskāwikanēhwēw ᐦᐦᐃᑲᓀᐦᐧᐤ
VTA s/he breaks s.o.'s back (*e.g.* by shot)

kaskāwikanēnēw ᐦᐦᐃᑲᓀᓀᐤ
VTA s/he breaks s.o.'s back by hand

kaskāwikanēsin ᐦᐦᐃᑲᓀᓯᐣ
VAI s/he has a broken back (from falling), s/he breaks his/her back falling

kaskēw ᐦᐊᐤ
VAI s/he goes overland

kaskēwēhtahēw ᐦᐊᐧᐤᐦᑕᐦᐧᐤ
VTA s/he crosses a portage carrying s.o. on his/her own back

kaskēwēhtatāw ᐦᐊᐧᐤᐦᑕᑖᐤ
VAIt s/he crosses a portage carrying s.t. on his/her own back

kaskēwēpahtāw ᐦᐊᐧᐤᐸᐦᑖᐤ
VAI s/he runs while crossing the portage

kaskēwētowatēw ᐦᐊᐧᐤᑐᐊᐧᑌᐤ
VAI s/he crosses a portage with goods on his/her own back

kaskēwēw ᐦᐊᐧᐤ
VAI s/he crosses over a portage, s/he goes across land

kaskēyihtam ᐦᐊᔨᐦᑕᒼ
VTI s/he is sad (over s.t.), s/he is lonesome, s/he has a longing, s/he is sad and impatient

kaskēyihtamihēw ᐦᐊᔨᐦᑕᒥᐦᐧᐤ
VTA s/he makes s.o. sad

kaskēyihtamihtāsow ᐦᐊᔨᐦᑕᒥᐦᑖᓱᐤ
VAI s/he makes things sad for everyone

kaskēyihtamowin ᐦᐊᔨᐦᑕᒧᐃᐧᐣ
NI loneliness

kaskēyihtamowinākosiw ᐦᐊᔨᐦᑕᒧᐃᐧᓈᑯᓯᐤ
VAI s/he looks sad and lonely

kaskēyihtamowinākwan ᐦᐊᔨᐦᑕᒧᐃᐧᓈᑲᐧᐣ
VII it looks sad and dismal, it looks depressing

kaskēyihtākosiw ᐦᐊᔨᐦᑖᑯᓯᐤ
VAI s/he is dreary, s/he is dismal, s/he is lonely

kaskēyihtākwan ᐦᐊᔨᐦᑖᑲᐧᐣ
VII it is sad, it is dreary, it is dismal

kaskēyimēw ᐦᐊᔨᒣᐤ
VTA s/he misses s.o., s/he yearns for s.o.

kaski- ᐦᐊ
IPV dense

kaski-tipiskāw ᐦᐊ ᑎᐱᐢᑳᐤ
VII it is pitch-black night

kaskicēwasināsosiw ᐦᐊᒋᐊᐧᓯᓈᓱᓯᐤ
VAI s/he has little black markings [*dim*]

kaskicēwāyowēs ᐦᐊᒋᐊᐧᔪᐧᐢ
NA black tail weasel

kaskicihcēyiw ᐦᐊᒋᐦᒉᔨᐤ
VAI s/he clenches his/her own fist

kaskihēw ᐦᐊᐧᐤ
VTA s/he is able to deal with s.o.; s/he manages, s/he controls s.o., s/he convinces s.o., s/he makes s.o. do something; s/he is able to seduce s.o.; s/he earns s.o. (*i.e.* money)

kaskihcikwanēhwēw ᐦᐃᒋᑲᐧᓀᐦᐧᐤ
VTA s/he breaks s.o.'s knee (*e.g.* by shot)

kaskihcikwanēskikāsow ᐦᐃᒋᑲᐧᓀᐢᑭᑳᓱᐤ
VAI s/he has knees broken

kaskihisow ᐦᐃᐦᐃᓱᐤ
VAI s/he succeeds for him/herself

kaskihkotēw ᐦᐃᐦᑯᑌᐤ
VTA s/he cuts s.o. (tobacco) fine

kaskihow ᐦᐃᐦᐅᐤ
VAI s/he has the ability to do s.t., s/he is able, s/he is competent; s/he escapes; [*slang:*] he scores (sexually)

kaskihowin ᐦᐃᐦᐅᐃᐧᐣ
NI achievement; ability; ability to seduce

kaskihtamawēw ᐦᐃᐦᑕᒪᐧᐤ
VTA s/he earns (it) for s.o.; s/he makes (it) possible for s.o.

kaskihtamākēwin ᐦᐃᐦᑕᒫᑫᐃᐧᐣ
NI ability to earn

kaskihtamāsow ᐦᐃᐦᑕᒫᓱᐤ
VAI s/he is able to do for him/herself, s/he accomplishes (it) for him/herself, s/he gets (it) for him/herself, s/he earns (it) for him/herself; s/he deserves what s/he gets (good or bad)

kaskihtāw ᐦᐃᐦᑖᐤ
VAIt s/he manages s.t., s/he controls s.t.; s/he is able to do s.t., s/he is competent at s.t.

kaskihtāwin ᐦᐃᐦᑖᐃᐧᐣ
NI ability to do s.t.; competence; power

kaskikātēsin ᐦᐃᑳᑌᓯᐣ
VAI s/he breaks his/her own leg falling

kaskikwācikan ᐦᐃᑲᐧᒋᑲᐣ
NI sewing machine; item being sewn

kaskikwācikēw ᐦᐃᑲᐧᒋᑫᐤ
VAI s/he sews things

kaskikwāsonāpisk ᐦᐃᑲᐧᓱᓈᐱᐢᐠ
NA thimble [*pl*: -wak]

kaskikwāsopaýihcikanis ᐦᐃᑲᐧᓱᐸᔨᐦᒋᑲᓂᐢ
NI sewing machine [*dim*]

kaskikwāsopaýihcikākēw ᐦᐃᑲᐧᓱᐸᔨᐦᒋᑳᑫᐤ
VAI s/he does machine-sewing with something; s/he uses something to machine-sew

kaskikwāsopaýis ᐦᐃᑲᐧᓱᐸᔨᐢ
NI sewing machine

kaskikwāsow ᐦᐃᑲᐧᓱᐤ
VAI s/he sews, s/he does his/her own sewing; s/he sews s.t.

kaskikwāsowin ᐦᐃᑲᐧᓱᐃᐧᐣ
NI doing one's sewing, the art of sewing

kaskikwāsowināpisk ᐦᐃᑲᐧᓱᐃᐧᓈᐱᐢᐠ
NA thimble [*pl*: -wak]

kaskikwāsowināpiskos ᐦᐃᑲᐧᓱᐃᐧᓈᐱᐢᑯᐢ
NA small thimble [*dim*]

kaskikwāswākan ᑲᐢᑭᑳᐧᓵᐧᑲᐣ
NI sewing machine

kaskikwāswākēw ᑲᐢᑭᑳᐧᓵᐧᑫᐤ
VAI s/he sews with something, s/he uses something in sewing

kaskikwāswēw ᑲᐢᑭᑳᐧᓭᐧᐤ
VTA s/he sews s.o. [*cf.* kaskikwāsow, kaskikwātēw]

kaskikwātam ᑲᐢᑭᑳᐧᑕᒼ
VTI s/he sews s.t.

kaskikwātamawēw ᑲᐢᑭᑳᐧᑕᒪᐁᐧᐤ
VTA s/he sews (it/him) for s.o.

kaskikwātamāsow ᑲᐢᑭᑳᐧᑕᒫᓱᐤ
VAI s/he sews (it/him) for him/herself

kaskikwātēw ᑲᐢᑭᑳᐧᑌᐤ
VII it is sewn

kaskikwātēw ᑲᐢᑭᑳᐧᑌᐤ
VTA s/he sews s.o. (*e.g.* pants); s/he sews for s.o. [*cf.* kaskikwāswēw]

kaskikwātisow ᑲᐢᑭᑳᐧᑎᓱᐤ
VAI s/he sews for him/herself

kaskikwēnam ᑲᐢᑭᑫᐧᓇᒼ
VTI s/he breaks s.t.'s neck (*e.g.* bottle)

kaskikwēnēw ᑲᐢᑭᑫᐧᓀᐤ
VTA s/he breaks s.o.'s neck by hand, s/he rings s.o.'s neck

kaskikwēnisow ᑲᐢᑭᑫᐧᓂᓱᐤ
VAI s/he breaks his/her own neck, it breaks it's own neck

kaskikwēpitēw ᑲᐢᑭᑫᐧᐱᑌᐤ
VTA s/he breaks s.o's neck by a pull

kaskikwēsin ᑲᐢᑭᑫᐧᓯᐣ
VAI s/he breaks his/her own neck falling (in an accident)

kaskimēw ᑲᐢᑭᒣᐤ
VTA s/he persuades s.o.

kaskipitaham ᑲᐢᑭᐱᑕᐦᐊᒼ
VTI s/he ties s.t. shut

kaskipitākan ᑲᐢᑭᐱᑖᑲᐣ
NA tobacco pouch

kaskipitēw ᑲᐢᑭᐱᑌᐤ
NI thing tied shut [*cf.* kaskipitēw *VII*]

kaskipitēw ᑲᐢᑭᐱᑌᐤ
VII it is tied shut [*cf.* kaskipitēw *NI*]

kaskitahtahkwanēhwēw ᑲᐢᑭᑕᐦᑕᐦᑲᐧᓀᐦᐁᐧᐤ
VTA s/he breaks s.o.'s wing (*e.g.* by shot)

kaskitāpiskanēsin ᑲᐢᑭᑖᐱᐢᑲᓀᓯᐣ
VAI s/he has a broken jaw (from falling)

kaskitēhkwēw ᑲᐢᑭᑌᐦᑫᐧᐤ
VAI s/he blackens his/her own face

kaskitēmin ᑲᐢᑭᑌᒥᐣ
NA prune; black bead

kaskitēmin ᑲᐢᑭᑌᒥᐣ
NI blackberry

kaskitēmināhtik ᑲᐢᑭᑌᒥᓈᐦᑎᐠ
NA blackberry bush [*pl*: -wak]

kaskitēnam ᑲᐢᑭᑌᓇᒼ
VTI s/he blackens s.t. by hand

kaskitēsip ᑲᐢᑭᑌᓯᑊ
NA black duck

kaskitēsitēw ᑲᐢᑭᑌᓯᑌᐤ
VAI it has black feet (*e.g.* an animal)

kaskitēsiw ᑲᐢᑭᑌᓯᐤ
VAI s/he is black

kaskitētahtahkwanēw ᑲᐢᑭᑌᑕᐦᑕᐦᑲᐧᓀᐤ
VAI it has black wings

kaskitēw ᑲᐢᑭᑌᐤ
NI gunpowder; piece of coal, cinder

kaskitēw-maskwa-maskosis ᑲᐢᑭᑌᐤ ᒪᐢᑲᐧ ᒪᐢᑯᓯᐢ
NA Little Black Bear [*Cree chief*]

kaskitēw-osāwāw ᑲᐢᑭᑌᐤ ᐅᓵᐋᐧᐤ
VII it is brown

kaskitēw-osāwisiw ᑲᐢᑭᑌᐤ ᐅᓵᐃᐧᓯᐤ
VAI s/he is brown

kaskitēwacāp ᑲᐢᑭᑌᐊᐧᒑᑊ
NA person with dark eyes; person with a black eye

kaskitēwacāpiw ᑲᐢᑭᑌᐊᐧᒑᐱᐤ
VAI s/he has dark eyes; s/he has a black eye

kaskitēwahkēsiw ᑲᐢᑭᑌᐊᐧᐦᑫᓯᐤ
NA black fox

kaskitēwahow ᑲᐢᑭᑌᐊᐧᐦᐅᐤ
VAI s/he dresses in black [*cf.* kaskitēwihow, kaskitēwisīhow]

kaskitēwahwēw ᑲᐢᑭᑌᐊᐧᐦᐁᐧᐤ
VTA s/he blackens s.o.

kaskitēwasākay ᑲᐢᑭᑌᐊᐧᓵᑲᐩ
NI black coat

kaskitēwaskisin ᑲᐢᑭᑌᐊᐧᐢᑭᓯᐣ
NI black shoe

kaskitēwastim ᑲᐢᑭᑌᐊᐧᐢᑎᒼ
NA black horse [*pl*: -wak]

kaskitēwatim ᑲᐢᑭᑌᐊᐧᑎᒼ
NA dark horse, black horse, black dog [*pl*: -wak]

kaskitēwatisikan ᑲᐢᑭᑌᐊᐧᑎᓯᑲᐣ
NI black dye

kaskitēwatiswēw ᑲᐢᑭᑌᐊᐧᑎᓭᐧᐤ
VTA s/he dyes s.o. (*e.g.* stocking) black

kaskitēwaýasit ᑲᐢᑭᑌᐊᐧᔭᓯᐟ
NA Blackfoot Indian

kaskitēwayān ᑲᐢᑭᑌᐊᐧᔮᐣ
NI black pelt, black clothing

kaskitēwākamiw ᑲᐢᑭᑌᐋᐧᑲᒥᐤ
VII it is black liquid [*also* kaskitēwākamin]

kaskitēwāniskwēw ᑲᐢᑭᑌᐋᐧᓂᐢᑫᐧᐤ
VAI s/he has black hair

kaskitēwāpahtēw ᑲᐢᑭᑌᐋᐧᐸᐦᑌᐤ
VII it gives off black smoke

kaskitēwāpēkan ᑲᐢᑭᑌᐋᐧᐯᑲᐣ
VII it is a dark, long object

kaskitēwāpēkisiw ᑲᐢᑭᑌᐋᐧᐯᑭᓯᐤ
VAI s/he is a dark, slim person; it is a dark, long object (*e.g.* animal pelt)

kaskitēwāpisk ᑲᐢᑭᑌᐋᐧᐱᐢᐠ
NI black metal [*pl*: -wa]

kaskitēwāskisow ᑲᐢᑭᑌᐋᐧᐢᑭᓱᐤ
VAI it is burnt black

kaskitēwāskitēw ᑲᐢᑭᑌᐋᐧᐢᑭᑌᐤ
NI burnt black area (in woods)

kaskitēwāskitēw ᑲᐢᑭᑌᐋᐧᐢᑭᑌᐤ
VII it is burnt black

kaskitēwāw ᑲᐢᑭᑌᐋᐧᐤ
VII it is black

kaskitēwāýowēw ᑲᐢᑭᑌᐋᐧᔪᐁᐧᐤ
VAI s/he has a dark tail

kaskitēwēkin ᑲᐢᑭᑌᐁᐧᑭᐣ
NI black cloth, black material

kaskitēwi- ᑲᐢᑭᑌᐃᐧ
IPV black

kaskitēwihēw ᑲᐢᑭᑌᐃᐧᐦᐁᐤ
VTA s/he blackens s.o. (by paint or dress)

kaskitēwihkwēw ᑲᐢᑭᑌᐃᐧᐦᑫᐧᐤ
VAI s/he has a black face

kaskitēwihow ᑲᐢᑭᑌᐃᐧᐦᐅᐤ
VAI s/he dresses in black [*cf.* kaskitēwahow, kaskitēwisīhow]

kaskitēwihtāw ᑲᐢᑭᑌᐃᐧᐦᑖᐤ
VAIt s/he blackens s.t.

kaskitēwikanakāpiw ᑲᐢᑭᑌᐃᐧᑲᓇᑳᐱᐤ
VAI s/he blackens his/her own face round the eyes

kaskitēwikātēw ᑲᐢᑭᑌᐃᐧᑳᑌᐤ
VAI s/he is black at the leg, s/he has black legs

kaskitēwinākosiw ᑲᐢᑭᑌᐃᐧᓈᑯᓯᐤ
VAI s/he looks black, s/he appears black

kaskitēwinākwan ᑲᐢᑭᑌᐃᐧᓈᑲᐧᐣ
VII it looks black, it appears black

kaskitēwinikan ᑲᐢᑭᑌᐃᐧᓂᑲᐣ
NI blackening agent, something to blacken with

kaskitēwisīhow ᑲᐢᑭᑌᐃᐧᓰᐦᐅᐤ
VAI s/he dresses in black [*cf.* kaskitēwahow, kaskitēwihow]

kaskitēwistikwān ᑲᐢᑭᑌᐃᐧᐢᑎᑳᐧᐣ
NA brunette, one with dark hair

kaskitēwistikwānēw ᑲᐢᑭᑌᐃᐧᐢᑎᑳᐧᓀᐤ
VAI s/he has dark hair

kaskitēwiyās ᑲᐢᑭᑌᐃᐧᔮᐢ
NA negro, Black man, African

kaskitihtimanēsin ᑲᐢᑭᑎᐦᑎᒪᓀᓯᐣ
VAI s/he has a broken shoulder (from falling)

kaskitokanēsin ᑲᐢᑭᑐᑲᓀᓯᐣ
VAI s/he has a broken hip (from falling)

kaskitokanēskawēw ᑲᐢᑭᑐᑲᓀᐢᑲᐍᐤ
VTA s/he breaks s.o.'s hip by foot or body

kaskīhkocikan ᑲᐢᑮᐦᑯᒋᑲᐣ
NI cut tobacco

kaspāhcikēw ᑲᐢᐹᐦᒋᑫᐤ
VAI s/he chews with a crunchy noise, s/he makes a crunchy noise while chewing

katawa ᑲᑕᐘ
IPC properly

katawasisin ᑲᑕᐘᓯᓯᐣ
VII it is beautiful

katawasisiw ᑲᑕᐘᓯᓯᐤ
VAI s/he is beautiful, s/he is good-looking

katawasisiwin ᑲᑕᐘᓯᓯᐏᐣ
NI beauty

katawasisīhēw ᑲᑕᐘᓯᓰᐦᐁᐤ
VTA s/he makes s.o. beautiful, s/he beautifies s.o.

katawasisīhtāw ᑲᑕᐘᓯᓰᐦᑖᐤ
VAIt s/he beautifies s.t.

katawēýihtam ᑲᑕᐍᔨᐦᑕᒼ
VTI s/he thinks s.t. pretty

katawēýimēw ᑲᑕᐍᔨᒣᐤ
VTA s/he thinks s.o. pretty

katāc ᑲᑖᐨ
IPC insistently; [*in negative clauses*:] necessarily, just in this way [*cf.* kākatāc]

katikoniw ᑲᑎᑯᓂᐤ
VAI s/he stays out overnight, s/he sleeps over, s/he spends the night

katisk ᑲᑎᐢᐠ
IPC just now, a moment ago; exactly, completely; [*in negative clauses*:] not merely [*wC*: katiskāw; *cf.* kētisk]

katōhpinēw ᑲᑑᐦᐱᓀᐤ
VAI s/he has tuberculosis, s/he has TB

kawacihkwamiw ᑲᐘᒋᐦᑿᒥᐤ
VAI s/he is cold while sleeping

kawacipaýiw ᑲᐘᒋᐸᔨᐤ
VAI s/he gets chilled, s/he gets cold

kawaciw ᑲᐘᒋᐤ
VAI s/he is cold, s/he experiences cold, s/he suffers from cold

kawaciwin ᑲᐘᒋᐏᐣ
NI coldness; of or pertaining to being cold

kawaciyawēpaýiw ᑲᐘᒋᔭᐍᐸᔨᐤ
VAI s/he has the chills

kawaham ᑲᐘᐦᐊᒼ
VTI s/he chops s.t. down, s/he fells s.t.

kawahikēw ᑲᐘᐦᐃᑫᐤ
VAI s/he chops down trees

kawahtam ᑲᐘᐦᑕᒼ
VTI s/he bites s.t. until it falls, s/he eats s.t. until it falls

kawahwēw ᑲᐘᐦᐍᐤ
VTA s/he fells s.o. by tool or shot

kawamēw ᑲᐘᒣᐤ
VTA it gnaws s.o. down (*e.g.* a beaver to a tree)

kawatāpāwēw ᑲᐘᑖᐹᐍᐤ
VAI s/he freezes immersed, s/he is wet to prostration

kawatihtāw ᑲᐘᑎᐦᑖᐤ
VAIt s/he gets (it/him) chilled, s/he gets s.t. cold

kawatimēw ᑲᐘᑎᒣᐤ
VTA s/he makes s.o. cold, s/he gets s.o. cold, s/he exposes s.o. to cold; s/he freezes s.o. to prostration

kawatimisow ᑲᐘᑎᒥᓱᐤ
VAI s/he gets him/herself cold

kawatin ᑲᐘᑎᐣ
VII it is cold

kawāhkatastimwēw ᑲᐚᐦᑲᑕᐢᑎᒷᐤ
VAI s/he has lean horses

kawāhkatēw ᑲᐚᐦᑲᑌᐤ
VAI s/he is starving; s/he is so hungry as to keel over from hunger

kawāhkatos ᑲᐚᐦᑲᑐᐢ
NA "Poor Man"; Kawacatoose or Poor Man's Reserve, SK [*personal and place name*; *cf.* kawāhkatosow]

kawāhkatosow ᑲᐚᐦᑲᑐᓱᐤ
VAI s/he is skinny; s/he is weak from hunger

kawāhotēw ᑲᐚᐦᐅᑌᐤ
VII it tips over in drifting

kawāhtik ᑲᐚᐦᑎᐠ
NA fallen tree [*pl*: -wak]

kawāhtikwēw ᑲᐚᐦᑎᑵᐤ
VAI s/he fells trees

kawākonēw ᑲᐚᑯᓀᐤ
VAI s/he falls down in deep snow; s/he falls down from the snow being too deep

kawāsiw ᑲᐚᓯᐤ
VAI it is blown down

kawihkwasiw ᑲᐏᐦᑿᓯᐤ
VAI s/he dozes, s/he dozes off; s/he is weak, s/he falls from sleepiness; s/he falls over while sleeping

kawihkwēýiw ᑲᐏᐦᑵᔨᐤ
VAI s/he frowns

kawihtakāw ᑲᐏᐦᑕᑳᐤ
VII there is a mass of fallen trees [*sg only*]

kawikaham ᑲᐏᑲᐦᐊᒼ
VTI s/he chops s.t. down, s/he cuts s.t. down

kawikahikan ᑲᐏᑲᐦᐃᑲᐣ
NI felled tree; tool for felling trees

kawikahwēw ᑲᐏᑲᐦᐍᐤ
VTA s/he chops s.o. down

kawikīhkāw ᑲᐏᑮᐦᑳᐤ
VAI s/he lies down with age, s/he is bent with age

kawikīhkāw ᑲᐏᑮᐦᑳᐤ
VAI s/he is very old, s/he is elderly; s/he is bent with age; s/he lies down with age; s/he is so old as to keel over with age, s/he is feeble with great age

kawikīhkāwin ᑲᐏᑮᐦᑳᐏᐣ
NI old age, lifetime

kawinam ᑲᐏᓇᒼ
VTI s/he breaks s.t. down, s/he demolishes s.t., s/he puts s.t. down

kawinamawēw ᑲᐏᓇᒪᐍᐤ
VTA s/he moves (it/him) down for s.o., s/he moves (it/him) down onto s.o.

kawinēw ᑲᐏᓀᐤ
VTA s/he wrestles s.o. down, s/he prostrates s.o. by hand; s/he breaks s.o. down

kawipaýihow ᑲᐏᐸᔨᐦᐅᐤ
VAI s/he throws him/herself down

kawipaýiw ᑲᐏᐸᔨᐤ
VAI s/he falls over, s/he falls over suddenly

kawipaýiw ᑲᐏᐸᔨᐤ
VII it falls over suddenly

kawipēw ᑲᐏᐯᐤ
VAI s/he falls from drunkenness

kawipitam ᑲᐏᐱᑕᒼ
VTI s/he pulls s.t. down

kawipitēw ᑲᐏᐱᑌᐤ
VTA s/he pulls s.o. down

kawipitisow ᑲᐏᐱᑎᓱᐤ
VAI s/he pulls him/herself down

kawisimonahēw ᑲᐏᓯᒧᓇᐦᐁᐤ
VTA s/he puts s.o. to bed, s/he places s.o. as if that one had lain down

kawisimonihkawēw ᑲᐏᓯᒧᓂᐦᑲᐍᐤ
VTA s/he prepares a bed for s.o.

kawisimonihkēw ᑲᐏᓯᒧᓂᐦᑫᐤ
VAI s/he gets ready for bed

kawisimopaýihow ᑲᐏᓯᒧᐸᔨᐦᐅᐤ
VAI s/he throws him/herself into bed

kawisimototawēw ᑲᐏᓯᒧᑐᑕᐍᐤ
VTA s/he lies down with s.o.; s/he goes to bed with s.o.

kawisimow ᑲᐏᓯᒧᐤ
VAI s/he goes to bed, s/he lies down; s/he gets ready for bed

kawiskam ᑲᐏᐢᑲᒼ
VTI s/he tramps s.t. down, s/he leans on s.t. so that it falls

kawiskawēw ᑲᐃᐧᐢᑲᐁᐧᐤ
VTA s/he knocks s.o. down by kick

kawiskosow ᑲᐃᐧᐢᑯᓱᐤ
VAI s/he falls under a burden

kawiwēpaham ᑲᐃᐧᐁᐧᐸᐦᐊᒼ
VTI s/he knocks s.t. down by tool

kawiwēpahwēw ᑲᐃᐧᐁᐧᐸᐦᐁᐧᐤ
VTA s/he knocks s.o. down by tool

kawiwēpinam ᑲᐃᐧᐁᐧᐱᓇᒼ
VTI s/he throws s.t. down, s/he pushes s.t. down

kawiwēpinēw ᑲᐃᐧᐁᐧᐱᓀᐤ
VTA s/he throws s.o. down, s/he pushes s.o. down

kawiwēpinitowak ᑲᐃᐧᐁᐧᐱᓂᑐᐊᐧᐠ
VAI they throw one another down

kawiwēpiskam ᑲᐃᐧᐁᐧᐱᐢᑲᒼ
VTI s/he knocks s.t. down by foot

kawiwēpiskawēw ᑲᐃᐧ ᐁᐧᐱᐢᑲᐁᐧᐤ
VTA s/he knocks s.o. down by foot

kayāhtē ᑲᔮᐦᑌ
IPC before, formerly; the same as it was previously; already

kayām ᑲᔮᒼ
IPC quietly, tranquilly; all right, nevermind [*cf.* kiyām]

kayās ᑲᔮᐢ
IPC long ago, of old, in earlier days; previously

kayās ēkwa ᑲᔮᐢ ᐁᑲᐧ
IPC it is a long time now

kayās māskōc ᑲᔮᐢ ᒫᐢᑰᐨ
IPC it must have been a long time ago

kayās ohci ᑲᔮᐢ ᐅᐦᒋ
IPC from a long ways back

kayās-akohp ᑲᔮᐢ ᐊᑯᐦᑊ
NI old blanket

kayās-asām ᑲᔮᐢ ᐊᓵᒼ
NA old snowshoe

kayās-astis ᑲᔮᐢ ᐊᐢᑎᐢ
NA old glove, old mitt

kayās-astotin ᑲᔮᐢ ᐊᐢᑐᑎᐣ
NI old hat

kayās-ācimowin ᑲᔮᐢ ᐋᒋᒧᐃᐧᐣ
NI old-time story

kayās-āyāna ᑲᔮᐢ ᐋᔮᓇ
NI old clothing [*pl*]

kayās-āyi ᑲᔮᐢ ᐋᔨ
NI old thing [*pl*: -āya]

kayās-āyiwan ᑲᔮᐢ ᐋᔨᐊᐧᐣ
VII it is old

kayās-āyiwin ᑲᔮᐢ ᐋᔨᐃᐧᐣ
NI old, an old thing [*also* kayāsi-ayawin]

kayās-āyiwiw ᑲᔮᐢ ᐋᔨᐃᐧᐤ
VAI s/he is old

kayās-isīhcikēwin ᑲᔮᐢ ᐃᓰᐦᒋᑫᐃᐧᐣ
NI the old way of doing things, traditional culture

kayāsasākay ᑲᔮᓴᓵᑲᐩ
NI old jacket, old coat

kayāsaskisin ᑲᔮᓴᐢᑭᓯᐣ
NI old shoe

kayāsēs ᑲᔮᓭᐢ
IPC a while ago, quite long ago, formerly [*also* kayāsīs]

kayāsi- ᑲᔮᓯ
IPN old; long ago, old-time [*cf.* kayāsi- *IPV*]

kayāsi- ᑲᔮᓯ
IPV old [*cf.* kayāsi- *IPN*]

kayāsi-mēskanaw ᑲᔮᓯ ᒣᐢᑲᓇᐤ
NI old road, old trail

kayāsi-wāskahikan ᑲᔮᓯ ᐋᐧᐢᑲᐦᐃᑲᐣ
NI old-house

kayāsinākosiw ᑲᔮᓯᓈᑯᓯᐤ
VAI s/he looks old, it appears old or worn

kayāsinākwan ᑲᔮᓯᓈᑲᐧᐣ
VII it looks old, it appears old or worn

kayāsipakwa ᑲᔮᓯᐸᑲᐧ
NI withered leaves [*pl*]

kayēyisiw ᑲᔦᔨᓯᐤ
VAI s/he cheats, s/he is sly [*also* kayēsiw]

kayēyisiwin ᑲᔦᔨᓯᐃᐧᐣ
NI cheating, cunning [*also* kayēsiwin]

kayēyisīhēw ᑲᔦᔨᓰᐦᐁᐤ
VTA s/he cheats s.o. [*also* kayēsīhēw]

kayēyisīhtāw ᑲᔦᔨᓰᐦᑖᐤ
VAIt s/he cheats when doing s.t. [*also* kayēsīhtāw]

kayēyisīmēw ᑲᔦᔨᓰᒣᐤ
VTA s/he cheats s.o. by his/her own talk [*also* kayēsīmēw]

ᑳ

kā ᑳ
IPC oh! yes [*exclamation; accepting information*; *cf.* ka, kah]

kā- ᑳ
IPV [*grammatical preverb; defines a changed conjunct clause; often a relative clause, i.e.* "who, which"]

kā-āyimahk ᑳ ᐋᔨᒪᕽ
INM difficult times; depression [*cf.* āyiman *VII*]

kā-kīnikamoki ᑳ ᑮᓂᑲᒧᑭ
INM prickly pear cacti [*pl*]

kā-kīsiwēw ᑳ ᑮᓯᐁᐧᐤ
INM "Loud Voice" [*Cree/Saulteaux chief*; *also*: kā-kīšiwē]

kā-kīskwēhēw ᑳ ᑮᐢᑫᐧᐦᐁᐤ
VTA s/he makes s.o. crazy by love medicine or other negative means [*rdpl*]

kā-kīspisit ᑳ ᑮᐢᐱᓯᐟ
INM bear [*cf.* kīspisiw *VAI*]

kā-kotikonamihk ᑳ ᑯᑎᑯᓇᒥᕽ
INM double-barrelled shotgun [*cf.* kotikonam]

kā-māyahkamikahk ᑳ ᒫᔮᐦᑲᒥᑲᕽ
INM The Riel Resistance of 1885 [*lit*: "when bad things happened"]

kā-mihkwaskīwahkāhk ᑳ ᒥᐦᑲᐧᐢᑮᐊᐧᐦᑳᕽ
INM Red Earth, SK [*cf.* mihkwaskīwahkāw *VII*]

kā-mihkwaskwāki ᑳ ᒥᐦᑲᐧᐢᑳᐧᑭ
INM beets [*pl*]

kā-miýosicik kinosēwak ᑳ ᒥᔪᓯᒋᐠ ᑭᓄᓭᐊᐧᐠ
INM Good Fish Lake, SK

kā-miýosisicik kinosēwak sākahikan ᑳ ᒥᔪᓯᓯᒋᐠ ᑭᓄᓭᐊᐧᐠ ᓵᑭᐦᐃᑲᐣ
INM Good Fish Lake, SK

kā-nahahcāpīw ᑳ ᓇᐦᐊᐦᒑᐲᐤ
INM "Making Ready the Bow" [*Cree chief*]

kā-nēhiýawēsicik ᑳ ᓀᐦᐃᔭᐁᐧᓯᒋᐠ
INM Cheyennes, Cheyenne Indians [*pl*; *lit*: "ones who speak a little Cree"]

kā-nihcāwāhcawēpaýīsis ᑳ ᓂᐦᒑᐋᐧᐦᒐᐁᐧᐸᔩᓯᐢ
NA squirrel [*see also* anikwacās]

kā-nikamōmakahk ᑳ ᓂᑲᒨᒪᑲᕽ
INM record player, phonograph [*cf.* nikamōmakan]

kā-nīkānīt ᑳ ᓃᑳᓃᐟ
INM Nekaneet, "Foremost Man" [*Cree chief and reserve name*]

kā-nīmihitocik ᑳ ᓃᒥᐦᐃᑐᒋᐠ
INM Northern Lights, aurora borealis [*proper name*: "they who are dancing"; *wC*: wāwāhtēwa]

kā-ohpawakāstahk
INM Flying Dust, SK [*Cree reserve name*; *lit*: "where the dust flies up"]

kā-osihkosiwayāniw ᑳ ᐅᓯᐦᑯᓯᐊᐧᔮᓂᐤ
INM Ermineskin, "Has-an-Ermineskin" [*male personal name*; *Cree chief*; *band name*; *also*: k-ōsihkosiwayāniw]

kā-otasiskīkamikowak ᑳ ᐅᑕᓯᐢᑮᑲᒥᑯᐊᐧᐠ
INM Missouri River Indians [*probably* MANDAN *and/or* HIDATSA; *cf.* otasiskīkamiko- *VAI* "have a mud dwelling"]

kā-pēyakwāskonam ᑳ ᐯᔭᑳᐧᐢᑯᓇᒼ
INM One Arrow [*Cree chief and reserve name*]

kā-piskihtahastāhk ᑳ ᐱᐢᑭᐦᑕᐦᐊᐢᑖᕽ
INM province

kā-pitikonāhk ᑳ ᐱᑎᑯᓈᕽ
INM Thunderchild Reserve, SK [*loc*; *lit*: "among *kā-pitikow*'s people"]

kā-pitikow ᑳ ᐱᑎᑯᐤ
INM Thunderchild [*personal name of Cree chief*; *lit*: "one who rolls up"]

kā-tahkāk ᑳ ᑕᐦᑳᐠ
INM ice cream [*cf.* cahkās, tahkāw]

kā-tēpwēwisīpīwiýiniwak ᑳ ᑌᐻᐏᓰᐲᐏᔨᓂᐘᐠ
NA Calling River People [*pl*; *division of the Cree*]

kā-tipēýihcikēt ᑳ ᑎᐯᔨᐦᒋᑫᐟ
INM The Lord; Creator [*Christian*; *lit*: "one who owns"]

kācikan ᑳᒋᑲᐣ
NI bead used in "hide and guess" game [*cf.* kātikan]

kācikātēw ᑳᒋᑳᑌᐤ
VII it is hidden

kāciwaswēw ᑳᒋᐘᓷᐤ
VTA s/he cooks s.o. along

kāh- ᑳᐦ
IPV would, ought to; likely to [*cf.* tāh-]

kāh-kapē- ᑳᐦ ᑲᐯ
IPV all the time

kāh-kawihkwasiw ᑳᐦ ᑲᐏᐦᑿᓯᐤ
VAI s/he dozes off (periodically) [*rdpl*]

kāh-kākīcihēw ᑳᐦ ᑳᑮᒋᐦᐁᐤ
VTA s/he consoles s.o. [*rdpl*]

kāh-kākīcihiwēw ᑳᐦ ᑳᑮᒋᐦᐃᐍᐤ
VAI s/he consoles (people) [*rdpl*]

kāh-kimiwan ᑳᐦ ᑭᒥᐘᐣ
VII it rains periodically, there are periodic rain showers [*rdpl*]

kāh-kipīhci ᑳᐦ ᑭᐲᐦᒋ
IPC stopping now and then [*rdpl*]

kāh-kinwēs ᑳᐦ ᑭᓊᐢ
IPC quite a long time, for a very long time [*rdpl*]

kāh-kitow ᑳᐦ ᑭᑐᐤ
VAI s/he hoots (*e.g.* owl); s/he calls repeatedly [*rdpl*]

kāh-kitowak ᑳᐦ ᑭᑐᐘᐠ
VAI there is thunder; they (the thunderbirds) thunder; they are calling [*rdpl*; *also* piyēsiwak kāh-kitowak]

kāh-kiýāskiw ᑳᐦ ᑭᔮᐢᑭᐤ
VAI s/he tells lies repeatedly [*rdpl*]

kāh-kīhtwām ᑳᐦ ᑮᐦᑣᒼ
IPC again and again, over and over, repeatedly [*rdpl*; *also* kā-kihtwām]

kāh-kīhtwāmipēw ᑳᐦ ᑮᐦᑣᒥᐯᐤ
VAI s/he drinks over and over [*rdpl*]

kāh-kīskwēhpinēw ᑳᐦ ᑮᐢᑵᐦᐱᓀᐤ
VAI s/he is delirious [*rdpl*]

kāh-kīskwēstikwānēw ᑳᐦ ᑮᐢᑵᐢᑎᒁᓀᐤ
VAI s/he has a migraine [*rdpl*]

kāh-kīmwēw ᑳᐦ ᑮᒵᐤ
VAI s/he whispers [*rdpl*; *cf.* kīmwēw]

kāh-kocīw ᑳᐦ ᑯᒌᐤ
VAI s/he exercises, s/he drills [*rdpl*; *also* kociw]

kāh-kwēkwask ᑳᐦ ᑵᑿᐢᐠ
IPC back and forth; criss-crossed [*rdpl*]

kāh-kwīwīstahāw ᑳᐦ ᑹᐑᐢᑕᐦᐋᐤ
INM "he flies around", Kahkewistahaw [*Cree chief and reserve name*]

kāhcitinam ᑳᐦᒋᑎᓇᒼ
VTI s/he catches s.t., s/he procures s.t.; s/he holds s.t., s/he seizes s.t.; s/he reaches s.t., s/he gets s.t. with effort by hand [*English loan*: catch]

kāhcitinēw ᑳᐦᒋᑎᓀᐤ
VTA s/he catches s.o., s/he procures s.o. (as money); s/he holds s.o., s/he seizes s.o. [*English loan*: catch]

kāhcitinikēw ᑳᐦᒋᑎᓂᑫᐤ
VAI s/he catches (things) [*cf.* kāhcitiniwēw]

kāhcitiniwēw ᑳᐦᒋᑎᓂᐍᐤ
VAI s/he catches (people, animals) [*cf.* kāhcitinikēw]

kāhkatikwanāskiy ᑳᐦᑲᑎᑿᓈᐢᑭᕀ
NA acreage, square block of land

kāhkākiw ᑳᐦᑳᑭᐤ
NA raven [*also* kahkākiw]

kāhkākiwaciýiniw ᑳᐦᑳᑭᐘᒋᔨᓂᐤ
NA Crow Indian [*also* kāhkākiwaciýin]

kāhkākīs ᑳᐦᑳᑮᐢ
NA young raven [*dim*]

kāhkākīsip ᑳᐦᑳᑮᓯᑊ
NA cormorant, crow duck

kāhkākīsipis ᑳᐦᑳᑮᓯᐱᐢ
NA young cormorant, young crow duck [*dim*]

kāhkākīsis ᑳᐦᑳᑮᓯᐢ
NA baby raven [*dim*]

kāhkākīwāhtik ᑳᐦᑳᑮᐚᐦᑎᐠ
NA juniper; raven-wood [*pl*: -wak; *also* kāhkākiwāhtik; *see also* āhāsīmināhtik]

kāhkēwak ᑳᐦᑫᐘᐠ
NI dried meat, dried venison [*pl*: -wa; *wC*: kāthkīwak]

kāhkēwakohkēw ᑳᐦᑫᐘᑯᐦᑫᐤ
VAI s/he makes dry meat [*wC*: kāthkīwakohkīw]

kāhkēwakos ᑳᐦᑫᐘᑯᐢ
NI piece of dried venison, dried meat [*dim*; *wC*: kāthkīwakos]

kāhkwāskwahikan ᑳᐦᒁᐢᑿᐦᐃᑲᐣ
NI pole which opens and closes the smoke hole on a tipi

kāhkwēskinēw ᑳᐦᑵᐢᑭᓀᐤ
VTA s/he turns s.o. around

kāhkwētipinam ᑳᐦᑵᑎᐱᓇᒼ
VTI s/he turns s.t. over repeatedly

kāhkwētipinēw ᑳᐦᑵᑎᐱᓀᐤ
VTA s/he turns s.o. over repeatedly

kāhkwētipipaýiw ᑳᐦᑵᑎᐱᐸᔨᐤ
VII it turns over repeatedly

kāhkwēýihtam ᑳᐦᑵᔨᐦᑕᒼ
VTI s/he is jealous in marriage (over s.t.); s/he is jealous of s.t.

kāhkwēýihtamowin ᑳᐦᑵᔨᐦᑕᒧᐏᐣ
NI jealousy

kāhkwēýihtaskiw ᑳᐦᑵᔨᐦᑕᐢᑭᐤ
VAI s/he is given to jealousy in marriage

kāhkwēýimēw ᑳᐦᑵᔨᒣᐤ
VTA s/he is jealous of s.o.; s/he is jealous in marriage about s.o.

kāhtinam ᑳᐦᑎᓇᒼ
VTI s/he pushes s.t.

kāhtinēw ᑳᐦᑎᓀᐤ
VTA s/he pushes s.o.

kākatāc ᑳᑲᑖᐨ
IPC insistently; [*in negative clauses*:] necessarily [*cf.* katāc]

kākā ᑳᑳ
IPC bowel waste; baby talk for anything dirty

kākēswān ᑳᑫᔂᐣ
IPC coincidentally; as it happened [*cf.* kēswān]

kākikē ᑳᑭᑫ
IPC forever, all the time, always

kākito ᑳᑭᑐ
IPC be quiet! [*imperative*; *cf.* ēkāwiya kito "don't make a sound!"]

kākīcihēw ᑳᑮᒋᐦᐁᐤ
VTA s/he consoles s.o.

kākīsimototawēw ᑳᑮᓯᒧᑐᑕᐍᐤ
VTA s/he supplicates s.o.

kākīsimow ᑳᑮᓯᒧᐤ
VAI s/he prays, s/he pleads, s/he chants [*ceremonial connotations, associated with the pipe ceremony*]

kākītisiw ᑳᑮᑎᓯᐤ
VAI s/he aches

kākosis ᑳᑯᓯᐢ
NA baby porcupine [*dim*]

kākwa ᑳᑿ
NA porcupine

kākwakos ᑳᑿᑯᐢ
NA half-grown porcupine

kākwayān ᗱᗱ·ᐤᑊ
  NI porcupine pelt
kākwayiwat ᗱᗱ·ᐱ<ᑊ·
  NI bag or birch-bark basket
  decorated with coloured
  porcupine quills
kāmwāci ᗱᒚ·ᕒ
  IPC quietly [cf. kāmwāci-
  IPV]
kāmwāci- ᗱᒚ·ᕒ
  IPV quietly [cf. kāmwāci
  IPC]
kāmwātan ᗱᒚ·ᑕᑊ
  VII it is quiet, it is quiet and
  peaceful
kāmwātapiw ᗱᒚ·ᑕᐱᐤ
  VAI s/he sits quietly, s/he
  sits dejectedly
kāmwātastēw ᗱᒚ·ᑕᔅᑌᐤ
  VII it lies quietly
kāmwātēyihtam ᗱᒚ·ᐅᔭ·ᕁᑕᒻ
  VTI s/he thinks in loneliness
kāmwātēyimow ᗱᒚ·ᐅᔭᒍ
  VAI s/he feels dejected
kāmwātisiw ᗱᒚ·ᓂᕒᐤ
  VAI s/he is quiet, s/he has a
  calm disposition
kānata ᗱᐊᑕ
  INM Canada [place name;
  also kānāta]
kāpōs ᐁᑤᐣ
  NA caboose; small mobile
  cabin on skis, pulled by a
  team of horses [English loan]
kāsak ᗱᔅᕽ
  NA tapeworm
kāsakēs ᗱᔅᑫᐣ
  NA glutton; cat
kāsakēw ᗱᔅᑫᐤ
  VAI s/he is gluttonous
kāsakēwin ᗱᔅᑫᐊᐤᑊ
  NI greediness
kāsāpiskāw ᗱᔅᐊᑊᑫᐤ
  VII there are an abundance
  of sharp rocks; it is an area
  of many sharp rocks
kāsāpiskisiw ᗱᔅᐊᑊᑭᔭᐤ
  VAI it is sharp (e.g. rock)
kāsāpitēw ᗱᔅᐊᐱᑌᐤ
  VAI s/he has sharp teeth
kāsāw ᗱᔅᐤ
  VII it is sharp
kāsikasēw ᗱᕒᑲᔭᐤ
  VAI s/he has sharp nails, it
  has sharp claws
kāsipocikan ᗱᕒᐳᕒᗱᑊ
  NI a file
kāsipotāw ᗱᕒᐳᐨᐤ
  VAIt s/he sharpens s.t. to a
  point
kāsisikin ᗱᕒᕒᑭᑊ
  VII it grows prickly
kāsisin ᗱᕒᕒᑊ
  VII it is sharp, it is pointed
  (e.g. a knife)
kāsisiw ᗱᕒᕒᐤ
  VAI it is sharply pointed; it

is sharp, it is scratchy (e.g.
wool)
kāsiskihtwān ᗱᕒᑊᑫᐤᐨᑊ
  VII it is prickly
kāsispokocin ᗱᕒᐳᑦᒋᑊ
  VAI s/he leaps beyond
kāsitēskanēw ᗱᕒᐅᑊᒐᐤ
  VAI it has pointed horns, it
  has sharp horns
kāsicihcenēw ᗱᕒᒋᕁᔭᑌᐤ
  VTA s/he washes the hands
  of s.o.; s/he washes s.o.'s
  hands
kāsicihcēw ᗱᕒᒋᕁᔭ°
  VAI s/he washes his/her own
  hands, s/he wipes his/her own
  hands
kāsicihtēw ᗱᕒᒋᕁᑌ°
  VAI s/he washes his/her own
  hands [cf. kāsicihcēw]
kāsīham ᗱᕒᐊᑊ
  VTI s/he wipes s.t. up, s/he
  washes s.t.
kāsīhamawēw ᗱᕒᐊᒪᐁᐡᐤ°
  VTA s/he wipes (it/him) for
  s.o., s/he washes (it/him) for
  s.o.
kāsihiyākanāpoy ᗱᕒᐊᔭᑲᐊᐱ°ᑊ
  NI dishwater
kāsihiyākanēw ᗱᕒᐊᔭᑲᑌ°
  VAI s/he washes dishes [cf.
  kāsiyākanēw]
kāsīhkwākan ᗱᕒᐊᑊᑲᐊᑊ
  NI towel
kāsīhkwākanis ᗱᕒᐊᑊᑲᐊᓯᑊ
  NI face-cloth, face towel
  [dim]
kāsīhkwākēw ᗱᕒᐊᑊᑲᑭᑊᐤ°
  VAI s/he washes his/her own
  face with something, s/he
  uses something to wash
  his/her own face
kāsīhkwēhon ᗱᕒᐊᑊᑫᑊᑕᑊᑊ
  NI towel
kāsīhkwēnēw ᗱᕒᐊᑊᑫᑊᑌᐤ°
  VTA s/he washes s.o.'s face,
  s/he wipes s.o.'s face
kāsīhkwēw ᗱᕒᐊᑊᑫᑊᐤ°
  VAI s/he washes his/her own
  face, s/he wipes his/her own
  face
kāsīhkwēwiyākan ᗱᕒᐊᑊᑫᑊᐊᐱᑊᑲᑊ
  NI wash-basin; sink
kāsīhtitāw ᗱᕒᐊᑊᐣᑕᑊᐤ°
  VAIt s/he wipes s.t. on
  something
kāsīhwēw ᗱᕒᐊᑊᐁᐤ°
  VTA s/he wipes s.o., s/he
  washes s.o.
kāsīnam ᗱᕒᐊᐊᑊ
  VTI s/he erases s.t., s/he
  wipes s.t.
kāsīnamawēw ᗱᕒᐊᐊᒪᐁᐤ°
  VTA s/he wipes (it/him) off
  for s.o.; [Christian:] s/he
  forgives s.o.
kāsinamāsow ᗱᕒᐊᐊᒪᒍ°
  VAI s/he wipes (it/him) off

for him/herself; [Christian:]
s/he has his/her sins forgiven,
s/he obtains forgiveness
kāsīnamātowak ᗱᕒᐊᐊᒪᐅᑐᐊᐣ
  VAI they wipe (it/him) off
  for one another; [Christian:]
  they forgive one another
kāsisimēw ᗱᕒᕒᒥᑌ°
  VTA s/he wipes s.o. on
  (it/him)
kāsīsinaham ᗱᕒᕒᓇᕁᐊᒼᐊᑊ
  VTI s/he writes over s.t.,
  s/he blots s.t. out in writing
kāsīskam ᗱᕒᐣᑲᒻ
  VTI s/he rubs s.t. out by
  foot, s/he wipes s.t. by foot
kāsīyākanēw ᗱᕒᐊᐱᑲᑌ°
  VAI s/he washes dishes, s/he
  wipes the dishes, s/he does
  the dishes
kāsīyākanēwiyākan
  ᗱᕒᐊᐱᑲᑌᐊᐱᑊᑲᑊ
  NI kitchen sink
kāsīyāpiskaham ᗱᕒᐊᐱᑊᑲᑊᐊᒻᑊᐊᑊ
  VTI s/he wipes s.t. as a
  metal
kāsīyāpahwēw ᗱᕒᐊᐱᑊᐤᐊᑊᐁᐤ°
  VTA s/he wipes s.o.'s eyes
kāsīyāpiw ᗱᕒᐊᐱᐱᑊ°
  VAI s/he wipes his/her own
  eyes
kāskaham ᗱᑊᑲᕁᐊᑊ
  VTI s/he scrapes s.t., s/he
  scrapes s.t. off
kāskahikan ᗱᑊᑲᕁᐊᕁᐁᑊ
  NI scraper
kāskahikēw ᗱᑊᑲᕁᐊᑭ°
  VAI s/he scrapes things
kāskahwēw ᗱᑊᑲᕁᐁᐤ°
  VTA s/he scrapes s.o.
kāskatāwahkinikēw
  ᗱᑊᑲᐨᐊᑊᐊᑊᑭᓂᑭ°
  VAI s/he scrapes on ground
  with his/her own hand
kāskāskaham ᗱᑊᑲᑊᑲᕁᐊᑊᑊ
  VTI s/he scrapes s.t. [rdpl]
kāskāskihkotēw ᗱᑊᑲᑊᑭᕁᑊᐣᑌᐤ
  VTA s/he scrapes s.o. (e.g.
  touchwood) off [rdpl]
kāskāskomināna ᗱᑊᑲᑊᒍᒥᓇᐊ
  NI holly berries [pl; rdpl]
kāskāskominēw ᗱᑊᑲᑊᒍᒥᑌᐤ°
  VAI s/he breaks off berries
  [rdpl]
kāskicin ᗱᑊᑭᒋᑊ
  VAI s/he has a scrape, s/he
  has an abrasion
kāskikwācikanis ᗱᑊᑭᑊᑲᒋᑲᓂᐣ
  NI rake [dim]
kāskikwācikēw ᗱᑊᑭᑊᑲᒋᑭᑭ°
  VAI s/he rakes
kāskipāson ᗱᑊᑭᑊᐸᐨᐱᑊ
  NI razor
kāskipāsow ᗱᑊᑭᑊᐸᐨᐱᒍ°
  VAI he shaves
kāskipātisow ᗱᑊᑭᑊᐸᐨᓂᒍ°
  VAI he shaves himself

kāskipitam ᕁᐢᑭᐊᑌᐨ
VTI s/he scratches s.t., s/he
pulls s.t. scraping

kāskipitēw ᕁᐢᑭᐊᐅᐤ
VTA s/he scratches s.o., s/he
pulls s.o. scraping

kāsōhikan ᕁᒎᐦᐃᑲᐣ
NI hunting blind

kāsōstam ᕁᒍᐣᐦᐨ
VTI s/he hides from s.t.

kāsōstawēw ᕁᒍᐣᐦᐨᐁᐧ ᐤ
VTA s/he hides from s.o.

kāsōstātowak ᕁᒍᐣᐦᐨᐦᐃᐧᐠ
VAI they hide from one
another

kāsōstātowin ᕁᒍᐣᐦᐨᐦᐃᐧᐣ
NI hide and seek game

kāsōw ᕁᒍᐤ
VAI s/he hides [also kāsow]

kāspahtam ᕁᐢᐸᐦᐨ ᐨ
VTI s/he crunches s.t. while
eating

kāspamēw ᕁᐢᐸᒣᐤ
VTA s/he crunches s.o. while
eating

kāspataham ᕁᐢᐸᑕᐦ ᐊᐨ
VTI s/he crunches s.t. by
pounding

kāspatahwēw ᕁᐢᐸᑕᐦ ᐦᐁᐧ ᐤ
VTA s/he gets the better of
s.o. in a deal, s/he gyps s.o.;
s/he crunches s.o. by
pounding

kāspāw ᕁᐢᐸᐤ
VII it is brittle

kāspi- ᕁᐢᐱ
IPN crunchy

kāspi- ᕁᐢᐱ
IPV crunching

kāspi-pahkwēsikan
ᕁᐢᐱ ᐸᐦ ᑫᐧ ᓯᑲᐣ
NA biscuit

kāspihkasam ᕁᐢᐱᐦ ᑲᓴᐨ
VTI s/he heats s.t. until
crisp, s/he cooks s.t. until
crisp

kāspihkasow ᕁᐢᐱᐦ ᑲᓱᐤ
VAI it is cooked until crisp

kāspisam ᕁᐢᐱᓴᐨ
VTI s/he heats s.t. until crisp

kāspisikan ᕁᐢᐱᓯᑲᐣ
NI coffee [see also
pihkātēwāpoy]

kāspisiw ᕁᐢᐱᓯᐤ
VAI s/he is brittle

kātamawēw ᕁ ᑕᒪᐁᐧ ᐤ
VTA s/he hides (it/him) from
s.o. [also kātawēw]

kātanohk ᕁ ᑕᓄᐠ
IPC secret hiding place

kātāw ᕁ ᑖᐤ
VAIt s/he hides s.t.

kātēw ᕁᑌᐤ
VII it hides, it is hidden

kātēw ᕁᑌᐤ
VTA s/he hides s.o.

kātikan ᕁ ᑎᑲᐣ
NI bead used in "hide and
guess" game [cf. kācikan]

kāwi ᕁᐊᐧ ·
IPC again; back, in return
[restoring a former state; cf.
kāwi- IPV]

kāwi- ᕁᐊᐧ ·
IPV again; back, in return
[restoring a former state; cf.
kāwi IPC]

kāwiy ᕁᐊᐧ ·ᐧ
NA porcupine-quill [pl
generally: kāwiyak]

kāwiya ᕁᐊᐧ ·ᐩ
IPC don't; no; not [in
conjunct and imperative
clauses; cf. ēkā, ēkāwiya,
ēkāy, ēkāya, kāya]

kāwiyātam ᕁᐊᐧ ·ᐩᐨ
VTI s/he puts quills on s.t.

kāya ᕁᐩ
IPC no, not; do not, don't
[in conjunct and imperative
clauses; cf. ēkā, ēkāwiýa,
ēkāy, ēkāya, kāwiýa]

kāya kīkway ᕁᐩ ᑭ ᑲᐧ ·ᐧ
IPH nothing

ᕁ

kē- ᕁ
IPV [grammatical preverb;
future, conditional: "shall";
defines a changed conjunct
clause]

kēcatayēnēw ᕁᒌ ᑕᔦ ᓀᐤ
VTA s/he takes out s.o.'s
entrails

kēcicihcēnēw ᕁᒋ ᒌᐦ ᒉ ᓀᐤ
VTA s/he takes (it/him) from
s.o.'s hand

kēcicihcēpitēw ᕁᒋᒌᐦ ᒉ ᐱᑌᐤ
VTA s/he pulls (it/him) from
s.o.'s hand

kēcikonam ᕁᒋ ᑯ ᓇᐨ
VTI s/he takes s.t. (clothing)
off [cf. kēcikoskam,
kēciskam]

kēcikonēw ᕁᒋ ᑯ ᓀᐤ
VTA s/he takes s.o.
(clothing) off; s/he removes
s.o. (e.g. from a trap) [cf.
kēcikoskawēw, kēciskawēw]

kēcikonēwēnēw ᕁᒋ ᑯ ᓀᐁᐧ ᓀᐤ
VTA s/he takes (it/him) out
of s.o.'s mouth

kēcikopayiw ᕁᒋ ᑯ ᐸᔨᐤ
VAI it comes off

kēcikopitam ᕁᒋ ᑯ ᐱᐨ
VTI s/he pulls s.t. free, s/he
pulls s.t. out

kēcikoskam ᕁᒋ ᑯᐢᑲᐨ
VTI s/he takes s.t. off (e.g.
clothing) [cf. kēcikonam,
kēciskam]

kēcikoskawēw ᕁᒋ ᑯᐢᑲᐁᐧ ᐤ
VTA s/he takes s.o. off, s/he
steps out of s.o. (e.g.
clothing) [cf. kēcikonēw,
kēciskawēw]

kēcikwaham ᕁᒋ ᒁ ·ᐧᐊᐨ
VTI s/he removes s.t. by tool

kēcikwāpitēpitēw ᕁᒋ ᒁ ·ᐧᐱᑌ ᐱᑌᐤ
VTA s/he pulls s.o.'s teeth

kēcikwāstan ᕁᒋ ᒁ ·ᐢᑕᐣ
VII it blows off

kēciskam ᕁᒋᐢᑲᐨ
VTI s/he takes s.t. off [cf.
kēcikonam, kēcikoskam]

kēciskawēw ᕁᒋᐢᑲᐁᐧ ᐤ
VTA s/he takes s.o. off [cf.
kēcikonēw, kēcikoskawēw]

kēcitāsēnēw ᕁᒋ ᑖ ᓭ ᓀᐤ
VTA s/he takes s.o.'s pants
off

kēcitāsēpitēw ᕁᒋ ᑖ ᓭ ᐱᑌᐤ
VTA s/he pulls s.o.'s pants
off

kēcitāsēw ᕁᒋ ᑖ ᓭᐤ
VAI s/he takes his/her own
pants off

kēcitāsiw ᕁᒋ ᑖ ᓯᐤ
VAI s/he is blown loose

kēcīw ᕁᒌᐤ
VAI s/he undresses

kēcīpitēw ᕁᒌ ᐱᑌᐤ
VTA s/he pulls s.o. out of
that one's clothes

kēhcē-ayiwiw ᕁᐦ ᒉ ᐊᔨᐃᐧᐤ
VAI s/he is an elder, s/he is
old [dim; cf. kēhtē-ayiwiw]

kēhcik ᕁᐦ ᒋᐠ
IPC nevertheless

kēhcinā ᕁᐦ ᒋ ᓈ
IPC of course, for sure;
certainly; perhaps, maybe [cf.
kēhcināc, kēhcinās, kēhtināc,
kēsinā]

kēhcināc ᕁᐦ ᒋ ᓈ-
IPC surely [cf. kēhcinā,
kēhcinās, kēhtināc, kēsinā]

kēhcināhow ᕁᐦ ᒋ ᓈᐦ ᐅᐤ
VAI s/he is certain, s/he is
sure; s/he makes sure

kēhcināhowin ᕁᐦ ᒋ ᓈᐦ ᐅᐃᐧᐣ
NI certainty, positiviness

kēhcinās ᕁᐦ ᒋ ᓈᐢ
IPC assuredly, definitely;
maybe, perhaps [cf. kēhcinā,
kēhcināc, kēhtināc, kēsinā]

kēhciwāk ᕁᐦ ᒋ ·ᐧᐊᐠ
IPC near, nearby; without
mediation, by immediate
contact

kēhkēhk ᕁᐦ ᑫ ᐦᐠ
NA hawk, sparrow hawk;
falcon [pl: -wak]

kēhkēhkowiw ᕁᐦ ᑫ ᐦ ᑯ ·ᐃᐧᐤ
VAI s/he is a hawk

kēhtē- ᕁᐦ ᑌ
IPN old, respected by age
[see also kayāsi-]

kēhtē-amisk ᕁᐦ ᑌ ᐊ ᒥᐢᐠ
NA old beaver [pl: -wak]

kēhtē-aya ᕁᐦ ᑌ ᐊᐩ
NA elder, old-one, old
person; [pl:] elders, the old

kēhtē-ayiwiw ᕁᐦ ᑌ ᐊᔨᐃᐧᐤ
VAI s/he is an elder, s/he is
old, s/he is an old person;
s/he is in his/her old age
[also kēhtēyiwiw, cf.
kēhtēwiw]

kēhtē-iskwēw ᘱᐦᐅ ᐃᔅᕀᐤ
NA old woman [*cf.*
kēhtēskwēw]

kēhtē-wēmistikōsiw
ᘱᐦᐅ ᗠᒡ^ᐣᑰᓯ°
NA an old Frenchman;
[*archaic*:] the king of France

kēhtēnākosiw ᘱᐦᐅ᐀ᐋᑯᓯ°
VAI s/he looks old

kēhtēnākwan ᘱᐦᐅᐋᑯᐸᐣ
VII it looks old

kēhtēskwēw ᘱᐦᐅ^ᕀᐤ
NA old woman [*cf.*
kēhtē-iskwēw]

kēhtēskwēwiw ᘱᐦᐅ^ᕀᐤᐃ°
VAI she is an old woman

kēhtēstim ᘱᐦᐅ^ᐣᐨ
NA old horse; old dog [*pl*:
-wak]

kēhtēwiw ᘱᐦᐅᐊᐧ°
VAI s/he is old [*cf.*
kēhtē-ayiwiw]

kēhtēyātisiw ᘱᐦᐅᐰᐟᓯ°
VAI s/he acts like an elderly
person

kēhtēyiniw ᘱᐦᐅᐸᔮ°
NA old man, old person

kēhtināc ᘱᐦᐋ-
IPC surely [*cf.* kēhcinā,
kēhcināc, kēhcinās, kēsinā]

kēhtinēw ᘱᐦᐊᐧᐤ°
VTA s/he treats s.o. with
respect or deference

kēkā ᘱᑫ
IPC almost, in immediate
prospect, impendingly [*cf.*
kēkāc, kēkāt]

kēkā-mitātaht ᘱᑫ ᒥᒐᐦ᷄
IPC nine

kēkā-mitātahtomitanaw
ᘱᑫ ᒥᒐᐦᑐᒋᓇᐤ°
IPC ninety

kēkā-mitātahtomitanawāw
ᘱᑫ ᒥᒐᐦᑐᒋᓇᐁᐧ°
IPC ninety times

kēkā-mitātahtosāp
ᘱᑫ ᒥᒐᐦᑐᓴᑊᐧ
IPC nineteen [*also*:
kēkā-mitātosāp, *see also*
kēkā-nīsitanaw]

kēkā-mitātahtwāpisk
ᘱᑫ ᒥᒐᐦᐟᐋᑉᐢ
IPC nine dollars

kēkā-mitātahtwāw
ᘱᑫ ᒥᒐᐦᐟᐋᐧ°
IPC nine times

kēkā-nistomitanaw
ᘱᑫ ᓂᐢᑐᒋᓇᐤ°
IPC twenty-nine [*cf.*
kēkāc-nistomitanaw, *see also*
nīstanaw-kēkā-mitātahtosāp]

kēkā-nīsitanaw ᘱᑫ ᓂᐟᒋᓇᐤ°
IPC nineteen [*see also*
kēkā-mitātahtosāp; *cf.*
kēkāc-nīsitanaw]

kēkāc ᘱᑫ-
IPC just about, almost,
nearly [*cf.* kēkā, kēkāt]

kēkāc-ayinānēmitanaw
ᘱᑫ- ᐊᐱᐋᓀᒥᒐᓇᐤ°
IPC seventy-nine

kēkāc-kēkā-mitātahtomitanaw
ᘱᑫ- ᘱᑫ ᒥᒐᐦᑐᒋᓇᐤ°
IPC eighty-nine

kēkāc-mitātaht ᘱᑫ- ᒥᒐᐦ᷄
IPC nine

kēkāc-nēmitanaw ᘱᑫ- ᐁᒋᓇᐤ°
IPC thirty-nine [*also*
kēkāc-nēwomitanaw]

kēkāc-nikotwāsomitanaw
ᘱᑫ- ᓂᑯᒡᐁᐧᓱᒋᓇᐤ°
IPC fifty-nine

kēkāc-nistomitanaw
ᘱᑫ- ᓂᐢᑐᒋᓇᐤ°
IPC twenty-nine [*also*
kēkā-nistomitanaw]

kēkāc-niyānanomitanaw
ᘱᑫ- ᓂᔭᐊᐧᓱᒋᓇᐤ°
IPC forty-nine [*also*
kēkāc-niyānomitanaw]

kēkāc-nīsitanaw ᘱᑫ- ᓂᐟᒋᓇᐤ°
IPC nineteen [*see also*
kēkā-mitātahtosāp, *also*
kēkā-nīsitanaw]

kēkāc-tēpakohpomitanaw
ᘱᑫ- ᐅᐸᑯᐦᐳᒋᓇᐤ°
IPC sixty-nine

kēkāci- ᘱᑫ
IPV almost

kēkāt ᘱᑫᐧ
IPC just about, almost [*cf.*
kēkā, kēkāc]

kēkēcipitēw ᘱᑫᕀᐱᑌᐤ°
VTA s/he pulls s.o. out of
that one's clothes [*rdpl*; *cf.*
kēcipitēw]

kēkētaskisinēw ᘱᑫᐟᐊᐢᕀᓯᓀᐤ°
VAI s/he takes off his/her
own moccasins, shoes [*rdpl*;
cf. kētaskisinēw]

kēkētaskisinēpahtāw
ᘱᑫᐟᐊᐢᕀᓯᓀᐸᐦᑖᐤ°
VAI s/he runs dropping
his/her own moccasins, shoes
[*rdpl*; *cf.* kētaskisinēpahtāw]

kēkisēp ᘱᕀᓴᑊᐧ
IPC this morning [*cf.*
kīkisēp]

kēko ᘱᑯ
PR which? what kind?

kēkoc ᘱᑯ-
IPC in proper person,
oneself

kēkwas ᘱᑯᐧ^
IPC back and forth

kēkwask ᘱᑯᐧ^ᐣ
IPC back and forth

kēkwāy ᘱᑯᐧᐧ
PR what [*sC*: kēkwān; *cf.*
kīkwāy]

kēmā ᘱᒫ
IPC or, or else [*Saulteaux
loan*]

kēposkāw ᘱᐳᐢᑳᐤ°
VII there are an abundance
of reeds

kēsinā ᘱᓯᓈ
IPC surely [*cf.* kēcinās,
kēhcinā, kēhcināc]

kēsiskam ᘱᓯᐢᑲᒼᐨ
VTI s/he comes in time for
s.t.; s/he reaches s.t. in time,
s/he arrives in time

kēsiskaw ᘱᓯᐢᑲ°
IPC quickly, right away

kēsiskawēw ᘱᓯᐢᑲᐁᐧ°
VTA s/he comes in time for
s.o., s/he comes upon s.o.;
s/he reaches s.o. in time (*e.g.*
before departure)

kēsiskawihkasikan
ᘱᓯᐢᑲᐃᐦᑲᓯᑲᐣ
NI microwave oven

kēsiskotātowak ᘱᓯᐢᑯᑖᑐᐊᐧᐠ
VAI they come upon one
another

kēsiyākēw ᘱᓯᔭᑫᐤ°
VAI s/he cheats

kēsiyohwēw ᘱᓯᔪᐦᐁᐧ°
VTA s/he cheats s.o.

kēstinam ᘱᐢᑎᓇᒼᐨ
VTI s/he catches s.t. in time

kēswān ᘱᐢᐋᐧᐣ
IPC by coincidence [*cf.*
kākēswān]

kēt- ᘱ
IPV take off, remove

kētahikan ᘱᑕᐦᐃᑲᐣ
NI ramrod

kētahtawē ᘱᑕᐦᑕᐁᐧ
IPC at one time, sometime,
in the future; once in a while;
suddenly [*cf.* kitahtawē]

kētasākēnēw ᘱᑕᓴᑫᓀᐤ°
VTA s/he takes the coat
(dress, etc.) off s.o.

kētasākēpayihow ᘱᑕᓴᑫᐸᔨᐦᐅᐤ°
VAI s/he pulls his/her own
coat (dress, etc.) off quickly

kētasākēpayiw ᘱᑕᓴᑫᐸᔨᐤ°
VAI s/he has his/her own
coat (dress, etc.) fall off

kētasākēpiw ᘱᑕᓴᑫᐱᐤ°
VAI s/he sits with his/her
own coat (dress, etc.) off

kētasākēw ᘱᑕᓴᑫᐤ°
VAI s/he takes his/her own
coat (dress, etc.) off

kētasāmēnēw ᘱᑕᓴᒣᓀᐤ°
VTA s/he takes the
snowshoes off s.o.

kētasāmēw ᘱᑕᓴᒣᐤ°
VAI s/he takes his/her own
snowshoes off

kētasikanēw ᘱᑕᓯᑲᓀᐤ°
VAI s/he takes his/her own
socks off

kētaskisinēnēw ᘱᑕᐢᕀᓯᓀᓀᐤ°
VTA s/he takes s.o.'s shoes
(moccasins, boots, etc.) off
by hand

kētaskisinēpahtāw
ᘱᑕᐢᕀᓯᓀᐸᐦᑖᐤ°
VAI s/he runs dropping
his/her own moccasins, shoes

kētaskisinēpayิw ᐧᑕᐦᑭᓯᓀᐸᔨᐤ
VAI s/he has his/her own
shoes, moccasins fall off

kētaskisinēpitēw ᐧᑕᐦᑭᓯᐧᐸᐅᐤ
VTA s/he pulls his/her own
shoes, moccasins off s.o.

kētaskisinēpiw ᐧᑕᐦᑭᓯᐧᐸᐤ
VAI s/he sits with his/her
own shoes, moccasins off

kētaskisinēw ᐧᑕᐦᑭᓯᐤᐤ
VAI s/he takes his/her own
shoes (moccasins, boots, etc.)
off

kētaspastākanēw ᐧᑕᐦᐸᐢᑕᐦᒐᐧᐤ
VAI s/he takes his/her own
apron off

kētastisēw ᐧᑕᐦᑎᓯᐤ
VAI s/he takes his/her own
mitts off

kētastotinēnēw ᐧᑕᐦᐄᑎᓀᐧᐤ
VTA s/he takes the hat off
s.o.

kētastotinēpayิw ᐧᑕᐦᐄᑎᓀᐸᐧᐄᐤ
VAI s/he has his/her own hat
fall off

kētastotinēpiw ᐧᑕᐦᐄᑎᓀᐸᐤ
VAI s/he sits with his/her
own hat off

kētastotinēpitēw ᐧᑕᐦᐄᑎᓀᐸᐅᐤ
VTA s/he pulls the hat off
s.o.

kētastotinēw ᐧᑕᐦᐄᑎᓀᐧᐤ
VAI s/he takes his/her own
hat off

kētayiwinisēw ᐧᑕᔪᐄᓂᓯᐤ
VAI s/he takes his/her own
clothes off

kētāspisow ᐧᑕᐦᐄᓱ
VAI s/he undresses

kētikonam ᐧᑎᑯᓇᐨ
VTI s/he takes s.t. off [cf.
kēcikonam]

kētikoskawēw ᐧᑎᑯᐢᑲᐧᐄᐤ
VTA s/he steps out of s.o.
(e.g. clothing), s/he takes s.o.
off [cf. kēcikoskawēw]

kētisk ᐧᑎᐢᐠ
IPC just barely, hardly;
fully, by exact measure

kētiskāwi ᐧᑎᐢᑲᐧ·
IPC to full measure

kētiski- ᐧᑎᐢᑭ
IPV to exact measure

kētitāsēw ᐧᑎᒐᓯᐤ
VAI s/he takes his/her own
pants off

kētowatēw ᐧᑐᐊᐅᐤ
VAI s/he takes off and puts
down his/her own burden

kēýakisīw ᐧᔦᑭᓰᐤ
VAI s/he itches, s/he is itchy
[cf. kiýakisiw]

kēyāpic ᐧᔦᐱᐨ
IPC still, yet, in continuity,
more [cf. ēyāpic, kēyāpit]

kēyāpit ᐧᔦᐱᐟ
IPC still, more [cf. ēyāpic,
kēyāpic]

kēyiwē ᐧᔦᐁ·
IPC that will help, that's
better than nothing [cf.
kēyiwēhk]

kēyiwēhk ᐧᔦᐁ·ᕽ
IPC fairly well, as well as
may be, at any rate [cf.
kēyiwē]

ᐱ

kici- ᐱᒉ
IPV so that [grammatical
preverb with conjunct clause]

kicikānēsīs ᐱᒉᑳᓀᓰᐢ
NA winter sunbird

kicikīskosīs ᐱᒉᑮᐢᑯᓰᐢ
NA chickadee [cf. kiciskosīs]

kicimākānēs ᐱᒉᒫᑳᓀᐢ
NA poor guy, pitiful person

kicimākinākosiw ᐱᒉᒫᑭᓈᑯᓯᐤ
VAI s/he is cute

kiciskinam ᐱᒉᐢᑭᓇᐨ
VTI s/he drops s.t. [cf.
kitiskinam]

kiciskinēw ᐱᒉᐢᑭᓀᐤ
VTA s/he drops s.o. [cf.
kitiskinēw]

kiciskaham ᐱᒉᐢᑲᐦᐊᐨ
VTI s/he makes s.t. creak

kicīskosīs ᐱᒉᐢᑯᓰᐢ
NA chickadee [cf.
kicikīskosīs]

kihawēma ᐱᐦᐊᐁᒪ
IPC too far, in excess [cf.
kīhyawēma]

kihc-ōkimānāhk ᐱᐦᐅᑭᒫᓈᕽ
INM the government, federal
government [cf.
kihci-okimānāhk]

kihcapiwin ᐱᐦᓵᐱᐧᐃᐣ
NI seat (in government)

kihcēkosīw ᐱᐦᒉᑯᓰᐤ
VAI s/he climbs up high (on
s.t.)

kihcēkosīwināhtik
ᐱᐦᒉᑯᓰᐄᓈᐦᑎᐠ
NI ladder [pl: -wa]

kihcēýihtam ᐱᐦᒉᔨᐦᑕᐨ
VTI s/he respects s.t.; s/he is
proud of s.t.; s/he thinks
highly of s.t.

kihcēýihtamawēw ᐱᐦᒉᔨᐦᑕᒪᐧᐄᐤ
VTA s/he thinks highly of
(it/him) for s.o.

kihcēýihtākosiw ᐱᐦᒉᔨᐦᑖᑯᓯᐤ
VAI s/he is esteemed; s/he is
knowledgeable and respected

kihcēýihtākwan ᐱᐦᒉᔨᐦᑖ�44ᐧᐤ
VII it is respected; it is
highly thought of; it is held
sacred; it is of the utmost
importance

kihcēýimēw ᐱᐦᒉᔨᒣᐤ
VTA s/he respects s.o.; s/he
thinks highly of s.o.

kihcēýimow ᐱᐦᒉᔨᒧ
VAI s/he is conceited, s/he is
proud; s/he thinks a lot of
him/herself

kihcēýiniw ᐱᐦᒉᔨᓂ
NA elder, important person
[an asset to an area]

kihci ᐱᐦᒉ
IPC the best; main one
IPN great, big
IPV great, big, important

kihci-atāwēwikamikowiýiniw
ᐱᐦᒉ ᐊᑖᐧᐁᐄ·ᐃᑲᒥᑯᐄᔨᓂ
NA store manager, post
manager, Hudson's Bay
Company factor [also
kihc-atāwēwikamikowiýiniw]

kihci-atāwēwikamik
ᐱᐦᒉ ᐊᑖᐧᐁᐄ·ᐃᑲᒥᐠ
NI department store;
Hudson's Bay Company
store [pl: -wa; also
kihc-atāwēwikamik]

kihci-awasi-otākosīhk
ᐱᐦᒉ ᐊᐊᓯ ᐅᑖᑯᓰᕽ
IPC two days before
yesterday

kihci-ayamihāwin
ᐱᐦᒉ ᐊᔭᒥᐦᐋᐄ·ᐣ
NI special prayer [also
kihc-āyamihāwin]

kihci-ayamihēwikamik
ᐱᐦᒉ ᐊᔭᒥᐦᐁᐄ·ᐁᐃᑲᒥᐠ
NI cathedral, temple, church
[pl: -wa]

kihci-ayamihēwiýiniw
ᐱᐦᒉ ᐊᔭᒥᐦᐁᐄ·ᔨᓂ
NA bishop [also
kihc-āyamihēwiýiniw]

kihci-aýisiýiniw ᐱᐦᒉ ᐊᔨᓯᔨᓂ
NA man of importance

kihci-aýisiýiniwiw
ᐱᐦᒉ ᐊᔨᓯᔨᓂᐄ·ᐤ
VAI he is a man of
importance, he is a great man

kihci-āpihtāwāni-kīsikāw
ᐱᐦᒉ ᐊᐱᐦᑖᐧᐋᓂ ᑮᓯᑳᐤ
VII it is Thursday, it is
mid-week; it is high noon
[see also nēwo-kīsikāw;
āpihtā-kīsikāw]

kihci-itwēw ᐱᐦᒉ ᐃᐅᐤ
VAI s/he takes an oath, s/he
swears an oath

kihci-itwēwin ᐱᐦᒉ ᐃᐅᐄ·ᐃᐟ
NI oath-taking (on the
Bible)

kihci-kiskinwahamātowikamik
ᐱᐦᒉ ᑭᐢᑭᐣᐊᐦᒫᑐᐄ·ᐃᑲᒥᐠ
NI university [pl: -wa; also
kihci-kiskinahamātowikamik,
kihci-kiskinohamātowikamik]

kihci-kīsik ᐱᐦᒉ ᑮᓯᐠ
NI heaven; outer space [loc:
-ohk]

kihci-kīsikāw ᐱᐦᒉ ᑮᓯᑳᐤ
VII it is an important day
(e.g. Christmas, New Year)

kihci-kīsikow ᑭᐦᒋ ᑮᓯᑰ
NA angel

kihci-kīsikōwiw ᑭᐦᒋ ᑮᓯᑰᐏᐤ
VAI s/he is an angel

kihci-manitow ᑭᐦᒋ ᒪᓂᑐᐤ
NA Great Spirit, God

kihci-manitōwiw ᑭᐦᒋ ᒪᓂᑑᐏᐤ
VAI s/he is the Great Spirit, s/he is God

kihci-masinahikan ᑭᐦᒋ ᒪᓯᓇᐦᐃᑲᐣ
NI Bible, good book

kihci-masinahikēwin ᑭᐦᒋ ᒪᓯᓇᐦᐃᑫᐏᐣ
NI holy scripture

kihci-māmawapiwin ᑭᐦᒋ ᒫᒪᐘᐱᐏᐣ
NI large conference, large meeting; religious gathering

kihci-mēskanaw ᑭᐦᒋ ᒣᐢᑲᓇᐤ
NI highway

kihci-mihti ᑭᐦᒋ ᒥᐦᑎ
NI big club, big stick [*pl*: -mihta]

kihci-mitātahtomitanaw ᑭᐦᒋ ᒥᑖᑕᐦᑐᒥᑕᓇᐤ
IPC thousand, one thousand [*preceded by* "times" *numeral*; *cf.* pēyakwāw-kihci-mitātahtomi tanaw "one thousand"]

kihci-mōhkomān ᑭᐦᒋ ᒨᐦᑯᒫᐣ
NA American [*lit*: "great-knife"]
NI a big knife

kihci-mōhkomānaskiy ᑭᐦᒋ ᒨᐦᑯᒫᓇᐢᑭᕀ
NI the USA [*lit*: "great-knife-land"; *see also* awasi-tipahaskān]

kihci-mōhkomāninâhk ᑭᐦᒋ ᒨᐦᑯᒫᓂᓈᕽ
INM (in the) United States [*lit*: "among the great knives"; *see also* awasi-tipahaskān]

kihci-mōhkomāniwiw ᑭᐦᒋ ᒨᐦᑯᒫᓂᐏᐤ
VAI s/he is an American

kihci-niska ᑭᐦᒋ ᓂᐢᑲ
NA Canada goose

kihci-okimāhkān ᑭᐦᒋ ᐅᑭᒫᐦᑳᐣ
NA great chief

kihci-okimāhkāniwiw ᑭᐦᒋ ᐅᑭᒫᐦᑳᓂᐏᐤ
VAI he is a great chief

kihci-okimāhkātēw ᑭᐦᒋ ᐅᑭᒫᐦᑳᑌᐤ
VTA s/he makes s.o. a great chief, s/he appoints s.o. to be governor

kihci-okimānâhk ᑭᐦᒋ ᐅᑭᒫᓈᕽ
INM the government [*cf.* kihc-ōkimānâhk]

kihci-okimāskwēw ᑭᐦᒋ ᐅᑭᒫᐢᑵᐤ
NA queen [*also* kihc-ōkimāskwēw]

kihci-okimāw ᑭᐦᒋ ᐅᑭᒫᐤ
NA king; government [*cf.* kihc-ōkimānâhk "the government"; *also* kihc-ōkimāw]

kihci-okimāw-apiwin ᑭᐦᒋ ᐅᑭᒫᐤ ᐊᐱᐏᐣ
NI throne, royal throne

kihci-okimāw-astotin ᑭᐦᒋ ᐅᑭᒫᐤ ᐊᐢᑐᑎᐣ
NI crown

kihci-okimāwiw ᑭᐦᒋ ᐅᑭᒫᐏᐤ
VAI he is king

kihci-okimāwikamik ᑭᐦᒋ ᐊᑭᒫᐏᑲᒥᐠ
NI palace, castle; royal residence [*pl*: -wa]

kihci-okimāwiwin ᑭᐦᒋ ᐅᑭᒫᐏᐏᐣ
NI royalty; royal blood

kihci-okiniy ᑭᐦᒋ ᐅᑭᓂᕀ
NA tomato [*cf.* okiniy "rose-hip"; *also* kihc-ōkiniy]

kihci-onīkānohtēw ᑭᐦᒋ ᐅᓃᑳᓄᐦᑌᐤ
NA lead-dog (in a sled team); leader on foot [*also* kihc-ōnīkānohtēw]

kihci-oýākan ᑭᐦᒋ ᐅᔮᑲᐣ
NI large dish

kihci-ōtēnaw ᑭᐦᒋ ᐆᑌᓇᐤ
NI city

kihci-sākiy
NI great inlet; Kitsakie, SK [*wC reserve name*; *part of La Ronge Indian Band*]

kihci-sōniyāw ᑭᐦᒋ ᓲᓂᔮᐤ
NA pound sterling (used in Treaty)

kihci-wīkiw ᑭᐦᒋ ᐑᑭᐤ
VAI s/he lives formally; s/he lives in residence

kihci-wīkihtow ᑭᐦᒋ ᐑᑭᐦᑐᐤ
VAI s/he is formally married in church

kihci-wīkihtowin ᑭᐦᒋ ᐑᑭᐦᑐᐏᐣ
NI formal marriage, Holy Matrimony

kihci-wīkihtowin-āhcanis ᑭᐦᒋ ᐑᑭᐦᑐᐏᐣ ᐋᐦᒐᓂᐢ
NA wedding ring

kihci-wīkimēw ᑭᐦᒋ ᐑᑭᒣᐤ
VTA s/he marries s.o. formally in church

kihcihtwāwi- ᑭᐦᒋᐦᑤᐏ
IPN of exalted character; venerable, holy [*cf.* kihcihtwāwi-mēriy "Holy Mary"]

kihcikamiy ᑭᐦᒋᑲᒥᕀ
NI sea, ocean; a great body of water

kihcikamīhk ᑭᐦᒋᑲᒦᕽ
IPC in the sea [*loc*]

kihcikamīwaskosiy ᑭᐦᒋᑲᒦᐘᐢᑯᓯᕀ
NI seaweed

kihcikamīwaskwa ᑭᐦᒋᑲᒦᐘᐢᑿ
NI bullrushes [*pl*]

kihcikamīwiýin ᑭᐦᒋᑲᒦᐏᔨᐣ
NA Ocean Man [*Cree name of Nakota chief*; *possibly a loan translation from English*: "Ocean Man", *originally from Nakota* ošiyã mani "man walking pitifully"]

kihcikanisiw ᑭᐦᒋᑲᓂᓯᐤ
VAI s/he holds a ceremony; s/he spends Christmas

kihcinākosiw ᑭᐦᒋᓈᑯᓯᐤ
VAI s/he looks important, s/he appears important

kihcinākwan ᑭᐦᒋᓈᑿᐣ
VII it looks impressive, it appears important

kihcinisk ᑭᐦᒋᓂᐢᐠ
NI right hand

kihciniskēhk ᑭᐦᒋᓂᐢᑫᕽ
IPC right, the right side, at the right

kihciniskin ᑭᐦᒋᓂᐢᑭᐣ
IPC right-hand side

kihciwē ᑭᐦᒋᐍ
IPC directly, without intermediary

kihciýiniw ᑭᐦᒋᔨᓂᐤ
NA head man, leader

kihēw ᑭᐦᐁᐤ
NA eagle; thunderbird [*cf.* kihīw]

kihiwayān ᑭᐦᐃᐘᔮᐣ
NA eagle feather garment

kihiwīkwan ᑭᐦᐃᐑᑿᐣ
NA eagle feather

kihīw ᑭᐦᐄᐤ
NA eagle [*also* kihiw; *cf.* kihēw]

kihtānam ᑭᐦᑖᓇᒼ
VTI s/he immerses s.t. by hand, s/he dips s.t. in the water

kihtānēw ᑭᐦᑖᓀᐤ
VTA s/he immerses s.o. by hand; s/he submerges s.o., s/he pushes s.o. under the water; s/he dips s.o. in the water

kihtāpaýihow ᑭᐦᑖᐸᔨᐦᐅᐤ
VAI s/he throws him/herself under water

kihtāpaýiw ᑭᐦᑖᐸᔨᐤ
VAI s/he goes under water

kihtēýihtākosiw ᑭᐦᑌᔨᐦᑖᑯᓯᐤ
VAI s/he is esteemed, s/he is well thought of

kihtimapiw ᑭᐦᑎᒪᐱᐤ
VAI s/he is tired of sitting, s/he is tired from sitting

kihtimēyihtam ᑭᐦᑎᒣᔨᐦᑕᒼ
VTI s/he is tired of s.t.

kihtimēyimēw ᑭᐦᑎᒣᔨᒣᐤ
VTA s/he is tired of s.o.

kihtimikan ᑭᐦᑎᒥᑲᐣ
NA lazy person, lazy-bones

kihtimikanēw ᑭᐦᑎᒥᑲᓀᐤ
VAI s/he is lazy, s/he is idle; s/he is a lazy-bones

kihtimiskiw ᑭᐦᑎᒥᐢᑭᐤ
VAI s/he is often lazy, s/he is lazy all the time [*hab*]

kihtimiw ᑭᐦᑎᒥᐤ
VAI s/he is lazy

kihtimiwin ᑭᐦᑎᒥᐏᐣ
NI laziness

kihtohtēw ᑭᐦᑐᐦᑌᐤ
VAI s/he walks despite being tired of it, s/he is tired of walking

kika- ᑭᑲ
IPV [*grammatical preverb*; *future*; *cf.* ka-, kita-, ta-, tita-]

kikamohtāw ᑭᑲᒧᐦᑖᐤ
VAIt s/he fastens s.t. on, s/he attaches s.t.; s/he puts s.t. on something

kikamon ᑭᑲᒧᐣ
VII it is attached, it is on something [*cf.* kikamow]

kikamow ᑭᑲᒧᐤ
VAI it clings, it sticks; it is fastened on

kikamow ᑭᑲᒧᐤ
VII it is attached [*cf.* kikamon]

kikamōhēw ᑭᑲᒨᐦᐁᐤ
VTA s/he fastens s.o. on, s/he attaches s.o.; s/he puts s.o. (*e.g.* yarn) on something

kikasāmēhtēw ᑭᑲᓵᒣᐦᑌᐤ
VAI s/he walks with snowshoes

kikasāmēw ᑭᑳᓵᒣᐤ
VAI s/he has snowshoes on, s/he wears snowshoes

kikaskisinēw ᑭᑲᐢᑭᓯᓀᐤ
VAI s/he wears (his/her own) shoes, s/he has (his/her own) shoes on

kikaskisinihkwāmiw ᑭᑲᐢᑭᓯᓂᐦᑳᒥᐤ
VAI s/he sleeps with (his/her own) shoes on

kikastotinēpiw ᑭᑲᐢᑐᑎᓀᐱᐤ
VAI s/he sits with his/her own hat on

kikastotinēw ᑭᑲᐢᑐᑎᓀᐤ
VAI s/he wears his/her own hat

kikawinam ᑭᑲᐏᓇᒼ
VTI s/he mixes s.t. into something, s/he sprinkles s.t. over something

kikawinēw ᑭᑲᐏᓀᐤ
VTA s/he mixes s.o. (*e.g.* tobacco) together by hand

kikāpōhkēw ᑭᑳᐴᐦᑫᐤ
VAI s/he adds s.t. to the soup

kiki ᑭᑭ
IPC for, with [*used for ingredients in cooking*]

kikinam ᑭᑭᓇᒼ
VTI s/he adds s.t. (*e.g.* baking powder) in, s/he mixes s.t. in, s/he includes s.t; s/he puts s.t. on something

kikinēw ᑭᑭᓀᐤ
VTA s/he adds s.o. (*e.g.* tobacco) in, s/he mixes s.o. in, s/he includes s.t.

kikinikātēw ᑭᑭᓂᑳᑌᐤ
VII it is included, it is mixed in, it is added in

kikiskam ᑭᑭᐢᑲᒼ
VTI s/he wears s.t.; s/he has s.t. as an intimate possession

kikiskamohēw ᑭᑭᐢᑲᒧᐦᐁᐤ
VTA s/he puts (it/him) on s.o.

kikiskawāwasow ᑭᑭᐢᑲᐚᐘᓱᐤ
VAI s/he is with child, s/he is pregnant

kikiskawēw ᑭᑭᐢᑲᐍᐤ
VTA s/he wears s.o. (*e.g.* stocking, ring); s/he is with child

kikitāsēw ᑭᑭᑖᓭᐤ
VAI s/he wears pants, breeches

kikowatēsin ᑭᑯᐘᑌᓯᐣ
VAI s/he lies with his/her own load on, s/he lies on his/her own baggage

kimisāhēw ᑭᒥᓵᐦᐁᐤ
VTA s/he wipes s.o.'s anus (*e.g.* a child's)

kimisāhow ᑭᒥᓵᐦᐅᐤ
VAI s/he wipes his/her own anus

kimisāhowinēkin ᑭᒥᓵᐦᐅᐏᓀᑭᐣ
NI toilet paper

kimiwan ᑭᒥᐘᐣ
NI rain [*cf.* kimiwan *VII*]

kimiwan ᑭᒥᐘᐣ
VII it rains, it is raining, it is rainy

kimiwanasākay ᑭᒥᐘᓇᓵᑲᕀ
NI raincoat

kimiwanāpoy ᑭᒥᐘᓈᐳᕀ
NI rain water

kimiwanēyāpiy ᑭᒥᐘᓀᔮᐱᕀ
NI rainbow [*see also* pīsimwēyāpiy]

kimiwanisiw ᑭᒥᐘᓂᓯᐤ
VAI it has rain, it receives rain; s/he is caught in the rain

kimiwasin ᑭᒥᐘᓯᐣ
VII it rains a little; it is drizzling [*dim*]

kimiwaskin ᑭᒥᐘᐢᑭᐣ
VII it rains frequently [*hab*]

kimosōm-pwātināhk ᑭᒧᓲᒼ ᐚᑎᓈᕽ
INM Deschambeault Lake, SK [*loc*; *lit*: "among the grandfather Sioux"]

kimotamawēw ᑭᒧᑕᒪᐍᐤ
VTA s/he steals (it/him) from s.o., s/he robs s.o. of (it/him)

kimotastotinēw ᑭᒧᑕᐢᑐᑎᓀᐤ
VAI s/he steals a hat, headgear

kimotisk ᑭᒧᑎᐢᐠ
NA thief

kimotiskiw ᑭᒧᑎᐢᑭᐤ
VAI s/he is a thief, s/he steals habitually [*hab*]

kimotiw ᑭᒧᑎᐤ
VAI s/he steals (it/him); s/he is a thief [*rdpl*: kāh-kimotiw]

kimotiwin ᑭᒧᑎᐏᐣ
NI theft; thing stolen

kinanāskomitin ᑭᓇᓈᐢᑯᒥᑎᐣ
IPC thank you, I am grateful to you [*cf.* nanāskom- *VTA*; *see also* kitatamihin]

kinēpik ᑭᓀᐱᐠ
NA snake [*pl*: -wak]

kinēpikos ᑭᓀᐱᑯᐢ
NA little snake [*dim*]

kinēpikosis ᑭᓀᐱᑯᓯᐢ
NA tiny snake [*dim*]

kinēpikoskāw ᑭᓀᐱᑯᐢᑳᐤ
VII there are an abundance of snakes

kinēpikowiýiniw ᑭᓀᐱᑯᐏᔨᓂᐤ
NA Snake Indian

kinēpikoýiniw ᑭᓀᐱᑯᔨᓂᐤ
NA Snake Indian

kinikinik ᑭᓂᑭᓂᐠ
NI shrub mixture (red willow bark and green leaves) used as traditional tobacco for the pipe

kinīpiko-sākahikanihk ᑭᓃᐱᑯ ᓵᑲᐦᐃᑲᓂᕽ
INM Pinehouse Lake, SK [*loc*; *lit*: "at snake lake"; *wC community*; *cf.* kinēpik]

kino- ᑭᓄ
IPN long, length

kino-miýēstawānēw ᑭᓄ ᒥᔦᐢᑕᐚᓀᐤ
VAI he has a long beard [*also* -mīhēstawānēw, -mihýēstawānēw; *cf.* miýēstawēw]

kinocihcān ᑭᓄᒋᐦᒑᐣ
NI middle finger

kinocihcēw ᑭᓄᒋᐦᒉᐤ
VAI s/he has a long hand

kinocihciy ᑭᓄᒋᐦᒋᕀ
NI long hand

kinocihcīs ᑭᓄᒋᐦᒌᐢ
NI long finger; middle finger

kinohēw ᑭᓄᐦᐁᐤ
VTA s/he lengthens s.o. (*e.g.* pants)

kinohkwēw ᑭᓄᐦᑵᐤ
VAI s/he has a long face

kinohtawakēw ᑭᓄᐦᑕᐘᑫᐤ
VAI s/he has long ears

kinohtāw ᑭᓄᐦᑖᐤ
VAIt s/he lengthens s.t.

kinokamāw ᑭᓄᑲᒫᐤ
VII it is a long lake

kinokasēw ᑭᓄᑲᓭᐤ
VAI s/he has long nails; it has long claws

kinokāpawiw ᑭᓄᑳᐸᐏᐤ
VAI s/he stands tall

kinokātēw ᑭᓄᑳᑌᐤ
VAI s/he has long legs

kinokohtāw ᑭᓄᑯᐦᑖᐤ
VAIt s/he lengthens s.t. by stretching

kinokohtēw ᑭᓄᑯᐦᑌᐤ
VAI s/he takes long steps

kinokot ᑭᓄᑯᐟ
NA long-nosed person

kinokotam ᑭᓄᑯᑕᒼ
VTI s/he cuts s.t. long (*e.g.* strips of hide for laces)

kinokotēw ᑭᓄᑯᑌᐤ
VAI s/he has a long nose; it has a long beak

kinokwanēw ᑭᓄᑲᐧᓀᐤ
VAI it has long feathers

kinokwayaw ᑭᓄᑲᐧᔭᐤ
NI a long neck

kinokwayawēw ᑭᓄᑲᐧᔭᐍᐤ
VAI s/he has a long neck

kinopayiw ᑭᓄᐸᔨᐤ
VII it stretches

kinopiskwanēw ᑭᓄᐱᐢᑲᐧᓀᐤ
VAI s/he has a long back

kinopitonēw ᑭᓄᐱᑐᓀᐤ
VAI s/he has long arms

kinosākay ᑭᓄᓵᑲᐩ
NI long dress, coat

kinosākēw ᑭᓄᓵᑫᐤ
VAI s/he has a long dress (coat, etc.)

kinosēsis ᑭᓄᓭᓯᐢ
NA little fish [*dim*]

kinosēskāw ᑭᓄᓭᐢᑳᐤ
VII there are an abundance of fish

kinosēw ᑭᓄᓭᐤ
NA fish

kinosēw-sākahikan ᑭᓄᓭᐤ ᓵᑲᐦᐃᑲᐣ
NI Saulteaux Reserve, SK [*lit*: "fish lake"; *Cree/ Saulteaux reserve name*]

kinosēwan ᑭᓄᓭᐘᐣ
VII there are many fish

kinosēwāpoy ᑭᓄᓭᐚᐳᐩ
NI fish broth

kinosēwēw ᑭᓄᓭᐍᐤ
VAI s/he fishes, s/he catches fish [*cf.* nōcikinosēwēw]

kinosēwikamik ᑭᓄᓭᐏᑲᒥᐠ
NI fish plant, fish storage house [*pl*: -wa]

kinosēwikamikohkēw ᑭᓄᓭᐏᑲᒥᑯᐦᑫᐤ
VAI s/he builds a fish plant

kinosēwimākosiw ᑭᓄᓭᐏᒫᑯᓯᐤ
VAI s/he smells fishy

kinosēwimākwan ᑭᓄᓭᐏᒫᑲᐧᐣ
VII it smells fishy

kinosēwipimiy ᑭᓄᓭᐏᐱᒥᐩ
NI fish oil; cod-liver oil

kinosēwiw ᑭᓄᓭᐏᐤ
VAI s/he is a fish

kinosisiw ᑭᓄᓯᓯᐤ
VAI s/he is a bit taller [*dim*]

kinositēw ᑭᓄᓯᑌᐤ
VAI s/he has long feet

kinosiw ᑭᓄᓯᐤ
VAI s/he is long, s/he is tall

kinotahtahkwanēw ᑭᓄᑕᐦᑕᐦᑲᐧᓀᐤ
VAI it has long wings [*cf.* mitahtahkwan]

kinotēskanēw ᑭᓄᑌᐢᑲᓀᐤ
VAI it has long horns

kinoyawēw ᑭᓄᔭᐍᐤ
VAI s/he has a long body

kinwāhtawēw ᑭᓈᐧᐦᑕᐍᐤ
VTA s/he lengthens (it/him) for s.o.

kinwāniskwēw ᑭᓈᐧᓂᐢᑫᐧᐤ
VAI s/he has long hair

kinwāpēkan ᑭᓈᐧᐯᑲᐣ
VII it is long (*e.g.* string)

kinwāpēkasākay ᑭᓈᐧᐯᑲᓵᑲᐩ
NI long coat, skirt

kinwāpēkasākēw ᑭᓈᐧᐯᑲᓵᑫᐤ
VAI she wears long skirts; s/he wears long clothing

kinwāpēkihkwēw ᑭᓈᐧᐯᑭᐦᑫᐧᐤ
VAI s/he has a long face (*e.g.* horse)

kinwāpēkihtawakay ᑭᓈᐧᐯᑭᐦᑕᐘᑲᐩ
NA long-eared creature

kinwāpēkikwayaw ᑭᓈᐧᐯᑭᑲᐧᔭᐤ
NA Longneck [*personal name*]; long-necked creature
NI long neck

kinwāpēkikwayawēw ᑭᓈᐧᐯᑭᑲᐧᔭᐍᐤ
VAI s/he has a long neck

kinwāpēkisiw ᑭᓈᐧᐯᑭᓯᐤ
VAI it is long (*e.g.* snake)

kinwāsin ᑭᓈᐧᓯᐣ
VII it is a bit long [*dim*]

kinwāskicēs ᑭᓈᐧᐢᑭᒉᐢ
NI tin-can [*dim*]

kinwāskosiw ᑭᓈᐧᐢᑯᓯᐤ
VAI s/he is tall; it is a tall tree, it is a long stick

kinwāskwan ᑭᓈᐧᐢᑲᐧᐣ
VII it is tall, it is long (*e.g.* board)

kinwāw ᑭᓈᐧᐤ
VII it is long, it is tall

kinwāyowēw ᑭᓈᐧᔪᐍᐤ
VAI it is long-tailed [*also* kinoyowēw]

kinwēs ᑭᓀᐧᐢ
IPC a long while; for a long time [*cf.* kinwēsk]

kinwēsīs ᑭᓀᐧᓰᐢ
IPC for a while, for quite a long time [*dim*]

kinwēsk ᑭᓀᐧᐢᐠ
IPC a long while; for a long time [*cf.* kinwēs]

kinwēstawēw ᑭᓀᐧᐢᑕᐍᐤ
VAI he has a long beard [*also* kinostawēw]

kipaham ᑭᐸᐦᐊᒼ
VTI s/he closes s.t., s/he obstructs s.t.

kipahamawēw ᑭᐸᐦᐊᒪᐍᐤ
VTA s/he closes (it/him) for s.o.

kipahāhpowān ᑭᐸᐦᐋᐦᐳᐚᐣ
NI gun wad

kipahikan ᑭᐸᐦᐃᑲᐣ
NI obstruction, dam, weir; cover, lid, stopper; cork

kipahikanihk ᑭᐸᐦᐃᑲᓂᕽ
INM Fort Qu'Appelle, SK; at the weir; jail [*see also* kipahotowikamik]

kipahikanis ᑭᐸᐦᐃᑲᓂᐢ
NI little cork, lid, stopper [*dim*]

kipahikāsow ᑭᐸᐦᐃᑳᓱᐤ
VAI s/he is obstructed, it is closed; s/he is closed in; s/he is in jail

kipahikātēw ᑭᐸᐦᐃᑳᑌᐤ
VII it is closed

kipahipānis ᑭᐸᐦᐃᐹᓂᐢ
NI fontanelle [*soft, boneless area of a baby's skull which later closes by forming bone*]

kipahon ᑭᐸᐦᐅᐣ
NI midriff, diaphragm (between chest and belly) [*cf.* kipahowin]

kipahotowikamik ᑭᐸᐦᐅᑐᐏᑲᒥᐠ
NI jail [*pl*: -wa; *cf.* kipahikanihk]

kipahotowin ᑭᐸᐦᐅᑐᐏᐣ
NI mutual imprisoning; imprisonment

kipahowin ᑭᐸᐦᐅᐏᐣ
NI diaphragm [*cf.* kipahon]

kipahwēw ᑭᐸᐦᐍᐤ
VTA s/he closes s.o. in, s/he imprisons s.o., s/he locks s.o. up

kipahwākan ᑭᐸᐦᐚᑲᐣ
NA prisoner

kipatāhtam ᑭᐸᑖᐦᑕᒼ
VTI s/he is short of breath, s/he is breathless

kipatāhtamowin ᑭᐸᑖᐦᑕᒧᐏᐣ
NI feeling faint; shortness of breath

kipatāmoskawēw ᑭᐸᑖᒧᐢᑲᐍᐤ
VTA s/he cuts off s.o.'s breath by foot or body; smother s.o.

kipāpiskaham ᑭᐹᐱᐢᑲᐦᐊᒼ
VTI s/he locks s.t., s/he bars s.t., s/he closes s.t. with or as a metal

kipāpiskahikan ᑭᐹᐱᐢᑲᐦᐃᑲᐣ
NI lock [*see also* āpāpiskahikan, kaskāpiskahikan]

kipāpiskahikanis ᑭᐹᐱᐢᑲᐦᐃᑲᓂᐢ
NI small lock [*dim*]

kipāpiskahikēw ᑭᐹᐱᐢᑲᐦᐃᑫᐤ
VAI s/he locks (things)

kipāpiskahwēw ᑭᐹᐱᐢᑲᐦᐍᐤ
VTA s/he locks s.o. in

kipēýihtamiskākow ᑭᐯᔩᐦᑕᒥᐢᑳᑯᐤ
VAI s/he over-eats and feels badly

kipi- ᑭᐱ
IPV blocking

kipi-wēpinam ᑭᐱ ᐍᐱᓇᒼ
VTI s/he throws s.t. shut

kipihcipaýiw ᑭᐱᐦᒋᐸᔩᐤ
VII it stops suddenly

kipihcipaýiwin ᑭᐱᐦᒋᐸᔩᐏᐣ
NI stop sign, detour sign

kipihcīw ᑭᐱᐦᒌᐤ
VAI s/he stops, s/he comes to a standstill; s/he quits

kipihkitonēhpisow ᑭᐱᐦᑭᑐᓀᐦᐱᓱᐤ
VAI s/he is tied choking

kipihkitonēhpitisow ᑭᐱᐦᑭᑐᓀᐦᐱᑎᓱᐤ
VAI s/he hangs or chokes him/herself

kipihkitonēnēw ᑭᐱᐦᑭᑐᓀᓀᐤ
VTA s/he strangles s.o. by hand

kipihkwēstēw ᑭᐱᐦᑫᐢᑌᐤ
VII it is loaded

kipihtawakēw ᑭᐱᐦᑕᐘᑫᐤ
VAI s/he is unable to hear, s/he has a blockage of the ear [*see also* kakēpihtēw]

kipihtēw ᑭᐱᐦᑌᐤ
VAI s/he is hard of hearing

kipihtēwin ᑭᐱᐦᑌᐏᐣ
NI deafness

kipihtinam ᑭᐱᐦᑎᓇᒼ
VTI s/he stops s.t. by hand

kipihtinamawēw ᑭᐱᐦᑎᓇᒪᐍᐤ
VTA s/he stops (it/him) for s.o.

kipihtinēw ᑭᐱᐦᑎᓀᐤ
VTA s/he stops s.o. by hand; s/he keeps s.o. in

kipihtowēw ᑭᐱᐦᑐᐍᐤ
VAI s/he stops calling, s/he stops talking

kipihtowēwin ᑭᐱᐦᑐᐍᐏᐣ
NI silence

kipikāpawiw ᑭᐱᑳᐸᐏᐤ
VAI s/he stands in the way

kipipaýiw ᑭᐱᐸᔩᐤ
VII it closes up quickly

kipipitam ᑭᐱᐱᑕᒼ
VTI s/he pulls s.t. shut

kipisiw ᑭᐱᓯᐤ
VAI it is obstructed (*e.g.* pipe)

kipiskam ᑭᐱᐢᑲᒼ
VTI s/he is in the way, s/he blocks the way of s.t.

kipiskawēw ᑭᐱᐢᑲᐍᐤ
VTA s/he blocks the way for s.o. [*cf.* kakēpiskawēw]

kipiskwā ᑭᐱᐢᒁ
IPC in the doorway

kipiskwāhc ᑭᐱᐢᒁᐦᐨ
IPC in the doorway

kipiskwāhtapiw ᑭᐱᐢᒁᐦᑕᐱᐤ
VAI s/he sits blocking the door

kipistanēhwēw ᑭᐱᐢᑕᓀᐦᐍᐤ
VTA s/he gives s.o. a nosebleed by striking with an instrument

kipistanēw ᑭᐱᐢᑕᓀᐤ
VAI s/he has a nose-bleed [*also* kipistaniw; pikistaniw]

kipitōnēw ᑭᐱᑑᓀᐤ
VAI s/he closes his/her own mouth; s/he does not speak

kipitōnēwin ᑭᐱᑑᓀᐏᐣ
NI closure of the mouth; not speaking

kipocāpinēw ᑭᐳᒑᐱᓀᐤ
VTA s/he holds his/her own hands over s.o.'s eyes

kipocāpinisow ᑭᐳᒑᐱᓂᓱᐤ
VAI s/he holds his/her own hands over his/her own eyes

kipocāpiwahpisow ᑭᐳᒑᐱᐘᐦᐱᓱᐤ
VAI s/he is blindfolded [*also* kipwacāpahpisow]

kipocāpiwahpitēw ᑭᐳᒑᐱᐘᐦᐱᑌᐤ
VTA s/he blindfolds s.o. [*also* kipwacāpahpitēw]

kipokin ᑭᐳᑭᐣ
VII it grows shut, it heals

kipokohtākanēpaýiw ᑭᐳᑯᐦᑖᑲᓀᐸᔩᐤ
VAI s/he has laryngitis

kipokwātam ᑭᐳᒁᑕᒼ
VTI s/he sews s.t. closed or together

kipokwātēw ᑭᐳᒁᑌᐤ
VTA s/he sews s.o. closed or together

kiponam ᑭᐳᓇᒼ
VTI s/he covers s.t. with his/her own hand; s/he holds s.t. closed (by hand)

kiponēw ᑭᐳᓀᐤ
VTA s/he holds s.o. in (by hand); s/he closes the outlet blocking s.o. (by hand)

kipopitam ᑭᐳᐱᑕᒼ
VTI s/he pulls s.t. closed quickly

kiposin ᑭᐳᓯᐣ
VAI s/he lies in the passageway; s/he lies so as to block passage

kiposiw ᑭᐳᓯᐤ
VAI it has no opening

kiposkam ᑭᐳᐢᑲᒼ
VTI s/he stands over a hole; s/he blocks s.t. from getting out

kipostaham ᑭᐳᐢᑕᐦᐊᒼ
VTI s/he sews s.t. shut

kipostahikēw ᑭᐳᐢᑕᐦᐃᑫᐤ
VAI s/he sews things shut

kipostahwēw ᑭᐳᐢᑕᐦᐍᐤ
VTA s/he sews s.o. shut

kipotēkātam ᑭᐳᑌᑳᑕᒼ
VTI s/he knocks s.t. over

kipwahpitam ᑭᐘᐦᐱᑕᒼ
VTI s/he ties s.t. closed in (in a sack); s/he pulls s.t. closed

kipwahpitēw ᑭᐘᐦᐱᑌᐤ
VTA s/he ties s.o. closed in (in a sack)

kipwatāmahpisow ᑭᐘᑖᒪᐦᐱᓱᐤ
VAI s/he smothers; s/he has s.t. tied over his/her own mouth

kipwatāmāpasow ᑭᐘᑖᒫᐸᓱᐤ
VAI s/he suffocates with smoke

kipwatāmoskawēw ᑭᐘᑖᒧᐢᑲᐍᐤ
VTA s/he cuts off s.o.'s breath by foot

kipwatāmow ᑭᐘᑖᒧᐤ
VAI s/he smothers, s/he suffocates

kipwāw ᑭᐚᐤ
VII it closes; it has no opening; it is closed

kisācimēw ᑭᓵᒋ�ᒣᐤ
VTA s/he convinces s.o. to stay

kisācimiwēw ᑭᓵᒋᒥᐍᐤ
VAI s/he tells people to stay put

kisācinam ᑭᓵᒋᓇᒼ
VTI s/he keeps s.t. there, s/he refuses to part with s.t. [*cf.* kisātinam]

kisācinēw ᑭᓵᒋᓀᐤ
VTA s/he detains s.o. [*cf.* kisātinēw]

kisākamicēwāpōs ᑭᓵᑲᒥᒉᐚᐴᐢ
NI warm water [*dim*]

kisākamisam ᑭᓵᑲᒥᓴᒼ
VTI s/he heats s.t. up as liquid

kisākamisikan ᑭᓵᑲᒥᓯᑲᐣ
NI tea kettle

kisākamisikēw ᑭᓵᑲᒥᓯᑫᐤ
VAI s/he heats water, s/he heats a liquid; s/he makes tea

kisākamitēhkwēw ᑭᓵᑲᒥᑌᐦᑫᐤ
VAI s/he drinks hot liquid

kisākamitēw ᑭᓵᑲᒥᑌᐤ
VII it is a hot liquid, it is heated (as liquid)

kisākamitēwāpoy ᑭᓵᑲᒥᑌᐚᐳᕀ
NI hot water

kisāpiskisam ᑭᓵᐱᐢᑭᓴᒼ
VTI s/he heats s.t. (*e.g.* metal)

kisāpiskisow ᑭᓵᐱᐢᑭᓱᐤ
VAI it is heated as stone or metal; it is hot metal

kisāpiskiswēw ᑭᓵᐱᐢᑭᐡᐍᐤ
VTA s/he heats s.o. as stone or metal

kisāpiskitēw ᑭᓵᐱᐢᑭᑌᐤ
VII it is hot (*e.g.* metal)

kisāpiskiwān ᐱᓵᐱᐢᑭᐊᐧᐣ
NA heated stone

kisāstaw ᐱᓵᐢᑕᐤ
IPC sort of, kind of, to appearance, by seeming; it might be

kisāstēw ᐱᓵᐢᑌᐤ
VII it is hot weather, it is sultry weather

kisāstēwāpoy ᐱᓵᐢᑌᐊᐧᐳᕀ
NI pop, soft drink [see also sīwāpoy]

kisātam ᐱᓵᑕᒼ
VTI s/he stays by s.t., s/he stays with s.t., s/he holds fast to s.t.

kisātēw ᐱᓵᑌᐤ
VTA s/he stays by s.o. (in spite of choice to leave); s/he stays with s.o., s/he refuses to leave s.o.

kisātinam ᐱᓵᑎᓇᒼ
VTI s/he keeps s.t. there, s/he refuses to part with s.t. [cf. kisātinam]

kisātinēw ᐱᓵᑎᓀᐤ
VTA s/he detains s.o.; s/he keeps s.o. there [cf. kisācinēw]

kisci- ᐱᐢᒋ
IPV big [cf. kihci-]

kiscikānis ᐱᐢᒋᑳᓂᐢ
NA single grain, seed [dim]

kiscikānis ᐱᐢᒋᑳᓂᐢ
NI garden; vegetable, potato [dim; also kistikānis; cf. kistikān]

kiscikēpayīs ᐱᐢᒋᑫᐸᔩᐢ
NI seeder, drill [dim]

kiscikēsiw ᐱᐢᒋᑫᓯᐤ
VAI s/he plants seeds; s/he has a small garden [dim]

kisciýiniw ᐱᐢᒋᔨᓂᐤ
NA old man

kisē- ᐱᓭ
IPV great, gentle

kisē-aya ᐱᓭ ᐊᔭ
NA old person

kisē-manitow ᐱᓭ ᒪᓂᑐᐤ
NA Great Spirit, God; [Christian:] Merciful God

kisē-manitowaskisin ᐱᓭ ᒪᓂᑐᐊᐧᐢᑭᓯᐣ
NI sandal

kisē-manitowi-pīkiskwēwin ᐱᓭ ᒪᓂᑐᐃᐧ ᐲᑭᐢᑫᐧᐃᐧᐣ
NI God's word

kisē-manitōwiw ᐱᓭ ᒪᓂᑑᐃᐧᐤ
VAI s/he is God, s/he is the Great Spirit

kisē-pīsim ᐱᓭ ᐲᓯᒼ
NA Great Moon; January

kisēpānēhkwēw ᐱᓭᐸᓀᐦᑫᐧᐤ
VAI s/he breakfasts, s/he eats breakfast

kisēpānēhkwēwin ᐱᓭᐸᓀᐦᑫᐧᐃᐧᐣ
NI breakfast [see also kīkisēpā-micisowin]

kisēpāyāki ᐱᓭᐸᔮᑭ
IPC in the morning, when it's morning [cf. kīkisēpāyāki]

kisēpāyāw ᐱᓭᐸᔮᐤ
VII it is morning [cf. kīkisēpāyāw]

kisēwātisitotawēw ᐱᓭᐊᐧᑎᓯᑐᑕᐁᐧᐤ
VTA s/he is kind and generous to s.o.

kisēwātisiw ᐱᓭᐊᐧᑎᓯᐤ
VAI s/he is merciful, s/he is kind, s/he is gentle, s/he is of compassionate disposition

kisēwātisiwin ᐱᓭᐊᐧᑎᓯᐃᐧᐣ
NI kindness, compassion, goodness

kisēýiniw ᐱᓭᔨᓂᐤ
NA old man, male elder [cf. -kisēyinim- NDA; in some areas of wC: kisitiniw]

kisēýinīpan ᐱᓭᔨᓃᐸᐣ
NA deceased old man

kisēýinīsis ᐱᓭᔨᓃᓯᐢ
NA little old man [dim]

kisēýinīwatim ᐱᓭᔨᓃᐊᐧᑎᒼ
NA old dog, old horse [pl: -wak]

kisēýinīwānēs ᐱᓭᔨᓃᐊᐧᓀᐢ
NA little old man

kisēýinīwinākosiw ᐱᓭᔨᓃᐊᐧᐃᐧᓈᑯᓯᐤ
VAI he looks old, he looks like an old man

kisēýinīwiw ᐱᓭᔨᓃᐃᐧᐤ
VAI he is an old man

kisik ᐱᓯᐠ
IPC as, while, at the same time, simultaneously; and also, along with

kisin ᐱᓯᐣ
NI the cold [cf. kisin VII]

kisin ᐱᓯᐣ
VII it is cold weather, it is very cold weather [term preferred in Alberta; see also tahkāyāw]

kisināsin ᐱᓯᓈᓯᐣ
VII it is a bit chilly

kisinātin ᐱᓯᓈᑎᐣ
NI cold wind [also kisinatin, kisinōtin]

kisināw ᐱᓯᓈᐤ
VII it is cold weather, it is bitterly cold weather

kisipanohk ᐱᓯᐸᓄᕽ
IPC at the edge, at the end; back up against the wall

kisipaskamikāw ᐱᓯᐸᐢᑲᒥᑳᐤ
VII it is the end of land

kisipayiw ᐱᓯᐸᔨᐤ
VII it ends, it terminates

kisipayiwin ᐱᓯᐸᔨᐃᐧᐣ
NI end, termination

kisipāpēkastāw ᐱᓯᐹᐯᑲᐢᑖᐤ
VAIt s/he places s.t. ending (e.g. string)

kisipāw ᐱᓯᐹᐤ
VII it ends, it terminates

kisipi- ᐱᓯᐱ
IPV end, finish, ending

kisipihkotam ᐱᓯᐱᐦᑯᑕᒼ
VTI s/he whittles s.t. to an end

kisipikahcēw ᐱᓯᐱᑲᐦᒉᐤ
VAI s/he is constipated

kisipikamāw ᐱᓯᐱᑲᒫᐤ
VII it is the end of the lake

kisipipayin ᐱᓯᐱᐸᔨᐣ
VII it comes to an end, it runs out

kisipipitam ᐱᓯᐱᐱᑕᒼ
VTI s/he pulls s.t. (e.g. string) all the way to its end

kisipisiw ᐱᓯᐱᓯᐤ
VAI it ends, it terminates

kisipiskawēw ᐱᓯᐱᐢᑲᐁᐧᐤ
VTA s/he comes to the end of s.o.

kisisam ᐱᓯᓴᒼ
VTI s/he heats s.t. up, s/he warms s.t. up (i.e. food)

kisisamawēw ᐱᓯᓴᒪᐁᐧᐤ
VTA s/he heats (it/him) for s.o.

kisisimēw ᐱᓯᓯᒉᐤ
VTA s/he impales s.o., s/he causes s.o. to get a splinter

kisisin ᐱᓯᓯᐣ
VAI s/he gets a splinter, s/he gets impaled; s/he pierces his/her own skin (e.g. stepping on a nail), s/he suffers pierced skin

kisiskā- ᐱᓯᐢᑳ
IPV fast, quickly

kisiskāciwan ᐱᓯᐢᑳᒋᐊᐧᐣ
VII it flows fast

kisiskāciwani-sīpiy ᐱᓯᐢᑳᒋᐊᐧᓂ ᓰᐱᕀ
NI Saskatchewan River, swift-flowing river

kisiskāhtēw ᐱᓯᐢᑳᐦᑌᐤ
VAI s/he walks fast

kisiskāpahtāw ᐱᓯᐢᑳᐸᐦᑖᐤ
VAI s/he runs fast

kisiskāpayihow ᐱᓯᐢᑳᐸᔨᐦᐅᐤ
VAI s/he moves fast

kisiskāpayiw ᐱᓯᐢᑳᐸᔨᐤ
VAI s/he goes fast

kisisow ᐱᓯᓱᐤ
VAI s/he is warm, s/he is hot; s/he is feverish, have a fever

kisisowāspinēw ᐱᓯᓱᐊᐧᐢᐱᓀᐤ
VAI s/he has pneumonia; s/he has a high fever

kisisowin ᐱᓯᓱᐃᐧᐣ
NI fever; body heat

kisiswēw ᐱᓯᓷᐤ
VTA s/he heats s.o., s/he warms s.o. (i.e. food)

kisitēw ᐱᓯᑌᐤ
VII it is hot

kisiwaskatēskawēw ᑭᓯᐘᐢᑲᑌᐢᑲᐍᐤ
VTA s/he gives s.o. a stomach-ache or indigestion [*commonly inanimate actor*: kisiwaskatēskākow "it gives s.o. indigestion"]
kisiwaskatēw ᑭᓯᐘᐢᑲᑌᐤ
VAI s/he has a stomach-ache, s/he has indigestion [*cf.* māýaskatēw]
kisiwaskatēwin ᑭᓯᐘᐢᑲᑌᐏᐣ
NI colic; indigestion
kisiwāhēw ᑭᓯᐚᐦᐁᐤ
VTA s/he angers s.o., s/he makes s.o. angry
kisiwāk ᑭᓯᐚᐠ
IPC near, nearby, close by
kisiwākiwiw ᑭᓯᐚᑭᐏᐤ
VII it is near, it is nearby, it is close by
kisiwāsihkāsow ᑭᓯᐚᓯᐦᑳᓱᐤ
VAI s/he pretends to be angry
kisiwāsiw ᑭᓯᐚᓯᐤ
VAI s/he is angry
kisiwāsiwin ᑭᓯᐚᓯᐏᐣ
NI anger, wrath
kisiwāsīstawēw ᑭᓯᐚᓰᐢᑕᐍᐤ
VTA s/he is angry at s.o.
kisiwi- ᑭᓯᐏ
IPV anger
kisiwihkwēýiw ᑭᓯᐏᐦᑵᔩᐤ
VAI s/he frowns
kisiwipaýiw ᑭᓯᐏᐸᔩᐤ
VAI s/he gets angry, s/he becomes angry suddenly
kisiwitisahwēw ᑭᓯᐏᑎᓴᐦᐍᐤ
VTA s/he chases s.o. so as to anger that one
kisiwiyow ᑭᓯᐏᔪᐤ
VAI s/he complains about work, s/he is angry about his/her own work
kisīhkwasiw ᑭᓰᐦᑿᓯᐤ
VAI s/he wakes angry
kisīkitotēw ᑭᓰᑭᑐᑌᐤ
VTA s/he speaks to s.o. in anger
kisīkocin ᑭᓰᑯᒋᐣ
VAI s/he flies fast, s/he speeds along
kisīmēw ᑭᓰᒣᐤ
VTA s/he angers s.o. by speech [*also* kisimēw]
kisīmow ᑭᓰᒧᐤ
VAI s/he speaks angrily
kisīpahtāw ᑭᓰᐸᐦᑖᐤ
VAI s/he runs fast, s/he runs quickly
kisīpaýiw ᑭᓰᐸᔩᐤ
VAI s/he goes fast, s/he travels fast, s/he drives fast
kisīpaýiw ᑭᓰᐸᔩᐤ
VII it goes fast, it travels fast
kisīpēkahtakinikēw ᑭᓰᐯᑲᐦᑕᑭᓂᑫᐤ
VAI s/he washes the floor [*also* kisīpēkihtakinikēw]

kisīpēkastēnēw ᑭᓰᐯᑲᐢᑌᓀᐤ
VTA s/he gives s.o. a bath
kisīpēkastēnisow ᑭᓰᐯᑲᐢᑌᓂᓱᐤ
VAI s/he gives him/herself a bath, s/he bathes him/herself
kisīpēkastēwi-mahkahk ᑭᓰᐯᑲᐢᑌᐏ ᒪᐦᑲᐦᐠ
NI bathtub [*pl*: -wa]
kisīpēkāpitēhon ᑭᓰᐯᑳᐱᑌᐦᐅᐣ
NI toothbrush [*cf.* kisīpēkinapitēwākan]
kisīpēkāpitēw ᑭᓰᐯᑳᐱᑌᐤ
VAI s/he brushes his/her own teeth
kisīpēkicihcēnēw ᑭᓰᐯᑭᒋᐦᒉᓀᐤ
VTA s/he washes s.o.'s hands
kisīpēkicihcēw ᑭᓰᐯᑭᒋᐦᒉᐤ
VAI s/he washes his/her own hands
kisīpēkihtakinikēw ᑭᓰᐯᑭᐦᑕᑭᓂᑫᐤ
VAI s/he washes a wooden floor, s/he washes floor-boards; s/he scrubs the floor, s/he scrubs floors [*also* kisēpēkihtakinikēw]
kisīpēkikwayawēw ᑭᓰᐯᑭᑿᔭᐍᐤ
VAI s/he washes his/her own neck
kisīpēkinam ᑭᓰᐯᑭᓇᒼ
VTI s/he washes s.t. (*e.g.* clothing) [*also* kisēpēkinam]
kisīpēkinamawēw ᑭᓰᐯᑭᓇᒪᐍᐤ
VTA s/he washes (it/him) for s.o.
kisīpēkinayiwinisēw ᑭᓰᐯᑭᓇᔨᐏᓂᓭᐤ
VAI s/he washes clothing
kisīpēkināpitēwākan ᑭᓰᐯᑭᓈᐱᑌᐚᑲᐣ
NI toothbrush [*cf.* kisīpēkāpitēhon]
kisīpēkinēw ᑭᓰᐯᑭᓀᐤ
VTA s/he washes s.o.; s/he bathes s.o. [*also* kisēpēkinēw]
kisīpēkini-mahkahk ᑭᓰᐯᑭᓂ ᒪᐦᑲᐦᐠ
NI washer, washing machine [*pl*: -wa]
kisīpēkinicihcēw ᑭᓰᐯᑭᓂᒋᐦᒉᐤ
VAI s/he washes his/her own hands
kisīpēkinikan ᑭᓰᐯᑭᓂᑲᐣ
NI soap [*also* kisēpēkinikan]
kisīpēkinikanihkawēw ᑭᓰᐯᑭᓂᑲᓂᐦᑲᐍᐤ
VTA s/he makes soap for s.o.
kisīpēkinikanihkēw ᑭᓰᐯᑭᓂᑲᓂᐦᑫᐤ
VAI s/he makes soap
kisīpēkinikākan ᑭᓰᐯᑭᓂᑳᑲᐣ
NI washing machine [*see also* kisīpēkinikēpayīs]
kisīpēkinikātēw ᑭᓰᐯᑭᓂᑳᑌᐤ
VII it is washed
kisīpēkinikēpaýīs ᑭᓰᐯᑭᓂᑫᐸᔩᐢ
NI washing machine [*see also* kisīpēkinikākan]

kisīpēkinikēw ᑭᓰᐯᑭᓂᑫᐤ
VAI s/he washes clothes, s/he does laundry [*also* kisēpēkinikēw]
kisīpēkinikēw-mahkahk ᑭᓰᐯᑭᓂᑫᐤ ᒪᐦᑲᐦᐠ
NI washtub [*pl*: -wa]
kisīpēkinikēwikamik ᑭᓰᐯᑭᓂᑫᐏᑲᒥᐠ
NI laundromat [*pl*: -wa]
kisīpēkinikēwin ᑭᓰᐯᑭᓂᑫᐏᐣ
NI laundry, the wash; doing the laundry, clothes-washing [*also* kisēpēkinikēwin]
kisīpēkinisitēw ᑭᓰᐯᑭᓂᓯᑌᐤ
VAI s/he washes his/her own feet
kisīpēkinisow ᑭᓰᐯᑭᓂᓱᐤ
VAI s/he washes him/herself [*also* kisēpēkinisow]
kisīpēkisitēnēw ᑭᓰᐯᑭᓯᑌᓀᐤ
VTA s/he washes s.o.' feet
kisīpēkisitēnisow ᑭᓰᐯᑭᓯᑌᓂᓱᐤ
VAI s/he washes his/her own feet for him/herself
kisīpēkisitēw ᑭᓰᐯᑭᓯᑌᐤ
VAI s/he washes his/her own feet
kisīpēkistikwānākēw ᑭᓰᐯᑭᐢᑎᒁᓈᑫᐤ
VAI s/he washes his/her own head with something, s/he uses something to wash his/her own head
kisīpēkistikwānēnēw ᑭᓰᐯᑭᐢᑎᒁᓀᓀᐤ
VTA s/he washes s.o.'s head
kisīpēkistikwānēw ᑭᓰᐯᑭᐢᑎᒁᓀᐤ
VAI s/he washes his/her own head
kisīpēkiýākanēw ᑭᓰᐯᑭᔮᑲᓀᐤ
VAI s/he washes dishes [*cf.* *wC*: sīpīkithākanīw]
kisīpēkīw ᑭᓰᐯᑮᐤ
VAI s/he bathes
kisīpēýākanikan ᑭᓰᐯᔮᑲᓂᑲᐣ
NI dishwasher
kisīpiciw ᑭᓰᐱᒋᐤ
VAI s/he moves camp fast
kisīstam ᑭᓰᐢᑕᒼ
VTI s/he is angry at s.t.
kisīstawēw ᑭᓰᐢᑕᐍᐤ
VTA s/he is angry with s.o., s/he stays angry with s.o.
kisīstākēwin ᑭᓰᐢᑖᑫᐏᐣ
NI angry mood [*not speaking to anyone*]
kisīstātowak ᑭᓰᐢᑖᑐᐘᐠ
VAI they are angry at one another
kisīstātowin ᑭᓰᐢᑖᑐᐏᐣ
NI mutual ill feeling
kisītāpāsow ᑭᓰᑖᐹᓱᐤ
VAI s/he drives fast
kisīw ᑭᓰᐤ
VAI s/he is cross and guards his/her own young from harm

kisīwē-tēpwēw ᑭᓰᐍ ᑌᐻᐤ
VAI s/he calls loudly

kisīwēw ᑭᓰᐍᐤ
VAI s/he speaks loudly, s/he sings loudly; s/he makes a loud vocalization; s/he speaks angrily

kisīwēyihtam ᑭᓰᐍᔨᐦᑕᒼ
VTI s/he is mentally angry

kisīwi- ᑭᓰᐎ
IPV angrily, in anger

kisīwinākosiw ᑭᓰᐎᓈᑯᓯᐤ
VAI s/he looks angry, s/he appears angry

kisīyāsiw ᑭᓰᔮᓯᐤ
VAI s/he sails fast

kisīyāstan ᑭᓰᔮᐢᑕᐣ
VII it sails fast (in the wind)

kiskahikēw ᑭᐢᑲᐦᐃᑫᐤ
VAI s/he points things out

kiskānak ᑭᐢᑳᓇᐠ
NA bitch [*pl*: -wak]

kiskēyihtam ᑭᐢᑫᔨᐦᑕᒼ
VTI s/he knows s.t., s/he knows s.t. of his/her own experience

kiskēyihtamāsow ᑭᐢᑫᔨᐦᑕᒫᓱᐤ
VAI s/he knows (it) for him/herself

kiskēyihtamāw ᑭᐢᑫᔨᐦᑕᒫᐤ
VAI s/he has spiritual knowledge

kiskēyihtamohēw ᑭᐢᑫᔨᐦᑕᒧᐦᐁᐤ
VTA s/he makes s.o. know (it); s/he makes (it/him) known to s.o.

kiskēyihtamohkāsow ᑭᐢᑫᔨᐦᑕᒧᐦᑳᓱᐤ
VAI s/he pretends to know (s.t.)

kiskēyihtamowin ᑭᐢᑫᔨᐦᑕᒧᐎᐣ
NI knowledge, experience, learning

kiskēyihtākosiw ᑭᐢᑫᔨᐦᑖᑯᓯᐤ
VAI s/he is known

kiskēyihtākwan ᑭᐢᑫᔨᐦᑖᑿᐣ
VII it is known

kiskēyihtowak ᑭᐢᑫᔨᐦᑐᐘᐠ
VAI they know one another

kiskēyimēw ᑭᐢᑫᔨᒣᐤ
VTA s/he knows s.o., s/he knows about s.o.

kiskēyimisowin ᑭᐢᑫᔨᒥᓱᐎᐣ
NI self-knowledge

kiskimēw ᑭᐢᑭᒣᐤ
VTA s/he makes an appointment with s.o.; s/he reminds s.o.

kiskiman ᑭᐢᑭᒪᐣ
NI file, rasp

kiskimanis ᑭᐢᑭᒪᓂᐢ
NI small file [*dim*]

kiskimow ᑭᐢᑭᒧᐤ
VAI s/he makes an appointment

kiskinawācihcikācēsiw ᑭᐢᑭᓇᐚᒋᐦᒋᑳᒉᓯᐤ
VII it is made symbolically, it is a manufactured little image [*dim*]

kiskinawācihon ᑭᐢᑭᓇᐚᒋᐦᐅᐣ
NI emblem

kiskinawācihowinis ᑭᐢᑭᓇᐚᒋᐦᐅᐎᓂᐢ
NI decorative, symbolic jewellry [*dim*]

kiskinawācihōkispison ᑭᐢᑭᓇᐚᒋᐦᐆᑭᐢᐱᓱᐣ
NA bracelet, charm-bracelet

kiskinawācihtāw ᑭᐢᑭᓇᐚᒋᐦᑖᐤ
VAIt s/he puts a mark on s.t.

kiskinoham ᑭᐢᑭᓄᐦᐊᒼ
VTI s/he marks s.t.; s/he guides s.t.; s/he points s.t. out

kiskinohtahēw ᑭᐢᑭᓄᐦᑕᐦᐁᐤ
VTA s/he shows s.o. the way; s/he guides s.o., s/he directs s.o.; s/he gives s.o. directions

kiskinohtahiwēw ᑭᐢᑭᓄᐦᑕᐦᐃᐍᐤ
VAI s/he guides, s/he guides people [*also* kiskinōhtahiwēw]

kiskinowācihcikan ᑭᐢᑭᓄᐚᒋᐦᒋᑲᐣ
NI beacon light, sign

kiskinowācihēw ᑭᐢᑭᓄᐚᒋᐦᐁᐤ
VTA s/he decorates s.o. to be seen; s/he puts a sign on s.o. to be known

kiskinowācihon ᑭᐢᑭᓄᐚᒋᐦᐅᐣ
NI rosette, flower as lapel decoration

kiskinowācihtamawēw ᑭᐢᑭᓄᐚᒋᐦᑕᒪᐍᐤ
VTA s/he decorates (it/him) for s.o.

kiskinowācihtawēw ᑭᐢᑭᓄᐚᒋᐦᑕᐍᐤ
VTA s/he decorates (it/him) for s.o.

kiskinowācihtāw ᑭᐢᑭᓄᐚᒋᐦᑖᐤ
VAIt s/he decorates s.t. to be seen

kiskinowāpahkēw ᑭᐢᑭᓄᐚᐸᐦᑫᐤ
VAI s/he looks on at people to learn

kiskinowāpahtam ᑭᐢᑭᓄᐚᐸᐦᑕᒼ
VTI s/he learns by watching s.t., s/he looks on to learn s.t.

kiskinowāpahtihēw ᑭᐢᑭᓄᐚᐸᐦᑎᐦᐁᐤ
VTA s/he teaches s.o. by example, s/he teaches s.o. by showing the way; s/he sets an example for s.o. by his/her own conduct; s/he shows s.o. by example

kiskinowāpahtihiwēw ᑭᐢᑭᓄᐚᐸᐦᑎᐦᐃᐍᐤ
VAI s/he teaches people by example, s/he teaches by showing the way

kiskinowāpahtihiwēwin ᑭᐢᑭᓄᐚᐸᐦᑎᐦᐃᐍᐎᐣ
NI example

kiskinowāpamēw ᑭᐢᑭᓄᐚᐸᒣᐤ
VTA s/he learns from watching s.o., s/he learns from observing s.o.; s/he imitates s.o., s/he uses s.o.'s tactics; s/he watches s.o.'s example

kiskinowāpiw ᑭᐢᑭᓄᐚᐱᐤ
VAI s/he observes, s/he learns by observing

kiskinowātasinaham ᑭᐢᑭᓄᐚᑕᓯᓇᐦᐊᒼ
VTI s/he writes the original copy; s/he writes s.t. as the original copy; s/he writes s.t. as teaching material

kiskinowātasinahikan ᑭᐢᑭᓄᐚᑕᓯᓇᐦᐃᑲᐣ
NI original example, teaching material, textbook

kiskinowātasinahikēw ᑭᐢᑭᓄᐚᑕᓯᓇᐦᐃᑫᐤ
VAI s/he writes the original copy, s/he writes teaching material

kiskinwahamawākan ᑭᐢᑭᓌᐦᐊᒪᐚᑲᐣ
NA student [*cf.* okiskinahamawākan; *also* kiskinahamawākan, kiskinohamawākan]

kiskinwahamawēw ᑭᐢᑭᓌᐦᐊᒪᐍᐤ
VTA s/he teaches s.o., s/he teaches (it) to s.o. [*also* kiskinahamawēw, kiskinohamawēw]

kiskinwahamākēw ᑭᐢᑭᓌᐦᐊᒫᑫᐤ
NA teacher [*cf.* okiskinwahamākēw; *also* kiskinahamākēw, kiskinohamākēw]

kiskinwahamākēw ᑭᐢᑭᓌᐦᐊᒫᑫᐤ
VAI s/he teaches, s/he teaches things, s/he teaches (it) to people [*also* kiskinahamākēw, kiskinohamākēw]

kiskinwahamākēwikamik ᑭᐢᑭᓌᐦᐊᒫᑫᐎᑲᒥᐠ
NI school building [*pl*: -wa; *also* kiskinohamākēwikamik]

kiskinwahamākēwikamikohkēw ᑭᐢᑭᓌᐦᐊᒫᑫᐎᑲᒥᑯᐦᑫᐤ
VAI s/he builds a school [*also* kiskinohamākēwikamikohkēw]

kiskinwahamākēwin ᑭᐢᑭᓌᐦᐊᒫᑫᐎᐣ
NI teaching, education; lessons, instructions [*also* kiskinohamākēwin]

kiskinwahamākēwiskwēw ᑭᐢᑭᓌᐦᐊᒫᑫᐎᐢᑵᐤ
NA school mistress [*also* kiskinohamākēwiskwēw]

kiskinwahamākosiw
ᐱᐢᑭᓇᐧᐊᒫᑯᓯᐤ
VAI s/he learns; s/he is a
student, s/he attends school;
s/he is taught [*also*
kiskinahamākosiw,
kiskinohamākosiw]

kiskinwahamākosiwin
ᐱᐢᑭᓇᐧᐊᒫᑯᓯᐃᐧᐣ
NI learning, being a student,
attending school;
schoolwork, homework [*also*
kiskinohamākosiwin]

kiskinwahamākowisiw
ᐱᐢᑭᓇᐧᐊᒫᑯᐃᐧᓯᐤ
VAI s/he is taught by higher
powers

kiskinwahamāsow ᐱᐢᑭᓇᐧᐊᒫᓱᐤ
VAI s/he is taught, s/he is in
school, s/he attends school,
s/he is a student; s/he teaches
(it to) him/herself [*also*
kiskinohamāsow]

kiskinwahamāsowin
ᐱᐢᑭᓇᐧᐊᒫᓱᐃᐧᐣ
NI self instruction

kiskinwahamātowak
ᐱᐢᑭᓇᐧᐊᒫᑐᐊᐧᐠ
VAI they teach (it to) one
another [*also*
kiskinohamātowak]

kiskinwahamātowikamik
ᐱᐢᑭᓇᐧᐊᒫᑐᐃᐧᑲᒥᐠ
NI school, school-house [*pl*:
-wa; *also*
kiskinahamātowikamik,
kiskinohamātowikamik]

kiskinwahamātowin
ᐱᐢᑭᓇᐧᐊᒫᑐᐃᐧᐣ
NI teaching one another,
learning; education [*also*
kiskinohamātowin]

kiskinwahamātōtāpānāsk
ᐱᐢᑭᓇᐧᐊᒫᑑᑖᐹᓈᐢᐠ
NA school bus [*pl*: -wak;
also kiskinohamātōtāpānāsk]

kiskinwahamāwasow
ᐱᐢᑭᓇᐧᐊᒫᐊᐧᓱᐤ
VAI s/he teaches (his/her
own) children

kiskinwāswēwitam
ᐱᐢᑭᓈᐢᐤᐁᐧᐃᐧᑕᒼ
VTI s/he speaks in a manner
to refer to the teachings of a
ceremony

kiskisis ᐱᐢᑭᓯᐢ
NA female animal, mare

kiskisitotam ᐱᐢᑭᓯᑐᑕᒼ
VTI s/he remembers s.t.

kiskisitotawēw ᐱᐢᑭᓯᑐᑕᐁᐧᐤ
VTA s/he remembers s.o.,
s/he remembers (it) about
s.o.; s/he remind s.o. of
something [*cf.*
kiskisototawēw]

kiskisiw ᐱᐢᑭᓯᐤ
VAI s/he remembers, s/he
remembers s.t.; s/he recalls

kiskisiwin ᐱᐢᑭᓯᐃᐧᐣ
NI remembrance, memory

kiskisohtowak ᐱᐢᑭᓲᐟᑐᐊᐧᐠ
VAI they remind one another

kiskisomēw ᐱᐢᑭᓲᒣᐤ
VTA s/he reminds s.o. [*also*
kiskisōmēw]

kiskisomitowak ᐱᐢᑭᓲᒥᑐᐊᐧᐠ
VAI they remind one another
[*also* kiskisōmitowak]

kiskisomitowin ᐱᐢᑭᓲᒥᑐᐃᐧᐣ
NI reminder

kiskisopayiw ᐱᐢᑭᓱᐸᔨᐤ
VAI s/he recollects, s/he
thinks of something, s/he
suddenly remembers

kiskisopayiwin ᐱᐢᑭᓱᐸᔨᐃᐧᐣ
NI recollections

kiskisototawēw ᐱᐢᑭᓱᑐᑕᐁᐧᐤ
VTA s/he remembers s.o. [*cf.*
kiskisitotawēw]

kiskiwēham ᐱᐢᑭᐁᐧᐦᐊᒼ
VTI s/he utters s.t. as a
prophecy, s/he utters
prophecies

kiskiwēhamāsow ᐱᐢᑭᐁᐧᐦᐊᒫᓱᐤ
VAI s/he marks (it) for
him/herself (*i.e.* in the bush)

kiskiwēhon ᐱᐢᑭᐁᐧᐦᐊᐣ
NI flag [*cf.* kiskiwēkin]

kiskiwēhonāhtik ᐱᐢᑭᐁᐧᐦᐊᓈᐦᑎᐠ
NA flagstaff [*pl*: -wak]

kiskiwēhwēw ᐱᐢᑭᐁᐧᐦᐊᐧᐤ
VTA s/he utters prophecies
to s.o., s/he utters prophecies
about s.o.

kiskiwēkin ᐱᐢᑭᐁᐧᑭᐣ
NI flag [*pl*: -wa; *cf.*
kiskiwēhon]

kisowi-kanawāpahtam
ᐱᓱᐃᐧᑲᓇᐋᐧᐸᐦᑕᒼ
VTI s/he frowns at s.t.

kisowi-kanawāpamēw
ᐱᓱᐃᐧᑲᓇᐋᐧᐸᒣᐤ
VTA s/he frowns at s.o.

kisowinākosiw ᐱᓱᐃᐧᓈᑯᓯᐤ
VAI s/he frowns

kispakahcīw ᐱᐢᐸᑲᐦᕀᐤ
VAI s/he is constipated

kispakasākay ᐱᐢᐸᑲᓵᑲᐩ
NI thick coat

kispakasēw ᐱᐢᐸᑲᓭᐤ
VAI s/he has thick skin

kispakaskitēw ᐱᐢᐸᑲᐢᑭᑌᐤ
VII it stands, it grows thick
(*e.g.* crop of grain)

kispakatin ᐱᐢᐸᑲᑎᐣ
VII it is frozen thick; it is
thick ice

kispakākamihtāw ᐱᐢᐸᑳᑲᒥᐦᑖᐤ
VAIt s/he thickens s.t.

kispakākamin ᐱᐢᐸᑳᑲᒥᐣ
VII it is a thick liquid

kispakākamisin ᐱᐢᐸᑳᑲᒥᓯᐣ
VII it is a rather thick liquid

kispakāpiskāw ᐱᐢᐸᑳᐱᐢᑳᐤ
VII it is a piece of thick
metal

kispakāpiskisiw ᐱᐢᐸᑳᐱᐢᑭᓯᐤ
VAI it is thick metal (*e.g.*
stove)

kispakāw ᐱᐢᐸᑳᐤ
VII it is thick

kispakēkan ᐱᐢᐸᑫᑲᐣ
VII it is thick (e.g. cloth,
paper)

kispakēkihtin ᐱᐢᐸᑫᑭᐦᑎᐣ
VII it lies in thick folds

kispakēkin ᐱᐢᐸᑫᑭᐣ
NI thick cloth

kispakihtin ᐱᐢᐸᑭᐦᑎᐣ
VII it lies thick

kispakikwātam ᐱᐢᐸᑭᒁᑕᐣ
VTI s/he sews s.t. thickly

kispakisiw ᐱᐢᐸᑭᓯᐤ
VAI s/he is thick

kispakiwēsākay ᐱᐢᐸᑭᐧᐁᓵᑲᐩ
NI thick coat

kispēwātam ᐱᐢᐯᐋᐧᑕᐨ
VTI s/he defends s.t., s/he is
overprotective of s.t.

kispēwātēw ᐱᐢᐯᐋᐧᑌᐤ
VTA s/he defends s.o., s/he
is overprotective of s.o.

kispēwēw ᐱᐢᐯᐁᐧᐤ
VAI s/he defends, s/he is
overpotective of his/her own
children

kispēwēwin ᐱᐢᐯᐁᐧᐃᐧᐣ
NI defence

kistahiyākanēw ᐱᐢᑕᐦᐃᔮᑲᓀᐤ
VAI s/he washes dishes, s/he
wipes dishes [*also*
kicistahiyākanēw]

kistapinān ᐱᐢᑕᐱᓈᐣ
NI Prince Albert, SK [*place
name; cf.* kistapinānihk]

kistapinānihk ᐱᐢᑕᐱᓈᓂᕽ
INM Prince Albert, SK [*loc*]

kistataham ᐱᐢᑕᑕᐦᐊᐨ
VTI s/he forces s.t. into the
ground (by tool)

kistatahikan ᐱᐢᑕᑕᐦᐃᑲᐣ
NI picket, post [*something
pounded into the ground*]

kistatāham ᐱᐢᐨᑕᐦᐊᐨ
VTI s/he makes a beaten
path

kistatamon ᐱᐢᐨᑕᒧᐣ
VII it is well-beaten (*i.e.* a
path)

kistāpawacikēw ᐱᐢᐨᐸᐊᐧᒋᑫᐤ
VAI s/he does washing, s/he
washes, s/he wipes [*also*
kicistāpawacikēw]

kistāpawatāw ᐱᐢᐨᐸᐊᐧᑖᐤ
VAIt s/he washes s.t. [*also*
kicistāpawatāw]

kistāpawayēw ᐱᐢᐨᐸᐊᐧᔦᐤ
VTA s/he washes s.o. [*also*
kicistāpawayēw]

kistāpawayōw ᐱᐢᐨᐸᐊᐧᔫᐤ
VAI s/he washes him/herself
[*also* kicistāpawayōw]

kistāpitēhow ᐱᐢᐨᐱᑌᐦᐅᐤ
VAI s/he cleans his/her own
teeth [*also* kicistāpitēhow]

kistēýihtam ᑭᐢᑌᕀᐦᑕᒼᐨ
VTI s/he has high regard for s.t.; s/he respects s.t., s/he esteems s.t., s/he glorifies s.t.

kistēýihtākosiw ᑭᐢᑌᕀᐦᑖᑯᓯᐤ
VAI s/he is well-respected, s/he is highly thought of; s/he is important

kistēýihtākwan ᑭᐢᑌᕀᐦᑖᑲᐧᐣ
VII it is highly thought of, it is important

kistēýikomēhisow ᑭᐢᑌᕀᑯᒣᐦᓱᐤ
VAI s/he wipes his/her own nose [*also* kicistēyikomēsow]

kistēýimēw ᑭᐢᑌᕀᒣᐤ
VTA s/he respects s.o., s/he esteems s.o., s/he glorifies s.o.; s/he has high regard for s.o.

kistēýimow ᑭᐢᑌᕀᒧᐤ
VAI s/he is conceited, s/he is proud [*see also* kihcēyimow]

kistēýimowin ᑭᐢᑌᕀᒧᐊᐧᐣ
NI pride, self-esteem

kistihtakinikēw ᑭᐢᑎᐦᑕᑭᓂᑫᐤ
VAI s/he scrubs the floor [*also* kicistihtakinikēw]

kistikācikan ᑭᐢᑎᑳᒋᑲᐣ
NI seed, plant for transplanting

kistikān ᑭᐢᑎᑳᐣ
NA grain, wheat, seed; sheaf of grain [*cf. dim*: kiscikānis]

kistikān ᑭᐢᑎᑳᐣ
NI field, arable land; farm; garden [*cf. dim*: kiscikānis]

kistikān-āpacihcikan ᑭᐢᑎᑳᐣ ᐋᐸᒋᐦᒋᑲᐣ
NI garden tool

kistikānikamik ᑭᐢᑎᑳᓂᑲᒥᐠ
NI grain elevator, granary [*pl*: -wa]

kistikātam ᑭᐢᑎᑳᑕᒼᐨ
VTI s/he plants s.t., s/he sows s.t.

kistikātamawēw ᑭᐢᑎᑳᑕᒪᐌᐤ
VTA s/he plants (it/him) for s.o.

kistikātēw ᑭᐢᑎᑳᑌᐤ
VII it is planted

kistikātēw ᑭᐢᑎᑳᑌᐤ
VTA s/he plants s.o., s/he sows s.o.

kistikēw ᑭᐢᑎᑫᐤ
VAI s/he farms; s/he plants things, s/he seeds things; s/he harvests

kistikēwin ᑭᐢᑎᑫᐏᐣ
NI farming

kistikēwiýiniw ᑭᐢᑎᑫᐏᔨᓂᐤ
NA farmer, farm instructor

kistikēwiýiniwiw ᑭᐢᑎᑫᐏᔨᓂᐃᐧᐤ
VAI he is a farmer

kistonēwēw ᑭᐢᑐᓀᐌᐤ
VAI s/he washes his/her own mouth, s/he has a mouthwash

kistonēwēwin ᑭᐢᑐᓀᐌᐏᐣ
NI mouthwash

kiswāspinēw ᑭᐢᐧᐋᐢᐱᓀᐤ
VAI s/he has typhoid fever

kita- ᑭᑕ
IPV [*grammatical preverb*; *future*: "will, shall"; *infinitive*; *optative*: "ought, should"; *cf*. ka-, kika-, ta-, tita-]

kita-kī- ᑭᑕ ᑮ
IPV can, be able to; may; ought to [*cf*. ka-kī-, ta-kī-]

kitahamawēw ᑭᑕᐦᐊᒪᐌᐤ
VTA s/he warns s.o. against (it/him), s/he advises s.o. against (it/him); s/he forbids (it to) s.o.; s/he disciplines s.o. (*i.e*. children)

kitahamākēw ᑭᑕᐦᐊᒫᑫᐤ
VAI s/he forbids people, s/he forbids (things); s/he disciplines children

kitahamāwēw ᑭᑕᐦᐊᒫᐌᐤ
VAI s/he forbids; s/he disciplines

kitamawēw ᑭᑕᒪᐌᐤ
VTA s/he eats it all on s.o.

kitamwēw ᑭᑕᒷᐤ
VTA s/he eats s.o. up, s/he eats all of s.o.; s/he smokes s.o. done

kitatamihin ᑭᑕᑕᒥᐦᐃᐣ
IPC thank you, you make me smile, you please me [*cf*. atamihēw *VTA*; *see also* kinanāskomitin]

kitānawēw ᑭᑖᓇᐌᐤ
VAI s/he eats all of it, s/he eats all of his/her own food

kitāpahkan ᑭᑖᐸᐦᑲᐣ
NI spyglass

kitāpahkēw ᑭᑖᐸᐦᑫᐤ
VAI s/he looks at people

kitāpahtam ᑭᑖᐸᐦᑕᒼᐨ
VTI s/he looks at s.t.

kitāpahtamākēw ᑭᑖᐸᐦᑕᒫᑫᐤ
VAI s/he looks at (it) for people

kitāpamēw ᑭᑖᐸᒣᐤ
VTA s/he looks at s.o.

kitāpaminākosiw ᑭᑖᐸᒥᓈᑯᓯᐤ
VAI s/he appears as when looked at

kitāpaýihtamawēw ᑭᑖᐸᔨᐦᑕᒪᐌᐤ
VTA s/he eats (it/him) up on s.o.

kitāpaýihtāw ᑭᑖᐸᔨᐦᑖᐤ
VAIt s/he swallows all of s.t.

kitāstapiwēw ᑭᑖᐢᑕᐱᐌᐤ
VAI s/he goes along rapidly

kitāw ᑭᑖᐤ
VAIt s/he eats all of s.t.; s/he eats s.t. up, s/he devours s.t. completely; s/he eats all of the food

kitimahēw ᑭᑎᒪᐦᐁᐧ
VTA s/he is rough on s.o.; s/he treats s.o. badly; s/he is

mean to s.o.; s/he ruins s.o., s/he reduces s.o. to ruin, s/he destroys s.o.

kitimahihkaswēw ᑭᑎᒪᐦᐃᐦᑲᓴᐌᐤ
VTA s/he burns s.o. to ruin

kitimahisow ᑭᑎᒪᐦᐃᓱᐤ
VAI s/he ruins him/herself

kitimahitowak ᑭᑎᒪᐦᐃᑐᐊᐧᐠ
VAI they are rough on one another; they treat one another badly; they are mean to one another; they ruin one another

kitimahow ᑭᑎᒪᐦᐅᐤ
VAI s/he is rough on him/herself, s/he ruins him/herself

kitimākan ᑭᑎᒫᑲᐣ
VII it is a state of destitution, it is a poor area

kitimākaskatēw ᑭᑎᒫᑲᐢᑲᑌᐤ
VTA s/he outruns s.o. in pitiful way

kitimākawāsis ᑭᑎᒫᑲᐚᓯᐢ
NA poor child

kitimākāpēw ᑭᑎᒫᑳᐯᐤ
NA poor man [*cf*. kitimāki-nāpēw]

kitimākēýihcikēw ᑭᑎᒫᑫᔨᐦᒋᑫᐤ
VAI s/he feels sorry for others

kitimākēýihcikēwin ᑭᑎᒫᑫᔨᐦᒋᑫᐏᐣ
NI compassion; pity

kitimākēýihtam ᑭᑎᒫᑫᔨᐦᑕᒼᐨ
VTI s/he takes pity on s.t.

kitimākēýihtākosiw ᑭᑎᒫᑫᔨᐦᑖᑯᓯᐤ
VAI s/he is pitiable

kitimākēýihtowak ᑭᑎᒫᑫᔨᐦᑐᐊᐧᐠ
VAI they are kind to one another, they love one another; they feel pity towards one another

kitimākēýihtowin ᑭᑎᒫᑫᔨᐦᑐᐃᐧᐣ
NI being kind to one another, loving one another; feeling pity towards one another

kitimākēýimēw ᑭᑎᒫᑫᔨᒣᐤ
VTA s/he pities s.o., s/he takes pity on s.o.; s/he feels sorry for s.o.; s/he has sympathy for s.o.; s/he loves s.o.; s/he blesses s.o.

kitimākēýimisow ᑭᑎᒫᑫᔨᒥᓱᐤ
VAI s/he feels sorry for him/herself

kitimākēýimisowin ᑭᑎᒫᑫᔨᒥᓱᐃᐧᐣ
NI self-pity

kitimākēýimow ᑭᑎᒫᑫᔨᒧᐤ
VAI s/he feels pitiable, s/he feels sorry for him/herself, s/he takes pity on him/herself

kitimākēýimowin ᑭᑎᒫᑫᔨᒧᐊᐧᐣ
NI sympathy

kitimāki- ᐲᓂᒫᑊ
IPV pitiable, pitiably

kitimāki-nāpēw ᐲᓂᒫᑊ ᐋᐯᐤ
NA poor man [cf. kitimākāpēw]

kitimāki-ohpikihēw ᐲᓂᒫᑉᐤᐱᑭᐦᐁᐤ
VTA s/he raises s.o. in poverty; s/he raises s.o. as an orphan [also kitimāk-ōhpikihēw]

kitimākihitowak ᐲᓂᒫᑊᐦᐃᑐᐊᐠ
VAI they make one another miserable; they are mean to one another

kitimākihtamēw ᐲᓂᒫᑊᐦᑕᒣᐤ
VTA s/he hears s.o. with pity; s/he feels sorry for s.o. upon hearing circumstances

kitimākihtākosiw ᐲᓂᒫᑊᐦᑖᑯᓯᐤ
VAI s/he sounds pitiable

kitimākimēw ᐲᓂᒫᑭᒣᐤ
VTA s/he belittles s.o.

kitimākinawēw ᐲᓂᒫᑭᓇᐌᐤ
VTA s/he pities s.o., s/he looks with pity upon s.o.; s/he lovingly tends s.o.; s/he regards s.o. with respect

kitimākinākēw ᐲᓂᒫᑭᓈᑫᐤ
VAI s/he sympathizes

kitimākinākēwin ᐲᓂᒫᑭᓈᑫᐏᐣ
NI compassion, sympathy

kitimākinākosiw ᐲᓂᒫᑭᓈᑯᓯᐤ
VAI s/he looks pitiable, s/he appears pitiful

kitimākinākowisiw ᐲᓂᒫᑭᓈᑯᐏᓯᐤ
VAI s/he is pitied by higher powers

kitimākināsow ᐲᓂᒫᑭᓈᓱᐤ
VAI s/he pities him/herself, s/he feels sorry for him/herself

kitimākisiw ᐲᓂᒫᑭᓯᐤ
VAI s/he is poor, s/he is pitiable, s/he is unfortunate

kitimākisiwin ᐲᓂᒫᑭᓯᐏᐣ
NI poverty

kitimākiýiniw ᐲᓂᒫᑭᕀᓂᐤ
NA poor, bereaved, crippled, poverty-stricken man

kitinēw ᐲᓂᓀᐤ
VTA s/he holds s.o. back

kitiskahwēw ᐲᓂᐢᑲᐦᐌᐤ
VTA s/he grazes s.o. with a shot

kitiskatahwēw ᐲᓂᐢᑲᑕᐦᐌᐤ
VTA s/he hits s.o. a glancing blow

kitiskinam ᐲᓂᐢᑭᓇᐢ
VTI s/he drops s.t. accidentally [cf. kiciskinam]

kitiskinēw ᐲᓂᐢᑭᓀᐤ
VTA s/he drops s.o. accidentally; s/he fumble s.o. (e.g. ball) [cf. kiciskinēw]

kitiskipayēw ᐲᓂᐢᑭᐸᔦᐤ
VTA s/he escapes from s.o.'s grasp

kitiskipitam ᐲᓂᐢᑭᐱᑕᒼ
VTI s/he has s.t. slip from his/her own hand; s/he fails to catch s.t.

kitiskipitamawēw ᐲᓂᐢᑭᐱᑕᒪᐌᐤ
VTA s/he pulls (it/him) from s.o.

kitohēw ᐲᑐᐦᐁᐤ
VTA s/he makes s.o. call out (as a bird or animal); s/he makes s.o. sound (car, horn, etc.)

kitohcikan ᐲᑐᐦᒋᑲᐣ
NI musical instrument; radio

kitohcikan kā-natohtamihk ᐲᑐᐦᒋᑲᐣ ᑳ ᓇᑐᐦᑕᒥᕽ
INM radio [cf. natohtam]

kitohcikanāhtik ᐲᑐᐦᒋᑲᓈᐦᑎᐠ
NI fiddle bow [pl: -wa]

kitohcikanēyāpiy ᐲᑐᐦᒋᑲᓀᔮᐱᕀ
NI guitar string, violin string

kitohcikanihkēw ᐲᑐᐦᒋᑲᓂᐦᑫᐤ
VAI s/he makes musical instruments

kitohcikanis ᐲᑐᐦᒋᑲᓂᐢ
NI flute; small musical instrument [dim; also kicohcikanis]

kitohcikēsiw ᐲᑐᐦᒋᑫᓯᐤ
VAI s/he plays a little on a musical instrument [dim]

kitohcikēskiw ᐲᑐᐦᒋᑫᐢᑭᐤ
VAI s/he plays often on a musical instrument [hab]

kitohcikēw ᐲᑐᐦᒋᑫᐤ
VAI s/he makes music, s/he plays a musical instrument

kitohcikēwin ᐲᑐᐦᒋᑫᐏᐣ
NI music

kitohtākan ᐲᑐᐦᑖᑲᐣ
NI organ (musical instrument)

kitohtāw ᐲᑐᐦᑖᐤ
VAIt s/he plays music on s.t.

kitosiwēw ᐲᑐᓯᐌᐤ
VAI s/he talks to people

kitotam ᐲᑐᑕᒼ
VTI s/he addresses s.t., s/he talk to s.t., s/he speaks to s.t.

kitotēw ᐲᑐᑌᐤ
VTA s/he addresses s.o., s/he talks to s.o., s/he speaks to s.o., s/he lectures s.o. [also kitōtēw]

kitotitowak ᐲᑐᑎᑐᐊᐠ
VAI they talk to one another

kitow ᐲᑐᐤ
VAI it makes a sound, it utters a sound, it calls, it cries, it hoots, it make noises (e.g. a bird or animal) [cf. kāh-kitow]

kitowē-āciwasow ᐲᑐᐍ ᐋᒋᐊᓱᕀ
VII it boils hard (so the cover rattles); it whistles in boiling

kitowē-āpiskahikan ᐲᑐᐍ ᐋᐱᐢᑲᐦᐃᑲᐣ
NI sounding metal

kitowēhkwāmiw ᐲᑐᐍᐦᒁᒥᐤ
VAI s/he snores

kitowēhtāw ᐲᑐᐍᐦᑖᐤ
VAIt s/he makes noise (on s.t.)

kitowēw ᐲᑐᐍᐤ
VII it makes a sound; a sound is heard

kitowēýēkāstan ᐲᑐᐍᔦᑳᐢᑕᐣ
VII it flaps noisily as cloth

kitowin ᐲᑐᐃᐣ
NI cry, call (of a bird or animal)

kitōpicikākan ᐲᑘᐱᒋᑳᑲᐣ
NA horn (musical instrument)

kiýa ᑭᕀ
PR you [second person sg; wC: kītha, sC: kina]

kiýa māka ᑭᕀ ᒫᑲ
IPH and you?

kiýakasēw ᑭᕀᑲᓭᐤ
VAI s/he has eczema; s/he has the itch, s/he has scabies [also kēýakasēw]

kiýakāspinēw ᑭᕀᑳᐢᐱᓀᐤ
VAI s/he has the itch [also kēýakāspinēw]

kiýakicēnēw ᑭᕀᑭᒉᓀᐤ
VTA s/he tickles s.o. [also kēýakicēnēw]

kiýakicihcēw ᑭᕀᑭᒋᐦᒉᐤ
VAI s/he has itchy hands [also kēýakicihcēw]

kiýakihtawakēw ᑭᕀᑭᐦᑕᐊᑫᐤ
VAI s/he has itchy ears [also kēýakihtawakēw]

kiýakinēw ᑭᕀᑭᓀᐤ
VTA s/he tickles s.o. [also kēýakinēw]

kiýakisitēw ᑭᕀᑭᓯᑌᐤ
VAI s/he has itchy feet [also kēýakisitēw]

kiýakisiw ᑭᕀᑭᓯᐤ
VAI s/he itches, s/he is itchy [also kēýakisiw]

kiýakisiwin ᑭᕀᑭᓯᐏᐣ
NI itchiness; seven-year itch [also kēýakisiwin]

kiýakistikwānēw ᑭᕀᑭᐢᑎᒁᓀᐤ
VAI s/he has an itchy head [also kēýakistikwānēw]

kiýaskoc ᑭᕀᐢᑯᐨ
IPC your turn [cf. kiýaskot]

kiýaskociwāw ᑭᕀᐢᑯᒋᐋᐤ
IPC your (pl) turn

kiýaskot ᑭᕀᐢᑯᐟ
IPC your turn [cf. kiýaskoc]

kiýatowahk ᑭᕀᑐᐊᕽ
IPC your sort [cf. kiýa itowahk]

kiýawāw ᑭᕀᐋᐤ
PR you [second person pl]

kiýām ᑭᕀᒼ
IPC oh well, it's okay, never

mind, think nothing of it; so
much for this; anyway,
rather; let it be, let there be
no further delay; please; let's
go then; do so; quietly

kiyām āta ᑭᔭᒻ ᐋᑕ
IPH even though

kiyāmapihēw ᑭᔭᒪᐱᐦᐁᐤ
VTA s/he makes s.o. sit still

kiyāmapiw ᑭᔭᒪᐱᐤ
VAI s/he is quiet, s/he keeps
quiet, s/he sits quietly, s/he
sits still [*from:* kiyām api
"nevermind, sit!"]

kiyāmatapiw ᑭᔭᒪᑕᐱᐤ
VAI s/he sits still

kiyāmayāwin ᑭᔭᒪᔭᐃᐧᐣ
NI stillness

kiyāmēwan ᑭᔭᒣᐊᐧᐣ
VII it is a quiet, peaceful
area

kiyāmēwisiw ᑭᔭᒣᐃᐧᓯᐤ
VAI s/he is bashful; s/he is
of a quiet, peaceful nature;
s/he does not fool around

kiyāmēwisiwin ᑭᔭᒣᐃᐧᓯᐃᐧᐣ
NI peacefulness, quietness

kiyāmēyihtākosiw ᑭᔭᒣᔨᐦᑖᑯᓯᐤ
VAI s/he is known to be
quiet

kiyāmihkwāmiw ᑭᔭᒥᐦᒁᒥᐤ
VAI s/he sleeps quietly

kiyāmikāpawiw ᑭᔭᒥᑳᐸᐃᐧᐤ
VAI s/he stands quietly

kiyānaw ᑭᔭᓇᐤ
PR we, us; we-and-you [*first
person pl inclusive*]

kiyāpac ᑭᔭᐸᐨ
IPC more, still [*cf.* kēyāpic]

kiyāsk ᑭᔭᐢᐠ
NA sea gull [*pl:* -wak]

kiyāskihēw ᑭᔭᐢᑭᐦᐁᐤ
VTA s/he makes s.o. lie

kiyāskimēw ᑭᔭᐢᑭᒣᐤ
VTA s/he falsely reports s.o.

kiyāskiskiw ᑭᔭᐢᑭᐢᑭᐤ
VAI s/he is a liar [*hab*]

kiyāskiw ᑭᔭᐢᑭᐤ
VAI s/he lies, s/he tells a lie

kiyāskiwin ᑭᔭᐢᑭᐃᐧᐣ
NI lie, falsehood

kiyāskīmēw ᑭᔭᐢᑮᒣᐤ
VTA s/he lies to s.o. [*cf.*
kiyāskistawēw]

kiyāskīmowin ᑭᔭᐢᑮᒧᐃᐧᐣ
NI untruth

kiyāskīstawēw ᑭᔭᐢᑮᐢᑕᐁᐧᐤ
VTA s/he lies to s.o. [*cf.*
kiyāskimēw]

kiyāskīwācimēw ᑭᔭᐢᑮᐋᐧᒋᒣᐤ
VTA s/he tells false tales
about s.o.

kiyāskīwācimostawēw
ᑭᔭᐢᑮᐋᐧᒋᒧᐢᑕᐁᐧᐤ
VTA s/he tells lies to s.o.

kiyāskīwācimow ᑭᔭᐢᑮᐋᐧᒋᒧᐤ
VAI s/he tells false news

kiyāskos ᑭᔭᐢᑯᐢ
NA little sea gull [*dim*]

kiyē- ᑭᔦ
IPV [*grammatical preverb;
future; in changed conjunct
clauses*]

kiyētohtēw ᑭᔦᑐᐦᑌᐤ
VAI s/he wanders about

kiyi- ᑭᔨ
IPV [*grammatical preverb;
future; defines a conjunct
clause*]

kiyikaw ᑭᔨᑲᐤ
IPC all over, pell mell;
every kind

kiyikaw ᑭᔨᑲᐤ
IPC in addition, additionally

kiyipa ᑭᔨᐸ
IPC quickly; soon, hurry up
[*cf.* kīhipa]

kiyipikin ᑭᔨᐱᑭᐣ
VII it grows quickly

kiyipikiw ᑭᔨᐱᑭᐤ
VAI s/he grows quickly

kiyipīw ᑭᔨᐲᐤ
VAI s/he is quick

kiyisin ᑭᔨᓯᐣ
VAI s/he slips

kiyokawēw ᑭᔪᑲᐍᐤ
VTA s/he visits s.o.

kiyokātowak ᑭᔪᑲᑐᐊᐧᐠ
VAI they visit one another

kiyokēw ᑭᔪᑫᐤ
VAI s/he visits, s/he visits
people, s/he pays a visit

kiyomā ᑭᔪᒫ
IPC continually

kiyomānākosiw ᑭᔪᒫᓈᑯᓯᐤ
VAI s/he is in full sight

kiyōtēw ᑭᔫᑌᐤ
VAI s/he visits afar, s/he
travels to visit; s/he visits for
a long duration

kiyōtēwin ᑭᔫᑌᐃᐧᐣ
NI visiting afar

ᑭ

kī- ᑭ
IPV [*grammatical preverb;
past, completion*]

kīhēw ᑮᐦᐁᐤ
VTA s/he gets away from
s.o.

kīhcēkosī-wēpinam
ᑮᐦᒉᑯᓯ ᐍᐱᓇᒼ
VTI s/he flings s.t. onto a
high thing

kīhcēkosī-wēpinēw
ᑮᐦᒉᑯᓯ ᐍᐱᓀᐤ
VTA s/he flings s.o. onto a
high thing

kīhcēkosīpayihow
ᑮᐦᒉᑯᓯᐸᔨᐦᐅᐤ
VAI s/he throws him/herself
to climbing

kīhcēkosīw ᑮᐦᒉᑯᓯᐤ
VAI s/he climbs up or in

kīhcēkosīw-ōhpīw
ᑮᐦᒉᑯᓯᐤ ᐆᐦᐲᐤ
VAI s/he clambers up, s/he
climbs up

kīhcēkosīwināhtik
ᑮᐦᒉᑯᓯᐃᐧᓈᐦᑎᐠ
NI ladder [*pl:* -wa]

kīhcēkosīyāmow ᑮᐦᒉᑯᓯᔮᒧᐤ
VAI s/he flees climbing

kīhcitahāskwān ᑮᐦᒋᑕᐦᐋᐢᒁᐣ
NI hitching post

kīhcitawākonēnam
ᑮᐦᒋᑕᐋᐧᑯᓀᓇᒼ
VTI s/he jabs s.t. into the
snow

kīhcitāskamawēw ᑮᐦᒋᑖᐢᑲᒪᐍᐤ
VTA s/he jabs (it/him) into
s.o.

kīhikosimow ᑮᐦᐃᑯᓯᒧᐤ
VAI s/he fasts

kīhikosimowin ᑮᐦᐃᑯᓯᒧᐃᐧᐣ
NI fasting

kīhipa ᑮᐦᐃᐸ
IPC quickly, in a hurry;
hurry up [*cf.* kiyipa]

kīhisahow ᑮᐦᐃᓴᐦᐅᐤ
VAI s/he restrains
him/herself

kīhkāhtowak ᑮᐦᑳᐦᑐᐊᐧᐠ
VAI they argue with one
another, they quarrel with
one another

kīhkāmēw ᑮᐦᑳᒣᐤ
VTA s/he scolds s.o., s/he
reviles s.o.; s/he argues with
s.o.

kīhkānākosiw ᑮᐦᑳᓈᑯᓯᐤ
VAI s/he is clearly visible,
s/he looks sharp and clear,
s/he is seen distinctly

kīhkānākwan ᑮᐦᑳᓈᑲᐧᐣ
VII it is clearly visible, it
looks sharp and clear, it is
seen distinctly

kīhkātēyihtākwan ᑮᐦᑳᑌᔨᐦᑖᑲᐧᐣ
VII it is held in high esteem,
it is prominent

kīhkātēyimēw ᑮᐦᑳᑌᔨᒣᐤ
VTA s/he holds s.o. in high
esteem

kīhkāw ᑮᐦᑳᐤ
NA old person

kīhkāwitam ᑮᐦᑳᐃᐧᑕᒼ
VTI s/he is cross and
scolding in a loud voice

kīhkāwitaskiw ᑮᐦᑳᐃᐧᑕᐢᑭᐤ
VAI s/he is scolding all the
time

kīhkāyāsowēw ᑮᐦᑳᔮᓱᐁᐧᐤ
VAI s/he shines clearly

kīhkēhtakāhk ᑮᐦᑫᐦᑕᑳᕽ
IPC in the corner

kīhkēw ᑮᐦᑫᐤ
VII it heals up

kīhkihtowak ᑮᐦᑭᐦᑐᐊᐧᐠ
VAI they antagonize one
another, they quarrel

kīhkīhk ᐱᑊᐱˣ
IPC in spite, nevertheless
kīhkīhkan ᐱᑊᐱᐣ
VII it is so in spite of all
kīhkīhkimēw ᐱᑊᐱᑊᐱᑎᐤ
VTA s/he persuades s.o.
against that one's will
kīhkīhtow ᐱᑊᐱᑉᑐ
VAI s/he discusses s.t.; s/he
talks about s.t.
kīhkwahāhkēw ᐱᑊᐳᐦᐋᐦᑲᐤ
NA wolverine
kīhtwām ᐱᑊᒐᐧ
IPC again; another, once
more [also kihtwām]
kīhtwām ka-wāpamitin
ᐱᑊᒐᐧ ᑲ ᐊᐧᐸᒥᑎᐣ
IPH good-bye, see you
again
kīhyawēma ᐱᑊᔭᐁᐧᒪ
IPC in excess, extremely [cf.
kihawēma]
kīkisēp ᐱᐱᐢ
IPC in the morning; this past
morning
kīkisēpā ᐱᐱᐢᐋ
IPC in the morning, early in
the morning
kīkisēpā-atoskēwin
ᐱᐱᐢᐋ ᐊᑐᐢᑫᐃᐧᐣ
NI morning chores
kīkisēpā-mīcisow ᐱᐱᐢᐋ ᒦᒋᓱ
VAI s/he eats breakfast
kīkisēpā-mīcisowin
ᐱᐱᐢᐋ ᒦᒋᓱᐃᐧᐣ
NI breakfast
kīkisēpā-mīciwin ᐱᐱᐢᐋ ᒦᒋᐃᐧᐣ
NI cereal, porridge;
breakfast food
kīkisēpāki ᐱᐱᐢᐋᑭ
IPC in the morning, when
it's morning [cf. kīkisēpāw,
kīkisēpāyāki]
kīkisēpāw ᐱᐱᐢᐋᐤ
VII it is morning, it is dawn,
it is near morning
kīkisēpāwahcikēwin
ᐱᐱᐢᐋᐧᐦᒋᑫᐃᐧᐣ
NI breakfast
kīkisēpāyāki ᐱᐱᐢᐋᔭᑭ
IPC in the morning, when
it's morning
kīkisēpāyāw ᐱᐱᐢᐋᔭᐤ
VII it is morning, it is dawn,
it is near morning
kīko ᐱᑯ
PR which, what one; what
kind
kīko-pīsim ᐱᑯ ᐱᓯᒼ
IPC what month (is it)
kīkw-āya ᐱᐠᔭ
NA which one; what kind
kīkway ᐱᐠᐤ
NA thing, something; what?
what sort?
kīkway ᐱᐠᐤ
NI thing, something; what?
what sort? [only non-locative
forms]

kīkway ᐱᐠᐤ
PR something, some, thing;
[in negative phrases:]
anything, any [indefinite;
usually both sg and pl may
be expressed by kīkway; also
kēkway]
kīkwayi ᐱᐠᔨ
PR what sort of thing?
kīkwayiwiw ᐱᐠᔨᐃᐧᐤ
VAI s/he is what sort
kīkwāhtik ᐱᐠᐋᐦᑎ
NI what tree, which tree [pl:
-wak; or IPC kīkwāhtik]
kīkwāhtikowiw ᐱᐠᐋᐦᑎᑯᐃᐧᐤ
VAI it is what kind of tree
[or IPC kīkwāhtikowiw
"what kind of tree is it?"]
kīkwākani ᐱᐠᐋᑲᓂ
PR what can it have been?
kīkwāyihkān ᐱᐠᐋᔨᐦᑲᐣ
PR what sort of thing? [sC:
kēkwāñihkān]
kīkwāpoy ᐱᐠᐋᐳᐤ
IPC what kind of liquid?
kīkwās ᐱᐠᐋᐢ
PR something, some, thing;
something little; [in negative
clauses:] anything, any [dim;
indefinite]
kīkwāy ᐱᐠᐋᐤ
PR what [anim prox and
inan sg; interrogative;
usually both sg and pl may
be expressed by kīkwāy]
kīkwāy ētikwē ᐱᐠᐋᐤ ᐁᑎᑵ
IPH I don't know what it is;
I wonder what it is
kīkwāy ōma ᐱᐠᐋᐤ ᐆᒪ
IPH what is this
kīkwāy piko ᐱᐠᐋᐤ ᐱᑯ
IPH the only thing is
[predicative]
kīkwāya ᐱᐠᐋᔭ
PR what [anim obv / inan
pl]
kīkwāyak ᐱᐠᐋᔭᐠ
PR what [anim prox pl]
kīkwāyihkān ᐱᐠᐋᔨᐦᑲᐣ
PR what odd thing is this?
kīmāmow ᐱᒫᒧ
VAI s/he flees by stealth
kīmāpahkēw ᐱᒫᐸᐦᑫᐤ
VAI s/he watches secretly,
s/he spies
kīmāpahtam ᐱᒫᐸᐦᑕᒼ
VTI s/he spies on s.t., s/he
watches s.t. secretly
kīmāpamēw ᐱᒫᐸᒣᐤ
VTA s/he spies on s.o., s/he
watches s.o. secretly
kīmāpiw ᐱᒫᐱᐤ
VAI s/he watches secretly
kīminatēw ᐱᒥᓇᑌᐤ
VTA s/he assails s.o.
stealthily
kīminēw ᐱᒥᓅ
VTA s/he touches or feels

s.o. sexually, s/he cops a feel;
s/he touches s.o.'s genitals
kīminikēw ᐱᒥᓂᑫᐤ
VAI s/he touches or feels
people sexually, s/he sneaks
a feel
kīminīcākan ᐱᒥᓃᒐᑲᐣ
NA bastard; illegitimate
child
kīminīcākanihkēw ᐱᒥᓃᒐᑲᓂᐦᑫᐤ
VAI s/he makes an
illegitimate child; she gives
birth to an illegitimate child
kīmīw ᐱᒦᐤ
VAI s/he sneaks away, s/he
escapes
kīmōc ᐱᒨ
IPC secretly, stealthily, slyly,
by stealth
kīmōci- ᐱᒨᒋ
IPV secretly, by stealth
kīmōcihēw ᐱᒨᒋᐦᐁᐤ
VTA s/he sneaks around on
s.o.; s/he conceals (it/him)
from s.o.
kīmōcisiw ᐱᒨᒋᓯᐤ
VAI s/he is sly; s/he conceals
his/her own slyness
kīmōtan ᐱᒨᑕᐣ
VII it is kept as a secret, it is
something which is not
talked about
kīmōtāpahtam ᐱᒨᑖᐸᐦᑕᒼ
VTI s/he watches s.t. slyly,
on the sly
kīmōtāpamēw ᐱᒨᑖᐸᒣᐤ
VTA s/he watches s.o. slyly,
on the sly
kīmōtāpiw ᐱᒨᑖᐱᐤ
VAI s/he looks secretly
kīmōtātisiw ᐱᒨᑖᑎᓯᐤ
VAI s/he is known to be sly
kīmōtisiw ᐱᒨᑎᓯᐤ
VAI s/he has an illicit affair
kīmwēw ᐱᒷᐤ
VAI s/he whispers
kīnāpiskāw ᐱᐋᐱᐢᑳᐤ
VII it is sharp or pointed
metal
kīnikaham ᐱᓂᑲᐦᐊᒼ
VTI s/he hews s.t. to an edge
kīnikamon ᐱᓂᑲᒧᐣ
VII it adheres sharply [cf.
kā-kīnikamoki]
kīnikatahamawēw
ᐱᓂᑲᑕᐦᐊᒪᐁᐧᐤ
VTA s/he makes pickets for
s.o.
kīnikatahikēw ᐱᓂᑲᑕᐦᐃᑫᐤ
VAI s/he makes pickets; s/he
hews things to points
kīnikatos ᐱᓂᑲᑐᐢ
NA pointed arrow [cf. atos]
kīnikāw ᐱᓂᑳᐤ
NI sharp edge, cutting tool
[cf. kīnikāw VII]
kīnikāw ᐱᓂᑳᐤ
VII it is sharp, it is pointed

kīnikihkotam ᐲᓯᑭᐦᒍᑕᒻ
VTI s/he whittles s.t. to an
edge

kīnikokotam ᐲᓯᑯᑯᑕᒻ
VTI s/he whittles s.t. to a
point

kīnikokotēw ᐲᓯᑯᑯᑌᐤ
VTA s/he whittles s.o. to a
point

kīnikotēw ᐲᓯᑯᑌᐤ
VAI s/he has a pointed nose

kīnikwānipayiw ᐲᓯᐠᐃᓂᐸᔨᐤ
VII it revolves, it rotates, it
spins

kīnikwāyowēwisip
ᐲᓯᐠᐋᔪᐁᐃᓯᑊ
NA spoonbill duck; pintail
duck [lit: "sharptail duck";
possibly also
kinokwayawēwisip
"longneck duck"]

kīnipocikan ᐲᓯᐳᓯᑲᐣ
NA stone for sharpening;
grindstone

kīnipocikēw ᐲᓯᐳᓯᑫᐤ
VAI s/he sharpens things

kīnipohēw ᐲᓯᐳᐦᐁᐤ
VTA s/he sharpens s.o. (with
a grindstone)

kīnipotāw ᐲᓯᐳᑖᐤ
VAIt s/he grinds s.t. sharp,
s/he sharpens s.t. (e.g. with
a file, grindstone)

kīnipotēw ᐲᓯᐳᑌᐤ
VTA s/he grinds s.o. sharp

kīpa ᐲᐸ
IPC soon; early

kīpan ᐲᐸᐣ
VII it goes quickly, it takes
no time at all

kīpēhtāw ᐲᐍᐦᑖᐤ
VAIt s/he does s.t. quickly

kīpi- ᐲᐱ
IPV quickly

kīpikin ᐲᐱᑭᐣ
VII it grows quickly

kīpikiw ᐲᐱᑭᐤ
VAI s/he grows quickly

kīpikwāsow ᐲᐱᐠᐋᓱᐤ
VAI s/he sews quickly

kīpikwātam ᐲᐱᐠᐋᑕᒼ
VTI s/he sews s.t. quickly

kīpikwātēw ᐲᐱᐠᐋᑌᐤ
VTA s/he sews s.o. quickly

kīpinam ᐲᐱᓇᒼ
VTI s/he uses s.t. quickly

kīpinēw ᐲᐱᓀᐤ
VTA s/he uses s.o. quickly;
s/he uses s.o. as money

kīpipayihow ᐲᐱᐸᔨᐦᐅᐤ
VAI s/he throws him/herself
over

kīpipayiw ᐲᐱᐸᔨᐤ
VAI s/he falls over, s/he
tumbles over; s/he goes
quickly, s/he passes quickly

kīpipitēw ᐲᐱᐱᑌᐤ
VTA s/he pulls s.o. so as to
make that one fall

kīpiskam ᐲᐱᐢᑲᒼ
VTI s/he wears s.t. out
(quickly)

kīpiskawēw ᐲᐱᐢᑲᐍᐤ
VTA s/he knocks s.o. over
(by foot or body)

kīpiskawēw ᐲᐱᐢᑲᐍᐤ
VTA s/he wears s.o. out
(quickly)

kīpiwēpahwēw ᐲᐱᐍᐸᐦᐁᐤ
VTA s/he knocks s.o. down
with a tool

kīpiwēpiskam ᐲᐱᐍᐱᐢᑲᒼ
VTI s/he kicks s.t. over

kīpiwēpiskawēw ᐲᐱᐍᐱᐢᑲᐍᐤ
VTA s/he kicks s.o. over

kīpiyahkinēw ᐲᐱᔭᐦᑭᓀᐤ
VTA s/he pushes s.o. forward

kīpīw ᐲᐲᐤ
VAI s/he goes quickly, s/he
goes in a hurry

kīs-ācimow ᐲᐢᐋᓯᒧᐤ
VAI s/he finishes a story
[also kīsi-ācimow]

kīs-āyāw ᐲᐢᐋᔮᐤ
VAI s/he is finished, s/he is
through [also kīsi-ayāw]

kīsahēw ᐲᐢᐊᐦᐁᐤ
VTA s/he finishes placing
s.o., s/he finishes putting s.o.
in place

kīsahkamikisiw ᐲᐢᐊᐦᑲᒥᑭᓯᐤ
VAI s/he finishes

kīsahpitam ᐲᐢᐊᐦᐱᑕᒼ
VTI s/he finishes tying s.t.

kīsahpitēw ᐲᐢᐊᐦᐱᑌᐤ
VTA s/he finishes tying s.o.
(hide); s/he finishes
harnessing s.o.

kīsapihkātam ᐲᐢᐊᐱᐦᑳᑕᒼ
VTI s/he braids s.t. to
completion, s/he knits s.t. to
completion

kīsapwēnāyāw ᐲᐢᐊᐘᐍᓈᔮᐤ
VII it turns milder, it
becomes milder

kīsapwēnipayiw ᐲᐢᐊᐘᐍᓂᐸᔨᐤ
VII it turns milder, it quickly
becomes milder [also
kīsapwēnipayin]

kīsapwēw ᐲᐢᐊᐘᐍᐤ
VII it is warm weather

kīsapwēyāw ᐲᐢᐊᐘᐍᔮᐤ
VII it is warm

kīsasinaham ᐲᐢᐊᓯᓇᐦᐊᒼ
VTI s/he finishes writing s.t.

kīsasinahikēw ᐲᐢᐊᓯᓇᐦᐃᑫᐤ
VTI s/he finishes writing

kīsasiwātam ᐲᐢᐊᓯᐚᑕᒼ
VTI s/he completes making a
law, s/he rules about s.t.; s/he
decides about s.t.

kīsastāw ᐲᐢᐊᐢᑖᐤ
VAIt s/he finishes placing
s.t., s/he finishes putting s.t.
in place; s/he finishes piling
s.t. [also kis-āstāw or
kīsi-astāw]

kīsatisohēw ᐲᐢᐊᑎᓱᐦᐁᐤ
VTA s/he fully ripens s.o.
[also kīs-ātisohēw or
kīsi-atisohēw]

kīsatisow ᐲᐢᐊᑎᓱᐤ
VAI s/he is fully ripe [also
kīs-ātisow or kīsi-atisow]

kīsāc ᐲᓵ-
IPC right away, at once; at
the same time

kīsāpēw ᐲᓵᐯᐤ
VAI he comes to manhood

kīsāspin ᐲᓵᐢᐱᐣ
IPC if [cf. kīspin]

kīsāspinē ᐲᓵᐢᐱᓀ
IPC might as well

kīsēyihtam ᐲᓭᔨᐦᑕᒼ
VTI s/he decides s.t., s/he
decides on s.t.; s/he
completes his/her own plan
of s.t.

kīsi- ᐲᓯ
IPV finish; completely, to
completion; completing,
having done

kīsi-atoskātam ᐲᓯ ᐊᑐᐢᑳᑕᒼ
VTI s/he is through working
on s.t., s/he finishes working
on s.t. [also kīs-ātoskātam]

kīsi-atoskēw ᐲᓯ ᐊᑐᐢᑫᐤ
VAI s/he is through working,
s/he finishes working [also
kīs-ātoskēw]

kīsi-masinahikēw ᐲᓯ ᒪᓯᓇᐦᐃᑫᐤ
VAI s/he finishes writing

kīsi-mānokēw ᐲᓯ ᒫᓄᑫᐤ
VAI s/he finishes setting up a
tent

kīsi-mētawēw ᐲᓯ ᒣᑕᐍᐤ
VAI s/he finishes playing

kīsi-mīcisow ᐲᓯ ᒦᓯᓱᐤ
VAI s/he finishes eating

kīsi-tipiskāw ᐲᓯ ᑎᐱᐢᑳᐤ
VII it is completely night

kīsi-wawēyīw ᐲᓯ ᐘᐍᔩᐤ
VAI s/he finishes getting
dressed

kīsihcikātēw ᐲᓯᐦᓯᑳᑌᐤ
VTA s/he finishes doing
business with s.o.

kīsihcikātēw ᐲᓯᐦᓯᑳᑌᐤ
VII it is finished, it is
accomplished

kīsihēw ᐲᓯᐦᐁᐤ
VTA s/he completes s.o. (e.g.
stocking), s/he finishes
preparing s.o.

kīsihtamawēw ᐲᓯᐦᑕᒪᐍᐤ
VTA s/he finishes (it/him)
for s.o.

kīsihtamākēw ᐲᓯᐦᑕᒫᑫᐤ
VAI s/he finishes (it/him) for
people

kīsihtāw ᐲᓯᐦᑖᐤ
VAIt s/he completes s.t., s/he
finishes s.t., s/he finishes
work on s.t. [also kīsihtāw]

kīsik ᐲᓯᐠ
NI sky [pl: -wa; loc: -ohk]

kīsikānam ᑮᓯᑳᓇᒼ
VTI s/he sees (s.t. as) daylight

kīsikānākwan ᑮᓯᑳᓈᑲᐧᐣ
VII it appears as daylight

kīsikāsiw ᑮᓯᑳᓯᐤ
VII there is a bit of daylight left

kīsikāstēskamawēw ᑮᓯᑳᐢᑌᐢᑲᒪᐌᐤ
VTA s/he makes it daylight for s.o. by going

kīsikāstēw ᑮᓯᑳᐢᑌᐤ
VII it is moonlight [*see also* nīpāyāstēw]

kīsikāw ᑮᓯᑳᐤ
NI day [*also NA*; *cf.* kīsikāw *VII*]

kīsikāw ᑮᓯᑳᐤ
VII it is day, it is daylight

kīsikāwacāhk ᑮᓯᑳᐘᒑᕽ
NA Day Star [*obv*: -wa; *Cree chief and reserve name*]

kīsikāwi-pīsim ᑮᓯᑳᐃᐧ ᐲᓯᒼ
NA sun [*pl*: -wak]

kīsikāwihkwāmiw ᑮᓯᑳᐏᐦᑳᐧᒥᐤ
VAI s/he takes a nap during the day

kīsikāyāpan ᑮᓯᑳᔮᐸᐣ
VII it is day-break [*cf.* wāpan]

kīsikāyāstēw ᑮᓯᑳᔮᐢᑌᐤ
VII it is dawn, it is first light; it is moonlight so bright as to be light as day [*see also* nīpāyāstēw]

kīsikohk ᑮᓯᑯᕽ
IPC in the sky; in heaven

kīsikwāsow ᑮᓯᑳᐧᓱᐤ
VAI s/he finishes his/her own sewing

kīsikwātam ᑮᓯᑳᐧᑕᒼ
VTI s/he finishes sewing s.t.

kīsikwātēw ᑮᓯᑳᐧᑌᐤ
VTA s/he finishes sewing s.o.

kīsinam ᑮᓯᓇᒼ
VTI s/he tans s.t.; s/he finishes tanning

kīsināc ᑮᓯᓈᐨ
IPC too bad; unfortunately

kīsinācihēw ᑮᓯᓈᒋᐦᐁᐤ
VTA s/he puts s.o. in an unfortunate dilemma

kīsinācihikowisiw ᑮᓯᓈᒋᐦᐃᑯᐏᓯᐤ
VAI s/he is made sad by higher powers

kīsinācipayiw ᑮᓯᓈᒋᐸᔨᐤ
VAI s/he falls into unfortunate circumstances

kīsinātakocin ᑮᓯᓈᑕᑯᒋᐣ
VAI s/he makes an unfortunate leap

kīsinātēyihtam ᑮᓯᓈᑌᔨᐦᑕᒼ
VTI s/he is grieved about s.t.; s/he regrets s.t.

kīsinātēyihtamawēw ᑮᓯᓈᑌᔨᐦᑕᒪᐌᐤ
VTA s/he regrets (it) deeply for s.o.

kīsinātēyihtamowin ᑮᓯᓈᑌᔨᐦᑕᒧᐏᐣ
NI regretfulness

kīsinātēyimēw ᑮᓯᓈᑌᔨᒣᐤ
VTA s/he regrets s.o.'s actions; s/he feels sorry for s.o.

kīsinātisiw ᑮᓯᓈᑎᓯᐤ
VAI s/he is unfortunate

kīsinēw ᑮᓯᓀᐤ
VTA s/he tans s.o.

kīsinikātēw ᑮᓯᓂᑳᑌᐤ
VII it is tanned

kīsinikow ᑮᓯᓂᑯᐤ
VAI s/he tans

kīsipayiw ᑮᓯᐸᔨᐤ
VII it ends, it terminates

kīsipayiwin ᑮᓯᐸᔨᐏᐣ
NI end, termination

kīsisam ᑮᓯᓴᒼ
VTI s/he cook s.t., s/he bakes s.t. to completion, s/he completes s.t. by heat

kīsisamawēw ᑮᓯᓴᒪᐌᐤ
VTA s/he cooks (it/him) for s.o.

kīsisikātēw ᑮᓯᓯᑳᑌᐤ
VII it is cooked, it is baked

kīsisikēw ᑮᓯᓯᑫᐤ
VAI s/he cooks

kīsisiw ᑮᓯᓯᐤ
VAI s/he is mature

kīsiskwēwiw ᑮᓯᐢᑫᐧᐏᐤ
VAI she comes to womanhood

kīsisow ᑮᓯᓱᐤ
VAI it is cooked to completion

kīsiswēw ᑮᓯᓭᐧᐤ
VTA s/he cooks s.o., s/he bakes s.o. to completion

kīsitēpotēw ᑮᓯᑌᐳᑌᐤ
VTA s/he cooks for s.o.

kīsitēpow ᑮᓯᑌᐳᐤ
VAI s/he cooks, s/he finishes cooking

kīsitēpowin ᑮᓯᑌᐳᐏᐣ
NI cooking

kīsitēw ᑮᓯᑌᐤ
VII it is cooked to completion; it burns, it is burnt

kīsīhow ᑮᓰᐦᐅᐤ
VAI s/he is finished dressing

kīskacayāskwahwēw ᑮᐢᑲᒐᔮᐢᑲᐧᐦᐍᐤ
VTA s/he cuts s.o.'s belly by tool [*with* "tree, wood" *as actor*; *humorous connotations*]

kīskacināsin ᑮᐢᑲᒋᓈᓯᐣ
VII it is a bit steep [*dim*]

kīskaham ᑮᐢᑲᐦᐊᒼ
VTI s/he chops s.t. through or off; s/he breaks s.t. apart (by tool)

kīskahamawēw ᑮᐢᑲᐦᐊᒪᐌᐤ
VTA s/he cuts s.o.'s hair

kīskahamāsow ᑮᐢᑲᐦᐊᒫᓱᐤ
VAI s/he cuts his/her own hair

kīskahcāw ᑮᐢᑲᐦᒑᐤ
VII it is steep (*e.g.* hill, bank)

kīskahikanisihk ᑮᐢᑲᐦᐃᑲᓂᓯᕽ
INM Molanosa, SK [*loc*]

kīskahtam ᑮᐢᑲᐦᑕᒼ
VTI s/he bites s.t. through or off

kīskahwēw ᑮᐢᑲᐦᐍᐤ
VTA s/he cuts s.o. through; s/he cuts from s.o.

kīskamēw ᑮᐢᑲᒣᐤ
VTA s/he bites s.o. through or off; s/he breaks a piece off s.o. (by teeth)

kīskanakēwasākay ᑮᐢᑲᓇᑫᐘᓵᑲᕀ
NI waistcoat

kīskanakēwayān ᑮᐢᑲᓇᑫᐘᔮᐣ
NI waistcoat

kīskasākay ᑮᐢᑲᓵᑲᕀ
NI skirt

kīskasākās ᑮᐢᑲᓵᑳᐢ
NI skirt [*dim*]

kīskasākēw ᑮᐢᑲᓵᑫᐤ
VAI s/he wears a skirt

kīskataham ᑮᐢᑲᑕᐦᐊᒼ
VTI s/he chops s.t. with an axe, s/he hews s.t. through or off; s/he chops s.t. in two

kīskatahikan ᑮᐢᑲᑕᐦᐃᑲᐣ
NI treestump

kīskatahikātēw ᑮᐢᑲᑕᐦᐃᑳᑌᐤ
VII it is cut in two

kīskatahikēw ᑮᐢᑲᑕᐦᐃᑫᐤ
VAI s/he limbs trees, s/he lops the limbs off trees

kīskatahwēw ᑮᐢᑲᑕᐦᐍᐤ
VTA s/he hews s.o. through or off

kīskatawēhamān ᑮᐢᑲᑕᐍᐦᐊᒫᐣ
NI forelock, bangs (in hair)

kīskatawēhamāw ᑮᐢᑲᑕᐍᐦᐊᒫᐤ
VAI s/he wears a forelock; s/he has bangs

kīskatāhtikwēw ᑮᐢᑲᑖᐦᑎᑫᐧᐤ
VAI s/he cuts logs

kīskatāwahkāw ᑮᐢᑲᑖᐘᐦᑳᐤ
NI steep bank [*cf.* kīskatāwahkāw *VII*]

kīskatāwahkāw ᑮᐢᑲᑖᐘᐦᑳᐤ
VII it is a steep river bank; it is an abrupt drop, it is a long way down

kīskatāwahkihtin ᑮᐢᑲᑖᐘᐦᑭᐦᑎᐣ
VII it flows between steep banks

kīskatināw ᑮᐢᑲᑎᓈᐤ
VII it is a short, jagged, mountainous hill

kīskāpiskāw ᑮᐢᑳᐱᐢᑳᐤ
NI cliff [*cf.* kīskāpiskāw *VII*]
kīskāpiskāw ᑮᐢᑳᐱᐢᑳᐤ
VII it is cut off rock; it is a rocky perpendicular area, it is a cliff
kīskāw ᑮᐢᑳᐤ
VII it is cut off, it is edged
kīskāýawāw ᑮᐢᑳᔭᐚᐤ
VII it is deep
kīskāýowēpitam ᑮᐢᑳᔪᐍᐱᑕᒼ
VTI s/he pulls s.t.'s tail off
kīskāýowēpitēw ᑮᐢᑳᔪᐍᐱᑌᐤ
VTA s/he pulls s.o.'s tail off
kīskāýowēswēw ᑮᐢᑳᔪᐍᔃᐤ
VTA s/he cuts off s.o.'s tail
kīskāýowēw ᑮᐢᑳᔪᐍᐤ
VAI it is cut off at the tail; it has a bobtail, it has a short tail
kīskēýisin ᑮᐢᑫᔨᓯᐣ
VAI s/he lies with a hard object under one
kīski- ᑮᐢᑭ
IPN severed, amputated, cut off
kīski- ᑮᐢᑭ
IPV severing, breaking, cutting off
kīski-wēpaham ᑮᐢᑭᐍᐸᐦᐊᒼ
VTI s/he knocks s.t. off (by tool); s/he breaks s.t. off
kīski-wēpahwēw ᑮᐢᑭᐍᐸᐦᐍᐤ
VTA s/he knocks s.o. off (by tool); s/he breaks s.o. off
kīskicāsis ᑮᐢᑭᒑᓯᐢ
NA pair of shorts, cut-offs
kīskicihcān ᑮᐢᑭᒋᐦᒑᐣ
NI amputated thumb
kīskicihcēpitēw ᑮᐢᑭᒋᐦᒉᐱᑌᐤ
VTA s/he tears s.o.'s hand off, s/he tears s.o.'s finger off
kīskicihcēw ᑮᐢᑭᒋᐦᒉᐤ
VAI s/he is cut off at the hand or finger; s/he has an amputated had or finger
kīskicihcīs ᑮᐢᑭᒋᐦᒌᐢ
NI amputated finger
kīskicin ᑮᐢᑭᒋᐣ
VAI s/he has a cut (from a sharp object)
kīskihcakos ᑮᐢᑭᐦᒐᑯᐢ
NI cut off stick [*dim*]
kīskihkomān ᑮᐢᑭᐦᑯᒫᐣ
NI cut off knife; Cutknife [*personal name of Sarcee chief*]
kīskihkomānaciy ᑮᐢᑭᐦᑯᒫᓇᒋᐩ
NI Cutknife Hill, SK
kīskihkomānihk
INM Poundmaker Reserve, SK [*loc*; *lit*: "at Cutknife"]
kīskihkwēsimēw ᑮᐢᑭᐦᑵᓯᒣᐤ
VTA s/he throws s.o. breaking that one's face
kīskihtawakay ᑮᐢᑭᐦᑕᐘᑲᐩ
NA creature which is cut off at the ear; one-eared person
kīskihtawakayēw ᑮᐢᑭᐦᑕᐘᑲᔦᐤ
VAI s/he is cut off at the ear
kīskihtawakēswēw ᑮᐢᑭᐦᑕᐘᑫᔃᐤ
VTA s/he cuts off s.o.'s ear
kīskikaham ᑮᐢᑭᑲᐦᐊᒼ
VTI s/he chops s.t. through or off
kīskikahwēw ᑮᐢᑭᑲᐦᐍᐤ
VTA s/he chops s.o. through or off
kīskikāt ᑮᐢᑭᑳᐟ
NA creature which has a cut-off leg
kīskikātēsam ᑮᐢᑭᑳᑌᓴᒼ
VTI s/he cuts the legs off s.t.
kīskikātēswēw ᑮᐢᑭᑳᑌᔃᐤ
VTA s/he amputates s.o.'s leg, s/he cuts the leg(s) off s.o.
kīskikātēw ᑮᐢᑭᑳᑌᐤ
VAI s/he is cut off at the leg; s/he has an amputated leg
kīskikotēswēw ᑮᐢᑭᑯᑌᔃᐤ
VTA s/he cuts off s.o.'s nose
kīskikotēw ᑮᐢᑭᑯᑌᐤ
VAI s/he is cut off at the nose
kīskikwēhwēw ᑮᐢᑭᑵᐦᐍᐤ
VTA s/he breaks s.o.'s neck (by tool)
kīskikwēnēw ᑮᐢᑭᑵᓀᐤ
VTA s/he rings s.o.'s neck; s/he breaks s.o.'s neck off (by hand)
kīskikwēpitēw ᑮᐢᑭᑵᐱᑌᐤ
VTA s/he jerks s.o.'s head off
kīskikwēsāwātēw ᑮᐢᑭᑵᓵᐚᑌᐤ
VTA s/he slices off s.o.'s head
kīskikwēsikēw ᑮᐢᑭᑵᓯᑫᐤ
VAI s/he cuts throats, s/he severs necks
kīskikwēsin ᑮᐢᑭᑵᓯᐣ
VAI s/he breaks his/her own neck (in falling)
kīskikwēswēw ᑮᐢᑭᑵᔃᐤ
VTA s/he cuts s.o.'s throat, s/he severs s.o.'s neck, s/he cuts off s.o.'s head (by cutting edge)
kīskikwētahwēw ᑮᐢᑭᑵᑕᐦᐍᐤ
VTA s/he severs s.o.'s neck by axe, s/he chops off s.o.'s head
kīskikwēwēpahwēw ᑮᐢᑭᑵᐍᐸᐦᐍᐤ
VTA s/he severs s.o.'s neck by throwing a missile, s/he knocks off s.o.'s head
kīskimitās ᑮᐢᑭᒥᑖᐢ
NA pair of shorts, cut-offs
kīskinakwēwayān ᑮᐢᑭᓇᑵᐘᔮᐣ
NI vest
kīskinam ᑮᐢᑭᓇᒼ
VTI s/he cuts s.t. off
kīskipaýiw ᑮᐢᑭᐸᔨᐤ
VAI s/he comes apart; it is split, it is cracked
kīskipitam ᑮᐢᑭᐱᑕᒼ
VTI s/he pulls s.t. apart; s/he pulls a piece off s.t.; s/he tears s.t. through or off
kīskipitēw ᑮᐢᑭᐱᑌᐤ
VTA s/he pulls s.o. apart; s/he pulls a part off s.o.
kīskipiton ᑮᐢᑭᐱᑐᐣ
NA one with a severed or amputated arm
kīskipitonēw ᑮᐢᑭᐱᑐᓀᐤ
VAI s/he is cut off at the arm; s/he has only one arm; s/he has a partial arm, s/he has an amputated arm
kīskipocikan ᑮᐢᑭᐳᒋᑲᐣ
NI saw, cross-cut saw
kīskipocikanis ᑮᐢᑭᐳᒋᑲᓂᐢ
NI cross-cut saw [*dim*]
kīskipocikēw ᑮᐢᑭᐳᒋᑫᐤ
VAI s/he saws things
kīskipotam ᑮᐢᑭᐳᑕᒼ
VTI s/he saws s.t. into lengths
kīskipotamawēw ᑮᐢᑭᐳᑕᒪᐍᐤ
VTA s/he saws (it/him) for s.o.
kīskipotamākēw ᑮᐢᑭᐳᑕᒫᑫᐤ
NA one who saws (for others)
kīskipotāw ᑮᐢᑭᐳᑖᐤ
VAIt s/he saws into lengths, s/he saws s.t. through
kīskipotēw ᑮᐢᑭᐳᑌᐤ
VTA s/he saws s.o.
kīskisam ᑮᐢᑭᓴᒼ
VTI s/he cuts s.t. through or off
kīskisamawēw ᑮᐢᑭᓴᒪᐍᐤ
VTA s/he cuts (it/him) off for s.o.; s/he offers (it/him) (*i.e.* tobacco) to s.o.
kīskisin ᑮᐢᑭᓯᐣ
VAI s/he has a cut (from falling)
kīskiswēw ᑮᐢᑭᔃᐤ
VTA s/he cuts s.o. through or off; s/he plays s.o. (card)
kīskitās ᑮᐢᑭᑖᐢ
NA woman's leggings
kīskīskwēhkāniskwēw ᑮᐢᑮᐢᑵᐦᑳᓂᐢᑵᐤ
NA silly woman [*rdpl*; *cf.* kīskwēhkāniskwēw]
kīskosīw ᑮᐢᑯᓰᐤ
VAI s/he whistles [*also* kwīskosīw; *cf.* kwēskosīw]
kīskowēmohēw ᑮᐢᑯᐍᒧᐦᐁᐤ
VTA s/he makes s.o. stop crying
kīskowēw ᑮᐢᑯᐍᐤ
VAI s/he stops talking or crying
kīskwēhēw ᑮᐢᑵᐦᐁᐤ
VTA s/he makes s.o. crazy, s/he drives s.o. insane

kīskwēhkān Ρ∩ᑫᐧᕁᑳᐣ
NA fool; mentally sick person

kīskwēhkāniskwēw Ρ∩ᑫᐧᕁᑳᓂᑫᐧᐤ
NA silly woman [cf. kiskīskwēhkāniskwēw]

kīskwēhkāniskwēwiw Ρ∩ᑫᐧᕁᑳᓂᑫᐧᐄᐧᐤ
VAI she is a foolish woman

kīskwēhkāniwiw Ρ∩ᑫᐧᕁᑳᓂᐤᐄᐧᐤ
VAI s/he is a mentally sick person

kīskwēhkwasiskiw Ρ∩ᑫᐧᕁᑿᓯᐢᑭᐤ
VAI s/he is given to sleep-walking [hab]

kīskwēhkwasiw Ρ∩ᑫᐧᕁᑿᓯᐤ
VAI s/he talks in his/her sleep, s/he walks in his/her sleep

kīskwēhkwasīhkāsow Ρ∩ᑫᐧᕁᑿᓰᕁᑳᓱᐤ
VAI s/he pretends to be sleep-walking

kīskwēhpinēw Ρ∩ᑫᐧᕁᐱᓀᐤ
VAI s/he is delirious

kīskwēhtākwan Ρ∩ᑫᐧᕁᑖᑾᐣ
VII it is a maddening sound

kīskwēmēw Ρ∩ᑫᐧᒣᐤ
VTA s/he drives s.o. crazy by his/her own foolish talk

kīskwēpēhēw Ρ∩ᑫᐧᐯᐦᐁᐤ
VTA s/he gets s.o. drunk

kīskwēpēhkāsow Ρ∩ᑫᐧᐯᕁᑳᓱᐤ
VAI s/he pretends to be drunk

kīskwēpēsk Ρ∩ᑫᐧᐯᐢᐠ
NA drunkard

kīskwēpēskākow Ρ∩ᑫᐧᐯᐢᑳᑯᐤ
VTA it makes s.o. drunk [inanimate actor VTA, cf. kīskwēpēskaw-]

kīskwēpēskiw Ρ∩ᑫᐧᐯᐢᑭᐤ
VAI s/he is a drunkard; s/he drinks habitually, s/he gets drunk all the time [hab]

kīskwēpēw Ρ∩ᑫᐧᐯᐤ
VAI s/he is drunk

kīskwēpēwin Ρ∩ᑫᐧᐯᐃᐧᐣ
NI intoxication, drunkenness; drinking

kīskwēpēwiyiniw Ρ∩ᑫᐧᐯᐃᐧᔨᓂᐤ
NA drinking man

kīskwēpiw Ρ∩ᑫᐧᐱᐤ
VAI s/he sits reeling

kīskwēsin Ρ∩ᑫᐧᓯᐣ
VAI s/he loses his/her senses in a fall or accident; s/he is disoriented from falling

kīskwēw Ρ∩ᑫᐧᐤ
VAI s/he is mentally disturbed, s/he is mad, s/he is crazy, s/he is insane, s/he is out of his/her mind; s/he is silly

kīskwēwēpahwēw Ρ∩ᑫᐧᐁᐧᐸᐦᐧᐁᐤ
VTA s/he knocks s.o. silly

kīskwēwikamik Ρ∩ᑫᐧᐃᐧᑲᒥᐠ
NI mental hospital [pl: -wa]

kīskwēwinākosiw Ρ∩ᑫᐧᐃᐧᓈᑯᓯᐤ
VAI s/he looks crazy, s/he appears crazy; s/he looks foolish, s/he appears foolish

kīskwēwinākwan Ρ∩ᑫᐧᐃᐧᓈᑿᐣ
VII it looks foolish, it appears foolish

kīskwēyāpamow Ρ∩ᑫᐧᔮᐸᒧᐤ
VAI s/he is dizzy

kīskwēyātis Ρ∩ᑫᐧᔮᑎᐢ
NA wild, immoral person; person living immorally, wildly

kīskwēyātisiw Ρ∩ᑫᐧᔮᑎᓯᐤ
VAI s/he is wild and giddy; s/he is mentally deranged, s/he is of a crazy nature

kīskwēyātisiwin Ρ∩ᑫᐧᔮᑎᓯᐃᐧᐣ
NI wild, riotous living

kīskwēyāwin Ρ∩ᑫᐧᔮᐃᐧᐣ
NI foolishness, madness [also kīskwē-ayāwin]

kīskwēyēýihtam Ρ∩ᑫᐧᔦᕁᐦᑕᒼ
VTI s/he is disturbed (by worry or sadness)

kīsokēw Ρᓱᑫᐤ
VAI s/he completes his/her own dwelling

kīsopwē- Ρᓱᐻ
IPV with hot weather [cf. kisāpwēw]

kīsopwēni-pipon Ρᓱᐻᓂ ᐱᐳᐣ
VII it is a mild winter

kīsopwēw Ρᓱᐻᐤ
VII it is warm weather, it is hot weather [cf. kisāpwēw]

kīsopwēyāw Ρᓱᐻᔮᐤ
VII it is warmish weather

kīso- Ρᓱ
IPN warmth [also kiso-]

kīsō-pīhtawēyān Ρᓱ ᐲᕁᑕᐌᐧᔮᐣ
NA warm undergarment

kīsōcihcēw Ρᓱᒋᐦᒉᐤ
VAI s/he has warm hands

kīsōhēw Ρᓱᐦᐁᐤ
VTA s/he keeps s.o. warm (as with a blanket)

kīsōhkwāmiw Ρᓱᕁᑿᒥᐤ
VAI s/he sleeps warmly

kīsōhowin Ρᓱᐦᐅᐃᐧᐣ
NI warm article of clothing; [pl:] warm clothing

kīsōhpīhkēw Ρᓱᕁᐲᕁᑫᐤ
VAI s/he makes water from snow

kīsōhtāw Ρᓱᕁᑖᐤ
VAIt s/he makes s.t. warm (e.g. house, by insulating)

kīsōnam Ρᓱᓇᒼ
VTI s/he warms s.t. (by holding)

kīsōnēw Ρᓱᓀᐤ
VTA s/he warms s.o. (by holding)

kīsōsimēw Ρᓱᓯᒣᐤ
VTA s/he lies s.o. down and covers him warmly

kīsōsimow Ρᓱᓯᒧᐤ
VAI s/he is lying warmly (in bed)

kīsōsitēw Ρᓱᓯᑌᐤ
VAI s/he has warm feet

kīsōsiw Ρᓱᓯᐤ
VAI s/he is warm, s/he is warmed

kīsōskawēw Ρᓱᐢᑲᐁᐧᐤ
VTA s/he warms s.o.

kīsōwahēw Ρᓱᐊᐧᐦᐁᐤ
VTA s/he places s.o. so as to warm him; s/he dresses s.o. warmly

kīsōwahon Ρᓱᐊᐧᐦᐅᐣ
NI warm clothes; warm parka

kīsōwahow Ρᓱᐊᐧᐦᐅᐤ
VAI s/he dresses warmly

kīsōwahpison Ρᓱᐊᐧᕁᐱᓱᐣ
NA scarf

kīsōwahpisow Ρᓱᐊᐧᕁᐱᓱᐤ
VAI s/he has a warm scarf, s/he wears a warm scarf

kīsōwahpisowin Ρᓱᐊᐧᕁᐱᓱᐃᐧᐣ
NI warm scarf

kīsōwākamin Ρᓱᐋᑲᒥᐣ
VII it is warm (as liquid)

kīsōwāw Ρᓱᐋᐤ
VII it is warm, it is warmed; it provides warmth [also kīsiwāw]

kīsōwāyāw Ρᓱᐋᔮᐤ
VII it is warm weather; it is mild

kīsōwihkasow Ρᓱᐃᐧᕁᑲᓱᐤ
VAI s/he warms him/herself by fire, s/he keeps him/herself warm by fire

kīsōwiyawēw Ρᓱᐃᐧᔭᐁᐧᐤ
VAI s/he has a warm body

kīspin Ρᐢᐱᐣ
IPC if, in case; whether [conditional conjunction; cf. kīsāspin]

kīspin ēkā Ρᐢᐱᐣ ᐁᑲ
IPH if not

kīspin ēsa Ρᐢᐱᐣ ᐁᓴ
IPH if it was, if ever

kīspinacikēmakan Ρᐢᐱᓇᒋᑫᒪᑲᐣ
VII it earns; it receives in return

kīspinacikēw Ρᐢᐱᓇᒋᑫᐤ
VAI s/he earns money, wages; s/he receives, s/he reaps in return

kīspinamākosiw Ρᐢᐱᓇᒫᑯᓯᐤ
VAI s/he is rewarded (for his/her own deeds)

kīspinatam Ρᐢᐱᓇᑕᒼ
VTI s/he earns enough to buy s.t.

kīspinatamawēw Ρᐢᐱᓇᑕᒪᐁᐧᐤ
VTA s/he earns (it/him) for s.o.

kīspinatēw Ρᐢᐱᓇᑌᐤ
VTA s/he earns enough to buy s.o. (e.g. horse)

kīspisiw ᐹᐣᐱᓯᐤ
VAI s/he is chapped, s/he is rough

kīsponēw ᐹᐣᐳᐁᐧᐤ
VII it is full

kīsposkākow ᐹᐣᐳᐢᑳᑯᐤ
VTA it filled s.o. up, it was a filling meal for s.o. [inanimate actor VTA, cf. kisposkaw-]

kīspow ᐹᐣᐳᐤ
VAI s/he is full, s/he has enough to eat

kīspōhēw ᐹᐣᐳᐦᐁᐧᐤ
VTA s/he makes s.o. full, s/he feeds s.o. until full, s/he gets s.o. (e.g. horse) fully fed, s/he gives s.o. enough to eat

kīspōhisow ᐹᐣᐳᐦᐃᓱᐤ
VAI s/he gives him/herself enough to eat

kīsta ᐹᐣᑕ
PR you, too [second person sg]

kīstanaw ᐹᐣᑕᓇᐤ
PR we, too; we-and-you, too [first person pl inclusive]

kīstawāw ᐹᐣᑕᐚᐤ
PR you (pl) too; you (pl) by contrast; you yourselves [second person pl]

kītahtawē ᐹᒋᐦᑕᐍ
IPC at one time, at a certain point in time, sometime; at times, sometimes, once in a while; all at once, suddenly, soon [cf. kētahtawē]

kītimihkawisiw ᐹᒋᒥᐦᑲᐃᐧᓯᐤ
VAI s/he has a sore place on his/her own back

kītiskawēw ᐹᒋᐢᑲᐁᐧᐤ
VTA s/he hurts s.o.'s sore place by stepping on him

kīwāc ᐹᐚᐨ
IPC alone; going astray

kīwāci- ᐹᐚᒋ
IPN lonely, desolate, bereaved

kīwāci- ᐹᐚᒋ
IPV orphaned, stray; lonely, desolately

kīwāci-awāsis ᐹᐚᒋ ᐊᐚᓯᐢ
NA orphan [also kīwāc-āwāsis]

kīwāci-iskwēw ᐹᐚᒋ ᐃᐢᑫᐧᐤ
NA bereaved woman, woman without relatives

kīwāci-nāpēw ᐹᐚᒋ ᓈᐯᐤ
NA bereaved man, man without relatives

kīwācihēw ᐹᐚᒋᐦᐁᐧᐤ
VTA s/he makes s.o. an orphan

kīwātan ᐹᐚᑕᐣ
VII it is a lonely, desolate area

kīwātēyihtam ᐹᐚᑌᔨᐦᑕᒼ
VTI s/he feels lonely, alone

kīwātēyimēw ᐹᐚᑌᔨᒣᐤ
VTA s/he feels sorry for s.o., s/he feels s.o. is alone

kīwātēyimow ᐹᐚᑌᔨᒧᐤ
VAI s/he feels lonely and depressed

kīwātēyimowin ᐹᐚᑌᔨᒧᐃᐧᐣ
NI loneliness, depression

kīwātis ᐹᐚᕙ
NA orphan, bereaved person

kīwātisiw ᐹᐚᕙᓯᐤ
VAI s/he is orphaned, s/he is an orphan

kīwē- ᐹᐁᐧ
IPV back, homeward

kīwēcimēw ᐹᐁᐧᒋᒣᐤ
VAI s/he goes home by boat

kīwēcitāpātēw ᐹᐁᐧᒋᑖᐹᑌᐤ
VTA s/he drags s.o. home

kīwēcitāpēw ᐹᐁᐧᒋᑖᐯᐤ
VAI s/he drags (something) home

kīwēciwan ᐹᐁᐧᒋᐊᐧᐣ
VII the tide is going out; it flows northward

kīwēhāw ᐹᐁᐧᐦᐋᐤ
VAI s/he flies back; s/he flies home, s/he goes home by plane

kīwēhow ᐹᐁᐧᐦᐅᐤ
VAI s/he goes home (by water)

kīwēhoyēw ᐹᐁᐧᐦᐅᔦᐤ
VTA s/he takes s.o. home (by water)

kīwēhtacikēw ᐹᐁᐧᐦᑕᒋᑫᐤ
VAI s/he takes things home

kīwēhtahēw ᐹᐁᐧᐦᑕᐁᐧᐤ
VTA s/he takes s.o. home, s/he carries s.o. back home; [inanimate actor:] it takes s.o. back, it reminds s.o. of bygone days

kīwēhtahiskwēwēw ᐹᐁᐧᐦᑕᐃᐢᑫᐧᐁᐧᐤ
VAI s/he takes a woman home with him

kīwēhtahisow ᐹᐁᐧᐦᑕᐃᐦᓱᐤ
VAI s/he takes him/herself home

kīwēhtahiwēw ᐹᐁᐧᐦᑕᐃᐦᐁᐧᐤ
VAI s/he takes people home with him/her

kīwēhtatamawēw ᐹᐁᐧᐦᑕᑕᒪᐁᐧᐤ
VTA s/he takes (it/him) home for s.o.

kīwēhtatāw ᐹᐁᐧᐦᑕᑖᐤ
VAIt s/he takes s.t. home, s/he carries s.t. back home with him/her

kīwēhtin ᐹᐁᐧᐦᑎᐣ
VII it is a north wind [cf. kīwētin]

kīwēkitāsow ᐹᐁᐧᑭᑖᓱᐤ
VAI s/he goes home in a huff, s/he goes home angry, upset

kīwēkosiw ᐹᐁᐧᑯᓯᐤ
VAI it sets (e.g. star)

kīwēpahēw ᐹᐁᐧᐸᐦᐁᐧᐤ
VTA s/he takes s.o. home (by vehicle, running, etc.)

kīwēpahtāw ᐹᐁᐧᐸᐦᑖᐤ
VAI s/he runs back home

kīwēpayiw ᐹᐁᐧᐸᔨᐤ
VAI s/he goes back home, s/he drives back home, s/he rides back home

kīwēpiciw ᐹᐁᐧᐱᒋᐤ
VAI s/he moves camp back home

kīwētāpēw ᐹᐁᐧᑖᐯᐤ
VAI s/he drags (something) home [rdpl: ka-kīwētāpēw]

kīwētin ᐹᐁᐧᑎᐣ
NI north wind; the north [loc: -ohk; also kīwēhtin]

kīwētinohk ᐹᐁᐧᑎᓄᕽ
IPC north, northwards, in the north [towards the north wind]

kīwētinohk isi ᐹᐁᐧᑎᓄᕽ ᐃᓯ
IPH northward, towards the north

kīwētinohk ohci ᐹᐁᐧᑎᓄᕽ ᐅᐦᒋ
IPH from the north

kīwētinōtāhk ᐹᐁᐧᑎᓄᑖᕽ
IPC in the north

kīwētinōtāwiýiniw ᐹᐁᐧᑎᓄᑖᐃᐧᔨᓂᐤ
NA northern Cree

kīwētisaham ᐹᐁᐧᑎᓴᐦᐊᒼ
VTI s/he sends s.t. home

kīwētisahwēw ᐹᐁᐧᑎᓴᐦᐁᐧᐤ
VTA s/he drives s.o. back home, s/he sends s.o. back home

kīwētotam ᐹᐁᐧᑐᑕᒼ
VTI s/he goes back to s.t., s/he returns home to s.t.

kīwētotawēw ᐹᐁᐧᑐᑕᐁᐧᐤ
VTA s/he goes back to s.o., s/he returns home to s.o.

kīwētowatēw ᐹᐁᐧᑐᐊᐧᑌᐤ
VAI s/he carries his/her own burden (e.g. backpack) home on his/her back

kīwētowātam ᐹᐁᐧᑐᐚᑕᒼ
VTI s/he returns with s.t. on his/her own back

kīwētowātēw ᐹᐁᐧᑐᐚᑌᐤ
VTA s/he returns with s.o. on his/her own back

kīwēw ᐹᐁᐧᐤ
VAI s/he goes home, s/he returns home

kīwēyahkahwēw ᐹᐁᐧᔭᐦᑲᐦᐁᐧᐤ
VTA s/he pushes s.o. home by tool

kīwēyāmohkēw ᐹᐁᐧᔮᒧᐦᑫᐤ
VAI s/he scares people home

kīwēyāmow ᐹᐁᐧᔮᒧᐤ
VAI s/he flees back home; s/he goes home to escape (s.t.)

kīwēyāsiw ᐹᐁᐧᔮᓯᐤ
VAI s/he is blown back home

kīwinēw ᑮᐎᓀᐤ
VAI it gives a dying spasm

ᑯ

kocawākanis ᑯᒐᐚᑲᓂᐢ
NI match [*dim*; *often pl*]
kocawānis ᑯᒐᐚᓂᐢ
NA campfire [*dim*]
koci- ᑯᒋ
IPV try to [*see also* kakwē-]
kocipaýihēw ᑯᒋᐸᔨᐦᐁᐤ
VTA s/he tries s.o. (*e.g.* motorized vehicle)
kocipaýihtāw ᑯᒋᐸᔨᐦᑖᐤ
VAIt s/he tries s.t. (*e.g.* computer)
kocispitam ᑯᒋᐢᐱᑕᒼ
VTI s/he tastes s.t.
kocispitēw ᑯᒋᐢᐱᑌᐤ
VTA s/he tastes s.o.
kocīhēw ᑯᒌᐦᐁᐤ
VTA s/he tries s.o. [*also* kocihēw]
kocīhikowisiw ᑯᒌᐦᐃᑯᐎᓯᐤ
VAI s/he is tried by the powers [*also* kocihikowisiw]
kocīhikowisiwin ᑯᒌᐦᐃᑯᐎᓯᐏᐣ
NI hardship [*also* kocihikowisiwin]
kocīhowin ᑯᒌᐦᐅᐏᐣ
NI exam
kocīhtāw ᑯᒌᐦᑖᐤ
VAIt s/he tries s.t., s/he tries to do s.t.; s/he fits s.t. in [*also* kocihtāw]
kocīw ᑯᒌᐤ
VAI s/he tries, s/he tries s.t.; s/he makes an effort [*rdpl*: kāh-kocīw]
kohcipaýihcikanēyāpiy ᑯᐦᒋᐸᔨᐦᒋᑲᓀᔮᐲ
NI gullet, esophagus [*proposed term*]
kohcipaýihēw ᑯᐦᒋᐸᔨᐦᐁᐤ
VTA s/he swallows s.o.
kohcipaýihtāw ᑯᐦᒋᐸᔨᐦᑖᐤ
VAIt s/he swallows s.t. [*cf.* kohtāpaýihtāw]
kohkohkohow ᑯᐦᑯᐦᑯᐦᐅᐤ
NA small owl [*Saulteaux loan*]
kohkominānihk ᑯᐦᑯᒥᓈᓂᕽ
INM Grandmother's Bay, SK [*cf.* kohkom "your grandmother"]
kohkomipaninaw ᑯᐦᑯᒥᐸᓂᓇᐤ
NA our deceased grandmother; cucumber [*used as a sound-alike for French* "cocombre"]
kohkōs ᑯᐦᑰᐢ
NA pig [*also* kōhkōs]
kohkōsi-pimiy ᑯᐦᑰᓯ ᐱᒦ
NI lard (from a pig)
kohkōsi-pīway ᑯᐦᑰᓯ ᐲᐘᕀ
NI pig bristle(s)
kohkōsis ᑯᐦᑰᓯᐢ
NA piglet [*dim*]
kohkōsiwikamik ᑯᐦᑰᓯᐏᑲᒥᐠ
NI pig barn; pig pen [*pl*: -wa]
kohkōsiwiyās ᑯᐦᑰᓯᐏᔮᐢ
NI pork
kohkōsiwiýin ᑯᐦᑰᓯᐏᔨᐣ
NA bacon [*pl*: -wak]
kohkōsiýākan ᑯᐦᑰᓯᔮᑲᐣ
NI pig trough
kohkōsopwām ᑯᐦᑰᓱᐻᒼ
NI ham [*count noun*]
kohkōsowasakay ᑯᐦᑰᓱᐘᓴᑲᕀ
NA pigskin
kohtaskwahikan ᑯᐦᑕᐢᑿᐦᐃᑲᐣ
NI stovepipe
kohtānēw ᑯᐦᑖᓀᐤ
VTA s/he immerses s.o. in liquid
kohtāpaýihtāw ᑯᐦᑖᐸᔨᐦᑖᐤ
VAIt s/he swallows s.t. [*cf.* kohcipaýihtāw]
konit-ācimowinis ᑯᓂᑖᒋᒧᐎᓂᐢ
NI just a little story [*dim*]
konita ᑯᓂᑕ
IPC merely, just for nothing, in vain, vainly, without reason, without purpose, at random; without further ado [*cf.* pikonita, pikwanita; *wC*: pakwanita]
konita-kīkway ᑯᓂᑕ ᑮᑾᕀ
NI something or other [*only non-locative forms*]
kosā ᑯᓵ
IPC making it superfluous
kosāpahcikamikos ᑯᓵᐸᐦᒋᑲᒥᑯᐢ
NI shaking lodge [*dim*]
kosāpahcikan ᑯᓵᐸᐦᒋᑲᐣ
NI shaking lodge; television
kosāpahcikēw ᑯᓵᐸᐦᒋᑫᐤ
VAI s/he communicates with the spirits
kosāpahcikēwin ᑯᓵᐸᐦᒋᑫᐏᐣ
NI communication with the spirits
kosāpahcikēwiýiniw ᑯᓵᐸᐦᒋᑫᐎᔨᓂᐤ
NA one who communicates with spirits, one who holds the shaking lodge
kosāpahtam ᑯᓵᐸᐦᑕᒼ
VTI s/he uses the shaking lodge; s/he knows future events; s/he finds out about s.t. through the spirits
kosāpahtamowin ᑯᓵᐸᐦᑕᒧᐏᐣ
NI communication with the spirits
kosāpamēw ᑯᓵᐸᒣᐤ
VTA s/he finds out about s.o. through the spirits
kosāskwatos ᑯᓵᐢᑿᑐᐢ
NI Saskatoon willow [*cf.* misāskwatos]
kosāwēkocin ᑯᓵᐍᑯᒋᐣ
VAI s/he hangs in the air
kosikosiw ᑯᓯᑯᓯᐤ
VAI s/he is heavy [*also* kosokosiw; *cf.* kosikwatiw]
kosikwan ᑯᓯᑿᐣ
IPC pounds [*measurement*]
kosikwan ᑯᓯᑿᐣ
VII it is heavy
kosikwanis ᑯᓯᑿᓂᐢ
IPC ounces [*measurement*]
kosikwasin ᑯᓯᑿᓯᐣ
VII it is a little heavy [*dim*]
kosikwatiw ᑯᓯᑿᑎᐤ
VAI s/he is heavy [*cf.* kosikosiw]
kosisān ᑯᓯᓵᐣ
NA male child, son
koskohēw ᑯᐢᑯᐦᐁᐤ
VTA s/he surprises s.o., s/he startles s.o. [*also* kōskohēw]
koskohiwēw ᑯᐢᑯᐦᐃᐍᐤ
VAI s/he startles people
koskomēw ᑯᐢᑯᒣᐤ
VTA s/he startles s.o. by a call [*also* kōskomēw]
koskonēw ᑯᐢᑯᓀᐤ
VTA s/he wakes s.o. up, s/he startles s.o. by hand [*also* kōskonēw]
koskopaýihtāw ᑯᐢᑯᐸᔨᐦᑖᐤ
VAIt s/he shakes s.t.
koskopaýiw ᑯᐢᑯᐸᔨᐤ
VAI s/he wakes up; it bursts; it goes loose; it shakes [*also* kōskopaýiw]
koskopaýiw ᑯᐢᑯᐸᔨᐤ
VII it bursts [*also* kōskopaýiw]
koskopitam ᑯᐢᑯᐱᑕᒼ
VTI s/he shakes s.t. by a pull
koskopitēw ᑯᐢᑯᐱᑌᐤ
VTA s/he shakes s.o. to awaken
koskoskoham ᑯᐢᑯᐢᑯᐦᐊᒼ
VTI s/he juggles s.t. with a stick
koskoskonēw ᑯᐢᑯᐢᑯᓀᐤ
VTA s/he startles s.o. awake, s/he wakes s.o. by hand [*rdpl*, *cf.* koskonēw]
koskoskopaýiw ᑯᐢᑯᐢᑯᐸᔨᐤ
VII it goes loose, it shakes [*rdpl*, *cf.* koskopaýiw *VII*]
koskoskopitam ᑯᐢᑯᐢᑯᐱᑕᒼ
VTI s/he shakes s.t. by a pull [*rdpl*, *cf.* koskopitam]
koskoskoýahkahwēw ᑯᐢᑯᐢᑯᔭᐦᑲᐦᐍᐤ
VTA s/he prods s.o. awake [*rdpl*, *cf.* koskoýahkahwēw]
koskoskwaham ᑯᐢᑯᐢᑿᐦᐊᒼ
VTI s/he makes a startling noise on s.t. by tool [*rdpl*, *cf.* koskwaham]
koskoskwāw ᑯᐢᑯᐢᒁᐤ
VII it rocks a bit (*e.g.* boat)
koskowātapiw ᑯᐢᑯᐚᑕᐱᐤ
VAI s/he sits still, s/he sits quietly

koskowātēyihtākwan ᑯᐢᑯᐋᐧᑌᔨᐦᑖᑲᐧᐣ
VII it is quiet, it is tranquil
koskowēpinēw ᑯᐢᑯᐁᐧᐱᓀᐤ
VTA s/he shakes s.o. to awaken; s/he jiggles s.o.'s bed to awaken
koskowihēw ᑯᐢᑯᐃᐧᐦᐁᐤ
VTA s/he startles s.o.
koskoýahkahwēw ᑯᐢᑯᔭᐦᑲᐦᐁᐧᐤ
VTA s/he prods s.o. awake
koskwaham ᑯᐢᑲᐧᐦᐊᒼ
VTI s/he makes a startling noise on s.t. by tool
koskwāpisin ᑯᐢᑳᐧᐱᓯᐣ
VAI s/he is startled by the sight of something
koskwāwātan ᑯᐢᑳᐧᐋᐧᑕᐣ
VII it is all quiet and in order
koskwēýihtam ᑯᐢᑫᐧᔨᐦᑕᒼ
VTI s/he is surprised by or at s.t.; s/he has inspiring thoughts about s.t.
koskwēýimēw ᑯᐢᑫᐧᔨᒣᐤ
VTA s/he is surprised by or at s.o.; s/he has frightening thoughts about s.o.
kospāhtawīw ᑯᐢᐹᐦᑕᐄᐧᐤ
VAI s/he goes upstairs [*see also* āmaciwēw]
kospāpēkinēw ᑯᐢᐹᐯᑭᓀᐤ
VTA s/he pulls s.o. away, s/he pulls s.o. out by a line
kospāyihk ᑯᐢᐹᔨᕽ
IPC away from the thing, away from lodge fire
kospihtahēw ᑯᐢᐱᐦᑕᐦᐁᐤ
VTA s/he takes s.o. up a bank
kospihtatāw ᑯᐢᐱᐦᑕᑖᐤ
VAIt s/he takes s.t. up a bank
kospiwēpinēw ᑯᐢᐱᐁᐧᐱᓀᐤ
VTA s/he flings s.o. off
kospīw ᑯᐢᐲᐤ
VAI s/he goes off (into the woods); s/he goes away from the water [*also* kospiw]
kospohtahēw ᑯᐢᐳᐦᑕᐦᐁᐤ
VTA s/he carries s.o. away from water
kospohtēw ᑯᐢᐳᐦᑌᐤ
VAI s/he walks away from the water, s/he walks up a bank and into the trees
kostam ᑯᐢᑕᒼ
VTI s/he fears s.t., s/he is afraid of s.t.
kostācihkwāmiw ᑯᐢᑖᒋᐦᑳᐧᒥᐤ
VAI s/he has a nightmare
kostācihkwāmiwin ᑯᐢᑖᒋᐦᑳᐧᒥᐃᐧᐣ
NI nightmare
kostācikosiw ᑯᐢᑖᒋᑯᓯᐤ
VAI s/he is frightening, s/he is scarey
kostācinākosiw ᑯᐢᑖᒋᓈᑯᓯᐤ
VAI s/he looks frightening
kostācinākwan ᑯᐢᑖᒋᓈᑲᐧᐣ
VII it looks frightening
kostāciýawēw ᑯᐢᑖᒋᔭᐁᐧᐤ
VAI s/he is in fear
kostācīskawēw ᑯᐢᑖᒌᐢᑲᐁᐧᐤ
VTA s/he frightens s.o. by going to that one
kostācīskiw ᑯᐢᑖᒌᐢᑭᐤ
VAI s/he is easily frightened [*hab*]
kostācīw ᑯᐢᑖᒌᐤ
VAI s/he is afraid, s/he is frightened [*also* kostāciw]
kostācīwin ᑯᐢᑖᒌᐃᐧᐣ
NI fear
kostākan ᑯᐢᑖᑲᐣ
NA enemy
kostāmikwan ᑯᐢᑖᒥᑲᐧᐣ
VII it is a blizzard
kostātēýihtākosiw ᑯᐢᑖᑌᔨᐦᑖᑯᓯᐤ
VAI s/he is feared, s/he is frightening
kostātēýihtākwan ᑯᐢᑖᑌᔨᐦᑖᑲᐧᐣ
VII it is feared, it is frightening
kostātikosiw ᑯᐢᑖᑎᑯᓯᐤ
VAI s/he is terrible, s/he is fearful
kostātikwan ᑯᐢᑖᑎᑲᐧᐣ
VII it is fearsome, it is awe-inspiring; it is scarey
kostēw ᑯᐢᑌᐤ
VTA s/he fears s.o., s/he is afraid of s.o.
kostitowak ᑯᐢᑎᑐᐊᐧᐠ
VAI they frighten one another
kotahāskwācikan ᑯᑕᐦᐋᐢᑳᐧᒋᑲᐣ
NI target, bull's-eye
kotahāskwātam ᑯᑕᐦᐋᐢᑳᐧᑕᒼ
VTI s/he uses s.t. as a target; s/he aims at s.t., s/he shoots at s.t.
kotahāskwātēw ᑯᑕᐦᐋᐢᑳᐧᑌᐤ
VTA s/he uses s.o. as a target; s/he aims at s.o., s/he shoots at s.o.
kotahāskwēw ᑯᑕᐦᐋᐢᑫᐧᐤ
VAI s/he shoots at a target; s/he tries target-shooting
kotahāskwēwin ᑯᑕᐦᐋᐢᑫᐧᐃᐧᐣ
NI target practice
kotahpisow ᑯᑕᐦᐱᓱᐤ
VAI s/he tries tying him/herself, s/he tries on a belt
kotak ᑯᑕᐠ
PR other, another [*anim prox sg / inan sg*]
kotak ispaýiki ᑯᑕᐠ ᐃᐢᐸᔨᑭ
IPH next week
kotak mīna ᑯᑕᐠ ᒦᓇ
PR another
kotak pīsim ᑯᑕᐠ ᐲᓯᒼ
IPH next month
kotaka ᑯᑕᑲ
PR other [*anim obv / inan pl*]
kotakak ᑯᑕᑲᐠ
PR other [*anim prox pl*]
kotakihk ᑯᑕᑭᕽ
IPC in another place, elsewhere
kotakiya ᑯᑕᑭᔭ
PR other one, the other one [*anim prox sg*; *archaic*]
kotakiyak ᑯᑕᑭᔭᐠ
PR other ones, the other ones [*anim prox pl*; *archaic*]
kotakiýiw ᑯᑕᑭᔨᐤ
PR other one, the other one [*inan obv*; *archaic*]
kotapinam ᑯᑕᐱᓇᒼ
VTI s/he overturns s.t. [*cf.* kwatapinam]
kotapinēw ᑯᑕᐱᓀᐤ
VTA s/he overturns s.o. [*cf.* kwatapinēw]
kotapipaýiw ᑯᑕᐱᐸᔨᐤ
VAI s/he overturns while riding in a vehicle (or boat) [*cf.* kwatapipaýiw]
kotapiskam ᑯᑕᐱᐢᑲᒼ
VTI s/he overturns s.t. by stepping into a boat
kotapīw ᑯᑕᐲᐤ
VAI s/he overturns, s/he turns over, s/he tips over [*cf.* kwatapīw]
kotawān ᑯᑕᐋᐧᐣ
NA campfire, bonfire; fireplace [*also NI*]
kotawānāpisk ᑯᑕᐋᐧᓈᐱᐢᐠ
NI stove, oven [*also NA*; *pl*: -wa(k)]
kotawēw ᑯᑕᐁᐧᐤ
VAI s/he builds a fire
kotāpacihtāw ᑯᑖᐸᒋᐦᑖᐤ
VAIt s/he tries using s.t.
kotāwahcinam ᑯᑖᐊᐧᐦᒋᓇᒼ
VTI s/he sinks into s.t. as s/he steps
kotāwaskamikīw ᑯᑖᐊᐧᐢᑲᒥᑮᐤ
VAI s/he sinks into the ground
kotāwinam ᑯᑖᐃᐧᓇᒼ
VTI s/he pushes s.t. under (out of sight)
kotāwinēw ᑯᑖᐃᐧᓀᐤ
VTA s/he makes s.o. sink into the ground; s/he pushes s.o. underground (out of sight)
kotāwipaýiw ᑯᑖᐃᐧᐸᔨᐤ
VAI s/he sinks into the ground (*e.g.* soft mud)
kotāwīw ᑯᑖᐄᐧᐤ
VAI s/he sinks into the ground; it digs him/herself under soil (*e.g.* a turtle)
kotāwīwi-pīsim ᑯᑖᐄᐧᐃᐧ ᐲᓯᒼ
NA eclipse [*pl*: -wak]
kotēskāmow ᑯᑌᐢᑳᒧᐤ
VAI s/he flees to shelter
kotēyihtam ᑯᑌᔨᐦᑕᒼ
VTI s/he tries s.t.

kotikonam ᑯᑎᑯᓇᐨ
VTI s/he pulls s.t. back
kotikonēw ᑯᑎᑯᓀᐤ
VTA s/he dislocates s.o., s/he cripples s.o.
kotikonikan ᑯᑎᑯᓂᑲᐣ
NI breech-loading gun
kotikonikātēw ᑯᑎᑯᓂᑳᑌᐤ
VII it is pulled back
kotikopaýiw ᑯᑎᑯᐸᔨᐤ
VAI s/he sprains him/herself while running
kotikopitēw ᑯᑎᑯᐱᑌᐤ
VTA s/he dislocates s.o. (while wrestling)
kotikosin ᑯᑎᑯᓯᐣ
VAI s/he sprains (a joint), s/he puts his/her own joint out of place; s/he falls breaking a limb
kotikoswēw ᑯᑎᑯᓭᐤ
VTA s/he cuts a limb from s.o.
kotinam ᑯᑎᓇᐨ
VTI s/he tests s.t. by hand
kotinēw ᑯᑎᓀᐤ
VTA s/he tests s.o. by hand
kotiskam ᑯᑎᐢᑲᐨ
VTI s/he tries s.t. on (*e.g.* article of clothing); s/he tries stepping on or into s.t.
kotiskawēw ᑯᑎᐢᑲᐍᐤ
VTA s/he tries s.o. on (*e.g.* article of clothing); s/he tries going with s.o.
kotiskāwēw ᑯᑎᐢᑳᐍᐤ
VAI s/he races; it gallops
kotiskāwēwatim ᑯᑎᐢᑳᐍᐘᑎᐨ
NA race-horse [*pl*: -wak]
kotispitam ᑯᑎᐢᐱᑕᐨ
VTI s/he samples s.t., s/he tastes s.t. [*cf.* kocispitam]
kotispitēw ᑯᑎᐢᐱᑌᐤ
VTA s/he tastes s.o. [*cf.* kocispitēw]
kotokonam ᑯᑐᑯᓇᐨ
VTI s/he sprains his/her own hand
kotokosin ᑯᑐᑯᓯᐣ
VAI s/he sprains, s/he dislocates s.t. (from falling)
kotokositēw ᑯᑐᑯᓯᑌᐤ
VAI s/he has a club-foot, s/he is club-footed

ᑰ

kōhtākan ᑰᐦᑖᑲᐣ
NI windpipe, throat [*cf.* -kōhtākan- *NDI*]
kōkiyāhokow ᑰᑭᔮᐦᐅᑯᐤ
VAI s/he is drawn under by current or waves
kōkīnam ᑰᑮᓇᐨ
VTI s/he holds s.t. underwater
kōkīpaýihow ᑰᑮᐸᔨᐦᐅᐤ
VAI s/he dives quickly
kōkīpaýiw ᑰᑮᐸᔨᐤ
VAI s/he goes underwater
kōkīw ᑰᑮᐤ
VAI s/he dives
kōkom! ᑰᑯᐨ
NDA Grandma! [*voc, familiar form*; *cf.* nohkō!, nohkom; *cf.* kohkom "your grandmother"]
kōna ᑰᓇ
NA snow [*prox sg and obv only*]
kōnikamik ᑰᓂᑲᒥᐠ
NI snow house [*pl*: -wa]
kōniwan ᑰᓂᐘᐣ
VII it is covered with snow, there is snow on the ground
kōniwāpoy ᑰᓂᐚᐳᐩ
NI water from melted snow, meltwater
kōniwiw ᑰᓂᐏᐤ
VII it is snowy; it is covered with snow
kōta- ᑰᑕ
IPV long for, be deprived of
kōtamāw ᑰᑕᒫᐤ
VAI s/he is in want
kōtatē- ᑰᑕᑌ
IPV at a loss, making no attempt
kōtawēýihtam ᑰᑕᐍᔨᐦᑕᐨ
VTI s/he misses s.t., s/he longs for s.t. [*cf.* kwētawēýihtam]
kōtawēýimēw ᑰᑕᐍᔨᒣᐤ
VTA s/he misses s.o., s/he longs for s.o. [*cf.* kwētawēýimēw]
kōwiýīkwanēw ᑰᐏᔩᑿᓀᐤ
NA yellow feather with black tip

ᑿ

kwataki- ᑿᑕᑭ
IPV distressing, tormenting, tortuous [*see* kakwātaki- *and related derivations*]
kwatapinam ᑿᑕᐱᓇᐨ
VTI s/he tips s.t. over [*cf.* kotapinam]
kwatapinēw ᑿᑕᐱᓀᐤ
VTA s/he tips s.o. over [*cf.* kotapinēw]
kwatapipaýiw ᑿᑕᐱᐸᔨᐤ
VII it tips over (*e.g.* canoe) [*cf.* kotapipaýiw]
kwatapisimēw ᑿᑕᐱᓯᒣᐤ
VTA s/he turns s.o. over, s/he tips s.o. over
kwatapiwēpinēw ᑿᑕᐱᐍᐱᓀᐤ
VTA s/he flips s.o. over, s/he throws s.o. over
kwatapīw ᑿᑕᐲᐤ
VAI s/he tips over (*e.g.* vehicle) [*cf.* kotapīw]
kwatapīw ᑿᑕᐲᐤ
VII it tips over (*e.g.* canoe)
kwayahikow ᑿᔭᐦᐃᑯᐤ
VAI s/he acts quickly
kwaýako- ᑿᔭᑯ
IPV taking out, directly
kwaýakoham ᑿᔭᑯᐦᐊᐨ
VTI s/he pries s.t. out
kwaýakohtitāw ᑿᔭᑯᐦᑎᑖᐤ
VAIt s/he gets s.t. out by shaking
kwaýakonam ᑿᔭᑯᓇᐨ
VTI s/he takes s.t. out by hand; s/he takes s.t. out of an opening
kwaýakonēw ᑿᔭᑯᓀᐤ
VTA s/he takes s.o. out of an opening
kwaýakopaýin ᑿᔭᑯᐸᔨᐣ
VII it falls out
kwaýakopitam ᑿᔭᑯᐱᑕᐨ
VTI s/he pulls s.t. out
kwaýakopitēw ᑿᔭᑯᐱᑌᐤ
VTA s/he pulls s.o. out
kwaýakosimēw ᑿᔭᑯᓯᒣᐤ
VTA s/he knocks s.o. (pipe) clean
kwaýakow ᑿᔭᑯᐤ
VAI it crawls out of a hole or den
kwaýakwahwēw ᑿᔭᑿᐦᐍᐤ
VTA s/he knocks s.o. (pipe) clean against something
kwaýakwatēhtam ᑿᔭᑿᑌᐦᑕᐨ
VTI s/he takes s.t. out of his/her own mouth
kwayas ᑿᔭᐢ
IPC right, properly, correct [*cf.* kwayask]
kwaýasitē-wēpinēw ᑿᔭᓯᑌ ᐍᐱᓀᐤ
VTA s/he tosses s.o. in
kwaýasitē-ýahkinēw ᑿᔭᓯᑌ ᔭᐦᑭᓀᐤ
VTA s/he pushes s.o. into a hole
kwaýasitēw ᑿᔭᓯᑌᐤ
VAI s/he goes into a hole or den
kwayask ᑿᔭᐢᐠ
IPC right, properly, straight, correct, by rights [*cf.* kwayas]
kwayask ēwako ᑿᔭᐢᐠ ᐁᐘᑯ
IPH that's right; that one would do right
kwayask-ispaýiw ᑿᔭᐢᐠ ᐃᐢᐸᔨᐤ
VII it works out properly [*also two words*]
kwayask-itamon ᑿᔭᐢᐠ ᐃᑕᒧᐣ
VII it is straight [*also two words*]
kwayask-itastēw ᑿᔭᐢᐠ ᐃᑕᐢᑌᐤ
VII it is proper or legal [*also two words*]
kwayask-itātisiw ᑿᔭᐢᐠ ᐃᑖᑎᓯᐤ
VAI s/he is well behaved; s/he is honest

kwayask-itēyihtākwan ᑲᐧᔭᐢᐠ ᐃᑌᔨᐦᑖᑲᐧᐣ
VII it is believed to be right [*also two words*]

kwayask-itōtam ᑲᐧᔭᐢᐠ ᐃᑑᑕᒼ
VTI s/he does s.t. right [*also two words*]

kwayask-itōtamowin ᑲᐧᔭᐢᐠ ᐃᑑᑕᒧᐏᐣ
NI just or legal dealing

kwayaskapiw ᑲᐧᔭᐢᑲᐱᐤ
VAI s/he sits properly

kwayaskastāw ᑲᐧᔭᐢᑲᐢᑖᐤ
VAIt s/he places s.t. properly

kwayaskastēw ᑲᐧᔭᐢᑲᐢᑌᐤ
VII it is right, correct

kwayaski- ᑲᐧᔭᐢᑭ
IPV properly [*cf.* kwayasko-]

kwayasko- ᑲᐧᔭᐢᑯ
IPV straight; properly, correctly [*cf.* kwayaski-]

kwayaskoham ᑲᐧᔭᐢᑯᐦᐊᒼ
VTI s/he pushes s.t. in place (with a pole)

kwayaskohēw ᑲᐧᔭᐢᑯᐦᐁᐤ
VTA s/he straightens s.o. out

kwayaskohtāw ᑲᐧᔭᐢᑯᐦᑖᐤ
VAIt s/he straightens s.t. out, s/he straightens the edges

kwayaskokāpawiw ᑲᐧᔭᐢᑯᑳᐸᐏᐤ
VAI s/he stands straight, s/he stands tall

kwayaskomohtāw ᑲᐧᔭᐢᑯᒧᐦᑖᐤ
VAIt s/he applies s.t. in its proper place

kwayaskopayiw ᑲᐧᔭᐢᑯᐸᔨᐤ
VAI s/he stands up properly

kwayaskosam ᑲᐧᔭᐢᑯᓴᒼ
VTI s/he cuts s.t. straight

kwayaskosāwācikan ᑲᐧᔭᐢᑯᓵᐚᒋᑲᐣ
NI board with lines cut through it

kwayaskosiw ᑲᐧᔭᐢᑯᓯᐤ
VAI s/he is straight; s/he stands upright

kwayaskowāpiskinam ᑲᐧᔭᐢᑯᐚᐱᐢᑭᓇᒼ
VTI s/he straightens s.t. (metal; *e.g.* wire) by hand

kwayaskwamon ᑲᐧᔭᐢᑲᐧᒧᐣ
VII it is a straight road

kwayaskwan ᑲᐧᔭᐢᑲᐧᐣ
VII it is straight; it stands upright

kwayaskwātisiw ᑲᐧᔭᐢᑳᐧᑎᓯᐤ
VAI s/he is honest and just

kwayaskwāw ᑲᐧᔭᐢᑳᐧᐤ
VII it is straight (*e.g.* a board)

kwayāc ᑲᐧᔮᐨ
IPC ready, prepared; already, beforehand [*cf.* kwayāci]

kwayāci ᑲᐧᔮᒋ
IPC already; beforehand [*cf.* kwayāc]

kwayāci- ᑲᐧᔮᒋ
IPV in readiness, already; in preparation; beforehand

kwayāci-sikwatahikātēw ᑲᐧᔮᒋ ᓯᑲᐧᑕᐦᐃᑳᑌᐤ
VII it is previously pounded (*e.g.* meat); it is minute steak

kwayācihtamawēw ᑲᐧᔮᒋᐦᑕᒪᐍᐤ
VTA s/he prepares (it/him) for s.o.

kwayācihtāw ᑲᐧᔮᒋᐦᑖᐤ
VAIt s/he gets s.t. ready, s/he prepares s.t.

kwayācikāpawiw ᑲᐧᔮᒋᑳᐸᐏᐤ
VAI s/he stands ready

kwayāhow ᑲᐧᔮᐦᐅᐤ
VAI s/he hurries, s/he hurries up [*cf.* kakwayāhow]

kwayātan ᑲᐧᔮᑕᐣ
VII it is ready

kwayātapiw ᑲᐧᔮᑕᐱᐤ
VAI s/he is ready, s/he sits ready

kwayātastamawēw ᑲᐧᔮᑕᐢᑕᒪᐍᐤ
VTA s/he puts (it/him) aside in readiness for s.o.

kwayātastamāsow ᑲᐧᔮᑕᐢᑕᒫᓱᐤ
VAI s/he puts (it/him) aside in readiness for him/herself

kwayātastāw ᑲᐧᔮᑕᐢᑖᐤ
VAIt s/he places s.t. in readiness, s/he puts s.t. aside in readiness

kwayātastēw ᑲᐧᔮᑕᐢᑌᐤ
VII it is placed in readiness

kwayātinam ᑲᐧᔮᑎᓇᒼ
VTI s/he holds s.t. ready in hand

kwayātinēw ᑲᐧᔮᑎᓀᐤ
VTI s/he holds s.o. ready in hand

kwayātisiw ᑲᐧᔮᑎᓯᐤ
VAI s/he is ready

ᑳᐧ

kwāhci- ᑳᐧᐦᒋ
IPV far off

kwāhci-wēpinam ᑳᐧᐦᒋᐍᐱᓇᒼ
VTI s/he flings s.t. aside

kwāhci-wēpinēw ᑳᐧᐦᒋᐍᐱᓀᐤ
VTA s/he flings s.o. aside

kwāhkonēw ᑳᐧᐦᑯᓀᐤ
VTA s/he pushes s.o. over

kwāhkosow ᑳᐧᐦᑯᓱᐤ
VAI s/he burns, s/he is burning, s/he catches on fire

kwāhkotēnikēw ᑳᐧᐦᑯᑌᓂᑫᐤ
VAI s/he starts a fire, s/he sets things aflame

kwāhkotē-wēpaham ᑳᐧᐦᑯᑌ ᐍᐸᐦᐊᒼ
VTI s/he rubs s.t. to make fire

kwāhkotēw ᑳᐧᐦᑯᑌᐤ
NI blaze [*cf.* kwāhkotēw *VII*]

kwāhkotēw ᑳᐧᐦᑯᑌᐤ
VII it catches fire, it burns, it blazes, it is in flames

kwāhko-wēpinēw ᑳᐧᐦᑯ ᐍᐱᓀᐤ
VTA s/he throws s.o. into the fire

kwāhtāhotēw ᑳᐧᐦᑖᐦᐅᑌᐤ
VII it drifts far away

kwāhtohtēw ᑳᐧᐦᑐᐦᑌᐤ
VAI s/he wanders far away [*also* kwahtohtēw]

kwāpaham ᑳᐧᐸᐦᐊᒼ
VTI s/he dips for s.t., s/he dips s.t. up (*i.e.* a liquid); s/he dips s.t. out

kwāpahamawēw ᑳᐧᐸᐦᐊᒪᐍᐤ
VTA s/he dips water for s.o.

kwāpahikan ᑳᐧᐸᐦᐃᑲᐣ
NA ladle

kwāpahikēw ᑳᐧᐸᐦᐃᑫᐤ
VAI s/he scoops things out, s/he scoops liquid out

kwāpahipān ᑳᐧᐸᐦᐃᐹᐣ
NI dipper, jug [*also* kwāpahōpān]

kwāpahōpākan ᑳᐧᐸᐦᐆᐹᑲᐣ
NA dipper

kwāpahwēw ᑳᐧᐸᐦᐍᐤ
VTA s/he scoops s.o. up (*e.g.* grain), s/he mines s.o. (*e.g.* gold)

kwāpatahwēw ᑳᐧᐸᑕᐦᐍᐤ
VTA s/he thrashes s.o.

kwāpikamawēw ᑳᐧᐱᑲᒪᐍᐤ
VTA s/he fetches water for s.o.

kwāpikākan ᑳᐧᐱᑳᑲᐣ
NI bucket

kwāpikākēw ᑳᐧᐱᑳᑫᐤ
VAI s/he uses something to dip water

kwāpikēskanaw ᑳᐧᐱᑫᐢᑲᓇᐤ
NI path to the watering place

kwāpikēw ᑳᐧᐱᑫᐤ
VAI s/he goes for water; s/he draws water, s/he fetches water, s/he hauls water

kwāsihēw ᑳᐧᓯᐦᐁᐤ
VTA s/he kidnaps s.o.; s/he runs off with s.o.; s/he seduces s.o.

kwāsihtawēw ᑳᐧᓯᐦᑕᐍᐤ
VTA s/he steals (it/him) from s.o.; he seduces s.o.'s wife

kwāsihtāw ᑳᐧᓯᐦᑖᐤ
VAIt s/he runs off with s.t.; s/he runs off with s.t.

kwāsihtwākēw ᑳᐧᓯᐦᑖᐧᑫᐤ
VAI s/he steals things from people

kwāsihtwāw ᑳᐧᓯᐦᑖᐧᐤ
VAI s/he is stolen from; s/he is seduced

kwāsiskwēwēw ᑳᐧᓯᐢᑫᐧᐍᐤ
VAI he steals a wife for himself

kwāskohcisīs ᑳᐧᐢᑯᐦᒋᓰᐢ
NA grasshopper [*cf.* kwāskohcīsis]

kwāskohcīsis ᑳᐧᐢᑯᐦᒌᓯᐢ
NA grasshopper [*cf.* kwāskohcisīs]

kwāskohtitotam ᑳᐧᐢᑯᐦᑎᑐᑕᒼ
VTI s/he jumps up for s.t.

kwāskohtiw ᑳᐧᐢᑯᐦᑎᐤ
VAI s/he jumps, s/he makes a jump

kwāskwahamawēw ᑳᐧᐢᑲᐧᐦᐊᒪᐍᐤ
VTA s/he knocks (it/him) into the air for s.o.

kwāskwāskinatowēw ᑳᐧᐢᑳᐧᐢᑭᓇᑐᐍᐤ
VAI s/he plays lacrosse [*rdpl*]

kwāskwāskohtiw ᑳᐧᐢᑳᐧᐢᑯᐦᑎᐤ
VAI s/he jumps [*rdpl, also* kwāhkwāskohtiw; *cf.* kwāskohtiw]

kwāskwāskotihpēw ᑳᐧᐢᑳᐧᐢᑯᑎᐦᐯᐤ
NI heartstring [*rdpl*]

kwāskwāskwanipīhkēw ᑳᐧᐢᑳᐧᐢᑲᐧᓂᐲᐦᑫᐤ
NI big vein from heart [*rdpl*]

kwāskwāskwēpaýihow ᑳᐧᐢᑳᐧᐢᑫᐧᐸᔨᐦᐅᐤ
VAI s/he throws him/herself leaping [*rdpl*]

kwāskwē- ᑳᐧᐢᑫᐧ
IPV upwards

kwāskwēkocin ᑳᐧᐢᑫᐧᑯᒋᐣ
VAI s/he leaps, s/he speeds through the air; s/he jumps from fright

kwāskwēkotēw ᑳᐧᐢᑫᐧᑯᑌᐤ
VII it jumps up, it leaps up

kwāskwēnitowān ᑳᐧᐢᑫᐧᓂᑐᐚᐣ
NA ball (for kicking), football [*also* kwāskwēnatowān]

kwāskwēpahwēw ᑳᐧᐢᑫᐧᐸᐦᐍᐤ
VTA s/he tosses s.o. by tool

kwāskwēpaýihow ᑳᐧᐢᑫᐧᐸᔨᐦᐅᐤ
VAI s/he throws him/herself leaping; s/he jumps

kwāskwēpaýihōs ᑳᐧᐢᑫᐧᐸᔨᐦᐆᐢ
NA jumping deer [*dim*]

kwāskwēpaýiw ᑳᐧᐢᑫᐧᐸᔨᐤ
VAI s/he leaps; it bounces

kwāskwēpicikan ᑳᐧᐢᑫᐧᐱᒋᑲᐣ
NI fishing-rod; fish hook, hook and line

kwāskwēpicikanēyāpiy ᑳᐧᐢᑫᐧᐱᒋᑲᓀᔮᐱᐩ
NI fishing line

kwāskwēpicikanis ᑳᐧᐢᑫᐧᐱᒋᑲᓂᐢ
NI fish-hook; small fishing-rod [*dim*]

kwāskwēpicikēw ᑳᐧᐢᑫᐧᐱᒋᑫᐤ
VAI s/he angles, s/he fishes (with rod and reel)

kwāskwēpicikēwin ᑳᐧᐢᑫᐧᐱᒋᑫᐃᐧᐣ
NI angling

kwāskwēpimosinēw ᑳᐧᐢᑫᐧᐱᒧᓯᓀᐤ
VTA s/he throws s.t. far

kwāskwēpitam ᑳᐧᐢᑫᐧᐱᑕᒼ
VTI s/he catches s.t., s/he grabs s.t.; s/he hooks s.t., s/he jerks s.t. quickly

kwāskwēpitamawēw ᑳᐧᐢᑫᐧᐱᑕᒪᐍᐤ
VTA s/he angles for s.o., s/he catches fish for s.o.

kwāskwēpitēw ᑳᐧᐢᑫᐧᐱᑌᐤ
VTA s/he catches s.o., s/he grabs s.o.; s/he hooks s.o., s/he jerks s.o. quickly (*e.g.* catching a fish)

kwāskwēpitisow ᑳᐧᐢᑫᐧᐱᑎᓱᐤ
VAI s/he catches him/herself on the hook

kwāskwēsin ᑳᐧᐢᑫᐧᓯᐣ
VAI s/he bounces

kwāskwēwēpahwēw ᑳᐧᐢᑫᐧᐍᐸᐦᐍᐤ
VTA s/he knocks s.o. aloft (by tool), s/he knocks s.o. into the air

kwāskwēwēpinēw ᑳᐧᐢᑫᐧᐍᐱᓀᐤ
VTA s/he flings s.o. aloft

kwāskwēyāciwasow ᑳᐧᐢᑫᐧᔮᒋᐊᐧᓱᐤ
VAI it is at a full boil (*e.g.* kettle)

kwāskwēyāstitāw ᑳᐧᐢᑫᐧᔮᐢᑎᑖᐤ
VAIt s/he makes s.t. flare up in the wind

kwātaki- ᑳᐧᑕᑭ
IPV distressing, tormenting, tortuous [*see also* kakwātaki- *for other derivations*]

ᑫᐧ

kwēcihkēmow ᑫᐧᒋᐦᑫᒧᐤ
VAI s/he asks [*cf.* kakwēcihkēmow]

kwēh-kwēkwask ᑫᐧᐦ ᑫᐧᑲᐧᐢᐠ
IPC back and forth [*rdpl*]

kwēkwēkocīs ᑫᐧᑫᐧᑯᒌᐢ
NA firefly

kwēs ᑫᐧᐢ
IPC come here! (call to dog team)

kwēskaham ᑫᐧᐢᑲᐦᐊᒼ
VTI s/he changes s.t.'s position; s/he turns s.t. with a fork (as in frying meat); s/he turns s.t. (using an instrument)

kwēskahcāhk ᑫᐧᐢᑲᐦᒑᕽ
IPC at the other side of the hill

kwēskahēw ᑫᐧᐢᑲᐦᐁᐤ
VTA s/he changes s.o.'s position in lying or sitting

kwēskahwēw ᑫᐧᐢᑲᐦᐍᐤ
VTA s/he turns s.o. over (using an instrument)

kwēskakihcikēw ᑫᐧᐢᑲᑭᐦᒋᑫᐤ
VAI s/he changes the prices

kwēskakihtam ᑫᐧᐢᑲᑭᐦᑕᒼ
VTI s/he changes the price of s.t.

kwēskakocin ᑫᐧᐢᑲᑯᒋᐣ
VAI s/he turns to the other side as s/he falls

kwēskapatēskwēw ᑫᐧᐢᑲᐸᑌᐢᑫᐧᐤ
VAI s/he turns the meat in the kettle

kwēskapiw ᑫᐧᐢᑲᐱᐤ
VAI s/he turns as s/he sits

kwēskastāw ᑫᐧᐢᑲᐢᑖᐤ
VAIt s/he places s.t. turning; s/he changes the position of s.t.

kwēskawēw ᑫᐧᐢᑲᐍᐤ
VAI s/he turns colour, s/he changes colour

kwēskāhtik ᑫᐧᐢᑳᐦᑎᐠ
IPC at the other side of the grove

kwēskātisiw ᑫᐧᐢᑳᑎᓯᐤ
VAI s/he repents; s/he changes his/her way of life

kwēskātisiwin ᑫᐧᐢᑳᑎᓯᐃᐧᐣ
NI conversion

kwēskāyihk ᑫᐧᐢᑳᔨᕽ
IPC at the other side of the place

kwēskēýihtam ᑫᐧᐢᑫᔨᐦᑕᒼ
VTI s/he changes his/her mind (about s.t.)

kwēski ᑫᐧᐢᑭ
IPC at the other side, changing

kwēski- ᑫᐧᐢᑭ
IPV turning

kwēskihtatin ᑫᐧᐢᑭᐦᑕᑎᐣ
VII there is a change in the wind

kwēskihtākosiw ᑫᐧᐢᑭᐦᑖᑯᓯᐤ
VAI s/he sounds differently (in voice)

kwēskihtākwan ᑫᐧᐢᑭᐦᑖᑲᐧᐣ
VII it changes sound, it sounds differently

kwēskihtin ᑫᐧᐢᑭᐦᑎᐣ
VII there is a turn in the wind

kwēskihtinipaýiw ᑫᐧᐢᑭᐦᑎᓂᐸᔨᐤ
VII there is a sudden change in the wind

kwēskikāpawiw ᑫᐧᐢᑭᑳᐸᐃᐧᐤ
VAI s/he turns standing; s/he turns around (when standing)

kwēskinam ᑫᐧᐢᑭᓇᒼ
VTI s/he turns s.t. over (the other way)

kwēskinamawēw ᑫᐧᐢᑭᓇᒪᐍᐤ
VTA s/he turns (it/him) once sideways for s.o.

kwēskinākohēw ᑫᐧᐢᑭᓈᑯᐦᐁᐤ
VTA s/he changes s.o.'s appearance

kwēskinākohtāw ᑫᐧᐢᑭᓈᑯᐦᑖᐤ
VAIt s/he changes s.t.'s appearance

kwēskinākosiw ᑴᐢᑭᓈᑯᓯᐤ
  VAI s/he looks different, s/he looks changed

kwēskinēw ᑴᐢᑭᓀᐤ
  VTA s/he turns s.o. over

kwēskiniskēpayihow ᑴᐢᑭᓂᐢᑫᐸᔨᐦᐅᐤ
  VAI s/he throws his/her own arm the other way

kwēskipayihow ᑴᐢᑭᐸᔨᐦᐅᐤ
  VAI s/he turns him/herself around, s/he throws him/herself around

kwēskipayiw ᑲᐢᑭᐸᔨᐤ
  VAI s/he twists round

kwēskipayiw ᑴᐢᑭᐸᔨᐤ
  VII it turns around; it changes suddenly

kwēskipimātisiw ᑴᐢᑭᐱᒫᑎᓯᐤ
  VAI s/he changes his/her life

kwēskipimātisīhēw ᑴᐢᑭᐱᒫᑎᓰᐦᐁᐤ
  VTA s/he converts s.o., s/he makes s.o. change lifestyle

kwēskipitam ᑴᐢᑭᐱᑕᒼ
  VTI s/he jerks s.t. around

kwēskipitēw ᑴᐢᑭᐱᑌᐤ
  VTA s/he pulls s.o. the other way

kwēskisimēw ᑴᐢᑭᓯᒣᐤ
  VTA s/he turns s.o. in that one's own bed

kwēskisin ᑴᐢᑭᓯᐣ
  VAI s/he turns over in bed, s/he turns as s/he lies

kwēskiskwēpayihow ᑴᐢᑭᐢᑴᐸᔨᐦᐅᐤ
  VAI s/he turns him/herself to face the other way

kwēskiskwēw ᑴᐢᑭᐢᑴᐤ
  VAI s/he turns his/her own head

kwēskiskwēyiw ᑴᐢᑭᐢᑴᔨᐤ
  VAI s/he turns his/her own head

kwēskiyowēw ᑴᐢᑭᔪᐌᐤ
  VII there is a change in the wind

kwēskīmow ᑴᐢᑮᒧᐤ
  VAI s/he changes his/her own shape or form

kwēskīstam ᑴᐢᑮᐢᑕᒼ
  VTI s/he turns toward s.t.

kwēskīstawēw ᑴᐢᑮᐢᑕᐌᐤ
  VTA s/he turns toward s.o.

kwēskīw ᑴᐢᑮᐤ
  VAI s/he turns, s/he turns about, s/he turns around

kwēskosīmēw ᑴᐢᑯᓰᒣᐤ
  VTA s/he whistles to s.o.

kwēskosītotawēw ᑴᐢᑯᓰᑐᑕᐌᐤ
  VTA s/he whistles to or at s.o.

kwēskosiw ᑴᐢᑯᓯᐤ
  VAI s/he whistles [*also* kwēskosiw; *cf.* kīskosiw]

kwēskosīwin ᑴᐢᑯᓰᐃᐣ
  NI whistling [*cf.* kīskosīwin]

kwēskosīyāstan ᑴᐢᑯᓰᔮᐢᑕᐣ
  VII there is a whistling wind

kwēskosīyowēw ᑴᐢᑯᓰᔪᐌᐤ
  VII there is a whistle in the wind

kwēskwēskastāw ᑴᐢᑴᐢᑲᐢᑖᐤ
  VAIt s/he places s.t. turning a number of times [*rdpl, cf.* kwēskastāw]

kwēskwēski ᑴᐢᑴᐢᑭ
  IPC at the other side, changing [*rdpl, cf.* kwēski]

kwēskwēskinam ᑴᐢᑴᐢᑭᓇᒼ
  VTI s/he repeatedly turns s.t. the other way [*rdpl, cf.* kwēskinam]

kwētamāw ᑴᑕᒫᐤ
  VAI s/he is in need

kwētamāwin ᑴᑕᒫᐃᐣ
  NI neediness

kwētapipayiw ᑴᑕᐱᐸᔨᐤ
  VAI s/he capsizes [*cf.* kotapipayiw, kwatapipayiw]

kwētapipayiw ᑴᑕᐱᐸᔨᐤ
  VII it capsizes [*cf.* kotapipayiw, kwatapipayiw]

kwētawēyihtam ᑴᑕᐌᔨᐦᑕᒼ
  VTI s/he misses s.t., s/he is at a loss for what to do about s.t. [*cf.* kōtawēyihtam]

kwētawēyimēw ᑴᑕᐌᔨᒣᐤ
  VTA s/he misses s.o., s/he wonders about s.o.'s whereabouts [*cf.* kōtawēyimēw]

kwētawi- ᑴᑕᐪ
  IPV doubtful

kwētawi-astāw ᑴᑕᐪ ᐊᐢᑖᐤ
  VAIt s/he places things doubtfully

kwētawi-itwēw ᑴᑕᐪ ᐃᐪᐌᐤ
  VAI s/he says s.t. doubtfully, s/he is at a loss for what to say

kwētawi-tōtam ᑴᑕᐪ ᑑᑕᒼ
  VTI s/he does s.t. hesitantly; s/he is not sure how to do s.t.

kwētawitēyihtam ᑴᑕᐪᑌᔨᐦᑕᒼ
  VTI s/he is doubtful, s/he is not sure

kwētawitēyihtamowin ᑴᑕᐪᑌᔨᐦᑕᒧᐃᐣ
  NI doubt

kwētipahtin ᑴᑎᐸᐦᑎᐣ
  VII it is tipped over

kwētipastāw ᑴᑎᐸᐢᑖᐤ
  VAI s/he turns bottom side up

kwētipawēpiskam ᑴᑎᐸᐌᐱᐢᑲᒼ
  VTI s/he knocks s.t. over

kwētipāhotēw ᑴᑎᐹᐦᑴᐤ
  VII it is tipped over by the current or waves

kwētipāskonam ᑴᑎᐹᐢᑯᓇᒼ
  VTI s/he turns s.t. over

kwētipāskonēw ᑴᑎᐹᐢᑯᓀᐤ
  VTA s/he turns s.o. over

kwētipinam ᑴᑎᐱᓇᒼ
  VTI s/he rolls s.t.

kwētipinēw ᑴᑎᐱᓀᐤ
  VTA s/he rolls s.o. over and over (*e.g.* a tree)

kwētipipayihow ᑴᑎᐱᐸᔨᐦᐅᐤ
  VAI s/he throws him/herself over to one side

kwētipipayiw ᑴᑎᐱᐸᔨᐤ
  VII it rolls over by itself

kwētipiskwēnēw ᑴᑎᐱᐢᑵᓀᐤ
  VTA s/he turns s.o.'s head to one side for that one

kwētipiwēpaham ᑴᑎᐱᐌᐸᐦᐊᒼ
  VTI s/he rolls s.t. over (with a pole)

kwētipiwēpahwēw ᑴᑎᐱᐌᐸᐦᐤᐁᐤ
  VTA s/he knocks s.o. over to one side; s/he upsets s.o., s/he rolls s.o. over (with a pole)

kwēyātapiw ᑴᔮᑕᐱᐤ
  VAI s/he is ready [*cf.* kwayātapiw]

kwēyātisiw ᑴᔮᑎᓯᐤ
  VAI s/he is ready [*cf.* kwayātisiw]

ᑮ

kwīhkwīsiw ᑮᐦᑮᓯᐤ
  NA Canada jay, whiskey jack, blue jay

kwīhtawēyihtam ᑮᐦᑕᐌᔨᐦᑕᒼ
  VTI s/he misses s.t., s/he yearns for s.t.

kwīhtawēyimēw ᑮᐦᑕᐌᔨᒣᐤ
  VTA s/he misses s.o., s/he yearns for s.o., s/he pines for s.o.

kwītatē ᑮᑌ
  IPC not even trying; wondering what to do

kwītawēyihcikātēw ᑮᑕᐌᔨᐦᒋᑳᑌᐤ
  VII it is missed, it is in short supply

kwītawi- ᑮᑕᐪ
  IPV impatiently

kwītāpacihtāw ᑮᑖᐸᒋᐦᑖᐤ
  VAIt s/he is short of s.t. to use; s/he lacks tools

kwītonam ᑮᑐᓇᒼ
  VTI s/he seeks s.t. in vain

kwītonēw ᑮᑐᓀᐤ
  VTA s/he seeks s.o. in vain

m

ᒪ

ma cī ᒪ ᒌ
IPC is it not the case? was it not? not so? [*cf.* nama cī]
ma kīkway ᒪ ᑮᑲᐧᐩ
PR nothing, not; zero, nil [*cf.* nama kīkway, namōýa kīkway]
ma nā ᒪ ᓈ
IPC is that not so [*sC*; *cf.* ma cī]
mac-ācimēw ᒪᒑᒋᒣᐤ
VTA s/he tells bad things of s.o., s/he tells hurtful gossip of s.o. [*also* maci-ācimēw]
mac-ācimoskiw ᒪᒑᒋᒧᐢᑭᐤ
VAI s/he always tells bad news, s/he is in the habit of telling hurtful gossip [*hab*; *also* maci-ācimoskiw]
mac-ācimow ᒪᒑᒋᒧᐤ
VAI s/he tells bad news [*also* maci-ācimow]
mac-ācimowin ᒪᒑᒋᒧᐃᐧᐣ
NI slander, evil report, hurtful gossip [*also* maci-ācimowin]
mac-āyisiw ᒪᒑᔨᓯᐤ
VAI s/he is bad, s/he is devilish; s/he is temperamental, cruel, wicked [*also* maci-ayisiw]
mac-āyisiwiw ᒪᒑᔨᓯᐃᐧᐤ
VAI s/he is a devil, he is the Devil [*also* maci-ayisiwiw]
mac-āyisiyiniw ᒪᒑᔨᓯᔨᓂᐤ
NA bad person, evil person; [*pl*:] bad people, evil people [*also* maci-ayisiyiniw]
mac-āyiwiw ᒪᒑᔨᐃᐧᐤ
VAI s/he is bad, s/he is mean, s/he is evil, s/he is wicked, s/he is a wicked person; s/he has a bad temper; s/he is a dangerous being [*cf.* maci-ayiwiw]
macan ᒪᒐᐣ
VII it is bad, it is evil, it is ugly
macastēhamānakēwin ᒪᒐᐢᑌᐦᐊᒫᓇᑫᐃᐧᐣ
NI ceremonial offering
macastim ᒪᒐᐢᑎᒼ
NA bad dog, nasty cur [*pl*: -wak]
macācisiw ᒪᒑᒋᓯᐤ
VAI s/he is wicked, s/he is a sinner [*cf.* macātisiw]
macāhpinēw ᒪᒑᐦᐱᓀᐤ
VAI s/he has a sexually transmitted disease (STD), s/he has a venereal disease (VD), s/he has a bad disease [*cf.* macāspinēw]
macānēs ᒪᒑᓀᐢ
NA member of a dance society [*pl generally*: macānēsak "worthless"]
NI game piece which is not worth the play
macāpahtam ᒪᒑᐸᐦᑕᒼ
VTI s/he dislikes the look of s.t.
macāpamēw ᒪᒑᐸᒣᐤ
VTA s/he dislikes the look of s.o.
macāpisin ᒪᒑᐱᓯᐣ
VAI s/he disapproves of what s/he sees
macāpoy ᒪᒑᐳᐩ
NI bad liquid
macāspinēw ᒪᒑᐢᐱᓀᐤ
VAI s/he has a sexually transmitted disease (STD), s/he has venereal disease (VD); s/he has a bad disease [*cf.* macāhpinēw]
macāspinēwin ᒪᒑᐢᐱᓀᐃᐧᐣ
NI sexually transmitted disease (STD), venereal disease (VD)
macātis ᒪᒑᑎᐢ
NA bad person
macātisiw ᒪᒑᑎᓯᐤ
VAI s/he is bad, s/he is evil, s/he is wicked [*cf.* macācisiw]
macātisiwin ᒪᒑᑎᓯᐃᐧᐣ
NI wickedness, sinfulness
macēkin ᒪᒉᑭᐣ
NI tipi
macēýihtam ᒪᒉᔨᐦᑕᒼ
VTI s/he despises s.t., s/he hates s.t.; s/he is suspicious of s.t.
macēýihtamowin ᒪᒉᔨᐦᑕᒧᐃᐧᐣ
NI hatred, contempt; suspicion
macēýihtākosiw ᒪᒉᔨᐦᑖᑯᓯᐤ
VAI s/he is mean, s/he is nasty, s/he is despicable
macēýihtākwan ᒪᒉᔨᐦᑖᑲᐧᐣ
VII it is despicable, it is shameful
macēýimēw ᒪᒉᔨᒣᐤ
VTA s/he thinks s.o. to be of no account, s/he hates s.o.; s/he suspects s.o.
maci- ᒪᒋ
IPV bad, evil, wicked, wrong, ill [*cf.* mac-...]
maci-awāsis ᒪᒋ ᐊᐋᐧᓯᐢ
NA bad child [*also* mac-āwāsis]
maci-isīhcikēw ᒪᒋ ᐃᓰᐦᒋᑫᐤ
VAI s/he does wicked things [*also* mac-īsīhcikēw]
maci-iskwēw ᒪᒋ ᐃᐢᑵᐤ
NA bad woman [*also* mac-īskwēw]
maci-iskwēwiw ᒪᒋ ᐃᐢᑵᐃᐧᐤ
VAI she is a bad woman [*also* mac-īskwēwiw]
maci-itēw ᒪᒋ ᐃᑌᐤ
VTA s/he tells bad things about s.o.
maci-itēýihtam ᒪᒋ ᐃᑌᔨᐦᑕᒼ
VTI s/he suspects evil, s/he thinks evil
maci-itēýihtamowin ᒪᒋ ᐃᑌᔨᐦᑕᒧᐃᐧᐣ
NI evil thoughts, wishing evil
maci-itwēw ᒪᒋ ᐃᑵᐤ
VAI s/he uses profane language [*see also* wiyahkwēw]
maci-itwēwin ᒪᒋ ᐃᑵᐃᐧᐣ
NI swearing, profanity [*see also* wiyahkwēwin]
maci-kīkway ᒪᒋ ᑮᑲᐧᐩ
NI bad thing, things [*only non-locative forms*]
maci-kīsikāw ᒪᒋ ᑮᓯᑳᐤ
VII it is bad weather, it is a bad day
maci-manitow ᒪᒋ ᒪᓂᑐᐤ
NA evil spirit; devil, Satan
maci-manitowan ᒪᒋ ᒪᓂᑐᐊᐧᐣ
VII it is devilish; it has evil spirits

maci-manitowēýihcikan ᒪᒋ ᒪᓂᑐᐍᔦᐦᒋᑲᐣ
NI evil mind [*cf.* maci-māmitonēýihcikan]

maci-manitowēýihtam ᒪᒋ ᒪᓂᑐᐍᔦᐦᑕᒼ
VTI s/he thinks evil

maci-manitowi- ᒪᒋ ᒪᓂᑐᐏ
IPV evil, devilish; Devil's

maci-manitōwiw ᒪᒋ ᒪᓂᑑᐏᐤ
VAI s/he is evil, s/he is devilish; s/he is the Devil

maci-maskihkiy ᒪᒋ ᒪᐢᑭᐦᑭᕀ
NI bad medicine, evil medicine

maci-maskosiy ᒪᒋ ᒪᐢᑯᓯᕀ
NI stink weed

maci-māmitonēýihcikan ᒪᒋ ᒫᒥᑐᓀᔦᐦᒋᑲᐣ
NI evil mind [*cf.* maci-manitowēýihcikan]

maci-nāpēsis ᒪᒋ ᓈᐯᓯᐢ
NA bad boy

maci-nāpēsisiwiw ᒪᒋ ᓈᐯᓯᓯᐏᐤ
VAI he is a bad boy

maci-nāpēw ᒪᒋ ᓈᐯᐤ
NA bad man

maci-nāpēwiw ᒪᒋ ᓈᐯᐏᐤ
VAI he is a bad man

maci-pawāmiw ᒪᒋ ᐸᐚᒥᐤ
VAI s/he has an evil dream spirit; s/he has a bad dream, s/he has a nightmare

maci-pīkiskwēw ᒪᒋ ᐲᑭᐢᑵᐤ
VAI s/he speaks evil, s/he uses bad language

maci-pīkiskwēwin ᒪᒋ ᐲᑭᐢᑵᐏᐣ
NI blasphemous language

maci-wēpisiw ᒪᒋ ᐍᐱᓯᐤ
VAI s/he behaves badly, s/he is bad

macihitowak ᒪᒋᐦᐃᑐᐘᐠ
VAI they do ill to one another (*i.e.* with bad medicine)

macihkiwis ᒪᒋᐦᑭᐏᐢ
NA Silly-Fellow; the oldest brother [*personal name of a legendary figure*]

macihow ᒪᒋᐦᐅᐤ
VAI s/he has his/her things in a mess; s/he has a tendency to be lewd

macihtiw ᒪᒋᐦᑎᐤ
VAI s/he sins, s/he commits sin

macihtiwin ᒪᒋᐦᑎᐏᐣ
NI sin

macihtwāw ᒪᒋᐦᑘᐤ
VAI s/he uses bad medicine, s/he is an evil person; s/he is of a bad disposition

macihtwāwin ᒪᒋᐦᑘᐏᐣ
NI sin, wickedness, bad temper, disobedience

macikosisān ᒪᒋᑯᓯᓵᐣ
NA bad son

macikosisāniwiw ᒪᒋᑯᓯᓵᓂᐏᐤ
VAI he is a bad son

macikwanās ᒪᒋᑿᓈᐢ
NI garbage, rubbish; weed [*also* macikonās]

macikwanāsi-maskimot ᒪᒋᑿᓈᓯ ᒪᐢᑭᒧᐟ
NI garbage bag [*also* macikonāsi-maskimot]

macikwanāsiwan ᒪᒋᑿᓈᓯᐘᐣ
VII it is weedy; it is piled with rubbish

macinākosiw ᒪᒋᓈᑯᓯᐤ
VAI s/he is ugly in appearance

macinākwan ᒪᒋᓈᑿᐣ
VII it looks bad, it is ugly in appearance

macipakoskāw ᒪᒋᐸᑯᐢᑳᐤ
VII it is infested with weeds, there are many weeds

macipakwa ᒪᒋᐸᑿ
NI bad weeds; bad herbs [*pl generally*]

macipaýin ᒪᒋᐸᔨᐣ
VII it goes ill, it runs poorly, it runs improperly

macipaýiw ᒪᒋᐸᔨᐤ
VAI s/he fares ill, s/he drives poorly

macipaýiwin ᒪᒋᐸᔨᐏᐣ
NI bad experience

macispakosiw ᒪᒋᐢᐸᑯᓯᐤ
VAI it tastes bad, it tastes awful, it has a bad taste

macispakosiwin ᒪᒋᐢᐸᑯᓯᐏᐣ
NI bad taste

macispakwan ᒪᒋᐢᐸᑿᐣ
VII it tastes bad, it tastes awful, it has a bad taste

macitēhēw ᒪᒋᑌᐦᐁᐤ
VAI s/he is cruel and unkind, s/he has a wicked heart

macitēhēwin ᒪᒋᑌᐦᐁᐏᐣ
NI cruelty, wickedness

macitōnēw ᒪᒋᑑᓀᐤ
VAI s/he has a foul mouth; s/he swears continually

macitōnēwin ᒪᒋᑑᓀᐏᐣ
NI swearing, foul language [*see also* wiyahkwēwin]

macostēham ᒪᒍᐢᑌᐦᐊᒼ
VTI s/he throws s.t. into the fire, s/he puts s.t. to burn

macostēhikan ᒪᒍᐢᑌᐦᐃᑲᐣ
NI incense, something to be burned (as incense)

macostēhwēw ᒪᒍᐢᑌᐦᐍᐤ
VTA s/he throws s.o. into the fire, s/he puts s.o. to burn

macostēpaýiw ᒪᒍᐢᑌᐸᔨᐤ
VAI s/he falls into the fire

macostēwēpaham ᒪᒍᐢᑌᐍᐸᐦᐊᒼ
VTI s/he pushes s.t. into the fire (with a pole)

macostēwēpahwēw ᒪᒍᐢᑌᐍᐸᐦᐍᐤ
VTA s/he pushes s.o. into the fire (with a pole)

macostēwēpinam ᒪᒍᐢᑌᐍᐱᓇᒼ
VTI s/he throws s.t. into the fire

macostēwēpinēw ᒪᒍᐢᑌᐍᐱᓀᐤ
VTA s/he throws s.o. into the fire

macostiwēham ᒪᒍᐢᑎᐍᐦᐊᒼ
VTI s/he throws s.t. in the fire, s/he lights s.t. up with fire

macwēwēs ᒪᒓᐍᐢ
NI repeating gun, machine gun [*dim*; *cf.* matwēwēw]

mah ᒪᐦ
IPC listen, hark

mahcāminis ᒪᐦᒑᒥᓂᐢ
NA kernel of corn [*dim*; *cf.* mahtāmin]

mahci ᒪᐦᒋ
IPC come, let's see [*dim*; *cf.* mahti]

mahihkan ᒪᐦᐃᐦᑲᐣ
NA wolf; grey wolf, timber wolf [*also*: mahīhkan]

mahihkanāhtik ᒪᐦᐃᐦᑲᓈᐦᑎᐠ
NA wolf willow [*pl*: -wak]

mahihkani-wāti ᒪᐦᐃᐦᑲᓂ ᐚᑎ
NI wolf-hole, wolf den [*pl*: -wāta]

mahihkaniminānāhtik ᒪᐦᐃᐦᑲᓂᒥᓈᓈᐦᑎᐠ
NA wolf willow (a tree) [*pl*: -wak]

mahihkaniwayān ᒪᐦᐃᐦᑲᓂᐘᔮᐣ
NA wolfskin, wolf pelt

mahihkaniwiw ᒪᐦᐃᐦᑲᓂᐏᐤ
VAI s/he is a wolf

mahkacāpiw ᒪᐦᑲᒑᐱᐤ
VAI s/he has large eyes

mahkahk ᒪᐦᑲᕽ
NI tub, barrel; box [*also NA*; *pl*: -wa(k)]

mahkahkohkākēw ᒪᐦᑲᐦᑯᐦᑳᑫᐤ
VAI s/he makes barrels from s.t.

mahkahkohkēw ᒪᐦᑲᐦᑯᐦᑫᐤ
VAI s/he makes barrels

mahkahkos ᒪᐦᑲᐦᑯᐢ
NI keg, bushel, small barrel [di*m*]

mahkasākēw ᒪᐦᑲᓵᑫᐤ
VAI s/he has a large coat, s/he wears a large coat

mahkasāmēw ᒪᐦᑲᓵᒣᐤ
VAI s/he has large snowshoes, s/he wears large snowshoes

mahkasinaham ᒪᐦᑲᓯᓇᐦᐊᒼ
VTI s/he writes s.t. large

mahkasinahikēw ᒪᐦᑲᓯᓇᐦᐃᑫᐤ
VAI s/he writes large

mahkaskisinēw ᒪᐦᑲᐢᑭᓯᓀᐤ
VAI s/he has large shoes, s/he wears large shoes

mahkastāw ᒪᐦᑲᐢᑖᐤ
VAIt s/he places s.t. in a large pile

mahkastēwa ᒪᐦᑲᐢᑌᐘ
VII they are placed in a large quantity [*pl generally*]
mahkastisēw ᒪᐦᑲᐢᑎᓭᐤ
VAI s/he has large mitts, s/he wears large mitts
mahkastotinēw ᒪᐦᑲᐢᑐᑎᓀᐤ
VAI s/he has a large hat, s/he wears a large hat
mahkatayēw ᒪᐦᑲᑕᔦᐤ
VAI s/he has a large stomach, belly; she is far along in her pregnancy
mahkatāhtam ᒪᐦᑲᑖᐦᑕᒼ
VTI s/he gives a deep sigh
mahkatāmow ᒪᐦᑲᑖᒧᐤ
VAI s/he sighs deeply
mahkāhan ᒪᐦᑳᐦᐊᐣ
VII it is rough, it is wavy [*cf.* mamahkāhan]
mahkāpiskāw ᒪᐦᑳᐱᐢᑳᐤ
VII it is a large piece of metal; there are many large rocks about
mahkāpitān ᒪᐦᑳᐱᑖᐣ
NI big tooth [*sg*; *pl generally*]
mahkāpitēw ᒪᐦᑳᐱᑌᐤ
VAI s/he has large teeth
mahkāskwēyāw ᒪᐦᑳᐢᑵᔮᐤ
VII there is a big grove
mahkāýowēw ᒪᐦᑳᔪᐍᐤ
VAI s/he has a large tail
mahkēsiw ᒪᐦᑫᓯᐤ
NA fox, large species of fox; coyote [*see also* mēstacākanis]
mahkēsīs ᒪᐦᑫᓰᐢ
NA fox [*dim*]
mahkēsīsi-wanihikan ᒪᐦᑫᓰᓯ ᐘᓂᐦᐃᑲᐣ
NI fox trap
mahkēsīsi-wāti ᒪᐦᑫᓰᓯ ᐚᑎ
NI fox hole [*pl*: -wāta]
mahkēsīsiwayān ᒪᐦᑫᓰᓯᐘᔮᐣ
NA fox pelt, fox skin [*also* mahkēsīwayān]
mahkēsīskāw ᒪᐦᑫᓰᐢᑳᐤ
VII there are many foxes around
mahki ᒪᐦᑭ
IPN big, large
mahki-miyēsāpiwinēw ᒪᐦᑭ ᒥᔦᓵᐱᐏᓀᐤ
VAI s/he has large eyelashes
mahkicihcēw ᒪᐦᑭᒋᐦᒉᐤ
VAI s/he has large hands
mahkihkwēw ᒪᐦᑭᐦᑵᐤ
VAI s/he has a large face
mahkihtawakēw ᒪᐦᑭᐦᑕᐘᑫᐤ
VAI s/he has large ears
mahkikamāw ᒪᐦᑭᑲᒫᐤ
VII it is a large body of water
mahkikasēw ᒪᐦᑭᑲᓭᐤ
VAI s/he has large nails, it has large hooves or claws
mahkikātēw ᒪᐦᑭᑳᑌᐤ
VAI s/he has large legs
mahkikotēw ᒪᐦᑭᑯᑌᐤ
VAI s/he has a large nose; s/he has a large beak
mahkikwayawēw ᒪᐦᑭᑿᔭᐍᐤ
VAI s/he has a large neck
mahkipakāw ᒪᐦᑭᐸᑳᐤ
VII there are big leaves; the leaves are big
mahkipitonēw ᒪᐦᑭᐱᑐᓀᐤ
VAI s/he has large arms
mahkipwāmēw ᒪᐦᑭᑇᒣᐤ
VAI s/he has large thighs
mahkisitēw ᒪᐦᑭᓯᑌᐤ
VAI s/he has large feet
mahkiskam ᒪᐦᑭᐢᑲᒼ
VTI s/he makes big footprints or tracks, s/he makes a big footprint (on s.t.); s/he stretches s.t. (*e.g.* clothing) through wear
mahkiskīsik ᒪᐦᑭᐢᑮᓯᐠ
NI big eye [*pl*: -wa]
mahkisōkanēw ᒪᐦᑭᓲᑲᓀᐤ
VAI s/he has a large derriere or bum
mahkistikwān ᒪᐦᑭᐢᑎᒁᐣ
NI large head
mahkistikwānēw ᒪᐦᑭᐢᑎᒁᓀᐤ
VAI s/he has a large head
mahkitiyēw ᒪᐦᑭᑎᔦᐤ
VAI s/he has a large bum, buttocks, derriere
mahkitohtōsimēw ᒪᐦᑭᑐᐦᑑᓯᒣᐤ
VAI she has large breasts; it has large teats
mahkitōnēw ᒪᐦᑭᑑᓀᐤ
VAI s/he has a large mouth, s/he has a big mouth
mahkwan ᒪᐦᑲᐧᐣ
NDI heel
mahkwanēyāpiy ᒪᐦᑲᐧᓀᔮᐱᕀ
NDI achilles tendon, tendon at back of heel
mahkwanikan ᒪᐦᑲᐧᓂᑲᐣ
NDI heelbone
mahtāmin ᒪᐦᑖᒥᐣ
NA corn, ear of corn, cob of corn; kernel of corn
mahtāmini-kistikān ᒪᐦᑖᒥᓂ ᑭᐢᑎᑳᐣ
NI corn field
mahtāminask ᒪᐦᑖᒥᓇᐢᐠ
NI corn husk [*pl*: -wa]
mahti ᒪᐦᑎ
IPC well, then, please; come, let's see [*hortatory*; *cf.* mahci]
mahti ēsa ᒪᐦᑎ ᐁᓴ
IPH please; let's see [*also* maht ēsa]
mahti māka ᒪᐦᑎ ᒫᑲ
IPH well ... [*colloquial*]
mahýakohēw ᒪᐦᔭᑯᐦᐁᐤ
VTA s/he gives s.o. bad luck
mahýakomēw ᒪᐦᔭᑯᒣᐤ
VTA s/he gives s.o. bad luck by speech
mahýakosiw ᒪᐦᔭᑯᓯᐤ
VAI s/he has bad luck; s/he is under evil influence
makosēhiwēw ᒪᑯᓭᐦᐃᐍᐤ
VAI s/he gives a feast
makosēw ᒪᑯᓭᐤ
VAI s/he feasts; s/he has a feast
makosī-kīsikani-pīsim ᒪᑯᓰ ᑮᓯᑲᓂ ᐲᓯᒼ
NA December [*wC*; *see also* manitowi-kīsikani-pīsim, pawācakinasīsi-pīsim]
makwahcāw ᒪᑿᐦᒑᐤ
NI knoll
mamahkāhan ᒪᒪᐦᑳᐦᐊᐣ
VII it is rough water, it is wavy water [*rdpl*; *cf.* mahkāhan]
mamahkāpōwēw ᒪᒪᐦᑳᐴᐍᐤ
VAI she has much milk (*e.g.* a cow) [*rdpl*]
mamahkāskāw ᒪᒪᐦᑳᐢᑳᐤ
VII it runs in big waves, there are large waves [*rdpl*; *cf.* mahkāhan, mamahkahan]
mamahkipakāw ᒪᒪᐦᑭᐸᑳᐤ
VII it has large leaves, the leaves are large [*rdpl*; *cf.* mahkipakāw]
mamahkisitēw ᒪᒪᐦᑭᓯᑌᐤ
VAI s/he has big feet [*rdpl*; *cf.* mahkisitēw]
mamāhcikokanēpaýiw ᒪᒫᐦᒋᑯᑲᓀᐸᔨᐤ
VAI s/he is crippled by arthritis; s/he wobbles when walking [*rdpl*]
mamāhcikonam ᒪᒫᐦᒋᑯᓇᒼ
VTI s/he holds s.t. down [*rdpl*]
mamāhcikonēw ᒪᒫᐦᒋᑯᓀᐤ
VTA s/he holds s.o. down, s/he holds s.o. immobile [*rdpl*]
mamāhcikwahpitam ᒪᒫᐦᒋᑿᐦᐱᑕᒼ
VTI s/he ties s.t. down [*rdpl*]
mamāhcikwahpitēw ᒪᒫᐦᒋᑿᐦᐱᑌᐤ
VTA s/he ties s.o. down [*rdpl*]
mamāhpinēw ᒪᒫᐦᐱᓀᐤ
VAI s/he moans in pain, s/he groans in pain repeatedly [*rdpl*]
mamāhtākosiw ᒪᒫᐦᑖᑯᓯᐤ
VAI s/he is glad; s/he is gifted, s/he is spiritually talented
mamāhtāwēýihtam ᒪᒫᐦᑖᐍᔨᐦᑕᒼ
VTI s/he thinks s.t. strange, supernatural or extraordinary
mamāhtāwēýihtawēw ᒪᒫᐦᑖᐍᔨᐦᑕᐍᐤ
VTA s/he hears s.o. with surprise, s/he thinks s.o.

strange, supernatural or extraordinary

mamāhtāwēýihtākosiw ᒪᒫᐦᑖᐍᔨᐦᑖᑯᓯᐤ
VAI s/he is thought strange, s/he is thought supernatural or extraordinary

mamāhtāwēýihtākwan ᒪᒫᐦᑖᐍᔨᐦᑖᑿᐣ
VII it is thought strange, it is thought supernatural or extraordinary

mamāhtāwēýimēw ᒪᒫᐦᑖᐍᔨᒣᐤ
VTA s/he thinks s.o. is strange, s/he thinks s.o. is supernatural or extraordinary; s/he thinks s.o. is a genius

mamāhtāwinākosiw ᒪᒫᐦᑖᐏᓈᑯᓯᐤ
VAI s/he looks strange, s/he looks wondrous, s/he looks supernatural

mamāhtāwinākwan ᒪᒫᐦᑖᐏᓈᑿᐣ
VII it looks strange and wonderful

mamāhtāwisiw ᒪᒫᐦᑖᐏᓯᐤ
VAI s/he has supernatural power, s/he is gifted spiritually; s/he does magic

mamāhtāwisiwin ᒪᒫᐦᑖᐏᓯᐏᐣ
NI spiritual power, talent; giftedness

mamāhtāwisīhcikēw ᒪᒫᐦᑖᐏᓰᐦᒋᑫᐤ
VAI s/he performs extraordinary feats, s/he makes extraordinary things; s/he performs miracles

mamāhtāwisīhcikēwin ᒪᒫᐦᑖᐏᓰᐦᒋᑫᐏᐣ
NI extraordinary feat; miracle

mamāhtāwisīhow ᒪᒫᐦᑖᐏᓰᐦᐅᐤ
VAI s/he dresses oddly, s/he dresses strangely; s/he dresses for ceremonial purposes

mamākonam ᒪᒫᑯᓇᒼ
VTI s/he kneads, s/he kneads s.t. [*rdpl*]

mamākonikēw ᒪᒫᑯᓂᑫᐤ
VAI s/he kneads, s/he presses things [*rdpl*]

mamākonikēwin ᒪᒫᑯᓂᑫᐏᐣ
NI kneading, pressure [*rdpl*]

mamākwahcikēw ᒪᒫᑿᐦᒋᑫᐤ
VAI s/he chews continually (*e.g.* a cow with her cud) [*rdpl*]

mamākwahtam ᒪᒫᑿᐦᑕᒼ
VAI s/he chews s.t. continually (*e.g.* a cow with her cud) [*rdpl*]

mamākwamēw ᒪᒫᑿᒣᐤ
VTA s/he chews s.o. continually [*rdpl*]

mamāýīw ᒪᒫᔩᐤ
VAI s/he is poor at s.t., s/he does s.t. poorly; s/he is inefficient [*rdpl*]

mamēciminēw ᒪᒣᒋᒥᓀᐤ
VTA s/he holds s.o. fast [*rdpl*; *cf.* miciminēw]

mamēhcikāpahtam ᒪᒣᐦᒋᑳᐸᐦᑕᒼ
VTI s/he stares in awe at s.t.

mamēhcikāpamēw ᒪᒣᐦᒋᑳᐸᒣᐤ
VTA s/he stares in awe at s.o.

mamēhkocinēw ᒪᒣᐦᑯᒋᓀᐤ
VAI s/he goes bare-legged [*see also* sāsākanikātēw]

mamēnaskwāw ᒪᒣᓇᐢᒁᐤ
VII it is partly cloudy

mamēsiwan ᒪᒣᓯᐘᐣ
VII it is scarce

mamiýwēýimēw ᒪᒥᔦᐧᔨᒣᐤ
VTA s/he desires s.o. [*rdpl*; *cf.* miýwēýimēw; *see also* akāwātēw]

mamihcihēw ᒪᒥᐦᒋᐦᐁᐤ
VTA s/he gladdens s.o. through deed or accomplishment, s/he boasts about s.o.; s/he makes s.o. proud

mamihcihtam ᒪᒥᐦᒋᐦᑕᒼ
VTI s/he praises s.t.

mamihcimēw ᒪᒥᐦᒋᒣᐤ
VTA s/he praises s.o., s/he boasts about s.o.

mamihcimisow ᒪᒥᐦᒋᒥᓱᐤ
VAI s/he brags about him/herself, s/he boasts about him/herself

mamihcimisowin ᒪᒥᐦᒋᒥᓱᐏᐣ
NI self praise

mamihcimoskiw ᒪᒥᐦᒋᒧᐢᑭᐤ
VAI s/he is boastful, s/he brags all the time [*hab*; *see also* kakihcimoskiw]

mamihcimostamawēw ᒪᒥᐦᒋᒧᐢᑕᒪᐍᐤ
VTA s/he boasts about (it/him) for s.o.

mamihcimow ᒪᒥᐦᒋᒧᐤ
VAI s/he boasts, s/he brags about him/herself, s/he is boastful [*see also* kakihcimow]

mamihcimowin ᒪᒥᐦᒋᒧᐏᐣ
NI boasting [*see also* kakihcimowin]

mamihcisiw ᒪᒥᐦᒋᓯᐤ
VAI s/he is proud

mamihcisiwin ᒪᒥᐦᒋᓯᐏᐣ
NI pride

mamisimēw ᒪᒥᓯᒣᐤ
VTA s/he tells on s.o., s/he tattles on s.o., s/he rats on s.o. [*rdpl*]

mamisītotam ᒪᒥᓰᑐᑕᒼ
VTI s/he trusts in s.t., s/he depends on s.t.

mamisītotamowin ᒪᒥᓰᑐᑕᒧᐏᐣ
NI confidence

mamisītotawēw ᒪᒥᓰᑐᑕᐍᐤ
VTA s/he relies on s.o., s/he depends on s.o.; s/he places spiritual hope in s.o.; s/he trusts s.o.

mamisīw ᒪᒥᓰᐤ
VAI s/he relies on (it/him), s/he places reliance, s/he places dependence and trust on (it/him); s/he places spiritual hope

mamisīwin ᒪᒥᓰᐏᐣ
NI dependence, trust

mamiýawihtam ᒪᒥᔭᐏᐦᑕᒼ
VTI s/he hears well [*rdpl*]

mamiýōsēw ᒪᒥᔫᓭᐤ
VAI she is a good breeder (*e.g.* cow), s/he is fertile; he is virile; s/he makes good offspring [*rdpl*]

mamiýwē ᒪᒥᔦᐧ
IPC easily

mamīskonēw ᒪᒦᐢᑯᓀᐤ
VTA s/he finds s.o. with his/her hand; s/he gropes s.o. [*rdpl*; *cf.* mīskonēw]

mamōhcw-āyihtiw ᒪᒨᐦᒗᔨᐦᑎᐤ
VAI s/he is retarded; s/he is silly

mamwēsahkīw ᒪᒵᓴᐦᑮᐤ
VAI s/he goes naked [*see also* mostāpēkasēw]

manaham ᒪᓇᐦᐊᒼ
VTI s/he skims s.t., s/he skims s.t. off a liquid

manahikan ᒪᓇᐦᐃᑲᐣ
NI cream; skimmer (for cream)

manahikākan ᒪᓇᐦᐃᑳᑲᐣ
NI cream separator

manahipēmātam ᒪᓇᐦᐃᐯᒫᑕᒼ
VTI s/he skims fat off s.t. (*e.g.* a liquid)

manahipēmēw ᒪᓇᐦᐃᐯᒣᐤ
VAI s/he skims off the fat

manahiskowēw ᒪᓇᐦᐃᐢᑯᐍᐤ
VAI s/he collects spruce gum

manahkwatatahwēw ᒪᓇᐦᑿᑕᑕᐦᐍᐤ
VTA s/he peels s.o. (as bark from a tree)

manahow ᒪᓇᐦᐅᐤ
VAI s/he takes, s/he gathers

manahýapēw ᒪᓇᐦᔭᐯᐤ
VAI s/he draws in the net, s/he takes up his/her net [*also* manaýapēw]

manakāskisitān ᒪᓇᑳᐢᑭᓯᑖᐣ
NI sole of moccasin

manakisow ᒪᓇᑭᓱᐤ
VAI s/he distributes food (after a kill) [*see also* mātinawēw]

manaskwamēw ᒪᓇᐢᑿᒣᐤ
VAI s/he gets ice, s/he cuts ice for use

manaspahcikanēw ᒪᓇᐢᐸᐦᒋᑲᓀᐤ
VAI s/he uses a relish or condiment (as fat with meat)
manastimwēw ᒪᓇᐢᑎᒣᐧᐤ
VAI s/he rounds up horses, s/he selects a horse or dog; he goes on a horse-raid
manā- ᒪᓈ
IPV beware of, careful not to, avoid doing
manācihcikēw ᒪᓈᒋᐦᒋᑫᐤ
VAI s/he is economical, s/he saves things; s/he is miserly, s/he is stingy
manācihcikēwin ᒪᓈᒋᐦᒋᑫᐏᐣ
NI economy, frugalness
manācihēw ᒪᓈᒋᐦᐁᐤ
VTA s/he is careful with s.o., s/he is protective about s.o., s/he avoids hurting s.o.; s/he spares s.o.; s/he respects s.o., s/he treats s.o. with respect; s/he uses s.o. carefully
manācihitowak ᒪᓈᒋᐦᐃᑐᐘᐠ
VAI they are careful with one another, they are protective about one another, they avoid hurting one another
manācihtāw ᒪᓈᒋᐦᑖᐤ
VAIt s/he is careful of s.t., s/he uses s.t. carefully, s/he spares s.t., s/he treats s.t. with respect
manācimākan ᒪᓈᒋᒫᑲᐣ
NA parent- or child-in-law; person to whom speech is avoided
manācimēw ᒪᓈᒋᒣᐤ
VTA s/he is careful how s/he speaks to s.o. out of respect; s/he avoids speaking to s.o.
manācimowinēw ᒪᓈᒋᒧᐏᓀᐤ
VAI s/he collects a story
manāskwēw ᒪᓈᐢᑫᐧᐤ
VAI s/he takes up (wooden) weapons
manātisihēw ᒪᓈᑎᓯᐦᐁᐤ
VTA s/he spares s.o.; s/he is careful of s.o.
manātisihtāw ᒪᓈᑎᓯᐦᑖᐤ
VAIt s/he is careful of s.t.
manātisiw ᒪᓈᑎᓯᐤ
VAI s/he acts discreetly
manāwēw ᒪᓈᐍᐤ
VAI s/he takes eggs from nests, s/he gathers eggs
manēhpwāw ᒪᓀᐦᐹᐧᐤ
VAI s/he is in want of smoking, s/he runs out of cigarettes
manēpaýiw ᒪᓀᐸᔨᐤ
VAI s/he runs short, s/he is lacking
manēsiw ᒪᓀᓯᐤ
VAI s/he is in need of s.t., s/he is in want of s.t., s/he lacks s.t., s/he has run out of s.t.; s/he is poor

manēsiwin ᒪᓀᓯᐏᐣ
NI want, neediness; poverty
manēwaskiy ᒪᓀᐘᐢᑭᕀ
NI poor land
mani- ᒪᓂ
IPV with the intent of, with the purpose of
manicōs ᒪᓂᒍᐢ
NA little worm; crawling insect, bug [*dim*]
manicōsiskāw ᒪᓂᒍᓯᐢᑳᐤ
VAI there are many insects
manicōsiwan ᒪᓂᒍᓯᐘᐣ
VII there are many insects; it is maggoty [*see also* ocēsiwan]
manihkomānēw ᒪᓂᐦᑯᒫᓀᐤ
VAI s/he takes a knife from somewhere, s/he gets a knife
manikātēpitēw ᒪᓂᑳᑌᐱᑌᐤ
VTA s/he pulls s.o.'s legs off
manikātēswēw ᒪᓂᑳᑌᓭᐧᐤ
VTA s/he cuts s.o.'s legs off
manimisāskwatwēw ᒪᓂᒥᓵᐢᑲᐧᑌᐧᐤ
VAI s/he gathers Saskatoon willows
maninam ᒪᓂᓇᒼ
VTI s/he takes s.t. off with his/her fingers
maninēw ᒪᓂᓀᐤ
VTA s/he takes s.o. off with his/her fingers
manipaýiw ᒪᓂᐸᔨᐤ
VAI it comes loose, it come off
manipaýiw ᒪᓂᐸᔨᐤ
VII it comes loose, it comes off
manipitam ᒪᓂᐱᑕᒼ
VTI s/he obtains s.t. by pulling; s/he pulls s.t. out (*e.g.* tooth), s/he pulls s.t. loose, s/he pulls s.t. free, s/he tears s.t. off; s/he picks s.t. (*i.e.* a plant)
manipitamawēw ᒪᓂᐱᑕᒪᐍᐤ
VTA s/he pulls (it/him) loose for s.o.
manipitēw ᒪᓂᐱᑌᐤ
VTA s/he pulls s.o. (*e.g.* a thorn) out; s/he pulls s.o. loose
manipīhtwāhēw ᒪᓂᐲᐦᑖᐧᐦᐁᐤ
VTA s/he (usually) provides smokes for s.o.
manisam ᒪᓂᓴᒼ
VTI s/he cuts s.t., s/he cuts s.t. to take; s/he mows s.t. (*e.g.* grass)
manisamawēw ᒪᓂᓴᒪᐍᐤ
VTA s/he cuts (it/him) from or for s.o.
manisāwēw ᒪᓂᓵᐍᐤ
VAI s/he cuts meat into strips [*see also* pānisāwēw]
manisikan ᒪᓂᓯᑲᐣ
NI mower, binder, scythe

manisikātēw ᒪᓂᓯᑳᑌᐤ
VII it is cut, it is mowed
manisikēw ᒪᓂᓯᑫᐤ
VAI s/he mows, s/he cuts things, s/he is haying
manisikēwin ᒪᓂᓯᑫᐏᐣ
NI cutting (*e.g.* hay); haying
manisosow ᒪᓂᓱᓱᐤ
VAI s/he has a cut, s/he cuts him/herself
maniswēw ᒪᓂᓭᐧᐤ
VTA s/he cuts s.o., s/he cuts s.o. to take; s/he cuts from s.o. [*unspecified actor form denotes surgery*: *e.g.* maniswāw "s/he has surgery; s/he is cut"]
manitow ᒪᓂᑐᐤ
NA spirit, spirit being; God [*poss*: -manitōm- *NDA*]
manitowakēýimow ᒪᓂᑐᐘᑫᔨᒧᐤ
VAI s/he thinks him/herself blessed with spirit power
manitowan ᒪᓂᑐᐘᐣ
VII it is of spirit nature, it is spiritual
manitowēkin ᒪᓂᑐᐍᑭᐣ
NI broadcloth, shroud
manitowēkinos ᒪᓂᑐᐍᑭᓄᐢ
NI small piece of cloth, scrap [*dim*]
manitowēpīwāpisk ᒪᓂᑐᐍᐲᐚᐱᐢᐠ
NI tempered steel [*pl*: -wa]
manitowēýimēw ᒪᓂᑐᐍᔨᒣᐤ
VTA s/he thinks s.o. supernatural
manitowi-kīsikani-pīsim ᒪᓂᑐᐏ ᑮᓯᑲᓂ ᐲᓯᒼ
NA God's month, Christmas moon; December [*see also* makosī-kīsikani-pīsim, pawācakinasīsi-pīsim]
manitowi-kīsikāw ᒪᓂᑐᐏ ᑮᓯᑳᐤ
VII it is Christmas Day [*cf.* kisē-manitowi-kīsikāw]
manitowi-masinahikan ᒪᓂᑐᐏ ᒪᓯᓇᐦᐃᑲᐣ
NI God's book, the Bible
manitowikosisān ᒪᓂᑐᐏᑯᓯᓵᐣ
NA Son of God
manitōhkān ᒪᓂᑑᐦᑳᐣ
NA image, idol
manitōhkāsow ᒪᓂᑑᐦᑳᓱᐤ
VAI s/he pretends to have supernatural powers
manitōhkēw ᒪᓂᑑᐦᑫᐤ
VAI s/he worships idols
manitōhkēwin ᒪᓂᑑᐦᑫᐏᐣ
NI spiritual communication
manitōmin ᒪᓂᑑᒥᐣ
NA wild currant, black currant
manitōmināhtik ᒪᓂᑑᒥᓈᐦᑎᐠ
NI black currant bush [*pl*: -wa]

manitōskātāsk Lᒍᐦᕽᐨᐠ
NA poison carrot, water hemlock [*pl*: -wak]

manitōwiw Lᓂᒍᐃ·°
VAI s/he is a spirit; s/he has spirit power

maniway Lᓂᐊ·ᐟ
NDI cheek [*also* manaway]

maniwēpaham Lᓂᐯ·ᐸᐦᐊᒼ
VTI s/he knocks s.t. off (with a stick)

maniwēpahwēw Lᓂᐯ·ᐸᐦᐁ·°
VTA s/he knocks s.o. off (like nuts from a tree)

manōminak Lᓄᒥᓇᐠ
NA wild rice [*pl*]

masakay Lᓴᑲᐟ
NDA skin

masaskonam Lᐢᑯᓇᒼ
VTI s/he gathers s.t. up wholly

masaskonēw Lᐢᑯᓀ°
VTA s/he strips s.o. of all that one owns

masān Lᓵᐣ
NA nettle; thistle

masānāhtik Lᓵᐦᐟᐠ
NA nettle stalk [*pl*: -wak]

masinaham Lᓯᓇᐦᐊᐨ
VTI s/he writes s.t.; s/he marks s.t. by tool; s/he draws s.t.

masinahamawēw Lᓯᓇᐦᐊᒪᐁ·°
VTA s/he writes (it) to s.o., s/he writes (it) for s.o.; s/he owes (it) it s.o., s/he owes s.o. money

masinahamāsow Lᓯᓇᐦᐊᒫᓱ°
VAI s/he writes (it) for him/herself, s/he writes him/herself; s/he draws (it) for him/herself

masinahamātowak Lᓯᓇᐦᐊᒫᑐᐊᐠ
VAI they write to one another; they owe one another

masinahamātowin Lᓯᓇᐦᐊᒫᑐᐃᐣ
NI correspondence; debt

masinahikan Lᓯᓇᐦᐃᑲᐣ
NI book; letter; written document, report, paper; magazine; will

masinahikanāhcikos Lᓯᓇᐦᐃᑲᓈᐦᒋᑯᐢ
NA pencil [*dim*; *also NI*]

masinahikanāhtik Lᓯᓇᐦᐃᑲᓈᐦᐟᐠ
NA pencil, pen [*pl*: -wak; *also NI, pl*: -wa]

masinahikanāpisk Lᓯᓇᐦᐃᑲᓈᐱᐢᐠ
NA slate; pen [*pl*: -wak]

masinahikanāpiskos Lᓯᓇᐦᐃᑲᓈᐱᐢᑯᐢ
NA pen [*dim*]

masinahikanāpoy Lᓯᓇᐦᐃᑲᓈᐳᐟ
NI ink

masinahikanēkin Lᓯᓇᐦᐃᑲᓀᐠᐤ
NI paper; wrapping paper; tar paper roofing [*pl*: -(w)a; *see also* asisiwēkin]

masinahikanēkinos Lᓯᓇᐦᐃᑲᓀᐠᐤᓄᐢ
NI small wrapping paper [*dim*]

masinahikanihkawēw Lᓯᓇᐦᐃᑲᓂᐦᑲᐁ·°
VTA s/he makes a book for s.o.

masinahikanihkākēw Lᓯᓇᐦᐃᑲᓂᐦᑳᑫ°
VAI s/he makes a book from s.t.

masinahikanihkēw Lᓯᓇᐦᐃᑲᓂᐦᑫ°
VAI s/he makes books, s/he publishes

masinahikanipicikēw Lᓯᓇᐦᐃᑲᓂᐱᒋᑫ°
VAI s/he types

masinahikanis Lᓯᓇᐦᐃᑲᓂᐢ
NI little book, booklet, pad [*dim*]

masinahikaniwiyiniw Lᓯᓇᐦᐃᑲᓂᐃᔨᓂ°
NA letter carrier, postman

masinahikaniwiyinīwiw ᓯᓇᐦᐃᑲᓂᐃᔨᓃ·°
VAI s/he is a letter carrier, s/he is a postman

masinahikākēw Lᓯᓇᐦᐃᑳᑫ°
VAI s/he uses (it) to write with

masinahikāsow Lᓯᓇᐦᐃᑳᓱ°
VAI it is written on; s/he is marked, it is pictured on

masinahikātēw Lᓯᓇᐦᐃᑳᑌᐤ°
VII it is written on; it has writing, it has marks, it is marked, it is pictured on

masinahikēhēw Lᓯᓇᐦᐃᑫᐦᐁ·°
VTA s/he hires s.o., s/he employs s.o., s/he gives s.o. work

masinahikēhiwēw Lᓯᓇᐦᐃᑫᐦᐃᐁ·°
NA employer

masinahikēhkāsow Lᓯᓇᐦᐃᑫᐦᑳᓱ°
VAI s/he pretends to type

masinahikēsiw Lᓯᓇᐦᐃᑫᓯ°
VAI s/he writes a bit [*dim*]

masinahikēsīs Lᓯᓇᐦᐃᑫᓰᐢ
NA stenographer, office clerk, secretary, [*pl*:] office personnel

masinahikēsīsiwiw Lᓯᓇᐦᐃᑫᓰᓯᐃᐁ·°
VAI s/he is a stenographer, s/he is an office clerk, s/he is a secretary, s/he is a writer

masinahikēstamawēw Lᓯᓇᐦᐃᑫᐢᑕᒪᐁ·°
VTA s/he writes (it) for s.o.

masinahikēw Lᓯᓇᐦᐃᑫ°
VAI s/he writes, s/he writes things, s/he is literate; s/he owes; s/he takes employment; s/he gives credit; s/he gets credit

masinahikēwin Lᓯᓇᐦᐃᑫᐃᐣ
NI writing; letter, character; debt, thing given on credit

masinahikēwināhtik Lᓯᓇᐦᐃᑫᐃᓈᐦᐟᐠ
NI writing table, desk [*pl*: -wa]

masinahikēwipayiw Lᓯᓇᐦᐃᑫᐃᐸᔨ°
VAI s/he gets credit, s/he suddenly is allowed credit

masinahikēwiyiniw Lᓯᓇᐦᐃᑫᐃᔨᓂ°
NA clerk

masinahwēw Lᓯᓇᐦᐁ·°
VTA s/he marks s.o., s/he pictures s.o.

masināpiskahikēw Lᓯᐋᐱᐢᑲᐦᐃᑫ°
VAI s/he makes marks on rocks; s/he takes pictures, s/he takes photographs

masināpiskinēw Lᓯᐋᐱᐢᑭᓀ°
VTA s/he marks s.o. on or as a rock

masināskisikan Lᓯᐋᐢᑭᓯᑲᐣ
NI branding iron; brand

masināskisow Lᓯᐋᐢᑭᓱ°
VAI s/he is branded

masināsow Lᓯᐋᓱ°
VAI s/he is marked, s/he is striped; s/he is branded

masināsowatim Lᓯᐋᓱᐊᑎᒼ
NA pinto; zebra [*pl*: -wak]

masināsowin Lᓯᐋᓱᐃᐣ
NI state of being marked, striped or coloured

masināstēw Lᓯᐋᐢᑌ°
VII it is marked, it is striped, it is coloured

masinihtatāw Lᓯᐣᐦᑕᑖ°
VAIt s/he traces s.t., s/he uses s.t. as a pattern

masinikocikēw Lᓯᓄᒋᑫ°
VAI s/he carves a pattern

masinikotam Lᓯᓄᑕᒼ
VTI s/he carves s.t.

masinikotēw Lᓯᓄᑌ°
VTA s/he carves s.o.

masinipayiw Lᓯᓇᐸᔨ°
VAI s/he has his/her picture taken; s/he is in a picture, s/he is photographed

masinipayiwin Lᓯᓇᐸᔨᐃᐣ
NI picture, photograph

masinipēham Lᓯᓇᐯᐦᐊᐨ
VTI s/he paints s.t.

masinipēhikan Lᓯᓇᐯᐦᐃᑲᐣ
NI paint

masinipēhikanāhtik Lᓯᓇᐯᐦᐃᑲᓈᐦᐟᐠ
NI paint brush handle [*pl*: -wa]

masinipēhikātēw Lᓯᓇᐯᐦᐃᑳᑌ°
VII it is painted

masinipēhikēw ᒪᓯᓂᐯᐦᐃᑫᐤ
VAI s/he colours, s/he paints (things)
masinipēhikēwin ᒪᓯᓂᐯᐦᐃᑫᐃᐧᐣ
NI painting
masinipēhikotam ᒪᓯᓂᐯᐦᐃᑯᑕᒼ
VTI s/he carves s.t.
masinisāwācikan ᒪᓯᓂᓵᐋᐧᒋᑲᐣ
NI cut-out pattern
masinisāwān ᒪᓯᓂᓵᐋᐧᐣ
NI pattern
masinisin ᒪᓯᓂᓯᐣ
VAI s/he is pictured, s/he is represented in embroidery
masinistaham ᒪᓯᓂᐢᑕᐦᐊᒼ
VTI s/he embroiders s.t.
masinistahikan ᒪᓯᓂᐢᑕᐦᐃᑲᐣ
NI embroidered article
masinistahikākēw ᒪᓯᓂᐢᑕᐦᐃᑳᑫᐤ
VAI s/he uses s.t. for embroidering
masinistahikēw ᒪᓯᓂᐢᑕᐦᐃᑫᐤ
VAI s/he embroiders
masinistahikēwin ᒪᓯᓂᐢᑕᐦᐃᑫᐃᐧᐣ
NI embroidery, embroidered work
masiwēw ᒪᓯᐁᐧᐤ
VAI s/he has sexual intercourse
masiwēwin ᒪᓯᐁᐧᐃᐧᐣ
NI sexual intercourse
maskahcihēw ᒪᐢᑲᐦᒋᐦᐁᐤ
VTA s/he takes (it/him) from s.o.
maskahtowak ᒪᐢᑲᐦᑐᐊᐧᐠ
VAI they seize from one another
maskahtwān ᒪᐢᑲᐦᑖᐧᐣ
NI something taken from an opponent
maskahtwēw ᒪᐢᑲᐦᑌᐧᐤ
VAI s/he robs, s/he takes by force, s/he grabs, s/he seizes things (from others)
maskahtwēwin ᒪᐢᑲᐦᑌᐧᐃᐧᐣ
NI robbery, proceeds of robbery
maskamēw ᒪᐢᑲᒣᐤ
VTA s/he grabs (it/him) from s.o., s/he robs s.o. (of it/him), s/he takes (it/him) away from s.o.
maskasiy ᒪᐢᑲᓯᐩ
NDA fingernail; claw
maskatay ᒪᐢᑲᑕᐩ
NDI stomach-covering; abdominal-wall, belly (of an animal)
maskatēpwēw ᒪᐢᑲᑌᐯᐧᐤ
VAI s/he broils on coals, s/he barbecues
maskawacistin ᒪᐢᑲᐊᐧᒋᐢᑎᐣ
VII there is a hard crust on snow
maskawahcāw ᒪᐢᑲᐊᐧᐦᒑᐤ
VII it is hard ground
maskawahkāw ᒪᐢᑲᐊᐧᐦᑳᐤ
VII it is in a hard lump (as clay)
maskawāhtik ᒪᐢᑲᐋᐧᐦᑎᐠ
NI hard wood [*pl*: -wa]
maskawāhtikwan ᒪᐢᑲᐋᐧᐦᑎᑲᐧᐣ
VII it is hard wood
maskawākamin ᒪᐢᑲᐋᐧᑲᒥᐣ
VII it is a strong liquid (as tea) [*also* maskawākamiw]
maskawākonakāw ᒪᐢᑲᐋᐧᑯᓇᑳᐤ
VII it is hard snow, it is hard-packed snow
maskawākonēw ᒪᐢᑲᐋᐧᑯᓀᐤ
VAI it is hard-crusted snow; it has a hard crust (as snow)
maskawāpēkan ᒪᐢᑲᐋᐧᐯᑲᐣ
VII it is strong (as twine)
maskawāpiskāw ᒪᐢᑲᐋᐧᐱᐢᑳᐤ
VII it is hard metal (*i.e.* cast iron)
maskawāpiskisiw ᒪᐢᑲᐋᐧᐱᐢᑭᓯᐤ
VAI it is hard metal (*e.g.* pail)
maskawāsin ᒪᐢᑲᐋᐧᓯᐣ
VII it is quite hard [*dim*, *cf.* maskawāw]
maskawāskamikāw ᒪᐢᑲᐋᐧᐢᑲᒥᑳᐤ
VII it is an area of hard ground
maskawāskatin ᒪᐢᑲᐋᐧᐢᑲᑎᐣ
VII it is frozen hard
maskawātisiw ᒪᐢᑲᐋᐧᑎᓯᐤ
VAI s/he is strong, s/he is healthy; it is a strong creature
maskawātisiwin ᒪᐢᑲᐋᐧᑎᓯᐃᐧᐣ
NI strength, hardiness
maskawāw ᒪᐢᑲᐋᐧᐤ
VII it is strong, it is hard
maskawihkomān ᒪᐢᑲᐃᐧᐦᑯᒫᐣ
NI strong knife
maskawihtāw ᒪᐢᑲᐃᐧᐦᑖᐤ
VAIt s/he hardens s.t., s/he strengthen s.t.
maskawisihtāw ᒪᐢᑲᐃᐧᓯᐦᑖᐤ
VAIt s/he strengthens s.t.
maskawisīw ᒪᐢᑲᐃᐧᓰᐤ
VAI s/he is strong, s/he is powerful; it is trump (card), it takes the trick
maskawisīwin ᒪᐢᑲᐃᐧᓰᐃᐧᐣ
NI strength, power
maskawitēhēw ᒪᐢᑲᐃᐧᑌᐦᐁᐤ
VAI s/he has a strong heart
maskawitēhēwin ᒪᐢᑲᐃᐧᑌᐦᐁᐃᐧᐣ
NI hard heartedness; strength of heart
maskawīmakan ᒪᐢᑲᐄᐧᒪᑲᐣ
VII it is powerful
maskēk ᒪᐢᑫᐠ
NI muskeg, swamp [*pl*: -wa]
maskēko-sākahikan ᒪᐢᑫᑯ ᓵᑲᐦᐃᑲᐣ
NI Fishing Lake, SK, "Muskeg Lake"
maskēko-sākahikanihk ᒪᐢᑫᑯ ᓵᑲᐦᐃᑲᓂᕽ
INM Muskeg Lake Cree Nation, SK [*loc*; *lit*: "at muskeg lake"]
maskēkohk ᒪᐢᑫᑯᕽ
IPC in the muskeg, in the swamp
maskēkomin ᒪᐢᑫᑯᒥᐣ
NI muskeg berry [*also* maskēkōmin]
maskēkomināna ᒪᐢᑫᑯᒥᓈᓇ
NI cranberries [*pl*; *see also* nīpiminān, wīsakīmin]
maskēkopakwa ᒪᐢᑫᑯᐸᑲᐧ
NI muskeg tea; native tea plant known as the Labrador tea plant [*pl*]
maskēkowan ᒪᐢᑫᑯᐊᐧᐣ
VII it is muskeg, it is swampy
maskēkowaskiy ᒪᐢᑫᑯᐊᐧᐢᑭᐩ
NI muskeg, swampland
maskēkowiýiniw ᒪᐢᑫᑯᐃᐧᔨᓂᐤ
NA Swampy Cree person; person from Muskeg Lake; [*pl*:] Swampy Crees; Muskeg-people, Muskeg Lake First Nation
maskēkwāpoy ᒪᐢᑫᑳᐧᐳᐩ
NI Labrador tea, "muskeg tea"
maskihkiy ᒪᐢᑭᐦᑭᐩ
NI herb, plant; medicine; chemicals
maskihkīs ᒪᐢᑭᐦᑮᐢ
NI candy, sweet; chocolate; medicine; pill [*dim*; *also NA*]
maskihkīwan ᒪᐢᑭᐦᑮᐊᐧᐣ
VII there are medicines present, it has medicinal properties
maskihkīwin ᒪᐢᑭᐦᑮᐃᐧᐣ
VII it has medicinal properties
maskihkīwāhtik ᒪᐢᑭᐦᑮᐋᐧᐦᑎᐠ
NI poverty weed, ragweed; medicinal plant [*pl*: -wa]
maskihkīwāpoy ᒪᐢᑭᐦᑮᐋᐧᐳᐩ
NI tea; liquid medicine
maskihkīwāpōhkēw ᒪᐢᑭᐦᑮᐋᐧᐴᐦᑫᐤ
VAI s/he makes tea; s/he makes medicine, s/he boils medicine
maskihkīwāspinēw ᒪᐢᑭᐦᑮᐋᐧᐢᐱᓀᐤ
VAI s/he is sick through bad medicine, evil spell
maskihkīwikamik ᒪᐢᑭᐦᑮᐃᐧᑲᒥᐠ
NI clinic; pharmacy; hospital [*see also* āhkosīwikamik]
maskihkīwimākwan ᒪᐢᑭᐦᑮᐃᐧᒫᑲᐧᐣ
VII it smells like medicine
maskihkīwin ᒪᐢᑭᐦᑮᐃᐧᐣ
NI medicine; medicinal ingredient
maskihkīwiskwēw ᒪᐢᑭᐦᑮᐃᐧᐢᑫᐧᐤ
NA nurse

maskihkīwiskwēwikamik
ᒪᐢᑭᐦᑮᐃᐧᐢᑵᐏᑲᒥᐠ
NI nursing station; clinic [*pl*:
-wa]

maskihkīwiwat ᒪᐢᑭᐦᑮᐃᐧᐊᐟ
NI medicine bag

maskihkīwiyiniw ᒪᐢᑭᐦᑮᐃᐧᔨᓂᐤ
NA doctor, physician,
medicine man

maskimocis ᒪᐢᑭᒧᒋᐢ
NA bean [*dim*]

maskimocis ᒪᐢᑭᒧᒋᐢ
NI little bag, small sack;
pocket [*dim*]

maskimot ᒪᐢᑭᒧᐟ
NI bag, sack

maskimotēkin ᒪᐢᑭᒧᑌᑭᐣ
NI sacking, cloth from
flour-sacks [*pl*: -wa]

maskimotihkākēw ᒪᐢᑭᒧᑎᐦᑳᑫᐤ
VAI s/he makes a bag from
s.t.

maskimotihkēw ᒪᐢᑭᒧᑎᐦᑫᐤ
VAI s/he makes bags

maskisin ᒪᐢᑭᓯᐣ
NI moccasin; shoe [*also NA*]

maskisinēyāpiy ᒪᐢᑭᓯᓀᔮᐱᕀ
NI moccasin string, shoelace

maskisinihkawēw ᒪᐢᑭᓯᓂᐦᑲᐌᐤ
VTA s/he makes moccasins
or shoes for s.o.

maskisinihkākēw ᒪᐢᑭᓯᓂᐦᑳᑫᐤ
VAI s/he makes moccasins
or shoes from something

maskisinihkēw ᒪᐢᑭᓯᓂᐦᑫᐤ
VAI s/he makes moccasins,
s/he makes shoes

maskisinihkēwin ᒪᐢᑭᓯᓂᐦᑫᐏᐣ
NI making or supply of
moccasins or shoes

maskisinis ᒪᐢᑭᓯᓂᐢ
NI little moccasin, child's
shoe [*dim*]

maskisiniw ᒪᐢᑭᓯᓂᐤ
VAI s/he has moccasins or
shoes

maskohkān ᒪᐢᑯᐦᑳᐣ
NA teddy bear

maskomin ᒪᐢᑯᒥᐣ
NI bearberry [*pl*]

maskominānāhtik ᒪᐢᑯᒥᓈᓈᐦᑎᐠ
NA bearberry bush [*pl*:
-wak]

maskosimow ᒪᐢᑯᓯᒧᐤ
VAI s/he dances the bear
dance

maskosimowin ᒪᐢᑯᓯᒧᐏᐣ
NI bear dance

maskosis ᒪᐢᑯᓯᐢ
NA little bear, bear cub
[*dim*]

maskosiy ᒪᐢᑯᓯᕀ
NI blade of grass; [*pl*:]
grass, hay [*also* maskwasiy]

maskosiyokān ᒪᐢᑯᓯᔪᑳᐣ
NI grass lodge

maskosīhkēw ᒪᐢᑯᓰᐦᑫᐤ
VAI s/he makes hay

maskosīmina ᒪᐢᑯᓰᒥᓇ
NI wild rice [*pl*]

maskosīs ᒪᐢᑯᓰᐢ
NI small amount of straw,
short grass [*dim*]

maskosīskāw ᒪᐢᑯᓰᐢᑳᐤ
VII there is a lot of hay
around

maskosīwan ᒪᐢᑯᓰᐊᐧᐣ
VII it is grassy

maskosīwastotin ᒪᐢᑯᓰᐊᐧᐢᑐᑎᐣ
NI straw hat

maskosīwān ᒪᐢᑯᓰᐋᐧᐣ
NI a water reed with edible
stem

maskosīwānikamāw
ᒪᐢᑯᓰᐋᐧᓂᑲᒫᐤ
VII it is a reedy lake

maskosīwikamik ᒪᐢᑯᓰᐃᐧᑲᒥᐠ
NI hayloft; straw hut [*pl*:
-wa]

maskotēw ᒪᐢᑯᑌᐤ
NI prairie; plain; Muskoday
First Nation, SK

maskotēw-askiy ᒪᐢᑯᑌᐤ ᐊᐢᑭᕀ
NI prairies, plains

maskotēwan ᒪᐢᑯᑌᐊᐧᐣ
VII it is an open prairie or
plain

maskotēwiyiniw ᒪᐢᑯᑌᐃᐧᔨᓂᐤ
NA plains Indian

maskotēwiyinīwiw
ᒪᐢᑯᑌᐃᐧᔨᓃᐃᐧᐤ
VAI he is a plains Indian

maskwa ᒪᐢᑿ
NA bear, black bear [*poss*:
-maskom- *NDA*]

maskwacīs ᒪᐢᑳᐧᒌᐢ
NI Hobbema, AB, "Bear
Hills" [*place name*; *also*
maskocīs]

maskwacīsihk ᒪᐢᑳᐧᒌᓯᕽ
INM Hobbema, AB; "at the
Bear Hills" [*loc*]

maskwamiy ᒪᐢᑿᒥᕀ
NA ice [*cf.* miskwamiy]

maskwaskāw ᒪᐢᑲᐧᐢᑳᐤ
VII there are many bears
around

maskwayān ᒪᐢᑲᐧᔮᐣ
NA bear skin

mastaw ᒪᐢᑕᐤ
IPC newly, recent, recently,
lately; not here before; later,
more recently; since

mastā- ᒪᐢᑖ
IPV later

matahkamikisiw ᒪᑕᐦᑲᒥᑭᓯᐤ
VAI s/he carries on in an evil
way; s/he carries on in a
cheeky way

matakwan ᒪᑕᑲᐧᐣ
VII it is not here [*cf.*
namatakwan]

matay ᒪᑕᕀ
NDI stomach, belly [*dim*:
macās]

matāwisipahtāw ᒪᑖᐃᐧᓯᐸᐦᑖᐤ
VAI s/he runs to an open
area or clearing

matāwisipiciw ᒪᑖᐃᐧᓯᐱᒋᐤ
VAI s/he travels in the open,
s/he moves camp out in the
open

matāwisipitam ᒪᑖᐃᐧᓯᐱᑕᒼ
VTI s/he pulls s.t. out into an
open area or clearing

matāwisipitēw ᒪᑖᐃᐧᓯᐱᑌᐤ
VTI s/he pulls s.o. out into
an open area or clearing

matāwisiw ᒪᑖᐃᐧᓯᐤ
VAI s/he comes into an open
area or clearing (from a trail)

matēw ᒪᑌᐤ
VTA he has sexual
intercourse with s.o.

matokahp ᒪᑐᑲᐦᑊ
NI campsite; empty camp,
messy campsite

matotisān ᒪᑐᑎᓵᐣ
NI sweat-lodge

matotisānihkēw ᒪᑐᑎᓵᓂᐦᑫᐤ
VAI s/he builds a
sweat-lodge

matotisiw ᒪᑐᑎᓯᐤ
VAI s/he goes into a
sweat-lodge, s/he sweats
him/herself; s/he takes a
steam bath

matwān ᒪᑜᐣ
IPC I wonder; can it really
be? [*discourse particle*]

matwān cī ᒪᑜᐣ ᒌ
IPH I wonder, I wonder if; I
believe; perhaps

matwē- ᒪᑜ
IPV audibly, visibly;
perceptibly; loudly; heard or
seen from a distance

matwē-ācimow ᒪᑜ ᐋᒋᒧᐤ
VAI s/he is heard from a
distance telling news

matwē-kitow ᒪᑜ ᑭᑐᐤ
VAI s/he is heard calling (as
a bird) from a distance

matwē-mātow ᒪᑜ ᒫᑐᐤ
VAI s/he cries loudly, s/he
cries so as to be heard, s/he
is heard crying from a
distance

matwē-nikamow ᒪᑜ ᓂᑲᒧᐤ
VAI s/he sings loudly, s/he is
heard singing from a distance

matwē-nipāw ᒪᑜ ᓂᐹᐤ
VAI s/he snores; s/he is
heard from a distance while
sleeping [*see also*
matwēhkwāmiw]

matwē-tēpwēw ᒪᑜ ᑌᐻᐤ
VAI s/he calls loudly (so as
to be heard at a distance)

matwēham ᒪᑜᐦᐊᒼ
VTI s/he hammers s.t.
causing a sound audible at a
distance

matwēhikātēw ᒪᑑᐦᐱᐦᑲᑌᐅᐤ
VII it is hammered, it is pounded to make a sound audible at a distance

matwēhikēw ᒪᑑᐦᐱᐊᑫᐤ
VAI s/he bangs things, s/he hammers things, s/he is heard hammering at a distance

matwēhikēwin ᒪᑑᐦᐱᐊᑫᐎᐣ
NI hammering, pounding audible at a distance

matwēhkasow ᒪᑑᐦᐸᑯᐤ
VAI it burns audibly or visibly at a distance

matwēhkwāmiw ᒪᑑᐦᐸᑊᒋᐤ
VAI s/he snores, s/he sleeps loudly, s/he makes sounds while sleeping audible at a distance [see also matwē-nipāw]

matwēhkwāmiwin ᒪᑑᐦᐸᑊᒋᐊᐎᐣ
NI snoring

matwēhtin ᒪᑑᐦᐟᐣ
VII it falls audibly; the sound of a door slamming is heard from a distance

matwēhtitāw ᒪᑑᐦᐟᒉᐤ
VAIt s/he knocks s.t. on (something), s/he hits s.t. against (something); s/he drops s.t. audibly to be heard at a distance

matwēhwēw ᒪᑑᐦᑌᐤ
VTA s/he bangs s.o. (e.g. drum); s/he hammers s.o., s/he pounds s.o., s/he hits s.o. audibly to be heard at a distance

matwēkahikēw ᒪᑑᐸᐦᐊᑫᐤ
VAI s/he chops noisily, s/he makes chopping sounds heard at a distance

matwēkahikēwin ᒪᑑᐸᐦᐊᑫᐊᐎᐣ
NI sounds of chopping heard at a distance

matwēpitam ᒪᑑᐱᑕᒼ
VTI s/he pulls s.t. audibly, s/he pulls s.t. hard and makes it snap so as to be heard at a distance

matwēsikēw ᒪᑑᕒᑫᐤ
VAI s/he is heard shooting at a distance

matwēsin ᒪᑑᕒᐢ
VAI s/he falls or steps audibly at a distance; s/he is heard falling down (as a clock striking is heard)

matwēskopayiw ᒪᑑᐣᐚᐸᔪᐤ
VII it cracks audibly from a distance

matwētahikēmakan ᒪᑑᐧᐨᐦᐊᑫᒪᑲᐣ
VII it makes detonations heard from a distance

matwētayēhkasow ᒪᑑᐧᐨᐧᓬᐦᐸᔪᐤ
VAI it pops at the belly from heat

matwēwasikēw ᒪᑑᐧᐊᕒᑫᐤ
VAI s/he is heard making cracklings

matwēwēsikēw ᒪᑑᐧᐁᕒᑫᐤ
VAI s/he is heard firing shots from a distance

matwēwēw ᒪᑑᐧᐁᐤ
VII it detonates; there is an audible report of a gun heard from a distance

matwēyāpiskaham ᒪᑑᔭᐱᐢᑲᐦᐊᒼ
VTI s/he strikes s.t. metal (e.g. steel triangle) so as to be heard at a distance

matwēyāpiskahikan ᒪᑑᔭᐱᐢᑲᐦᐃᑲᐣ
NI sounding triangle; cymbal

matwēyāpiskahikēw ᒪᑑᔭᐱᐢᑲᐦᐃᑫᐤ
VAI s/he hits a steel triangle

mawapiw ᒪᐧᐊᐱᐤ
VAI s/he visits [sC; see also kiyokēw]

mawimoscikākēw ᒪᐊᐧᒍᐢᒋᑲᑫᐤ
VAI s/he makes an offering and entreaty

mawimoscikēw ᒪᐊᐧᒍᐢᒋᑫᐤ
VAI s/he prays, s/he chants, s/he worships, s/he prays to God, s/he makes an entreaty

mawimoscikēwikamik ᒪᐊᐧᒍᐢᒋᑫᐃᐧᑲᒥᐠ
NI house of worship [pl: -wa]

mawimoscikēwin ᒪᐊᐧᒍᐢᒋᑫᐃᐧᐣ
NI entreaty, worship, praying, prayer to the Great Spirit; religion

mawimosk ᒪᐊᐧᒍᐢᐠ
NA one who cries out, wails

mawimoskiw ᒪᐊᐧᒍᐢᑭᐤ
VAI s/he cries out, wails all the time [hab]

mawimostam ᒪᐊᐧᒍᐢᑕᒼ
VTI s/he worships s.t.

mawimostawēw ᒪᐊᐧᒍᐢᑕᐁᐧᐤ
VTA s/he implores s.o., s/he wails before s.o.; s/he worships s.o., s/he prays to s.o. for help, s/he exhorts s.o.

mawimow ᒪᐊᐧᒍᐤ
VAI s/he cries out; s/he wails, s/he squeals, s/he entreats

mawimowin ᒪᐊᐧᒍᐊᐧᐣ
NI dissatisfaction, complaining; cry of pain

mawinēham ᒪᐊᐧᓀᐦᐊᒼ
VTI s/he challenges, s/he attacks s.t.

mawinēhikēw ᒪᐊᐧᓀᐦᐊᑫᐤ
VAI s/he challenges

mawinēhotowak ᒪᐊᐧᓀᐦᐅᑐᐊᐧᐠ
VAI they challenge one another

mawinēhotowin ᒪᐊᐧᓀᐦᐅᑐᐃᐧᐣ
NI challenge

mawinēhwēw ᒪᐊᐧᓀᐦᐁᐧᐤ
VTA s/he challenges s.o. to a contest

mawinēskomēw ᒪᐊᐧᓀᐢᑯᒣᐤ
VTA s/he challenges s.o.

mawisow ᒪᐊᐧᓱᐤ
VAI s/he picks berries, s/he gathers berries; s/he gathers food (by hand above ground)

mawisowin ᒪᐊᐧᓱᐃᐧᐣ
NI berry picking

mawisōstamawēw ᒪᐊᐧᓲᐢᑕᒪᐁᐧᐤ
VTA s/he gathers berries for s.o.

mawiswākan ᒪᐊᐧᔃᑲᐣ
NI berry basket; berry patch, area of berries

mawiswātam ᒪᐊᐧᔃᑕᒼ
VTI s/he picks the bush clean of berries, s/he picks all the berries on the bush

mawīhkātam ᒪᐄᐦᑲᑕᒼ
VTI s/he laments for s.t., s/he cries for s.t., s/he mourns for s.t. [also mowihkātam]

mawīhkātamawēw ᒪᐄᐦᑲᑕᒪᐁᐧᐤ
VTA s/he begs s.o. for (it/him) with tears

mawīhkātamowin ᒪᐄᐦᑲᑕᒧᐃᐧᐣ
NI crying, mourning

mawīhkātēw ᒪᐄᐦᑲᑌᐤ
VTA s/he begs s.o. with tears; s/he cries for s.o., s/he mourns for s.o.; s/he is sad to see s.o. go [also mowihkātēw]

may´akask ᒪᭆᑲᐢᐠ
NDI palate [pl: -wa]

mayakāpisin ᒪᔭᑲᐱᓯᐣ
VAI s/he is left in surprise at the sight of sight [cf. māmaskātāpisin]

mayaw ᒪᔭᐤ
IPC as soon as; straight, exact, on time [cf. mayawāc]

mayawāc ᒪᔭᐧᐋᐨ
IPC as soon as [cf. mayaw]

may´āskam ᒪᭆᐢᑲᒼ
VTI s/he passes s.t. walking [cf. miyāskam]

may´āskawēw ᒪᭆᐢᑲᐁᐧᐤ
VTA s/he passes s.o. walking [cf. miyāskawēw]

may´āwaham ᒪᭆᐊᐧᐦᐊᒼ
VTI s/he passes s.t. by water [cf. miyāwaham]

may´āwahwēw ᒪᭆᐊᐧᐦᐁᐧᐤ
VTA s/he passes s.o. by water [cf. miyāwahwēw]

maywēs ᒪᐁᐧᐢ
IPC before [also moyēs; cf. maywēsk, pāmwayēs]

maywēsk ᒪᐁᐧᐢᐠ
IPC before [cf. maywēs, pāmwayēs]

ᒫ

mā ᒫ
IPC surely, surely not

mā-mitātaht ᒫ ᒥᑖᑕᐦᐟ
IPC ten each; ten times [*cf.* mitātahtwāw]

mā-mitātahtomitanaw ᒫ ᒥᑖᑕᐦᑐᒥᑕᓇᐤ
IPC one hundred each

māci- ᒫᒋ
IPN beginning

māci- ᒫᒋ
IPV begin to, start to; commencement; initially

māci-atoskēw ᒫᒋ ᐊᑐᐢᑫᐤ
VAI s/he starts working [*also* māc-ātoskēw; *cf.* mātatoskēw]

māci-ayamihāw ᒫᒋ ᐊᔭᒥᐦᐋᐤ
VAI s/he starts praying [*also* māc-āyamihāw]

māci-ayamihcikēw ᒫᒋ ᐊᔭᒥᐦᒋᑫᐤ
VAI s/he starts reading [*also* māc-āyamihcikēw]

māci-āhkosiw ᒫᒋ ᐋᐦᑯᓯᐤ
VAI s/he is getting sick; s/he is beginning labour [*also* māc-āhkosiw]

māci-mīcisow ᒫᒋ ᒦᒋᓱᐤ
VAI s/he starts eating

māci-nīmihitow ᒫᒋ ᓃᒥᐦᐃᑐᐤ
VAI s/he starts dancing

māci-nikamow ᒫᒋ ᓂᑲᒧᐤ
VAI s/he starts singing

māci-nipāw ᒫᒋ ᓂᐹᐤ
VAI s/he starts sleeping

māci-pimipahtāw ᒫᒋ ᐱᒥᐸᐦᑖᐤ
VAI s/he starts running

māci-pīkiskwēw ᒫᒋ ᐲᑭᐢᑵᐤ
VAI s/he starts speaking

mācihtahēw ᒫᒋᐦᑕᐦᐁᐤ
VTA s/he starts s.o.

mācihtāw ᒫᒋᐦᑖᐤ
VAIt s/he starts, s/he starts s.t., s/he starts to do s.t., s/he starts making s.t.; s/he begins to operate s.t. [*also* mācīhtāw]

mācika ᒫᒋᑲ
IPC for instance, as it now appears; so [*weak concessive*]

mācikiw ᒫᒋᑭᐤ
VAI s/he starts to grow

mācikōci ᒫᒋᑰᒋ
IPC look, you will see for yourself that it is so

mācikōcicāk ᒫᒋᑰᒋᒑᐠ
IPC for example

mācikōcicān ᒫᒋᑰᒋᒑᐣ
IPC look, let me show you [*dim*; *pl*: mācikōcicānitik]

mācikōtān ᒫᒋᑰᑖᐣ
IPC you will see for yourself that it is so

mācikōtitāk ᒫᒋᑰᑎᑖᐠ
IPC let me show you (*pl*)

mācikōtitān ᒫᒋᑰᑎᑖᐣ
IPC look, let me show you; you will see [*optional pl*: mācikōtitāk]

mācipaýihtāw ᒫᒋᐸᔨᐦᑖᐤ
VAIt s/he starts s.t. up

mācipaýin ᒫᒋᐸᔨᐣ
VII it begins to run (*e.g.* tape-recorder), it starts to operate [*cf.* mācipaýiw]

mācipaýiw ᒫᒋᐸᔨᐤ
VII it starts to operate [*cf.* mācipaýin]

mācipaýiwin ᒫᒋᐸᔨᐎᐣ
NI the beginning

mācisam ᒫᒋᓴᒼ
VTI s/he cuts s.t.

mācistan ᒫᒋᐢᑕᐣ
VII it is a thawing river

māciswēw ᒫᒋᔃᐤ
VTA s/he cuts s.o. open [*cf.* mātiswēw]

mācīhkāsow ᒫᒌᐦᑳᓱᐤ
VAI s/he pretends to go hunting

mācīhtahēw ᒫᒌᐦᑕᐦᐁᐤ
VTA s/he takes s.o. hunting

mācīhtāniwan ᒫᒌᐦᑖᓂᐘᐣ
VII it is started (*e.g.* construction) [*VAI unspecified actor*]

mācīpiciw ᒫᒌᐱᒋᐤ
VAI s/he moves camp to hunt

mācīs ᒫᒌᐢ
NI a match [*dim*; *English loan*: "match"]

mācītisahwēw ᒫᒌᑎᓴᐦᐍᐤ
VTA s/he drives s.o. to hunt

mācītotawēw ᒫᒌᑐᑕᐍᐤ
VTA s/he hunts for s.o.

mācīw ᒫᒌᐤ
VAI s/he hunts, s/he goes hunting, s/he hunts big game

mācīwin ᒫᒌᐎᐣ
NI hunting, the hunt

mācīwinihkēw ᒫᒌᐎᓂᐦᑫᐤ
VAI s/he organizes a hunt

mācosiw ᒫᒍᓯᐤ
VAI s/he cries a little [*dim*]

māham ᒫᐦᐊᒼ
VTI s/he canoes downriver, s/he paddles downstream, s/he rows downstream, s/he goes downstream (by canoe)

māh-māwaci ᒫᐦ ᒫᐗᒋ
IPC the most, the best [*rdpl*; *cf.* māwaci]

māh-mēskoc ᒫᐦ ᒣᐢᑯᐨ
IPC each in turn, take turns [*rdpl*; *also* māh-mēskot, *cf.* mēskoc, mīskoc]

māh-mēskotonamātowak ᒫᐦ ᒣᐢᑯᑐᓇᒫᑐᐘᐠ
VAI they exchange things with one another [*rdpl*]

māh-mihkwaskāpiw ᒫᐦ ᒥᐦᑿᐢᑳᐱᐤ
VAI s/he has red eyes, s/he has conjunctivitis

māh-misimēw ᒫᐦ ᒥᓯᒣᐤ
VTA s/he reports s.o. repeatedly, s/he tells on s.o. repeatedly [*rdpl*]

māh-mīnomēw ᒫᐦ ᒦᓄᒣᐤ
VTA s/he corrects s.o.'s behaviour or attitude [*rdpl*; *cf.* mīnomēw]

māh-mīsaham ᒫᐦ ᒦᓴᐦᐊᒼ
VTI s/he mends s.t. in several places [*rdpl*]

māh-mīsahwēw ᒫᐦ ᒦᓴᐦᐍᐤ
VTA s/he mends s.o. in several places [*rdpl*]

māhāpaýiw ᒫᐦᐋᐸᔨᐤ
VAI s/he drifts downstream

māhāpocikāna ᒫᐦᐋᐳᒋᑳᓇ
NI raft of logs afloat [*pl*]

māhāpocikēw ᒫᐦᐋᐳᒋᑫᐤ
VAI s/he drives logs, s/he floats logs downstream

māhāpokow ᒫᐦᐋᐳᑯᐤ
VAI s/he canoes downstream

māhāpotāw ᒫᐦᐋᐳᑖᐤ
VAI s/he drifts logs downstream

māhāpoýow ᒫᐦᐋᐳᔪᐤ
VAI s/he drifts downstream

māhāpwēwēw ᒫᐦᐋᐻᐌᐤ
VAI s/he paddles downstream

māhāstan ᒫᐦᐋᐢᑕᐣ
VII it sails downstream, it is blown downstream

māhcikonēw ᒫᐦᒋᑯᓀᐤ
VTA s/he holds s.o. down (so that one is helpless)

māhcikwahpicikēw ᒫᐦᒋᑿᐦᐱᒋᑫᐤ
VAI s/he binds things, s/he ties things down

māhcikwahpisowin ᒫᐦᒋᑿᐦᐱᓱᐎᐣ
NI binder, bond, hobble

māhcikwahpitam ᒫᐦᒋᑿᐦᐱᑕᒼ
VTI s/he ties s.t. down

māhcikwahpitēw ᒫᐦᒋᑿᐦᐱᑌᐤ
VTA s/he ties s.o. down (so that one cannot move)

māhi- ᒫᐦᐃ
IPV downstream

māhihk ᒫᐦᐃᕽ
IPC in the east; in the downstream direction [*cf.* māmihk]

māhipiciw ᒫᐦᐃᐱᒋᐤ
VAI s/he moves camp downstream

māhiskam ᒫᐦᐃᐢᑲᒼ
VTI s/he goes downstream to trading post for supplies; s/he goes to the store

māhmākwahcikanēyāpiy ᒫᐦᒫᑿᐦᒋᑲᓀᔮᐱᕀ
NI rawhide rope [*rdpl*]

māhohtēw i"ᐅ"ᑌᐤ
VAI s/he walks downstream

māhpinēsiw i"ᐱᐧᑊᔦᐤ
VAI s/he groans a little (from fear or pain) [dim]

māhpinēw i"ᐱᐧᑊᐤ
VAI s/he groans in pain; s/he is cowardly [cf. mamāhpinēw]

māhpinēwin i"ᐱᐧᐸᐃᐧᐣ
NI groan, groaning; cry of pain

māhtakoskam i"ᒋᐨᐧᐸᑊ
VTI s/he steps on s.t.; s/he lies on s.t.; s/he sits on s.t.

māhtakoskawēw i"ᒋᐨᐧᐸᑊᐯᐧ·ᐤ
VTA s/he steps on s.o.; s/he lies on s.o.; s/he sits on s.o.

māhtāhitowak i"ᒋᐦ"ᐊᑐᐊᐧᐠ
VAI they organize a give-away feast, they give a potlatch

māhtāhitowin i"ᒋᐦ"ᐊᑐᐊᐤ
NI give-away feast, potlatch

māhtāhitowinihkēw
i"ᒋᐦ"ᐊᑐᐊᐧ·ᓂᐦᐧ·ᐦ9ᐤ
VAI s/he arranges a give-away feast or potlatch

māhtāw-askiy i"ᒋ" ᐊᓂᑊᐱᐟ
NI wondrous land, strange land; wondrous country, strange country

māhtāwakēýimēw i"ᒋ◁·9ᐱᔨᐤ
VTA s/he considers s.o. wondrous, s/he considers s.o. strange

māhtāwi-sīpiy i"ᒋᐧ· ᓯᐱᐟ
NI Churchill River [lit: "difficult, wondrous river"]

māhtāwinākosiw i"ᒋᐧ·ᐊᐦᐨᐤ
VAI s/he looks wondrous, s/he looks strange [cf. mamāhtawi-]

māhtāwinākwan i"ᒋᐧ·ᐊᐦᑊᐤ
VII it looks wondrous, it looks strange [cf. mamāhtawi-]

māhtāwisiw i"ᒋᐧ·ᔨᐤ
VAI s/he has mysterious ways, s/he has wondrous ways, s/he has strange ways [cf. mamāhtāwisiw]

māhtāwisiwin i"ᒋᐧ·ᔨᐊᐤ
NI mysterious ways, wondrous ways, strange ways [cf. mamāhtāwisiwin]

māhtāwisīhcikēw i"ᒋᐧ·ᔨᐦᐦ9ᐤ
VAI s/he does things wondrously, s/he does things strangely

māhtāwisīhcikēwin
i"ᒋᐧ·ᔨᐦ"ᐸ9ᐊᐤ
NI mysterious act, wondrous act, strange act

māhtāwitēýihtam i"ᒋᐧ·ᐸᔨᐸᐦ"ᐸᐨ
VTI s/he considers s.t. wondrous, s/he considers s.t. strange [cf. mamāhtāwitēýihtam]

māhtāwitēýihtākosiw
i"ᒋᐧ·ᐸᔨᐸᐦ"ᐸᐨᐤᐤ
VAI s/he is known to have mysterious ways, s/he is known to have wondrous ways

māhtāwitotam i"ᒋᐧ·ᐅᒋᐨ
VTI s/he performs spiritual rites, s/he does wondrous things

māhtāwitōtawēw i"ᒋᐧ·ᐅᒋᐯᐧ·ᐤ
VTA s/he does strange things to s.o.

māhtinam i"ᓇᐢᐨ
VTI s/he moves s.t.

māhtinēw i"ᓇ ᐧᐤ
VTA s/he moves s.o.

māka ᐃᐦ
IPC but, then; still

māka awa ᐃᐦ ◁◁·
IPH but here s/he is, speak of the devil [also māk āwa]

māka mīna ᐃᐦ ᒋᐟ
IPH as usual

māka ōma ᐃᐦ ᐅᒐ
IPH but here it is [also māk ōma]

mākohēw ᐃᐨ"ᐁᐤ
VTA s/he presses hard on s.o.; s/he pressures s.o., s/he torments s.o., s/he threatens s.o., s/he bothers s.o.

mākohikēwin ᐃᐨ"ᐊ9ᐊᐤ
NI threat

mākohiwēw ᐃᐨ"ᐊ ᐁ·ᐤ
VAI s/he threatens people

mākonam ᐃᐤᐨᐨ
VTI s/he presses s.t. (hard, by hand); s/he squeezes s.t.

mākonēw ᐃᐤᐃᐤᐤ
VTA s/he presses s.o., s/he presses s.o.'s hand; s/he kneads s.o. (e.g. bread)

mākonikan ᐃᐤᐦᐧᐸᑊ
NI bread dough; rolling pin

mākonikēw ᐃᐤᐃᐃ9ᐤ
VAI s/he kneads bread; s/he rolls pastry dough

mākoniskēpaýiw ᐃᐤᐃᐢᑊ9ᐱᐤ
VAI s/he wrings his/her own hands

mākopaýiw ᐃᐤ9ᐱᐤ
VII it becomes flat (from being pressed)

mākoskam ᐃᐤᐢᑊᑊ
VTI s/he steps on s.t., s/he presses s.t. down

mākoskawēw ᐃᐤᐢᑊᐯᐧ·ᐤ
VTA s/he presses upon s.o., s/he tramples on s.o.; s/he presses s.o. down with his/her weight

mākowiw ᐃᐤᐃᐧ·ᐤ
VAI it is a loon [cf. mwākowiw]

mākōhkasow ᐃᐤ"ᑊᔨᐤ
VAI s/he is oppressed by heat

mākwa ᐃᐸ·
NA loon [cf. mwākwa]

mākwa-sākahikan ᐃᐸ· ᐢᑊ"ᐊᐠ
NI Loon Lake, SK; Makwa Lake, SK [loc generally]

mākwaciw ᐃᐸ·ᒐᐤ
VAI s/he is oppressed by cold

mākwaham ᐃᐸᐧ·◁ᐨ
VTI s/he presses s.t. down (by tool)

mākwahcikēnikan ᐃᐸᐧ"ᒐ9ᐤᐠᐤ
NI vice, vice-grip; pliers; thongs

mākwahcikēw ᐃᐸᐧ"ᒐ9ᐤ
VAI s/he chews

mākwahikan ᐃᐸ·"ᐊᐠ
NI cheese; press

mākwahikanis ᐃᐸ·"ᐊᐠᐤᐣ
NI small press (e.g. to extract juice) [dim]

mākwahpitam ᐃᐸ·"ᐱᐨᐨ
VTI s/he ties s.t. up, s/he ties s.t. solidly

mākwahpitēw ᐃᐸ·"ᐱᐁᐤ
VTA s/he ties s.o. up; s/he immobilizes s.o. by tying

mākwahtam ᐃᐸ·"ᐸᐨ
VTI s/he bites s.t., s/he gnaws on s.t., s/he chews on s.t. [rdpl: mā-mākwahtam]

mākwahwēw ᐃᐸ·"ᐁ·ᐤ
VTA s/he presses s.o. close by tool or with horns [cf. mākwāham]

mākwamēw ᐃᐸ·ᒐ9ᐤ
VTA s/he bites s.o., s/he chews on s.o., s/he seizes s.o. hard with teeth or mouth [also mākomēw]

mākwastēnikan ᐃᐸ·ᓇᐅᐧᐸᑊ
NI trigger

mākwāskwahwēw ᐃᐸ·ᐢᑊᐧ·"ᐁ·ᐤ
VTA s/he presses s.o. close with a stick; it oppresses s.o. [e.g. "tree" as actor; also mākwāskohwēw]

mākwēýihtam ᐃ9·ᔨᐸ"ᐨᐨ
VTI s/he is frightened of s.t.

mākwēýimow ᐃ9·ᔨᐃᔨᐤ
VAI s/he is afraid; s/he feels pressed upon, s/he feels oppressed

mākwēýimowin ᐃ9·ᔨᐸᔨᐊᐤ
NI fright; fear

māmacikastēw ᐃᒐᒋᐸᑊᐅ·ᐤ
VAI s/he is proud, s/he is conceited

māmaskāc ᐃᒐᐢᑊ·ᐸ·
IPC surprising; wonderful and strange; amazing!

māmaskācinākosiw ᐃᒐᐢᑊᐧ·ᐊᐦᐨᐤ
VAI s/he looks strange or amazing

māmaskācinākwan ᐃᒐᐢᑊᐧ·ᐊᐦᐸᐤ
VII it looks strange (e.g. an area)

māmaskācitōtam ᐃᒐᐢᑊᐧ·ᒋᐅᒋᐨ
VTI s/he works in strange ways

mämaskäsäpahtam ᒫᒪᐢᑳᓴᐸᐦᑕᒼ
VTI s/he looks on s.t. with wonder

mämaskäsäpamēw ᒫᒪᐢᑳᓴᐸᒣᐤ
VTA s/he looks on s.o. with wonder

mämaskätam ᒫᒪᐢᑳᑕᒼ
VTI s/he is surprised at s.t., s/he finds s.t. strange, s/he finds s.t. incomprehensible, s/he wonders at s.t.

mämaskätamowin ᒫᒪᐢᑳᑕᒧᐃᐧᐣ
NI wonder, amazement; mystery

mämaskätäpisin ᒫᒪᐢᑳᑖᐱᓯᐣ
VAI s/he is surprised or amazed at the sight of sight [*cf.* mayakäpisin]

mämaskätēw ᒫᒪᐢᑳᑌᐤ
VTA s/he is surprised by s.o.; s/he wonders at or about s.o.; s/he finds s.o. strange, s/he finds s.o. incomprehensible

mämaskätēýihtam ᒫᒪᐢᑳᑌᔨᐦᑕᒼ
VTI s/he thinks s.t. strange; s/he is amazed

mämaskätēýihtamowin ᒫᒪᐢᑳᑌᔨᐦᑕᒧᐃᐧᐣ
NI astonishment

mämaskätēýihtäkosiw ᒫᒪᐢᑳᑌᔨᐦᑖᑯᓯᐤ
VAI s/he is thought strange

mämaskätēýihtäkwan ᒫᒪᐢᑳᑌᔨᐦᑖᒁᐣ
VII it is amazing, it is surprising

mämaw-ōhtäwimäw ᒫᒧᐦᑖᐑᒫᐤ
NA All Father, Father-of-All, Creator, God [*cf.* mämawi-ohtäwimäw]

mämawaci ᒫᒪᐊᐧᒋ
IPC most, the very most [*superlative*]

mämawaci-kayäs ᒫᒪᐊᐧᒋ ᑲᔮᐢ
IPC at the very earliest time [*cf.* mämawo-kayäs]

mämawapiwak ᒫᒪᐊᐧᐱᐊᐧᐠ
VAI they have a meeting [*pl*; *also* mämawōpiwak]

mämawapiwin ᒫᒪᐊᐧᐱᐃᐧᐣ
NI meeting [*also* mämawōpiwin]

mämawaskitēwa ᒫᒪᐊᐧᐢᑭᑌᐊᐧ
VII they stand in a cluster (*e.g.* plants) [*pl*]

mämawatoskēwak ᒫᒪᐊᐧᑐᐢᑫᐊᐧᐠ
VAI they work together [*pl*]

mämawēyas ᒫᒪᐊᐧᔭᐢ
IPC where all are assembled

mämawēyatiwak ᒫᒪᐊᐧᔭᑎᐊᐧᐠ
VAI they go together, they proceed together; they are assembled [*pl*]

mämawi- ᒫᒪᐃᐧ
IPV together; in full number of them all, altogether, all together as a group [*also* mämäwi]

mämawi-akihcikēw ᒫᒪᐃᐧ ᐊᑭᐦᒋᑫᐤ
VAI s/he adds all together

mämawi-atoskēwak ᒫᒪᐃᐧ ᐊᑐᐢᑫᐊᐧᐠ
VAI they work altogether

mämawi-ayamihäwak ᒫᒪᐃᐧ ᐊᔭᒥᐦᐋᐊᐧᐠ
VAI they pray altogether

mämawi-ayamihcikēwak ᒫᒪᐃᐧ ᐊᔭᒥᐦᒋᑫᐊᐧᐠ
VAI they read altogether

mämawi-aýwēpiwak ᒫᒪᐃᐧ ᐊᔦᐧᐱᐊᐧᐠ
VAI they rest altogether

mämawi-äcimowak ᒫᒪᐃᐧ ᐋᒋᒧᐊᐧᐠ
VAI they tell stories altogether

mämawi-itohtēwak ᒫᒪᐃᐧ ᐃᑐᐦᑌᐊᐧᐠ
VAI they walk altogether

mämawi-kiyokēwak ᒫᒪᐃᐧ ᑭᔪᑫᐊᐧᐠ
VAI they visit altogether

mämawi-mäciwak ᒫᒪᐃᐧ ᒫᒋᐊᐧᐠ
VAI they hunt altogether

mämawi-mätowak ᒫᒪᐃᐧ ᒫᑐᐊᐧᐠ
VAI they cry altogether

mämawi-micisowak ᒫᒪᐃᐧ ᒥᒋᓱᐊᐧᐠ
VAI they eat altogether

mämawi-nikamowak ᒫᒪᐃᐧ ᓂᑲᒧᐊᐧᐠ
VAI they sing altogether

mämawi-nipäwak ᒫᒪᐃᐧ ᓂᐹᐊᐧᐠ
VAI they sleep altogether

mämawi-nimihitowak ᒫᒪᐃᐧ ᓃᒥᐦᐃᑐᐊᐧᐠ
VAI they dance altogether

mämawi-ohtäwimäw ᒫᒪᐃᐧ ᐅᐦᑖᐑᒫᐤ
NA All Father, Father-of-All, Creator, God [*cf.* mämaw-ōhtäwimäw]

mämawi-pihtwäwak ᒫᒪᐃᐧ ᐲᐦᒡᐋᐊᐧᐠ
VAI they smoke altogether

mämawi-pikiskwēwak ᒫᒪᐃᐧ ᐲᑭᐢᑵᐊᐧᐠ
VAI they speak altogether

mämawi-wicihitowin ᒫᒪᐃᐧ ᐄᐧᒋᐦᐃᑐᐃᐧᐣ
NI all helping together, general cooperation

mämawi-wikiwak ᒫᒪᐃᐧ ᐄᐧᑭᐊᐧᐠ
VAI they live altogether

mämawihitowak ᒫᒪᐃᐧᐦᐃᑐᐊᐧᐠ
VAI they are altogether in one group, they gather in a group

mämawinam ᒫᒪᐃᐧᓇᒼ
VTI s/he holds s.t. together

mämawinitowak ᒫᒪᐃᐧᓂᑐᐊᐧᐠ
VAI they unify, they bring one another together

mämawinitowin ᒫᒪᐃᐧᓂᑐᐃᐧᐣ
NI unification

mämawipaýihowak ᒫᒪᐊᐧᐸᔨᐦᐅᐊᐧᐠ
VAI they gather quickly

mämawipaýiwa ᒫᒪᐊᐧᐸᔨᐊᐧ
VII they mix together

mämawipaýiwak ᒫᒪᐊᐧᐸᔨᐊᐧᐠ
VAI they gather in one place

mämawipaýiwin ᒫᒪᐊᐧᐸᔨᐃᐧᐣ
NI togetherness; a union, gathering

mämawo-kayäs ᒫᒪᐅᐧ ᑲᔮᐢ
IPC at the very earliest time [*cf.* mämawaci-kayäs]

mämawohkamätowak ᒫᒪᐅᐧᐦᑲᒫᑐᐊᐧᐠ
VAI they do things together, they cooperate; they work (at it/him) together as a group

mämawohkamätowin ᒫᒪᐅᐧᐦᑲᒫᑐᐃᐧᐣ
NI cooperation

mämawohkawēwak ᒫᒪᐅᐧᐦᑲᐁᐧᐊᐧᐠ
VTA they present a unified front against s.o.; they go at s.o. in full numbers

mämawō ᒫᒪᐅᐧ
IPC all together

mämawōkihtam ᒫᒪᐅᐧᑭᐦᑕᒼ
VTI s/he counts s.t. all together

mämawōpaýiwak ᒫᒪᐅᐧᐸᔨᐊᐧᐠ
VAI they get together, they have a meeting, they assemble, they go in a body

mämawōpiwak ᒫᒪᐅᐧᐱᐊᐧᐠ
VAI they sit assembled, they sit together, they hold a meeting [*cf.* mämawapiwak]

mämawōpiwin ᒫᒪᐅᐧᐱᐃᐧᐣ
NI meeting [*cf.* mämawapiwin]

mämäkwahtam ᒫᒫᒁᐦᑕᒼ
VTI s/he chews s.t. [*rdpl*]

mämäkwamēw ᒫᒫᒁᒣᐤ
VTA s/he chews s.o. [*rdpl*]

mämäsis ᒫᒫᓯᐢ
IPC poorly done; hurriedly done, low quality work

mämäwacēyas ᒫᒫᐊᐧᒉᔭᐢ
IPC most, moreso; beyond others [*also* mämäwaciyas; *cf.* mämawaci]

mämēscihtäsow ᒫᒣᐢᒋᐦᑖᓱᐤ
VAI s/he exterminates (*e.g.* insects) [*rdpl*]

mämihk ᒫᒥᕽ
IPC downriver; east [*cf.* mähihk]

mämihkiýiniwak
NA Downstream People [*pl*; *division of the Cree, including* kä-tēpwēwisipiwiýiniwak "Calling River People", posäkanaciwiýiniwak "Touchwood Hills People" *and* wäposwayänak "Rabbitskin People"]

māmiskōmēw ᒫᒥᐢᑯᒣᐤ
VTA s/he talks about s.o., s/he discusses s.o., s/he mentions s.o., s/he speaks of s.o. [*also* māmiskomēw]

māmiskōmisow ᒫᒥᐢᑯᒥᓱᐤ
VAI s/he speaks of him/herself

māmiskōtam ᒫᒥᐢᑯᑕᒼ
VTI s/he talks about s.t., s/he discusses s.t., s/he expounds s.t., s/he speaks of s.t.

māmiskōtamawēw ᒫᒥᐢᑯᑕᒪᐍᐤ
VTA s/he tells s.o. about (it/him), s/he discusses (it/him) for s.o.

māmitonēýihcikan ᒫᒥᑐᓀᔨᐦᒋᑲᐣ
NI mind; a thought; [*pl*:] thoughts

māmitonēýihcikēw ᒫᒥᑐᓀᔨᐦᒋᑫᐤ
VAI s/he thinks, s/he meditates

māmitonēýihtam ᒫᒥᑐᓀᔨᐦᑕᒼ
VTI s/he thinks about s.t., s/he ponders s.t., s/he ponders over s.t., s/he considers s.t., s/he wonders about s.t.; s/he worries about s.t.

māmitonēýihtamimēw ᒫᒥᑐᓀᔨᐦᑕᒥᒣᐤ
VTA s/he gives s.o. (s.t.) to think about

māmitonēýihtamowin ᒫᒥᑐᓀᔨᐦᑕᒧᐏᐣ
NI thought

māmitonēýihtēstamāsow ᒫᒥᑐᓀᔨᐦᑌᐢᑕᒫᓱᐤ
VAI s/he thinks about (it/him) for him/herself, s/he plans for him/herself

māmitonēýimēw ᒫᒥᑐᓀᔨᒣᐤ
VTA s/he thinks about s.o., s/he ponders over s.o., s/he has s.o. on his/her mind, s/he meditates on s.o.

māmiýākācihtowak ᒫᒥᔮᑳᒋᐦᑐᐘᐠ
VAI they argue with one another; they question one another

māmiýwākācimow ᒫᒥᔼᑳᒋᒧᐤ
VAI s/he questions, s/he argues

māmwayēs ᒫᒷᔦᐢ
IPC before; sooner than [*cf.* mwayēs, pāmwayēs]

māna ᒫᓇ
IPC usually, habitually, generally, always; used to

māna ᒫᓇ
IPC to be feared, trouble ahead

mānahtēw ᒫᓇᐦᑌᐤ
VAI s/he gets his/her pelts, s/he gets furs

māni ᒫᓂ
IPC to be feared, trouble ahead

māni māka ᒫᓂ ᒫᑲ
IPH possibly, it could be; for sure; (if) it were to [*wC*; *hypothetical*]

mānihtoýāsk ᒫᓂᐦᑐᔮᐢᐠ
NI hide-scraping tool made of bone, axe for scraping-hides

māninakis ᒫᓂᓇᑭᐢ
IPC on and on [*cf.* māninakisk]

māninakisk ᒫᓂᓇᑭᐢᐠ
IPC on and on; then, right away, vigorously, entirely, just like that, without hesitation [*cf.* māninakis; *also* mānakisk, āninakisk]

mānināk ᒫᓂᓈᐠ
IPC without hesitation, entirely

māninākisk ᒫᓂᓈᑭᐢᐠ
IPC without hesitation, entirely

māninākisko- ᒫᓂᓈᑭᐢᑯ
IPV without hesitation, entirely

māninis ᒫᓂᓂᐢ
IPC I really believe (surprise)

mānokawēw ᒫᓄᑲᐍᐤ
VTA s/he sets up a tent or tipi for s.o., s/he makes a house for s.o.

mānokēw ᒫᓄᑫᐤ
VAI s/he camps; s/he puts up a tent, s/he sets up a tipi; s/he makes a ceremonial lodge

māsamēkos ᒫᓴᒣᑯᐢ
NA speckled trout [*dim*]

māsihēw ᒫᓯᐦᐁᐤ
VTA s/he wrestles with s.o., s/he fights s.o.

māsihitowak ᒫᓯᐦᐃᑐᐘᐠ
VAI they wrestle with one another, they wrestle together

māsihitowin ᒫᓯᐦᐃᑐᐏᐣ
NI wrestling

māsihkēskiw ᒫᓯᐦᑫᐢᑭᐤ
VAI s/he is fond of wrestling [*hab*]

māsihkēw ᒫᓯᐦᑫᐤ
VAI s/he wrestles, s/he is a wrestler

māsihkēwin ᒫᓯᐦᑫᐏᐣ
NI wrestling match

māsihtāw ᒫᓯᐦᑖᐤ
VAIt s/he wrestles with s.t., s/he fights with s.t.; s/he undertakes a tough job

māsikīsk ᒫᓯᑮᐢᐠ
NI cedar, cedar bush [*pl*: -wa]

māsiskānitās ᒫᓯᐢᑳᓂᑖᐢ
NI bib overalls

māskahkān ᒫᐢᑲᐦᑳᐣ
NI worn-out tool

māskāw ᒫᐢᑳᐤ
VII it is imperfect, it is defective

māskāwikan ᒫᐢᑳᐏᑲᐣ
NA one who has a crippled back
NI a crippled back

māskāwikanēw ᒫᐢᑳᐏᑲᓀᐤ
VAI s/he has a deformed back; s/he is hunchbacked

māski- ᒫᐢᑭ
IPN crippled, lame; deformed
IPV crippled; defective, deformed

māski-mahkēsīs ᒫᐢᑭ ᒪᐦᑫᓰᐢ
NA lame fox

māskicēhēsiw ᒫᐢᑭᒉᐦᐁᓯᐤ
VAI s/he has a defective heart (as an infant) [*dim*, *cf.* māskitēhēw]

māskicihcēw ᒫᐢᑭᒋᐦᒉᐤ
VAI s/he has a deformed hand

māskicihciy ᒫᐢᑭᒋᐦᒋᐩ
NI crippled hand

māskihcikwan ᒫᐢᑭᐦᒋᑿᐣ
NI deformed knee

māskihēw ᒫᐢᑭᐦᐁᐤ
VTA s/he wounds s.o. [*see also* miswēw]

māskikan ᒫᐢᑭᑲᐣ
NDI chest, breast

māskikanēw ᒫᐢᑭᑲᓀᐤ
VAI s/he has a deformed chest

māskikanis ᒫᐢᑭᑲᓂᐢ
NDI small chest, small breast [*dim*]

māskikāt ᒫᐢᑭᑳᐟ
NA one with a deformed leg
NI deformed leg

māskikātēw ᒫᐢᑭᑳᑌᐤ
VAI s/he has a lame leg

māskikiw ᒫᐢᑭᑭᐤ
VAI s/he grows deformed

māskipaýiw ᒫᐢᑭᐸᔨᐤ
VAI s/he limps; s/he is lame, s/he goes lame

māskipaýiwin ᒫᐢᑭᐸᔨᐏᐣ
NI limping

māskipiw ᒫᐢᑭᐱᐤ
VAI s/he is sitting crippled

māskipiskwanēw ᒫᐢᑭᐱᐢᑿᓀᐤ
VAI s/he has a deformed back

māskipitonēw ᒫᐢᑭᐱᑐᓀᐤ
VAI s/he has a deformed arm

māskisitēw ᒫᐢᑭᓯᑌᐤ
VAI s/he has a lame foot, has a deformed foot

māskisiw ᒫᐢᑭᓯᐤ
VAI s/he is lame, s/he is crippled, s/he is deformed

māskitēhēw ᒫᐢᑭᑌᐦᐁᐤ
VAI s/he has a defective heart

māskōc ᒫᐢᑯᐨ
IPC perhaps, maybe, I suppose; probably, it's likely, it's a reasonably likely

possibility [*cf.* māskōt; *see also* ahpō ētikwē]
māskōt ᒫᐢᑰᐟ
IPC perhaps, maybe, I suppose; probably, it's likely, it's a reasonably likely possibility [*cf.* māskōc; *see also* ahpō ētikwē]
mātaham ᒫᑕᐦᐊᒼ
VTI s/he works s.t. (*e.g.* hide); s/he scrapes the fur off s.t.
mātahikan ᒫᑕᐦᐃᑲᐣ
NI hide scraper; scraper for fur
mātahikanāhtik ᒫᑕᐦᐃᑲᓈᐦᑎᐠ
NI frame for stretching hides in winter [*pl*: -wa]
mātahikākēw ᒫᑕᐦᐃᑳᑫᐤ
VAI s/he scrapes hides with something
mātahikēw ᒫᑕᐦᐃᑫᐤ
VAI s/he scrape hides, s/he scrapes the fur off
mātahpinatēw ᒫᑕᐦᐱᓇᑌᐤ
VTA s/he starts hitting or slaughtering s.o.
mātahtam ᒫᑕᐦᑕᒼ
VTI s/he starts to eat s.t.
mātahwēw ᒫᑕᐦᐍᐤ
VTA s/he works s.o. (*e.g.* hide)
mātakihtam ᒫᑕᑭᐦᑕᒼ
VTI s/he starts counting s.t.
mātakimēw ᒫᑕᑭᒣᐤ
VTA s/he starts counting s.o.
mātamēw ᒫᑕᒣᐤ
VTA s/he starts to eat s.o.
mātatoskēw ᒫᑕᑐᐢᑫᐤ
VAI s/he begins to work [*cf.* māci-atoskēw]
mātayak ᒫᑕᔭᐠ
IPC ahead of time, beforehand
mātāhēw ᒫᑖᐦᐁᐤ
VTA s/he comes upon s.o.'s track, s/he sees s.o.'s footprints; s/he tracks s.o. [*possibly also* mātāhwēw]
mātāhpinēw ᒫᑖᐦᐱᓀᐤ
VAI s/he begins to feel sick or pain; she begins to feel labour pains
mātāhpinēwin ᒫᑖᐦᐱᓀᐏᐣ
NI first pains, onset of labour pains
mātāpohtēwak ᒫᑖᐳᐦᑌᐘᐠ
VAI they walk abreast [*pl*; *see also* nīpitēhtēw]
mātāposinwak ᒫᑖᐳᓯᓇᐧᐠ
VAI they lie in a row [*pl*]
mātinamawēw ᒫᑎᓇᒪᐍᐤ
VTA s/he deals (it/him) out to s.o.; s/he portions out food to s.o., s/he passes food to s.o.
mātinamākēw ᒫᑎᓇᒫᑫᐤ
VAI s/he shares, s/he distributes food
mātinamātowak ᒫᑎᓇᒫᑐᐘᐠ
VAI they share (it/him) with one another, they give one another food
mātinawēw ᒫᑎᓇᐍᐤ
VAI s/he serves food, s/he passes food around, s/he portions out food [*see also* manakisow]
mātinawē-kīsikāw
ᒫᑎᓇᐍ ᑮᓯᑳᐤ
VII it is Saturday [*lit*: "ration-day"; *see also* nikotwāso-kīsikāw; *cf.* mātinawi-kīsikāw]
mātinawē-kīsikāsin
ᒫᑎᓇᐍ ᑮᓯᑳᓯᐣ
VII it is Friday [*dim*]
mātinawi-kīsikāw
ᒫᑎᓇᐏ ᑮᓯᑳᐤ
VII it is Saturday [*lit*: "ration-day"; *see also* nikotwāso-kīsikāw; *cf.* mātiniwē-kīsikāw]
mātisam ᒫᑎᓴᒼ
VTI s/he cuts s.t. open, s/he starts to cut s.t.
mātisāwātam ᒫᑎᓵᐚᑕᒼ
VTI s/he starts to cut s.t.
mātisāwātēw ᒫᑎᓵᐚᑌᐤ
VTA s/he starts to cut s.o.
mātisikēw ᒫᑎᓯᑫᐤ
VAI s/he starts to cut (as a pattern)
mātiswēw ᒫᑎᔃᐤ
VTA s/he cuts s.o. open [*cf.* māciswēw]
mātitāpihtēpisow ᒫᑎᑖᐱᐦᑌᐱᓱᐤ
VAI s/he starts to wear earrings
mātohkāsow ᒫᑐᐦᑳᓱᐤ
VAI s/he pretends to weep
mātopahtāw ᒫᑐᐸᐦᑖᐤ
VAI s/he cries while running
mātosk ᒫᑐᐢᐠ
NA crybaby
mātoskiw ᒫᑐᐢᑭᐤ
VAI s/he cries easily, s/he cries often [*hab*; *see also* wāhkēmow]
mātow ᒫᑐᐤ
VAI s/he cries, s/he wails, s/he weeps [*rdpl*: mā-mātow]
mātowin ᒫᑐᐏᐣ
NI crying, weeping
mātowināpoy ᒫᑐᐏᓈᐳᐩ
NI tear, tears [*see also* ohcikawāpoy]
māwacēyas ᒫᐘᒉᔭᐢ
IPC moreso, extremely so; beyond others [*cf.* māmāwacēyas]
māwaci ᒫᐘᒋ
IPC best, most, extremely; all [*superlative*]
māwaci iýikohk ᒫᐘᒋ ᐃᔨᑯᕽ
IPH best, most [*superlative*]
māwaci-kihci-mitātahtomitanaw
ᒫᐘᒋ ᑭᐦᒋ ᒥᑖᑕᐦᑐᒥᑕᓇᐤ
IPC one million, 1,000,000 [*lit*: "an extreme-great-hundred; an extreme thousand"]
māwacihcikan ᒫᐘᒋᐦᒋᑲᐣ
NI savings, accumulation of what has been saved
māwacihcikēw ᒫᐘᒋᐦᒋᑫᐤ
VAI s/he conserves, s/he saves, s/he gathers, s/he collects things
māwacihcikēwin ᒫᐘᒋᐦᒋᑫᐏᐣ
NI conservation
māwacihēw ᒫᐘᒋᐦᐁᐤ
VTA s/he saves s.o., s/he preserves s.o.; s/he assembles s.o., s/he gathers s.o.
māwacihitowak ᒫᐘᒋᐦᐃᑐᐘᐠ
VAI they assemble
māwacihtamawēw ᒫᐘᒋᐦᑕᒪᐍᐤ
VTA s/he assembles (them) for s.o.
māwacihtamāsow ᒫᐘᒋᐦᑕᒫᓱᐤ
VAI s/he assembles (them) for him/herself
māwacihtāw ᒫᐘᒋᐦᑖᐤ
VAIt s/he saves s.t., s/he preserves s.t., s/he conserves s.t.; s/he assembles s.t., s/he collects s.t.
māwacīs ᒫᐘᒌᐢ
IPC all
māwasako ᒫᐘᓴᑯ
IPC all together [*also* mawasako; *cf. all derivatives*]
māwasakonam ᒫᐘᓴᑯᓇᒼ
VTI s/he collects s.t., s/he gathers all of s.t.
māwasakonēw ᒫᐘᓴᑯᓀᐤ
VTA s/he collects s.o., s/he gather s.o. (*e.g.* wheat) [*cf.* *wC*: mawasokonēw, māwasokonēw]
māwasakopaýinwa ᒫᐘᓴᑯᐸᔨᓇᐘ
VII they collect together
māwasakopicikan ᒫᐘᓴᑯᐱᒋᑲᐣ
NI rake
māwasakopicikēw ᒫᐘᓴᑯᐱᒋᑫᐤ
VAI s/he rakes things up
māwasakopitam ᒫᐘᓴᑯᐱᑕᒼ
VTI s/he rakes s.t. in a heap, s/he rakes s.t. up
māwasakopitēw ᒫᐘᓴᑯᐱᑌᐤ
VTA s/he rakes s.o. in a heap
māwasakostaham ᒫᐘᓴᑯᐢᑕᐦᐊᒼ
VTI s/he sews s.t. together
māwasakostahwēw
ᒫᐘᓴᑯᐢᑕᐦᐍᐤ
VTA s/he sews s.o. together
māwasakotisahwēw
ᒫᐘᓴᑯᑎᓴᐦᐍᐤ
VTA s/he rounds s.o. up
māwasakwahēw ᒫᐘᓴᑿᐦᐁᐤ
VTA s/he piles s.o. up

māwasakwastāw ᒫᐘᓴᑿᐢᑖᐤ
VAIt s/he piles s.t. up, s/he gathers s.t in a heap
māwikan ᒫᐏᑲᐣ
NDI backbone, spine; back
māýacihkos ᒫᔭᒋᐦᑯᐢ
NA lamb, small sheep [*dim*; *cf.* māýatihk]
māýacihkos ᒫᔭᒋᐦᑯᐢ
NA lamb
māýacihkwayān ᒫᔭᒋᐦᑾᔮᐣ
NA sheepskin [*cf.* māýatihkwayān]
māýacihkwayānasākay ᒫᔭᒋᐦᑾᔮᓇᓵᑲᐩ
NI sheepskin coat
māýahkamikan ᒫᔭᐦᑲᒥᑲᐣ
VII it is a bad deed, it is a bad situation, there are evil doings [*cf.* kā-māýahkamikahk "Riel Resistance"]
māýahkamikisiw ᒫᔭᐦᑲᒥᑭᓯᐤ
VAI s/he does wrong
māýakohēw ᒫᔭᑯᐦᐁᐤ
VTA s/he brings bad luck to s.o.
māýakohow ᒫᔭᑯᐦᐅᐤ
VAI s/he brings bad luck on him/herself
māýakosiw ᒫᔭᑯᓯᐤ
VAI s/he is unlucky
māýakoskawēw ᒫᔭᑯᐢᑲᐍᐤ
VTA s/he sends bad luck in hunting to s.o. [*wC*: māthakoskawiw]
māýamahcihow ᒫᔭᒪᐦᒋᐦᐅᐤ
VAI s/he feels poorly, s/he feels badly, s/he feels ill, s/he is sick; s/he fares ill [*cf.* māýimahcihow]
māýamēk ᒫᔭᒣᐠ
NA catfish [*pl*: -wak]
māýaskatēw ᒫᔭᐢᑲᑌᐤ
VAI s/he has an upset stomach [*cf.* kisiwaskitēw]
māýatihk ᒫᔭᑎᕽ
NA sheep [*pl*: -wak]
māýatihkokamik ᒫᔭᑎᐦᑯᑲᒥᐠ
NI sheep barn [*pl*: -wa]
māýatihkokamikohkēw ᒫᔭᑎᐦᑯᑲᒥᑯᐦᑫᐤ
VAI s/he makes a sheep barn
māýatihkopīway ᒫᔭᑎᐦᑯᐲᐘᐩ
NI sheep's fleece; wool
māýatihkowiyās ᒫᔭᑎᐦᑯᐏᔮᐢ
NI mutton
māýāci- ᒫᔮᒋ
IPV bad
māýācimēw ᒫᔮᒋᒣᐤ
VTA s/he speaks ill of s.o., s/he tells bad news of s.o. [*also* māyi-ācimēw]
māýācimow ᒫᔮᒋᒧᐤ
VAI s/he tells bad news [*also* māyi-ācimow]
māýācimowin ᒫᔮᒋᒧᐏᐣ
NI bad news
māýācitēhēw ᒫᔮᒋᑌᐦᐁᐤ
VAI s/he is angry, s/he has a bad heart, s/he has evil intent in his/her heart
māýāhpinēw ᒫᔮᐦᐱᓀᐤ
VTA s/he is ill, s/he feels ill
māýāspinēw ᒫᔮᐢᐱᓀᐤ
VAI s/he has a serious disease
māýātan ᒫᔮᑕᐣ
VII it is bad, it is evil; it is ugly
māýātis ᒫᔮᑎᐢ
NA one who is ugly
māýātisiw ᒫᔮᑎᓯᐤ
VAI s/he is bad, s/he is evil; s/he is ugly
māýātisiwin ᒫᔮᑎᓯᐏᐣ
NI ugliness
māýēýihcikēw ᒫᔦᔨᐦᒋᑫᐤ
VAI s/he has no respect, s/he is disrespectful
māýēýihcikēwin ᒫᔦᔨᐦᒋᑫᐏᐣ
NI disrespect
māýēýihtam ᒫᔦᔨᐦᑕᒼ
VTI s/he despises s.t.
māýēýihtākosiw ᒫᔦᔨᐦᑖᑯᓯᐤ
VAI s/he is hateful, s/he is disrespectful
māýēýihtākosiwin ᒫᔦᔨᐦᑖᑯᓯᐏᐣ
NI contempt, scorn
māýēýihtākwan ᒫᔦᔨᐦᑖᑿᐣ
VII it is hateful
māýēýihtowin ᒫᔦᔨᐦᑐᐏᐣ
NI contempt, despising
māýēýimēw ᒫᔦᔨᒣᐤ
VTA s/he despises s.o.
māýi ᒫᔨ
IPN bad, ugly, nasty, evil, wicked
IPV bad, evil; badly, evilly, wickedly
māýi-kīkway ᒫᔨ ᑮᑿᐩ
NI bad thing, something bad
māýi-kīsikanisiw ᒫᔨ ᑮᓯᑲᓂᓯᐤ
VAI s/he has a bad day, s/he has bad weather (as one who is travelling)
māýi-kīsikāw ᒫᔨ ᑮᓯᑳᐤ
VII it is a bad day; it is nasty, it is bad weather; it is a storm, it is storming
māýi-masinahikēw ᒫᔨ ᒪᓯᓇᐦᐃᑫᐤ
VAI s/he writes poorly, s/he writes badly
māýi-mītos ᒫᔨ ᒦᑐᐢ
NA black poplar [*also* māýi-mētos]
māýi-pipon ᒫᔨ ᐱᐳᐣ
VII it is a bad winter
māýi-pīkiskwēw ᒫᔨ ᐲᑭᐢᑵᐤ
VAI s/he speaks poorly, s/he has difficulty with his/her speech
māýi-tōtam ᒫᔨ ᑑᑕᒼ
VTI s/he does a bad thing, s/he imposes a curse; s/he does s.t. wrongly; s/he does s.t. evil [*rdpl*: māh-māýi-tōtam]
māýi-tōtawēw ᒫᔨ ᑑᑕᐍᐤ
VTA s/he does a bad thing to s.o., s/he does evil to s.o., s/he makes s.o. sick, s/he puts a curse on s.o., s/he does s.o. wrong
māýicihcēw ᒫᔨᒋᐦᒉᐤ
VAI s/he has a bad hand
māýihkwēýistam ᒫᔨᐦᑵᔨᐢᑕᒼ
VTI s/he makes a face at s.t., s/he sneers at s.t.
māýihkwēstawēw ᒫᔨᐦᑵᐢᑕᐍᐤ
VTA s/he makes a face at s.o., s/he sneers at s.o.
māýihkwēw ᒫᔨᐦᑵᐤ
VAI s/he makes a face; s/he has a bad face
māýihtākosiw ᒫᔨᐦᑖᑯᓯᐤ
VAI s/he is hoarse, s/he is difficult to hear plainly; s/he sounds bad
māýihtākwan ᒫᔨᐦᑖᑿᐣ
VII it appears bad; it sounds bad [*cf.* nawac māýihtākwan "it sounds worse"]
māýihtin ᒫᔨᐦᑎᐣ
VII it spoils (*e.g.* food)
māýikwāsow ᒫᔨᒁᓱᐤ
VAI s/he sews badly
māýikwāsowin ᒫᔨᒁᓱᐏᐣ
NI bad sewing, poorly done sewing
māýimahcihow ᒫᔨᒪᐦᒋᐦᐅᐤ
VAI s/he feels poorly, s/he feels badly, s/he feels ill [*cf.* māýamahcihow]
māýimākosiw ᒫᔨᒫᑯᓯᐤ
VAI s/he smells bad
māýimākwan ᒫᔨᒫᑿᐣ
VII it smells bad
māýimāsow ᒫᔨᒫᓱᐤ
VAI s/he smells something bad on him/herself (*e.g.* tripe)
māýinam ᒫᔨᓇᒼ
VTI s/he finds s.t. ugly
māýinākosiw ᒫᔨᓈᑯᓯᐤ
VAI s/he looks sick, s/he has a sick look
māýinākwan ᒫᔨᓈᑿᐣ
VII it looks bad (*e.g.* a storm)
māýinikēhkātowak ᒫᔨᓂᑫᐦᑳᑐᐘᐠ
VAI they act badly towards one another, they act harmfully towards one another
māýinikēw ᒫᔨᓂᑫᐤ
VAI s/he has ill befall him/her, s/he has bad luck, s/he has misfortune; she becomes pregnant out of wedlock; s/he acts badly, s/he

acts harmfully, s/he does harmful things; s/he handles things badly [*rdpl*: māh-māýinikēw]
māýinikēwin ᒫᔨᓂᑫᐏᐣ
NI wrong-doing, evil deed; bad luck
māýinikwan ᒫᔨᓂᑿᐣ
VII it is difficult walking because of too much snow
māýipaýiw ᒫᔨᐸᔨᐤ
VAI s/he suffers ill, s/he fares ill, s/he fares badly; s/he suffers a death, s/he is bereaved (by the loss of s.o.)
māýipaýiwin ᒫᔨᐸᔨᐏᐣ
NI misfortune
māýisikow ᒫᔨᓯᑯᐤ
VII it has rough ice (as a lake); it is a lake with rough ice
māýisin ᒫᔨᓯᐣ
VAI s/he lies awkwardly; it spoils (*e.g.* food)
māýiskākow ᒫᔨᐢᑳᑯᐤ
VTA it affects s.o. badly, it has an adverse effect on s.o.; it makes s.o. ill, it makes s.o. react allergically [*usually only in forms of the inverse VTA paradigm*; *cf.* māýiskawēw]
māýiskwēsisāhtik ᒫᔨᐢᑵᓯᓵᐦᑎᐠ
NA black poplar, "naughty girl tree" [*pl*: -wak]
māýispakosiw ᒫᔨᐢᐸᑯᓯᐤ
VAI it tastes bad
māýispakwan ᒫᔨᐢᐸᑿᐣ
VII it tastes bad
māýispwākan ᒫᔨᐢᑷᑲᐣ
NA poor pipe
māýistācīhkawēw ᒫᔨᐢᑖᒌᐦᑲᐍᐤ
VTA s/he bothers s.o.

ᒣ

mēcawākanis ᒣᒐᐚᑲᓂᐢ
NI small toy [*dim*]
mēcawēsiw ᒣᒐᐍᓯᐤ
VAI s/he plays a little; s/he plays a children's game [*dim*]
mēcimosiw ᒣᒋᒧᓯᐤ
VAI s/he is stuck
mēcimwāci- ᒣᒋᒹᒋ
IPV permanently, for good
mēcimwātihtin ᒣᒋᒹᑎᐦᑎᐣ
VII it becomes stuck
mēkinawēw ᒣᑭᓇᐍᐤ
VAI s/he gives up his/her losings
mēkiskiw ᒣᑭᐢᑭᐤ
VAI s/he is liberal, s/he is fond of giving [*hab*]
mēkiskwēmēw ᒣᑭᐢᑵᒣᐤ
VTA s/he gives s.o. (female) away in an arranged marriage
mēkiskwēwāniw ᒣᑭᐢᑵᐚᓂᐤ
VAI she is given away in an arranged marriage
mēkiskwēwēw ᒣᑭᐢᑵᐍᐤ
VAI s/he gives a woman away in an arranged marriage
mēkiw ᒣᑭᐤ
VAI s/he gives, s/he gives away; s/he gives s.t. away; s/he releases s.t.; he gives her in marriage
mēkiwin ᒣᑭᐏᐣ
NI gift, free gift, something given [*see also* miýitowin]
mēkwan ᒣᑿᐣ
NA feather [*cf.* mīkwan]
mēkwayāhtik ᒣᑿᔮᐦᑎᐠ
IPC among the trees
mēkwayēs ᒣᑿᔦᐢ
IPC among
mēkwā- ᒣᒁ
IPV currently, presently, right now; while, during, in the meantime, in the act or place [*cf.* mēkwāc]
mēkwā-kīsikāw ᒣᒁ ᑮᓯᑳᐤ
VII while it is daylight
mēkwā-pimātisiw ᒣᒁ ᐱᒫᑎᓯᐤ
VAI while s/he lives, s/he is living presently, during his/her lifespan
mēkwā-tipiskāw ᒣᒁ ᑎᐱᐢᑳᐤ
VII while it is dark, nighttime
mēkwāc ᒣᒁᐨ
IPC currently, presently, right now; while, during, in the course of, in the meantime, during the time; ago [*cf.* mēkwā]
mēkwāham ᒣᒁᐦᐊᒼ
VTI s/he goes through s.t. by air or water
mēkwānohk ᒣᒁᓄᕽ
IPC amongst, amidst
mēkwāskawēw ᒣᒁᐢᑲᐍᐤ
VTA s/he gets there at the same time with s.o.; s/he catches s.o. in the act
mēmēkwēsiw ᒣᒣᑵᓯᐤ
NA little person, one of the sacred little people
mēmihtāciwin ᒣᒥᐦᑖᒋᐏᐣ
NI thing regretted, lost in gambling
mēmohci ᒣᒧᐦᒋ
IPC in particular, above all
mēnikan ᒣᓂᑲᐣ
NI fence
mēnikanāhtik ᒣᓂᑲᓈᐦᑎᐠ
NI fence-rail [*pl*: -wa]
mēnikanihk ᒣᓂᑲᓂᕽ
IPC in the corral; on the fence [*loc*; *cf.* mēnikan]
mēnikanihkawēw ᒣᓂᑲᓂᐦᑲᐍᐤ
VTA s/he makes a fence for s.o.
mēnikanihkākēw ᒣᓂᑲᓂᐦᑳᑫᐤ
VAI s/he makes fences from something, s/he makes rails for fencing
mēnikanihkēw ᒣᓂᑲᓂᐦᑫᐤ
VAI s/he makes fences
mēnikanis ᒣᓂᑲᓂᐢ
NI short fence [*dim*; *see also* mēnis, mēnisk]
mēnikātam ᒣᓂᑳᑕᒼ
VTI s/he fences s.t. in
mēnikātēw ᒣᓂᑳᑌᐤ
VTA s/he fences s.o. in
mēnis ᒣᓂᐢ
NI short fence [*see also* mēnikanis]
mēnisk ᒣᓂᐢᐠ
NI trench, earthwork, fortification
mēniskihkēw ᒣᓂᐢᑭᐦᑫᐤ
VAI s/he makes an earthwork, s/he digs a trench
mēsakwanipipon ᒣᓴᑿᓂᐱᐳᐣ
IPC every winter, year
mēscacākanis ᒣᐢᒐᒑᑲᓂᐢ
NA coyote [*cf.* mēstacākanis]
mēscakāsa ᒣᐢᒐᑳᓴ
NDI hair; short hair [*pl*; *dim*; *sg*: mēscakās]
mēsci- ᒣᐢᒋ
IPV exhaustively, till all is gone
mēsciham ᒣᐢᒋᐦᐊᒼ
VTI s/he gets rid of all of s.t.
mēscihēw ᒣᐢᒋᐦᐁᐤ
VTA s/he kills s.o. off, s/he annihilates s.o., s/he exterminates s.o.
mēscihtāsow ᒣᐢᒋᐦᑖᓱᐤ
VAI s/he exterminates s.t. for him/herself
mēscihtāw ᒣᐢᒋᐦᑖᐤ
VAIt s/he does away with all of s.t.
mēscihtitāw ᒣᐢᒋᐦᑎᑖᐤ
VAIt s/he wears s.t. out
mēscinēwak ᒣᐢᒋᓀᐘᐠ
VAI they die out [*pl*]
mēscipaýihēw ᒣᐢᒋᐸᔨᐦᐁᐤ
VTA s/he uses s.o. up, s/he wears s.o. out; s/he consumes s.o.
mēscipaýihtāw ᒣᐢᒋᐸᔨᐦᑖᐤ
VAIt s/he consumes s.t.
mēscipaýin ᒣᐢᒋᐸᔨᐣ
VII it runs out, it winds down (as a tape-recorder)
mēscipaýiw ᒣᐢᒋᐸᔨᐤ
VAI s/he is worn out
mēscipaýiw ᒣᐢᒋᐸᔨᐤ
VII it is worn out; it is all gone (as water from a leaking barrel)
mēscipimīw ᒣᐢᒋᐱᒦᐤ
VAI s/he is out of gas; s/he is out of lard, grease

mēscipitam ᒣᐢᒋᐸᑕᒼ
VTI s/he uses s.t. up entirely,
s/he pulls s.t. out entirely;
s/he exhausts all resources

mēscipitēw ᒣᐢᒋᐸᑌᐤ
VTA s/he pulls s.o. out
entirely (e.g. carrots)

mēscisimēw ᒣᐢᒋᓯᒣᐤ
VTA s/he wears s.o. out on
things

mēsciskam ᒣᐢᒋᐢᑲᒼ
VTI s/he wears s.t. out

mēsciwēpaham ᒣᐢᒋᐌᐸᐦᐊᒼ
VTI s/he knocks s.t. (meat)
right off

mēsciwasow ᒣᐢᒋᐊᓱᐤ
VAI it melts or boils away

mēsciwatēw ᒣᐢᒋᐊᑌᐤ
VII it melts or boils away

mēskanaw ᒣᐢᑲᓇᐤ
NI road, path

mēskanawin ᒣᐢᑲᓇᐃᐧ
VII it is a road

mēskanāhkan ᒣᐢᑲᐋᐦᑲᐣ
NI graded road

mēskanāhkātam ᒣᐢᑲᐋᐦᑳᑕᒼ
VTI s/he builds a road to s.t.

mēskanāhkātēw ᒣᐢᑲᐋᐦᑳᑌᐤ
VTA s/he builds a road for
s.o.

mēskanāhkēsiw ᒣᐢᑲᐋᐦᑫᓯᐤ
VAI s/he builds a path [dim]

mēskanāhkēw ᒣᐢᑲᐋᐦᑫᐤ
VAI s/he builds a road

mēskanāhkēwin ᒣᐢᑲᐋᐦᑫᐃᐧ
NI roadbuilding

mēskanās ᒣᐢᑲᐋᐢ
NI trail, path, little road
[dim]

mēskoc ᒣᐢᑯ
IPC instead, in exchange;
unlike [cf. miskoc]

mēskocipayiw ᒣᐢᑯᒋᐸᔨᐤ
VII it changes into
something else

mēskocīw ᒣᐢᑯᐄᐤ
VAI s/he changes clothes [cf.
mēskotayiwinisēw]

mēskotapistawēw ᒣᐢᑯᑕᐱᐢᑕᐌᐤ
VTA s/he exchanges seats
with s.o.

mēskotayiwinisēw
ᒣᐢᑯᑕᔨᐃᐧᓂᓭᐤ
VAI s/he changes his/her
clothes [cf. mēskocīw]

mēskotāpinam ᒣᐢᑯᑖᐱᓇᒼ
VTI s/he changes s.t. (e.g.
the water) in boiling

mēskotāsayikēw ᒣᐢᑯᑖᓴᔨᑫᐤ
VAI s/he changes diapers,
s/he changes pants [also
miskotāsayikēw; wC:
miskotāsathihkīw]

mēskotāsiyānihkēw
ᒣᐢᑯᑖᓯᔮᓂᐦᑫᐤ
VAI s/he changes diapers; he
changes breech-cloths

mēskotinam ᒣᐢᑯᑎᓇᒼ
VTI s/he changes s.t., s/he
exchanges s.t. [cf.
mēskotōnam]

mēskotōnam ᒣᐢᑯᑑᓇᒼ
VTI s/he exchanges s.t. [cf.
miskotōnam]

mēskotōnamawēw ᒣᐢᑯᑑᓇᒪᐌᐤ
VTA s/he exchanges (it/him)
with s.o.

mēskotōnamātowak
ᒣᐢᑯᑑᓇᒫᑐᐊᐧ
VAI they exchange (it/him)
with one another

mēskotōnēw ᒣᐢᑯᑑᓀᐤ
VTA s/he exchanges s.o.

mēskotōnikan ᒣᐢᑯᑑᓂᑲᐣ
NI exchanged article

mēskotōnikākēw ᒣᐢᑯᑑᓂᑳᑫᐤ
VAI s/he gives s.t. in
exchange

mēskotōnikēw ᒣᐢᑯᑑᓂᑫᐤ
VAI s/he exchanges things

mēskwacipayin ᒣᐢᒀᒋᐸᔨᐣ
VII it changes

mēstacākan ᒣᐢᑖᒑᑲᐣ
NA coyote

mēstacākanis ᒣᐢᑖᒑᑲᓂᐢ
NA coyote; coyote pup [dim;
cf. mēscacākanis]

mēstahcihkwasiw ᒣᐢᑕᐦᒋᐦᒁᓯᐤ
VAI s/he is sleepy from
rising early

mēstahōsiw ᒣᐢᑕᐦᐆᓯᐤ
VAI s/he is worn out, s/he is
burnt out

mēstahōtēw ᒣᐢᑕᐦᐆᑌᐤ
VII it is worn out, it is burnt
out

mēstakaya ᒣᐢᑕᑲᔭ
NDI hair [pl]

mēstakocin ᒣᐢᑕᑯᒋᐣ
VAI it is out of the sky (as
the moon), it is the last
quarter moon; it is hanging
used or burnt up, it has hung
its last

mēstahtam ᒣᐢᑕᐦᑕᒼ
VTI s/he eats all of s.t.

mēstamēw ᒣᐢᑕᒣᐤ
VTA s/he eats all of s.o.

mēstan ᒣᐢᑕᐣ
NA edible gummy sap of
tree; inner bark

mēstan-pīwayān ᒣᐢᑕᐣ ᐲᐊᐧᔮᐣ
NI down of geese or ducks

mēstanāpoy ᒣᐢᑕᓈᐳᕀ
NI juice of trees

mēstasinaham ᒣᐢᑕᓯᓇᐦᐊᒼ
VTI s/he writes it all down;
s/he uses s.t. up in writing

mēstasīhkawēwak
ᒣᐢᑕᓰᐦᑲᐌᐊᐧ
VTA they ostracize s.o. [pl
generally]

mēstaskisinēw ᒣᐢᑕᐢᑭᓯᓀᐤ
VAI s/he wears out all the
moccasins or shoes

mēstasow ᒣᐢᑕᓱᐤ
VAI s/he saps trees, s/he
takes the juice of trees by
scraping the inner bark [cf.
mīstasow]

mēstawihēw ᒣᐢᑕᐃᐧᐦᐁᐧᐤ
VTA s/he uses up all of s.o.'s
resources, s/he exhausts all
of s.o.'s resources

mēstawihikēw ᒣᐢᑕᐃᐧᐦᐃᑫᐤ
VAI s/he uses up his/her own
resources, s/he exhausts
his/her own resources

mēstāciwasow ᒣᐢᒑᒋᐊᓱᐤ
VAI it boils dry

mēstāciwatēw ᒣᐢᒑᒋᐊᑌᐤ
VII it boils dry [cf.
mēsciwatēw]

mēstāpāwaham ᒣᐢᒑᐹᐊᐧᐦᐊᒼ
VTI s/he wears s.t. away by
repeated action

mēstāpāwahwēw ᒣᐢᒑᐹᐊᐧᐦᐌᐤ
VTA s/he wears s.o. away by
repeated action

mēstāskisam ᒣᐢᒑᐢᑭᓴᒼ
VTI s/he burns s.t. out

mēstāskiswēw ᒣᐢᒑᐢᑭᓷᐤ
VTA s/he burns s.o. out, s/he
burns s.o. away (e.g. log)

mēstāskisow ᒣᐢᒑᐢᑭᓱᐤ
VAI it is burnt up, it is burnt
out

mēstāskitēw ᒣᐢᒑᐢᑭᑌᐤ
VII it is burnt out, it is
totally destroyed by burning

mēstāskow ᒣᐢᒑᐢᑯ
VAI s/he uses up all the
wood

mēstāskwēsin ᒣᐢᒑᐢᒬᓯᐣ
VAI s/he is left without
weapons, bullets or arrows;
s/he has used up all his/her
ammunition [originally,
wooden arrows in particular]

mēstātaham ᒣᐢᒑᑕᐦᐊᒼ
VTI s/he scrapes s.t. all
away

mēstātayōhkanēsin
ᒣᐢᒑᑕᔫᐦᑲᓀᓯᐣ
VAI s/he runs out of sacred
stories, s/he has no more
sacred stories

mēstāwatēw ᒣᐢᒑᐊᑌᐤ
VAI s/he takes (it) all away
with him/her

mēsti- ᒣᐢᑎ
IPV it is used up, it is burnt
out, it is spent

mēstihkahtēw ᒣᐢᑎᐦᑲᐦᑌᐤ
VII it burns all up, it is burnt
up, there is nothing left, it
burns down completely

mēstihkasam ᒣᐢᑎᐦᑲᓴᒼ
VTI s/he burns s.t. down,
s/he burns s.t. all up

mēstihkasamawēw ᒣᐢᑎᐦᑲᓴᒪᐌᐤ
VTA s/he burns (it/him) all
up for s.o.

mēstihkasow ᒣᐢᑎᐦᑲᓱᐤ
VAI s/he burns all up, s/he melts away
mēstihkaswēw ᒣᐢᑎᐦᑲᓭᐧᐤ
VTA s/he burns s.o. all up
mēstinam ᒣᐢᑎᓇᒼ
VTI s/he uses s.t. up, s/he uses all of s.t.
mēstinamawēw ᒣᐢᑎᓇᒪᐁᐧᐤ
VTA s/he uses (it/him) all up on s.o.; s/he leaves none of (it/him) for s.o.
mēstinēw ᒣᐢᑎᓀᐤ
VTA s/he uses s.o. up (*e.g.* money)
mēstinikātēw ᒣᐢᑎᓂᑳᑌᐤ
VII it is used up
mēstinikēw ᒣᐢᑎᓂᑫᐤ
VAI s/he uses things up; s/he exhausts things, s/he wastes things; s/he spends, s/he spends it all
mēstinikēwin ᒣᐢᑎᓂᑫᐃᐧᐣ
NI expense, spending; waste
mēstisam ᒣᐢᑎᓴᒼ
VTI s/he burns s.t. up
mēstiskam ᒣᐢᑎᐢᑲᒼ
VTI s/he tramples s.t. to nothing, s/he wears s.t. out (*e.g.* shoes)
mēstiskawēw ᒣᐢᑎᐢᑲᐁᐧᐤ
VTA s/he tramples s.o. to nothing, s/he wears s.o. out (*e.g.* pants)
mētawākan ᒣᑕᐋᐧᑲᐣ
NI toy, plaything [*cf.* mētawēwinākan]
mētawākātam ᒣᑕᐋᐧᑳᑕᒼ
VTI s/he plays with s.t.; s/he makes light of s.t., s/he toys with s.t., s/he denigrates s.t., s/he disrespects s.t., s/he makes light of s.t., s/he makes a mockery of s.t.
mētawākātēw ᒣᑕᐋᐧᑳᑌᐤ
VTA s/he plays (with things) with s.o.; s/he toys with s.o., s/he denigrates s.o., s/he shows s.o. disrespect, s/he makes light of s.o., s/he makes a mockery of s.o. [*sexual connotations*: "he uses a woman"]
mētawākēw ᒣᑕᐋᐧᑫᐤ
VAI s/he plays with things; s/he toys with things, s/he denigrates things, s/he disrespects things, s/he makes light of things, s/he makes a mockery of things
mētawēhēw ᒣᑕᐁᐧᐦᐁᐤ
VTA s/he makes s.o. play
mētawēhisow ᒣᑕᐁᐧᐦᐃᓱᐤ
VAI s/he amuses him/herself
mētawēmēw ᒣᑕᐁᐧᒣᐤ
VTA s/he plays with s.o. [*cf.* wīci-mētawēmēw]
mētawēskiw ᒣᑕᐁᐧᐢᑭᐤ
VAI s/he likes to play, s/he plays a lot [*hab*]
mētawēw ᒣᑕᐁᐧᐤ
VAI s/he plays; s/he gambles, s/he contests
mētawēwikamik ᒣᑕᐁᐧᐃᐧᑲᒥᐠ
NI gymnasium, gym; recreation center; poolroom; theatre, playhouse [*pl*: -wa]
mētawēwin ᒣᑕᐁᐧᐃᐧᐣ
NI game, contest, sport; dialogue
mētawēwinākan ᒣᑕᐁᐧᐃᐧᓈᑲᐣ
NI toy [*cf.* mētawākan]
mētawēwinihkēw ᒣᑕᐁᐧᐃᐧᓂᐦᑫᐤ
VAI s/he organizes games
mētokēta ᒣᑐᑫᑕ
IPC not likely
mētoni ᒣᑐᓂ
IPC very, *really [rhetorically distorted emphatic,cf.* mitoni]
mētwēyānē ᒣᑌᐧᔮᓀ
IPC as was my foreboding, as I felt in my bones
mēyākwām ᒣᔮᑳᐧᒼ
IPC be careful
mēyi ᒣᔨ
NI stool, excrement, dung, manure [*pl*: mēya]
mēyisimin ᒣᔨᓯᒥᐣ
NI cactus berry
mēyiwan ᒣᔨᐊᐧᐣ
VII it is smeared with dung
mēyiwiw ᒣᔨᐃᐧᐤ
VAI it is full of dung, s/he is smeared with dung
mēyiwiw ᒣᔨᐃᐧᐤ
VII it is full of dung

ᒥ

micakisīs ᒥᒐᑭᓰᐢ
NI intestine; sausage; [*slang*:] penis [*dim, cf.* mitakisiy]
micēstatay ᒥᒉᐢᑕᑕᐩ
NDI muscle
micēstatayēyāpiy ᒥᒉᐢᑕᑕᔦᔮᐱᐩ
NDI ligament
micicāskay ᒥᒋᒑᐢᑲᐩ
NDI crotch
micihciy ᒥᒋᐦᒋᐩ
NDI hand
micihcīs ᒥᒋᐦᒌᐢ
NDI finger; little hand [*dim*; *cf.* yiyīkicihcān, yiyīkicihcīs]
micimahpisow ᒥᒋᒪᐦᐱᓱᐤ
VAI s/he is tied, s/he is bound
micimahpisowina ᒥᒋᒪᐦᐱᓱᐃᐧᓇ
NI manacles, handcuffs [*pl generally*]
micimāhikanis ᒥᒋᒫᐦᐃᑲᓂᐢ
NI screw
micimāpēkinēw ᒥᒋᒫᐯᑭᓀᐤ
VTA s/he holds s.o. by a rope, s/he leads s.o. by a rope
micimāpiskahikan ᒥᒋᒫᐱᐢᑲᐦᐃᑲᐣ
NI iron bar (used to bar a door)
micimāskohtin ᒥᒋᒫᐢᑯᐦᑎᐣ
VII it is jammed by it's length; it is too long to go in
micimāskwaham ᒥᒋᒫᐢᑲᐧᐦᐊᒼ
VTI s/he bars the door shut, s/he fastens s.t. as or to a solid by tool
micimāskwahikan ᒥᒋᒫᐢᑲᐧᐦᐃᑲᐣ
NI bar to hold a door or gate shut or open
micimāskwahwēw ᒥᒋᒫᐢᑲᐧᐦᐁᐧᐤ
VTA s/he bars s.o. in, s/he holds s.o. in place (as or by wood)
micimihkwāmiw ᒥᒋᒥᐦᑳᐧᒥᐤ
VAI s/he sleeps soundly
miciminam ᒥᒋᒥᓇᒼ
VTI s/he holds s.t. fast, s/he holds s.t. in place, s/he grasps s.t.
miciminamawēw ᒥᒋᒥᓇᒪᐁᐧᐤ
VTA s/he holds (it/him) fast for s.o., s/he holds on to (it/him) for s.o.
miciminamāsow ᒥᒋᒥᓇᒫᓱᐤ
VAI s/he holds (it/him) for him/herself
miciminamōhēw ᒥᒋᒥᓇᒨᐦᐁᐤ
VTA s/he makes s.o. hold on to (it/him)
miciminēw ᒥᒋᒥᓀᐤ
VTA s/he holds s.o. fast, s/he holds s.o. in place, s/he takes hold of s.o., s/he holds on to s.o.
miciminikan ᒥᒋᒥᓂᑲᐣ
NI handle, door knob
miciminikēw ᒥᒋᒥᓂᑫᐤ
VAI s/he takes hold, s/he grips (things) hard
miciminisow ᒥᒋᒥᓂᓱᐤ
VAI s/he holds him/herself fast
micimīmakan ᒥᒋᒦᒪᑲᐣ
VII it clings on (as a repair made)
micimīw ᒥᒋᒦᐤ
VAI s/he holds on (with the hands); s/he clings on
micimohow ᒥᒋᒧᐦᐅᐤ
VAI s/he is stuck fast
micimohpitam ᒥᒋᒧᐦᐱᑕᒼ
VTI s/he ties s.t. fast
micimohpitēw ᒥᒋᒧᐦᐱᑌᐤ
VTA s/he ties s.o. fast
micimohtin ᒥᒋᒧᐦᑎᐣ
VII it sticks fast (as it does not fit)
micimosin ᒥᒋᒧᓯᐣ
VAI s/he sticks fast (as s/he is too big to enter)

micimoskiwakiw ᒥᒋᒧᐢᑭᐘᑭᐤ
VAI s/he gets bogged down, s/he gets stuck in a bog or mud

micimoskiwēw ᒥᒋᒧᐢᑭᐍᐤ
VAI s/he is stuck in mud or in gum

micimōhēw ᒥᒋᒨᐦᐁᐤ
VTA s/he causes a problem for s.o., s/he stumps s.o.; s/he causes s.o. to be stuck

micimōsow ᒥᒋᒨᓱᐤ
VAI s/he is stuck in mud

micimōtāw ᒥᒋᒨᑖᐤ
VAIt s/he gets s.t. stuck

micimwākonēw ᒥᒋᒹᑯᓀᐤ
VAI s/he gets stuck in snow

micimwāskosow ᒥᒋᒹᐢᑯᓱᐤ
VAI s/he gets snagged

micisk ᒥᒋᐢᐠ
NDI anus [*also used derogatorily in name-calling*]

miciskakisiy ᒥᒋᐢᑲᑭᓯᕀ
NDI rectum (lower end)

miciskēyāpiy ᒥᒋᐢᑫᔮᐱᕀ
NDI rectum (full length)

miciwāmihtowak ᒥᒋᐚᒥᐦᑐᐘᐠ
VAI they are brothers, sisters, cousins, blood brothers; they are related as ociwāmimāwak or ociwāmiskwēmimāwak

miciyawēsiw ᒥᒋᔭᐍᓯᐤ
VAI s/he is sorry

micīhcīkom ᒥᒌᐦᒌᑯᒼ
NDA wart

micohcōsimis ᒥᒍᐦᒎᓯᒥᐢ
NDA nipple (of a breast); small breast [*dim*]

mihcāpēkisiw ᒥᐦᒑᐯᑭᓯᐤ
VAI it is a large strand (of thread or wool)

mihcāskokātēw ᒥᐦᒑᐢᑯᑳᑌᐤ
VAI s/he has stout legs

mihcāskopitonēw ᒥᐦᒑᐢᑯᐱᑐᓀᐤ
VAI s/he has stout arms

mihcāskosiw ᒥᐦᒑᐢᑯᓯᐤ
VAI it is a big tree, it is big around (as a tree)

mihcāskoýaw ᒥᐦᒑᐢᑯᔭᐤ
NA large bodied person

mihcāskoýawēw ᒥᐦᒑᐢᑯᔭᐍᐤ
VAI s/he has a large stout body; s/he has a large waistline

mihcāskwan ᒥᐦᒑᐢᑿᐣ
VII it is large, it is big around (as wood)

mihcēcis ᒥᐦᒉᒋᐢ
IPC fairly many [*dim*; *cf.* mihcēt; *wC*: mihcīcis]

mihcēnwa ᒥᐦᒉᓌ
VII they are numerous, they are many [*cf.* mihcētinwa]

mihcēt ᒥᐦᒉᐟ
IPC many, much; a good number

mihcētastimwēw ᒥᐦᒉᑕᐢᑎᒵᐤ
VAI s/he has many horses or dogs, s/he owns many horses or dogs [*cf.* mihcētwastimwēw]

mihcēti ᒥᐦᒉᑎ
IPC many times

mihcētinwa ᒥᐦᒉᑎᓌ
VII they are numerous, they are many [*cf.* mihcēnwa]

mihcētipakāw ᒥᐦᒉᑎᐸᑳᐤ
VII it is leafy; it has many leaves

mihcētiwak ᒥᐦᒉᑎᐘᐠ
VAI they are numerous, they are many, they are plentiful

mihcētiwān ᒥᐦᒉᑎᐚᐣ
IPC many kinds

mihcētokamikosiw ᒥᐦᒉᑐᑲᒥᑯᓯᐤ
VAI s/he has many houses

mihcētokamikwa ᒥᐦᒉᑐᑲᒥᒁ
IPC many lodges

mihcētokātēw ᒥᐦᒉᑐᑳᑌᐤ
VAI it has many legs

mihcētowihkātam ᒥᐦᒉᑐᐏᐦᑳᑕᒼ
VTI s/he calls s.t. by many names, s/he gives s.t. many names

mihcētowihkātēw ᒥᐦᒉᑐᐏᐦᑳᑌᐤ
VTA s/he calls s.o. by many names, s/he give s.o. many names

mihcētōsēw ᒥᐦᒉᑑᓭᐤ
VAI she has many children; she has many young ones, it has numerous offspring

mihcētōskisina ᒥᐦᒉᑑᐢᑭᓯᓇ
IPC many moccasins

mihcētwastimwēw ᒥᐦᒉᑘᐢᑎᒵᐤ
VAI s/he has many horses or dogs, s/he owns many horses or dogs [*cf.* mihcētastimwēw]

mihcētwayak ᒥᐦᒉᑘᔭᐠ
IPC in a lot of ways, in many ways

mihcētwāw ᒥᐦᒉᑚᐤ
IPC many times, often, frequently

mihcikwan ᒥᐦᒋᑿᐣ
NDI knee [*cf.* 3: ohcikwan "his/her knee"; *also* mīhcikwān; *cf.* 3: wīhcikwan]

mihcikwanikan ᒥᐦᒋᑿᓂᑲᐣ
NDI kneebone [*cf.* 3: ohcikwanikan "his/her kneebone"; *also* mīhcikwanikan; *cf.* 3: wīhcikwanikan]

mihcis ᒥᐦᒋᐢ
NI split wood, small firewood, stick [*dim*; *pl generally*: mihcisa]

mihkawakīw ᒥᐦᑲᐘᑮᐤ
VAI s/he is a fast runner [*also* mihkawikīw]

mihkihkwan ᒥᐦᑭᐦᑿᐣ
NI hide scraper

mihkināhk ᒥᐦᑭᓈᕽ
NA turtle [*pl*: -wak; *cf.* miskināhk]

mihkitam ᒥᐦᑭᑕᒼ
VTI s/he scrapes s.t. (meat) off the hide

mihkiw ᒥᐦᑭᐤ
VAI s/he scrapes hide

mihko ᒥᐦᑯ
NI blood [*sg only*; *wC*: misko, mithko]

mihko- ᒥᐦᑯ
IPV red [*wC*: misko, mithko]

mihko-atisikan ᒥᐦᑯ ᐊᑎᓯᑲᐣ
NI red dye [*wC*: misko-]

mihko-sīpihkosiw ᒥᐦᑯ ᓰᐱᐦᑯᓯᐤ
VAI s/he is purple [*see also* nīpāmāyātisiw]

mihko-sīpihkwāw ᒥᐦᑯ ᓰᐱᐦᒁᐤ
VII it is purple [*see also* nīpāmāyātan]

mihkocēskiwakās ᒥᐦᑯᒉᐢᑭᐘᑳᐢ
NI jam

mihkocihcēw ᒥᐦᑯᒋᐦᒉᐤ
VAI s/he has bloody hands, s/he has red hands

mihkohēw ᒥᐦᑯᐦᐁᐤ
VTA s/he makes s.o. bleed; s/he reddens s.o., s/he makes s.o. red

mihkohkwēw ᒥᐦᑯᐦᑵᐤ
VAI s/he has a red face

mihkokātēw ᒥᐦᑯᑳᑌᐤ
VAI s/he has red legs

mihkokotēw ᒥᐦᑯᑯᑌᐤ
VAI s/he has a red nose

mihkokwan ᒥᐦᑯᑿᐣ
NA red feather

mihkokwaniy ᒥᐦᑯᑿᓂᕀ
NI rose

mihkokwayawēw ᒥᐦᑯᑿᔭᐍᐤ
NI redneck; Whiteman

mihkokwayawēw ᒥᐦᑯᑿᔭᐍᐤ
VAI s/he has a red neck

mihkomina ᒥᐦᑯᒥᓇ
NI redberries

mihkomināpoy ᒥᐦᑯᒥᓈᐳᕀ
NI red wine

mihkominis ᒥᐦᑯᒥᓂᐢ
NI small redberry, a certain red berry [*dim*]

mihkonākosiw ᒥᐦᑯᓈᑯᓯᐤ
VAI s/he looks reddish

mihkonākwan ᒥᐦᑯᓈᑿᐣ
VII it looks reddish

mihkonikātēw ᒥᐦᑯᓂᑳᑌᐤ
VII it is painted red

mihkopaýin ᒥᐦᑯᐸᔨᐣ
VII it reddens, it turns red

mihkopaýiw ᒥᐦᑯᐸᔨᐤ
VAI s/he reddens; s/he has his/her face redden, s/he blushes

mihkopēmak ᒥᐦᑯᐯᒪᐠ
NA red willow [*sg/pl*; *cf.* mihkwāpēmakwa]

mihkopiscipowin ᒥᐦᑯᐱᐢᒋᐳᐏᐣ
NI blood poison [*cf.* pihcipowin]

mihkosihow ᒥᐦᑯᓯᐦᐅᐤ
VAI s/he is painted red

mihkosihtak ᒥᐦᑯᓯᐦᑕᐠ
NI a dried-up pine tree (with red needles)

mihkosikan ᒥᐦᑯᓯᑲᐣ
NI red pigment

mihkosiw ᒥᐦᑯᓯᐤ
VAI s/he is red [*wC*: miskosiw, mithkosiw]

mihkosīhow ᒥᐦᑯᓰᐦᐅᐤ
VAI s/he is dressed in red

mihkospwākan ᒥᐦᑯᐢᐹᑲᐣ
NI red pipestone pipe [*wC*: mithkospwākan]

mihkostikwānēwisip ᒥᐦᑯᐢᑎᑳᓀᐏᓯᑊ
NA red-headed duck [*wC*: mithkostikwānīwisip]

mihkotāpānāsk ᒥᐦᑯᑖᐹᓈᐢᐠ
NA red car [*pl*: -wak; *wC*: miskotāpānāsk]

mihkotāsēw ᒥᐦᑯᑖᓭᐤ
VAI s/he has red pants

mihkowan ᒥᐦᑯᐘᐣ
VII it is bloody, it is blood-stained

mihkowayān ᒥᐦᑯᐘᔮᐣ
NI red cloth, red material

mihkowi- ᒥᐦᑯᐏ
IPN bloody

mihkowihtakāw ᒥᐦᑯᐏᐦᑕᑳᐤ
VII it is a bloody board or floor

mihkowiw ᒥᐦᑯᐏᐤ
VII it is bloody; it bleeds, it is bleeding

mihkowiýiniw ᒥᐦᑯᐏᔨᓂᐤ
NA Blood Indian (of the Blackfoot Confederacy)

mihkwahikātēw ᒥᐦᑲᐦᐃᑳᑌᐤ
VII it is made red

mihkwan ᒥᐦᑲᐣ
VII it is red [*cf.* mihkwāw]

mihkwasakēw ᒥᐦᑲᓴᑫᐤ
VAI s/he has red skin

mihkwasākay ᒥᐦᑲᓵᑲᕀ
NI red coat

mihkwasākēw ᒥᐦᑲᓵᑫᐤ
VAI s/he has a red coat, s/he wears a red coat

mihkwasēw ᒥᐦᑲᓭᐤ
VAI s/he has the measles

mihkwasēwin ᒥᐦᑲᓭᐏᐣ
NI measles, red measles

mihkwasināsow ᒥᐦᑲᓯᓈᓱᐤ
VAI s/he has red marks, red spots, red stripes

mihkwasināstēw ᒥᐦᑲᓯᓈᐢᑌᐤ
VII it has red marks, red spots, red stripes

mihkwaskamikāw ᒥᐦᑲᐢᑲᒥᑳᐤ
VII it is red ground, it is red earth

mihkwaskāpiw ᒥᐦᑲᐢᑳᐱᐤ
VAI s/he is red-eyed

mihkwaskāw ᒥᐦᑲᐢᑳᐤ
VII it is a red sky, there are red clouds at sunset

mihkwaskīwakāhk ᒥᐦᑲᐢᑮᐘᑳᕽ
INM Red Earth, SK [*loc*; *Cree reserve name*; *cf.* kā-mihkwaskīwakāhk]

mihkwawēw ᒥᐦᑲᐍᐤ
VAI it has a red coat (*e.g.* animal)

mihkwāhtik ᒥᐦᑳᐦᑎᐠ
NA a certain tree [*pl*: -wak]

mihkwākamin ᒥᐦᑳᑲᒥᐣ
VII it is a red liquid

mihkwākamiw ᒥᐦᑳᑲᒥᐤ
VII it is a red liquid, it is red water

mihkwākamīw-sīpiy ᒥᐦᑳᑲᒦᐤ ᓰᐱᕀ
NI Red River

mihkwākan ᒥᐦᑳᑲᐣ
NDI face [*dim*: mihkwākanis; *cf.* 3: ohkwākan "his/her face"; *also*: mīhkwākan; *cf.* 3: wīhkwākan]

mihkwākanihkān ᒥᐦᑳᑲᓂᐦᑳᐣ
NI mask

mihkwāpakwanīw ᒥᐦᑳᐸᑲᓃᐤ
VII it has red flowers [*also* mihkwāpakonīw]

mihkwāpēmakohp ᒥᐦᑳᐯᒪᑯᐦᑊ
NA red willow bark

mihkwāpēmakomin ᒥᐦᑳᐯᒪᑯᒥᐣ
NI berry of red willow

mihkwāpēmakw-āya ᒥᐦᑳᐯᒪᑳᔭ
IPC "red willow" stuff [*pl*]

mihkwāpēmakwa ᒥᐦᑳᐯᒪᑲ
NI "red willow" scrapings; red willow [*pl generally*; *presumably the stringy cambium or "inner bark" of red-osier dogwood*; *wC*: mithkwāpēmakwa; *cf.* mihkopēmak]

mihkwāpēmakwāhtik ᒥᐦᑳᐯᒪᑳᐦᑎᐠ
NA red willow tree [*pl*: -wak]

mihkwāpiskāw ᒥᐦᑳᐱᐢᑳᐤ
VII it is red (metal or rock)

mihkwāpiskisiw ᒥᐦᑳᐱᐢᑭᓯᐤ
VAI it is red hot (*e.g.* a stove)

mihkwāpiskiswēw ᒥᐦᑳᐱᐢᑭᓷᐤ
VTA s/he reddens s.o. (*e.g.* stone) by heat

mihkwāpowēyān ᒥᐦᑳᐳᐍᔮᐣ
NI red blanket

mihkwāpoy ᒥᐦᑳᐳᕀ
NI blood soup; red liquid

mihkwāsin ᒥᐦᑳᓯᐣ
VII it is quite red (as a bruise)

mihkwāskikanēw ᒥᐦᑳᐢᑭᑲᓀᐤ
VAI it has a red breast (*e.g.* a robin)

mihkwāw ᒥᐦᑳᐤ
VII it is red [*wC*: miskwāw, mithkwāw]

mihkwēkin ᒥᐦᑫᑭᐣ
NI red cloth

mihkwēkinwētās ᒥᐦᑫᑭᓌᑖᐢ
NA red cloth breeches

mihkwēyāpiy ᒥᐦᑫᔮᐱᕀ
NI vein, blood-vessel

mihkwēyāpīs ᒥᐦᑫᔮᐲᐢ
NI small blood-vessel [*dim*]

mihtamipaýiw ᒥᐦᑕᒥᐸᔨᐤ
VAI it goes tight

mihtamisiw ᒥᐦᑕᒥᓯᐤ
VAI it is tight

mihtawakay ᒥᐦᑕᐘᑲᕀ
NDI ear [*dim*: mihcawakās; *cf.* 3: ohtawakay "his/her ear"; *also* mīhtawakay; *cf.* 3: wīhtawakay]

mihtawēskiw ᒥᐦᑕᐍᐢᑭᐤ
VAI s/he pouts all the time; s/he is prone to dissatisfaction [*hab*]

mihtawēw ᒥᐦᑕᐍᐤ
VAI s/he is dissatisfied, s/he grumbles; s/he pouts [*also* mīhtawēw]

mihtātam ᒥᐦᑖᑕᒼ
VTI s/he regrets s.t., s/he is sorry about s.t., s/he grieves over s.t.

mihtātēw ᒥᐦᑖᑌᐤ
VTA s/he mourns for s.o., s/he grieves for s.o., s/he longs for s.o.

mihtēýimēw ᒥᐦᑌᔨᒣᐤ
VTA s/he grumbles at s.o.

mihti ᒥᐦᑎ
NI piece of wood, piece of firewood

mihtihkān ᒥᐦᑎᐦᑳᐣ
NI wood-pile

mihtikonikan ᒥᐦᑎᑯᓂᑲᐣ
NI raft

mihtikowāhp ᒥᐦᑎᑯᐚᐦᑊ
NI wooden lodge

mihtikwan ᒥᐦᑎᑲᐣ
NI pile of firewood

mihtimiýēhēw ᒥᐦᑎᒥᔦᐦᐁᐤ
VAI s/he has laboured breathing [*cf.* ýēhýēw; *wC*: mihtimithīthīw]

mihtiskāw ᒥᐦᑎᐢᑳᐤ
VII it is wooded land; there is an abundance of wood, there is plenty of firewood in the area

mihtos ᒥᐦᑐᐢ
NI raft [*also* mihtot]

mihýawē- ᒥᐦᔭᐍ
IPV with fur or body hair [*also* miýawē, mīhawē]

mihýawēhkwēw ᒥᐦᔭᐍᐦᑫᐤ
VAI he has hair on his face

mihýawēpitonēw ᒥᐦᔭᐍᐱᑐᓀᐤ
VAI he has hairy arms

mihýawēsākay ᒥᐦᔭᐍᓵᑲᕀ
NI fur coat

mihýawēsiw ᒥᐦᔭᐍᓯᐤ
VAI he has body hair, it has fur

mihýawēstis ᒥᐦᔭᐍᐢᑎᐢ
NA fur glove or mitten

mihýawēstotin ᒥᐦᔭᐍᐢᑐᑎᐣ
NI fur cap

mihýawēýiniw ᒥᐦᔭᐍᔨᓂᐤ
NA hairy man

mikēhkwan ᒥᑫᐦᑿᐣ
NI tanning tool, to remove fat and gristle [*cf.* mīhkīhkwan]

mikisimoskiw ᒥᑭᓯᒧᐢᑭᐤ
VAI it is always barking [*hab*]

mikisimow ᒥᑭᓯᒧᐤ
VAI it barks (*i.e.* a dog)

mikisiw ᒥᑭᓯᐤ
NA eagle, bald eagle; golden eagle; small eagle

mikisiw-wacīhk ᒥᑭᓯᐤ ᐘᒌᕽ
INM Red Pheasant Reserve, SK; Eagle Hills [*loc*; *lit*: "at eagle hills"; *also* mikisiwacīhk]

mikisiwi-pīsim ᒥᑭᓯᐏ ᐲᓯᒼ
NA Eagle Moon; February

mikiskon ᒥᑭᐢᑯᐣ
VII it is early fall

mikitam ᒥᑭᑕᒼ
VTI it barks at s.t.

mikitēw ᒥᑭᑌᐤ
VTA it barks at s.o.

mikitik ᒥᑭᑎᐠ
NDI kneecap; knee [*pl*: -wa; *see also* mihcikwan]

mikiw ᒥᑭᐤ
VAI it barks

mikohcaskwayēyāpīsa
ᒥᑯᐦᒐᐢᑿᔦᔮᐲᓴ
NDI bronchial tubes [*pl*; *proposed term*]

mikohtaskway ᒥᑯᐦᑕᐢᑿᐩ
NDI throat

mikohtaskwayēyāpiy
ᒥᑯᐦᑕᐢᑿᔦᔮᐱᐩ
NDI windpipe [*proposed term*]

mikohtākan ᒥᑯᐦᑖᑲᐣ
NDI throat

mikosiskācihēw ᒥᑯᓯᐢᑳᒋᐦᐁᐤ
VTA s/he disturbs s.o., s/he agitates s.o.

mikosiskācihiwēw
ᒥᑯᓯᐢᑳᒋᐦᐃᐍᐤ
NA teaser, annoyer; one who teases

mikoskācihēw ᒥᑯᐢᑳᒋᐦᐁᐤ
VTA s/he bothers s.o., s/he gives s.o. trouble

mikoskācihtākosiw
ᒥᑯᐢᑳᒋᐦᑖᑯᓯᐤ
VAI s/he makes a disturbing noise, s/he disturbs by being loud; s/he sounds annoying

mikoskācihtākwan ᒥᑯᐢᑳᒋᐦᑖᑿᐣ
VII it makes a disturbing noise

mikoskācihtāw ᒥᑯᐢᑳᒋᐦᑖᐤ
VAIt s/he bothers s.t.

mikoskācikēwin ᒥᑯᐢᑳᒋᑫᐏᐣ
NI disturbance, trouble

mikoskācimēw ᒥᑯᐢᑳᒋᒣᐤ
VTA s/he disturbs s.o., s/he annoys s.o. (by speech)

mikoskātamikisiw ᒥᑯᐢᑳᑕᒥᑭᓯᐤ
VAI s/he annoys and disturbs the community

mikoskātēýihtam ᒥᑯᐢᑳᑌᔨᐦᑕᒼ
VTI s/he is annoyed by s.t., s/he is perplexed by s.t., s/he worries about s.t. [*also* mikwaskātēýihtam]

mikoskātēýihtamihēw
ᒥᑯᐢᑳᑌᔨᐦᑕᒥᐦᐁᐤ
VTA s/he makes s.o. worry (about it/him)

mikoskātēýihtamowin
ᒥᑯᐢᑳᑌᔨᐦᑕᒧᐏᐣ
NI troubled mind; annoyance

mikoskātēýihtākosiw
ᒥᑯᐢᑳᑌᔨᐦᑖᑯᓯᐤ
VAI s/he is troublesome [*also* mikwaskātēýihtākosiw]

mikoskātēýihtākwan
ᒥᑯᐢᑳᑌᔨᐦᑖᑿᐣ
VII it is troublesome [*also* mikwaskātēýihtākwan]

mikoskātēýimēw ᒥᑯᐢᑳᑌᔨᒣᐤ
VTA s/he worries about s.o. [*also* mikwaskātēýimēw]

mikoskātisiw ᒥᑯᐢᑳᑎᓯᐤ
VAI s/he is bothersome, s/he is annoying, s/he is a trouble maker

mikoskātisiwin ᒥᑯᐢᑳᑎᓯᐏᐣ
NI annoyance, disturbance

mikot ᒥᑯᐟ
NDI nose; beak [*see also* miskiwan]

mikwayaw ᒥᑿᔭᐤ
NDI neck

mikwayawikan ᒥᑿᔭᐏᑲᐣ
NDI neck-bone [*proposed term*]

mikwāskonēw ᒥᒁᐢᑯᓀᐤ
NDI chin

mikwāskonēwikan ᒥᒁᐢᑯᓀᐏᑲᐣ
NDI chin

mimikonam ᒥᒥᑯᓇᒼ
VTI s/he shakes s.t.

mimikonēw ᒥᒥᑯᓀᐤ
VTA s/he shakes s.o.

mimikopēkinam ᒥᒥᑯᐯᑭᓇᒼ
VTI s/he rubs s.t. in the water

mimikopēkinēw ᒥᒥᑯᐯᑭᓀᐤ
VTA s/he washes s.o. (by hand), s/he rubs s.o. in the water

mimikopitam ᒥᒥᑯᐱᑕᒼ
VTI s/he rubs s.t.

mimikopitēw ᒥᒥᑯᐱᑌᐤ
VTA s/he rubs s.o.

mimikwās ᒥᒥᒁᐢ
NA butterfly [*see also* kamāmak]

minahēw ᒥᓇᐦᐁᐤ
VTA s/he gives s.o. a drink or broth; s/he gives s.o. (it) to drink

minahik ᒥᓇᐦᐃᐠ
NA pine; spruce tree; tamarack [*pl*: -wak; *see also* sihta, wākinākan]

minahikoskāw ᒥᓇᐦᐃᑯᐢᑳᐤ
NI pine forest, spruce grove

minahikoskāw ᒥᓇᐦᐃᑯᐢᑳᐤ
VII it is a pine forest, it is a spruce grove

minahikowiw ᒥᓇᐦᐃᑯᐏᐤ
VAI it is a pine

minahikwāhtik ᒥᓇᐦᐃᒁᐦᑎᐠ
NA pine tree; spruce tree [*pl*: -wak; *see also* sihta]

minahisow ᒥᓇᐦᐃᓱᐤ
VAI s/he gives him/herself a drink

minahiwēw ᒥᓇᐦᐃᐍᐤ
VAI s/he gives people drinks

minahow ᒥᓇᐦᐅᐤ
VAI s/he hunts an animal, s/he kills an animal, s/he kills game, s/he makes a kill, s/he has a successful hunt

minahowin ᒥᓇᐦᐅᐏᐣ
NI kill of game, successful hunt

minahōstamawēw ᒥᓇᐦᐆᐢᑕᒪᐍᐤ
VTA s/he kills game for s.o., s/he kills an animal for s.o., s/he makes a kill for s.o.

minahōstamāsow ᒥᓇᐦᐆᐢᑕᒫᓱᐤ
VAI s/he kills game for him/herself, s/he kills an animal for him/herself, s/he makes a kill for him/herself

minahtāw ᒥᓇᐦᑖᐤ
VAIt s/he kills s.t. as game

minastēw ᒥᓇᐢᑌᐤ
NI cord of wood

minihkwācikan ᒥᓂᐦᒁᒋᑲᐣ
NI glass, cup, mug, drinking vessel

minihkwācikanis ᒥᓂᐦᒁᒋᑲᓂᐢ
NI cup, small cup [*dim*]

minihkwākan ᒥᓂᐦᒁᑲᐣ
NI cup, glass

minihkwātam ᒥᓂᐦᒁᑕᒼ
VTI s/he drinks s.t.

minihkwātēw ᒥᓂᐦᒁᑌᐤ
VTA s/he trades s.o. for a drink; s/he drinks s.o. all up (as money)

minihkwēsiw ᒥᓂᐦᑵᓯᐤ
VAI s/he drinks a little [*dim*]

minihkwēskiw ᒥᓂᐦᑵᐢᑭᐤ
VAI s/he makes a habit of drinking, s/he is a drinker, s/he is a chronic abuser of alcohol, s/he is an alcoholic [*hab*]

minihkwēw ᒥᓂᐦᑫᐤ
VAI s/he drinks, s/he has a drink; s/he drinks s.t.; s/he drinks, s/he abuses alcohol [*rdpl*: māh-minihkwēw]
minihkwēwikamik ᒥᓂᐦᑫᐃᑲᒥᐠ
NI bar, pub, saloon, tavern [*pl*: -wa]
minihkwēwin ᒥᓂᐦᑫᐏᐣ
NI drink, beverage, alcoholic beverage; drinking, alcoholic abuse
minihkwēwinis ᒥᓂᐦᑫᐏᓂᐢ
NI beverage, pop of any flavour [*dim*]
minihkwēwiýākanis ᒥᓂᐦᑫᐏᔮᑲᓂᐢ
NI glass [*dim*]
miniscikos ᒥᓂᐢᒋᑯᐢ
NI small island [*dim*]
miniskwahpicikan ᒥᓂᐢᑲᐦᐱᒋᑲᐣ
NI rein, line
miniskwēpicikan ᒥᓂᐢᑫᐱᒋᑲᐣ
NI rein, line
ministik ᒥᓂᐢᑎᐠ
NI island [*pl*: -wa]
ministikowiw ᒥᓂᐢᑎᑯᐏᐤ
VII it has islands
ministikwan ᒥᓂᐢᑎᑿᐣ
INM Ministikwan, SK [*also VII*; *lit*: "it is an island"; *Cree reserve name*]
minōs ᒥᓅᐢ
NA cat [*French loan*]
minōsis ᒥᓅᓯᐢ
NA kitten, little cat [*dim*; *French loan*]
mipwām ᒥᑇᒼ
NDI thigh
mipwāmikan ᒥᑇᒥᑲᐣ
NDI femur [*proposed term*]
misacimosis ᒥᓴᒋᒧᓯᐢ
NA little horse, pony, foal, colt [*dim*]
misahci ᒥᓴᐦᒋ
IPC in great numbers
misahkamik ᒥᓴᐦᑲᒥᐠ
IPC many, in great number, all [*also* misāhkamik]
misahtastāw ᒥᓴᐦᑕᐢᑖᐤ
VAIt s/he makes a large pile of s.t.
misakāmē ᒥᓴᑳᒣ
IPC entirely, all the way; all the way across the whole area
misakāmē- ᒥᓴᑳᒣ
IPV all the way
misakāmēpaýiw ᒥᓴᑳᒣᐸᔨᐤ
VAI s/he goes across from one side to another
misakāmēsohtin ᒥᓴᑳᒣᓱᐦᑎᐣ
VII it extends all the way
misakāmēýāsiw ᒥᓴᑳᒣᔮᓯᐤ
VAI s/he sails across from one side to the other, s/he is blown across
misakāw ᒥᓴᑳᐤ
VAI s/he lands on shore, s/he comes to shore
misamiýēhēw ᒥᓴᒥᔦᐦᐁᐤ
VAI s/he has laboured breathing [*cf.* ýēhýēw; *wC*: misamithīthīw]
misasiniy ᒥᓴᓯᓂᕀ
NA big stone [*cf.* mistasiniy]
misatim ᒥᓴᑎᒼ
NA horse [*pl*: -wak; *cf.* mistatim]
misatimokamik ᒥᓴᑎᒧᑲᒥᐠ
NI horse-barn, stable [*pl*: -wa]
misatimosimow ᒥᓴᑎᒧᓯᒧᐤ
VAI he dances the horse dance, he dances the mounted dance
misatimosimowin ᒥᓴᑎᒧᓯᒧᐏᐣ
NI horse dance; mounted dance
misatimositēw ᒥᓴᑎᒧᓯᑌᐤ
VAI s/he has horse feet
misatimwas ᒥᓴᑎᒷᐢ
NI saddlebag [*also* misatimwat; *cf.* misatimwaskimot]
misatimwaskasiy ᒥᓴᑎᒷᐢᑲᓯᕀ
NA hoof, horse's hoof [*also* misatimoskasiy]
misatimwaskimot ᒥᓴᑎᒷᐢᑭᒧᐟ
NI saddlebag [*cf.* misatimwas]
misatimwaýow ᒥᓴᑎᒷᔪᐤ
NI horse-tail; tail-hair of a horse
misawāc ᒥᓴᐚᐨ
IPC anyway, at any rate, in any case, whatever might be though; no doubt it is the case
misawihēw ᒥᓴᐏᐦᐁᐤ
VTA s/he defeats s.o. conclusively
misāhcinēham ᒥᓵᐦᒋᓀᐦᐊᒼ
VTI s/he buys s.t.
misāhtāw ᒥᓵᐦᑖᐤ
VAIt s/he makes s.t. big, s/he makes s.t. bigger [*cf.* misihtāw]
misāsin ᒥᓵᓯᐣ
VII it is rather large [*dim*]
misāskwacosihk ᒥᓵᐢᑲᒍᓯᕽ
IPC among the saskatoon willows [*loc*; *dim*]
misāskwat ᒥᓵᐢᑲᐟ
NA saskatoon willow [*pl*: -wak]
misāskwatōmina ᒥᓵᐢᑲᑑᒥᓇ
NI saskatoon berries [*pl*]
misāskwatōmināhtik ᒥᓵᐢᑲᑑᒥᓈᐦᑎᐠ
NA saskatoon willow [*pl*: -wak]
misāskwatōminihk ᒥᓵᐢᑲᑑᒥᓂᕽ
INM Saskatoon, SK [*loc*; *lit*: "at the Saskatoon berry"]
misāskwatōminiskāhk ᒥᓵᐢᑲᑑᒥᓂᐢᑳᕽ
INM Saskatoon, SK [*loc*; *lit*: "the place of many Saskatoon berries"; *see also* mīnisihk]
misāskwatwāhtik ᒥᓵᐢᑲᑣᐦᑎᐠ
NA saskatoon willow [*pl*: -wak]
misāw ᒥᓵᐤ
VII it is big
misāýēkisiw ᒥᓵᔦᑭᓯᐤ
VAI it is wide (*e.g.* material, as a shawl)
miscacimosis ᒥᐢᒐᒋᒧᓯᐢ
NA pony; little horse [*dim*; *cf.* misacimosis, mistatim]
miscahīs ᒥᐢᒐᐦᐄᐢ
IPC a good deal; quite greatly, quite a bit, a fair amount [*dim*; *cf.* mistahi]
miscahīs-kīkway ᒥᐢᒐᐦᐄᐢ ᑮᑿᕀ
IPC quite a lot [*sometimes pl as if NI*]
miscanikwacās ᒥᐢᒐᓂᑿᒑᐢ
NA gopher [*dim*; *also* miscanikocās; *cf.* mistanikwacās; *see also* ocīskimow]
miscanikwacāsōsōsa ᒥᐢᒐᓂᑿᒑᓲᓲᓴ
NI horsetail grass; "gopher tails" [*dim*; *pl generally*]
miscikowacis ᒥᐢᒋᑯᐊᒋᐢ
NI small box [*dim*; *cf.* mistikowat]
miscikōsis ᒥᐢᒋᑰᓯᐢ
NI wooden boat [*dim*]
miscikwānis ᒥᐢᒋᒁᓂᐢ
NDI little head, baby's head [*dim*; *cf.* mistikwān]
misēkin ᒥᓭᑭᐣ
VII it is an expanse of ice; it is a big hide, it is a large piece of material [*pl*: -wa]
misēkisiw ᒥᓭᑭᓯᐤ
VAI it is a big hide
misi ᒥᓯ
IPN big, large, great [*cf.* misi *IPV*]
misi- ᒥᓯ
IPV big, greatly; much, a lot; very, extremely, to the extreme [*cf.* misi *IPN*]
misi-ayamihāw ᒥᓵᔭᒥᐦᐋᐤ
VAI s/he holds mass, s/he celebrates high mass [*also* mis-āyamihāw]
misi-ayiwāk ᒥᓯ ᐊᔨᐚᐠ
IPC much more
misi-kinēpik ᒥᓯ ᑭᓀᐱᐠ
NA large snake, serpent [*pl*: -wak]
misi-kitow ᒥᓯ ᑭᑐᐤ
VAI s/he calls out loudly; s/he makes a loud call; [*pl*:] there is thunder [*cf.* piyēsiwak misi-kitowak "Thunderbirds call loudly"]
misi-kitowak ᒥᓯ ᑭᑐᐘᐠ
VAI there is thunder [*pl*; *cf.* piyēsiwak misi-kitowak "Thunderbirds call loudly"]

misi-minōs ᕑᕀ ᕑᐤᐣ
  NA large cat
misi-mohkāhāsiw ᕑᕀ ᒍᐦᑲᐦᐊᓯᐤ
  NA heron
misi-omikīwin ᕑᕀ ᐅᕑᑭᐅᐤ
  NI smallpox [*also* mis-ōmikīwin]
misi-pāwistik ᕑᕀ ᐸᐄᔅᑎᐠ
  NI large rapid [*pl*: -wa]
misi-pāwistikohk ᕑᕀ ᐸᐄᔅᑎᑯᐦᐠ
  INM Grand Rapids, MB [*loc*]
misi-pisiw ᕑᕀ ᐱᓯᐤ
  NA large lynx, cougar;
  mythical water-lynx
misi-pīminahkwān ᕑᕀ ᐱᒥᓇᐦᑾᐣ
  NI large rope
misi-pītos ᕑᕀ ᐱᑐᐣ
  IPC very different
misi-pōnam ᕑᕀ ᐳᓇᐨ
  VTI s/he makes a large fire
misi-pōnamawēw ᕑᕀ ᐳᓇᒪᐍᐤ
  VTA s/he makes a large fire
  for s.o.
misi-sāponikan ᕑᕀ ᓴᐳᓂᑲᐣ
  NI large needle
misi-sīsīp ᕑᕀ ᓰᓰᑊ
  NA large duck
misi-tawāw ᕑᕀ ᑕᐊᐧᐤ
  VII there is plenty of room;
  there is a large open space
misi-tāwinam ᕑᕀ ᑖᐃᐧᓇᐨ
  VTI s/he makes a large
  opening, s/he opens it wide
misi-ýōtin ᕑᕀ ᔪᐦᑎᐣ
  VII it is very windy, there is
  a strong wind
misicāhk ᕑᕀᐦᐠ
  NA horsefly [*pl*: -wak; *cf.*
  misasāhk, misisāhk]
misicihcān ᕑᕀᐦᐦ
  NI thumb
misihēw ᕑᕀᐦᐍᐤ
  NA turkey; chicken; eagle,
  hawk [*also* misihýēw; *wC*:
  misihthīw]
misihēw ᕑᕀᐦᐍᐤ
  VTA s/he gets s.o. in trouble,
  s/he exposes s.o., s/he
  betrays s.o.
misihkēmos ᕑᕀᐦᑫᒧᐢ
  NA tattle tale
misihkēmosk ᕑᕀᐦᑫᒧᐢᐠ
  NA tattle tale
misihkēmow ᕑᕀᐦᑫᒧᐤ
  VAI s/he tattle, s/he tells on,
  s/he reveals the truth
misihkēmowin ᕑᕀᐦᑫᒧᐃᐧᐣ
  NI exposition, revealing the
  truth, tattling
misihtak ᕑᕀᐦᑕᐠ
  IPC a large floor
misikamāw ᕑᕀᑲᒫᐤ
  VII it is a big expanse of
  water, it is a big lake
misikitisiw ᕑᕀᑭᑎᓯᐤ
  VAI s/he is quite large [*dim*]
misikitiw ᕑᕀᑭᑎᐤ
  VAI s/he is big, s/he is large

(in height or girth); s/he is a
big person
misikwāyowēwisip
ᕑᕀᑳᔪᐍᐃᐧᓯᑊ
  NA canvas back duck
misimēw ᕑᕀᒣᐤ
  VTA s/he tells on s.o. [*cf.*
  mamisimēw]
misimiýawēw ᕑᕀᒥᔭᐍᐤ
  VAI s/he has a large body
misinihēw ᕑᕀᓂᐦᐍᐤ
  VTA s/he defeats s.o.
misipīk ᕑᕀᐲᐠ
  NA the ace of spades
misipocikēw ᕑᕀᐳᒋᑫᐤ
  VAI s/he runs things (e.g.
  hide) over a sharp edge
misipotākanēyāpiy
ᕑᕀᐳᑖᑲᓀᔮᐲᕀ
  NI string for stretching hide
misipotāw ᕑᕀᐳᑖᐤ
  VAIt s/he stretches s.t. (e.g.
  hide) [*see also* taswēkipitam]
misisāhk ᕑᕀᓴᐦᐠ
  NA horsefly [*pl*: -wak; *wC*:
  misasāhk; *also* misicāhk]
misisihtāw ᕑᕀᓯᐦᑖᐤ
  VAIt s/he makes s.t. big
misisitān ᕑᕀᓯᑖᐣ
  NI big toe
misit ᕑᕀ
  IPC foot [*measurement*]
misit ᕑᕀ
  NDI foot [*dim*: misicis]
misitakisiy ᕑᕀᑕᑭᓯᕀ
  NI large intestine, colon
misiwanācihcikēskiw
ᕑᕀᐊᐧᐋᒋᐦᒋᑫᐢᑭᐤ
  VAI s/he spoils things, s/he
  destroys things habitually,
  s/he fails to be careful with
  things [*hab*; *cf.*
  nisiwanācihcikēskiw; *all
  derivatives listed below
  begin with "nisi-" in sC, and
  in some areas of pC and wC*]
misiwanācihcikēw ᕑᕀᐊᐧᐋᒋᐦᒋᑫᐤ
  VAI s/he spoils things, s/he
  destroys things [*cf.*
  nisiwanācihcikēw]
misiwanācihēw ᕑᕀᐊᐧᐋᒋᐦᐍᐤ
  VTA s/he ruins s.o., s/he
  destroys s.o., s/he wastes s.o.
  [*cf.* nisiwanācihēw]
misiwanācihēwin ᕑᕀᐊᐧᐋᒋᐦᐍᐃᐧᐣ
  NI destruction
misiwanācihisow ᕑᕀᐊᐧᐋᒋᐦᐃᓱᐤ
  VAI s/he ruins him/herself,
  s/he destroys him/herself;
  s/he commits suicide
misiwanācihisowin
ᕑᕀᐊᐧᐋᒋᐦᐃᓱᐃᐧᐣ
  NI self-destruction; suicide
misiwanācihitowak
ᕑᕀᐊᐧᐋᒋᐦᐃᑐᐊᐧᐠ
  VAI they destroy one another
misiwanācihow ᕑᕀᐊᐧᐋᒋᐦᐅᐤ
  VAI s/he destroys
  him/herself

misiwanācihowin
ᕑᕀᐊᐧᐋᒋᐦᐅᐃᐧᐣ
  NI self-corruption
misiwanācihtamawēw
ᕑᕀᐊᐧᐋᒋᐦᑕᒪᐍᐤ
  VTA s/he ruins (it/him) for
  s.o., s/he destroys (it/him) for
  s.o.
misiwanācihtāw ᕑᕀᐊᐧᐋᒋᐦᑖᐤ
  VAIt s/he ruins s.t., s/he
  destroys s.t., s/he wastes s.t.
  [*cf.* nisiwanācihtāw]
misiwanācisiw ᕑᕀᐊᐧᐋᒋᓯᐤ
  VAI s/he is ruined
misiwanācisīmakan
ᕑᕀᐊᐧᐋᒋᓰᒪᑲᐣ
  VII it is ruined; it causes
  ruin, destruction
misiwanāpēw ᕑᕀᐊᐧᐋᐱᐤ
  NA bad man
misiwanātahkamikisiw
ᕑᕀᐊᐧᐋᑕᐦᑲᒥᑭᓯᐤ
  VAI s/he makes a mess of
  things, s/he destroys
misiwanātan ᕑᕀᐊᐧᐋᑕᐣ
  VII it is ruined, it is
  destroyed, it is spoiled, it
  decays
misiwanātisiw ᕑᕀᐊᐧᐋᑎᓯᐤ
  VAI s/he is ruined, s/he is
  destroyed, it is spoiled, it
  decays
misiwanātisiwin ᕑᕀᐊᐧᐋᑎᓯᐃᐧᐣ
  NI decaying, spoiling
misiwē ᕑᕀᐍ
  IPC all over, everywhere,
  the entire place, on the whole
  body
misiwē ita ᕑᕀᐍ ᐃᑕ
  IPH everywhere, all over
  [*also* misiw ita]
misiwē itē ᕑᕀᐍ ᐃᑌ
  IPH everywhere, all over, to
  every place [*also* misiw itē]
misiwē-ayiwinisa
ᕑᕀᐍ ᐊᔨᐃᐧᓂᓴ
  NI coveralls, skidoo suit
misiwēminakinikātēw
ᕑᕀᐍᒥᓇᑭᓂᑳᑌᐤ
  VII it is fully beaded, it is
  covered in beads, it is beaded
  all over
misiwēminakinam ᕑᕀᐍᒥᓇᑭᓇᐨ
  VTI s/he puts beads all over
  s.t.; s/he covers s.t. with beads
misiwēpaýihcikan ᕑᕀᐍᐸᔨᐦᒋᑲᐣ
  NI pill, medication
misiwēpaýihcikanis
ᕑᕀᐍᐸᔨᐦᒋᑲᓂᐢ
  NI pill [*dim*]
misiwēpaýihēw ᕑᕀᐍᐸᔨᐦᐍᐤ
  VTA s/he swallows s.o.
  whole
misiwēpaýihtāw ᕑᕀᐍᐸᔨᐦᑖᐤ
  VAIt s/he swallows s.t. whole
misiwēsiw ᕑᕀᐍᓯᐤ
  VAI it is all in one piece, it
  is entire, it is whole

misiwēskamik ᕆ᙮ᐁᐧ•ᐣᑲᒥᐟᐧ
IPC all over the land, all over the world

misiwētāpānāsk ᕆ᙮ᐁᐧ•ᒐ᙮ᐸᓈᐢᐠ
NA van [*pl*: -wak]

misiwētās ᕆ᙮ᐁᐧ•ᒐᐣ
IPC overall

misiwēyāhtik ᕆ᙮ᐁᐧ᙮ᐧᓯᐣᐧ
IPC the entire length of a log

misiwēyāw ᕆ᙮ᐁᐧ᙮ᐧᔪ°
VII it is whole

misiwēyēkin ᕆ᙮ᐁᐧ•ᓯᐯᐧ
NI full piece of cloth

misiyāpiskāw ᕆᐧᔭᐱᐢᑳ°
NI rust

misiyāpiskāw ᕆᐧᔭᐱᐢᑳᐧ°
VII it is rusty, it is rusted

misīhēw ᕆᐧᐦᐁ°
VTA s/he makes s.o. larger

misīhtam ᕆᐧᐦᒐᐨ
VTI s/he chews s.t.

misīhtawikāpawiwak
ᕆᐧᐦᒐᐁᐧ•ᐣᑲ᙮ᐯᐧ•ᐃᐧᐊ᙮ᐣ
VAI they stand in numbers [*pl*]

misīhtāw ᕆᐧᐦᒐ°
VAIt s/he makes s.t. big, larger

misīmēw ᕆᐧᒥ°
VTA s/he chews s.o. (*e.g.* tobacco)

misīmiskiwēw ᕆᐧᕆᐢᑭᐁᐧ•°
VAI s/he chews gum, s/he chews snuff

miskam ᒥᐢᑲᐨ
VTI s/he finds s.t.

miskamawēw ᒥᐢᑲᒪᐁᐧ•°
VTA s/he finds (it/him) for s.o.

miskamāsow ᒥᐢᑲᒪᐧᐧ°
VAI s/he finds (it/him) for him/herself

miskan ᒥᐢᑲᐣ
NDI bone [*cf.* oskan]

miskanis ᒥᐢᑲᓂᐢ
NDI small bone [*dim*]

miskawēw ᒥᐢᑲᐁᐧ•°
VTA s/he finds s.o.

miskawihkomān ᒥᐢᑲᐃᐧᐦᑯᒫᐣ
NI knife that is found

miskāhtik ᒥᐢᑳᐦᐣᐧ
NDI forehead [*pl*: -wa; *also* miskahtik]

miskāhtikwanikan ᒥᐢᑳᐦᐣᑲᐧᓂ•ᐢᓂᑲᐧᐣ
NDI frontal bone of skull [*proposed term*]

miskākaniw ᒥᐢᑳᑲᓂᐧ°
VII it is found

miskāt ᒥᐢᑳᐟ
NDI leg

miskātikan ᒥᐢᑲᓂᑲᐣ
NDI legbone

miskātowak ᒥᐢᑳᐟᐅᐊᐧ•ᐣ
VAI they find one another [*cf.* miskotātowak]

miskikātēw ᒥᐢᐱᑳᑌᐧ°
VII it is found

miskināhk ᒥᐢᐱᓈᐦᔅ
NA turtle [*pl*: -wak; *primarily* wC; *cf.* mihkināhk]

miskiwan ᒥᐢᐱᐊᐧᐧ
NDI nose, snout [*see also* mikot]

miskiwanikan ᒥᐢᐱᐊᐧᓂ•ᐢᓂᑲᐣ
NDI nasal bone [*proposed term*]

miskīsik ᒥᐢᐱᓯᐢᐧ
NDI eye [*pl*: -wa; *dim*: miskīsikos]

miskīsiko-mohtēw ᒥᐢᐱᓯᐧᐧ ᒍᐧᐅᐧ°
NA sty

miskīsikohkāna ᒥᐢᐱᓯᐧᐧᐧᐧᓂᐊᐧ
NDI eye glasses [*pl only*]

miskīsikwāpitān ᒥᐢᐱᓯᐧᐧ•ᐱ•ᐱᒐᐧ
NDI eye-tooth [*proposed term*]

miskocākās ᒥᐢᐧᑲᓯᐢᐧ
NDI small coat, jacket; dress; short skirt [*dim, cf.* miskotākay]

miskocēnam ᒥᐢᐧᑌᐣᐊᐧᐨ
VTI s/he finds s.t.'s whole body with his/her hand (*e.g.* in the dark)

miskon ᒥᐢᐧᐧ
NDI liver

miskonam ᒥᐢᐧᑕᐧᐨ
VTI s/he finds s.t. with his/her hand (*e.g.* in the dark)

miskonēw ᒥᐢᐧᑕ°°
VTA s/he finds s.o. with his/her hand (*e.g.* in the dark)

miskoskam ᒥᐢᐧᑕᐢᐧᐨ
VTI s/he comes upon s.t.; s/he finds s.t. (with his/her foot or body)

miskoskawēw ᒥᐢᐧᑕᐢᑲᐁᐧ•°
VTA s/he comes upon s.o.; s/he finds s.o. (with his/her foot or body) [*rdpl*: māh-miskōskawēw]

miskotākay ᒥᐢᐧᑕᒐᑲᐧᐟ
NDI coat, jacket; dress; skirt [*dim*: miskocākās]

miskotākihkawēw ᒥᐢᐧᑕᒐᐱᐦᑲᐁᐧ•°
VTA s/he makes a coat for s.o.

miskotākihkākēw ᒥᐢᐧᑕᒐᐱᐦᑳᐱ°
VAI s/he makes a coat from s.t.

miskotātowak ᒥᐢᐧᑕᒐᐟᐅᐊᐧ•ᐣ
VAI they find one another [*cf.* miskātowak]

miskwamēw ᒥᐢᑲᐧᒥ•ᐧ°
VTA s/he finds s.o. by biting

miskwamiy ᒥᐢᑲᐧᒥᐧ•ᕆᐧ
NA ice [*cf.* maskwamiy]

miskwamī-manahikan
ᒥᐢᑲᐧᒥᐧᕆ ᒪ᙮ᐧᐊᐱᑲᐧᐧ
NI ice cream [*loan translation; see also* cahkās, kā-tahkāk]

miskwamī-pahkisin
ᒥᐢᑲᐧᒥᐧᕆ ᐸᐧᐧᐱᕆᐧ
VAI it hails, it is hailing; ice is falling

miskwamīs ᒥᐢᑲᐧᒥᐧᐧᐧ
NA ice [*dim*]

miskwamīwikamik ᒥᐢᑲᐧ•ᒥᐧᐃᐧᐧᓂᑲᐧᐧ
NI ice-house [*pl*: -wa]

miskwamīwiw ᒥᐢᑲᐧ•ᒥᐧ᙮ᐃᐧ°
VII it is icy

miskwēyihtam ᒥᐢᐧᑊᓂ᙮ᐢᐧᐨᐨᐣ
VTI s/he finds s.t. out, s/he solves s.t.; s/he thinks of a plan for s.t.

miskwēyihtamipayīw
ᒥᐢᐧᑊᓂ᙮ᐢᐧᒐᒥᐧᐸᐧᐧ°
VAI s/he realizes s.t., s/he solves s.t. suddenly; s/he has a sudden inspiration

misōkan ᒥᐧᐧᑲᐣ
NDI tail-bone; rear-end, buttocks

mispayowak ᒥᐢᐧ•ᐸᐧᑕᐧ•ᐣᐧ
NDA ovaries [*pl*]

mispiconis ᒥᐢᐧᐱᐧᐧᓂᐢᐧ
NDI little arm; fore-arm of a small animal [*dim, cf.* mispiton]

mispikay ᒥᐢᐧᐱᑲᐧᐧ
NDI rib [*cf.* mispikēkan]

mispikēkan ᒥᐢᐧᐱᐧᑳᑲᐧ
NDI rib, rib-bone [*cf.* mispikay]

mispiskwan ᒥᐢᐧᐱᐢᑲᐧᐧ
NDI back

mispiton ᒥᐢᐧᐱᐧᐧ
NDI arm

mispon ᒥᐢᐧᐧ
VII it snows, it is snowing

misponisiw ᒥᐢᐧᐧᐧᐧᕆᐧ°
VAI s/he has snowfall, s/he has snow overtake him/her, s/he receives snow

misposin ᒥᐢᐧᐧᕆᐧ
VII it snows a little [*dim*]

misposkin ᒥᐢᐧᐧᐧᐧᐱᐧ
VII it snows often [*hab*]

mistah-āya ᒥᐢᒐ᙮ᐧᐧᓯᐧ
NA bear [*lit*: "big one"; *pl*: -k]

mistahāpēw ᒥᐢᒐ᙮᙮ᐧᐧᐁᐧ°
NA giant [*cf.* mistāpēw]

mistahcikēw ᒥᐢᒐ᙮᙮ᕆᐧ°
VAI s/he eats a lot

mistahi ᒥᐢᒐ᙮ᐧ
IPC much, greatly, a great deal, a lot, lots; very, very many; very much so [*also IPV*]

mistahi-kīkway ᒥᐢᒐ᙮ᐧᐧ ᐱ᙮ᑲᐧ•ᐧ
IPC many things, a great deal [*sometimes pl as if NI*]

mistahi-maskwa ᒥᐢᒐ᙮ᐧᐧ ᐧᐧᐱ᙮
INM Big Bear [*prominent Cree chief*]

mistahi-sākahikan
ᒥᐢᒐ᙮ᐧᐧ ᓯᐧᑲᐧ᙮ᐧᐱᑲᐧᐧ
NI Lac La Ronge

mistahi-sākahikanihk
ᒥᐢᒐ᙮ᐧᐧ ᓯᐧᑲᐧ᙮ᐧᐱᑲᐧᐧᐧ
INM Lac La Ronge, SK; La Ronge, SK [*loc*; wC *community*]

mistahi-sīpīhk ᒥᐢᑕᕁᐊ ᓯᐲᕁ
  INM Big River, SK [*loc;
Cree reserve name*]

mistahiminis ᒥᐢᑕᕁᐃᒥᓂᐢ
  NI peach

mistahkēsiw ᒥᐢᑕᕁᑫᓯᐤ
  NA lion

mistakihtēw ᒥᐢᑕᑭᐦᑌᐤ
  VII it is counted for much, it
is expensive [*see also*
sohkakihtēw]

mistakisow ᒥᐢᑕᑭᓱᐤ
  VAI it is expensive; s/he is in
a high social position

mistamēk ᒥᐢᑕᒣᐠ
  NA whale [*pl*: -wak]

mistanask ᒥᐢᑕᓇᐢᐠ
  NA badger [*pl*: -wak]

mistanaskwayān ᒥᐢᑕᓇᐢᑲᐊᔮᐣ
  NA badger skin

mistanikwacās ᒥᐢᑕᓂᑲᐊᒐᐢ
  NA gopher [*also*
mistanikocās; *cf.*
miscanikwacās]

mistanikwacāsāýow
ᒥᐢᑕᓂᑲᐊᒐᓴᔪᐤ
  NI skunk grass, "gopher
tail"

mistanikwacāsiwayān
ᒥᐢᑕᓂᑲᐊᒐᓯᐊᔮᐣ
  NA gopher skin

mistasiniy ᒥᐢᑕᓯᓂᐩ
  NA big stone [*cf.* misasiniy]

mistaskihk ᒥᐢᑕᐢᑭᕁ
  NA large pail, kettle [*pl*:
-wak]

mistaskosīmin ᒥᐢᑕᐢᑯᓯᒥᐣ
  NI wild turnip; wild onion

mistaskosīminān ᒥᐢᑕᐢᑯᓯᒥᓈᐣ
  NI bed of wild turnips

mistatay ᒥᐢᑕᑕᕀ
  NI big stomach

mistatayēpaýiw ᒥᐢᑕᑕᔦᐸᔨᐤ
  VAI s/he has his/her stomach
swell

mistatayēw ᒥᐢᑕᑕᔦᐤ
  VAI s/he is big at the belly,
s/he has a big belly, s/he has
a large stomach

mistatim ᒥᐢᑕᑎᐨ
  NA horse [*pl*: -wak; *cf.*
misatim]

mistatimosoy ᒥᐢᑕᑎᒧᓱᕀ
  NI horse-tail

mistatimotāpānāsk
ᒥᐢᑕᑎᒧᑖᐸᓈᐢᐠ
  NA sled, sleigh, wagon,
horse-drawn vehicle [*pl*:
-wak]

mistawāsis ᒥᐢᑕᐊᓯᐢ
  NA Mistawasis [*lit*: "big-
child"; *prominent Cree chief
and SK reserve name*]

mistākayāsiw ᒥᐢᒑᑲᔮᓯᐤ
  NA big Englishman

mistāpēw ᒥᐢᒑᐯᐤ
  NA giant, large man; large
bull

mistāpēwiw ᒥᐢᒑᐯᐅᐤ
  VAI he is a large man, it is a
large bull

mistāpos ᒥᐢᒑᐳᐢ
  NA jackrabbit [*pl*: -wak]

mistihkomān ᒥᐢᑎᐦᑯᒫᐣ
  NI big, large knife;
hunting-knife

mistik ᒥᐢᑎᐠ
  IPC miles [*unit of
measurement*]

mistik ᒥᐢᑎᐠ
  NA tree [*pl*: -wak]

mistik ᒥᐢᑎᐠ
  NI stick, log, pole, post,
wood, wooden rail [*pl*: -wa]

mistiko- ᒥᐢᑎᐠᐅ
  IPV wood

mistiko-kipahikan
ᒥᐢᑎᐠᐅ ᑭᐸᐦᐃᑲᐣ
  NI wooden plug

mistiko-nāpēw ᒥᐢᑎᐠᐅ ᓈᐯᐤ
  NA carpenter

mistiko-nāpēwikamik
ᒥᐢᑎᐠᐅ ᓈᐯᐅᑲᒥᐠ
  NI carpentry shop [*pl*: -wa]

mistiko-nāpēwiw ᒥᐢᑎᐠᐅ ᓈᐯᐅᐤ
  VAI he is a carpenter

mistiko-pakamahākan
ᒥᐢᑎᐠᐅ ᐸᑲᒪᐦᐋᑲᐣ
  NI mallet

mistiko-wanihikēw
ᒥᐢᑎᐠᐅ ᐊᓂᐦᐃᑫᐤ
  VAI s/he uses wooden traps

mistikohkān ᒥᐢᑎᐠᐅᐦᑳᐣ
  NI totem pole

mistikokamik ᒥᐢᑎᐠᐅᑲᒥᐠ
  NI log-house, wooden house
[*pl*: -wa]

mistikokāt ᒥᐢᑎᐠᐅᑳᐟ
  NA person with wooden leg

mistikomin ᒥᐢᑎᐠᐅᒥᐣ
  NA acorn

mistikomināhtik ᒥᐢᑎᐠᐅᒥᓈᐦᑎᐠ
  NA oak tree [*pl*: -wak]

mistikos ᒥᐢᑎᐠᐅᐢ
  NA small tree [*dim; cf.*
miscikos, mistik]

mistikoskātāsk ᒥᐢᑎᐠᐅᐢᑳᑖᐢᐠ
  NA dried up carrot, carrot
that has gone wooden with
age [*pl*: -wak]

mistikoskāw ᒥᐢᑎᐠᐅᐢᑳᐤ
  NI wooded area, heavily
treed area

mistikospwākan ᒥᐢᑎᐠᐅᐢᑊᐋᑲᐣ
  NA wooden pipe

mistikow ᒥᐢᑎᐠᐅᐤ
  VAI it is a tree

mistikowacis ᒥᐢᑎᐠᐅᐊᒋᐢ
  NI small box, small trunk or
chest [*dim; cf.* miscikowacis]

mistikowan ᒥᐢᑎᐠᐅᐊᐣ
  VII it is wooden, it is made
of wood

mistikowas ᒥᐢᑎᐠᐅᐊᐢ
  NI box, trunk [*cf.*
mistikowat]

mistikowat ᒥᐢᑎᐠᐅᐊᐟ
  NI box, trunk, chest; wagon
box [*loc*: mistikowatihk; *cf.*
mistikowas]

mistikowatihkawēw
ᒥᐢᑎᐠᐅᐊᑎᐦᑲᐁᐤ
  VTA s/he makes a trunk for
s.o.

mistikowiw ᒥᐢᑎᐠᐅᐃᐤ
  VAI s/he is wooden, s/he is
made of wood

mistikoýākan ᒥᐢᑎᐠᐅᔮᑲᐣ
  NI wooden bowl

mistikōsi ᒥᐢᑎᐠᐅᓯ
  NI boat, wooden boat

mistikōsiw ᒥᐢᑎᐠᐅᓯᐤ
  NA Frenchman, French
person [*cf.* wēmistikōsiw]

mistikwaskihk ᒥᐢᑎᐠᐊᐢᑭᕁ
  NA drum [*pl*: -wak]

mistikwaskihkos ᒥᐢᑎᐠᐊᐢᑭᐦᑯᐢ
  NA small drum [*dim*]

mistikwaskihkwāhtik
ᒥᐢᑎᐠᐊᐢᑭᐦᑾᐦᑎᐠ
  NI wooden part of drum,
drum box [*pl*: -wa]

mistikwaskisin ᒥᐢᑎᐠᐊᐢᑭᓯᐣ
  NA Dutchman [*also*
wēmistikwaskiniw]
  NI shoe, heavy work boot;
army boot; wooden shoe

mistikwaskisinis ᒥᐢᑎᐠᐊᐢᑭᓯᓂᐢ
  NI small work boot [*dim*]

mistikwatēhikan ᒥᐢᑎᐠᐊᑌᐦᐃᑲᐣ
  NI wagon box

mistikwāhtik ᒥᐢᑎᐠᐋᐦᑎᐠ
  NI wooden stick [*pl*: -wa]

mistikwān ᒥᐢᑎᐠᐋᐣ
  NDI head; mind [*dim*:
miscikwānis, mistikwānis]

mistikwānaskatihkway
ᒥᐢᑎᐠᐋᓇᐢᑲᑎᐦᑾᕀ
  NDI top of skull, parietal
bone

mistikwānikan ᒥᐢᑎᐠᐋᓂᑲᐣ
  NDI skull

mistikwāskwēyāw ᒥᐢᑎᐠᐋᐢᑵᔮᐤ
  VII there is a bluff of
evergreen trees

mistikwēmihkwān ᒥᐢᑎᐠᐁᒥᐦᑾᐣ
  NA wooden spoon

mistiýākan ᒥᐢᑎᔮᑲᐣ
  NI big dish, platter, large
bowl

miswākan ᒥᐢᐊᑲᐣ
  NA wounded person,
wounded soldier, wounded
animal

miswākanikātēw ᒥᐢᐊᑲᓂᑳᑌᐤ
  VTA s/he wounds s.o.

miswākaniwiw ᒥᐢᐊᑲᓂᐃᐤ
  VAI s/he is a wounded
person or animal

miswāw ᒥᐢᐊᐤ
  VAI s/he is wounded [*or
VTA unspecified actor*]

miswēw ᒥᐢᐁᐤ
  VTA s/he wounds s.o., s/he

wounds s.o. with a missile
[*see also* māskihēw]

mitahtahkwan ᒥᑕᐦᑕᐦᒁᐣ
NI wing [*or NDI*]

mitakay ᒥᑕᑲᐩ
NDI penis

mitakikom ᒥᑕᑭᑯᒼ
NDA mucus, snot, rheum
[*cf.* akik]

mitakisiya ᒥᑕᑭᓯ�␣
NDI intestines [*pl*]

mitanaw ᒥᑕᓇᐤ
IPC decade

mitapiskohkan ᒥᑕᐱᐢᑯᐦᑲᐣ
NDI back of skull, occipital
bone

mitasiskitān ᒥᑕᓯᐢᑭᑖᐣ
NDI calf of the leg; ligament

mitākay ᒥᑖᑲᐩ
NDA vagina, vulva

mitāpiskan ᒥᑖᐱᐢᑲᐣ
NDI jaw; chin [*see also*
mikwāskonēw]

mitās ᒥᑖᐢ
NDA pair of pants [*dim*
micāsis]
NDI legging, gaiter

mitāsihkawēw ᒥᑖᓯᐦᑲᐚᐤ
VTA s/he makes trousers for
s.o.

mitāsihkākēw ᒥᑖᓯᐦᑳᑫᐤ
VAI s/he makes trousers
from s.t.

mitāsihkēw ᒥᑖᓯᐦᑫᐤ
VAI s/he makes trousers

mitātaht ᒥᑖᑕᐦᐟ
IPC ten

mitātahtasiwak ᒥᑖᑕᐦᑕᓯᐚᐠ
VAI they are ten in number
[*cf.* mitātasiwak]

mitātahtomitanaw
ᒥᑖᑕᐦᑐᒥᑕᓇᐤ
IPC a hundred [*preceded by*
"times" *numeral*; *cf.*
pēyakwāw-mitātahtomitanaw
"one hundred"]

mitātahtomitanaw-maskimot
ᒥᑖᑕᐦᑐᒥᑕᓇᐤ ᒪᐢᑭᒧᐟ
IPC a hundred bags, one
hundred bags

mitātahtomitanawāw
ᒥᑖᑕᐦᑐᒥᑕᓇᐚᐤ
IPC one hundred times

mitātahtwāpisk ᒥᑖᑕᐦᑤᐱᐢᐠ
IPC ten dollars

mitātahtwāw ᒥᑖᑕᐦᑤᐤ
IPC ten times

mitātasiwak ᒥᑖᑕᓯᐚᐠ
VAI they are ten in number
[*cf.* mitātahtasiwak]

mitēh ᒥᑌᐦ
NDI heart [*dim*: micēhis]

mitēhimina ᒥᑌᐦᐃᒥᓇ
NI strawberries [*pl*; *see also*
otēhimina]

mitēskan ᒥᑌᐢᑲᐣ
NDA horn; antler [*cf.* ēskan,
-(t)ēskan- *NDA*]

mitēw ᒥᑌᐤ
NA participant in the
Mitewin, medicine lodge

mitēwikamik ᒥᑌᐏᑲᒥᐠ
NI medicine lodge [*pl*: -wa]

mitēwiw ᒥᑌᐏᐤ
NA participant in the
Mitewin, medicine lodge

mitēwiw ᒥᑌᐏᐤ
VAI he takes part in the
Mitewin, medicine lodge

mitēwiwin ᒥᑌᐏᐃᐧᐣ
NI Mitewin Society,
Medicine Society

mitēyikom ᒥᑌᔨᑯᒼ
NDI nostril

mitēyiniy ᒥᑌᔨᓂᐩ
NDI tongue [*also* mitēyaniy]

mitēyiniyāpiy ᒥᑌᔨᓂᔮᐱᐩ
NDI tongue string [*also*
mitēyaniyāpiy]

mitihcikēw ᒥᑎᐦᒋᑫᐤ
VAI s/he follows trails

mitihcipayistawēw
ᒥᑎᐦᒋᐸᔨᐢᑕᐍᐤ
VTA s/he pursues s.o. by that
one's trail

mitihtam ᒥᑎᐦᑕᒼ
VTI s/he tracks s.t., s/he
follows s.t. (road, path) as a
trail

mitihtamawēw ᒥᑎᐦᑕᒪᐍᐤ
VTA s/he trails (it/him) for
s.o.

mitihtēw ᒥᑎᐦᑌᐤ
VTA s/he trails s.o., s/he
tracks s.o.

mitihtihkos ᒥᑎᐦᑎᐦᑯᐢ
NDA kidney

mitihtihkosiw ᒥᑎᐦᑎᐦᑯᓯᐤ
NDA kidney

mitihtihkosiy ᒥᑎᐦᑎᐦᑯᓯᐩ
NDA kidney

mitihtikon ᒥᑎᐦᑎᑯᐣ
NDI armpit [*pl*: -wa]

mitihtiman ᒥᑎᐦᑎᒪᐣ
NDI shoulder

mitihtimanikan ᒥᑎᐦᑎᒪᓂᑲᐣ
NDI shoulder-bone

mitimēw ᒥᑎᒣᐤ
VAI s/he follows a trail, s/he
follows tracks, s/he follows
footprints

mitimēyāhtawēw ᒥᑎᒣᔮᐦᑕᐍᐤ
VAI s/he climbs on the
gunwale

mitisiy ᒥᑎᓯᐩ
NDI navel, belly-button

mitisiyēyāpiy ᒥᑎᓯᔦᔮᐱᐩ
NDI umbilical chord

mitiskwēspiy ᒥᑎᐢᑵᐢᐱᐩ
NDI bottom rib

mitisowayak ᒥᑎᓱᐘᔭᐠ
NDA testicles [*pl*]

mitiy ᒥᑎᐩ
NDI bum; buttocks

mitīhikan ᒥᑏᐦᐃᑲᐣ
NDI shoulder-blade

mitīhiy ᒥᑏᐦᐃᐩ
NDA shoulder-blade

mitīhkōkan ᒥᑏᐦᑰᑲᐣ
NDI armpit

mitohtōsim ᒥᑐᐦᑑᓯᒼ
NDA breast, nipple [*also*
mitōhtōsim; *cf.*
micohcōsimis]

mitokan ᒥᑐᑲᐣ
NDI hip [*also* mitōkan]

mitonēyihcikan ᒥᑐᓀᔨᐦᒋᑲᐣ
NI reflection, object of
meditation [*cf.*
māmitonēyihcikan]

mitonēyihtam ᒥᑐᓀᔨᐦᑕᒼ
VTI s/he ponders over s.t.
[*cf.* māmitonēyihtam]

mitonēyimēw ᒥᑐᓀᔨᒣᐤ
VTA s/he meditates upon s.o.
[*cf.* māmitonēyimēw]

mitoni ᒥᑐᓂ
IPC very, really, intensively,
fully, completely, to full
degree; quite; much, a lot;
well [*cf.* mētoni; *also IPV*]

mitōn ᒥᑑᐣ
NDI mouth

mitōskwan ᒥᑑᐢᑲᐧᐣ
NDI elbow [*dim*:
micōskwanis]

miý-ōtinēw ᒥᔾᐆᑎᓀᐤ
VTA s/he takes s.o. in, s/he
accepts s.o. [*also* miýo-
otinēw]

miyaw ᒥᔭᐤ
NDI body; corpse, dead
body [*cf.* 3: wiyaw]

miýahciwānāna ᒥᔭᐦᒋᐚᓈᓇ
NI pubic hair [*pl*]

miýawācihēw ᒥᔭᐚᒋᐦᐁᐤ
VTA s/he cures s.o.

miýawātam ᒥᔭᐚᑕᒼ
VTI s/he celebrates (s.t.),
s/he rejoices (over s.t.), s/he
enjoys s.t.; s/he has fun, s/he
is joyful

miýawātamowin ᒥᔭᐚᑕᒧᐃᐧᐣ
NI amusement; fun,
joyfulness

miýawātikwan ᒥᔭᐚᑎᑲᐧᐣ
VII it is a celebration

miýawēsiw ᒥᔭᐍᓯᐤ
VAI s/he is hairy

miýay ᒥᔭᐩ
NA mariah fish [*wC*:
mathay]

miýāhcikan ᒥᔮᐦᒋᑲᐣ
NI smelling salts

miýāhcikēw ᒥᔮᐦᒋᑫᐤ
VAI s/he smells things, s/he
tests his/her sense of smell

miýāhkasam ᒥᔮᐦᑲᓴᒼ
VTI s/he burns s.t. as
incense

miýāhkasamawēw ᒥᔮᐦᑲᓴᒪᐍᐤ
VTA s/he burns (it/him as)
incense for s.o.

miýāhkasikan ⌐ᐅᐟᑊᑲᐳᑲᐳ
  NI incense; sweetgrass,
  cedar, sage

miýāhkasikākēw ⌐ᐅᐟᑊᑲᐳᑲᐳᑫᑯ
  VAI s/he uses something as
  incense; s/he uses something
  as a scented lure (*e.g.* in
  trapping)

miýāhkasikēw ⌐ᐅᐟᑊᑲᐳᑭᑯ
  VAI s/he smudges with
  sweetgrass, s/he burns
  incense

miýāhkasow ⌐ᐅᐟᑊᑲᐳᐤ
  VAI it gives off a cooking
  smell

miýāhkohkasikan ⌐ᐅᐟᑯᐟᑊᑲᐳᑲᐳ
  NI incense

miýāhkosiw ⌐ᐅᐟᑊᑯᑭᑯ
  VAI s/he has an odour

miýāhkwan ⌐ᐅᐟᑊᑲᐳ
  VII it has an odour

miýāhtam ⌐ᐅᐟᑊᐨᐨ
  VTI s/he smells s.t., s/he
  sniffs s.t. [*also* miýahtam]

miýākohon ⌐ᐅᑯᐟᑊᐅᐳ
  NI scent, perfume

miýākohow ⌐ᐅᑯᐟᑊᐅᐤ
  VAI s/he scents his/her
  breath [*traditionally*
  accomplished by chewing
  willow pith]

miýākohtāw ⌐ᐅᑯᐟᑊᐨᐨ
  VAIt s/he perfumes s.t.

miýākohwākēw ⌐ᐅᑯᐟᑊᐊᐧ·ᑲᑯ
  VAI s/he perfumes

miýākwan ⌐ᐅᑲᐳ
  VII it smells, it emits an
  odour

miýāmay ⌐ᐅᒪᐞᐩ
  IPC surely, without doubt
  [*cf.* miýāmā, miýamāc]

miýāmā ⌐ᐅᒪᐞ
  IPC I believe [*cf.* miýāmay,
  miýamāc]

miýamāc ⌐ᐅᒪᐞᑊ
  IPC assuredly; I do believe
  so [*cf.* miýāmay, miýāmā]

miýāmēw ⌐ᐅᒪᐞᑯ
  VTA s/he smells s.o., s/he
  sniffs s.o.

miýānam ⌐ᐅᓇᑊ
  VTI s/he leaves fresh tracks

miýāskam ⌐ᐅᐢᑲᐨ
  IPC past; gone beyond (*e.g.*
  the hour)

miýāskam ⌐ᐅᐢᑲᐨ
  VTI s/he passes s.t., s/he
  passes s.t. walking; s/he
  transgresses s.t. [*also*
  maýāskam]

miýāskawēw ⌐ᐅᐢᑲᐁᑯ
  VTA s/he passes s.o., s/he
  passes s.o. walking, s/he goes
  past s.o. [*also* maýāskawēw]

miýāskotātowak ⌐ᐅᑯᐟᐨᐅᐊᐧᐣ
  VAI they pass one another

miýāwaham ⌐ᐅᐊᐧᐟᐨᐊᐨ
  VTI s/he passes s.t. by water
  [*also* maýāwaham]

miýāwahwēw ⌐ᐅᐊᐧᐟᐨᐁ·ᐤ
  VTA s/he passes s.o. by
  water [*also* maýāwahwēw]

miýēsāpiwinān ⌐ᐠᐁᐱᐅ·ᐅᐳ
  NI eyelash, eyebrow [*also*
  mīsāpiwinān]

miýēstawān ⌐ᐠᐠᐨᐊᐳ
  NI beard [*wC*: mīthistowān]

miýēstawēw ⌐ᐠᐠᐨᐁ·ᐤ
  VAI he has a beard [*wC*:
  mīthistowīw]

miýēw ⌐ᐠᐤ
  VTA s/he gives (it/him) to
  s.o. [*wC*: mīthiw]

miyi ⌐ᐳ
  NI pus

miýikosiwin ⌐ᐳᑯᑭᐅᐳ
  NI gift [*wC*: mīthikosiwin]

miýikowisiw ⌐ᐳᑯᐅᑭᐤ
  VAI s/he has (it/him) given
  by the powers, God; s/he is
  given (it/him) by the powers;
  s/he receives (it/him) from
  the powers; s/he is given
  spiritual relief [*wC*:
  mīthikowisiw]

miýikowisiwin ⌐ᐳᑯᐅᑭᐅᐳ
  NI gift from higher power;
  bestowed gift [*wC*:
  mīthikowisiwin]

miýimāwahcāw ⌐ᐳᒪᐞᐊᐧᐟᐨᐠᐳ
  NI damp ground

miýimāwāw ⌐ᐳᒪᐞᐊᐧᐤ
  VII it is damp, it is moist

miýimāwisiw ⌐ᐳᒪᐞᐊᐧᑭᐤ
  VAI it is damp (*e.g.* tobacco)

miýisow ⌐ᐳᑯᐤ
  VAI s/he gives (it/him) to
  him/herself [*wC*: mīthisow]

miýitowak ⌐ᐳᐅᐊᐧᐣ
  VAI they give (it/him) to one
  another [*wC*: mīthitowak]

miýitowin ⌐ᐳᐅᐳᐳ
  NI gift, exchange of gifts
  [*wC*: mīthitowin; *see also*
  mēkiwin]

miýiwan ⌐ᐳᐊᐧᐳ
  VII it has pus, it has a
  discharge

miýiwin ⌐ᐳᐊᐧᐳ
  NI discharge from infection

miýiwipiskwanēw ⌐ᐳᐊᐧᐱᐢᑲᐧᐳ·ᐁᐤ
  VAI s/he has tuberculosis,
  s/he has TB

miýiwiw ⌐ᐳᐊᐧᐤ
  VAI s/he has an open
  infection, s/he has discharge,
  s/he has pus

miýo- ⌐ᐁ
  IPN good, well

miýo- ⌐ᐁ
  IPV good, well, beautiful,
  valuable

miýo-akohpēw ⌐ᐁ ᐊᑯᐟᑊᐁᑯ
  VAI s/he has good blankets

miýo-atoskēw ⌐ᐁ ᐊᐟᐢᑫᐟᑯ
  VAI s/he works well [*cf.*
  miýwatoskēw]

miýo-atoskēwin ⌐ᐁ ᐊᐟᐢᑫᐅᐳ
  NI good work, a fine job [*cf.*
  miýwatoskēwin]

miýo-ācimēw ⌐ᐁ ᐊᐨᑐᑯ
  VTA s/he speaks well of s.o.

miýo-ācimow ⌐ᐁ ᐊᐨᑐᐤ
  VAI s/he tells good news

miýo-ācimowin ⌐ᐁ ᐊᐨᑐᐅᐳ
  NI good news [*cf.*
  miýwācimowin]

miýo-āpacihēw ⌐ᐁ ᐊᐸᐨᑊᐁᐤ
  VTA s/he uses s.o. well, s/he
  makes good use of s.o.

miýo-āpacihtāw ⌐ᐁ ᐊᐸᐨᐨᑊᐨ
  VAIt s/he uses s.t. well, s/he
  makes good use of s.t.

miýo-isihcikēw ⌐ᐁ ᐊᐟᑊᑫᐟᑯ
  VAI s/he does well, s/he acts
  well

miýo-isihcikēwin ⌐ᐁ ᐊᐟᑊᑫᐳᐳ
  NI good deed

miýo-isiwēpisiw ⌐ᐁ ᐊᐟᐁᐱᐟᑯ
  VAI s/he has a good character

miýo-isiwēpisiwin
  ⌐ᐁ ᐊᐟᐁ·ᐱᐟᑯᐳ
  NI good conduct

miýo-itātisiw ⌐ᐁ ᐊᐨᐳᐟᑯ
  VAI s/he is naturally good

miýo-kakēskihkēmowin
  ⌐ᐁ ᑲᐟᑊᑲᐟᑊᒪᐤᐳ
  NI good counselling, good
  preaching

miýo-kanawāpahtam
  ⌐ᐁ ᑲᓇᐊᐧᐸᐟᑊᐨᐨ
  VTI s/he regards s.t. with
  favour

miýo-kanawāpamēw
  ⌐ᐁ ᑲᓇᐊᐧᐸᒪᑯ
  VTA s/he regards s.o. with
  favour

miýo-kanawāpamikowisiwin
  ⌐ᐁ ᑲᓇᐊᐧᐸᒪᑯᐅᑭᐅᐳ
  NI good treatment (from the
  powers)

miýo-kīkway ⌐ᐁ ᑭᑲᐧᐩ
  IPC something good, a good
  thing [*sometimes pl as if NI*]

miýo-kīsihēw ⌐ᐁ ᑭᑭᐟᑊᐤ
  VTA s/he finishes s.o. well;
  s/he educates s.o. well

miýo-kīsikāw ⌐ᐁ ᑭᑭᑲᐤ
  VII it is a nice day, it is a
  fine day; it is good weather

miýo-nāpēw ⌐ᐁ ᓇᐱᑯ
  NA good man

miýo-nāpēwiw ⌐ᐁ ᓇᐱᐅᐤ
  VAI he is a good man, he is
  a handsome man [*cf.*
  miýwāpēwiw]

miýo-nikamow ⌐ᐁ ᓂᑲᒪᐤ
  VAI s/he sings well

miýo-nōcihtāw ⌐ᐁ ᓄᐨᐨᑊᐨ
  VAI s/he pursues good
  things; [*in negative clauses*:]
  s/he is bad, s/he is evil

miýo-ohpikihāwasowin
  ⌐ᐁ ᐅᐟᑊᐱᑲᐟᐊᐧᐟᐊᐧᐳᐳ
  NI good-child-rearing [*also*
  miy-ōhpikihāwasowin]

miýo-pimātisiw ᒥᔪ ᐱᒫᑎᓯᐤ
VAI s/he lives a good life, s/he is well, s/he keeps well
miýo-pimātisiwin ᒥᔪ ᐱᒫᑎᓯᐃᐧᐣ
NI good behavior, good life
miýo-pīkiskwēwin ᒥᔪ ᐲᑭᐢᑫᐧᐃᐧᐣ
NI good speech; [*Christian*:] the good news
miýo-tipiskāw ᒥᔪ ᑎᐱᐢᑳᐤ
VII it is a fine night, it is a good night
miýo-tōtam ᒥᔪ ᑑᑕᒼ
VTI s/he does a good thing, s/he does s.t. good
miýo-tōtamowin ᒥᔪ ᑑᑕᒧᐃᐧᐣ
NI good deed, good works
miýo-tōtawēw ᒥᔪ ᑑᑕᐁᐧᐤ
VTA s/he does s.o. good, s/he does s.o. a good turn, s/he affects s.o. beneficially, s/he does a charitable deed for s.o.
miýo-tōtākēw ᒥᔪ ᑑᑖᑫᐤ
VAI s/he does good things, s/he comforts and consoles
miýo-tōtākēwin ᒥᔪ ᑑᑖᑫᐃᐧᐣ
NI advantage, benefit
miýo-wāhkōmēw ᒥᔪ ᐋᐧᐦᑰᒣᐤ
VTA s/he gets on well with s.o.
miýo-wīcēhtam ᒥᔪ ᐄᐧᒉᐦᑕᒼ
VTI s/he is supportive of s.t.; s/he is cooperative
miýo-wīcēhtowak ᒥᔪ ᐄᐧᒉᐦᑐᐊᐧᐠ
VAI they get along well with one another, they get along well together
miýo-wīcēhtowin ᒥᔪ ᐄᐧᒉᐦᑐᐃᐧᐣ
NI living in harmony together
miýo-wīcēwēw ᒥᔪ ᐄᐧᒉᐁᐧᐤ
VTA s/he gets along well with s.o.
miýohēw ᒥᔪᐦᐁᐤ
VTA s/he puts s.o. in a good position
miýohkwāmiw ᒥᔪᐦᑳᐧᒥᐤ
VAI s/he sleeps well
miýohkwēw ᒥᔪᐦᑫᐧᐤ
VAI s/he has a pleasant face, s/he has a nice face
miýohkwēwin ᒥᔪᐦᑫᐧᐃᐧᐣ
NI good looks
miýohow ᒥᔪᐦᐅᐤ
VAI s/he is well-dressed; s/he dresses well
miýohowin ᒥᔪᐦᐅᐃᐧᐣ
NI fine apparel
miýohtahēw ᒥᔪᐦᑕᐦᐁᐤ
VTA s/he guides s.o. well
miýohtam ᒥᔪᐦᑕᒼ
VTI s/he likes the sound of s.t., s/he likes how s.t. is said
miýohtawēw ᒥᔪᐦᑕᐁᐧᐤ
VTA s/he likes the sound of s.o., s/he hears s.o. with pleasure
miýohtākosiw ᒥᔪᐦᑖᑯᓯᐤ
VAI s/he sounds pleasant
miýohtākwan ᒥᔪᐦᑖᑲᐧᐣ
VII it sounds pleasant
miýohtāw ᒥᔪᐦᑖᐤ
VAIt s/he makes s.t. fit well
miýohtwāw ᒥᔪᐦᑖᐧᐤ
VAI s/he is kind, s/he is good-natured, s/he is of pleasant character; s/he acts well
miýohtwāwin ᒥᔪᐦᑖᐧᐃᐧᐣ
NI goodness, good-naturedness
miýokāmow ᒥᔪᑳᒧᐤ
VAI s/he is fat
miýokihtāw ᒥᔪᑭᐦᑖᐤ
VAIt s/he is good at growing s.t.
miýokiw ᒥᔪᑭᐤ
VAI s/he grows well
miýokosisān ᒥᔪᑯᓯᓵᐣ
NI fine son
miýokosisāniwiw ᒥᔪᑯᓯᓵᓂᐃᐧᐤ
VAI he is a fine son
miýokwāsow ᒥᔪᑳᐧᓱᐤ
VAI s/he sews well
miýokwātam ᒥᔪᑳᐧᑕᒼ
VTI s/he sews s.t. well
miýokwātēw ᒥᔪᑳᐧᑌᐤ
VTA s/he sews s.o. well
miýomahcihow ᒥᔪᒪᐦᒋᐦᐅᐤ
VAI s/he feels fine, s/he feels well, s/he feels healthy, s/he is in good health or spirit; s/he feels pleased; s/he fares well
miýomahcihowin ᒥᔪᒪᐦᒋᐦᐅᐃᐧᐣ
NI good health, good feelings
miýomāhtam ᒥᔪᒫᐦᑕᒼ
VTI s/he likes the smell of s.t.
miýomākosiw ᒥᔪᒫᑯᓯᐤ
VAI s/he smells good, s/he smells fragrant
miýomākwan ᒥᔪᒫᑲᐧᐣ
VII it smells good, it smells fragrant
miýomāsow ᒥᔪᒫᓱᐤ
VAI it smells good in cooking
miýomēw ᒥᔪᒣᐤ
VTA s/he speaks well of s.o.
miýomisow ᒥᔪᒥᓱᐤ
VAI s/he speaks well of him/herself
miýomon ᒥᔪᒧᐣ
VII it fits well (as a window in a frame) [*also* miýwamon; *cf. wC*: mithwamon]
miýonam ᒥᔪᓇᒼ
VTI s/he has a good hold on s.t.; s/he likes the looks of s.o.
miýonawēw ᒥᔪᓇᐁᐧᐤ
VTA s/he likes the way s.o. looks; s/he likes the appearance of s.o. (looks, clothing)
miýonākohcikēw ᒥᔪᓈᑯᐦᒋᑫᐤ
VAI s/he has his/her property look nice, s/he has things look prosperous
miýonākohēw ᒥᔪᓈᑯᐦᐁᐤ
VTA s/he makes s.o. look good; s/he adorn s.o., s/he improves the looks of s.o.
miýonākohow ᒥᔪᓈᑯᐦᐅᐤ
VAI s/he makes him/herself look good; s/he adorns him/herself, s/he improves his/her own looks
miýonākohtāw ᒥᔪᓈᑯᐦᑖᐤ
VAIt s/he improves the looks of s.t. (as a yard)
miýonākosiw ᒥᔪᓈᑯᓯᐤ
VAI s/he is beautiful, s/he looks good
miýonākosiwin ᒥᔪᓈᑯᓯᐃᐧᐣ
NI good looks
miýonākwan ᒥᔪᓈᑲᐧᐣ
VII it is beautiful, it looks good, it has a nice appearance, it looks prosperous
miýonēw ᒥᔪᓀᐤ
VTA s/he holds s.o. nicely (as a mother holds her child); s/he has a good hold on s.o.
miýonikwan ᒥᔪᓂᑲᐧᐣ
VII it is good walking
miýopaýihēw ᒥᔪᐸᔨᐦᐁᐤ
VTA s/he makes s.o. fare well; s/he gives s.o. good luck
miýopaýin ᒥᔪᐸᔨᐣ
VII it runs well, it runs smoothly; it works well [*cf.* miýopaýiw]
miýopaýiw ᒥᔪᐸᔨᐤ
VAI s/he has good luck; s/he fares well, s/he has things go well, s/he has things go smoothly; s/he works well
miýopaýiw ᒥᔪᐸᔨᐤ
VII it goes well, it goes smoothly; it works well [*cf.* miýopaýin]
miýopaýiwin ᒥᔪᐸᔨᐃᐧᐣ
NI good luck; welfare; prosperity; good heart
miýopitam ᒥᔪᐱᑕᒼ
VTI s/he pulls s.t. straight
miýosisiw ᒥᔪᓯᓯᐤ
VAI s/he is nice [*dim*]
miýosiw ᒥᔪᓯᐤ
VAI s/he is good, s/he is nice, s/he is pretty, s/he is handsome, s/he is beautiful
miýosiwin ᒥᔪᓯᐃᐧᐣ
NI beauty
miýosīhow ᒥᔪᓰᐦᐅᐤ
VAI s/he dresses well, s/he is dressed well

miýosīhtāw ᒥᔪᓰᐦᑖᐤ
VAIt s/he makes s.t. good, s/he makes s.t. beautiful
miýoskam ᒥᔪᐢᑲᒼ
VTI s/he has a good fit of s.t., s/he fits s.t. well
miýoskamikāw ᒥᔪᐢᑲᒥᑳᐤ
NI rich land
miýoskamiki ᒥᔪᐢᑲᒥᑭ
IPC next early spring; when it's early spring
miýoskamikohk ᒥᔪᐢᑲᒥᑯᕽ
IPC in the early spring [*past*]
miýoskamin ᒥᔪᐢᑲᒥᐣ
VII it is early spring, it is springtime, it is ice break-up [*lit*: "good ground"; *see also* sīkwan]
miýoskaminowi-pīsimwak ᒥᔪᐢᑲᒥᓄᐃᐧ ᐲᓯᒷᐠ
NA spring months [*pl*; *i.e.* March, April, and May]
miýoskamiw ᒥᔪᐢᑲᒥᐤ
NI early spring
miýoskamiw ᒥᔪᐢᑲᒥᐤ
VII it is early spring [*cf.* miýoskamin]
miýoskamīhk ᒥᔪᐢᑲᒦᕽ
IPC last spring [*also* miýoskamik]
miýoskawēw ᒥᔪᐢᑲᐍᐤ
VAI s/he fits s.o. (*e.g.* clothing) nicely; s/he is well-suited to s.o.
miýoskākow ᒥᔪᐢᑳᑯᐤ
VTA it goes through s.o.'s body with good affect, it does s.o. good (*e.g.* animate food as actor); it fits s.o. well (*e.g.* pants) [*inverse VTA paradigm*; *cf.* miýoskawēw]
miýoskwēw ᒥᔪᐢᑵᐤ
NA fine woman
miýoskwēwiw ᒥᔪᐢᑵᐃᐧᐤ
VAI she is a fine woman
miýosow ᒥᔪᓱᐤ
VAI it burns well, it smokes well (*e.g.* tobacco)
miýospakosiw ᒥᔪᐢᐸᑯᓯᐤ
VAI it tastes good, it tastes nice, it has a fine taste
miýospakwan ᒥᔪᐢᐸᑿᐣ
VII it tastes good, it tastes nice, it has a fine taste
miýostāw ᒥᔪᐢᑖᐤ
VAIt s/he arranges s.t. nicely [*cf.* miýwastāw]
miýostēw ᒥᔪᐢᑌᐤ
VII it is arranged nicely [*cf.* miýwastēw]
miýotamon ᒥᔪᑕᒧᐣ
VII it is a good road; it is a well-beaten path
miýotākosin ᒥᔪᑖᑯᓯᐣ
VII it is a fine evening
miýotāmow ᒥᔪᑖᒧᐤ
VAI s/he has a melodious voice [*also* miýwatāmow]

miýotēhēw ᒥᔪᑌᐦᐁᐤ
VAI s/he is good-hearted, s/he has a good heart
miýotēhēw ᒥᔪᑌᐦᐁᐤ
VTA s/he gives s.o. a good feeling at heart; s/he consoles and enlightens s.o.
miýotēhēwin ᒥᔪᑌᐦᐁᐃᐧᐣ
NI good-heartedness, kindness; consolation
miýowēw ᒥᔪᐍᐤ
VAI it has good fur, s/he has good hair
miýoýihkāsow ᒥᔪᔨᐦᑳᓱᐤ
VAI s/he has a good name
miýōw ᒥᔫᐤ
VAI s/he does well, s/he is skillful, s/he is good at something; s/he is dexterous, s/he is agile
miýw-āyāw ᒥᔼᔮᐤ
VAI s/he is well, s/he is in good health, s/he is in good shape
miýw-āyāwin ᒥᔼᔮᐃᐧᐣ
NI good health, prosperity
miýwahcihow ᒥᔺᐦᒋᐦᐅᐤ
VAI s/he is in good health
miýwahcikēw ᒥᔺᐦᒋᑫᐤ
VAI s/he has good eating
miýwakisow ᒥᔺᑭᓱᐤ
VAI it is well-priced
miýwanohk ᒥᔺᓄᕽ
IPC in a kind way
miýwapiw ᒥᔺᐱᐤ
VAI s/he sits well; s/he is well-off
miýwasinaham ᒥᔺᓯᓇᐦᐊᒼ
VTI s/he writes s.t. well
miýwasinahikēw ᒥᔺᓯᓇᐦᐃᑫᐤ
VAI s/he writes well, s/he has good hand-writing
miýwasinahikēwin ᒥᔺᓯᓇᐦᐃᑫᐃᐧᐣ
NI good hand-writing
miýwasināsow ᒥᔺᓯᓈᓱᐤ
VAI s/he is marked nicely, s/he is shaded nicely
miýwasināstēw ᒥᔺᓯᓈᐢᑌᐤ
VII it is marked nicely, s/he is shaded nicely
miýwaskisinēw ᒥᔺᐢᑭᓯᓀᐤ
VAI s/he has good moccasins, s/he has good shoes
miýwastāw ᒥᔺᐢᑖᐤ
VAIt s/he places s.t. well [*cf.* miýostāw]
miýwastēw ᒥᔺᐢᑌᐤ
VII it is placed well [*cf.* miýostēw]
miýwatoskēw ᒥᔺᑐᐢᑫᐤ
VAI s/he works well
miýwatoskēwin ᒥᔺᑐᐢᑫᐃᐧᐣ
NI good work
miýwācimowin ᒥᔼᒋᒧᐃᐧᐣ
NI good news [*cf.* miýo-ācimowin]

miýwāhtik ᒥᔼᐦᑎᐠ
NA good tree, log [*pl*: -wak]
miýwāpēwiw ᒥᔼᐯᐃᐧᐤ
VAI he is handsome, he is a handsome man [*cf.* miýo-nāpēwiw]
miýwāpin ᒥᔼᐱᐣ
NI pleasing sight
miýwāpisin ᒥᔼᐱᓯᐣ
VAI s/he likes the look of something
miýwāsin ᒥᔼᓯᐣ
NI good thing
miýwāsin ᒥᔼᓯᐣ
VII it is good, it is nice, it is pretty, it is beautiful; it is valuable; [*in negative clauses*:] it is bad, it is evil
miýwāsisiw ᒥᔼᓯᓯᐤ
VAI s/he is good, s/he is fine
miýwātamowin ᒥᔼᑕᒧᐃᐧᐣ
NI amusement; happiness [*cf.* miýawātamowin]
miýwātisiw ᒥᔼᑎᓯᐤ
VAI s/he is good
miýwātisiwin ᒥᔼᑎᓯᐃᐧᐣ
NI good naturedness
miýwēýihcikātēw ᒥᔰᔨᐦᒋᑳᑌᐤ
VII it is well thought of; it feels good
miýwēýihtam ᒥᔰᔨᐦᑕᒼ
VTI s/he is glad, s/he is happy, s/he is pleased; s/he is glad about s.t.; s/he likes s.t., s/he thinks well of s.t., s/he considers s.t. good
miýwēýihtamihēw ᒥᔰᔨᐦᑕᒥᐦᐁᐤ
VTA s/he pleases s.o.; s/he makes s.o. glad
miýwēýihtamowin ᒥᔰᔨᐦᑕᒧᐃᐧᐣ
NI happiness, pleasure, cheerfulness, merriment
miýwēýihtākosiw ᒥᔰᔨᐦᑖᑯᓯᐤ
VAI s/he is well-liked; s/he is pleasant, s/he is good-natured
miýwēýihtākwan ᒥᔰᔨᐦᑖᑿᐣ
VII it is enjoyable, it is pleasant; it is well-liked
miýwēýihtowak ᒥᔰᔨᐦᑐᐘᐠ
VAI they like one another
miýwēýimēw ᒥᔰᔨᒣᐤ
VTA s/he likes s.o., s/he thinks well of s.o.; s/he is pleased with s.o., s/he considers s.o. good
miýwēýimisow ᒥᔰᔨᒥᓱᐤ
VAI s/he likes him/herself
miýwēýimow ᒥᔰᔨᒧᐤ
VAI s/he thinks well of him/herself; s/he likes people
miýwēýimowin ᒥᔰᔨᒧᐃᐧᐣ
NI happiness; self-satisfaction [*cf.* miýwēýihtamowin]

ᐦ

mīcaskosīs ᒦᐦᒃᑯᓰᐢ
   NA swallow (bird)
mīcim ᒦᒋᒼ
   NI food
mīcimāpoy ᒦᒋᒫᐳᕀ
   NI soup, broth
mīcimāpōhkākēw ᒦᒋᒫᐳᐦᑳᑫᐤ
   VAI s/he makes broth out of
   things
mīcimāpōhkān ᒦᒋᒫᐳᐦᑳᐣ
   NI stew
mīcimāpōhkēw ᒦᒋᒫᐳᐦᑫᐤ
   VAI s/he makes stew, s/he
   makes broth
mīcimāpōs ᒦᒋᒫᐳᐢ
   NI soup [*dim*]
mīcimīhkācikan ᒦᒋᒦᐦᑳᒋᑲᐣ
   NI bait
mīcimīhkācikēsiw ᒦᒋᒦᐦᑳᒋᑫᓯᐤ
   VAI s/he uses s.t. as bait
   [*dim*]
mīcimīhkācikēwān ᒦᒋᒦᐦᑳᒋᑫᐚᐣ
   NI bait
mīcimīhkātam ᒦᒋᒦᐦᑳᑕᒼ
   VTI s/he puts bait on the
   trap; s/he sets bait for s.t.
mīcimīhkātēw ᒦᒋᒦᐦᑳᑌᐤ
   VTA s/he sets bait for s.o.
mīcimōc ᒦᒋᒨᐨ
   IPC right from the
   beginning
mīcisohēw ᒦᒋᓱᐦᐁᐤ
   VTA s/he gives s.o. to eat;
   s/he makes s.o. eat
mīcisohkāsow ᒦᒋᓱᐦᑳᓱᐤ
   VAI s/he pretends to eat
mīcisosiw ᒦᒋᓱᓯᐤ
   VAI s/he eats a little [*dim*]
mīcisoskiw ᒦᒋᓱᐢᑭᐤ
   VAI s/he eats often, s/he eats
   all the time [*hab*]
mīcisow ᒦᒋᓱᐤ
   VAI s/he eats, s/he has a
   meal
mīcisowamahcihow ᒦᒋᓱᐊᒪᐦᒋᐦᐅᐤ
   VAI s/he feels like eating
mīcisowēkin ᒦᒋᓱᐍᑭᐣ
   NI tablecloth
mīcisowikamik ᒦᒋᓱᐏᑲᒥᐠ
   NI restaurant; dining room
   [*pl*: -wa]
mīcisowin ᒦᒋᓱᐏᐣ
   NI meal; eating, eating
   habits, food
mīcisowināhcikos ᒦᒋᓱᐏᓈᐦᒋᑯᐢ
   NI small table [*dim*]
mīcisowināhtik ᒦᒋᓱᐏᓈᐦᑎᐠ
   NI table, dining table [*pl*:
   -wa; *also* mīcisōnāhtik]
mīcisowināhtikohkawēw ᒦᒋᓱᐏᓈᐦᑎᑯᐦᑲᐍᐤ
   VTA s/he makes tables for
   s.o.

mīcisowināhtikohkēw ᒦᒋᓱᐏᓈᐦᑎᑯᐦᑫᐤ
   VAI s/he makes tables
mīcisowinihkēw ᒦᒋᓱᐏᓂᐦᑫᐤ
   VAI s/he prepares a meal,
   s/he prepares meals [*also*
   mīcisonihkēw]
mīcisowinis ᒦᒋᓱᐏᓂᐢ
   NI lunch, small meal; light
   meal, snack [*dim*]
mīciswākan ᒦᒋᐢᐚᑲᐣ
   NI back tooth [*pl*:
   mīciswākana; *proposed term*]
mīcitēw ᒦᒋᑌᐤ
   VTA s/he soils s.o. with
   excrement [*also wC*:
   mīsātēw; *cf.* mititēw]
mīcitisow ᒦᒋᑎᓱᐤ
   VAI s/he soils him/herself
   with excrement [*cf.*
   mītitisow]
mīciw ᒦᒋᐤ
   VAIt s/he eats s.t.
mīciwin ᒦᒋᐏᐣ
   NI food, groceries; meal
mīciwinis ᒦᒋᐏᓂᐢ
   NI bit of food
mīcīminak ᒦᒋᒥᓇᐦ
   NA peas [*pl*]
mīhawēsākay ᒦᐦᐊᐧᐁᐧᓵᑲᕀ
   NI fur coat [*cf.*
   mihyāwēsākay]
mīhawēstotin ᒦᐦᐊᐧᐁᐧᐢᑑᑎᐣ
   NI fur cap [*cf.*
   mihyāwēstotin]
mīhcikēw ᒦᐦᒋᑫᐤ
   NI muskrat spear
mīhistowān ᒦᐦᐃᐢᑑᐚᐣ
   NI (single) hair of beard
   [*wC*: mīthistowān; *cf.*
   miyēstawān]
mīhistowēw ᒦᐦᐃᐢᑑᐍᐤ
   VAI he has beard hairs [*wC*:
   mīthistowīw; *cf.*
   miyēstawēw]
mīhkawikiw ᒦᐦᑲᐏᑭᐤ
   VAI s/he runs fast [*also*
   mīhkawikiw]
mīhkīhkotam ᒦᐦᑮᐦᑯᑕᐨ
   VTI s/he uses a tanning tool
mīhkīhkwan ᒦᐦᑮᐦᑿᐣ
   NI tanning tool for taking fat
   or grizzle off [*cf.*
   mikēhkwan]
mīkis ᒦᑭᐢ
   NA bead [*poss*: -im]
mīkisasākay ᒦᑭᓴᓵᑲᕀ
   NI beaded jacket, beaded
   coat, beaded dress
mīkisaskisin ᒦᑭᓴᐢᑭᓯᐣ
   NI beaded moccasin
mīkisayiwinisa ᒦᑭᓴᔨᐏᓂᓴ
   NI beaded clothing [*pl
   generally*]
mīkisāpiy ᒦᑭᓵᐱᕀ
   NI string of beads
mīkisihkahcikēw ᒦᑭᓯᐦᑲᐦᒋᑫᐤ
   VAI s/he does beadwork,
   s/he beads things

mīkisihkahcikēwin ᒦᑭᓯᐦᑲᐦᒋᑫᐏᐣ
   NI beadwork, beading
mīkisihkahtam ᒦᑭᓯᐦᑲᐦᑕᒼ
   VTI s/he beads s.t., s/he puts
   beads on s.t.
mīkisihkahtēw ᒦᑭᓯᐦᑲᐦᑌᐤ
   VII it is beaded
mīkisis ᒦᑭᓯᐢ
   NA bead [*dim*]
mīkisistaham ᒦᑭᓯᐢᑕᐦᐊᒼ
   VTI s/he beads s.t.; s/he puts
   beadwork on s.t.; s/he adorns
   s.t. with beadwork, s/he
   works beads on s.t.
mīkisistahikan ᒦᑭᓯᐢᑕᐦᐃᑲᐣ
   NI bead ornament, beaded
   article
mīkisistahikēw ᒦᑭᓯᐢᑕᐦᐃᑫᐤ
   VAI s/he beads, s/he does
   beadwork
mīkisistahikēwin ᒦᑭᓯᐢᑕᐦᐃᑫᐏᐣ
   NI doing beadwork
mīkisistikwān ᒦᑭᓯᐢᑎᒁᐣ
   NA person with beads on
   head
mīkisistikwānēw ᒦᑭᓯᐢᑎᒁᓀᐤ
   VAI s/he has beads on
   his/her head
mīkisiwi-pakwahtēhon ᒦᑭᓯᐏ ᐸᑿᐦᑌᐦᐅᐣ
   NI beaded belt
mīkisiwiw ᒦᑭᓯᐏᐤ
   VII it is beaded
mīkisiyākan ᒦᑭᓯᔮᑲᐣ
   NI earthenware crockery,
   dish
mīkiwahp ᒦᑭᐘᐦᑊ
   NI tipi, lodge [*also*
   mīkiwāhp]
mīkiwahpēskān ᒦᑭᐘᐦᐯᐢᑳᐣ
   NI tipi campground
mīkiwahpihkēw ᒦᑭᐘᐦᐱᐦᑫᐤ
   VAI s/he makes a tipi
mīkiwahpis ᒦᑭᐘᐦᐱᐢ
   NI tipi, lodge, wigwam,
   cabin, house
mīkiwām ᒦᑭᐚᒼ
   NI home
mīkwan ᒦᑿᐣ
   NA feather [*cf.* mēkwan]
mīna ᒦᓇ
   IPC and, plus; and also,
   again, furthermore
mīna apisīs ᒦᓇ ᐊᐱᓰᐢ
   IPH and a quarter, 15
   minutes or so [*measurement
   of time; also* min āpisīs]
mīna āpihtāw ᒦᓇ ᐋᐱᐦᑖᐤ
   IPH and a half, half-hour,
   half past the hour
   [*measurement of time; also*
   min āpihtaw]
mīnahokan ᒦᓇᐦᐅᑲᐣ
   NI movable tent-pole for
   opening smoke hole
mīnis ᒦᓂᐢ
   NI berry [*usually pl*: mīnisa]

mīnisāhtik ᒦᓂᖬᐦᑎᐠ
NI fruit tree, berry bush [pl: -wa]

mīnisāpoy ᒦᓂᖬᐳᐩ
NI berry, fruit juice; berry broth

mīnisāpōhkān ᒦᓂᖬᐴᐦᑳᐣ
NI jam (made of fruit)

mīnisihk ᒦᓂᓯᕁ
INM Saskatoon, SK [loc; lit: "at the berry"; see also misāskwatōminihk, misāskwatōminiskāhk]

mīnisiskāw ᒦᓂᓯᐢᑳᐤ
VII there are many berries, berries are abundant

mīnisiwan ᒦᓂᓯᐗᐣ
VII it bears fruit

mīnisiwat ᒦᓂᓯᐗᐟ
NI berry bag

mīnisiwiw ᒦᓂᓯᐃᐤ
VAI it bears fruit (as a tree)

mīnisīhkān ᒦᓂᓯᐦᑳᐣ
NI grape

mīnisīhkēs ᒦᓂᓯᐦᑫᐢ
NA Seneca root

mīnohtāw ᒦᓄᐦᒑᐤ
VAIt s/he corrects s.t.

mīnomēw ᒦᓄᒣᐤ
VTA s/he straightens s.o. out, s/he corrects s.o. verbally, s/he corrects s.o.'s behaviour or attitude [rdpl: māh-mīnomēw]

mīnoskam ᒦᓄᐢᑲᐣ
VTI s/he rectifies s.t. by foot

mīnopayīw ᒦᓄᐸᔩᐤ
VAI s/he settles s.t., s/he balances s.t.

mīnosinaham ᒦᓄᓯᓇᐦᐊᐠ
VTI s/he corrects s.t., s/he rewrites s.t.

mīnoskwēpicikan ᒦᓄᐢᒀᐱᒋᑲᐣ
NI bridle

mīnoskwēpicikanēyāpiy ᒦᓄᐢᒀᐱᒋᑲᓀᔮᐱᕀ
NI bridle rein (by which a horse is guided)

mīpicikan ᒦᐱᒋᑲᐣ
NDI gums

mīpit ᒦᐱᐟ
NDI tooth

mīpitāpoy ᒦᐱᑖᐳᐩ
NI saliva (from teething)

mīpitihkāna ᒦᐱᑎᐦᑳᓇ
NDI false teeth, dentures [pl]

mīsaham ᒦᓴᐦᐊᐟ
VTI s/he mends s.t., s/he repairs s.t., s/he patches s.t.

mīsahikan ᒦᓴᐦᐃᑲᐣ
NI patch

mīsahikākēw ᒦᓴᐦᐃᑳᑫᐤ
VAI s/he uses s.t. as a patch

mīsahikāsow ᒦᓴᐦᐃᑳᓱᐤ
VAI it is mended

mīsahikātēw ᒦᓴᐦᐃᑳᑌᐤ
VII it is mended

mīsahikēw ᒦᓴᐦᐃᑫᐤ
VAI s/he mends things, s/he patches things

mīsahwēw ᒦᓴᐦᐍᐤ
VTA s/he mends s.o., s/he patches s.o. (e.g. pants)

mīsākan ᒦᓴᑲᐣ
NI anus

mīsihtāw ᒦᓯᐦᒑᐤ
VAIt s/he has (s.t. as) a supply of food

mīsiyāpiskisiw ᒦᓯᔮᐱᐢᑭᓯᐤ
VAI it is rusty

mīsiyāpiskāw ᒦᓯᔮᐱᐢᑳᐤ
VII it is rusty

mīsīhkasow ᒦᓰᐦᑲᓱᐤ
VAI s/he is made to defecate from the heat

mīsīhkāsow ᒦᓰᐦᑳᓱᐤ
VAI s/he pretends to defecate

mīsīw ᒦᓰᐤ
VAI s/he defecates, s/he has a bowel movement

mīsīwākan ᒦᓰᐚᑲᐣ
NI anus

mīsīwikamik ᒦᓰᐃᑲᒥᐠ
NI lavatory, washroom; outhouse, toilet [pl: -wa; see also waýawistamāsowikamik]

mīsīwin ᒦᓰᐃᐣ
NI evacuation of bowels, defecation

mīsīwoýākan ᒦᓰᐅᔮᑲᐣ
NI toilet bowl; bed pan

mīskaw ᒦᐢᑲᐤ
IPC occasionally, now and then

mīskoc ᒦᐢᑯᐨ
IPC in return, in exchange; by retaliation [cf. mēskoc]

mīskonam ᒦᐢᑯᓇᐠ
VTI s/he feels s.t. [often used with sexual connotations]

mīskonēw ᒦᐢᑯᓀᐤ
VTA s/he feels s.o. (by hand) [often used with sexual connotations]

mīskonisow ᒦᐢᑯᓂᓱᐤ
VAI s/he feels him/herself; s/he masturbates

mīskoskam ᒦᐢᑯᐢᑲᐠ
VTI s/he reverts to s.t. in turn (exchange)

mīskotahpititowak ᒦᐢᑯᑕᐦᐱᑎᑐᐗᐠ
VAI they tie one another in turn

mīskotayiwinisēw ᒦᐢᑯᑕᔨᐃᓂᓭᐤ
VAI s/he changes his/her clothes

mīskotinam ᒦᐢᑯᑎᓇᐠ
VTI s/he changes s.t., s/he replaces s.t. [cf. mēskotinam]

mīskotinamawēw ᒦᐢᑯᑎᓇᒪᐍᐤ
VTA s/he changes (it/him) for s.o.

mīskotinēw ᒦᐢᑯᑎᓀᐤ
VTA s/he changes s.o., s/he replaces s.o.

mīskotōnam ᒦᐢᑯᑑᓇᐨ
VTI s/he exchanges s.t. [cf. mēskotōnam]

mīskotōnamawēw ᒦᐢᑯᑑᓇᒪᐂᐤ
VTA s/he exchanges (it/him) with, to or for s.o.

mīskotōnamātowak ᒦᐢᑯᑑᓇᒫᑐᐗᐧ
VAI they exchange with one another

mīskotōnēw ᒦᐢᑯᑑᓀᐤ
VTA s/he exchanges s.o.

mīskotōnikan ᒦᐢᑯᑑᓂᑲᐣ
NA substitute performer in rite; stand-in

mīskwaham ᒦᐢᑳᐦᐊᐟ
VTI s/he hits s.t., s/he strikes s.t., s/he discovers s.t. (by tool; as in water searching for an article)

mīskwahwēw ᒦᐢᑳᐦᐍᐤ
VTA s/he hits s.o., s/he strikes s.o., s/he discovers s.o. (by tool; as in water searching for an article)

mīskwāpahtam ᒦᐢᑳᐸᐦᑕᐨ
VTI s/he notices s.t., s/he catches a glimpse of s.t.

mīskwāpamēw ᒦᐢᑳᐸᒣᐤ
VTA s/he notices s.o., s/he catches a glimpse of s.o.

mīstasow ᒦᐢᑕᓱᐤ
VAI s/he eats poplar bast; s/he gets sap, s/he taps a tree for sap [cf. mēstasow]

mītihkwāmiw ᒦᑎᐦᑳᒥᐤ
VAI s/he defecates while sleeping; s/he soils his/her bed with excrement while sleeping [also wC: misihkwāmiw]

mītihp ᒦᑎᐦᵐ
NDI brain

mītitēw ᒦᑎᑌᐤ
VTA s/he soils s.o. with excrement [also wC: mīsātēw; cf. mīcitēw]

mītitisow ᒦᑎᑎᓱᐤ
VAI s/he soils him/herself with excrement [cf. mīcitisow]

mītos ᒦᑐᐢ
NA tree; white poplar

mītosihk ᒦᑐᓯᕁ
IPC in the tree [loc]

mītosiskāw ᒦᑐᓯᐢᑳᐤ
NI poplar thicket [cf. mitosiskāw VII]

mītosiskāw ᒦᑐᓯᐢᑳᐤ
VII there are many trees, it is a poplar thicket

mīwipiskwanēw ᒦᐃᐱᐢᑳᓀᐤ
VAI s/he has consumption, tuberculosis, TB

ᒧ

mohci ᒧᐦᒋ
IPC on the ground
mohcihk ᒧᐦᒋᕽ
IPC on the bare ground; on the floor; to the ground
mohcihtak ᒧᐦᒋᐦᑕᐠ
IPC on the floor
mohcihtakāhk ᒧᐦᒋᐦᑕᑳᕽ
IPC on the floor
mohciyāhtik ᒧᐦᒋᔮᐦᑎᐠ
NI pine stem [*pl*: -wa]
mohkahasiw ᒧᐦᑲᐦᐊᓯᐤ
NA blue heron, bittern [*also*: mohkahosiw, mohkōsiw; *cf.* mōhkahasiw]
mohkicēw ᒧᐦᑭᒉᐤ
VAI s/he exposes him/herself indecently
mohkiciwanipēw ᒧᐦᑭᒋᐘᓂᐯᐤ
VII it is a spring (of water)
mohtāskikanēhosow ᒧᐦᑖᐢᑭᑲᓀᐦᐅᓱᐤ
VAI s/he wounds him/herself in the chest
mohtāskikanēhwēw ᒧᐦᑖᐢᑭᑲᓀᐦᐍᐤ
VTA s/he wounds s.o. in the chest
mohtēmiw ᒧᐦᑌᒥᐤ
VAI s/he has a pimple; s/he has a boil
mohtēw ᒧᐦᑌᐤ
NA pimple; boil
mohtēw ᒧᐦᑌᐤ
NA worm, caterpillar, maggot
mohtēwiskāw ᒧᐦᑌᐏᐢᑳᐤ
VII there is a caterpillar plague, there are many caterpillars
mohtēwiw ᒧᐦᑌᐏᐤ
VAI it is maggoty
mohtēwiyās ᒧᐦᑌᐏᔮᐢ
NI maggoty meat
mohýāpiciskān ᒧᐦᔮᐱᒋᐢᑳᐣ
NI piece of hide with fur turned in
mohýāpitasēkan ᒧᐦᔮᐱᑕᓭᑲᐣ
NI coat with fur turned in
mohýāpitasēkow ᒧᐦᔮᐱᑕᓭᑯᐤ
VAI s/he wears clothes with fur turned in
mosawaham ᒧᓭᐘᐦᐊᒼ
VTI s/he bares s.t. (by tool)
mosci ᒧᐢᒋ
IPC just, merely, plainly, singly, without instrumentality; free
mosci- ᒧᐢᒋ
IPV just, merely, plainly, simply, directly, without mediation, without instrumentality; by hand
mosci-mēkiwin ᒧᐢᒋ ᒣᑭᐏᐣ
NI free gift
moscikwāsow ᒧᐢᒋᒁᓱᐤ
VAI s/he sews by hand
moscikwātam ᒧᐢᒋᒁᑕᒼ
VTI s/he sew s.t. by hand
moscikwātēw ᒧᐢᒋᒁᑌᐤ
VTA s/he sew s.o. by hand
moscitōn ᒧᐢᒋᑑᐣ
IPC gratuitously by speech, without adding a gift or offering
moscos ᒧᐢᑯᐢ
NA cow [*pl*: -(w)ak; *dim*; *cf.* mostos]
moscosis ᒧᐢᑯᓯᐢ
NA calf
mosē ᒧᓭ
IPC openly
mosēkātēw ᒧᓭᑳᑌᐤ
VAI s/he has bare legs
mosēpitēw ᒧᓭᐱᑌᐤ
VTA s/he uncovers s.o.
mosēsin ᒧᓭᓯᐣ
VAI s/he lies uncovered
mosēskatēnēw ᒧᓭᐢᑲᑌᓀᐤ
VTA s/he undresses s.o.
mosēskatēpiw ᒧᓭᐢᑲᑌᐱᐤ
VAI s/he sits naked
mosēskatēw ᒧᓭᐢᑲᑌᐤ
VAI s/he is naked
mosēskatēwin ᒧᓭᐢᑲᑌᐏᐣ
NI nudity
mosēspitonēw ᒧᓭᐢᐱᑐᓀᐤ
VAI s/he has bare arms, s/he goes with bare arms
mosēstikwānēw ᒧᓭᐢᑎᒁᓀᐤ
VAI s/he has a bare head, s/he goes without a hat
mosētiýēhkwāmiw ᒧᓭᑎᔦᐦᒁᒥᐤ
VAI s/he sleeps with bare buttocks
mosētiýēw ᒧᓭᑎᔦᐤ
VAI s/he has a bare buttocks
mosis ᒧᓯᐢ
IPC plain to perception, visibly, done in the open
mósom! ᒧᓱᒼ
INM Grandpa! [*voc, with uncharacteristic stress on first syllable*; *familiar form*; *cf.* nimosō!, nimosōm]
mostakocīs ᒧᐢᑕᑯᒌᐢ
NI automobile [*see also* sēhkēpayīs]
mostaskamik ᒧᐢᑕᐢᑲᒥᐠ
IPC on the surface of the ground
mostaskamikāw ᒧᐢᑕᐢᑲᒥᑳᐤ
VII it is bare ground
mostaskamikohk ᒧᐢᑕᐢᑲᒥᑯᕽ
IPC in the ground
mostastāw ᒧᐢᑕᐢᑖᐤ
VAIt s/he places s.t. simply on bare ground
mostāhtak ᒧᐢᑖᐦᑕᐠ
IPC on bare ground
mostāhtakāw ᒧᐢᑖᐦᑕᑳᐤ
NI bare ground
mostāpēkasēpiw ᒧᐢᑖᐯᑲᓭᐱᐤ
VAI s/he sits naked
mostāpēkasēw ᒧᐢᑖᐯᑲᓭᐤ
VAI s/he is bare, s/he is naked, s/he is nude; s/he goes naked [*see also* mamwēsahkīw]
mostapēkikātēw ᒧᐢᑖᐯᑭᑳᑌᐤ
VAI s/he is bare-legged, s/he has bare legs [*see also* sāsākinikātēw]
mostātwēwitam ᒧᐢᑖᑍᐏᑕᒼ
VTI s/he speaks without effect; s/he makes a nuisance of him/herself speaking
mostāwahtāw ᒧᐢᑖᐘᐦᑖᐤ
VII it is bare ground
mostihkwāmiw ᒧᐢᑎᐦᒁᒥᐤ
VAI s/he sleeps alone; s/he sleeps on bare ground
mostinam ᒧᐢᑎᓇᒼ
VTI s/he takes s.t. with bare hands
mostinēw ᒧᐢᑎᓀᐤ
VTA s/he takes s.o. by actual seizure; s/he catches s.o. in the act of taking
mostohtēw ᒧᐢᑐᐦᑌᐤ
VAI s/he walks without aid or conveyance; s/he merely walks, s/he travels on foot
mostos ᒧᐢᑐᐢ
NA cow; buffalo; [*pl*:] cattle [*pl*: -(w)ak; *cf.* moscos]
mostos-wapāsihk ᒧᐢᑐᐢ ᐘᐹᓯᕽ
INM Buffalo Narrows, SK [*loc*]
mostoso-kwāskohtisīs ᒧᐢᑐᓱ ᒁᐢᑯᐦᑎᓰᐢ
NA a certain grasshopper
mostosokamik ᒧᐢᑐᓱᑲᒥᐠ
NI cow barn [*pl*: -wa]
mostososimow ᒧᐢᑐᓱᓯᒧᐤ
VAI he dances the Buffalo Society dance
mostososimowin ᒧᐢᑐᓱᓯᒧᐏᐣ
NI Buffalo Society dance
mostosonāhk ᒧᐢᑐᓱᓈᕽ
IPC in the buffalo country
mostosostikwān ᒧᐢᑐᓱᐢᑎᒁᐣ
NI buffalo head
mostosowiyās ᒧᐢᑐᓱᐏᔮᐢ
NI beef
mostosw-āya ᒧᐢᑐᐢᐚᔭ
IPC of a cow, of cattle
mostoswaskasiy ᒧᐢᑐᓷᐢᑲᓯᐩ
NA buffalo hoof
mostoswayān ᒧᐢᑐᓷᔮᐣ
NA cow-hide; buffalo robe
mostoswēkin ᒧᐢᑐᓷᑭᐣ
NI cow-hide [*pl*: -(w)a]
mowac ᒧᐘᐨ
IPC most [*cf.* māwaci, nawac]
mowāhkwēw ᒧᐚᐦᑵᐤ
VAI s/he eats roe
mowākonēw ᒧᐚᑯᓀᐤ
VAI s/he eats snow
mowēw ᒧᐍᐤ
VTA s/he eats s.o. (*e.g.*

bread) [*rdpl*: māh-mowēw; *also* mōwēw]
mowiskwamēw ᒧᐏᐢᑿᒣᐤ
VAI s/he eats ice
mowitowak ᒧᐏᑐᐘᐠ
VAI they eat one another

ᒨ

mōcēyāpiskos ᒨᒉᔮᐱᐢᑯᐢ
NI little bottle [*dim*]
mōcikan ᒨᒋᑲᐣ
VII it is fun
mōcikāw ᒨᒋᑳᐤ
VAI s/he has fun
mōcikēýihtam ᒨᒋᑫᔨᐦᑕᒼ
VTI s/he is merry, s/he is happy; s/he is thrilled by s.t.; s/he rejoices
mōcikihcāsiw ᒨᒋᑭᐦᒑᓯᐤ
VAI s/he has a little fun [*dim*]
mōcikihēw ᒨᒋᑭᐦᐁᐤ
VTA s/he makes s.o. happy
mōcikihtāw ᒨᒋᑭᐦᑖᐤ
VAI s/he has fun; s/he has a good time (over s.t.)
mōcikihtāwin ᒨᒋᑭᐦᑖᐏᐣ
NI having fun; party
mōcikihtāwinihkēw ᒨᒋᑭᐦᑖᐏᓂᐦᑫᐤ
VAI s/he throws a party
mōcikipēw ᒨᒋᑭᐯᐤ
VAI s/he has fun (from drink)
mōhcitonāmow ᒨᐦᒋᑐᓈᒧᐤ
VAI s/he talks foolishly
mōhco- ᒨᐦᒍ
IPV silly, crazy
mōhcohkān ᒨᐦᒍᐦᑳᐣ
NA clown; lout
mōhcohkāsow ᒨᐦᒍᐦᑳᓱᐤ
VAI s/he acts silly, s/he behaves foolishly; s/he pretends to be silly, s/he pretends to be crazy
mōhcohkēw ᒨᐦᒍᐦᑫᐤ
VAI s/he uses love medicine
mōhcowisiw ᒨᐦᒍᐏᓯᐤ
VAI s/he is silly, s/he is crazy
mōhcowiw ᒨᐦᒍᐏᐤ
VAI s/he is mad, s/he is crazy; s/he is stupid, s/he is foolish, s/he is silly
mōhcowiyāw ᒨᐦᒍᐏᔮᐤ
VAI s/he is silly
mōhcōyinīwiw ᒨᐦᒎᔨᓃᐏᐤ
VAI he is a crazy man
mōhēw ᒨᐦᐁᐤ
VTA s/he makes s.o. cry, s/he makes s.o. weep
mōhkahasiw ᒨᐦᑲᐦᐊᓯᐤ
NA heron [*cf.* mohkahasiw]
mōhkahcāw ᒨᐦᑲᐦᒑᐤ
VII it is bare hilly land
mōhkiciwanipēk ᒨᐦᑭᒋᐘᓂᐯᐠ
NI spring of water
mōhkitapiw ᒨᐦᑭᑕᐱᐤ
VAI s/he sits with improper exposure
mōhkitohtēw ᒨᐦᑭᑐᐦᑌᐤ
VAI s/he walks with improper exposure
mōhkocikan ᒨᐦᑯᒋᑲᐣ
NI carpenter's plane
mōhkocikākēw ᒨᐦᑯᒋᑳᑫᐤ
VAI s/he planes wood with s.t.
mōhkocikātēw ᒨᐦᑯᒋᑳᑌᐤ
VII it is whittled, it is sharpened (as a pencil); it is planed
mōhkocikēw ᒨᐦᑯᒋᑫᐤ
VAI s/he whittles, s/he planes things
mōhkocikēwākan ᒨᐦᑯᒋᑫᐚᑲᐣ
NI plane (for lumber)
mōhkocikēwin ᒨᐦᑯᒋᑫᐏᐣ
NI planing
mōhkomān ᒨᐦᑯᒫᐣ
NI knife
mōhkomānatos ᒨᐦᑯᒫᓇᑐᐢ
NI arrowhead
mōhkomānatosāpisk ᒨᐦᑯᒫᓇᑐᓵᐱᐢᐠ
NI stone or metal arrowhead [*pl*: -wa]
mōhkomānāhtik ᒨᐦᑯᒫᓈᐦᑎᐠ
NI knife handle [*pl*: -wa]
mōhkomānāpisk ᒨᐦᑯᒫᓈᐱᐢᐠ
NI knife-blade [*pl*: -wa]
mōhkomānihkān ᒨᐦᑯᒫᓂᐦᑳᐣ
NI cutter, blade
mōhkomānis ᒨᐦᑯᒫᓂᐢ
NI little knife; table knife, paring knife, pocket knife [*dim*]
mōhkomānitōskwanēw ᒨᐦᑯᒫᓂᑑᐢᑿᓀᐤ
VAI s/he has knife edges on elbows
mōhkotam ᒨᐦᑯᑕᒼ
VTI s/he whittles s.t., s/he planes s.t.
mōhkotākan ᒨᐦᑯᑖᑲᐣ
NI carpenter's plane, draw knife
mōhkotēw ᒨᐦᑯᑌᐤ
VTA s/he planes s.o.
mōhkwākanēw ᒨᐦᒁᑲᓀᐤ
VAI it bucks, it gallops [*rdpl*: māmōhkwākanēw]
mōhkwākanēýiw ᒨᐦᒁᑲᓀᔨᐤ
VAI it bucks [*rdpl*: māmōhkwākanēýiw]
mōminēw ᒨᒥᓀᐤ
VAI s/he eats berries from the bush, s/he eats berries as s/he picks [*rdpl*: māh-mōminēw]
mōnaham ᒨᓇᐦᐊᒼ
VTI s/he digs s.t., s/he digs for s.t., s/he digs s.t. out
mōnahaskwān ᒨᓇᐦᐊᐢᒁᐣ
NI digger; rooter
mōnahaskwēw ᒨᓇᐦᐊᐢᑵᐤ
VAI s/he harvests; s/he roots
mōnahicēpihkākan ᒨᓇᐦᐃᒉᐱᐦᑳᑲᐣ
NI digging tool (for roots)
mōnahicēpihkēw ᒨᓇᐦᐃᒉᐱᐦᑫᐤ
VAI s/he digs roots out
mōnahikanāhtik ᒨᓇᐦᐃᑲᓈᐦᑎᐠ
NI stick for digging roots [*pl*: -wa]
mōnahikākan ᒨᓇᐦᐃᑳᑲᐣ
NI spade, shovel
mōnahikātam ᒨᓇᐦᐃᑳᑕᒼ
VTI s/he digs s.t.
mōnahikēsiw ᒨᓇᐦᐃᑫᓯᐤ
VAI s/he digs a small hole [*dim*]
mōnahikēstamawēw ᒨᓇᐦᐃᑫᐢᑕᒪᐍᐤ
VTA s/he digs for s.o.
mōnahikēw ᒨᓇᐦᐃᑫᐤ
VAI s/he harvests; s/he digs, s/he digs things
mōnahipān ᒨᓇᐦᐃᐹᐣ
NI a well
mōnahipēpicikan ᒨᓇᐦᐃᐯᐱᒋᑲᐣ
NI drill (for wells)
mōnahipēpicikēw ᒨᓇᐦᐃᐯᐱᒋᑫᐤ
VAI s/he drills wells
mōnahipēpitam ᒨᓇᐦᐃᐯᐱᑕᒼ
VTI s/he digs a well, s/he drills a well
mōnahiskiwākan ᒨᓇᐦᐃᐢᑭᐚᑲᐣ
NI pick
mōnahwēw ᒨᓇᐦᐍᐤ
VTA s/he digs for s.o., s/he digs s.o. out (*e.g.* tree) [*also* mōnahēw]
mōnipitam ᒨᓂᐱᑕᒼ
VTI s/he pulls s.t. up from the ground
mōnisōniyāwēw ᒨᓂᓲᓂᔮᐍᐤ
VAI s/he digs for gold or silver; s/he prospects
mōniyāhkāsow ᒨᓂᔮᐦᑳᓱᐤ
VAI s/he is like a White-Man, s/he acts like a White-Man
mōniyās ᒨᓂᔮᐢ
NA a White-Man, the Whites; little White-Man; Canadian [*dim*; *sometimes derogatory*; *cf.* mōniyāw]
mōniyāskwēw ᒨᓂᔮᐢᑵᐤ
NA a White woman, Canadian woman
mōniyāw ᒨᓂᔮᐤ
IPN White, White-Man's
mōniyāw ᒨᓂᔮᐤ
NA White-Man; non-Indian; Canadian [*cf.* mōniyās]
mōniyāw-āyi ᒨᓂᔮᐚᔨ
IPC White-Man stuff, White-Man article [*sometimes pl as if NI*: mōniyāw-āya]

mōniyāw-iyiniw ᒧᓂᔮ° ᐃᔨᓂᵒ
NA Canadian, White-Man
[*cf.* mōniyāw]

mōniyāw-kiskēyihtamowin
ᒧᓂᔮ° ᑭᐢᑫᕀᐦᑕᒧᐃᐧᐣ
NI White-Man knowledge

mōniyāw-kīkway ᒧᓂᔮ° ᑮᐠᐧᐩ
NI White-Man stuff,
White-Man things [*only
non-locative forms*]

mōniyāwi ᒧᓂᔭᐄᐧ
IPN White-Man's

mōniyāwi-cistēmāw
ᒧᓂᔭᐄᐧ ᒋᐢᑌᒫᵒ
NA White-Man's tobacco,
trade tobacco

mōniyāwi-itwēw ᒧᓂᔭᐄᐧ ᐃᑐᐧᐧᐤ
VAI s/he says the White
word, s/he says the English
word

mōniyāwi-sākahikanihk
ᒧᓂᔭᐄᐧ ᓵᑲᐦᐃᑲᓂᕽ
INM Montreal Lake, SK
[*loc; wC community*]

mōniyāwiw ᒧᓂᔭᐄᐧᐤ
VAI he is a White-Man, s/he
is White

mōniyāwīhtwāwin
ᒧᓂᔮᐦᑤᐃᐧᐣ
NI White-Man's way,
White-Man's custom

mōsak ᒧᓴᐠ
IPC always

mōsāhkamēw ᒧᓵᐦᑲᒣᐤ
VTA it gathers up s.o. to eat,
it picks up s.o. to eat (as a
chicken picks at grain on the
ground)

mōsāhkinam ᒧᓵᐦᑭᓇᒼ
VTI s/he picks s.t., s/he
picks s.t. up, s/he gathers s.t.
up [*also* mōsahkinam]

mōsāhkinēw ᒧᓵᐦᑭᓀᐤ
VTA s/he picks s.o. up, s/he
gathers s.o. up [*also*
mōsahkinēw]

mōsāhkinikēw ᒧᓵᐦᑭᓂᑫᐤ
VAI s/he gathers (things)

mōsāhkinikēwin ᒧᓵᐦᑭᓂᑫᐃᐧᐣ
NI collection

mōsāhkipitam ᒧᓵᐦᑭᐱᑕᒼ
VTI s/he gathers s.t. quickly

mōsāhkipitēw ᒧᓵᐦᑭᐱᑌᐤ
VTA s/he gathers s.o. quickly

mōsākamin ᒧᓵᑲᒥᐣ
VII it is a weak liquid (as
tea)

mōsāpēw ᒧᓵᐯᐤ
NA spouseless man,
bachelor, widower

mōsāpēwiw ᒧᓵᐯᐃᐧᐤ
VAI he is a single man, he is
a spouseless man, he is a
bachelor, he is an unmarried
man, he is a widower

mōsihēw ᒧᓯᐦᐁᐤ
VTA s/he senses s.o., s/he
feels s.o., s/he perceives
s.o.'s presence or coming

mōsihow ᒧᓯᐦᐅᐤ
VAI s/he feels s.t. is coming;
s/he has the sensation of
feeling

mōsihowin ᒧᓯᐦᐅᐃᐧᐣ
NI sensation of feeling

mōsihowinis ᒧᓯᐦᐅᐃᐧᓂᐢ
NI nerve [*pl:* mōsihowinisa;
proposed term]

mōsihowiniw ᒧᓯᐦᐅᐃᐧᓂᐤ
VAI s/he has feelings; s/he is
a seer, s/he is psychic

mōsihtāw ᒧᓯᐦᑖᐤ
VAIt s/he feels s.t., s/he
senses s.t.; s/he perceives
s.t.'s presence or coming

mōsiskwēw ᒧᓯᐢᑵᐤ
NA single woman, widow

mōsiskwēwiw ᒧᓯᐢᑵᐃᐧᐤ
VAI she is a single woman,
she is a spinster, she is a
widow

mōskatāwahkiskawēw
ᒧᐢᑲᑖᐊᐧᐦᑭᐢᑲᐍᐤ
VTA s/he uncovers s.o. as
that one steps

mōskākonēpitam ᒧᐢᑳᑯᓀᐱᑕᒼ
VTI s/he pulls s.t. out of the
snow

mōskākonēpitēw ᒧᐢᑳᑯᓀᐱᑌᐤ
VTA s/he pulls s.o. out of the
snow

mōskiciwan ᒧᐢᑭᒋᐊᐧᐣ
VII it flows out (as a spring)

mōskinēw ᒧᐢᑭᓀᐤ
VII it is full, it overflows

mōskinēw ᒧᐢᑭᓀᐤ
VTA s/he uncovers s.o., s/he
removes s.o. from
concealment, s/he exposes
s.o.

mōskipayiw ᒧᐢᑭᐸᔨᐤ
VAI s/he has a rash, s/he
breaks out in a rash, s/he
breaks out in sores (*e.g.* with
thrush)

mōskipēw ᒧᐢᑭᐯᐤ
VAI s/he emerges from
water, s/he comes to the
surface

mōskipēw ᒧᐢᑭᐯᐤ
VII it is a spring of water

mōskipitam ᒧᐢᑭᐱᑕᒼ
VTI s/he pulls s.t. forth; s/he
uncovers s.t., s/he pulls s.t.
out from concealment

mōskipitēw ᒧᐢᑭᐱᑌᐤ
VTA s/he uncovers and
removes s.o., s/he reveals s.o.
by uncovering

mōskiwēpiskam ᒧᐢᑭᐍᐱᐢᑲᒼ
VTI s/he uncovers s.t. by a
kick

mōskīscikēw ᒧᐢᑮᐢᒋᑫᐤ
VAI s/he attacks things

mōskīstam ᒧᐢᑮᐢᑕᒼ
VTI s/he attacks s.t., s/he
rushes at s.t.

mōskīstamawēw ᒧᐢᑮᐢᑕᒪᐍᐤ
VTA s/he attacks (it/him) for
s.o.

mōskīstamātowak ᒧᐢᑮᐢᑕᒫᑐᐊᐧᐠ
VAI they attack (it/him) for
one another

mōskīstawēw ᒧᐢᑮᐢᑕᐍᐤ
VTA s/he attacks s.o., s/he
rushes at s.o.

mōskīstākēw ᒧᐢᑮᐢᑖᑫᐤ
VAI s/he attacks people

mōskīstātowak ᒧᐢᑮᐢᑖᑐᐊᐧᐠ
VAI they attack one another

mōskīw ᒧᐢᑮᐤ
VAI s/he comes forth

mōskomēw ᒧᐢᑯᒣᐤ
VTA s/he moves s.o. to tears
by weeping or speaking; s/he
makes s.o. cry, s/he makes
s.o. weepy, s/he makes s.o.
become emotional

mōskomow ᒧᐢᑯᒧᐤ
VAI s/he makes him/herself
cry (by speech), s/he talks
him/herself into crying, s/he
cries while talking

mōskopēw ᒧᐢᑯᐯᐤ
VAI s/he cries from drinking

mōskowāhkatisow ᒧᐢᑯᐚᐦᑲᑎᓱᐤ
VAI s/he cries from hunger

mōskowēpahwēw ᒧᐢᑯᐍᐸᐦᐊᐧᐤ
VTA s/he makes s.o. cry by
hitting

mōskwamēw ᒧᐢᒁᒣᐤ
VTA s/he makes s.o. cry by
biting

mōskwaskopitēw ᒧᐢᑲᐧᐢᑯᐱᑌᐤ
VTA s/he pulls s.o. out from
under grass

mōskwāpāwēw ᒧᐢᒁᐹᐍᐤ
VAI s/he cries because of
water; s/he is made to cry by
water

mōso-pahkēkin ᒧᓱ ᐸᐦᑫᑭᐣ
NI finished moose-hide

mōso-tāpiskanihk ᒧᓱ ᑖᐱᐢᑲᓂᕽ
INM Moose Jaw, SK [*loc;
back translation from
English*]

mōsocihtin ᒧᓱᒋᐦᑎᐣ
NI moose toe

mōsokot ᒧᓱᑯᐟ
NI moose nose

mōsomin ᒧᓱᒥᐣ
NI low bush cranberry,
moose berry

mōsominihk ᒧᓱᒥᓂᕽ
INM Moosomin Reserve,
SK [*named for a Cree chief*];
Moosomin, SK [*named for
the cranberry*]

mōsosis ᒧᓱᓯᐢ
NA little moose, moose calf
[*dim*]

mōsoskāw ᒧᓱᐢᑳᐤ
VII there are many moose in
the area

mōsotowin ᒧᓱᑐᐃᐧᐣ
NI scissors [*cf.* mōswākan]

mōsowiw ᒨᓱᐃᐤ
VAI it is a moose
mōsowiyās ᒨᓱᐃᔮᐢ
NI moose-meat
mōswa ᒨᐢᐘ
NA moose [*pl*: -k]
mōswacīhk ᒨᐢᐘᒌᕁ
INM White Bear First
Nation, SK [*loc*; *lit*: "at
Moose Mountain"]
mōswasiniy ᒨᐢᐘᓯᓂᕀ
NI shell, bullet (for moose);
303 or 30-30 shell [*also*
mōsosiniy]
mōswasinis ᒨᐢᐘᓯᓂᐢ
NI 22 shell, bullet [*dim*]
mōswasinīwi-pāskisikan
ᒨᐢᐘᓯᓃᐘ ᐹᐢᑭᓯᑲᐣ
NI shotgun
mōswaskāw ᒨᐢᐘᐢᑳᐤ
VII there are lots of moose
mōswayān ᒨᐢᐘᔮᐣ
NA moose hide, moose skin
mōswākan ᒨᐢᐘᑲᐣ
NI pair of scissors [*cf.*
mōsotowin]
mōswēkin ᒨᐢᐍᑭᐣ
NI moose hide, leather [*pl*:
-wa]
mōtēyāpisk ᒨᐦᐁᔮᐱᐢᐠ
NI bottle, jar, jug, flask [*pl*:
-wa; *also* mōtēwāpisk,
mōtayāpisk; *the latter*
especially wC]
mōtēyāpiskos ᒨᐦᐁᔮᐱᐢᑯᐢ
NI small bottle, small flask
[*dim*]
mōy ᒨᐩ
IPC no, not
mōy cēskwa ᒨᐩ ᒉᐢᑲ·
IPH not yet [*cf.* nama
cēskwa, namōya cēskwa;
also mōcēskwa]
mōy kakētihk ᒨᐩ ᑲᑫᑎᕁ
IPH a great many
mōy konita ᒨᐩ ᑯᓂᒐ
IPH not in vain [*cf.* namōya
pikonita]
mōy nānitaw ᒨᐩ ᓈᓂᑕᐤ
IPH it's fine, all right [*cf.*
mōya nānitaw]

mōy nānitaw itē ᒨᐩ ᓈᓂᑕᐤ ᐃᑌ
IPH nowhere [*also*
mōnānitawitē]
mōy wīhkāc ᒨᐩ ᐑᐦᑳᐦᐨ
IPH never [*cf.* mōy wīhkāt]
mōy wīhkāt ᒨᐩ ᐑᐦᑳᐟ
IPH never [*cf.* mōy wīhkāc]
mōya ᒨᔭ
IPC not [*cf.* namōya]
mōya ahpō ᒨᔭ ᐊᐦᐴ
IPH not even
mōya awiyak ᒨᔭ ᐊᐃᔭᐠ
PR no-one, nobody
mōya cī ᒨᔭ ᒌ
IPH isn't that so? [*cf.* ma cī]
mōya nānitaw ᒨᔭ ᓈᓂᑕᐤ
IPH it's fine, all right [*cf.*
mōy nānitaw]
mōyēyihtam ᒨᔦᔨᐦᑕᒼ
VTI s/he senses s.t., s/he
realises s.t., s/he becomes
aware of s.t.; s/he suspects s.t.
mōyēyimēw ᒨᔦᔨᒣᐤ
VTA s/he becomes aware of
s.o.; s/he suspects s.o.

ᒪ

mwayēs ᒪᐌᐢ
IPC just before [*cf.* mwayī,
pāmwayēs]
mwayī- ᒪᐎ
IPV before, prior to [*cf.*
mwayēs]

ᒫ

mwāc ᒫᐨ
IPC not [*cf.* mwāt *IPC*,
namwāc *IPC*]
mwāc ahpō ᒫᐨ ᐊᐦᐴ
IPH not even; no
mwākowiw ᒫᑯᐃᐤ
VAI s/he is a loon [*cf.*
mākowiw]
mwākwa ᒫᐠᐘ
NA loon [*cf.* mākwa]
mwāsi ᒫᓯ
IPC [*in negative clauses*
only:] not much, not often

mwāskēsiwān ᒫᐢᑫᓯᐚᐣ
NI a water-reed with edible
stem; bullrush stalk
mwāt ᒫᐟ
IPC not [*cf.* mwāc, namwāc]

ᒣ

mwēhci ᒣᐦᒋ
IPC just; just then, exactly
then; just after; just like;
exactly
mwēsiskam ᒣᓯᐢᑲᒼ
VTI s/he comes just too late
for s.t.
mwēsiskawēw ᒣᓯᐢᑲᐚᐤ
VTA s/he misses s.o.; s/he is
too late for s.o., s/he comes
just too late for s.o.
mwēstas ᒣᐢᑕᐢ
IPC after, afterwards, later,
subsequently; late
mwēstasin ᒣᐢᑕᓯᐣ
VII it is late
mwēstasisin ᒣᐢᑕᓯᓯᐣ
VAI s/he is late
mwēstacimēw ᒣᐢᑕᒋᒣᐤ
VTA s/he wears s.o. out by
speech; s/he tells all the
relating about s.o.
mwēstacīhkam ᒣᐢᑕᒌᕽᑲᒼ
VTI s/he bothers s.t., s/he
hangs around a place
mwēstasihtam ᒣᐢᑕᓯᐦᑕᒼ
VTI s/he is tired of listening
to s.t.
mwēstāsihtawēw ᒣᐢᑕᓯᐦᑕᐚᐤ
VTA s/he is tired of listening
to s.o.
mwēstātēw ᒣᐢᑕᑌᐤ
VTA s/he is tired of s.o., s/he
is fed up with s.o.
mwēstinam ᒣᐢᑎᓇᒼ
VTI s/he is too late to catch
s.t.
mwēstinēw ᒣᐢᑎᓀᐤ
VTA s/he is too late to catch
s.o.

n

ᓇ

na ᓇ
IPC here! here it is, take it! [*deictic use*: *in giving*; *cf.* nah]

na-napwahpisow ᓇ ᓇᐸᐧᐦᐱᓱᐤ
VAI s/he is hobbled [*rdpl*]

na-napwahpitēw ᓇ ᓇᐸᐧᐦᐱᑌᐤ
VTA s/he hobbles s.o. [*rdpl*]

na-nāh-nēstopaýiw
ᓇ ᓈᐦ ᓀᐢᑐᐸᔨᐤ
VAI s/he is lethargic [*rdpl*]

na-nēpēwihēw ᓇ ᓀᐯᐃᐧᐦᐁᐤ
VSA s/he embarrasses s.o.; s/he shames s.o. [*rdpl*]

na-nēpēwihtākwan
ᓇ ᓀᐯᐃᐧᐦᑖᑲᐧᐣ
VII it sounds shameful; it sounds disgraceful [*rdpl*]

na-nēpēwisiw ᓇ ᓀᐯᐃᐧᓯᐤ
VAI s/he is ashamed, s/he is embarrassed; s/he is bashful [*rdpl*]

na-nēsowisiw ᓇ ᓀᓱᐃᐧᓯᐤ
VAI s/he is weak [*rdpl*]

na-nitohtam ᓇ ᓂᑐᐦᑕᒼ
VTI s/he listens to s.t. [*rdpl*]

na-nīswascēyāpēs
ᓇ ᓃᓴᐧᐢᒉᔮᐯᐢ
NA bear [*rdpl*; *constellation legend*]

nah ᓇᐦ
IPC here, here it is, take it *(when handing an object to someone)*; *cf.* na]

nahahēw ᓇᐦᐊᐦᐁᐤ
VTA s/he puts s.o. away [*also* nahahýēw; *cf.* *wC*: nahahthīw]

nahapiw ᓇᐦᐊᐱᐤ
VAI s/he sits down, s/he sits down in his/her place, s/he is properly seated

nahapīhēw ᓇᐦᐊᐲᐦᐁᐤ
VTA s/he makes s.o. sit, s/he seats s.o. [*also* nahapihēw]

nahapīstam ᓇᐦᐊᐲᐢᑕᒼ
VTI s/he sits down by s.t., s/he sits down to s.t.

nahapīstawēw ᓇᐦᐊᐲᐢᑕᐁᐧᐤ
VTA s/he sits down by s.o.

nahascikēw ᓇᐦᐊᐢᒋᑫᐤ
VAI s/he puts things away, s/he puts things into place; s/he tidies up [*wC*: nahāscikīw]

nahastamawēw ᓇᐦᐊᐢᑕᒪᐁᐧᐤ
VTA s/he puts (it/him) away for s.o.; s/he places (it/him) right for s.o. [*also* nahastawēw]

nahastamāsow ᓇᐦᐊᐢᑕᒫᓱᐤ
VAI s/he puts (it/him) away for him/herself

nahastāsimonihkawēw
ᓇᐦᐊᐢᑖᓯᒧᓂᐦᑲᐁᐧᐤ
VTA s/he prepares a bed for s.o.

nahastāsimonihkātam
ᓇᐦᐊᐢᑖᓯᒧᓂᐦᑳᑕᒼ
VTI s/he makes s.t. up (as a bed)

nahastāsimonihkēw
ᓇᐦᐊᐢᑖᓯᒧᓂᐦᑫᐤ
VAI s/he prepares beds

nahastāsow ᓇᐦᐊᐢᑖᓱᐤ
VAI s/he places things for him/herself, s/he straightens s.t. out; s/he makes the beds

nahastāw ᓇᐦᐊᐢᑖᐤ
VAIt s/he puts s.t. away; s/he puts s.t. in its place, s/he places s.t. right; s/he stores, caches s.t.; s/he buries s.t.

nahawēkinam ᓇᐦᐊᐁᐧᑭᓇᒼ
VTI s/he folds s.t. neatly

nahawēkinēw ᓇᐦᐊᐁᐧᑭᓀᐤ
VTA s/he folds s.o. neatly (*e.g.* pants)

nahāhkaniskwēw ᓇᐦᐋᐦᑲᓂᐢᑫᐧᐤ
NA daughter-in-law [*cf.* -nahāhkaniskwēm- *NDA*]

nahāhkapiw ᓇᐦᐋᐦᑲᐱᐤ
VAI he lives with his wife's people or his wife's parents

nahāhkis ᓇᐦᐋᐦᑭᐢ
NA son-in-law; bridegroom [*cf.* -nahāhkisīm- *NDA*, 1: ninahāhkisīm "my son-in-law"]

nahāpahtam ᓇᐦᐋᐸᐦᑕᐣ
VTI s/he sees s.t. clearly, readily; s/he sees s.t. favourably

nahāpamēw ᓇᐦᐋᐸᒣᐤ
VTA s/he sees s.o. clearly, readily; s/he sees s.o. favourably

nahāpasow ᓇᐦᐋᐸᓱᐤ
VAI s/he smells right, properly, well

nahāpiw ᓇᐦᐋᐱᐤ
VAI s/he sees clearly, s/he sees well; s/he has good vision

nahāsiw ᓇᐦᐋᓯᐤ
VAI s/he is keen of perception; s/he is a good shot

nahāwakihtam ᓇᐦᐋᐊᐧᑭᐦᑕᒼ
VTI s/he counts s.t. carefully

nahāwakimēw ᓇᐦᐋᐊᐧᑭᒣᐤ
VTA s/he counts s.o. carefully

nahāwascikēw ᓇᐦᐋᐊᐧᐢᒋᑫᐤ
VAI s/he places things in order, nicely, neatly; s/he arranges things neatly

nahāwastāw ᓇᐦᐋᐊᐧᐢᑖᐤ
VAIt s/he places s.t. in order, s/he arranges s.t. in order

nahāwastēw ᓇᐦᐋᐊᐧᐢᑌᐤ
VII it is placed in order, it is neat and proper

nahāwihtam ᓇᐦᐋᐃᐧᐦᑕᒼ
VTI s/he hears well; s/he hears s.t. well

nahāwihtawēw ᓇᐦᐋᐃᐧᐦᑕᐁᐧᐤ
VTA s/he hears s.o. well

nahāwinikēw ᓇᐦᐋᐃᐧᓂᑫᐤ
VAI s/he is orderly; s/he puts things compactly

nahāwinikēwin ᓇᐦᐋᐃᐧᓂᑫᐃᐧᐣ
NI compact storage (of cargo)

nahēkāc ᓇᐦᐁᑳᐨ
IPC sparingly [*also* nahihkāc]

nahēkācihtāw ᓇᐦᐁᑳᒋᐦᑖᐤ
VAIt s/he is sparing of s.t.

nahēkinam ᓇᐦᐁᑭᓇᒼ
VTI s/he folds s.t. up properly (well)

nahēýihtam ᓇᐦᐁᔨᐦᑕᒼ
VTI s/he is satisfied with s.t., s/he is pleased with s.t., s/he is content

nahēýihtamihēw ᓇᐦᐁᔨᐦᑕᒥᐦᐁᐤ
VTA s/he makes s.o. feel good, at home, s/he makes s.o. feel content [*also* nahēýihtamohēw]

nahēýihtamowin ᓇᐦᐁᔨᐦᑕᒧᐃᐧᐣ
NI contentment; satisfaction

nahēýihtawēýihtam
ᓇᐦᐁᔨᐦᑕᐁᐧᔨᐦᑕᒼ
VTI s/he has good sense in reasoning

nahēýihtākwan ᓇᐦᐁᔩᐦᑖᑿᐣ
VII it is satisfactory, well
nahēýihtowak ᓇᐦᐁᔩᐦᑐᐗᐠ
VAI they agree with one another
nahēýihtowin ᓇᐦᐁᔩᐦᑐᐎᐣ
NI satisfactory agreement
nahēýimēw ᓇᐦᐁᔩᒣᐤ
VTA s/he is fond of s.o., s/he is pleased with s.o.
nahi- ᓇᐦᐃ
IPV well, fair
nahihēw ᓇᐦᐃᐦᐁᐤ
VTA s/he satisfies s.o.
nahihow ᓇᐦᐃᐦᐅᐤ
VAI s/he is satisfied
nahihtam ᓇᐦᐃᐦᑕᒼ
VTI s/he listens well to s.t.; s/he obeys s.t.; s/he heeds s.t.; s/he hears s.t. well
nahihtawēw ᓇᐦᐃᐦᑕᐍᐤ
VTA s/he heeds s.o. well, s/he obeys s.o.
nahihtāhēw ᓇᐦᐃᐦᑖᐦᐁᐤ
VTA s/he makes s.o. listen, s/he makes s.o. pay attention
nahihtātowak ᓇᐦᐃᐦᑖᑐᐗᐠ
VAI they heed well one another's speech
nahikāpawiw ᓇᐦᐃᑳᐸᐏᐤ
VAI s/he stands in position
nahikāpawīstawēw ᓇᐦᐃᑳᐸᐑᐢᑕᐍᐤ
VTA s/he stands in place by s.o.; he acts as s.o.'s best man at a wedding [*see also* nīpawīstawēw]
nahikohtākanēmow ᓇᐦᐃᑯᐦᑖᑲᓀᒧᐤ
VAI s/he clears his/her throat
nahinam ᓇᐦᐃᓇᒼ
VTI s/he buries s.t.
nahinēw ᓇᐦᐃᓀᐤ
VTA s/he buries s.o.; s/he has a funeral for s.o.; s/he puts s.o. in place
nahinikēwin ᓇᐦᐃᓂᑫᐎᐣ
NI burial
nahipaýiw ᓇᐦᐃᐸᔩᐤ
VAI s/he has things work properly
nahipaýiw ᓇᐦᐃᐸᔩᐤ
VII it fits well (*e.g.* a door on a frame)
nahisin ᓇᐦᐃᓯᐣ
VAI s/he lies properly, comfortably; it fits well in something
nahiskam ᓇᐦᐃᐢᑲᒼ
VTI s/he has s.t. fit well, s/he fits s.t. well; s/he looks nice in s.t.; s/he looks nicely dressed; s/he wears s.t. becomingly
nahiskawēw ᓇᐦᐃᐢᑲᐍᐤ
VTA s/he has s.o. fit well, s/he fits s.o. well; s/he looks nice in s.o. (*e.g.* pants); s/he looks nicely dressed; s/he wears s.o. becomingly (*e.g.* pants); s/he looks good with s.o.
nahiskātomakanwa ᓇᐦᐃᐢᑳᑐᒪᑲᓈ
VII they match, they look nice together [*pl generally*]
nahiskātomakisiwak ᓇᐦᐃᐢᑳᑐᒪᑭᓯᐗᐠ
VAI they match, they look nice together [*pl generally; said of objects, not people or animals*]
nahiskātowak ᓇᐦᐃᐢᑳᑐᐗᐠ
VAI they match (people), they look good together
nahitāk ᓇᐦᐃᑖᐠ
IPC just in time, by chance
nahitōtam ᓇᐦᐃᑑᑕᒼ
VTI s/he does s.t. carefully or accurately
nahiýikohk ᓇᐦᐃᔩᑯᕽ
IPC to the proper degree, to the proper extent, just enough, just right, fittingly, appropriately; exact quantity, exact number; evenly; better
nahītikitiw ᓇᐦᐄᑎᑭᑎᐤ
VAI s/he is of an exact size, s/he is just the right size
nahīw ᓇᐦᐄᐤ
VAI s/he is good (at something); s/he is often right on the mark
nahkawēw ᓇᐦᑲᐍᐤ
VAI s/he speaks Saulteaux
nahkawēwin ᓇᐦᑲᐍᐎᐣ
NI speaking Saulteaux, the Saulteaux language
nahkawimow ᓇᐦᑲᐏᒧᐤ
VAI s/he speaks Saulteaux
nahkawiskwēw ᓇᐦᑲᐏᐢᑵᐤ
NA Saulteaux woman
nahkawiýiniw ᓇᐦᑲᐏᔨᓂᐤ
NA Saulteaux, Ojibway; Saulteaux person, Ojibway person [*also* nahkawīnaw]
nahkawiýinīnāhk ᓇᐦᑲᐏᔨᓃᓈᕽ
INM Saulteaux country, Saulteaux reserve; Ojibway country
nahkawiýinīs ᓇᐦᑲᐏᔨᓃᐢ
NA little Saulteaux [*dim*]
nahkawiýinīwiw ᓇᐦᑲᐏᔨᓃᐏᐤ
VAI s/he is a Saulteaux Indian
nahkwan ᓇᐦᑿᐣ
NDI my heel
nahkwanēyāpiy ᓇᐦᑿᓀᔮᐱᕀ
NDI my achilles tendon, tendon at back of my heel
nahkwanikan ᓇᐦᑿᓂᑲᐣ
NDI my heelbone
nahtā- ᓇᐦᑖ
IPV able; good at, competent, practised, experienced, skillful at, expert at, known as one who does s.t. habitually; well [*cf.* nihtā-]
nakacihēw ᓇᑲᒋᐦᐁᐤ
VTA s/he is familiar with s.o.'s character, s/he knows s.o. well, s/he is able to get along with s.o. through proper observation of his/her character; s/he observes s.o. well
nakacihiwēwin ᓇᑲᒋᐦᐃᐍᐎᐣ
NI the ability to read people and get along with them
nakacihtāw ᓇᑲᒋᐦᑖᐤ
VAIt s/he knows well how to do s.t., s/he is familiar with doing s.t., s/he is practised at s.t., s/he is skilled (through experience); s/he is used to s.t.'s ways
nakacipahēw ᓇᑲᒋᐸᐦᐁᐤ
VTA s/he runs away from s.o.; s/he leaves s.o. alone, behind by running; s/he outdistances s.o.
nakacipiciscikātēw ᓇᑲᒋᐱᒋᐢᒋᑳᑌᐤ
VII it is left when camp is moved, it is moved away from
nakacipicistam ᓇᑲᒋᐱᒋᐢᑕᒼ
VTI s/he moves camp leaving s.t. behind
nakacipicistawēw ᓇᑲᒋᐱᒋᐢᑕᐍᐤ
VTA s/he moves camp leaving s.o. behind
nakahāskwān ᓇᑲᐦᐋᐢᒁᐣ
NA shield [*see also* pahpahāhkwān]
nakahcāw ᓇᑲᐦᒑᐤ
NI steep hill, cliff
nakahcāw ᓇᑲᐦᒑᐤ
VII it is a steep hill, it is a cliff
nakahpēhan ᓇᑲᐦᐯᐦᐊᐣ
VII there is a west wind
nakahpēhanohk ᓇᑲᐦᐯᐦᐊᓄᕽ
IPC west, in the west [*loc*]
nakamow ᓇᑲᒧᐤ
VAI s/he sings [*cf.* nikamow]
nakasitowak ᓇᑲᓯᑐᐗᐠ
VAI they leave one another behind, each in turn; they race [*cf.* nakatitowak]
nakasiwēw ᓇᑲᓯᐍᐤ
VAI s/he is ahead; s/he outdistances people, s/he outruns everyone
nakatahwēw ᓇᑲᑕᐦᐍᐤ
VTA s/he leaves s.o. behind by canoe, boat, car
nakatam ᓇᑲᑕᒼ
VTI s/he leaves s.t., s/he abandons s.t., s/he leaves s.t. behind; s/he goes away from s.t.

nakatamawēw ᓇᑲᑕᒪᐍᐤ
VTA s/he leaves (it/him) behind for s.o.

nakataskēw ᓇᑲᑕᐢᑫᐤ
VAI s/he leaves the earth behind, s/he departs the world, s/he dies

nakatēw ᓇᑲᑌᐤ
VTA s/he leaves s.o., s/he abandons s.o., s/he leaves s.o. behind; s/he goes away from s.o.; s/he dies and leaves s.o. behind

nakatisahwēw ᓇᑲᑎᓴᐦᐍᐤ
VTA s/he sends s.o. away; s/he drives s.o. to leave, s/he forces s.o. to leave

nakatisamawēw ᓇᑲᑎᓴᒪᐍᐤ
VTA s/he drives (it/him) away for s.o.

nakatisihtam ᓇᑲᑎᓯᐦᑕᒼ
VTI s/he leaves s.t. lying

nakatisimēw ᓇᑲᑎᓯᒣᐤ
VTA s/he leaves s.o. lying

nakatitowak ᓇᑲᑎᑐᐘᐠ
VAI they race one another [*cf.* nakasitowak]

nakaýāhēw ᓇᑲᔮᐦᐁᐤ
VTA s/he tames s.o., s/he trains s.o., s/he breaks s.o. (*e.g.* horse); s/he gets s.o. accustomed to something

nakaýāskam ᓇᑲᔮᐢᑲᒼ
VTI s/he is used to s.t., s/he is accustomed to s.t., s/he is comfortable with s.t.

nakaýāskawēw ᓇᑲᔮᐢᑲᐍᐤ
VTA s/he is used to s.o., s/he is familiar with s.o.; s/he is accustomed to s.o., s/he is comfortable with s.o.

nakācikanēhpicikan ᓇᑳᒋᑲᓀᐦᐱᒋᑲᐣ
NI martingale [*forked strap of a horse's harness passing from the noseband to the girth between the forelegs*]

nakāhikana ᓇᑳᐦᐃᑲᓇ
NI brakes [*pl*]

nakāhtwāw ᓇᑳᐦᑤᐤ
VAI s/he wins

nakānam ᓇᑳᓇᒼ
VTI s/he holds s.t. back [*cf.* nakinam]

nakānēw ᓇᑳᓀᐤ
VTA s/he stops s.o.; s/he detains s.o. [*cf.* nakinēw]

nakānikan ᓇᑳᓂᑲᐣ
NI fence, gate; stopper [*see also* mēnikan]

nakāpitam ᓇᑳᐱᑕᒼ
VTI s/he pulls s.t. to a stop

nakāpitēw ᓇᑳᐱᑌᐤ
VTA s/he pulls s.o. to a stop

nakāsin ᓇᑳᓯᐣ
VAI s/he is unable to continue because of blockage; s/he stops [*wC*: nakisin]

nakāwāskwēsinam ᓇᑳᐚᐢᑵᓯᓇᒼ
VTI s/he stops dead from running into s.t.

nakēhkwasow ᓇᑫᐦᑿᓱᐤ
VAI s/he is stopped from going further by fire

nakēstiw ᓇᑫᐢᑎᐤ
VAI s/he stops

nakēwihēw ᓇᑫᐏᐦᐁᐤ
VTA s/he stops s.o. from leaving by blocking the way

naki- ᓇᑭ
IPV stopping

nakinam ᓇᑭᓇᒼ
VTI s/he stops s.t. [*cf.* nakānam]

nakinēw ᓇᑭᓀᐤ
VTA s/he stops s.o. [*cf.* nakānēw]

nakipaýiw ᓇᑭᐸᔨᐤ
VAI s/he stops travelling, s/he stops driving

nakinikēw ᓇᑭᓂᑫᐤ
VAI s/he stops things

nakipaýiw ᓇᑭᐸᔨᐤ
VII it stops working (automatically)

nakipicikēw ᓇᑭᐱᒋᑫᐤ
VAI s/he stops his/her team; s/he stops machinery

nakiskam ᓇᑭᐢᑲᒼ
VTI s/he meets s.t. [*cf.* nakiskātēw]

nakiskamohtahēw ᓇᑭᐢᑲᒧᐦᑕᐦᐁᐤ
VTA s/he introduces s.o.

nakiskawēw ᓇᑭᐢᑲᐍᐤ
VTA s/he meets s.o., s/he encounters s.o. [*imperative form used as an introductory exclamation*: nakiskaw ... "meet ..."]

nakiskākēw ᓇᑭᐢᑳᑫᐤ
VAI s/he meets people

nakiskātam ᓇᑭᐢᑳᑕᒼ
VTI s/he meets s.t. [*cf.* nakiskam]

nakiskātowak ᓇᑭᐢᑳᑐᐘᐠ
VAI they meet one another

nakiskātowin ᓇᑭᐢᑳᑐᐏᐣ
NI meeting (one another)

nakiskotātowak ᓇᑭᐢᑯᑖᑐᐘᐠ
VAI they meet one another unexpectedly

nakīstam ᓇᑮᐢᑕᒼ
VTI s/he stops before s.t., s/he stops by s.t., s/he stops for s.t.

nakīstawēw ᓇᑮᐢᑕᐍᐤ
VTA s/he stops before s.o., s/he stops by s.o., s/he stops for s.o.

nakīw ᓇᑮᐤ
VAI s/he stops, s/he comes to a stop; s/he parks

nakīwaciy ᓇᑮᐘᒋᐩ
NI Sweetgrass Reserve, SK [*lit*: "hill's end"]

nakīwacīhk ᓇᑮᐘᒌᕽ
INM Sweetgrass Reserve, SK [*loc*; *lit*: "at hill's end"]

nakīwin ᓇᑮᐏᐣ
NI stop, stopping place

nakwataýēhpicikan ᓇᑿᑕᔦᐦᐱᒋᑲᐣ
NI girth, belly band (of horse's harness)

nakwākan ᓇᒁᑲᐣ
NI snare [*see also* tāpakwān]

nakwāsow ᓇᒁᓱᐤ
VAI s/he is snared, s/he is stopped by a snare

nakwātēw ᓇᒁᑌᐤ
VTA s/he snares s.o.

nakwātisow ᓇᒁᑎᓱᐤ
VAI s/he snares him/herself, s/he catches him/herself in a snare

nama ᓇᒪ
IPC not [*negator in nominal phrases*]

nama awiya ᓇᒪ ᐊᐏᔭ
PR no-one, nobody [*anim obv; also* nam āwiya]

nama awiyak ᓇᒪ ᐊᐏᔭᐠ
PR no-one, nobody [*anim prox; also* nam āwiyak]

nama cī ᓇᒪ ᒌ
IPH is it not the case? isn't it that? wasn't that so? right [*predicative*; *cf.* ma cī]

nama kīkway ᓇᒪ ᑮᑿᐩ
IPH nothing; not at all; there is none [*predicative*; *cf.* ma kīkway, namōya kīkway, namakīkwāw]

nama mayaw ᓇᒪ ᒪᔭᐤ
IPH not soon enough; not immediately, later

nama nānitaw ᓇᒪ ᓈᓂᑕᐤ
IPH not much, not anything; nothing; that's alright

nama wīhkāc ᓇᒪ ᐑᐦᑳᐨ
IPH never [*cf.* namōya wīhkāc]

namahcīhk ᓇᒪᐦᒌᕽ
IPC left; the left side; to the left [*cf.* namahtinihk]

namahcīs ᓇᒪᐦᒌᐢ
NA lefthander, left-handed person

namahcīw ᓇᒪᐦᒌᐤ
VAI s/he is left-handed

namahcīwin ᓇᒪᐦᒌᐏᐣ
NI left-handedness

namahcīwiýiniw ᓇᒪᐦᒌᐏᔨᓂᐤ
NA lefthander

namahtin ᓇᒪᐦᑎᐣ
IPC left side, the left one

namahtinihk ᓇᒪᐦᑎᓂᕽ
IPC left, on the left, at the left; the left side [*cf.* namahcīhk]

namahtinisk ᓇᒪᐦᑎᓂᐢᐠ
NI left hand

namakīkwāw ᓇᒪᑮᑳᐤ
VII it disappears, it is nothing [*cf.* nama kīkway]
namakīkwāýiwiw ᓇᒪᑮᑳᔨᐏᐤ
VAI s/he comes to nothing
namastēw ᓇᒪᐢᑌᐤ
VII it is wrong, incorrect
namatakon ᓇᒪᑕᑯᐣ
VII it is absent, it is gone; it disappears
namatēw ᓇᒪᑌᐤ
VAI s/he is absent, s/he is gone; s/he is nonexistent, s/he has disappeared; s/he disappears
namayēw ᓇᒪᔦᐤ
VAI s/he did not arrive on time; s/he did not accomplish his/her task in time
namayēw ᓇᒪᔦᐤ
VII it did not occur in time
namēhpin ᓇᒣᐦᐱᐣ
NI wild ginger
namēhtāw ᓇᒣᐦᑖᐤ
VAI s/he leaves tracks
namēkos ᓇᒣᑯᐢ
NA lake trout
namēkosis ᓇᒣᑯᓯᐢ
NA small fish; small trout [*dim*]
namēkosiskāw ᓇᒣᑯᓯᐢᑳᐤ
VII there are many trout
namēpiñ ᓇᒣᐱᐣ
NA suckerfish [*sC and pC*; *cf. wC*: namīpith, namīpin; *cf.* namēpiý *in some areas of pC*]
namēpiý ᓇᒣᐱᕀ
NA sucker; carp [*cf.* namēpiñ]
namēpīsis ᓇᒣᐲᓯᐢ
NA small sucker [*dim*; *also* namēpisis]
namēs ᓇᒣᐢ
NA fish; small sturgeon [*dim*; *cf.* namēw]
namēsiwan ᓇᒣᓯᐘᐣ
VII there are sturgeon
namēskwa ᓇᒣᐢᑿ
IPC not yet [*cf.* namoýa cēskwa]
namēstēk ᓇᒣᐢᑌᐠ
NA dried fish; fillets, sucker fillets [*pl*: -wak]
namēstēkohkēw ᓇᒣᐢᑌᑯᐦᑫᐤ
VAI s/he makes dried fish; s/he makes fillets, s/he makes sucker fillets
namēw ᓇᒣᐤ
NA sturgeon
namikēstawēw ᓇᒥᑫᐢᑕᐍᐤ
VTA s/he curtsies for s.o.
namikēýiw ᓇᒥᑫᔦᐤ
VAI s/he curtsies
naminās ᓇᒥᓈᐢ
NI syrup; molasses [*French loan*: "la mélasse"]
namipaýihow ᓇᒥᐸᔨᐦᐅᐤ
VAI s/he shakes him/herself; s/he shivers [*rdpl generally*: nanamipaýihow]
namipaýiw ᓇᒥᐸᔨᐤ
VAI s/he shakes, s/he shivers [*rdpl generally*: nanamipaýiw]
namipaýiw ᓇᒥᐸᔨᐤ
VII it shakes [*rdpl generally*: nanamipaýiw]
namiskwēstawēw ᓇᒥᐢᑵᐢᑕᐍᐤ
VTA s/he nods to s.o. [*rdpl generally*: nanamiskwēstawēw]
namiskwēýiw ᓇᒥᐢᑵᔨᐤ
VAI s/he puts his/her own head down
namīpithi-sīpīhk ᓇᒦᐱᖨ ᓰᐲᕽ
INM Sucker River, SK [*loc*; *wC community*; *cf.* namēpiñ]
namīwi-sākahikanihk ᓇᒦᐏ ᓵᑲᐦᐃᑲᓂᕽ
INM Sturgeon Lake, SK [*loc*; *wC community*; *cf.* namēw *NA*]
namīwi-sīpīhk ᓇᒦᐏ ᓰᐲᕽ
INM Sturgeon Landing, SK [*loc*; *lit*: "at sturgeon lake"; *wC community*; *cf.* namēw *NA*]
namōy ᓇᒨᕀ
IPC not [*in independent clauses*; *cf.* mōy, mōýa, namōýa]
namōy wīhkāc ᓇᒨᕀ ᐑᐦᑳᐨ
IPH never [*cf.* namōýa wīhkāc]
namōýa ᓇᒨᔭ
IPC no; not [*negator in independent and certain conjunct clauses*; *cf.* mōy, mōýa, namōy; *wC*: namōtha, *sC*: namōña]
namōýa ahpō ᓇᒨᔭ ᐊᐦᐴ
IPH not even
namōýa apisīs ᓇᒨᔭ ᐊᐱᓰᐢ
IPH not a little, quite a bit
namōýa awiyak ᓇᒨᔭ ᐊᐏᔭᐠ
PR no-one, nobody [*cf.* nama awiyak]
namōýa cēskwa ᓇᒨᔭ ᒉᐢᑿ
IPH not yet [*cf.* mōy cēskwa]
namōýa cī ᓇᒨᔭ ᒌ
IPH could it be? is it not?
namōýa ēkwaýikohk ᓇᒨᔭ ᐁᑿᔨᑯᕽ
IPH not so, not as much, not that much [*negative comparative*]
namōýa kakētihk ᓇᒨᔭ ᑲᑫᑎᕽ
IPH extremely, a great deal, a great many
namōýa kīkway ᓇᒨᔭ ᑮᑿᕀ
PR nothing, none [*cf.* ma kīkway, nama kīkway]
namōýa nānitaw ᓇᒨᔭ ᓈᓂᑕᐤ
IPH fine, I'm fine, all right, okay; insignificant, of little account; nowhere [*cf.* nama nānitaw]
namōýa nānitawitē ᓇᒨᔭ ᓈᓂᑕᐏᑌ
IPH nowhere
namōýa wāpiw ᓇᒨᔭ ᐚᐱᐤ
VAI s/he is blind [*neg*; *see also* pāskāpiw; *cf.* wāpiw]
namōýa wiýa ᓇᒨᔭ ᐏᔭ
IPH not him, not her
namōýa wīhkāc ᓇᒨᔭ ᐑᐦᑳᐨ
IPH never [*cf.* namōý wīhkāc]
namwāc ᓇᒹᐨ
IPC not; by no means, not at all [*cf.* mwāc, mwāt]
namwāc ēkwaýikohk ᓇᒹᐨ ᐁᑿᔨᑯᕽ
IPH not so, not as much, not that much [*negative comparative*]
nanahihtam ᓇᓇᐦᐃᐦᑕᒼ
VTI s/he listens obediently to s.t., s/he listens well to s.t.; s/he obeys s.t.; s/he hears well, s/he has good hearing [*rdpl*]
nanahihtawēw ᓇᓇᐦᐃᐦᑕᐍᐤ
VTA s/he listens well to s.o.; s/he obeys s.o. [*rdpl*]
nanahihtāw ᓇᓇᐦᐃᐦᑖᐤ
VAIt s/he puts s.t. in order, s/he makes s.t. look tidy [*rdpl*]
nanamaciw ᓇᓇᒪᒋᐤ
VAI s/he shivers with cold, s/he is shivering
nanamaskamikēpaýiw ᓇᓇᒪᐢᑲᒥᑫᐸᔨᐤ
VII there is an earthquake; the earth trembles
nanamāspinēw ᓇᓇᒫᐢᐱᓀᐤ
VAI s/he has palsy
nanamāspinēwin ᓇᓇᒫᐢᐱᓀᐏᐣ
NI palsy (a sickness)
nanamāstan ᓇᓇᒫᐢᑕᐣ
VII it is shaken by the wind
nanamipaýiw ᓇᓇᒥᐸᔨᐤ
VAI s/he shakes; s/he has his/her entire body shake
nanamipaýīs ᓇᓇᒥᐸᔩᐢ
NI jelly [*dim*]
nanamipitam ᓇᓇᒥᐱᑕᒼ
VTI s/he shakes s.t.
nanamipitēw ᓇᓇᒥᐱᑌᐤ
VTA s/he shakes s.o.
nanamiskwēstawēw ᓇᓇᒥᐢᑵᐢᑕᐍᐤ
VTA s/he bows to s.o. (with the head only like a nod); s/he bows his/her own head to s.o.
nanamiskwēýiw ᓇᓇᒥᐢᑵᔨᐤ
VAI s/he nods his/her own head, s/he shakes his/her own head
nanamitāpiskanēw ᓇᓇᒥᑖᐱᐢᑲᓀᐤ
VAI s/he has his/her own jaw tremble

nanamitāpiskanēwaciw ᓇᓇᒥᑖᐱᐢᑲᓀᐊᐧᒋᐤ
VAI s/he has his/her own jaw tremble from cold

nanamwēw ᓇᓇᒣᐧᐤ
VAI s/he stutters [*see also* nānakiwēpaýiw]

nanapakicihciy ᓇᓇᐸᑭᒋᐦᒋᕀ
NA bear [*rdpl*; *lit*: "flatpaw"]

nanapotōkanēskawēw ᓇᓇᐳᑑᑲᓀᐢᑲᐁᐧᐤ
VTA s/he kicks s.o.'s rump crooked [*rdpl*]

nanapotōkanēw ᓇᓇᐳᑑᑲᓀᐤ
VAI s/he has a crooked rump [*rdpl*]

nanayēhtāwipaýiw ᓇᓇᔦᐦᑖᐃᐧᐸᔨᐤ
VAI s/he suffers misfortune, s/he has a breakdown [*wC*: nanahīhtāwipathiw]

nanayēhtāwipaýiwin ᓇᓇᔦᐦᑖᐃᐧᐸᔨᐃᐧᐣ
NI misfortune, breakdown [*wC*: nanahīhtāwipathiwin]

nanācohkikwācēs ᓇᓈᒍᐦᑭᑳᐧᒉᐢ
NI patchwork quilt [*dim*]

nanānis ᓇᓈᓂᐢ
IPC among; in various places, in various directions, in all directions

nanāniscipaýiw ᓇᓈᓂᐢᒋᐸᔨᐤ
VAI s/he breaks apart in pieces

nanāniscipitam ᓇᓈᓂᐢᒋᐱᑕᒼ
VTI s/he pulls s.t. into bits

nanāniscipitēw ᓇᓈᓂᐢᒋᐱᑌᐤ
VTA s/he pulls s.o. into pieces, bits

nanānistinam ᓇᓈᓂᐢᑎᓇᒼ
VTI s/he takes s.t. apart

nanānistinēw ᓇᓈᓂᐢᑎᓀᐤ
VTA s/he takes s.o. apart (as a clock)

nanāskomēw ᓇᓈᐢᑯᒣᐤ
VTA s/he thanks s.o., s/he gives thanks to s.o., s/he is grateful to s.o., s/he speaks words of thanks to s.o. [*cf.* kinanāskomitin "thank you"]

nanāskomow ᓇᓈᐢᑯᒧᐤ
VAI s/he is grateful, s/he is thankful; s/he gives thanks, s/he expresses thanks

nanāskomowin ᓇᓈᐢᑯᒧᐃᐧᐣ
NI thankfulness, gratitude

nanāskotam ᓇᓈᐢᑯᑕᒼ
VTI s/he is thankful (for s.t.)

nanāspisihtāw ᓇᓈᐢᐱᓯᐦᑖᐤ
VAIt s/he copies s.t. [*rdpl*]

nanātatwēwēmēw ᓇᓈᑕᑌᐧᐁᐧᒣᐤ
VTA s/he calls for his/her spirit helper by song

nanātawāpahtam ᓇᓈᑕᐋᐧᐸᐦᑕᒼ
VTI s/he looks for s.t., s/he search for s.t.; s/he looks out for s.t. [*rdpl*]

nanātawāpamēw ᓇᓈᑕᐋᐧᐸᒣᐤ
VTA s/he looks around for s.o., s/he searches for s.o.; s/he looks out for s.o. [*rdpl*]

nanātawāpiw ᓇᓈᑕᐋᐧᐱᐤ
VAI s/he looks around [*rdpl*]

nanātawāpōhkān ᓇᓈᑕᐋᐧᐴᐦᑳᐣ
NI medicinal drink

nanātawāpōhkēw ᓇᓈᑕᐋᐧᐴᐦᑫᐤ
VAI s/he prepares a medicinal drink

nanātawihēw ᓇᓈᑕᐃᐧᐦᐁᐤ
VTA s/he treats s.o. (medically); s/he doctors s.o., s/he heals s.o.

nanātawihisow ᓇᓈᑕᐃᐧᐦᐃᓱᐤ
VAI s/he doctors him/herself

nanātawihitowin ᓇᓈᑕᐃᐧᐦᐃᑐᐃᐧᐣ
NI doctoring, healing

nanātawihiwākēw ᓇᓈᑕᐃᐧᐦᐃᐋᐧᑫᐤ
VAI s/he doctors people with something, s/he uses something to doctor people

nanātawihiwēw ᓇᓈᑕᐃᐧᐦᐃᐁᐧᐤ
VAI s/he treats people, s/he heals people, s/he doctors people

nanātawihiwēwin ᓇᓈᑕᐃᐧᐦᐃᐁᐧᐃᐧᐣ
NI doctoring; healing (day after day for a long time)

nanātawihow ᓇᓈᑕᐃᐧᐦᐅᐤ
VAI s/he treats him/herself (medically); s/he doctors him/herself, s/he heals him/herself

nanātawihowin ᓇᓈᑕᐃᐧᐦᐅᐃᐧᐣ
NI remedy; curing ceremony; healing

nanātawimēw ᓇᓈᑕᐃᐧᒣᐤ
VTA s/he examines s.o.

nanātohk ᓇᓈᑐᕽ
IPC different, variously, all kinds, of various kinds, different items

nanātohk isi ᓇᓈᑐᕽ ᐃᓯ
IPH in various ways

nanātohk kīkway ᓇᓈᑐᕽ ᑮᑲᐧᕀ
IPH different, all kinds of things

nanātohkinākwan ᓇᓈᑐᐦᑭᓈᑲᐧᐣ
VII it is many-coloured

nanātohkisiwak ᓇᓈᑐᐦᑭᓯᐊᐧᐠ
VAI they are many different kinds [*pl*]

nanātohkokwāsow ᓇᓈᑐᐦᑯᑳᐧᓱᐤ
VAI s/he sews patchwork blankets

nanātohkomēw ᓇᓈᑐᐦᑯᒣᐤ
VTA s/he teases s.o. (by joking and talking); s/he says all kinds of things to s.o.; s/he is verbally cheeky to s.o.

nanātohkōskān ᓇᓈᑐᐦᑰᐢᑳᐣ
IPC all kinds of things, different kinds

nanātohkwāpakwanīw ᓇᓈᑐᐦᑳᐧᐸᑲᐧᓃᐤ
VII it has many-coloured flowers

nanātostahikēw ᓇᓈᑐᐢᑕᐦᐃᑫᐤ
VAI s/he uses different stitches

nanēhtahkāw ᓇᓀᐦᑕᐦᑳᐤ
VII it is twilight

nanimaham ᓇᓂᒪᐦᐊᒼ
VTI s/he canoes against the wind

naniway ᓇᓂᐊᐧᕀ
NDI my cheek [*also* nanaway]

naniwēyitwēw ᓇᓂᐁᐧᔨᑌᐧᐤ
VAI s/he jokes, s/he tells a joke

nanīcikanēw ᓇᓃᒋᑲᓀᐤ
VAI s/he has lumps on his/her joints

nanīmiskam ᓇᓃᒥᐢᑲᒼ
VTI s/he walks against the wind

nanīsānan ᓇᓃᓵᓇᐣ
VII it is difficult [*archaic*]

nanīskāpiw ᓇᓃᐢᑳᐱᐤ
VAI s/he has watery eyes

nanōcihēw ᓇᓅᒋᐦᐁᐤ
VTA s/he whips s.o., s/he punishes s.o. physically [*rdpl*]

nanōcihtāw ᓇᓅᒋᐦᑖᐤ
VAIt s/he whips s.t.; s/he works hard at s.t. [*rdpl*]

nanōsawāpamēw ᓇᓅᓴᐋᐧᐸᒣᐤ
VTA s/he escorts s.o., s/he accompanies s.o. a ways as that one departs

nanōýacihēw ᓇᓅᔭᒋᐦᐁᐤ
VTA s/he teases s.o.

nanōýacihitowak ᓇᓅᔭᒋᐦᐃᑐᐊᐧᐠ
VAI they tease one another

nanwēýacihēw ᓇᓀᐧᔭᒋᐦᐁᐤ
VTA s/he harrasses s.o.; s/he provokes s.o.

nanwēýacihitowak ᓇᓀᐧᔭᒋᐦᐃᑐᐊᐧᐠ
VAI they harrass one another

napakamēkos ᓇᐸᑲᒣᑯᐢ
NA gold eye (fish)

napakaskisin ᓇᐸᑲᐢᑭᓯᐣ
NI flat moccasin, flat shoe

napakastāw ᓇᐸᑲᐢᑖᐤ
VAIt s/he places s.t. flat, upside down

napakataham ᓇᐸᑲᑕᐦᐊᒼ
VTI s/he flattens s.t. with a stick, s/he pounds s.t. flat

napakatayēw ᓇᐸᑲᑕᔦᐤ
VAI s/he has a flat belly

napakāhtik ᓇᐸᑳᐦᑎᐠ
NA plank; toboggan [*pl*: -wak]

napakāhtik ᓇᐸᑳᐦᑎᐠ
NI flat board, sled [*pl*: -wa]

napakāpiskāw ᓇᐸᑳᐱᐢᑳᐤ
VII it is a flat metal

napakāpiskisiw ᓇᐸᑳᐱᐢᑭᓯᐤ
VAI it is a flat stone, it is a flat metal

napakāsiht ᓇᐸᑳᓯᐦᐟ
NA balsam pine; cedar [*cf.* sihta, napakāsihtak]

napakāsihtak ᓇᐸᑳᓯᐦᑕᐠ
NA balsam pine, silver pine [*pl*: -wak; *also* napakosistak]

napakāsihtak ᓇᐸᑳᓯᐦᑕᐠ
NI cedar plank [*pl*: -wa]

napakāsin ᓇᐸᑳᓯᐣ
VII it is rather flat [*dim*]

napakāskitiýēw ᓇᐸᑳᐢᑭᑎᔦᐤ
VAI s/he has flat buttocks

napakāw ᓇᐸᑳᐤ
VII it is flat

napakēyāpiy ᓇᐸᑫᔮᐱᕀ
NA belt [*see also* pakwahtēhon]

napaki- ᓇᐸᑭ
IPV flat

napakihkomān ᓇᐸᑭᐦᑯᒫᐣ
NI flat (two edged) knife (for war)

napakihtak ᓇᐸᑭᐦᑕᐠ
NI board, flat lumber, flat wooden object [*pl*: -wa]

napakikamik ᓇᐸᑭᑲᒥᐠ
NI wall tent [*pl*: -wa]

napakikamikos ᓇᐸᑭᑲᒥᑯᐢ
NI flat-roofed log-house, small wall tent [*dim*]

napakikotēw ᓇᐸᑭᑯᑌᐤ
VAI s/he has a flat nose

napakinam ᓇᐸᑭᓇᒼ
VTI s/he makes s.t. flat, s/he flattens s.t., s/he presses s.t. flat

napakinēw ᓇᐸᑭᓀᐤ
VTA s/he flattens s.o., s/he presses s.o. flat

napakisam ᓇᐸᑭᓴᒼ
VTI s/he cuts s.t. flat (*e.g.* meat into chops)

napakisin ᓇᐸᑭᓯᐣ
VAI s/he lies flat, prone

napakisitēw ᓇᐸᑭᓯᑌᐤ
VAI s/he has flat feet, s/he is flat-footed

napakisiw ᓇᐸᑭᓯᐤ
VAI s/he is flat

napakistikwān ᓇᐸᑭᐢᑎᒁᐣ
NA Flathead Indian

napakitāpānāsk ᓇᐸᑭᑖᐹᓈᐢᐠ
NA toboggan, sled [*pl*: -wak]

napakiýākan ᓇᐸᑭᔮᑲᐣ
NI plate, flat dish

napakiýākanis ᓇᐸᑭᔮᑲᓂᐢ
NI saucer, bread and butter plate [*dim*]

napatāk ᓇᐸᑖᐠ
NI potato [*pl*: -wa; *French loan*: "la patate"; *pl generally*: napatākwa]

napatē ᓇᐸᑌ
IPC on one side; one side, sideways

napatē-nipowipaýiw ᓇᐸᑌ ᓂᐳᐏᐸᔨᐤ
VAI s/he is becoming paralyzed on one side

napatēcihcēw ᓇᐸᑌᒋᐦᒉᐤ
VAI s/he has only one hand

napatēhkasikan ᓇᐸᑌᐦᑲᓯᑲᐣ
NA pie (single crust)

napatēhkāpiw ᓇᐸᑌᐦᑳᐱᐤ
VAI s/he winks one eye, s/he squints one eye

napatēhkāpīstawēw ᓇᐸᑌᐦᑳᐲᐢᑕᐍᐤ
VTA s/he winks at s.o.

napatēkām ᓇᐸᑌᑳᒼ
IPC on one bank

napatēkātēw ᓇᐸᑌᑳᑌᐤ
VAI s/he has only one leg

napatēnisk ᓇᐸᑌᓂᐢᐠ
IPC with one arm, at one arm

napatēniskēw ᓇᐸᑌᓂᐢᑫᐤ
VAI s/he uses one arm

napatēpitonēw ᓇᐸᑌᐱᑐᓀᐤ
VAI s/he has only one arm

napatēpocikan ᓇᐸᑌᐳᒋᑲᐣ
NI plane, planer

napatēstāwikēw ᓇᐸᑌᐢᑖᐏᑫᐤ
VAI s/he builds a lean-to

napatēyāpiw ᓇᐸᑌᔮᐱᐤ
VAI s/he looks with one eye; s/he has only one eye

napatēyāsiw ᓇᐸᑌᔮᓯᐤ
VAI s/he is blown to one side

napatēyāstan ᓇᐸᑌᔮᐢᑕᐣ
VII it is blown to one side

napācihēw ᓇᐹᒋᐦᐁᐤ
VTA s/he fixes s.o., s/he repairs s.o. [*cf.* nānapācihēw]

napācihtāw ᓇᐹᒋᐦᑖᐤ
VAIt s/he fixes s.t., s/he repairs s.t. [*cf.* nānapācihtāw]

napāwi ᓇᐹᐏ
IPC too late [*cf.* nānapāwi, nānapāwisk]

naponam ᓇᐳᓇᒼ
VTI s/he folds s.t. together

naponēw ᓇᐳᓀᐤ
VTA s/he folds s.o. together

napopaýiw ᓇᐳᐸᔨᐤ
VII it folds over (automatically)

napotokan ᓇᐳᑐᑲᐣ
NA knock-kneed person

napotokanēw ᓇᐳᑐᑲᓀᐤ
VAI s/he is knock-kneed

napotōkanēw ᓇᐳᑑᑲᓀᐤ
VAI s/he is crooked at the rump

napotōkanēkocin ᓇᐳᑑᑲᓀᑯᒋᐣ
VAI s/he stalks with crooked rump

napwahpisow ᓇᐘᐦᐱᓱᐤ
VAI s/he is hobbled [*often rdpl*]

napwahpisowin ᓇᐘᐦᐱᓱᐏᐣ
NI hobble

napwahpitēw ᓇᐘᐦᐱᑌᐤ
VTA s/he hobbles s.o. (*e.g.* a horse) [*often rdpl*]

napwēkinam ᓇᐍᑭᓇᒼ
VTI s/he folds s.t. double, s/he folds s.t. in half

napwēkinēw ᓇᐍᑭᓀᐤ
VTA s/he folds s.o. in half

napwēkipitam ᓇᐍᑭᐱᑕᒼ
VTI s/he folds s.t. flat

napwēkipitēw ᓇᐍᑭᐱᑌᐤ
VTA s/he folds s.o. flat

napwēkiskam ᓇᐍᑭᐢᑲᒼ
VTI s/he tramples s.t. up; s/he flattens s.t.

napwēkiskawēw ᓇᐍᑭᐢᑲᐍᐤ
VTA s/he tramples s.o. up; s/he flattens s.o.

napwēn ᓇᐍᐣ
NA frying pan, skillet [*French loan*: "la poele"; *also* nāpwēn; *see also* sāsāpiskisikan, sāsēskihkwān]

napwēnis ᓇᐍᓂᐢ
NA little frying pan [*dim*]

nasakay ᓇᓴᑲᕀ
NDA my skin

nasihkāc ᓇᓯᐦᑳᐨ
IPC slowly [*cf.* nisihkāc]

naskasiy ᓇᐢᑲᓯᕀ
NDA my fingernail; my claw

naskatay ᓇᐢᑲᑕᕀ
NDI my stomach-covering; my abdominal-wall

naskomēw ᓇᐢᑯᒣᐤ
VTA s/he answers s.o.

naskomitowak ᓇᐢᑯᒥᑐᐘᐠ
VAI they answer one another

naskomow ᓇᐢᑯᒧᐤ
VAI s/he responds, s/he answers, s/he makes a verbal response

naskomowin ᓇᐢᑯᒧᐏᐣ
NI answer

naskonēw ᓇᐢᑯᓀᐤ
VTA s/he answers s.o. (favourably)

naskotam ᓇᐢᑯᑕᒼ
VTI s/he answers s.t. (favourably)

naskwahamawēw ᓇᐢᑿᐦᐊᒪᐍᐤ
VTA s/he responds to s.o.; s/he sings in response to s.o.

naskwahamākēw ᓇᐢᑿᐦᐊᒫᑫᐤ
VAI s/he accompanies people (dancers) by song; s/he acts as a back-up singer

naskwāhkēw ᓇᐢᒄᐦᑫᐤ
VAI s/he fights back

naskwāw ᓇᐢᒁᐤ
VAI s/he retaliates, s/he fights back; s/he resists

naskwēham ᓇᐢᑵᐦᐊᒼ
VTI s/he sings to s.t.

naskwēhamawēw ᓇᐢᑵᐦᐊᒪᐍᐤ
VTA s/he sings along with s.o.
naskwēhamākēwin ᓇᐢᑵᐦᐊᒫᑫᐏᐣ
NI response; an accompaniment
naskwēhamātowak ᓇᐢᑵᐦᐊᒫᑐᐘᐠ
VAI they sing together; they accompany one another singing
naskwēhtawēw ᓇᐢᑵᐦᑕᐍᐤ
VTA s/he answers s.o.
naskwēnam ᓇᐢᑵᓇᒼ
VTI s/he catches s.t. as it comes by
naskwēnēw ᓇᐢᑵᓀᐤ
VTA s/he picks s.o. up; s/he catches s.o. as that one comes by
naskwēpitam ᓇᐢᑵᐱᑕᒼ
VTI s/he seizes s.t. as it passes
naskwēpitēw ᓇᐢᑵᐱᑌᐤ
VTA s/he seizes s.o. as that one passes
naskwēwasihtwāwin ᓇᐢᑵᐘᓯᐦᑣᐏᐣ
NI answer
naskwēwasimēw ᓇᐢᑵᐘᓯᒣᐤ
VTA s/he answers s.o.
naspāc ᓇᐢᐹᐨ
IPC opposite; in a different way, contrarily, wrongly
naspāci- ᓇᐢᐹᒋ
IPV opposite, contrarily
naspāci-nihtāwikihāwasow ᓇᐢᐹᒋ ᓂᐦᑖᐏᑭᐦᐋᐘᓱᐤ
VAI she gives birth to a breech baby, she has a breech birth
naspāci-nihtāwikiw ᓇᐢᐹᒋ ᓂᐦᑖᐏᑭᐤ
VAI s/he is a breech birth
naspāciskam ᓇᐢᐹᒋᐢᑲᒼ
VTI s/he wears s.t. the wrong way (*e.g.* shoes on the wrong feet; a coat inside out)
naspācitōtam ᓇᐢᐹᒋᑑᑕᒼ
VTI s/he does s.t. the wrong way
naspātinam ᓇᐢᐹᑎᓇᒼ
VTI s/he holds s.t. the wrong way
naspātinēw ᓇᐢᐹᑎᓀᐤ
VTA s/he holds s.o. the wrong way
naspātiskam ᓇᐢᐹᑎᐢᑲᒼ
VTI s/he wears s.t. inside out
naspātiskawēw ᓇᐢᐹᑎᐢᑲᐍᐤ
VTA s/he wears s.o. inside out
naspitam ᓇᐢᐱᑕᒼ
VTI s/he resembles s.t.
naspitamohisow ᓇᐢᐱᑕᒧᐦᐃᓱᐤ
VAI s/he makes him/herself into a likeness
naspitawēw ᓇᐢᐱᑕᐍᐤ
VTA s/he resembles s.o., s/he bears a resemblence to s.o., s/he looks like s.o.
naspitākēwin ᓇᐢᐱᑖᑫᐏᐣ
NI resemblence
naspitohtam ᓇᐢᐱᑐᐦᑕᒼ
VTI s/he imitates the sound of s.t.
naspitohtawēw ᓇᐢᐱᑐᐦᑕᐍᐤ
VTA s/he imitates the sound of s.o.
nataham ᓇᑕᐦᐊᒼ
VTI s/he canoes upstream, s/he paddles upstream
natahipahtāw ᓇᑕᐦᐃᐸᐦᑖᐤ
VAI s/he runs up river
nataminahow ᓇᑕᒥᓇᐦᐅᐤ
VAI s/he goes on a hunt
natawēýihtam ᓇᑕᐍᔨᐦᑕᒼ
VTI s/he wants s.t. [*cf.* nitawēyihtam]
natawēýihtākosiw ᓇᑕᐍᔨᐦᑖᑯᓯᐤ
VAI s/he is necessary, s/he is required
natawēýihtākwan ᓇᑕᐍᔨᐦᑖᑿᐣ
VII it is necessary, it is required
natawēýimēw ᓇᑕᐍᔨᒣᐤ
VTA s/he wants s.o. [*cf.* nitawēyimēw]
natawi- ᓇᑕᐏ
IPV go to [*cf.* nitawi]
natawi-asamēw ᓇᑕᐏ ᐊᓴᒣᐤ
VTA s/he goes to feed s.o.
natawi-kanawāpahtam ᓇᑕᐏ ᑲᓇᐚᐸᐦᑕᒼ
VTI s/he goes to take a look at s.t.
natawi-kapēsiw ᓇᑕᐏ ᑲᐯᓯᐤ
VAI s/he goes to pitch camp
natay ᓇᑕᕀ
NDI my stomach, my belly [*dim:* nacās]
natayipaýihow ᓇᑕᔨᐸᔨᐦᐅᐤ
VAI it spawns; s/he travels upstream
natimihk ᓇᑎᒥᕽ
IPC upstream, up river; inland; in the west
natimihk isi ᓇᑎᒥᕽ ᐃᓯ
IPH upstream; inland; towards the west
natimīwiýiniwak ᓇᑎᒦᐏᔨᓂᐘᐠ
NA upriver Cree, western Cree; Upstream people [*pl; division of the Cree including* amiskowacīwiýiniwak "Beaver Hills People", paskohkopāwiýiniwak "Parklands People", sīpīwiýiniwak "River People", *and* wāskahikaniwiýiniwak "House People"; *also* natimiýiniwak]
natocikēw ᓇᑐᒋᑫᐤ
VAI s/he asks for things; s/he places an order (for supplies), s/he sends for supplies
natohtam ᓇᑐᐦᑕᒼ
VTI s/he listens to s.t. [*cf.* nitohtam]
natohtawēw ᓇᑐᐦᑕᐍᐤ
VTA s/he listens to s.o. [*cf.* nitohtawēw]
natomācikēw ᓇᑐᒫᒋᑫᐤ
VAI s/he smells around for a scent (as a dog) [*also* natamiyāhcikēw]
natomēw ᓇᑐᒣᐤ
VTA s/he calls s.o., s/he invites s.o., s/he asks s.o. to come [*cf.* nitomēw]
natonam ᓇᑐᓇᒼ
VTI s/he looks for s.t., s/he seeks s.t., s/he searches for s.t. [*cf.* nitonam]
natonawēw ᓇᑐᓇᐍᐤ
VTA s/he looks for s.o., s/he seek s.o., s/he searches for s.o. [*cf.* nitonaw]
natonikēw ᓇᑐᓂᑫᐤ
VAI s/he searches
natopaýiw ᓇᑐᐸᔨᐤ
VAI s/he goes scouting around [*cf.* nitopaýiw]
natopaýiwin ᓇᑐᐸᔨᐏᐣ
NI scouting party
natotam ᓇᑐᑕᒼ
VTI s/he asks for s.t.
natotamawēw ᓇᑐᑕᒪᐍᐤ
VTA s/he asks s.o. for (it/him)
natotamākēw ᓇᑐᑕᒫᑫᐤ
VAI s/he makes a request
nawac ᓇᐘᐨ
IPC by comparison; better, more; before; instead, rather, somewhat [*cf.* nawat]
nawac apisīs ᓇᐘᐨ ᐊᐱᓰᐢ
IPH less
nawac ēkosi ᓇᐘᐨ ᐁᑯᓯ
IPH that's better
nawac ēkosi isi ᓇᐘᐨ ᐁᑯᓯ ᐃᓯ
IPH that's better that way
nawac kwayask ᓇᐘᐨ ᑿᔭᐢᐠ
IPH better
nawac mistahi ᓇᐘᐨ ᒥᐢᑕᐦᐃ
IPH more, even more
nawac piko ᓇᐘᐨ ᐱᑯ
IPH sort of, kind of, approximately; more or less; even a little
nawaci- ᓇᐘᒋ
IPV better
nawacīhisow ᓇᐘᒌᐦᐃᓱᐤ
VAI s/he roasts (it) for him/herself
nawacīstamawēw ᓇᐘᒌᐢᑕᒪᐍᐤ
VTA s/he cooks (it/him) for s.o., s/he roasts (it/him) for s.o.
nawacīstamāsow ᓇᐘᒌᐢᑕᒫᓱᐤ
VAI s/he cooks (it/him) for

him/herself, s/he roasts (it/him) for him/herself
nawacīswēw ᓇᐘᒌᓭᐧᐤ
VTA s/he roasts s.o.
nawacīw ᓇᐘᒌᐤ
VAI s/he roasts s.t., s/he cooks s.t. (*i.e.* in a wood stove or on a fire)
nawacīwātēw ᓇᐘᒌᐚᑌᐤ
VTA s/he makes a roast of s.o., s/he roasts s.o. (*e.g.* rabbit)
nawacīwin ᓇᐘᒌᐏᐣ
NI roast
nawakapiw ᓇᐘᑲᐱᐤ
VAI s/he sits with his/her own head and body bent down
nawakipahtāw ᓇᐘᑭᐸᐦᑖᐤ
VAI s/he runs with his/her own body bent
nawakipaýihow ᓇᐘᑭᐸᔨᐦᐅᐤ
VAI s/he ducks his/her own head, s/he bends down quickly
nawakiskwēnēw ᓇᐘᑭᐢᑫᐧᓀᐤ
VTA s/he bends down s.o.'s head
nawakiskwēpiw ᓇᐘᑭᐢᑫᐧᐱᐤ
VAI s/he sits with his/her own head down
nawakiskwēýiw ᓇᐘᑭᐢᑫᐧᔨᐤ
VAI s/he hangs his/her own head down, s/he bends down his/her own head
nawakīstawēw ᓇᐘᑮᐢᑕᐍᐤ
VTA s/he bows to s.o.
nawakīw ᓇᐘᑮᐤ
VAI s/he bends over, s/he bends down, s/he bends forward; s/he stoops, s/he bends
nawasawāpamow ᓇᐘᓴᐚᐸᒧᐤ
VAI s/he makes his/her choice by sight
nawasōnam ᓇᐘᓲᓇᒼ
VTI s/he chooses s.t.
nawasōnamawēw ᓇᐘᓲᓇᒪᐍᐤ
VTA s/he chooses (it/him) for s.o.; s/he makes a choice for s.o.
nawasōnākan ᓇᐘᓲᓈᑲᐣ
NA chosen person
nawasōnēw ᓇᐘᓲᓀᐤ
VTA s/he chooses s.o.; s/he picks s.o. out
nawasōnikan ᓇᐘᓲᓂᑲᐣ
NI chosen thing
nawasōnikēw ᓇᐘᓲᓂᑫᐤ
VAI s/he chooses
nawasōnikēwin ᓇᐘᓲᓂᑫᐏᐣ
NI choosing
nawaswāsiwēw ᓇᐘᓵᐧᓯᐍᐤ
VAI s/he chases after a person, people; s/he pursues a person, people
nawaswātam ᓇᐘᓵᐧᑕᒼ
VTI s/he chases after s.t., s/he pursues s.t.
nawaswātēw ᓇᐘᓵᐧᑌᐤ
VTA s/he chases after s.o., s/he pursues s.o.
nawaswātitowak ᓇᐘᓵᐧᑎᑐᐘᐠ
VAI they chase one another
nawaswēw ᓇᐘᓭᐧᐤ
VAI s/he gives chase, s/he chases game; s/he is in pursuit, s/he pursues
nawat ᓇᐘᐟ
IPC by comparison; better, more [*cf.* nawac]
nawataham ᓇᐘᑕᐦᐊᒼ
VTI s/he hits s.t. in mid-air, as it flies by
nawatahwēw ᓇᐘᑕᐦᐍᐤ
VTA s/he hits s.o. in mid-air, as it flies by
nawatāskitēw ᓇᐘᑖᐢᑭᑌᐤ
VII it catches on fire, it is reached by flames, it catches fire
nawatinam ᓇᐘᑎᓇᒼ
VTI s/he grabs s.t., s/he seizes s.t.; s/he catches s.t. in his/her hand
nawatinamawēw ᓇᐘᑎᓇᒪᐍᐤ
VTA s/he takes hold of (it/him) for s.o.
nawatinēw ᓇᐘᑎᓀᐤ
VTA s/he grabs s.o., s/he seizes s.o.; s/he catches s.o. in his/her hand (*e.g.* a ball)
nawēkamik ᓇᐍᑲᒥᐠ
NI lean-to shelter [*pl*: -wa]
nawēkocin ᓇᐍᑯᒋᐣ
VAI s/he hangs slanted (as a clock on the wall)
nawēkotēw ᓇᐍᑯᑌᐤ
VII it hangs slanted (as a picture)
nawēyāsiw ᓇᐍᔮᓯᐤ
VAI s/he leans into the wind, it leans against the wind
nawēyāskosin ᓇᐍᔮᐢᑯᓯᐣ
VAI it lies crosswise or slanting (as wood)
nawēyāskwaham ᓇᐍᔮᐢᑲᐧᐦᐊᒼ
VTI s/he makes s.t. lean by using a stick
nawēyicihēw ᓇᐍᔨᒋᐦᐁᐤ
VTA s/he teases s.o.
nawēyicimēw ᓇᐍᔨᒋᒣᐤ
VTA s/he teases s.o. verbally
nayahcikan ᓇᔭᐦᒋᑲᐣ
NI sacred bundle; pack for carrying on back; back pack
nayahcikanēyāpiy ᓇᔭᐦᒋᑲᓀᔮᐱᐩ
NI braces for carrying; pack strap
nayahcikēw ᓇᔭᐦᒋᑫᐤ
VAI s/he carries things on his/her back [*cf.* nayōhcikēw]
nayahcikēwin ᓇᔭᐦᒋᑫᐏᐣ
NI thing carried on back [*cf.* nayōhcikēwin]
nayahtahēw ᓇᔭᐦᑕᐦᐁᐤ
VTA s/he makes s.o. carry (it/him) on his back; s/he gives s.o. a pack, s/he puts a pack on s.o.'s back [*cf.* nayōhtahēw]
nayahtam ᓇᔭᐦᑕᒼ
VTI s/he carries s.t. on his/her back, s/he bears s.t. [*also* nayāhtam; *cf.* nayōhtam]
nayahtowak ᓇᔭᐦᑐᐘᐠ
VAI they take turns carrying one another on their backs; they ride up on one another (*e.g.* beads)
naýakask ᓇᔭᑲᐢᐠ
NDI my palate [*pl*: -wa]
nayawapiw ᓇᔭᐘᐱᐤ
VAI s/he is tired, s/he is out of breath
nayawāmohkēw ᓇᔭᐚᒧᐦᑫᐤ
VAI s/he scares off the game and loses it
nayawiskōsow ᓇᔭᐏᐢᑰᓱᐤ
VAI s/he is weary under the burden
nayawispim ᓇᔭᐏᐢᐱᒼ
IPC at a dizzy height
nayawīhēw ᓇᔭᐑᐦᐁᐤ
VTA s/he tires s.o. out
nayawīw ᓇᔭᐑᐤ
VAI s/he is tired
nayēhtāw-āyāw ᓇᔦᐦᑖᐤ ᐋᔮᐤ
VAI s/he is troubled, s/he has problems (*e.g.* health problems)
nayēhtāwamahcihow ᓇᔦᐦᑖᐘᒪᐦᒋᐦᐅᐤ
VAI s/he is troubled in health
nayēhtāwan ᓇᔦᐦᑖᐘᐣ
VII it is difficult, problematical, awkward, troublesome, inconvenient [*also* nayihtāwan]
nayēhtāwēýihtam ᓇᔦᐦᑖᐍᔨᐦᑕᒼ
VTI s/he finds s.t. difficult, s/he finds s.t. troublesome, annoying
nayēhtāwēýimēw ᓇᔦᐦᑖᐍᔨᒣᐤ
VTA s/he finds s.o. difficult, s/he finds s.o. troublesome, annoying
nayēhtāwipaýin ᓇᔦᐦᑖᐏᐸᔨᐣ
VII there is trouble, there are problems
nayēhtāwipaýiw ᓇᔦᐦᑖᐏᐸᔨᐤ
VAI s/he runs into difficulties, s/he experiences trouble, s/he is hindered in his/her progress
nayēhtāwisiw ᓇᔦᐦᑖᐏᓯᐤ
VAI s/he is hard to manage; s/he is hard to get along with
nayēhtāwīw ᓇᔦᐦᑖᐑᐤ
VAI s/he is hindered, s/he has a difficult time doing something; s/he is awkward at something

nayēstaw ᓇᔦᐢᑕᐤ
IPC only, exclusively; it is only that; instead of [*often predicative*]

nayēwac ᓇᔦᐚᐨ
IPC somewhere along the way

nayēwācimow ᓇᔦᐚᒋᒧᐤ
VAI s/he speaks along the way

nayōhcikēw ᓇᔫᐦᒋᑫᐤ
VAI s/he packs; s/he carries things on his/her back [*cf.* nayahcikēw]

nayōhcikēwin ᓇᔫᐦᒋᑫᐏᐣ
NI thing carried on back

nayōhtam ᓇᔫᐦᑕᒼ
VTI s/he carries s.t. on his/her back

nayōmēw ᓇᔫᒣᐤ
VTA s/he carries s.o. on his/her back

ᓈ

nā ᓈ
IPC [*question marker; follows a clause-initial word or phrase; non-Plains dialects; cf.* cī]

nāci- ᓈᒋ
IPV getting

nācikātēw ᓈᒋᑳᑌᐤ
VII it is fetched, brought

nācimihtēw ᓈᒋᒥᐦᑌᐤ
VAI s/he fetches firewood, s/he gets wood, s/he gets firewood [*cf. wC:* nācinihtīw]

nācimostoswēw ᓈᒋᒧᐢᑐᐢᐍᐤ
VAI s/he goes for the cattle

nācinēhikēw ᓈᒋᓀᐦᐃᑫᐤ
VAI s/he gets spiritual help, assistance or counselling (from s.o.) by offering appropriate gifts or payment

nācipahāw ᓈᒋᐸᐦᐋᐤ
VAI s/he rounds up buffalo to lead to a pound, buffalo jump or enclosure

nācipahēw ᓈᒋᐸᐦᐁᐤ
VTA s/he goes quickly for s.o.; s/he fetches s.o. quickly

nācipahtāw ᓈᒋᐸᐦᑖᐤ
VAIt s/he goes for s.t. at a run

nācitāpēw ᓈᒋᑖᐯᐤ
VAI s/he goes and drags s.t. back, s/he fetches s.t. by cart; s/he drags s.t. home [*cf.* nātitāpēw]

nāciwanihikanēw ᓈᒋᐘᓂᐦᐃᑲᓀᐤ
VAI s/he goes for his/her own trap

nāciwanihikēw ᓈᒋᐘᓂᐦᐃᑫᐤ
VAI s/he checks his/her own traps, s/he gets his/her own traps, s/he goes to look at his/her own traps

nāciyōscikēw ᓈᒋᔫᐢᒋᑫᐤ
VAI s/he creeps up, s/he creeps towards things

nāciyōstam ᓈᒋᔫᐢᑕᒼ
VTI s/he creeps towards s.t.

nāciyōstawēw ᓈᒋᔫᐢᑕᐍᐤ
VTA s/he creeps up to s.o., s/he creeps towards s.o.

nāh ᓈᐦ
IPC not so! [*expression of disagreement; also* nā]

nāh-nahihtawēw
ᓈᐦ ᓇᐦᐃᐦᑕᐍᐤ
VTA s/he listens obediently to s.o. [*rdpl*]

nāh-nakīw ᓈᐦ ᓇᑮᐤ
VAI s/he stops now and then [*rdpl*]

nāh-nanamikātēpaýiw
ᓈᐦ ᓇᓇᒥᑳᑌᐸᔩᐤ
VAI s/he has trembling legs [*rdpl*]

nāh-nanamiskwēkāpawiw
ᓈᐦ ᓇᓇᒥᐢᑵᑳᐸᐏᐤ
VAI s/he stands with shaking head [*rdpl*]

nāh-nanamispitonēpaýiw
ᓈᐦ ᓇᓇᒥᐢᐱᑐᓀᐸᔩᐤ
VAI s/he has trembling arms [*rdpl*]

nāh-nanamitēhēw
ᓈᐦ ᓇᓇᒥᑌᐦᐁᐤ
VAI s/he has heart palpitations [*rdpl*]

nāh-naponam ᓈᐦ ᓇᐳᓇᒼ
VTI s/he folds s.t. together [*rdpl*]

nāh-naponēw ᓈᐦ ᓇᐳᓀᐤ
VTA s/he folds s.o. together [*rdpl*]

nāh-napwahpisow
ᓈᐦ ᓇᐸᐦᐱᓱᐤ
VAI s/he is hobbled [*rdpl*]

nāh-napwahpitam
ᓈᐦ ᓇᐸᐦᐱᑕᒼ
VTI s/he hobbles s.t., s/he ties s.t. together [*rdpl*]

nāh-napwahpitēw
ᓈᐦ ᓇᐸᐦᐱᑌᐤ
VTA s/he hobbles s.o. [*rdpl*]

nāh-napwēkinam ᓈᐦ ᓇᐯᑭᓇᒼ
VTI s/he folds s.t.

nāh-napwēkinēw ᓈᐦ ᓇᐯᑭᓀᐤ
VTA s/he folds s.o. (*e.g.* pair of pants)

nāh-naspitātowak
ᓈᐦ ᓇᐢᐱᑖᑐᐘᐠ
VAI they resemble one another; they emulate, copy one another [*rdpl*]

nāh-nawaswātitowak
ᓈᐦ ᓇᐘᓵᑎᑐᐘᐠ
VAI they pursue one another [*rdpl*]

nāh-nāskonēw ᓈᐦ ᓈᐢᑯᓀᐤ
VTA s/he tows s.o. in (by rope or stick) [*rdpl*]

nāh-nāspicimow ᓈᐦ ᓈᐢᐱᒋᒧᐤ
VAI s/he has whooping-cough; s/he has an uncontrollable cough [*rdpl*]

nāh-nāway ᓈᐦ ᓈᐘᐩ
IPC one behind the other, one after another in a series [*rdpl; also* nā-nāway, nāh-nāwaýi]

nāh-nāwaýōhpisowak
ᓈᐦ ᓈᐘᔫᐦᐱᓱᐘᐠ
VAI they are tied in a sequence, they are tied one behind the other [*rdpl*]

nāh-nēpēwihēw
ᓈᐦ ᓀᐯᐏᐦᐁᐤ
VTA s/he continually embarrases s.o. [*rdpl*]

nāh-nēwo ᓈᐦ ᓀᐓ
IPC by fours [*rdpl*]

nāh-nikotwāsik ᓈᐦ ᓂᑯᑖᓯᐠ
IPC by sixes [*rdpl*]

nāh-nisto ᓈᐦ ᓂᐢᑐ
IPC by threes [*rdpl*]

nāh-nitonam ᓈᐦ ᓂᑐᓇᒼ
VTI s/he goes to look for s.t. [*rdpl; cf.* natonam]

nāh-nitonawēw ᓈᐦ ᓂᑐᓇᐍᐤ
VTA s/he goes to look for s.o. [*rdpl; cf.* natonawēw]

nāh-niyānan ᓈᐦ ᓂᔮᓇᐣ
IPC by fives [*rdpl*]

nāh-nīsiwak ᓈᐦ ᓃᓯᐘᐠ
VAI they are in pairs, they are two in number [*rdpl*]

nāh-nīso ᓈᐦ ᓃᓱ
IPC by twos [*rdpl*]

nāh-nīsohtēwak ᓈᐦ ᓃᓱᐦᑌᐘᐠ
VAI they go in pairs, they walk in pairs [*rdpl*]

nāh-nōmi-mōsihow
ᓈᐦ ᓅᒥ ᒨᓯᐦᐅᐤ
VAI s/he feels labour starting [*rdpl*]

nāha ᓈᐦᐊ
PR that one yonder, that further [*anim prox sg; demonstrative*]

ñāhkāstimon ᓈᐦᑳᐢᑎᒧᐣ
VII it sails lightly [*sC*]

nākacihtāw ᓈᑲᒋᐦᑖᐤ
VAIt s/he attends to s.t., s/he looks after s.t.; s/he observes s.t.

nākasohtamohkāsow
ᓈᑲᓱᐦᑕᒧᐦᑳᓱᐤ
VAI s/he pretends to pay attention

nākataweýimēw ᓈᑲᑕᐍᔨᒣᐤ
VTA s/he takes care of s.o.; s/he thinks of s.o. [*cf.* nākatēýimēw]

nākatēýihtam ᓈᑲᑌᔨᐦᑕᒼ
VTI s/he is careful; s/he cares for s.t.; s/he looks after s.t.

nākatēýimēw ᓈᑲᑌᔨᒣᐤ
VTA s/he cares for s.o.; s/he

looks after s.o. [*cf.*
nākatawēyimēw]

nākatohkawēw ᐋᐸᑐᕝᐹᐧᐅ
VTA s/he takes care of s.o.,
s/he looks after s.o.

nākatohkātam ᐋᐸᑐᕻᐹᑕᐨ
VTI s/he is interested in s.t.,
s/he pays attention to s.t.,
s/he looks out for s.t.

nākatohkātēw ᐋᐸᑐᕻᕡᐤ
VTA s/he is interested in s.o.,
s/he pays attention to s.o.,
s/he looks out for s.o.

nākatohkātisow ᐋᐸᑐᕻᐸᐣᓯᐧ
VAI s/he pays attention to
his/her own needs, s/he looks
out for him/herself

nākatohkātitowak
ᐋᐸᑐᕻᐸᐣᑐᐊᐧᐢ
VAI they keep a careful eye
on one another, they look out
for one another

nākatohkēw ᐋᐸᑐᕻᖑᐤ
VAI s/he notices people, s/he
pays attention to people; s/he
cares for people, s/he looks
after people, s/he attends to
people; s/he listens
attentively

nākē ᐋᖑ
IPC later, later on

nāmiwan ᐋᒥᐊᐧᐣ
IPC from the windward

nāmiwanaham ᐋᒥᐊᐧᐊᐧᐦᐊᐨ
VTI s/he canoes with the
wind to his/her rear

nāmiwanāw ᐋᒥᐊᐧᐋᐧ
VII there is a wind from the
rear

nānahitāk ᐋᐊᐧᕻᐃᑖᐢ
IPC just in time, by chance
[*rdpl*]

nānahwēw ᐋᐊᐧᕻᐧᐅ
VTA s/he trims s.o. along the
edge

nānakiwēpayiw ᐋᐊᐧᑭᐯᐸᔨᐧ
VAI s/he stutters [*rdpl*; *also*
nānakwēpayiw; *see also*
nanamwēw]

nānapācihēw ᐋᐊᐧᐸᒋᕻᐧᐅ
VTA s/he mends s.o., s/he
doctors s.o.; s/he tends to
s.o.; s/he tidies s.o.

nānapācihisow ᐋᐊᐧᐸᒋᕻᐃᐧᐧᐅ
VAI s/he fixes him/herself
up; s/he mends him/herself,
s/he doctors him/herself; s/he
tidies him/herself

nānapācihow ᐋᐊᐧᐸᒋᕻᐅᐧ
VAI s/he mends him/herself,
s/he dresses his/her own
wounds

nānapācihtamawēw
ᐋᐊᐧᐸᒋᕻᑕᒪᐧᐅ
VTA s/he repairs (it/him) for
s.o. [*cf.* nānapācihtawēw]

nānapācihtawēw ᐋᐊᐧᐸᒋᕻᑕᐧᐅ
VTA s/he repairs (it/him) for
s.o. [*cf.* nānapācihtamawēw]

nānapācihtāw ᐋᐊᐧᐸᒋᕻᑖᐤ
VAIt s/he repairs s.t., s/he
fixes s.t.; s/he tidies s.t.

nānapāwi ᐋᐊᐧᐸᐧᐋᐧ
IPC it's too late now

nānapāwis ᐋᐊᐧᐸᐧᐃᐧᐢ
IPC it's too late, why does
he come now

nānapāwisk ᐋᐊᐧᐸᐧᐃᐧᐢᐠ
IPC oh, sure, now he gets
here! [*used to express
frustration that someone
shows up now, rather than at
some earlier more convenient
time*]

nānapēc ᐋᐊᐧᐯᐨ
IPC all of a sudden; finally;
too late

nānaskwāhtawīw ᐋᐊᐧᐢᐠᐧᐋᕻᑕᐧᐄ
VAI s/he crawls across
(water) on a log

nānāhtētēw ᐋᐋᕻᐚᐤ
VII it is a heat mirage

nānāhtēw ᐋᐋᕻᐚᐤ
VII it is a mirage, dazzling
sunlight

nānāspicipayiw ᐋᐋᐢᐱᒋᐸᔨᐧ
VAI s/he shakes
uncontrollably; s/he has a
convulsion

nānāwayōkāpawiwak
ᐋᐋᐊᐧᔪᑳᐸᐃᐧᐊᐧᐢ
VAI they stand in single file,
they stand one behind the
other

nānāwayōpayiwak
ᐋᐋᐊᐧᔪᐸᔨᐊᐧᐢ
VAI they go in single file

nānāwayōstāw ᐋᐋᐊᐧᔫᐢᑖᐤ
VAIt s/he places s.t. one
behind the other [*also*
nāh-nāway astāw]

nāni ᐋᓂ
IPC even

nānihkisiw ᐋᓂᕻᑭᓯᐧ
VAI s/he is in haste, s/he is
in a hurry

nānikaskwa ᐋᓂᐠᐊᐢᐠᐊᐧ
NI broad hay, broad expanse
of hay, a meadow of hay [*pl*]

nānistipitam ᐋᓂᐢᑎᐱᑕᐨ
VTI s/he tears s.t. up

nānistipitamawēw
ᐋᓂᐢᑎᐱᑕᒪᐧᐅ
VTA s/he tears (it/him) up
for s.o.

nānistipitamāsow ᐋᓂᐢᑎᐱᑕᒫᓱᐧ
VAI s/he tears (it/him) up for
him/herself

nānistipitamātowak
ᐋᓂᐢᑎᐱᑕᒫᑐᐊᐧᐢ
VAI they tear (it/him) up for
one another

nānistipitēw ᐋᓂᐢᑎᐱᑌᐤ
VTA s/he tears s.o. up

nānitaw ᐋᓂᑕᐤ
IPC simply; something;
something bad; somewhere;

anyhow; in some way [*with
numbers:*] about,
approximately; [*in negative
clauses:*] anything, anything
bad [*usually with negative
presupposition; cf.* nānitaw-]

nānitaw- ᐋᓂᑕᐤ
IPV [*in negative clauses:*]
any [*cf.* nānitaw]

nānitaw isi ᐋᓂᑕᐤ ᐃᓯ
IPH in some way, in any
way; in various ways; if by
any chance, just in case
[*usually with negative
presupposition*]

nānitaw ita ᐋᓂᑕᐤ ᐃᑕ
IPH somewhere

nānitaw itē ᐋᓂᑕᐤ ᐃᑌ
IPH somewhere

nānitawāpahtam ᐋᓂᑕᐊᐧᐸᕻᑕᐨ
VTI s/he looks around for
s.t. [*rdpl; cf.* nitawāpahtam]

nānitawāpamēw ᐋᓂᑕᐊᐧᐸᒣᐧ
VTA s/he looks around for
s.o., s/he searches for s.o.
[*rdpl; cf.* nitawāpamēw]

nānitawāpiw ᐋᓂᑕᐊᐧᐱᐧ
VAI s/he looks around [*rdpl;
cf.* nitawāpiw]

nāpē- ᐋᐯ
IPN male, maleness

nāpē-atoskēyākan
ᐋᐯ ᐊᑐᐢᖑᔮᐠᐊᐣ
NA male servant

nāpē-aya ᐋᐯ ᐊᕀ
NA male animal [*pl*: -k]

nāpē-kohkōs ᐋᐯ ᑯᕻᑰᐢ
NA boar

nāpē-minōs ᐋᐯ ᒥᓅᐢ
NA tomcat

nāpē-pāhkahahkwān
ᐋᐯ ᐹᕻᑲᕻᐊᐧᐣ
NA rooster

nāpēhkān ᐋᐯᕻᑳᐣ
NA one who acts like a man,
one who pretends to be a
man; brave; mannequin,
robot

nāpēhkāsow ᐋᐯᕻᑳᓱᐧ
VAI he is brave, he acts
bravely, he pretends to be
brave; he pretends to be a
man [*compliment to a boy,
insult to a man*]

nāpēmēk ᐋᐯᒣᐠ
NA male fish [*pl*: -wak]

nāpēs ᐋᐯᐢ
NA boy [*dim*]

nāpēsip ᐋᐯᓯᑊ
NA drake, male duck

nāpēsis ᐋᐯᓯᐢ
NA boy, little boy [*dim*]

nāpēstim ᐋᐯᐢᑎᐨ
NA stallion, male horse;
male dog [*pl*: -wak]

nāpēw ᐋᐯᐤ
NA man, male adult, male
being; husband

nāpēw-āya ᓈᐯᐚᔭ
IPC men's stuff, men's clothing [*sometimes pl as if NI*]
nāpēwasākay ᓈᐯᐘᓵᑲᐩ
NI man's coat
nāpēwasikan ᓈᐯᐘᓯᑲᐣ
NA man's sock
nāpēwin ᓈᐯᐏᐣ
NI maleness
nāpēwinākosiw ᓈᐯᐏᓈᑯᓯᐤ
VAI s/he looks like a man, it is of human appearance
nāpēwiw ᓈᐯᐏᐤ
VAI he is a man; he is brave
nāpēyāpos ᓈᐯᔮᐳᐢ
NA male rabbit [*pl*: -wak]
nāpihkwān ᓈᐱᐦᒁᐣ
NI ship
nāpihkwānis ᓈᐱᐦᒁᓂᐢ
NI motor boat [*dim*]
nāsic ᓈᓯᐨ
IPC very, very much
nāsipahēw ᓈᓯᐸᐦᐁᐤ
VTA s/he fetches s.o. [*cf.* nācipahēw]
nāsipahtāw ᓈᓯᐸᐦᑖᐤ
VAIt s/he runs to fetch s.t. [*cf.* nācipahtāw]
nāsipēhtahēw ᓈᓯᐯᐦᑕᐦᐁᐤ
VTA s/he takes s.o. down to the edge of the water
nāsipēhtatāw ᓈᓯᐯᐦᑕᑖᐤ
VAIt s/he takes s.t. down to the edge of the water
nāsipēpahtāw ᓈᓯᐯᐸᐦᑖᐤ
VAI s/he runs down to the edge of the water
nāsipētāw ᓈᓯᐯᑖᐤ
VAIt s/he takes s.t. down to the water
nāsipēw ᓈᓯᐯᐤ
VAI s/he goes down to the water
nāsiwēw ᓈᓯᐍᐤ
VAI s/he fetches people
nāskikan ᓈᐢᑭᑲᐣ
NDI my chest, my breast [*dim*: nāskikanis]
nāspic ᓈᐢᐱᐨ
IPC forever, for good, beyond return, beyond reach; continuous [*also* nāspici]
nāspitahwēw ᓈᐢᐱᑕᐦᐍᐤ
VTA s/he knocks s.o. unconscious, s/he clubs s.o. to death
nāspitamohtāw ᓈᐢᐱᑕᒧᐦᑖᐤ
VAIt s/he fastens s.t. permanently
nāspitatāmow ᓈᐢᐱᑕᑖᒧᐤ
VAI s/he succumbs, s/he gives up his/her last breath
nāspitihkwāmiw ᓈᐢᐱᑎᐦᒁᒥᐤ
VAI s/he is in a trance, coma; s/he sleeps forever, s/he sleeps for a long period of time

nāspitohtēw ᓈᐢᐱᑐᐦᑌᐤ
VAI s/he goes never to return
nātaham ᓈᑕᐦᐊᒼ
VTI s/he fetches s.t. by water, s/he goes to get s.t. by boat
nātahapēw ᓈᑕᐦᐊᐯᐤ
VAI s/he checks his/her own nets [*cf.* nātahýapēw; *wC*: nātathapīw; *sC*: nātañapēw]
nātahāhtēw ᓈᑕᐦᐋᐦᑌᐤ
VTA s/he goes for s.o. by following that one's tracks
nātahākonēw ᓈᑕᐦᐋᑯᓀᐤ
VAI s/he fetches snow
nātahipēw ᓈᑕᐦᐃᐯᐤ
VAI s/he fetches water
nātahtawātam ᓈᑕᐦᑕᐚᑕᒼ
VTI s/he climbs to fetch s.t.
nātahtawātēw ᓈᑕᐦᑕᐚᑌᐤ
VTA s/he climbs to fetch s.o.
nātahwēw ᓈᑕᐦᐍᐤ
VTA s/he fetches s.o. by water
nātahýapēw ᓈᑕᐦᔭᐯᐤ
VAI s/he goes to look at the nets [*cf.* nātahapēw]
nātakaham ᓈᑕᑲᐦᐊᒼ
VTI s/he beaches s.t. paddling
nātakām ᓈᑕᑳᒼ
IPC across the water; towards land, towards shore; in the bush country
nātakāmēpitam ᓈᑕᑳᒣᐱᑕᒼ
VTI s/he pulls s.t. to shore
nātakāmēpitēw ᓈᑕᑳᒣᐱᑌᐤ
VTA s/he pulls s.o. to shore
nātakāmēyāsiw ᓈᑕᑳᒣᔮᓯᐤ
VAI s/he sails or is blown across toward shore
nātakāmēyāstan ᓈᑕᑳᒣᔮᐢᑕᐣ
VII it sails or is blown across toward shore
nātakāsi- ᓈᑕᑳᓯ
IPV into the bush country
nātakāsiw ᓈᑕᑳᓯᐤ
VAI s/he goes to the bush country
nātakohpēw ᓈᑕᑯᐦᐯᐤ
VAI s/he fetches the blankets
nātakwēw ᓈᑕᑵᐤ
VAI s/he checks his/her own snares
nātam ᓈᑕᒼ
VTI s/he fetches s.t.; s/he goes for s.t., s/he goes to get s.t.
nātamawēw ᓈᑕᒪᐍᐤ
VTA s/he fetches (it/him) for s.o., s/he gets (it/him) for s.o.; s/he helps s.o. to get (it/him)
nātamākēw ᓈᑕᒫᑫᐤ
VAI s/he helps, s/he assists the needy; s/he takes up (for s.o.), s/he sticks up for people

nātamākēwin ᓈᑕᒫᑫᐏᐣ
NI help, support
nātamāsow ᓈᑕᒫᓱᐤ
VAI s/he fetches (it/him) for him/herself
nātamātowak ᓈᑕᒫᑐᐘᐠ
VAI they help one another fetch (it)
nātasākēw ᓈᑕᓵᑫᐤ
VAI s/he goes for his/her coat
nātasāmawēw ᓈᑕᓵᒪᐍᐤ
VTA s/he gets snowshoes for s.o.
nātaskihkwēw ᓈᑕᐢᑭᐦᑵᐤ
VAI s/he goes for a pail
nātaskosīwēw ᓈᑕᐢᑯᓰᐍᐤ
VAI s/he fetches hay
nātastimwēw ᓈᑕᐢᑎᒷᐤ
VAI s/he fetches horses or dogs, s/he goes for the horses or dogs
nātastotinēw ᓈᑕᐢᑐᑎᓀᐤ
VAI s/he goes for his/her own hat
nātawāpahtam ᓈᑕᐚᐸᐦᑕᒼ
VTI s/he goes to see s.t., s/he fetches s.t. [*cf.* nitawāpahtam]
nātawāpamēw ᓈᑕᐚᐸᒣᐤ
VTA s/he goes to see s.o., s/he fetches s.o. [*cf.* nitawāpamēw]
nātawēw ᓈᑕᐍᐤ
NA Iroquois person, Iroquois Indian
nātawihcikan ᓈᑕᐏᐦᒋᑲᐣ
NI thermometer
nātawimēw ᓈᑕᐏᒣᐤ
VTA s/he examines s.o.
nātaýapēw ᓈᑕᔭᐯᐤ
VAI s/he goes for his/her net [*cf.* nātahapēw]
nātāmostawēw ᓈᑖᒧᐢᑕᐍᐤ
VTA s/he flees to s.o. for help, protection; s/he seeks advice from s.o.
nātāmototam ᓈᑖᒧᑐᑕᒼ
VTI s/he goes to s.t. for help; s/he flees to s.t.
nātāmototawēw ᓈᑖᒧᑐᑕᐍᐤ
VTA s/he flees to s.o., s/he seeks refuge with s.o.
nātāwatāw ᓈᑖᐘᑖᐤ
VAIt s/he goes and hauls s.t.
nātāwēw ᓈᑖᐍᐤ
VAI s/he fetches eggs
nātēw ᓈᑌᐤ
VTA s/he fetches s.o.; s/he goes for s.o., s/he goes to get s.o.
nātipēw ᓈᑎᐯᐤ
VAI s/he fetches a liquid, s/he goes for water; s/he goes for liquor
nātisaham ᓈᑎᓴᐦᐊᒼ
VTI s/he sends for s.t., s/he orders s.t.

nātisahikēw ᐋᐣᓴᐦᐃᐠᐊᔫ
VAI s/he sends for things, s/he orders things

nātisahikēwin ᐋᐣᓴᐦᐃᐠᐊᔫᐃᐧᐣ
NI an order (for things), catalogue order, requisition

nātisahwēw ᐋᐣᓴᐦᐤᐁᐧᐤ
VTA s/he sends for s.o.; s/he drives s.o. in

nātiskwēwēw ᐋᐣᐢᑫᐧᐍᐤ
VAI he fetches women, he goes for his wife or girlfriend

nātisōniyāhkēw ᐋᐣᓱᓂᔮᐦᑫᐧᐤ
VAI s/he goes to make money [*also* nācisōniyāhkēw]

nātisōniyāwēw ᐋᐣᓱᓂᔮᐍᐤ
VAI s/he fetches money (*e.g.* get treaty money) [*also* nācisōniyāwēw]

nātitāpēw ᐋᐣᑖᐯᐤ
VAI s/he goes and drags (it) back, s/he fetches (it) by cart [*cf.* nācitāpēw]

nātitisaham ᐋᐣᑎᓴᐦᐊᒼᐊᐨ
VTI s/he sends for s.t., s/he orders s.t.

nātitisahikēw ᐋᐣᑎᓴᐦᐃᐠᐊᔫ
VAI s/he sends for things

nātitisahwēw ᐋᐣᑎᓴᐦᐤᐁᐧᐤ
VTA s/he sends for s.o.

nātitowak ᐋᐣᑐᐊᐧᐠ
VAI they make for one another, they go for one another

nātōpēw ᐋᑑᐯᐤ
VAI s/he goes for a drink; s/he goes for liquor [*also* nātopēw]

nātwāham ᐋᒋᐦᐊᒼᐊᐨ
VTI s/he splits s.t. by tool, s/he chops s.t. off something; s/he breaks s.t. in two

nātwāhimihtēw ᐋᒋᐦᐃᒥᐦᑌᐤ
VAI s/he splits wood [*see also* tāskihtakahikēw; *cf.* nātwāhinihtēw]

nātwāhinihtēw ᐋᒋᐦᐃᓂᐦᑌᐤ
VAI s/he splits wood [*see also* tāskihtakahikēw; *cf.* nātwāhimihtēw]

nātwāhtin ᐋᒋᐦᑎᐣ
VII it breaks in two from falling

nātwāhtitāw ᐋᒋᐦᑎᑖᐤ
VAIt s/he breaks s.t. in two by knocking it on something

nātwākaham ᐋᒋᑲᐦᐊᐨ
VTI s/he breaks s.t. with a hammer

nātwānam ᐋᒋᐊᒼ
VTI s/he snaps s.t. apart; s/he breaks s.t. off by hand

nātwānamawēw ᐋᒋᐊᒪᐍᐤ
VTA s/he breaks (it/him) off by hand for s.o.

nātwānēw ᐋᒋᓅ
VTA s/he breaks s.o. in two; s/he breaks s.o. off by hand

nātwāpayiw ᐋᒋᐸᔨᐤ
VII it breaks in two; it breaks off (as in a high wind)

nātwāpitam ᐋᒋᐱᑦᐠ
VTI s/he breaks s.t. off (by pulling and bending)

nātwāpitēw ᐋᒋᐱᑌᐤ
VTA s/he breaks s.o. off (by pulling and bending)

nātwāsimēw ᐋᒋᓯᒥᐤ
VTA s/he breaks s.o. (by throwing him against something)

nātwāsin ᐋᒋᓯᐣ
VAI s/he breaks (by falling)

nātwāskam ᐋᒋᐢᑲᐨ
VTI s/he breaks s.t. by a kick

nātwāskihkasow ᐋᒋᐢᑭᐦᑳᓱᐤ
VAI it is broken in fire (*i.e.* tree)

nātwāskikāsow ᐋᒋᐢᑭᑳᓱᐤ
VAI it is broken, it has a limb broken (*i.e.* tree)

nātwāwēpaham ᐋᒋᐧᐁᐸᐦᐊᐨ
VTI s/he breaks s.t. (by hitting with a tool)

nātwāwēpiskam ᐋᒋᐧᐁᐱᐢᑲᐨ
VTI s/he breaks s.t. with a violent kick

nātwāyāsiw ᐋᒋᔮᓯᐤ
VAI s/he breaks in the wind (as a tree)

nātwāyāstan ᐋᒋᔮᐢᑕᐣ
VII it breaks in the wind

nāway ᐋᐊᐧᕀ
IPC in back, behind, at the rear; past, in the past [*e.g. behind one another*]

nāwayawi- ᐋᐊᐧᔭᐃᐧ
IPV one behind the other, in a row

nāwayēs ᐋᐊᐧᔦᐢ
IPC a bit behind

nāwayimēw ᐋᐊᐧᔨᒣᐤ
VTA s/he follows behind s.o.

nāwaýōhpitam ᐋᐊᐧᔪᐦᐱᑦᐨ
VTI s/he ties s.t. in a sequence

nāwaýōhpitēw ᐋᐊᐧᔪᐦᐱᑌᐤ
VTA s/he ties s.o. in a sequence

nāwikan ᐋᐃᐧᑲᐣ
NDI my backbone, my spine; my back

ᐅᐦ

nēha ᓀᐦᐊ
PR those yonder [*anim prox pl; cf.* nēki]

nēhi ᓀᐦᐃ
PR those yonder, that yonder [*inan pl / anim obv*]

nēhiýaw ᓀᐦᐃᔭᐤ
NA Cree, Cree man, Cree Indian, Indian [*cf. wC:* nīhithaw, *sC:* nēhiñaw]

nātwāpayiw ᐋᒋᐸᔨᐤ — *see above*

nēhiýaw-askiy ᓀᐦᐃᔭᐤ ᐊᐢᑭᕀ
NI Cree reserve, Cree land

nēhiýaw-askīhk ᓀᐦᐃᔭᐤ ᐊᐢᑮᕁ
IPC Cree reserve, on Cree land [*loc*]

nēhiýaw-aýisiýiniw ᓀᐦᐃᔭᐤ ᐊᔨᓯᔨᓂᐤ
NA a Cree person

nēhiýaw-isīhcikēwin ᓀᐦᐃᔭᐤ ᐃᓰᐦᒋᑫᐧᐃᐧᐣ
NI Cree culture, Cree ceremony; Indian culture, Indian ceremony [*see also* nēhiýawīhcikēwin, nēhiýawihtwāwin]

nēhiýaw-iskonikan ᓀᐦᐃᔭᐤ ᐃᐢᑯᓂᑲᐣ
IPC Cree reserve, Cree land

nēhiýaw-iskwēsis ᓀᐦᐃᔭᐤᐃᐢᑫᐧᓯᐢ
NA Cree girl

nēhiýaw-iskwēw ᓀᐦᐃᔭᐤᐃᐢᑫᐧᐤ
NA a Cree woman, Cree Indian woman

nēhiýaw-kīkway ᓀᐦᐃᔭᐤ ᑮᑲᐧᕀ
IPC Cree things [*sometimes pl as if NI*]

nēhiýaw-masinīwin ᓀᐦᐃᔭᐤ ᒪᓯᓃᐃᐧᐣ
NI Cree design, Cree motif, Indian design, Indian motif

nēhiýaw-maskihkiy ᓀᐦᐃᔭᐤ ᒪᐢᑭᐦᑭᕀ
NI Cree medicine; Indian medicine

nēhiýaw-mawimoscikēwin ᓀᐦᐃᔭᐤ ᒪᐃᐧᒧᐢᒋᑫᐧᐃᐧᐣ
NI Cree ceremony, Cree prayer

nēhiýaw-nitotamāwin ᓀᐦᐃᔭᐤ ᓂᑐᑕᒫᐃᐧᐣ
NI the Cree way of supplication

nēhiýaw-pwātak ᓀᐦᐃᔭᐤ ᐹᑕᐠ
NA Piapot Band [*pl; band of mixed Cree and Dakota*]

nēhiýaw-pwātināhk ᓀᐦᐃᔭᐤ ᐹᑎᓈᕁ
INM Piapot Reserve, SK [*loc; lit:* "among the Cree-Dakota"]

nēhiýaw-wapāsihk ᓀᐦᐃᔭᐤ ᐊᐧᑳᓯᕁ
INM Canoe Lake, SK [*loc; lit:* "at Cree narrows"]

nēhiýawascikēw ᓀᐦᐃᔭᐊᐧᐢᒋᑫᐧᐤ
VAI s/he writes Cree

nēhiýawascikēwin ᓀᐦᐃᔭᐊᐧᐢᒋᑫᐧᐃᐧᐣ
NI writing in Cree, translation into Cree

nēhiýawasinahikēw ᓀᐦᐃᔭᐊᐧᓯᓇᐦᐃᐠᐊᔫ
VAI s/he writes in Cree

nēhiýawasinahikēwin ᓀᐦᐃᔭᐊᐧᓯᓇᐦᐃᐠᐊᔫᐃᐧᐣ
NI Cree writing

nēhiýawastāw ᓀᐦᐃᔭᐊᐧᐢᑖᐤ
VAIt s/he writes s.t. in Cree, s/he translates s.t. into Cree

nēhiýawātisiw ᓀᐦᐃᔭᐚᑎᓯᐤ
VAI s/he has the Cree cultural tradition, s/he lives a traditional Cree life

nēhiýawēmototawēw ᓀᐦᐃᔭᐍᒧᑐᑕᐍᐤ
VTA s/he speaks Cree to s.o. [*cf.* nēhiýawimototawēw]

nēhiýawēw ᓀᐦᐃᔭᐍᐤ
VAI s/he speaks Cree

nēhiýawēwin ᓀᐦᐃᔭᐍᐏᐣ
NI the Cree language; speaking Cree

nēhiýawi- ᓀᐦᐃᔭᐏ
IPN Cree

nēhiýawi- ᓀᐦᐃᔭᐏ
IPV Cree, in Cree

nēhiýawi-kiskinwahamawēw ᓀᐦᐃᔭᐏ ᑭᐢᑭᓊᐦᐊᒪᐍᐤ
VTA s/he teaches s.o. Cree, Cree ways [*cf.* kiskinwahamawēw]

nēhiýawi-kiskinwahamākosiw ᓀᐦᐃᔭᐏ ᑭᐢᑭᓊᐦᐊᒫᑯᓯᐤ
VAI s/he learns Cree, Cree ways; s/he attends Cree school [*cf.* kiskinwahamākosiw]

nēhiýawi-pīkiskwēw ᓀᐦᐃᔭᐏ ᐲᑭᐢᑵᐤ
VAI s/he speaks Cree, s/he uses Cree words

nēhiýawi-wīhowin ᓀᐦᐃᔭᐏ ᐑᐦᐅᐏᐣ
NI Cree name, Indian name

nēhiýawimototawēw ᓀᐦᐃᔭᐏᒧᑐᑕᐍᐤ
VTA s/he speaks Cree to s.o. [*cf.* nēhiýawēmototawēw]

nēhiýawiýīhkāsow ᓀᐦᐃᔭᐏᔩᐦᑳᓱᐤ
VAI s/he is called so in Cree, s/he has a Cree name, s/he has an Indian name

nēhiýawiýīhkātam ᓀᐦᐃᔭᐏᔩᐦᑳᑕᒼ
VTI s/he calls s.t. so in Cree

nēhiýawiýīhkātēw ᓀᐦᐃᔭᐏᔩᐦᑳᑌᐤ
VTA s/he calls s.o. so in Cree [*cf.* nēhiyawīhkātēw *VTA*]

nēhiýawiýīhkātēw ᓀᐦᐃᔭᐏᔩᐦᑳᑌᐤ
VII it is called so in Cree

nēhiýawīhcikēwin ᓀᐦᐃᔭᐑᐦᒋᑫᐏᐣ
NI Cree culture; Indian culture [*see also* nēhiýaw-isīhcikēwin, nēhiýawihtwāwin]

nēhiýawīhkātēw ᓀᐦᐃᔭᐑᐦᑳᑌᐤ
VTA s/he calls s.o. so in Cree [*cf.* nēhiýawiýīhkātēw *VTA*]

nēhiýawīhtwāwin ᓀᐦᐃᔭᐑᐦᑛᐏᐣ
NI the Cree way, Cree culture; Cree custom [*also* nēhiýawihtwāwin-]

nēhiýānāhk ᓀᐦᐃᔮᓈᕽ
IPC Cree country; in the Cree country

nēhiýāsis ᓀᐦᐃᔮᓯᐢ
NA young Cree, Cree boy, Cree child; young Indian [*dim*]

nēhiýāwiw ᓀᐦᐃᔮᐏᐤ
VAI s/he is Cree, s/he is a Cree Indian; s/he is an Indian

nēhiýāwiwin ᓀᐦᐃᔮᐏᐏᐣ
NI being Cree, Cree identity, Creeness; Indianness

nēhpamīw ᓀᐦᐸᒦᐤ
VAI s/he is ready

nēhpēkāpawiw ᓀᐦᐯᑳᐸᐏᐤ
VAI s/he stands in readiness

nēhpēmahēw ᓀᐦᐯᒪᐦᐁᐤ
VTA s/he puts s.o. in readiness

nēhpēmapiw ᓀᐦᐯᒪᐱᐤ
VAI s/he sits in readiness

nēhpēmastāw ᓀᐦᐯᒪᐢᑖᐤ
VAIt s/he places s.t. in readiness; s/he puts or sets s.t. at hand

nēhpēmastēw ᓀᐦᐯᒪᐢᑌᐤ
VII it is placed in readiness

nēhpēmēw ᓀᐦᐯᒣᐤ
VAI s/he is ready, s/he stands by

nēhpēmikāpawiw ᓀᐦᐯᒥᑳᐸᐏᐤ
VAI s/he stands in readiness

nēhpēminam ᓀᐦᐯᒥᓇᒼ
VTI s/he holds s.t. in readiness, s/he holds s.t. ready

nēhpēminēw ᓀᐦᐯᒥᓀᐤ
VTA s/he holds s.o. in readiness

nēkā! ᓀᑳ
NDA mother! [*voc*; *also* nikā; *cf.* nikāwiy]

nēki ᓀᑭ
PR those yonder [*anim prox pl*]

nēkik ᓀᑭᐠ
PR those yonder [*anim prox pl*; *sC*; *cf.* nēki]

nēma ᓀᒪ
PR that yonder [*inan sg*]

nēmitanaw ᓀᒥᑕᓇᐤ
IPC forty [*cf.* nēwomitanaw]

nēmīta ᓀᒦᑕ
IPC there it is [*inan sg*; *cf.* nēma ita]

nēmow ᓀᒧᐤ
VAI s/he growls

nēnāpos ᓀᓈᐳᐢ
NA Nenapos, the Saulteaux culture hero [*also* nānapos; *see also* wīsahkēcāhk]

nēpēmēw ᓀᐯᒣᐤ
VTA s/he shames s.o. by speech, s/he embarrasses s.o. by speech [*cf.* nēpēwimēw]

nēpēwihēw ᓀᐯᐏᐦᐁᐤ
VTA s/he makes s.o. ashamed, s/he shames s.o., s/he puts s.o. to shame; s/he makes s.o. become shy

nēpēwihtākwan ᓀᐯᐏᐦᑖᑿᐣ
VII it sounds shameful; it sounds disgraceful

nēpēwimēw ᓀᐯᐏᒣᐤ
VTA s/he shames s.o. by speech, s/he embarrasses s.o. by speech [*cf.* nēpēmēw]

nēpēwimow ᓀᐯᐏᒧᐤ
VAI s/he shames him/herself (by speech), s/he embarrasses him/herself

nēpēwinākosiw ᓀᐯᐏᓈᑯᓯᐤ
VAI s/he looks shy, s/he looks embarrassed

nēpēwinākwan ᓀᐯᐏᓈᑿᐣ
VII it looks disgraceful, shameful

nēpēwisiw ᓀᐯᐏᓯᐤ
VAI s/he is bashful, s/he is shy; s/he is ashamed, s/he is shamed, s/he is embarrassed

nēpēwisiwin ᓀᐯᐏᓯᐏᐣ
NI bashfulness; shame; embarrassment

nēpēwisīstam ᓀᐯᐏᓰᐢᑕᒼ
VTI s/he is ashamed of s.t., s/he is bashful about s.t.

nēpēwisīstawēw ᓀᐯᐏᓰᐢᑕᐍᐤ
VTA s/he is bashful about s.o.

nēpōminānāhtik ᓀᐴᒥᓈᓈᐦᑎᐠ
NA snake-root tree [*pl*: -wak]

nēscakāsa ᓀᐢᒐᑳᓴ
NDI my hair, my short hair [*dim*; *pl generally*; *sg*: nēscakās]

nēsowan ᓀᓱᐘᐣ
VII it is weak

nēsowātisiw ᓀᓱᐚᑎᓯᐤ
VAI s/he is weak, s/he has a weak constitution, s/he appears in a weak state; s/he is on the verge of dying

nēsowātisiwin ᓀᓱᐚᑎᓯᐏᐣ
NI weakness

nēsowāw ᓀᓱᐚᐤ
VII it is weak

nēsowisiw ᓀᓱᐏᓯᐤ
VAI s/he is weak, s/he is weary, s/he is sickly; s/he is extremely weak, s/he is near death

nēsowisiwin ᓀᓱᐏᓯᐏᐣ
NI poor health

nēsowitēhēw ᓀᓱᐏᑌᐦᐁᐤ
VAI s/he has a weak heart; s/he is timid

nēsowitēhēwin ᓀᓱᐏᑌᐦᐁᐏᐣ
NI timidity

nēstakaya ᓀᐢᑕᑲᔭ
NDI my hair [*pl generally*]

nēstocihcēnēw ᓀᐢᑐᒋᐦᒉᓀᐤ
VTA s/he tires out s.o.'s hand

nēstocihcēnisow ᓀᐢᑐᒋᐦᒉᓂᓱᐤ
VAI s/he tires out his/her own hand

nēstohkwasiw ᓀᐢᑐᐦᑿᓯᐤ
VAI s/he is weary with sleepiness

nēstohkwastimēw ᓀᐢᑐᐦᑿᐢᑎᒣᐤ
VTA s/he tires s.o. out with sleepiness

nēstohkwēkawiw ᓀᐢᑐᐦᑵᑲᐏᐤ
VAI s/he is weak from loss of blood; s/he bleeds to exhaustion; s/he bleeds to death

nēstohtēw ᓀᐢᑐᐦᑌᐤ
VAI s/he is tired from walking

nēstokāpawiw ᓀᐢᑐᑳᐸᐏᐤ
VAI s/he is tired from standing

nēstokātēw ᓀᐢᑐᑳᑌᐤ
VAI s/he has tired legs

nēstonāmow ᓀᐢᑐᓈᒧᐤ
VAI s/he is tired of talking

nēstosin ᓀᐢᑐᓯᐣ
VAI s/he is tired of lying about

nēstosiw ᓀᐢᑐᓯᐤ
VAI s/he is tired

nēstosiwin ᓀᐢᑐᓯᐏᐣ
NI tiredness, fatigue

nēstoskawēw ᓀᐢᑐᐢᑲᐍᐤ
VTA s/he tires s.o. by his/her weight

nēstoskwastimwēw ᓀᐢᑐᐢᑿᐢᑎᒷᐤ
VAI s/he tires out his/her horses

nēstotipiskwēw ᓀᐢᑐᑎᐱᐢᑵᐤ
VAI s/he is tired from being up at night

nēstwatāhtam ᓀᐢᑘᑖᐦᑕᒼ
VTI s/he is out of breath (from running)

nēstwākonāmow ᓀᐢᑚᑯᓈᒧᐤ
VAI s/he is tired from fleeing in snow

nēta ᓀᑕ
IPC yonder, thereabouts

nētē ᓀᑌ
IPC over there, over yonder, in that direction

nētē ohci ᓀᑌ ᐅᐦᒋ
IPH from over there

nētināw ᓀᑎᓈᐤ
VII it is a sharply projecting hill

nēwahtay ᓀᐘᐦᑕᐩ
NA four dollars [*lit*: "four-pelts"]

nēwayak ᓀᐘᔭᐠ
IPC in four ways, fourfold; in four places

nēwayakihtāw ᓀᐘᔭᑭᐦᑖᐤ
VAIt s/he divides s.t. in four [*cf.* nēwohtāw, nēwowihtāw]

nēwāpēwak ᓀᐚᐯᐘᐠ
VAI they are four brothers

nēwāpisk ᓀᐚᐱᐢᐠ
IPC four dollars

nēwāw ᓀᐚᐤ
IPC four times [*also* nēwowāw, nēyowāw]

nēwinisk ᓀᐏᓂᐢᐠ
IPC four fathoms

nēwinwa ᓀᐏᓌ
VII they are four in number

nēwiwak ᓀᐏᐘᐠ
VAI they are four in number [*also* nēyowak]

nēwo ᓀᐓ
IPC four [*also* nēyo]

nēwo-kīsikāw ᓀᐓ ᑮᓯᑳᐤ
VII it is Thursday [*lit*: "it is the fourth day"]

nēwo-sōniyās ᓀᐓ ᓲᓂᔮᐢ
IPC one (silver) dollar; four quarters

nēwo-tipiskāw ᓀᐓ ᑎᐱᐢᑳᐤ
IPC four nights

nēwohēw ᓀᐓᐦᐁᐤ
VTA s/he quarters s.o.; s/he partitions s.o. in four

nēwohtāw ᓀᐓᐦᑖᐤ
VAIt s/he divides s.t. in four [*cf.* nēwayakihtāw, nēwowihtāw]

nēwokāciwēpayīs ᓀᐓᑳᒋᐍᐸᔩᐢ
NI buggy

nēwokātēw ᓀᐓᑳᑌᐤ
NA wagon

nēwokātēw ᓀᐓᑳᑌᐤ
VAI s/he is four-legged

nēwokātēw ᓀᐓᑳᑌᐤ
VII it is four panels wide (as a tent)

nēwomitanaw ᓀᐓᒥᑕᓇᐤ
IPC forty [*cf.* nēmitanaw]

nēwomitanawāw ᓀᐓᒥᑕᓇᐚᐤ
IPC forty times

nēwopēhikan ᓀᐓᐯᐦᐃᑲᐣ
NA dollar

nēwosāp ᓀᐓᓵᑊ
IPC fourteen

nēwosimow ᓀᐓᓯᒧᐤ
VAI s/he dances as one of four (in a fiddle-dance, square-dance); s/he square-dances

nēwotāpānāsk ᓀᐓᑖᐹᓈᐢᐠ
IPC four wagonloads

nēwowanwa ᓀᐓᐘᓌ
VII they are four in number [*also* nēyowanwa]

nēwowayak ᓀᐓᐘᔭᐠ
IPC in four places [*also* nēyowayak]

nēwowihtāw ᓀᐓᐏᐦᑖᐤ
VAIt s/he divides s.t. in four places [*also* nēyowihtāw; *cf.* nēwayakihtāw, nēwohtaw]

nēwōnikiw ᓀᐕᓂᑭᐤ
NI four of a kind (at cards)

nēwōsēmihkēw ᓀᐕᓭᒥᐦᑫᐤ
VAI s/he delivers quadruplets

nēwōtēmihkēw ᓀᐕᑌᒥᐦᑫᐤ
VAI it has four puppies

nēyāhtakāw ᓀᔮᐦᑕᑳᐤ
VII the trees are just right (for setting snares, etc.)

nēyāskwēyāw ᓀᔮᐢᑵᔮᐤ
VII it is a point of the woods

nēyāw ᓀᔮᐤ
VII it is a promontory, a tip of land, a peninsula

ᓂ

nicawāsimis ᓂᒐᐚᓯᒥᐢ
NDA my child; my fetus [*dim*; *cf.* awāsis, nitawāsimis]

nicāhkos ᓂᒑᐦᑯᐢ
NDA my female cross-cousin; my sister-in-law [*used by a female speaker only*; *voc*: nicāhkosē!]

nicāhkosē! ᓂᒑᐦᑯᓭ
NDA female cross-cousin!; sister-in-law! [*voc*; *cf.* nicāhkos; *used by a female speaker only*]

nicāpān ᓂᒑᐹᐣ
NDA my great grandparent; my great grandchild [*also* nocāpān; *cf.* cāpān, nitāpān]

nicāpānis ᓂᒑᐹᓂᐢ
NDA my (very small) great grandchild [*dim*; *also* nocāpānis; *cf.* cāpān, nitāpān]

nicēhcāwāw ᓂᒉᐦᒑᐚᐤ
NDA my co-parent-in-law [*cf.* nitihtāwāw]

nicēhis ᓂᒉᐦᐃᐢ
NDI my little heart [*dim*; *as endearment*: "my dear heart"]

nicēmisis ᓂᒉᒥᓯᐢ
NDA my pup, my puppy; my little horse [*cf.* acimosis]

nicēstatay ᓂᒉᐢᑕᑕᐩ
NDI my muscle

nicēstatayēyāpiy ᓂᒉᐢᑕᑕᔦᔮᐱᐩ
NDI my ligament

nici ᓂᒋ
IPC at that time, at sometime in the future [*cf.* ici]

nicicāskay ᓂᒋᒑᐢᑲᐩ
NDI my crotch, my pubic region [*in some areas, possibly restricted to use by female speakers only*; *cf.* nitayān]

nicihciy ᓂᒋᐦᒋᐩ
NDI my hand

nicihcīs ᓂᒋᐦᒌᐢ
NDI my finger; my little hand [*dim*; *cf.* ýiýīkicihcān, ýiýīkicihcīs]

nicisk ᓂᒋᐢᐠ
NDI my anus

niciskakisiy ᓂᒋᐢᑲᑭᓯᕀ
NDI my rectum (lower end)

niciskēyāpiy ᓂᒋᐢᑫᔮᐱᕀ
NDI my rectum (full length)

niciwā! ᓂᒋᐚ
NDA brother!; male parallel cousin!; friend!; rival! [*voc*; *cf.* niciwām; *used by a male speaker only*]

niciwām ᓂᒋᐚᒼ
NDA my brother; my friend; my male parallel cousin; husband of my female cross-cousin; my rival; [*pl*:] brethren (in Christian sense) [*used by a male speaker only*; *dim*: niciwāmis; *voc*: niciwā!]

niciwāmiskwēm ᓂᒋᐚᒥᐢᑵᒼ
NDA my female parallel cousin; wife of my male cross-cousin; my father's brother's daughter, my mother's sister's daughter; my fellow tribeswoman; my sister-in-law [*used by a female speaker only*]

nicīhcīkom ᓂᒌᐦᒌᑯᒼ
NDA my wart

nicohcōsimis ᓂᒍᐦᒎᓯᒥᐢ
NDA my nipple [*also* nicōhcōsimis]

nihc-āyihk ᓂᐦᒑᔨᕽ
IPC down, downstairs

nihcikwan ᓂᐦᒋᑿᐣ
NDI my knee [*cf.* 3: ohcikwan "his/her knee"; *also* nīhcikwan; *cf.* 3: wīhcikwan]

nihcikwanikan ᓂᐦᒋᑿᓂᑲᐣ
NDI my kneebone [*cf.* 3: ohcikwanikan "his/her kneebone"; *also* nīhcikwānikan; *cf.* 3: wīhcikwanikan; *see also* nikitik]

nihkwākan ᓂᐦᒁᑲᐣ
NDI my face [*dim*: nihkwākanis; *cf.* 3: ohkwākan; *also* nīhkwākan; *cf.* 3: wīhkwākan]

nihtawakay ᓂᐦᑕᐘᑲᕀ
NDI my ear [*dim*: nihcawakās; *cf.* 3: ohtawakay; *also* nīhtawakay; *cf.* 3: wīhtawakay]

nihtā- ᓂᐦᑖ
IPV able; good at, competent, practised, experienced, skillful at, expert at, known as one who does s.t. habitually; well

nihtā-atoskēw ᓂᐦᑖ ᐊᑐᐢᑫᐤ
VAI s/he is a good worker

nihtā-ācimow ᓂᐦᑖ ᐋᒋᒧᐤ
VAI s/he tells good stories; s/he is a good talker

nihtā-kitohcikēw ᓂᐦᑖ ᑭᑐᐦᒋᑫᐤ
VAI s/he plays music well

nihtā-kiýāskiw ᓂᐦᑖ ᑭᔮᐢᑭᐤ
VAI s/he is good at telling lies; s/he is known as a habitual liar [*not typically in a derogatory sense*; *cf.* kiýāskiskiw]

nihtā-kīsitēpow ᓂᐦᑖ ᑮᓯᑌᐳᐤ
VAI s/he cooks well [*cf.* nihtāwitēpow]

nihtā-kīskipocikēw ᓂᐦᑖ ᑮᐢᑭᐳᒋᑫᐤ
VAI s/he saws well

nihtā-masinahikēw ᓂᐦᑖ ᒪᓯᓇᐦᐃᑫᐤ
VAI s/he writes well

nihtā-minahow ᓂᐦᑖ ᒥᓇᐦᐅᐤ
VAI s/he is a good hunter

nihtā-mīcisow ᓂᐦᑖ ᒦᒋᓱᐤ
VAI s/he has a good appetite; s/he is a habitual eater

nihtā-mīkisistahikēw ᓂᐦᑖ ᒦᑭᓯᐢᑕᐦᐃᑫᐤ
VAI s/he is good at beading

nihtā-nikamow ᓂᐦᑖ ᓂᑲᒧᐤ
VAI s/he sings well

nihtā-nīmihitow ᓂᐦᑖ ᓃᒥᐦᐃᑐᐤ
VAI s/he dances well

nihtā-nōtinikēw ᓂᐦᑖ ᓅᑎᓂᑫᐤ
VAI s/he is a good fighter, s/he is known as a habitual fighter

nihtā-pakāsimow ᓂᐦᑖ ᐸᑳᓯᒧᐤ
VAI s/he swims well

nihtā-ýāhýānam ᓂᐦᑖ ᔮᐦᔮᓇᒼ
VTI s/he swims well

nihtāwāhtawīw ᓂᐦᑖᐚᐦᑕᐑᐤ
VAI s/he climbs well, s/he is a good climber

nihtāwēw ᓂᐦᑖᐍᐤ
VAI s/he is able to talk well; s/he speaks well [*commonly used of children learning to speak*; *derogatory if applied to fluent adult speakers*]

nihtāwēýihtam ᓂᐦᑖᐍᔨᐦᑕᒼ
VTI s/he is resourceful; s/he has knowledge for doing; s/he is clever (about s.t.), s/he is able to solve problems; s/he is content

nihtāwicimēw ᓂᐦᑖᐏᒋᒣᐤ
VAI s/he uses a boat and paddles well

nihtāwihtāw ᓂᐦᑖᐏᐦᑖᐤ
VAIt s/he does s.t. well; s/he is smart

nihtāwikihākan ᓂᐦᑖᐏᑭᐦᐋᑲᐣ
NA child

nihtāwikihāwasow ᓂᐦᑖᐏᑭᐦᐋᐘᓱᐤ
VAI s/he gives birth to a child

nihtāwikihcikan ᓂᐦᑖᐏᑭᐦᒋᑲᐣ
NI field, garden

nihtāwikihcikanihk ᓂᐦᑖᐏᑭᐦᒋᑲᓂᕽ
INM James Smith Reserve, SK [*loc*]

nihtāwikihcikanis ᓂᐦᑖᐏᑭᐦᒋᑲᓂᐢ
NI small field, small garden [*dim*]

nihtāwikihcikanisihk ᓂᐦᑖᐏᑭᐦᒋᑲᓂᓯᕽ
INM James Smith Reserve, SK [*loc*]

nihtāwikihcikēw ᓂᐦᑖᐏᑭᐦᒋᑫᐤ
VAI s/he farms, s/he makes a garden

nihtāwikihcikēwiýiniw ᓂᐦᑖᐏᑭᐦᒋᑫᐏᔨᓂᐤ
NA farmer

nihtāwikihēw ᓂᐦᑖᐏᑭᐦᐁᐤ
VTA she gives birth to s.o., s/he aids s.o.'s birth

nihtāwikināwasow ᓂᐦᑖᐏᑭᓈᐘᓱᐤ
VAI s/he gives birth to a child

nihtāwikiw ᓂᐦᑖᐏᑭᐤ
VAI s/he is born

nihtāwikiwin ᓂᐦᑖᐏᑭᐏᐣ
NI birthday

nihtāwikwāsow ᓂᐦᑖᐏᒁᓱᐤ
VAI s/he sews well, s/he is a good seamstress; s/he does fancy sewing

nihtāwikwāsowin ᓂᐦᑖᐏᒁᓱᐏᐣ
NI fancy sewing

nihtāwikwātam ᓂᐦᑖᐏᒁᑕᒼ
VTI s/he sews s.t. well

nihtāwikwātēw ᓂᐦᑖᐏᒁᑌᐤ
VTA s/he sews s.o. well; s/he sews well for s.o.

nihtāwiminakinikēw ᓂᐦᑖᐏᒥᓇᑭᓂᑫᐤ
VAI s/he is good at sewing on beads

nihtāwisīhcikēw ᓂᐦᑖᐏᓰᐦᒋᑫᐤ
VAI s/he is good at making things

nihtāwitēpow ᓂᐦᑖᐏᑌᐳᐤ
VAI s/he is good at cooking

nihtāwitōtam ᓂᐦᑖᐏᑑᑕᒼ
VTI s/he does s.t. well; s/he is capable

nihtāwōsēw ᓂᐦᑖᐒᓭᐤ
VAI s/he raises a good family

nihtiy ᓂᐦᑎᕀ
NI tea

nihtīhkēw ᓂᐦᑏᐦᑫᐤ
VAI s/he makes tea

nihtīwaskihk ᓂᐦᑏᐘᐢᑭᕽ
NA tea kettle [*pl*: -wak]

nikamoham ᓂᑲᒧᐦᐊᒼ
VTI s/he sings about s.t.; s/he plays the record player

nikamohēw ᓂᑲᒧᐦᐁᐤ
VTA s/he makes s.o. sing; s/he teaches s.o. songs

nikamon ᓂᑲᒧᐣ
NI song; hymn [*cf.* nikamowin]

nikamoskiw ᓂᑲᒧᐢᑭᐤ
VAI s/he sings habitually, s/he sings often [*hab*]

nikamostamawēw ᓂᐸᒍᐢᒐᒪᐍᐤ
VTA s/he sings for s.o.

nikamostamākēw ᓂᐸᒍᐢᒐᒫᑫᐤ
VAI s/he sings for people, s/he makes music for people

nikamow ᓂᐸᒍᐤ
VAI s/he sings [cf. nakamow]

nikamowin ᓂᐸᒍᐃᐤ
NI song, singing [cf. nakamowin, nikamon]

nikamōmakan ᓂᐸᒍᒫᐸᐣ
VII it sings [cf. kā-nikamōmakahk "record player, phonograph"]

nikayāsim ᓂᐸᔮᓯᒼ
NDA my old flame, my former sweetheart

nikā! ᓂᐸ
NDA mother! [voc; also nēkā!; wC: nīkā; cf. nikāwiy]

nikāwiy ᓂᐸᐃᐧ
NDA my mother; my mother's sister [voc: nēkā!, nikā!; see also nimāmā]

nikāwīs ᓂᐸᐄᐢ
NDA my parallel aunt; my mother's sister, my father's brother's wife; my godmother; my stepmother [dim: "my dear mother"; cf. nikāwiy]

nikēhtē-ayim ᓂᕱᐦᑌ ᐊᔨᒼ
NDA my elder; my parent, my grandparent

nikihci-āniskotāpān ᓂᑭᐦᒋ ᐋᓂᐢᑯᑖᐹᐣ
NDA my great great great grandparent; my great great great grandchild; my ancestor

nikik ᓂᑭᐠ
NA otter [pl: -wak]

nikikomin ᓂᑭᑯᒥᐣ
NI wild black currant [pl generally; lit: "otter-berry"]

nikikopīway ᓂᑭᑯᐲᐊᐧᐤ
NI (single) hair of otter

nikikowāsāhk ᓂᑭᑯᐋᓵᕽ
INM Otter Rapids [loc]

nikikwayān ᓂᑭᐠᐊᐧᔭᐣ
NA otter pelt, otterskin

nikisēyinim ᓂᑭᓭᔨᓂᒼ
NDA my old man, my husband [cf. kisēyiniw]

nikitik ᓂᑭᑎᐠ
NDI my kneecap; my knee [pl: -wa; see also nihcikwan]

nikocāk ᓂᑯᒑᐠ
NDA my wife's former partner, my wife's ex; [archaic:] my fellow husband [used by male speaker only; cf. nikocāsiskwēm]

nikocāsiskwēm ᓂᑯᒑᓯᐢᑫᐧᒼ
NDA my husband's former partner, my husband's ex;

[archaic:] my fellow wife [used by female speaker only; cf. nikocāk; see also niskwa]

nikocwāsaskanōs ᓂᑯᒑᓴᐢᑲᓅᐢ
NA six shooter [dim]

nikohcaskwayēyāpisa ᓂᑯᐦᒐᐢᑫᐧᔦᔮᐱᓴ
NDI my bronchial tube [pl; proposed term]

nikohtamawēw ᓂᑯᐦᑕᒪᐍᐤ
VTA s/he chops wood for s.o.

nikohtaskway ᓂᑯᐦᑕᐢᑲᐧᐩ
NDI my throat

nikohtaskwayēyāpiy ᓂᑯᐦᑕᐢᑫᐧᔦᔮᐱᐩ
NDI my windpipe [proposed term; also nikohtaskwayāpiy]

nikohtākan ᓂᑯᐦᑖᐸᐣ
NDI my throat

nikohtātam ᓂᑯᐦᑖᑕᒼ
VTI s/he chops s.t. for firewood

nikohtēmakan ᓂᑯᐦᑌᒪᐸᐣ
VII it prepares firewood

nikohtēstamawēw ᓂᑯᐦᑌᐢᑕᒪᐍᐤ
VTA s/he makes firewood for s.o., s/he prepares s.o.'s firewood

nikohtēstamāsow ᓂᑯᐦᑌᐢᑕᒫᓱᐤ
VAI s/he makes firewood for him/herself, s/he makes his/her own firewood

nikohtēw ᓂᑯᐦᑌᐤ
VAI s/he cuts wood, s/he chops wood; s/he gets, gathers, collects, prepares firewood

nikohtēwin ᓂᑯᐦᑌᐃᐧᐣ
NI making firewood

nikosē! ᓂᑯᓭ
NDA son! [voc; cf. nikosis]

nikosim ᓂᑯᓯᒼ
NDA my nephew; [male speaker:] my brother's son; husband of my sister's daughter; [female speaker:] my sister's son, husband of my brother's daughter [cf. nikosis]

nikosis ᓂᑯᓯᐢ
NDA my son; my parallel nephew, [male speaker:] my brother's son; [female speaker:] my sister's son [cf. nikosim, nitōsim; voc: nikosē!]

nikot ᓂᑯᐟ
NDI my nose [see also niskiwan]

nikotwāsik ᓂᑯᐟᐋᐧᓯᐠ
IPC six

nikotwāsik-askiy ᓂᑯᐟᐋᐧᓯᐠ ᐊᐢᑭᕀ
IPC six years

nikotwāsiko-kīsikāw ᓂᑯᐟᐋᐧᓯᑯ ᑮᓯᑳᐤ
VII it is Saturday [cf. nikotwāso-kīsikāw]

nikotwāsikwāw ᓂᑯᐟᐋᐧᓯᑾᐤ
IPC six times [cf. nikotwāswāw]

nikotwāsiwak ᓂᑯᐟᐋᐧᓯᐊᐧᐠ
VAI they are six in number

nikotwāso-kīsikāw ᓂᑯᐟᐋᐧᓱ ᑮᓯᑳᐤ
VII it is Saturday [cf. nikotwāsiko-kīsikāw]

nikotwāsomitanaw ᓂᑯᐟᐋᐧᓲᒥᑕᓇᐤ
IPC sixty [wC: nikotwāsikomitanaw]

nikotwāsomitanaw-askiy ᓂᑯᐟᐋᐧᓲᒥᑕᓇᐤ ᐊᐢᑭᕀ
IPC sixty years

nikotwāsosāp ᓂᑯᐟᐋᐧᓱᓵᑊ
IPC sixteen

nikotwāswāpisk ᓂᑯᐟᐋᐧᓴᐧᐱᐢᐠ
IPC six dollars

nikotwāswāw ᓂᑯᐟᐋᐧᓴᐧᐤ
IPC six times [cf. nikotwāsikwāw]

nikotwāw ᓂᑯᐟᐋᐧᐤ
IPC either one, anyone, any, any choice; anytime

nikwatis ᓂᑲᐧᑎᐢ
IPC somewhere

nikwatisow ᓂᑲᐧᑎᓱᐤ
VAI s/he fetches meat from the killing place [wC: nakwatisow]

nikwatisowin ᓂᑲᐧᑎᓱᐃᐧᐣ
NI communal activity of sharing in the kill (e.g. of moose) [wC: nakwatisowin]

nikwayaw ᓂᑲᐧᔭᐤ
NDI my neck

nikwayawikan ᓂᑲᐧᔭᐃᐧᐸᐣ
NDI my neck-bone [proposed term]

nikwāskonēw ᓂᑲᐧᐢᑯᓀᐤ
NDI my chin

nikwāskonēwikan ᓂᑲᐧᐢᑯᓀᐃᐧᐸᐣ
NDI my chin

nikwēmē! ᓂᑫᐧᒣ
NDA namesake! [voc; kinship term: addressing one whom you are named after, one who is named after you, or simply one who shares the same name; cf. nikwēmēs]

nikwēmēs ᓂᑫᐧᒣᐢ
NDA my namesake, my friend [voc: nikwēmē!]

nimaham ᓂᒪᐦᐊᒼ
VTI s/he shakes his/her own fist at s.t.

nimahwēw ᓂᒪᐦᐍᐤ
VTA s/he threatens s.o. with a weapon; s/he shakes his/her own fist at s.o.

nimanācimākan ᓂᒪᓈᒋᒫᐸᐣ
NDA [female speaker:] my father-in-law; [male speaker:] my mother-in-law; [person to whom speech is avoided]

nimanitōm ᓂᒪᓂᑑᒼ
NDA my god; my Lord [cf. manitow]

nimāmā ᓂᒫᒫ
NDA my mom, my mother

[*European loan*; *voc*: nimāmā!; *see also* nikāwiy]
niminōsimis ᓂᒥᓅᓯᒥᐢ
NDA my kitten [*dim*; *cf.* minōsis]
nimis ᓂᒥᐢ
NDA my older sister; my older female parallel cousin (*i.e.* daughter of mother's sister or father's brother) [*voc*: nimisē!]
nimisē! ᓂᒥᓭ
NDA older sister! [*voc*; *cf.* nimis]
nimisīwihēw ᓂᒥᓰᐏᐦᐁᐤ
VTA s/he threatens s.o.
nimistikom ᓂᒥᐢᑎᑯᒼ
NDI my cane, my stick [*see also* saskahon]; [*slang*:] my penis [*cf.* mistik *NI*]
nimitaham ᓂᒥᑕᐦᐊᒼ
VTI it rubs its own horns on wood (speaking of a deer)
nimitaw ᓂᒥᑕᐤ
IPC to the open country
nimitawaham ᓂᒥᑕᐘᐦᐊᒼ
VTI s/he canoes to the open water; s/he canoes to the prairie, open country
nimitāsipiciw ᓂᒥᑖᓯᐱᒋᐤ
VAI s/he moves camp to the open country [*wC*: "s/he moves camp away from shore"]
nimitāsiw ᓂᒥᑖᓯᐤ
VAI s/he goes to the open country [*wC*: "s/he heads away from shore"]
nimitāsiýahkahwēw ᓂᒥᑖᓯᔭᐦᑲᐦᐍᐤ
VTA s/he pushes s.o. with stick to the open country or away from shore
nimitāwaham ᓂᒥᑖᐘᐦᐊᒼ
VTI s/he goes out to sea; s/he goes out into the lake
nimitāwi ᓂᒥᑖᐏ
IPC in the water away from shore
nimitāwiýāsiw ᓂᒥᑖᐏᔮᓯᐤ
VAI s/he blows from land out into water
nimitāwiýāstan ᓂᒥᑖᐏᔮᐢᑕᐣ
VII it blows from land out into water
nimiýēsāpiwinān ᓂᒥᔦᓵᐱᐏᓈᐣ
NDI my eyebrow [*also* nimiýēsāpiwin, nimīhēsāpiwinān]
nimiýēsāpiwinānis ᓂᒥᔦᓵᐱᐏᓈᓂᐢ
NDI my eyelash [*dim*; *also*: nimiýēsāpiwinis, nimīhēsāpiwinānis]
nimosō! ᓂᒧᓲ
NDA grandfather! [*voc*; *cf.* mósom!, nimosōm]
nimosōm ᓂᒧᓲᒼ
NDA my grandfather [*reference extended to all related males of grandfather's generation*; *term for any respected male elder*; *voc*: nimosō! mósom!]
nimosōmipan ᓂᒧᓲᒥᐸᐣ
NDA my deceased grandfather, my late grandfather
nimwāhkohkēw ᓂᒷᐦᑯᐦᑫᐤ
NDI my arm muscle, my biceps [*also* nimākohkēw]
ninahāhkim ᓂᓇᐦᐋᐦᑭᒼ
NDA my son-in-law [*cf.* ninahāhkisīm]
ninahāhkisīm ᓂᓇᐦᐋᐦᑭᓰᒼ
NDA my son-in-law [*cf.* ninahāhkim]
ninahākaniskwēm ᓂᓇᐦᐋᑲᓂᐢᑵᒼ
NDA my daughter-in-law [*used by female speaker only*; *cf.* nahākaniskwēw]
nināpēm ᓂᓈᐯᒼ
NDA my husband, my lover [*cf.* nāpēw]
ninipīm ᓂᓂᐲᒼ
NDI my amniotic fluid; my urine; my glass of water [*cf.* nipiy]
ninīkānimihk ᓂᓃᑳᓂᒥᕽ
IPC in front of me
ninīkihik ᓂᓃᑭᐦᐃᐠ
NDA my parent; my blood relative [*pl generally*: -wak; *cf.* nīkihik]
ninōtokwēm ᓂᓅᑐᑵᒼ
NDA my old woman, my wife [*also* ninōtikwēm; *cf.* nōtokwēw]
nipahaciw ᓂᐸᐦᐊᒋᐤ
VAI s/he freezes to death
nipahatāhtam ᓂᐸᐦᐊᑖᐦᑕᒼ
VTI s/he is overcome by loss of breath and dies
nipahāhkatēw ᓂᐸᐦᐋᐦᑲᑌᐤ
VAI s/he is extremely hungry, s/he perishes from hunger [*cf.* nipahāskatēw]
nipahāhkatosohēw ᓂᐸᐦᐋᐦᑲᑐᓱᐦᐁᐤ
VTA s/he starves s.o. to death
nipahāhkatosow ᓂᐸᐦᐋᐦᑲᑐᓱᐤ
VAI s/he starves to death, s/he dies from starvation, s/he perishes from hunger
nipahāhkwan ᓂᐸᐦᐋᐦᑿᐣ
VII it is powerful (*e.g.* medicine)
nipahāpasow ᓂᐸᐦᐋᐸᓱᐤ
VAI s/he dies from smoke, s/he is smoked to death
nipahāpākwēw ᓂᐸᐦᐋᐹᑵᐤ
VAI s/he dies of thirst; s/he is extremely thirsty
nipahāskatēw ᓂᐸᐦᐋᐢᑲᑌᐤ
VAI s/he is extremely hungry, s/he perishes from hunger [*cf.* nipahāhkatēw]
nipahāskwaciw ᓂᐸᐦᐋᐢᑾᒋᐤ
VAI s/he is extremely cold, s/he freezes, s/he freezes to death
nipahcikākēw ᓂᐸᐦᒋᑳᑫᐤ
VAI s/he kills with something
nipahēw ᓂᐸᐦᐁᐤ
VTA s/he kills s.o. [*rdpl*: na-nipahēw]
nipahi- ᓂᐸᐦᐃ
IPV really, very, extremely [*emphatic*]; to prostration or death [*common with descriptions of temperature, as well as likes and dislikes*]
nipahi-sākihēw ᓂᐸᐦᐃ ᓵᑭᐦᐁᐤ
VTA s/he loves s.o. a great deal
nipahi-ýōtin ᓂᐸᐦᐃ ᔫᑎᐣ
VII it is very windy
nipahihkasow ᓂᐸᐦᐃᐦᑲᓱᐤ
VAI s/he is burned to death, s/he is scalded to death; s/he is extremely hot
nipahihkaswēw ᓂᐸᐦᐃᐦᑲᓷᐤ
VTA s/he burns s.o. to death, s/he scalds s.o. to death
nipahikanēw ᓂᐸᐦᐃᑲᓀᐤ
VAI s/he is extremely lazy
nipahikīhkāw ᓂᐸᐦᐃᑮᐦᑳᐤ
VAI s/he dies of old age
nipahimikīw ᓂᐸᐦᐃᒥᑮᐤ
VAI s/he dies of smallpox
nipahinēw ᓂᐸᐦᐃᓀᐤ
VTA s/he squeezes s.o. to death by hand
nipahipahtāw ᓂᐸᐦᐃᐸᐦᑖᐤ
VAI s/he runs until s/he falls down [*rdpl*: nāh-nipahipahtāw]
nipahipāwanīw ᓂᐸᐦᐃᐹᐘᓃᐤ
VAI s/he is extremely skinny, lean
nipahisimēw ᓂᐸᐦᐃᓯᒣᐤ
VTA s/he throws s.o. to death; s/he drops s.o. (*e.g.* a baby) accidentally causing death
nipahisin ᓂᐸᐦᐃᓯᐣ
VAI s/he falls to death, s/he is killed by a fall; s/he lies dead
nipahiskawēw ᓂᐸᐦᐃᐢᑲᐍᐤ
VTA s/he kicks s.o. to death, s/he tramples s.o. to death; s/he kills s.o. by rolling over onto him
nipahisow ᓂᐸᐦᐃᓱᐤ
VAI s/he kills him/herself, s/he commits suicide [*see also* misiwanācihisow, nisiwanācihisow]
nipahisowin ᓂᐸᐦᐃᓱᐏᐣ
NI suicide
nipahitowak ᓂᐸᐦᐃᑐᐘᐠ
VAI they kill one another

nipahiwēmakan σ<"ᐃᐁ·Ⴑᑿ
   VII it is deadly

nipahiwēw σ<"ᐃᐁ·°
   VAI s/he kills people, s/he
   murders people

nipahtamawēw σ<"Cⴑᐁ·°
   VTA s/he kills (it/him) for
   s.o., s/he makes a kill for s.o.
   [*cf.* nipahtawēw]

nipahtamāsow σ<"Cᒷᒍ°
   VAI s/he kills (it/him) for
   him/herself

nipahtawēw σ<"CᐁV·°
   VTA s/he kills (it/him) for
   s.o. [*cf.* nipahtamawēw]

nipahtākēskiw σ<"ᒡᑫˆᑭ°
   VAI s/he murders frequently
   [*hab*]

nipahtākēw σ<"ᒡᑫ°
   VAI s/he kills people, s/he
   murders people

nipahtākēwin σ<"ᒡᑫᐃ·ᐣ
   NI murder

nipahtāw σ<"ᒡ°
   VAIt s/he kills s.t.

nipahtwāsow σ<"ᒡᒍ°
   VAI s/he kills (it/him) for
   him/herself

nipawākan σ<ᐃ·ᑿᑊ
   NDA my dream spirit

nipākēw σᐸᑫ°
   VAI s/he uses something as
   sleepwear

nipākwēsimow σᐸᑫᐧᒴᒍ°
   VAI s/he attends a Sundance,
   s/he participates in a
   Sundance; s/he attends a
   Rain Dance, s/he participates
   in a Rain Dance

nipākwēsimowikamik
   σᐸᑫᐧᒴᒍᐃ·ᑲᒥᐠ
   NI Sundance-Lodge [*pl:*
   -wa]

nipākwēsimowin σᐸᑫᐧᒴᒍᐃ·ᐣ
   NI Sundance

nipākwēsimowinihkēw
   σᐸᑫᐧᒴᒍᐃ·σ"ᑫ°
   VAI s/he gives a Sundance,
   s/he holds a Sundance

nipāpā σᐸᐸ
   NDA my dad, my father
   [*European loan*; *voc*:
   nipāpā!; *cf.* nohtāwiy]

nipāsiw σᐸᓯ°
   VAI s/he dozes, naps, sleeps
   a little [*dim*]

nipāsk σᐸᐢᐠ
   NA sleepyhead; sleeper

nipāskākow σᐸˆᑲᑯ°
   VTA it makes one sleep
   [*restricted, inanimate actor
   form of VTA* *nipāskaw-; *cf.*
   nipēskākow]

nipāskiw σᐸˆᑭ°
   VAI s/he sleeps all the time,
   s/he sleeps constantly, s/he
   likes to sleep [*hab*]

nipātwēwitam σᐸᑌᐤ·ᐃ·Cᐨ
   VTI s/he talks constantly

nipāw σᐸ°
   VAI s/he sleeps, s/he is
   asleep

nipāwin σᐸᐃ·ᐣ
   NI sleeping, sleep

nipē-wīci-ispīhcisimākan
   σᐁ ᐩᐧ ᐃˆ᐀"ᒥᒡᑿ
   NDA my age-mate from
   there on down [*also*
   nipē-wīc-īspīhcisimākan]

nipēhēw σᐁ"ᐁ°
   VTA s/he makes s.o. sleep,
   s/he puts s.o. to sleep

nipēhkāsow σᐁ"ᑿᒍ°
   VAI s/he pretends to sleep
   [*also* nipāhkāsow]

nipēminak σᐁᒥᑕ·ᑊ
   NDI my shin, my calf

nipēpayiw σᐁᐸᔆ°
   VAI s/he falls asleep, s/he
   dozes off

nipēpīm σᐁᐩᐨ
   NDA my baby [*European
   loan*]

nipēskākēmakan σᐁˆᑲᑫᒪᑿᑊ
   VII it causes sleep

nipēskakow σᐁˆᑲᑯ°
   VTA it makes s.o. sleep
   [*restricted, inanimate actor
   form of* *nipēskaw- *VTA*; *cf.*
   nipāskākow]

nipēwayāna σᐁᐊ·ᔭᓇ
   NI pyjamas, nightgown [*pl
   generally*]

nipēwapiwin σᐁᐊ·ᐱᐃ·ᐣ
   NI lazy-boy recliner,
   davenport

nipēwāpoy σᐁᐊ·ᐳᐟ
   NI anaesthetic

nipēwāspinēw σᐁᐊ·ˆᐱˆ°
   VAI s/he has a sleeping
   disorder, s/he has narcolepsy

nipēwāspinēwin σᐁᐊ·ˆᐱˆᐃ·ᐣ
   NI sleeping disorder;
   narcolepsy

nipēwikamik σᐁᐃ·ᑲᒥᐠ
   NI bedroom [*pl*: -wa]

nipēwin σᐁᐃ·ᐣ
   NI bed

nipēwināhtik σᐁᐃ·ᐤ"ᐣᐟ
   NI bedframe; headboard;
   bedpost [*pl*: -wa]

nipēwinis σᐁᐃ·σᐢ
   NI cradle, crib; cot, small
   bed; bed [*dim*; *see also*
   tihkinākan]

nipēyakokosisān σᐁᔆᑯᑯᓯᓴᐣ
   NDA my only son

nipiskēw σᐱˆᑫ°
   VAI s/he doctors using
   traditional rites

nipiw σᐱ°
   VAI s/he dies; s/he is dead
   [*in some areas, restricted to
   non-human reference*]

nipiwin σᐱᐃ·ᐣ
   NI death; vital spot

nipiy σᐱᐩ
   NI water

nipīhkawēw σᐱ"ᑲᐁ·°
   VTA s/he melts snow to
   make water for s.o.

nipīhkātam σᐱ"ᑲCᐨ
   VTI s/he melts s.t. to make
   water

nipīhkēw σᐱ"ᑫ°
   VAI s/he melts snow to make
   water

nipīhtawāwikanān
   σᐱ"Cᐊ·ᐃ·ᑲᐨ
   NDI my spinal chord

nipīmakan σᐱᒪᑿᑊ
   VII it dies, it dies out; it is
   dead [*cf.* nipōmakan]

nipīs σᐱˆ
   NI small amount of water
   [*dim*]

nipīskāw σᐱˆᑲ°
   VII there is a lot of water
   around

nipīwan σᐱᐊ·ᐣ
   VII it is wet, it is dripping
   wet

nipīwēpicikan σᐱᐁ·ᐱᒋᑲᐣ
   NI water mill

nipīwiw σᐱᐃ·°
   VII there is water, it has
   water, it is watery, it contains
   water (*e.g.* watermelon)

nipowipayiw σᐳᐃ·ᐸᔆ°
   VAI s/he is becoming
   paralyzed

nipowisiw σᐳᐃ·ᓯᒍ°
   VAI s/he is paralyzed, s/he
   is crippled by a stroke; it is
   withered (*e.g.* a tree)

nipōhkāsow σᐳ"ᑿᒍ°
   VAI s/he pretends to be dead

nipōmakan σᐳᒪᑿᑊ
   VII it dies, it is dead [*cf.*
   nipīmakan]

nipōstamawēw σᐳˆᐣCⴑᐁᐤ·
   VTA s/he dies for s.o.

nipōwāpiw σᐳᐊ·ᐱᐧ°
   VAI s/he has weak eyes

nipōwinākosiw σᐳᐃ·ᓈᑯᒍᒍ°
   VAI s/he looks like death,
   s/he looks as if dead

nipōwinākwan σᐳᐃ·ᓈᑿᐣ
   VII it looks like death, it
   looks as if dead

nipwāhkāw σᐧᐊ·"ᑲ°
   VAI s/he is clever

nipwāhkāwin σᐧᐊ·"ᑲᐃ·ᐣ
   NI cleverness

nipwām σᐧᐊ·ᐨ
   NDI my thigh

nipwāmikan σᐧᐊ·ᒥᑲᑊ
   NDI my femur [*proposed
   term*]

nisēkipatwān σᔆᑭᐸᐧCᐨ
   NDI my braid [*see also*
   apihkān]

nisēkitikom σᔆᑭᐳᐨᐨ
   NDI my tangled hair, my
   knotted hair, my uncombed
   hair

nisihk ᓂᓯᕽ
IPC quietly, a little

nisihkāc ᓂᓯᐦᑳᐨ
IPC slowly, gently; without trouble [*cf.* nisīhkāc]

nisihkēpaýiw ᓂᓯᐦᑫᐸᔨᐤ
VAI s/he trots

nisikatisiw ᓂᓯᑲᑎᓯᐤ
VAI s/he dwells off alone with his/her family [*also* nisikēcisiw]

nisikos ᓂᓯᑯᐢ
NDA my aunt, my cross-aunt; my father's sister, my mother's brother's wife; my mother-in-law [*voc*: nisikosē!; *see also* nimanācikan]

nisikosē! ᓂᓯᑯᓭ
NDA aunt!, cross-aunt!; father's sister!, mother's brother's wife!; mother-in-law! [*voc*; *cf.* nisikos]

nisikwākan ᓂᓯᒁᑲᐣ
NDI the back of my knee

nisis ᓂᓯᐢ
NDA my uncle, my cross-uncle; my mother's brother, my father's sister's husband; my father-in-law [*voc*: nisisē!; *see also* nimanācimākan]

nisisē! ᓂᓯᓭ
NDA uncle!, cross-uncle!; mother's brother!, father's sister's husband!; father-in-law! [*voc*; *cf.* nisis]

nisit ᓂᓯᐟ
NDI my foot [*dim*: nisicis]

nisitaw ᓂᓯᑕᐤ
IPC satisfactorily (suitable)

nisitawēýihcikātēw ᓂᓯᑕᐍᔨᐦᒋᑳᑌᐤ
VII it is recognized

nisitawēýihtam ᓂᓯᑕᐍᔨᐦᑕᒼ
VTI s/he knows s.t., s/he recognizes s.t., s/he is acquainted with s.t.

nisitawēýihtākosiw ᓂᓯᑕᐍᔨᐦᑖᑯᓯᐤ
VAI s/he is known, s/he is recognized

nisitawēýihtākwan ᓂᓯᑕᐍᔨᐦᑖᑿᐣ
VII it is known, it is recognized

nisitawēýimēw ᓂᓯᑕᐍᔨᒣᐤ
VTA s/he knows s.o., s/he recognizes s.o., s/he is acquainted with s.o.

nisitawihtam ᓂᓯᑕᐏᐦᑕᒼ
VTI s/he recognizes s.t. by sound

nisitawihtawēw ᓂᓯᑕᐏᐦᑕᐍᐤ
VTA s/he recognizes s.o. by sound

nisitawinam ᓂᓯᑕᐏᓇᒼ
VTI s/he recognizes s.t. by sight

nisitawinawēw ᓂᓯᑕᐏᓇᐍᐤ
VTA s/he recognizes s.o. by sight

nisitohtam ᓂᓯᑐᐦᑕᒼ
VTI s/he understands; s/he understands s.t.

nisitohtamohkāsow ᓂᓯᑐᐦᑕᒧᐦᑳᓱᐤ
VAI s/he pretends to understand (it/him)

nisitohtamowin ᓂᓯᑐᐦᑕᒧᐏᐣ
NI understanding

nisitohtamōhēw ᓂᓯᑐᐦᑕᒨᐦᐁᐤ
VTA s/he makes s.o. understand (it/him)

nisitohtawēw ᓂᓯᑐᐦᑕᐍᐤ
VTA s/he understands s.o.

nisitohtākosiw ᓂᓯᑐᐦᑖᑯᓯᐤ
VAI s/he is recognized by sound

nisitohtākwan ᓂᓯᑐᐦᑖᑿᐣ
VII it is recognized by sound, it is recognizable in sound

nisitohtātowak ᓂᓯᑐᐦᑖᑐᐘᐠ
VAI they understand one another

nisitospitam ᓂᓯᑐᐢᐱᑕᒼ
VTI s/he recognizes s.t. by taste

nisitospitēw ᓂᓯᑐᐢᐱᑌᐤ
VTA s/he recognizes s.o. by taste

nisiwanācihēw ᓂᓯᐘᓈᒋᐦᐁᐤ
VTA s/he ruins s.o. [*cf.* misiwanācihēw]

nisiwanācihisow ᓂᓯᐘᓈᒋᐦᐃᓱᐤ
VAI s/he destroys him/herself; s/he commits suicide [*cf.* misiwanācihisow; *see also* nipahisow]

nisiwanācihitowak ᓂᓯᐘᓈᒋᐦᐃᑐᐘᐠ
VAI they destroy one another [*cf.* misiwanācihitowak]

nisiwanācihtāw ᓂᓯᐘᓈᒋᐦᑖᐤ
VAIt s/he ruins s.t. [*cf.* misiwanācihtāw]

nisiwanātahkamikisiw ᓂᓯᐘᓈᑕᐦᑲᒥᑭᓯᐤ
VAI s/he is destructive [*cf.* misiwanātahkamikisiw]

nisiwanātan ᓂᓯᐘᓈᑕᐣ
VII it is spoiled, be destroyed [*cf.* misiwanātan]

nisiwanātisiw ᓂᓯᐘᓈᑎᓯᐤ
VAI s/he perishes, s/he is ruined [*cf.* misiwanācisiw]

nisīhkāc ᓂᓰᐦᑳᐨ
IPC gently, softly, carefully, slowly; quietly [*cf.* nisihkāc]

nisīhkāci- ᓂᓰᐦᑳᒋ
IPV gently, carefully, slowly [*cf.* nisihkāc]

nisīm ᓂᓰᒼ
NDA my younger sibling (brother or sister) [*voc*: nisīmē!]

nisīmē! ᓂᓰᒣ
NDA younger sibling! [*voc*; *pl*: nisīmitik!; *cf.* nisīm(is)]

nisīmis ᓂᓰᒥᐢ
NDA my younger sibling (brother or sister) [*dim*; *cf.* nisīm]

niska ᓂᐢᑲ
NA goose [*sg*: niska; *cf.* -niskim- *NDA*]

niskan ᓂᐢᑲᐣ
NDI my bone [*dim*: niskanis]

niskasiniya ᓂᐢᑲᓯᓂᔭ
NI birdshot, buckshot, shotgun shells [*pl generally*]

niskaskwa ᓂᐢᑲᐢᑿ
NI goose grass [*pl*]

niskāhtik ᓂᐢᑳᐦᑎᐠ
NDI my forehead [*pl*: -wa; *also* niskahtik]

niskāhtikwanikan ᓂᐢᑳᐦᑎᑿᓂᑲᐣ
NDI my frontal bone [*proposed term*]

niskāt ᓂᐢᑳᐟ
NDI my leg

niskātikan ᓂᐢᑳᑎᑲᐣ
NDI my legbone

niski-pimiy ᓂᐢᑭ ᐱᒥᕀ
NI goose oil

niski-pīsim ᓂᐢᑭ ᐲᓯᒼ
NA Goose Moon; March [*obv*: -wa]

niski-pīway ᓂᐢᑭ ᐲᐘᕀ
NI goose down

niskihkān ᓂᐢᑭᐦᑳᐣ
NA goose decoy

niskimin ᓂᐢᑭᒥᐣ
NI gooseberry [*see also* sāpōmin]

niskisis ᓂᐢᑭᓯᐢ
NA gosling

niskiskāw ᓂᐢᑭᐢᑳᐤ
VII there is an abundance of geese

niskiwan ᓂᐢᑭᐘᐣ
NDI my nose, my snout [*see also* nikot]

niskiwanikan ᓂᐢᑭᐘᓂᑲᐣ
NDI my nasal bone [*proposed term*]

niskiwiw ᓂᐢᑭᐏᐤ
VAI s/he is a goose

niskīsik ᓂᐢᑮᓯᐠ
NDI my eye [*pl*: -wa; *dim*: niskīsikos]

niskīsikohkāna ᓂᐢᑮᓯᑯᐦᑳᓇ
NDI my eyeglasses, my glasses, my spectacles [*pl*]

niskīsikwāpitān ᓂᐢᑮᓯᒁᐱᑖᐣ
NDI my eye-tooth [*proposed term*]

niskon ᓂᐢᑯᐣ
NDI my liver

niskotākay ᓂᐢᑯᑖᑲᕀ
NDI my coat, my jacket; my dress; my skirt [*dim*: niskocākās]

nisoy ᓂᓱᐩ
NDI my tail [*dim*: nisōs]
nisōkan ᓂᓲᑲᐣ
NDI my tail-bone; my rear-end, my buttocks
nispayowak ᓂᐢᐸᔪᐊᐧᐠ
NDA my ovaries [*pl*]
nispikay ᓂᐢᐱᑲᐩ
NDI my rib [*cf.* nispikēkan]
nispikēkan ᓂᐢᐱᑫᑲᐣ
NDI my rib, my rib bone
nispiskwan ᓂᐢᐱᐢᑲᐧᐣ
NDI my back
nispiton ᓂᐢᐱᑐᐣ
NDI my arm [*dim*: nispiconis]
nistam ᓂᐢᑕᒼ
IPC first; at first, for the first time, initially, originally
nistam māwacēyas
ᓂᐢᑕᒼ ᒫᐊᐧᒉᔭᐢ
IPH first, earliest, oldest
nistamāpitān ᓂᐢᑕᒫᐱᑖᐣ
NI baby tooth [*pl*: nistamāpitāna]
nistamosān ᓂᐢᑕᒧᓵᐣ
NA first born
nistamosāniwēwin
ᓂᐢᑕᒧᓵᓂᐁᐧᐃᐧᐣ
NI birth right of the first born
nistamosāniwiw ᓂᐢᑕᒧᓵᓂᐃᐧᐤ
VAI s/he is first born
nistāpāwahēw ᓂᐢᑖᐹᐊᐧᐦᐁᐤ
VTA s/he drowns s.o. [*cf.* mistāpāwahēw]
nistāpāwēw ᓂᐢᑖᐹᐁᐧᐤ
VAI s/he drowns, s/he gets drowned [*cf.* mistāpawēw]
nistāpāwēwin ᓂᐢᑖᐹᐁᐧᐃᐧᐣ
NI drowning [*cf.* mistāpāwēwin]
nistāsihkawēw ᓂᐢᑖᓯᐦᑲᐁᐧᐤ
VTA s/he gives s.o. good company
nistēs ᓂᐢᑌᐢ
NDA my older brother, my older male parallel cousin (*i.e.* son of mother's sister or father's brother) [*voc*: nistēsē!]
nistēsē! ᓂᐢᑌᓭ
NDA older brother! [*voc*; *cf.* nistēs]
nistikwān ᓂᐢᑎᑳᐧᐣ
NDI my head; my mind [*dim*: niscikwānis, nistikwānis]
nistikwānaskatihkway
ᓂᐢᑎᑳᐧᓇᐢᑲᑎᐦᑲᐧᐩ
NDI top of my skull, my parietal bone
nistikwānikan ᓂᐢᑎᑳᐧᓂᑲᐣ
NDI my skull
nistim ᓂᐢᑎᒼ
NDA my niece, my cross-niece; my daughter-in-law; [*male speaker*:] my sister's daughter; [*female speaker*:] my brother's daughter
nistimihkāwin ᓂᐢᑎᒥᐦᑳᐃᐧᐣ
NDA my common-law daughter-in-law
nistinwa ᓂᐢᑎᓇᐧ
VII they are three in number
nistiwak ᓂᐢᑎᐊᐧᐠ
VAI they are three in number
nisto ᓂᐢᑐ
IPC three
nisto kīsikāw ᓂᐢᑐ ᑮᓯᑳᐤ
IPH three days
nisto tipahikan ᓂᐢᑐ ᑎᐸᐦᐃᑲᐣ
IPH three o'clock; three yards
nisto tipiskāw ᓂᐢᑐ ᑎᐱᐢᑳᐤ
IPH three nights
nisto-kīsikāw ᓂᐢᑐ ᑮᓯᑳᐤ
VII it is Wednesday
nisto-sōniyās ᓂᐢᑐ ᓲᓂᔮᐢ
IPC three quarters, seventy-five cents
nisto-tipiskwēw ᓂᐢᑐ ᑎᐱᐢᑫᐧᐤ
VAI s/he is away from home for three nights
nistocihc ᓂᐢᑐᒋᐦᐨ
IPC three inches
nistohkwāmiwak ᓂᐢᑐᐦᑳᐧᒥᐊᐧᐠ
VAI they sleep three in a bed
nistohtāw ᓂᐢᑐᐦᑖᐤ
VAIt s/he divides s.t. in three
nistokamik ᓂᐢᑐᑲᒥᐠ
IPC three houses (near one another)
nistokāt ᓂᐢᑐᑳᐟ
NA three-legged being (*e.g.* a dog who has lost a leg)
nistokātēw ᓂᐢᑐᑳᑌᐤ
VAI it has three legs, it is three-legged
nistokātēwēyāw ᓂᐢᑐᑳᑌᐁᐧᔮᐤ
VII it has three legs (as a stool)
nistokātis ᓂᐢᑐᑳᑎᐢ
NA three-legged iron kettle (of long ago)
nistokēwak ᓂᐢᑐᑫᐊᐧᐠ
VAI they are three living together
nistomitanaw ᓂᐢᑐᒥᑕᓇᐤ
IPC thirty
nistomitanaw tahtwāpisk
ᓂᐢᑐᒥᑕᓇ ᑕᐦᑖᐧᐱᐢᐠ
IPH thirty dollars
nistopiponwēw ᓂᐢᑐᐱᐳᓀᐧᐤ
VAI s/he is three years old [*also* nistopiponēw]
nistosāp ᓂᐢᑐᓵᑊ
IPC thirteen
nistosinwak ᓂᐢᑐᓯᓇᐧᐠ
VAI they lie as three
nistoskisin ᓂᐢᑐᐢᑭᓯᐣ
IPC three pairs of shoes
nistohtēw ᓂᐢᑐᐦᑌᐤ
VAI s/he travels in a family of three
nistoyawēw ᓂᐢᑐᔭᐁᐧᐤ
VAI s/he shoots three of them with one shot
nistōsēmihkēw ᓂᐢᑑᓭᒥᐦᑫᐤ
VAI s/he delivers triplets
nistōskān ᓂᐢᑑᐢᑳᐣ
NI three of a kind (at cards)
nistōskwēwēw ᓂᐢᑑᐢᑫᐧᐁᐧᐤ
VAI he has three wives
nistōtēmihkēw ᓂᐢᑑᑌᒥᐦᑫᐤ
VAI it has three puppies
nistw-āskiy ᓂᐢᑐ ᐋᐢᑭᐩ
IPC three years [*also* nisto askiy]
nistwahpisowak ᓂᐢᑕᐧᐦᐱᓱᐊᐧᐠ
VAI they are harnessed in threes
nistwayak ᓂᐢᑕᐧᔭᐠ
IPC three places, three kinds, three ways; Nistowiak, SK [*place name*]
nistwāpēwak ᓂᐢᑖᐧᐯᐊᐧᐠ
VAI they are three men, they are three brothers
nistwāpisk ᓂᐢᑖᐧᐱᐢᐠ
IPC three dollars
nistwāskaciwak ᓂᐢᑖᐧᐢᑲᒋᐊᐧᐠ
VAI they are three frozen together
nistwāw ᓂᐢᑖᐧᐤ
IPC third time; three times
nitakay ᓂᑕᑲᐩ
NDI my penis
nitaki ᓂᑕᑭ
IPC yeah, right! not by any chance; just in time [*also* nitaka; *cf.* nitakis, nitakisa]
nitakikom ᓂᑕᑭᑯᒼ
NDA my mucus, my snot [*cf.* akik, mitakikom]
nitakis ᓂᑕᑭᐢ
IPC yeah, right! not by any chance [*cf.* nitaki, nitakisa]
nitakisa ᓂᑕᑭᓴ
IPC yeah, right! not by any chance [*cf.* nitaki, nitakis]
nitakisiya ᓂᑕᑭᓯᔭ
NDI my intestines, my bowels, my guts, my entrails [*pl*]
nitasiskitān ᓂᑕᓯᐢᑭᑖᐣ
NDI calf of my leg; my ligament
nitaskihkom ᓂᑕᐢᑭᐦᑯᒼ
NDA my pail, my kettle [*cf.* askihk]
nitaw-āyamihāw ᓂᑕᐋᐧᔭᒥᐦᐋᐤ
VAI s/he attends church [*also* nitawi-ayamihāw]
nitawahcikēw ᓂᑕᐊᐧᐦᒋᑫᐤ
VAI s/he sniffs at things for food
nitawastimwēw ᓂᑕᐊᐧᐢᑎᒣᐧᐤ
VAI s/he goes for horses or dogs; s/he looks for his/her own horses or dogs
nitawāc ᓂᑕᐋᐧᐨ
IPC in spite of everything,

as the best thing to do;
instead

nitawāpahkēw ᓂᑕᐋᐧᐸᐦᑫᐤ
VAI s/he goes and watches;
s/he observes things, s/he
watches things; s/he goes to
see people, s/he tries to see
people

nitawāpahtam ᓂᑕᐋᐧᐸᐦᑕᒼ
VTI s/he goes to see s.t., s/he
tries to see s.t.

nitawāpamēw ᓂᑕᐋᐧᐸᒣᐤ
VTA s/he goes and sees s.o.,
s/he tries to see s.o., s/he
goes to visit s.o.

nitawāpēnawēw ᓂᑕᐋᐧᐸᐁᐧᓇᐁᐧᐤ
VTA s/he goes to see about
s.o. (e.g. a sick person); s/he
checks on s.o.

nitawāpēnākēw ᓂᑕᐋᐧᐸᐁᐧᓈᑫᐤ
VAI s/he visits the sick; s/he
checks on people

nitawāpēnāsow ᓂᑕᐋᐧᐸᐁᐧᓈᓱ
VAI s/he examines his/her
own infirmities, s/he checks
on his/her own injuries

nitawāpēnikēw ᓂᑕᐋᐧᐸᐁᐧᓂᑫᐤ
VAI s/he checks up on
people/things, s/he inspects
symptoms

nitawāpiw ᓂᑕᐋᐧᐱᐤ
VAI s/he looks, s/he takes a
look

nitawāsimis ᓂᑕᐋᐧᓯᒥᐢ
NDA my child; my fetus
[also nitawāsim; cf. awāsis,
nicawāsimis]

nitawāwēw ᓂᑕᐋᐧᐁᐧᐤ
VAI s/he goes looking for
eggs, s/he goes to collect
eggs

nitawēmā! ᓂᑕᐁᐧᒫ
NDA cross-sibling! [voc; cf.
nitawēmāw]

nitawēmāw ᓂᑕᐁᐧᒫᐤ
NDA my cross-sibling, my
sibling or parallel cousin of
opposite gender; [male
speaker:] my sister; my
female parallel cousin (i.e.
daughter of my mother's
sister or my father's brother;
[female speaker:] my
brother; my male parallel
cousin (i.e. son of my
mother's sister or my father's
brother [voc: nitawēmā!]

nitawēyihcikēw ᓂᑕᐁᐧᔨᐦᒋᑫᐤ
VAI s/he desires things

nitawēyihtam ᓂᑕᐁᐧᔨᐦᑕᒼ
VTI s/he wants s.t., s/he
desires s.t.

nitawēyihtamawēw
ᓂᑕᐁᐧᔨᐦᑕᒪᐁᐧᐤ
VTA s/he wants (it/him) for
s.o., s/he wants (it/him) from
s.o., s/he desires (it/him) of
s.o.

nitawēyihtākosiw
ᓂᑕᐁᐧᔨᐦᑖᑯᓯᐤ
VAI s/he is desired, s/he is
wanted; s/he is necessary

nitawēyihtākwan ᓂᑕᐁᐧᔨᐦᑖᑾᐣ
VII it is desired, it is wanted;
it is necessary

nitawēyimēw ᓂᑕᐁᐧᔨᒣᐤ
VTA s/he wants s.o., s/he
desires s.o., s/he desires
(it/him) from s.o.

nitawi- ᓂᑕᐃᐧ
IPV go and, go to; engaged
in [also nitō-, tō-]

nitawi-ayamihāw
ᓂᑕᐃᐧ ᐊᔭᒥᐦᐋᐤ
VAI s/he goes to church, s/he
attends church, s/he goes to
pray

nitawi-ayamihcikēw
ᓂᑕᐃᐧ ᐊᔭᒥᐦᒋᑫᐤ
VAI s/he goes to school, s/he
attends school [lit: "s/he goes
to read"]

nitawi-mīcisow ᓂᑕᐃᐧ ᒦᒋᓱ
VAI s/he goes to eat

nitawiminēw ᓂᑕᐃᐧᒥᓀᐤ
VAI s/he goes berry-picking,
s/he goes for berries

nitawiskwēwēw ᓂᑕᐃᐧᐢᑫᐧᐁᐧᐤ
VAI he looks for a woman

nitayān ᓂᑕᔮᐣ
NDI my crotch, my pubic
region [in some areas,
possibly restricted to use by
male speakers only; cf.
nicicāskay; cf. nitayān "I
have it", first person singular
inflected form of ayā- VAI];
my vagina

nitayīsiyinīm ᓂᑕᔩᓯᔨᓃᒼ
NDA my partner; [pl:] my
people, my followers [cf.
ayīsiyiniw]

nitāhtāmēw ᓂᑖᐦᑖᒣᐤ
VTA s/he borrows (it/him)
from s.o., s/he seeks to
borrow from s.o.

nitāhtāmow ᓂᑖᐦᑖᒧ
VAI s/he borrows, s/he seeks
to borrow

nitākay ᓂᑖᑲᐩ
NDA my vagina, my vulva

nitāmisow ᓂᑖᒥᓱ
VAI s/he pick berries, gather
berries

nitān! ᓂᑖᐣ
NDA daughter! [voc; cf.
nitānis]

nitānis ᓂᑖᓂᐢ
NDA my daughter; [male
speaker:] my brother's
daughter; [female speaker:]
my sister's daughter [dim:
nicānis; voc: nitān!]

nitāniskocāpān ᓂᑖᓂᐢᑯᒑᐹᐣ
NDA my great great
grandchild; my great great

grandparent [dim; cf.
nitāniskocāpānis,
nitāniskotāpān]

nitāniskocāpānis ᓂᑖᓂᐢᑯᒑᐹᓂᐢ
NDA my (very small) great
great grandchild [dim; cf.
nitāniskocāpān,
nitāniskotāpān]

nitāniskotāpān ᓂᑖᓂᐢᑯᑖᐹᐣ
NDA my great great
grandparent; my great great
grandchild [cf.
nitāniskocāpān,
nitāniskocāpānis]

nitāpān ᓂᑖᐹᐣ
NDA my great grandparent;
my great grandchild [also
notāpān; cf. cāpān, nicāpān,
nicāpānis]

nitāpiskan ᓂᑖᐱᐢᑲᐣ
NDI my jaw; my chin

nitāpiskohkēw ᓂᑖᐱᐢᑯᐦᑫᐤ
NDI back of my skull, my
occipital bone

nitās ᓂᑖᐢ
NDA my pair of pants,
trousers [dim: nicāsis, nitāsis]

nitās ᓂᑖᐢ
NDI my legging, my gaiter

nitāyim ᓂᑖᔨᒼ
NDA my fellow wife

nitēh ᓂᑌᐦ
NDI my heart [cf. dim:
nicēhis]

nitēm ᓂᑌᒼ
NDA my dog; my horse [pl:
-ak; cf. atim, misatim]

nitēyikom ᓂᑌᔨᑯᒼ
NDI my nostril

nitēyiniy ᓂᑌᔨᓂᐩ
NDI my tongue [also
nitēyaniy]

nitēyiniyāpiy ᓂᑌᔨᓂᔮᐱᐩ
NDI my tongue string

nitihkom ᓂᑎᐦᑯᒼ
NDA my louse [cf. ihkwa]

nitihkomātēw ᓂᑎᐦᑯᒫᑌᐤ
VTA s/he picks lice from s.o.
[cf. nōtihkomātēw]

nitihkwatim ᓂᑎᐦᑲᐧᑎᒼ
NDA my nephew, my
cross-nephew (i.e. son of
sibling of opposite gender);
my son-in-law; [male
speaker:] my sister's son;
[female speaker:] my
brother's son [voc: nitihkwā!;
also nitēhkwā!]

nitihkwā! ᓂᑎᐦᑾ
NDA nephew!,
cross-nephew!; son-in-law!
[voc; also nitēhkwā; cf.
nitihkwatim]

nitihtāwāw ᓂᑎᐦᑖᐋᐧᐤ
NDA my co-parent-in-law
[cf. nicēhcāwāw]

nitihtihkos ᓂᑎᐦᑎᐦᑯᐢ
NDA my kidney

nitihtihkosiw ᓂᑎᐦᑎᐦᑯᓯᐤ
NDA my kidney
nitihtihkosiy ᓂᑎᐦᑎᐦᑯᓯᕀ
NDA my kidney
nitihtikon ᓂᑎᐦᑎᑯᐣ
NDI my armpit [*pl*: -wa; *see also* nitīhkōkan]
nitihtiman ᓂᑎᐦᑎᒪᐣ
NDI my shoulder
nitihtimanikan ᓂᑎᐦᑎᒪᓂᑲᐣ
NDI my shoulder-bone
nitisiy ᓂᑎᓯᕀ
NDI my navel, my belly-button
nitisiyēyāpiy ᓂᑎᓯᔦᔮᐱᕀ
NDI my umbilical chord
nitiskwēm ᓂᑎᐢᑵᒼ
NDA my wife, my woman [*cf.* iskwēw]
nitiy ᓂᑎᕀ
NDI my buttocks
nitiýinīmak ᓂᑎᔨᓃᒪᐠ
NDA my people, my followers [*pl*]
nitīhikan ᓂᑏᐦᐃᑲᐣ
NDI my shoulder-blade
nitīhiy ᓂᑏᐦᐃᕀ
NDA my shoulder-blade
nitīhkōkan ᓂᑏᐦᑰᑲᐣ
NDI my armpit [*see also* nitihtikon]
nitohkēmow ᓂᑐᐦᑫᒧᐤ
VAI s/he asks people, s/he invites people
nitohtam ᓂᑐᐦᑕᒼ
VTI s/he listens to s.t., s/he listens for s.t.; s/he tries to hear s.t. [*cf.* natohtam]
nitohtawēw ᓂᑐᐦᑕᐍᐤ
VTA s/he listens to s.o., s/he listens for s.o.; s/he obeys s.o. [*cf.* natohtawēw]
nitohtākowisiw ᓂᑐᐦᑖᑯᐏᓯᐤ
VAI s/he is heard by the powers
nitohtātowak ᓂᑐᐦᑖᑐᐘᐠ
VAI they call one another
nitohtowak ᓂᑐᐦᑐᐘᐠ
VAI they call one another
nitohtōsim ᓂᑐᐦᑑᓯᒼ
NDA my breast, my nipple [*also* nitōhtōsim]
nitokan ᓂᑐᑲᐣ
NDI my hip [*also* nitōkan]
nitomēw ᓂᑐᒣᐤ
VTA s/he invites s.o., call s.o.
nitomiskwēwātēw ᓂᑐᒥᐢᑵᐚᑌᐤ
VTA he asks for s.o.'s hand (*i.e.* a woman)
nitomiskwēwēw ᓂᑐᒥᐢᑵᐍᐤ
VAI he asks for a woman's hand in marriage
nitonam ᓂᑐᓇᒼ
VTI s/he seeks s.t., s/he looks for s.t. [*cf.* natonam]
nitonamawēw ᓂᑐᓇᒪᐍᐤ
VTA s/he seeks (it/him) for s.o.; [*slang*:] s/he feels s.o.'s genitals
nitonawēw ᓂᑐᓇᐍᐤ
VTA s/he seeks s.o., s/he looks for s.o. [*cf.* natonawēw; nitonēw]
nitonēw ᓂᑐᓀᐤ
VTA s/he seeks s.o., s/he looks for s.o. (by hand) [*cf.* nitonawēw]
nitonikātēw ᓂᑐᓂᑳᑌᐤ
VII it is looked for
nitonikēw ᓂᑐᓂᑫᐤ
VAI s/he takes a look; s/he seeks things, s/he looks for things, s/he gropes for things
nitopahtwāw ᓂᑐᐸᐦᑣᐤ
VAIt s/he searches for s.t.
nitopaýiw ᓂᑐᐸᔨᐤ
VAI he goes on the warpath; s/he goes seeking
nitopaýiwin ᓂᑐᐸᔨᐏᐣ
NI warpath, raid
nitopaýiwinihkēw ᓂᑐᐸᔨᐏᓂᐦᑫᐤ
VAI he leads a war-party, he conducts a war-party; he arranges a raid
nitopaýīstawēw ᓂᑐᐸᔩᐢᑕᐍᐤ
VTA s/he makes war on s.o.
nitosk-āyim ᓂᑐᐢᑳᔨᒼ
NDA my young person, my child, my grandchild [*also* nitoski-ayim]
nitoskinīkīmis ᓂᑐᐢᑭᓃᑮᒥᐢ
NDA my young man, my hired man [*dim*; *cf.* oskinīkiw, oskinīkīs]
nitosowayak ᓂᑐᓱᐘᔭᐠ
NDA my testicles [*pl*]
nitostikwānim ᓂᑐᐢᑎᒁᓂᒼ
NDI my severed head (used as lodge emblem) [*archaic*]
nitotam ᓂᑐᑕᒼ
VTI s/he asks for s.t.
nitotamawēw ᓂᑐᑕᒪᐍᐤ
VTA s/he asks s.o. for (it/him)
nitotamākēstawēw ᓂᑐᑕᒫᑫᐢᑕᐍᐤ
VTA s/he makes demands for (it/him) for s.o.
nitotamākēw ᓂᑐᑕᒫᑫᐤ
VAI s/he requests things, s/he asks for things, s/he prays for things; s/he demands things
nitotamāw ᓂᑐᑕᒫᐤ
VAIt s/he requests s.t., s/he asks for s.t., s/he prays for s.t.; s/he demands things
nitōn ᓂᑑᐣ
NDI my mouth [*dim*: nicōnis]
nitōnāstēw ᓂᑑᓈᐢᑌᐤ
VAI s/he looks for lice
nitōsim ᓂᑑᓯᒼ
NDA my nephew, my parallel nephew; [*male speaker:*] my brother's son; husband of my sister's daughter; [*female speaker*:] my sister's son; husband of my brother's daughter [*cf.* nikosim, nikosis]
nitōsim ᓂᑑᓯᒼ
NDI my boat, my canoe [*cf.* ōsi, 3: otōsim; "his/her canoe"; *dialectal variant*: -(t)ōt-, *cf.* 1: nitōt "my canoe", 3: otōt "his/her canoe"]
nitōsimiskwēm ᓂᑑᓯᒥᐢᑵᒼ
NA my niece, my parallel niece; [*male speaker*:] my brother's daughter, wife of my sister's son; [*female speaker*:] my sister's daughter, wife of my brother's son [*cf.* nitānis]
nitōsis ᓂᑑᓯᐢ
NDA my aunt, my parallel aunt, my mother's sister, my father's brother's wife [*see also* nikāwīs]
nitōskam ᓂᑑᐢᑲᒼ
VTI s/he seeks s.t.
nitōskawēw ᓂᑑᐢᑲᐍᐤ
VTA s/he seeks s.o.
nitōskwan ᓂᑑᐢᑿᐣ
NDI my elbow [*dim*: nicōskwanis]
nitōt ᓂᑑᐟ
NDI my boat, my canoe [*cf.* ōsi; 3 *sg*: otōt; *cf.* nitōsim *NDI*; *see also* cīmān]
nitōtēm ᓂᑑᑌᒼ
NDA my friend, my kinsman [*voc*: nitōtēm!]
nitōwāhkawēw ᓂᑑᐚᐦᑲᐍᐤ
VAI s/he plays Indian poker (card game)
nitōwin ᓂᑑᐏᐣ
NI trump card
nitwahāhcikēw ᓂᑘᐦᐋᐦᒋᑫᐤ
VAI s/he seeks trails
niwāhkōmākan ᓂᐚᐦᑰᒫᑲᐣ
NDA my relative
niwiyihkosak ᓂᐏᔨᐦᑯᓴᐠ
NDA my glands [*pl*; *dim*; *cf.* niyihkosak]
niwiyihkwak ᓂᐏᔨᐦᑿᐠ
NDA my glands [*sg*: niwiyihk; *cf.* 3: (o)wiyihkwa "his/her gland(s)"; *cf.* niyihkwak]
niwīcēwākan ᓂᐑᒉᐚᑲᐣ
NDA my spouse; my companion, my partner, my buddy, my friend
niwīcēwākanis ᓂᐑᒉᐚᑲᓂᐢ
NDA my companion [*dim*]
niwīkimākan ᓂᐑᑭᒫᑲᐣ
NDA my spouse, my wife, my husband; my housemate [*cf.* wīkimākan]

niwītatoskēmākan ᓂᐑᑕᑐᐢᑫᒫᑲᐣ
NDA my fellow worker, my co-worker

niýa ᓂᔭ
PR I, me, mine [*first person sg*]

niýa wiýa ᓂᔭ ᐏᔭ
PR for my part, as for me; I myself

niýanān ᓂᔭᓈᐣ
PR we, us, our [*first person pl exclusive*]

niýatowihk ᓂᔭᑐᐏᕽ
IPC like me, my kind

niyaw ᓂᔭᐤ
NDI my body [*cf.* 3: wiyaw]

niyā ᓂᔮ
IPC go ahead, go on, be off! [*also pl*: niyāk; *imperative usage only*]

niyāk ᓂᔮᐠ
IPC for the future, in the future

niyānan ᓂᔮᓇᐣ
IPC five

niyānaniwa ᓂᔮᓇᓂᐘ
VII they are five in number

niyānaniwak ᓂᔮᓇᓂᐘᐠ
VAI they are five in number

niyānano-kīsikāw ᓂᔮᓇᓄ ᑮᓯᑳᐤ
VII it is Friday [*also* niyāno-kīsikāw]

niyānanomitanaw ᓂᔮᓇᓄᒥᑕᓇᐤ
IPC fifty

niyānanosāp ᓂᔮᓇᓄᓵᑊ
IPC fifteen [*also* niyānosāp]

niyānanosāpwāw ᓂᔮᓇᓄᓵᐺᐤ
IPC fifteen times

niyānanwāpisk ᓂᔮᓇᓌᐱᐢᐠ
IPC five dollars

niyānanwāw ᓂᔮᓇᓌᐤ
IPC five times

niyāw ᓂᔮᐤ
VII it is a point of land [*cf.* nēyāw]

niyihkwak ᓂᔨᐦᑿᐠ
NDA my glands [*sg*: niyihk; *cf.* 3: oyihkwa "his/her gland(s); *cf.* niwiyihkwak]

ᓃ

nīc-āyis ᓃᒑᔨᐢ
NDA my fellow youngster, my young age-mate [*also* nīci-ayis]

nīci-atoskēyākan ᓃᒋ ᐊᑐᐢᑫᔮᑲᐣ
NDA my fellow employee

nīci-aýisiýiniw ᓃᒋ ᐊᔨᓯᔨᓂᐤ
NDA my fellow human [*cf.* nīci-aýisiýinīm; *also* nīc-āýisiýiniw]

nīci-aýisiýinīm ᓃᒋ ᐊᔨᓯᔨᓃᒼ
NDA my fellow human [*cf.* nīci-aýisiýiniw; *also* nīc-āýisiýinīm]

nīci-kisēýin ᓃᒋ ᑭᓭᔨᐣ
NDA my fellow old man, my co-elder [*prox sg and voc only*; *cf.* nīci-kisēýiniw]

nīci-kisēýiniw ᓃᒋ ᑭᓭᔨᓂᐤ
NDA my fellow old man, my co-elder [*cf.* nīci-kisēýin]

nīci-kiskinwahamawākan ᓃᒋ ᑭᐢᑭᓊᐦᐊᒪᐚᑲᐣ
NDA my fellow student, my school-mate [*also* -kiskinoh-]

nīci-nahāhkis ᓃᒋ ᓇᐦᐋᐦᑭᐢ
NDA my brother-in-law

nīci-nāpēw ᓃᒋ ᓈᐯᐤ
NDA my fellow man

nīci-nēhiýaw ᓃᒋ ᓀᐦᐃᔭᐤ
NDA my fellow Cree, my fellow Indian person; my blood brother

nīci-nōnimākan ᓃᒋ ᓅᓂᒫᑲᐣ
NDA my foster sibling [*lit*: "my fellow suckling"]

nīcimos ᓃᒋᒧᐢ
NDA my sweetheart, my lover [*dim*; *familiar and more intimate form of* nītim]

nīcisān ᓃᒋᓵᐣ
NDA my sibling [*dim*: nīcisānis; *cf.* nītisan]

nīhc-āyihk ᓃᐦᒑᔨᕽ
IPC below; down, downstairs; in the low place [*also* nīhcāyihk; *from*: nīhci-ayihk]

nīhci- ᓃᐦᒋ
IPV down, downwards; bottom

nīhci-kwāskohtiw ᓃᐦᒋ ᑹᐢᑯᐦᑎᐤ
VAI s/he jumps down

nīhci-wēpaham ᓃᐦᒋ ᐌᐸᐦᐊᒼ
VTI s/he knocks s.t. down by tool; s/he knocks s.t. down off (of something), s/he pushes s.t. down off (of something)

nīhci-wēpahwēw ᓃᐦᒋ ᐌᐸᐦᐌᐤ
VTA s/he knocks s.o. down by a shot or by tool; s/he knocks s.o. down off (of something), s/he pushes s.o. down off (of something)

nīhci-wēpinam ᓃᐦᒋ ᐌᐱᓇᒼ
VTI s/he throws s.t. down, off

nīhci-wēpinamawēw ᓃᐦᒋ ᐌᐱᓇᒪᐌᐤ
VTA s/he throws (it/him) down for s.o.

nīhci-wēpinēw ᓃᐦᒋ ᐌᐱᓀᐤ
VTA s/he throws s.o. down, off

nīhci-ýahkaham ᓃᐦᒋ ᔭᐦᑲᐦᐊᒼ
VTI s/he pushes s.t. down by tool

nīhci-ýahkahwēw ᓃᐦᒋ ᔭᐦᑲᐦᐌᐤ
VTA s/he pushes s.o. down by tool

nīhcikahwēw ᓃᐦᒋᑲᐦᐌᐤ
VTA s/he sends s.o. down by cutting

nīhcikāpawiw ᓃᐦᒋᑳᐸᐏᐤ
VAI s/he steps down

nīhcikwāskwēsin ᓃᐦᒋᑹᐢᑵᓯᐣ
VAI s/he is bounced out of something (*e.g.* a buggy or wagon)

nīhcipaýihow ᓃᐦᒋᐸᔨᐦᐅᐤ
VAI s/he jumps down, s/he jumps off; s/he throws him/herself down

nīhcipaýiw ᓃᐦᒋᐸᔨᐤ
VAI s/he comes down, s/he falls down, s/he falls off

nīhcipicikātēw ᓃᐦᒋᐱᒋᑳᑌᐤ
VII it is pulled down

nīhcipitam ᓃᐦᒋᐱᑕᒼ
VTI s/he pulls s.t. down, s/he drags s.t. down

nīhcipitēw ᓃᐦᒋᐱᑌᐤ
VTA s/he pulls s.o. down, s/he drags s.o. down

nīhtaciwē- ᓃᐦᑕᒋᐍ
IPV downhill, down

nīhtaciwē-ýahkinam ᓃᐦᑕᒋᐍ ᔭᐦᑭᓇᒼ
VTI s/he pushes s.t. down the hill or stairs

nīhtaciwē-ýahkinēw ᓃᐦᑕᒋᐍ ᔭᐦᑲᓀᐤ
VTA s/he pushes s.o. down the hill or stairs

nīhtaciwēhcāw ᓃᐦᑕᒋᐌᐦᒑᐤ
VII it is downhill land

nīhtaciwēhtahēw ᓃᐦᑕᒋᐌᐦᑕᐦᐁᐤ
VTA s/he takes s.o. downwards

nīhtaciwēhtatāw ᓃᐦᑕᒋᐌᐦᑕᑖᐤ
VAIt s/he takes s.t. downwards

nīhtaciwēpahtāw ᓃᐦᑕᒋᐌᐸᐦᑖᐤ
VAI s/he runs down (*e.g.* stairs, hill)

nīhtaciwēpaýiw ᓃᐦᑕᒋᐌᐸᔨᐤ
VAI s/he goes downhill, s/he goes down, s/he drives downhill

nīhtaciwēpitam ᓃᐦᑕᒋᐌᐱᑕᒼ
VTI s/he pulls s.t. downhill

nīhtaciwēpitēw ᓃᐦᑕᒋᐌᐱᑌᐤ
VTA s/he pulls s.o. downhill

nīhtaciwētāpāsow ᓃᐦᑕᒋᐌᑖᐹᓱᐤ
VAI s/he drives downhill, s/he rides downhill

nīhtaciwēw ᓃᐦᑕᒋᐌᐤ
VAI s/he climbs down, s/he walks down; s/he goes downstairs, s/he descends a hill, stairs, etc.

nīhtaciwēýāhtawīw ᓃᐦᑕᒋᐌᔮᐦᑕᐑᐤ
VAI s/he climbs down, s/he descends on wood

nīhtakocin ᐛᐦᒐᑯᒋᐣ
VAI s/he falls down through air

nīhtakosīw ᐛᐦᒐᑯᓯᐤ
VAI s/he dismounts, s/he climbs down, s/he gets down, s/he gets off

nīhtaskamik ᐛᐦᒐᐢᑲᒥᐠ
IPC underground, down below ground

nīhtaskēw ᐛᐦᒐᐢᑫᐤ
VAI s/he descends to the ground

nīhtataham ᐛᐦᒐᒐᐦᐋᐨ
VTI s/he knocks s.t. down off something

nīhtatahwēw ᐛᐦᒐᒐᐦᐍᐤ
VTA s/he knocks s.o. down off something

nīhtāhtawīpahtāw
ᐛᐦᒐᐦᒐᐏᐸᐦᑖᐤ
VAI s/he climbs down at a run

nīhtāhtawīw ᐛᐦᒐᐦᒐᐏᐤ
VAI s/he climbs down

nīhtāmatin ᐛᐦᒐᒥᓂᐣ
IPC at the bottom of the bank, bottom of the hill

nīhtāpēkinam ᐛᐦᒐᐯᑭᓇᐨ
VTI s/he lowers s.t. by a rope

nīhtāpēkinēw ᐛᐦᒐᐯᑭᓀᐤ
VTA s/he lowers s.o. by a rope; s/he leads s.o. down by rope

nīhtāpēkipitam ᐛᐦᒐᐯᑭᐱᑕᐨ
VTI s/he pulls s.t. down by rope, s/he lets s.t. down on a rope

nīhtāpēkipitēw ᐛᐦᒐᐯᑭᐱᑌᐤ
VTA s/he pulls down by rope, s/he lets s.o. down on a rope

nīhtāpokow ᐛᐦᒐᐳᑯᐤ
VAI s/he slides downhill

nīhtāsiw ᐛᐦᒐᓯᐤ
VAI s/he is blown down

nīhtāskocin ᐛᐦᒐᐢᑯᒋᐣ
VAI s/he gets hooked and falls down

nīhtāskwaham ᐛᐦᒐᐢᑿᐦᐊᐨ
VTI s/he takes s.t. down with a tool (e.g. stick)

nīhtāskwahwēw ᐛᐦᒐᐢᑿᐦᐍᐤ
VTA s/he takes s.o. down with a tool (e.g. stick)

nīhtāstan ᐛᐦᒐᐢᑕᐣ
VII it is blown down

nīhtinam ᐛᐦᐱᓇᐨ
VTI s/he takes s.t. down or off; s/he lowers s.t., s/he unloads s.t.; s/he hands s.t. down, s/he lifts s.t. down

nīhtinamawēw ᐛᐦᐱᓇᒪᐍᐤ
VTA s/he takes (it/him) down for s.o.

nīhtinēw ᐛᐦᐱᓀᐤ
VTA s/he takes s.o. down or off, s/he lowers s.o., s/he puts s.o. down

nīhtinikēw ᐛᐦᐱᓂᑫᐤ
VAI s/he takes things down or off, s/he unloads things

nīhtinisow ᐛᐦᐱᓂᓱᐤ
VAI s/he lets him/herself down, s/he lowers him/herself

nīhtowatēnam ᐛᐦᑐᐊᐁᓇᐨ
VTI s/he takes s.t. down as a load

nīhtowatēnēw ᐛᐦᑐᐊᐁᓀᐤ
VTA s/he takes s.o. down as a load

nīhtowatēnikēw ᐛᐦᑐᐊᐁᓂᑫᐤ
VAI s/he takes down a load

nīkān ᓃᑳᐣ
IPC first, in front, ahead, at the head; lead, in the lead [primarily spatial, can be extended to temporal meaning]

nīkān-ayāw ᓃᑳᐩ ᐊᔮᐤ
VAI s/he is in the front [also two words]

nīkān-wīhtam ᓃᑳᐩ ᐄᐦᑕᐨ
VTI s/he tells s.t. first [also two words]

nīkān-wīhtamawēw
ᓃᑳᐩ ᐄᐦᑕᒪᐍᐤ
VTA s/he tells s.o. (about it/him) first [also two words]

nīkānakimēw ᓃᑳᓇᑭᒣᐤ
VTA s/he counts s.o. in first position, s/he holds s.o. (tobacco) to be a prime element

nīkānapiw ᓃᑳᓇᐱᐤ
VAI s/he sits in the lead; s/he is head of the department

nīkānahēw ᓃᑳᓇᐦᐁᐤ
VTA s/he puts s.o. in front

nīkānastamawēw ᓃᑳᓇᐢᑕᒪᐍᐤ
VTA s/he puts (it/him) forward for s.o.

nīkānastamākēwin
ᓃᑳᓇᐢᑕᒫᑫᐏᐣ
NI leadership

nīkānastāw ᓃᑳᓇᐢᑖᐤ
VAIt s/he puts s.t. in front

nīkānēs ᓃᑳᓀᐢ
IPC a ways ahead, at the head

nīkānēyihtam ᓃᑳᓀᔨᐦᑕᐨ
VTI s/he thinks s.t. superior, a priority

nīkānēyihtākosiw ᓃᑳᓀᔨᐦᑖᑯᓯᐤ
VAI s/he is thought of as superior, a priority

nīkānēyihtākwan ᓃᑳᓀᔨᐦᑖᑿᐣ
VII it is thought of as superior, a priority

nīkānēyimēw ᓃᑳᓀᔨᒣᐤ
VTA s/he thinks s.o. superior

nīkānēyimow ᓃᑳᓀᔨᒧᐤ
VAI s/he thinks him/herself superior

nīkāni- ᓃᑳᓂ
IPV in front, ahead, at the head, in the future

nīkānihk ᓃᑳᓂᕽ
IPC in the future

nīkānikāt ᓃᑳᓂᑳᐟ
NI front leg

nīkāninikāsow ᓃᑳᓂᓂᑳᓱᐤ
VAI s/he takes precedence, s/he is of the first rank; it is the prime element

nīkānipahtāw ᓃᑳᓂᐸᐦᑖᐤ
VAI s/he runs ahead

nīkānipayiw ᓃᑳᓂᐸᔨᐤ
VAI s/he goes at the head, s/he rides at the head, s/he runs ahead

nīkānitwēwin ᓃᑳᓂᑤᐃᐏᐣ
NI preface, foreword (of a book)

nīkānimakan ᓃᑳᓂᒪᑲᐣ
VII it is first, best, favorite; it leads

nīkānīw ᓃᑳᓃᐤ
VAI s/he is first, best, favorite; s/he leads, s/he is ahead, s/he is at the head

nīkānīwiw ᓃᑳᓃᐃᐤ
VII it is in the future [also nīkāniwiw]

nīkānohtahēw ᓃᑳᓄᐦᑕᐦᐁᐤ
VTA s/he takes s.o. ahead, s/he takes s.o. in the front to walk

nīkānohtawēw ᓃᑳᓄᐦᑕᐍᐤ
VTA s/he walks ahead of s.o.

nīkānohtēw ᓃᑳᓄᐦᑌᐤ
VAI s/he walks at the head, s/he walks ahead

nīki ᓃᑭ
NDI my home, my dwelling

nīkihcanakwēwisip
ᓃᑭᐦᒐᓇᑵᐃᐏᐢ
NA blue wing duck

nīkihik ᓃᑭᐦᐃᐠ
NA parent [pl: -wak; commonly pl and NDA: ninīkihikwak "my parents"]

nīkihikomāw ᓃᑭᐦᐃᑯᒫᐤ
NA parent

nīkis ᓃᑭᐢ
NDI my small home; my cabin [dim]

nīmāhēw ᓃᒪᐦᐁᐤ
VTA s/he gives s.o. provisions for the journey, s/he makes lunch for s.o. to take, s/he makes s.o. take a lunch

nīmāhisow ᓃᒪᐦᐃᓱᐤ
VAI s/he makes lunch for him/herself to take

nīmākohpēw ᓃᒪᑯᐦᐯᐤ
VAI s/he takes his/her blankets along (when on a trip) [also nimakohpēw]

nīmāsiw ᓃᒪᓯᐤ
VAI s/he takes a little lunch along [dim]

nīmāskwaham ᓃᒫᐢᑲᐧᐦᐊᒼ
VTI s/he puts s.t. on a spit
nīmāskwawinēw ᓃᒫᐢᑲᐧᐃᐧᓀᐤ
VTA s/he takes weapons along for s.o.
nīmāskwākan ᓃᒫᐢᑳᐧᑲᐣ
NI weapon
nīmāskwān ᓃᒫᐢᑳᐧᐣ
NI weapon(s); gun carried along with one
nīmāskwēw ᓃᒫᐢᑫᐧᐤ
VAI s/he carries a gun, weapons; s/he is armed
nīmāskwēwin ᓃᒫᐢᑫᐧᐃᐧᐣ
NI armour, weapons
nīmāw ᓃᒫᐤ
VAI s/he packs a lunch, s/he takes provisions on the way
nīmāwin ᓃᒫᐃᐧᐣ
NI lunch, provisions for the way
nīmāwinihkēw ᓃᒫᐃᐧᓂᐦᑫᐤ
VAI s/he prepares provisions
nīmāwiniwat ᓃᒫᐃᐧᓂᐊᐧᐟ
NI grub box; a lunchbox
nīmi- ᓃᒥ
IPV take along
nīmicīkahikanēw ᓃᒥ ᒌᑲᐦᐃᑲᓀᐤ
VAI s/he carries an axe along
nīmihēw ᓃᒥᐦᐁᐤ
VTA s/he makes s.o. dance
nīmihitow ᓃᒥᐦᐃᑐᐤ
VAI s/he dances, s/he joins in the dancing; [*pl*:] they make one another dance, they dance with one another, they dance
nīmihitohēw ᓃᒥᐦᐃᑐᐦᐁᐤ
VTA s/he makes s.o. dance
nīmihitoskiw ᓃᒥᐦᐃᑐᐢᑭᐤ
VAI s/he is fond of dancing [*hab*]
nīmihitowikamik ᓃᒥᐦᐃᑐᐃᐧᑲᒥᐠ
NI dance-lodge; dance hall [*pl*: -wa]
nīmihitowin ᓃᒥᐦᐃᑐᐃᐧᐣ
NI dance
nīmihitowinihkēw ᓃᒥᐦᐃᑐᐃᐧᓂᐦᑫᐤ
VAI s/he organizes a dance, s/he holds a dance
nīmihiwēw ᓃᒥᐦᐃᐍᐤ
VAI s/he gives a dance
nīmikwāsow ᓃᒥᑳᐧᓱᐤ
VAI s/he takes his/her own sewing along
nīminam ᓃᒥᓇᒼ
VTI s/he holds s.t. aloft
nīminamawēw ᓃᒥᓇᒪᐍᐤ
VTA s/he holds (it/him) aloft for s.o.; s/he performs funeral rites for s.o.
nīminān ᓃᒥᓈᐣ
NI dance
nīmināniwan ᓃᒥᓈᓂᐊᐧᐣ
VII it is a dance, a time of dancing
nīminēw ᓃᒥᓀᐤ
VTA s/he holds s.o. aloft
nīminikēw ᓃᒥᓂᑫᐤ
VAI s/he prays over the food (at a feast); s/he holds things aloft; s/he performs a funeral
nīmipāskisikanēw ᓃᒥᐹᐢᑭᓯᑲᓀᐤ
VAI s/he carries a gun along
nīmipīhtatwānēw ᓃᒥᐲᐦᑕᑖᐧᓀᐤ
VAI s/he carries a quiver
nīmiskotēnēw ᓃᒥᐢᑯᑌᓀᐤ
VTA s/he holds s.o. aloft over the fire
nīmiw ᓃᒥᐤ
VAI s/he dances
nīmiwin ᓃᒥᐃᐧᐣ
NI a dance, Indian dance
nīmōpēw ᓃᒨᐯᐤ
VAI s/he carries a supply of water; s/he takes a drink along
nīni ᓃᓂ
NDI my bone-marrow [*commonly 3rd person form only*: wīni]
nīpawihēw ᓃᐸᐃᐧᐦᐁᐤ
VTA s/he makes s.o. stand up
nīpawipaýihow ᓃᐸᐃᐧᐸᔨᐦᐅᐤ
VAI s/he stands up suddenly
nīpawiw ᓃᐸᐃᐧᐤ
VAI s/he stands, s/he stands up, s/he stands erect, s/he stands there, s/he stands fast
nīpawiwinihk ᓃᐸᐃᐧᐃᐧᓂᕽ
INM Nipawin, SK [*loc*; *lit*: "at the standing place", *in reference to looking out over the valley*]
nīpawīstam ᓃᐸᐄᐧᐢᑕᒼ
VTI s/he stands s.t., s/he endures s.t.
nīpawīstamawēw ᓃᐸᐄᐧᐢᑕᒪᐍᐤ
VTA s/he stands up for s.o., s/he is a witness (*e.g.* at wedding) for s.o.
nīpawīstawēw ᓃᐸᐄᐧᐢᑕᐍᐤ
VTA s/he stands by s.o. [*see also* nahikāpawīstawēw]
nīpawīstātowak ᓃᐸᐄᐧᐢᑖᑐᐊᐧᐠ
VAI they stand by one another
nīpā- ᓃᐹ
IPV at night, in the dark
nīpā-ayamihāw ᓃᐹ ᐊᔭᒥᐦᐋᐤ
VAI s/he celebrates midnight mass (at Christmas)
nīpā-itohtēw ᓃᐹ ᐃᑐᐦᑌᐤ
VAI s/he goes during the night
nīpā-tipisk ᓃᐹ ᑎᐱᐢᐠ
IPC in the dark of the night, at night, during the night
nīpāhow ᓃᐹᐦᐅᐤ
VAI s/he canoes in the dark
nīpāhtēw ᓃᐹᐦᑌᐤ
VAI s/he walks in the dark, s/he comes home late at night
nīpāmāýātan ᓃᐹᒫᔮᑕᐣ
VII it is purple
nīpāmāýātastotin ᓃᐹᒫᔮᑕᐢᑐᑎᐣ
NI purple hat
nīpāmāýātisiw ᓃᐹᒫᔮᑎᓯᐤ
VAI s/he is purple
nīpāyāstēw ᓃᐹᔮᐢᑌᐤ
VII it is moonlight, be a moonlit night [*also* nīpāhāstēw]
nīpēpiw ᓃᐯᐱᐤ
VAI s/he has a wake, s/he holds a wake; s/he sits up with someone dead or dying
nīpēpīstamawēw ᓃᐯᐲᐢᑕᒪᐍᐤ
VTA s/he sits up with s.o. who has passed on
nīpēpīstawēw ᓃᐯᐲᐢᑕᐍᐤ
VTA s/he sits up with s.o. who has passed on
nīpicikan ᓃᐱᒋᑲᐣ
NDI my gums
nīpihki ᓃᐱᐦᑭ
IPC next summer; when it's summer
nīpiminānа ᓃᐱᒥᓈᓇ
NI highbush cranberries [*pl*]
nīpiminānāhtik ᓃᐱᒥᓈᓈᐦᑎᐠ
NI cranberry bush [*also NA*; *pl*: -wa(k)]
nīpin ᓃᐱᐣ
VII it is summer
nīpin-aya ᓃᐱᐣ ᐊᔭ
NA summer bird, summer animal [*pl*: -k]
nīpinaskamikāw ᓃᐱᓇᐢᑲᒥᑳᐤ
NI bare ground after snow melts
nīpinēsīs ᓃᐱᓀᓰᐢ
NA small summer bird [*dim*]
nīpinisiw ᓃᐱᓂᓯᐤ
VAI s/he camps for the summer
nīpinisiwin ᓃᐱᓂᓯᐃᐧᐣ
NI summer camp; summer resort
nīpinitāpānāsk ᓃᐱᓂᑖᐹᓈᐢᐠ
NA stone boat; wagon [*pl*: -wak]
nīpinohk ᓃᐱᓄᕽ
IPC last summer
nīpisiy ᓃᐱᓯᕀ
NI willow, willow bush [*also NA*]
nīpisīhkopāw ᓃᐱᓰᐦᑯᐹᐤ
NI stand of willows, willow-patch, willow grove
nīpisīhkopāw ᓃᐱᓰᐦᑯᐹᐤ
VII it is a willow grove
nīpisīhkopāwiýiniw ᓃᐱᓰᐦᑯᐹᐃᐧᔨᓂᐤ
NA Willow Cree person
nīpisīhkopāwiýinināhk ᓃᐱᓰᐦᑯᐹᐃᐧᔨᓂᓈᕽ
INM Beardy's and Okemasis [*loc*; *lit*: "among the Willow Cree"; *SK Cree reserve*]
nīpisīhtak ᓃᐱᓰᐦᑕᐠ
NI willow stick, willow piece, willow trunk [*pl*: -wa]

nīpisīs ᓃᐱᓰᐢ
NI willow branch, willow switch; little willow [dim]

nīpisīskāw ᓃᐱᓰᐢᑳᐤ
NI willow grove

nīpisīwāsaskwētow ᓃᐱᓰᐚᓴᐢᑴᑐᐤ
NI willow cone; fungus on willow

nīpit ᓃᐱᐟ
NDI my tooth

nīpitē ᓃᐱᑌ
IPC all in a row

nīpitēhēw ᓃᐱᑌᐦᐁᐤ
VTA s/he puts s.o. in a row

nīpitēhtēw ᓃᐱᑌᐦᑌᐤ
VAI s/he walks abreast; [pl:] they walk in a row

nīpitēpiwak ᓃᐱᑌᐱᐘᐠ
VAI they sit in a row

nīpitēsinaham ᓃᐱᑌᓯᓇᐦᐊᒼ
VTI s/he writes s.t. down in a row

nīpitēsinwak ᓃᐱᑌᓯᓄᐘᐠ
VAI they lie in a line [pl generally]

nīpitēstāw ᓃᐱᑌᐢᑖᐤ
VAIt s/he puts s.t. in a row

nīpitēstēwa ᓃᐱᑌᐢᑌᐘ
VII they are in a row [pl generally]

nīpitihkāna ᓃᐱᑎᐦᑳᓇ
NDI my false teeth, my dentures [pl]

nīpiy ᓃᐱᕀ
NI leaf; blade of grass; [pl:] leaves; salad

nīpīs ᓃᐲᐢ
NI little leaf

nīpīskāw ᓃᐲᐢᑳᐤ
VII there are many leaves

nīpīwiw ᓃᐲᐏᐤ
VII it has leaves

niscās ᓂᐢᒑᐢ
NDA my male cross-cousin; my father's sister's son, my mother's brother's son, my brother-in-law [dim; familiar form of nīstāw; used by male speaker only; voc: niscās!; cf. nīstāw]

nīsinwa ᓃᓯᓇ
VII they are two in number

nīsitanaw ᓃᓯᑕᓇᐤ
IPC twenty [also nīstanaw]

nīsitanaw tahtwāpisk ᓃᓯᑕᓇᐤ ᑕᐦᑖᐱᐢᐠ
IPH twenty dollars [also nīstanaw...]

nīsitanawāw ᓃᓯᑕᓇᐚᐤ
IPC twenty times [also nīstanawāw]

nīsitanawitowak ᓃᓯᑕᓇᐃᑐᐘᐠ
VAI they are twenty in number

nīsiwak ᓃᓯᐘᐠ
VAI they are two in number; both

nīskāw ᓃᐢᑳᐤ
VII it is damp

nīskāyāw ᓃᐢᑳᔮᐤ
VII it is damp weather

nīskisiw ᓃᐢᑭᓯᐤ
VAI s/he is damp

nīskwa ᓃᐢᑿ
NDA my husband's former wife, my husband's ex; [archaic:] my fellow wife [see also nikocāsiskwēm]

nīso ᓃᓱ
IPC two

nīso- ᓃᓱ
IPV two

nīso-kīkway ᓃᓱ ᑮᒁᐧ
IPC two things [sometimes pl as if NI]

nīso-kīsikāw ᓃᓱ ᑮᓯᑳᐤ
IPC two days

nīso-kīsikāw ᓃᓱ ᑮᓯᑳᐤ
VII it is Tuesday

nīso-sōniyās ᓃᓱ ᓲᓂᔮᐢ
IPC two quarters, fifty cents [dim]

nīso-tipiskāw ᓃᓱ ᑎᐱᐢᑳᐤ
IPC two nights

nīso-tipiskāw ᓃᓱ ᑎᐱᐢᑳᐤ
VII it is Tuesday night

nīso-tipiskāwa ᓃᓱ ᑎᐱᐢᑳᐘ
IPC two nights

nīso-tipiskwēw ᓃᓱ ᑎᐱᐢᑴᐤ
VAI s/he fasts for two days and nights; s/he is away two nights, s/he goes for two nights

nīsocihc ᓃᓱᒋᐦᐨ
IPC two fingers, with two fingers

nīsohkwāmiwak ᓃᓱᐦᑿᒥᐘᐠ
VAI they sleep two in a bed

nīsohtāw ᓃᓱᐦᑖᐤ
VAIt s/he makes s.t. two

nīsohtēwak ᓃᓱᐦᑌᐘᐠ
VAI they walk together in twos

nīsokamik ᓃᓱᑲᒥᐠ
IPC two buildings

nīsokamikisiwak ᓃᓱᑲᒥᑭᓯᐘᐠ
VAI they live two in a house, they live in two houses; [sg:] s/he lives in two houses

nīsokācis ᓃᓱᑳᒋᐢ
NI bicycle [dim; lit: "little two-leg"]

nīsokāpawiwak ᓃᓱᑳᐸᐑᐘᐠ
VAI they stand in pairs [pl generally]

nīsokātēw ᓃᓱᑳᑌᐤ
VAI s/he has two legs

nīsokēwak ᓃᓱᑳᐧᐠ
VAI they camp together in twos

nīsonam ᓃᓱᓇᒼ
VTI s/he holds two of s.t. together

nīsonēw ᓃᓱᓀᐤ
VTA s/he holds two of s.o. together (in one hand)

nīsonisk ᓃᓱᓂᐢᐠ
IPC two fathoms

nīsoniskēyiw ᓃᓱᓂᐢᑫᔨᐤ
VAI s/he reaches with both arms

nīsonitowak ᓃᓱᓂᑐᐘᐠ
VAI they hold one another

nīsopiponwēw ᓃᓱᐱᐳᓌᐤ
VAI s/he is two years old [also nīsopiponēw]

nīsopīwāpisk ᓃᓱᐲᐚᐱᐢᐠ
NI double rail [pl: -wa]

nīsosākēw ᓃᓱᓵᑫᐤ
VAI s/he has two coats

nīsosāp ᓃᓱᓵᑊ
IPC twelve

nīsosimow ᓃᓱᓯᒧᐤ
VAI s/he jigs, s/he dances as one of two; [pl:] they dance in twos; they jig

nīsoskawēw ᓃᓱᐢᑲᐁᐤ
VAI s/he wears two pairs

nīsoskwēwēw ᓃᓱᐢᑴᐁᐤ
VAI he has two women, wives

nīsostahwēw ᓃᓱᐢᑕᐦᐁᐤ
VTA s/he gets two of s.o. in one shot

nīsotak ᓃᓱᑕᐠ
NA two canoes [pl]

nīsotāpānāsk ᓃᓱᑖᐹᓈᐢᐠ
NA two outfits, two wagons [pl: -wak]

nīsotēskanēw ᓃᓱᑌᐢᑲᓀᐤ
VAI it has two horns

nīsowēwak ᓃᓱᐍᐘᐠ
VAI they speak together, at once

nīsoyawēw ᓃᓱᔭᐁᐤ
VTA s/he shoots two of s.o. with a single shot

nīsoyīhkāsow ᓃᓱᔩᐦᑳᓱᐤ
VAI s/he has two names

nīsoyīhkātēw ᓃᓱᔩᐦᑳᑌᐤ
VII it has two names

nīsōcēsis ᓃᓲᒉᓯᐢ
NA twin [dim]

nīsōhkamawēw ᓃᓲᐦᑲᒪᐁᐤ
VTA s/he helps s.o., s/he gives s.o. assistance

nīsōhkamākēwin ᓃᓲᐦᑲᒫᑫᐏᐣ
NI assistance; help

nīsōhkamātowak ᓃᓲᐦᑲᒫᑐᐘᐠ
VAI they work together at (it/him) as two

nīsōhkamātowin ᓃᓲᐦᑲᒫᑐᐏᐣ
NI mutual assistance

nīsōhkawēwak ᓃᓲᐦᑲᐁᐘᐠ
VTA they fight s.o. two against one

nīsōhkonisk ᓃᓲᐦᑯᓂᐢᐠ
IPC with both hands

nīsōhkoniskēw ᓃᓲᐦᑯᓂᐢᑫᐤ
VAI s/he uses both hands

nīsōskān ᓃᓲᐢᑳᐣ
IPC two pairs

nīsōtēmihkēw ᓃᓲᑌᒥᐦᑫᐤ
VAI s/he has twins, it has two offspring

nīsōtēw ᐅᐩᒍᐤ
NA twin

nīsta ᐅᐣᐨ
PR I, too; I by contrast; I myself *[first person sg]*

nīstamik ᐅᐣᒍᕐ
IPC before (s.t.), first

nīstanān ᐅᐣᒐᐣ
IPC we, too; we by contrast; we ourselves *[first person pl exclusive]*

nīstāw ᐅᐣᒍᐤ
NDA my male cross-cousin; my father's sister's son, my mother's brother's son; my brother-in-law *[used by male speaker only; cf.* niscās*]*

nīsw-āskiy ᐅᐩᐢᑭᐩ
IPC two years *[also* nīso-askiy*]*

nīsw-āya ᐅᐩᔭ
IPC two of s.t., two things

nīsw-āyamihēwi-kīsikāw
ᐅᐩᐧᐊᐧᒥᐦᐁᐧᐄᐧ ᑭᓯᑲᐤ
IPC two weeks

nīsw-āyihk ᐅᐩᕐᐤ
IPC in two places *[cf.* niswayak*]*

nīswahpisowak ᐅᐩᐦᐱᓱᐊᐧᐠ
VAI they are harnessed as two, they are a team of two; they are tied in a pair

nīswahpitam ᐅᐩᐦᐱᑕᒼ
VTI s/he ties s.t. together as two (*e.g.* bones)

nīswahpitēw ᐅᐩᐦᐱᑌᐤ
VTA s/he ties s.o. together as two (*e.g.* horses)

nīswapiw ᐅᐩᐊᐱᐤ
VAI s/he sits as two, be situated as two, come together as two

nīswaskanōs ᐅᐩᐢᑲᓅᐢ
NI double-barreled gun

nīswaskisin ᐅᐩᐢᑭᓯᐣ
IPC two pair of shoes

nīswaskitēwa ᐅᐩᐢᑭᑌᐊᐧ
VII they are two standing together

nīswastāw ᐅᐩᐢᒍᐤ
VAIt s/he puts two of s.t. together

nīswastēw ᐅᐩᐢᑌᐤ
VII it is doubled

nīswatōspow ᐅᐩᒍᐢᐳᐤ
VAI s/he eats with another from same dish

nīswayak ᐅᐩᔭᐠ
IPC simultaneously; in two ways, in two places *[cf.* nīsw-āyihk*]*

nīswāhtik ᐅᐩᐦᑎᐠ
IPC two sticks

nīswāpēk ᐅᐩᐁᐧᐠ
IPC in two strings

nīswāpēkinam ᐅᐩᐁᐧᑭᓇᒼ
VTI s/he doubles the strand; s/he doubles s.t.

nīswāpēkinēw ᐅᐩᐁᐧᑭᓀᐤ
VTA s/he doubles s.o.

nīswāpisk ᐅᐩᐊᐱᐢᐠ
IPC two dollars

nīswāskisowak ᐅᐩᐢᑭᓱᐊᐧᐠ
VAI they stands in pairs (as trees) *[pl generally]*

nīswāskwēw ᐅᐩᐢᑫᐧᐤ
VAI s/he uses two solids (in game)

nīswāw ᐅᐩᐤ
IPC twice, two times; double

nīswāw-mitātahtomitanaw
ᐅᐩᐤ ᒥᒐᐦᑐᒥᑕᓇᐤ
IPC two hundred

nīswēskisinēw ᐅᐩᐢᑭᓯᓀᐤ
VAI s/he has double moccasins

nītihp ᐅᐣᐦ
NDI my brain

nītim ᐅᐣᒼ
NDA my cross-cousin of the opposite gender; *[male speaker:]* daughter of my father's sister or my mother's brother; my sister-in-law (*i.e.* wife of male sibling or parallel cousin); *[female speaker:]* son of my father's sister or my mother's brother; my brother-in-law (*i.e.* husband of female sibling or parallel cousin) *[pl: -wak; cf.* nīcimos*]*

nītisān ᐅᐣᓯᐣ
NDA my sibling; my brother or sister *[cf.* nīcisān(is)*]*

nīwa ᐅᐊ
NDA my wife *[commonly third person form only:* wiwa*]*

nīwahikan ᐅᐊᐦᐃᑲᐣ
NDA my pounded meat *[also* niyīwahikan; *cf.* īwahikan, yīwahikan*]*

nīwas ᐅᐊᐢ
NDI my sacred pack, my sacred bundle *[pl:* nīwata; *loc:* nīwatihk*]*

ᐅ
---

nohcāwīs ᐅᐦᒑᐃᐧᐢ
NDA my parallel uncle; my father's brother, my mother's sister's husband; my godfather; my stepfather *[dim: "my dear father"; also* nōhcāwīs; *see also* nohkomis; *cf.* nohtāwiy*]*

nohkom ᐅᐦᑯᒼ
NDA my grandmother *[reference extended to all related females of grandmother's generation; term for any respected*

female elder; *also* nōhkom; *cf.* 3: ohkoma "his/her grandmother(s)," *also* ōhkoma; *voc:* nohkō!, kōkom!*]*

nohkomipan ᐅᐦᑯᒥᐸᐣ
NDA my deceased grandmother, my late grandmother *[also* nōhkomipan*]*

nohkomis ᐅᐦᑯᒥᐢ
NDA my uncle, my parallel uncle; my father's brother, my mother's sister's husband *[also* nōhkomis; *see also* nohcāwis*]*

nohkō! ᐅᐦᑰ
NDA grandmother! *[voc; also* nōhkō!, kōkom!; *cf.* nohkom*]*

nohpan ᐅᐦᐸᐣ
NDI my lung *[also* nōhpan; *cf.* 3: ohpana "his/her lungs"*]*

nohtā! ᐅᐦᒐ
NDA father! *[voc; also:* nōhtā!; *cf.* nohtāwiy; *in some areas, this has been restricted in Christian reference to God]*

nohtāwiy ᐅᐦᒐᐃᐧᐩ
NDA my father; *[Christian:]* Heavenly Father *[also* nōhtawiy; *cf.* 3: ohtāwiya "his/her father"; *voc:* nohtā!*]*

nohtāwīhkāwin ᐅᐦᒐᐃᐧᐦᑲᐃᐧᐣ
NDA my godfather, my step-father *[also* nōhtāwīhkāwin*]*

nohtāwīpan ᐅᐦᒐᐃᐧᐸᐣ
NDA my deceased father, my late father *[also* nōhtāwīpan*]*

nosonēham ᐅᓱᓅᐦᐊᒼ
VTI s/he follows s.t.

nosonēhwēw ᐅᓱᓅᐦᐁᐧᐤ
VTA s/he follows s.o.

ᐆ
---

nōcacaskwēw ᐆᒐᒐᐢᑫᐧᐤ
VAI s/he hunts muskrats *[cf.* nōtacaskwēw*]*

nōcihēw ᐆᒋᐦᐁᐧᐤ
VTA s/he beats s.o. up; s/he hunts s.o., s/he pursues s.o.; s/he traps s.o. (*e.g.* beaver, muskrat); s/he whips s.o., s/he gives s.o. the strap

nōcihcikēw ᐆᒋᐦᒋᑫᐧᐤ
VAI s/he traps, s/he traps things; s/he hunts

nōcihcikēwaskiy ᐆᒋᐦᒋᑫᐧᐊᐧᐢᑭᐩ
NI trapping territory, trapline

nōcihcikēwin ᐆᒋᐦᒋᑫᐧᐃᐧᐣ
NI trapline; trapping, hunting

nōcihiskwēwēsk ᓅᒋᐦᐃᐢᑵᐍᐢᐠ
NA womanizer, man given to chasing women

nōcihiskwēwēw ᓅᒋᐦᐃᐢᑵᐍᐤ
VAI he courts women, he chases women

nōcihiskwēwēwin ᓅᒋᐦᐃᐢᑵᐍᐏᐣ
NI flirting; chasing women

nōcihito-pīsim ᓅᒋᐦᐃᑐ ᐲᓯᒼ
NA Mating Moon, Rutting Moon, September [*obv*: -wa]

nōcihitowak ᓅᒋᐦᐃᑐᐘᐠ
VAI they pursue each other; they mate, they mate with one another, they find mates [*in reference to animals*]

nōcihitowi-pīsim ᓅᒋᐦᐃᑐᐏ ᐲᓯᒼ
NA Mating Moon, Rutting Moon, September [*obv*: -wa; *cf.* onōcihitowi-pīsim]

nōcihitowin ᓅᒋᐦᐃᑐᐏᐣ
NI mating; rutting; courting

nōcihtāw ᓅᒋᐦᑖᐤ
VAIt s/he pursues s.t., s/he works on s.t.; s/he hunts for s.t.

nōcikinosēwēw ᓅᒋᑭᓄᓭᐍᐤ
VAI s/he fishes, s/he goes fishing, s/he goes for fish; s/he is engaged in fishing

nōcikinosēwiýiniw ᓅᒋᑭᓄᓭᐏᔨᓂᐤ
NA fisherman

nōcikinosēwiýinīwiw ᓅᒋᑭᓄᓭᐏᔨᓃᐏᐤ
VAI he is a fisherman

nōcikinosēwīstamawēw ᓅᒋᑭᓄᓭᐑᐢᑕᒪᐍᐤ
VTA s/he fishes for s.o.

nōcikwēsiw ᓅᒋᑵᓯᐤ
NA old woman, wife [*dim*; *cf.* nōcokwēsiw, nōtikwēw, nōtokwēsiw, nōtokwēw]

nōcināpēwēskiw ᓅᒋᓈᐯᐍᐢᑭᐤ
VAI she is a flirt; she is fond of chasing men [*hab*]

nōcināpēwēw ᓅᒋᓈᐯᐍᐤ
VAI she chases men, she looks for men

nōcinīwihēsiw ᓅᒋᓃᐏᐦᐁᓯᐤ
NA duck hawk

nōcisipēw ᓅᒋᓯᐯᐤ
VAI s/he hunts ducks, s/he is engaged in duck-hunting

nōcīhkamawēw ᓅᒌᐦᑲᒪᐍᐤ
VTA he seduces s.o.'s wife

nōcīhkawēw ᓅᒌᐦᑲᐍᐤ
VTA s/he seduces s.o.; s/he feels s.o. up (as in foreplay)

nōcokwēsiw ᓅᒍᑵᓯᐤ
NA old woman, old lady, wife [*dim*; *cf.* nōcikwēsiw, nōtikwēw, nōtokwēsiw, nōtokwēw]

nōhāwasow ᓅᐦᐋᐘᓱᐤ
VAI she suckles her child, she nurses her children

nōhcimihk ᓅᐦᒋᒥᕽ
IPC inland, in the woods, on the inside; away from the water, up in the woods; at the far end [*also* nohcimihk]

nōhēw ᓅᐦᐁᐤ
VTA she suckles s.o., she nurses s.o., she breastfeeds s.o.; she allows s.o. to suck

nōhisow ᓅᐦᐃᓱᐤ
VAI s/he nurses (*i.e.* a child)

nōhkwācikēw ᓅᐦᒁᒋᑫᐤ
VAI s/he licks (*e.g.* a dish)

nōhkwātam ᓅᐦᒁᑕᒼ
VTI s/he licks s.t.

nōhkwātēw ᓅᐦᒁᑌᐤ
VTA s/he licks s.o.

nōhtaw ᓅᐦᑕᐤ
IPC short of (in length, time); too soon; before

nōhtē- ᓅᐦᑌ
IPV want to, desire to; lack [*also* nohtē-]

nōhtē-apiw ᓅᐦᑌ ᐊᐱᐤ
VAI s/he would like to sit

nōhtē-atoskēw ᓅᐦᑌ ᐊᑐᐢᑫᐤ
VAI s/he would like to work

nōhtē-kīwēw ᓅᐦᑌ ᑮᐍᐤ
VAI s/he would like to go home

nōhtē-mātow ᓅᐦᑌ ᒫᑐᐤ
VAI s/he would like to cry

nōhtē-mīcisow ᓅᐦᑌ ᒦᒋᓱᐤ
VAI s/he is hungry; s/he wants to eat, s/he would like to eat

nōhtē-nikamow ᓅᐦᑌ ᓂᑲᒧᐤ
VAI s/he would like to sing

nōhtē-nipāw ᓅᐦᑌ ᓂᐹᐤ
VAI s/he would like to sleep

nōhtē-pwākomow ᓅᐦᑌ ᐺᑯᒧᐤ
VAI s/he is nauseated

nōhtēhēw ᓅᐦᑌᐦᐁᐤ
VTA s/he makes s.o. give out, s/he tires s.o. out

nōhtēhkasow ᓅᐦᑌᐦᑲᓱᐤ
VAI it is not hot enough, s/he is in need of warmth

nōhtēhkatēw ᓅᐦᑌᐦᑲᑌᐤ
VAI s/he is hungry, s/he wants food

nōhtēhkatēwin ᓅᐦᑌᐦᑲᑌᐏᐣ
NI hunger

nōhtēhkwasipaýiw ᓅᐦᑌᐦᑿᓯᐸᔨᐤ
VAI s/he becomes sleepy

nōhtēhkwasiw ᓅᐦᑌᐦᑿᓯᐤ
VAI s/he is sleepy

nōhtēhkwastimēw ᓅᐦᑌᐦᑿᐢᑎᒣᐤ
VTA s/he makes s.o. sleepy, s/he tires s.o. out causing sleepiness

nōhtēhtēw ᓅᐦᑌᐦᑌᐤ
VAI s/he fails to walk all the way

nōhtēpaýihēw ᓅᐦᑌᐸᔨᐦᐁᐤ
VTA s/he causes s.o. to lack (s.t.); s/he causes s.o. to run short (of s.t.)

nōhtēpaýihow ᓅᐦᑌᐸᔨᐦᐅᐤ
VAI s/he is in want (for him/herself)

nōhtēpaýiw ᓅᐦᑌᐸᔨᐤ
VAI s/he lacks (s.t.); s/he falls short, s/he runs short (of s.t.); s/he is in want

nōhtēpaýiw ᓅᐦᑌᐸᔨᐤ
VII it is insufficient, it falls short

nōhtēsimēw ᓅᐦᑌᓯᒣᐤ
VTA s/he tires s.o. out, s/he leaves s.o. on the way (as that one is tired)

nōhtēsin ᓅᐦᑌᓯᐣ
VAI s/he is played out, s/he is tired; s/he falls on the way, s/he has his/her strength fail

nōhtēskam ᓅᐦᑌᐢᑲᒼ
VTI s/he falls short of pacing a distance (measurement)

nōhtēyāpākwēw ᓅᐦᑌᔮᐹᑵᐤ
VAI s/he is thirsty

nōhtēyāpākwēwin ᓅᐦᑌᔮᐹᑵᐏᐣ
NI thirst

nōkohāwasow ᓅᑯᐦᐋᐘᓱᐤ
VAI she gives birth [*lit*: "she causes her child to appear"]

nōkohcikēw ᓅᑯᐦᒋᑫᐤ
VAI s/he shows things

nōkohēw ᓅᑯᐦᐁᐤ
VTA s/he brings s.o. into appearance

nōkohtāw ᓅᑯᐦᑖᐤ
VAIt s/he lets s.t. appear, s/he shows s.t.; s/he is a capable person

nōkosiw ᓅᑯᓯᐤ
VAI s/he appears, s/he comes into view, s/he is visible, s/he is seen; s/he is born

nōkwan ᓅᑿᐣ
VII it appears, it becomes visible, it is seen [*rdpl*: na-nōkwan]

nōmakēs ᓅᒪᑫᐢ
IPC for awhile, for quite a while

nōmanakēs ᓅᒪᓇᑫᐢ
IPC for awhile, for quite a while

nōmiskam ᓅᒥᐢᑲᒼ
VTI s/he goes part of the way

nōnācikan ᓅᓈᒋᑲᐣ
NI nursing bottle; a soother

nōnācikanis ᓅᓈᒋᑲᓂᐢ
NI nipple (on a bottle) [*dim*]

nōnācikēhēw ᓅᓈᒋᑫᐦᐁᐤ
VTA s/he gives s.o. (baby) a bottle to suck; s/he makes s.o. suckle

nōnācikēsīs ᓅᓈᒋᑫᓰᐢ
NA sucker (fish) [*dim*]

nōnācikēw ᓅᓈᒋᑫᐤ
VAI s/he sucks, s/he sucks a bottle

nōnācikēwin ᓅᓈᒋᑫᐎᐣ
NI sucking; suction

nōnātam ᓅᓈᑕᒼ
VTI s/he sucks s.t.

nōnātēw ᓅᓈᑌᐤ
VTA s/he sucks s.o. (an animal that is suckled)

nōnihtahisow ᓅᓂᐦᑖᐦᐃᓱ
VAI s/he puts him/herself to suckle

nōniskiw ᓅᓂᐢᑭᐤ
VAI s/he is constantly sucking [hab]

nōniw ᓅᓂᐤ
VAI s/he is nursing, s/he is breastfeeding, s/he sucks at the breast

nōsē- ᓅᓭ
IPN female

nōsē-aya ᓅᓭ ᐊᔭ
NA female being [pl: -k]

nōsē-kōhkōs ᓅᓭ ᑰᐦᑰᐢ
NA sow

nōsē-minōs ᓅᓭ ᒥᓅᐢ
NA female cat

nōsē-mistāhkēsiw ᓅᓭ ᒥᐢᑖᐦᑫᓯᐤ
NA lioness

nōsē-pāhkahahkwān ᓅᓭ ᐹᐦᑲᐦᐊᐦᑲᐣ
NA hen

nōsē-pihēw ᓅᓭ ᐱᐦᐁᐤ
NA female partridge

nōsē-wāpos ᓅᓭ ᐋᐳᐢ
NA doe, female rabbit [pl: -wak]

nōsēmēk ᓅᓭᒣᐠ
NA spawn [pl: -wak]

nōsēsip ᓅᓭᓯᑊ
NA female duck

nōsēstim ᓅᓭᐢᑎᒼ
NA bitch; mare [pl: -wak; cf. kiskānak]

nōsisē! ᓅᓯᓭ
NDA grandchild! [voc; cf. nōsisim]

nōsisim ᓅᓯᓯᒼ
NDA my grandchild [dim: nōsisimis; voc: nōsisē!]

nōsōskam ᓅᓱᐢᑲᒼ
VTI s/he follows after s.t.

nōsōskawēw ᓅᓱᐢᑲᐍᐤ
VTA s/he follows after s.o.

nōtacaskwēw ᓅᑕᒐᐢᑵᐤ
VAI s/he hunts muskrats [cf. nōcacaskwēw]

nōtamēsēw ᓅᑕᒣᓭᐤ
VAI s/he is fishing, s/he goes fishing

nōtamiskwēw ᓅᑕᒥᐢᑵᐤ
VAI s/he hunts beavers

nōtasāwākanēw ᓅᑕᓵᐋᑲᓀᐤ
VAI s/he hunts to get furs

nōtatāwākanēw ᓅᑕᑖᐋᑲᓀᐤ
VAI s/he hunts for furs

nōtāposwēw ᓅᑖᐳᐢᐍᐤ
VAI s/he hunts rabbits

nōtihkomātēw ᓅᑎᐦᑯᒫᑌᐤ
VTA s/he hunts for lice on s.o.'s head [cf. nitihkomātēw]

nōtihkomēw ᓅᑎᐦᑯᒣᐤ
VAI s/he hunts for lice

nōtikwēw ᓅᑎᑵᐤ
NA old woman, wife [cf. nōcikwēsiw, nōcokwēsiw, nōtokwēsiw, nōtokwēw]

nōtimāw ᓅᑎᒫᐤ
VII it is round [see also wāwiyēyāw]

nōtimisiw ᓅᑎᒥᓯᐤ
VAI s/he is round [see also wāwiyēsiw]

ñōtin ᓅᑎᐣ
VII there is a wind, it is windy [sC; cf. ẏōtin; cf. nōtinēw]

nōtinam ᓅᑎᓇᒼ
VTI s/he fights s.t., s/he fights with s.t

nōtinastimwēw ᓅᑎᓇᐢᑎᒭᐤ
VAI s/he is cruel to horses

nōtinākan ᓅᑎᓈᑲᐣ
NA enemy

nōtinēw ᓅᑎᓀᐤ
VTA s/he fights s.o., s/he fights with s.o.; s/he seizes s.o.

nōtinikēskiw ᓅᑎᓂᑫᐢᑭᐤ
VAI s/he fights often, s/he is a habitual fighter [hab; used derogatorily]

nōtinikēstamawēw ᓅᑎᓂᑫᐢᑕᒪᐍᐤ
VTA s/he fights (people) for s.o.

nōtinikēstamāsow ᓅᑎᓂᑫᐢᑕᒫᓱ
VAI s/he fights (people) for him/herself

nōtinikēw ᓅᑎᓂᑫᐤ
VAI s/he fights people, s/he puts up a fight; s/he takes part in war (e.g. World War II)

nōtinikēwin ᓅᑎᓂᑫᐎᐣ
NI fight; war

nōtinikēwiẏiniw ᓅᑎᓂᑫᐎᔨᓂᐤ
NA warrior

nōtiniskwēwēw ᓅᑎᓂᐢᑵᐍᐤ
VAI he fights his wife

nōtinito-sīpiy ᓅᑎᓂᐟ ᓰᐱᕀ
NI Battle River, SK [also nōtinitowi-sīpiy]

nōtinito-sīpīhk ᓅᑎᓂᐟ ᓰᐲᕽ
INM Battleford, SK [loc]

nōtinitowak ᓅᑎᓂᐟᐊᐠ
VAI they fight, they fight one another

nōtinitowi-sīpīhk ᓅᑎᓂᐟᐅᐄ ᓰᐲᕽ
INM North Battleford, SK; Battleford, SK [loc]

nōtinitowin ᓅᑎᓂᐟᐅᐃᐣ
NI fight, fighting; war

nōtisin ᓅᑎᓯᐣ
VAI s/he is too big (to enter an opening); s/he fails to fit in

nōtisipēw ᓅᑎᓯᐯᐤ
VAI s/he hunts ducks

nōtiskam ᓅᑎᐢᑲᒼ
VTI s/he fails to fit s.t. as it is too small

nōtiskawēw ᓅᑎᐢᑲᐍᐤ
VTA s/he fails to fit s.o. (e.g. pants) as it is too small

nōtiskwēwātēw ᓅᑎᐢᑵᐋᑌᐤ
VTA he courts s.o. (i.e. a woman)

nōtiskwēwēskiw ᓅᑎᐢᑵᐍᐢᑭᐤ
VAI he is a woman chaser [hab]

nōtiskwēwēw ᓅᑎᐢᑵᐍᐤ
VAI he courts a woman

nōtokēsiw ᓅᑐᑫᓯᐤ
NA old woman, old lady

nōtokēw ᓅᑐᑫᐤ
NA old woman

nōtokēwihkomān ᓅᑐᑫᐎᐦᑯᒫᐣ
NI dull knife

nōtokēwikamikos ᓅᑐᑫᐎᑲᒥᑯᐢ
NI old woman's hut [dim]

nōtokēwiw ᓅᑐᑫᐎᐤ
VAI she is an old woman [cf. nōtokwēwiw]

nōtokwēs ᓅᑐᑵᐢ
NA little old lady

nōtokwēsiw ᓅᑐᑵᓯᐤ
NA old woman, old lady, wife [cf. nōcikwēsiw, nōcokwēsiw, nōtikwēw, nōtokwēw; also nōtokēsiw]

nōtokwēw ᓅᑐᑵᐤ
NA old woman, wife [cf. nōcikwēsiw, nōcokwēsiw, nōtikwēw, nōtokwēsiw]

nōtokwēwānak ᓅᑵᐋᓇᐠ
NA old mare [pl: -wak]

nōtokwēwiw ᓅᑐᑵᐎᐤ
VAI she is an old woman [cf. nōtokēwiw]

O

▷

ocahkisēhikaniw ▷ᒧ"ᑭᣔ"ᐃᑲᣔᣞ°
　VAI s/he has a flint
ocakisīmisiw ▷ᒪᑭᣔᒥᣔᣞ°
　VAI s/he has appendicitis
　[*proposed term*]
ocapihkēsīs ▷ᒪᐱ"ᑫᣔᣔ
　NA spider [*dim*]
ocasinīmisiw ▷ᒪᣔᓂᒥᣔᣞ°
　VAI s/he has gall-stones
ocawāsimisiw ▷ᒪᐊᣔᒥᣔᣞ°
　VAI s/he has a child, s/he
　has (s.o. as) a child [*dim*; *cf.*
　otawāsimisiw]
ocayisinākēs ▷ᒪᣔᣔᐊᣗ
　NA monkey [*dim*; *see also*
　onaspicākēs]
ocāhkosimāw ▷ᒧ"ᑯᣔᒪ°
　NA sister-in-law; eldest of
　all sisters-in-law
ocāhkosiw ▷ᒧ"ᑯᣔ°
　VAI s/he has (s.o. as) a
　sister-in-law
ocāpahtam ▷ᒪᐸ"ᑕᐦ
　VTI s/he is alive to see s.t.
ocāpahtowak ▷ᒪᐸ"ᗄᐧᐣ
　VAI they are alive to see one
　another
ocāpahtowin ▷ᒪᐸ"ᗄᐧᐩ
　NI being alive to see one
　another
ocāpamēw ▷ᒪᐸᒧ°
　VTA s/he is alive to see s.o.
ocāpānāskos ▷ᒪᐸᣕᣔᑯᣔ
　NA buggy; small wagon
　[*dim*; *cf.* otāpānāsk]
ocāpowēs ▷ᒪᐳᐁᣔ
　NA Ochapowace, "one who
　recites from memory" [*Cree
　chief and SK reserve name*;
　alternatively: ocāpahwēs
　"one who unties"]
ocēhpīw ▷ᑊ"ᐱ°
　VAI s/he is active and
　nimble; s/he is light-footed
　[*cf.* wacēhpīw]
ocēhtam ▷ᑊ"ᑕᐦ
　VTI s/he kisses s.t.
ocēhtowak ▷ᑊ"ᗄᐧᐣ
　VAI they kiss one another
ocēhtowi-kīsikāw
　▷ᑊ"ᗄᐧ· ᑭᣔᑲᣔ°
　VII it is New Year's Day
ocēhtowin ▷ᑊ"ᗄᐧᐩ
　NI kissing, the act of kissing

ocēk ▷ᑫᣔ
　NA fisher (*i.e.* mammal) [*pl*:
　-wak]
ocēkatāhk ▷ᑫᑲᒑᕽ
　NA the Big Dipper, the
　Great Bear (constellation)
　[*obv*: -wa]
ocēkowayān ▷ᑫᑯᐊᣕᣔᐩ
　NA fisher pelt
ocēmāwasow ▷ᑫᒪᐊᐧᓱ°
　VAI s/he kisses his/her child
　or children
ocēmēw ▷ᑫᒧ°
　VTA s/he kisses s.o.
ocēpihk ▷ᑫᐱᕽ
　NI root [*pl*: -(w)a; *cf. dim*:
　ocēpihkis *or* ocēpihkos]
ocēpihkis ▷ᑫᐱᐦᑭᣔ
　NI little root [*dim*; *cf.*
　ocēpihkos]
ocēpihkos ▷ᑫᐱᐦᑯᣔ
　NI herb, root [*dim*; *cf.*
　ocēpihkis]
ocēpihkowan ▷ᑫᐱᐦᑯᐊᐧᐣ
　VII it has roots
ocēpihkowiw ▷ᑫᐱᐦᑯᐃᐧ°
　VAI it has roots
ocēskanihkēs ▷ᑫᔅᑲᓂᐦᑫᣔ
　NA a water plant with edible
　root
ocēstatay ▷ᑫᔅᑕᑕᐩ
　NI gristle; muscle [*cf.*
　-cēstatay- *NDI*]
ocēstatēyāpiy ▷ᑫᔅᑕᑌᐊᣕᐱᐩ
　NI tendon
ocicāhk ▷ᒋᒑᕽ
　NA crane; wild turkey [*pl*:
　-wak]
ocicāhkos ▷ᒋᒑᐦᑯᣔ
　NA young or small crane
　[*dim*]
ocicāhkoskāw ▷ᒋᒑᐦᑯᔅᑲᣔ°
　VII cranes are numerous,
　there are numerous cranes
ocicāmacēsis ▷ᒋᒑᒪᒉᓯᣔ
　NA unborn puppy or calf
　[*dim*]
ocicāskāhk ▷ᒋᒑᔅᑲᕽ
　IPC between the legs, in the
　crotch [*also* ocicāskā; *cf.*
　-cicāskay- *NDI*]
ocihci- ▷ᒋᐦᒋ
　IPV back in time; far back;
　from before, earlier; having

lived long enough for
something; chance to, live to,
live to see
ocihci-kiskisiw ▷ᒋᐦᒋ ᑭᔅᑭᓯ°
　VAI s/he remembers things,
　s/he has memories far back
ocihcihkwanapiw ▷ᒋᐦᒋᐦᑲ·ᐊᓇᐱ°
　VAI s/he kneels, s/he sits on
　his/her own knees [*cf.*
　ocihkwanapiw]
ocihcihkwanapīhēw
　▷ᒋᐦᒋᐦᑲ·ᐊᓇᐱᐦᐁ°
　VTA s/he makes s.o. kneel
ocihciminam ▷ᒋᐦᒋᒥᓇᐦ
　VTI s/he holds s.t. there, at
　that spot
ocihciminikācēs ▷ᒋᐦᒋᒥᓂᑲᒉᣔ
　NI butt of gun
ocihciminikātēw ▷ᒋᐦᒋᒥᓂᑲᑌᐤ
　VII it is held at that spot
ocihcipaýin ▷ᒋᐦᒋᐸᔨᐩ
　VII it comes to pass, it
　occurs [*also* ocihcipaýiw]
ocihcipisīs ▷ᒋᐦᒋᐱᓯᣔ
　NA yellow-throated bunting
ocihkomēs ▷ᒋᐦᑯᒣᣔ
　NA one who has lice; mangy
　wolf
ocihkomisīs ▷ᒋᐦᑯᒥᓯᣔ
　NA member of a dancing
　society [*lit*: "little lousy
　one"]
ocihkwanapiw ▷ᒋᐦᑲ·ᐊᓇᐱ°
　VAI s/he kneels, s/he kneels
　in prayer [*cf.*
　ocihcihkwanapiw]
ocihkwanapīstawēw
　▷ᒋᐦᑲ·ᐊᓇᐱᔅᑕᐁ°
　VTA s/he kneels before s.o.
ocikana ▷ᒋᑲᓇ
　NI beaver food (provisions
　for winter) [*pl*]
ocikicihcēw ▷ᒋᑭᒋᐦᒉ°
　VAI s/he has a scarred hand
ocikicihciy ▷ᒋᑭᒋᐦᒋᐩ
　NI scarred hand
ocikicisk ▷ᒋᑭᒋᔅᐠ
　NI scarred buttocks
ocikiciskēw ▷ᒋᑭᒋᔅᑫ°
　VAI s/he is scarred on the
　buttocks
ocikihkwēw ▷ᒋᑭᐦᑫ·°
　VAI s/he is scarred on the
　face

ocikihkwēwin ᐅᒋᑭᐦᑴᐎᐣ
NI scars on the face
ocikikwayaw ᐅᒋᑭᑲᔭᐤ
NI scarred neck
ocikikwayawēw ᐅᒋᑭᑲᔭᐍᐤ
VAI s/he has a scarred neck
ocikisiw ᐅᒋᑭᓯᐤ
VAI s/he is scarred
ocikisiwin ᐅᒋᑭᓯᐎᐣ
NI scarredness, having scars
ocikispiton ᐅᒋᑭᐢᐱᑐᐣ
NI scarred arm
ocikispitonēw ᐅᒋᑭᐢᐱᑐᓀᐤ
VAI s/he has a scarred arm
ocipicikanāhkosa ᐅᒋᐱᒋᑲᓈᐦᑯᓴ
NI double trees (in harness), crossbar on a wagon, carriage or plow [*always pl*; *dim*]
ocipicikanāhtik ᐅᒋᐱᒋᑲᓈᐦᑎᐠ
NI shaft, wagon pole [*pl*: -wa]
ocipicikanāpisk ᐅᒋᐱᒋᑲᓈᐱᐢᐠ
NI metal traces (in harness) [*pl*: -wa]
ocipicikanēyāpiy ᐅᒋᐱᒋᑲᓀᔮᐱᕀ
NI harness, leather straps of harness
ocipicikātēw ᐅᒋᐱᒋᑳᑌᐤ
VII it is pulled, it is pulled out
ocipitam ᐅᒋᐱᑕᒼ
VTI s/he pulls s.t., s/he pulls s.t. out, towards
ocipitamawēw ᐅᒋᐱᑕᒪᐍᐤ
VTA s/he pulls (it/him) for s.o., s/he pulls (it/him) out for s.o.
ocipitamāsow ᐅᒋᐱᑕᒫᓱᐤ
VAI s/he pulls (it/him) for him/herself, s/he pulls (it/him) out for him/herself
ocipitēw ᐅᒋᐱᑌᐤ
VTA s/he pulls s.o., s/he pulls s.o. out, towards; s/he wins from s.o.
ocipitikow ᐅᒋᐱᑎᑯᐤ
VAI s/he has a seizure, s/he has fits; s/he has cramps
ocipitikowaskatēw ᐅᒋᐱᑎᑯᐘᐢᑲᑌᐤ
VAI s/he has stomach cramps
ocipitikowin ᐅᒋᐱᑎᑯᐎᐣ
NI cramps
ocipitisow ᐅᒋᐱᑎᓱᐤ
VAI s/he pulls him/herself up or along (with a rope)
ocipohkasam ᐅᒋᐳᐦᑲᓴᒼ
VTI s/he shrinks s.t. (with heat)
ocipohkaswēw ᐅᒋᐳᐦᑲᓷᐤ
VTA s/he shrinks s.o. (with heat)
ocipwēw ᐅᒋᐍᐤ
NA Ojibway Indian
ocipwēwiw ᐅᒋᐍᐏᐤ
VAI s/he is an Ojibway

ocistēmāw ᐅᒋᐢᑌᒫᐤ
VAI s/he has tobacco, s/he has (it/him) as tobacco
ociwāmihtowak ᐅᒋᐚᒥᐦᑐᐘᐠ
VAI they are brothers or cousins to one another
ociwāmihtowin ᐅᒋᐚᒥᐦᑐᐎᐣ
NI blood relationship, brotherly relationship, treating or taking one another as brothers
ociwāmimāw ᐅᒋᐚᒥᒫᐤ
NA brother, cousin
ociwāmiw ᐅᒋᐚᒥᐤ
VAI he has a brother, cousin [*in reference to a male only*]
ocīhcīkomiw ᐅᒌᐦᒌᑯᒥᐤ
VAI s/he has warts [*cf.* cīhcīkomiw; *also* ocihcīkomiw]
ocīkahikaniw ᐅᒌᑲᐦᐃᑲᓂᐤ
VAI s/he has an axe
ocīkwahikan ᐅᒌᑿᐦᐃᑲᐣ
NI sewing rod for pleating moccasins
ocīkwēhikan ᐅᒌᑵᐦᐃᑲᐣ
NI pleated moccasin, moccasin with gathered top
ocīsiciskēw ᐅᒌᓯᒋᐢᑫᐤ
VAI s/he has a burn (scar) on the buttocks
ocīsihkwēw ᐅᒌᓯᐦᑴᐤ
VAI s/he has a burn (scar) on the face
ocīsisiw ᐅᒌᓯᓯᐤ
VAI s/he is scarred by burning
ocīskimow ᐅᒌᐢᑭᒧᐤ
NA gopher [*see also* miscanikwacās]
ocīstahāsēponiw ᐅᒌᐢᑕᐦᐋᓭᐳᓂᐤ
VAI s/he has a fork
ocīstahikaniw ᐅᒌᐢᑕᐦᐃᑲᓂᐤ
VAI s/he has an awl; s/he has a fork
ohcāwīsimāw ᐅᐦᒑᐑᓯᒫᐤ
NA uncle; father's brother, mother's sister's husband
ohci ᐅᐦᒋ
IPC from there, thence, out of; with, by means of; because of; for; from then; about [*enclitic*; *cf.* ohci *IPV*]
ohci- ᐅᐦᒋ
IPV from there; with, by means of; because, for that reason, therefore, thence [*grammatical preverb*; *past preverb in negative clauses*; *cf.* ohci *IPC*, ō *IPV*; ōh- *IPV*]
ohci-kāhcitinam ᐅᐦᒋ ᑳᐦᒋᑎᓇᒼ
VTI s/he catches s.t. from there
ohci-kāhcitinēw ᐅᐦᒋ ᑳᐦᒋᑎᓀᐤ
VTA s/he catches s.o. from there
ohci-waýawīw ᐅᐦᒋ ᐘᔭᐑᐤ
VAI s/he comes out of (there)

ohciciwan ᐅᐦᒋᒋᐘᐣ
VII it flows thence, it flows from there
ohcihēw ᐅᐦᒋᐦᐁᐤ
VTA s/he stops s.o., s/he holds s.o. away
ohcikawāpiw ᐅᐦᒋᑲᐚᐱᐤ
VAI s/he sheds tears; s/he has tears dropping
ohcikawāpiwin ᐅᐦᒋᑲᐚᐱᐎᐣ
NI tears, tear drop
ohcikawāpoy ᐅᐦᒋᑲᐚᐳᕀ
NI tears [*see also* mātowināpoy]
ohcikawihtāw ᐅᐦᒋᑲᐏᐦᑖᐤ
VAIt s/he makes s.t. drip, leak
ohcikawiw ᐅᐦᒋᑲᐏᐤ
VII it drips, it flows from there; it leak
ohcinatēw ᐅᐦᒋᓇᑌᐤ
VTA s/he fights s.o. over something; s/he fights s.o. on account of something
ohcinākosiw ᐅᐦᒋᓈᑯᓯᐤ
VAI s/he is seen from there
ohcinākwan ᐅᐦᒋᓈᑿᐣ
VII it is seen from there
ohcinēw ᐅᐦᒋᓀᐤ
VAI s/he suffers in retribution for something
ohcipahtāw ᐅᐦᒋᐸᐦᑖᐤ
VAI s/he runs from there
ohcipaýin ᐅᐦᒋᐸᔨᐣ
VII it comes from there, it results from that [*cf.* ohcipaýiw *VII*]
ohcipaýiw ᐅᐦᒋᐸᔨᐤ
VAI s/he moves thence, s/he rides thence
ohcipaýiw ᐅᐦᒋᐸᔨᐤ
VII it moves thence, it rides thence; it come from there [*cf.* ohcipaýin *VII*]
ohcipicihēw ᐅᐦᒋᐱᒋᐦᐁᐤ
VTA s/he moves s.o.'s household from there, s/he helps s.o. move from somewhere
ohcipiciw ᐅᐦᒋᐱᒋᐤ
VAI s/he moves from somewhere
ohcipitam ᐅᐦᒋᐱᑕᒼ
VTI s/he pulls s.t. from somewhere
ohcipitēw ᐅᐦᒋᐱᑌᐤ
VTA s/he pulls s.o. from somewhere
ohcisin ᐅᐦᒋᓯᐣ
VAI s/he lies on that side
ohciskanawēw ᐅᐦᒋᐢᑲᓇᐍᐤ
VAI s/he leaves tracks from there, s/he leaves a trail from there
ohcistin ᐅᐦᒋᐢᑎᐣ
VII it leaks
ohcitaw ᐅᐦᒋᑕᐤ
IPC on purpose, purposely,

deliberately; it has to be, it's necessary; as expected; without fail; by all means; expressly, specifically [*predicative*; *cf.* ohtitaw]

ohcitawitēýikomēw ᐅᐦᒋᑕᐏᑌᔨᑯᒣᐤ
VAI s/he runs at the nose, s/he has a runny nose

ohciyawēw ᐅᐦᒋᔭᐍᐤ
VTA s/he wins from, over s.o. (with things)

ohciyākēw ᐅᐦᒋᔮᑫᐤ
VAI s/he wins from, over people (with things); s/he scores a win

ohcīhkamawēw ᐅᐦᒌᐦᑲᒪᐍᐤ
VTA s/he attempts to win (it/him) from s.o.; he woos s.o.'s wife

ohcīw ᐅᐦᒌᐤ
VAI s/he is from there, s/he comes from there; s/he exists thence, therefore

ohkohkēw ᐅᐦᑯᐦᑫᐤ
VAI it barks (*e.g.* dog)

ohkomimāw ᐅᐦᑯᒥᒫᐤ
NA grandmother

ohkomisimāw ᐅᐦᑯᒥᓯᒫᐤ
NA uncle [*more common in sC*; *see also* ohcāwīsimāw]

ohkomiw ᐅᐦᑯᒥᐤ
VAI s/he has a grandmother, s/he has s.o. as a grandmother

ohpaham ᐅᐦᐸᐦᐊᒼ
VTI s/he pries s.t. up; s/he sets traps

ohpahamawēw ᐅᐦᐸᐦᐊᒪᐍᐤ
VTA s/he sets traps for s.o.

ohpahikēw ᐅᐦᐸᐦᐃᑫᐤ
VAI s/he sets traps

ohpahipēw ᐅᐦᐸᐦᐃᐯᐤ
VII it floats to the top (*e.g.* drowned body)

ohpahow ᐅᐦᐸᐦᐅᐤ
VAI s/he flies up, s/he rises, s/he flies away, it flies from its perch

ohpahowi-pīsim ᐅᐦᐸᐦᐅᐏ ᐲᓯᒼ
NA Flying-Up Moon; August

ohpakocin ᐅᐦᐸᑯᒋᐣ
VAI it bounces up into the air, s/he darts into the air

ohpan ᐅᐦᐸᐣ
NDI lung; his/her lung [*cf.* 1: nohpan; *also* nōhpan]

ohpastēw ᐅᐦᐸᐢᑌᐤ
VII it is higher than ground level

ohpatināw ᐅᐦᐸᑎᓈᐤ
VII it is a high hill

ohpāpēkipicikēw ᐅᐦᐹᐯᑭᐱᒋᑫᐤ
VAI s/he hoists things with a machine, pulley

ohpāpēkipitam ᐅᐦᐹᐯᑭᐱᑕᒼ
VTI s/he pulls s.t. up by a string, s/he hoists s.t. (as a flag)

ohpāpēkipitēw ᐅᐦᐹᐯᑭᐱᑌᐤ
VTA s/he pulls s.o. up by a string; s/he hoists s.o.

ohpāsiw ᐅᐦᐹᓯᐤ
VAI s/he is raised by the wind (as a kite); s/he blows off the ground and into the air

ohpāskwaham ᐅᐦᐹᐢᑿᐦᐊᒼ
VTI s/he lifts s.t. with a stick, s/he raises s.t. (with a bar or pole)

ohpāskwahikan ᐅᐦᐹᐢᑿᐦᐃᑲᐣ
NI lifter

ohpāskwahwēw ᐅᐦᐹᐢᑿᐦᐍᐤ
VTA s/he raises s.o. (with a bar or pole)

ohpihāw ᐅᐦᐱᐦᐋᐤ
VAI s/he flies up

ohpihkasikan ᐅᐦᐱᐦᑲᓯᑲᐣ
NI baking powder; yeast; bread

ohpikihākan ᐅᐦᐱᑭᐦᐋᑲᐣ
NA foster child, adopted child; person raised

ohpikihāwasow ᐅᐦᐱᑭᐦᐋᐘᓱᐤ
VAI s/he raises a family, s/he raises children

ohpikihcikēw ᐅᐦᐱᑭᐦᒋᑫᐤ
VAI s/he raises things, s/he grows things

ohpikihcikēwin ᐅᐦᐱᑭᐦᒋᑫᐏᐣ
NI raising, rearing

ohpikihēw ᐅᐦᐱᑭᐦᐁᐤ
VTA s/he raises s.o., s/he rears s.o.

ohpikihitowak ᐅᐦᐱᑭᐦᐃᑐᐘᐠ
VAI they raise one another (*i.e.* orphans)

ohpikihtamāsow ᐅᐦᐱᑭᐦᑕᒫᓱᐤ
VAI s/he makes (it/him) grow for him/herself

ohpikihtāw ᐅᐦᐱᑭᐦᑖᐤ
VAIt s/he raises s.t., s/he grows s.t., s/he makes s.t. grow

ohpikin ᐅᐦᐱᑭᐣ
VII it grows, it grows up [*cf.* ohpikīmakan]

ohpikināwasow ᐅᐦᐱᑭᓈᐘᓱᐤ
VAI s/he raises his/her children

ohpikiw ᐅᐦᐱᑭᐤ
VAI s/he grows, s/he grows up; s/he is raised [*rdpl*: ay-ohpikiw]

ohpikiwin ᐅᐦᐱᑭᐏᐣ
NI growing up

ohpikīmakan ᐅᐦᐱᑮᒪᑲᐣ
VII it grows up [*cf.* ohpikin]

ohpim ᐅᐦᐱᒼ
IPC off to the side, away

ohpimē ᐅᐦᐱᒣ
IPC off, away, to the side; at another place, elsewhere, somewhere else

ohpimēhpisow ᐅᐦᐱᒣᐦᐱᓱᐤ
VAI s/he is tied a ways off

ohpinam ᐅᐦᐱᓇᒼ
VTI s/he lifts s.t., s/he lifts s.t. up, s/he hoists s.t. up

ohpinamawēw ᐅᐦᐱᓇᒪᐍᐤ
VTA s/he lifts (it/him) up for s.o., s/he raises (it/him) for s.o.

ohpinamākēw ᐅᐦᐱᓇᒫᑫᐤ
VAI s/he lifts (it/him) for others

ohpinamāsow ᐅᐦᐱᓇᒫᓱᐤ
VAI s/he lifts (it/him) for him/herself

ohpinēw ᐅᐦᐱᓀᐤ
VTA s/he lifts s.o., s/he lifts s.o. up, s/he raises s.o. (*e.g.* pipe), s/he hoists s.o. up

ohpinikēw ᐅᐦᐱᓂᑫᐤ
VAI s/he lifts things up

ohpinikēwin ᐅᐦᐱᓂᑫᐏᐣ
NI weightlifting; act of lifting things

ohpiniskēw ᐅᐦᐱᓂᐢᑫᐤ
VAI s/he raises his/her own arms

ohpinisow ᐅᐦᐱᓂᓱᐤ
VAI s/he raises him/herself up

ohpipaýihow ᐅᐦᐱᐸᔨᐦᐅᐤ
VAI s/he starts up; s/he jumps up

ohpipaýiw ᐅᐦᐱᐸᔨᐤ
VAI it rises (as yeast bread); s/he floats to the top

ohpipitam ᐅᐦᐱᐱᑕᒼ
VTI s/he pulls s.t. up, s/he raises s.t. (by rope)

ohpipitēw ᐅᐦᐱᐱᑌᐤ
VTA s/he pulls s.o. up, s/he raises s.o. (by rope)

ohpipwāmēýiw ᐅᐦᐱᑹᒣᔨᐤ
VAI s/he lifts his/her own thigh

ohpisikan ᐅᐦᐱᓯᑲᐣ
NA yeast

ohpisin ᐅᐦᐱᓯᐣ
VAI s/he rises (as bread rises)

ohpiskāw ᐅᐦᐱᐢᑳᐤ
VAI s/he goes upward; s/he ascends [*Christian*: *in relation to Jesus ascending to heaven*]

ohpiskāwin ᐅᐦᐱᐢᑳᐏᐣ
NI ascension

ohpiskwēpaýihow ᐅᐦᐱᐢᑵᐸᔨᐦᐅᐤ
VAI s/he throws up his/her own head

ohpiskwēýiw ᐅᐦᐱᐢᑵᔨᐤ
VAI s/he lifts his/her own head, s/he raises his/her head

ohpiwēpinam ᐅᐦᐱᐍᐱᓇᒼ
VTI s/he throws s.t. aloft

ohpiwēpinēw ᐅᐦᐱᐍᐱᓀᐤ
VTA s/he throws s.o. aloft

ohpīstam ▷"ᐧᐞᐱᒐ
VTI s/he jumps at s.t.; s/he jumps at a chance

ohpīstawēw ▷"ᐱᒐᐠᐁᐧ·ᵒ
VTA s/he jumps at s.o.

ohpīw ▷"ᐱᵒ
VAI s/he jumps up, s/he goes up

ohpīw ▷"ᐱᵒ
VII it goes up, it jumps

ohpīwātam ▷"ᐱᐊᐧᒐ
VTI s/he jumps, s/he rises in direction to s.t.

ohpīwātēw ▷"ᐱᐊᐧᐁᵒ
VTA s/he jumps, s/he rises in direction to s.o.

ohpwēnam ▷"ᐯᐧᐊᒡ
VTI s/he makes s.t. fly up (e.g. dust)

ohpwēnēw ▷"ᐯᐧᐁᵒ
VTA s/he makes s.o. fly up (e.g. startling ducks)

ohpwēstikwānēwāsiw
▷"ᐯᐧᐢᑎᒃᐧᐋᐁᐧᐋᓯᐤ
VAI s/he has messy, wind-blown hair [cf. sēkwēstikwāniwāsiw]

ohpwēýawāhkāstan
▷"ᐯᐧᐩᐊᐧᐋᐦᑳᐢᑕᐣ
VII there is a sandstorm

ohtaham ▷"ᑕᐦᐊᒼ
VTI s/he brings s.t. from there by tool

ohtahipēw ▷"ᑕᐦᐃᐯᵒ
VAI s/he draws water from there

ohtahtam ▷"ᑕᐦᑕᒼ
VTI s/he eats s.t. from there; s/he slurps s.t. up

ohtahwēw ▷"ᑕᐦᐁᐧᵒ
VTA s/he brings s.o. from there by tool

ohtakocin ▷"ᑕᑯᒋᐣ
VAI s/he flies from there, s/he falls from there; s/he arrives by water from there

ohtamēw ▷"ᑕᒣᵒ
VTA s/he eats s.o. (e.g. food) from there; s/he slurps s.o. up

ohtamēýihtam ▷"ᑕᒣᐩᐦᑕᒼ
VTI s/he is delayed by anxiety, s/he is anxious about s.t.

ohtamēýimēw ▷"ᑕᒣᐩᒥᐁᵒ
VTA s/he is anxious about s.o., s/he thinks of s.o. as one who is sick

ohtamihow ▷"ᑕᒥᐦᐅᵒ
VAI s/he is delayed by something

ohtapiw ▷"ᑕᐱᵒ
VAI s/he sits on that side, there

ohtapiwin ▷"ᑕᐱᐪ
NI seat

ohtaskatēw ▷"ᑕᐢᑲᑌᵒ
VTA s/he leaves s.o., s/he

walks out on s.o., s/he leaves s.o. behind going from there

ohtatāmēw ▷"ᒐᑖᒣᵒ
VTA s/he takes s.o. into his/her own mouth; s/he inhales s.o. (e.g. tobacco)

ohtatāmototam ▷"ᒐᑖᒧᑐᒐ
VTI s/he inhales s.t.

ohtatāmow ▷"ᒐᑖᒧᵒ
VAI s/he inhales

ohtawakayēw ▷"ᒐᐊᐧᑲᔦᵒ
VAI s/he has ears [also ohtawakēw]

ohtawakēhow ▷"ᒐᐊᐧᑫᐦᐅᵒ
NA large horned owl

ohtācihow ▷"ᒌᒋᐦᐅᵒ
VAI s/he makes his/her living from there, that source; s/he travels from there

ohtāpamihēw ▷"ᒌᐸᒥᐦᐁᵒ
VTA s/he nourishes s.o. from that source [also ohci-pamihēw]

ohtāpamihow ▷"ᒌᐸᒥᐦᐅᵒ
VAI s/he gets his/her own food from that source [also ohci-pamihow]

ohtāpēkamohtāw ▷"ᒌᐯᑲᒧᐦᑖᵒ
VAIt s/he fastens s.t. from there as string

ohtāstan ▷"ᒌᐢᑕᐣ
VII it is blown by the wind from there

ohtāwīmāw ▷"ᒌᐋᐧᐄᒫᵒ
NA father [cf. 1: nohtāwiy "my father"]

ohtāwīmēw ▷"ᒌᐋᐧᐄᒣᵒ
VTA s/he regards s.o. as his/her own father

ohtāwīw ▷"ᒌᐋᐧᐄᵒ
VAI s/he has (s.o. as) a father [cf. oyohtāwī-]

ohtāyihk ▷"ᒌᔦᕽ
IPC from the place

ohtēpayiw ▷"ᐸᔦᐧᵒ
VII it boils (e.g. water), it bubbles; it fizzes, it foams (e.g. water in falls or rapids)

ohtēw ▷"ᐅᵒ
VII it boils

ohtēýihtam ▷"ᐅᔦᐩᐦᑕᒼ
VTI s/he is jealous on account of s.t., s/he is envious

ohtēýihtamowin ▷"ᐅᔦᐩᐦᑕᒧᐎᐪ
NI jealousy, envy

ohtēýimēw ▷"ᐅᔦᐩᒥᐁᵒ
VTA s/he is jealous of s.o., s/he envies s.o.

ohtin ▷"ᐣᐪ
VII there is wind blowing from that way

ohtinam ▷"ᐣᐊᒡ
VTI s/he gets s.t. from there, s/he takes s.t. from there, s/he obtains s.t. from there, s/he accepts s.t. from there

ohtinamawēw ▷"ᐣᐊᒪᐧ·ᵒ
VTA s/he takes (it/him) from there for s.o.

ohtinamākēwin ▷"ᐣᐊᒪᑫᐊᐧᐪ
NI provisions

ohtinamāsow ▷"ᐣᐊᒪᓱᵒ
VAI s/he gets (it/him) from there for him/herself, s/he takes (it/him) from there for him/herself, s/he obtains (it/him) from there for him/ herself

ohtinēw ▷"ᐣᐁᵒ
VTA s/he gets s.o. from there, s/he takes s.o. from there, s/he obtains s.o. from there

ohtinikēw ▷"ᐣᓀᑯᵒ
VAI s/he gets things from there, s/he takes things from there, s/he obtains things from there

ohtisiw ▷"ᐣᓯᵒ
VAI s/he receives s.t. from there, s/he obtains s.t. (e.g. money) from there; s/he receives benefit from there, s/he profits

ohtisiwin ▷"ᐣᓯᐃᐧᐠ
NI gain; profit, wages

ohtiskaw ▷"ᐣᐢᑲᵒ
IPC before it; in front of it

ohtiskawapiw ▷"ᐣᐢᑲᐊᐧᐱᵒ
VAI s/he sits facing; s/he sits in front (facing an audience) [also ohtāstawapiw]

ohtiskawapīstam
▷"ᐣᐢᑲᐊᐧᐱᐞᑕᒼ
VTI s/he sits in front of and facing s.t.

ohtiskawapīstawēw
▷"ᐣᐢᑲᐊᐧᐱᐞᑕᐧ·ᵒ
VTA s/he sits in front of and facing s.o.

ohtiskawi- ▷"ᐣᐢᑲᐃᐧ·
IPV facing

ohtiskawikāpawiw
▷"ᐣᐢᑲᐃᐧᑳᐸᐧ<ᐃᐧ·ᵒ
VAI s/he stands in front (facing an audience)

ohtiskawinam ▷"ᐣᐢᑲᐃᐧᓇᒡ
VTI s/he holds s.t. in front (facing)

ohtiskawinamawēw
▷"ᐣᐢᑲᐃᐧᓇᒪᐧ·ᵒ
VTA s/he holds (it/him) in front of, for s.o.

ohtiskawinēw ▷"ᐣᐢᑲᐃᐧᓇᐁᐧᵒ
VTA s/he holds s.o. in front (facing)

ohtiskawisin ▷"ᐣᐢᑲᐃᐧᓯᐪ
VAI s/he lies facing someone

ohtiskawisinōstam
▷"ᐣᐢᑲᐃᐧᓯᓄᐞᑕᒼ
VTI s/he lies facing s.t.

ohtiskawisinōstawēw
▷"ᐣᐢᑲᐃᐧᓯᓄᐞᑕᐧ·ᵒ
VTA s/he lies facing s.o.

ohtitaw ▷"∩C°
  IPC by nature, of necessity,
  for real [*cf.* ohcitaw]

ohtohtahēw ▷"⊃"C"∇°
  VTA s/he brings s.o. along
  from there

ohtohtēw ▷"⊃"∪°
  VAI s/he comes from there,
  s/he is coming from there,
  s/he walks from there; s/he
  arrives from there [*rdpl*:
  wāh-ohtohtēw]

ohtosāpahcikēw ▷"⊃ᒡ<"ᕐᑫ°
  NA foreteller [*see also*
  okosāpahcikēw]

okakayēsisiw ▷ᏏᏏᐧᏒᏒᏒ°
  NA cheater [*rdpl*; *also*
  okakayēyisiw]

okanawāpokēw ▷Ꮟᐁᐧᐋᐧ>ᕐᑫ°
  NA house-sitter; one who
  watches the camp

okakēpātis ▷Ꮟᑫ<∩ᐠ
  NA stupid person, fool,
  nuisance [*cf.* kakēpācis]

okakihcimosk ▷Ꮟᑭ"ᒐᐠ
  NA boaster, braggart [*hab*]

okakiyāskisk ▷Ꮟᑭᐟᐢᐠ
  NA liar [*hab*; *cf. rdpl*:
  ka-kiyāskiw]

okakiyāskiwācimon
▷Ꮟᑭᐟᐢᑭᐋᐧᒋᒧᐣ
  NI tale of falsehoods [*cf.*
  rdpl: ka-kiyāskiw "s/he keeps
  lying"]

okanawēwitipiskwēw
▷Ꮟᐁᐧᐁᐧᐃᐧ∩ᐱᐢᑫᐧ°
  NA night watchman

okanawēyihcikēw
▷Ꮟᐁᐧᔮᐧ"ᕐᑫ°
  NA guard; caretaker;
  resource officer

okanawēyimatihkowēw
▷Ꮟᐁᐧᔮᐧᒪ∩"ᑯᐋᐧ°
  NA shepherd [*cf.*
  okanawēyimāᐧyatihkwēw]

okanawēyimāwasow
▷Ꮟᐁᐧᔮᐧᒫᐧᐋᐧ°
  NA babysitter

okanawēyimāᐧyatihkwēw
▷Ꮟᐁᐧᔮᐧᒫᐧ∩"ᑫᐧ°
  NA shepherd [*cf.*
  okanawēyimatihkowēw]

okanawēyimostosowēw
▷Ꮟᐁᐧᔮᐧᒧᐢ⊃ᓱᐋᐧ°
  NA cattle herder

okanawēyiskwāhtēmiwēw
▷Ꮟᐁᐧᔮᐧᐃᐧᐢᑲᐧ"ᑌᒥᐋᐧ°
  NA doorkeeper; goaltender,
  goalkeeper

okaskikwācikēw ▷Ꮟᐢᑭᑲᐧᒋᑫ°
  NA seamstress; tailor

okawikīhkāw ▷Ꮟᐃᐧᑮ"ᑳ°
  NA extremely old person

okawiy ▷Ꮟᐃᐧᐧ
  NA porcupine quill

okāhkākicihiwēw
▷Ꮟ"ᑳᑭᒋᐦᐃᐧᐁᐧ°
  NA one who consoles others,
  a thoughtful person

okāhkwāskwahikaniw
▷Ꮟ"ᏏᐧᐢᏏᐧᐦᐃᏏᐧᓂᐤ°
  VAI s/he has a totem sign

okāminakasiy ▷ᏏᒥᏒᏏᐧᐧ
  NA thorn-tree, brier [*cf.*
  akwāminakasiy]

okāminakasīskāhk ▷ᏏᒥᏒᏏᐧᐧᐢᑳᐦᐠ
  INM in a thorn thicket [*loc*]

okāminakasīskāw ▷ᏏᒥᏒᏏᐧᐧᐢᑳᐤ°
  VII there are many
  thornbushes

okāminakasīwāhtik
▷ᏏᒥᏒᏏᐧᐧᐋᐧᐦᑎ
  NA thorn-tree [*pl*: -wak]

okāsakēw ▷ᏏᐦᏏᑫ°
  NA glutton, one who eats a
  lot

okāsakimiw ▷ᏏᐦᏏᒥᐧ°
  VAI s/he has a tapeworm

okāsikāk ▷ᏏᐦᏏᐠ
  IPC just a little while ago;
  yesterday [*see also*
  otākosīhk]

okāsīcihkomēs ▷Ꮟᐧᒋᐦᑯᒣᐢ
  NA kindergarten pupil [*wC
  term*]

okāskipāsowēw ▷Ꮟᐢᑭᐸᐧᓱᐋᐧ°
  NA barber; one who uses a
  razor

okāskiskahwān ▷ᏏᐢᑭᐢᏏᐧ"ᐋᐧᐣ
  NI shoulder (of moose)

okāw ▷Ꮟᐤ°
  NA pickerel; walleye; perch

okāwīmāw ▷Ꮟᐋᐧᐃᐧᒫᐤ°
  NA mother [*cf. 1*: nikāwiy
  "my mother"]

okāwīmāwaskiy ▷Ꮟᐋᐧᐃᐧᒫᐧᐢᑭᐧ
  NI mother earth

okāwimēw ▷Ꮟᐋᐧᐃᐧᒣᐤ°
  VTA s/he regards s.o. as
  his/her own mother

okāwiw ▷Ꮟᐋᐧᐃᐧ°
  VAI s/he has (s.o. as) a
  mother

okīskimanasiw ▷ᐱᐢᑭᒪᏏᐧᐧ°
  NA kingfisher [*also family
  name*]

okihcihtāw ▷ᐱ"ᒋ"ᒡ°
  NA warrior, worthy young
  man

okihcihtāwikamik
▷ᐱ"ᒋ"ᒡᐃᐧᏏᒥ
  NI lodge of warriors' society
  [*pl*: -wa]

okihciniskihk ▷ᐱ"ᒋᓂᐢᑭᐠ
  IPC on the right [*cf.*
  kihciniskēhk]

okihciniskiw ▷ᐱ"ᒋᓂᐢᑭᐧ°
  VAI s/he has a right hand

okihciwāw ▷ᐱ"ᒋᐋᐧᐧ°
  NA member of a certain
  society or clan

okihtimēwiýiniw ▷ᐱ"∩ᒣᐃᐧᐧ∆ᐱᓂᐤ°
  NA lazy person, idler

okihtimiskiw ▷ᐱ"∩ᒥᐢᑭᐧ°
  NA one who is lazy, one
  who makes no effort to
  survive [*hab*]

okihtimiw ▷ᐱ"∩ᒥᐧ°
  NA lazy person, one who is
  lazy

okimāhkān ▷ᐱ"Ꮟᐣ°
  NA chief; elected or
  appointed chief; reserve
  chief; band council leader;
  pretend leader [*cf.* okimāw]

okimāhkāniwin ▷ᐱ"Ꮟᓂᐃᐧᐣ°
  NI chieftaincy

okimāhkāniwiw ▷ᐱ"Ꮟᓂᐃᐧ°
  VAI s/he is chief, s/he serves
  as elected chief; s/he is a
  government-appointed chief

okimāhkāsow ▷ᐱ"Ꮟᓱᐧ°
  VAI s/he pretends to be chief

okimāhkātēw ▷ᐱ"Ꮟᑌᐤ°
  VTA s/he makes s.o. chief

okimānāhk ▷ᐱᏏᐦᐠ
  IPC government, federal or
  provincial government; Band
  Council, Band authorities [*cf.*
  okimāw, okimāwiwin]

okimāsis ▷ᐱᏒᐢ
  NA little chief, boss; office
  clerk; prince; [*in jest*:]
  "noble"; Littlechief [*personal
  and family name*]; Okemasis
  [*personal name of Cree chief
  and SK reserve; see*
  BEARDY'S AND OKEMASIS]

okimāskwēhkāsow ▷ᐱᏒᑫᐦᏏᓱᐧ°
  VAI she tries to act like a
  queen

okimāskwēsis ▷ᐱᏒᑫᐧᐢ
  NA chief's daughter;
  daughter of anyone known as
  "okimāw"; princess

okimāskwēw ▷ᐱᏒᑫᐧ°
  NA queen; female boss,
  female of high position;
  chief's wife, wife of anyone
  known as "okimāw"

okimāw ▷ᐱᏒ°
  NA chief, leader, head
  person, man of high position;
  king; boss; one's superior
  [*also a personal name*; *cf.*
  okimāhkān; *poss*:
  -(t)ōkimām-, *cf. 1*:
  nitōkimām "my chief"]

okimāwastotin ▷ᐱᏒᐧᐢ⊃∩ᐣ°
  NI crown

okimāwayān ▷ᐱᏒᐧᐧᐋᐧᐣ
  NA chief's robe, bearskin;
  ermine pelt; king or queen's
  robe

okimāwēyihtākosiw
▷ᐱᏒᐧᔮᐧᐦᑖᑯᐢ
  VAI s/he is honourable; s/he
  is highly respected

okimāwēyimēw ▷ᐱᏒᐧᔮᐧᒣᐤ°
  VTA s/he honours s.o. as a
  chief or governor

okimāwikamik ▷ᐱᏒᐃᐧᏏᒥ
  NI governor's residence [*pl*:
  -wa]

okimāwikosisān ▷ᐱᏒᐃᐧᑯᓯᐋᐧᐣ
  NA son of a chief, prince

okimāwiw ᐅᑭᒫᐏᐤ
VAI s/he is a chief, leader, head person, boss; he is the master

okimāwiwin ᐅᑭᒫᐏᐏᐣ
NI chieftaincy; social status; government

okimotiskiw ᐅᑭᒧᑎᐢᑭᐤ
NA thief, kleptomaniac

okimotiw ᐅᑭᒧᑎᐤ
NA thief

okiniy ᐅᑭᓇᐩ
NA rose-bush berry, rose hip; thorn berry; tomato [*cf.* kihc-ōkiniy]

okinīs ᐅᑭᓃᐢ
NA little rose-hip; Okanese [*dim*; *Cree/Saulteaux chief and SK reserve name*]

okinīwāhcikos ᐅᑭᓈᐚᐦᒋᑯᐢ
NA thorn bush, small wild rose tree [*dim*]

okinīwāhtik ᐅᑭᓃᐚᐦᑎᐠ
NI wild rose tree [*pl*: -wa]

okinīwāhtikoskāw ᐅᑭᓃᐚᐦᑎᑯᐢᑳᐤ
NI grove of thorn trees [*or VII* "there are many thorn trees"]

okinīwiw ᐅᑭᓈᐏᐤ
VAI it is a thorn tree

okinosēmiw ᐅᑭᓄᓭᒥᐤ
VAI s/he has fish

okinwāpēkikwayaw ᐅᑭᓈᐧᐯᑭᑲᐧᔮᐤ
NA Longneck [*personal name*; *cf.* kinwāpēkikwayawēw]

okipahowēsiw ᐅᑭᐸᐦᐅᐍᓯᐤ
NA policeman; prison guard [*dim*; *see also* simākanis]

okipahowēw ᐅᑭᐸᐦᐅᐍᐤ
NA jailer, prison guard; goalie, goalkeeper, goaltender

okisēwātis ᐅᑭᓭᐚᑎᐢ
NA kind person

okisēwātisiw ᐅᑭᓭᐚᑎᓯᐤ
NA kind person [*cf.* kisēwātisiw]

okisēwātisiwiniw ᐅᑭᓭᐚᑎᓯᐏᓂᐤ
VAI s/he has kindness

okisīpēkihtakinikēw ᐅᑭᓰᐯᑭᐦᑕᑭᓂᑫᐤ
NA floorwasher, janitor

okisīpēkinikēw ᐅᑭᓰᐯᑭᓂᑫᐤ
NA laundry person

okiskimaniw ᐅᑭᐢᑭᒪᓂᐤ
VAI s/he has a file (for sharpening tools)

okiskinohtahiwēw ᐅᑭᐢᑭᓄᐦᑕᐦᐃᐍᐤ
NA leader, guide

okiskinwahamawākan ᐅᑭᐢᑭᓇᐧᐦᐊᒪᐚᑲᐣ
NA student, one who is taught [*cf.* kiskinwahamawākan; *also* okiskinahamawākan, okiskinohamawākan]

okiskinwahamākan ᐅᑭᐢᑭᓇᐧᐦᐊᒫᑲᐣ
NA student, scholar; one being taught [*cf.* kiskinwahamākan; *also* okiskinahamākan, okiskinohamākan]

okiskinwahamākēw ᐅᑭᐢᑭᓇᐧᐦᐊᒫᑫᐤ
NA teacher, instructor [*also* okiskinohamākēw]

okiskinwahamākēwiw ᐅᑭᐢᑭᓇᐧᐦᐊᒫᑫᐏᐤ
VAI s/he is a teacher [*also* okiskinohamākēwiw]

okiskiwēhikēw ᐅᑭᐢᑭᐍᐦᐃᑫᐤ
NA prophet; traffic controller

okispēwēw ᐅᑭᐢᐯᐍᐤ
NA defender, one who defends and takes part

okistakēwi ᐅᑭᐢᑕᑫᐏ
IPC much, many

okistatōwān ᐅᑭᐢᑕᑑᐚᐣ
NA grizzly bear [*also* okistatowān]

okistikānikamikow ᐅᑭᐢᑎᑳᓂᑲᒥᑯᐤ
VAI s/he has a granary

okistikāniw ᐅᑭᐢᑎᑳᓂᐤ
VAI s/he has a field or garden

okistikēw ᐅᑭᐢᑎᑫᐤ
NA farmer

okistikēwiýiniw ᐅᑭᐢᑎᑫᐏᔨᓂᐤ
NA farm instructor (from Indian Affairs)

okistikēwiýinīwin ᐅᑭᐢᑎᑫᐏᔨᓃᐏᐣ
NI farming

okistikēwiýinīwiw ᐅᑭᐢᑎᑫᐏᔨᓃᐏᐤ
VAI s/he is a farmer, s/he is engaged in agriculture

okitahamākēw ᐅᑭᑕᐦᐊᒫᑫᐤ
NI one who forbids

okitimākinākēw ᐅᑭᑎᒫᑭᓈᑫᐤ
NA sympathizer

okitimākis ᐅᑭᑎᒫᑭᐢ
NA poor person, materially or mentally challenged; [*pl*:] the poor

okitimākisiw ᐅᑭᑎᒫᑭᓯᐤ
NA person in need, one who is poor

okitohcikaniw ᐅᑭᑐᐦᒋᑲᓂᐤ
VAI s/he has musical instruments

okitohcikēw ᐅᑭᑐᐦᒋᑫᐤ
NA musician; [*pl*:] orchestra

okiyokēw ᐅᑭᔪᑫᐤ
NA visitor

okiyōtēw ᐅᑭᔫᑌᐤ
NA visitor from a great distance [*cf.* okiyōtēwiw]

okiyōtēwiw ᐅᑭᔫᑌᐏᐤ
VAI s/he is a visitor from a great distance [*cf.* okiyōtēw]

okīhikosimow ᐅᑮᐦᐃᑯᓯᒧᐤ
NA faster, one who fasts

okīhkwahāhkēw ᐅᑮᐦᑲᐧᐦᐋᐦᑫᐤ
NA wolverine

okīmāpahkēw ᐅᑮᒫᐸᐦᑫᐤ
NA peeping tom; spy

okīmōtāpahkēw ᐅᑮᒨᑖᐸᐦᑫᐤ
NA peeping tom; spy

okīnipocikaniw ᐅᑮᓂᐳᒋᑲᓂᐤ
VAI s/he has a file (for sharpening saws)

okīnipocikēw ᐅᑮᓂᐳᒋᑫᐤ
NA filer; one who files saws

okīsikow ᐅᑮᓯᑯᐤ
NA angel

okīskwēpēsk ᐅᑮᐢᑵᐯᐢᐠ
NA habitual drunkard, alcoholic [*hab*]

okīskwēpēw ᐅᑮᐢᑵᐯᐤ
NA drunkard

okīskwēw ᐅᑮᑵᐤ
NA madman, insane person

okīskwēyātis ᐅᑮᐢᑵᔮᑎᐢ
NA mentally ill person

okocawākanisiw ᐅᑯᒐᐚᑲᓂᓯᐤ
VAI s/he has matches

okosāpahcikēw ᐅᑯᓵᐸᐦᒋᑫᐤ
NA foreteller; one who communicates with the spirits [*see also* ohtosāpahcikēw]

okosimān ᐅᑯᓯᒫᐣ
NI cucumber

okosisimāw ᐅᑯᓯᓯᒫᐤ
NA son [*cf.* 1: nikosis "my son"]

okosisimāw ᐅᑯᓯᓯᒫᐤ
NA womb, uterus

okosisimāwiw ᐅᑯᓯᓯᒫᐏᐤ
VAI he is a son

okosisimēw ᐅᑯᓯᓯᒣᐤ
VTA s/he has s.o. as son

okosisimiw ᐅᑯᓯᓯᒥᐤ
VAI s/he has (s.o. as) a son; he fathers a son; s/he takes s.o. as his/her own son

okosisiw ᐅᑯᓯᓯᐤ
VAI s/he has (s.o. as) a son

okoskohiwēw ᐅᑯᐢᑯᐦᐃᐍᐤ
NA startler, one who startles others [*see also* pihēw; *cf.* ātaýōhkan: "wīsahkēcāhk *and the Startlers*"]

okotawāniw ᐅᑯᑕᐚᓂᐤ
VAI s/he has a campfire

okotākanaskwa ᐅᑯᑖᑲᓇᐢᑿ
NI goose grass [*pl*]

okōhtakanaskwa ᐅᑰᐦᑕᑲᓇᐢᑿ
NI water-reeds [*pl*]

okōhtaskisahikan ᐅᑰᐦᑕᐢᑭᓴᐦᐃᑲᐣ
NI stovepipe

okōhtāskwahikan ᐅᑰᐦᑖᐢᑲᐧᐦᐃᑲᐣ
NI stovepipe

okwāskohcīs ▷�579"ᒥᐣ
 NA grasshopper [*also* okwāskohcis, *cf.* kwāskohcisis]

okwāskohcīsikāt ▷ᑲ·ᐨᑯ"ᕆᕐᑲᐧ
 NI pocket knife

okwāskwāskotēpēw ▷ᑲ·ᑲ·ᐊᑌᑌᐁᐤ
 NI white muscle in the heart

okwāskwēpayihōs ▷ᑲ·ᐧᕠ·ᐸᐧᐅᒥᐣ
 NA jumping deer [*dim*]

okwāskwēpicikanēyāpiy ▷ᑲ·ᐧᕠ·ᐱᐦᐋᑲᐅᐊᐸᐧ
 NI angling line, fishing line

okwāskwēpicikēw ▷ᑲ·ᐧᕠ·ᐱᐦᐋᐧ
 NA angler, fisherman, one who fishes with hook and line

okwēmēsiw ▷ᐧᒣᐟᐅ
 VAI s/he is named after s.o.; s/he has (s.o. as) a namesake; s/he has the same name (as s.o.)

omacātis ▷ᒪᕈᐣ
 NA wicked person; nasty, miserable person

omacihtiw ▷ᒪᐦᐧᐣ
 NA sinner

omanaskosīwākan ▷ᓚᐣᒍᐊᐧᑲᐧ
 NI mower (for cutting hay); mowing machine

omanaskosīwēw ▷ᓚᐣᒍᐊᐧᐅᐤ
 NA one who mows; mower

omanācimākaniw ▷ᒪᕮᒪᑲᐅᐤ
 NA s/he has relatives-in-law

omanicōsimiw ▷ᓚᕬᒍᕆᐅ
 VAI s/he has worms

omanisikēw ▷ᓚᐅᕐᐧᐅᐧ
 NA swather, reaper, one who swathes or reaps

omanitōmimēw ▷ᓚᕬᒍᕮᐅ
 VTA s/he has or addresses s.o. as god

omanitōmiw ▷ᓚᕬᒍᕆᐅ
 VAI s/he has (s.o. as) a god

omanitōwiw ▷ᓚᕬᒍᐅᐧᐅ
 NA person with supernatural power

omasinahikaniw ▷ᒪᕐᐊᐦᐊᑲᐧ
 VAI s/he has paper, letters, books

omasinahikēsīs ▷ᒪᕐᐊᐦᐅᕮᐣ
 NA clerk, office worker, office typist, secretary

omasinahikēw ▷ᒪᕐᐊᐦᐅᐧ
 NA writer

omaskahtwēsk ▷ᒪᑲᐦᐅᐊᐣ
 NA purse snatcher; mugger; one who steals another's partner, wife or husband [*hab*]

omaskihkīmiw ▷ᒪᐢᐱ"ᕆᐅ
 VAI s/he has medicine

omaskisiniw ▷ᒪᐢᐱᕬᐅ
 VAI s/he has shoes

omaskisinihkēw ▷ᒪᐢᐱᕬᐅ"ᐧᐅ
 NA shoemaker

omaskosīhkēw ▷ᒪᐢᒍᕆ"ᐊᐧ
 NA hay maker

omaskosīmiw ▷ᒪᐢᒍᕆᐅ
 VAI s/he has hay

omawimostamākēw ▷ᒪᐊ·ᒍᐢᑕᒣᑲᐧᐧ
 NA participant in ceremonial rite; petitioner

omawisow ▷ᒪᐊ·ᐅᐟ
 NA berry-picker

omācīw ▷ᒪᐦᐅ
 NA hunter

omāham ▷ᒪ"ᐊᐨ
 NA voyageur, one who canoes downriver [*pl*: -wak]

omāhamow ▷ᒪ"ᐊᒍᐧ
 NA voyageur, boatman, one who goes downriver

omāmāw ▷ᒪᒪᐅ
 VAI s/he has (s.o. as) a mother

omāmāwiw ▷ᒪᒪᐅᐊᐧᐅ
 VAI s/he has (s.o. as) a mother

omāmihkwēw ▷ᒪᕆ"ᐧᐧ
 NA Stoney, Assiniboine, Nakota woman

omānisīsis ▷ᒪᕬᕆᐣ
 NA puppy, calf [*dim*]

omātahikaniw ▷ᒪᐨᐊᐦᐊᑲᐅᐧ
 VAI s/he has a hide-scraper

omāw ▷ᒪᐧ
 NI "bible", manyplies, omasum, third stomach of ruminant, digestive organ of a moose or cow's stomach

omāwacihcikēw ▷ᒪᐊᕬᐦᐅ"ᐧᐧ
 NA collector

omāwatinikēw ▷ᒪᐊᐧᐊᑎᓂᐧᐧ
 NA collector, one who gathers a collection

omihtawēw ▷ᕆᐦᐊᐧᐅᐧ
 NA sulker, one who sulks, pouts, expresses regret

omihtimiw ▷ᕆᐦᐣᕆᐅ
 VAI s/he has (it as) his/her own firewood, s/he has wood, s/he has firewood

omikiy ▷ᕆᐱᐧ
 NI scab, sore; scale; rash

omikiýiniw ▷ᕆᐱᕬᐅ
 NA Scabby [*personal name*]

omikiw ▷ᕆᐱᐅ
 VAI s/he has a sore, s/he has a scab; s/he has excema

omikiwāspinēw ▷ᕆᐱᐊᐧᐊᐢᐱᕬᐅᐧ
 VAI s/he has chicken-pox

omisihkēmōs ▷ᕆᐧᕆ"ᐧᐊᐟ
 NA teller of tall tales, tattle tale

omisi ▷ᕆᐧ
 IPC thus, in this way, as follows, like this [*cf.* ōmisi]

omisi isi ▷ᕆᐧ ᐃᐧ
 IPH like this, in this way; this is how it is [*also* omis isi, ōmis isi]

omisimās ▷ᕆᕆᒪᐣ
 NA eldest sister [*dim*; *cf*. 1: nimis "my older sister"; *cf.* omisimāw]

omisimāw ▷ᕆᕆᒪᐅ
 NA eldest sister, oldest sister [*cf*. 1: nimis "my older sister"; *cf.* omisimās]

omisimāwiw ▷ᕆᕆᒪᐊ·ᐅ
 VAI s/he is the oldest girl in the family

omisimiw ▷ᕆᕆᕆᐅ
 VAI s/he has (s.o. as) an older sister

omisiw ▷ᕆᕆᐅ
 VAI s/he has (s.o. as) an older sister

omistatimomiw ▷ᕆᐢᑕᑎᒍᕆᐅ
 VAI s/he has (it as) a horse

omistikomiw ▷ᕆᐢᑎᑯᕆᐅ
 VAI s/he has a cane

omīcaskosīs ▷ᕆᒪᐢᒍᕆᐣ
 NA swallow (bird) [*dim*]

omīcaskosīsiwiw ▷ᕆᒪᐢᒍᕆᕆᐊ·ᐤ
 VAI it is a swallow

omīciwiniw ▷ᕆᕆᐊ·ᕬᐅᐧ
 VAI s/he has food

omīhkawikīw ▷ᕆᕆ"ᑲᐊ·ᐱᐧᐅ
 NA sprinter, fast runner

omīkiwahpihkēw ▷ᕆᕆᐱᐊ·"ᐊᐧᐧ
 NA one who sews tipis, one who makes tipis

omīmīsis ▷ᕆᕆᕆᐣ
 NA young pigeon, young dove

omīmīw ▷ᕆᕆᕆᐅ
 NA pigeon, dove [*cf*. mīmēw, *Saulteaux* omīmī]

omosōmimāw ▷ᒍᕆᕆᒪᐅ
 NA grandfather

omosōmiw ▷ᒍᕆᕆᐅ
 VAI s/he has (s.o. as) a grandfather

omostosomiw ▷ᒍᐢᒍᕆᐅ
 VAI s/he has buffalo, s/he has cattle, s/he has (it as) a cow

omōhkocikēw ▷ᒍ"ᑯᕆᑲᐧᐧ
 NA one who planes

omōhkomāniw ▷ᒍ"ᑯᒪᕬᐅ
 VAI s/he has a knife

omōnisōniyāwēw ▷ᒍᕬᒍᕬᐅᑲᐅ·ᐤ
 NA prospector

omōsāhkinikēw ▷ᒍᐢᐊ"ᐱᕬᐊᐧ
 NA collector

omōtay ▷ᒍᐊᐨ
 NI crop of a chicken or partridge

omōtēyāpiskomiw ▷ᒍᐅᐸᐢᐱᕬᒍᕆᐅ
 VAI s/he has a bottle

onahāhkimiw ▷ᓇ"ᐧᕆᐅ
 VAI s/he has a son-in-law

onahāhkisimiw ▷ᓇ"ᐧᐱᕆᕆᐅ
 VAI s/he has a son-in-law

onakinikēs ▷ᓇᐱᕬᐧᐊ
 NA one who puts a stop to proceedings

onanātawihowēw ▷ᓇᕮᑕᐊ·"ᐅᐧᐁᐅ·ᐤ
 NA doctor, healer

onanēskwēw ᐅᓇᓀᐢᑫᐧᐤ
VAI s/he fills the kettle

onaskwahamākēw ᐅᓇᐢᑲᐧᐦᐊᒫᑫᐤ
NA back-up singer

onaspicākēs ᐅᓇᐢᐱᒑᑫᐢ
NA monkey [*dim*; *see also* ocayisinākēs]

onāpēhkāsow ᐅᓈᐯᐦᑳᓱᐤ
NA brave man; one who pretends to be brave, one who puts up a front

onāpēmihkawēw ᐅᓈᐯᒥᐦᑲᐁᐧᐤ
VTA she makes a husband of s.o.

onāpēmihkāw ᐅᓈᐯᒥᐦᑳᐤ
VAI she lives common-law

onāpēmihkēw ᐅᓈᐯᒥᐦᑫᐤ
VAI she lives common-law; she makes a husband (of s.o.)

onāpēmimāw ᐅᓈᐯᒥᒫᐤ
NA husband

onāpēmimēw ᐅᓈᐯᒥᒣᐤ
VTA she has s.o. as a husband

onāpēmiw ᐅᓈᐯᒥᐤ
VAI she has (s.o. as) a husband, she gets a husband, she is a married woman

onātamākēw ᐅᓈᑕᒫᑫᐤ
NA defender (interceding for s.o.); mediator

onātawihowēw ᐅᓈᑕᐃᐧᐦᐅᐁᐧᐤ
NA doctor, healer

onēpēwisiwiniw ᐅᓀᐯᐃᐧᓯᐧᐃᐧᓂᐤ
VAI s/he has shame

onihcāwāhcawēpaýihosīs
ᐅᓂᐦᒑᐚᐦᒐᐁᐧᐸᔨᐦᐅᓰᐢ
NA chipmunk [*dim*]

onihcikiskwapiwinihk
ᐅᓂᐦᒋᑭᐢᑲᐧᐱᐃᐧᓂᕽ
INM Saddle Lake, AB [*loc*]

onihtāwikihcikaniw
ᐅᓂᐦᑖᐃᐧᑭᐦᒋᑲᓂᐤ
VAI s/he has a field, garden

onikamow ᐅᓂᑲᒧᐤ
NA singer

onikāhp ᐅᓂᑳᐦᑊ
NI portage

onikēw ᐅᓂᑫᐤ
VAI s/he portages in a canoe; s/he carries s.t. across his/her own shoulder

onikohtēw ᐅᓂᑯᐦᑌᐤ
NA woodcutter

onimiskīskāw ᐅᓂᒥᐢᑮᐢᑳᐤ
VII there is plenty of thunder

onipahiwēw ᐅᓂᐸᐦᐃᐁᐧᐤ
NA murderer

onipahtākēw ᐅᓂᐸᐦᑖᑫᐤ
NA killer, murderer; executioner

onipēwiniw ᐅᓂᐯᐃᐧᓂᐤ
VAI s/he has a bed

onipiw ᐅᓂᐱᐤ
NA dead person

onipiwiniw ᐅᓂᐱᐃᐧᓂᐤ
VAI s/he has a death, s/he has a vital spot [*also* onipōwiniw]

onipīmiw ᐅᓂᐲᒥᐤ
VAI s/he has water

oniskimiw ᐅᓂᐢᑭᒥᐤ
VAI s/he has geese

onitopaýiw ᐅᓂᑐᐸᔨᐤ
NA person on warpath

onīcāniw ᐅᓃᒑᓂᐤ
NA cow, female moose, female animal

onīkāniskāt ᐅᓃᑳᓂᐢᑳᐟ
NI front leg

onīkānīw ᐅᓃᑳᓃᐤ
NA headman, leader [*also* onīkāniw]

onīkānohtēw ᐅᓃᑳᓄᐦᑌᐤ
NA leader, one who walks at the head of a group

onīkihikomāw ᐅᓃᑭᐦᐃᑯᒫᐤ
NA parent [*cf.* -nīkihikw-*NDA*]

onīmihitow ᐅᓃᒥᐦᐃᑐᐤ
NA dancer

onōcihcikēw ᐅᓅᒋᐦᒋᑫᐤ
NA trapper; hunter

onōcihitowi-pīsim
ᐅᓅᒋᐦᐃᑐᐃᐧ ᐲᓯᒼ
NA Rutting Moon; Mating Moon September [*cf.* nōcihitowi-pīsim]

onōcikinēpikwēsiw
ᐅᓅᒋᑭᓀᐱᑫᐧᓯᐤ
NA snake hawk

onōcikinosēwēw ᐅᓅᒋᑭᓄᓭᐁᐧᐤ
NA fisherman

onōtāposwēw ᐅᓅᑖᐳᓭᐧᐤ
NA rabbit hunter

onōtinikēsk ᐅᓅᑎᓂᑫᐢᐠ
NA fighter; boxer [*hab*]

onōtinikēskiw ᐅᓅᑎᓂᑫᐢᑭᐤ
NA fighting man [*hab*]

onōtinikēw ᐅᓅᑎᓂᑫᐤ
NA warrior [*pl*:] army

onōtinikēwiýiniw
ᐅᓅᑎᓂᑫᐃᐧᔨᓂᐤ
NA warrior

onōtinikēwokimāwiw
ᐅᓅᑎᓂᑫᐅᐧᑭᒫᐃᐧᐤ
VAI he is a chief of warriors; s/he is an officer

opahkēkinihkēw ᐅᐸᐦᑫᑭᓂᐦᑫᐤ
NA tanner, processor of hides

opahkēkiniw ᐅᐸᐦᑫᑭᓂᐤ
VAI s/he has leather, hide

opahkwēsikanihkēw
ᐅᐸᐦᑫᐧᓯᑲᓂᐦᑫᐤ
NA baker

opahkwēsikanimiw
ᐅᐸᐦᑫᐧᓯᑲᓂᒥᐤ
VAI s/he has bannock, bread, flour

opakatinikēw ᐅᐸᑲᑎᓂᑫᐤ
NA one who plants grain, a garden

opakitahwāw ᐅᐸᑭᑕᐦᐋᐧᐤ
NA fisherman (using nets)

opakitahwāwiw ᐅᐸᑭᑕᐦᐋᐧᐃᐧᐤ
VAI s/he is a fisherman

opakosihtāsk ᐅᐸᑯᓯᐦᑖᐢᐠ
NA beggar [*hab*]

opamihiwēw ᐅᐸᒥᐦᐃᐁᐧᐤ
NA servant; attendant

opaminikēw ᐅᐸᒥᓂᑫᐤ
NA governess; steward; boss, leader; administrator

opapāmācihōs ᐅᐸᐹᒫᒋᐦᐆᐢ
NA traveller

opapāmāmōs ᐅᐸᐹᒫᒨᐢ
NA fugitive

opapāmohtēw ᐅᐸᐹᒧᐦᑌᐤ
NA wanderer; prostitute

opapāsīw ᐅᐸᐹᓰᐤ
NA speedy person, person who does things quickly

opasastēhikaniw ᐅᐸᓴᐢᑌᐦᐃᑲᓂᐤ
VAI s/he has a whip

opasastēhiwēw ᐅᐸᓴᐢᑌᐦᐃᐁᐧᐤ
NA one who whips others

opaskosowēw ᐅᐸᐢᑯᓱᐁᐧᐤ
NA barber

opaskostikwānēw ᐅᐸᐢᑯᐢᑎᑳᐧᓀᐤ
NA bald person

opaskowi-pīsim ᐅᐸᐢᑯᐃᐧ ᐲᓯᒼ
NA Moulting Moon; July [*cf.* paskowi-pīsim]

opawahikaniw ᐅᐸᐊᐧᐦᐃᑲᓂᐤ
VAI s/he has a threshing machine, s/he has a combine

opawahikēw ᐅᐸᐊᐧᐦᐃᑫᐤ
NA thresher, one who threshes grain, one who combines

opawākanēyāspinatēw
ᐅᐸᐋᐧᑲᓀᔮᐢᐱᓇᑌᐤ
VTA s/he harms s.o. by means of dream spirits

opawāmiw ᐅᐸᐋᐧᒥᐤ
VAI s/he has a dream spirit [*cf.* pawāmiw]

opāpāw ᐅᐹᐹᐤ
VAI s/he has (s.o. as) a father

opāpāwiw ᐅᐹᐹᐃᐧᐤ
VAI s/he has (s.o. as) a father

opāskāwēhowi-pīsim
ᐅᐹᐢᑳᐁᐧᐦᐅᐃᐧ ᐲᓯᒼ
NA Egg-Hatching Moon; June [*cf.* paskāwihowi-pīsim]

opāskisikaniw ᐅᐹᐢᑭᓯᑲᓂᐤ
VAI s/he has a gun

opāskwēyāw ᐅᐹᐢᑫᐧᔮᐤ
NI Le Pas, MB [*place name*; *loc generally*: opāskwēyāhk]

opāstāmow ᐅᐹᐢᑖᒧᐤ
NA slanderer; blasphemer; one who brings curses upon him/herself through improper speech or action

opēpīmiw ᐅᐯᐲᒥᐤ
VAI s/he has (s.o. as) a baby

opimācihiwēw ᐅᐱᒫᒋᐦᐃᐁᐧᐤ
NA saviour

opiminawasow ▷ᐱᕁᐊᐧᔪ
NA chef; cook [*also* opaminawasow]

opimipiciw ▷ᐱᒥᐱᕁ
NA traveller; nomad

opimīhkānimiw ▷ᐱᶠᵇᐢᒣ
VAI s/he has pemmican

opimīmiw ▷ᐱᶠᒥ
VAI s/he has lard, oil, fat

opimohtahiwēw ▷ᐱᒍᐦᒅᐁᐧ
NA bus driver; transporter

opimotahkwēw ▷ᐱᒍᑫᐧ
NA archer, one who shoots with bow and arrows

opiniyāwēhowi-pīsim ▷ᐱᓂᔮᐯᐦᐅ ᐱᓯᑦ
NA Egg-Laying Moon; May

opīhtawēsākān ▷ᐱᐦᑕᐯᓵᑳᐣ
NI petticoat [*cf.* pihtawēsākay]

opīhtawēsākānimiw ▷ᐱᐦᑕᐯᓵᑳᓂᒥ
VAI s/he has a petticoat

opīhtwākaniw ▷ᐱᐦᒄᑳᓂ
VAI s/he has a pipe, tobacco

opīkopicikēw ▷ᐱᑯᐱᒋᑫᐧ
NA one who ploughs

opīma ▷ᐱᒪ
INM Hobbema, AB [*see also* maskwacis]

opīminahkwānimiw ▷ᐱᒥᓇᐦᒄᑫᒣ
VAI s/he has rope

opīsākanēyāpīmiw ▷ᐱᓵᑲᓀᔮᐱᒥ
VAI s/he has a rawhide rope

opīsimōhkānimiw ▷ᐱᓯᒨᐦᑳᓂᒣ
VAI s/he has a clock

opīsimōhkānisiw ▷ᐱᓯᒨᐦᑳᓂᓯ
VAI s/he has a watch

opītatowēw ▷ᐱᑕᑐᐁᐧ
NA Ukrainian; European

opīwayakohp ▷ᐱᐊᐧᔭᑯᐦᑊ
NI feather or down quilt

opīwāpiskoýākanēw ▷ᐱᐋᐧᐱᐢᑯᔮᑲᓀᐧ
VAI s/he has a metal plate, cup

opiwās ▷ᐱᐊᐧᐢ
NI fur [*dim*]

opōtācikaniw ▷�ᑕᒋᑲᓂ
VAI s/he has a trumpet, flute, wind instrument

opōtācikēs ▷ᑐᒅᒋᑫᐢ
NA mole [*dim*]

opōtācikēsīs ▷ᑐᒅᒋᑫᓯᐢ
NA mole [*dim*]

opōtācikēw ▷ᑐᒅᒋᑫᐧ
NA trumpeter; flutist

opwām ▷ᐧᐋᒼ
NA thigh of meat; ham [*cf* mipwām *NDI*; 3 *poss*: opwām "his/her thigh"]

opwēýakatāmēw ▷ᐯᔭᑲᑖᒣᐧ
NI tree felled by a beaver

opwēýakatowēw ▷ᐯᔭᑲᑐᐁᐧ
NA one who peels and gnaws (*e.g.* a beaver)

osakahikaniw ▷ᓴᑲᐦᐃᑲᓂ
VAI s/he has nails

osakāskwahoniw ▷ᓴᑳᐢᒁᐦᐅᓂ
VAI s/he has a brooch, clasp

osam ▷ᓴᒼ
VTI s/he boils s.t., s/he keeps s.t. (*e.g.* water) at the boil

osaskahoniw ▷ᓴᐢᑲᐦᐅᓂ
VAI s/he has a cane

osaskamow ▷ᓴᐢᑲᒍ
NA one who receives sacrament or communion

osaskamowin ▷ᓴᐢᑲᒍᐃᐧᐣ
NI sacrament, communion

osākohcihiwēw ▷ᓵᑯᐦᒋᐦᐃᐁᐧ
NA victor; one who wins

osākotēhēw ▷ᓵᑯᑌᐦᐁᐧ
NA coward; timid person

osām ▷ᓵᒼ
IPC too much, excessively; because, since, for; because of excess [*causal conjunction*]

osām apisīs ▷ᓵᒼ ᐊᐱᓰᐢ
IPH too little, less than enough

osām mistahi ▷ᓵᒼ ᒥᐢᑕᐦᐃ
IPH too much, more than enough

osām piko ▷ᓵᒼ ᐱᑯ
IPH mainly, mostly; more or less

osāmakocin ▷ᓵᒪᑯᒋᐣ
VAI s/he drives too far, s/he drives past his/her destination

osāmaskinahtāw ▷ᓵᒪᐢᑭᓇᐦᑖᐧ
VAIt s/he overfills s.t., s/he puts too much into s.t.

osāmaskinēw ▷ᓵᒪᐢᑭᓀᐧ
VAI s/he is overfilled, s/he is too full of food, s/he has overeaten

osāmāhkatosow ▷ᓵᒫᐦᑲᑐᓱ
VAI s/he is too lean, slender, thin

osāmāhpinēw ▷ᓵᒫᐦᐱᓀᐧ
VAI s/he dies of illness

osāmāskaciw ▷ᓵᒫᐢᑲᒋ
VAI s/he is frozen too hard

osāmēyatinwa ▷ᓵᒣᔭᑎᓇᐧ
VII they are too numerous [*pl*]

osāmēyatiwak ▷ᓵᒣᔭᑎᐊᐧᐠ
VAI they are too numerous [*pl*]

osāmi- ▷ᓵᒥ
IPV too much; because of excess, for

osāmi-pōnam ▷ᓵᒥ ᑑᓇᒼ
VTI s/he puts on too much firewood, s/he puts too much on the fire

osāmihēw ▷ᓵᒥᐦᐁᐧ
VTA s/he does too much with s.o.

osāmihkahtēw ▷ᓵᒥᐦᑲᐦᑌᐧ
VII it is overcooked

osāmihkanitēpow ▷ᓵᒥᐦᑲᓂᑌᐳ
VAI s/he cooks too much

osāmihkasam ▷ᓵᒥᐦᑲᓴᒼ
VTI s/he overcooks s.t.

osāmihkasow ▷ᓵᒥᐦᑲᓱ
VAI it is overcooked

osāmihkaswēw ▷ᓵᒥᐦᑲ� ᐢᐁᐧ
VTA s/he overcooks s.o.

osāmihkwāmiw ▷ᓵᒥᐦᒁᒥ
VAI s/he oversleeps

osāmihow ▷ᓵᒥᐦᐅ
VAI s/he has more than enough

osāmihtāw ▷ᓵᒥᐦᑖᐧ
VAIt s/he overdoes s.t.

osāmipaýiw ▷ᓵᒥᐸᔨ
VAI s/he goes beyond s.t., s/he goes past s.t.

osāmipēw ▷ᓵᒥᐯᐧ
VAI s/he drinks too much; s/he is drunk

osāmipitam ▷ᓵᒥᐱᑕᒼ
VTI s/he exaggerates s.t., s/he makes a tall tale of s.t.; s/he overdoes s.t., s/he exceeds s.t.

osāmisiw ▷ᓵᒥᓯ
VAI s/he has an over-bearing personality, s/he always has to be first or in the center of activity; s/he is excessive

osāmiskōýow ▷ᓵᒥᐢᑰᔪ
VAI s/he overeats, s/he stuffs him/herself

osāmitōn ▷ᓵᒥᑑᐣ
NA gossip, mouthy person; tattle-tale, tattler

osāmitōnēw ▷ᓵᒥᑑᓀᐧ
VAI s/he gossips, s/he talks too much, s/he is too talkative [*also* osāmitonēw]

osāpahcikan ▷ᓵᐸᐦᒋᑲᐣ
NI binoculars; telescope

osāpahkēw ▷ᓵᐸᐦᑫᐧ
VAI s/he watches people from there [*also* ohtāpahkēw]

osāpahtam ▷ᓵᐸᐦᑕᒼ
VTI s/he watches s.t. from there [*also* ohtāpahtam]

osāpahtēw ▷ᓵᐸᐦᑌᐧ
VII there is smoke or haze coming from that direction [*also* ohtāpahtēw]

osāpamēw ▷ᓵᐸᒣᐧ
VTA s/he watches s.o. from there, s/he looks at s.o. from there [*also* ohtāpamēw]

osāpiw ▷ᓵᐱᐧ
VAI s/he watches from there, s/he looks from there [*also* ohtāpiw]

osāponikaniw ▷ᓵᑐᓂᑲᓂ
VAI s/he has a needle

osāwahkēsiw ▷ᓵᐊᐧᐦᑫᓯ
NA red fox

osāwasapāp ▷ᓵᐊᐧᓴᐹᑊ
NA yellow thread

osāwasākay ᐅᓵᐘᓵᑲᐩ
NI yellow dress, coat
osāwasēstak ᐅᓵᐘᓭᐢᑕᐠ
NA yellow yarn [*pl*: -wak]
osāwasiskīwastēnam ᐅᓵᐘᓯᐢᑮᐘᐢᑌᓇᒼ
VTI s/he plasters or paints s.t. with yellow clay
osāwasiskīwastēnēw ᐅᓵᐘᓯᐢᑮᐘᐢᑌᓀᐤ
VTA s/he plasters or paints s.o. with yellow clay
osāwasiskīwastēnisow ᐅᓵᐘᓯᐢᑮᐘᐢᑌᓂᓱᐤ
VAI s/he paints him/herself with yellow clay
osāwasiskīwasow ᐅᓵᐘᓯᐢᑮᐘᓱᐤ
VAI s/he is painted with yellow clay
osāwasiskīwastēw ᐅᓵᐘᓯᐢᑮᐘᐢᑌᐤ
VII it is painted with yellow clay
osāwaski- ᐅᓵᐘᐢᑭ
IPV green, blue-green [*not common in western dialects*]
osāwaskosiw ᐅᓵᐘᐢᑯᓯᐤ
VAI s/he is blue-green [*not common in western dialects*]
osāwask ᐅᓵᐘᐢᐠ
NA brown bear [*pl*: -wak]
osāwaskwa ᐅᓵᐘᐢᑲᐧ
NI yellow grass [*pl*]
osāwaskwan ᐅᓵᐘᐢᑲᐧᐣ
VII it is a yellow sky (*e.g.* sunset, fire in the distance)
osāwaskwāpēs ᐅᓵᐘᐢᑳᐧᐯᐢ
NA jackfish [*see also* iýinito-kinosēw]
osāwaskwāw ᐅᓵᐘᐢᑳᐧᐤ
VII it is blue-green
osāwastim ᐅᓵᐘᐢᑎᒼ
NA sorrel horse [*pl*: -wak]
osāwastotin ᐅᓵᐘᐢᑐᑎᐣ
NI yellow hat
osāwatisikan ᐅᓵᐘᑎᓯᑲᐣ
NI yellow dye
osāwākamin ᐅᓵᐚᑲᒥᐣ
VII it is a yellow liquid [*also* osāwākamiw]
osāwāniskwēw ᐅᓵᐚᓂᐢᑫᐧᐤ
VAI s/he has brown hair
osāwāpakwanīs ᐅᓵᐚᐸᑲᐧᓃᐢ
NI yellow flower
osāwāpān ᐅᓵᐚᐹᐣ
NI bile (a yellow liquid) [*cf.* osāwāpoy]
osāwāpisk ᐅᓵᐚᐱᐢᐠ
NI brass; copper
osāwāpiskāw ᐅᓵᐚᐱᐢᑳᐤ
VII it is golden, copper, brass
osāwāpiskisiw ᐅᓵᐚᐱᐢᑭᓯᐤ
VAI s/he is yellow (metal, stone)
osāwāpoy ᐅᓵᐚᐳᐩ
NI bile liquid (which one vomits) [*cf.* osāwāpān]

osāwās ᐅᓵᐚᐢ
NA orange [*dim*]
osāwās ᐅᓵᐚᐢ
NI wild mustard [*dim*]
osāwāsāpoy ᐅᓵᐚᓵᐳᐩ
NI orange juice, orange pop
osāwāw ᐅᓵᐚᐤ
VII it is yellow; it is orange
osāwēkin ᐅᓵᐍᑭᐣ
NI yellow material; yellow cloth [*pl*: -wa]
osāwi- ᐅᓵᐏ
IPV yellow, brown
osāwi-mihkosiw ᐅᓵᐏ ᒥᐦᑯᓯᐤ
VAI s/he is orange
osāwi-mihkwāw ᐅᓵᐏ ᒥᐦᑳᐧᐤ
VII it is orange
osāwi-mīkis ᐅᓵᐏ ᒦᑭᐢ
NA yellow bead
osāwi-piyēsīs ᐅᓵᐏ ᐱᔦᓰᐢ
NA yellow bird; canary
osāwi-sēnipān ᐅᓵᐏ ᓭᓂᐹᐣ
NA yellow ribbon
osāwi-sōniyāw ᐅᓵᐏ ᓲᓂᔮᐤ
NA gold
osāwi-sōniyāwāpisk ᐅᓵᐏ ᓲᓂᔮᐚᐱᐢᐠ
IPC copper; gold
osāwi-sōniyāwāpisk ᐅᓵᐏ ᓲᓂᔮᐚᐱᐢᐠ
NA gold ore, gold coin [*obv*: -wa]
osāwi-sōniyāwēw ᐅᓵᐏ ᓲᓂᔮᐍᐤ
VAI s/he has gold
osāwi-sōniyāwiw ᐅᓵᐏ ᓲᓂᔮᐏᐤ
VII it contains gold; it is made of gold
osāwihēw ᐅᓵᐏᐦᐁᐤ
VTA s/he makes s.o. yellow; s/he colours s.o. yellow
osāwihtāw ᐅᓵᐏᐦᑖᐤ
VAIt s/he makes s.t. yellow, s/he colours s.t. yellow
osāwinākosiw ᐅᓵᐏᓈᑯᓯᐤ
VAI s/he looks yellowish or brownish; s/he looks jaundiced
osāwinākwan ᐅᓵᐏᓈᑲᐧᐣ
VII it looks yellowish or brownish
osāwipak ᐅᓵᐏᐸᐠ
NA pumpkin [*pl*: -wak]
osāwipaýiw ᐅᓵᐏᐸᔨᐤ
VAI s/he has jaundice
osāwipēskwan ᐅᓵᐏᐯᐢᑲᐧᐣ
VII it is a sky with yellow spots
osāwisip ᐅᓵᐏᓯᑊ
NA brown duck [*also a personal name*]
osāwisiw ᐅᓵᐏᓯᐤ
VAI s/he is yellow; s/he is orange; s/he is brown; it is an orange (fruit) [*cf.* k-ōsāwisicik "oranges"]

osāwistikwān ᐅᓵᐏᐢᑎᑳᐧᐣ
NA yellow head, blonde; a fair-haired person
osāwitās ᐅᓵᐏᑖᐢ
NA a yellow or orange pair of pants
oscikwānis ᐅᐢᒋᑳᐧᓂᐢ
NA (his/her) little head [*dim; also a female personal name*]
oscoscocasiw ᐅᐢᒍᐢᒍᒐᓯᐤ
VAI s/he coughs a little [*dim; cf.* ostostotam]
osēhcāw ᐅᓭᐦᒑᐤ
VII it is a rise in the land, it is a hill
osēkitikomiw ᐅᓭᑭᑎᑯᒥᐤ
VAI s/he has a tangle of hair, s/he has tangled hair; s/he has a braid
osēskicēs ᐅᓭᐢᑭᒉᐢ
NI roach (traditional men's pow-wow headdress made of porcupine quills) [*cf.* sēskicēs]
osētināw ᐅᓭᑎᓈᐤ
VII it is a ridge or knoll
osihkihpimiw ᐅᓯᐦᑭᐦᐱᒥᐤ
VAI s/he has a helldiver
osihtēw ᐅᓯᐦᑌᐤ
VAI s/he has the power of hearing; [*in negative clauses*:] s/he is deaf
osikanātam ᐅᓯᑲᓈᑕᒼ
VTI s/he boils (s.t. as) a bone for grease
osikanēw ᐅᓯᑲᓀᐤ
VAI s/he boils bones (for grease)
osikiýās ᐅᓯᑭᔮᐢ
NA lizard, water dog
osikiýāwis ᐅᓯᑭᔮᐏᐢ
NA lizard, water dog
osikosimāw ᐅᓯᑯᓯᒫᐤ
NA mother-in-law; paternal aunt, wife of maternal uncle [*cf.* 1: nisikos "my aunt/ mother-in-law"]
osikosimiw ᐅᓯᑯᓯᒥᐤ
VAI s/he has (s.o. as) a mother-in-law
osikosiw ᐅᓯᑯᓯᐤ
VAI s/he has (s.o. as) a mother-in-law
osikow ᐅᓯᑯᐤ
VAI s/he suffers a miscarriage by fall or injury
osikw-āyāhēw ᐅᓯᑳᐧᔮᐦᐁᐤ
VTA s/he procures an abortion for her
osikw-āyāw ᐅᓯᑳᐧᔮᐤ
VAI s/he has a miscarriage or abortion
osikwānāsam ᐅᓯᑳᐧᓈᓴᒼ
VTI s/he smoke-dries s.t.
osikwānāsow ᐅᓯᑳᐧᓈᓱᐤ
VAI it is smoke-dried
osikwānāstēw ᐅᓯᑳᐧᓈᐢᑌᐤ
VII it is smoke-dried

osikwānāswēw ▷ᒃᐷᐧᐦᐧᓵᔪᐧᐤ
VTA s/he smoke-dries s.o.

osipēham ▷ᓯᐯᐦᐊᒼ
VTI s/he writes, s/he writes
s.t. (with ink) [*possible
Saulteaux loan*]

osipēhikanāhtik ▷ᓯᐯᐦᐃᑲᓈᐦᑎᐠ
NI pen, pencil [*pl*: -wa; *see
also* masinahikanāhtik]

osipēhwēw ▷ᓯᐯᐦᐧᐁᐧᐤ
VTA s/he paints a picture of
s.o.

osisahamawēw ▷ᓯᓴᐦᐊᒪᐧᐁᐧᐤ
VTA s/he startles the game
for s.o.; s/he drives off the
game on s.o. [*also*
osahamawēw]

osisahikēw ▷ᓯᓴᐦᐃᑫᐧᐤ
VAI s/he frightens the
animals (when hunting) [*also*
osahikēw]

osisahwēw ▷ᓯᓴᐦᐧᐁᐧᐤ
VTA s/he scares s.o. off, s/he
startles s.o. [*also* osahwēw]

osisimāw ▷ᓯᓯᒫᐤ
NA father-in-law; maternal
uncle, husband of paternal
aunt [*cf.* 1: nisis "my
uncle/father-in-law"]

osisiw ▷ᓯᓯᐧᐤ
VAI s/he has (s.o. as) a
father-in-law

osiskwēpayihow ▷ᓯᐢᑫᐧᐸᔨᐦᐅᐧᐤ
VAI s/he pokes his/own head
up out of something (*e.g.*
gopher hole)

osīhcikan ▷ᓰᐦᒋᑲᐣ
NI that which is made,
manufactured item

osīhcikākēw ▷ᓰᐦᒋᑲᑫᐧᐤ
VAI s/he makes things from
s.t., s/he prepares things from
s.t.

osīhcikāsow ▷ᓰᐦᒋᑲᓱᐧᐤ
VAI s/he is created, it is
prepared

osīhcikātēw ▷ᓰᐦᒋᑲᑌᐧᐤ
VII it is built, it is made, it is
prepared

osīhcikēw ▷ᓰᐦᒋᑫᐧᐤ
VAI s/he manufactures
things, s/he makes things

osīhcikēwin ▷ᓰᐦᒋᑫᐧᐃᐣ
NI what is made, handiwork,
product; making,
manufacture

osīhēw ▷ᓰᐦᐧᐁᐧᐤ
VTA s/he makes s.o., s/he
arranges s.o., s/he prepares
s.o. (*e.g.* porcupine-quill)
[*also* osihēw]

osīhisow ▷ᓰᐦᐃᓱᐧᐤ
VAI s/he arranges
him/herself, s/he gets dressed

osīhkihpimiw ▷ᓰᐦᑭᐦᐱᒥᐧᐤ
VAI s/he has a boil

osīhtamawēw ▷ᓰᐦᑕᒪᐧᐁᐧᐤ
VTA s/he makes (it/him) for

s.o., s/he arranges (it/him) for
s.o., s/he prepares (it/him) for
s.o.

osīhtamāsow ▷ᓰᐦᑕᒫᓱᐧᐤ
VAI s/he makes (it/him) for
him/herself, s/he arranges
(it/him) for him/herself, s/he
prepares (it/him) for
him/herself

osīhtamowinihkēw
▷ᓰᐦᑕᒧᐧᐃᓂᐦᑫᐧᐤ
VAI s/he has s.t. made

osīhtāw ▷ᓰᐦᑖᐧᐤ
VAIt s/he makes s.t., s/he
prepares s.t., s/he builds s.t.

osīkinikēw ▷ᓰᑭᓂᑫᐧᐤ
NA bartender

osīmihtowak ▷ᓰᒥᐦᑐᐧᐊᐠ
VAI they are brothers,
siblings

osīmimās ▷ᓰᒥᒫᐢ
NA youngest sibling [*dim*;
cf. osimimāw]

osīmimāw ▷ᓰᒥᒫᐤ
NA youngest sibling,
youngest brother or sister [*cf.*
osimimās, 1: nisim "my
younger sibling"]

osīmimāwiw ▷ᓰᒥᒫᐧᐃᐧᐤ
VAI s/he is the youngest
sibling

osīmisimāw ▷ᓰᒥᓯᒫᐤ
NA younger sibling [*cf.* 1:
nisimis "my younger
sibling"]

osīmisiw ▷ᓰᒥᓯᐧᐤ
VAI s/he has (s.o. as) a
younger sibling

osīsipāskwatimiw ▷ᓰᓯᐸᐢᑲᐧᑎᒥᐧᐤ
VAI s/he has some maple
sugar [*cf.* sīsipāskwat]

osk-āya ▷ᐢᑲᔭ
NA young one, young
person, young creature; the
young [*pl*: -k; *also* oski-aya]

osk-āyi ▷ᐢᑲᔨ
NI new thing, young
creature [*pl*: osk-āya; *also*
oski-ayi]

osk-āyis ▷ᐢᑲᔨᐢ
NA young one; young
animal, young bird [*also*
oski-ayis]

osk-āyisis ▷ᐢᑲᔨᓯᐢ
NA young creature [*dim*;
also oski-ayisis]

osk-āyisiyiniw ▷ᐢᑲᔨᓯᔨᓂᐧᐤ
NA young person [*also*
oski-ayisiyiniw]

osk-āyiwan ▷ᐢᑲᔨᐧᐊᐣ
VII it is new [*also*
oski-ayiwan]

osk-āyiwiw ▷ᐢᑲᔨᐧᐃᐧᐤ
VAI s/he is young, s/he is a
young person, s/he is a
young creature [*also*
oski-ayiwiw]

osk-īskwēw ▷ᐢᑮᐢᑫᐧᐤ
NA young woman [*also*
oski-iskwēw]

osk-īyinīs ▷ᐢᑮᔨᓃᐢ
NA young person, young
Indian person [*also*
osk-īyinīs]

oskac ▷ᐢᑲᐨ
IPC at first

oskacānisip ▷ᐢᑲᒑᓂᓯᑊ
NA mudhen

oskahtāmin ▷ᐢᑲᐦᑖᒥᐣ
NA young kernel or stone
(of fruit)

oskakimēw ▷ᐢᑲᑭᒣᐧᐤ
VTA s/he counts anew from
s.o. (*i.e.* the new moon)
[*often in unspecified actor
VTA form*: oskakimāw "it is
counted anew"]

oskakocin ▷ᐢᑲᑯᒋᐣ
VAI it hangs new; it is a new
moon

oskan ▷ᐢᑲᐣ
NI bone; his/her bone [*cf.*
miskan]

oskana kā-asastēki
▷ᐢᑲᓇ ᑳ ᐊᓴᐢᑌᑭ
INM Regina, SK; [*lit*:
"where the bones are piled",
"pile-of-bones"]

oskanēw ▷ᐢᑲᓀᐧᐤ
NA bull finch

oskani-pimiy ▷ᐢᑲᓂ ᐱᒥᕀ
NI bone-marrow; oil taken
after boiling bones

oskaninēw ▷ᐢᑲᓂᓀᐧᐤ
VAI s/he has arthritis or
rheumatism

oskaniwan ▷ᐢᑲᓂᐧᐊᐣ
VII it is bony, it has bones

oskaniwiw ▷ᐢᑲᓂᐧᐃᐧᐤ
VAI s/he is bony; it is bony

oskasakay ▷ᐢᑲᓴᑲᕀ
NA new skin

oskasākay ▷ᐢᑲᓵᑲᕀ
NI new garment (*e.g.* dress,
coat, jacket)

oskasikan ▷ᐢᑲᓯᑲᐣ
NA new sock

oskaskihk ▷ᐢᑲᐢᑭᐦᐠ
NA new pail, new kettle [*pl*:
-wak]

oskaskisin ▷ᐢᑲᐢᑭᓯᐣ
NI new shoe, new moccasin,
new boot

oskaskosiya ▷ᐢᑲᐢᑯᓯᔭ
NI new grass, fresh hay [*pl*]

oskaskosīwinākosiw
▷ᐢᑲᐢᑯᓰᐧᐃᓈᑯᓯᐧᐤ
VAI s/he looks green, s/he
has a green appearance

oskaskosīwinākwan
▷ᐢᑲᐢᑯᓰᐧᐃᓈᑾᐣ
VII it looks green, it has a
green appearance

oskastimowiw ▷ᐢᑲᐢᑎᒧᐧᐃᐧᐤ
VAI it is a young horse

oskastimwēw ᐅᐢᑲᐢᑎᒷᐤ
VAI s/he has a young horse

oskastis ᐅᐢᑲᐢᑎᐢ
NA new glove, new mitt

oskawāsis ᐅᐢᑲᐚᓯᐢ
NA newborn baby, infant, young child

oskayiwinis ᐅᐢᑲᔨᐏᓂᐢ
NI new article of clothing [*pl generally*]

oskācāskos ᐅᐢᑳᒑᐢᑯᐢ
NA carrot [*dim*]

oskācik ᐅᐢᑳᒋᐠ
NI awl [*pl*: -wa]

oskāhtak ᐅᐢᑳᐦᑕᐠ
NA jackpine [*pl*: -wak]

oskāhtako-pihēw ᐅᐢᑳᐦᑕᑯ ᐱᐦᐁᐤ
NA spruce partridge

oskāhtakoskāw ᐅᐢᑳᐦᑕᑯᐢᑳᐤ
VII there are many pines, there is an abundance of pines around

oskāhtikosiskāw ᐊᐢᑳᐦᑎᑯᓯᐢᑳᐤ
NI land full of young trees, jackpines

oskāhtikosiskāw ᐊᐢᑳᐦᑎᑯᓯᐢᑳᐤ
VII it is a land full of young trees, jackpines

oskānak ᐅᐢᑳᓇᐠ
NA bitch, female dog [*pl*: -wak]

oskānēsiw ᐅᐢᑳᓀᓯᐤ
VAI s/he is of a tribe or race

oskāpēwis ᐅᐢᑳᐯᐏᐢ
NA elder's helper, helper at ceremonies

oskāpitēw ᐅᐢᑳᐱᑌᐤ
VAI s/he has a new tooth (as a baby); s/he has new teeth

oskātāsk ᐅᐢᑳᑖᐢᐠ
NA carrot [*pl*: -wak]

oskātāsko-sīpīhk ᐅᐢᑳᑖᐢᑯ ᓰᐲᕽ
INM Carrot River, SK [*loc*]

oski ᐅᐢᑭ
IPN young, new, fresh [*cf.* oski *IPV*]

oski- ᐅᐢᑭ
IPV new, young, first [*cf.* oski *IPN*]

oski-aýisiýiniw ᐅᐢᑭ ᐊᔨᓯᔨᓂᐤ
NA young person [*cf.* osk-āyisiyiniw; *also* oskayisiyiniw]

oski-iskwēw ᐅᐢᑭ ᐃᐢᑵᐤ
NA young woman [*cf.* osk-īskwēw]

oski-iýinīs ᐅᐢᑭ ᐃᔨᓃᐢ
NA young person, young Indian person [*dim*; *cf.* osk-īýinīs]

oski-mīnis ᐅᐢᑭ ᒦᓂᐢ
NI fresh berry [*pl generally*]

oski-ōsi ᐅᐢᑭ ᐆᓯ
NI new boat [*pl*: oski-ōsa]

oski-pimiy ᐅᐢᑭ ᐱᒥᕀ
NI fresh lard, fresh grease

oski-wāwi ᐅᐢᑭ ᐚᐏ
NI fresh egg [*pl*: oski-wāwa]

oski-wiýasiwēwin ᐅᐢᑭ ᐏᔭᓯᐍᐏᐣ
NI new commandment

oski-wiyās ᐅᐢᑭ ᐏᔮᐢ
NI fresh meat

oskiciy ᐅᐢᑭᒋᕀ
NI pipestem, ceremonial pipe [*cf.* oskitiy]

oskicīhkān ᐅᐢᑭᒌᐦᑳᐣ
NI stovepipe

oskihtēkom ᐅᐢᑭᐦᑌᑯᒼ
NA seed (*e.g.* apple)

oskihtēpak ᐅᐢᑭᐦᑌᐸᐠ
NI plant [*pl*: -wa]

oskimisk ᐅᐢᑭᒥᐢᐠ
NA bud; leaf bud

oskinākosiw ᐅᐢᑭᓈᑯᓯᐤ
VAI s/he looks young, it looks new

oskinākwan ᐅᐢᑭᓈᑿᐣ
VII it looks new, it looks fresh

oskinīkiskwēhkāsow ᐅᐢᑭᓃᑭᐢᑵᐦᑳᓱᐤ
VAI s/he pretends to be a young woman

oskinīkiskwēmakisiw ᐅᐢᑭᓃᑭᐢᑵᒪᑭᓯᐤ
VAI she acts appropriately for a young woman

oskinīkiskwēs ᐅᐢᑭᓃᑭᐢᑵᐢ
NA female youth, teenage girl [*dim*]

oskinīkiskwēsis ᐅᐢᑭᓃᑭᐢᑵᓯᐢ
NA teenage girl [*dim*]

oskinīkiskwēw ᐅᐢᑭᓃᑭᐢᑵᐤ
NA young woman; maiden; virgin

oskinīkiskwēwiw ᐅᐢᑭᓃᑭᐢᑵᐏᐤ
VAI she is a young woman

oskinīkiw ᐅᐢᑭᓃᑭᐤ
NA young man, male youth

oskinīkīhkāsow ᐅᐢᑭᓃᑮᐦᑳᓱᐤ
VAI s/he pretends to be a young man, s/he tries to appear to be a young man

oskinīkīs ᐅᐢᑭᓃᑮᐢ
NA youth, boy, teenage boy [*dim*]

oskinīkīsiw ᐅᐢᑭᓃᑮᓯᐤ
VAI he is a teenage boy

oskinīkīwiw ᐅᐢᑭᓃᑮᐏᐤ
VAI he is a young man, youth

oskinīkiwiýinīsiwiw ᐅᐢᑭᓃᑮᐏᔨᓃᓯᐏᐤ
VAI he is a young man

oskisiw ᐅᐢᑭᓯᐤ
VAI it is new, fresh

oskiskwēwēw ᐅᐢᑭᐢᑵᐍᐤ
VAI he has a new wife, he has a recent wife, he has a young wife

oskitiy ᐅᐢᑭᑎᕀ
NI pipestem, ceremonial pipe [*cf.* oskiciy]

oskitiyāhtik ᐅᐢᑭᑎᔮᐦᑎᐠ
NI pipestem [*pl*: -wa]

oskīsikow ᐅᐢᑮᓯᑯᐤ
VAI s/he has eyes

oskonāhpinēwin ᐅᐢᑯᓈᐦᐱᓀᐏᐣ
NI liver disease [*proposed term*; *cf.* oskon "his/her liver"]

oskotākāw ᐅᐢᑯᑖᑳᐤ
VAI s/he has a coat, dress

oskoyēwiw ᐅᐢᑯᔦᐏᐤ
VAI she comes to reproductive maturity [*female reference only*]

oskwatim ᐅᐢᑿᑎᒼ
NI beaver dam [*pl*: -wa; *see also* amisko-wīsti]

osow ᐅᓱᐤ
VAI it is at a boil (*e.g.* cracklings), it comes to a boil (*e.g.* kettle), it boils

osoy ᐅᓱᕀ
NDI tail; its tail [*cf.* misoy]

osōniyāmiw ᐅᓲᓂᔮᒥᐤ
VAI s/he has money

osōs ᐅᓲᐢ
NDI tail; its little tail [*dim*; *cf.* misōs]

osōsimānisiw ᐅᓲᓯᒫᓂᓯᐤ
VAI s/he has a snow-dart

osōsiw ᐅᓲᓯᐤ
VAI s/he has a little tail

osōskwahikaniw ᐅᓲᐢᑿᐦᐃᑲᓂᐤ
VAI s/he has an iron, steam iron, pressing iron

osōwiw ᐅᓲᐏᐤ
VAI s/he has a tail [*dim*]

ospiskwanāspinēw ᐅᐢᐱᐢᑿᓈᐢᐱᓀᐤ
VAI s/he has a back-ache

ospitoniw ᐅᐢᐱᑐᓂᐤ
VAI s/he has arms, s/he has an arm

ospwākan ᐅᐢᐽᑲᐣ
NA pipe

ospwākanāpisk ᐅᐢᐽᑲᓈᐱᐢᐠ
NI black pipestone [*pl*: -wa]

ospwākanēhikan ᐅᐢᐽᑲᓀᐦᐃᑲᐣ
NI stovepipe

ospwākanihkān ᐅᐢᐽᑲᓂᐦᑳᐣ
NI stovepipe

ospwākanis ᐅᐢᐽᑲᓂᐢ
NA little pipe [*dim*]

ospwākaniw ᐅᐢᐽᑲᓂᐤ
VAI s/he has a pipe

ostēsimāw ᐅᐢᑌᓯᒫᐤ
NA oldest brother, eldest brother, firstborn male [*cf.* 1: nistēs "my older brother"]

ostēsimāwasinahikan ᐅᐢᑌᓯᒫᐘᓯᓇᐦᐃᑲᐣ
NI treaty, constitution

ostēsimāwasinahikēwin ᐅᐢᑌᓯᒫᐘᓯᓇᐦᐃᑫᐏᐣ
NI writing or negotiating a treaty, constitution

ostēsimāwiw ᐅᐢᑌᓯᒫᐏᐤ
VAI he is the oldest brother

ostēsimāwoýasiwēwin ᐅᐢᑌᓯᒫᐓᔭᓯᐍᐏᐣ
NI constitution; treaty

ostikwānāpisk ᐅᐢᑎᑳᓈᐱᐢᐠ
NI helmet (of metal) [*pl*: -wa]
ostimimāw ᐅᐢᑎᒥᒫᐤ
NA daughter-in-law; niece [*cf.* 1: nistim "my niece/daughter-in-law"]
ostostotam ᐅᐢᑐᐢᑐᑕᒼ
VTI s/he coughs; s/he coughs s.t. up
ostostotamopaýiw ᐅᐢᑐᐢᑐᑕᒧᐸᔨᐤ
VAI s/he has a coughing fit
ostostotamowi-maskihkiy ᐅᐢᑐᐢᑐᑕᒧᐏ ᒪᐢᑭᐦᑭᕀ
NI cough medicine, cough syrup, cough remedy
ostostotamowin ᐅᐢᑐᐢᑐᑕᒧᐎᐣ
NI cough
ostostotaskiw ᐅᐢᑐᐢᑐᑕᐢᑭᐤ
VAI s/he coughs a lot [*hab*]
oswēw ᐅᓷᐤ
VTA s/he brings s.o. (*e.g.* cracklings) to the boil, s/he boils s.o., s/he keeps s.o. at the boil [*rdpl*: oy-oswēw]
otahkonāwasow ᐅᑖᐦᑯᓈᐘᓱᐤ
NA one who carries a child; a nursing mother [*also* otahkwanāwasow]
otahkwētawēskikēsk ᐅᑕᐦᑫᑕᐍᐢᑭᑫᐢᐠ
NA one who habitually wears several layers of clothing [*hab*]
otahowēw ᐅᑕᐦᐅᐍᐤ
VAI s/he wins, s/he wins in gambling
otahowēwin ᐅᑕᐦᐅᐍᐎᐣ
NI winnings
otahtahkwan ᐅᑕᐦᑕᐦᑲᐣ
NDI his/her wing [*cf.* mitahtahkwan]
otahwēw ᐅᑕᐦᐍᐤ
VTA s/he draws s.o. by tool, s/he catches s.o. (*e.g.* fish) in a net; s/he beats s.o. in a game or contest
otakikomiw ᐅᑕᑭᑯᒥᐤ
VAI s/he has a cold, s/he has the common cough; s/he has a discharge from the nose
otakikomiwin ᐅᑕᑭᑯᒥᐎᐣ
NI cold
otakisīhkān ᐅᑕᑮᓰᐦᑳᐣ
NI sausage
otakohpiw ᐅᑕᑯᐦᐱᐤ
VAI s/he has a blanket
otakwanāniw ᐅᑕᑲᓈᓂᐤ
VAI s/he has a shawl
otakwāhoniw ᐅᑕᒁᐦᐅᓂᐤ
VAI s/he has a shawl
otakwāhonēwisimowin ᐅᑕᒁᐦᐅᓀᐏᓯᒧᐎᐣ
NI Fancy Shawl Dance
otamāw ᐅᑕᒫᐤ
VAIt s/he draws, s/he takes a puff
otamēw ᐅᑕᒣᐤ
VTA s/he draws on s.o. (as a pipe one is smoking)
otamēýihtam ᐅᑕᒣᔨᐦᑕᒼ
VTI s/he is delayed by caring for s.t.
otamēýimēw ᐅᑕᒣᔨᒣᐤ
VTA s/he is delayed by caring for s.o.
otami- ᐅᑕᒥ
IPV busy, occupied, delayed
otami-atoskēw ᐅᑕᒥ ᐊᑐᐢᑫᐤ
VAI s/he is occupied, s/he has his/her time taken
otami-mīcisow ᐅᑕᒥ ᒦᒋᓱᐤ
VAI s/he is occupied with eating
otami-mētawēw ᐅᑕᒥ ᒣᑕᐍᐤ
VAI s/he is occupied with play
otamihēw ᐅᑕᒥᐦᐁᐤ
VTA s/he hinders s.o.; s/he interrupts s.o., s/he delays s.o., s/he hinders s.o., s/he keeps s.o. busy
otamihow ᐅᑕᒥᐦᐅᐤ
VAI s/he is busy, s/he keeps busy, s/he busies him/herself, s/he is preoccupied; s/he is delayed [*also* otamiyow]
otamihtwāsow ᐅᑕᒥᐦᑤᓱᐤ
VAI s/he delays him/herself with work
otamimēw ᐅᑕᒥᒣᐤ
VTA s/he delays s.o. by speech
otaminēw ᐅᑕᒥᓀᐤ
VTA s/he plays with s.o., s/he amuses s.o.
otamiskay ᐅᑕᒥᐢᑲᕀ
NI hide-scrapings, meat scraped from hide [*pl generally*]
otapāhtēýimow ᐅᑕᐹᐦᑌᔨᒧᐤ
NA meek, humble person
otapoýihkēw ᐅᑕᐳᔨᐦᑫᐤ
NA paddle maker [*also* otapōhkēw]
otasahkēw ᐅᑕᓴᐦᑫᐤ
NA the one who distributes rations; Indian agent
otasawāpiw ᐅᑕᓴᐚᐱᐤ
NA watchman
otasāmēw ᐅᑕᓵᒣᐤ
VAI s/he has snowshoes
otasāmihkēw ᐅᑕᓵᒥᐦᑫᐤ
NA snowshoe maker
otasihkēw ᐅᑕᓯᐦᑫᐤ
NA resident
otasikaniw ᐅᑕᓯᑲᓂᐤ
VAI s/he has socks
otaskīw ᐅᑕᐢᑮᐤ
VAI s/he has land, s/he has a farm
otaspastākaniw ᐅᑕᐢᐸᐢᑖᑲᓂᐤ
VAI s/he has an apron
otaspiskwēsimoniw ᐅᑕᐢᐱᐢᑵᓯᒧᓂᐤ
VAI s/he has a pillow
otastēnam ᐅᑕᐢᑌᓇᒼ
VTI s/he cocks a gun
otastinwāniw ᐅᑕᐢᑎᓌᓂᐤ
VAI s/he has sinew
otastisiw ᐅᑕᐢᑎᓯᐤ
VAI s/he has mitts
otatāwēw ᐅᑕᑖᐍᐤ
NA store-keeper, store-manager; buyer; trader
otatāwēwiw ᐅᑕᑖᐍᐏᐤ
VAI s/he is a store-keeper, s/he is a store-manager
otatoskēw ᐅᑕᑐᐢᑫᐤ
NA worker, labourer
otawāsimisiw ᐅᑕᐚᓯᒥᓯᐤ
VAI s/he has children [*cf.* ocawāsimisiw]
otawāsisīhkāniw ᐅᑕᐚᓯᓰᐦᑳᓂᐤ
VAI s/he has a doll
otayamihāw ᐅᑕᔭᒥᐦᐋᐤ
NA Christian, adherent of Christianity; one who prays
otayānisiwiw ᐅᑕᔮᓂᓯᐏᐤ
VAI s/he has clothing, possessions
otayāniw ᐅᑕᔮᓂᐤ
VAI s/he has clothing, possessions
otaýisiýinīmiw ᐅᑕᔨᓯᔨᚹᒥᐤ
VAI s/he has people (as a chief, leader)
otāhcanisiw ᐅᑖᐦᒐᓂᓯᐤ
VAI s/he has a ring
otāhk ᐅᑖᕽ
IPC behind, in the back, in the rear, at the back of something
otāhk ispaýiw ᐅᑖᕽ ᐃᐢᐸᔨᐤ
IPH last week
otāhkikāt ᐅᑖᐦᑭᑳᐟ
NI hind leg, hindquarters [*also* otāhkokāt]
otāhkosiw ᐅᑖᐦᑯᓯᐤ
NA sick person, patient
otākosiki ᐅᑖᑯᓯᑭ
IPC in the evening, when it's evening
otākosin ᐅᑖᑯᓯᐣ
VII it is evening
otākosinēhkwēw ᐅᑖᑯᓯᓀᐦᑵᐤ
VAI s/he has supper
otākosī ᐅᑖᑯᓰ
IPC yesterday [*cf.* otākosīhk]
otākosīhk ᐅᑖᑯᓰᕽ
IPC yesterday [*cf.* otākosī]
otākwan-acāhkos ᐅᑖᑲᐣ ᐊᒑᐦᑯᐢ
NA evening star
otākwani-mīcisow ᐅᑖᑲᓂ ᒦᒋᓱᐤ
VAI s/he eats supper, s/he eats an evening meal
otākwani-mīcisowin ᐅᑖᑲᓂ ᒦᒋᓱᐎᐣ
NI supper, evening meal

otākwani-mīcisowinihkawēw ᐅᑖᑿᓂ ᒦᒋᓱᐏᓂᐦᑲᐍᐤ
VTA s/he makes supper for s.o.

otākwani-mīcisowinihkēw ᐅᑖᑿᓂ ᒦᒋᓱᐏᓂᐦᑫᐤ
VAI s/he makes supper

otāmaham ᐅᑖᒪᐦᐊᒼ
VTI s/he strikes s.t.

otāmahikan ᐅᑖᒪᐦᐃᑲᐣ
NI hammer [*see also* pakamākan]

otāmahwēw ᐅᑖᒪᐦᐍᐤ
VTA s/he strikes s.o. with a weapon

otānāhk ᐅᑖᓈᕽ
IPC behind

otānisimāw ᐅᑖᓂᓯᒫᐤ
NA daughter [*only in non-possessed form*]

otānisiw ᐅᑖᓂᓯᐤ
VAI s/he has (s.o. as) a daughter

otāniyihk ᐅᑖᓂᔨᕽ
IPC on his (*obv*) hind part

otāpahākan ᐅᑖᐸᐦᐋᑲᐣ
NA horse, dog, ox used for pulling things; driving horse

otāpahākaniw ᐅᑖᐸᐦᐋᑲᓂᐤ
VAI s/he has a draft animal

otāpahēw ᐅᑖᐸᐦᐁᐤ
VTA s/he makes s.o. drag something; s/he drives s.o. (*e.g.* horse)

otāpān ᐅᑖᐹᐣ
NI wagon

otāpānāsk ᐅᑖᐹᓈᐢᐠ
NA vehicle; toboggan, sled, car, wagon [*pl*: -wak]

otāpānāskow ᐅᑖᐹᓈᐢᑯᐤ
VAI s/he has a wagon, sled

otāpānēyāpiy ᐅᑖᐹᓀᔮᐱᐩ
NI harness [*pl generally*: otāpānēyāpiya]

otāpānēyāpīwikamik ᐅᑖᐹᓀᔮᐲᐏᑲᒥᐠ
NI harness shop [*pl*: -wa]

otāpāsow ᐅᑖᐹᓱᐤ
VAI s/he rides in a vehicle, s/he drives

otāpātam ᐅᑖᐹᑕᒼ
VTI s/he gives s.t. a ride; s/he pulls s.t.

otāpātēw ᐅᑖᐹᑌᐤ
VTA s/he drags s.o.; s/he serves as draft animal; s/he gives s.o. a ride in a sled, s/he pulls s.o. in a sled; s/he pulls s.o.

otāpēw ᐅᑖᐯᐤ
VAI s/he drags s.t. [*rdpl*: oy-otāpēw]

otāpēyāpiy ᐅᑖᐯᔮᐱᐩ
NI drag net

otāpiskākanēsīs ᐅᑖᐱᐢᑳᑲᓀᓰᐢ
NA killdeer

otāpiskākaniw ᐅᑖᐱᐢᑳᑲᓂᐤ
VAI s/he has a tie, necklace, handkerchief

otāpwēhtam ᐅᑖᐻᐦᑕᒼ
NA believer [*pl*: -wak]

otāsiw ᐅᑖᓯᐤ
VAI s/he has pants, trousers, leggings

otāskwaham ᐅᑖᐢᑿᐦᐊᒼ
VTI s/he draws s.t. in by a stick

otāskwahamawēw ᐅᑖᐢᑿᐦᐊᒪᐍᐤ
VTA s/he draws (it/him) in for s.o. by a stick

otāskwahwēw ᐅᑖᐢᑿᐦᐍᐤ
VTA s/he draws s.o. in by a stick

otāstawēhikēw ᐅᑖᐢᑕᐍᐦᐃᑫᐤ
NA firefighter

otēhāspinēw ᐅᑌᐦᐋᐢᐱᓀᐤ
VAI s/he has heart disease

otēhimin ᐅᑌᐦᐃᒥᐣ
NI strawberry [*see also* mitēhimin]

otēhimināni-cēpihk ᐅᑌᐦᐃᒥᓈᓂ ᒉᐱᕽ
NI strawberry root [*pl*: -wa; *cf.* ocēpihk]

otēhipak ᐅᑌᐦᐃᐸᐠ
NI cabbage [*pl*: -wa]

otēhtapiw ᐅᑌᐦᑕᐱᐤ
NA rider, horseman

otēhtapīwatimomiw ᐅᑌᐦᑕᐲᐘᑎᒧᒥᐤ
VAI s/he has (s.o. for) a riding horse

otēmihēw ᐅᑌᒥᐦᐁᐤ
VTA s/he gives s.o. a dog or horse

otēmiw ᐅᑌᒥᐤ
VAI s/he has (s.o. as) a dog or horse

otēpwēstamākēw ᐅᑌᐻᐢᑕᒫᑫᐤ
NA herald, announcer

otēskaniw ᐅᑌᐢᑲᓂᐤ
VAI s/he has horns

otēskimin ᐅᑌᐢᑭᒥᐣ
NI banana [*lit*: "horn berry"; *see also* wākās]

oti ᐅᑎ
IPC in fact [*emphasizes preceding word or phrase*]

otihkomiw ᐅᑎᐦᑯᒥᐤ
VAI s/he has lice

otihkwatimimāw ᐅᑎᐦᑿᑎᒥᒫᐤ
NA nephew; son-in-law [*also* mitihkwatimimāw; *cf.* -tihkwatim-]

otihtaham ᐅᑎᐦᑕᐦᐊᒼ
VTI s/he reaches s.t.

otihtahēw ᐅᑎᐦᑕᐦᐁᐤ
VTA s/he brings s.o. up to something

otihtahikan ᐅᑎᐦᑕᐦᐃᑲᐣ
NI compass

otihtam ᐅᑎᐦᑕᒼ
VTI s/he reaches s.t., s/he comes to where s.t. is, s/he arrives at s.t., s/he encounters s.t.

otihtapinahisin ᐅᑎᐦᑕᐱᓇᐦᐃᓯᐣ
VAI s/he moves to lie face-down

otihtapipaýihow ᐅᑎᐦᑕᐱᐸᔨᐦᐅᐤ
VAI s/he crouches face down to the ground

otihtapisimēw ᐅᑎᐦᑕᐱᓯᒣᐤ
VTA s/he lays s.o. on that one's stomach

otihtapisin ᐅᑎᐦᑕᐱᓯᐣ
VAI s/he lies prone, s/he lies on his/her own stomach face down to the ground

otihtapiskwēýiw ᐅᑎᐦᑕᐱᐢᑵᔨᐤ
VAI s/he lowers his/her own head

otihtawēw ᐅᑎᐦᑕᐍᐤ
VTA s/he reaches s.o., s/he gets to s.o.; s/he comes upon s.o., s/he approaches s.o. [*in inverse or inanimate actor*: otihtākow "s/he contracts s.t. (*e.g.* disease), s/he receives s.t."; *cf.* otihtēw]

otihtēw ᐅᑎᐦᑌᐤ
VTA s/he reaches s.o., s/he gets to s.o.; s/he comes upon s.o., s/he approaches s.o. [*in inverse or inanimate actor*: otihtikow "s/he contracts s.t. (*e.g.* disease), s/he receives s.t."; *cf.* otihtawēw]

otihtinam ᐅᑎᐦᑎᓇᒼ
VTI s/he catches s.t.; s/he grabs s.t., s/he seizes s.t.

otihtinēw ᐅᑎᐦᑎᓀᐤ
VTA s/he catches s.o.; s/he grabs s.o., s/he seizes s.o.; he rapes s.o.

otihtinikēsk ᐅᑎᐦᑎᓂᑫᐢᐠ
NA rapist [*hab*]

otihtinikēw ᐅᑎᐦᑎᓂᑫᐤ
VAI s/he seizes things; he rapes

otihtinikēwin ᐅᑎᐦᑎᓂᑫᐏᐣ
NI rape; assault

otihtinitowak ᐅᑎᐦᑎᓂᑐᐘᐠ
VAI they seize one another, they grab one another

otihtitowak ᐅᑎᐦᑎᑐᐘᐠ
VAI they reach one another

otinam ᐅᑎᓇᒼ
VTI s/he takes s.t., s/he steals s.t.; s/he chooses s.t.; s/he purchases s.t.

otinamawēw ᐅᑎᓇᒪᐍᐤ
VTA s/he takes (it/him) for s.o., s/he buys (it/him) for s.o.

otinamāsow ᐅᑎᓇᒫᓱᐤ
VAI s/he takes (it/him) for him/herself; s/he steals (it/him); s/he buys (it/him) for him/herself

otinamātowak ᐅᑎᓇᒫᑐᐘᐠ
VAI they take (it/him) for or from one another; they steal

(it/him) for or from one
another; they buy (it/him) for
or from one another

otinākan ⊃∩ᴖ·ᑫᑊ
NA captive [cf. otinikan]

otinākaniwiw ⊃∩ᴖ·ᑫᑕᐁᐧᐤ
VAI it is a thing taken; s/he
is a captive

otinēw ⊃∩ᓎᐤ
VTA s/he takes s.o., s/he
chooses s.o.; s/he purchases
s.o.; s/he takes s.o. for
(it/him), s/he steals s.o.

otinikan ⊃∩ᓂᑫᑊ
NA captive [cf. otinākan]

otinikātēw ⊃∩ᓂᑫᐪᐁᐤ
VII it is taken, it is
purchased

otinikēmakan ⊃∩ᓂᓎᑫᒪᑫᑊ
VII it acts to take away; it
takes away

otinikēw ⊃∩ᓂᓎᐊᑫᐤ
VAI s/he makes a purchase,
s/he buys things; s/he takes
things, s/he steals things

otinikēwin ⊃∩ᓂᓎᐊᐁᐧᐣ
NI shopping, articles
purchased

otinikowisiw ⊃∩ᓂᑯᐃᐧᓯᐤ
VAI s/he is taken by the
powers, s/he passes away

otinitowak ⊃∩ᓂᑐᐊᐧᐠ
VAI they take one another;
they marry each other

otipahaskēw ⊃∩ᐸᐦᐊᐢᑫᐤ
NA surveyor

otipēýihcikēw ⊃∩ᐯᔨᐦᒋᑫᐤ
NA owner; manager; lord
[cf. kā-tipēýihcikēt]

otipēýimisow ⊃∩ᐯᔨᒥᓱᐤ
NA independent person

otisāpahtam ⊃∩ᓵᐸᐦᑕᒼ
VTI s/he sees s.t. arriving,
s/he has lived long enough to
see s.t., s/he lives long
enough to see s.t. again

otisāpamēw ⊃∩ᓵᐸᒣᐤ
VTA s/he sees s.o. coming in
the distance

otisīhkān ⊃∩ᓰᐦᑳᐣ
NI turnip [also otisihkān]

otisīhkāniw ⊃∩ᓰᐦᑳᓂᐤ
VAI s/he has turnips

otisīhkānipak ⊃∩ᓰᐦᑳᓂᐸᐠ
NI turnip top [pl: -wa]

otitāmiyaw ⊃∩ᑖᒥᔭᐤ
NI innards [cf. atāmiyaw]

otitwēstamākēw ⊃∩ᑤᐢᑕᒫᑫᐤ
NA interpreter

otohpinikēw ⊃ᐤᐦᐱᓂᑫᐤ
NA weightlifter

otōkimāmiw ⊃ᐅᑭᒫᒥᐤ
VAI s/he has (s.o. as) a boss,
master

otōnapiy ⊃ᐅᓇᐱᕀ
NA tullibee (fish) [pC and
sC; wC: otōthapiy, dim:
ocōthapis]

otōniw ⊃ᐅᓂᐤ
VAI s/he has a mouth

otōsimimāw ⊃ᐅᓯᒥᒫᐤ
NA nephew; a man's
brother's son or woman's
sister's son [cf. 1: nitōsim
"my nephew"]

otōskinīkiskwēmiw ⊃ᐅᐢᑭᓃᑭᐢᑵᒥᐤ
VAI s/he has a young woman
(as partner, servant or
employee)

otōskwanihk ⊃ᐅᐢᑿᓂᐦᐠ
INM Calgary, AB [loc; lit:
"at (his/her) elbow", in
reference to the Bow River]

otōspwākaniw ⊃ᐅᐢᑅᐃᐧᑫᐤ
VAI s/he has a pipe

otōtēmimāw ⊃ᐅᑌᒥᒫᐤ
NA friend

otōtēmimēw ⊃ᐅᑌᒥᒣᐤ
VTA s/he makes friends with
s.o.; s/he has s.o. as a friend

otōtēmimiw ⊃ᐅᑌᒥᒥᐤ
VAI s/he has (s.o. as) a
friend

otōtēmitowak ⊃ᐅᑌᒥᑐᐊᐧᐠ
VAI they become friends
with one another

otōtēmiw ⊃ᐅᑌᒥᐤ
VAI s/he is friendly; s/he has
(s.o. as) a friend or kinsman

otōtēmiwēwin ⊃ᐅᑌᒥᐁᐧᐃᐧᐣ
NI friendship

otōýākaniw ⊃ᐅᔮᑲᓂᐤ
VAI s/he has a dish

owacistwaniw ᐅᐊᐧᒋᐢᑤᓂᐤ
VAI s/he has a nest

owanihikaniw ᐅᐊᐧᓂᐦᐃᑲᓂᐤ
VAI s/he has traps

owanihikēw ᐅᐊᐧᓂᐦᐃᑫᐤ
NA trapper

owaninēw ᐅᐊᐧᓂᓀᐤ
NA crazy person

owatapīwatēw ᐅᐊᐧᑕᐲᐊᐧᑌᐤ
VAI s/he has a birch-bark
basket

owācihkēsis ᐅᐋᒋᐦᑫᓯᐢ
NA badger [dim]

owāhkicān ᐅᐋᐦᑭᒐᐣ
NI an edible plant [exact
identity not yet established]

owāskahikanihkēw ᐅᐋᐢᑲᐦᐃᑲᓂᐦᑫᐤ
NA house-builder

owāskahikaniw ᐅᐋᐢᑲᐦᐃᑲᓂᐤ
VAI s/he has a house

owāspisonihkēw ᐅᐋᐢᐱᓱᓂᐦᑫᐤ
NA moss-bag maker

owāspisoniw ᐅᐋᐢᐱᓱᓂᐤ
VAI s/he has a moss bag

owātiw ᐅᐋᑎᐤ
VAI s/he has a den, lair

owāwiw ᐅᐋᐃᐧᐤ
VAI she lays eggs; s/he has
eggs

owēpahikaniw ᐅᐁᐧᐸᐦᐃᑲᓂᐤ
VAI s/he has a broom

owēstakēw ᐅᐁᐧᐢᑕᑫᐤ
VAI s/he has hair

owēstakēyiw ᐅᐁᐧᐢᑕᑫᔨᐤ
VAI s/he has hair

owiýasiwēw ᐅᐃᐧᔭᓯᐁᐧᐤ
NA judge; lawyer

owiýasiwēw-apiwin ᐅᐃᐧᔭᓯᐁᐧᐊᐧᐱᐃᐧᐣ
NI judge's seat

owiýasiwēwikimāw ᐅᐃᐧᔭᓯᐁᐧᐃᐧᑭᒫᐤ
NI magistrate; governor

owiyāsimiw ᐅᐃᐧᔮᓯᒥᐤ
VAI s/he has meat

owīcēwākanimēw ᐅᐄᒉᐧᐋᑲᓂᒣᐤ
VTA s/he makes s.o. a
buddy, partner

owīcēwākaniw ᐅᐄᒉᐧᐋᑲᓂᐤ
VAI s/he has (s.o. as) a
companion or partner

owīcimosiw ᐅᐄᒋᒧᓯᐤ
VAI s/he has (s.o. as) a
lover; he has a girlfriend, she
has a boyfriend

owīhkohkēw ᐅᐄᐦᑯᐦᑫᐤ
NA one who makes a feast

owīhowiniw ᐅᐄᐦᐅᐃᐧᓂᐤ
VAI s/he has a name, s/he
has (it) as a name

owīkihtow ᐅᐄᑭᐦᑐᐤ
NA bridegroom; bride

owīkimākaniw ᐅᐄᑭᒫᑲᓂᐤ
VAI s/he has (s.o. as) a
spouse, wife, husband

owīkiw ᐅᐄᑭᐤ
VAI s/he lives there, s/he has
a home there [cf. wīkiw]

owītisāniw ᐅᐄᑎᓵᓂᐤ
VAI s/he has (s.o. as) a
sibling [cf. witisāniw]

oýahākan ᐅᔭᐦᐋᑲᐣ
NA person placed

oýahēw ᐅᔭᐦᐁᐤ
VTA s/he sets s.o. in place

oýahisow ᐅᔭᐦᐃᓱᐤ
NA blacksmith

oýahisowikamik ᐅᔭᐦᐃᓱᐃᐧᑲᒥᐠ
NI smithy, blacksmith shop
[pl: -wa]

oýahpicikēw ᐅᔭᐦᐱᒋᑫᐤ
VAI s/he harnesses [cf.
wiýahpicikēw]

oýahpisow ᐅᔭᐦᐱᓱᐤ
VAI it is harnessed, saddled
[cf. wiýahpisow]

oýahpitam ᐅᔭᐦᐱᑕᒼ
VTI s/he ties s.t. in place [cf.
wiýahpitam]

oýahpitamawēw ᐅᔭᐦᐱᑕᒪᐁᐧᐤ
VTA s/he ties (it/him) for
s.o., s/he saddles s.o.'s horse
[cf. wiýahpitamawēw]

oýahpitastimwēw ᐅᔭᐦᐱᑕᐢᑎᒼᐁᐧᐤ
VAI s/he hitches up his/her
own horses [cf.
wiýahpitastimwēw]

oýahpitēw ᐅᔭᐦᐱᑌᐤ
VTA s/he ties s.o. in place
[cf. wiýahpitēw]

oýakēsk ▷ᐅᑫᐣᐢ
 NI pan, dish, bowl [*pl*: -wa]

oýakihtam ▷ᐅᑭᑊᐦᑕᐨ
 VTI s/he prices s.t.

oýaman ▷ᐅᒪᐣ
 NA vermillion, colored paint

oýamanask ▷ᐅᒪᓇᐢᐢ
 NI love medicine [*pl*: -wa]

oýapiw ▷ᐅᐱᐤ
 VAI s/he sits in place

oýascikēw ▷ᐅᐢᒋᑫᐤ
 VAI s/he arranges things, s/he sets things in order; s/he sets the table

oýasiwātam ▷ᐅᓯᐚᑕᐨ
 VTI s/he makes a law of s.t., for s.t., s/he judges s.t. [*cf.* oýasiwātām]

oýasiwātāw ▷ᐅᓯᐚᑖᐤ
 VAIt s/he makes a law of s.t., for s.t. [*cf.* oýasiwātam]

oýasiwātēw ▷ᐅᓯᐚᑌᐤ
 VTA s/he makes a law for s.o.; s/he judges s.o., s/he tries s.o. in court

oýasiwēw ▷ᐅᓯᐌᐤ
 VAI s/he makes laws; s/he judges

oýasiwēwin ▷ᐅᓯᐌᐃᐣ
 NI law, decision, commandment; laws of the country [*also* wiýasiwēwin]

oýasiwēwiýiniw ▷ᐅᓯᐌᐃᔨᓂᐤ
 NA band counsellor

oýaskinahēw ▷ᐅᐢᑲᓇᐦᐁᐤ
 VTA s/he fills s.o. (e.g. pipe); s/he gets s.o. ready by filling

oýaskinahtawēw ▷ᐅᐢᑲᐦᑕᐌᐤ
 VTA s/he fills (it/him) (e.g. pipe) for s.o.

oýastāsow ▷ᐅᐢᑖᓱᐤ
 VAI s/he sets the table; s/he orders things, s/he puts things in order

oýastāw ▷ᐅᐢᑖᐤ
 VAIt s/he sets the table; s/he orders things, s/he puts things in order; s/he edits s.t.

oýatahikāsow ▷ᐅᑕᐦᐃᑳᓱᐤ
 VAI it is hewn to shape

oýatahwēw ▷ᐅᑕᐦᐌᐤ
 VTA s/he hews s.o. to shape

oýākan ▷ᐅᑳᐣ
 NI plate, dish, pan; bowl

oýākanikamik ▷ᐅᑳᓂᑲᒥᐠ
 NI kitchen cabinet, pantry [*pl*: -wa]

oýākanis ▷ᐅᑳᓂᐢ
 NI cup; little plate, small dish [*dim*]

oýākonēham ▷ᐅᑳᐅᓀᐦᐊᐨ
 VTI s/he places s.t. carefully in snow

oýāpicikēw ▷ᐅᑳᐱᒋᑫᐤ
 VAI s/he muddles things up; s/he fails to put things back in place

oýāpiskātahikan ▷ᐅᑳᐱᐢᑳᑕᐦᐃᑲᐣ
 NI anvil

oýāpiw ▷ᐅᑳᐱᐤ
 VAI s/he looks on

oýāpīhkātam ▷ᐅᑳᐱᐦᑳᑕᐨ
 VTI s/he arranges s.t. on a string, s/he threads s.t. on a string

oýāskwaham ▷ᐅᑳᐢᑲᐦᐊᐨ
 VTI s/he arranges s.t. on wood or stick

oýāskwahwēw ▷ᐅᑳᐢᑲᐦᐌᐤ
 VTA s/he arranges s.o. on wood or stick

oýāskwan ▷ᐅᑳᐢᑲᐣ
 VII it is arranged on wood or stick

oýipēhamawēw ▷ᐅᐱᐦᐊᒪᐌᐤ
 VTA s/he writes (it) to s.o.

oýisam ▷ᐅᓯᐢ
 VTI s/he cuts s.t. to shape

oyōhpikihēw ▷ᐅᐦᐱᑭᐦᐁᐤ
 VTA s/he raises s.o. over a long period of time [*rdpl*]

oyōsēw ▷ᐅᓱᐤ
 VAI she is fertile

oyōýow ▷ᐅᔪᐤ
 VAI s/he howls (as a wolf, coyote); s/he neighs (as a horse) [*also* ōýow; *wC*: ōthow]

ō
ᐆ

ō- ᐆ
   IPV from there, for that reason; with, by means of; [*grammatical preverb*; *cf.* ohci *IPV*, ōh *IPV*]

ōcēnās ᐆᒉᓈᐢ
   NI town; village [*dim*]

ōcēs ᐆᒉᐢ
   NA housefly [*dim*]

ōcēsis ᐆᒉᓯᐢ
   NA small fly; insect [*dim*]

ōcēw ᐆᒉᐤ
   NA housefly, maggot [*also* ocēw]

ōcēwan ᐆᒉᐘᐣ
   VII there are many flies; it is maggoty

ōcēwātam ᐆᒉᐚᑕᒼ
   VTI s/he makes s.t. maggoty

ōcēwātēw ᐆᒉᐚᑌᐤ
   VTA s/he makes s.o. maggoty

ōcēwiw ᐆᒉᐏᐤ
   VAI s/he is a fly

ōh ᐆᐦ
   IPC oh! [*exclamation*]

ōh- ᐆᐦ
   IPV from there, for that reason; with, by means of [*past preverb in negative clauses*; *cf.* ohci *IPV*]

ōhi ᐆᐦᐃ
   PR this [*inan pl/anim obv*; *wC:* ōho]

ōhīta ᐆᐦᐃᑕ
   IPC here they are, here it is [*inan pl / anim obv*; *cf.* ōhi ita; *wC:* ōhōta]

ōhkomiw ᐆᐦᑯᒥᐤ
   VAI s/he has (s.o. as) a grandmother [*cf.* nōhkom, nohkom]

ōhow ᐆᐦᐅᐤ
   NA owl [*also* ōhōw]

ōhōsimow ᐆᐦᐆᓯᒧᐤ
   VAI s/he dances the owl dance

ōhōsimowaham ᐆᐦᐆᓯᒧᐘᐦᒪᐧ
   VTI s/he sings the owl dance

ōhōsis ᐆᐦᐆᓯᐢ
   NA owlet, young owl [*dim*]

ōki ᐆᑭ
   PR these [*anim prox pl*; *wC:* ōko; *sC:* ōkik]

ōkīkwa ᐆᑮᒁ
   NI gills (of fish) [*pl*]

ōkīta ᐆᑮᑕ
   IPC here they are [*anim prox pl*; *cf.* ōki ita; *wC:* ōkōta]

ōma ᐆᒪ
   IPC it is this; the fact that; then; when; as it is, actually [*factive*; *also predicative*; *cf.* ōma *PR*]

ōma ᐆᒪ
   PR this [*inan sg*; *cf.* ōma *IPC*]

ōmatowahk ᐆᒪᑐᐚᕽ
   IPC of this kind, like this [*often accompanied by a gesture*]

ōmatowihk ᐆᒪᑐᐃᕽ
   IPC right here, in this place; like this [*often accompanied by a gesture*]

ōmayīkohk ᐆᒪᔦᑯᕽ
   IPC this much, to this degree, to this extent, this far [*often accompanied by a gesture*]

ōmē ᐆᒣ
   IPC over here [*archaic*]

ōmēyīkohk ᐆᒣᔦᑯᕽ
   IPC this much, this far

ōmēyiw ᐆᒣᔨᐤ
   PR this [*inan obv*; *archaic in pC*; *cf. wC:* omīthiw]

ōmīta ᐆᒦᑕ
   IPC here it is [*inan sg*; *cf.* ōma ita]

ōsi ᐆᓯ
   NI boat; canoe [*pl*: ōsa]

ōta ᐆᑕ
   IPC here

ōtāhkimihk ᐆᒐᐦᑭᒥᕽ
   IPC at his/her rear, behind him/her [*loc*]

ōtē ᐆᐅ
   IPC over here; over there

ōtē isi ᐆᐅ ᐊᓯ
   IPH over this way

ōtēnaw ᐆᐅᓇᐤ
   NI town, camp-circle, settlement; city

ōtēnawihtāw ᐆᐅᓇᐃᐦᑖᐤ
   VAIt s/he forms a village

ōtēnāhk ᐆᐅᓈᕽ
   IPC in town, in the city [*loc*; *cf.* ōtēnaw]

ōtēnāwiwin ᐆᐅᓈᐏᐃᐧᐣ
   NI township; realm

ōti ᐆᓂ
   IPC that is to say, at any rate [*cf.* oti *IPC*]

ōyā ᐆᔮ
   PR that one no longer here [*anim prox sg*; *archaic*; *also:* ōyāpan]

ōyē ᐆᔦ
   PR that one no longer here [*inan sg*; *archaic*]

ōyēhā ᐆᔦᐦᐋ
   PR those ones no longer here, that one no longer here [*inan pl / anim obv*; *archaic*]

ōyēhkāk ᐆᔦᐦᑳᐠ
   PR those ones no longer here [*anim prox pl*; *archaic*]

p

ᐸ

pa-pakamahwēsiw ᐸ ᐸᑲᒪᐦᐍᓯᐤ
VTA s/he pats s.o. on the head [*rdpl*; *dim*; *cf.* pakamahwēw, pakamahwēsiw]

pa-pakamahwēw ᐸ ᐸᑲᒪᐦᐍᐤ
VTA s/he beats s.o. [*rdpl*]

pa-pasakwāpiw ᐸ ᐸᓴᑳᐧᐱᐤ
VAI s/he blinks, s/he closes his/her eyes [*rdpl*, *cf.* pasakwāpiw]

pa-pasastēham ᐸ ᐸᓴᐢᑌᐦᐊᒼ
VTI s/he thrashes s.t. (with a flail) [*rdpl*; *cf.* pasastēhēw]

pa-pāstāmow ᐸ ᐹᐢᑖᒧᐤ
VAI s/he blasphemes [*rdpl*; *cf.* pāstāmow]

pa-pēhēw ᐸ ᐯᐦᐁᐤ
VTA s/he is still waiting for s.o. [*rdpl*; *cf.* pēhēw]

pa-pimātisiw ᐸ ᐱᒫᑎᓯᐤ
VAI s/he is alive and well [*rdpl*]

pa-pimohtēw ᐸ ᐱᒧᐦᑌᐤ
VAI s/he walks along [*rdpl*]

paci- ᐸᒋ
IPV wrongly, in error

paci-sīkinam ᐸᒋ ᓰᑭᓇᒼ
VTI s/he misses pouring a liquid; s/he spills a liquid) [*cf.* patisīkinam]

paci-tōtawēw ᐸᒋ ᑑᑕᐍᐤ
VTA s/he wrongs s.o.

pacipaýihtāw ᐸᒋᐸᔨᐦᑖᐤ
VAIt s/he makes s.t. miss

pacipaýiw ᐸᒋᐸᔨᐤ
VAI s/he misses (*e.g.* a chair); s/he falls off the main track

paciýawēhēw ᐸᒋᔭᐍᐦᐁᐤ
VTA s/he provokes s.o.'s anger; s/he wrongs s.o. by one's utterance

pahkacimēw ᐸᐦᑲᒋᒣᐤ
VTA s/he tricks s.o. into doing something, s/he tricks s.o. into a commitment

pahkaham ᐸᐦᑲᐦᐊᒼ
VTI s/he has a pulse

pahkahokow ᐸᐦᑲᐦᐅᑯᐤ
VAI s/he has a heart beat

pahkahokowin ᐸᐦᑲᐦᐅᑯᐏᐣ
NI pulse

pahkēkin ᐸᐦᑫᑭᐣ
NI hide; tanned hide, dressed hide, finished hide, leather [*pl*: -wa]

pahkēkinohkēw ᐸᐦᑫᑭᓄᐦᑫᐤ
VAI s/he makes dressed hides, s/he makes leather

pahkēkinos ᐸᐦᑫᑭᓄᐢ
NI small dressed hide, small piece of leather [*dim*]

pahkēkinowat ᐸᐦᑫᑭᓄᐗᐟ
NI leather bag

pahkēkinwēsākay ᐸᐦᑫᑭᓀᐧᓵᑲᐩ
NI leather coat, leather jacket [*also* pahkēkinwasākay]

pahkēkinwēskisin ᐸᐦᑫᑭᓀᐧᐢᑭᓯᐣ
NI leather moccasin [*also* pahkēkinwaskisin]

pahkēkinwēskisinihkēw ᐸᐦᑫᑭᓀᐧᐢᑭᓯᓂᐦᑫᐤ
VAI s/he makes moccasins

pahki- ᐸᐦᑭ
IPV portion of

pahkihtin ᐸᐦᑭᐦᑎᐣ
VII it falls, it falls down

pahkihtitāw ᐸᐦᑭᐦᑎᑖᐤ
VAIt s/he drops s.t. accidently

pahkihtitēw ᐸᐦᑭᐦᑎᑌᐤ
VTA s/he drops s.o. accidently

pahkikawin ᐸᐦᑭᑲᐏᐣ
VII it drips (*e.g.* water) [*cf.* pahkikawiw]

pahkikawinam ᐸᐦᑭᑲᐏᓇᒼ
VTI s/he lets s.t. drip, s/he lets s.t. fall drop by drop

pahkikawiw ᐸᐦᑭᑲᐏᐤ
VII it is dripping (*i.e.* a liquid) [*cf.* pahkikawin]

pahkipēstāw ᐸᐦᑭᐯᐢᑖᐤ
VII it is a shower, there are large raindrops falling, there are raindrops falling gently

pahkipēstin ᐸᐦᑭᐯᐢᑎᐣ
VII it drips (as from a roof)

pahkisam ᐸᐦᑭᓴᒼ
VTI s/he bombs s.t.; s/he explodes s.t.

pahkisimēw ᐸᐦᑭᓯᒣᐤ
VTA s/he lets s.o. fall (*e.g.* pants), s/he drops s.o. down

pahkisimon ᐸᐦᑭᓯᒧᐣ
NI sunset [*cf.* pahkisimow, pahkisimon *VII*]

pahkisimon ᐸᐦᑭᓯᒧᐣ
VII it is sunset [*cf.* pahkisimow, pahkisimon *NI*]

pahkisimotāhk ᐸᐦᑭᓯᒧᑖᕽ
IPC west; in, to the west, "towards the sunset"

pahkisimow ᐸᐦᑭᓯᒧᐤ
VAI it sets (*i.e.* the sun), the sun is setting [*cf.* pahkisimon *NI*, *VII*]

pahkisimowin ᐸᐦᑭᓯᒧᐏᐣ
NI sunset

pahkisin ᐸᐦᑭᓯᐣ
VAI s/he falls, s/he falls down

pahkisow ᐸᐦᑭᓱᐤ
VAI s/he explodes; there is an explosion

pahkitēw ᐸᐦᑭᑌᐤ
VII it explodes; embers are crackling

pahkitēwāpoy ᐸᐦᑭᑌᐚᐳᐩ
NI gasoline

pahkonam ᐸᐦᑯᓇᒼ
VTI s/he skins s.t.

pahkonēw ᐸᐦᑯᓀᐤ
VTA s/he skins s.o., s/he takes s.o.'s pelt

pahkonikēw ᐸᐦᑯᓂᑫᐤ
VAI s/he skins an animal, s/he skins animals

pahkopēhēw ᐸᐦᑯᐯᐦᐁᐤ
VTA s/he makes s.o. walk into water

pahkopēpahtāw ᐸᐦᑯᐯᐸᐦᑖᐤ
VAI s/he runs into water

pahkopēpaýihow ᐸᐦᑯᐯᐸᔨᐦᐅᐤ
VAI s/he goes quickly into water

pahkopēpaýiw ᐸᐦᑯᐯᐸᔨᐤ
VAI s/he slips into water

pahkopēw ᐸᐦᑯᐯᐤ
VAI s/he wades, s/he walks into water

pahkwacipaýihcikēw ᐸᐦᑲᐧᒋᐸᔨᐦᒋᑫᐤ
VAI s/he brings up mucus

pahkwacipaýihtāw ᐸᐦᑲᐧᒋᐸᔨᐦᑖᐤ
VAIt s/he loosens s.t. (*e.g.* mucus)

pahkwacipaýiw <"ᑊᑲᑌᐸᔩ°
VAI it loosens and falls off

pahkwacipitam <"ᑊᑲᑌᐱᐊᐨ
VTI s/he loosens and pulls s.t. off

pahkwacipitēw <"ᑊᑲᑌᐱᐁ°
VTA s/he loosens and pulls s.o. off

pahkwaciwēpaham <"ᑊᑲᑌᐠᐁᐸ<"ᐊᐨ
VTI s/he knocks s.t. off, s/he pries s.t. off (*e.g.* hide-scrapings)

pahkwaciwēpahwēw <"ᑊᑲᑌᐠᐁ<"ᐁ°
VTA s/he knocks s.o. off, s/he pries s.o. off (*e.g.* wood-tick)

pahkwataham <"ᑊᑲ·ᐨ"ᐊᐨ
VTI s/he knocks s.t. off; s/he peels s.t. off with a knife

pahkwatahwēw <"ᑊᑲ·ᐨ"ᐁ°
VTA s/he knocks s.o. off; s/he peels s.o. off with a knife

pahkwatinam <"ᑊᑲᓇᐟᐨ
VTI s/he takes s.t. off by hand, s/he loosens s.t. by hand

pahkwatinēw <"ᑊᑲᓇᐟ°
VTA s/he takes s.o. off by hand, s/he loosens s.o. by hand

pahkwācīs <"ᑊᑲᑌᐣ
NA bat [*cf.* apahkwācīs]

pahkwācīsiskāw <"ᑊᑌᐣᐢᑲᐧ°
VII there is an abundance of bats, there are numerous bats [*also* apahkwācīsiskāw]

pahkwātihpēpitēw <"ᑊᑲᓇ"ᐯᐱᐁ°
VTA s/he scalps s.o. [*lit:* "s/he peel s.o.'s head and pulls"]

pahkwēham <"ᖃ"ᐊᐨ
VTI s/he breaks a piece off s.t. by tool (as a piece of a dish)

pahkwēhtam <"ᖃ"ᐨᐨ
VTI s/he bites a piece from s.t.

pahkwēhwēw <"ᖃ"ᐁ°
VTA s/he breaks a piece off s.o. by tool

pahkwēmēw <"ᖃ·ᐁᐟ°
VTA s/he bites a piece from s.o.

pahkwēnam <"ᖃ·ᐊᐨ
VTI s/he breaks a piece off s.t. by hand

pahkwēnamawēw <"ᖃ·ᐊᐟᐁ°
VTA s/he portions (it/him) for s.o.; s/he breaks a piece off (of it/him) for s.o.

pahkwēnēw <"ᖃ·ᐁ°
VTA s/he breaks a piece off s.o. (*e.g.* bread) by hand

pahkwēpayín <"ᖃ·ᐸᔑᐣ
VII it has a piece break off; it breaks into pieces

pahkwēpayíw <"ᖃ·ᐸᔑ°
VAI it breaks off

pahkwēpitam <"ᖃ·ᐱᐨᐨ
VTI s/he breaks a piece off s.t., s/he tears a piece off s.t.

pahkwēpitēw <"ᖃ·ᐱᐁ°
VTA s/he breaks a piece off s.o., s/he tears a piece off s.o.

pahkwēsam <"ᖃᔕᐨ
VTI s/he cuts a piece off s.t., s/he cuts a piece from s.t.

pahkwēsamawēw <"ᖃᔕᒧᐁ°
VTA s/he cuts a piece off (it/him) for s.o.

pahkwēsāwācikan <"ᖃᓯᐌᑌᑲᐣ
NA slice of bread

pahkwēsāwātam <"ᖃᓯᐌᐊᐨᐨ
VTI s/he slices s.t. off, s/he cuts a piece off s.t.

pahkwēsāwātēw <"ᖃᓯᐌᐊᐱᐁ°
VTA s/he slices s.o. off, s/he cuts a piece off s.o.

pahkwēsikan <"ᖃᕐᐸᐣ
NA bannock, bread; flour [*see also* sikwāwakinikan]

pahkwēsikani-kīsikāw <"ᖃᕐᐸᐢ ᑭᕐᑲᐧ
VII it is Friday [*lit:* "flour-day"; *see also* niyānano-kisikāw]

pahkwēsikanihkawēw <"ᖃᕐᐸᐢᐢᑕᐁ°
VTA s/he makes bread for s.o.

pahkwēsikanihkān <"ᖃᕐᐸᐢᐢᑲᐣ
NA flour

pahkwēsikanihkēw <"ᖃᕐᐸᐢᐢᑲᐁᐧ
VAI s/he makes bannock, bread

pahkwēsikanis <"ᖃᕐᐸᐢᓯᐣ
NA cookie; small bannock, bit of bread; bit of flour [*dim*]

pahkwēsikaniwat <"ᖃᕐᐸᐢᓯᐧᐊᐧ
NI flour-bag

pahkwēsiw <"ᖃᕐᔨ°
VAI it has a portion missing, it is gone from it

pahkwēswēw <"ᖃᔕᔨ°
VTA s/he cuts a piece off s.o.

pahpahāhkwān <"<"ᐊᐣ"ᑲᐣ
NA shield [*see also* nakahāskwān]

pahpawaham <"<ᐊᐧ"ᐊᐧ
VTI s/he beats s.t., s/he shakes s.t. out by tool; s/he dusts s.t. off

pahpawahwēw <"<ᐊᐧ"ᐁ°
VTA s/he beats s.o., s/he shakes s.o. out by tool; s/he dusts s.o. off

pahpawipayíhēw <"<ᐃᐧᐸᔑ"ᐁᐧ°
VTA s/he shakes s.o.

pahpawipayíhow <"<ᐃᐧᐸᔑ"ᐃᐧᐅ°
VAI s/he shakes him/herself (*e.g.* a dog)

pahpawipayíhtāw <"<ᐃᐧᐸᔑ"ᐨ°
VAIt s/he shakes s.t.

pahpawisimēw <"<ᐃᐧᓯᐟᐁᐧᐟ°
VTA s/he knocks s.o. (*e.g.* pipe) against something to empty it

pahpawiwēpinam <"<ᐃᐧᐁᐧᐱᐊᐧ
VTI s/he shakes s.t. out by hand

pahpawiwēpinēw <"<ᐃᐧᐁᐧᐱᐊᐧ°
VTA s/he shakes s.o. out by hand

pahpawīw <"<ᐃᐧᐊᐧ·°
VAI s/he shakes him/herself

pahtakoskam <"Cᑯᐢᑲᐨ
VTI s/he sits on s.t., s/he presses s.t. down, s/he flattens s.t.

pahtakoskawēw <"Cᑯᐢᑲᐁ·°
VTA s/he sits on s.o., s/he presses s.o. down, s/he flattens s.o.

pahtakwātimātēw <"Cᑲᓇᑌᐁᐧ°
VTA s/he stamps s.o. on ground by snowshoe

pakahamān <ᑲ"ᐊᐧᐩ
NA drum

pakahamānāhtik <ᑲ"ᐊᐧᓇᐧ"ᐣᐠ
NI drum stick [*pl:* -wa]

pakahkam <ᑲ"ᑲᐨ
IPC I think, I believe, apparently; perhaps, maybe; surely, it's very likely, to judge by appeal [*expectation; contrast* ēsa *and* ētikwē, ētokwē; *also* pakāhkam]

pakamaham <ᑲᒪ"ᐊᐩ
VTI s/he hits s.t., s/he pounds s.t., s/he strikes s.t.

pakamahākanis <ᑲᒪ"ᐋᑲᓇᐣ
NI hammer [*dim*]

pakamahikan <ᑲᒪ"ᐃᑲᐩ
NI threshing machine [*see also* pawahikan]

pakamahikāsow <ᑲᒪ"ᐃᑲᓴᐧᐟ°
VAI s/he is beaten, s/he receives blows

pakamahikātēw <ᑲᒪ"ᐃᑲᐱᐁ°
VII it is hit

pakamahikēw <ᑲᒪ"ᐃᖃ°
VAI s/he strikes, s/he hits, s/he hammers; s/he boxes

pakamahwēsiw <ᑲᒪ"ᐁ·ᔨ°
VTA s/he gives s.o. a gentle pat [*dim*]

pakamahwēw <ᑲᒪ"ᐁ·°
VTA s/he hits s.o., s/he pounds s.o., s/he strikes s.o., s/he beats s.o.

pakamākan <ᑲᒪᑲᐩ
NI bat (*i.e.* baseball), club, sledge-hammer

pakamākanis <ᗷᒉᗷᓯᐣ
NI hammer [dim]
pakamāpahwēw <ᗷᒉ<ᐦᐁᐧᐅ·ᵒ
VTA s/he strikes s.o.'s eye
by tool
pakamāpiskahikēw
<ᗷᒉᐱᐦᑫᐦᐃᐠᐁᐧᵒ
VAI s/he is a blacksmith;
s/he hits rocks or metal
pakamāskwēw <ᗷᒉᐢᒀᐧᵒ
VAI s/he hits wood
pakamāstan <ᗷᒉᐢᐨᐣ
VII it is hit against
something by the wind
pakamicihcihamāw
<ᗷᒉᒥᐦᒋᐦᐊᒪᐧᵒ
VAI s/he claps his/her hands
pakamicihcīhēw <ᗷᒉᒥᐦᒋᐦᐃᐧᵒ
VTA s/he claps s.o.'s hands
for that one, s/he makes s.o.
clap that's one's hands
pakamihkwēhwēw <ᗷᒉᐦᒀᐦᐁᐧᐅ·ᵒ
VTA s/he strikes s.o. on the
face
pakamihtatāw <ᗷᒉᐦᐨᐦᐨᐧᵒ
VAIt s/he hammers s.t., s/he
bangs s.t., s/he hits s.t.
against something
pakamihtin <ᗷᒉᐦᐨᐣ
VII it falls against something
pakamipayiw <ᗷᒉᐱᐊᐧᐸᵒ
VII it bumps against
something
pakamisin <ᗷᒉᐢᐣ
VAI s/he falls against things;
s/he falls down with a thud
pakamisimēw <ᗷᒉᐢᒥᐧᵒ
VTA s/he strikes s.o. to the
ground, s/he throws s.o.
down on the ground
pakamiskam <ᗷᒉᐢᐠᐊᐨ
VTI s/he bumps s.t. with
his/her body
pakamiskawēw <ᗷᒉᐢᐠᐊᐧᐅ·ᵒ
VTA s/he bumps s.o. with
his/her body
pakaski <ᗷᐢᑭ
IPC brightly coloured; very
clearly, fluently
pakaski-nēhiyawēw
<ᗷᐢᑭ ᓀᐦᐃᔭᐧᐅ·ᵒ
VAI s/he speaks Cree very
fluently, s/he speaks Cree
extremely well
pakaskinam <ᗷᐢᑭᓇᐨ
VTI s/he sees s.t. clearly
pakaskinākosiw <ᗷᐢᑭᓈᑯᓯᐧᵒ
VAI s/he is clear, visible
pakaskinākwan <ᗷᐢᑭᓈᒀᐣ
VII it is clear, visible
pakastawēham <ᗷᐢᑕᐧᐁᐦᐊᐨ
VTI s/he puts, places s.t. in
water, s/he drops s.t. in the
water
pakastawēhwēw <ᗷᐢᑕᐧᐁᐦᐧᐅ·ᵒ
VTA s/he puts, places s.o. in
water, s/he sets s.o. in the
water (e.g. a net)

pakastawēpayin <ᗷᐢᑕᐧᐁᐸᐊᐧᐸᐣ
VII it falls into the water
pakastawēpayiw <ᗷᐢᑕᐧᐁᐸᐊᐧᐸᐧᵒ
VAI s/he falls into the water
pakastawēpinam <ᗷᐢᑕᐧᐁᐱᓇᐨ
VTI s/he throws s.t. into the
water [also
pakastawēwēpinam]
pakastawēpinēw <ᗷᐢᑕᐧᐁᐱᓀᐧᵒ
VTA s/he throws s.o. into the
water [also
pakastawēwēpinēw]
pakāhcikēw <ᗷᐦᒋᐠᐧᵒ
VAI s/he boils things in
water
pakāhtāw <ᗷᐦᐨᐧᵒ
VAIt s/he boils s.t. in water
pakāhtēw <ᗷᐦᐁᐧᵒ
VII it is boiled in water
pakān <ᗷᐣ
NA nut
pakānāhtik <ᗷᐊᐧᐦᐨᐠ
NA nut tree [pl: -wak]
pakāsimēw <ᗷᐊᔭᒥᐧᵒ
VTA s/he boils s.o. in water;
s/he immerses s.o. in water
pakāsimow <ᗷᐊᔭᒧᐧᵒ
VAI s/he swims [in some
areas of sC: kapāsimow]
pakāsimonahēw <ᗷᐊᔭᒧᓇᐦᐁᐧᵒ
VTA s/he bathes s.o., s/he
immerses s.o.
pakāsimonahāwasow
<ᗷᐊᔭᒧᓇᐦᐊᐧᐧᐊᓱᔭᵒ
VAI s/he bathes his/her
children, s/he immerses
his/her children
pakāsow <ᗷᐊᔭᓱᐧᵒ
VAI s/he is boiled in water
pakēsēw <ᐸᑫᓴᔨᵒ
VAI s/he gambles with dice
(Indian game)
pakici-wēpinam <ᐸᒋ ᐧᐁ·ᐱᓇᐨ
VTI s/he lets go of s.t., s/he
abandons s.t.
pakici-wēpinēw <ᐸᒋ ᐧᐁ·ᐱᓀᐧᵒ
VTA s/he lets go of s.o., s/he
abandons s.o.
pakiciw <ᐸᒋᐧᵒ
VAI s/he lets go,
releases; s/he quits
pakisāpahtam <ᐸᑭᐊᐧᐸᐦᐨᐨ
VTI s/he lets s.t. out of sight
pakisāpamēw <ᐸᑭᐊᐧᐸᒥᐧᵒ
VTA s/he lets s.o. out of
sight
pakitahwākan-sākahikan
NI Sturgeon Lake [lit:
"fishing-net lake"; see also
namīwi-sākahikanihk]
pakitahwāw <ᐸᐸᐨᐦᐊᐧᐧᵒ
VAI s/he fishes by net; s/he
sets nets (i.e. for fishing)
pakitahwāwin <ᐸᐸᐨᐦᐊᐧᐧᐊᐧᐃᐧᐣ
NI commercial fishing;
netting for fish

pakitatāmow <ᐸᒋᐨᑕᒧᔭᵒ
VAI s/he lets his/her breath
out, s/he breathes his/her last
pakitatāmowin <ᐸᒋᐨᑕᒧᒋᐊᐧᐸᔭ
NI last breath
pakitāpēkinam <ᐸᒋᐨᐸᑫᐱᐣᐊᓇᐨ
VTI s/he lowers s.t. (by
rope)
pakitāpēkinēw <ᐸᒋᐨᐸᑫᐱᐣᐧᵒ
VTA s/he lowers s.o. (by
rope)
pakitāskwahwēw <ᐸᒋᐨᐢᐠᐊᐦᐧᐅ·ᵒ
VTA s/he lets s.o. go by tool
["tree" as actor]
pakitēyihtam <ᐸᐅᔭᐱᐦᐨᐨᐨ
VTI s/he gives up hope, s/he
gives s.t. up
pakitēyimēw <ᐸᐅᔭᒥᐧᵒ
VTA s/he gives s.o. up, s/he
tries to forget s.o.; s/he
forgives s.o.
pakitēyimisow <ᐸᐅᔭᒥᓯᔭᵒ
VAI s/he gives him/herself
up, s/he resigns him/herself;
s/he forgives him/herself
pakitinam <ᐸᐱᓇᐧᐊᐨ
VTI s/he lets s.t. go; s/he
releases s.t., s/he sets s.t.
down by hand; s/he allows
s.t., s/he provides s.t.; s/he
leaves s.t. behind; s/he sows
s.t., s/he puts s.t. in (e.g. seed
potatoes)
pakitinamawēw <ᐸᐱᓇᒪᐧᐊᐧᐅ·ᵒ
VTA s/he lets s.o., s/he
allows s.o.; s/he sets (it/him)
down for s.o. (by hand); s/he
lets s.o. have (it/him); s/he
sows (it/him) for s.o.
pakitinamākowisiw
<ᐸᐱᓇᒪᐧᐃᒋᐊ·ᔭᵒ
VAI s/he is permitted
(it/him) by the powers
pakitināsow <ᐸᐱᓈᐧᐊᓱᔭᵒ
VAI s/he gives an offering
(in a collection plate), s/he
tithes
pakitināsowin <ᐸᐱᓈᐧᐊᓱᐊᐧᐸᔭ
NI sacrifice; offering, tithe
pakitinēw <ᐸᐱᓀᐧᵒ
VTA s/he lets s.o. go, s/he
releases s.o.; s/he sets s.o.
down by hand; s/he lets s.o.,
s/he allows s.o., s/he gives
permission to s.o., s/he
permits (it) to s.o.; s/he sets
s.o. free
pakitinikan <ᐸᐱᓂᐠᐣ
NA seed [see also kiscikānis
NA]
pakitinikāsow <ᐸᐱᓂᐠᐊᓱᔭᵒ
VAI s/he is allowed, s/he has
permission; s/he is released
pakitinikātēw <ᐸᐱᓂᐠᐊᐸᐅᔭᵒ
VII it is permitted
pakitinikēw <ᐸᐱᓂᐠᐧᵒ
VAI s/he sows seeds; s/he
gives an offering

pakitinikēwiýākan
<ᐸᏆᓂ�−ᕋᐃ᠎ᐧᕁᑳᐸ᠊>
NI collection plate

pakitinikowisiw <ᐸᏆᓂᑯᐃᐧᓯᐤ>
VAI s/he is released, s/he is let go by the powers, s/he is set down by the powers; s/he is permitted by the powers

pakitiniskwēwēw <ᐸᏆᓂ᠊ᑫᐧᐁᐧᐤ>
VAI he gives his wife up, he divorces his wife

pakitinisow <ᐸᏆᓂᓱᕁ>
VAI s/he lets him/herself go; s/he releases him/herself; s/he gives him/herself up

pakocenēw <ᐸᑯᓈᐧᕈ>
VTA s/he cuts s.o. open, s/he draws s.o. out (*e.g.* intestines from a chicken) [*wC*: pakohcinīw]

pakocēpaýiw <ᐸᑯᓈᐸᕁᐤ>
VAI s/he has a rupture [*wC*: pakohcīpathiw]

pakonēham <ᐸᑯ᠊ᐦᐊ᠊ᐧ>
VTI s/he bores s.t., s/he makes a hole in s.t.

pakonēhikan <ᐸᑯ᠊ᐦᐃᑲᐸ᠊>
NI awl, boring tool [*see also* oskācik]

pakonēhisiw <ᐸᑯ᠊ᐦᐃᓯᐤ>
VAI s/he is punctured

pakonēhwēw <ᐸᑯ᠊ᐦᐧᐁᐤ>
VTA s/he bores s.o., s/he makes a hole in s.o.

pakonēsin <ᐸᑯᓯᐧ>
VAI s/he punctures him/herself (by falling on something)

pakonēskam <ᐸᑯ᠊ᓐᑊᐨ>
VTI s/he wears a hole in s.t. (*e.g.* moccasin)

pakonēskawēw <ᐸᑯ᠊ᓐᑊᐸᐧᐁᐧᐤ>
VTA s/he wears a hole in s.o. (*e.g.* sock)

pakonēýāw <ᐸᑯᓈᕁ᠊>
VII it has a hole in it

pakonipēkīw <ᐸᑯᓂᐯᑭᐧᐤ>
VAI s/he makes blisters on his/her hands or feet [*cf.* pāpakonēw]

pakosēýihtam <ᐸᑯᕁᐋ᠊ᐦ᠊ᐨᐨ>
VTI s/he expects s.t., s/he hopes for s.t.

pakosēýihtākosiw <ᐸᑯᕁᐋᐦᑳᐨᑯᕁᐤ>
VAI s/he is expected, desired, hoped for

pakosēýimēw <ᐸᑯᕁᐋᒣ᠊ᐤ>
VTA s/he wishes s.o. (to get well), s/he wishes (it) for s.o.

pakosēýimow <ᐸᑯᕁᐋᒧᐤ>
VAI s/he has expectation, desire, hope; s/he wishes for something

pakosēýimowin <ᐸᕁᐋᒧᐃᐧᐣ>
NI hope, desire

pakosīhēw <ᐸᑯᒋᐦᐧᐁᐧᐤ>
VTA s/he begs s.o. (for something)

pakosīhtāsk <ᐸᑯᒋᐦᐨᐊᕁ>
NA beggar [*hab; also* opakosīhtāsk]

pakosīhtāw <ᐸᑯᒋᐦᐨᐧᐤ>
VAIt s/he begs, s/he begs for s.t

pakosīhtāwin <ᐸᑯᒋᐦᐨᐋᐃᐧᐣ>
NI begging

pakowayān <ᐸᑯᐊᐧᕁᐣ>
NI shirt [*cf.* papakiwayān]

pakwahcēhonis <ᐸᐧᐦᐧᑊᐦᐅᓂᐢ>
NI child's belt; small belt, small girdle [*dim*]

pakwahtēham <ᐸᐧᐦᐨᐁᐧᐦᐊᐨ>
VTI s/he puts a belt on s.t.

pakwahtēhēw <ᐸᐧᐦᐨᐁᐧᐦᐧᐁᐧᐤ>
VTA s/he puts a belt on s.o.

pakwahtēhon <ᐸᐧᐦᐨᐁᐧᐦᐅᐣ>
NI belt; girdle

pakwahtēhow <ᐸᐧᐦᐨᐁᐧᐦᐅᐤ>
VAI s/he has a belt on

pakwanaw <ᐸᐧᐊᐧᐤ>
IPC instinctively

pakwāc-āya <ᐸᐧᐄᕁ>
NA wild beast, wild creature [*also* pakwāci-aya; *cf.* pikwāci]

pakwāc-āyihk <ᐸᐧᐄᕁ᠊ᕁ᠊ᕁ>
IPC nature; rough [*loc; also* pakwāci-ayihk]

pakwāc-āyis <ᐸᐧᐄᕁ᠊ᐢ>
NA small wild animal or bird [*dim; also* pakwāci-ayis; *cf.* pikwāci]

pakwācaskiy <ᐸᐧᐄᕁᐢᑊᑊᐟ>
NI uninhabited land, desert, hinterland [*cf.* pikwāci]

pakwāci <ᐸᐧᐟᐧᕁ>
IPC wild [*also* pakwaci; *cf.* pikwāci]

pakwāci-pisiskiw <ᐸᐧᐟ ᐱᓯᐢᑭᐤ>
NA wild animal [*cf.* pikwāci]

pakwācikan <ᐸᐧᐟᕁᐸ᠊>
NA enemy, hated one [*cf.* pikwaci]

pakwānikamik <ᐸᐧᐊᓂᑲᒥᐠᐸ᠊>
NI tent [*pl:* -wa; *cf.* pakowayān; *from* papakiwayānikamik]

pakwānikamikohk <ᐸᐧᐊᓂᑲᒥᑯᕁᐠ>
IPC in the tent [*loc*]

pakwānikamikos <ᐸᐧᐊᓂᑲᒥᑯᐢ>
NI a small tent [*dim*]

pakwānikamikwēkin
<ᐸᐧᐊᓂᑲᒥᑲᐧᐃᐧᑭᐣᐸ᠊>
NI canvas [*lit:* "tent-material"; *cf.* pakowayān; *see also* apahkwāson]

pakwāno- <ᐸᐧᐊᓄ>
IPV from memory

pakwānomēw <ᐸᐧᐊᓄᒣ᠊ᐤ>
VTA s/he talks behind s.o.'s back

pakwānomēwēwin <ᐸᐧᐊᓄᒣ᠊ᐧᐁᐧᐃᐧᐣ>
NI for nothing talk, gossip

pakwāsiwēwin <ᐸᐧᐊᓯᐧᐁᐧᐃᐧᐣ>
NI hatred

pakwātam <ᐸᐧᐋᑕᐨ>
VTI s/he hates s.t., s/he dislikes s.t., s/he disapproves of s.t.

pakwātamawēw <ᐸᐧᐋᑕᒪ᠊ᐃᐧᐋᐧᐤ>
VTA s/he hates (it/him) for s.o., s/he dislikes (it/him) for s.o.

pakwātāhtik <ᐸᐧᐋᐨᐦᐨᐣᕁ>
NA tree growing in the desert or desolate area [*pl:* -wa]

pakwātēw <ᐸᐧᐋᑌᐤ>
VTA s/he hates s.o., s/he dislikes s.o., s/he disapproves of s.o.

pakwātikosiw <ᐸᐧᐋᐣᑯᕁᐤ>
VAI s/he is hateful

pakwātikwan <ᐸᐧᐋᐣᑲᐧᐣ>
VII it is hateful, it is hated

pakwātitowak <ᐸᐧᐋᐣᑐᐧᐊᕁ>
VAI they hate one another

pakwātitowin <ᐸᐧᐋᐣᑐᐃᐧᐣ>
NI hatred, mutual disgust

pakwātōsān <ᐸᐧᐋᑐᕁᐣ>
NA bastard, illegitimate child

pakwātōsānēw <ᐸᐧᐋᑐᕁᐧᐤ>
VAI s/he has a child out of wedlock, s/he has an illegitimate child

pakwātōsānihkēw <ᐸᐧᐋᑐᕁᓯ᠊ᐦᑫᐧᐤ>
VAI he causes a woman to have a child out of wedlock, he causes a woman to have an illegitimate child

pakwātōsēw <ᐸᐧᐋᑐᕁᐤ>
VAI s/he gives birth to a child out of wedlock, s/he has an illegitimate child

pamihēw <ᐸᒥᐦᐧᐁᐧᐤ>
VTA s/he takes care of s.o., s/he looks after s.o., s/he helps s.o., s/he gives aid to s.o., s/he attends to s.o., s/he tends s.o., s/he serves s.o.; s/he drives s.o. (*e.g.* horse, car)

pamihastimwēw <ᐸᒥᐦᐊᐢᑎᒼᐧᐁᐧᐤ>
VAI s/he drives the horses; s/he drives the dog-sled

pamihcikēw <ᐸᒥᐦᐳᑫᐧᐤ>
VAI s/he drives; s/he tends things

pamihisow <ᐸᒥᐦᐃᓱᐤ>
VAI s/he looks after him/herself, s/he tends him/herself, s/he waits on him/herself, s/he supports him/herself

pamihiwēw <ᐸᒥᐦᐃᐧᐁᐧᐤ>
VAI s/he looks after others, s/he attends others, s/he serves others; s/he is a mid-wife

pamihiwēwin <ᐸᒥᐦᐃᐧᐁᐧᐃᐧᐣ>
NI personal services

pamihow <ᑊᒲᐅ°
VAI s/he is well off; s/he is well looked after

pamihtamawēw <ᒪᑊᒪᐦᑕ·ᐤ
VTA s/he tends to (it/him) for s.o., s/he looks after (it/him) for s.o.; s/he drives (it) for s.o.; s/he manages (it) for s.o. (e.g. a store)

pamihtamāsow <ᒪᑊᒪᐃ·ᒍ°
VAI s/he tends to (it/him) for or by him/herself, s/he looks after (it/him) for or by him/herself; s/he drives (it) for him/herself; s/he manages (it) for him/herself (e.g. a store)

pamihtamātowak <ᒪᑊᒪᐃᐳᐊ·ᐩ
VAI they tend (it/him) for one another, they look after (it/him) for one another

pamihtāw <ᒪᑊᐨ°
VAIt s/he takes care of s.t., s/he looks after s.t., s/he attends to s.t., s/he tends s.t.; s/he drives s.t.; s/he manages s.t. (e.g. a business)

paminam <ᒪᓇᕻ
VTI s/he tends to s.t., s/he looks after s.t.

paminamawēw <ᒪᓇᒪᐊ·ᐤ
VTA s/he tends to (it/him) for s.o., s/he handles (it/him) for s.o.; s/he fosters (him) for s.o., s/he supports (it/him) for s.o., s/he looks after (it/him) for s.o.

paminawasow <ᒪᓇ·ᐊ·ᒍ°
VAI s/he cooks, s/he prepares a meal [cf. piminawasow]

pamināwasow <ᒪᐃ·ᐊ·ᒍ°
VAI s/he looks after his/her child, s/he takes care of children

paminēw <ᒪᓄ°
VTA s/he tends to s.o., s/he handles s.o.; s/he fosters s.o., s/he supports s.o., s/he looks after s.o.; s/he guides s.o.

paminikēw <ᒪᓂᒉᐊ°
VAI s/he fosters care; s/he takes care of things, s/he looks after things

paminikēwin <ᒪᓂᒉᐃᐧ
NI mode of support

paminisow <ᒪᓂᒍ°
VAI s/he tends to him/herself, s/he looks after him/herself

paminiwēw <ᒪᓂᐧ·°
VAI s/he tends to people, s/he looks after people

pamīstākēw <ᒥᐢᐨᒉᐊ°
VAI s/he attends others, s/he serves others

pamīstākēwin <ᒥᐢᐨᒉᐊᐧ
NI service

panicāyisihk <ᓂᒑᔨᓯᕽ
INM Punnichy, SK [loc]

papakāhtikwān <ᐸᑲᐦᑎᑿᐣ
NI thin side of skull, temporal bone

papakāsin <ᐸᑲᓯᐣ
VII it is thin, it is rather thin (e.g. cloth or paper) [dim; also pakāsin]

papakāw <ᐸᑲ°
VII it is thin, it is not thick (e.g. a board)

papakisam <ᐸᑭᓴᕻ
VTI s/he slices s.t. thinly

papakisāwātam <ᐸᑭᓵᐘᑕᕻ
VTI s/he cuts s.o. into thin slices

papakisāwātēw <ᐸᑭᓵᐘᑌ°
VTA s/he cuts s.t. into thin slices

papakisiw <ᐸᑭᓯ°
VAI it is thin [non-human reference only]

papakiswēw <ᐸᑭᔁ·°
VTA s/he slices s.o. thinly (e.g. a loaf of bread, turkey)

papakitin <ᐸᑭᑎᐣ
VII it freezes thin, it is thin ice

papakiwayān <ᐸᑭᐊ·ᔮᐣ
NI shirt; blouse [rdpl: also pakowayān, papakowayān]

papakiwayānēkin <ᐸᑭᐊ·ᔮᓀᑭᐣ
NI thin cloth, fabric; cotton; canvas; shirting [pl: -wa; cf. pakwayānēkin]

papakiwayānihkawēw
<ᐸᑭᐊ·ᔮᓂᐦᑲᐤ·°
VTA s/he makes shirts for s.o. [also pakowayānihkawēw]

papakiwayānihkākēw
<ᐸᑭᐊ·ᔮᓂᐦᑳᑫ°
VAI s/he makes shirts from s.t. [also pakowayānihkākēw]

papakiwayānihkēw
<ᐸᑭᐊ·ᔮᓂᐦᑫ°
VAI s/he makes shirts [also pakowayānihkēw]

papakiwayānikamik
<ᐸᑭᐊ·ᔮᓂᑲᒥᐠ
NI tent [pl: -wa; cf. pakwayānikamik]

papakwatēýihtākosiw
<ᐸᑿᑌᔨᐦᑖᑯᓯ°
VAI s/he is amusing

papakwatēýihtākwan
<ᐸᑿᑌᔨᐦᑖᑿᐣ
VII it is amusing

papakwatēýimow <ᐸᑿᑌᔨᒧ°
VAI s/he is amused

papaýēkitōn <ᐸᔦᑭᑑᐣ
NA bigmouth, mouthy person

papā- <<ᐸ
IPV go around, about, all over [cf. papāmi-]

papām-ācimēw <<ᒫᐊᒋᒣ°
VTA s/he goes around telling news of s.o.

papām-ācimow <<ᒫᐊᒋᒧ°
VAI s/he goes around telling news

papām-ātotam <<ᒫᐊᐳᑕᕻ
VTI s/he goes around talking about s.t.

papām-āyāw <<ᒫᐊᔮ°
VAI s/he stays here and there; s/he bums around; s/he is unstable

papāmapiw <<ᒫᐊᐱ°
VAI s/he goes sitting here and there

papāmaskatēw <<ᒫᓴᑲᑌ°
VTA s/he goes along leaving s.o. outdistanced

papāmastāw <<ᒫᓴᐨ°
VAIt s/he puts s.t. here and there

papāmastēw <<ᒫᓴᑌ°
VII it lies along; it is here and there, it is littered about

papāmatoskēw <<ᒫᐊᐳᐢᑫ°
VAI s/he works in different locations, s/he works about

papāmācihow <<ᒫᐊᒋᑊᐅ°
VAI s/he travels, s/he wanders, s/he goes here and there; s/he is unstable

papāmāhokow <<ᒫᐊᐦᐅᑯ°
VAI s/he drifts about, s/he floats around, s/he sails about by the wind [also papāmāwokow]

papāmāhtawiw <<ᒫᐊᐦᑕ·°
VAI s/he climbs about [also papāmāhtawēw]

papāmāmohkawēw <<ᒫᐊᒧᐦᑲᐤ·°
VTA s/he chases after and harrass s.o. for a long duration

papāmāmow <<ᒫᐊᒧ°
VAI s/he flees about

papāmāpēkamow <<ᒫᐊᐯᑲᒧ°
VII it is strung about, it is clinging

papāmāsiw <<ᒫᐊᓯ°
VAI s/he is blown about, s/he sails about by the wind

papāmāskawēw <<ᒫᐊᐢᑲᐤ·°
VTA s/he follows s.o. about

papāmāstan <<ᒫᐊᐢᑕᐣ
VII it is blown about with the wind

papāmātisiw <<ᒫᐊᑎᓯ°
VAI s/he leads a nomadic life

papāmātisiwin <<ᒫᐊᑎᓯᐧ
NI leading a nomadic life

papāmēýimow <<ᒫᔦᔨᒧ°
VAI s/he goes about thinking well of him/herself

papāmi- <<ᒫ
IPV around, about, all over, here and there, hither and thither [rdpl; cf. pimi-]

papāmi-piciw <<ᒥ ᐱᕀ°
VAI s/he travels around, s/he moves around with his/her camp, s/he treks about, s/he camps here and there

papāmicimēw <<ᒥᒋᒥᐟ°
VAI s/he canoes about, s/he moves about on the water by vehicle

papāmihāmakan <<ᒥ"ᐋᒪᑲᐤ
VII it flies about

papāmihāw <<ᒥ"ᐋ°
VAI s/he flies around, about [*cf. wC:* papāmithāw; *sC:* papāmiñaw]

papāmipahtāw <<ᒥ<"ᐨ°
VAI s/he runs about; s/he runs around, s/he is promiscuous [*rdpl:* pāh-papāmipahtāw]

papāmipayihēw <<ᒥ<ᐱ"ᐁ°
VTA s/he takes s.o. about (by car or horse)

papāmipayiw <<ᒥ<ᐱ°
VAI s/he rides around, s/he rides about (by car or horse)

papāmiskāw <<ᒥᐢᑲ°
VAI s/he paddles about, s/he canoes about; it swims around (*e.g.* an animal)

papāmitācimow <<ᒥᑖᒋᒧ°
VAI s/he crawls around, about

papāmitāpāsow <<ᒥᑖᐸᓱ°
VAI s/he rides around, about; s/he drives about

papāmitisaham <<ᒥᑎᐢ"ᐊᐨ
VTI s/he follows s.t. around, about

papāmitisahikēskiw
<<ᒥᑎᐢ"ᐊᐟᐯ°
VAI s/he always wants to tag along (*e.g.* accompanying a spouse), s/he constantly follows people about [*hab*]

papāmitisahikēw <<ᒥᑎᐢ"ᐊᐟ°
VAI s/he follows people about

papāmitisahwēw <<ᒥᑎᐢ"ᐁ·°
VTA s/he runs after s.o.; s/he follows s.o. around, s/he chases s.o. about

papāmitohtahēw <<ᒥᑐ"ᒣ"ᐁ°
VTA s/he takes s.o. around, s/he takes s.o. for a walk, s/he takes s.o. about on his/her travels

papāmitohtatāw <<ᒥᑐ"ᒣᐨ°
VAIt s/he takes s.t. around, s/he takes s.t. about on his/her travels

papāmiwēpāsiw <<ᒥᐁ·ᐱᐟ°
VAI s/he blows about with the wind

papāmiwēpāstan <<ᒥᐁ·ᐟᐣᐨ
VII it blows about with the wind

papāmiwihēw <<ᒥᐃ·"ᐁ°
VTA s/he carries s.o. about

papāmohcēsiw <<ᒧ"ᐟᓯ°
VAI s/he walks about a little (*e.g.* a small child) [*dim*]

papāmohtahēw <<ᒧ"ᒣ"ᐁ°
VTA s/he carries s.o. about, s/he walks s.o. about, s/he takes s.o. about, s/he takes s.o. here and there

papāmohtatāw <<ᒧ"ᒣᐨ°
VAIt s/he carries s.t. about, s/he takes s.t. about, s/he takes s.t. here and there

papāmohtēskiw <<ᒧ"ᒥᐟᐯ°
VAI s/he walks about a lot, s/he likes walking around [*hab*]

papāmohtēw <<ᒧ"ᐃ°
VAI s/he wanders, s/he walks around, s/he walks about, s/he goes here and there; s/he runs around, s/he is promiscuous

papāmohtēwākēw <<ᒧ"ᐃ ᐋᐧᑫ°
VAI s/he walks about with the help of s.t. (*e.g.* crutches)

papāmowacis <<ᒧᐧᕀᐢ
NI backpack [*dim*]

papāmowatāw <<ᒧᐧᐨ°
VAIt s/he carries s.t. about on his/her back

papāmowatēw <<ᒧᐧᐃ°
VAI s/he carries a load about on his/her back

papāsi- <<ᓯ
IPV fast, in a hurry, quick

papāsitisahwēw <<ᓯᑎᐢ"ᐁ°
VTA s/he drives s.o. onward hastily, s/he hurries s.o.

papāsiwihēw <<ᓯᐃ·"ᐁ°
VTA s/he bothers s.o.

papāsīw <<ᓯ°
VAI s/he hurries, s/he is in a great haste

papāsīwin <<ᓯᐃ·ᐣ
NI haste

papāstamēw <<ᐢᑕᒣ°
VTA s/he breaks s.o. with his/her teeth

papātinikēw <<ᐱᓂᑫ°
VAI s/he sticks his/her head out [*e.g.* from cover, hiding]

papēciw <ᐯᒋ°
VAI s/he is slow [*cf.* papētisiw]

papēciwin <ᐯᒋᐃ·ᐣ
NI tardiness, slow in action

papēskomina <ᐯᐢᑯᒥᓇ
NI pepper [*pl generally; see also* askiwi-siwihtākan, pēskōmina, wīsakat]

papēskwacistin <ᐯᐢᐱᕀᐢᑎᐣ
VII it is a snowdrift, it is snowdrifting

papēskwatāstan <ᐯᐢᐱᐨ·ᐠ ᐣᐨ
VII it is drifting into snowbanks

papēstin <ᐯᐢᑎᐣ
VII it is a drift from the wind

papētan <ᐯᑕᐣ
VII it is slow

papētisiw <ᐯᑎᓯ°
VAI s/he is slow [*cf.* papēciw]

papēwē <ᐯᐁ·
NA Lucky Man [*name of Cree chief and SK reserve*]

papēwēhēw <ᐯᐁ·"ᐁ°
VTA s/he makes s.o. lucky

papēwēw <ᐯᐁ·°
VAI s/he is lucky, fortunate (in the hunt)

papēyāhtak <ᐯᐩ"ᐨ
IPC slowly, carefully [*rdpl*]

papimīwāpōwēw <ᐱᒥᐃ·ᐋᐳᐁ·°
VAI she has fatty milk (*e.g.* cow)

papitikohkahtēw <ᐱᑎᑯ"ᐠ"ᐅ°
VII it burns shriveling [*rdpl; also* papētikohkahtēw]

papitikonam <ᐱᑎᑯᑕᒼ
VTI s/he bundles and ties s.t. up [*rdpl; also* papētikonam]

papitikonēw <ᐱᑎᑯᐟ°
VTA s/he bundles and ties s.o. up [*rdpl; also* papētikonēw]

papitikopayihow <ᐱᑎᑯᐸᐱ"ᐅ°
VAI s/he doubles him/herself up, s/he crouches [*rdpl; also* papētikopayihow]

papitikosin <ᐱᑎᑯᓯᐣ
VAI s/he lies curled up, s/he lies rolled up [*rdpl; also* papētikosin]

papitikwapiw <ᐱᑎᑲᐧᐱᐧᐃᐯ·ᐱ
VAI s/he sits hunched [*rdpl; also* papētikwapiw]

papitikwēkinēw <ᐱᑎᑲᐧᐯᐟ°
VTA s/he rolls s.o. small as cloth [*rdpl; also* papētikwēkinēw]

papimiskwēsisitēw
<ᐱᕀᐧᓯᓯᑎᐅ°
VAI s/he is pigeon-toed [*rdpl*]

pasaham <ᐦᐊᐨ
VTI s/he hews and squares s.t.

pasahcāw <ᐦᐃ·ᐦ°
VII it is a valley, it is a long hollow

pasahikēw <ᐦ"ᐊᑫ°
VAI s/he is hewing logs

pasahikēwi-cīkahikan
<ᐦ"ᐊᑫᐧ· ᒌᑲᐦᐃᑲᐣ
NI axe used for hewing

pasahkāpiw <ᐦ"ᑲᐱᐧ
VAI s/he blinks his/her eyes [*cf.* pasakwāpiw "s/he closes his/her own eyes"]

pasakāpiw <ᐦᑲᐱᐧ
VAI s/he has gummy eyes

pasakocēskiwakāw
<ᐦᑯᒋᐢᑭᐧᐊᑲᐤ
VII it is sticky mud

pasakosiw ⊲ˋᑯᔑ°
   VAI it is sticky (*e.g.*
   adhesive, tar)
pasakwaham ⊲ˋbᵘᐧᐁᶜ
   VTI s/he glues s.t. together;
   s/he pastes s.t. on (the wall)
pasakwahikan ⊲ˋbᵘᐧᐃᐣ
   NI glue, paste
pasakwahikēw ⊲ˋbᵘᐧᐁˢ°
   VAI s/he is pasting or gluing
pasakwahwēw ⊲ˋbᵘᐁᐧ°
   VTA s/he pastes s.o. on
pasakwamow ⊲ˋbᐧᒍ°
   VII it adheres, it sticks
pasakwatāmow ⊲ˋbᐧᒼᒍ°
   VAI s/he has thick mucus,
   phlegm
pasakwāpiw ⊲ˋbᐧᐱ°
   VAI s/he closes his/her eyes
pasakwāpisimow ⊲ˋbᐧᐱᔑᒍ°
   VAI s/he dances with eyes
   shut, s/he dances the
   Shut-Eye Dance
pasakwāpisimowin
   ⊲ˋbᐧᐱᔑᒍᐃᐧᐣ
   NI Shut-Eye Dance
pasakwāpisimowinihkēw
   ⊲ˋbᐧᐱᔑᒍᐃᐧ-ᓄᐦᑫ°
   VAI s/he gives a Shut-Eye
   Dance
pasakwāw ⊲ˋbᐧ°
   VII it is sticky
pasascēhikanis ⊲ˋᓓᐦᐃᑲᓂ
   NI small whip [*dim*]
pasastēham ⊲ˋᓴᑌᐦᐊᒼ
   VTI s/he whips s.t.
pasastēhikan ⊲ˋᓴᑌᐦᐃᑲᐣ
   NI whip
pasastēhikanihkēw
   ⊲ˋᓴᑌᐦᐃᑲᓂᐦᑫ°
   VAI s/he makes a whip
pasastēhikēw ⊲ˋᓴᑌᐦᐃᑫ°
   VAI s/he whips
pasastēhokowin ⊲ˋᓴᑌᐦᐅᑯᐃᐧᐣ
   NI stripe; welt
pasastēhwēw ⊲ˋᓴᑌᐦᐧ°
   VTA s/he whips s.o.
pasastēpicikan ⊲ˋᓴᑌᐱᒋᑲᐣ
   NI slingshot
pasastēpicikanēyāpiy
   ⊲ˋᓴᑌᐱᒋᑲᓀᔮᐱ
   NI rubber used for slingshot
pasastēpicikēw ⊲ˋᓴᑌᐱᒋᑫ°
   VAI s/he shoots with a
   slingshot
pasān ⊲ˋᐣ
   NA bullrush; cattail
pasātihpēhwēw ⊲ˋᓯᐦᑊᐁᐧᐦᐧ°
   VTA s/he slaps s.o. on the
   head
pasicihcēhwēw ⊲ˋᒋᐦᒉᐦᐧ°
   VTA s/he slaps s.o. on the
   hand
pasihkān ⊲ˋᐦᑳᐣ
   NI bullrush
pasikō- ⊲ˋᑯ
   IPV get up (from sitting)

pasikō-kwāskohtiw
   ⊲ˋᑯ ᑳˢᑯᐦᑎ°
   VAI s/he jumps up (from
   sitting)
pasikōnam ⊲ˋᑯᓇᶜ
   VTI s/he sets s.t. up (after it
   fell)
pasikōnēw ⊲ˋᑯᓀ°
   VTA s/he helps s.o. up, s/he
   helps s.o. to stand
pasikōpahtāw ⊲ˋᑯᐸᐦᑖ°
   VAI s/he jumps up hurriedly
pasikōpitam ⊲ˋᑯᐱᑕᒼ
   VTI s/he pulls s.t. upright
   (after it fell)
pasikōpitēw ⊲ˋᑯᐱᑌ°
   VTA s/he pulls s.o. up to a
   standing position
pasikōw ⊲ˋᑯ°
   VAI s/he gets up, s/he arises
   (from sitting); s/he is uplifted
pasiposōs ⊲ˋᐳᓲᐢ
   NA reach [*lengthwise bar
   under the wagon-box to
   which axles are attached*]
pasisāwēw ⊲ˋᓴᐧ°
   VII it is a prairie fire, it is (a
   field) set on fire
pasitēw ⊲ˋᑌ°
   VII it is on fire, it is a prairie
   fire
pasīhkwētahwēw ⊲ˋᐦᒃᐧᑌᐦᐧ°
   VTA s/he slaps s.o. on the
   face
paskahtam ⊲ˋᑲᐦᒼᶜ
   VTI s/he bites through s.t.
paskamēw ⊲ˋᑲᒣ°
   VTA s/he bites s.o. through,
   s/he breaks s.o. by biting
   (*e.g.* yarn)
paskāpēkiw ⊲ˋᑳᐯᑭ°
   VAI s/he breaks the water
   (*i.e.* the baby); she has her
   water break birthing [*cf.*
   ē-paskāpēkit "her water
   broke"]
paskē ⊲ˋᑫ
   IPC off on one side
paskē-cakisīs ⊲ˋᑫ ᒐᑭᓰᐢ
   NI appendix
paskēhēw ⊲ˋᑫᐦᐁ°
   VTA s/he leads s.o. aside,
   s/he makes s.o. go to the side
paskēhitowin ⊲ˋᑫᐦᐃᑐᐃᐧᐣ
   NI separation; agreement to
   part, separation agreement
paskēhtin ⊲ˋᑫᐦᑎᐣ
   VII it is a small river
   branching off (from the
   main)
paskēkohtākanēw ⊲ˋᑫᑯᐦᑖᑲᓀ°
   VAI s/he is hoarse
paskēmon ⊲ˋᑫᒧᐣ
   VII it branches off, it is a
   fork in the road; [*pl*:] divide,
   separate
paskēpayiw ⊲ˋᑫᐸᔪ°
   VAI s/he branches off, s/he

   moves off; s/he stops off
   there
paskēsēwin ⊲ˋᑫᓭᐃᐧᐣ
   NI limb
paskēskanaw ⊲ˋᑫˢᑲᓇ°
   NI side road
paskētahēw ⊲ˋᑫᑕᐦᐁᐧ°
   VTA s/he takes s.o. on the
   side road
paskētāpāsow ⊲ˋᑫᑖᐹᓱ°
   VAI s/he pulls over to one
   side
paskētisahwēw ⊲ˋᑫᑎᓴᐦᐧ°
   VTA s/he drives s.o. off from
   the herd
paskēw ⊲ˋᑫ°
   VAI s/he goes onto the side
   road; s/he leaves, s/he
   departs, s/he goes off; s/he
   leaves home; s/he goes out
   on his/her own
paskēwihēw ⊲ˋᑫᐃᐧᐦᐁᐧ°
   VTA s/he parts company
   with s.o.
paskēwihitowak ⊲ˋᑫᐃᐧᐦᐃᑐᐊᐧᐠ
   VAI they separate from one
   another; they leave from one
   another; they separate, they
   divorce
paskēwihitowin ⊲ˋᑫᐃᐧᐦᐃᑐᐃᐧᐣ
   NI separation (in a
   marriage); divorce
paskicāwikanēhikanis
   ⊲ˋᑭᒑᐧᐃᑲᓀᐦᐃᑲᓂᐢ
   NI backband of harness
   [*dim*]
paskicēs ⊲ˋᑭᒉᐢ
   NI spark
paskicēsikan ⊲ˋᑭᒉᓯᑲᐣ
   NI spark plug
paskici-wēpinam ⊲ˋᑭᒋ ᐌᐱᓇᶜ
   VTI s/he throws s.t. over, on
   top of (it/him)
paskici-wēpinēw ⊲ˋᑭᒋ ᐌᐱᓀ°
   VTA s/he throws s.o. over,
   on top of (it/him)
paskicipayihow ⊲ˋᑭᒋᐸᔨᐦᐅ°
   VAI s/he hangs over (a rail
   fence)
paskicipayihtāw ⊲ˋᑭᒋᐸᔨᐦᑖ°
   VAIt s/he hangs s.t. over (a
   rail fence)
paskicipayiw ⊲ˋᑭᒋᐸᔪ°
   VII it falls and hangs over
   (the fence)
paskinam ⊲ˋᑭᓇᶜ
   VTI s/he breaks s.t. off
paskinēw ⊲ˋᑭᓀ°
   VTA s/he breaks s.o. off (*e.g.*
   thread)
paskipayiw ⊲ˋᑭᐸᔪ°
   VAI it snaps (when pulled;
   as thread)
paskipayiw ⊲ˋᑭᐸᔪ°
   VII it snaps (when pulled; as
   rope)
paskipitam ⊲ˋᑭᐱᑕᒼ
   VTI s/he pulls and breaks s.t.
   (*e.g.* rope)

paskipitēw <ˆPᴧU°
VTA s/he pulls and breaks
s.o. (*e.g.* yarn)

paskisam <ˆPᒪᶜ
VTI s/he cuts s.t. through

paskisosow <ˆPᒉᒉ°
VAI s/he cuts him/herself
free

paskisow <ˆPᒉ°
VAI s/he explodes, it ignites

paskiswēw <ˆPᒪᵛ·°
VTA s/he cuts s.o. through
(*e.g.* yarn)

paskitēw <ˆPU°
VII it sparks, it has sparks
come from it

paskiýawēw <ˆPᒪ▽·°
VTA s/he beats s.o. in a
contest, s/he overpowers s.o.;
s/he wins from s.o.

paskiýākēw <ˆPᒪ9°
VAI s/he wins things, s/he is
the winner

paskohkopāwiýiniwak
<ˆdᵘᒉᐸᐃ·ᣖᖊᐊ·ᐠ
NA Parklands People [*pl*;
division of the Cree]

paskopicikēw <ˆdᒐᒉ9°
VAI s/he is plucking fowl or
weeds from the garden

paskopitam <ˆdᴧᐸᐨᶜ
VTI s/he plucks s.t. (e.g.
weeds)

paskopitēw <ˆdᴧU°
VTA s/he plucks s.o. (birds),
s/he defeathers s.o.

paskos <ˆdˆ
NA bald one [*Cree chief and
personal name; see also*
wāpimostosis]

paskosam <ˆdᒪᶜ
VTI s/he cuts hair off s.t.;
s/he cuts the grass

paskostikwān <ˆdˆᑎᑲᒉ
NA bald person

paskostikwān <ˆdˆᑎᑲᒉ
NI bald head

paskostikwānēw <ˆdˆᑎᑲ·ᵛ°
VAI s/he is bald, s/he has a
bald head

paskoswēw <ˆdᒪ·°
VTA s/he cuts s.o.'s hair

paskow <ˆd°
VAI it moults

paskowi-pīsim <ˆdᐁ· ᐱᣖᶜ
NA Moulting Moon, July
[*obv:* -wa; *also* pasko-pīsim;
cf. opaskowi-pīsim]

paskwacās <ˆb·ᒥˆ
NI bare belly [*dim*]

paskwahamātowin
<ˆbᵓᐧᐊᒧᐅᐁᐧ
NI scissors [*see also*
mōswākan]

paskwahtam <ˆbᵓᐧᐨᶜ
VTI s/he bites through s.t.
(e.g. string); s/he cleans or
clears s.t. by mouth

paskwamēw <ˆbᐧᒼ°
VTA s/he cleans or clears
s.o. by mouth

paskwatahikēw <ˆbᐧᐸᐧᐃᐧ△9°
VAI s/he chops and clears
land

paskwatāwahkāw <ˆbᐧᐪᐊᵓᐧᒃᐅ°
NI bare ground, treeless
place

paskwatāwahkinam
<ˆbᐧᐪᐊᵓᐧᒃᐸᑫᶜ
VTI s/he clears s.t. (as
ground)

paskwāpisk <ˆbᐧ·ᐱᣖˆ
IPC bare mountain

paskwātihpēw <ˆbᐧ·ᑎᵓᐧᵛ°
VAI s/he is bald, s/he is
bald-headed; s/he has a
shaven head [*see also*
paskostikwānēw]

paskwāw <ˆbᐧ·°
NI prairie, plains

paskwāw <ˆbᐧ·°
VII it is prairie

paskwāw-askīhk <ˆbᐧ·° ᐊˆᑉˣ
INM Little Red River [*loc*;
lit: "at the prairie or bald
plain"; *SK Cree reserve
name*]

paskwāwaskosiya <ˆbᐧ·ᐊᐧᒉᒃ
NI prairie grass, prairie
weeds [*pl generally*]

paskwāwi-moscosis
<ˆbᐧ·ᐊ· ᒍᒉˆ
NA buffalo calf [*also*
paskwāwi-moscosos]

paskwāwi-mostos <ˆbᐧ·ᐊ· ᒍᒍˆ
NA buffalo, bison [*pl:* -wak;
also paskwāmostos]

paskwāwi-mostosowiýās
<ˆbᐧ·ᐊ· ᒍᒍᒉᐊ·ᣖˆ
NI buffalo meat

paskwāwi-sākahikanihk
<ˆbᐧ·ᐊ· ᣖᑲᵓᐊᑲ◦ˣ
INM Meadow Lake, SK
[*loc*; *Cree reserve name*]

paskwāwihkwaskwa
<ˆbᐧ·ᐊ·ᵓᐧbᐧbᐧ
NI sage [*pl generally*]

paskwāwinīmowin
<ˆbᐧ·ᐊ·ᐧᒋ ᒍᐊᐧ
NI Plains Cree, "Y"-dialect

paskwāwiýiniw <ˆbᐧ·ᐊ·ᣖᖊᖑ°
NA Plains Cree

paskwāwiýinīnāhk
<ˆbᐧ·ᐊ·ᣖᖊᐊᐧˣ
IPC in Plains Cree country
[*loc*]

paskwāyāw <ˆbᐧ·ᣖ°
VII it is open country

pasow <ᒉ°
VAI s/he smells s.t., s/he
catches a scent, s/he catches
a fragrance

paspaskiw <ˆ<ˆP°
NA partridge, wood
partridge, birch grouse,
ruffed grouse; quail

paspāmow <ˆᐸᒍ°
VAI s/he escapes through an
opening

paspāpahtam <ˆᐸᐸᵓᐧᐨᶜ
VTI s/he peeps at s.t.
through a crack

paspāpamēw <ˆᐸᐸ◦ᒼ°
VTA s/he peeps at s.o.
through a crack

paspāpiw <ˆᐸᐱᣖ°
VAI s/he looks out (e.g. a
window); s/he peeps through
a crack

paspi- <ˆᐱ
IPV through narrow opening

paspikāpawiw <ˆᐱᑲ<ᐊ·°
VAI s/he stands in a narrow
opening

paspinam <ˆᐱᑫᶜ
VTI s/he takes a risk and
goes through

paspinatēw <ˆᐱᑫU°
VTA s/he almost causes
s.o.'s death, s/he barely
misses s.o. (by shooting, in a
car, etc.)

paspinatikow <ˆᐱᑫᑎd°
VAI s/he has a narrow
escape, s.t. just misses
him/her [*inanimate actor
form of VTA* paspinat-; *cf.*
paspinatēw]

paspināsow <ˆᐱᑫᒉ°
VAI s/he almost kills
him/herself (accidentally)

paspinēw <ˆᐱᒍ°
VAI s/he has a close
encounter with death

paspiskwēýiw <ˆᐱˆ9ᣖ°
VAI s/he sticks his/her head
through narrow opening

paspitisēnam <ˆᐱᑎᒉᑫᶜ
VTI s/he puts s.t. through an
open window

paspitisēnēw <ˆᐱᑎᒉᒍ°
VTA s/he puts s.o. through
an open window

paspīhēw <ˆᐱᐧᵛ°
VTA s/he rescues s.o., s/he
helps s.o. out

paspīw <ˆᐱᣖ°
VAI s/he escapes, s/he gets
free

paspīwin <ˆᐱᐊᐧ
NI escape, close call

paswātam <ᒉᐊᐧᐨᶜ
VTI s/he smells s.t. [*see also*
miyāhtam]

paswēskōyow <ᒪᒣᑯᒉ°
VAI s/he gets sick from
eating excessively fatty food

paswēw <ᒪ·°
VTA s/he smells s.o. [*see
also* miyāmēw]

paswēyāw <ᒪᣖ°
VII it is excessively fatty, it
is fat and greasy

pataham <C"◁ᶜ
   VTI s/he misses s.t. (by tool
   or shot); s/he misses the
   target, s/he misses the mark

patahēw <C"▽°
   VTA s/he places, handles s.o.
   so as to miss

patahikākēw <C"Δᑲ9°
   VAI s/he misses with
   something in shooting

patahikēw <C"Δᑫ°
   VAI s/he misses

patahotowak <C"ᐅ◁·ᐣ
   VAI they miss one another
   with tool or shot

patahtam <C"Cᶜ
   VTI s/he misses s.t. (when
   trying to bite it)

patahwēw <C"▽·°
   VTA s/he misses s.o. (by tool
   or shot)

patamēw <Cᒣ°
   VTA s/he misses s.o. (when
   trying to bite him)

patapāýowēw <C◁ᐟ▽·°
   VAI it lets its own tail hang

patapiskwēýiw <CΛᐢᑫ·ᐟ°
   VAI s/he hangs his/her own
   head down [*see also*
   tapahtiskwēýiw,
   tipahtiskwēýiw]

patāhtawēkanēsin
   <Ċ"C▽·ᑲᐟ
   VAI s/he has a dislocation,
   s/he is out of joint (from
   falling)

patāpahtam <Ċ<"Cᶜ
   VTI s/he fails to notice s.t.,
   s/he overlooks s.t.

patāpahtamowin <Ċ<"CJΔ·ᐤ
   NI oversight, mistake

patāpamēw <Ċᒣ°
   VTA s/he overlooks s.o., s/he
   fails to notice s.o.

patāsokēw <Ċᔆ9°
   VAI s/he slips off a log or
   bridge

patinam <∩ᘁᶜ
   VTI s/he drops s.t., s/he
   misses s.t. by hand

patinēw <∩ᐤ°
   VTA s/he drops s.o., s/he
   misses s.o. (*e.g.* a ball) by
   hand

patinikēw <∩ᓂ9°
   VAI s/he errs, s/he makes a
   mistake, s/he takes a wrong
   step, s/he transgresses; s/he
   sins

patisīkinam <∩ᓯᘁᶜ
   VTI s/he misses pouring a
   liquid (*i.e.* spill a liquid) [*cf.*
   paci-sīkinam]

patiskatēmēw <∩ᐢᑲᑌ°
   VTA s/he drops s.o. from
   his/her mouth [*see also*
   patamēw]

patotē <ᐅU
   IPC off alone, away from
   the band; aside, on one side

patotēpahtāw <ᐅU<"Ċ°
   VAI s/he runs aside or off
   the trail

patotēpaýiw <ᐅU<ᐟ°
   VII it runs off the track or
   line

patotēpitam <ᐅUΛCᶜ
   VTI s/he pulls s.t. aside, s/he
   pulls s.t. off the track

patotēpitēw <ᐅUΛU°
   VTA s/he pulls s.o. aside,
   s/he pulls s.o. off the track

patotēpiw <ᐅUΛ°
   VAI s/he misses sitting on
   his/her chair

pawaham <◁·"◁ᶜ
   VTI s/he beats s.t., s/he
   shakes s.t. out, s/he brushes
   s.t. off by tool; s/he threshes
   s.t.

pawahamawēw <◁·"◁L▽·°
   VTA s/he threshes (it/him)
   for s.o.

pawahikan <◁·"Δᑲᐠ
   NI threshing-machine;
   combine

pawahikēw <◁·"Δᑫ°
   VAI s/he threshes, s/he
   threshes grain, s/he combines

pawahiminēw <◁·"Δᒥᓓ°
   VAI s/he knocks off berries

pawahokēw <◁·"ᐅᑫ°
   VAI s/he beats the tent walls
   or the house

pawahwēw <◁·"▽·°
   VTA s/he brushes s.o. off by
   tool; s/he threshes s.o. (*e.g.*
   grain)

pawācakinasīs <◁·ᒪᑲᘁᓯᐢ
   NA December [*wC*:
   "blizzard"; *cf.*
   pāh-pīwahcakinasīs; *also*
   pawaca..., pawahca...,
   pawāhca...]

pawācakinasīsi-pīsim
   <◁·ᒪᑲᘁᓯᐟ ᐱᔑ
   NA Frost-Exploding Trees
   Moon, Blizzard Moon,
   December [*obv:* -wa; *see
   also* makosī-kīsikani-pīsim,
   manitowi-kīsikani-pīsim]

pawākan <◁·ᑲᐠ
   NA dream spirit

pawāmēw <◁·ᒣ°
   VTA s/he dreams of s.o.

pawāmiw <◁·ᒥ°
   VAI s/he dreams; s/he has a
   dream spirit [*cf.* opawāmiw]

pawāmiwin <◁·ᒥΔᐤ
   NI spirit power, dream
   power

pawāpiskaham <◁·Λᑊᑲ"◁ᶜ
   VTI s/he brushes s.t. with
   metal or stone; s/he cleans
   s.t. out with metal or stone

pawāpiskahwēw <◁·Λᑊᑲ"▽·°
   VTA s/he brushes s.o. (*e.g.*
   pipe, stove) with or as metal
   or stone; s/he cleans s.o. out
   with or as metal or stone

pawātam <◁·Cᶜ
   VTI s/he dreams about s.t.

pawātamowin <◁·CJΔ·ᐤ
   NI dream

pawātaskiw <◁·Cᘁᒃ°
   VAI s/he is a dreamer, s/he
   dreams often [*hab*]

pawātākan <◁·Ċᑲᐟ
   NA dream guardian

pawātēw <◁·U°
   VTA s/he dreams about s.o.

pawinam <Δ·ᘁᶜ
   VTI s/he shakes s.t. out

pawinēw <Δ·ᐤ°
   VTA s/he shakes s.o. out

paýāk <ᐟ
   IPC without foreskin [*a
   derisive term, used as a
   curse directed towards a
   male*]

paýēkwac <ᔦᑲ·ᐟ
   IPC in solitude

paýipaham <ᐟ<"◁ᶜ
   VTI s/he bores a hole in s.t.

paýipahtam <ᐟ<"Cᶜ
   VTI s/he bites a hole in s.t.

paýipahwēw <ᐟ<"▽·°
   VTA s/he bores a hole
   through s.o.

paýipāw <ᐟ<°
   VII it has a hole through it

paýipēýikom <ᐟᐯᐟᒃᶜ
   NA Nez-Percé Indian

paýipihtēw <ᐟΛ"U°
   VAI s/he has pierced ears

paýipisam <ᐟΛᔅᶜ
   VTI s/he cuts s.t. out, s/he
   cuts a hole in s.t., s/he
   perforates s.t.

paýipisikan <ᐟΛᔑᑲᐟ
   NI perforation, hole; tool
   that perforates, hole-punch

paýipisikātēw <ᐟΛᔑᑲᕒU°
   VII it is perforated

paýipiswēw <ᐟΛᔅᐧ°
   VTA s/he cuts s.o. out, s/he
   cuts a hole in s.o., s/he
   perforates s.o.

paýipwāt <ᐟᐧᐟ
   NA Chief Piapot, "Hole-in-
   the-Sioux" [*prominent Cree
   chief of the* nēhiýaw-pwātak
   or Piapot band]

ᐸ

pāh-pahki ᐸ" <"ᑭ
   IPC part of this, part of that;
   here and there [*rdpl*]

pāh-pakamaham ᐸ" ᑕᒪ"◁ᶜ
   VTI s/he raps s.t. repeatedly
   [*rdpl*]

pāh-pakamahwēw ᐹᐦ ᐸᑲᒪᐦᐍᐤ
VTA s/he hits s.o. repeatedly [*rdpl*]

pāh-pakwacihēw ᐹᐦ ᐸᑿᒋᐦᐁᐤ
VTA s/he amuses s.o. [*rdpl*]

pāh-pakwacihow ᐹᐦ ᐸᑿᒋᐦᐅᐤ
VAI s/he amuses him/herself [*rdpl*]

pāh-pakwatēýihtam ᐹᐦ ᐸᑿᑌᔨᐦᑕᒼ
VTI s/he is amused by s.t. [*rdpl*]

pāh-pakwatēýihtākosiw ᐹᐦ ᐸᑿᑌᔨᐦᑖᑯᓯᐤ
VAI s/he is very amusing [*rdpl*]

pāh-pakwatēýihtākwan ᐹᐦ ᐸᑿᑌᔨᐦᑖᑿᐣ
VII it is very amusing [*rdpl*]

pāh-pakwatēýimēw ᐹᐦ ᐸᑿᑌᔨᒣᐤ
VTA s/he is amused by s.o. [*rdpl*]

pāh-pasakwāpiw ᐹᐦ ᐸᓴᒁᐱᐤ
VAI s/he opens and closes his/her eyes repeatedly, s/he blinks [*rdpl*]

pāh-pasīhkwēhwēw ᐹᐦ ᐸᓰᐦᑵᐦᐁᐤ
VTA s/he slaps s.o.'s face repeatedly [*rdpl*]

pāh-pawaham ᐹᐦ ᐸᐘᐦᐊᒼ
VTI s/he beats s.t., s/he shakes s.t. out by tool; s/he dusts s.t. (with a brush) [*rdpl*]

pāh-pawahikēw ᐹᐦ ᐸᐘᐦᐃᑫᐤ
VAI s/he knocks things clean, s/he beats things clean; s/he dusts (*e.g.* furniture) [*rdpl*]

pāh-pawahwēw ᐹᐦ ᐸᐘᐦᐍᐤ
VTA s/he dusts s.o. (with a brush) [*rdpl*]

pāh-pawāstitāw ᐹᐦ ᐸᐚᐢᑎᑖᐤ
VAIt s/he hangs s.t. in the wind to dust it [*rdpl*]

pāh-pawihtitāw ᐹᐦ ᐸᐏᐦᑎᑖᐤ
VAIt s/he dusts s.t. by shaking and hitting it on something; s/he shakes s.t. (s/he hits on s.t. to dust) [*rdpl*]

pāh-pawinipēhēw ᐹᐦ ᐸᐏᓂᐯᐦᐁᐤ
VTA s/he causes s.o. to have palpitations [*rdpl*]

pāh-pākikātēpaýiw ᐹᐦ ᐹᑭᑳᑌᐸᔨᐤ
VAI s/he has swollen legs, s/he has edema, s/he has water retention in her legs [*rdpl*]

pāh-pēkatēw ᐹᐦ ᐯᑲᑌᐤ
VAI s/he is belching, s/he belches now and again [*rdpl*]

pāh-pēyak ᐹᐦ ᐯᔭᐠ
IPC each individually, one each; singly, one at a time, one by one [*rdpl*]

pāh-pēyakwan ᐹᐦ ᐯᔭᑿᐣ
IPC the same, all of them [*rdpl*]

pāh-piscimēw ᐹᐦ ᐱᐢᒋᒣᐤ
VTA s/he hurts s.o.'s feelings without meaning to; s/he strikes a nerve with s.o. [*rdpl*; *cf.* pāhpisimēw]

pāh-piskihc ᐹᐦ ᐱᐢᑭᐦᐨ
IPC each separately, in separate divisions [*rdpl*]

pāh-piskihcastāw ᐹᐦ ᐱᐢᑭᐦᒐᐢᑖᐤ
VAIt s/he places s.t. in separate places [*rdpl*]

pāh-piskihcastēw ᐹᐦ ᐱᐢᑭᐦᒐᐢᑌᐤ
VII it is in separate places [*rdpl*]

pāh-piskihcayāw ᐹᐦ ᐱᐢᑭᐦᒐᔮᐤ
VAI it is divided, it is partitioned [*rdpl*]

pāh-piskokanēpaýiw ᐹᐦ ᐱᐢᑯᑲᓀᐸᔨᐤ
VAI s/he has arthritis [*rdpl*]

pāh-piskwahcāw ᐹᐦ ᐱᐢᑿᐦᒑᐤ
VII it is uneven ground [*rdpl*]

pāh-piskwāw ᐹᐦ ᐱᐢᒁᐤ
VII it is lumpy in places [*rdpl*]

pāh-pītos ᐹᐦ ᐲᑐᐢ
IPC very different; different from one another, each differently; separate [*rdpl*]

pāh-pītosēýimēw ᐹᐦ ᐲᑐᓭᔨᒣᐤ
VTA s/he has a different opinion about s.o. [*rdpl*]

pāhk-ōstostotam ᐹᐦᑰᐢᑐᐢᑐᑕᒼ
VTI s/he has a dry cough [*also* pāhko-ostostotam]

pāhkaci- ᐹᐦᑲᒋ
IPV fixed, not moving; locked in to a previously stated obligation

pāhkaciw ᐹᐦᑲᒋᐤ
VAI s/he freezes up, s/he does not move

pāhkahāhkwān ᐹᐦᑲᐦᐋᐦᒁᐣ
NA chicken [*cf.* pāhpahāhkwān]

pāhkahāhkwānis ᐹᐦᑲᐦᐋᐦᒁᓂᐢ
NA chick [*dim*; *cf.* pāhpahāhkwānis]

pāhkahāhkwāniwiyās ᐹᐦᑲᐦᐋᐦᒁᓂᐏᔮᐢ
NI chicken meat

pāhkahkos ᐹᐦᑲᐦᑯᐢ
NA Bony Spectre, Hunger Spirit, spirit being

pāhkahkosiwiw ᐹᐦᑲᐦᑯᓯᐏᐤ
VAI s/he is a bony spectre (*i.e.* in a dance or ceremony)

pāhkahkowiw ᐹᐦᑲᐦᑯᐏᐤ
VAI s/he is a bony spectre (*i.e.* in a dance or ceremony)

pāhko- ᐹᐦᑯ
IPV dry

pāhkocihcēhosow ᐹᐦᑯᒋᐦᒉᐦᐅᓱᐤ
VAI s/he dries his/her own hands

pāhkocihcēhow ᐹᐦᑯᒋᐦᒉᐦᐅᐤ
VAI s/he dries his/her own hands

pāhkocihcēhwēw ᐹᐦᑯᒋᐦᒉᐦᐍᐤ
VTA s/he dries s.o.'s hands

pāhkocihcēw ᐹᐦᑯᒋᐦᒉᐤ
VAI s/he has dry hands

pāhkohkwēhon ᐹᐦᑯᐦᑵᐦᐅᐣ
NI towel, face towel [*see also* kāsīhkwēhon]

pāhkohkwēhonis ᐹᐦᑯᐦᑵᐦᐅᓂᐢ
NI small towel, face-cloth [*dim*]

pāhkohkwēhow ᐹᐦᑯᐦᑵᐦᐅᐤ
VAI s/he dries his/her own face

pāhkohkwēhwēw ᐹᐦᑯᐦᑵᐦᐍᐤ
VTA s/he dries s.o.'s face

pāhkokanēhwēw ᐹᐦᑯᑲᓀᐦᐍᐤ
VTA s/he crushes s.o.'s bone by tool

pāhkopaýihow ᐹᐦᑯᐸᔨᐦᐅᐤ
VAI s/he dries him/herself (as a dog shaking itself)

pāhkopaýiw ᐹᐦᑯᐸᔨᐤ
VAI s/he gets dry, s/he dries out, s/he dries (by warmth or wind)

pāhkositēhosow ᐹᐦᑯᓯᑌᐦᐅᓱᐤ
VAI s/he dries his/her own feet

pāhkositēhwēw ᐹᐦᑯᓯᑌᐦᐍᐤ
VTA s/he dries s.o.'s feet

pāhkosiw ᐹᐦᑯᓯᐤ
VAI s/he dries, it dries off (*e.g.* bacon strips)

pāhkw-āyamihāw ᐹᐦᒁᔭᒥᐦᐋᐤ
VAI s/he is a Roman Catholic

pāhkw-āyamihāwin ᐹᐦᒁᔭᒥᐦᐋᐏᐣ
NI Roman Catholic religion [*also* pāhko-ayamihēwin, pāhkw-āyamihēwin]

pāhkw-āyamihēwiýiniw ᐹᐦᒁᔭᒥᐦᐁᐏᔨᓂᐤ
NA Roman Catholic priest

pāhkwaham ᐹᐦᑿᐦᐊᒼ
VTI s/he dries s.t., s/he wipes s.t. dry

pāhkwahamawēw ᐹᐦᑿᐦᐊᒪᐍᐤ
VTA s/he dries (it/him) for s.o.; s/he wipes (it/him) dry for s.o.

pāhkwahākosiw ᐹᐦᑿᐦᐋᑯᓯᐤ
VAI s/he is dried off (by something)

pāhkwahcāw ᐹᐦᑿᐦᒑᐤ
NI dry land

pāhkwahcāw ᐹᐦᑿᐦᒑᐤ
VII it is dry ground

pāhkwahwēw ᐹᐦᑿᐦᐍᐤ
VTA s/he dries s.o., s/he wipes s.o. dry

pāhkwasakātihpēhwēw ᐹᐦᑿᓴᑳᑎᐦᐯᐦᐍᐤ
VTA s/he crushes s.o.'s head by a tool

pāhkwastēwinikan ᐹᐦᑿᐢᑌᐏᓂᑲᐣ
NI clothes dryer

pāhkwatāmow ᐹᐦᑿᑖᒧᐤ
VAI s/he has a dry throat, s/he is very thirsty

pāhkwaýīk ᐹᐦᑿᔩᐠ
NA frog heard during a dry spell

pāhkwāpiw ᐹᐦᒁᐱᐤ
VAI s/he dries his/her eyes, s/he has dry eyes

pāhkwāsin ᐹᐦᒁᓯᐣ
VII it is shallow, it is the bottom of water [*dim*]

pāhkwāw ᐹᐦᒁᐤ
VII it is dry; it is shallow water, it is almost dried up

pāhkwāw-sākahikanihk ᐹᐦᒁᐤ ᓵᑲᐦᐃᑲᓂᕽ
INM Shoal Lake, SK [*loc*]

pāhkwēkan ᐹᐦᑵᑲᐣ
NA night-owl

pāhpahāhkwān ᐹᐦᐸᐦᐋᐦᒁᐣ
NA chicken, domestic chicken [*cf.* pāhkahāhkwān]

pāhpahāhkwāni-mīcimāpoy ᐹᐦᐸᐦᐋᐦᒁᓂ ᒦᒋᒫᐳᐩ
NI chicken soup

pāhpahāhkwānis ᐹᐦᐸᐦᐋᐦᒁᓂᐢ
NA chick [*dim*; *cf.* pāhkahāhkwānis]

pāhpakowēwayān ᐹᐦᐸᑯᐍᐘᔮᐣ
NI hide with thick hair on it

pāhpawēw ᐹᐦᐸᐍᐤ
VAI s/he shakes him/herself (as a dog out of water)

pāhpawi-wēpinam ᐹᐦᐸᐏ ᐍᐱᓇᒼ
VTI s/he shakes s.t. out (to remove contents)

pāhpawi-wēpinēw ᐹᐦᐸᐏ ᐍᐱᓀᐤ
VTA s/he shakes s.o. out

pāhpawipaýihtāw ᐹᐦᐸᐏᐸᔨᐦᑖᐤ
VAIt s/he shakes s.t. out

pāhpāscēs ᐹᐦᐹᐢᒉᐢ
NA small (species of) woodpecker [*dim*]

pāhpāstēw ᐹᐦᐹᐢᑌᐤ
NA large woodpecker

pāhpāwēhcahikēsis ᐹᐦᐹᐍᐦᒐᐦᐃᑫᓯᐢ
NA woodpecker

pāhpāwēhikēw ᐹᐦᐹᐍᐦᐃᑫᐤ
VAI s/he knocks, s/he knocks on the door [*also* pāhpawahikēw; *see also* pakamahikēw]

pāhpihēw ᐹᐦᐱᐦᐁᐤ
VTA s/he laughs at s.o., s/he derides s.o.; s/he jokes with s.o.; s/he makes s.o. laugh

pāhpihkwēw ᐹᐦᐱᐦᑵᐤ
VAI s/he smiles

pāhpihtam ᐹᐦᐱᐦᑕᒼ
VTI s/he laughs at s.t. [*cf.* pāhpihtāw]

pāhpihtāw ᐹᐦᐱᐦᑖᐤ
VAIt s/he laughs at s.t., s/he derides s.t. [*cf.* pāhpihtam]

pāhpihtākosiw ᐹᐦᐱᐦᑖᑯᓯᐤ
VAI s/he is laughable

pāhpihtākwan ᐹᐦᐱᐦᑖᑿᐣ
VII it is laughable

pāhpinākosiw ᐹᐦᐱᓈᑯᓯᐤ
VAI s/he smiles; s/he looks as if s/he is laughing [*cf.* pāhpiwinākosiw]

pāhpisihēw ᐹᐦᐱᓯᐦᐁᐤ
VTA s/he teases s.o.

pāhpisihitowak ᐹᐦᐱᓯᐦᐃᑐᐘᐠ
VAI they tease one another

pāhpisimēw ᐹᐦᐱᓯᒣᐤ
VTA s/he teases s.o. by speech, s/he jeers s.o., s/he makes fun of s.o. [*cf.* pāh-piscimēw]

pāhpisiw ᐹᐦᐱᓯᐤ
VAI s/he smiles, s/he laughs a little [*dim*]

pāhpiskiw ᐹᐦᐱᐢᑭᐤ
VAI s/he laughs a lot; s/he is a joker [*hab*]

pāhpiw ᐹᐦᐱᐤ
VAI s/he laughs, s/he is laughing, s/he smiles

pāhpiwin ᐹᐦᐱᐏᐣ
NI laughter, glee

pāhpiwinākosiw ᐹᐦᐱᐏᓈᑯᓯᐤ
VAI s/he smiles; s/he looks as if s/he is laughing [*cf.* pāhpinākosiw]

pāhpīhkāsow ᐹᐦᐲᐦᑳᓱᐤ
VAI s/he pretends to laugh

pākahatowān ᐹᑲᐦᐊᑐᐚᐣ
NA ball [*cf.* pākāhtowān]

pākahatowānāhtik ᐹᑲᐦᐊᑐᐚᓈᐦᑎᐠ
NI baseball bat; lacrosse stick [*pl*: -wa]

pākahatowēw ᐹᑲᐦᐊᑐᐍᐤ
VAI s/he plays ball, baseball, lacrosse [*cf.* pākāhtowēw]

pākan ᐹᑲᐣ
VII it is swollen [*cf.* pākāw]

pākāhcowānis ᐹᑳᐦᒍᐚᓂᐢ
NA softball; child's ball [*dim*]

pākāhtowān ᐹᑳᐦᑐᐚᐣ
NA ball; soccer ball; basketball; baseball [*cf.* pākahatowān]

pākāhtowēw ᐹᑳᐦᑐᐍᐤ
VAI s/he plays ball, baseball, soccer [*cf.* pākahatowēw]

pākāpitēw ᐹᑳᐱᑌᐤ
VAI s/he has swollen gums

pākāpiw ᐹᑳᐱᐤ
VAI s/he has swollen eyes

pākāw ᐹᑳᐤ
VII it is swollen [*cf.* pākan]

pākikanēpaýiw ᐹᑭᑲᓀᐸᔨᐤ
VAI s/he has swollen limbs; s/he has gout

pākikātēpaýiw ᐹᑭᑳᑌᐸᔨᐤ
VAI s/he swells at the leg suddenly

pākikātēw ᐹᑭᑳᑌᐤ
VAI s/he has a swollen leg

pākikotēw ᐹᑭᑯᑌᐤ
VAI s/he has a swollen nose

pākipaýiw ᐹᑭᐸᔨᐤ
VAI s/he swells, s/he has a swelling

pākipaýiwin ᐹᑭᐸᔨᐏᐣ
NI swelling

pākisitēpaýiw ᐹᑭᓯᑌᐸᔨᐤ
VAI s/he swells at the foot suddenly

pākisitēw ᐹᑭᓯᑌᐤ
VAI s/he has a swollen foot

pākiýihkwēpaýiw ᐹᑭᔨᐦᑵᐸᔨᐤ
VAI s/he has swollen glands

pāmwayēs ᐹᒷᔦᐢ
IPC before; go toward, to [*temporal conjunction*; *also* pāmayas, pāmoyēs; *see also* maywēs]

pānaham ᐹᓇᐦᐊᒼ
VTI s/he clears the snow from s.t.

pānahākonam ᐹᓇᐦᐋᑯᓇᒼ
VTI s/he clears s.t. of snow

pānahākonamawēw ᐹᓇᐦᐋᑯᓇᒪᐍᐤ
VTA s/he clears (it/him) of snow for s.o., s/he clears snow away from (it/him) for s.o.

pānahākonēw ᐹᓇᐦᐋᑯᓀᐤ
VAI s/he clears away snow

pānahikēw ᐹᓇᐦᐃᑫᐤ
VAI s/he clears away snow

pānahkoskēw ᐹᓇᐦᑯᐢᑫᐤ
VAI s/he kicks the snow aside

pānahkoskikēw ᐹᓇᐦᑯᐢᑭᑫᐤ
VAI s/he kicks the snow aside

pānahwēw ᐹᓇᐦᐍᐤ
VTA s/he clears the snow from s.o.

pānisam ᐹᓂᓴᒼ
VTI s/he cuts s.t. into sheets, s/he cuts s.t. (*e.g.* meat) for use; s/he cuts and prepares meat

pānisāwēw ᐹᓂᓵᐍᐤ
VAI s/he prepares meat cut into sheets, s/he slices meat to dry [*cf.* manisāwēw]

pāniswēw ᐹᓂᐢᐍᐤ
VTA s/he cuts s.o. into sheets; s/he cuts (it) from s.o.

pāpahtāw ᐹᐸᐦᑖᐤ
VAI s/he comes running

pāpakonam ᐹᐸᑯᓇᒼ
VTI s/he makes blisters

pāpakonēw ᐹᐸᑯᓀᐤ
VTA s/he bruises or blisters s.o. (by hitting)

pāpakwātahwēw ᐹᐸᒁᑕᐦᐍᐤ
VTA s/he blisters s.o., s/he causes s.o. to blister

pāpaýihēw ᐹᐸᔨᐦᐁᐤ
VTA s/he vomits s.o. up; s/he makes s.o. come here

pāpaýihtāw ᐹᐸᔨᐦᑖᐤ
VAIt s/he vomits s.t. up; s/he makes s.t. come here

pāpaýiw ᐹᐸᔨᐤ
VAI s/he comes driving along; s/he moves here, s/he drives here; s/he is seen coming (by horse or vehicle)

pāpiciw ᐹᐱᒋᐤ
VAI s/he moves camp here

pāsam ᐹᓴᒼ
VTI s/he dries s.t. (by warmth)

pāsci- ᐹᐢᒋ
IPV over, beyond [*cf.* pāsici-]

pāsci-kwāskohtiw ᐹᐢᒋ ᒁᐢᑯᐦᑎᐤ
VAI s/he jumps over (as a human); s/he leaps

pāsci-ohpīw ᐹᐢᒋ ᐅᐦᐲᐤ
VAI s/he jumps over (as an animal)

pāsci-tahkoskēw ᐹᐢᒋ ᑕᐦᑯᐢᑫᐤ
VAI s/he steps over

pāsci-wēpinam ᐹᐢᒋ ᐍᐱᓇᒼ
VTI s/he takes and throws s.t. over (something)

pāsci-wēpinēw ᐹᐢᒋ ᐍᐱᓀᐤ
VTA s/he takes and throws s.o. over (something)

pāscipaýihow ᐹᐢᒋᐸᔨᐦᐅᐤ
VAI s/he goes over (without leaping)

pāscipaýiw ᐹᐢᒋᐸᔨᐤ
VAI it bursts; it is overfilled, it goes over (as a pail of water)

pāscipēw ᐹᐢᒋᐯᐤ
VII it overflows

pāsici- ᐹᓯᒋ
IPV stepping over, skipping [*cf.* pāsci-]

pāsikan ᐹᓯᑲᐣ
NI dryer

pāsikātēw ᐹᓯᑳᑌᐤ
VII it is dried

pāsikwātan ᐹᓯᒁᑕᐣ
VII it is stormy

pāsimināna ᐹᓯᒥᓈᓇ
NI dried berries [*pl generally*]

pāsiminēw ᐹᓯᒥᓀᐤ
VAI s/he dries berries

pāsitahkoskēw ᐹᓯᑕᐦᑯᐢᑫᐤ
VAI s/he steps over solids; s/he straddles

pāsitohtēw ᐹᓯᑐᐦᑌᐤ
VAI s/he goes over, across; s/he walks over s.t. (as a heap on the ground)

pāskac ᐹᐢᑲᐨ
IPC even, on top of it all, to top it all off; coincidentally; besides; to that point

pāskaciwaswēw ᐹᐢᑲᒋᐘᔃᐤ
VAI it boils

pāskaham ᐹᐢᑲᐦᐊᒼ
VTI s/he breaks s.t. open (*e.g.* an egg)

pāskahwēw ᐹᐢᑲᐦᐍᐤ
VTA s/he bursts s.o.

pāskatayēpaýiw ᐹᐢᑲᑕᔦᐸᔨᐤ
VAI s/he bursts at the belly

pāskatayēpitēw ᐹᐢᑲᑕᔦᐱᑌᐤ
VTA s/he tears s.o. open at the belly

pāskatayēskawēw ᐹᐢᑲᑕᔦᐢᑲᐍᐤ
VTA s/he kicks s.o. open at the belly

pāskākonēw ᐹᐢᑳᑯᓀᐤ
VAI s/he makes tracks in the fresh snow

pāskāpahwēw ᐹᐢᑳᐸᐦᐍᐤ
VTA s/he bursts s.o.'s eye, s/he puts out s.o.'s eye by tool

pāskāpatahwēw ᐹᐢᑳᐸᑕᐦᐍᐤ
VTA s/he puts out s.o.'s eye by stick or beak

pāskāpicin ᐹᐢᑳᐱᒋᐣ
VAI s/he bursts his/her own eye (by running into a sharp stick)

pāskāpisin ᐹᐢᑳᐱᓯᐣ
VAI s/he bursts his/her own eye (by falling on something)

pāskāpiw ᐹᐢᑳᐱᐤ
VAI s/he has a ruptured eye; s/he has only one eye, s/he is one-eyed; s/he is unable to see, s/he is blind; s/he opens his/her own eyes [*see also* namoýa wāpiw]

pāskāwēhow ᐹᐢᑳᐍᐦᐅᐤ
VAI it bursts the shell (*e.g.* hatching bird)

pāskāwihow ᐹᐢᑳᐏᐦᐅᐤ
VAI it hatches

pāskāwihowi-pīsim ᐹᐢᑳᐏᐦᐅᐏ ᐲᓯᒼ
NA Egg-Hatching Moon, June [*obv*: -wa; *cf.* opāskāwēhowi-pīsim]

pāskicēnam ᐹᐢᑭᒉᓇᒼ
VTI s/he bursts s.t. (by fingers) (*e.g.* an egg)

pāskicēnēw ᐹᐢᑭᒉᓀᐤ
VTA s/he bursts s.o. (by fingers)

pāskihkwēnēw ᐹᐢᑭᐦᑵᓀᐤ
VTA s/he uncovers s.o.'s face for him

pāskihkwēýiw ᐹᐢᑭᐦᑵᔨᐤ
VAI s/he uncovers his/her own face

pāskihtēpaýin ᐹᐢᑭᐦᑌᐸᔨᐣ
VII it goes open (*e.g.* door)

pāskihtēpaýiw ᐹᐢᑭᐦᑌᐸᔨᐤ
VAI it goes open

pāskinam ᐹᐢᑭᓇᒼ
VTI s/he uncovers s.t., s/he turns s.t. over; s/he turns the page

pāskinamawēw ᐹᐢᑭᓇᒪᐍᐤ
VTA s/he uncovers (it/him) for s.o.; s/he opens (it/him) for s.o.

pāskinēw ᐹᐢᑭᓀᐤ
VTA s/he uncovers s.o.

pāskinokēw ᐹᐢᑭᓄᑫᐤ
VAI s/he breaks up camp

pāskipaýihow ᐹᐢᑭᐸᔨᐦᐅᐤ
VAI s/he uncovers him/herself

pāskipaýiw ᐹᐢᑭᐸᔨᐤ
VAI s/he uncovers (as the wind blows it off)

pāskisam ᐹᐢᑭᓴᒼ
VTI s/he shoots s.t. with a gun, s/he shoots at s.t.; s/he hits s.t. with lightning

pāskisamawēw ᐹᐢᑭᓴᒪᐍᐤ
VTA s/he shoots (it/him) for s.o.

pāskisikan ᐹᐢᑭᓯᑲᐣ
NI gun

pāskisikanāhtik ᐹᐢᑭᓯᑲᓈᐦᑎᐠ
NI gun stock [*pl*: -wa]

pāskisikanāpisk ᐹᐢᑭᓯᑲᓈᐱᐢᐠ
NI gun barrel [*pl*: -wa]

pāskisikanis ᐹᐢᑭᓯᑲᓂᐢ
NI revolver, pistol [*dim*]

pāskisikēw ᐹᐢᑭᓯᑫᐤ
VAI s/he shoots; s/he fires a shot

pāskisikēwin ᐹᐢᑭᓯᑫᐏᐣ
NI shooting; target practice; ammunition

pāskisosow ᐹᐢᑭᓱᓱᐤ
VAI s/he shoots him/herself

pāskisotowak ᐹᐢᑭᓱᑐᐘᐠ
VAI they shoot one another

pāskiswēw ᐹᐢᑭᔃᐤ
VTA s/he shoots s.o. with a gun, s/he shoots at s.o.; s/he hits s.o. with lightning

pāskiwēpaham ᐹᐢᑭᐍᐸᐦᐊᒼ
VTI s/he uncovers s.t. (with a tool)

pāskiwēpahwēw ᐹᐢᑭᐍᐸᐦᐍᐤ
VTA s/he uncovers s.o. (with a tool)

pāskīw ᐹᐢᑮᐤ
VAI s/he comes out from under covers, s/he uncovers him/herself

pāsonāson ᐹᓱᓈᓱᐣ
NI clothesline

pāsonāsow ᐹᓱᓈᓱᐤ
VAI s/he dries his/her clothes

pāsosow ᐹᓱᓱᐤ
VAI s/he dries him/herself

pāsow ᐹᓱᐤ
VAI s/he is dry

pāstaham ᐹᐢᑕᐦᐊᒼ
VTI s/he cracks s.t. (by pressure)
pāstahtam ᐹᐢᑕᐦᑕᒼ
VTI s/he breaks s.t. (by biting, with teeth) [*cf.* pāstahtāw]
pāstahtāw ᐹᐢᑕᐦᑖᐤ
VAIt s/he cracks s.t. (with his/her teeth) [*cf.* pāstahtam]
pāstahwēw ᐹᐢᑕᐦᐍᐤ
VTA s/he cracks s.o. (by pressure)
pāstamēw ᐹᐢᑕᒣᐤ
VTA s/he cracks s.o. (by biting, with teeth)
pāstataham ᐹᐢᑕᑕᐦᐊᒼ
VTI s/he breaks s.t. (*e.g.* bones) by tool or shot
pāstāciwahtēw ᐹᐢᑖᒋᐘᐦᑌᐤ
VII it boils over
pāstāciwasow ᐹᐢᑖᒋᐘᓱᐤ
VAI s/he boils over (as a tea kettle)
pāstāham ᐹᐢᑖᐦᐊᒼ
VTI s/he brings evil to s.t.
pāstāhēw ᐹᐢᑖᐦᐁᐤ
VTA s/he brings evil to s.o.
pāstāhow ᐹᐢᑖᐦᐅᐤ
VAI s/he brings evil upon him/herself; s/he is killed by lightning; s/he breaches the natural order, s/he transgresses; s/he uses bad medicine; s/he sins, s/he is a sinner, s/he does evil
pāstāhowin ᐹᐢᑖᐦᐅᐏᐣ
NI transgression, breach of the natural order; use of bad medicine; sin, evil doings
pāstāmēw ᐹᐢᑖᒣᐤ
VTA s/he curses s.o.; s/he gives s.o. bad luck by evil incantation [*cf.* pāstāmwēw]
pāstāmoskiw ᐹᐢᑖᒧᐢᑭᐤ
VAI s/he is a blasphemer [*hab*]
pāstāmototam ᐹᐢᑖᒧᑐᑕᒼ
VTI s/he blasphemes s.t.
pāstāmototawēw ᐹᐢᑖᒧᑐᑕᐍᐤ
VTA s/he blasphemes s.o.
pāstāmow ᐹᐢᑖᒧᐤ
VAI s/he curses; s/he sins by his/her speech
pāstāmowin ᐹᐢᑖᒧᐏᐣ
NI curse; blasphemy, cursing, cursewords
pāstāmwēw ᐹᐢᑖᒷᐤ
VTA s/he curses s.o.; s/he gives s.o. bad luck by evil incantation [*cf.* pāstāmēw]
pāstāskow ᐹᐢᑖᐢᑯᐤ
VAI s/he steps over s.t. (as a fence)
pāstāsow ᐹᐢᑖᓱᐤ
VAI s/he breaks bones for marrow
pāstāstawīw ᐹᐢᑖᐢᑕᐑᐤ
VAI s/he climbs over (as a fence)
pāstē-wiyās ᐹᐢᑌ ᐃᔮᐢ
NI dried meat
pāstēw ᐹᐢᑌᐤ
VII it dries, it is dried (in warmth), it is dry
pāstēwaskiy ᐹᐢᑌᐘᐢᑮ
NI dry land, drought
pāstēwāhtik ᐹᐢᑌᐚᐦᑎᐠ
NA dry tree [*pl*: -wak]
NI dry wood [*pl*: -wa]
pāstēwi-mihti ᐹᐢᑌᐏ ᒥᐦᑎ
NI dry wood (for the stove) [*pl*: pāstēwi-mihta]
pāstihtin ᐹᐢᑎᐦᑎᐣ
VAI s/he cracks (by falling)
pāstihtitāw ᐹᐢᑎᐦᑎᑖᐤ
VAIt s/he smashes s.t. (against something)
pāstinam ᐹᐢᑎᓇᒼ
VTI s/he crushes s.t. by hand, s/he cracks s.t.
pāstinēw ᐹᐢᑎᓀᐤ
VTA s/he crushes s.o. by hand, s/he cracks s.o.
pāstipaýin ᐹᐢᑎᐸᔨᐣ
VII it breaks, it bursts (*e.g.* bottle, head)
pāstipaýiw ᐹᐢᑎᐸᔨᐤ
VII it is smashed; it cracks (as a glass in hot water)
pāstiskam ᐹᐢᑎᐢᑲᒼ
VTI s/he breaks s.t. by foot
pāstiskawēw ᐹᐢᑎᐢᑲᐍᐤ
VTA s/he breaks s.o. by foot
pāstiwēpaham ᐹᐢᑎᐍᐸᐦᐊᒼ
VTI s/he breaks s.t. by missile
pāstiwēpahwēw ᐹᐢᑎᐍᐸᐦᐍᐤ
VTA s/he breaks s.o. by missile
pāswēw ᐹᓷᐤ
VTA s/he dries s.o. (in warmth) (*e.g.* a pelt)
pātimā ᐹᑎᒫ
IPC by and by; then, later; until [*cf.* pitamā]
pātimā ici ᐹᑎᒫ ᐃᒋ
IPH later on, o.k.? [*cf.* *wC*: pātimā nici]
pātimā itāp ᐹᑎᒫ ᐃᑖᑊ
IPH later on, o.k.? [*cf.* *wC*: pātimā nitāp]
pātos ᐹᑐᐢ
IPC only later; then, later
pātos-āyihk ᐹᑐᓭᔨᕽ
INM outside area, uninhabited land
pāwanīw ᐹᐘᓃᐤ
VAI s/he is thin, s/he is lean
pāwiscikos ᐹᐏᐢᒋᑯᐢ
NI small rapid or waterfall [*dim*]
pāwistik ᐹᐏᐢᑎᐠ
NI rapids, waterfall; Brandon, MB [*pl*: -wa; *place name*]
pāwistikociwan ᐹᐏᐢᑎᑯᒋᐘᐣ
VII it flows with rapids
pāwistikowan ᐹᐏᐢᑎᑯᐘᐣ
VII there are a series of rapids
pāwistikowiýiniw ᐹᐏᐢᑎᑯᐏᔨᓂᐤ
NA Atsina, Gros Ventre [*pl*: pāwistikowiýiniwak "people of the rapids"]

ᐯ

pē- ᐯ
IPV come and; towards, approaching; hither; thence, from there on down [*towards focus*]
pē-apiw ᐯ ᐊᐱᐤ
VAI s/he comes and sits
pē-atoskēw ᐯ ᐊᑐᐢᑫᐤ
VAI s/he comes to work
pē-ispahkēnam ᐯ ᐃᐢᐸᐦᑫᓇᒼ
VTI s/he comes and raises s.t.
pē-itisaham ᐯ ᐃᑎᓴᐦᐊᒼ
VTI s/he sends s.t here
pē-itisahwēw ᐯ ᐃᑎᓴᐦᐍᐤ
VTA s/he sends s.o. here
pē-itohtahēw ᐯ ᐃᑐᐦᑕᐦᐁᐤ
VTA s/he walks s.o. hither, s/he brings s.o.
pē-itohtatamawēw ᐯ ᐃᑐᐦᑕᑕᒪᐍᐤ
VTA s/he brings (it/him) for s.o.
pē-itohtatāw ᐯ ᐃᑐᐦᑕᑖᐤ
VAIt s/he brings s.t.
pē-itohtēw ᐯ ᐃᑐᐦᑌᐤ
VAI s/he comes walking, s/he comes over here
pē-kisīpaýin ᐯ ᑭᓰᐸᔨᐣ
VII it comes quickly (by sailing)
pē-kisīpaýiw ᐯ ᑭᓰᐸᔨᐤ
VAI s/he comes quickly (by horse or car)
pē-kiyokēw ᐯ ᑭᔪᑫᐤ
VAI s/he comes and visits
pē-kīwēhtahēw ᐯ ᑮᐍᐦᑕᐦᐁᐤ
VTA s/he brings s.o. home, back
pē-kīwēhtatāw ᐯ ᑮᐍᐦᑕᑖᐤ
VAIt s/he brings s.t. home, back
pē-kīwēpahtāw ᐯ ᑮᐍᐸᐦᑖᐤ
VAI s/he runs home, s/he comes running home
pē-kīwēw ᐯ ᑮᐍᐤ
VAI s/he comes home, s/he returns
pē-mētawēw ᐯ ᒣᑕᐍᐤ
VAI s/he comes and plays
pē-mīcisow ᐯ ᒦᒋᓱᐤ
VAI s/he comes and eats
pē-nāsipēw ᐯ ᓈᓯᐯᐤ
VAI s/he comes down to the shore

pē-nātam ᐯ ᓈᑕᒼ
VTI s/he comes to get s.t.
pē-nātēw ᐯ ᓈᑌᐤ
VTA s/he comes for s.o., s/he comes to get s.o.
pē-nipāw ᐯ ᓂᐹᐤ
VAI s/he comes and sleeps
pē-nīhtaciwēw ᐯ ᓃᐦᑕᒋᐍᐤ
VAI s/he comes down (as from stairs or a hill)
pē-nīhtakosīw ᐯ ᓃᐦᑕᑯᓰᐤ
VAI s/he comes climbing down (out of a tree or off a ladder)
pē-nōkosiw ᐯ ᓅᑯᓯᐤ
VAI s/he comes into sight, s/he is seen
pē-nōkwan ᐯ ᓅᑲᐣ
VII it comes in sight, it is seen; it comes to pass
pē-ohtohtēw ᐯ ᐅᐦᑐᐦᑌᐤ
VAI s/he arrives from over there
pē-otihtam ᐯ ᐅᑎᐦᑕᒼ
VTI s/he comes to s.t., s/he arrives at his/her destination
pē-otihtēw ᐯ ᐅᑎᐦᑌᐤ
VTA s/he comes to s.o.
pē-pīhtikwēw ᐯ ᐲᐦᑎᑵᐤ
VAI s/he comes in; s/he comes and enters [*also* pīhtokēw, pīhtokwēw]
pē-pīkiskwēw ᐯ ᐲᑭᐢᑵᐤ
VAI s/he comes and speaks
pē-sāminēw ᐯ ᓵᒥᓀᐤ
VTA s/he comes and touches s.o.
pē-takosin ᐯ ᑕᑯᓯᐣ
VAI s/he arrives, s/he comes
pē-waýawī-pimosinēw ᐯ ᐘᔭᐑ ᐱᒧᓯᓀᐤ
VAI s/he throws s.t. outside (towards the speaker)
pē-waýawīhtahēw ᐯ ᐘᔭᐑᐦᑕᐦᐁᐤ
VTA s/he brings s.o. outside
pē-waýawīhtatāw ᐯ ᐘᔭᐑᐦᑕᑖᐤ
VAIt s/he brings s.t. outside
pē-waýawīw ᐯ ᐘᔭᐑᐤ
VAI s/he comes outside
pē-wāpahtam ᐯ ᐚᐸᐦᑕᒼ
VTI s/he comes and sees s.t.
pē-wāpamēw ᐯ ᐚᐸᒣᐤ
VTA s/he comes and sees s.o.
pē-wīhkwacipitam ᐯ ᐑᐦᑲᒋᐱᑕᒼ
VTI s/he comes and pulls s.t. out (of a mud hole), s/he comes and pulls s.t. free
pē-wīhkwacipitēw ᐯ ᐑᐦᑲᒋᐱᑌᐤ
VTA s/he comes and pulls s.o. out (of a mud hole); s/he comes and pulls s.o. free
pē-ýahkinam ᐯ ᔭᐦᑭᓇᒼ
VTI s/he comes and pushes s.t.
pē-ýahkinēw ᐯ ᔭᐦᑭᓀᐤ
VTA s/he comes and pushes s.o.
pē-yāsipaýiw ᐯ ᔮᓯᐸᔨᐤ
VAI s/he comes sliding down
pē-yāsipaýiw ᐯ ᔮᓯᐸᔨᐤ
VII it comes sliding down
pē-ýōhtēnam ᐯ ᔫᐦᑌᓇᒼ
VTI s/he comes and opens s.t.
pēci ᐯᒋ
IPC hither, to here; thence, from there on down; approach
pēci-nāway ᐯᒋ ᓈᐘᕀ
IPC from back then; down from the distant past
pēcicimēw ᐯᒋᒋᒣᐤ
VAI s/he paddles hither
pēciciwan ᐯᒋᒋᐘᐣ
VII there is water flowing in, there is water coming in, it is the tide
pēciciwanihkawēw ᐯᒋᒋᐘᓂᐦᑲᐍᐤ
VTA s/he digs a ditch for s.o. (for irrigation)
pēciciwanihkātam ᐯᒋᒋᐘᓂᐦᑳᑕᒼ
VTI s/he digs and makes the water flow
pēciciwanihkēw ᐯᒋᒋᐘᓂᐦᑫᐤ
VAI s/he makes a ditch for water
pēcihāw ᐯᒋᐦᐋᐤ
VAI s/he flies toward (us), s/he approaches by flight
pēcikātēw ᐯᒋᑳᑌᐤ
VII it is brought
pēcikēw ᐯᒋᑫᐤ
VAI s/he brings things
pēcimēw ᐯᒋᒣᐤ
VTA s/he calls s.o. hither
pēcimihtēw ᐯᒋᒥᐦᑌᐤ
VAI s/he brings firewood
pēcinākosiw ᐯᒋᓈᑯᓯᐤ
VAI s/he is seen approaching
pēcinākwan ᐯᒋᓈᑲᐣ
VII it is seen approaching
pēcipēham ᐯᒋᐯᐦᐊᒼ
VTI s/he writes s.t. hither
pēcipēhamawēw ᐯᒋᐯᐦᐊᒪᐍᐤ
VTA s/he writes (it) hither to s.o.
pēcipitam ᐯᒋᐱᑕᒼ
VTI s/he pulls s.t. here
pēcipitēw ᐯᒋᐱᑌᐤ
VTA s/he pulls s.o. here
pēcitāpāsow ᐯᒋᑖᐹᓱᐤ
VAI s/he drives hither, s/he comes driving
pēcitāpēw ᐯᒋᑖᐯᐤ
VAI s/he drags (it) hither
pēciwatāw ᐯᒋᐘᑖᐤ
VAIt s/he brings s.t. hither on his/her back
pēciwatēw ᐯᒋᐘᑌᐤ
VTA s/he brings s.o. hither on his/her back
pēciýawēmow ᐯᒋᔭᐍᒧᐤ
VAI s/he feels enthusiasm coming on
pēh-pēyak ᐯᐦ ᐯᔭᐠ
IPC one by one, individually [*cf.* pāh-pēyak]
pēhēw ᐯᐦᐁᐤ
VTA s/he waits for s.o.
pēhkācihow ᐯᐦᑳᒋᐦᐅᐤ
VAI s/he keeps him/herself clean
pēhkihcikēw ᐯᐦᑭᐦᒋᑫᐤ
VAI s/he cleans up
pēhkihēw ᐯᐦᑭᐦᐁᐤ
VTA s/he cleans s.o., s/he cleanses s.o.
pēhkihow ᐯᐦᑭᐦᐅᐤ
VAI s/he keeps him/herself clean
pēhkihtāw ᐯᐦᑭᐦᑖᐤ
VAIt s/he cleans s.t., s/he cleanses s.t.
pēhkisiw ᐯᐦᑭᓯᐤ
VAI s/he is clean
pēhonān ᐯᐦᐅᓈᐣ
NI waiting place; Fort a la Corne, SK; Fort Carlton, SK; Prince Albert, SK [*place name*]
pēhonānihk ᐯᐦᐅᓈᓂᕽ
INM waiting place; Fort Carlton, SK [*loc*]
pēhow ᐯᐦᐅᐤ
VAI s/he waits; s/he expects, s/he is in expectation (of someone's arrival)
pēhowikamik ᐯᐦᐅᐏᑲᒥᐠ
NI railway station; waiting room [*pl*: -wa]
pēhowin ᐯᐦᐅᐏᐣ
NI waiting; expecting someone
pēhpēkahākan ᐯᐦᐯᑲᐦᐋᑲᐣ
NI stone in leather as war-club
pēhtam ᐯᐦᑕᒼ
VTI s/he hears s.t. [*rdpl*: pa-pēhtam]
pēhtamowin ᐯᐦᑕᒧᐏᐣ
NI what is heard; hearing
pēhtawēw ᐯᐦᑕᐍᐤ
VTA s/he hears s.o. [*rdpl*: pāh-pēhtawēw]
pēhtākaniwiw ᐯᐦᑖᑲᓂᐏᐤ
VII it is heard
pēhtākēw ᐯᐦᑖᑫᐤ
VAI s/he hears with something
pēhtākosiw ᐯᐦᑖᑯᓯᐤ
VAI s/he is heard, s/he makes him/herself heard
pēhtākwan ᐯᐦᑖᑲᐣ
VII it is audible, it is heard; it is noisy
pēhtāsow ᐯᐦᑖᓱᐤ
VAI s/he hears him/herself
pēkatēskākow ᐯᑲᑌᐢᑳᑯᐤ
VTA it makes him/her belch,

burp [*inanimate actor form of VTA* pēkatēskaw-]

pēkatēskiw ᐯᑲᐟᐁᐢᑭᐤ
VAI s/he belches, burps frequently [*hab*]

pēkatēw ᐯᑲᐟᐁᐤ
VAI s/he belches, burps

pēkatēwin ᐯᑲᐅᐠᐧ
NI belching, burping

pēkohēw ᐯᑯᐦᐁᐤ
VTA s/he wakes s.o.

pēkomēw ᐯᑯᒣᐤ
VTA s/he wakes s.o. by speech

pēkopayiw ᐯᑯᐸᔨᐤ
VAI s/he wakes up, s/he awakens

pēkopēw ᐯᑯᐯᐤ
VAI s/he comes up from under water, s/he emerges from water

pēkopēwin ᐯᑯᐯᐃᐧ
NI emerging place (for water animals)

pēkopitēw ᐯᑯᐱᐟᐁᐤ
VTA s/he pulls s.o. awake [*not wC; see also* pikopitēw]

pēkwatāmow ᐯᑿᑖᒧᐤ
VAI s/he comes up through breathing hole

pēpēsiskāw ᐯᐯᓰᐢᑳᐤ
VAI s/he goes slowly [*rdpl; cf.* pēsiskāw]

pēpēskōmina ᐯᐯᐢᑰᒥᓇ
NI pepper beans [*pl generally; English loan base*]

pēpisis ᐯᐱᓯᐢ
NA baby [*dim; English loan*]

pēsēkin ᐯᓭᑭᐣ
NI salvage material, cloth

pēsinam ᐯᓯᓇᒼ
VTI s/he has a cut hand (from a blade)

pēsiskāw ᐯᓯᐢᑳᐤ
VAI s/he goes slowly

pēsiwēw ᐯᓯᐍᐤ
VTA s/he brings s.o., s/he brings s.o. hither [*rdpl*: pa-pēsiwēw]

pēskis ᐯᐢᑭᐢ
IPC at the same time, simultaneously; also, besides, as well

pēskōmina ᐯᐢᑰᒥᓇ
NI pepper [*pl generally; see also* askīwisiwihtākan, papēskōmina, pēpēskōmina, wīsakat]

pēsohtam ᐯᓱᐦᑕᒼ
VTI s/he hears s.t. close by

pēsonākosiw ᐯᓱᓈᑯᓯᐤ
VAI s/he is coming near, s/he appears to be near

pēsonākwan ᐯᓱᓈᑿᐣ
VII it appears to be near

pēsowan ᐯᓱᐊᐧᐣ
VII it is near, it is a short distance

pēswāpahtam ᐯᐢᐚᐸᐦᑕᒼ
VTI s/he sees s.t. at close range, nearby

pēswāpamēw ᐯᐢᐚᐸᒣᐤ
VTA s/he sees s.o. at close range, nearby

pēsweyihtam ᐯᐢᐁᐧᔨᐦᑕᒼ
VTI s/he thinks s.t. is near

pēsweyimēw ᐯᐢᐁᐧᔨᒣᐤ
VTA s/he thinks s.o. is near

pētahiskwēwēw ᐯᑕᐦᐃᐢᑵᐍᐤ
VAI he bring a woman by canoe, he brings his wife by canoe

pētakocin ᐯᑕᑯᒋᐣ
VAI s/he comes through the air, s/he comes swiftly by water

pētakotēw ᐯᑕᑯᐟᐁᐤ
VII it comes through the air

pētamawēw ᐯᑕᒪᐍᐤ
VTA s/he brings (it/him) to, for s.o.

pētamāsow ᐯᑕᒫᓱᐤ
VAI s/he brings (it/him) for him/herself

pētasinahikēw ᐯᑕᓯᓇᐦᐃᑫᐤ
VAI s/he writes hither; s/he comes in search of mail, books

pētaskosīwēw ᐯᑕᐢᑯᓰᐍᐤ
VAI s/he brings hay

pētastimwēw ᐯᑕᐢᑎᒼᐍᐤ
VAI s/he brings horses, dogs

pētatāmow ᐯᑕᑖᒧᐤ
VAI s/he blows hither, s/he breathes forth; s/he has his/her breathing return

pētawēw ᐯᑕᐍᐤ
VTA s/he brings (it/him) to or for s.o. [*cf.* pētamawēw]

pētācimēw ᐯᑖᒋᒣᐤ
VTA s/he comes with news of s.o.; s/he tells news of s.o. coming

pētāhotēw ᐯᑖᐦᐅᐟᐁᐤ
VII it is carried hither by current or waves

pētāmisow ᐯᑖᒥᓱᐤ
VAI s/he comes from berrying

pētāmohkawēw ᐯᑖᒧᐦᑲᐍᐤ
VTA s/he flees hither to s.o. for help

pētāmohkēw ᐯᑖᒧᐦᑫᐤ
VAI s/he flees hither for help

pētāmow ᐯᑖᒧᐤ
VAI s/he comes in flight, s/he flees here for shelter, s/he flees here for help

pētāpan ᐯᑖᐸᐣ
VII it is dawn, it is daybreak, it becomes dawn

pētāpēkamowak ᐯᑖᐯᑲᒧᐊᐧᐠ
VAI they come in a line hither, they come here on a string [*pl*]

pētāpēkipahēw ᐯᑖᐯᑭᐸᐦᐁᐤ
VTA s/he runs s.o. hither on a string

pētāpahtam ᐯᑖᐸᐦᑕᒼ
VTI s/he sees s.t. coming

pētāpamēw ᐯᑖᐸᒣᐤ
VTA s/he sees s.o. coming

pētāpiw ᐯᑖᐱᐤ
VAI s/he looks hither, s/he looks in this direction

pētāsiw ᐯᑖᓯᐤ
VAI s/he sails this way; s/he blows this way (in the wind)

pētāstamohtēw ᐯᑖᐢᑕᒧᐦᑌᐤ
VAI s/he comes walking hither

pētāstan ᐯᑖᐢᑕᐣ
VII it blows this way

pētāstēw ᐯᑖᐢᑌᐤ
VII it is blown here by the wind

pētātakāw ᐯᑖᑕᑳᐤ
VAI s/he swims hither; s/he wades hither

pētātāmow ᐯᑖᑖᒧᐤ
VAI s/he arrives crying

pētāw ᐯᑖᐤ
VAIt s/he brings s.t., s/he brings s.t. hither

pētāwahēw ᐯᑖᐊᐧᐦᐁᐤ
VTA s/he hauls s.o. in

pētāwatāw ᐯᑖᐊᐧᑖᐤ
VAIt s/he hauls s.t. in; s/he brings, s/he handles s.t.

pētisaham ᐯᑎᓴᐦᐊᒼ
VTI s/he drives or sends s.t. hither

pētisahamawēw ᐯᑎᓴᐦᐊᒪᐍᐤ
VTA s/he drives or sends (it/him) hither for s.o.

pētisahwēw ᐯᑎᓴᐦᐍᐤ
VTA s/he drives or sends s.o. hither

pētisāpahtam ᐯᑎᓵᐸᐦᑕᒼ
VTI s/he sees s.t. coming

pētisāpamēw ᐯᑎᓵᐸᒣᐤ
VTA s/he sees s.o. coming

pētiskwēwēw ᐯᑎᐢᑵᐍᐤ
VAI s/he brings a woman

pētonawān ᐯᑐᓇᐚᐣ
NI ceremonial food

pētonawēw ᐯᑐᓇᐍᐤ
VAI s/he gives ceremonial food

pētowatēw ᐯᑐᐊᐧᑌᐤ
VAI s/he brings a load, s/he carries a load on his/her back

pētowēkotēw ᐯᑐᐍᑯᑌᐤ
VII it comes noisily flying

pētwēwēnam ᐯᑤᐍᓇᒼ
VTI s/he walks audibly, s/he steps audibly

pētwēwēsin ᐯᑤᐍᓯᐣ
VAI s/he comes stepping with noise

pētwēwētāhtam ᐯᑤᐍᑖᐦᑕᒼ
VTI s/he comes breathing loudly

pētwēwitam ᐯᑘᐏᑕᒼ
VTI s/he comes speaking noisily

pēyak ᐯᔭᐠ
IPC one; alone, single; the only one

pēyak-askiy ᐯᔭᐠ ᐊᐢᑭᐩ
IPC one year

pēyak-ispayin ᐯᔭᐠ ᐃᐢᐸᔨᐣ
IPC one week

pēyak-kosikwan ᐯᔭᐠ ᑯᓯᑿᐣ
IPC one pound

pēyak-kosikwanis ᐯᔭᐠ ᑯᓯᑿᓂᐢ
IPC one ounce [*dim*]

pēyak-misicisikan ᐯᔭᐠ ᒥᓯᒋᓯᑲᐣ
IPC one inch [*dim*; *cf.* misit *IPC*]

pēyak-misit ᐯᔭᐠ ᒥᓯᐟ
IPC one foot [*cf.* misit *IPC*]

pēyak-pīsim ᐯᔭᐠ ᐲᓯᒼ
IPC one moon, one month

pēyak-sōniyās ᐯᔭᐠ ᓲᓂᔮᐢ
IPC one quarter, twenty-five cents [*dim*]

pēyak-tipahōpān ᐯᔭᐠ ᑎᐸᐦᐴᐹᐣ
IPC one gallon

pēyak-tipiskāw ᐯᔭᐠ ᑎᐱᐢᑳᐤ
IPC one night

pēyako- ᐯᔭᑯ
IPV alone, only; as one

pēyako-itēýihtamwak ᐯᔭᑯ ᐃᑌᔨᐦᑕᒷᐠ
VTI they think as one, they are unanimous [*pl*]

pēyako-kīsikāw ᐯᔭᑯ ᑮᓯᑳᐤ
VII it is Monday [*cf.* pōni-āyamihēwi-kīsikāw]

pēyako-nīmāskwēwinēw ᐯᔭᑯ ᓃᒫᐢᑵᐏᓀᐤ
VAI s/he has only one weapon, s/he took only one weapon along

pēyako-nīpawiw ᐯᔭᑯ ᓃᐸᐏᐤ
VAI s/he stands alone (without aid)

pēyako-piponwēw ᐯᔭᑯ ᐱᐳᓊᐤ
VAI s/he is one year old [*also* -piponēw]

pēyako-tipiskāw ᐯᔭᑯ ᑎᐱᐢᑳᐤ
IPC one night

pēyako-tipiskwēw ᐯᔭᑯ ᑎᐱᐢᑵᐤ
VAI s/he stays one night

pēyakocihcēw ᐯᔭᑯᒋᐦᒉᐤ
VAI s/he has one hand

pēyakohēw ᐯᔭᑯᐦᐁᐤ
VTA s/he deals only with s.o., s/he deals with s.o. alone

pēyakohkam ᐯᔭᑯᐦᑲᒼ
VTI s/he tends s.t. alone

pēyakohkawēw ᐯᔭᑯᐦᑲᐌᐤ
VTA s/he tends s.o. alone; s/he goes at s.o. single-handed

pēyakohkwāmiw ᐯᔭᑯᐦᒀᒥᐤ
VAI s/he sleeps alone

pēyakohtāw ᐯᔭᑯᐦᑖᐤ
VAI s/he keeps to one area

pēyakokamikosiw ᐯᔭᑯᑲᒥᑯᓯᐤ
VAI s/he lives in a lone lodge

pēyakokāpawiw ᐯᔭᑯᑳᐸᐏᐤ
VAI s/he stands alone (without others around)

pēyakokāt ᐯᔭᑯᑳᐟ
NA one-legged person

pēyakokātēw ᐯᔭᑯᑳᑌᐤ
VAI s/he has one leg, s/he is one-legged

pēyakokēw ᐯᔭᑯᑫᐤ
VAI s/he dwells alone, s/he lives alone

pēyakonēham ᐯᔭᑯᓀᐦᐊᒼ
VTI s/he brings s.t. as only thing

pēyakonēhow ᐯᔭᑯᓀᐦᐅᐤ
VAI s/he things brings alone

pēyakonēw ᐯᔭᑯᓀᐤ
VTA s/he holds s.o. apart, alone

pēyakonisk ᐯᔭᑯᓂᐢᐠ
IPC one fathom

pēyakopēhikan ᐯᔭᑯᐯᐦᐃᑲᐣ
NI playing card; ace; [*pl*:] cards, deck of cards, game of cards

pēyakopēhikēw ᐯᔭᑯᐯᐦᐃᑫᐤ
VAI s/he plays cards

pēyakosāp ᐯᔭᑯᓵᑊ
IPC eleven

pēyakosāpwāw ᐯᔭᑯᓵᐺᐤ
IPC eleven times

pēyakosimow ᐯᔭᑯᓯᒧᐤ
VAI s/he lies down alone; s/he hides; s/he dances alone

pēyakosisān ᐯᔭᑯᓯᓵᐣ
NA only son

pēyakosisāniwiw ᐯᔭᑯᓯᓵᓂᐏᐤ
VAI he is an only son

pēyakotās ᐯᔭᑯᑖᐢ
IPC enough for one pair of leggings

pēyakotēskanēw ᐯᔭᑯᑌᐢᑲᓀᐤ
VAI s/he has one antler

pēyakow ᐯᔭᑯᐤ
VAI s/he is alone; s/he is the only one

pēyakowiw ᐯᔭᑯᐏᐤ
VAI s/he is the same

pēyakōskān ᐯᔭᑰᐢᑳᐣ
NA one family; one pair (at cards)

pēyakōskānēsiwak ᐯᔭᑰᐢᑳᓀᓯᐘᐠ
VAI they are one tribe, one nation [*pl*]

pēyakw-āya ᐯᔭᒁᔭ
NA a single one (*e.g.* stocking) [*pl*: pēyakw-āyak:] a single pair

pēyakwahpicikēw ᐯᔭᑿᐦᐱᒋᑫᐤ
VAI s/he drives one horse

pēyakwahpicikēw-aya ᐯᔭᑿᐦᐱᒋᑫᐘᔭ
NA cart pulled by a single horse

pēyakwahpitēw ᐯᔭᑿᐦᐱᑌᐤ
VTA s/he harnesses s.o. singly

pēyakwahtay ᐯᔭᑿᐦᑕᐩ
NI one fur

pēyakwan ᐯᔭᑿᐣ
IPC same, the same, just the same; similar

pēyakwan ᐯᔭᑿᐣ
VII it is one, it is the same [*cf.* pēyakwan *IPC*]

pēyakwanohk ᐯᔭᑿᓄᕽ
IPC in one place, the same spot

pēyakwapiw ᐯᔭᑿᐱᐤ
VAI s/he is alone; s/he sits, stays alone at home

pēyakwaskan ᐯᔭᑿᐢᑲᐣ
VII it is for one shot, it is single-barreled

pēyakwaskanōs ᐯᔭᑿᐢᑲᓅᐢ
NI single-barreled gun [*dim*]

pēyakwaskisin ᐯᔭᑿᐢᑭᓯᐣ
IPC one pair of shoes

pēyakwaskisow ᐯᔭᑿᐢᑭᓱᐤ
VAI it grows alone (*e.g.* a tree)

pēyakwaskokāpawiw ᐯᔭᑿᐢᑯᑳᐸᐏᐤ
VII it stands as one blade or stem

pēyakwatahikan ᐯᔭᑿᑕᐦᐃᑲᐣ
NI one piece as chopped

pēyakwayak ᐯᔭᑿᔭᐠ
IPC in one place, in a certain place; in the same place; one way, one kind

pēyakwayiwinisa ᐯᔭᑿᔨᐏᓂᓴ
NI suit [*pl generally*]

pēyakwāpisk ᐯᔭᒁᐱᐢᐠ
IPC one dollar, silver dollar

pēyakwāw ᐯᔭᒁᐤ
IPC once, once more

pēyakwāw ēsa ᐯᔭᒁᐤ ᐁᓴ
IPC once upon a time, one time

pēyakwēkan ᐯᔭᑵᑲᐣ
VII it is a single piece (*i.e.* cloth)

pēyakwēýimisow ᐯᔭᑵᔨᒥᓱᐤ
VAI s/he thinks only of him/herself, s/he is selfish, s/he is self-centered

pēyāhtak ᐯᔮᐦᑕᐠ
IPC quietly, slowly; s/he takes it easy [*cf.* pēyāhtik]

pēyāhtakēyimowin ᐯᔮᐦᑕᑫᔨᒧᐏᐣ
NI peace

pēyāhtakisiw ᐯᔮᐦᑕᑭᓯᐤ
VAI s/he is quiet, s/he is careful

pēyāhtakotosiw ᐯᔮᐦᑕᑯᑐᓯᐤ
VAI s/he is slow getting around

pēyāhtakowēw ᐯᔮᐦᑕᑯᐍᐤ
VAI s/he talks slowly, carefully; s/he chooses his/her words carefully

pēyāhtakowisiw ᐯᔮᐦᑕᑯᐏᓯᐤ
VAI s/he moves slowly, carefully

pēyāhtik ᐯᔮᐦᑎᐠ
IPC quietly, softly, slowly, carefully [*cf.* pēyāhtak]

pēyāsiw ᐯᔮᓯᐤ
VAI s/he comes down through the air

ᐱ

piciw ᐱᒋᐤ
VAI s/he moves, s/he moves camp; s/he moves his/her belongings and family; s/he travels, s/he goes on a trek

picihēw ᐱᒋᐦᐁᐤ
VTA s/he moves s.o., s/he moves camp for s.o., s/he moves s.o. away, s/he helps s.o. to move

picihtāw ᐱᒋᐦᑖᐤ
VAIt s/he moves camp, s/he moves all, s/he moves s.t.

picikīskosīs ᐱᒋᑮᐢᑯᓰᐢ
NA chickadee, wren

picikwās ᐱᒋᒁᐢ
NA apple

piciwin ᐱᒋᐏᐣ
NI trek, moving of camp

piciwinihkēw ᐱᒋᐏᓂᐦᑫᐤ
VAI s/he arranges for the moving of camp; s/he makes a trip

picwastēw ᐱᒓᐢᑌᐤ
VII it lies around

pihcipohtāw ᐱᐦᒋᐳᐦᑖᐤ
VAIt s/he poisons s.t. [*cf.* piscipohtāw]

pihcipow ᐱᐦᒋᐳᐤ
VAI s/he is poisoned [*cf.* piscipow]

pihcipowin ᐱᐦᒋᐳᐏᐣ
NI poison [*cf.* piscipowin]

pihēsis ᐱᐦᐁᓯᐢ
NA little prairie-chicken [*dim*; *wC*: pithīsis; *sC*: piñēsis]

pihēsiw ᐱᐦᐁᓯᐤ
NA thunderbird [*cf.* piyēsiw; *wC*: pithīsiw; *sC*: piñēsiw]

pihēskāw ᐱᐦᐁᐢᑳᐤ
VII there are many partridges [*wC*: pithīskāw; *sC*: piñēskāw]

pihēw ᐱᐦᐁᐤ
NA prairie chicken; grouse; partridge [*cf.* pihýēw; *wC*: pithīw; *sC*: piñēw]

pihēw-motay ᐱᐦᐁᐤ ᒧᑕᐩ
NI partridge's crop

pihēwaýasit ᐱᐦᐁᐘᔭᓯᐟ
NI club (at cards) [*also* pihēwosit; *cf.* pihēw osit "prairie chicken's foot"]

pihēwiw ᐱᐦᐁᐏᐤ
VAI it is a partridge, it is a prairie chicken [*wC*: pithīwiw; *sC*: piñēwiw]

pihēwokas ᐱᐦᐁᐓᑲᐢ
NA partridge claw [*legendary male personal name*]

pihkahcēwāpōs ᐱᐦᑲᐦᒉᐚᐴᐢ
NI coffee [*dim*]

pihkahtēw ᐱᐦᑲᐦᑌᐤ
VII it is burnt (as a roast)

pihkahtēwāhtik ᐱᐦᑲᐦᑌᐚᐦᑎᐠ
NA burnt stick [*obv*: -wa; *legendary female personal name*]

pihkasam ᐱᐦᑲᓴᒼ
VTI s/he toasts s.t.

pihkasikan ᐱᐦᑲᓯᑲᐣ
NA toast

pihkasikanāpoy ᐱᐦᑲᓯᑲᓈᐳᐩ
NI coffee [*see also* kāspisikan, pihkātēwāpoy]

pihkasikātēw ᐱᐦᑲᓯᑳᑌᐤ
VII it is toasted, it is burnt

pihkasow ᐱᐦᑲᓱᐤ
VAI s/he is burnt

pihkaswēw ᐱᐦᑲᓭᐤ
VTA s/he toasts s.o., s/he burns s.o.

pihkatēwāpoy ᐱᐦᑲᑌᐚᐳᐩ
NI coffee [*also* pihkahtēwāpoy; *see also* kāspisikan]

pihkihkomānis ᐱᐦᑭᐦᑯᒫᓂᐢ
NI pocket knife [*dim*]

pihko ᐱᐦᑯ
NI soot, ashes, wood ashes, dust [*mass noun, always sg*]

pihkohisow ᐱᐦᑯᐦᐃᓱᐤ
VAI s/he frees him/herself

pihkohitowak ᐱᐦᑯᐦᐃᑐᐘᐠ
VAI they free one another

pihkohkēw ᐱᐦᑯᐦᑫᐤ
VAI s/he makes ashes

pihkohow ᐱᐦᑯᐦᐅᐤ
VAI s/he gets loose, s/he gets free, s/he frees him/herself, s/he escapes; s/he gets there, s/he gets along

pihkohtāw ᐱᐦᑯᐦᑖᐤ
VAIt s/he accomplishes s.t., s/he achieves s.t., s/he manages to do s.t.

pihkohtēwāpoy ᐱᐦᑯᐦᑌᐚᐳᐩ
NI lye solution (ashes and water)

pihkohtēwāpōhkākēw ᐱᐦᑯᐦᑌᐚᐴᐦᑳᑫᐤ
VAI s/he makes lye from s.t. (*e.g.* wood ashes)

pihkohtēwāpōhkēw ᐱᐦᑯᐦᑌᐚᐴᐦᑫᐤ
VAI s/he makes wood ash lye

pihkohtēwāpōstamawēw ᐱᐦᑯᐦᑌᐚᐴᐢᑕᒪᐍᐤ
VTA s/he makes wood ash lye for s.o.

pihkonākosiw ᐱᐦᑯᓈᑯᓯᐤ
VAI s/he is grey, s/he is ashen

pihkonākwan ᐱᐦᑯᓈᑿᐣ
VII it is grey, it is ashen

pihkos ᐱᐦᑯᐢ
NA gnat; sandfly

pihkosiskāw ᐱᐦᑯᓯᐢᑳᐤ
VII there are many sandflies

pihkowan ᐱᐦᑯᐘᐣ
VII it is covered with ashes

pihkwan ᐱᐦᑿᐣ
VII it is coarse

pihkwāpoy ᐱᐦᒁᐳᐩ
NI lye

pihpihcēw ᐱᐦᐱᐦᒉᐤ
NA robin [*also* pihpihciw]

pihýēw ᐱᐦᔦᐤ
NA partridge, prairie chicken [*cf.* pihēw; *wC*: pithīw; *sC*: piñēw]

pikihtawētāmow ᐱᑭᐦᑕᐍᑖᒧᐤ
VAI s/he breathes steaming (as in cold weather)

pikihtēw ᐱᑭᐦᑌᐤ
VII it smokes, it sends up smoke, it is burning; it sends up fog (as water cooling)

pikiskatin ᐱᑭᐢᑲᑎᐣ
VII it is decayed; it is rotten [*see also* sikwatatin, wīnihtin]

pikiskatiw ᐱᑭᐢᑲᑎᐤ
VAI it is rotten; it is decayed (*e.g.* tree, apple) [*see also* sikwatatiw]

pikiw ᐱᑭᐤ
NA gum, pitch, resin, tar; rubber

pikiwaskāpiw ᐱᑭᐘᐢᑳᐱᐤ
VAI s/he has gummy eyes

pikiwēkin ᐱᑭᐍᑭᐣ
NI rubberized cloth, tarpaulin

pikīhkēkātam ᐱᑮᐦᑫᑳᑕᒼ
VTI s/he smears pitch on s.t.; s/he waterproofs s.t. by smearing pitch on it

pikīhkēw ᐱᑮᐦᑫᐤ
VAI s/he makes pitch

pikīkāhtam ᐱᑮᑳᐦᑕᒼ
VTI s/he caulks s.t.

pikīwaskisin ᐱᑮᐘᐢᑭᓯᐣ
NI rubber boot, rubber golosh [*also* pikiwaskisin]

piko ᐱᑯ
IPC must, have to [*also* poko; *clause-initial predicative*; *obligation* (*modal*); *immediately preceding conjunct verb with future preverb*]

piko ᐱᑯ
IPC only; for sure, without a

doubt [*follows emphasized word*]
piko ani ᐱᑯ ᐊᓂ
IPH anyway [*also* pikw āni]
piko awiyak ᐱᑯ ᐊᐃᐧᔭᕽ
PR everyone, everybody [*also* pikw āwiyak]
piko ispī ᐱᑯ ᐃᐢᐲ
IPH anytime [*also* pikw īspī]
piko ita ᐱᑯ ᐃᑕ
IPH anywhere, in any place; everywhere [*cf.* piko itē; *also* pikw īta]
piko itē ᐱᑯ ᐃᑌ
IPH anywhere; all over, everywhere [*also* pikw ītē; *cf.* piko ita]
piko itē isi ᐱᑯ ᐃᑌ ᐃᓯ
IPH in any direction
piko itowahk ᐱᑯ ᐃᑐᐘᕽ
IPH of any kind, of all kinds [*wC*: pokītowahk]
piko itowihk ᐱᑯ ᐃᑐᐏᕽ
IPH in any place, in all places
piko iýikohk ᐱᑯ ᐃᔨᑯᕽ
IPH any amount
piko īyiwas ᐱᑯ ᐄᔨᐘᐢ
IPH entirely
piko kīkway ᐱᑯ ᑮᑲᐧᕀ
IPH something or other; anything at all, everything [*cf.* piko kīkwās]
piko kīkwās ᐱᑯ ᑮᑲᐧᐢ
IPH something or other; anything at all [*dim*; *sometimes pl as if NI*; *cf.* piko kīkway]
pikohkwēsikan ᐱᑯᐦᑫᐧᓯᑲᐣ
NI sharp knife, lancet (for blood-letting)
pikohkwēswēw ᐱᑯᐦᑫᐧᓭᐤ
VTA s/he cuts s.o., s/he lances s.o.; s/he bleeds s.o.
pikonita ᐱᑯᓂᑕ
IPC wasted efforts [*also* pakonita; *wC*: pakwanita; *cf.* konita, pikwanita]
pikoýikohk ᐱᑯᔨᑯᕽ
IPC no matter how much, to any extent [*cf.* piko iýikohk]
pikōwanipiy ᐱᑰᐘᓂᐱᕀ
NI spring of water
pikwanāhtik ᐱᑲᐧᓈᐦᑎᐠ
NA wild rhubarb [*pl*: -wak; *lr. Burdock, arctium lappa*]
pikwanita ᐱᑲᐧᓂᑕ
IPC without reason; all for nothing [*also* pakwanita; *cf.* konita, pikonita]
pikwāci ᐱᑳᐧᒋ
IPC wild; desolate [*also* pikwaci; *cf.* pakwāci]
pikwāhtin ᐱᑳᐧᐦᑎᐣ
VII it is dull
pikwāhwēw ᐱᑳᐧᐦᐍᐤ
VTA s/he pierces s.o. with tool or bullet
pikwāskawēw ᐱᑳᐧᐢᑲᐍᐤ
VTA s/he pierces s.o. by foot or body movement
pikwāstahwēw ᐱᑳᐧᐢᑕᐦᐍᐤ
VTA s/he pierces s.o.'s skin
pikwātahwēw ᐱᑳᐧᑕᐦᐍᐤ
VTA s/he pricks s.o.
pikwātastim ᐱᑳᐧᑕᐢᑎᒼ
NA unbroken horse, wild horse [*pl*: -wak]
pikwātayēhwēw ᐱᑳᐧᑕᔦᐦᐍᐤ
VTA s/he pierces s.o. in the belly by tool
pikwātōsān ᐱᑳᐧᑑᓵᐣ
NA illegitimate child; bastard [*cf.* pakwātōsān]
pikwīta ᐱᑹᑕ
IPC anywhere [*cf.* piko ita]
pikwītowahk ᐱᑹᑐᐘᕽ
IPC any kind [*cf.* piko itowahk]
pimaham ᐱᒪᐦᐊᒼ
VTI s/he travels down the river
pimahokow ᐱᒪᐦᐅᑯᐤ
VAI s/he drifts
pimahotēw ᐱᒪᐦᐅᑌᐤ
VII it drifts
pimakocin ᐱᒪᑯᒋᐣ
VAI s/he flies past; s/he moves along, s/he goes by; it works, it is in working order (*e.g.* clock, car)
pimakotēw ᐱᒪᑯᑌᐤ
VII it flies past; it runs along, it operates, it works, it is in working order (*e.g.* tape-recorder)
pimamon ᐱᒪᒧᐣ
VII it runs along, it passes along [*cf.* pimamow]
pimamow ᐱᒪᒧᐤ
VII it passes along [*cf.* pimamon]
pimapiw ᐱᒪᐱᐤ
VAI s/he sits along a place
pimaskatēw ᐱᒪᐢᑲᑌᐤ
VTA s/he goes along leaving s.o. outdistanced
pimastēw ᐱᒪᐢᑌᐤ
VII it is placed in linear fashion, it runs along, it lies along
pimācihāwasow ᐱᒫᒋᐦᐋᐘᓱᐤ
VAI s/he makes a living for his/her children
pimācihēw ᐱᒫᒋᐦᐁᐤ
VTA s/he saves s.o., s/he revives s.o., s/he restores s.o.; s/he makes s.o. live, s/he gives life to s.o., s/he keeps s.o. alive, s/he lets s.o. live; s/he makes a living for s.o., s/he sustains s.o.
pimācihisow ᐱᒫᒋᐦᐃᓱᐤ
VAI s/he makes a living for him/herself, s/he is able to support him/herself; s/he restores him/herself to life, s/he cures him/herself; s/he makes him/herself live
pimācihisowin ᐱᒫᒋᐦᐃᓱᐏᐣ
NI vocation, that from which one makes a living
pimācihiwēw ᐱᒫᒋᐦᐃᐍᐤ
VAI s/he gives people life
pimācihiwēwin ᐱᒫᒋᐦᐃᐍᐏᐣ
NI giving of life; way of life, way of making a living
pimācihow ᐱᒫᒋᐦᐅᐤ
VAI s/he travels; s/he lives, s/he makes him/herself live, s/he makes a living (from s.t.)
pimācihowin ᐱᒫᒋᐦᐅᐏᐣ
NI travel, journey; living, way of life, livelihood, earning a living; culture
pimācihtāw ᐱᒫᒋᐦᑖᐤ
VAIt s/he keeps s.t. alive (*e.g.* a plant)
pimāhtawātēw ᐱᒫᐦᑕᐚᑌᐤ
VTA s/he climbs along on s.o., s/he crosses over on s.o.
pimāhtawīw ᐱᒫᐦᑕᐑᐤ
VAI s/he climbs along [*also* pimāhtawēw]
pimāmow ᐱᒫᒧᐤ
VAI s/he flees along, s/he flees past
pimāpahtēw ᐱᒫᐸᐦᑌᐤ
VII it floats along as smoke, it is smoke blowing a long way
pimāpakow ᐱᒫᐸᑯᐤ
VAI s/he floats downstream with the current
pimāpamēw ᐱᒫᐸᒣᐤ
VTA s/he sees s.o. pass
pimāpēkamow ᐱᒫᐯᑲᒧᐤ
VII it is strung about clinging to things
pimāpotēw ᐱᒫᐳᑌᐤ
VII it flows along
pimāsiw ᐱᒫᓯᐤ
VAI s/he sails; s/he is blown about by the wind
pimāsiwin ᐱᒫᓯᐏᐣ
NI sailing (with sailing equipment)
pimāskohtin ᐱᒫᐢᑯᐦᑎᐣ
VII it lies on the ground (*e.g.* a log)
pimāskosin ᐱᒫᐢᑯᓯᐣ
VAI s/he lies along the road (*e.g.* a fallen tree or person)
pimāstamahcāw ᐱᒫᐢᑕᒪᐦᒑᐤ
VII it is a hill facing sideways
pimāstan ᐱᒫᐢᑕᐣ
VII it is blown about by the wind, it sails about in the wind
pimātakāskow ᐱᒫᑕᑳᐢᑯᐤ
VAI s/he walks on ice

pimātakāw ᐱᒫᑕᑳᐤ
VAI s/he swims along, s/he swims by; s/he wades by

pimātan ᐱᒫᑕᐣ
VII it has life, it lives

pimātisihtāw ᐱᒫᑎᓯᐦᑖᐤ
VAIt s/he keeps s.t. alive

pimātisiw ᐱᒫᑎᓯᐤ
VAI s/he lives, s/he is alive [*cf.* pōni-pimātisiw]

pimātisiwin ᐱᒫᑎᓯᐏᐣ
NI life

pimātisiwiniwiw ᐱᒫᑎᓯᐏᓂᐏᐤ
VII it is life

pimātisītotam ᐱᒫᑎᓰᑐᑕᒼ
VTI s/he lives his/her life; s/he lives his/her life by s.t.

pimēýihtam ᐱᒣᔨᐦᑕᒼ
VTI s/he keeps s.t. in mind

pimēýimēw ᐱᒣᔨᒣᐤ
VTA s/he keeps s.o. in mind

pimēýimow ᐱᒣᔨᒧᐤ
VAI s/he goes about thinking well of him/herself

pimi- ᐱᒥ
IPV along, in linear progression; while moving in linear progression [*through time and/or space*; *cf. rdpl*: papāmi]

pimi-cikāstēpaýiw
ᐱᒥ ᒋᑳᐢᑌᐸᔨᐤ
VAI s/he has his/her shadow pass by; s/he casts a shadow in passing

pimi-kwāskohtiw ᐱᒥ ᒁᐢᑯᐦᑎᐤ
VAI s/he jumps along

pimi-pakitinam ᐱᒥ ᐸᑭᑎᓇᒼ
VTI s/he drops s.t. (along the way)

pimi-tahkonam ᐱᒥ ᑕᐦᑯᓇᒼ
VTI s/he goes past carrying s.t.

pimi-tahkonēw ᐱᒥ ᑕᐦᑯᓀᐤ
VTA s/he goes past carrying s.o.

pimi-waýawīhtahēw
ᐱᒥ ᐘᔭᐑᐦᑕᐁᐤ
VTA s/he goes past taking s.o. outside

pimi-waýawīhtatāw
ᐱᒥ ᐘᔭᐑᐦᑕᑖᐤ
VAIt s/he goes past taking s.t. outside

pimic ᐱᒥᐨ
IPC crosswise, from side, at right angle; alongside

pimic-āyihk ᐱᒋᑳᔨᕽ
IPC beside, alongside [*loc*; *also* pimicāyihk]

pimicascēs ᐱᒥᒐᐢᒉᐢ
NI railway tie [*dim*; *also* pimitastēs]

pimicaskēkās ᐱᒥᒐᐢᑫᑳᐢ
INM Leask, SK [*place name*]

pimicastāw ᐱᒥᒐᐢᑖᐤ
VAIt s/he puts s.t. alongside

pimicastēw ᐱᒥᒐᐢᑌᐤ
VII it is set alongside

pimicāskwēyāsihk ᐱᒥᒑᐢᑵᔮᓯᕽ
INM Lloydminster, SK [*loc*]

pimici- ᐱᒥᒋ
IPV crosswise, from side, at right angle

pimicimēw ᐱᒥᒋᒣᐤ
VAI s/he canoes along, paddle along; it swims (*e.g.* animal, not human)

pimicipaýiw ᐱᒥᒋᐸᔨᐤ
VAI s/he goes, s/he rides sidewise, across

pimiciwan ᐱᒥᒋᐘᐣ
VII it flows, it flows along (as a stream)

pimiciýowēw ᐱᒥᒋᔪᐍᐤ
VII it blows from the side

pimihamowi-pīsim
ᐱᒥᐦᐊᒧᐏ ᐲᓯᒼ
NA October [*obv*: -wa; *cf.* pimihāwi-pīsim; *see also* kaskatino-pīsim]

pimihaýaýihkēw ᐱᒥᐦᐊᔭᔨᐦᑫᐤ
VAI s/he covers s.t. with dirt

pimihākan ᐱᒥᐦᐋᑲᐣ
NI airplane [*also* pimihýākan, pimiýākan; *wC*: pimithākan, *sC*: pimiñākan]

pimihākanis ᐱᒥᐦᐋᑲᓂᐢ
NI small plane [*dim*; *also* pimihýākanis, pimiýākanis]

pimihāmakan ᐱᒥᐦᐋᒪᑲᐣ
VII it flies

pimihāw ᐱᒥᐦᐋᐤ
VAI s/he flies, s/he flies along [*also* pimihýāw; *wC*: pimithāw, *sC*: pimiñāw]

pimihāwi-pīsim ᐱᒥᐦᐋᐏ ᐲᓯᒼ
NA Migrating Moon; October [*obv*: -wa]

pimihtin ᐱᒥᐦᑎᐣ
VII it goes past, it goes along (*e.g.* river, trail); it streams, it flows by; it lies extended

pimikāpawiw ᐱᒥᑳᐸᐏᐤ
VAI s/he stands by

piminawasosiw ᐱᒥᓇᐘᓱᓯᐤ
VAI s/he cooks a little [*dim*]

piminawasow ᐱᒥᓇᐘᓱᐤ
VAI s/he cooks, s/he does the cooking [*cf.* paminawasow; *also* pininawasow]

piminawasowikamik
ᐱᒥᓇᐘᓱᐏᑲᒥᐠ
NI cookhouse, kitchen [*pl*: -wa]

piminawatēw ᐱᒥᓇᐘᑌᐤ
VTA s/he cooks for s.o., s/he cooks a meal for s.o.

pimipahcāsiw ᐱᒥᐸᐦᒑᓯᐤ
VAI s/he trots, s/he runs a little [*dim*]

pimipahci- ᐱᒥᐸᐦᒋ
IPV running, on the run

pimipahēw ᐱᒥᐸᐦᐁᐤ
VTA s/he carries s.o. along

pimipahtāhēw ᐱᒥᐸᐦᑖᐦᐁᐤ
VTA s/he makes s.o. run

pimipahtāw ᐱᒥᐸᐦᑖᐤ
VAI s/he runs

pimipahtāwaskisin
ᐱᒥᐸᐦᑖᐘᐢᑭᓯᐣ
NI running shoe

pimipahtāwin ᐱᒥᐸᐦᑖᐏᐣ
NI foot race; election

pimipahtāwipaýisiw
ᐱᒥᐸᐦᑖᐏᐸᔨᓯᐤ
VAI s/he breaks into a little run along [*dim*]

pimipaýihēw ᐱᒥᐸᔨᐦᐁᐤ
VTA s/he gives s.o. a trial run (*e.g.* car); s/he starts s.o., s/he starts the motor

pimipaýihow ᐱᒥᐸᔨᐦᐅᐤ
VAI s/he moves along, s/he run along

pimipaýihtāw ᐱᒥᐸᔨᐦᑖᐤ
VAIt s/he runs s.t., s/he operates s.t., (*e.g.* machine, program); s/he keeps s.t. up, s/he exercises s.t.; s/he conducts s.t.

pimipaýin ᐱᒥᐸᔨᐣ
VII it works, it goes, it functions; it runs, it runs along [*cf.* pimipaýiw *VII*]

pimipaýiw ᐱᒥᐸᔨᐤ
VAI s/he rides along, s/he moves along; it is on (*e.g.* motor, electricity); it exists currently

pimipaýiw ᐱᒥᐸᔨᐤ
VII it moves along; it runs by, it goes on; it is on, it operates [*cf.* pimipaýin]

pimipaýīs ᐱᒥᐸᔩᐢ
NA runner (on a sled) [*dim*]

pimipicēs ᐱᒥᐱᒉᐢ
NA motorized vehicle [*dim*]

pimipiciw ᐱᒥᐱᒋᐤ
VAI s/he moves camp, s/he travels, s/he goes past in a wagon with his/her belongings, s/he is moving

pimisēwēw ᐱᒥᓭᐍᐤ
VAI s/he is heard passing by (with bells on)

pimisimēw ᐱᒥᓯᒣᐤ
VTA s/he lays s.o. extended, s/he lays s.o. on the ground or bed

pimisimow ᐱᒥᓯᒧᐤ
VAI s/he dances by, s/he dances along

pimisin ᐱᒥᓯᐣ
VAI s/he lies, s/he lies down, s/he lies extended

pimiskanaw ᐱᒥᐢᑲᓇᐤ
NI trail

pimiskanawēw ᐱᒥᐢᑲᓇᐍᐤ
VAI s/he makes tracks

pimiskākan ᐱᒥᐢᑳᑲᐣ
NI paddle, oar, fin

pimiskāw ᐱᒥᐢᑳᐤ
VAI s/he swims by; s/he paddles by in a canoe, boat; s/he paddles, s/he rows

pimiskāwin ᐱᒥᐢᑳᐏᐣ
NI rowing; swimming

pimitahpicikan ᐱᒥᑕᐦᐱᒋᑲᐣ
NI cross bar or pole in tent

pimitakām ᐱᒥᑕᑳᒼ
IPC across the place, along the shore (in water)

pimitamon ᐱᒥᑕᒧᐣ
NI crossroad

pimitamow ᐱᒥᑕᒧᐤ
VII it is a crosswise road, it lies crosswise

pimitapiw ᐱᒥᑕᐱᐤ
VAI s/he sits across

pimitastāw ᐱᒥᑕᐢᑖᐤ
VAIt s/he places s.t. crosswise, across the way

pimitastēw ᐱᒥᑕᐢᑌᐤ
VII it lies sideways; it is a bunk (on a wagon) [*cf.* kā-pimitastēki "bunks"]

pimitācimosiw ᐱᒥᑖᒋᒧᓯᐤ
VAI s/he crawls a bit [*dim*]

pimitācimoskiw ᐱᒥᑖᒋᒧᐢᑭᐤ
VAI s/he crawls constantly [*hab*]

pimitācimow ᐱᒥᑖᒋᒧᐤ
VAI s/he crawls about, s/he crawls around, s/he creeps

pimitācimowin ᐱᒥᑖᒋᒧᐏᐣ
NI crawling, creeping

pimitāpāsow ᐱᒥᑖᐹᓱᐤ
VAI s/he drives about, s/he drives by, s/he drives around

pimitāskosin ᐱᒥᑖᐢᑯᓯᐣ
VAI it lies across

pimitāskostākan ᐱᒥᑖᐢᑯᐢᑖᑲᐣ
NI pole to dry fish on

pimitāskostāw ᐱᒥᑖᐢᑯᐢᑖᐤ
VAIt s/he lays s.t. across, crosswise

pimitāskwahikan ᐱᒥᑖᐢᑲᐧᐦᐃᑲᐣ
NI cross

pimitēhcikociskāwēstawēw ᐱᒥᑌᐦᒋᑯᒋᐢᑳᐍᐢᑕᐍᐤ
VTA s/he races along with s.o. on horseback

pimitēhcikociskāwēw ᐱᒥᑌᐦᒋᑯᒋᐢᑳᐍᐤ
VAI s/he races along on horseback

pimitēhcipayīstawēw ᐱᒥᑌᐦᒋᐸᔩᐢᑕᐍᐤ
VTA s/he rides along with s.o.

pimitēhtapiw ᐱᒥᑌᐦᑕᐱᐤ
VAI s/he goes past on horseback

pimitēw ᐱᒥᑌᐤ
NI broth [*archaic*]

pimitinam ᐱᒥᑎᓇᒼ
VTI s/he holds s.t. crosswise

pimitinēw ᐱᒥᑎᓀᐤ
VTA s/he holds s.o. crosswise

pimitisaham ᐱᒥᑎᓴᐦᐊᒼ
VTI s/he follows s.t.; s/he sends s.t.

pimitisahikēw ᐱᒥᑎᓴᐦᐃᑫᐤ
VAI s/he follows, s/he follows people, s/he tags along, s/he is a follower

pimitisahwēw ᐱᒥᑎᓴᐦᐍᐤ
VTA s/he follows behind s.o., s/he drives s.o. along; s/he sends s.o.

pimitohtēw ᐱᒥᑐᐦᑌᐤ
VAI s/he walks sidewise, across

pimitowatān ᐱᒥᑐᐘᑖᐣ
NA beam, housebeam

pimiwihēw ᐱᒥᐏᐦᐁᐤ
VTA s/he carries s.o. along; s/he takes s.o. along (*e.g.* clock, watch) [*also* pimowihēw]

pimiwitāw ᐱᒥᐏᑖᐤ
VAIt s/he carries s.t. along [*also* pimowitāw]

pimiy ᐱᒥᐩ
NI grease (rendered); lard; shortening; oil; butter; fat; crude petroleum; [*pl*:] variety of fats, lards, tallow, mazola [*sg generally*; *also male personal name*]

pimīcihcēw ᐱᒦᒋᐦᒉᐤ
VAI s/he has oily hands

pimīhēw ᐱᒦᐦᐁᐤ
VTA s/he makes s.o. oily

pimīhkawēw ᐱᒦᐦᑲᐍᐤ
VTA s/he renders fat for s.o., s/he makes grease for s.o.

pimīhkākēw ᐱᒦᐦᑳᑫᐤ
VAI s/he renders grease from s.t.

pimīhkān ᐱᒦᐦᑳᐣ
NI pemmican [*also* pimihkān]

pimīhkāniwas ᐱᒦᐦᑳᓂᐘᐢ
NI pemmican bag [*sg only*; *cf. pl*: pimihkāniwata]

pimīhkāniwat ᐱᒦᐦᑳᓂᐘᐟ
NI pemmican bag [*for some, pl only*: pimīhkāniwata; *cf. sg*: pimihkāniwas]

pimīhkēw ᐱᒦᐦᑫᐤ
VAI s/he makes pemmican

pimīs ᐱᒦᐢ
NI grease (rendered); small amount of oil, lard, grease [*dim*]

pimīwakan ᐱᒦᐘᑲᐣ
VII it smells greasy, oily

pimīwan ᐱᒦᐘᐣ
VII it contains oil; it is greasy

pimīwastēw ᐱᒦᐘᐢᑌᐤ
VII it forms fat

pimīwāhtik ᐱᒦᐚᐦᑎᐠ
NA olive tree [*pl*: -wak]

pimīwihtin ᐱᒦᐏᐦᑎᐣ
VII it settles and forms fat

pimocikan ᐱᒧᒋᑲᐣ
NA slingshot and stone

pimocikanis ᐱᒧᒋᑲᓂᐢ
NA little arrow [*dim*]

pimocikēw ᐱᒧᒋᑫᐤ
VAI s/he shoots arrows, s/he shoots with a slingshot

pimohcēsiw ᐱᒧᐦᒉᓯᐤ
VAI s/he begins to walk; s/he walks a little (as a child) [*dim*]

pimohtahēw ᐱᒧᐦᑕᐦᐁᐤ
VTA s/he takes s.o. along; s/he walks with s.o., s/he makes s.o. walk

pimohtatāw ᐱᒧᐦᑕᑖᐤ
VAIt s/he carries s.t., s/he takes s.t. along, s/he travels with s.t., s/he has s.t. along; s/he transports s.t.

pimohtākēwin ᐱᒧᐦᑖᑫᐏᐣ
NI walker (for babies, elderly, disabled, etc.)

pimohtēhon ᐱᒧᐦᑌᐦᐅᐣ
NI passage, travel through life

pimohtēhow ᐱᒧᐦᑌᐦᐅᐤ
VAI s/he travels

pimohtēmakan ᐱᒧᐦᑌᒪᑲᐣ
VII it goes on its own, it goes on, it functions

pimohtēmakisiw ᐱᒧᐦᑌᒪᑭᓯᐤ
VAI it goes, it is in use, it functions

pimohtēskanaw ᐱᒧᐦᑌᐢᑲᓇᐤ
NI walking path, foot path, trail

pimohtēskanawan ᐱᒧᐦᑌᐢᑲᓇᐘᐣ
VII it is a foot path or trail

pimohtēskanāhk ᐱᒧᐦᑌᐢᑲᓈᕽ
IPC on the travelled road [*loc*]

pimohtēw ᐱᒧᐦᑌᐤ
VAI s/he walks, s/he walks along; s/he goes along

pimohtēwin ᐱᒧᐦᑌᐏᐣ
NI walk, stroll; sidewalk

pimohwatān ᐱᒧᐦᐘᑖᐣ
NI packsack, backpack

pimosinātam ᐱᒧᓯᓈᑕᒼ
VTI s/he throws a stone (or object) at s.t.

pimosinātēw ᐱᒧᓯᓈᑌᐤ
VTA s/he throws a stone (or object) at s.o.

pimosinēw ᐱᒧᓯᓀᐤ
VAI s/he throws something (as a rock into the river) [*cf.* pimwasinēw]

pimotahkwēhēw ᐱᒧᑕᐦᑫᐧᐦᐁᐤ
VTA s/he makes s.o. shoot with bow and arrow

pimotahkwēw ᐱᒧᑕᐦᑫᐧᐤ
VAI s/he shoots with bow and arrow

pimotam ᐱᒧᑕᒼ
VTI s/he shoots an arrow at

s.t.; s/he shoots s.t. with an arrow

pimotākan ᐱᒧᑖᑲᐣ
NI bow and arrow

pimotātowin ᐱᒧᑖᑐᐎᐣ
NI Indian game of archery

pimotēw ᐱᒧᑌᐤ
VTA s/he shoots an arrow at s.o.

pimowatēw ᐱᒧᐊᐧᑌᐤ
VAI s/he carries a load

pimōsēwēw ᐱᒨᓭᐍᐤ
VAI s/he bears children regularly

pimwasinēw ᐱᒪᐧᓯᓀᐤ
VAI s/he throws something, s/he heaves something [*cf.* pimosinēw]

pimwēw ᐱ�districts
VTA s/he shoots s.o. with arrow

pinahēsēw ᐱᓇᐦᐁᓭᐤ
VAI s/he scales fish

pinahihkwān ᐱᓇᐦᐃᐦᑳᐧᐣ
NI fine comb; comb for delousing

pinahkwaýipicikan ᐱᓇᐦᑲᐧᔦᐱᒋᑲᐣ
NI harrow

pinahwēw ᐱᓇᐦᐍᐤ
VTA s/he scales s.o. (*i.e.* fish) [*sC*; *cf.* piyahwēw]

pinakocin ᐱᓇᑯᒋᐣ
VAI s/he falls down from aloft

pinasiwētisahwēw ᐱᓇᓯᐍᑎᓴᐦᐍᐤ
VTA s/he sends s.o. down, s/he chases s.o. down, s/he drives s.o. downward

pinasiwēw ᐱᓇᓯᐍᐤ
VAI s/he goes downward

pinawēwin ᐱᓇᐍᐎᐣ
NI dropped hair; animals shedding in spring

pināskowi-pīsim ᐱᓈᐢᑯᐎ ᐲᓯᒼ
NA Leaf-Falling Moon, October [*obv*: -wa; *see also* pimihāwi-pīsim]

pināwēw ᐱᓈᐍᐤ
VAI s/he lays eggs [*also* pinawēw]

pināwēwi-pīsim ᐱᓈᐍᐎ ᐲᓯᒼ
NA Egg-Laying Moon; June [*obv*: -wa]

pinikanēw ᐱᓂᑲᓀᐤ
VAI s/he is listless, s/he feels weak

pinipakāw ᐱᓂᐸᑳᐤ
VII it is leaf-fall

pinipaýihow ᐱᓂᐸᔨᐦᐅᐤ
VAI s/he throws him/herself down

pinipaýiw ᐱᓂᐸᔨᐤ
VAI s/he goes downward, s/he falls

pinipocikan ᐱᓂᐳᒋᑲᐣ
NI mill; [*pl*:] sawdust; refuse from a mill

pinipocikēw ᐱᓂᐳᒋᑫᐤ
VAI s/he grinds, s/he is grinding

pinipohēw ᐱᓂᐳᐦᐁᐤ
VTA s/he grinds s.o. (*e.g.* wheat)

pinipotāw ᐱᓂᐳᑖᐤ
VAIt s/he grinds s.t. (*e.g.* meat)

pipik ᐱᐱᐠ
NA flea [*pl*: -wak]

pipikos ᐱᐱᑯᐢ
NA small flea

pipikwan ᐱᐱᑲᐧᐣ
NI eagle bone whistle, flute

pipikwanāhtik ᐱᐱᑲᐧᓈᐦᑎᐠ
NA whistle-tree [*pl*: -wak; *name of two kinds of tree*]

pipikwatēhtēw ᐱᐱᑲᐧᑌᐦᑌᐤ
NA toad

pipohki ᐱᐳᐦᑭ
IPC next winter; when it's winter, if it's winter

pipon ᐱᐳᐣ
NI year, winter

pipon ᐱᐳᐣ
VII it is winter; is one year

pipon-ayi ᐱᐳᓇᔨ
NI article of winter clothing

pipon-ayis ᐱᐳᓇᔨᐢ
NA winter bird

pipon-āyis ᐱᐳᓈᔨᐢ
NA chicken hawk

piponasākay ᐱᐳᓇᓵᑲᐩ
NI winter jacket, winter coat

piponasiw ᐱᐳᓇᓯᐤ
NA winter hawk

piponaskisin ᐱᐳᓇᐢᑭᓯᐣ
NI winter boot

piponastotin ᐱᐳᓇᐢᑐᑎᐣ
NI winter hat

piponāsiw ᐱᐳᓈᓯᐤ
NA chicken hawk

piponāskos ᐱᐳᓈᐢᑯᐢ
NA yearling horse, colt

piponāspinēwin ᐱᐳᓈᐢᐱᓀᐎᐣ
NI polio [*proposed term*]

piponi-mēskanaw ᐱᐳᓂ ᒣᐢᑲᓇᐤ
NI winter road

piponihēwiw ᐱᐳᓂᐦᐁᐏᐤ
VAI s/he stays in winter

piponisiw ᐱᐳᓂᓯᐤ
VAI s/he camps for the winter

piponohk ᐱᐳᓄᕽ
IPC last winter, in the winter

piponwēw ᐱᐳᓊᐤ
VAI s/he is one winter old; s/he is one year old [*also* piponēw]

pisci- ᐱᐢᒋ
IPV accidentally, mistakenly, erroneously

pisci-otinam ᐱᐢᒋ ᐅᑎᓇᒼ
VTI s/he takes s.t. by accident

pisci-otinēw ᐱᐢᒋ ᐅᑎᓀᐤ
VTA s/he takes s.o. by accident

pisci-pakamiskawēw ᐱᐢᒋ ᐸᑲᒥᐢᑲᐍᐤ
VTA s/he bumps s.o. accidentally

pisci-sīkinam ᐱᐢᒋ ᓰᑭᓇᒼ
VTI s/he spills s.t. accidentally

pisci-tōtam ᐱᐢᒋ ᑑᑕᒼ
VTI s/he does s.t. by accident

pisci-tōtawēw ᐱᐢᒋ ᑑᑕᐍᐤ
VTA s/he does so to s.o. by accident

piscikahosow ᐱᐢᒋᑲᐦᐅᓱᐤ
VAI s/he chops him/herself by accident

piscipitam ᐱᐢᒋᐱᑕᒼ
VTI s/he accidentally drags s.t. along

piscipitēw ᐱᐢᒋᐱᑌᐤ
VTA s/he accidentally drags s.o. along

piscipohēw ᐱᐢᒋᐳᐦᐁᐤ
VTA s/he poisons s.o. [*cf.* pihcipohēw]

piscipohitowak ᐱᐢᒋᐳᐦᐃᑐᐊᐧᐠ
VAI they poison one another

piscipohtāw ᐱᐢᒋᐳᐦᑖᐤ
VAIt s/he poisons s.t.

piscipow ᐱᐢᒋᐳᐤ
VAI s/he is poisoned [*cf.* pihcipow]

piscipowin ᐱᐢᒋᐳᐎᐣ
NI poison [*cf.* pihcipowin]

piscipōskākow ᐱᐢᒋᐴᐢᑳᑯᐤ
VTA it poisons him/her [*inanimate actor form of VTA* piscipōskaw-]

pisik ᐱᓯᐠ
IPC always; continually [*cf.* pisisik]

pisikwācis ᐱᓯᑳᐧᒋᐢ
NA one who lives as a prostitute

pisikwātēýihtam ᐱᓯᑳᐧᑌᔨᐦᑕᒼ
VTI s/he thinks immorally

pisikwātēýimēw ᐱᓯᑳᐧᑌᔨᒣᐤ
VTA s/he thinks of s.o. as an adulterer/adulteress

pisikwātināpēw ᐱᓯᑳᐧᑎᓈᐯᐤ
NA pimp, male prostitute [*proposed term*]

pisikwātisiw ᐱᓯᑳᐧᑎᓯᐤ
VAI he is bold with women; she is bold with men; s/he commits adultery

pisikwātisiwin ᐱᓯᑳᐧᑎᓯᐎᐣ
NI adultery; prostitution

pisikwātiskwēw ᐱᓯᑳᐧᑎᐢᑵᐤ
NA whore, prostitute

pisin ᐱᓯᐣ
VAI s/he gets something in his/her eye

pisinē ᐱᓯᓀ
IPC as soon as

pisisik ᐱᓯᓯᐠ
IPC always, all the time, constantly, every time,

routinely; mere; nothing else
[*cf.* pisik]

pisisikwastēw ᐱᕆᓯᒃᐊᐢᑌᐤ
VII it stands empty

pisiskāpahtam ᐱᓯᐢᑳᐸᐦᑕᒼ
VTI s/he notices s.t., s/he
observes s.t.

pisiskāpamēw ᐱᓯᐢᑳᐸᒣᐤ
VTA s/he notices s.o., s/he
observes s.o.

pisiskēs ᐱᓯᐢᑫᐢ
NA raccoon

pisiskēyihcikēw ᐱᓯᐢᑫᔨᐦᒋᑫᐤ
VAI s/he regards things, s/he
looks after things

pisiskēyihtam ᐱᓯᐢᑫᔨᐦᑕᒼ
VTI s/he pays attention to
s.t., s/he cares for s.t., s/he
watches over s.t.

pisiskēyihtamawēw
ᐱᓯᐢᑫᔨᐦᑕᒪᐍᐤ
VTA s/he cares for (it/him)
for s.o.; s/he looks after
(it/him) for s.o.

pisiskēyihtamowin
ᐱᓯᐢᑫᔨᐦᑕᒧᐃᐣ
NI care; attention

pisiskēyimēw ᐱᓯᐢᑫᔨᒣᐤ
VTA s/he pays attention to
s.o., s/he takes care of s.o.;
s/he deals with s.o. [*rdpl:*
pā-pisiskēyimēw]

pisiskisīs ᐱᓯᐢᑭᓰᐢ
NA animal, small animal
(including birds) [*dim*]

pisiskiw ᐱᓯᐢᑭᐤ
NA animal, beast; domestic
animal

pisiskīwiw ᐱᓯᐢᑮᐃᐤ
VAI it is an animal [*also*
pisiskēwiw]

pisistōsis ᐱᓯᐢᑰᓯᐢ
NI small whirlwind [*cf.*
pistōs]

pisistōsiwan ᐱᓯᐢᑰᓯᐊᐣ
VII it is a small whirlwind

pisiw ᐱᓯᐤ
NA lynx; bobcat

pisiw-tāpakwān ᐱᓯᐤ ᒃᐸᑲᐣ
NI lynx snare

pisiwayān ᐱᓯᐊᔭᐣ
NA lynx skin, lynx pelt

pisiwāhtik ᐱᓯᐊᐦᑎᐠ
NI tree selected to set a trap
for lynx [*pl:* -wa]

piskihcastāw ᐱᐢᑭᐦᒐᐢᑖᐤ
VAIt s/he puts s.t. separately
[*cf.* piskihtastāw]

piskihcāsin ᐱᐢᑭᐦᒑᓯᐣ
VII it is a separate
compartment [*dim*]

piskihcāw ᐱᐢᑭᐦᒑᐤ
VII it is partitioned off

piskihcāyāw ᐱᐢᑭᐦᒑᔮᐤ
VII it is separate; it is by
itself

piskihci ᐱᐢᑭᐦᒋ
IPC separate; by itself

piskihci-kipaham
ᐱᐢᑭᐦᒋ ᑭᐸᐦᐊᒼ
VTI s/he partitions s.t.

piskihcikamik ᐱᐢᑭᐦᒋᑲᒥᐠ
NI separate room [*pl:* -wa]

piskihcikamikohkēw
ᐱᐢᑭᐦᒋᑲᒥᑯᐦᑫᐤ
VAI s/he makes a separate
room

piskihcikwātam ᐱᐢᑭᐦᒋᒀᑕᒼ
VTI s/he sews an extension
on s.t. (*e.g.* canvas)

piskihcikwātēw ᐱᐢᑭᐦᒋᒀᑌᐤ
VTA s/he sews an extension
on s.o. (*e.g.* pants)

piskihcisin ᐱᐢᑭᐦᒋᓯᐣ
VAI s/he lies by him/herself

piskihtahēw ᐱᐢᑭᐦᑕᐦᐁᐤ
VTA s/he puts s.o. separately

piskihtasinahikēwin
ᐱᐢᑭᐦᑕᓯᓇᐦᐃᑫᐃᐣ
NI paragraph

piskihtastāw ᐱᐢᑭᐦᑕᐢᑖᐤ
VAIt s/he puts s.t. separately
[*cf.* piskihcastāw]

piskihtinam ᐱᐢᑭᐦᑎᓇᒼ
VTI s/he holds s.t. separately

piskihtinēw ᐱᐢᑭᐦᑎᓀᐤ
VTA s/he holds s.o.
separately

piskihtisahwēw ᐱᐢᑭᐦᑎᓴᐦᐍᐤ
VTA s/he drives s.o. away
separately (as one cow from
the herd); s/he drives s.o.
apart

piskihtisiw ᐱᐢᑭᐦᑎᓯᐤ
VAI it is apart (as an orange
broken into sections)

piskokanān ᐱᐢᑯᑲᓈᐣ
NI wrist bone, knuckle bone,
joint

piskosiw ᐱᐢᑯᓯᐤ
VAI s/he has a lump, s/he
has a growth

piskwahcāw ᐱᐢᑲᐧᐦᒑᐤ
VII it is a knoll

piskwahpitāwin ᐱᐢᑲᐧᐦᐱᑖᐃᐣ
NI forelock, head dress

piskwahpitwāw ᐱᐢᑲᐧᐦᐱᑣᐤ
VAI s/he has his/her hair tied
in a knot

piskwatāpiskataham
ᐱᐢᑲᐧᑖᐱᐢᑲᑕᐦᐊᒼ
VTI s/he shapes a metal
knob on s.t.

piskwatāpiskatahwēw
ᐱᐢᑲᐧᑖᐱᐢᑲᑕᐦᐍᐤ
VTA s/he shapes a metal
knob on s.o.

piskwatināw ᐱᐢᑲᐧᑎᓈᐤ
VII it is a mound

piskwāw ᐱᐢᑲᐧᐤ
VII it is lumpy, it has a lump

piskwāwikanēw ᐱᐢᑲᐧᐃᑲᓀᐤ
VAI it has a lumpy back

piskwāwikanēwi-pisiskiw
ᐱᐢᑲᐧᐃᑲᓀᐃ ᐱᓯᐢᑭᐤ
NA camel

pisoham ᐱᓱᐦᐊᒼ
VTI s/he stumbles over s.t.

pisomēw ᐱᓱᒣᐤ
VTA s/he hurts s.o.'s feelings
by speech

pisosimēw ᐱᓱᓯᒣᐤ
VTA s/he makes s.o. stumble

pisosin ᐱᓱᓯᐣ
VAI s/he tumbles, s/he
stumbles

pisositēsin ᐱᓱᓯᑌᓯᐣ
VAI s/he stumbles over
his/her own feet

pisoskam ᐱᓱᐢᑲᒼ
VTI s/he stumbles over s.t.

pisoskawēw ᐱᓱᐢᑲᐍᐤ
VTA s/he hits against s.o.
with foot or body

pispāskwatowi-pakamākan
ᐱᐢᐸᐢᑲᐧᑐᐃ ᐸᑲᒪᑲᐣ
NI spiked club

pistaham ᐱᐢᑕᐦᐊᒼ
VTI s/he hits s.t. accidentally
(with an object)

pistahosow ᐱᐢᑕᐦᐅᓱᐤ
VAI s/he shoots or hits
him/herself by mistake

pistahowēw ᐱᐢᑕᐦᐅᐍᐤ
VAI s/he shoots people by
accident

pistahtam ᐱᐢᑕᐦᑕᒼ
VTI s/he bites s.t. by mistake

pistahwēw ᐱᐢᑕᐦᐍᐤ
VTA s/he shoots or knocks
s.o. by mistake, s/he hits s.o.
accidentally (with an object)

pistamēw ᐱᐢᑕᒣᐤ
VTA s/he bites s.o. by
mistake

pistinam ᐱᐢᑎᓇᒼ
VTI s/he takes s.t.
accidentally, by mistake

pistinēw ᐱᐢᑎᓀᐤ
VTA s/he takes s.o.
accidentally, by mistake

pistisam ᐱᐢᑎᓴᒼ
VTI s/he cuts s.t.
accidentally

pistiskam ᐱᐢᑎᐢᑲᒼ
VTI s/he steps on s.t.
accidentally, s/he bumps or
knocks into s.t. by mistake

pistiskawēw ᐱᐢᑎᐢᑲᐍᐤ
VTA s/he steps on s.o.
accidentally, s/he bumps or
knocks into s.o. by mistake

pistiskākēw ᐱᐢᑎᐢᑳᑫᐤ
VAI s/he steps on people by
accident

pistisosow ᐱᐢᑎᓱᓱᐤ
VAI s/he cuts him/herself
accidentally

pistiswēw ᐱᐢᑎᓴᐧᐤ
VTA s/he cuts s.o.
accidentally

pistōs ᐱᐢᑰᐢ
NI tornado; whirlwind [*cf.*
pisistōsis]

pistōsiw ᐱᐢᑑᓯᐤ
NI tornado; whirlwind [*also* pisistōsiw]

piswaham ᐱᔃᐦᐊᒼ
VTI s/he gets snagged on s.t.

piswahcahikēw ᐱᔃᐦᒐᐦᐃᑫᐤ
VAI s/he stumbles, s/he stumbles on things

pita ᐱᑕ
IPC first, for a while; before doing something else; wait, just a minute

pitamā ᐱᑕᒫ
IPC for now, just a while; in the meantime, first, prior to doing anything else [*cf.* pātimā]

pitanē ᐱᑕᓀ
IPC would that; I wish, I hope [*with conjunct mode*; *see also* tānika]

pitihkohtin ᐱᑎᐦᑯᐦᑎᐣ
VII it falls with a thud

pitihkopahtāw ᐱᑎᐦᑯᐸᐦᑖᐤ
VAI s/he runs thudding

pitihkopaýiw ᐱᑎᐦᑯᐸᔨᐤ
VAI s/he goes thudding

pitihkosin ᐱᑎᐦᑯᓯᐣ
VAI s/he makes a noise falling, s/he falls with a thud

pitihkow ᐱᑎᐦᑯᐤ
VAI s/he makes a noise

pitihkwaskamikisiw ᐱᑎᐦᑿᐢᑲᒥᑭᓯᐤ
VAI s/he makes crashing noises (*e.g.* breaking dishes)

pitihkwēkāstan ᐱᑎᐦᑵᑳᐢᑕᐣ
VII it flaps noisily in the wind

pitihkwēw ᐱᑎᐦᑵᐤ
VII it thuds, it makes a noise

pitikohkwēw ᐱᑎᑯᐦᑵᐤ
VAI s/he has a round face or snout

pitikokiw ᐱᑎᑯᑭᐤ
VAI s/he is growing round (*e.g.* chubby child); s/he is humped up

pitikomin ᐱᑎᑯᒥᐣ
NA dried prune

pitikonam ᐱᑎᑯᓇᒼ
VTI s/he shapes s.t., s/he forms s.t. into patties; s/he folds s.t. small; s/he holds s.t. in a bundle

pitikonēw ᐱᑎᑯᓀᐤ
VTA s/he shapes s.o., s/he forms s.o. into patties; s/he folds s.o. small; s/he holds s.o. in a bundle

pitikonikan ᐱᑎᑯᓂᑲᐣ
NI round raft; small float for clothes

pitikonikanāpoy ᐱᑎᑯᓂᑲᓈᐳᕀ
NI meatball soup

pitikonikātēw ᐱᑎᑯᓂᑳᑌᐤ
VII it is shaped, it is formed into patties

pitikopaýihow ᐱᑎᑯᐸᔨᐦᐅᐤ
VAI s/he doubles him/herself up, s/he crouches

pitikosiw ᐱᑎᑯᓯᐤ
VAI s/he is short and fat

pitikosin ᐱᑎᑯᓯᐣ
VAI s/he lies rolled up, s/he lies doubled up

pitikow ᐱᑎᑯᐤ
VAI s/he doubles him/herself up

pitikwahpitam ᐱᑎᑿᐦᐱᑕᒼ
VTI s/he ties s.t. in a bundle

pitikwahpitēw ᐱᑎᑿᐦᐱᑌᐤ
VTA s/he ties s.o. in a bundle

pitikwapiw ᐱᑎᑿᐱᐤ
VAI s/he sits hunched

pitikwaýasit ᐱᑎᑿᔭᓯᐟ
NA club foot

pitikwāw ᐱᑎᒀᐤ
VII it is all in a lump

pitikwēkinam ᐱᑎᑵᑭᓇᒼ
VTI s/he rolls s.t. small as cloth

pitikwēkinēw ᐱᑎᑵᑭᓀᐤ
VTA s/he rolls s.o. small as cloth

piýahwēw ᐱᔭᐦᐍᐤ
VTA s/he scrapes the scales from s.o.; s/he scales s.o. (*e.g.* fish) [*wC*: pihahwēw; *cf.* piñahwēw]

piýēsiw ᐱᔦᓯᐤ
NA thunderbird; thunder

piýēsiw-k-ōtēskanit ᐱᔦᓯᐤ ᑰᑌᐢᑲᓂᐟ
INM horned thunderer [*male personal name*]

piýēsiwa-k-ōyōhtāwīt ᐱᔦᓯᐘ ᑰᔫᐦᑖᐑᐟ
NA "One who has a thunderbird as father" [*male personal name*; *cf.* THUNDERCHILD]

piýēsiwacistwan ᐱᔦᓯᐘᒋᐢᑝᐣ
NI thunderer's nest

piýēsiwiw ᐱᔦᓯᐏᐤ
VII it is a thunderstorm

piýēsīs ᐱᔦᓰᐢ
NA bird, small bird [*wC*: pithīsis, *sC*: piñēsis]

piýēsīsikamik ᐱᔦᓰᓯᑲᒥᐠ
NI bird house, bird cage [*pl*: -wa]

piýēsīsis ᐱᔦᓰᓯᐢ
NA baby bird; hatchling [*dim*]

piýēsīskāw ᐱᔦᓰᐢᑳᐤ
VII there are an abundance of birds; birds are numerous

piýis ᐱᔨᐢ
IPC eventually, finally, in the end, at last; until [*cf.* piýisk]

piýisk ᐱᔨᐢᐠ
IPC eventually, finally, at last; until [*cf.* piýis; *wC*: pīthisk]

ᐲ

pīcicipaýiw ᐲᒋᒋᐸᔨᐤ
VAI s/he bursts forth

pīcicipitam ᐲᒋᒋᐱᑕᒼ
VTI s/he pulls s.t. forth

pīciciwikamik ᐲᒋᒋᐏᑲᒥᐠ
NI lodge for pow-wow [*pl*: -wa]

pīcicīw ᐲᒋᒌᐤ
VAI s/he Round Dances, s/he dances a Round Dance; s/he dances in the pow-wow

pīcicīwin ᐲᒋᒌᐏᐣ
NI Round Dance

pīcicīwinihkēw ᐲᒋᒌᐏᓂᐦᑫᐤ
VAI s/he organizes or holds a Round Dance

pīcitisin ᐲᒋᑎᓯᐣ
VAI s/he lies facing speaker

pīhawawāskwēyāw ᐲᐦᐊᐘᐚᐢᑵᔮᐤ
VII it is open land

pīhc-āyihk ᐲᐦᒑᔨᕽ
IPC inside, indoors [*also* pīhcāyihk]

pīhcaciwānis ᐲᐦᒐᒋᐚᓂᐢ
NA small quiver [*dim*]

pīhcawēsākānis ᐲᐦᒐᐍᓵᑳᓂᐢ
NI small petticoat [*dim*]

pīhcāsin ᐲᐦᒑᓯᐣ
VII it is quite a ways [*dim*]

pīhcāsowinis ᐲᐦᒑᓱᐏᓂᐢ
NI small shell, charge for a gun [*dim*]

pīhcāw ᐲᐦᒑᐤ
IPC for a long distance

pīhcāw ᐲᐦᒑᐤ
VII it extends far, it is far off, it is a long way

pīhci- ᐲᐦᒋ
IPV inside, in, within

pīhci-wēpinam ᐲᐦᒋ ᐍᐱᓇᒼ
VTI s/he throws s.t. into (something)

pīhci-wēpinēw ᐲᐦᒋ ᐍᐱᓀᐤ
VTA s/he throws s.o. into (something)

pīhcihāw ᐲᐦᒋᐦᐋᐤ
VAI s/he flies inside

pīhcihkomān ᐲᐦᒋᐦᑯᒫᐣ
NI knife case

pīhcihtin ᐲᐦᒋᐦᑎᐣ
VII it fits inside

pīhcikwanān ᐲᐦᒋᑿᓈᐣ
NI feather case, sacred bundle

pīhcipacikan ᐲᐦᒋᐸᒋᑲᐣ
NI funnel

pīhcipaýiw ᐲᐦᒋᐸᔨᐤ
VAI s/he falls into (something)

pīhcipihkwān ᐲᐦᒋᐱᐦᒀᐣ
NA shell; powder horn

pīhciýowēw ᐲᐦᒋᔪᐍᐤ
VII it blows in, it is a wind blowing in

pīhconēs ᐲᐦᒍᓀᐢ
NI blouse; vest
pīhcwākanis ᐲᐦᒞᑲᓂᐢ
NA cigarette [*dim*]
pīhcwāsiw ᐲᐦᒞᓯᐤ
VAI s/he smokes a little [*dim*]
pīhkinam ᐲᐦᑭᓇᒼ
VTI s/he bends s.t. over; s/he shapes s.t.
pīhkinēw ᐲᐦᑭᓀᐤ
VTA s/he bends s.o. over
pīhkipaýiw ᐲᐦᑭᐸᔨᐤ
VII it bends at an angle
pīhkipitonēw ᐲᐦᑭᐱᑐᓀᐤ
VAI s/he has a bent arm
pīhkipitonēýiw ᐲᐦᑭᐱᑐᓀᔨᐤ
VAI s/he bends his/her arm
pīhkohtāw ᐲᐦᑯᐦᑖᐤ
VAIt s/he earns s.t. (by working)
pīhkosin ᐲᐦᑯᓯᐣ
VAI s/he cuts him/herself on ice in falling
pīhkwāsin ᐲᐦᒁᓯᐣ
VII it is quite sharp [*dim*]
pīhkwātin ᐲᐦᒁᑎᐣ
VII it is sharp
pīhpīkisīs ᐲᐦᐲᑭᓰᐢ
NA sparrow hawk; Peepeekisis Reserve [*Cree chief and SK reserve name*]
pīhtamohtāw ᐲᐦᑕᒧᐦᑖᐤ
VAIt s/he fits s.t. inside another part
pīhtasinān ᐲᐦᑕᓯᓈᐣ
NI ammunition bag
pīhtasinānēyāpiy ᐲᐦᑕᓯᓈᓀᔮᐱᕀ
NI ammunition belt, gun belt
pīhtaskatēwān ᐲᐦᑕᐢᑲᑌᐚᐣ
NI powder horn
pīhtaskinēw ᐲᐦᑕᐢᑭᓀᐤ
VAI s/he is inside (a container or box)
pīhtatiwān ᐲᐦᑕᑎᐚᐣ
NA quiver, case for arrows
pīhtatiwānihkawēw ᐲᐦᑕᑎᐚᓂᐦᑲᐍᐤ
VTA s/he makes a quiver for s.o.
pīhtatiwānihkēw ᐲᐦᑕᑎᐚᓂᐦᑫᐤ
VAI s/he makes a quiver
pīhtaw ᐲᐦᑕᐤ
IPC besides, in the actual outcome; in the end, come to find out, as it appeared; exclamation expressing disappointment
pīhtawē- ᐲᐦᑕᐌ
IPV under; double
pīhtawē-papakiwayān ᐲᐦᑕᐌ ᐸᐸᑭᐘᔮᐣ
NI under shirt
pīhtawēkin ᐲᐦᑕᐌᑭᐣ
NI lining material; insulation
pīhtawēkinam ᐲᐦᑕᐌᑭᓇᒼ
VTI s/he lines s.t. (*i.e.* lining of a robe, jacket); s/he insulates s.t. (*e.g.* building)
pīhtawēkinēw ᐲᐦᑕᐌᑭᓀᐤ
VTA s/he lines s.o. (*e.g.* mitts, pants)
pīhtawēkwācikan ᐲᐦᑕᐌᒀᒋᑲᐣ
NI inside pocket
pīhtawēkwātam ᐲᐦᑕᐌᒀᑕᒼ
VTI s/he sews s.t. as lining into a garment; s/he sews s.t. in between covers, s/he sews covers on s.t.
pīhtawēkwātēw ᐲᐦᑕᐌᒀᑌᐤ
VTA s/he sews s.o. as lining into a garment; s/he sews s.o. in between covers, s/he sews covers on s.o.
pīhtawēnikan ᐲᐦᑕᐌᓂᑲᐣ
NI inner lining
pīhtawēpisam ᐲᐦᑕᐌᐱᓴᒼ
VTI s/he cuts a piece from the inside of s.t.
pīhtawēsākān ᐲᐦᑕᐌᓵᑳᐣ
NI slip, undergarment, petticoat
pīhtawētās ᐲᐦᑕᐌᑖᐢ
NA undershorts
pīhtawētāsān ᐲᐦᑕᐌᑖᓵᐣ
NA long-johns, long underwear; underwear, undershorts, drawers
pīhtawēwayiwinisa ᐲᐦᑕᐌᐘᔨᐏᓂᓴ
NI underwear, underclothes [*pl generally*]
pīhtawiskwāhtēm ᐲᐦᑕᐏᐢᒁᐦᑌᒼ
NI porch
pīhtākonēw ᐲᐦᑖᑯᓀᐤ
VAI s/he gets snow in his/her shoes; s/he loads snow
pīhtāpāwahēw ᐲᐦᑖᐹᐘᐦᐁᐤ
VTA s/he gives s.o. an enema
pīhtāpāwatāw ᐲᐦᑖᐹᐘᑖᐤ
VAIt s/he puts liquid into s.t.
pīhtāpēk ᐲᐦᑖᐯᐠ
NI lagoon
pīhtāsow ᐲᐦᑖᓱᐤ
VAI s/he loads, s/he loads his/her gun
pīhtāsowin ᐲᐦᑖᓱᐏᐣ
NI act of loading a gun; charge for a gun; pocket
pīhtēyas ᐲᐦᑌᔭᐢ
IPC in the center
pīhtēyask ᐲᐦᑌᔭᐢᐠ
IPC at the central circle of poles [*in a dance-lodge*]
pīhtikwē-āwacimihtēw ᐲᐦᑎᑵ ᐋᐘᒋᒥᐦᑌᐤ
VAI s/he hauls firewood inside
pīhtikwē-āwacimihtēwin ᐲᐦᑎᑵ ᐋᐘᒋᒥᐦᑌᐏᐣ
NI hauling firewood inside
pīhtikwēsitēw ᐲᐦᑎᑵᓯᑌᐤ
VAI s/he has inward feet, s/he is pigeon-toed
pīhtikwēw ᐲᐦᑎᑵᐤ
VAI s/he enters, s/he comes in [*cf.* pīhtikēw, pīhtokwēw]
pīhtikwēyāmow ᐲᐦᑎᑵᔮᒧᐤ
VAI s/he flees inside
pīhtokahān ᐲᐦᑐᑲᐦᐋᐣ
NI buffalo pound [*also* pīhtokahākan]
pīhtokahānapiwiýin ᐲᐦᑐᑲᐦᐋᓇᐱᐏᔨᐣ
NA Chief Poundmaker [*prominent Cree chief*]
pīhtokahēw ᐲᐦᑐᑲᐦᐁᐤ
VTA s/he brings s.o. inside [*cf.* pīhtokwahēw]
pīhtokamik ᐲᐦᑐᑲᒥᐠ
IPC inside, indoors, inside a house, tent, dwelling
pīhtokatāw ᐲᐦᑐᑲᑖᐤ
VAIt s/he brings s.t. in
pīhtokawēw ᐲᐦᑐᑲᐍᐤ
VTA s/he enters s.o.'s abode, s/he enters to visit s.o.
pīhtokākan ᐲᐦᑐᑳᑲᐣ
NA guest, caller
pīhtokē- ᐲᐦᑐᑫ
IPV entering to the inside, entering house
pīhtokē-wēpinam ᐲᐦᑐᑫ ᐍᐱᓇᒼ
VTI s/he throws s.t. in, s/he flings s.t. inside
pīhtokē-wēpinēw ᐲᐦᑐᑫ ᐍᐱᓀᐤ
VTA s/he throws s.o. in, s/he flings s.o. inside
pīhtokēhāw ᐲᐦᑐᑫᐦᐋᐤ
VAI s/he flies in
pīhtokēkocin ᐲᐦᑐᑫᑯᒋᐣ
VAI s/he flies in, s/he falls in
pīhtokēpahēw ᐲᐦᑐᑫᐸᐦᐁᐤ
VTA s/he runs in with s.o.
pīhtokēpaýihēw ᐲᐦᑐᑫᐸᔨᐦᐁᐤ
VTA s/he makes s.o. go in
pīhtokēpaýihow ᐲᐦᑐᑫᐸᔨᐦᐅᐤ
VAI s/he throws him/herself in
pīhtokēpaýiw ᐲᐦᑐᑫᐸᔨᐤ
VAI s/he goes in accidentally, s/he falls in
pīhtokēpitam ᐲᐦᑐᑫᐱᑕᒼ
VTI s/he pulls s.t. inside
pīhtokēpitēw ᐲᐦᑐᑫᐱᑌᐤ
VTA s/he pulls s.o. inside
pīhtokētācimow ᐲᐦᑐᑫᑖᒋᒧᐤ
VAI s/he crawls in
pīhtokētisahwēw ᐲᐦᑐᑫᑎᓴᐦᐍᐤ
VTA s/he sends s.o. in; s/he drives in, s/he chases s.o. in
pīhtokētisinam ᐲᐦᑐᑫᑎᓯᓇᒼ
VTI s/he hands s.t. in
pīhtokēw ᐲᐦᑐᑫᐤ
VAI s/he enters, s/he goes in [*cf.* pīhtokwēw]
pīhtokēyāmow ᐲᐦᑐᑫᔮᒧᐤ
VAI s/he flees indoors
pīhtokēyāstan ᐲᐦᑐᑫᔮᐢᑕᐣ
VII it is blown in

pīhtokēyāwatāw ᐲᐦᑐᑫᔮᐘᑖᐤ
VAIt s/he hauls s.t. inside

pīhtokēyāwatēw ᐲᐦᑐᑫᔮᐘᑌᐤ
VTA s/he hauls s.o. inside

pīhtokwahēw ᐲᐦᑐᑿᐦᐁᐤ
VTA s/he makes s.o. enter, s/he makes s.o. go inside, s/he takes s.o. inside, s/he brings s.o. inside; s/he allows s.o. to enter [*cf.* pīhtokahēw]

pīhtokwatamākēw ᐲᐦᑐᑿᑕᒫᑫᐤ
VAI s/he brings (it/him) inside for people

pīhtokwatāw ᐲᐦᑐᑿᑖᐤ
VAIt s/he brings s.t. inside

pīhtokwēhāw ᐲᐦᑐᑵᐦᐋᐤ
VAI s/he flies in

pīhtokwēhēw ᐲᐦᑐᑵᐦᐁᐤ
VTA s/he makes s.o. enter; s/he takes s.o. inside

pīhtokwēkocin ᐲᐦᑐᑵᑯᒋᐣ
VAI s/he flies inside, s/he comes flying inside

pīhtokwēmon ᐲᐦᑐᑵᒧᐣ
VII it goes into (as a door, gate, room); it enters (as a path), it runs in

pīhtokwēpahtāw ᐲᐦᑐᑵᐸᐦᑖᐤ
VAI s/he runs inside

pīhtokwēpaýiw ᐲᐦᑐᑵᐸᔨᐤ
VAI s/he falls in (as the door is opened)

pīhtokwēpihāw ᐲᐦᑐᑵᐱᐦᐋᐤ
VAI s/he flies inside, s/he enters by flying

pīhtokwētācimow ᐲᐦᑐᑵᑖᒋᒧᐤ
VAI s/he crawls inside

pīhtokwēw ᐲᐦᑐᑵᐤ
VAI s/he enters, s/he goes inside [*cf.* pīhtikwēw, pīhtokēw]

pīhtokwēyāmow ᐲᐦᑐᑵᔮᒧᐤ
VAI s/he runs into a building, s/he runs inside, s/he flees inside

pīhtonam ᐲᐦᑐᓇᒼ
VTI s/he peels s.t. by hand (*e.g.* tree bark)

pīhtonēw ᐲᐦᑐᓀᐤ
VTA s/he peels s.o. by hand (*e.g.* fruit)

pīhtopaýiw ᐲᐦᑐᐸᔨᐤ
VAI s/he peels (*e.g.* sunburnt skin), s/he sheds his/her skin; it sheds its bark (*e.g.* tree)

pīhtopitam ᐲᐦᑐᐱᑕᒼ
VTI s/he peels (it) from s.t.; s/he peels off s.t.'s skin

pīhtopitēw ᐲᐦᑐᐱᑌᐤ
VTA s/he peels, s/he pulls, s/he removes (*e.g.* skin or bark) from s.o.

pīhtosam ᐲᐦᑐᓴᒼ
VTI s/he peels s.t. with a knife

pīhtoswēw ᐲᐦᑐᓷᐤ
VTA s/he peels s.o. with a knife

pīhtowēskikanak ᐲᐦᑐᐍᐢᑭᑲᓇᐠ
NA long underwear, long-johns [*pl generally*]

pīhtwamēw ᐲᐦᑣᒣᐤ
VTA s/he eats the outer skin of s.o. (*i.e.* fruit)

pīhtwāhamākēwin ᐲᐦᑥᐦᐊᒫᑫᐏᐣ
NI smoking circle and meeting (offered to the spirits)

pīhtwāhēw ᐲᐦᑥᐦᐁᐤ
VTA s/he gives s.o. a smoke; s/he gives s.o. to smoke; s/he makes s.o. smoke

pīhtwāhkāsow ᐲᐦᑥᐦᑳᓱᐤ
VAI s/he pretends to smoke

pīhtwākan ᐲᐦᑥᑲᐣ
NA tobacco; pipe, cigarette holder

pīhtwākākēw ᐲᐦᑥᑳᑫᐤ
VAI s/he uses something to smoke with

pīhtwākēw ᐲᐦᑥᑫᐤ
VAI s/he smokes with something, s/he uses something in the pipe, s/he uses something as tobacco; s/he smokes things

pīhtwāskiw ᐲᐦᑥᐢᑭᐤ
VAI s/he is fond of smoking; s/he smokes continually [*hab*]

pīhtwātam ᐲᐦᑥᑕᒼ
VTI s/he smokes s.t.

pīhtwātēw ᐲᐦᑥᑌᐤ
VTA s/he smokes s.o. (*e.g.* tobacco)

pīhtwāw ᐲᐦᑥᐤ
VAI s/he smokes; s/he smokes the pipe, s/he uses the pipe; s/he has a pipe ceremony; s/he is a nicotine addict

pīhtwāwikamik ᐲᐦᑥᐏᑲᒥᐠ
NI smoking lodge; smoking room, lounge [*pl*: -wa]

pīhtwāwin ᐲᐦᑥᐏᐣ
NI smoking; smoking ceremony; [*Christian*:] cannabis abuse

pīhtwāwinihkēw ᐲᐦᑥᐏᓂᐦᑫᐤ
VAI s/he arranges a pipe ceremony; s/he gives a smoking ceremony

pīkanowiýiniw ᐲᑲᓄᐏᔨᓂᐤ
NA a Piegan Indian [*also* pīkanowinaw]

pīkanowiýinīnāhk ᐲᑲᓄᐏᔨᓃᓈᕽ
IPC in the Piegan country [*loc*]

pīkinaham ᐲᑭᓇᐦᐊᒼ
VTI s/he breaks lumps of s.t. into pieces

pīkinataham ᐲᑭᓇᑕᐦᐊᒼ
VTI s/he chops s.t. into pieces

pīkinatahwēw ᐲᑭᓇᑕᐦᐍᐤ
VTA s/he chops s.o. into pieces, s/he chops s.o. small

pīkinihkosow ᐲᑭᓂᐦᑯᓱᐤ
VAI s/he is cut into small pieces

pīkinikaham ᐲᑭᓂᑲᐦᐊᒼ
VTI s/he hews s.t. small

pīkinikahwēw ᐲᑭᓂᑲᐦᐍᐤ
VTA s/he hews s.o. small

pīkinipaýiw ᐲᑭᓂᐸᔨᐤ
VAI it crumbles; it breaks into pieces

pīkinisam ᐲᑭᓂᓴᒼ
VTI s/he cuts s.t. into small pieces

pīkiniswēw ᐲᑭᓂᓷᐤ
VTA s/he cuts s.o. into small pieces

pīkisēmahan ᐲᑭᓭᒪᐦᐊᐣ
VII it is foggy on the water

pīkisēnam ᐲᑭᓭᓇᒼ
VTI s/he has blurred vision

pīkisēwin ᐲᑭᓭᐏᐣ
NI steam; vapor

pīkisēyāw ᐲᑭᓭᔮᐤ
VII it is foggy, it is misty

pīkiskāci- ᐲᑭᐢᑳᒋ
IPV sorry, sad, lonely

pīkiskācihēw ᐲᑭᐢᑳᒋᐦᐁᐤ
VTA s/he makes s.o. lonely and sad

pīkiskācihtākosiw ᐲᑭᐢᑳᒋᐦᑖᑯᓯᐤ
VAI s/he sounds mournful, sad

pīkiskācihtākwan ᐲᑭᐢᑳᒋᐦᑖᑿᐣ
VII it sounds mournful, sad

pīkiskācimēw ᐲᑭᐢᑳᒋᒣᐤ
VTA s/he makes s.o. lonely (by speech)

pīkiskācinākosiw ᐲᑭᐢᑳᒋᓈᑯᓯᐤ
VAI s/he is lonely and sad

pīkiskācinākwan ᐲᑭᐢᑳᒋᓈᑿᐣ
VII it looks lonely and gloomy

pīkiskātam ᐲᑭᐢᑳᑕᒼ
VTI s/he is lonesome, lonely, s/he feels sad; s/he longs for s.t., s/he grieves for s.t., s/he finds (s.t.) lonely

pīkiskātamowin ᐲᑭᐢᑳᑕᒧᐏᐣ
NI loneliness; longing

pīkiskātēw ᐲᑭᐢᑳᑌᐤ
VTA s/he is lonesome for s.o., s/he longs for s.o., s/he grieves for s.o.

pīkiskātēýihtam ᐲᑭᐢᑳᑌᔨᐦᑕᒼ
VTI s/he is troubled and lonely (about s.t.)

pīkiskātēýimēw ᐲᑭᐢᑳᑌᔨᒣᐤ
VTA s/he is troubled and lonely because of s.o.

pīkiskātikosiw ᐲᑭᐢᑳᑎᑯᓯᐤ
VAI s/he is sad and lonely

pīkiskātikwan ᐲᑭᐢᑳᑎᑿᐣ
VII it is a sad situation

pīkiskātisiw ᐲᑭᐢᑳᑎᓯᐤ
VAI s/he is lonesome, s/he is sad, s/he suffers grief

pīkiskwātam ᐱᕀᐣᕑᐱᐧᐸᐟᐨ
    VTI s/he speaks to s.t., s/he talks to s.t.; s/he speaks about s.t.

pīkiskwātēw ᐱᕀᐣᕑᐱᐧᐅᐤ°
    VTA s/he speaks to s.o., s/he talks to s.o.; s/he speaks about s.o.

pīkiskwātisow ᐱᕀᐣᕑᐱᐧᐳᐣᑌ°
    VAI s/he speaks to him/herself, s/he speaks about him/herself

pīkiskwātitowak ᐱᕀᐣᕑᐱᐧᐳᐣᑎᐊᐧᐧ
    VAI they speak to one another

pīkiskwēhēw ᐱᕀᐣᕑᐧᐅ°
    VTA s/he makes s.o. speak, s/he gets s.o. to speak

pīkiskwēmakan ᐱᕀᐣᕑᐧᐸᐸᐤᐩ
    VII it speaks, it talks, it uses words

pīkiskwēpayiw ᐱᕀᐣᕑᐧᐸᐸᐳ°
    VAI s/he bursts into speech

pīkiskwēskiw ᐱᕀᐣᕑᐧᐸᐸᐟᐳ°
    VAI s/he is talkative [hab]

pīkiskwēstamawēw
    ᐱᕀᐣᕑᐧᐸᐟᐨᐸᐃᐧᐧᐸ°
    VTA s/he speaks for s.o., s/he speaks on s.o.'s behalf

pīkiskwēstamākēw
    ᐱᕀᐣᕑᐧᐸᐟᐨᐸᐃᐧᐧᐸ°
    VAI s/he speaks for other, s/he speaks on others' behalf

pīkiskwēstamāsow ᐱᕀᐣᕑᐧᐸᐟᐨᐸᐃᐧᐧᐳ°
    VAI s/he speaks for him/herself

pīkiskwēstawēw ᐱᕀᐣᕑᐧᐸᐟᐨᐸᐃᐧᐧᐸ°
    VTA s/he speaks for s.o., s/he speaks on s.o.'s behalf

pīkiskwēw ᐱᕀᐣᕑᐧᐸ°
    VAI s/he speaks, s/he talks, s/he use words, s/he makes a speech

pīkiskwēwin ᐱᕀᐣᕑᐧᐸᐃᐧᐧᐩ
    NI word, expression, phrase; what is being said, speech, talk, conversation; lecture; language; voice; syllable of syllabary

pīkiskwēyāpīsa ᐱᕀᐣᕑᐧᐸᐃᐧᐧᐸᐩ
    NI vocal cords [pl; proposed term]

pīkocin ᐱᕀᐣᕑᐳ
    VAI s/he is torn by thorns, slivers; s/he gets cut on a snag, thorn

pīkohkasam ᐱᕀᐣᕑᐸᐟᐨ
    VTI s/he burns s.t. to pieces

pīkohkaswēw ᐱᕀᐣᕑᐸᐳ°
    VTA s/he burns s.o. to pieces

pīkohkwēpayiw ᐱᕀᐣᕑᐸᐸᐳ°
    VAI s/he has pimples, acne

pīkohtin ᐱᕀᐣᕑᐳᐩ
    VII it is broken falling, it breaks while falling

pīkohtitam ᐱᕀᐣᕑᐳᐸᐟᐨ
    VTI s/he breaks s.t. by dropping

pīkohtitāw ᐱᕀᐣᕑᐳᐸᐟᐨ°
    VAIt s/he breaks s.t. by dropping

pīkohtitēw ᐱᕀᐣᕑᐳᐸᐤ°
    VTA s/he breaks s.o. by dropping

pīkokonēwēpayiw ᐱᕀᐣᐳᐧᐸᐧᐳ°
    VAI s/he has cracks in his/her mouth, s/he has his/her mouth break out in blisters (*e.g.* from thrush); s/he has canker sores

pīkonam ᐱᕀᐣᐳᐨ
    VTI s/he breaks s.t. by hand

pīkonēw ᐱᕀᐣᐳ°
    VTA s/he breaks s.o. by hand; s/he tames s.o.; s/he breaks up s.o.'s house

pīkonikātēw ᐱᕀᐣᐳᐸᐤ°
    VII it is broken, it is torn, it is broken down

pīkonikēmakan ᐱᕀᐣᐳᐸᐸᐤᐩ
    VII it causes things to break down

pīkonikēw ᐱᕀᐣᐳᐸ°
    VAI s/he breaks things; s/he is destructive

pīkopayin ᐱᕀᐣᐳᐸᐸᐳ
    VII it is broken; it breaks down [*cf.* pikopayiw *VII*]

pīkopayiw ᐱᕀᐣᐳᐸᐳ°
    VAI it is broken, torn; it breaks down; s/he is broke, s/he is without monetary funds

pīkopayiw ᐱᕀᐣᐳᐸᐳ°
    VAI s/he has chicken pox

pīkopayiw ᐱᕀᐣᐳᐸᐳ°
    VII it is broken [*cf.* pīkopayin]

pīkopicikan ᐱᕀᐣᐳᐸᐸᐩ
    NI plough

pīkopicikātēw ᐱᕀᐣᐳᐸᐸᐤ°
    VII it is ploughed soil, it is cultivated

pīkopicikēhēw ᐱᕀᐣᐳᐸᐸᐧᐅ°
    VTA s/he makes s.o. plough, s/he uses s.o. (*e.g.* oxen) in ploughing; s/he hires s.o. to plough

pīkopicikēstamawēw
    ᐱᕀᐣᐳᐸᐸᐧᐸᐟᐨᐸ°
    VTA s/he ploughs (land) for s.o.

pīkopicikēw ᐱᕀᐣᐳᐸᐸ°
    VAI s/he ploughs, s/he does the ploughing, s/he breaks land

pīkopicikēwin ᐱᕀᐣᐳᐸᐸᐃᐧᐧᐩ
    NI ploughing

pīkopitam ᐱᕀᐣᐳᐸᐟᐨ
    VTI s/he tears s.t., s/he breaks s.t. (*e.g.* soil), s/he ploughs s.t. (*e.g.* field)

pīkopitamawēw ᐱᕀᐣᐳᐸᐟᐨᐸ°
    VTA s/he breaks (it) for s.o., s/he ploughs (it) for s.o.

pīkopitēw ᐱᕀᐣᐳᐸᐤ°
    VTA s/he tears s.o. to pieces, s/he tears s.o. apart

pīkosam ᐱᕀᐣᐳᐟᐨ
    VTI s/he cuts s.t. to pieces, s/he cuts s.t. up, s/he ruins s.t. by cutting

pīkosikēw ᐱᕀᐣᐳᐸ°
    VAI s/he cuts things to pieces, s/he destroys by cutting

pīkosimēw ᐱᕀᐣᐳᐸᐤ°
    VTA s/he throws s.o. to break, s/he breaks s.o. on something, s/he breaks s.o. by dropping

pīkosin ᐱᕀᐣᐳᐸ
    VAI s/he is broken (by falling)

pīkoskam ᐱᕀᐣᐳᐸᐨ
    VTI s/he breaks s.t. (by foot or body)

pīkoskamawēw ᐱᕀᐣᐳᐸᐸᐸ°
    VTA s/he breaks (it/him) by foot or body for s.o.

pīkoskawēw ᐱᕀᐣᐳᐸᐸᐸ°
    VTA s/he breaks s.o. by foot movement; s/he wears s.o. out (by sitting; *i.e.* pants) [*idiomatic:* "s/he wears out his/her pants"]

pīkostikwānēsin ᐱᕀᐣᐳᐸᐸᐳᐳ
    VAI s/he falls and breaks his/her head

pīkoswēw ᐱᕀᐣᐳᐸᐤ°
    VTA s/he cuts s.o. up, s/he cuts s.o. to pieces, s/he cuts up s.o.'s house, s/he ruins s.o.

pīkowēpaham ᐱᕀᐣᐳᐸᐧᐸᐸᐸᐟᐨ
    VTI s/he breaks s.t. (by prying with a bar)

pīkowēpiskam ᐱᕀᐣᐳᐸᐧᐸᐳᐸᐨ
    VTI s/he breaks s.t. by a swift kick

pīkowēpiskawēw ᐱᕀᐣᐳᐸᐧᐸᐳᐸᐸ°
    VTA s/he breaks s.o. by a swift kick

pīkwaham ᐱᕀᐸᐸᐧᐸᐟᐨ
    VTI s/he breaks s.t. (with a bar)

pīkwahtam ᐱᕀᐸᐳᐸᐟᐨ
    VTI s/he breaks s.t. by mouth or teeth; s/he bites, s/he chews holes in s.t. [*also* pikohtam]

pīkwahtamawēw ᐱᕀᐸᐳᐸᐟᐨᐸ°
    VTA s/he breaks (it/him) by mouth or teeth for s.o.

pīkwahwēw ᐱᕀᐸᐳᐸ°
    VTA s/he breaks s.o. (by prying with a bar)

pīkwamēw ᐱᕀᐸᐳᐤ°
    VTA s/he breaks s.o. by mouth or teeth, s/he chews s.o. up, s/he chews holes in s.o.

pīkwaskisinēpaýiw ᐲᑿᐢᑭᓯᓀᐸᔨᐤ
VAI s/he goes with torn moccasins

pīkwaskisinēw ᐲᑿᐢᑭᓯᓀᐤ
VAI s/he tears his/her moccasin, s/he has a torn moccasin

pīkwataham ᐲᑿᑕᐦᐊᒼ
VTI s/he chops s.t. to pieces; s/he breaks s.t. by striking

pīkwatahikan ᐲᑿᑕᐦᐃᑲᐣ
NI chisel

pīkwatahwēw ᐲᑿᑕᐦᐍᐤ
VTA s/he breaks s.o. with axe; s/he breaks s.o. by striking

pīkwāsiw ᐲᒀᓯᐤ
VAI it breaks (in the wind)

pīkwāskawēw ᐲᒀᐢᑲᐍᐤ
VTA s/he breaks through s.o. (as ice)

pīkwāstan ᐲᒀᐢᑕᐣ
VII it breaks in the wind; it is blown to pieces

pīkwēýihtam ᐲᑵᔨᐦᑕᒼ
VTI s/he is worried about s.t., s/he is sad and troubled

pīkwēýihtamihēw ᐲᑵᔨᐦᑕᒥᐦᐁᐤ
VTA s/he causes s.o. mental anguish

pīkwēýihtamowin ᐲᑵᔨᐦᑕᒧᐏᐣ
NI mental anguish; anxiety

pīmaham ᐲᒪᐦᐊᒼ
VTI s/he twists s.t.

pīmahikan ᐲᒪᐦᐃᑲᐣ
NI screwdriver; auger; tourniquet

pīmahikēw ᐲᒪᐦᐃᑫᐤ
VAI s/he twists things

pīmahowi-sakahikan ᐲᒪᐦᐅᐏ ᓴᑲᐦᐃᑲᐣ
NI screw

pīmahōpakos ᐲᒪᐦᐆᐸᑯᐢ
NI chickweed [*dim*; *alsine media*]

pīmahōpakwa ᐲᒪᐦᐆᐸᑿ
NI wild buckwheat [*pl*; *polygonum convolvulus*]

pīmahwēw ᐲᒪᐦᐍᐤ
VTA s/he winds s.o. (as a clock); s/he twists s.o.

pīmakām ᐲᒪᑳᒼ
IPC not opposite; diagonally

pīmakāmēham ᐲᒪᑳᒣᐦᐊᒼ
VTI s/he goes diagonally across the water

pīmakāmēpisona ᐲᒪᑳᒣᐱᓱᓇ
NI suspenders [*pl generally*]

pīmakāmēpitēw ᐲᒪᑳᒣᐱᑌᐤ
VTA s/he straps s.o. on, s/he harnesses s.o.

pīmakāmēskam ᐲᒪᑳᒣᐢᑲᒼ
VTI s/he wears s.t. on a strap; s/he twists by foot

pīmastēhikan ᐲᒪᐢᑌᐦᐃᑲᐣ
NI spinning wheel

pīmastēhikēw ᐲᒪᐢᑌᐦᐃᑫᐤ
VAI s/he spins wool, yarn

pīmastēnam ᐲᒪᐢᑌᓇᒼ
VTI s/he twists s.t. (to twist a few times)

pīmastēnēw ᐲᒪᐢᑌᓀᐤ
VTA s/he twists s.o.; s/he pinches s.o.

pīmayiwinisēw ᐲᒪᔨᐏᓂᓭᐤ
VAI s/he makes a fold in his/her garment

pīmāpiskaham ᐲᒫᐱᐢᑲᐦᐊᒼ
VTI s/he screws s.t. in

pīmāpiskahikan ᐲᒫᐱᐢᑲᐦᐃᑲᐣ
NI gimlet, drill bit

pīmāpiskāw ᐲᒫᐱᐢᑳᐤ
VII it is crooked (something made of metal)

pīmāpiskisiw ᐲᒫᐱᐢᑭᓯᐤ
VAI it is twisted (something made of metal)

pīmāw ᐲᒫᐤ
VII it is twisted; it is not straight

pīmāwēnikēw ᐲᒫᐌᓂᑫᐤ
VAI s/he twists or braids his/her hair

pīmi- ᐲᒥ
IPV twisted

pīmiciwacis ᐲᒥᒋᐘᒋᐢ
NA bean

pīmihkwēw ᐲᒥᐦᑵᐤ
VAI s/he has a crooked face (as the effects of a stroke)

pīmihtakinam ᐲᒥᐦᑕᑭᓇᒼ
VTI s/he drives a screw into s.t. as wood

pīmihtakinikan ᐲᒥᐦᑕᑭᓂᑲᐣ
NI screw

pīmihtāw ᐲᒥᐦᑖᐤ
VAIt s/he makes s.t. twist

pīmikitam ᐲᒥᑭᑕᒼ
VTI s/he embroiders s.t. with quill-work

pīmikitēw ᐲᒥᑭᑌᐤ
VII it has quill-work

pīmikitēwayiwinisa ᐲᒥᑭᑌᐘᔨᐏᓂᓴ
NI embroidered clothing [*pl*]

pīmikwāsow ᐲᒥᒀᓱᐤ
VAI it is sewn crooked

pīmikwātam ᐲᒥᒀᑕᒼ
VTI s/he sews s.t. crooked

pīmikwātēw ᐲᒥᒀᑌᐤ
VTA s/he sews s.o. crooked

pīmikwātēw ᐲᒥᒀᑌᐤ
VII it is sewn crooked

pīmikwēnēw ᐲᒥᑵᓀᐤ
VTA s/he wrings and twists s.o.'s neck

pīmikwēpitēw ᐲᒥᑵᐱᑌᐤ
VTA s/he twists s.o.'s neck, s/he wrings s.o.'s neck

pīminahkwān ᐲᒥᓇᐦᒀᐣ
NI rope; cord

pīminahkwānis ᐲᒥᓇᐦᒀᓂᐢ
NI string; twine [*dim*]

pīminam ᐲᒥᓇᒼ
VTI s/he twists s.t. by hand, s/he unscrews s.t.; s/he turns s.t. down (*i.e.* in temperature)

pīminēw ᐲᒥᓀᐤ
VTA s/he twists s.o.

pīminikan ᐲᒥᓂᑲᐣ
NA twist-tobacco; wrench

pīminikanis ᐲᒥᓂᑲᓂᐢ
NI gimlet [*dim*]

pīmisāwātam ᐲᒥᓵᐚᑕᒼ
VTI s/he cuts s.t. crooked (not straight)

pīmisāwātēw ᐲᒥᓵᐚᑌᐤ
VTA s/he cuts s.o. crooked (not straight)

pīmisiw ᐲᒥᓯᐤ
VAI s/he is twisted (as a tree)

pīmiskam ᐲᒥᐢᑲᒼ
VTI s/he wears s.t. crooked; s/he wears s.t. wrong

pīmiskawēw ᐲᒥᐢᑲᐍᐤ
VTA s/he wears s.o. crooked; s/he wears s.o. wrong

pīmiskwēsitēw ᐲᒥᐢᑵᓯᑌᐤ
VAI s/he has twisted feet

pīmitahēw ᐲᒥᑕᐦᐁᐤ
VTA s/he places s.o. crosswise, across the way [*cf.* *wC*: pīmitathīw]

pīsahtam ᐲᓴᐦᑕᒼ
VTI s/he chews s.t. into little bits

pīsamēw ᐲᓴᒣᐤ
VTA s/he chews s.o. into little bits

pīsawācāsin ᐲᓴᐚᒑᓯᐣ
VII it is windy with rain

pīsākamāskāsin ᐲᓵᑲᒫᐢᑳᓯᐣ
VII the water is a bit rough

pīsākanāpiy ᐲᓵᑲᓈᐱᐩ
NI rawhide thong, rope

pīsākosiw ᐲᓵᑯᓯᐤ
VAI it contains much; it has a capacity for holding a lot

pīsākwan ᐲᓵᑿᐣ
VII it contains much; it has a capacity for holding a lot; it is abundant

pīsāpikwaniy ᐲᓵᐱᑿᓂᐩ
NI small flower

pīsāpikwanīwan ᐲᓵᐱᑿᓃᐘᐣ
VII it has small flowers

pīsi-kiscikānis ᐲᓯ ᑭᐢᒋᑳᓂᐢ
NI vegetable; seed

pīsi-kiscikānisi-mēskanās ᐲᓯ ᑭᐢᒋᑳᓂᓯ ᒣᐢᑲᓈᐢ
NI garden row

pīsim ᐲᓯᒼ
NA sun; moon; month [*pl*: -wak]

pīsimāspinēw ᐲᓯᒫᐢᐱᓀᐤ
VAI she has a menstrual period

pīsimohkān ᐲᓯᒧᐦᑳᐣ
NA clock, watch

pīsimohkānēyāpiy ᐲᓯᒧᐦᑳᓀᔮᐱᐩ
NI watch chain

pīsimohkānis ᐲᓯᒧᐦᑳᓂᐢ
NA watch [*dim*]

pīsimotāhk ᐲᓯᒧᑖᕽ
IPC towards the south

pīsimowan ᐱᕐᒧᐊᐣ
VII it is sunny; it is moonlight

pīsimowāsis ᐱᕐᒧᐊᕀᐢ
NA Sun Child [legendary male personal name]

pīsimowāyāw ᐱᕐᒧᐊᐧᔭᐤ
VII it is bright and sunny

pīsimowiw ᐱᕐᒧᐊᐤ
VII it has sun, it is sunny

pīsimoyāpiy ᐱᕐᒧᔭᐱᑦ
NI rainbow [cf. pīsimwēyāpiy]

pīsimoyāpis ᐱᕐᒧᔭᐱᐢ
NA Little Rainbow [dim; legendary personal name]

pīsimwāpakwaniy ᐱᕐᒋᐚᐸᐧᑲᓂᑦ
NI daisy

pīsimwēw ᐱᕐᒷᐤ
VAI s/he is one month old

pīsimwēyāpiy ᐱᕐᒷᔭᐱᑦ
NI rainbow; sunbeam; sundial [cf. pīsimoyāpiy]

pīsipakāw ᐱᕐᐸᑲᐤ
VII it has small leaves

pīskatahikēw ᐱᐢᑲᑕᐦᐃᑫᐤ
VAI s/he makes kindling

pīskwa ᐱᐢᑿ
NA mosquito-hawk; night-hawk [pl: -k; some dialects of sC and eastward have sg: pīsk; the name is onomatopoeic, the bird's call sounding as "pīsk, pīsk"]

pīstēw ᐱᐢᑌᐤ
NI foam, froth

pīstēwaciwahtāw ᐱᐢᑌᐊᐧᒋᐊᐧᐦᑖᐤ
VAIt s/he boils s.t. until a scum appears

pīstēwaciwahtēw ᐱᐢᑌᐊᐧᒋᐊᐧᐦᑌᐤ
VII it boils until a scum appears

pīstēwaciwasow ᐱᐢᑌᐊᐧᒋᐊᐧᓱᐤ
VAI it boils until a scum appears

pīstēwan ᐱᐢᑌᐊᐧᐣ
VII it has foam; it is foamy

pīstēwataham ᐱᐢᑌᐊᐧᑕᐦᐊᒼ
VTI s/he beats s.t. (as eggs with a beater)

pīstēwatahikan ᐱᐢᑌᐊᐧᑕᐦᐃᑲᐣ
NI egg-beater

pīstēwiw ᐱᐢᑌᐃᐧᐤ
VII it has froth or foam

pīswē-maskimot ᐱᐢᐧ ᒪᐢᑭᒧᐟ
NI flannel bag

pīswē-maskisin ᐱᐢᐧ ᒪᐢᑭᓯᐣ
NI "felt", woollen boot liner

pīswē-pīway ᐱᐢᐧ ᐱᐊᐧᑦ
NA down from geese or ducks

pīswē-pīwayān ᐱᐢᐧ ᐱᐊᐧᔮᐣ
NI raw wool

pīswēhkasikan ᐱᐢᐧᐦᑲᓯᑲᐣ
NA leavened bread; baking powder; yeast

pīswēhkasikanihkēw ᐱᐢᐧᐦᑲᓯᑲᓂᐦᑫᐤ
VAI s/he makes bread

pīswēhkasikanis ᐱᐢᐧᐦᑲᓯᑲᓂᐢ
NA bun [dim]

pīswēhkasow ᐱᐢᐧᐦᑲᓱᐤ
VAI it rises (e.g. bread)

pīswēkin ᐱᐢᐧᑭᐣ
NI woollen material

pīswēpayíw ᐱᐢᐧᐸᔩᐤ
VAI s/he has edema, s/he retains water; it is spongy, it is fluffy

pīswēpiw ᐱᐢᐧᐱᐤ
VAI s/he sits loose (e.g. snow)

pīswēsākās ᐱᐢᐧᓭᑲᐢ
NI sweater [dim]

pīswēskiwakāw ᐱᐢᐧᐢᑭᐊᐧᑲᐤ
VII it is a soft bog, it is quicksand

pīswēwastotin ᐱᐢᐧᐊᐧᐢᑑᑎᐣ
NI toque

pīswēwayān ᐱᐢᐧᐊᐧᔮᐣ
NI flannel

pīswēyān ᐱᐢᐧᔮᐣ
NI woollen garment (e.g. sweater)

pīswēyās ᐱᐢᐧᔮᐢ
NI cotton batting [dim]

pīswēyāw ᐱᐢᐧᔮᐤ
VII it is woolly and fleecy

pītatowēw ᐱᑕᑐ�Ꮙᐤ
NA European, immigrant

pītos ᐱᑐᐢ
IPC strange, strangely; different, differently; foreign

pītos mīna ᐱᑐᐢ ᒦᓇ
IPH different from

pītosēyíhtam ᐱᑐᐢᔩᐦᑕᒼ
VTI s/he thinks differently

pītosēyimēw ᐱᑐᐢᔨᒣᐤ
VTA s/he thinks of s.o. differently; s/he finds s.o. changed, different

pītosi- ᐱᑐᓯ
IPV different, foreign

pītosinākosiw ᐱᑐᓯᓈᑯᓯᐤ
VAI s/he looks different

pītosinākwan ᐱᑐᓯᓈᑳᐧᐣ
VII it looks different

pītosisiw ᐱᑐᓯᓯᐤ
VAI s/he is a stranger, s/he is an outsider, s/he is a foreigner

pītosiskwēw ᐱᑐᓯᐢᑵᐤ
NA foreign woman

pītosiýiniw ᐱᑐᓯᔨᓂᐤ
NA foreigner, enemy

pītotāpisin ᐱᑐᑖᐱᓯᐣ
VAI s/he sees strange sights

pītotēyíhtam ᐱᑐᑌᔩᐦᑕᒼ
VTI s/he thinks s.t. strange

pītotēýihtākosiw ᐱᑐᑌᔨᐦᑖᎤᓯᐤ
VAI s/he is thought strange, s/he is considered odd

pīwahcikan ᐱᐊᐧᐦᒋᑲᐣ
NI crumb; a bit of food

pīwahcikēw ᐱᐊᐧᐦᒋᑫᐤ
VAI s/he makes crumbs (while eating)

pīwan ᐱᐊᐧᐣ
VII it is drifting (i.e. snow); it is a blizzard

pīwaniýōtin ᐱᐊᐧᓂᔫᑎᐣ
VII it is a blizzard

pīwapiw ᐱᐊᐧᐱᐤ
VAI s/he lies around

pīwaskisow ᐱᐊᐧᐢᑭᓱᐤ
VII it is poor grain growth

pīwastāw ᐱᐊᐧᐢᑖᐤ
VAIt s/he scatters s.t. about

pīwastēw ᐱᐊᐧᐢᑌᐤ
VII it is scattered about [generally pl]

pīway ᐱᐊᐧᑦ
NI hair from a hide, fur, bristles; feathers, plumage [pl generally: pīwaya]

pīwāpisk ᐱᐚᐱᐢᐠ
NA metal, piece of metal; steel blade; iron; dollar [pl: -wak]

pīwāpisko-mēskanaw ᐱᐚᐱᐢᑯ ᒣᐢᑲᓇᐤ
NI railroad

pīwāpisko-miciminikan ᐱᐚᐱᐢᑯ ᒥᒋᒥᓂᑲᐣ
NI iron tongs

pīwāpisko-wanihikan ᐱᐚᐱᐢᑯ ᐊᐧᓂᐦᐃᑲᐣ
NI iron trap

pīwāpiskominis ᐱᐚᐱᐢᑯᒥᓂᐢ
NA bead of metal

pīwāpiskos ᐱᐚᐱᐢᑯᐢ
NA penny, cent; coin; wire; needle [dim; pl rarely used]

pīwāpiskowan ᐱᐚᐱᐢᑯᐊᐧᐣ
VII it is iron, it is metal

pīwāpiskowaskihk ᐱᐚᐱᐢᑯᐊᐧᐢᑭᕽ
NA iron or metal kettle [pl: -wak]

pīwāpiskowāsis ᐱᐚᐱᐢᑯᐚᓯᐢ
NA metal child [male personal name]

pīwāpiskowiw ᐱᐚᐱᐢᑯᐃᐧᐤ
VAI s/he is of iron

pīwāpiskowiw ᐱᐚᐱᐢᑯᐃᐧᐤ
VII it is of iron

pīwāpiskoýākan ᐱᐚᐱᐢᑯᔭᑲᐣ
NI iron or metal dish

pīwāpiskoýākanis ᐱᐚᐱᐢᑯᔭᑲᓂᐢ
NI small iron or metal dish [dim]

pīwāpiskwastotin ᐱᐚᐱᐢᑲᐧᐢᑑᑎᐣ
NA German

pīwāpiskwastotin ᐱᐚᐱᐢᑲᐧᐢᑑᑎᐣ
NI steel helmet

pīwāpiskwastotinēw ᐱᐚᐱᐢᑲᐧᐢᑑᑎᓀᐤ
VAI s/he has a helmet

pīwāpiskwēyāpiy ᐱᐚᐱᐢᑵᔭᐱᑦ
NI chain

pīwāstan ᐱᐧᐊᐢᒐᐣ
 VII it is scattered about by
 the wind
pīwēnam ᐱᐁᐧᐊᐨ
 VTI s/he scatters s.t. about
pīwēnēw ᐱᐁᐧᐄᐅᣞ
 VTA s/he scatters s.o. about
 (as grain when planted by
 hand)
pīwēpinam ᐱᐁᐧᐱᐊᐨ
 VTI s/he scatters s.t. about
 by throwing
pīwēpinēw ᐱᐁᐧᐱᐅᣞ
 VTA s/he scatters s.o. about
 by throwing
pīwēsikan ᐱᐁᐧᓯᑲᐣ
 NA sock
pīwēsikēw ᐱᐁᐧᓯᑫᣞ
 VAI s/he wears socks
pīwētaham ᐱᐁᐧᒐᐦᐊᐨ
 VTI s/he makes chips (while
 chopping wood)
pīwēwēpinam ᐱᐁᐧᐁᐧᐱᐊᐨ
 VTI s/he scatters s.t., s/he
 sprinkles in a pinch of s.t.
pīwēyāwahkwāw ᐱᐁᐧᔮᐊᐧᐦᐠᐋᐧᐤ
 VII it is powdery
pīwēyihtam ᐱᐁᐧᔨᐦᒐᐨ
 VTI s/he despises s.t.; s/he
 thinks little of s.t., s/he
 considers s.t. inferior
pīwēyihtākosiw ᐱᐁᐧᔨᐦᑖᑯᓯᐤ
 VAI s/he is despised, s/he is
 considered inferior
pīwēyihtākwan ᐱᐁᐧᔨᐦᑖᑲᐧᐣ
 VII it is despised, it is
 considered inferior
pīwēyimēw ᐱᐁᐧᔨᒣᐤ
 VTA s/he despises s.o.; s/he
 thinks little of s.o., s/he
 considers s.o. inferior
pīwēyimisow ᐱᐁᐧᔨᒥᓱᐤ
 VAI s/he despises him/
 herself; s/he thinks little of
 him/herself, s/he considers
 him/herself inferior, s/he
 feels inferior
pīwēyimow ᐱᐁᐧᔨᒧᐤ
 VAI s/he thinks little of
 him/herself, s/he has low
 self-esteem; s/he is humble
pīwi- ᐱᐄᐧ
 IPV small
pīwi-kiscikānis ᐱᐄᐧ ᑭᐢᒋᑳᓂᐢ
 NA garden seed [*dim*]
pīwi-kiscikānis ᐱᐄᐧ ᑭᐢᒋᑳᓂᐢ
 NI vegetable [*dim*]
pīwi-kistikān ᐱᐄᐧ ᑭᐢᑎᑲᐣ
 NI vegetable garden
pīwihkahikana ᐱᐄᐧᐦᑲᐦᐃᑲᓇ
 NI wood-chips, shavings [*pl
 generally*]
pīwihkotākana ᐱᐄᐧᐦᑯᑖᑲᓇ
 NI shavings [*pl generally*]
pīwihtakahikana ᐱᐄᐧᐦᑕᑲᐦᐃᑲᓇ
 NI shavings, wood-chips [*pl
 generally*]

pīwinam ᐱᐄᐧᐊᐨ
 VTI s/he scatters s.t. about
 (small articles)
pīwinēw ᐱᐄᐧᐅᣞ
 VTA s/he scatters s.o. about
 (e.g. beads)
pīwinikēw ᐱᐄᐧᓂᑫᣞ
 VAI s/he scatters things
 about (small articles)
pīwipayiw ᐱᐄᐧᐸᔨᐤ
 VII it lies scattered about
pīwipicikan ᐱᐄᐧᐱᒋᑲᐣ
 NI piece or remnant [*pl
 generally*]
pīwipicikēw ᐱᐄᐧᐱᒋᑫᣞ
 VAI s/he tears things and
 scatters them about; s/he
 makes it untidy
pīwipitam ᐱᐄᐧᐱᒐᐨ
 VTI s/he drops and scatters
 s.t. about
pīwipitēw ᐱᐄᐧᐱᑌᐤ
 VTA s/he drops and scatters
 s.o. about
pīwisam ᐱᐄᐧᓴᐨ
 VTI s/he cuts scraps off; s/he
 makes scraps
pīwisikan ᐱᐄᐧᓯᑲᐣ
 NI leftovers; scraps and
 clippings
pīwisikēw ᐱᐄᐧᓯᑫᣞ
 VAI s/he cuts things out and
 leaves remnants lying about
pīwiswēw ᐱᐄᐧᓴᐧᐤ
 VTA s/he cuts pieces off s.o.
pīwitam ᐱᐄᐧᒐᐨ
 VTI s/he shoots rapids
pīwiyiniwiw ᐱᐄᐧᔨᓂᐃᐧᐤ
 VAI he is a man of no
 account

>

pohciniskēyiw ᐳᐦᒋᓂᐢᑫᔨᐤ
 VAI s/he sticks his/her arm
 into a hole
pohcipayihow ᐳᐦᒋᐸᔨᐦᐅᐤ
 VAI s/he jumps into a hole
pohcipayin ᐳᐦᒋᐸᔨᐣ
 VII it falls into a hole
pohcipayiw ᐳᐦᒋᐸᔨᐤ
 VII it goes into a hole, it
 falls into a hole
pohciwēpaham ᐳᐦᒋᐁᐧᐸᐦᐊᐨ
 VTI s/he shovels s.t. in
pohciwēpahwēw ᐳᐦᒋᐁᐧᐸᐦᐊᐧᐤ
 VTA s/he shovels s.o. in
pohciwēpinam ᐳᐦᒋᐁᐧᐱᐊᐨ
 VTI s/he throws s.t. into a
 hole
pohciwēpinēw ᐳᐦᒋᐁᐧᐱᐅᣞ
 VTA s/he throws s.o. into a
 hole
pohtahēw ᐳᐦᑕᐦᐁᐤ
 VTA s/he inserts s.o.
pohtastāw ᐳᐦᑕᐢᒑᐤ
 VAIt s/he inserts s.t.

pohtastēw ᐳᐦᑕᐢᑌᐤ
 VII it is inserted
pohtātakinam ᐳᐦᒑᑕᑭᐊᐧᐨ
 VTI s/he stumbles stepping
 into a hole
pohtātakinikēw ᐳᐦᒑᑕᑭᓂᑫᣞ
 VAI s/he steps or falls into
 an unseen hole
posakāhkēpicikan ᐳᓴᑳᐦᑫᐱᒋᑲᐣ
 NA small feather for hat
posākan ᐳᓴᑲᐣ
 NA touchwood, tinder of
 birch fungus [*Fomes
 fomentarius*]
posākanaciy ᐳᓴᑲᓇᒋᕀ
 NI Touchwood Hills, SK
posākanacīhk
 INM Gordon's Reserve, SK
 [*loc*; *lit:* "at touchwood
 hills"]
posākanacīwiyiniwak
 ᐳᓴᑲᓇᒌᐃᐧᔨᓂᐊᐧᐠ
 NA Touchwood Hills People
 [*pl*; *division of the Cree*]
poscipayiw ᐳᐢᒋᐸᔨᐤ
 VAI it goes on (e.g. a ring)
poscipitam ᐳᐢᒋᐱᒐᐨ
 VTI s/he pulls s.t. on
posiskahcāw ᐳᓯᐢᑲᐦᒑᐤ
 NI long, narrow valley,
 gulley
posiskatināw ᐳᓯᐢᑲᑎᓈᐤ
 VII it is a steep gulley wall,
 it is a steep valley wall
positāsēw ᐳᓯᑖᓭᐤ
 VAI s/he puts on breeches
 [*cf.* postitāsēw]
postamōhēw ᐳᐢᑕᒧᐦᐁᐤ
 VTA s/he puts s.o. on; s/he
 fastens s.o. on; s/he hitches
 s.o. up
postasākahēw ᐳᐢᑕᓵᑲᐦᐁᐧᐤ
 VTA s/he makes s.o. put on a
 coat
postasākēhēw ᐳᐢᑕᓵᑫᐦᐁᐧᐤ
 VTA s/he puts a coat (or
 dress) on s.o.
postasākēw ᐳᐢᑕᓵᑫᐤ
 VAI s/he puts his/her own
 jacket (coat, vest, dress, etc.)
 on; s/he has a coat on
postasāmēw ᐳᐢᑕᓵᒣᐤ
 VAI s/he puts on his/her own
 snowshoes
postasikanēw ᐳᐢᑕᓯᑲᐅᣞ
 VAI s/he puts his/her own
 socks on; s/he has socks on
postaskisinahēw ᐳᐢᑕᐢᑭᓯᓇᐦᐁᐧᐤ
 VTA s/he makes s.o. put
 moccasins, shoes on
postaskisinēhēw ᐳᐢᑕᐢᑭᓯᓀᐦᐁᐧᐤ
 VTA s/he makes s.o. put
 moccasins, shoes on
postaskisinēw ᐳᐢᑕᐢᑭᓯᓀᐤ
 VAI s/he puts his/her own
 moccasins, shoes on
postaspastākanēw
 ᐳᐢᑕᐢᐸᐢᑖᑲᓀᐤ
 VAI s/he has an apron on

postastisēw >ᑊᑕᐣᔫ
  VAI s/he puts his/her own
  mitts on
postastotinēhēw >ᑊᑕᐣᑐᑎᐦᐁᐤ
  VTA s/he puts a hat on s.o.
postastotinēw >ᑊᑕᐣᑐᑎᐣᐤ
  VAI s/he puts his/her own
  hat, cap on
postayiwinisahēw
  >ᑊᑕᕈᐄᐧᓂᔕᐦᐁᐤ
  VTA s/he dresses s.o., s/he
  makes s.o. put clothes on;
  s/he clothes s.o., s/he makes
  clothes for s.o.
postayiwinisahisow
  >ᑊᑕᕈᐄᐧᓂᔕᐦᐃᓲᐤ
  VAI s/he dresses him/herself,
  s/he clothes him/herself, s/he
  makes clothes for him/herself
postayiwinisēw >ᑊᑕᕈᐄᐧᓂᔫ
  VAI s/he puts his/her own
  clothing on, s/he gets dressed
postiskam >ᑊᑎᐣᑲᒻ
  VTI s/he puts s.t. (clothing)
  on; s/he wears s.t.
postiskawēw >ᑊᑎᐣᑲᐁᐧᐤ
  VTA s/he puts s.o. (clothing)
  on, s/he wears s.o.
postitāsēw >ᑊᑎᑖᔫ
  VAI s/he puts his/her own
  pants, breeches on
poýakahtam >ᕉᑲᐦᑕᒻ
  VTI s/he peels s.t. with
  his/her teeth
poýakamēw >ᕉᑲᒣᐤ
  VTA s/he peels s.o. with
  his/her teeth (*e.g.* an orange)
  [*cf.* pwēýakamēw]
poýakinam >ᕉᑭᓇᒻ
  VTI s/he peels s.t. with
  his/her hands [*cf.*
  pwēýakinam]
poýakinēw >ᕉᑭᓈᐤ
  VTA s/he peels s.o. with
  his/her hands (*e.g.* an orange)
  [*cf.* pwēýakinēw]

> ᐳ

pōh-pōtātam ᐳᐦ ᐳᑖᑕᒻ
  VTI s/he blows on s.t. [*rdpl*]
pōh-pōtātēw ᐳᐦ ᐳᑖᑌᐤ
  VTA s/he blows on s.o.
  [*rdpl*]
pōmēhēw ᐳᒣᐦᐁᐤ
  VTA s/he discourages s.o.,
  s/he makes s.o. discouraged;
  s/he disappoints s.o.
pōmēmēw ᐳᒣᒣᐤ
  VTA s/he discourages s.o.
  (by speech)
pōmēnākwan ᐳᒣᓈᐧᐸᐣ
  VII it look discouraging
pōmēw ᐳᒣᐤ
  VAI s/he is discouraged, s/he
  gives up, s/he quits

pōn-ācimow ᐳᐣᐋᒋᒧᐤ
  VAI s/he is finished telling
  stories [*also* pōni-ācimow]
pōn-āhkosiw ᐳᐣᐋᐦᑯᓯᐤ
  VAI s/he recovers from
  his/her illness [*also*
  pōni-āhkosiw]
pōn-āpihtā-kīsikāki
  ᐳᐣᐋᐱᐦᑖ ᑮᓯᑳᑭ
  IPC in the afternoon, when
  it's afternoon
pōn-āpihtā-kīsikāw
  ᐳᐣᐋᐱᐦᑖ ᑮᓯᑳᐤ
  VII it is afternoon
pōn-āpihtā-tipiskāw
  ᐳᐣᐋᐱᐦᑖ ᑎᐱᐢᑳᐤ
  VII it is after midnight, it is
  very early morning
pōn-ātoskēw ᐳᐣᐋᑑᐢᑫᐤ
  VAI s/he is finished working
  [*also* pōni-atoskēw]
pōn-āyamihāw ᐳᐣᐋᕁᒥᐦᐋᐤ
  VAI s/he ceases praying
  [*also* pōni-ayamihāw]
pōn-āyamihēwi-kīsikāw
  ᐳᐣᐋᕁᒥᐦᐁᐧᐄ ᑮᓯᑳᐤ
  VII it is Monday [*see also*
  pēyako-kīsikāw]
pōnakiskātēw ᐳᓇᑭᐢᑳᑌᐤ
  VTA s/he doctors s.o. with a
  rattle
pōnam ᐳᓇᒻ
  VTI s/he builds a fire, s/he
  feeds the fire; s/he builds a
  fire with s.t., s/he puts (s.t.
  as) fuel on the fire [*cf.*
  pōnikātēw]
pōnamawēw ᐳᓇᒪᐁᐧᐤ
  VTA s/he makes a fire for
  s.o., s/he builds a fire for s.o.
pōnamāsow ᐳᓇᒫᓲᐤ
  VAI s/he keeps up his/her
  own fire
pōnāhpiw ᐳᓈᐦᐱᐤ
  VAI s/he stops laughing
pōnāmow ᐳᓈᒧᐤ
  VAI s/he quits fleeing
pōnāsiw ᐳᓈᓯᐤ
  VAI s/he stops being blown
  about
pōnēsin ᐳᓀᓯᐣ
  VAI s/he lands descending
pōnēw ᐳᓀᐤ
  VTA s/he puts s.o. as fuel on
  the fire
pōnēýihtam ᐳᓀᕈᐦᑕᒻ
  VTI s/he ceases thinking of
  s.t., s/he thinks no more of
  s.t., s/he forgets s.t.; s/he gets
  over a worrying
  preoccupation
pōnēýihtamawēw ᐳᓀᕈᐦᑕᒪᐁᐧᐤ
  VTA s/he forgives s.o. for
  (it)
pōnēýihtamāsow ᐳᓀᕈᐦᑕᒫᓲᐤ
  VAI s/he forgives
  him/herself

pōnēýihtamātowak
  ᐳᓀᕈᐦᑕᒫᑐᐊᐧᐠ
  VAI they forgive one another
pōnēýihtamowin ᐳᓀᕈᐦᑕᒧᐃᐧᐣ
  NI forgiveness
pōnēýimēw ᐳᓀᕈᒣᐤ
  VTA s/he gives up the
  thought of s.o.; s/he stops
  thinking about s.o.
pōni- ᐳᓂ
  IPV stop, terminate, cease;
  after
pōni-kimiwan ᐳᓂ ᑭᒥᐊᐧᐣ
  VII it stops raining
pōni-mātow ᐳᓂ ᒫᑑᐤ
  VAI s/he stops crying
pōni-mispon ᐳᓂ ᒥᐢᐳᐣ
  VII it stops snowing
pōni-mīcisow ᐳᓂ ᒥᒋᓲᐤ
  VAI s/he stops eating, s/he is
  finished eating
pōni-nōhēw ᐳᓂ ᓅᐦᐁᐤ
  VTA s/he stops nursing s.o.;
  s/he weans s.o.
pōni-nōkwan ᐳᓂ ᓅᐧᑲᐣ
  VII it disappears
pōni-pimātisiw ᐳᓂ ᐱᒫᑎᓯᐤ
  VAI s/he ceases living, s/he
  dies, s/he ceases to be alive,
  s/he is dead
pōni-pimātisiwin ᐳᓂ ᐱᒫᑎᓯᐃᐧᐣ
  NI death
pōni-ýēhēw ᐳᓂ ᔦᐦᐁᐤ
  VAI s/he stops breathing
  [*also* -ýēhyēw; *cf.* wC:
  thihthiw]
pōni-ýēhēwin ᐳᓂ ᔦᐦᐁᐃᐧᐣ
  NI end of existence; death
  [*also* -ýēhyēwin; *cf.* wC:
  thihthiwin]
pōnihēw ᐳᓂᐦᐁᐤ
  VTA s/he leaves s.o. alone,
  s/he leaves off from s.o.
pōnihkam ᐳᓂᐦᑲᒻ
  VTI s/he leaves s.t. alone
pōnihkawēw ᐳᓂᐦᑲᐁᐧᐤ
  VTA s/he stops bothering s.o.
pōnihtāw ᐳᓂᐦᑖᐤ
  VAIt s/he stops s.t., s/he
  ceases of (s.t.); s/he leaves
  off from s.t., s/he leaves s.t.
  alone
pōnihtin ᐳᓂᐦᑎᐣ
  VII it ceases to fall
pōnikākēw ᐳᓂᑳᑫᐤ
  VAI s/he makes fire with s.t.
pōnikātēw ᐳᓂᑳᑌᐤ
  VII it is burnt in a fire; it is
  made a fire of
pōnimēw ᐳᓂᒣᐤ
  VTA s/he leaves off talking
  to s.o.
pōnipaýin ᐳᓂᐸᕀᐣ
  VII it stops, it quits [*cf.*
  pōnipaýiw]
pōnipaýiw ᐳᓂᐸᕁᐤ
  VII it stops running, it stops
  operating, it ceases, it ceases
  to exist [*cf.* pōnipaýin]

pōnisimow ᐳᓯᒧᐤ
VAI s/he stops dancing

pōnisin ᐳᓯᓐ
VAI s/he stops falling, it stops falling (e.g. hail)

pōnīw ᐳᓃᐤ
NA bull [English loan]

pōnōsēw ᐳᓅᓭᐤ
VAI s/he is no longer of child-bearing age

pōnwēwitam ᐳᐃᐧᐁᐧᐃᑕᒼ
VTI s/he stops talking about s.t.; s/he ceases making noise

pōsahtawiw ᐳᓴᐦᑕᐃᐧᐤ
VAI s/he climbs aboard

pōsāhkwāmiw ᐳᓵᐦᒁᒥᐤ
VAI s/he sleeps a lot; s/he sleeps late, s/he sleeps soundly

pōsi-kwāskohtiw ᐳᓯ ᒁᐢᑯᐦᑎᐤ
VAI s/he jumps in (a vehicle)

pōsi-wēpaham ᐳᓯ ᐍᐸᐦᐊᒼ
VTI s/he throws s.t. on board (using a fork or stick)

pōsi-wēpahwēw ᐳᓯ ᐍᐸᐦᐁᐧᐤ
VTA s/he knocks s.o. aboard by tool; s/he throws s.o. aboard

pōsi-wēpinam ᐳᓯ ᐍᐱᓇᒼ
VTI s/he throws s.t. in (a vehicle), s/he throws s.t. on (a conveyance)

pōsi-wēpinēw ᐳᓯ ᐍᐱᓀᐤ
VTA s/he throws s.o. in (a vehicle)

pōsihcikēw ᐳᓯᐦᒋᑫᐤ
VAI s/he loads things

pōsihēw ᐳᓯᐦᐁᐧᐤ
VTA s/he gives s.o. a ride; s/he puts s.o. on board, s/he makes s.o. board a conveyance

pōsihtāsow ᐳᓯᐦᑖᓱᐤ
VAI s/he loads things up (in a truck or wagon)

pōsihtāsowin ᐳᓯᐦᑖᓱᐃᐧᐣ
NI cargo

pōsihtāswan ᐳᓯᐦᑖᐢᐧᐊᐣ
NI load, ton

pōsihtāw ᐳᓯᐦᑖᐤ
VAIt s/he puts s.t. on board, s/he loads s.t.

pōsināpāsk ᐳᓯᓈᐹᐢᐠ
NA bus [pl: -wak]

pōsipayīhow ᐳᓯᐸᔩᐦᐅᐤ
VAI s/he jumps on board

pōsipayīw ᐳᓯᐸᔩᐤ
VAI it goes or falls on board (e.g. a load)

pōsitisaham ᐳᓯᑎᓴᐦᐊᒼ
VTI s/he sends s.t. aboard

pōsitisahwēw ᐳᓯᑎᓴᐦᐁᐧᐤ
VTA s/he sends s.o. aboard

pōsiw ᐳᓯᐤ
VAI s/he boards, s/he gets aboard, s/he embarks; s/he rides (in a vehicle)

pōsiwas ᐳᓯᐊᐧᐢ
NI suitcase [sg only; cf. pl: pōsiwata]

pōsiwat ᐳᓯᐊᐧᐟ
NI suitcase [cf. pōsiwas]

pōsiwin ᐳᓯᐃᐧᐣ
NA passenger car, train

pōsiy ᐳᓯᕀ
NA domestic cat [English loan]

pōsīs ᐳᓰᐢ
NA cat; kitten [dim; English loan; see also minōs-]

pōsīw ᐳᓰᐤ
NA cat [English loan]

pōsko- ᐳᐢᑯ
IPP the same

pōsko-kīsik ᐳᐢᑯ ᑭᓯᐠ
IPC half day; the same day; during the day

pōsko-pīsim ᐳᐢᑯ ᐲᓯᒼ
IPC half a month; the same month; during the month

pōskohtin ᐳᐢᑯᐦᑎᐣ
VII it gets a hole through it (e.g. a canoe); it bursts (as a tire), it bursts from wearing out

pōskohtitāw ᐳᐢᑯᐦᑎᑖᐤ
VAIt s/he bursts s.t. (by wearing out)

pōskonam ᐳᐢᑯᓇᒼ
VTI s/he opens s.t., s/he bursts s.t. open

pōskonēw ᐳᐢᑯᓀᐤ
VTA s/he opens s.o., s/he bursts s.o. open

pōskopayīhēw ᐳᐢᑯᐸᔩᐦᐁᐧᐤ
VTA s/he bursts s.o.

pōskopayīhtāw ᐳᐢᑯᐸᔩᐦᑖᐤ
VAIt s/he bursts s.t.

pōskopayīw ᐳᐢᑯᐸᔩᐤ
VII it bursts

pōskopitam ᐳᐢᑯᐱᑕᒼ
VTI s/he tears a hole in s.t.

pōskopitēw ᐳᐢᑯᐱᑌᐤ
VTA s/he tears a hole in s.o.

pōskosam ᐳᐢᑯᓴᒼ
VTI s/he cuts s.t. to burst; s/he cuts a hole in s.t.

pōskosiw ᐳᐢᑯᓯᐤ
VAI it has a hole in it (e.g. pants)

pōskoskam ᐳᐢᑯᐢᑲᒼ
VTI s/he makes a hole in s.t. by stepping, s/he treads a hole in s.t.

pōskoskawēw ᐳᐢᑯᐢᑲᐍᐤ
VTA s/he makes a hole in s.o. by stepping, s/he treads a hole in s.o.

pōskoswēw ᐳᐢᑯᓯᐧᐤ
VTA s/he cuts s.o. to burst; s/he cuts a hole in s.o.

pōskwaham ᐳᐢᒁᐦᐊᐧᐟ
VTI s/he opens s.t. (by making a hole)

pōskwahikāsow ᐳᐢᒁᐦᐃᑳᓱᐤ
VAI it has holes put in it; s/he has his/her ears pierced; s/he has his/her body pierced

pōskwahikātēw ᐳᐢᒁᐦᐃᑳᑌᐤ
VII it has holes put in it; it is pierced

pōskwahwēw ᐳᐢᒁᐦᐁᐧᐤ
VTA s/he puts holes in s.o.; s/he opens by putting holes in s.o.; s/he breaks s.o. open (e.g. coconut)

pōskwataham ᐳᐢᑲᐧᑕᐦᐊᐧᐟ
VTI s/he puts holes in s.t. (by tool)

pōskwatahwēw ᐳᐢᑲᐧᑕᐦᐁᐧᐤ
VTA s/he puts holes in s.o. (by tool)

pōskwāw ᐳᐢᒁᐤ
VII it has a hole in it

pōtācikan ᐳᑖᒋᑲᐣ
NI horn, bugle, or whistle

pōtācikanihkēw ᐳᑖᒋᑲᓂᐦᑫᐤ
VAI s/he makes a horn, bugle, or whistle

pōtācikanis ᐳᑖᒋᑲᓂᐢ
NI flute [dim; also pōcācikanis]

pōtācikēsīs ᐳᑖᒋᑫᓰᐢ
NA mole

pōtācikēw ᐳᑖᒋᑫᐤ
VAI s/he blows

pōtācikēwin ᐳᑖᒋᑫᐃᐧᐣ
NI blowing a horn, whistle, or bugle

pōtātam ᐳᑖᑕᒼ
VTI s/he blows at s.o., s/he blows upon s.t.

pōtātēw ᐳᑖᑌᐤ
VTA s/he blows at s.o., s/he blows upon s.o.

pōtāwisiw ᐳᑖᐃᐧᓯᐤ
VAI s/he is bloated

pōti ᐳᑎ
IPC what was this! lo and behold! and here it was! then, as it turns out [precedes demonstrative pronouns; also poti]

pōyow ᐳᔪᐤ
VAI s/he stops, s/he ceases, s/he quits, s/he gives up

pwāhpinatam ᐘᐦᐱᓇᑕᒼ
VTI s/he fails attacking s.t.

pwāhpinatēw ᐘᐦᐱᓇᑌᐤ
VTA s/he fails attacking s.o.

pwākamahkwēw ᐘᑲᒪᐦᒁᐤ
VAI s/he vomits blood [also pwākomohkwēw]

pwākamohēw ᐘᑲᒧᐦᐁᐧᐤ
VTA s/he makes s.o. vomit [also pākomohēw]

pwākamosikan ᐘᑲᒧᓯᑲᐣ
NI medicine to induce vomiting

pwākamow ᐘᑲᒧᐤ
VAI s/he vomits; s/he is sick [also pākomow]

pwākamowāspinēw
ᐸᐧᐸᑯᐧᐊᐧᐱᐣᐁᐤ
  VAI s/he is vomiting

pwākamowin **ᐸᐧᐸᑯᐊᐧ**
  NI vomit [*also* pākomowin]

pwāna- **ᐸᐧᐊ**
  IPV unable, fail to

pwāsīmow **ᐸᐧᐪᒧ**
  NA Assiniboine, Assiniboine
  person, Nakota, Nakota
  person

pwāsīmow **ᐸᐧᐪᒧ**
  VAI s/he speaks Assiniboine,
  Nakota; s/he speaks Dakota,
  Sioux

pwāstawāc **ᐸᐧᐣᒐᐧ**
  IPC with too little speed or
  energy

pwāstāw **ᐸᐧᐣᒐᐤ**
  IPC slowly; too late

pwāstāwēw **ᐸᐧᐣᒐᐁᐧᐤ**
  VAI s/he is slow; s/he is late

pwāta **ᐸᐧᒐ**
  NA Dakota, Sioux Indian
  [*pl*: -k]

pwātaskisin **ᐸᐧᒐᐢᑭᓯᐧ**
  NI Sioux moccasin

pwātawi- **ᐸᐧᒐᐊᐧ**
  IPV unable to do, failing

pwātawihcikēw **ᐸᐧᒐᐊᐧᐦᒋᑫᐤ**
  VAI s/he is unable to finish

pwātawihēw **ᐸᐧᒐᐊᐧᐦᐁᐧᐤ**
  VTA s/he fails of s.o., s/he
  gives up in helping s.o.

pwātawihtāw **ᐸᐧᒐᐊᐧᐦᒐᐤ**
  VAIt s/he fails of s.t., s/he is
  thwarted at s.t.; s/he gives up
  trying to fix s.t.

pwātimow **ᐸᐧᑎᒧ**
  VAI s/he speaks Dakota, s/he
  speaks Sioux

pwātimowin **ᐸᐧᑎᒧᐊᐧ**
  NI Dakota language

pwātisimow **ᐸᐧᑎᕁᒧ**
  VAI s/he dances pow-wow,
  s/he dances the Grass Dance,
  s/he dances the Sioux Dance
  (a war dance)

pwātisimowin **ᐸᐧᑎᕁᒧᐊᐧ**
  NI the Grass Dance, pow-
  wow

pwātiwiw **ᐸᐧᑎᐊᐧᐤ**
  VAI s/he is a Dakota, Sioux
  Indian

pwāwatēw **ᐸᐧᐊᐧᑌᐤ**
  VAI s/he is overloaded, s/he
  is heavily burdened

pwāwatēwin **ᐸᐧᐊᐧᑌᐊᐧ**
  NI heavy burden

pwāwihēw **ᐸᐧᐊᐧᐦᐁᐧᐤ**
  VTA s/he is unable to carry
  s.o.

pwāwitisahwēw **ᐸᐧᐊᐧᑎᐢᐦᐁᐧᐤ**
  VTA s/he is unable to drive
  s.o.

pwāwīw **ᐸᐧᐊᐧᐤ**
  VAI s/he is pregnant, s/he is
  heavy with child

pwēkitow **ᐯᐧᑭᒍ**
  VAI s/he farts

pwēẏakamēw **ᐯᐧᕁᑲᒣᐤ**
  VTA s/he peels s.o. (by
  teeth) [*cf.* poẏakamēw]

pwēẏakataham **ᐯᐧᕁᑲᒐᐦᐊᐨ**
  VTI s/he peels s.t. (by a hard
  blow)

pwēẏakatahwēw **ᐯᐧᕁᑲᒐᐦᐁᐧᐤ**
  VTA s/he peels s.o. (by a
  hard blow)

pwēẏakinam **ᐯᐧᕁᑲᓇᐨ**
  VTI s/he peels s.t. [*cf.*
  poẏakinam]

pwēẏakinēw **ᐯᐧᕁᑭᐯᐤ**
  VTA s/he peels s.o. (as an
  orange or apple) [*cf.*
  poẏakinēw]

S

ᓴ

sa-sākiskwēw ᓴ ᓵᑭᐢᑵᐤ
VAI s/he pokes his/her own head out of a hole (as a gopher) [*rdpl*]

sa-sāpikanēw ᓴ ᓵᐱᑲᓀᐤ
VAI s/he has sturdy bones; s/he has strong bones [*rdpl*]

sa-sīhkimēw ᓴ ᓰᐦᑭᒣᐤ
VTA s/he urges s.o. on [*rdpl*]

sa-sīhtonam ᓴ ᓰᐦᑐᓇᒼ
VTI s/he supports s.t., s/he holds s.t. up [*rdpl*]

sa-sīhtonēw ᓴ ᓰᐦᑐᓀᐤ
VTA s/he supports s.o., s/he holds s.o. up [*rdpl*]

sa-sīhtosiw ᓴ ᓰᐦᑐᓯᐤ
VAI s/he is stiff (after exertion) [*rdpl*]

sa-sīpēýihtam ᓴ ᓰᐯᔨᐦᑕᒼ
VTI s/he is patient [*rdpl*]

sa-sīpēýimēw ᓴ ᓰᐯᔨᒣᐤ
VTA s/he is patient with s.o. [*rdpl*]

sahkwēw ᓴᐦᑵᐤ
VII it makes a crashing sound; it echoes

sakaham ᓴᑲᐦᐊᒼ
VTI s/he nails s.t., s/he fastens s.t. (by tool)

sakahikan ᓴᑲᐦᐃᑲᐣ
NI nail; spike

sakahikanis ᓴᑲᐦᐃᑲᓂᐢ
NI small nail; tack [*dim*]

sakahikēw ᓴᑲᐦᐃᑫᐤ
VAI s/he drives nails

sakahpisow ᓴᑲᐦᐱᓱᐤ
VAI s/he is tied fast, tightly

sakahpitam ᓴᑲᐦᐱᑕᒼ
VTI s/he ties s.t. fast, tightly

sakahpitēw ᓴᑲᐦᐱᑌᐤ
VII it is tied fast or tightly

sakahpitēw ᓴᑲᐦᐱᑌᐤ
VTA s/he ties s.o. fast or tightly, s/he tethers s.o.

sakahwēw ᓴᑲᐦᐍᐤ
VTA s/he nails s.o. onto something

sakamon ᓴᑲᒧᐣ
VII it adheres; it is caught or hooked, it is attached

sakamotēýanīwēw ᓴᑲᒧᑌᔭᓃᐍᐤ
VAI s/he mumbles; s/he holds his/her own tongue

sakamow ᓴᑲᒧᐤ
VAI s/he holds on; it is fastened on to something, it is attached

sakapwākan ᓴᑲᑇᑲᐣ
NI roasting hook

sakapwān ᓴᑲᑇᐣ
NI hook; roasted food

sakapwānāsk ᓴᑲᑇᓈᐢᐠ
NI stick for roasting [*pl*: -wa; *cf.* apwānāsk]

sakapwēw ᓴᑲᐻᐤ
VAI it roasts over a fire (by hanging, with string on stick)

sakatahtahkwanēnēw ᓴᑲᑕᐦᑕᐦᑿᓀᓀᐤ
VTA s/he seizes s.o. by the wing

sakatēhtam ᓴᑲᑌᐦᑕᒼ
VTI s/he holds s.t. between his/her own teeth

sakatēmēw ᓴᑲᑌᒣᐤ
VTA s/he holds s.o. between his/her own teeth

sakāhk ᓴᑳᕽ
IPC in the woods [*loc*; *cf.* sakāw]

sakāpātam ᓴᑳᐹᑕᒼ
VTI s/he attaches s.t. by sewing, s/he sews s.t. on

sakāpēkahpisow ᓴᑳᐯᑲᐦᐱᓱᐤ
VAI it is tethered, hitched

sakāpēkinēw ᓴᑳᐯᑭᓀᐤ
VTA s/he leads s.o., s/he holds s.o. by string in hand

sakāpēkipahēw ᓴᑳᐯᑭᐸᐦᐁᐤ
VTA s/he leads s.o.; s/he makes s.o. run on a rope (as on a lead)

sakāpīhkanis ᓴᑳᐲᐦᑲᓂᐢ
NI string [*dim*]

sakāpīhkātam ᓴᑳᐲᐦᑳᑕᒼ
VTI s/he ties s.t. fast

sakāpīhkātēw ᓴᑳᐲᐦᑳᑌᐤ
VTA s/he ties s.o. fast

sakās ᓴᑳᐢ
NI small bluff of trees [*dim*; *cf.* sakāw]

sakāskwaham ᓴᑳᐢᑿᐦᐊᒼ
VTI s/he pins s.t.; s/he buttons s.t. up; s/he fastens s.t.

sakāskwahamawēw ᓴᑳᐢᑿᐦᐊᒪᐍᐤ
VTA s/he pins (it/him) for s.o.; s/he buttons (it/him) for s.o.; s/he fastens (it/him) for s.o.

sakāskwahikan ᓴᑳᐢᑿᐦᐃᑲᐣ
NI pin for tent door

sakāskwahikanis ᓴᑳᐢᑿᐦᐃᑲᓂᐢ
NI clothes pin [*dim*]

sakāskwahon ᓴᑳᐢᑿᐦᐅᐣ
NA safety-pin; button; brooch; buckle; clasp

sakāskwahonis ᓴᑳᐢᑿᐦᐅᓂᐢ
NI hook and eye [*generally pl*]

sakāskwahwēw ᓴᑳᐢᑿᐦᐍᐤ
VTA s/he buttons s.o. up; s/he pins s.o.; s/he fastens s.o.

sakāw ᓴᑳᐤ
NI bush, woods, grove of trees, woodland, forest [*also VII*]

sakāwaskosiya ᓴᑳᐘᐢᑯᓯᔭ
NI forest grass [*pl generally*]

sakāwi-pihēw ᓴᑳᐏ ᐱᐦᐁᐤ
NA wood-cock, wood-partridge, wood chicken; spruce grouse [*cf.* pihēw, pihýēw; *wC*: pithīw]

sakāwiýiniw ᓴᑳᐏᔨᓂᐤ
NA Woods Cree, Woods Cree person

sakāwiýinīwiw ᓴᑳᐏᔨᓃᐏᐤ
VAI s/he is a Woods Cree

sakicihcēnēw ᓴᑭᒋᐦᒉᓀᐤ
VTA s/he seizes s.o.'s hand (by hand), s/he takes s.o. by the hand; s/he shakes hands with s.o.

sakicihcēnitowak ᓴᑭᒋᐦᒉᓂᑐᐘᐠ
VAI they take one another by hand; they shake hands with one another

sakicin ᓴᑭᒋᐣ
VAI s/he is caught on s.t.

sakikwēnam ᓴᑭᑵᓇᒼ
VTI s/he holds s.t. by the neck

sakikwēnēw ᓴᑭᑵᓀᐤ
VTA s/he seizes s.o.'s neck (by hand), s/he holds s.o. by the neck, s/he takes s.o. by the neck

sakikwēpisow ᓴᑭᑵᐱᓱᐤ
VAI it is tied by the neck, it is bridled

sakikwēpitēw ᓴᐱᖃ·ᐱᑌᐤ
   VTA s/he grabs s.o. by the neck

sakimēs ᓴᐱᔆ
   NA mosquito

sakimēsis ᓴᐱᔆᓯ
   NA small mosquito [*dim*]

sakimēskāw ᓴᐱᔆᑳᐳ
   VII there is an abundance of mosquitoes, it is infested with mosquitoes

sakimēw ᓴᐱᔆᐤ
   NA mosquito

sakimēw ᓴᐱᔆᐤ
   VTA s/he holds s.o. firmly (with the teeth)

sakimēwayān ᓴᐱᔆᐊ·ᐷ
   NI mosquito netting

sakimiyēstawānēnēw ᓴᐱᒋᐧᐨᑕᐃ·ᓇᓀᐤ
   VTA s/he seizes s.o. by the beard [*also* sakimīhistōwānēnēw]

sakinam ᓴᐱᓇᐨ
   VTI s/he hangs on to s.t. (by hand)

sakinamawēw ᓴᐱᓇᒪᐧᐤ
   VTA s/he seizes (it/him) for s.o.

sakinēw ᓴᐱᓀᐤ
   VTA s/he seizes s.o., s/he hangs on to s.o. (by hand)

sakiniskēnēw ᓴᐱᓂᐢᑫᓀᐤ
   VTA s/he seizes s.o.'s arm (by hand); s/he holds s.o.'s hand, s/he holds s.o. by the arm

sakiniskēnitowak ᓴᐱᓂᐢᑫᓂᑐᐊ·ᐠ
   VAI they hold hands, they hold hands with one another

sakiniskēpahēw ᓴᐱᓂᐢᑫᐸᐦᐤ
   VTA s/he runs s.o. by the arm

sakipāson ᓴᐱᐹᓱ
   NA button

sakipātam ᓴᐱᐹᑕᐨ
   VTI s/he buttons s.t.

sakipātēw ᓴᐱᐹᑌᐤ
   VTA s/he buttons s.o. (*e.g.* pants)

sakipitonēnēw ᓴᐱᐱᑐᓀᓀᐤ
   VTA s/he seizes s.o. by the arm

sakipitonēpitēw ᓴᐱᐱᑐᓀᐱᑌᐤ
   VTA s/he pulls s.o. by the arm

sakiskam ᓴᐱᐢᑲᐨ
   VTI s/he steps on s.t.

sakiskawēw ᓴᐱᐢᑲᐧᐤ
   VTA s/he steps on s.o.

sakiskēnēw ᓴᐱᐢᑫᓀᐤ
   VTA s/he takes s.o. by the hand

sakistikwānēcin ᓴᐱᐢᓂᐧᓇ·ᐨᕐ
   VAI s/he gets snagged by his/her own hair

sakistikwānēnēw ᓴᐱᐢᓂᐧᐧᐤ
   VTA s/he seizes s.o.'s head or hair (by hand)

sakistikwānēpitēw ᓴᐱᐢᓂᐧᐧᐱᑌᐤ
   VTA s/he pulls s.o. by the head or hair

sakwāskwaham ᓴᐧ·ᐢᐧᐦᐩᐊᐨ
   VTI s/he fastens s.t.; s/he zippers s.t. up

sakwāskwahon ᓴᐧ·ᐢᐧᐦᐅᐳ
   NA button [*see also* aniskamān]

samacīw ᓴᒪᒋᐤ
   VAI it rears up (*e.g.* horse)

samahcāw ᓴᒪᐦᒐᐤ
   VII it is steep

samakiskam ᓴᒪᐱᐢᑲᐨ
   VTI s/he weighs s.t. down

samakiskawēw ᓴᒪᐱᐢᑲᐧᐤ
   VTA s/he weighs s.o. down

samaskipayihow ᓴᒪᐢᐱᐸᔨᐦᐤ
   VAI s/he throws oneself flat

samaskisin ᓴᒪᐢᐱᓯᐣ
   VAI s/he lies flat

samaskīw ᓴᒪᐢᐱᐤ
   VAI s/he stays crouching flat

samatapiw ᓴᒪᑕᐱᐤ
   VAI s/he sits up

samatiskam ᓴᒪᓂᐢᑲᐨ
   VTI s/he sits on s.t. and flattens it

samatiskawēw ᓴᒪᓂᐢᑲᐧᐤ
   VTA s/he sits on s.o. and flattens it

samatiskwēyiw ᓴᒪᓂᐢᐧᐧᔨᐤ
   VAI s/he raises his/her own head

samiskamāsow ᓴᒋᐢᑲᒫᓱᐤ
   VAI s/he presses down for him/herself

sapiko ᓴᐱᐦ
   IPC actually; in fact [*cf.* ēsa piko, isapiko]

sasahkēmow ᓴᓴᐦᐱᐧᒧᐤ
   VAI s/he speaks boldly, brashly, bragging

sasawāpohtēw ᓴᓴᐊ·ᐳᐦᑌᐤ
   VAI s/he walks with wobbly knees

sasākisiw ᓴᓴᐱᓯᐤ
   VAI s/he is selfish, s/he is stingy

sasākisiwin ᓴᓴᐱᓯᐃ·ᐳ
   NI stinginess; miserliness

sasākosiw ᓴᓴᐦᑯᓯᐤ
   VAI s/he is slender

sasākwāw ᓴᓴᐧ·ᐤ
   VII it is narrow [*rdpl, cf.* sākwāw; *wC:* sākāwāw]

sasciwihēw ᓴᔆᒋᐃᐦᐧᐤ
   VTA s/he startles s.o.

sasīhciwihēw ᓴᔆᒋᐃᐦᐧᐤ
   VTA s/he makes s.o. ashamed, s/he embarrasses s.o.

sasīpihtam ᓴᔆᐱᐦᑕᐨ
   VTI s/he is disobedient, s/he disobeys s.t.; s/he is stubborn; s/he fails to listen (to s.t.)

sasīpihtamowin ᓴᔆᐱᐦᑕᒧᐃᐧᐤ
   NI disobedience

sasīpihtawēw ᓴᔆᐱᐦᑕᐧᐤ
   VTA s/he fails to listen to s.o., s/he disobeys s.o.

sasīpihtawakēw ᓴᔆᐱᐦᑕᐧᑫᐧᐤ
   VAI s/he is disobedient, s/he refuses to listen

saskaci- ᓴᐢᑲᒋ
   IPV weary, tired of

saskaham ᓴᐢᑲᐦᐊᐨ
   VTI s/he kindles s.t., s/he ignites s.t, s/he lights s.t. (*e.g.* a lamp); s/he sets s.t. on fire

saskahamawēw ᓴᐢᑲᐦᐊᒪᐧᐤ
   VTA s/he sets fire to (it/him) for s.o.; s/he lights (it/him) for s.o.

saskahamāsow ᓴᐢᑲᐦᐊᒫᓱᐤ
   VAI s/he lights (it/him) for him/herself (*e.g.* fire, pipe)

saskahispwākanēw ᓴᐢᑲᐦᐃᐢᐯᐧ·ᑲᓀᐤ
   VAI s/he lights the pipe

saskahohtākan ᓴᐢᑲᐦᐅᐦᑖᑲᐣ
   NI cane

saskahohtān ᓴᐢᑲᐦᐅᐦᑖᐣ
   NI cane

saskahohtēw ᓴᐢᑲᐦᐅᐦᑌᐤ
   VAI s/he walks with a cane

saskahon ᓴᐢᑲᐦᐅᐣ
   NI cane, staff, walking-stick

saskahow ᓴᐢᑲᐦᐅᐤ
   VAI s/he uses a cane

saskahowākēw ᓴᐢᑲᐦᐅᐧ·ᑫᐧᐤ
   VAI s/he uses s.t. as a cane; s/he uses s.t. when walking

saskahowin ᓴᐢᑲᐦᐅᐃᐧᐤ
   NI crutch; [*pl:*] crutches

saskahwēw ᓴᐢᑲᐦᐧᐤ
   VTA s/he kindles s.o., s/he ignites s.o., s/he sets s.o. on fire

saskamēw ᓴᐢᑲᔆᐤ
   VTA s/he puts s.o. into his/her own mouth

saskamohēw ᓴᐢᑲᒧᐦᐧᐤ
   VTA s/he puts (it/him) into s.o.'s mouth for that one, s/he gives s.o. a soother; s/he gives s.o. communion

saskamon ᓴᐢᑲᒧᐣ
   NI holy communion; sacrament

saskamow ᓴᐢᑲᒧᐤ
   VAI s/he puts (it/him) into his/her own mouth; s/he takes holy communion

saskamowēpinēw ᓴᐢᑲᒧᐧᐱᓀᐤ
   VTA s/he throws (it/him) into s.o.'s mouth for that one (*e.g.* mother bird feeding young)

saskan ᓴᐢᑲᐣ
   VII it thaws, it is melting, it is ice-break, it is a chinook; it is the thaw, it is a time of fast snow-melting

saskaniýōwēw ᓴᐢᑲᓂᔫᐍᐤ
VII it is a chinook

saskanōtin ᓴᐢᑲᓅᑎᐣ
NI chinook wind [*also VII* "it is a chinook wind"]

saskatahtam ᓴᐢᑲᑕᐦᑕᒼ
VTI s/he is tired of eating the same food

saskatēýihtam ᓴᐢᑲᑌᔨᐦᑕᒼ
VTI s/he is tired of s.t.; s/he is tired of his/her own surroundings and life

saskatēýimēw ᓴᐢᑲᑌᔨᒣᐤ
VTA s/he is tired of s.o.

saskatwēmopaýiw ᓴᐢᑲᑚᒧᐸᔨᐤ
VAI s/he takes s.t. into his/her own mouth with noise; s/he eats s.t. noisily, s/he slurps s.t.

saskisow ᓴᐢᑭᓱᐤ
VAI it catches on fire, it ignites, s/he is on fire

saskitēpaýiw ᓴᐢᑭᑌᐸᔨᐤ
VII it ignites; it catches on fire

saskitēw ᓴᐢᑭᑌᐤ
VII it catches on fire, it ignites, it is on fire

sawahamawēw ᓴᐘᐦᐊᒪᐍᐤ
VTA s/he spreads (it/him) for s.o.

sawāhpinēw ᓴᐚᐦᐱᓀᐤ
VAI s/he has unexplainable pain

sawānakēýihtam ᓴᐚᓇᑫᔨᐦᑕᒼ
VTI s/he is jealous of s.t., s/he is envious of s.t.

sawānakēýihtamowin ᓴᐚᓇᑫᔨᐦᑕᒧᐎᐣ
NI jealousy in the mind

sawānakēýimēw ᓴᐚᓇᑫᔨᒣᐤ
VTA s/he is jealous of s.o., s/he is envious of s.o.

sawānakēýimoskiw ᓴᐚᓇᑫᔨᒧᐢᑭᐤ
VAI s/he is habitually jealous [*hab*]

sawānakēýimow ᓴᐚᓇᑫᔨᒧᐤ
VAI s/he is jealous, s/he envies, s/he is envious

sawānakēýimowin ᓴᐚᓇᑫᔨᒧᐎᐣ
NI jealousy; envy

sawēsiw ᓴᐍᓯᐤ
VAI it has four sides

sawēsk ᓴᐍᐢᐠ
NI sword; bayonet [*pl*: -wa; *cf.* isawēsk]

sawēyāw ᓴᐍᔮᐤ
VII it has four sides

sawēýihcikēwin ᓴᐍᔨᐦᒋᑫᐎᐣ
NI a blessing

sawēýihtam ᓴᐍᔨᐦᑕᒼ
VTI s/he blesses s.t.

sawēýihtākosiw ᓴᐍᔨᐦᑖᑯᓯᐤ
VAI s/he is blessed

sawēýihtākosiwin ᓴᐍᔨᐦᑖᑯᓯᐎᐣ
NI blessedness; a blessing

sawēýihtākwan ᓴᐍᔨᐦᑖᑿᐣ
VII it is blessed

sawēýihtowak ᓴᐍᔨᐦᑐᐘᐠ
VAI they bless one another; they love one another

sawēýihtowin ᓴᐍᔨᐦᑐᐎᐣ
NI blessing; the act of blessing

sawēýimēw ᓴᐍᔨᒣᐤ
VTA s/he cherishes s.o., s/he loves s.o., s/he takes care of s.o., s/he looks out for s.o.; s/he is generous to s.o.; s/he blesses s.o.; s/he gives s.o. the last sacrament

sawēýimikowisiw ᓴᐍᔨᒥᑯᐏᓯᐤ
VAI s/he is blessed by the powers, God

ᓵ

sāh-sāposow ᓵᐦ ᓵᐳᓱᐤ
VAI s/he has frequent diarrhea [*rdpl*]

sāh-sīpīpitam ᓴ ᓰᐲᐱᑕᒼ
VTI s/he stretches s.t. repeatedly [*rdpl*]

sāh-sīpīpitēw ᓴ ᓰᐲᐱᑌᐤ
VTA s/he stretches s.o. repeatedly [*rdpl*]

sākaciwahtēw ᓵᑲᒋᐘᐦᑌᐤ
VII it sticks out at the top in boiling

sākaciwasow ᓵᑲᒋᐘᓱᐤ
VAI it sticks out at the top in boiling

sākahikan ᓵᑲᐦᐃᑲᐣ
NI lake

sākahikanis ᓵᑲᐦᐃᑲᓂᐢ
NI pond, small lake [*dim*]

sākahikanisis ᓵᑲᐦᐃᑲᓂᓯᐢ
NI pond, small lake [*dim*]

sākahikanisiwiw ᓵᑲᐦᐃᑲᓂᓯᐎᐤ
VII it is a small lake

sākahikaniwiw ᓵᑲᐦᐃᑲᓂᐎᐤ
VII it is a lake, it has lakes

sākamon ᓵᑲᒧᐣ
VII it sticks out, it projects [*cf.* sākamow]

sākamow ᓵᑲᒧᐤ
VAI s/he sticks out

sākamow ᓵᑲᒧᐤ
VII it sticks out [*cf.* sākamon]

sākaskāw ᓵᑲᐢᑳᐤ
VII it is the grass showing growth

sākaskinaham ᓵᑲᐢᑭᓇᐦᐊᒼ
VTI s/he fills s.t. up [*cf.* sākaskinahtāw]

sākaskinahēw ᓵᑲᐢᑭᓇᐦᐁᐤ
VTA s/he fills s.o. up, s/he fills s.o. (*e.g.* pail)

sākaskinahtamawēw ᓵᑲᐢᑭᓇᐦᑕᒪᐍᐤ
VTA s/he fills (it/him) for s.o.

sākaskinahtāw ᓵᑲᐢᑭᓇᐦᑖᐤ
VAIt s/he fills s.t. up, s/he makes s.t. full [*cf.* sākaskinaham]

sākaskinēmākwan ᓵᑲᐢᑭᓀᒫᑿᐣ
VII it is filled with a scent (*i.e.* a place)

sākaskinēpatāw ᓵᑲᐢᑭᓀᐸᑖᐤ
VAIt s/he fills s.t. to the brim

sākaskinēpiwak ᓵᑲᐢᑭᓀᐱᐘᐠ
VAI they are seated filled to capacity; they fill a place to capacity while seated

sākaskinēw ᓵᑲᐢᑭᓀᐤ
VAI s/he is full; it is in to the full

sākaskinēw ᓵᑲᐢᑭᓀᐤ
VII it is full; it is in to the full

sākaskinēyāpahtēw ᓵᑲᐢᑭᓀᔮᐸᐦᑌᐤ
VII it is filled with smoke

sākaskitēw ᓵᑲᐢᑭᑌᐤ
VII it projects out of the ground

sākatēhtam ᓵᑲᑌᐦᑕᒼ
VTI s/he holds s.t. with the teeth so as to project from his/her own mouth

sākatēmēw ᓵᑲᑌᒣᐤ
VTA s/he holds s.o. with the teeth so as to project from his/her own mouth

sākākonēkāpawiw ᓵᑳᑯᓀᑳᐸᐏᐤ
VAI s/he stands sticking out of the snow

sākākonēw ᓵᑳᑯᓀᐤ
VAI s/he sticks out of the snow

sākāpitēw ᓵᑳᐱᑌᐤ
VAI s/he is teething

sākāskitēw ᓵᑳᐢᑭᑌᐤ
VII flames are seen from a distance

sākāstēnāw ᓵᑳᐢᑌᓈᐤ
NI the east

sākāstēnāw ᓵᑳᐢᑌᓈᐤ
VAI it is sunrise, it rises (*e.g.* sun)

sākāstēnohk ᓵᑳᐢᑌᓄᕽ
IPC east, in the east [*lit*: "towards the sunrise"]

sākāstēnohk isi ᓵᑳᐢᑌᓄᕽ ᐃᓯ
IPH toward the east, eastward

sākāstēw ᓵᑳᐢᑌᐤ
NI sunrise

sākāstēw ᓵᑳᐢᑌᐤ
VII it is sunrise; it is sunny, it is day-light

sākāwāpisk ᓵᑳᐚᐱᐢᐠ
NI narrow stone or metal [*pl*: -wa]

sākāwāsin ᓵᑳᐚᓯᐣ
VII it is a bit narrow, it is rather narrow [*dim*]

sākāwāw ᓵᑳᐚᐤ
VII it is narrow

sākēkamon ᓵᑫᑲᒧᐣ
VII it sticks out as cloth, it projects as cloth

sākēwē- ᓵᑫᐍ·
IPV behind obstacle to vision, into view

sākēwēpahtāw ᓵᑫᐍ·ᐸᐦᑖᐤ
VAI s/he runs into view

sākēwēpayihow ᓵᑫᐍ·ᐸᔨᐦᐅᐤ
VAI s/he throws him/herself into view

sākēwēpayiw ᓵᑫᐍ·ᐸᔨᐤ
VAI s/he comes into view

sākēwēpiciw ᓵᑫᐍ·ᐱᒋᐤ
VAI s/he treks into view

sākēwētotam ᓵᑫᐍ·ᑐᑕᒼ
VTI s/he comes into view of s.t.

sākēwētotawēw ᓵᑫᐍ·ᑐᑕᐏᐤ
VTA s/he comes into view of s.o.

sākēwēw ᓵᑫᐍᐤ
VAI s/he comes into view

sākihākan ᓵᑭᐦᐋᑲᐣ
NA loved one; favourite one

sākihēw ᓵᑭᐦᐁᐤ
VTA s/he loves s.o., s/he prizes s.o., s/he is attached to s.o.

sākihikosiw ᓵᑭᐦᐃᑯᓯᐤ
VAI s/he is lovable

sākihisow ᓵᑭᐦᐃᓱᐤ
VAI s/he loves him/herself; s/he likes him/herself

sākihito-maskihkiy ᓵᑭᐦᐃᑐ ᒪᐢᑭᐦᑭᐩ
NI love medicine

sākihitowak ᓵᑭᐦᐃᑐᐊᐠ
VAI they love one another

sākihitowask ᓵᑭᐦᐃᑐᐊᐢᐠ
NI love medicine [*pl*: -wa]

sākihitowin ᓵᑭᐦᐃᑐᐃᐣ
NI love; mutual love; affection; charity

sākihiwēw ᓵᑭᐦᐃᐍᐤ
VAI s/he loves others

sākihiwēwin ᓵᑭᐦᐃᐍᐃᐣ
NI love; charity

sākihtam ᓵᑭᐦᑕᒼ
VTI s/he likes s.t., s/he loves s.t.; s/he has a strong attachment to s.t. [*cf.* sākihtāw]

sākihtamawēw ᓵᑭᐦᑕᒪᐍᐤ
VTA s/he keeps (it/him) from s.o.; s/he refuses (love to) s.o.

sākihtāw ᓵᑭᐦᑖᐤ
VAIt s/he loves s.t., s/he prizes s.t., s/he is attached to s.t.; s/he is stingy of s.t., s/he is selfish of s.t. [*cf.* sākihtam]

sākikin ᓵᑭᑭᐣ
VII it grows forth, it sprouts

sākikiw ᓵᑭᑭᐤ
VAI s/he grows forth, it sprouts

sākiniskēw ᓵᑭᓂᐢᑫᐤ
VAI s/he takes his/her own

hand out from under the covers, s/he sticks his/her own hand out from cover

sākipakāw ᓵᑭᐸᑳᐤ
VII it is budding, it is leaf-budding; it sprouts leaves; it is the time of leaf-budding

sākipakāwi-pīsim ᓵᑭᐸᑳ· ᐱᓰᒼ
NA Leaf-Budding Moon; May [*obv*: -wa]

sākiskwēkāpawiw ᓵᑭᐢᒀᑳᐸᐃᐤ
VAI s/he stands with head sticking out

sākiskwēpayihow ᓵᑭᐢᒀ·ᐸᔨᐦᐅᐤ
VAI s/he pokes his/her own head out; s/he throws him/herself so that his/her own head sticks out

sākiskwēw ᓵᑭᐢᒀᐤ
VAI s/he sticks his/her own head out

sākistikwānēnēw ᓵᑭᐢᑎᑲᐣᐁᓀᐤ
VTA s/he uncovers s.o.'s head

sākistikwānēw ᓵᑭᐢᑎᑲᐣᐁᐤ
VAI s/he has his/her own head out from under covers

sākitawāhk ᓵᑭᑕᐘᕽ
INM Ile à la Crosse, SK [*loc; place name given to a number of sites where waters meet; also* sākitawāk]

sākitawāhk ᓵᑭᑕᐘᕽ
IPC at the mouth of a river

sākitawāwiyiniw ᓵᑭᑕᐘ·ᐃᔨᓂᐤ
NA Ile à la Crosse Indian

sākitēyanīstam ᓵᑭᐟᕁᐊᓃᐢᑕᒼ
VTI s/he sticks his/her own tongue out at s.t.

sākitēyanīstawēw ᓵᑭᐟᕁᐊᓃᐢᑕᐍᐤ
VTA s/he sticks his/her own tongue out at s.o.

sākitēyanīw ᓵᑭᐟᕁᐊᓃᐤ
VAI s/he sticks his/her own tongue out

sākitēyanīwēw ᓵᑭᐟᕁᐊᓃᐍᐤ
VAI s/he sticks his/her own tongue out

sākiy ᓵᑭᐩ
NI inlet

sākiw ᓵᑭᐤ
NA crab; lobster [*cf.* asākiw]

sākohēw ᓵᑯᐦᐁᐤ
VTA s/he overcomes s.o., s/he overpowers s.o., s/he defeats s.o.

sākohitowak ᓵᑯᐦᐃᑐᐊᐠ
VAI they overpower one another

sākohtamawēw ᓵᑯᐦᑕᒪᐍᐤ
VTA s/he defeats (it/him) for s.o.

sākohtāw ᓵᑯᐦᑖᐤ
VAIt s/he overcomes s.t., s/he defeats s.t., s/he manages s.t.; s/he

accomplishes s.t., s/he is able to lift s.t. up; s/he is capable of defending

sākohtēw ᓵᑯᐦᑌᐤ
VAI s/he comes into view; it rises (*i.e.* the sun)

sākohtwāw ᓵᑯᐦᑤᐤ
VAI s/he overcomes, s/he is victorious

sākohtwāwin ᓵᑯᐦᑤᐃᐣ
NI victory

sākowātēw ᓵᑯᐚᑌᐤ
VTA s/he whoops at or over s.o.

sākowēstayawēw ᓵᑯᐍᐢᑕᔭᐁᐤ
VTA s/he yells for s.o., s/he encourages s.o.

sākowēw ᓵᑯᐍᐤ
VAI s/he calls, s/he yells

sākōc ᓵᑰᐨ
IPC really!

sākōcihēw ᓵᑰᒋᐦᐁᐤ
VTA s/he defeats s.o., s/he overcomes s.o., s/he beats s.o.

sākōcihitowak ᓵᑰᒋᐦᐃᑐᐊᐠ
VAI they defeat one another

sākōcihiwēw ᓵᑰᒋᐦᐃᐍᐤ
VAI s/he defeats people, s/he is victorious

sākōcihiwēwin ᓵᑰᒋᐦᐃᐍᐃᐣ
NI victory

sākōcihtāw ᓵᑰᒋᐦᑖᐤ
VAIt s/he conquers s.t.

sākōcihtowak ᓵᑰᒋᐦᑐᐊᐠ
VAI they talk one another down

sākōcihtwāw ᓵᑰᒋᐦᑤᐤ
VAI s/he is defeated

sākōcimēw ᓵᑰᒋᒣᐤ
VTA s/he convinces s.o. by speech; s/he talks s.o. down, s/he persuades s.o.

sākōcimiwēw ᓵᑰᒋᒥᐍᐤ
VAI s/he persuades people, s/he convinces people

sākōcimiwēwin ᓵᑰᒋᒥᐍᐃᐣ
NI persuasion

sākōtēhēw ᓵᑰᑌᐦᐁᐤ
VAI s/he is cowardly; s/he is timid

sākōtēhēwin ᓵᑰᑌᐦᐁᐃᐣ
NI cowardice

sākōtēyimēw ᓵᑰᑌᔨᒣᐤ
VTA s/he intimidates s.o.

sākwahtamow ᓵᒂᐦᑕᒧᐤ
NA large hawk [*also* sasākwatēmow, sahkwātamow]

sākwāskosimēw ᓵᒁᐢᑯᓯᒣᐤ
VTA s/he lays a child down under blankets with feet protruding

sākwēs ᓵᒉᐢ
NA mink [*cf.* sākwēsiw]

sākwēsis ᓵᒉᓯᐢ
NA baby mink [*dim*]

sākwēsiw ᓵᑵᓯᐤ
NA mink, full-grown mink [*cf.* sākwēs]
sākwēsiwayān ᓵᑵᓯᐘᔮᐣ
NA mink pelt, mink fur
sākwēýihtam ᓵᑵᔨᐦᑕᒼ
VTI s/he fears s.t. to be too difficult
sākwēýimēw ᓵᑵᔨᒣᐤ
VTA s/he doubts s.o.; s/he fears for s.o., s/he fears s.o. is not capable
sākwēýimow ᓵᑵᔨᒧᐤ
VAI s/he hesitates; s/he is unwilling
sākwēýimowin ᓵᑵᔨᒧᐏᐣ
NI hesitation
sāmaham ᓵᒪᐦᐊᒼ
VTI s/he touches s.t. with a tool
sāmahamawēw ᓵᒪᐦᐊᒪᐌᐤ
VTA s/he touches (it/him) with a tool for s.o.
sāmahtam ᓵᒪᐦᑕᒼ
VTI s/he tastes s.t., s/he touches s.t. with mouth
sāmahwēw ᓵᒪᐦᐌᐤ
VTA s/he touches s.o. with tool
sāmamēw ᓵᒪᒣᐤ
VTA s/he tastes s.o., s/he touches s.o. with mouth
sāmaskēhtin ᓵᒪᐢᑫᐦᑎᐣ
VII it lies or falls so as to touch ground
sāmaskēhtitāw ᓵᒪᐢᑫᐦᑎᑖᐤ
VAIt s/he places s.t. to touch the ground
sāmihtin ᓵᒥᐦᑎᐣ
VII it touches (as something touching the floor)
sāmihtitāw ᓵᒥᐦᑎᑖᐤ
VAIt s/he touches s.t.; s/he makes s.t. touch (as a dress touching the floor)
sāminam ᓵᒥᓇᒼ
VTI s/he touches s.t.
sāminēw ᓵᒥᓀᐤ
VTA s/he touches s.o.
sāmisin ᓵᒥᓯᐣ
VAI s/he touches (s.t.) with his/her own body
sāmiskam ᓵᒥᐢᑲᒼ
VTI s/he touches s.t. with foot
sāmiskawēw ᓵᒥᐢᑲᐌᐤ
VTA s/he touches s.o. with foot; s/he rubs against s.o.
sāpahcikanihk ᓵᐸᐦᒋᑲᓂᕽ
IPC opening for smoke at top of tipi
sāpēýihtam ᓵᐯᔨᐦᑕᒼ
VTI s/he is not keen on s.t.
sāpēýimēw ᓵᐯᔨᒣᐤ
VTA s/he is not keen on s.o.
sāpikanēw ᓵᐱᑲᓀᐤ
VAI s/he has strong bones
sāpo ᓵᐳ
IPC through
sāpo- ᓵᐳ
IPV fully, exhaustively, through, through and through, right through, from end to end; beyond
sāpo-itwēw ᓵᐳ ᐃᑵᐤ
VAI s/he recites s.t. through
sāpo-kiskinohtahēw ᓵᐳ ᑭᐢᑭᓄᐦᑕᐦᐁᐤ
VTA s/he guides s.o. all the way through
sāpo-pimiskanawēw ᓵᐳ ᐱᒥᐢᑲᓇᐌᐤ
VAI s/he goes cross country; s/he leaves tracks right through the territory
sāpo-pimohtēw ᓵᐳ ᐱᒧᐦᑌᐤ
VAI s/he walks past
sāpo-wāsitēw ᓵᐳ ᐚᓯᑌᐤ
VII lights are seen shining through, it shines through
sāpo-wēpinam ᓵᐳ ᐍᐱᓇᒼ
VTI s/he throws s.t. through
sāpo-wēpinēw ᓵᐳ ᐍᐱᓀᐤ
VTA s/he throws s.o. through
sāpocin ᓵᐳᒋᐣ
VAI s/he pierces him/herself through
sāpociwan ᓵᐳᒋᐘᐣ
VII it flows through
sāpohāw ᓵᐳᐦᐋᐤ
VAI s/he flies through a pane of glass; s/he flies right past without stopping
sāpohkwāmiw ᓵᐳᐦᒁᒥᐤ
VAI s/he sleeps in, s/he oversleeps; s/he sleeps right through the night
sāpohtak ᓵᐳᐦᑕᐠ
NI rifle [*pl*: -wa]
sāpohtawān ᓵᐳᐦᑕᐚᐣ
NI long lodge, long hall, hallway; buffalo lane [*cf.* sāpostawān]
sāpohtawēhtēw ᓵᐳᐦᑕᐍᐦᑌᐤ
VAI s/he walks through, s/he walks through an opening
sāpohtawēyāw ᓵᐳᐦᑕᐍᔮᐤ
VII it has an opening at each end
sāpohtēw ᓵᐳᐦᑌᐤ
VAI s/he walks through (s.t.), s/he goes right past; s/he passes through
sāpohýawāw ᓵᐳᐦᔭᐚᐤ
VII it has an opening (as a culvert)
sāpokēhcāw ᓵᐳᑫᐦᒑᐤ
NI wet ground
sāponam ᓵᐳᓇᒼ
VTI s/he puts or pierces through s.t.
sāponākosiw ᓵᐳᓈᑯᓯᐤ
VAI s/he is transparent; it is seen through (like a shawl can be seen through)
sāponākwan ᓵᐳᓈᑿᐣ
VII it is transparent
sāponēw ᓵᐳᓀᐤ
VTA s/he puts or pierces through s.o.
sāponikan ᓵᐳᓂᑲᐣ
NI needle
sāponikanis ᓵᐳᓂᑲᓂᐢ
NI small needle [*dim*]
sāpopacikēw ᓵᐳᐸᒋᑫᐤ
VAI s/he wets things
sāpopahēw ᓵᐳᐸᐦᐁᐤ
VTA s/he gets s.o. drenched, s/he makes s.o. wet (*e.g.* by spraying)
sāpopatāw ᓵᐳᐸᑖᐤ
VAIt s/he waters s.t.; s/he drenches s.t., s/he dips s.t., s/he gets s.t. thoroughly wet
sāpopaýiw ᓵᐳᐸᔨᐤ
VAI s/he is pierced, it is leaky
sāpopaýiw ᓵᐳᐸᔨᐤ
VII it is pierced, it is leaky; it goes through; it passes through
sāpopēcihcēw ᓵᐳᐯᒋᐦᒉᐤ
VAI s/he has wet hands
sāpopēkan ᓵᐳᐯᑲᐣ
VII it is soaking
sāpopēmēw ᓵᐳᐯᒣᐤ
VTA s/he wets s.o. with mouth
sāpopēskisinēw ᓵᐳᐯᐢᑭᓯᓀᐤ
VAI s/he has wet moccasins, shoes
sāpopētēhtam ᓵᐳᐯᑌᐦᑕᒼ
VTI s/he wets s.t. in his/her own mouth
sāpopēw ᓵᐳᐯᐤ
VAI s/he is wet, s/he is drenched
sāpopēw ᓵᐳᐯᐤ
VII it is wet, it is drenched
sāpopēyāw ᓵᐳᐯᔮᐤ
VII it is water-soaked (*e.g.* the ground)
sāpopitam ᓵᐳᐱᑕᒼ
VTI s/he pulls s.t. through
sāpopitēw ᓵᐳᐱᑌᐤ
VTA s/he pulls s.o. through
sāposci- ᓵᐳᐢᒋ
IPV through
sāposikan ᓵᐳᓯᑲᐣ
NI purgative, purge, laxative
sāposkam ᓵᐳᐢᑲᒼ
VTI s/he passes through s.t.; s/he pushes s.t. through by foot
sāposkākow ᓵᐳᐢᑳᑯᐤ
VTA it goes through s.o., it enters s.o.'s body; it purges s.o. [*inanimate actor form of VTA* sāposkaw-]
sāposkāwisiw ᓵᐳᐢᑳᐏᓯᐤ
VAI s/he has diarrhea
sāposow ᓵᐳᓱᐤ
VAI s/he has diarrhea, s/he has dysentery
sāposowāspinēw ᓵᐳᓱᐚᐢᐱᓀᐤ
VAI s/he has diarrhea

sāposowin ᓵᐳᓱᐃᐧᐣ
  NI diarrhea; dysentery
sāposōhpinēw ᓵᐳᓲᐦᐱᓀᐤ
  VAI s/he has diarrhea
sāpostaham ᓵᐳᐢᑕᐦᐊᒼ
  VTI s/he pierces s.t. through
  with a needle
sāpostahwēw ᓵᐳᐢᑕᐦᐯᐤ
  VTA s/he pierces s.o.
  through with a needle
sāpostamow ᓵᐳᐢᑕᒧᐤ
  VII it goes through [*cf.*
  kā-sāpostamoki "reaches (on
  a carriage)"]
sāpostawān ᓵᐳᐢᑕᐋᐧᐣ
  NI long lodge [*cf.*
  sāpohtawān]
sāpotawēw ᓵᐳᑕᐁᐧᐤ
  VAI s/he looks over a
  meadow
sāpowēýawihow ᓵᐳᐁᐧᔭᐃᐧᐦᐅᐤ
  VAI s/he flies through the
  body
sāpoýahkēw ᓵᐳᔭᐦᑫᐤ
  VAI s/he squeezes through
sāpoýahkinam ᓵᐳ ᔭᐦᑭᓇᒼ
  VTI s/he squeezes s.t.
  through
sāpoýahkinēw ᓵᐳ ᔭᐦᑭᓀᐤ
  VTA s/he squeezes s.o.
  through
sāpoýōwēw ᓵᐳᔾᐅᐁᐧᐤ
  VII it has the wind blowing
  through
sāpōmin ᓵᐳᒥᐣ
  NA gooseberry; current [*also*
  sāpomin]
sāpōmināhtik ᓵᐳᒥᓈᐦᑎᐠ
  NI gooseberry bush [*pl:* -wa]
sāpōminiskāw ᓵᐳᒥᓂᐢᑳᐤ
  VII there are many
  gooseberry bushes around
sāpwāpahcikan ᓵᐹᐧᐸᐦᒋᑲᐣ
  NI x-ray
sāpwāpahtam ᓵᐹᐧᐸᐦᑕᒼ
  VTI s/he sees through s.t.,
  s/he takes a x-ray of s.t
sāpwāpamēw ᓵᐹᐧᐸᒣᐤ
  VTA s/he sees through s.o.;
  s/he takes s.o.'s x-ray
sāpwāskonam ᓵᐹᐧᐢᑯᓇᒼ
  VTI s/he pushes s.t. through
  (as in a tube)
sāpwāskonēw ᓵᐹᐧᐢᑯᓀᐤ
  VTA s/he pushes s.o. through
  (as in a tube)
sāpwāsow ᓵᐹᐧᓱᐤ
  VAI s/he is transparent
sāpwāstan ᓵᐹᐧᐢᑕᐣ
  VII it is the wind blowing
  through
sāpwāstēw ᓵᐹᐧᐢᑌᐤ
  VII it is transparent
sāpwāstēwiýākan ᓵᐹᐧᐢᑌᐃᐧᔮᑲᐣ
  NI glass tumbler
sāsakici ᓵᓴᑭᒋ
  IPC backwards; supine, on
  one's back

sāsakici ᓵᓴᑭᒋ
  IPV backwards; supine
sāsakici-wēpaham
  ᓵᓴᑭᒋ ᐁᐧᐸᐦᐊᒼ
  VTI s/he knocks s.t. supine
  by a shot
sāsakici-wēpahwēw
  ᓵᓴᑭᒋ ᐁᐧᐸᐦᐁᐧᐤ
  VTA s/he knocks s.o. supine
  by a shot
sāsakici-wēpiskam
  ᓵᓴᑭᒋ ᐁᐧᐱᐢᑲᒼ
  VTI s/he kicks s.t. supine
sāsakici-wēpiskawēw
  ᓵᓴᑭᒋ ᐁᐧᐱᐢᑲᐁᐧᐤ
  VTA s/he kicks s.o. supine
sāsakicisin ᓵᓴᑭᒋᓯᐣ
  VAI s/he lies supine, s/he
  lies on his/her own back
sāsakiciýawēsiw ᓵᓴᑭᒋᔭᐁᐧᓯᐤ
  VAI s/he is furious; s/he has
  a tantrum, s/he falls on
  his/her own back from such
  anger
sāsakitastāw ᓵᓴᑭᑕᐢᑖᐤ
  VAI s/he places s.t. facing up
sāsakitastēw ᓵᓴᑭᑕᐢᑌᐤ
  VII it is placed facing up
sāsakitisin ᓵᓴᑭᑎᓯᐣ
  VAI s/he lies supine, s/he
  lies on his/her own back
sāsamīna ᓵᓴᒥᓇ
  IPC again; already [*cf.* āsay
  mīna]
sāsay ᓵᓴᕀ
  IPC already, before now [*cf.*
  āsay]
sāsākanikātēw ᓵᓴᑲᓂᑳᑌᐤ
  VAI s/he goes bare-legged
  [*see also* mamēhkocinēw]
sāsākawāpiskos ᓵᓴᑲᐋᐧᐱᐢᑯᐢ
  NA chipmunk; striped
  gopher [*cf.* sāsākwāpiskos]
sāsākihtēw ᓵᓴᑭᐦᑌᐤ
  VAI s/he walks barefoot
sāsākihtiw ᓵᓴᑭᐦᑎᐤ
  VAI s/he is barefoot, s/he
  goes barefoot
sāsākinicihcēw ᓵᓴᑭᓂᒋᐦᒉᐤ
  VAI s/he has bare hands
sāsākinikātēw ᓵᓴᑭᓂᑳᑌᐤ
  VAI s/he is bare-legged, s/he
  has bare legs [*cf.*
  mostāpēkikātēw]
sāsākinipitonēw ᓵᓴᑭᓂᐱᑐᓀᐤ
  VAI s/he has bare arms
sāsākinisitēw ᓵᓴᑭᓂᓯᑌᐤ
  VAI s/he goes barefoot, s/he
  has bare feet
sāsākwāpēwiw ᓵᓴᑲᐧᐋᐯᐃᐧᐤ
  VAI he is a slim man
sāsākwāpiskos ᓵᓴᑲᐧᐋᐱᐢᑯᐢ
  NA chipmunk; striped
  gopher [*cf.* sāsākawāpiskos]
sāsāpiskicikātēw ᓵᓵᐱᐢᑭᒋᑳᑌᐤ
  VII it is fried
sāsāpiskisam ᓵᓵᐱᐢᑭᓴᒼ
  VTI s/he fries s.t.

sāsāpiskisikan ᓵᓵᐱᐢᑭᓯᑲᐣ
  NA frying pan
sāsāpiskisikēw ᓵᓵᐱᐢᑭᓯᑫᐤ
  VAI s/he fries
sāsāpiskiswēw ᓵᓵᐱᐢᑭᓷᐧᐤ
  VTA s/he fries s.o.
sāsāpiskitēw ᓵᓵᐱᐢᑭᑌᐤ
  VII it is fried
sāsēskihkwān ᓵ� séÐk
  NA frying pan [*see also*
  napwēn]
sāsinikonastimwēw
  ᓵᓯᓂᑯᓇᐢᑎᒷᐧᐤ
  VAI s/he pets his/her own
  dog, s/he strokes his/her own
  dog
sāsinikwastimwēw ᓵᓯᓂᑲᐧᐢᑎᒷᐧᐤ
  VAI s/he pets his/her own
  dog
sāsipimēw ᓵᓯᐱᒣᐤ
  VAI s/he renders fat [*also*
  sāsipimiw]
sāsipimīhkasam ᓵᓯᐱᒦᐦᑲᓴᒼ
  VTI s/he renders s.t.
sāsipimīhkēw ᓵᓯᐱᒦᐦᑫᐤ
  VAI s/he renders fat
sāsisam ᓵᓯᓴᒼ
  VTI s/he fries s.t.
sāsiswēw ᓵᓯᓷᐧᐤ
  VTA s/he fries s.o. (*e.g.* fish)
sāsīnāhk ᓵᓰᓈᕽ
  IPC in the land of the
  Sarcee, at Sarcee Reserve
  [*loc*]
sāsīw ᓵᓰᐤ
  NA Sarcee
sāsīwiskwēw ᓵᓰᐃᐧᐢᑫᐧᐤ
  NA Sarcee woman [*also*
  sasiwiskwēw]
sāskwatōn ᓵᐢᑲᐧᑑᐣ
  INM Saskatoon, SK [*see*
  also misāskwatōminihk,
  mīnisihk]
sāwahtow ᓵᐊᐧᐦᑐᐤ
  VAI s/he extends his/her own
  legs
sāwaniýōtin ᓵᐊᐧᓂᔫᑎᐣ
  VII it is a south wind
sāwanohk ᓵᐊᐧᓄᕽ
  IPC south, in the south
sāwanohk isi ᓵᐊᐧᓄᕽ ᐃᓯ
  IPH southward, to the south

�

sēham ᓭᐦᐊᒼ
  VTI s/he swabs s.t. out (*e.g.*
  dish, bowl)
sēhispwākanān ᓭᐦᐃᐢᐹᐧᑲᓈᐣ
  NI pipe cleaner
sēhispwākanēw ᓭᐦᐃᐢᐹᐧᑲᓀᐤ
  VAI s/he cleans his/her pipe
sēhkē ᓭᐦᑫ
  IPC by itself, of own
  accord; move ahead of own
  accord; willingly

sēhkē-atoskēmakan ᓭᐦᑫ ᐊᑐᐢᑭᒪᑲᐣ
VII it works automatically

sēhkē-pimipaýīs ᓭᐦᑫ ᐱᒥᐸᔩᐢ
NA automobile, car [*dim*; *cf.* sēhkēpaýīs, sēhkēw]

sēhkēpaýiw ᓭᐦᑫᐸᔨᐤ
VII it goes forward quickly; it goes automatically

sēhkēpaýīs ᓭᐦᑫᐸᔩᐢ
NA automobile, car [*dim*; *cf.* sēhkē-pimipaýīs, sēhkēw]

sēhkēw ᓭᐦᑫᐤ
NA car [*cf.* sēhkēpaýīs]

sēkihēw ᓭᑭᐦᐁᐤ
VTA s/he scares s.o., s/he frightens s.o. [*rdpl*: sā-sēkihēw]

sēkihisow ᓭᑭᐦᐃᓱᐤ
VAI s/he frightens him/herself

sēkihiwēw ᓭᑭᐦᐃᐍᐤ
VAI s/he frightens people

sēkihtāw ᓭᑭᐦᑖᐤ
VAIt s/he frightens s.t.

sēkimēw ᓭᑭᒣᐤ
VTA s/he frightens s.o. by speech

sēkinākosiw ᓭᑭᓈᑯᓯᐤ
VAI s/he looks frightful, frightening; s/he looks frightened [*cf.* sēsēskinākosiw]

sēkinākwan ᓭᑭᓈᑲᐧᐣ
VII it looks frightful, frightening [*cf.* sēsēskinākwan]

sēkipatwān ᓭᑭᐸᑖᐧᐣ
NI braid of hair [*see also* apihkān]

sēkipatwānēyāpiy ᓭᑭᐸᑖᐧᓀᔮᐱᐩ
NI hair ribbon, ribbon for braids

sēkipatwāw ᓭᑭᐸᑖᐧᐤ
VAI s/he has a braid

sēkisiw ᓭᑭᓯᐤ
VAI s/he is afraid, s/he is scared

sēkisiwin ᓭᑭᓯᐎᐣ
NI fear; fright

sēkonam ᓭᑯᓇᒼ
VTI s/he puts s.t. under or between; s/he puts s.t. into the oven

sēkonēw ᓭᑯᓀᐤ
VTA s/he puts s.o. (*e.g.* a chicken) into the oven

sēkopaýihow ᓭᑯᐸᔨᐦᐅᐤ
VAI s/he goes in, under s.t.; s/he quickly hides from sight under s.t.

sēkopaýin ᓭᑯᐸᔨᐣ
VII it runs beneath, s/he goes underneath, s/he gets caught underneath

sēkopaýiw ᓭᑯᐸᔨᐤ
VAI s/he slips between or under

sēkowēpināpisk ᓭᑯᐍᐱᓈᐱᐢᐠ
NI oven [*pl*: -wa]

sēkoýahkinam ᓭᑯᔭᐦᑭᓇᒼ
VTI s/he pushes s.t. between or under

sēkoýahkinēw ᓭᑯᔭᐦᑭᓀᐤ
VTA s/he stores s.o. between things; s/he pushes s.o. between or under

sēkōw ᓭᑰᐤ
VAI s/he gets between something, s/he goes under something (*e.g.* blankets)

sēkwahkinam ᓭᑲᐧᐦᑭᓇᒼ
VTI s/he puts s.t. under ashes

sēkwahkinēw ᓭᑲᐧᐦᑭᓀᐤ
VTA s/he puts s.o. under ashes

sēkwamow ᓭᑲᐧᒧᐤ
VII it is underneath

sēkwasow ᓭᑲᐧᓱᐤ
VAI s/he carries things in his/her own belt

sēkwāmow ᓭᑳᐧᒧᐤ
VAI s/he flees and hides under something

sēkwāpiskinam ᓭᑳᐧᐱᐢᑭᓇᒼ
VTI s/he puts s.t. in an oven, s/he puts s.o. under the coals

sēkwāpiskinēw ᓭᑳᐧᐱᐢᑭᓀᐤ
VTA s/he puts s.o. in an oven

sēkwēstikwāniwāsiw ᓭᑫᐧᐢᑎᑳᐧᓂᐚᓯᐤ
VAI s/he has messy, wind-blown hair [*cf.* ohpēstikwāniwāsiw]

sēmāk ᓭᒫᐠ
IPC right now, right away, at once, immediately

sēmākipaýiw ᓭᒫᑭᐸᔨᐤ
VAI s/he goes past his/her destination, s/he drives right past his/her destination

sēmākohtēw ᓭᒫᑯᐦᑌᐤ
VAI s/he walks right past his/her destination

sēnipān ᓭᓂᐹᐣ
NA ribbon

sēnipānēkin ᓭᓂᐹᓀᑭᐣ
NI satin, silk

sēnipānis ᓭᓂᐹᓂᐢ
NA narrow ribbon, piece of silk [*dim*]

sēnipānisapāp ᓭᓂᐹᓂᓴᐹᑊ
NA silk thread

sēsāw-āyāw ᓭᓵᐋᐧᔮᐤ
VAIt s/he rests s.t. [*also* sēsāwi-ayāw]

sēsāwi- ᓭᓵᐏ
IPV stretching, exercising

sēsāwinēw ᓭᓵᐏᓀᐤ
VTA s/he stretches s.o., s/he exercises s.o.

sēsāwipahtāw ᓭᓵᐏᐸᐦᑖᐤ
VAI s/he jogs

sēsāwipaýiw ᓭᓵᐏᐸᔨᐤ
VAI s/he stretches, s/he becomes relaxed (after exercise)

sēsāwīhkasow ᓭᓵᐑᐦᑲᓱᐤ
VAI s/he refreshes him/herself by steam bath (*e.g.* sweat-lodge, sauna)

sēsāwīw ᓭᓵᐑᐤ
VAI s/he stretches him/herself, s/he takes exercise

sēsāwohtēw ᓭᓵᐓᐦᑌᐤ
VAI s/he refreshes him/herself by walking

sēscakos ᓭᐢᒐᑯᐢ
NI thread; one-ply yarn [*dim*; *also* sēstakos]

sēsēkwapitēhow ᓭᓭᑲᐧᐱᑌᐦᐅᐤ
VAI s/he picks his/her own teeth

sēsēsiw ᓭᓭᓯᐤ
NA snipe; snow snipe; long legged duck; yellow legs, plover; water bird

sēsēskinākosiw ᓭᓭᐢᑭᓈᑯᓯᐤ
VAI s/he has a frightening look [*rdpl*; *cf.* sēkisiw]

sēsēskinākosiwin ᓭᓭᐢᑭᓈᑯᓯᐎᐣ
NI frightful appearance [*rdpl*]

sēsēskinākwan ᓭᓭᐢᑭᓈᑲᐧᐣ
VII it looks dreadful, frightful [*rdpl*; *cf.* sēkisiw]

sēsēwiýākan ᓭᓭᐏᔮᑲᐣ
NA bell [*also* sēsēwihýākan; *cf.* sēwēýākan]

sēskāmow ᓭᐢᑳᒧᐤ
VAI s/he flees into bushes, the woods

sēskāpahtēw ᓭᐢᑳᐸᐦᑌᐤ
VII there is smoke blowing into the woods

sēskicēs ᓭᐢᑭᒉᐢ
NI roach, men's pow-wow head regalia [*cf.* osēskicēs]

sēskipaýihtāw ᓭᐢᑭᐸᔨᐦᑖᐤ
VAIt s/he beaches s.t. (using a motor)

sēskipaýiw ᓭᐢᑭᐸᔨᐤ
VAI s/he goes into woods; s/he runs off the road into a bluff

sēskipitam ᓭᐢᑭᐱᑕᒼ
VTI s/he beaches s.t., s/he pulls s.t. into the bush

sēskipitēw ᓭᐢᑭᐱᑌᐤ
VTA s/he beaches s.o., s/he pulls s.o. into the bush

sēskisiw ᓭᐢᑭᓯᐤ
VAI s/he is in the bush; s/he enters the bush, s/he goes into the woods

sēskitāpāsow ᓭᐢᑭᑖᐹᓱᐤ
VAI s/he drives into the bush (with horse and wagon)

sēstak ᓭᐢᑕᐠ
NA yarn, thread [*pl*: -wak]

sēstōyow ᓭᐢᑑᔪᐤ
VAI s/he puts on extra inner clothes

sēwēhtitāw ᒉᐁᐧᐦᑎᑖᐤ
  VAIt s/he shakes s.t. (*e.g.* a
  rattle); s/he rattles s.t.
sēwēpayiw ᒉᐁᐧᐸᔨᐤ
  VAI s/he jingles, s/he rattles
sēwēpayiw ᒉᐁᐧᐸᔨᐤ
  VII it jingles, s/he rattles
sēwēpicikan ᒉᐁᐧᐱᒋᑲᐣ
  NI phone, telephone
sēwēpicikēw ᒉᐁᐧᐱᒋᑫᐤ
  VAI s/he jingles things; s/he
  rings a bell
sēwēpitam ᒉᐁᐧᐱᑕᐣ
  VTI s/he jingles s.t., s/he
  rings s.t.; s/he phones
sēwēpitamawēw ᒉᐁᐧᐱᑕᒪᐁᐧᐤ
  VTA s/he phones s.o., s/he
  calls s.o. by phone
sēwēpitēw ᒉᐁᐧᐱᑌᐤ
  VTA s/he jingles s.o., s/he
  rings s.o. (*e.g.* a bell)
sēwēw ᒉᐁᐧᐤ
  VAI it rings
sēwēýakan ᒉᐁᐧᔭᑲᐣ
  NA bell [*cf.* sēsēwiýakan]
sēyāpitēw ᒉᔭᐱᑌᐤ
  VAI s/he grins and shows
  his/her own teeth

ᒋ

sihkaciw ᓯᐦᑳᒋᐤ
  VAI s/he is extremely cold
sihkihp ᓯᐦᑭᑊ
  NA water hen, hell-diver,
  diver duck, coot
sihkihp-sākahikan
  ᓯᐦᑭᑊ ᓵᑲᐦᐃᑲᐣ
  NI Waterhen, SK [*lit:*
  "waterhen lake"; *Cree
  reserve name*]
sihkos ᓯᐦᑯᐢ
  NA weasel; ermine
sihkosiw ᓯᐦᑯᓯᐤ
  NA weasel; ermine
sihkosiwayān ᓯᐦᑯᓯᐊᐧᔮᐣ
  NA weasel skin; ermine skin
sihkosiwayānasākay
  ᓯᐦᑯᓯᐊᐧᔮᓇᓵᑲᕀ
  NI weaselskin coat
sihkosiwayāninēsākay
  ᓯᐦᑯᓯᐊᐧᔮᓂᓀᓵᑲᕀ
  NI weaselskin coat
sihkosiwayāninētās
  ᓯᐦᑯᓯᐊᐧᔮᓂᓀᑖᐢ
  NA weaselskin breeches
sihkoskiw ᓯᐦᑯᐢᑭᐤ
  VAI s/he spits all the time
  [*hab*]
sihkow ᓯᐦᑯᐤ
  VAI s/he spits
sihkowin ᓯᐦᑯᐃᐧᐣ
  NI spittle, saliva
sihkwātam ᓯᐦᒀᑕᐣ
  VTI s/he spits on s.t.
sihkwātēw ᓯᐦᒀᑌᐤ
  VTA s/he spits on s.o.

sihta ᓯᐦᑕ
  NA spruce, evergreen [*pl:*
  -k]
sihtapihkwan ᓯᐦᑕᐱᐦᑲᐧᐣ
  NA button on fir tree branch;
  pine cone
sikaci- ᓯᑲᒋ
  IPV impatiently, bored with
  [*also* sikati-]
sikatēýihtam ᓯᑲᑌᔨᐦᑕᐣ
  VTI s/he is bored by s.t.
sikatēýimēw ᓯᑲᑌᔨᒣᐤ
  VTA s/he is bored by s.o.
sikāk ᓯᑳᐠ
  NA skunk [*pl:* -wak]
sikākomākosiw ᓯᑳᑯᒫᑯᓯᐤ
  VAI s/he has a skunk odour
sikākomākwan ᓯᑳᑯᒫᑲᐧᐣ
  VII it has a skunk odour
sikākos ᓯᑳᑯᐢ
  NA small, young skunk
  [*dim*]
sikihkwāmiw ᓯᑭᐦᒁᒥᐤ
  VAI s/he wets the bed, s/he
  urinates while sleeping
sikihkwāmisk ᓯᑭᐦᒁᒥᐢᐠ
  NA bed-wetter [*hab*]
sikihkwāmiskiw ᓯᑭᐦᒁᒥᐢᑭᐤ
  VAI s/he is a bed-wetter
  [*hab*]
sikitam ᓯᑭᑕᐣ
  VTI s/he urinates on s.t.
sikitēw ᓯᑭᑌᐤ
  VTA s/he urinates on s.o.
sikitisow ᓯᑭᑎᓱᐤ
  VAI s/he urinates on
  him/herself, s/he wets
  him/herself, s/he is
  incontinent
sikiw ᓯᑭᐤ
  VAI s/he urinates
sikiwin ᓯᑭᐃᐧᐣ
  NI urine
sikiýāsiw ᓯᑭᔮᓯᐤ
  VAI s/he is happy, glad
sikīwiwīhkway ᓯᑮᐃᐧᐄᐧᐦᑲᐧᕀ
  NI bladder [*proposed term*]
sikokaham ᓯᑯᑲᐦᐊᒼ
  VTI s/he chops s.t. small
sikokahwēw ᓯᑯᑲᐦᐍᐤ
  VTA s/he chops s.o. small
sikokāhtāw ᓯᑯᑳᐦᑖᐤ
  VAI s/he has hiccups
sikokocikan ᓯᑯᑯᒋᑲᐣ
  NA cut tobacco
sikonam ᓯᑯᓇᒼ
  VTI s/he crushes s.t. by hand
  until small
sikonēw ᓯᑯᓀᐤ
  VTA s/he crushes s.o. by
  hand (*e.g.* nuts)
sikopayiw ᓯᑯᐸᔨᐤ
  VII it is reduced to small
  bits, it is pulverized
sikopitam ᓯᑯᐱᑕᐣ
  VTI s/he tears s.t. to pieces
sikopitēw ᓯᑯᐱᑌᐤ
  VTA s/he tears s.o. to pieces

sikopocikan ᓯᑯᐳᒋᑲᐣ
  NI grinder [*cf.* sisikopicikan]
sikopotam ᓯᑯᐳᑕᒼ
  VTI s/he grinds s.t. up
sikopotēw ᓯᑯᐳᑌᐤ
  VTA s/he grinds s.o. up
sikosam ᓯᑯᓴᒼ
  VTI s/he chops s.t. small
sikosāwātam ᓯᑯᓵᐊᐧᑕᒼ
  VTI s/he slices s.t. small
sikoskam ᓯᑯᐢᑲᒼ
  VTI s/he breaks s.t. by foot;
  s/he tramps s.t. to bits
sikoskawēw ᓯᑯᐢᑲᐍᐤ
  VTA s/he breaks s.o. by foot;
  s/he crushes s.o. by stepping
sikoswēw ᓯᑯᐢᐍᐤ
  VTA s/he cuts s.o. up (*e.g.*
  tobacco)
sikowēpaham ᓯᑯᐁᐧᐸᐦᐊᒼ
  VTI s/he mashes s.t. with a
  fork
sikowēpahwēw ᓯᑯᐁᐧᐸᐦᐍᐤ
  VTA s/he mashes s.o. (*e.g.*
  loaf of bread, raspberries)
sikwaham ᓯᑲᐧᐦᐊᒼ
  VTI s/he crushes s.t. (by
  tool) until small; s/he mashes
  s.t.
sikwahcikēw ᓯᑲᐧᐦᒋᑫᐤ
  VAI s/he chews
sikwahcipicikan ᓯᑲᐧᐦᒋᐱᒋᑲᐣ
  NI harrow
sikwahcisikan ᓯᑲᐧᐦᒋᓯᑲᐣ
  NI disk (on plough)
sikwahcisikēw ᓯᑲᐧᐦᒋᓯᑫᐤ
  VAI s/he cultivates, s/he
  harrows
sikwahtam ᓯᑲᐧᐦᑕᒼ
  VTI s/he chews s.t. until
  small, s/he masticates s.t.
sikwamēw ᓯᑲᐧᒣᐤ
  VTA s/he chews s.o. until
  small
sikwataham ᓯᑲᐧᑕᐦᐊᒼ
  VTI s/he pounds s.t. (by tool
  with handle) until small, s/he
  crushes s.t. (by pounding)
sikwatahikan ᓯᑲᐧᑕᐦᐃᑲᐣ
  NI straw
sikwatahikanāpoy
  ᓯᑲᐧᑕᐦᐃᑲᓈᐳᕀ
  NI ground beef soup,
  hamburger soup
sikwatahikātēw ᓯᑲᐧᑕᐦᐃᑳᑌᐤ
  VII it is pounded until small
sikwatahikēw ᓯᑲᐧᑕᐦᐃᑫᐤ
  VAI s/he crushes (by
  pounding)
sikwatahwēw ᓯᑲᐧᑕᐦᐍᐤ
  VTA s/he crushes s.o. (by
  pounding); s/he pounds s.o.
  to pieces, pulp
sikwatakahikēw ᓯᑲᐧᑕᑲᐦᐃᑫᐤ
  VAI s/he prods, s/he jabs
  with a stick
sikwatatin ᓯᑲᐧᑕᑎᐣ
  VII it is rotten [*see also*
  pikiskatin, winihtin]

sikwatatiw ᓯᑲᐧᑕᑎᐤ
VAI it is rotten [*see also* pikiskatiw]

sikwāciwahtēw ᓯᑳᐧᒋᐊᐧᐦᑌᐤ
VII it is boiled so as to fall into small bits

sikwāciwasow ᓯᑳᐧᒋᐊᐧᓱᐤ
VAI it is boiled so as to fall into small bits

sikwāwakinikan ᓯᑳᐧᐊᐧᑭᓂᑲᐣ
NA flour [*see also* pahkwēsikan]

simaci- ᓯᒪᒋ
IPV upright; straightened

simacipaýiw ᓯᒪᒋᐸᔨᐤ
VII it turns upwards, it straightens up

simacīw ᓯᒪᒌᐤ
VAI s/he straightens up, it stands upright; it rears up (*e.g.* horse)

simatapiw ᓯᒪᑕᐱᐤ
VAI s/he sits up

simākan ᓯᒫᑲᐣ
NA policeman [*dim generally*, *cf.* simākanis]

simākanis ᓯᒫᑲᓂᐢ
NA policeman, officer; [*pl*:] police; soldiers; jack (at cards) [*dim*]

simākanisihkān ᓯᒫᑲᓂᓯᐦᑳᐣ
NA soldier; special constable; security officer

simākanisihkāniwiw ᓯᒫᑲᓂᓯᐦᑳᓂᐃᐧᐤ
VAI s/he is a soldier; s/he takes part in war

simākanisikimāw ᓯᒫᑲᓂᓯᑭᒫᐤ
NA officer, commanding officer

simākanisiwikamik ᓯᒫᑲᓂᓯᐃᐧᑲᒥᐠ
NI police station, police barracks [*pl*: -wa]

simākanisiwikimāw ᓯᒫᑲᓂᓯᐃᐧᑭᒫᐤ
NA officer

simākanisiwiw ᓯᒫᑲᓂᓯᐃᐧᐤ
VAI s/he is a police officer

simākaniskwēw ᓯᒫᑲᓂᐢᑫᐧᐤ
NA policewoman

sinikohcāpinēw ᓯᓂᑯᐦᒑᐱᓀᐤ
VTA s/he rubs s.o.'s eyes

sinikohcāpinisow ᓯᓂᑯᐦᒑᐱᓂᓱᐤ
VAI s/he rubs his/her own eyes

sinikohkitonēnēw ᓯᓂᑯᐦᑭᑐᓀᓀᐤ
VTA s/he rubs s.o. over the mouth

sinikohkitonēpitēw ᓯᓂᑯᐦᑭᑐᓀᐱᑌᐤ
VTA s/he pulls s.o. rubbing that one's mouth

sinikohkwēsin ᓯᓂᑯᐦᑫᐧᓯᐣ
VAI s/he falls scraping his/her own face

sinikohkwēpaýiw ᓯᓂᑯᐦᑫᐧᐸᔨᐤ
VAI s/he falls and scrapes his/her own face on the ground

sinikohtaham ᓯᓂᑯᐦᑕᐦᐊᒼ
VTI s/he scrubs s.t.

sinikohtahikan ᓯᓂᑯᐦᑕᐦᐃᑲᐣ
NI scrubbing brush, washboard

sinikohtakaham ᓯᓂᑯᐦᑕᑲᐦᐊᒼ
VTI s/he scrubs s.t. (as wood)

sinikohtakahikan ᓯᓂᑯᐦᑕᑲᐦᐃᑲᐣ
NI scrub-brush, floor-brush, brush for wood

sinikohtakahikanis ᓯᓂᑯᐦᑕᑲᐦᐃᑲᓂᐢ
NI small scrub-brush [*dim*]

sinikohtakahikēw ᓯᓂᑯᐦᑕᑲᐦᐃᑫᐤ
VAI s/he scrubs the floor; s/he is scrubbing

sinikohtakinikan ᓯᓂᑯᐦᑕᑭᓂᑲᐣ
NI wash-board; scrubber, brush

sinikohtatāw ᓯᓂᑯᐦᑕᑖᐤ
VAIt s/he rubs s.t. on the floor

sinikohtitāw ᓯᓂᑯᐦᑎᑖᐤ
VAIt s/he places s.t. rubbing

sinikonam ᓯᓂᑯᓇᒼ
VTI s/he rubs s.t., s/he strokes s.t.

sinikonamawēw ᓯᓂᑯᓇᒪᐁᐧᐤ
VTA s/he strokes or rubs (it/him) for s.o.

sinikonēw ᓯᓂᑯᓀᐤ
VTA s/he rubs s.o., s/he strokes s.o.

sinikonisow ᓯᓂᑯᓂᓱᐤ
VAI s/he rubs him/herself, s/he strokes him/herself

sinikosimow ᓯᓂᑯᓯᒧᐤ
VAI s/he rubs against something

sinikoskam ᓯᓂᑯᐢᑲᒼ
VTI s/he rubs against s.t.

sinikoskawēw ᓯᓂᑯᐢᑲᐁᐧᐤ
VTA s/he rubs his/her own body against s.o.

sinikotamēnēw ᓯᓂᑯᑕᒣᓀᐤ
VTA s/he strokes s.o. on the mouth (*e.g.* a baby's gums when teething)

sinikwaham ᓯᓂᑲᐧᐦᐊᒼ
VTI s/he rubs s.t. on (as linament on his/her own leg)

sinikwahwēw ᓯᓂᑲᐧᐦᐁᐧᐤ
VTA s/he rubs or washes s.o. with a cloth

sipwē- ᓯᐯᐧ
IPV leaving, departing, going away; starting out, commencement

sipwē-kisiwāsiw ᓯᐯᐧ ᑭᓯᐋᐧᓯᐤ
VAI s/he leaves sulking, s/he leaves angry

sipwē-tēhtapiw ᓯᐯᐧ ᑌᐦᑕᐱᐤ
VAI s/he rides away

sipwēcimēw ᓯᐯᐧᒋᒣᐤ
VAI s/he leaves by boat, s/he canoes away, s/he paddles away

sipwēham ᓯᐯᐧᐦᐊᒼ
VTI s/he utters s.t.; s/he begins to sing with accompaniment

sipwēhamawēw ᓯᐯᐧᐦᐊᒪᐁᐧᐤ
VTA s/he starts a tune for s.o.

sipwēhamākēw ᓯᐯᐧᐦᐊᒫᑫᐤ
NA lead singer; orchestra conductor

sipwēhtahēw ᓯᐯᐧᐦᑕᐦᐁᐤ
VTA s/he takes s.o. away; s/he leaves with s.o.

sipwēhtahiwēw ᓯᐯᐧᐦᑕᐦᐃᐁᐧᐤ
VAI s/he takes people away

sipwēhtatāw ᓯᐯᐧᐦᑕᑖᐤ
VAIt s/he takes s.t. away

sipwēhtēhkāsow ᓯᐯᐧᐦᑌᐦᑳᓱᐤ
VAI s/he pretends to go away

sipwēhtēpaýiw ᓯᐯᐧᐦᑌᐸᔨᐤ
VAI s/he goes quickly on his/her own way

sipwēhtēw ᓯᐯᐧᐦᑌᐤ
VAI s/he leaves, s/he goes off, s/he departs

sipwēkitāsow ᓯᐯᐧᑭᑖᓱᐤ
VAI s/he leaves sulking, s/he leaves angry

sipwēkocin ᓯᐯᐧᑯᒋᐣ
VAI s/he flies off, s/he departs flying; s/he leaves by water or air

sipwēmakan ᓯᐯᐧᒪᑲᐣ
VII it goes away

sipwēpahtāw ᓯᐯᐧᐸᐦᑖᐤ
VAI s/he leaves running; s/he runs off

sipwēpaýihtāw ᓯᐯᐧᐸᔨᐦᑖᐤ
VAIt s/he makes s.t. go, s/he makes s.t. start; s/he starts s.t. (*e.g.* a vehicle)

sipwēpaýin ᓯᐯᐧᐸᔨᐣ
VII it starts off to run (*e.g.* tape recorder); it goes off

sipwēpaýiw ᓯᐯᐧᐸᔨᐤ
VAI s/he leaves riding; s/he leaves by vehicle, s/he drives off, s/he goes away

sipwēpaýiw ᓯᐯᐧᐸᔨᐤ
VII it leaves (*e.g.* a vehicle)

sipwēpiciw ᓯᐯᐧᐱᒋᐤ
VAI s/he moves camp away, s/he moves away with all his/her own goods and family

sipwēpihāw ᓯᐯᐧᐱᐦᐋᐤ
VAI s/he leaves flying [*cf.* *wC*: sipwīpithāw]

sipwētatwēmow ᓯᐯᐧᑕᑌᐧᒧᐤ
VAI s/he goes off weeping

sipwētācimopahtāw ᓯᐯᐧᑖᒋᒧᐸᐦᑖᐤ
VAI s/he crawls off fast

sipwētāpāsow ᓯᐯᐧᑖᐹᓱᐤ
VAI s/he leaves with a team of horses, s/he travels away by team
sipwētāpēw ᓯᐯᐧᑖᐯᐤ
VAI s/he drags s.t. away
sipwētisaham ᓯᐯᐧᑎᓴᐦᐊᒼ
VTI s/he sends s.t. away, s/he mails s.t. away
sipwētisahwēw ᓯᐯᐧᑎᓴᐦᐁᐧᐤ
VTA s/he sends s.o. away, s/he expels s.o.; s/he drives s.o. to depart
sipwētowatēw ᓯᐯᐧᑐᐊᐧᑌᐤ
VAI s/he departs with a load on his/her own back
sipwēyāhokow ᓯᐯᐧᔮᐦᐅᑯᐤ
VAI s/he drifts away
sipwēyāhtawīw ᓯᐯᐧᔮᐦᑕᐄᐧᐤ
VAI s/he departs climbing [*also* sipwēyāhtawēw]
sipwēyāpēkamowak ᓯᐯᐧᔮᐯᑲᒧᐊᐧᐠ
VAI they file off; they go off in a line [*pl*]
sipwēýāsiw ᓯᐯᐧᔮᓯᐤ
VAI s/he blows away (as a boat with sails)
sipwēýāstan ᓯᐯᐧᔮᐢᑕᐣ
VII it blows away
sipwēýāstitāw ᓯᐯᐧᔮᐢᑎᑖᐤ
VAIt s/he starts s.t. sailing
sipwēyātakāw ᓯᐯᐧᔮᑕᑳᐤ
VAI s/he swims away, s/he wades away
sisikoc ᓯᓯᑯᐨ
IPC suddenly, all at once [*cf.* siskwac]
sisikoci- ᓯᓯᑯᒋ
IPV suddenly
sisikocimēw ᓯᓯᑯᒋᒣᐤ
VTA s/he surprises s.o. with speech
sisikocinēw ᓯᓯᑯᒋᓀᐤ
VAI s/he dies suddenly
sisikokahtāw ᓯᓯᑯᑲᐦᑖᐤ
VAI s/he hiccups
sisikopicikaniwiyās ᓯᓯᑯᐱᒋᑲᓂᐃᐧᔮᐢ
NI hamburger, ground beef [*cf.* sisikwac]
sisikotāhpinēw ᓯᓯᑯᑖᐦᐱᓀᐤ
VAI s/he dies suddenly (from a short illness)
sisikotēýihtam ᓯᓯᑯᑌᔨᐦᑕᒼ
VTI s/he is surprised, s/he is shocked
sisikotēýimēw ᓯᓯᑯᑌᔨᒣᐤ
VTA s/he is surprised at s.o., s/he is shocked by s.o.
sisikotiskēnam ᓯᓯᑯᑎᐢᑫᓇᒼ
VTI s/he grapples with s.t. by surprise with the hand
sisikotiskēnēw ᓯᓯᑯᑎᐢᑫᓀᐤ
VTA s/he grapples with s.o. by surprise with the hand
sisikwac ᓯᓯᑲᐧᐨ
IPC all of a sudden [*cf.* sisikoc]

sisikwacihēw ᓯᓯᑲᐧᒋᐦᐁᐤ
VTA s/he startles s.o.
sisiwē- ᓯᓯᐍ
IPV spread, scatter
sisiwēpaýihēw ᓯᓯᐍᐸᔨᐦᐁᐤ
VTA s/he scatters s.o.
sisiwēpaýihtāw ᓯᓯᐍᐸᔨᐦᑖᐤ
VAIt s/he scatters s.t.
sisiwēpaýin ᓯᓯᐍᐸᔨᐣ
VII it scatters
sisiwēpaýiw ᓯᓯᐍᐸᔨᐤ
VII it scatters
sisiwēpinam ᓯᓯᐍᐱᓇᒼ
VTI s/he scatters s.t. about by hand
sisiwēpinēw ᓯᓯᐍᐱᓀᐤ
VTA s/he scatters s.o. about by hand (such as grain)
sisiwēpinikātēw ᓯᓯᐍᐱᓂᑳᑌᐤ
VII it is scattered by hand
sisiwēpinikēw ᓯᓯᐍᐱᓂᑫᐤ
VAI s/he scatters things (*e.g.* seeds) by hand
sisiwēskam ᓯᓯᐍᐢᑲᒼ
VTI s/he scatters s.t. with his/her own feet
sisiwēskawēw ᓯᓯᐍᐢᑲᐍᐤ
VTA s/he scatters s.o. with his/her own feet
sisocēskiwakinikēw ᓯᓱᒉᐢᑭᐘᑭᓂᑫᐤ
VAI s/he plasters with mud (*e.g.* a log house)
sisonam ᓯᓱᓇᒼ
VTI s/he paints s.t. on by hand (*i.e.* not with a brush)
sisonē ᓯᓱᓀ
IPC along, alongside, along the edge
sisonēpēhk ᓯᓱᓀᐯᕽ
IPC along the water; edge of the lake [*also* sisonēpīhk]
sisonikan ᓯᓱᓂᑲᐣ
NI linament
sisopācikātēw ᓯᓱᐹᒋᑳᑌᐤ
VII it is sprayed upon
sisopātam ᓯᓱᐹᑕᒼ
VTI s/he licks s.t.; s/he spits s.t. spattering (*e.g.* in traditional healing practice of chewing herbs which are blown on a patient)
sisopātēw ᓯᓱᐹᑌᐤ
VTA s/he spreads (it/him) on s.o.; s/he spits (it/him) onto s.o. spattering (*e.g.* in traditional healing practice of chewing herbs which are blown on a patient)
sisopēkaham ᓯᓱᐯᑲᐦᐊᒼ
VTI s/he paints s.t.
sisopēkahikan ᓯᓱᐯᑲᐦᐃᑲᐣ
NI paint
sisopēkahikanāhcikos ᓯᓱᐯᑲᐦᐃᑲᓈᐦᒋᑯᐢ
NI small paintbrush [*dim*]
sisopēkahikanāhtik ᓯᓱᐯᑲᐦᐃᑲᓈᐦᑎᐠ
NI paintbrush [*pl*: -wa]

sisopēkahikēw ᓯᓱᐯᑲᐦᐃᑫᐤ
VAI s/he paints
sisopēkahwākēw ᓯᓱᐯᑲᐦᐚᑫᐤ
VAI s/he sprinkles people with something (*e.g.* priest sprinkling holy water)
sisopēkahwēw ᓯᓱᐯᑲᐦᐍᐤ
VTA s/he paints s.o.; s/he puts salve on s.o.
sisopēkinam ᓯᓱᐯᑭᓇᒼ
VTI s/he rubs s.t. with oil, fat, linament, etc.
sisopēkinēw ᓯᓱᐯᑭᓀᐤ
VTA s/he rubs s.o. with oil, fat, linament, etc.
sisoskiwakaham ᓯᓱᐢᑭᐘᑲᐦᐊᒼ
VTI s/he plasters s.t.
sisoskiwakahikēw ᓯᓱᐢᑭᐘᑲᐦᐃᑫᐤ
VAI s/he plasters
sisoskiwakinam ᓯᓱᐢᑭᐘᑭᓇᒼ
VTI s/he plasters s.t., s/he muds s.t. by hand
sisoskiwakinamāsow ᓯᓱᐢᑭᐘᑭᓇᒫᓱᐤ
VAI s/he plasters (it/him) for him/herself, s/he does the mudding for him/herself
sisoskiwakinēw ᓯᓱᐢᑭᐘᑭᓀᐤ
VTA s/he plasters s.o., s/he muds s.o. by hand
sisoskiwakinikātēw ᓯᓱᐢᑭᐘᑭᓂᑳᑌᐤ
VII it is plastered, it is mudded
sisoskiwakinikēw ᓯᓱᐢᑭᐘᑭᓂᑫᐤ
VAI s/he plasters by hand
sisowaham ᓯᓱᐘᐦᐊᒼ
VTI s/he paints s.t.
sisowahikan ᓯᓱᐘᐦᐃᑲᐣ
NI paint; linament; lotion [*also* siswahikan]
sisowahikanāhtik ᓯᓱᐘᐦᐃᑲᓈᐦᑎᐠ
NI paint brush handle [*pl*: -wa; *also* siswahikanāhtik]
sisowahwēw ᓯᓱᐘᐦᐍᐤ
VTA s/he paints s.o.
siswamēw ᓯᔆᐘᒣᐤ
VTA s/he sprinkles s.o.
siswēwēpinam ᓯᔆᐍᐍᐱᓇᒼ
VTI s/he sprinkles s.t. about (*e.g.* ashes in cleaning)
siyākēs ᓯᔮᑫᐢ
IPC better (in health), recovered

ᓰ

sīhcāw ᓰᐦᒑᐤ
VII it is tightly packed, it is crowded; it is tight, it is taut [*also* sihcāw]
sīhcihtāw ᓰᐦᒋᐦᑖᐤ
VAIt s/he has difficulty with s.t.; s/he makes s.t. tight or firm

sīhcihtin Ꮧᐦᕑᐱᖐ

VII it fits tightly (as in a box)

sīhcipayiw Ꮧᐦᕑᐸᔪ

VII it tightens

sīhcipitam Ꮧᐦᕑᐸᐨ

VTI s/he pulls s.t. tight (as a rope)

sīhcisiw Ꮧᐦᕑᓯ

VAI s/he is tightly packed, s/he fits tightly (as in a box)

sīhciw Ꮧᐦᕒ

VAI s/he has a difficult time

sīhcīw Ꮧᐦᕒ

VAI s/he puts great effort in doing something

sīhkaciw Ꮧᐦᑲᕒ

VAI s/he is very thin; s/he is lean

sīhkatimēw Ꮧᐦᑲᖐᒧ

VTA s/he puts s.o. on a diet to lose weight

sīhkawēw Ꮧᐦᑲᐁ

VTA s/he bothers s.o.

sīhkihkēmow Ꮧᐦᑭᐦᑫᒧ

VAI s/he gives orders; s/he urges others, s/he encourages others

sīhkihp Ꮧᐦᑭᑊ

NI boil, carbuncle [*cf.* sikihp]

sīhkihpimiw Ꮧᐦᑭᑊᐱᒥ

VAI s/he has a boil (sore)

sīhkimēw Ꮧᐦᑭᒧ

VTA s/he urges s.o., s/he orders s.o., s/he guides s.o. (by speech)

sīhkimitowak Ꮧᐦᑭᒥᑐᐊᐠ

VAI they encourage one another

sīhkimitowin Ꮧᐦᑭᒥᑐᐃᐣ

NI mutual encouragement

sīhkimiwēwin Ꮧᐦᑭᒥᐁᐃᐣ

NI persuasion; encouragement

sīhkinam Ꮧᐦᑭᓇᐨ

VTI s/he pushes s.t. on

sīhkinēw Ꮧᐦᑭᓀᐤ

VTA s/he pushes s.o. on

sīhkipicikākēw Ꮧᐦᑭᐱᒋᑳᑫᐤ

VAI s/he stretches hides with something

sīhkipitam Ꮧᐦᑭᐱᐨ

VTI s/he stretches s.t. (*e.g.* a hide)

sīhkipitākan Ꮧᐦᑭᐱᑖᑲᐣ

NI hide-stretching frame

sīhkipitākanēyāpiy Ꮧᐦᑭᐱᑖᑲᓀᔮᐱᕀ

NI string to tie hides onto a stretching frame

sīhkipitēw Ꮧᐦᑭᐱᑌᐤ

VTA s/he stretches s.o.

sīhkiskam Ꮧᐦᑭᐢᑲᐨ

VTI s/he pushes s.t., s/he supports or emphasizes an idea

sīhkiskawēw Ꮧᐦᑭᐢᑲᐁᐤ

VTA s/he incites s.o.; s/he urges s.o. bodily

sīhkitisahwēw Ꮧᐦᑭᖠᓴᐦᐁᐤ

VTA s/he drives s.o. ahead

sīhtaham Ꮧᐦᑕᐦᐊᐨ

VTI s/he tightens s.t. with a wrench

sīhtahamawēw Ꮧᐦᑕᐦᐊᒪᐁᐤ

VTA s/he tightens (it/him) for s.o.

sīhtahpitam Ꮧᐦᑕᐦᐱᐨ

VTI s/he ties s.t. tightly

sīhtahpitēw Ꮧᐦᑕᐦᐱᑌᐤ

VTA s/he ties s.o. tightly

sīhtahwēw Ꮧᐦᑕᐦᐁᐤ

VTA s/he winds s.o., s/he tightens s.o.

sīhtamohtāw Ꮧᐦᑕᒧᐦᑖ

VAIt s/he fastens s.t. tightly

sīhtapēkinam Ꮧᐦᑕᐯᑭᓇᐨ

VTI s/he pulls s.t. tight (*e.g.* rope)

sīhtapēkinēw Ꮧᐦᑕᐯᑭᓀᐤ

VTA s/he pulls s.o. tight (*e.g.* yarn, thread)

sīhtapiw Ꮧᐦᑕᐱ

VAI s/he sits crowded together, s/he sits clustered together

sīhtascāpēnam Ꮧᐦᑕᐢᒑᐯᓇᐨ

VTI s/he tightens his/her own bowstring

sīhtatoskawēw Ꮧᐦᑕᑐᐢᑲᐁᐤ

VTA s/he works hard on or for s.o.

sīhtatoskātam Ꮧᐦᑕᑐᐢᑳᐨ

VTI s/he works hard at s.t.

sīhtawaham Ꮧᐦᑕᐊᐦᐊᐨ

VTI s/he starches s.t.

sīhtawahikan Ꮧᐦᑕᐊᐦᐃᑲᐣ

NI starch

sīhtawahikēw Ꮧᐦᑕᐊᐦᐃᑫᐤ

VAI s/he starches things

sīhtawāskosin Ꮧᐦᑕᐋᐢᑯᓯᐣ

VAI s/he lies pinched between trees

sīhtawāw Ꮧᐦᑕᐋ

VII it is stiff

sīhtawihikan Ꮧᐦᑕᐱᐦᐃᑲᐣ

NI oakum (material for chinking, filling seams in boat planks)

sīhtawikaham Ꮧᐦᑕᐱᑲᐦᐊᐨ

VTI s/he chinks the log house, s/he patches s.t. tightly

sīhtawikwēhwēw Ꮧᐦᑕᐱ�·ᐁᐤ

VTA s/he holds s.o. tight on neck with tool

sīhtāpīhkēnam Ꮧᐦᑖᐲᐦᑫᓇᐨ

VTI s/he holds s.t. tight

sīhtāpīhkēnēw Ꮧᐦᑖᐲᐦᑫᓀᐤ

VTA s/he holds s.o. tight

sīhtāskikanēw Ꮧᐦᑖᐢᑭᑲᓀᐤ

VAI s/he has a congested chest; s/he experiences tightness in the chest

sīhtāskwahon Ꮧᐦᑖᐢᑲᐦᐅᐣ

NI girdle; corset

sīhtāskwahow Ꮧᐦᑖᐢᑲᐦᐅ

VAI s/he wears a girdle, corset

sīhtihkasam Ꮧᐦᖏᐦᑲᓴᐨ

VTI s/he tightens s.t. up by heat

sīhtihkaswēw Ꮧᐦᖏᐦᑲᐢᐁᐤ

VTA s/he tightens s.o. up by heat

sīhtihkokanāham Ꮧᐦᖏᐦᑯᑲᓈᐦᐊᐨ

VTI s/he holds s.t. tightly over his/her shoulder [*also* sīhtawihkokanāham]

sīhtihkokanāhwēw Ꮧᐦᖏᐦᑯᑲᓈᐦᐁᐤ

VTA s/he holds s.o. around the neck and shoulders (while being carried on that one's back) [*also* sīhtawihkokanāhwēw]

sīhtiskam Ꮧᐦᖏᐢᑲᐨ

VTI s/he fits s.t. tightly; s/he wears s.t. tight fitting; s/he wears s.t. too small

sīhtiskawēw Ꮧᐦᖏᐢᑲᐁᐤ

VTA s/he fits s.o. (*e.g.* pants) tightly; s/he wears s.o. tight fitting

sīhtonam Ꮧᐦᑐᓇᐨ

VTI s/he supports s.t. by holding

sīhtonēw Ꮧᐦᑐᓀᐤ

VTA s/he supports s.o. by holding

sīhtopayiw Ꮧᐦᑐᐸᔪ

VII it stiffens

sīhtwahpicikan Ꮧᐦ�ᐦᐱᒋᑲᐣ

NI bandage

sīhtwahpitam Ꮧᐦ� ᐦᐱᐨ

VTI s/he bandages s.t.

sīhtwahpitēw Ꮧᐦ� ᐦᐱᑌᐤ

VTA s/he bandages s.o.

sīhtwamohtāw Ꮧᐦ� ᒧᐦᑖ

VAIt s/he fits s.t. on tightly

sīhtwamon Ꮧᐦ� ᒧᐣ

VII it fits tightly, it is on tight

sīhtwamow Ꮧᐦ� ᒧ

VII it fits very tightly

sīhtwāskwaham Ꮧᐦ� ᐋᐢᑲᐦᐊᐨ

VTI s/he props s.t. up

sīhtwāskwahikan Ꮧᐦ� ᐋᐢᑲᐦᐃᑲᐣ

NI prop; pillar

sīhtwāskwahwēw Ꮧᐦ� ᐋᐢᑲᐦᐁᐤ

VTA s/he props s.o. up

sīkahasinēw Ꮧᑲᐦᐊᓯᓀᐤ

VAI s/he pours cement

sīkahāhcihēw Ꮧᑲᐦᐋᐦᒋᐁᐤ

VTA s/he pours water on s.o.

sīkahāhcikēw Ꮧᑲᐦᐋᐦᒋᑫᐤ

VAI s/he waters plants

sīkahāhtam Ꮧᑲᐦᐋᐦᑕᐨ

VTI s/he splashes or pours water on s.t.

sīkahāhtawēw Ꮧᑲᐦᐋᐦᑕᐁᐤ

VTA s/he sprinkles s.o., s/he

splashes s.o., s/he pours water onto s.o.; s/he baptizes s.o.

sīkahāhtāsow ᓰᑲᐦᐋᐦᑖᓱᐤ
VAI s/he splashes or pours water on him/herself; s/he is baptized

sīkahon ᓰᑲᐦᐅᐣ
NI comb [*also* sēkahon, sīkahowin]

sīkahosow ᓰᑲᐦᐅᓱᐤ
VAI s/he combs his/her own hair [*cf.* sīkahow]

sīkahow ᓰᑲᐦᐅᐤ
VAI s/he combs his/her own hair [*also* sēkahow]

sīkahowinis ᓰᑲᐦᐅᐃᐧᓂᐢ
NI small comb [*dim*; *also* sīkahonis]

sīkahwēw ᓰᑲᐦᐁᐧᐤ
VTA s/he combs s.o.'s hair

sīkawāhokow ᓰᑲᐋᐧᐦᐅᑯᐤ
VAI s/he is borne along in a flood, it (*e.g.* ice) is borne along in a flood

sīkawi- ᓰᑲᐃᐧ
IPV pouring, flooding

sīkawīpiciwak ᓰᑲᐄᐧᐱᒋᐊᐧᐠ
VAI they trek away [*pl*]

sīkawīstamawēw ᓰᑲᐄᐧᐢᑕᒪᐁᐧᐤ
VTA s/he clears (it/him) for s.o.

sīkawīwak ᓰᑲᐄᐧᐊᐧᐠ
VAI they go away in numbers [*pl only*]

sīkāwihow ᓰᑳᐃᐧᐦᐅᐤ
VAI s/he is in mourning

sīkāwiskwēw ᓰᑳᐃᐧᐢᑫᐧᐤ
NA widow

sīkāwiw ᓰᑳᐃᐧᐤ
VAI s/he is in mourning

sīkihp ᓰᑭᐦᑊ
NI boil, skin eruption [*cf.* sīhkihp]

sīkihtitāw ᓰᑭᐦᑎᑖᐤ
VAIt s/he pours s.t. out, s/he dumps s.t.

sīkinam ᓰᑭᓇᒼ
VTI s/he pours s.t.; s/he spills s.t.

sīkinamawēw ᓰᑭᓇᒪᐁᐧᐤ
VTA s/he pours (it/him) out for s.o.

sīkināpāwēw ᓰᑭᓈᐹᐁᐧᐤ
VAI s/he is drenched

sīkinēw ᓰᑭᓀᐤ
VTA s/he pours s.o.; s/he spills s.o.

sīkinikēw ᓰᑭᓂᑫᐤ
VAI s/he taps beer or liquor, s/he is a bartender

sīkipaýiw ᓰᑭᐸᔨᐤ
VII it spills; it is spilling

sīkipēstāw ᓰᑭᐯᐢᑖᐤ
VII it is a downpour; it is pouring rain, it showers

sīkipicikēw ᓰᑭᐱᒋᑫᐤ
VAI s/he spills things

sīkipitam ᓰᑭᐱᑕᒼ
VTI s/he spills s.t., s/he pours s.t.

sīkipitēw ᓰᑭᐱᑌᐤ
VTA s/he spills s.o.

sīkiskam ᓰᑭᐢᑲᒼ
VTI s/he spills s.t. by bumping

sīkiskawēw ᓰᑭᐢᑲᐁᐧᐤ
VTA s/he spills s.o. by bumping

sīkiskātowak ᓰᑭᐢᑳᑐᐊᐧᐠ
VAI they are overcrowded

sīkiwēpaham ᓰᑭᐁᐧᐸᐦᐊᒼ
VTI s/he knocks s.t. over spilling it

sīkiwēpahwēw ᓰᑭᐁᐧᐸᐦᐁᐧᐤ
VTA s/he knocks s.o. over spilling it

sīkiwēpinam ᓰᑭᐁᐧᐱᓇᒼ
VTI s/he pours s.t. out, s/he throws liquid out of a container, s/he pours s.t. away

sīkiwēpinēw ᓰᑭᐁᐧᐱᓀᐤ
VTA s/he throws a liquid out of s.o. (*e.g.* a pail)

sīkiwēpinikēw ᓰᑭᐁᐧᐱᓂᑫᐤ
VAI s/he is emptying water

sīkiwēpiskam ᓰᑭᐁᐧᐱᐢᑲᒼ
VTI s/he spills s.t. by foot

sīkiwēpiskawēw ᓰᑭᐁᐧᐱᐢᑲᐁᐧᐤ
VTA s/he spills s.o. by foot

sīkohkinam ᓰᑯᐦᑭᓇᒼ
VTI s/he empties s.t.

sīkohkinēw ᓰᑯᐦᑭᓀᐤ
VTA s/he empties s.o.

sīkonam ᓰᑯᓇᒼ
VTI s/he empties s.t.

sīkonēw ᓰᑯᓀᐤ
VTA s/he empties s.o.

sīkonikan ᓰᑯᓂᑲᐣ
NI piece of cloth for straining; [*pl*:] refuse

sīkopwātinam ᓰᑯᐹᐧᑎᓇᒼ
VTI s/he strains s.t., s/he sifts s.t.

sīkopwātinēw ᓰᑯᐹᐧᑎᓀᐤ
VTA s/he strains s.o., s/he sifts s.o.

sīkopwātinikan ᓰᑯᐹᐧᑎᓂᑲᐣ
NI strainer

sīkosākanak ᓰᑯᓵᑲᓇᐠ
NA cracklings; rendered fat [*pl generally*; *incompletely rendered pieces of fat or the solids remaining at the end of the process of rendering*]

sīkōpēsin ᓰᑰᐯᓯᐣ
VAI s/he spills a liquid in falling

sīkwahkasow ᓰᑲᐧᐦᑲᓱᐤ
VAI it spills in being heated, it boils over

sīkwan ᓰᑲᐧᐣ
NI grate for wood, plane

sīkwan ᓰᑲᐧᐣ
VII it is spring [*see also* miýoskamin]

sīkwanāpisk ᓰᑲᐧᓈᐱᐢᐠ
NI hone, whetstone [*pl*: -wa]

sīkwanohk ᓰᑲᐧᓄᕽ
IPC last spring

sīkwāhkatosow ᓰᑳᐧᐦᑲᑐᓱᐤ
VAI s/he is starved lean

sīkwāpān ᓰᑳᐧᐹᐣ
NI sleigh runner

sīkwāspinēwin ᓰᑳᐧᐢᐱᓀᐃᐧᐣ
NI spring fever

sīmihkwasiw ᓰᒥᐦᑲᐧᓯᐤ
VAI s/he is still sleepy

sīnam ᓰᓇᒼ
VTI s/he wrings s.t. out, s/he twists s.t.

sīnāskwaham ᓰᓈᐢᑲᐧᐦᐊᒼ
VTI s/he wrings s.t. out with a wooden tool

sīnāskwahikēw ᓰᓈᐢᑲᐧᐦᐃᑫᐤ
VAI s/he wrings things out with a wooden tool

sīnāskwahwēw ᓰᓈᐢᑲᐧᐦᐁᐧᐤ
VTA s/he wrings s.o. out with a wooden tool

sīnēw ᓰᓀᐤ
VTA s/he wrings s.o. out

sīnihkomēhēw ᓰᓂᐦᑯᒣᐦᐁᐤ
VTA s/he makes s.o. blow and wipe that one's nose

sīnihkomēw ᓰᓂᐦᑯᒣᐤ
VAI s/he blows his/her own nose

sīnikan ᓰᓂᑲᐣ
NI wringer

sīnikēw ᓰᓂᑫᐤ
VAI s/he wrings things out

sīnipātinam ᓰᓂᐹᑎᓇᒼ
VTI s/he wrings s.t. out

sīnipātinēw ᓰᓂᐹᑎᓀᐤ
VTA s/he wrings s.o. out

sīnipēkinam ᓰᓂᐯᑭᓇᒼ
VTI s/he wrings s.t. out

sīnipēkinēw ᓰᓂᐯᑭᓀᐤ
VTA s/he wrings s.o. out

sīnipēkinikēw ᓰᓂᐯᑭᓂᑫᐤ
VAI s/he wrings things out

sīpaham ᓰᐸᐦᐊᒼ
VTI s/he stretches s.t., s/he stretches s.t. on the stretcher to dry

sīpahikan ᓰᐸᐦᐃᑲᐣ
NI stretcher (for pelts)

sīpahikēw ᓰᐸᐦᐃᑫᐤ
VAI s/he stretches a fur, s/he stretches a pelt, s/he stretches things

sīpahwēw ᓰᐸᐦᐁᐧᐤ
VTA s/he stretches s.o. (*e.g.* pelt)

sīpan ᓰᐸᐣ
VII it is durable; it wears well

sīpaskitāw ᓰᐸᐢᑭᑖᐤ
VAIt s/he implants s.t. solidly

sīpaskitēw ᓰᐸᐢᑭᑌᐤ
VII it stands a long time (as a building)

sīpā ᒉᐸ
  IPC under, underneath, beneath [*cf.* sīpāhk, sīpāyihk]

sīpāhk ᒉᐸᕽ
  INM skids

sīpāhk ᒉᐸᕽ
  IPC under [*cf.* sīpā, sīpāyihk]

sīpāpaýihow ᒉᐸᐸᔭᐦᐅ
  VAI s/he ducks under

sīpāpaýiw ᒉᐸᐸᔭ
  VII it goes under

sīpāpicikan ᒉᐸᐱᒋᑲᐣ
  NI jigger, pole used to draw lines under water or ice

sīpāpicikēw ᒉᐸᐱᒋᑫ
  VAI s/he draws a jigger line under the ice

sīpāpitam ᒉᐸᐱᑕᒼ
  VTI s/he pulls s.t. under

sīpāpitēw ᒉᐸᐱᑌ
  VTA s/he pulls s.o. under; s/he pulls thread under the sewing machine

sīpāsiw ᒉᐸᓯ
  VAI s/he goes underneath, s/he passes under (a low overpass over the road)

sīpāskopicikan ᒉᐸᐢᑯᐱᒋᑲᐣ
  NA jigger

sīpāskosīhk ᒉᐸᐢᑯᓰᕽ
  IPC under the grass [*loc*]

sīpāýāhtik ᒉᐸᔭᐦᑎᐠ
  IPC under the tree

sīpāýākonakihēw ᒉᐸᔭᑯᓇᑭᐦᐁᐤ
  VTA s/he makes s.o. go under the snow

sīpāýākonakihtāw ᒉᐸᔭᑯᓇᑭᐦᑖ
  VAIt s/he makes s.t. go under the snow

sīpāýāsiw ᒉᐸᔭᓯ
  VAI s/he is blown under by the wind

sīpāyihk ᒉᐸᔨᕽ
  IPC under [*cf.* sīpā, sīpāhk]

sīpēkāskwaham ᒉᐺᑳᐢᑴᐦᐊᒼ
  VTI s/he stretches s.t. on sticks

sīpēkāskwahwēw ᒉᐺᑳᐢᑴᐦᐧᐁᐤ
  VTA s/he stretches s.o. on sticks

sīpēkinam ᒉᐺᑭᓇᒼ
  VTI s/he washes s.t. [*cf.* kisīpēkinam]

sīpēkinēw ᒉᐺᑭᓀᐤ
  VTA s/he washes s.o. [*cf.* kisīpēkinēw]

sīpēkipaýiw ᒉᐺᑭᐸᔭ
  VAI s/he stretches (as a garment)

sīpēkipaýiw ᒉᐺᑭᐸᔭ
  VII it stretches

sīpēkipitam ᒉᐺᑭᐱᑕᐨ
  VTI s/he stretches s.t.

sīpēkipitēw ᒉᐺᑭᐱᑌᐤ
  VTA s/he stretches s.o. (*e.g.* yarn)

sīpēkiskāwasākay ᒉᐺᑭᐢᑳᐘᓵᑲᕀ
  NI knit jacket, sweater

sīpēkiskāwasākās ᒉᐺᑭᐢᑳᐘᓵᑳᐢ
  NI sweater [*dim*]

sīpēkiskāwayān ᒉᐺᑭᐢᑳᐘᔮᐣ
  NI sweater

sīpēýāw ᒉᐺᔮ
  VII there is an open place in the woods; there is an opening from land to water

sīpēýihtam ᒉᐺᔨᐦᑕᒼ
  VTI s/he is patient; s/he bears s.t. without complaining

sīpēýihtamowin ᒉᐺᔨᐦᑕᒧᐃᐧᐣ
  NI patience

sīpēýimēw ᒉᐺᔨᒣᐤ
  VTA s/he is patient with s.o.

sīpi-kiskisiw ᒉᐱ ᑭᐢᑭᓯ
  VAI s/he remembers far back

sīpihkēýihtam ᒉᐱᐦᑫᔨᐦᑕᒼ
  VTI s/he endures s.t. by strength of mind; perseveres

sīpihkiskāwasākay ᒉᐱᐦᑭᐢᑳᐘᓵᑲᕀ
  NI sweater [*see also* pīswēsākās]

sīpihkiskāwascocinis ᒉᐱᐦᑭᐢᑳᐘᐢᒍᒋᓂᐢ
  NI toque [*dim; see also* pīswēwastotin]

sīpihko- ᒉᐱᐦᑯ
  IPN blue

sīpihko-papakiwayān ᒉᐱᐦᑯ ᐸᐸᑭᐘᔮᐣ
  NI blue shirt

sīpihkomin ᒉᐱᐦᑯᒥᐣ
  NI blueberry [*see also* nikikomin, iýinimin]

sīpihkosākay ᒉᐱᐦᑯᓵᑲᕀ
  NI blue coat

sīpihkosākēw ᒉᐱᐦᑯᓵᑫᐤ
  VAI s/he wears a blue coat

sīpihkosiw ᒉᐱᐦᑯᓯ
  VAI s/he is blue

sīpihkwasiw ᒉᐱᐦ�?ᓯ
  VAI s/he can go without sleep for a long time

sīpihkwāpowēýān ᒉᐱᐦ�್ᐘᐳᐁᔮᐣ
  NI blue blanket

sīpihkwāsin ᒉᐱᐦᑴᓯᐣ
  VII it is blueish [*dim*]

sīpihkwāw ᒉᐱᐦᑴ
  VII it is blue

sīpihkwēkin ᒉᐱᐦᑴᑭᐣ
  NI blue cloth [*pl:* -wa]

sīpikāpawiw ᒉᐱᑳᐸᐤ
  VAI s/he stands a long time without tiring

sīpinam ᒉᐱᓇᒼ
  VTI s/he makes s.t. last a long time

sīpinēw ᒉᐱᓀ
  VAI s/he is long-lived; s/he is hardy; s/he is hard to kill

sīpinēw ᒉᐱᓀ
  VTA s/he makes s.o. last a long time

sīpinēwin ᒉᐱᓀᐃᐧᐣ
  NI longevity; hardiness

sīpisiw ᒉᐱᓯ
  VAI s/he is strong and durable (*e.g.* fur)

sīpiy ᒉᐱ
  NI river

sīpiyawēsiw ᒉᐱᔭᐍᓯ
  VAI s/he is not easily provoked, s/he is tolerant

sīpiyawēsiwin ᒉᐱᔭᐍᓯᐃᐧᐣ
  NI long suffering; patience, tolerance

sīpīhkān ᒉᐲᐦᑳᐣ
  NI canal; irrigation ditch

sīpīhkānihkēw ᒉᐲᐦᑳᓂᐦᑫᐤ
  VAI s/he makes a ditch

sīpīhkānis ᒉᐲᐦᑳᓂᐢ
  NI small canal; small irrigation ditch [*dim*]

sīpīsis ᒉᐲᓯᐢ
  NI little river, creek, brook stream [*dim*]

sīpīsisihk ᒉᐲᓯᓯᕽ
  INM Beauval, SK [*loc; lit:* "at the creek"]

sīpīsisiwahcāw ᒉᐲᓯᓯᐘᐦᒑ
  VII it is an area of creeks

sīpīsisiwiw ᒉᐲᓯᓯᐃᐧ
  VII it is a creek, it has a creek

sīpīw ᒉᐲ
  VAI s/he stretches

sīpīwāpoy ᒉᐲᐘᐳᕀ
  NI river water

sīpīwiýiniwak ᒉᐲᐏᔨᓂᐘᐠ
  NA River People [*pl; division of the Cree*]

sīpostaham ᒉᐳᐢᑕᐦᐊᒼ
  VTI s/he sews s.t. up (as a rip in his/her own clothes)

sīpostahamawēw ᒉᐳᐢᑕᐦᐊᒪᐍᐤ
  VTA s/he sews (it/him) up for s.o.

sīpostahwēw ᒉᐳᐢᑕᐦᐧᐁᐤ
  VTA s/he sews s.o. up

sīpwēwēmow ᒉᐻᐍᒧ
  VAI s/he is long-winded in speech

sīsipāskwamin ᓰᓯᐸᐢᑲᒥᐣ
  VII it is sweet

sīsipāskwamiw ᓰᓯᐸᐢᑲᒥᐤ
  VAI s/he is sweet

sīsipāskwat ᓰᓯᐸᐢᑲᐟ
  NI maple sugar, soft sugar

sīsipāskwatāhtik ᓰᓯᐸᐢᑲᑖᐦᑎᐠ
  NA sugar maple [*pl:* -wak]

sīsipāskwatihkēw ᓰᓯᐸᐢᑲᑎᐦᑫᐤ
  VAI s/he makes maple sugar

sīsikan ᓰᓯᑲᐣ
  VII it hails [*also* miskwamiy pahkisin]

sīsīkomow ᓰᓰᑯᒧ
  VAI it whines (*e.g.* a dog)

sīsīkow ᓰᓰᑯ
  VAI it whines (*e.g.* a dog)

sīsīkwan ᓰᓰᑲᐧᐣ
  NA rattle

sīsīkwanihkēw ᓰᓰᑲᐧᓂᐦᑫᐤ
VAI s/he makes a rattle

sīsīkwanis ᓰᓰᑲᐧᓂᐢ
NA small rattle [*dim*; *cf.* sīsīkwanisak "the Little Rattles" dancing society]

sīsīkwēsis ᓰᓰᑫᐧᓯᐢ
NA little rattlesnake [*dim; also family name*]

sīsīkwēw ᓰᓰᑫᐧᐤ
NA rattlesnake

sīsīp ᓰᓰᑉ
NA duck

sīsīp-sākahikanihk ᓰᓰᑉ ᓵᑲᐦᐃᑲᓂᕽ
INM Duck Lake, SK [*loc*]

sīsīp-wāwi ᓰᓰᑉ ᐚᐏ
NI duck egg [*pl*: sīsīp-wāwa]

sīsīpaskihk ᓰᓰᐸᐢᑭᕽ
NA teapot, tea kettle, kettle with spout [*pl*: -wak]

sīsīpasiniy ᓰᓰᐸᓯᓂᕀ
NI duck shot [*generally pl*]

sīsīpi- ᓰᓰᐱ
IPN duck

sīsīpi-mīcimāpoy ᓰᓰᐱ ᒦᒋᒫᐳᕀ
NI duck soup

sīsīpi-pīway ᓰᓰᐱ ᐲᐘᕀ
NI duck feathers, duck-down

sīsīpis ᓰᓰᐱᐢ
NA small duck [*dim*]

sīsīpisis ᓰᓰᐱᓯᐢ
NA duckling [*dim*]

sīsīpiskāw ᓰᓰᐱᐢᑳᐤ
VII there are many ducks

sīsīpokāt ᓰᓰᐳᑳᐟ
NI gun hammer; the long head of the old N.W. guns

sīskēpison ᓰᐢᑫᐱᓱᐣ
NI garter; elastic

sīskēpisow ᓰᐢᑫᐱᓱᐤ
VAI s/he puts on a garter

sīskēpitisow ᓰᐢᑫᐱᑎᓱᐤ
VAI s/he garters him/herself

sīspopayiw ᓰᐢᐳᐸᔨᐤ
VAI s/he loses weight

sīwaham ᓰᐘᐦᐊᒼ
VTI s/he sweetens s.t., s/he salts s.t. [*cf.* sīwīhtākanaham]

sīwahcikēw ᓰᐘᐦᒋᑫᐤ
VAI s/he eats sweets

sīwahwēw ᓰᐘᐦᐍᐤ
VTA s/he sweetens s.o., s/he salts s.o. [*cf.* sīwīhtākanahēw]

sīwanos ᓰᐘᓄᐢ
NI sweet, candy [*also* sīwinōs]

sīwaskatēw ᓰᐘᐢᑲᑌᐤ
VAI s/he feels his/her own stomach is empty

sīwatēw ᓰᐘᑌᐤ
VAI s/he has an empty stomach

sīwākamisikan ᓰᐚᑲᒥᓯᑲᐣ
NI birch tree syrup

sīwākamisikēw ᓰᐚᑲᒥᓯᑫᐤ
VAI s/he makes birch tree syrup

sīwāpoy ᓰᐚᐳᕀ
NI soft drink, pop; any sweet drink; vinegar

sīwās ᓰᐚᐢ
NI candy [*dim*; *cf.* sīwanos]

sīwāsin ᓰᐚᓯᐣ
VII it is a bit sweet; it is a bit sour; it is a bit salty [*dim*]

sīwāw ᓰᐚᐤ
VII it is sweet; it is sour; it is salty

sīwicīs ᓰᐏᒌᐢ
NA piece of candy [*dim*]

sīwihkasikan ᓰᐏᐦᑲᓯᑲᐣ
NA cake; sweet baked goods

sīwinam ᓰᐏᓇᒼ
VTI s/he sweetens s.t.

sīwinēw ᓰᐏᓀᐤ
VTA s/he sweetens s.o.

sīwinikan ᓰᐏᓂᑲᐣ
NA sugar, sweetener [*see also* sōkāw]

sīwinikēw ᓰᐏᓂᑫᐤ
VAI s/he sweetens his/her own tea; s/he uses sugar

sīwipakwa ᓰᐏᐸᑲᐧ
NI rhubarb [*pl generally*]

sīwipīwiw ᓰᐏᐲᐏᐤ
VAI s/he has edema, water retention

sīwisiw ᓰᐏᓯᐤ
VAI s/he is sweet (*e.g.* watermelon)

sīwispakosiw ᓰᐏᐢᐸᑯᓯᐤ
VAI it tastes sweet; it tastes salty

sīwispakwan ᓰᐏᐢᐸᑲᐧᐣ
VII s/he tastes sweet; s/he tastes salty

sīwīhtākamin ᓰᐑᐦᑖᑲᒥᐣ
VII it is a salty liquid

sīwīhtākan ᓰᐑᐦᑖᑲᐣ
NI salt

sīwīhtākan-sāposikan ᓰᐑᐦᑖᑲᐣ ᓵᐳᓯᑲᐣ
NI epsom salts

sīwīhtākanaham ᓰᐑᐦᑖᑲᓇᐦᐊᒼ
VTI s/he salts s.t.; s/he rubs salt into s.t.

sīwīhtākanahēw ᓰᐑᐦᑖᑲᓇᐦᐁᐤ
VTA s/he salts s.o. (*e.g.* fish)

sīwīhtākanahikēw ᓰᐑᐦᑖᑲᓇᐦᐃᑫᐤ
VAI s/he cures meats or fish (in brine)

sīwīhtākanāpōhkēw ᓰᐑᐦᑖᑲᓈᐴᐦᑫᐤ
VAI s/he makes brine

sīwīhtākanēwāpoy ᓰᐑᐦᑖᑲᓀᐚᐳᕀ
NI brine

sīwīhtākani-sākahikan ᓰᐑᐦᑖᑲᓂ ᓵᑲᐦᐃᑲᐣ
NI salt-lake; Blaine Lake, SK [*place name*]

sīwīhtākani-sākahikanihk ᓰᐑᐦᑖᑲᓂ ᓵᑲᐦᐃᑲᓂᕽ
INM [*loc*: "at salt-lake"]; Blaine Lake, SK

sīwīhtākaniskiwakāw ᓰᐑᐦᑖᑲᓂᐢᑭᐘᑳᐤ
NI salt-marsh

sīwīhtāw ᓰᐑᐦᑖᐤ
VAIt s/he makes s.t. salty

ᓲ

sōhkahāt- ᓲᐦᑲᐦᐋᐟ
IPV greatly, powerfully

sōhkakihtam ᓲᐦᑲᑭᐦᑕᒼ
VTI s/he prices s.t. dear

sōhkakihtēw ᓲᐦᑲᑭᐦᑌᐤ
VII it is expensive [*see also* mistakihtēw]

sōhkakisow ᓲᐦᑲᑭᓱᐤ
VAI it is expensive [*see also* mistakisow]

sōhkan ᓲᐦᑲᐣ
VII it is strongly made, it is sturdy, it is firm, it is solid, it is strong [*also* sōhkān; *cf.* sōhkāw]

sōhkastāw ᓲᐦᑲᐢᑖᐤ
VAIt s/he places s.t. solidly

sōhkatin ᓲᐦᑲᑎᐣ
VII it freezes solidly

sōhkatoskēw ᓲᐦᑲᑐᐢᑫᐤ
VAI s/he works hard

sōhkāhtik ᓲᐦᑳᐦᑎᐠ
NA strong tree [*pl*: -wak]

sōhkāhtik ᓲᐦᑳᐦᑎᐠ
NI strong board [*pl*: -wa]

sōhkākamihtāw ᓲᐦᑳᑲᒥᐦᑖᐤ
VAIt s/he makes s.t. (*i.e.* liquid) strong (*e.g.* tea)

sōhkākamiw ᓲᐦᑳᑲᒥᐤ
VII it is a strong liquid (*e.g.* tea)

sōhkākonēw ᓲᐦᑳᑯᓀᐤ
VAI it is hard snow, it is snow packed hard enough to bear weight

sōhkāpēkan ᓲᐦᑳᐯᑲᐣ
VII it is strong (*e.g.* rope)

sōhkāpēkasin ᓲᐦᑳᐯᑲᓯᐣ
VII it is rather strong (*e.g.* twine, rope) [*dim*]

sōhkāpēkisiw ᓲᐦᑳᐯᑭᓯᐤ
VAI it is strong (*e.g.* thread, yarn)

sōhkāpiskāw ᓲᐦᑳᐱᐢᑳᐤ
VII it is strong (*i.e.* metal)

sōhkāpiskisiw ᓲᐦᑳᐱᐢᑭᓯᐤ
VAI it is strong (*i.e.* metal)

sōhkāskohtāw ᓲᐦᑳᐢᑯᐦᑖᐤ
VAIt s/he strengthens s.t. by poles, s/he reinforces s.t., s/he props s.t. with poles

sōhkāskosiw ᓲᐦᑳᐢᑯᓯᐤ
VAI s/he is strong (as a tree)

sōhkāskwahwēw ᓲᐦᑳᐢᑲᐧᐦᐍᐤ
VTA s/he props s.o. up to reinforce

sōhkāskwan ᓲᐦᑳᐢᑲᐣ
　VII it is strong (as wood-lumber)

sōhkāstan ᓲᐦᑳᐢᑕᐣ
　VII it blows away in a strong wind

sōhkātisiw ᓲᐦᑳᑎᓯᐤ
　VAI s/he is strong, s/he is powerful, s/he is sturdy, s/he is mighty

sōhkātisiwin ᓲᐦᑳᑎᓯᐃᐧᐣ
　NI strength; power

sōhkāw ᓲᐦᑳᐤ
　VII it is strong [cf. sōhkan]

sōhkēciwan ᓲᐦᑫᒋᐊᐧᐣ
　VII it flows strongly, it is a strong current [cf. sōhkiciwan]

sōhkēhtatāw ᓲᐦᑫᐦᑕᑖᐤ
　VAIt s/he throws s.t. hard, s/he throws s.t. down forcefully

sōhkēkan ᓲᐦᑫᑲᐣ
　VII it is strong (i.e. cloth)

sōhkēkin ᓲᐦᑫᑭᐣ
　NI strong cloth [pl: -wa]

sōhkēkocin ᓲᐦᑫᑯᒋᐣ
　VAI s/he travels at great speed

sōhkēkotēw ᓲᐦᑫᑯᑌᐤ
　VII it runs hard, it runs fast, it runs vigorously; it speeds well

sōhkēmow ᓲᐦᑫᒧᐤ
　VAI s/he speaks boldly, forcefully

sōhkēmowitotam ᓲᐦᑫᒧᐃᐧᑐᑕᐣ
　VTI s/he speaks about s.t. boldly, forcefully

sōhkēmowitotawēw ᓲᐦᑫᒧᐃᐧᑐᑕᐌᐤ
　VTA s/he speaks to s.o. boldly, forcefully

sōhkēpahtāw ᓲᐦᑫᐸᐦᑖᐤ
　VAI s/he runs hard, s/he runs fast

sōhkēpayin ᓲᐦᑫᐸᔨᐣ
　VII it is strong, it works effectively (e.g. machine, medicine)

sōhkēpayiw ᓲᐦᑫᐸᔨᐤ
　VII it moves surely and quickly

sōhkēpitam ᓲᐦᑫᐱᑕᐣ
　VTI s/he stands firmly behind s.t., s/he promotes s.t.; s/he pulls s.t. using strength

sōhkēpitēw ᓲᐦᑫᐱᑌᐤ
　VTA s/he stands firmly behind s.o., s/he promotes s.o.; s/he pulls s.o. using strength

sōhkēsimow ᓲᐦᑫᓯᒧᐤ
　VAI s/he dances hard, vigorously

sōhkēsis ᓲᐦᑫᓯᐢ
　IPC a little faster

sōhkēwēpinam ᓲᐦᑫᐍᐱᓇᐣ
　VTI s/he throws s.t. hard

sōhkēwēpinēw ᓲᐦᑫᐍᐱᓀᐤ
　VTA s/he throws s.o. hard

sōhkēyihtam ᓲᐦᑫᔨᐦᑕᐣ
　VTI s/he is steadfast, s/he is steadfast about s.t.

sōhkēyihtākosiw ᓲᐦᑫᔨᐦᑖᑯᓯᐤ
　VAI s/he is thought to be strong, s/he is rated as brave

sōhkēyihtākwan ᓲᐦᑫᔨᐦᑖᑿᐣ
　VII it is thought to be strong

sōhkēyimēw ᓲᐦᑫᔨᒣᐤ
　VTA s/he thinks s.o. brave; s/he is confident of s.o.

sōhkēyimisow ᓲᐦᑫᔨᒥᓱᐤ
　VAI s/he thinks him/herself brave

sōhkēyimisowin ᓲᐦᑫᔨᒥᓱᐃᐧᐣ
　NI self-confidence

sōhkēyimow ᓲᐦᑫᔨᒧᐤ
　VAI s/he is brave, s/he is bold, s/he is confident

sōhkēyimowin ᓲᐦᑫᔨᒧᐃᐧᐣ
　NI confidence; bravery

sōhki ᓲᐦᑭ
　IPC hard, strong [also sohki]

sōhki- ᓲᐦᑭ
　IPV hard, strongly, intensively, vigourously, properly [also sohki-]

sōhkiciwan ᓲᐦᑭᒋᐊᐧᐣ
　VII it flows strongly, it is a strong current or stream [cf. sōhkēciwan]

sōhkihēw ᓲᐦᑭᐦᐁᐤ
　VTA s/he makes s.o. strong, s/he fortifies s.o.

sōhkihtākosiw ᓲᐦᑭᐦᑖᑯᓯᐤ
　VAI s/he has a powerful voice or sound

sōhkihtākwan ᓲᐦᑭᐦᑖᑿᐣ
　VII it has a powerful sound

sōhkihtāw ᓲᐦᑭᐦᑖᐤ
　VAIt s/he builds s.t. strongly, s/he fortifies s.t.

sōhkikāpawiw ᓲᐦᑭᑳᐸᐃᐧᐤ
　VAI s/he stands firm

sōhkinākosiw ᓲᐦᑭᓈᑯᓯᐤ
　VAI s/he looks strong; it is built strong

sōhkinākwan ᓲᐦᑭᓈᑿᐣ
　VII it looks strong; it is built strong

sōhkisiw ᓲᐦᑭᓯᐤ
　VAI s/he is strong, s/he is stout; s/he has supernatural power

sōhkisiwin ᓲᐦᑭᓯᐃᐧᐣ
　NI strength

sōhkistimēw ᓲᐦᑭᐢᑎᒣᐤ
　VTA s/he soaks s.o.; s/he dilutes s.o.

sōhkistitāw ᓲᐦᑭᐢᑎᑖᐤ
　VAIt s/he soaks s.t.; s/he dilutes s.t.

sōhkitēhēw ᓲᐦᑭᑌᐦᐁᐤ
　VAI s/he is stout of heart, s/he has a strong heart

sōhkitēhēwin ᓲᐦᑭᑌᐦᐁᐃᐧᐣ
　NI courage; bravery

sōhkiýowēw ᓲᐦᑭᔪᐌᐤ
　VII it is very windy, it is a strong wind

sōkāw ᓲᑳᐤ
　NA sugar [European loan; sg generally; see also sīwinikan]

sōkāwāhtik ᓲᑳᐘᐦᑎᐠ
　NA sugar maple [pl: -wak]

sōkāwāspinēw ᓲᑳᐚᐢᐱᓀᐤ
　VAI s/he has diabetes

sōkāwiýākanis ᓲᑳᐏᔮᑲᓂᐢ
　NI sugar bowl [dim]

sōmin ᓲᒥᐣ
　NA grape, raisin

sōmin-pahkwēsikan ᓲᒥᐣ ᐸᐦᑲᐧᓯᑲᐣ
　NA raisin bannock, raisin bread; fruit bread

sōmināhtik ᓲᒥᓈᐦᑎᐠ
　NA berry tree; grape vine [pl: -wak]

sōmināpoy ᓲᒥᓈᐳᕀ
　NI wine

sōmināpōhkākēw ᓲᒥᓈᐳᐦᑳᑫᐤ
　VAI s/he makes wine from something

sōmināpōhkēw ᓲᒥᓈᐳᐦᑫᐤ
　VAI s/he makes wine

sōminis ᓲᒥᓂᐢ
　NA currant; little grape, raisin [dim]

sōniskwātahikēw ᓲᓂᐢᑾᑕᐦᐃᑫᐤ
　VAI s/he skates; s/he plays hockey; s/he skis

sōniskwātahikēwikamik ᓲᓂᐢᑾᑕᐦᐃᑫᐏᑲᒥᐠ
　NI arena, hockey rink [pl: -wa]

sōniskwātahikēwin ᓲᓂᐢᑾᑕᐦᐃᑫᐃᐧᐣ
　NI skating; hockey

sōniyāhkākēw ᓲᓂᔮᐦᑳᑫᐤ
　VAI s/he makes money out of s.t.

sōniyāhkātam ᓲᓂᔮᐦᑳᑕᐣ
　VTI s/he earns money from s.t., s/he makes money at s.t., s/he uses s.t. to make money

sōniyāhkātēw ᓲᓂᔮᐦᑳᑌᐤ
　VTA s/he earns money using s.o., s/he makes money from s.o. (e.g. bannock)

sōniyāhkēw ᓲᓂᔮᐦᑫᐤ
　VAI s/he earns money, s/he earns wages; s/he makes money, s/he creates money

sōniyās ᓲᓂᔮᐢ
　NA money; change; quarter dollar [dim; sg: sōniyās "a quarter; twenty-five cents"; pl rarely used; cf. sōniyāw]

sōniyāskāw ᓲᓂᔮᐢᑳᐤ
　VII it is Treaty Day; there is an abundance of money

sōniyāw ᒍᓂᔮᐤ
  NA money, wages; gold,
  silver [*cf.* sōniyās]
sōniyāw-kīsikāw ᒍᓂᔮᐤ ᑮᓯᑳᐤ
  VII it is Treaty Day
sōniyāw-masinahikan
  ᒍᓂᔮᐤ ᒪᓯᓇᐦᐃᑲᐣ
  NI money order or cheque
sōniyāw-okimāw ᒍᓂᔮᐤ ᐅᑭᒫᐤ
  NA Indian Agent,
  money-boss [*cf.*
  sōniyāwikimāw]
sōniyāw-okimāwiw ᒍᓂᔮᐤ ᐅᑭᒫᐃᐧᐤ
  VAI he is an Indian agent
sōniyāw-wāskahikan
  ᒍᓂᔮᐤ ᐋᐧᐢᑲᐦᐃᑲᐣ
  NI bank [*cf.* sōniyāwikamik]
sōniyāwacis ᒍᓂᔮᐊᐧᒋᐢ
  NI purse; change purse
  [*dim*]
sōniyāwan ᒍᓂᔮᐊᐧᐣ
  VII it is worth money; it
  consists of money
sōniyāwasinahikan
  ᒍᓂᔮᐊᐧᓯᓇᐦᐃᑲᐣ
  NI cheque; money order
sōniyāwāhkēsīs ᒍᓂᔮᐋᐦᑫᓰᐢ
  NA silver fox
sōniyāwāpisk ᒍᓂᔮᐋᐱᐢᐠ
  NA copper [*lit:*
  "money-metal"; *pl:* -wak]
sōniyāwāskosiw ᒍᓂᔮᐋᐢᑯᓯᐤ
  VAI it is a golden stick
sōniyāwi ᒍᓂᔮᐃᐧ
  IPC with respect to money,
  in finacial matters
sōniyāwi-pīwayēw
  ᒍᓂᔮᐃᐧ ᐲᐊᐧᔦᐤ
  VAI it has golden feathers
sōniyāwihkēw ᒍᓂᔮᐃᐧᐦᑫᐤ
  VAI s/he makes money from
  s.t.
sōniyāwikamik ᒍᓂᔮᐃᐧᑲᒥᐠ
  NI bank [*pl:* -wak]
sōniyāwikimāw ᒍᓂᔮᐃᐧᑭᒫᐤ
  NA Indian Agent [*cf.*
  sōniyāw-okimāw]
sōniyāwiw ᒍᓂᔮᐃᐧᐤ
  VII it is money, gold; it has
  money, gold
sōniyāwiwacis ᒍᓂᔮᐃᐧᐊᐧᒋᐢ
  NI purse; change purse
  [*dim*]
sōniyāwiwat ᒍᓂᔮᐃᐧᐊᐧᐟ
  NI cash box
sōpahcikēw ᒍᐸᐦᒋᑫᐤ
  VAI s/he eats good food and
  licks his/her own fingers;
  s/he eats finger-licking good
  food
sōpahtam ᒍᐸᐦᑕᒼ
  VTI s/he spits on s.t.; s/he
  laps s.t. up; s/he licks s.t. off
  the bone; s/he eats meat off
sōpamēw ᒍᐸᒣᐤ
  VTA s/he eats s.o. dunked or
  soaked in broth or milk (*e.g.*
  bannock)

sōpēkahikan ᒍᐯᑲᐦᐃᑲᐣ
  NI paint
sōsawihtāw ᓱᓴᐃᐧᐦᑖᐤ
  VAIt s/he defiles s.t.
sōsawiskam ᓱᓴᐃᐧᐢᑲᒼ
  VTI s/he defiles s.t. by
  stepping or wearing
sōsawiskawēw ᓱᓴᐃᐧᐢᑲᐁᐧᐤ
  VTA s/he defiles s.o. by
  stepping or wearing
sōsāsiw ᓱᓵᓯᐤ
  NA salmon
sōsimān ᓱᓯᒫᐣ
  NA snow-dart, ice throwing
  stick
sōsimēw ᓱᓯᒣᐤ
  VAI s/he plays at throwing
  snow-darts
sōsiniskwātaham ᓱᓯᓂᐢᑹᑕᐦᐊᒼ
  VTI s/he skates on s.t.
sōsiniskwātahikan
  ᓱᓯᓂᐢᑹᑕᐦᐃᑲᐣ
  NI skate; [*pl:*] pair of skates
sōsiniskwātahikēw
  ᓱᓯᓂᐢᑹᑕᐦᐃᑫᐤ
  VAI s/he is skating
sōskohtāw ᓱᐢᑰᐦᑖᐤ
  VAIt s/he makes s.t. smooth
  by sanding
sōskokaham ᓱᐢᑯᑲᐦᐊᐧᐨ
  VTI s/he hews s.t. smooth
sōskokahwēw ᓱᐢᑯᑲᐦᐁᐧᐤ
  VTA s/he hews s.o. smooth
sōskonam ᓱᐢᑯᓇᒼ
  VTI s/he lets s.t. slip out of
  his/her own hands
sōskonēw ᓱᐢᑯᓀᐤ
  VTA s/he lets s.o. slip out of
  his/her own hands
sōskopayihow ᓱᐢᑯᐸᔨᐦᐅᐤ
  VAI s/he flings him/herself
  to glide, s/he slides away
sōskopayiw ᓱᐢᑯᐸᔨᐤ
  VAI s/he slips, s/he slides
  down, s/he glides; s/he
  skidoos
sōskopayīs ᓱᐢᑯᐸᔩᐢ
  NA skidoo, snowmobile
sōskopicikēw ᓱᐢᑯᐱᒋᑫᐤ
  VAI s/he falls on smooth ice
sōskosin ᓱᐢᑯᓯᐣ
  VAI s/he slips
sōskosiw ᓱᐢᑯᓯᐤ
  VAI s/he is smooth, it is
  slippery
sōskoskam ᓱᐢᑯᐢᑲᒼ
  VTI s/he slips stepping on
  s.t.
sōskoskamikāw ᓱᐢᑯᐢᑲᒥᑳᐤ
  VII it is smooth ground, it is
  slippery ground
sōskoskawēw ᓱᐢᑯᐢᑲᐁᐧᐤ
  VTA s/he slips stepping on
  s.o.
sōskoyāpawiw ᓱᐢᑯᔮᐸᐃᐧᐤ
  VAI s/he skis
sōskwaciwēw ᓱᐢᑲᐧᒋᐁᐧᐤ
  VAI s/he slides downhill,
  s/he toboggans

sōskwaciwēwin ᓱᐢᑲᐧᒋᐁᐧᐃᐧᐣ
  NI slide (as action); hill for
  sliding [*used as a place
  name; also* sōskwaciwān]
sōskwaham ᓱᐢᑲᐧᐦᐊᒼ
  VTI s/he irons s.t.
sōskwahikan ᓱᐢᑲᐧᐦᐃᑲᐣ
  NI iron
sōskwahikēw ᓱᐢᑲᐧᐦᐃᑫᐤ
  VAI s/he irons, s/he irons
  things smooth, s/he presses
  things smooth
sōskwahwēw ᓱᐢᑲᐧᐦᐁᐧᐤ
  VTA s/he irons s.o. (*e.g.*
  pants)
sōskwanātaham ᓱᐢᑲᐧᓈᑕᐦᐊᐧᐨ
  VTI s/he skates
sōskwanātahikan ᓱᐢᑲᐧᓈᑕᐦᐃᑲᐣ
  NI skate
sōskwanātahikēw ᓱᐢᑲᐧᓈᑕᐦᐃᑫᐤ
  VAI s/he skates
sōskwanātahikēwin
  ᓱᐢᑲᐧᓈᑕᐦᐃᑫᐃᐧᐣ
  NI skating
sōskwanātahiwākan
  ᓱᐢᑲᐧᓈᑕᐦᐃᐋᐧᑲᐣ
  NI skate
sōskwāc ᓱᐢᑲᐧ-
  IPC just, regardless, no
  matter what the
  consequences; truly, surely;
  directly, immediately,
  straight away; simply,
  without further ado, without
  delay; [*in negative clauses:*]
  at all [*cf.* sōskwāt]
sōskwākamin ᓱᐢᑲᐧᑲᒥᐣ
  VII it is soft water
sōskwāpēkan ᓱᐢᑲᐧᐯᑲᐣ
  VII it is smooth (*i.e.* rope)
sōskwāpisk ᓱᐢᑲᐧᐱᐢᐠ
  NI hone [*pl:* -wa]
sōskwāpiskāw ᓱᐢᑲᐧᐱᐢᑳᐤ
  VII it is smooth (*i.e.* rock or
  metal)
sōskwāsiw ᓱᐢᑲᐧᓯᐤ
  VAI s/he is blown gliding
sōskwāskosiw ᓱᐢᑲᐧᐢᑯᓯᐤ
  VAI it is smooth (*i.e.* tall
  tree)
sōskwāskwan ᓱᐢᑲᐧᐢᑲᐧᐣ
  VII it is smooth (*i.e.* long
  pole)
sōskwāstimēw ᓱᐢᑲᐧᐢᑎᒣᐤ
  VTA s/he makes s.o. glide
  before the wind
sōskwāt ᓱᐢᑲᐧᐟ
  IPC just, regardless, no
  matter what the
  consequences; truly, surely;
  directly, straight away [*cf.*
  sōskwāc]
sōskwātahikēw ᓱᐢᑲᐧᑕᐦᐃᑫᐤ
  VAI s/he skates
sōskwāw ᓱᐢᑲᐧᐤ
  VII it is smooth, it is
  slippery (*e.g.* highway)
sōskwēkan ᓱᐢᑫᐧᑲᐣ
  VII it is smooth (*e.g.* velvet)

sōskwēkin ᓲᐢᑵᑭᐣ
NI velvet [*pl*: -wa]
sōsowacimos ᓲᓱᐘᒋᒧᐢ
NA young mule [*dim*]

sōsowatim ᓲᓱᐘᑎᒼ
NA mule [*pl*: -wak; *also* sōsōw-ātim]
sōsōsis ᓲᓲᓯᐢ
NA donkey [*dim*]

sōswēpaýiw ᓲᔅᐍᐸᔨᐤ
VII it scatters [*cf.* sisiwēpaýiw]
sōwahkēýiw ᓲᐘᐦᑫᔨᐤ
VAI s/he soars (as a bird)

t

c

ta- ᒐ
IPV [*grammatical preverb: future*; *infinitive*; *cf.* ka-, kika-, kita-, tita-]

ta-kī- ᒐ ᑭ
IPV can, be able to; should, ought to [*cf.* ka-kī-]

tacīwihēw ᒐᒋᐃᐧᐦᐁᐤ
VTA s/he gets ahead of s.o.

tacīwihtāw ᒐᒋᐃᐧᐦᑖᐤ
VAIt s/he gets ahead of s.t.

tahci- ᒐᐧᒋ
IPV coming apart, undone

tahcipaýihēw ᒐᐧᒋᐸᕿᐦᐁᐤ
VTA s/he loosens s.o. by applying pressure or weight

tahcipaýihow ᒐᐧᒋᐸᕿᐦᐅᐤ
VAI s/he breaks loose

tahcipaýiw ᒐᐧᒋᐸᕿᐤ
VII it becomes loose or unhooked

tahcipitam ᒐᐧᒋᐱᑕᒼ
VTI s/he undoes s.t. [*rdpl*: tāh-tahcipitam]

tahcipitēw ᒐᐧᒋᐱᑌᐤ
VTA s/he undoes s.o.

tahciwēpaham ᒐᐧᒋᐍᐸᐦᐊᒼ
VTI s/he springs the trap; s/he unlocks the trap

tahciwēpahwēw ᒐᐧᒋᐍᐸᐦᐍᐤ
VTA s/he frees s.o. (from a trap)

tahkaciw ᒐᐦᑲᒋᐤ
VAI s/he catches cold

tahkahcikan ᒐᐦᑲᐧᒋᑲᐣ
NI spear; dagger; pool cue, billiard cue

tahkahcikēw ᒐᐦᑲᐧᒋᑫᐤ
VAI s/he stabs; s/he plays pool, s/he plays billiards

tahkahtam ᒐᐦᑲᐦᑕᒼ
VTI s/he stabs s.t., s/he jabs s.t.; s/he stabs with s.t.

tahkamēw ᒐᐦᑲᒣᐤ
VTA s/he stabs s.o. [*rdpl*: tāh-tahkamēw]

tahkamisow ᒐᐦᑲᒥᓱᐤ
VAI s/he stabs him/herself

tahkapiw ᒐᐦᑲᐱᐤ
VAI s/he is cold (*e.g.* a goose from the oven)

tahkascikan ᒐᐦᒐᓯᑲᐣ
NI refrigerator [*see also* ahkwatihcikan]

tahkastāw ᒐᐦᑲᐢᑖᐤ
VAIt s/he cools s.t. by putting it in a cool place

tahkastēw ᒐᐦᑲᐢᑌᐤ
VII it is cold; it is cold indoors

tahkatēskācikan ᒐᐦᑲᑌᐢᑳᒋᑲᐣ
NI spur

tahkatēskācikēw ᒐᐦᑲᑌᐢᑳᒋᑫᐤ
VAI s/he applies spurs

tahkatin ᒐᐦᑲᑎᐣ
VII it is cool

tahkākamin ᒐᐦᑳᑲᒥᐣ
VII it is a cold liquid [*cf.* tahkikamin]

tahkākonakāw ᒐᐦᑳᑯᓇᑳᐤ
VII it is cold (by the snow)

tahkāpāwahēw ᒐᐦᑳᐹ�’ᐊᐧᐦᐁᐤ
VTA s/he cools s.o. in the water

tahkāpāwatāw ᒐᐦᑳᐹᐧᐊᑖᐤ
VAIt s/he cools s.t. in the water

tahkāpiskāw ᒐᐦᑳᐱᐢᑳᐤ
VII it is cold (*i.e.* metal)

tahkāpiskisiw ᒐᐦᑳᐱᐢᑭᓯᐤ
VAI s/he is cold (*i.e.* metal)

tahkāsin ᒐᐦᑳᓯᐣ
VII it is rather cold (to touch) [*dim*; *also*: cahkāsin]

tahkāsiw ᒐᐦᑳᓯᐤ
VAI s/he is cooled by the wind

tahkāw ᒐᐦᑳᐤ
VII it is cool, it is cold (to the touch)

tahkāýāsin ᒐᐦᑳᕹᓯᐣ
VII it is cool weather [*dim*; *also*: cahkāýāsin]

tahkāýāw ᒐᐦᑳᕹᐤ
VII it is cool weather

tahkēýihtam ᒐᐦᑫᕿᐦᑕᒼ
VTI s/he perceives the cold, s/he feels the cold

tahki ᒐᐦᑭ
IPC always, constantly, all the time, repeated action

tahki- ᒐᐦᑭ
IPV repeated action, always, constantly; receiving a chill, cold

tahki ayiwāk ᒐᐦᑭ ᐊᕠᐚᐠ
IPH increasingly, more and more; getting to be [*also* tahk āyiwāk]

tahkikamāpoy ᒐᐦᑭᑲᒫᐳᕀ
NI cold water

tahkikamāpōhkēw ᒐᐦᑭᑲᒫᐴᐦᑫᐤ
VAI s/he adds ice to water, cool the water

tahkikamin ᒐᐦᑭᑲᒥᐣ
VII it is a body of cold water

tahkikamiw ᒐᐦᑭᑲᒥᐤ
VII it is cold water

tahkimastāw ᒐᐦᑭᒪᐢᑖᐤ
VAIt s/he places s.t. (*e.g.* liquid) to cool [*also* tahkamastāw]

tahkinē ᒐᐦᑭ�
IPC always, forever [*see also* kākikē]

tahkipaýin ᒐᐦᑭᐸᕿᐣ
VII it cools, it cools off

tahkipaýiw ᒐᐦᑭᐸᕿᐤ
VAI s/he cools, s/he cools off

tahkipēstāw ᒐᐦᑭᐯᐢᑖᐤ
VII it is cold rain falling

tahkisitēw ᒐᐦᑭᓯᑌᐤ
VAI s/he has cold feet

tahkisiw ᒐᐦᑭᓯᐤ
VAI s/he is cold; s/he grows cool

tahkiskam ᒐᐦᑭᐢᑲᒼ
VTI s/he kicks s.t. [*cf.* tahkiskātam]

tahkiskawēw ᒐᐦᑭᐢᑲᐍᐤ
VTA s/he kicks s.o. [*cf.* tahkiskātēw]

tahkiskācikan ᒐᐦᑭᐢᑳᒋᑲᐣ
NA football, soccer ball

tahkiskācikēw ᒐᐦᑭᐢᑳᒋᑫᐤ
VAI s/he kicks

tahkiskātam ᒐᐦᑭᐢᑳᑕᒼ
VTI s/he kicks s.t. [*cf.* tahkiskam]

tahkiskātēw ᒐᐦᑭᐢᑳᑌᐤ
VTA s/he kicks s.o. [*cf.* tahkiskawēw]

tahkiskikēw ᒐᐦᑭᐢᑭᑫᐤ
VAI s/he kicks

tahkispiskwanēw ᒐᐦᑭᐢᐱᐢᑲᐧᓀᐤ
VAI s/he has a cold back

tahkispiskwanēwaciw ᒐᐦᑭᐢᐱᐢᑲᐧᓀᐧᐊᒋᐤ
VAI s/he has a freezing back,

s/he catches cold on his/her own back from a draft

tahkistikwānēw Cᵖᵖᑭ·ᐣᑊᐦ·ᐧ°
VAI s/he has a cold head

tahkiỳawēpaỳiw Cᵖᑭᐳᐁ·ᐊᐳᐦ·ᐊ·ᐸᐧ
VAI s/he feels cold in his/her own body

tahkiỳowēw Cᵖᑭᐪᐁ·°
VII it is a cold wind, it is cold air

tahko-miỳēw Cᐧᒃ ᒥᐊᐧ
VTA s/he gives s.o. extra [*also* tako-miỳēw; *wC*: -mīthīw]

tahkocihcēskawēw Cᐧᒋᐦᐦᔦᑲ·ᐧ°
VTA s/he steps on s.o.'s hand

tahkoham Cᐧᐦᐊᒼ
VTI s/he holds s.t., s/he steers s.t.

tahkohc Cᐧᐦ·
IPC top, on top; above [*cf.* tahkoht]

tahkohc-āyihk Cᐧᐦᐃ̇ᐠᐨ
IPC at the top, on top of the place [*loc*]

tahkohci- Cᐧᐦᒋ
IPV on top [*see also* tāhci-, tēhci-]

tahkohci-pahkisin Cᐧᐦᒋ ᐸᐦᑭᓯᐣ
VAI s/he falls on top

tahkohcikāpawiw Cᐧᐦᒋᑳᐸᐃ·°
VAI s/he stands on the top of something

tahkohcipaỳihow Cᐧᐦᒋᐸᐊᐳᐦᐅ°
VAI s/he throws him/herself up on top; s/he jumps on the top of something

tahkohcipaỳiw Cᐧᐦᒋᐸᐊᐳᐦ°
VII it falls on the top

tahkohcisin Cᐧᐦᒋᓯᐣ
VAI s/he lies on the top of something

tahkoht Cᐧᐦᐟ
IPC top, on top [*cf.* tahkohc]

tahkohtaciwēhtahēw Cᐧᐦᑕᒋᐁ·ᐧᐦᑕᐦᐁ·°
VTA s/he brings s.o. to the top of the hill or stairs

tahkohtaciwēhtatāw Cᐧᐦᑕᒋᐁ·ᐧᐦᑕᑖ°
VAIt s/he brings s.t. to the top of the hill or stairs

tahkohtaciwēw Cᐧᐦᑕᒋᐁ·°
VAI s/he goes to the top of the hill or stairs, s/he reaches the top

tahkohtastāw Cᐧᐦᑕᐢᑖ°
VAIt s/he places s.t. on top

tahkohtastēw Cᐧᐦᑕᐢᑌ°
VII it sits on top, it is on top

tahkohtāmatin Cᐧᐦᑖᒪᑎᐣ
VII it is at the top of the hill

tahkonam Cᐧᒐ·ᒃ
VTI s/he grasps s.t., s/he holds s.t.; s/he carries s.t.

tahkonamawēw Cᐧᒐ·ᒪᐊᐧ°
VTA s/he carries (it/him) for s.o.

tahkonāwasow Cᐧᒐ·ᐊ·ᐊᐧ°
VAI s/he carries an infant

tahkonēw Cᐧᐧ°
VTA s/he grasps s.o., s/he holds s.o.; s/he carries s.o.

tahkonikan Cᐧᐧᑊ
NI handle; shopping bag

tahkonikēw Cᐧᐧᑫ·°
VAI s/he carries things

tahkonikēwin Cᐧᐧᑫ·ᐧᐃᐧ
NI armful; carried things

tahkopicamānis Cᐧᐸᐱᒐ·ᓂᐢ
NI shoestring [*dim*]

tahkopicikan Cᐧᐸᐱᐦᑊ
NI cord, string

tahkopicikanēyāpiy Cᐧᐸᐱᑲᐧᐱ·ᐊ·ᐸ+
NI string, cord

tahkopicikākēw Cᐧᐸᐱᑳᑫ·°
VAI s/he uses s.t. to tie with

tahkopicikēpaỳin Cᐧᐸᐱᑫ·ᐊᐧᐸᐸᐧ
VII it has a knot form; it is tangled

tahkopicikēpaỳiw Cᐧᐸᐱᑫ·ᐊᐧᐸᐦ°
VAI it has a knot form; s/he gets tangled

tahkopicikēw Cᐧᐸᐱᑫ·°
VAI s/he ties, s/he ties things

tahkopicikēwin Cᐧᐸᐱᑫ·ᐃᐧᐧ
NI knot

tahkopisow Cᐧᐸᐱᐦᐅᐧ°
VAI s/he is tied fast

tahkopitam Cᐧᐸᐱᐟᒃ
VTI s/he ties s.t. fast

tahkopitamawēw Cᐧᐸᐱᑕᒪᐁ·°
VTA s/he ties (it/him) fast for s.o.

tahkopitamān Cᐧᐸᐱᑕᒐ·
NI moccasin string

tahkopitapasonāhtik Cᐧᐸᐱᑕᐸᓱᓇ·ᐦᐣ`
NI primary tent pole [*pl*: -wa]

tahkopitapasoyānāhtik Cᐧᐸᐱᑕᐸᓱᔭ·ᓇ·ᐦᐣ`
NI primary tent pole [*pl*: -wa]

tahkopitāwasow Cᐧᐸᐱᑖᐊᐧᐦ·ᐊᐧ°
VAI s/he ties his/her own child up in a moss-bag; s/he swaddles a child

tahkopitēw Cᐧᐸᐱᐁᐧ°
VII it is tied fast

tahkopitēw Cᐧᐸᐱᐁᐧ°
VTA s/he ties s.o. fast

tahkopitisow Cᐧᐸᐱᓱᐧ°
VAI s/he ties him/herself

tahkoskam Cᐧᐢᑊᐨ
VTI s/he treads on s.t. [*cf.* tahkoskātam]

tahkoskawēw Cᐧᐢᑲᐁᐧ·°
VTA s/he steps on s.o., s/he treads on s.o. [*cf.* tahkoskātēw]

tahkoskācikan Cᐧᐢᑳᒋᑊ
NI foot stool

tahkoskācikēw Cᐧᐢᑳᒋᑫᐧ°
VAI s/he treads on things

tahkoskātam Cᐧᐢᑳᐟᒃ
VTI s/he steps on s.t. [*cf.* tahkoskam]

tahkoskātēw Cᐧᐢᑳᐃᐧᐅᐧ
VTA s/he steps on s.o. [*cf.* tahkoskawēw]

tahkoskēw Cᐧᐢᑫᐧ°
VAI s/he steps; s/he steps on s.t., s/he kicks s.t.

tahkoskēwin Cᐧᐢᑫᐧ·ᐃᐧᐧ
NI step, pace, yard; footprint; [*pl*:] steps, footsteps

tahkwahcikēw Cᐧᐦ·ᐦᒐᑫᐧ°
VAI s/he bites, s/he clamps

tahkwahcikēmakan Cᐧᐦ·ᐦᒐᑫ·ᒪᑊ
VII it clamps, it bites

tahkwahkēskiw Cᐧᐦ·ᐦᑫᐢᑭ°
VAI s/he has a habit of biting [*hab*]

tahkwahkēw Cᐧᐦ·ᐦᑫ°
VAI s/he bites

tahkwahtam Cᐧᐦ·ᐦᑕᒃ
VTI s/he bites s.t.

tahkwamācikan Cᐧᐦ·ᒪ·ᒋᑊ
NI vice, press

tahkwamēw Cᐧᐦ·ᒪᐁᐧ
VTA s/he bites s.o.; s/he has s.o. in his/her own mouth

tahkwāskwēpitam Cᐧᐦ·ᐢᑫᐧ·ᐱᑕᐨ
VTI s/he ties s.t. fast to wood or solid

tahkwāskwēpitēw Cᐧᐦ·ᐢᑫᐧ·ᐱᑌᐅᐧ
VTA s/he ties s.o. fast to wood or solid

tahpisimina Cᐧᐱᓯᒥᓇ
NA necklace of beads [*pl*]

tahtakiw Cᐧᑭ°
NA crane, pelican [*cf.* cahcakiw]

tahtakosiw Cᐧᑕᑯᓯᐅᐧ°
VAI it is flat, level (e.g. snow)

tahtakwahcāw Cᐧᑕᑲᐧᐦ·ᒐ̇·
VII it is even, level land

tahtakwāw Cᐧᑕᑲᐧ·°
VII it is level, it is a flat area

tahtinam Cᐧᓇᑊᐨ
VTI s/he loosens s.t. (e.g. braid), s/he unties s.t.

tahtinēw Cᐧᓇᐧ°
VTA s/he sets s.o. free, s/he unties s.o., s/he looses s.o.

tahtinikan Cᐧᓇᐱᑊ
NI trigger

tahtinikātēw Cᐧᓇᐱᑳᐅᐧ°
VII it is taken off, it is loosened, it is untied

tahto Cᐧᑐ
IPC each, every; so many, so much; as many

tahto- Cᐧᑐ
IPV as many as

tahto-awāsisak ᑕᐦᑐ ᐊᐋᐧᓯᓴᐠ
IPC every child

tahto-iskwēwak ᑕᐦᑐ ᐃᐢᑫᐧᐊᐧᐠ
IPC every woman

tahto-kīsikāw ᑕᐦᑐ ᑮᓯᑳᐤ
IPC each day, every day, daily

tahto-misit ᑕᐦᑐ ᒥᓯᐟ
IPC that many feet

tahto-nāpēwak ᑕᐦᑐ ᓈᐯᐊᐧᐠ
IPC every man

tahto-pipon ᑕᐦᑐ ᐱᐳᐣ
IPC yearly, annually, every year

tahto-tipiskāw ᑕᐦᑐ ᑎᐱᐢᑳᐤ
IPC each night; every night

tahto-tipiskwēw ᑕᐦᑐ ᑎᐱᐢᑫᐧᐤ
VAI s/he sleeps out many nights

tahtocihcān ᑕᐦᑐᒋᐦᒑᐣ
IPC so many inches; so many thumbs

tahtonisk ᑕᐦᑐᓂᐢᐠ
IPC so many fathoms

tahtopiponwēw ᑕᐦᑐᐱᐳᓀᐧᐤ
VAI s/he is so many winters old [*also* tahtopiponēw; *cf.* itahtopiponwēw]

tahtoskānēsiwak ᑕᐦᑐᐢᑳᓀᓯᐊᐧᐠ
VAI they are of so many kinds, nations [*pl*]

tahtw-āskiy ᑕᐦᑖᐧᐢᑭᐩ
IPC so many years, as many years [*also* tahto-askiy]

tahtw-āya ᑕᐦᑖᐧᔭ
IPC so many [*also* tahto-aya]

tahtw-āyamihēwi-kīsikāw
ᑕᐦᑖᐧᔭᒥᐦᐁᐃᐧ ᑮᓯᑳᐤ
IPC every Sunday

tahtwayak ᑕᐦᑕᐧᔭᐠ
IPC at every place; in so many places, ways

tahtwānakisiwak ᑕᐦᑖᐧᓇᑭᓯᐊᐧᐠ
VAI they are of so many kinds

tahtwāpacihtāwinēw
ᑕᐦᑖᐧᐸᒋᐦᑖᐃᐧᓀᐤ
VAI s/he has so many tools

tahtwāpisk ᑕᐦᑖᐧᐱᐢᐠ
IPC dollar(s); so many dollars

tahtwāw ᑕᐦᑖᐧᐤ
IPC each time, every time; so many times

takahkahpicikēw ᑕᑲᐦᑲᐦᐱᒋᑫᐤ
VAI s/he has a good team (of horses)

takahkastim ᑕᑲᐦᑲᐢᑎᒼ
NA good horse; good dog [*pl*: -wak]

takahkastimwēw ᑕᑲᐦᑲᐢᑎᒣᐧᐤ
VAI s/he has a good horse, good dog

takahkatim ᑕᑲᐦᑲᑎᒼ
NA good horse; good dog [*pl*: -wak]

takahkāciwasomēw
ᑕᑲᐦᑳᒋᐊᐧᓱᒣᐤ
VTA s/he boils s.o. well (*e.g.* duck)

takahkāpāwēw ᑕᑲᐦᑳᐹᐁᐧᐤ
VII it is well washed; it washes well

takahkāpēwiw ᑕᑲᐦᑳᐯᐃᐧᐤ
VAI he is a good, strong, handsome man

takahkēýihtam ᑕᑲᐦᑫᔨᐦᑕᒼ
VTI s/he is glad, s/he is pleased; s/he thinks well of s.t., s/he likes s.t. [*rdpl*: tāh-takahkēýihtam]

takahkēýihtamihēw
ᑕᑲᐦᑫᔨᐦᑕᒥᐦᐁᐤ
VTA s/he pleases s.o.

takahkēýimēw ᑕᑲᐦᑫᔨᒣᐤ
VTA s/he thinks well of s.o., s/he likes s.o., s/he considers s.o. nice; s/he likes s.o.'s ways

takahkēýimow ᑕᑲᐦᑫᔨᒧᐤ
VAI s/he is pleased with him/herself

takahkēýimowin ᑕᑲᐦᑫᔨᒧᐃᐧᐣ
NI self-confidence

takahki ᑕᑲᐦᑭ
IPC good, nice; really good, great

takahki- ᑕᑲᐦᑭ
IPN good, nice

takahki- ᑕᑲᐦᑭ
IPV good, nice

takahkihkasam ᑕᑲᐦᑭᐦᑲᓴᒼ
VTI s/he bakes s.t. well

takahkihkaswēw ᑕᑲᐦᑭᐦᑲᓭᐧᐤ
VTA s/he bakes s.o. well

takahkihtākosiw ᑕᑲᐦᑭᐦᑖᑯᓯᐤ
VAI s/he sounds nice

takahkihtākwan ᑕᑲᐦᑭᐦᑖᑲᐧᐣ
VII it sounds nice

takahkimākosiw ᑕᑲᐦᑭᒫᑯᓯᐤ
VAI s/he smells good

takahkimākwan ᑕᑲᐦᑭᒫᑲᐧᐣ
VII it smells good

takahkinākohtāw ᑕᑲᐦᑭᓈᑯᐦᑖᐤ
VAIt s/he makes s.t. look good, nice, great

takahkinākosiw ᑕᑲᐦᑭᓈᑯᓯᐤ
VAI s/he looks good, nice, great

takahkinākwan ᑕᑲᐦᑭᓈᑲᐧᐣ
VII it looks good, nice, great

takahkipahtāw ᑕᑲᐦᑭᐸᐦᑖᐤ
VAI s/he runs really well

takahkipēw ᑕᑲᐦᑭᐯᐤ
VAI s/he feels good with drink, s/he feels intoxicated

takahkisiw ᑕᑲᐦᑭᓯᐤ
VAI s/he is polite, s/he is well-mannered

takahkisīhēw ᑕᑲᐦᑭᓰᐦᐁᐤ
VTA s/he dresses s.o. nicely; s/he makes s.o. look well with dress, s/he prepares s.o. (*e.g.* jewellry) well, nicely

takahkisīhow ᑕᑲᐦᑭᓰᐦᐅᐤ
VAI s/he is very well dressed

takahkisīhtāw ᑕᑲᐦᑭᓰᐦᑖᐤ
VAIt s/he makes s.t. nice, nicely, well

takahkispakosiw ᑕᑲᐦᑭᐢᐸᑯᓯᐤ
VAI s/he tastes good, delicious

takahkispakwan ᑕᑲᐦᑭᐢᐸᑲᐧᐣ
VII it tastes good, delicious

takahkwēwēhtitāw
ᑕᑲᐦᑫᐧᐁᐧᐦᑎᑖᐤ
VAIt s/he makes a nice drumming or tapping sound, s/he makes a nice drumming sound on s.t.

tako- ᑕᑯ
IPV in addition to, on top, over and above; with, having along, also

takohāw ᑕᑯᐦᐋᐤ
VAI s/he arrives by plane

takohēw ᑕᑯᐦᐁᐤ
VTA s/he joins s.o. to something, s/he adds to s.o.

takohtahēw ᑕᑯᐦᑕᐦᐁᐤ
VTA s/he arrives with s.o.; s/he takes s.o., s/he brings s.o. to a destination

takohtahiwēw ᑕᑯᐦᑕᐦᐃᐁᐧᐤ
VAI s/he arrives with people, s/he brings people

takohtatamawēw ᑕᑯᐦᑕᑕᒪᐁᐧᐤ
VTA s/he arrives with (it/him) for s.o.

takohtatāw ᑕᑯᐦᑕᑖᐤ
VAIt s/he arrives with s.t.; s/he arrives carrying s.t., s/he bring s.t. along

takohtēw ᑕᑯᐦᑌᐤ
VAI s/he arrives (walking)

takonam ᑕᑯᓇᒼ
VTI s/he adds more to s.t., s/he includes s.t., s/he adds s.t. to something

takonēw ᑕᑯᓀᐤ
VTA s/he adds on to s.o., s/he adds more to s.o., s/he adds (it/him) to s.o.; s/he includes s.o.; s/he holds s.o. close to something

takonikātēw ᑕᑯᓂᑳᑌᐤ
VII it is added in by hand

takopahtāw ᑕᑯᐸᐦᑖᐤ
VAI s/he arrives running, s/he arrives in a rush

takopaýiw ᑕᑯᐸᔨᐤ
VAI s/he arrives riding, s/he arrives by vehicle

takopaýiw ᑕᑯᐸᔨᐤ
VII it arrives (*e.g.* a vehicle)

takopaýiwin ᑕᑯᐸᔨᐃᐧᐣ
NI arrival

takopicikātēw ᑕᑯᐱᒋᑳᑌᐤ
VII it is tied along to something else

takopiciw ᑕᑯᐱᒋᐤ
VAI s/he arrives with his/her

own camp; s/he arrives with family and belongings

takopitam Cᗡᐱᐦ
VTI s/he ties s.t. along to something else

takopitēw Cᗡᐱ∪°
VII it is tied to something

takopitēw CᗡᐱU°
VTA s/he ties s.o. along to something else

takopotāw Cᗡ⟩Ċ°
VAI s/he adds more liquid

takosin Cᗡᒐ
VAI s/he arrives

takosinōmakan CᗡᒐᗒᏞᏏ
VII it arrives

takotāpātam CᗡĊ⟨ᐦ
VTI s/he arrives dragging s.t.

takotāpātēw CᗡĊ⟨∪°
VTA s/he arrives dragging s.o.

takotāpēw CᗡĊᐯ°
VAI s/he arrives dragging (s.t.)

takotēhtapiw CᗡU"Cᐱ°
VAI s/he arrives (riding)

takotisaham Cᗡᑎᔥᐦᐊ
VTI s/he drives or chases s.t. to arrive at a destination simultaneously

takotisahwēw Cᗡᑎᔥᐦᐁ°
VTA s/he drives or chases s.o. to arrive at a destination simultaneously

takowāc Cᗡ⊲·
IPC close by

takōtāni CᗡĊᓂ
IPC it is a good thing

takw-āhēw Cᑲᐦᐃᐁ°
VTA s/he puts more of s.o. in [*wC:* takw-āhthīw; *sC:* takw-ānēw; *also* tako-ahēw]

takw-āstāw CᑲᐦᏟ°
VAIt s/he puts more of s.t. in [*also* tako-astāw]

takwaham Cᑲᐦᐊ
VTI s/he crushes s.t. (by hand); s/he adds s.t. by tool; s/he pounds or presses s.t. with a heavy weight; s/he crushes berries

takwahamawēw Cᑲᐦᐊᒪᐁᐧ°
VTA s/he pounds (it/him) for s.o.

takwahikan Cᑲᐦᐃᑲ
NI chopper; press

takwahikēw Cᑲᐦᐃᐊᑫ°
VAI s/he grinds grains

takwahikēwikamik Cᑲᐦᐃᐊᑫᐃᑲᒥᐠ
NI place where grain is ground; mill [*pl:* -wa]

takwahikēwin Cᑲᐦᐃᐊᑫᐃ
NI grinding

takwahimināhtik Cᑲᐦᐃᒥᓈᐦᑎᐠ
NA chokecherry tree [*pl:* -wak]

takwahiminān Cᑲᐦᐃᒥᓈ
NI chokecherry [*also NA;* *also* takwahimin]

takwahiminānāhtik Cᑲᐦᐃᒥᓈᓈᐦᑎᐠ
NA chokecherry tree [*pl:* -wak]

takwahiminēw Cᑲᐦᐃᒥᓀ°
VAI s/he crushes berries

takwahwēw Cᑲᐦᐁᐧ°
VTA s/he crushes s.o.; s/he puts a weight on s.o.

takwakocin Cᑲᑯᒐ
VAI s/he arrives flying, s/he arrives by vehicle

takwanāw Cᑲᓇ°
NA bull

takwastāw CᑲᐢᏟ°
VAIt s/he adds s.t. on [*cf.* takw-āstāw]

takwāki-pīsim Cᑲᑭ ᐱᓯᒼ
NA Autumn Moon; September [*obv:* -wa; *see* *also* nōcihitowi-pīsim]

takwākiki Cᑲᑭᑭ
IPC next autumn; when it's autumn

takwākin Cᑲᑭ
VII it is autumn, it is fall

takwākisip Cᑲᑭᓯᑉ
NA fall duck

takwākohk Cᑲᑯᐦᐠ
IPC last autumn, last fall

takwāmow Cᑲᒧ°
VAI s/he arrives, s/he gets (there); s/he arrives in flight, s/he arrives fleeing

takwāpiskataham Cᑲᐱᐢᑲᑕᐦᐊ
VTI s/he smashes s.t. against stone with tool

takwāpiskatahwēw Cᑲᐱᐢᑲᑕᐦᐁᐧ°
VTA s/he smashes s.o. against stone with tool

takwāpōyow Cᑲᐳᔪ
VAI s/he arrives by rail, s/he arrives by train

takwāsin Cᑲᓯ
VAI s/he arrives by sail boat

takwāsiw Cᑲᓯ°
VAI s/he arrives by sailing

takwāw Cᑲ°
VII it is level

tapahtakocin C<"Cᑯᒐ
VAI s/he flies low, s/he hangs low

tapahtakotāw C<"CᑯĊ°
VAIt s/he hangs s.t. low

tapahtakotēw C<"Cᑯ∪°
VII it hangs low

tapahtakotēw C<"Cᑯ∪°
VTA s/he hangs s.o. low

tapahtēyihtam C<"Uᕄ"ᐦ
VTI s/he thinks lowly of s.t.

tapahtēyimēw C<"Uᕄᒣ°
VTA s/he thinks lowly of s.o.

tapahtēyimisow C<"Uᕄᒥᓱ°
VAI s/he is humble; s/he thinks little of him/herself

tapahtēyimisowin C<"Uᕄᒥᓱᐃ
NI humility

tapahtēyimohēw C<"Uᕄᒧᐦᐁᐧ°
VTA s/he makes s.o. think lowly of himself; s/he puts s.o. down

tapahtiskwēkāpawiw C<"ᑎᐢᑫᑳᐸᐃ°
VAI s/he stands humbly (with head bowed)

tapahtiskwēsin C<"ᑎᐢᑫᓯ
VAI s/he lies with lowered head

tapahtiskwēyiw C<"ᑎᐢᑫᕆ°
VAI s/he lowers his/her own head; s/he hangs his/her own head down; s/he bows [*cf.* tipahtiskwēyiw; *see also* patapiskwēyiw]

tapasīhēw C<ᒐᐦᐁᐧ°
VTA s/he flees from s.o., s/he runs away from s.o.; s/he flees with s.o., s/he runs away with s.o., s/he helps s.o. to flee

tapasīhtāw C<ᒐᐦĊ°
VAIt s/he flees with s.t.

tapasīstam C<ᒐᐢᐦ
VTI s/he flees from s.t.; s/he runs away from s.t.

tapasīstawēw C<ᒐᐢCᐁᐧ°
VTA s/he flees from s.o.; s/he runs away from s.o.

tapasīw C<ᒐ°
VAI s/he flees, s/he runs away

tapasīwin C<ᒐᐃ
NI escape

tasi Cᒐ
IPC there

tasi- Cᒐ
IPV for such a time, for the duration; an action at a time, while

tasi-pīkiskwēw Cᒐ ᐱᑫᐢᑫ°
VAI s/he speaks while others are speaking, s/he speaks simultaneously with others

tasinam Cᕁᐊᐦ
VTI s/he fires s.t. (*e.g.* gun); s/he released s.t., s/he untangles s.t.

tasinē Cᕁᐅ
IPC all the time [*cf.* tahkinē]

tasinikan Cᕁᓂᑲ
NI trigger

tasīhkam Cᒐ"ᑲᐦ
VTI s/he bothers with s.t., s/he is engaged in s.t., s/he is busy with s.t., s/he works at s.t. [*cf.* tasīhkātam]

tasīhkawēw Cᒐ"ᑲᐁᐧ°
VTA s/he works with s.o., s/he works on s.o., s/he is

busy with s.o. (as a doctor with a patient) [*cf.* tasīhkātēw]

tasīhkātam ᑕᓰᐦᑳᑕᒼ
VTI s/he is busy with s.t.; s/he tries to repair s.t. [*cf.* tasīhkam]

tasīhkātēw ᑕᓰᐦᑳᑌᐤ
VTA s/he is busy with s.o. [*cf.* tasīhkawēw]

tasīhkēw ᑕᓰᐦᑫᐤ
VAI s/he is busy

taskam ᑕᐢᑲᒼ
IPC straight across

taskamiham ᑕᐢᑲᒥᐦᐊᒼ
VTI s/he goes across the water

taskamihāw ᑕᐢᑲᒥᐦᐋᐤ
VAI s/he flies across

taskamipaýiw ᑕᐢᑲᒥᐸᔨᐤ
VAI s/he goes across

taskamohtēw ᑕᐢᑲᒧᐦᑌᐤ
VAI s/he walks across

tasokāpawiw ᑕᓱᑳᐸᐏᐤ
VAI s/he stands straight

tasokātēw ᑕᓱᑳᑌᐤ
VAI s/he straightens his/her own legs

tasonam ᑕᓱᓇᒼ
VTI s/he straightens s.t.

tasonēw ᑕᓱᓀᐤ
VTA s/he straightens s.o. by laying him down

tasopaýiw ᑕᓱᐸᔨᐤ
VAI s/he straightens up, s/he straightens him/herself out

tasopitam ᑕᓱᐱᑕᒼ
VTI s/he opens s.t. up (with a knife)

tasopitēw ᑕᓱᐱᑌᐤ
VTA s/he opens s.o. up (with a knife)

tasowisow ᑕᓱᐏᓱᐤ
VAI s/he traps him/herself; s/he catches him/herself in a trap [*cf.* tasōsow]

tasōhēw ᑕᓲᐦᐁᐤ
VTA s/he traps s.o. under something, s/he catches s.o. in a trap

tasōsow ᑕᓲᓱᐤ
VAI s/he is trapped under something

tasōtāw ᑕᓲᑖᐤ
VAIt s/he drops a tree on s.t. (as a deadfall); s/he traps s.t.

tasōtēw ᑕᓲᑌᐤ
VII it is caught (under a tree)

tasōw ᑕᓲᐤ
VAI s/he straightens up, s/he straightens him/herself

taspāsōwēw ᑕᐢᐹᓲᐍᐤ
VAI it shines brightly

tastakiskwēýiw ᑕᐢᑕᑭᐢᑵᔨᐤ
VAI s/he lifts his/her own head up

tastasāpahtam ᑕᐢᑕᓵᐸᐦᑕᒼ
VTI s/he looks up at s.t.

tastasāpamēw ᑕᐢᑕᓵᐸᒣᐤ
VTA s/he looks up at s.o.

tastasāpiw ᑕᐢᑕᓵᐱᐤ
VAI s/he looks up

tastaw ᑕᐢᑕᐤ
IPC in between

tastawahikan ᑕᐢᑕᐘᐦᐃᑲᐣ
NI forked pole for holding things up

tastawahikanapasoya ᑕᐢᑕᐘᐦᐃᑲᓇᐸᓱᔭ
NI main poles of the tipi [*pl generally*]

tastawahikēw ᑕᐢᑕᐘᐦᐃᑫᐤ
VAI s/he puts up his/her own tent pole

tastawasakay ᑕᐢᑕᐘᓴᑲᐩ
NA web, webbing of web-footed waterbirds

tastawaýakap ᑕᐢᑕᐘᔭᑲᑊ
IPC between the legs

tastawaýas ᑕᐢᑕᐘᔭᐢ
IPC in between, in the middle

tastawāpitēhikan ᑕᐢᑕᐚᐱᑌᐦᐃᑲᐣ
NI forked stick

tastawāpitēyāw ᑕᐢᑕᐚᐱᑌᔮᐤ
VII it is forked

tastawāyak ᑕᐢᑕᐚᔭᐠ
IPC in the middle

tastawāyihk ᑕᐢᑕᐚᔨᕽ
IPC in between [*loc*]

tastawēýas ᑕᐢᑕᐍᔭᐢ
IPC in between, in the place between

tastawic ᑕᐢᑕᐏᐨ
IPC between

tastawicihcān ᑕᐢᑕᐏᒋᐦᒑᐣ
NI middle finger

tastāpasikēw ᑕᐢᑖᐸᓯᑫᐤ
VAI s/he makes smoke to drive off insects (using buffalo grass) [*see also* tisamāw]

taswāskonam ᑕᓵᐧᐢᑯᓇᒼ
VTI s/he straightens s.t.

taswāskonēw ᑕᓵᐧᐢᑯᓀᐤ
VTA s/he straightens s.o.

taswāskosin ᑕᓵᐧᐢᑯᓯᐣ
VAI s/he lies extended as solid; s/he lies full length on his/her own back

taswāw ᑕᓵᐧᐤ
VII it is straight

taswēkakocin ᑕᓭᐧᑲᑯᒋᐣ
VAI it glides through air with outspread wings

taswēkanikwacās ᑕᓭᐧᑲᓂᑿᒑᐢ
NA flying squirrel [*wC:* tawēkwanikwacās]

taswēkastāw ᑕᓭᐧᑲᐢᑖᐤ
VAIt s/he spreads s.t. around, s/he spreads s.t. out (*e.g.* a blanket); s/he places s.t. spread out

taswēkataham ᑕᓭᐧᑲᑕᐦᐊᒼ
VTI s/he pounds s.t. flat, s/he flattens s.t.

taswēkatahwēw ᑕᓭᐧᑲᑕᐦᐍᐤ
VTA s/he pounds s.o. flat, s/he flattens s.o.

taswēkāpiskisiw ᑕᓭᐧᑳᐱᐢᑭᓯᐤ
VAI it is stone that is spread out

taswēkinam ᑕᓭᐧᑭᓇᒼ
VTI s/he spreads s.t. out (by hand), s/he spreads s.t. open

taswēkinēw ᑕᓭᐧᑭᓀᐤ
VTA s/he spreads s.o. out, s/he spreads s.o. open

taswēkipakēhtiw ᑕᓭᐧᑭᐸᑫᐦᑎᐤ
VII it grows spreading leaves

taswēkipaýiw ᑕᓭᐧᑭᐸᔨᐤ
VII it is opened by pulling, its spread out (*e.g.* material)

taswēkipitam ᑕᓭᐧᑭᐱᑕᒼ
VTI s/he spreads s.t. open

taswēkipitēw ᑕᓭᐧᑭᐱᑌᐤ
VTA s/he spreads s.o. open

taswēkisāwātam ᑕᓭᐧᑭᓵᐚᑕᒼ
VTI s/he cuts s.t. thinly, s/he slices s.t. to spread open

taswēkisāwātēw ᑕᓭᐧᑭᓵᐚᑌᐤ
VTA s/he cuts s.o. thinly, s/he slices s.o. to spread open

taswēkiwēpinam ᑕᓭᐧᑭᐍᐱᓇᒼ
VTI s/he throws s.t. spreading

taswēkiwēpinēw ᑕᓭᐧᑭᐍᐱᓀᐤ
VTA s/he throws s.o. spreading

tatahkamikisiw ᑕᑕᐦᑲᒥᑭᓯᐤ
VAI s/he has things to do; s/he is busy there, s/he is busy at s.t. [*cf.* itahkamikisiw]

tatāhpiw ᑕᑖᐦᐱᐤ
VAI s/he laughs there [*cf.* itāhpiw]

tatāstapiwēw ᑕᑖᐢᑕᐱᐍᐤ
VAI s/he talks fast [*rdpl*; *cf.* tāstapiwēw]

tatāstapīw ᑕᑖᐢᑕᐲᐤ
VAI s/he is quick [*rdpl*]

tatāstawāyihk ᑕᑖᐢᑕᐚᔨᕽ
IPC between this and that, in the spaces [*rdpl*]

tatāyawāw ᑕᑖᔭᐚᐤ
VII it is crowded

tatwēwitam ᑕᑌᐧᐏᑕᒼ
VTI s/he noises s.t., s/he makes noise while others are speaking [*cf.* itwēwitam]

tawaham ᑕᐘᐦᐊᒼ
VTI s/he slashes s.t. open (as a path), s/he clears or marks s.t. (as a line)

tawahcāw ᑕᐘᐦᒑᐤ
VII it is a narrow ravine

tawahikēw ᑕᐘᐦᐃᑫᐤ
VAI s/he slashes a path, s/he clears or marks a line, s/he clears the way of trees

tawahkahikēw ᑕᐘᐦᑲᐦᐃᑫᐤ
VAI s/he hews a road through the woods

tawapīstawēw ᑕᐊᐱᐢᑕᐊᐧᐤ
VTA s/he makes room for
s.o. to sit

tawaskisow ᑕᐊᐢᑭᓲᐤ
VAI it grows leaving a
passage (*e.g.* plants)

tawastēw ᑕᐊᐢᑌᐤ
VII it lies leaving a passage
through

tawataham ᑕᐊᑕᐦᐊᒼ
VTI s/he blazes a trail, s/he
slashes a path; s/he makes
room by tool

tawatahikan ᑕᐊᑕᐦᐃᑲᐣ
NI blazed trail

tawatināw ᑕᐊᑎᓈᐤ
VII it is a valley

tawayāw ᑕᐊᔮᐤ
VAI s/he leaves a passage,
s/he makes room

tawāpiskanēpitēw
ᑕᐋᐱᐢᑲᓀᐱᑌᐤ
VTA s/he pulls s.o. wide
open

tawāstēw ᑕᐋᐢᑌᐤ
VII it is a week

tawāw ᑕᐋᐤ
IPC come in, you're
welcome; there's room

tawāw ᑕᐋᐤ
VII it is open, it is an
opening; there is room, it has
room

tawāyihk ᑕᐋᔨᕽ
IPC between the places, in
the place between [*cf.*
tāwāyihk]

tawikaham ᑕᐃᑲᐦᐊᒼ
VTI s/he slashes, s/he
slashes s.t., s/he chops s.t.

tawikahikēw ᑕᐃᑲᐦᐃᑫᐤ
VAI s/he slashes or chops a
path

tawinam ᑕᐃᓇᒼ
VTI s/he opens s.t. by hand;
s/he clears the way as s/he
goes, s/he makes space

tawinamawēw ᑕᐃᓇᒪᐁᐧᐤ
VTA s/he opens (it/him) by
hand for s.o.; s/he makes
room for s.o.

tawinākwan ᑕᐃᓈᑾᐣ
VII it looks open ahead

tawinēw ᑕᐃᓀᐤ
VTA s/he opens s.o. by hand

tawinikēw ᑕᐃᓂᑫᐤ
VAI s/he makes a space, s/he
puts things aside; s/he makes
room for action

tawipayīhikow ᑕᐃᐸᔩᐦᐃᑯᐤ
VAI s/he has time [*inanimate
actor VTA* tawipayīh-]

tawipīstawēw ᑕᐃᐱᐢᑕᐁᐧᐤ
VTA s/he gives s.o. a place
to sit

tawitisahwēw ᑕᐃᑎᓴᐦᐁᐧᐤ
VTA s/he drives s.o. apart

tawīstam ᑕᐄᐢᑕᒼ
VTI s/he makes room for s.t.
to go by

tawīstawēw ᑕᐄᐢᑕᐁᐧᐤ
VTA s/he makes room for
s.o. to go by; s/he opens the
tent for s.o.

Ċ

tācikwēw ᒑᒋᑫᐧᐤ
VAI s/he yells; s/he screams

tācikwēwin ᒑᒋᑫᐧᐃᐧᐣ
NI scream

tāh- Ċᐦ
IPV would, ought to; likely
to [*cf.* kāh-]

tāh-tēpakohp Ċᐦ ᑌᐸᑯᐦᑉ
IPC seven each; by sevens
[*rdpl*]

tāh-tēpi Ċᐦ ᑌᐱ
IPC at regular intervals
[*rdpl*]

tāhci- Ċᐦᒋ
IPV on the top [*see also*
tahkohci-, tēhci-]

tāhcikāpawiw Ċᐦᒋᑳᐸᐃᐧᐤ
VAI s/he stands on the top

tāhcipayīhow Ċᐦᒋᐸᔩᐦᐅᐤ
VAI s/he jumps on the top

tāhcipohākan Ċᐦᒋᐳᐦᐋᑲᐣ
NA feeder cow or pig;
animal being fattened

tāhcipohēw Ċᐦᒋᐳᐦᐁᐤ
VTA s/he fattens s.o.

tāhcipohikan Ċᐦᒋᐳᐦᐃᑲᐣ
NI fattening element

tāhcipow Ċᐦᒋᐳᐤ
VAI s/he gains weight, s/he
becomes fat; it is in good
flesh from eating

tāhkinam Ċᐦᑭᓇᒼ
VTI s/he touches s.t., s/he
pokes s.t. to identify

tāhkinēw Ċᐦᑭᓀᐤ
VTA s/he touches s.o. or
pokes s.o. to get that one's
attention

tāhtakowāc Ċᐦᑕᑯᐋᒡ
IPC every little ways [*rdpl*]

tāhtāsaham Ċᐦᑖᓴᐦᐊᒼ
VTI s/he sharpens s.t., s/he
strops s.t. [*rdpl*]

tān-āna Ċᐊᓇ
PR which one [*anim prox
sg; also* tānāna]

tāna Ċᐊ
PR which; which one?
[*anim prox sg*]

tānā Ċᐊ
IPC would that

tānē Ċᐁ
IPC would that [*cf.* pitanē]

tānēhā Ċᐁᐦᐊ
IPC would that

tānēhki Ċᐁᐦᑭ
IPC why

tānēhki ana Ċᐁᐦᑭ ᐊᓇ
IPH why is that? what is the
matter with him/her?

tāni Ċᐊ
IPC which one [*anim prox
sg / inan sg*]

tānihi Ċᐊᐦᐃ
PR which ones, which one
[*inan pl / anim obv*]

tānika Ċᐊᑲ
IPC would that [*see also*
pitanē]

tāniki Ċᐊᑭ
PR which ones [*anim prox
pl*]

tānima Ċᐊᒪ
PR which one [*inan sg*]

tānima ēwako askiy
Ċᐊᒪ ᐁᐊᐧᑯ ᐊᐢᑭᕀ
IPH what year was it [*also*
tānim ēwakw āskiy]

tānimatahto Ċᐊᒪᑕᐦᑐ
IPC how many

tānimatahto-askīwinēw
Ċᐊᒪᑕᐦᑐ ᐊᐢᑮᐃᐧᓀᐤ
VAI s/he is how many years
old

tānimatowāhtik Ċᐊᒪᑐᐋᐦᑎᐠ
IPC what kind of tree
[*sometimes pl as if NA:*
-wak]

tānimatowihk Ċᐊᒪᑐᐃᐧᕽ
IPC in what sort of place

tānimayīkohk Ċᐊᒪᔩᑯᕽ
IPC how much, to what
extent; how far is it [*also*
tānimayīko]

tānimayīkohkēskamik
Ċᐊᒪᔩᑯᐦᑫᐢᑲᒥᐠ
IPC for how long

tānimā Ċᐊᒪ
PR where is s/he [*anim
prox; cf.* tāniwā]

tānimēyiw Ċᐊᒣᔨᐤ
PR which one [*inan obv;
archaic in pC*]

tānimi Ċᐊᒥ
PR which one [*inan sg*]

tānisi Ċᐊᓯ
IPC how, in what way;
hello, how are you

tānisi ēkwa Ċᐊᓯ ᐁᑾ
IPH how are you?

tānisi ētikwē Ċᐊᓯ ᐁᑎᑵ
IPH I don't know

tānispī Ċᐊᓂᐢᐱ
IPC when, at what point in
time [*cf.* tānispīhk]

tānispī ohci Ċᐊᓂᐢᐱ ᐅᐦᒋ
IPH how long

tānispīhk Ċᐊᓂᐢᐱᕽ
IPC when [*cf.* tānispī]

tānita Ċᐊᑕ
IPC where [*in a defined
area, precisely; cf.* tānitē]

tānita ohci Ċᐊᑕ ᐅᐦᒋ
IPH from where

tānitahto ᑖᓂᑕᐦᑐ
IPC how many; so many

tānitahto kīsikāw ᑖᓂᑕᐦᑐ ᑮᓯᑳᐤ
IPH what day (is it)

tānitahto tipahikan ᑖᓂᑕᐦᑐ ᑎᐸᐦᐃᑲᐣ
IPH what time (is it)

tānitahto-askiy ᑖᓂᑕᐦᑐ ᐊᐢᑭᕀ
IPC how many years [*cf.* tānitahtw-āskiy]

tānitahto-pīsim ᑖᓂᑕᐦᑐ ᐲᓯᒼ
IPC how many months; what month is it; [*predicative*:] so many months

tānitahto-tipiskāw ᑖᓂᑕᐦᑐ ᑎᐱᐢᑳᐤ
IPC how many nights

tānitahtopiponēw ᑖᓂᑕᐦᑐᐱᐳᓀᐤ
VAI s/he is how many years old [*interrogative only*; *cf.* itahtopiponēw]

tānitahtw-āskiy ᑖᓂᑕᐦᑖᐢᑭᕀ
IPC how many years [*cf.* tānitahto-askiy]

tānitahtw-āya ᑖᓂᑕᐦᑖᔭ
IPC how many kinds

tānitahtwasiyēk ᑖᓂᑕᐦᑘᓯᔦᐠ
INM there are how many of you (in the family)? [2p; *cf.* tānitahto, ihtasiw]

tānitahtwayak ᑖᓂᑕᐦᑘᔭᐠ
IPC in how many places, from how many sides; how many different kinds

tānitahtwāw ᑖᓂᑕᐦᑚᐤ
IPC how many times; so many times

tānitē ᑖᓂᑌ
IPC where, where over there, whither [*in an undefined area, in general*; *cf.* tānita]

tānitē ētikwē ᑖᓂᑌ ᐁᑎᑫ
IPH I don't know where; I wonder where

tānitowahk ᑖᓂᑐᐘᕽ
PR what kind, in what way [*also* tānitowa]

tānitowihk ᑖᓂᑐᐏᕽ
IPC where, in what place; what kind of thing

tāniwā ᑖᓂᐚ
PR where is s/he? [*anim prox sg*]

tāniwā ētikwē ᑖᓂᐚ ᐁᑎᑫ
IPH I do not know where s/he is, I wonder where s/he is [*cf.* tāniwātokē]

tāniwātokē ᑖᓂᐚᑐᑫ
IPC I do not know where s/he is, I wonder where s/he is [*cf.* tāniwā ētikwē]

tāniwē ᑖᓂᐍ
PR where is it [*inan sg*]

tāniwēhā ᑖᓂᐍᐦᐋ
PR where are they, where is it [*inan pl* / *anim obv*]

tāniwēhē ᑖᓂᐍᐦᐁ
PR where [*inan pl*; *cf.* tāniwēhā]

tāniwēhkāk ᑖᓂᐍᐦᑳᐠ
PR where are they? [*anim prox pl*]

tāniýiko ᑖᓂᔨᑯ
IPC how much, to what extent [*cf.* tāniýikohk]

tāniýikohk ᑖᓂᔨᑯᕽ
IPC how much, to what extent [*also* tānīkohk; *cf.* tāniýiko]

tānōtāni ᑖᓅᑖᓂ
IPC how much, how great

tāpakwamowēw ᑖᐸᑿᒧᐍᐤ
VTA s/he sets snares for s.o.

tāpakwān ᑖᐸᒁᐣ
NI snare

tāpakwāsow ᑖᐸᒁᓱᐤ
VAI s/he is snared

tāpakwātam ᑖᐸᒁᑕᒼ
VTI s/he snares s.t.

tāpakwātēw ᑖᐸᒁᑌᐤ
VTA s/he snares s.o.

tāpakwēstamawēw ᑖᐸᑵᐢᑕᒪᐍᐤ
VTA s/he sets snares on behalf of s.o.

tāpakwēw ᑖᐸᑵᐤ
VAI s/he snares, s/he sets snares

tāpakwēwēpinam ᑖᐸᑵᐍᐱᓇᒼ
VTI s/he lassoes s.t.

tāpakwēwēpinēw ᑖᐸᑵᐍᐱᓀᐤ
VTA s/he lassoes s.o.

tāpakwēwēpinikan ᑖᐸᑵᐍᐱᓂᑲᐣ
NI lasso

tāpapīstam ᑖᐸᐲᐢᑕᒼ
VTI s/he takes s.t.'s seat

tāpapīstamawēw ᑖᐸᐲᐢᑕᒪᐍᐤ
VTA s/he sits in s.o.'s place, s/he takes the seat that was vacated by s.o.; s/he succeeds s.o. in office

tāpasinahikan ᑖᐸᓯᓇᐦᐃᑲᐣ
NI copy, finished copy

tāpasinahikēpaýihcikan ᑖᐸᓯᓇᐦᐃᑫᐸᔨᐦᒋᑲᐣ
NI photocopier

tāpasinahikēpaýihtāw ᑖᐸᓯᓇᐦᐃᑫᐸᔨᐦᑖᐤ
VAIt s/he makes a photocopy of s.t., s/he photocopies s.t.

tāpasinahikēw ᑖᐸᓯᓇᐦᐃᑫᐤ
VAI s/he copies; s/he makes a copy

tāpastāw ᑖᐸᐢᑖᐤ
VAIt s/he replaces s.t.

tāpāhkōmēw ᑖᐹᐦᑰᒣᐤ
VTA s/he adopts s.o., s/he takes s.o. as a relative

tāpānaham ᑖᐹᓇᐦᐊᒼ
VTI s/he spies s.t. with a spy glass [*also* itāpānaham]

tāpānahikēw ᑖᐹᓇᐦᐃᑫᐤ
VAI s/he is spying; s/he looks through a spy glass [*also* itāpānahikēw]

tāpānahwēw ᑖᐹᓇᐦᐍᐤ
VTA s/he spies s.o. with a spy glass [*also* itāpānahwēw]

tāpāpēkinam ᑖᐹᐯᑭᓇᒼ
VTI s/he slings s.t. on by a string

tāpāpēkinēw ᑖᐹᐯᑭᓀᐤ
VTA s/he slings s.o. on by a string

tāpāskwēw ᑖᐹᐢᑵᐤ
VAI s/he fits wood into wood

tāpi- ᑖᐱ
IPV through the same place

tāpic ᑖᐱᐨ
IPC out at sea

tāpihēw ᑖᐱᐦᐁᐤ
VTA s/he replaces s.o.

tāpihtēpison ᑖᐱᐦᑌᐱᓱᐣ
NA earring

tāpihtēpisonāpisk ᑖᐱᐦᑌᐱᓱᓈᐱᐢᐠ
NI metal for earring [*pl*: -wa]

tāpihtēpisow ᑖᐱᐦᑌᐱᓱᐤ
VAI s/he wears earrings

tāpihtin ᑖᐱᐦᑎᐣ
VII it is inserted, it is fastened in

tāpihtitāw ᑖᐱᐦᑎᑖᐤ
VAIt s/he fits s.t. in; s/he puts a handle on s.t.

tāpikwatisow ᑖᐱᑿᑎᓱᐤ
VAI s/he brings home game

tāpipaýiw ᑖᐱᐸᔨᐤ
VII it fits all around

tāpipiw ᑖᐱᐱᐤ
VAI s/he takes another's place

tāpisaham ᑖᐱᓴᐦᐊᒼ
VTI s/he threads s.t. (*e.g.* needle)

tāpisahamawēw ᑖᐱᓴᐦᐊᒪᐍᐤ
VTA s/he threads (it) for s.o.

tāpisahamow ᑖᐱᓴᐦᐊᒧᐤ
VII it is threaded

tāpisahwēw ᑖᐱᓴᐦᐍᐤ
VTA s/he threads s.o. (*e.g.* bead)

tāpisi- ᑖᐱᓯ
IPV threading, inserting

tāpisikonam ᑖᐱᓯᑯᓇᒼ
VTI s/he pulls the trigger of s.t.

tāpisikopaýiw ᑖᐱᓯᑯᐸᔨᐤ
VAI s/he gets caught in something

tāpisikoskam ᑖᐱᓯᑯᐢᑲᒼ
VTI s/he steps into a hoop

tāpisimēw ᑖᐱᓯᒣᐤ
VTA s/he fits s.o. in

tāpisiminēw ᑖᐱᓯᒥᓀᐤ
VAI s/he threads beads

tāpisin ᑖᐱᓯᐣ
VAI it lies fit in or strung

tāpisitēpison Ċᐱᕒᑌᐱᕑ
NI stirrup

tāpiskahēw Ċᐱᵇᔅᐤᵒ
VTA s/he puts a necklace or collar on s.o.

tāpiskam Ċᐱᵇᒡ
VTI s/he wears s.t. around his/her own neck

tāpiskawēw Ċᐱᵇᐁᐧᵒ
VTA s/he wears s.o. (e.g. beads) around his/her own neck

tāpiskākan Ċᐱᵇᒼᕑ
NA scarf, necktie; necklace; handkerchief

tāpiskākan Ċᐱᵇᒼᕑ
NI collar, horse-collar; necklace

tāpiskākanāhtik Ċᐱᵇᒼᒼᐊᐦᐣ
NI neckyoke [pl: -wa]

tāpiskākanēkin Ċᐱᵇᒼᕑᐤᕑ
NA kerchief [pl: -wak]

tāpiskākanēmin Ċᐱᵇᒼᕑᐠ
NA bead from a necklace; [pl:] bead necklace, necklace of beads

tāpiskākanēsis Ċᐱᵇᒼᕑᐱᐟᐢ
NA meadowlark; killdeer [lit: "kerchief bird"]

tāpiskākanihkēw Ċᐱᵇᒼᕑᓂᐦᑫᐤ
VAI s/he knits a scarf

tāpiskākanis Ċᐱᵇᒼᕑᐢ
NA small handkerchief [dim]

tāpiskopayiw Ċᐱᐣᑯᐸᔨᐤ
VII it fits in, s/he falls into place

tāpiskopisow Ċᐱᐣᑯᐱᓱᐤ
VAI s/he is tied round and round; s/he is tied around the waist

tāpiskoskācikan Ċᐱᐣᑯᐢᑳᒋᑲᐣ
NI stirrup

tāpiskōc Ċᐱᐣᒍ
IPC like, for instance; just like, as if, in the same way; it seems, seemingly, apparently, similar to; equally [cf. tāpiskōt]

tāpiskōt Ċᐱᐣᒍᐟ
IPC like, for instance; as if, it seems [cf. tāpiskōc]

tāpiskōtastāw Ċᐱᐣᒍᐢᑖᐤ
VAIt s/he places s.t. alike; s/he duplicates s.t.

tāpiskwēkanēkin Ċᐱᐣᑴᑲᓀᑭᐣ
NA material for shawls or kerchiefs [pl: -wak]

tāpitaw Ċᐱᑕᐤ
IPC even if; always, all the time [cf. tāpitawi]

tāpitawākonakāw Ċᐱᑕᐋᑯᓇᑳᐤ
VII it is level snow

tāpitawāw Ċᐱᑕᐋᐤ
VII it is uniform; is even

tāpitawi Ċᐱᑕᐤ
IPC all the time, constantly, continually; in the same way [cf. tāpitaw]

tāpitawihtāw Ċᐱᑕᐃᐧᐦᑖᐤ
VAIt s/he evens s.t. all the way around

tāpitonēhpicikan Ċᐱᒍᐅᐦᐱᒋᑲᐣ
NI bridle; bit

tāpitonēhpicikanāpisk Ċᐱᒍᐅᐦᐱᒋᑲᓈᐱᐢ
NI bit [pl: -wa]

tāpitonēhpicikanēyāpiy Ċᐱᒍᐅᐦᐱᒋᑲᓀᔮᐱᐩ
NI bridle; reins

tāpowakēyihtam Ċᐳᐊᑫᔨᐦᑕᐣ
VTI s/he has faith in s.t.; s/he believes s.t.

tāpowēw Ċᐳᐁᐤ
VAI s/he recites; s/he repeats what s/he has heard

tāpowēwin Ċᐳᐁᐃᐧᐣ
NI recitation

tāpōkēyihcikēw Ċᐳᑫᔨᐦᒋᑫᐤ
VAI s/he believes [term used in traditional rites]

tāpōkēyihtam Ċᐳᑫᔨᐦᑕᐣ
VTI s/he believes s.t. [term used in traditional rites]

tāpōkēyimēw Ċᐳᑫᔨᒣᐤ
VTA s/he believes s.o. [term used in traditional rites]

tāpwē Ċᐁ
IPC in truth, truly, indeed, really, for sure

tāpwē piko ani Ċᐁ ᐱᑯ ᐊᓂ
IPH certainly, okay, go ahead [cf. piko ani]

tāpwē wiya Ċᐁ ᐃᐧᔭ
IPH it is a fact; oh, that one (guy, girl); how typical of that one

tāpwē wiya ani Ċᐁ ᐃᐧᔭ ᐊᓂ
IPH it is a fact

tāpwēhtam Ċᐁᐦᑕᐣ
VTI s/he believes s.t., s/he agrees with s.t.

tāpwēhtamawēw Ċᐁᐦᑕᒪᐁᐧᐤ
VTA s/he believes (it/him) for, from s.o.

tāpwēhtamowin Ċᐁᐦᑕᒧᐃᐧᐣ
NI belief; a belief

tāpwēhtawēw Ċᐁᐦᑕᐁᐧᐤ
VTA s/he believes s.o., s/he agrees with s.o.

tāpwēhtākēw Ċᐁᐦᑖᑫᐤ
VAI s/he believes people

tāpwēkam Ċᐁᑲᒼ
IPC seriously; as a matter of fact

tāpwēmakan Ċᐁᒪᑲᐣ
VII it speaks the truth

tāpwēmēw Ċᐁᒣᐤ
VTA s/he tells the truth about s.o. (generally about personality); s/he convinces s.o. to be truthful

tāpwēskiw Ċᐁᐢᑭᐤ
VAI s/he always speaks the truth [hab]

tāpwēw Ċᐁᐤ
VAI s/he speaks true, s/he speaks the truth

tāpwēwakēyihtam Ċᐁᐧᐊᑫᔨᐦᑕᐣ
VTI s/he believes in s.t., s/he regards s.t. positively, s/he holds s.t. to be true

tāpwēwin Ċᐁᐃᐧᐣ
NI truth, the truth; true speech

tāpwēyēyimēw Ċᐁᔦᔨᒣᐤ
VTA s/he believes in s.o.

tāsaham Ċᔅᐋᒼ
VTI s/he sharpens s.t.

tāsahamawēw Ċᔅᐊᒪᐁᐧᐤ
VTA s/he sharpens (it/him) for s.o.

tāsahikan Ċᔅᐊᐦᐃᑲᐣ
NA whetstone, file, grind stone

tāsawisāwātam Ċᔅᐊᐃᐧᓵᐚᑕᐣ
VTI s/he cuts into the middle of s.t., s/he slices s.t. open

tāsawisāwātēw Ċᔅᐊᐃᐧᓵᐚᑌᐤ
VTA s/he cuts into the middle of s.o., s/he slices s.o. open

tāsipwā Ċᕒᐚ
IPC surely, in fact [cf. tāsipwāw, tāspwāw]

tāsipwāw Ċᕒᐚᐤ
IPC as a matter of fact [cf. tāsipwā, tāspwāw]

tāskataham Ċᐢᑲᑕᐦᐊᒼ
VTI s/he splits s.t.

tāskatahikan Ċᐢᑲᑕᐦᐃᑲᐣ
NI split wood

tāskatahikēw Ċᐢᑲᑕᐦᐃᑫᐤ
VAI s/he splits wood with axe

tāskatahimihtēw Ċᐢᑲᑕᐦᐃᒥᐦᑌᐤ
VAI s/he splits firewood

tāskatahwēw Ċᐢᑲᑕᐦᐧᐁᐤ
VTA s/he splits s.o.

tāskāw Ċᐢᑳᐤ
VII it is split

tāskihikan Ċᐢᑭᐦᐃᑲᐣ
NI wedge

tāskihkotam Ċᐢᑭᐦᑯᑕᐣ
VTI s/he splits s.t. by knife

tāskihkotēw Ċᐢᑭᐦᑯᑌᐤ
VTA s/he splits s.o. by knife

tāskihtakahikēw Ċᐢᑭᐦᑕᑲᐦᐃᑫᐤ
VAI s/he splits wood [see also nātwāhimihtēw, nātwāhinihtēw]

tāskinam Ċᐢᑭᓇᒼ
VTI s/he divides s.t. by hand

tāskinamawēw Ċᐢᑭᓇᒪᐁᐧᐤ
VTA s/he divides (it/him) for s.o.; s/he divides (it/him) among s.o.

tāskinēw Ċᐢᑭᓀᐤ
VTA s/he divides s.o.

tāskipayiw Ċᐢᑭᐸᔨᐤ
VAI s/he splits open, s/he is split; s/he comes apart

tāskipitam Ċᐢᑭᐱᑕᐣ
VTI s/he tears s.t. in half, s/he tears s.t. in two

tāskipitēw Ċᐣᕀᐱᐁᐤ
  VTA s/he tears s.o. in two
tāskipocikan Ċᐣᕀᐳᕌᕝ
  NI rip saw
tāskipocikēw Ċᐣᕀᐳᕌᕐᖁ
  VAI s/he saws (lumber), s/he
  rips a board
tāskipocikēwikamik
  Ċᐣᕀᐳᕌᕐᖁᐃᐧᐸᕐᐠ
  NI sawmill [*pl*: -wa]
tāskipohēw Ċᐣᕀᐳᐳᐤᐧᐁᐤ
  VTA s/he saws s.o. with a rip
  saw
tāskipotāw ĊᐣᕀᐳᐳĊᐤ
  VAIt s/he saws s.t. with a rip
  saw
tāskisiw Ċᐣᕀᐞᐤ
  VAI it is split open
tāskisow Ċᐣᕀᐞᐤ
  VAI it is split, forked
tāskiswēw Ċᐣᕀᔫᐤ
  VTA s/he cuts s.o. into
  slices; s/he lashes s.o.
tāskiwēpaham Ċᐣᕀᐱᐁᐧᐸᐦᐊᒼ
  VTI s/he knocks s.t. splitting
  with tool
tāskiwēpahwēw Ċᐣᕀᐱᐁᐧᐸᐦᐃᐧᐁᐤ
  VTA s/he knocks s.o.
  splitting with tool
tāspwā Ċᐣᐧᐋ
  IPC for that reason; no
  wonder, so [*cf.* tāsipwā,
  tāsipwāw, tāspwāw]
tāspwāw Ċᐣᐧᐋᐤ
  IPC as a result, for that
  reason; as a matter of fact;
  no wonder [*cf.* tāsipwā,
  tāspwā, tāsipwāw]
tāstakoskwēyíiw Ċᐣὒᑯᐢᖁᐁᔨᐤ
  VAI s/he holds his/her own
  head back
tāstapiwēw Ċᐣᐸᐱᐁᐧᐤ
  VAI s/he speaks rapidly
tāstapīw Ċᐣᐸᐱᐤ
  VAI s/he hurries up; s/he is
  active and quick [*cf. dim*:
  cāstapīw]
tātonam Ċᐩᐅᐊᐧᒼ
  VTI s/he pulls s.t. to pieces
tātonēw Ċᐅᐟᐤ
  VTA s/he pulls s.o. to pieces
tātopayíiw Ċᐅᐸᔨᐤ
  VII it is ragged and torn
tātopicikan Ċᐅᐱᕌᕝ
  NI tool for ripping seams
tātopitam Ċᐅᐱᐊᐟᐨ
  VTI s/he rips s.t.; s/he tears
  s.t. (at the seams)
tātopitēw Ċᐅᐱᐁᐤ
  VTA s/he rips s.o.
tātoskam Ċᐅᐢᑲᒼ
  VTI s/he tears s.t. (with
  his/her own feet; *e.g.* shoes,
  moccasins)
tātoskawēw Ċᐅᐢᑲᐁᐧᐤ
  VTA s/he tears s.o. (with
  his/her own feet; *e.g.* pants)

tāwaciwan Ċᐊᐧᕆᐊᐧᐣ
  VII there is a midstream
  current
tāwaham Ċᐊᐧᐦᐊᐤᐊᐨ
  VTI s/he hits s.t. with a
  missile; s/he hits s.t. (as a
  target), s/he hits the mark;
  s/he bumps into s.t.
tāwahwēw Ċᐊᐧᐦᐅᐧᐁᐧᐤ
  VTA s/he hits s.o. (as a
  target); s/he pierces s.o. with
  a shot
tāwakām Ċᐊᐧᑳᒼ
  IPC out in the middle of the
  lake or water, midstream; in
  the middle of the expanse
tāwakihtin Ċᐊᐧᑭᐦᐟᐣ
  VII it bumps into something
tāwakisin Ċᐊᐧᑭᐢᐣ
  VAI s/he bumps into
  something
tāwatihēw Ċᐊᐧᐟᐦᐅᐧᐁᐧᐤ
  VTA s/he makes s.o.'s mouth
  open
tāwatinēw Ċᐊᐧᐟᐣᐤ
  VTA s/he opens s.o.'s mouth
  (by hand); s/he holds s.o.'s
  mouth open
tāwatipayíiw Ċᐊᐧᐟᐸᔨᐤ
  VAI s/he opens his/her own
  mouth suddenly
tāwatiw Ċᐊᐧᐟᐤ
  VAI s/he opens his/her own
  mouth; s/he yawns; s/he
  gapes
tāwāpiskanēpitam
  Ċᐊᐧᐱᐢᑲᐣᐯᐱᐊᐟᐨ
  VTI s/he jerks s.t. wide open
  at the jaw
tāwāpiskanēpitēw
  Ċᐊᐧᐱᐢᑲᐣᐯᐱᐁᐤ
  VTA s/he jerks s.o.'s jaw
  wide open
tāwāpitēw Ċᐊᐧᐱᐁᐤ
  VAI s/he has a missing tooth
  (in front)
tāwāskikan Ċᐊᐧᐢᑭᕝ
  IPC in the middle of the
  chest
tāwāyihk Ċᐊᐧᔨᕁ
  IPC in the centre, in the
  middle [*also* tāw-āyihk]
tāwic Ċᐃᐧ
  IPC away from shore; out in
  the water
tāwicēnam Ċᐃᐧᒉᐊᐧᐨ
  VTI s/he parts s.t. in the
  middle
tāwicēnikēw Ċᐃᐧᒉᐣᐃᑫᐧᐤ
  VAI s/he parts his/her own
  hair
tāwicihcān Ċᐃᐧᒋᐦᒑᐣ
  NI mid-finger
tāwicihcis Ċᐃᐧᒋᐦᒋᐢ
  NI middle finger [*dim*]
tāwihtak Ċᐃᐧᐦᐟᐠ
  IPC in the center of the

boards or floor; center of a
  canoe or boat
tāwikipayíihtāw Ċᐃᐧᑭᐸᔨᐦᐟᐤ
  VAIt s/he runs into s.t.
tāwikipayíimēw Ċᐃᐧᑭᐸᔨᒣᐤ
  VTA s/he runs into s.o.
tāwikisin Ċᐃᐧᑭᐢᐣ
  VAI s/he bumps into
  something
tāwikiskam Ċᐃᐧᑭᐢᑲᒼ
  VTI s/he knocks into s.t.
tāwikiskawēw Ċᐃᐧᑭᐢᑲᐁᐧᐤ
  VTA s/he knocks into s.o.
tāwikistikwānēsin
  Ċᐃᐧᑭᐢᑎᒁᐣᐢᐣ
  VAI s/he bumps his/her own
  head in a fall
tāwinam Ċᐃᐧᐊᐧᐨ
  VTI s/he encounters s.t., s/he
  bumps into s.t.
tāwinēw Ċᐃᐧᐟᐤ
  VTA s/he encounters s.o.,
  s/he bumps into s.o.
tāwisitān Ċᐃᐧᓯᐟᐣ
  NI middle toe
tāwiskam Ċᐃᐧᐢᑲᒼ
  VTI s/he encounters s.t., s/he
  comes upon s.t.
tāwiskawēw Ċᐃᐧᐢᑲᐁᐧᐤ
  VTA s/he bumps into s.o.,
  s/he encounters s.o., s/he
  comes into contact with s.o.
tāwiw Ċᐃᐧᐤ
  VAI s/he hits the mark
  (throwing a lance)
tāyispī Ċᐩᐢᐱ
  IPC when [*cf.* tānispī,
  tānispīhk]

U

tēham ᑌᐦᐊᐨ
  VTI s/he stirs s.t. [*cf.* itēham]
tēhamawēw ᑌᐦᐊᐧᐸᒪᐁᐧᐤ
  VTA s/he stirs (it/him) for
  s.o. [*cf.* itēhamawēw]
tēhamān ᑌᐦᐊᐧᐋᐣ
  NA playing card
tēhamāsow ᑌᐦᐊᐧᐋᓱᐤ
  VAI s/he stirs (it/him) for
  him/herself [*cf.* itēhamāsow]
tēhamāw ᑌᐦᐊᐧᐋᐤ
  VAI s/he plays cards [*also*
  tēnamāw]
tēhci- ᑌᐦᐨ
  IPV on, on top of something
  [*cf.* tahkohci-, tāhci-]
tēhcikāpawin ᑌᐦᐨᑲᐸᐃᐧᐣ
  NI step stool; stepladder
tēhcikāpawiw ᑌᐦᐨᑲᐸᐃᐧᐤ
  VAI s/he stands on
  something
tēhcipayíihow ᑌᐦᐨᕆᐸᔨᐦᐃᐧᐤ
  VAI s/he jumps on (a horse),
  s/he gets on top (of s.t.), s/he
  throws him/herself on top (of
  s.t.)

tēhcipaýiw U"ᒣ<ᔅ°
  VAI s/he springs to the top
tēhciwēpinam U"ᒣᵛ·ᐱᐊᒧᑊ
  VTI s/he throws s.t. on top
  of something
tēhciwēpinēw U"ᒣᵛ·ᐱᐄ°
  VTA s/he throws s.o. on top
  of something
tēhtahākan U"ᑕ"ᑕᐹᑊ
  NI shelf for storing meat;
  shelf
tēhtahēw U"ᑕ"ᑕᵛ°
  VTA s/he puts s.o. on
  surface, into saddle; s/he
  places s.o. on top (of
  something), s/he sets s.o.
  upon [*wC:* tīhtahthīw]
tēhtahokan U"ᑕ"ᐅᑲᑊ
  NI platform
tēhtakocin U"ᑕᑯᒋᓫᑊ
  VAI s/he slips on top of
  something
tēhtapahipēw U"ᑕᐸ"ᐃᐁᵛ°
  VAI s/he floats (upon the
  surface)
tēhtapahipēw U"ᑕᐸ"ᐃᐁᵛ°
  VII it floats (upon the
  surface)
tēhtapiw U"ᑕᐱᐱᐧ°
  VAI s/he mounts, s/he is
  mounted, s/he rides; s/he sits
  on horseback, s/he is on
  horseback; s/he sits on top
tēhtapiwaskisin U"ᑕᐱᐊᐧᔅᑭᓯᑊ
  NI riding boot
tēhtapiwin U"ᑕᐱᐃᑊ
  NA mount, horse
tēhtapiwin U"ᑕᐱᐃᑊ
  NI chair, seat; saddle
tēhtapīwitās U"ᑕᐱᐧᐃᐧᑕᔅᐣ
  NA riding legging, riding
  breeches
tēhtascikēwin U"ᑕᐢᒋᕟᐊᐱᐧᑊ
  NI shelf
tēhtastāw U"ᑕᐢᑕᐧᐧᑊ
  VAIt s/he places s.t. on top
  of something
tēhtastēw U"ᑕᐢᑕᐧᐤ°
  VII it is on top of something
tēnam Uᐊᒧᑊ
  VTI s/he mixes and stirs s.t.
  [*cf.* itēnam]
tēnamawēw Uᐊᒪᐁᐧ°
  VTA s/he deals cards for s.o.
  [*cf.* itēnamawēw]
tēnikan Uᓂᑲᑊ
  NA playing card [*cf.*
  itēnikan]
tēnikēw Uᓂᒀ°
  VAI s/he deals (cards) [*cf.*
  itēnikēw]
tēniki Uᓂᑭ
  IPC thanks, thank you
  [*English loan; more common
  outside of Plains Cree area;
  see also* kinanāskomitin,
  kitatamihin]

tēpakēýimow U<ᑫ᛬ᒧᔪ°
  VAI s/he is willing after
  much consideration
tēpakihcikēw U<ᑭ"ᒋᑫ᛬°
  VAI s/he adds enough; s/he
  has enough money, s/he is
  able to afford
tēpakihtam U<ᑭ"ᒐᒼ
  VTI s/he counts s.t. up
tēpakimēw U<ᑭᒣ°
  VTA s/he counts s.o. enough
tēpakohp U<ᑯ"ᑊ
  IPC seven
tēpakohp-askiy U<ᑯ"ᑊ ᐊᐢᑭᑊ
  IPC seven years
tēpakohp-tahtwāpisk
  U<ᑯ"ᑊ ᑕ"ᒐᐧᐱᐢᐠ
  IPC seven dollars
tēpakohpiwak U<ᑯ"ᐱᐊᐧᐠ
  VAI they are a group of
  seven
tēpakohpomitanaw
  U<ᑯ"ᐳᒥᑕᓇᐤ
  IPC seventy
tēpakohpopiponēw
  U<ᑯ"ᐳᐱᐳᓀᐧ°
  VAI s/he is seven years old
tēpakohposāp U<ᑯ"ᐳᓵᑊ
  IPC seventeen [*also*
  tēpakohptahtosāp]
tēpakohpwāw U<ᑯ"ᐧᐋᐤ°
  IPC seven times
tēpapiw U<ᐱᐧ°
  VAI s/he has room to sit;
  s/he has room to sit on one
  seat
tēpasākēw U<ᓵᑫ°
  VAI s/he has enough for a
  dress or coat
tēpastāw U<ᐢᑕᐧ°
  VAIt s/he places s.t. within
  reach; s/he has enough room
  for storage
tēpācimow U<ᒋᒧ°
  VAI s/he tells enough news
tēpāpahtam U<ᐸ"ᑕᒼ
  VTI s/he is able to see (all
  the way to) s.t.
tēpāskiskam U<ᐢᑭᐢᑲᒼ
  VTI s/he meets s.t. on
  crossing paths
tēpāskiskawēw U<ᐢᑭᐢᑲᐁᐧ°
  VTA s/he meets s.o. on
  crossing paths
tēpāskonam U<ᐢᑯᓇᒼ
  VTI s/he is able to reach
  around s.t.
tēpāskonēw U<ᐢᑯᓀᐧ°
  VTA s/he is able to reach
  around s.o.
tēpēýihtam Uᐯᔩᐟᑕᒼ
  VTI s/he is satisfied with
  s.t.; s/he has enough of s.t.;
  s/he considers s.t. enough
tēpēýihtamowin Uᐯᔩᐟᑕᒧᐃᐧᑊ
  NI contentment
tēpēýimēw Uᐯᔩᒣᐧ°
  VTA s/he is content with s.o.

tēpēýimow Uᐯᔩᒧᔪ°
  VAI s/he agrees, s/he agrees
  s/he can do s.t.; s/he is
  content, s/he is willing
tēpi- Uᐱ
  IPV sufficiently; enough,
  reaching
tēpi-māham Uᐱ ᒫᐦᐊᒼ
  VTI s/he travels enough (on
  water); s/he goes far enough
  downstream
tēpi-mētawēw Uᐱ ᒣᑕᐧᐁ·°
  VAI s/he plays enough
tēpi-mīcisow Uᐱ ᒦᒋᓱ°
  VAI s/he eats enough
tēpi-miýēw Uᐱ ᒥᔦᐧ°
  VTA s/he gives s.o. enough
  (of it/him)
tēpi-nayahtam Uᐱ ᓇᔭᐦᑕᒼ
  VTI s/he is tired of carrying
  s.t. on his/her own back
tēpi-nipāw Uᐱ ᓂᐹᐧ°
  VAI s/he has enough sleep
tēpi-nīmihitow Uᐱ ᓃᒥᐦᐃᑐ°
  VAI s/he has enough dancing
tēpi-tōtam Uᐱ ᑑᑕᒼ
  VTI s/he does enough
tēpihkwāmiw Uᐱ"ᒀᒥ°
  VAI s/he has enough sleep
tēpihtam Uᐱ"ᑕᒼ
  VTI s/he (is near enough
  and) hears s.t.
tēpihtawēw Uᐱ"ᑕᐁᐧ·°
  VTA s/he (is near enough
  and) hears s.o.
tēpinam Uᐱᓇᒼ
  VTI s/he is able to reach,
  hold, carry s.t
tēpinākosiw Uᐱᓈᑯᓯ°
  VAI s/he is still seen (in the
  distance), s/he is still in sight
tēpinākwan Uᐱᓈᑿᑊ
  VII it is still seen (in the
  distance), it is still in sight
tēpinēham Uᐱᓀᐦᐊᒼ
  VTI s/he has enough
  (money) to pay for s.t.
tēpinēhwēw Uᐱᓀ"ᐁᐧ·°
  VTA s/he has enough money
  to buy s.o.
tēpinēw Uᐱᓀᐧ°
  VTA s/he is able to reach,
  hold, carry s.o.
tēpipaýihēw Uᐱᐸᔨᐦᐁᐧ·°
  VTA s/he makes s.o. last
  (such as thread)
tēpipaýihtāw Uᐱᐸᔨᐦᑕᐧ°
  VAIt s/he makes s.t. last
tēpipaýiw Uᐱᐸᔨ°
  VAI s/he has enough, s/he is
  sufficient
tēpipaýiw Uᐱᐸᔨ°
  VII it is enough
tēpisin Uᐱᓯᑊ
  VAI s/he has room to lie or
  step
tēpiskam Uᐱᐢᑲᒼ
  VTI s/he fits s.t. (*e.g.* coat)

tēpiskawēw ᑌᐱᐢᑲᐯᐧᐤ
VTA s/he fits s.o. (*e.g.* pants)

tēpiskāk ᑌᐱᐢᑳᐠ
IPC last night [*changed conjunct; cf.* tipiskohk]

tēpiskātowak ᑌᐱᐢᑳᑐᐊᐧᐠ
VAI they have just enough room

tēpiýawēsiw ᑌᐱᔭᐁᐧᓯᐤ
VAI s/he gets over his/her own anger

tēpiýāhk ᑌᐱᔭᕽ
IPC the only thing; the most (if any); at least, at any rate, as long as; only if; just, just so, just barely; merely [*in negative phrases*:] all but

tēpwātam ᑌᕀᐋᑕᒼ
VTI s/he calls for s.t.

tēpwātēw ᑌᕀᐋᑌᐤ
VTA s/he calls to s.o., s/he calls for s.o., s/he yells at s.o.

tēpwēmakan ᑌᐻᒪᑲᐣ
VII it calls (train, whistling)

tēpwēstamawēw ᑌᐻᐢᑕᒪᐁᐧᐤ
VTA s/he acts as an announcer for s.o.

tēpwēstamākēw ᑌᐻᐢᑕᒫᑫᐧᐤ
VAI s/he announces, s/he acts as an announcer (for people)

tēpwēw ᑌᐻᐤ
VAI s/he calls, s/he yells, s/he hollers

tēpwēwin ᑌᐻᐃᐧᐣ
NI call, yell; calling

tēsipicikan ᑌᓯᐱᒋᑲᐣ
NI funeral platform; meat drying platform

tētipēwēpahtāw ᑌᑎᐯᐍᐸᐦᑖᐤ
VAI s/he runs round something

tētipēwēpaýihow ᑌᑎᐯᐍᐸᔮᐦᐅᐤ
VAI s/he quickly goes round something (to hide)

tētipēwēw ᑌᑎᐯᐍᐤ
VAI s/he goes round

tētipēwēýāmow ᑌᑎᐯᐍᔮᒧᐤ
VAI s/he flees around in a circle

tētipēwēýāpīhkēsin ᑌᑎᐯᐍᔮᐲᐦᑫᓯᐣ
VAI s/he lies as coiled string

tēwāpitēw ᑌᐋᐧᐱᑌᐤ
VAI s/he has a toothache

tēwāpitēwin ᑌᐋᐧᐱᑌᐃᐧᐣ
NI toothache

tēwēhikan ᑌᐯᐧᐦᐃᑲᐣ
NA drum [*cf. Saulteaux:* tēwēhikan; *see also* mistikwaskihk]

tēwihtawakēw ᑌᐃᐧᐦᑕᐊᐧᑫᐧᐤ
VAI s/he has an earache

tēwikanēw ᑌᐃᐧᑲᓀᐧᐤ
VAI s/he has aching bones, s/he has pain in his/her own bones

tēwikotēw ᑌᐃᐧᑯᑌᐤ
VAI s/he has an aching nose

tēwipitonēw ᑌᐃᐧᐱᑐᓀᐧᐤ
VAI s/he has aching arms

tēwisitēw ᑌᐃᐧᓯᑌᐤ
VAI s/he has aching feet

tēwistikwānēsin ᑌᐃᐧᐢᑎᑾᓀᓯᐣ
VAI s/he has a headache from falling

tēwistikwānēw ᑌᐃᐧᐢᑎᑾᓀᐧᐤ
VAI s/he has a headache

tēyakwac ᑌᔭᑿᐨ
IPC instead [*wC*: piyakwac]

tēyāpitēw ᑌᔮᐱᑌᐤ
VAI s/he has a toothache [*cf.* tēwāpitēw]

tēyāpitēwin ᑌᔮᐱᑌᐃᐧᐣ
NI toothache [*cf.* tēwāpitēwin]

tēyāskikanēw ᑌᔮᐢᑭᑲᓀᐧᐤ
VAI s/he has a pain in his/her own chest

tēyi- ᑌᔨ
IPV pain [*also* tēwi-]

tēyicihcēw ᑌᔨᒋᐦᐨᐤ
VAI s/he has aching hands; s/he has arthritis

tēyihtawakēw ᑌᔨᐦᑕᐊᐧᑫᐧᐤ
VAI s/he has pain in his/her own ears

tēyihtawakēwin ᑌᔨᐦᑕᐊᐧᑫᐧᐃᐧᐣ
NI earache

tēyikanēw ᑌᔨᑲᓀᐧᐤ
VAI s/he has aching bones

tēyikātēw ᑌᔨᑳᑌᐤ
VAI s/he has leg pains

tēyikotēw ᑌᔨᑯᑌᐤ
VAI s/he has a sore nose

tēyipitonēw ᑌᔨᐱᑐᓀᐧᐤ
VAI s/he has arm pains

tēyisitēw ᑌᔨᓯᑌᐤ
VAI s/he has foot pains

tēyisiw ᑌᔨᓯᐤ
VAI s/he has aches and pains

tēyisiwin ᑌᔨᓯᐃᐧᐣ
NI aches, pains

tēyistikwānēw ᑌᔨᐢᑎᑾᓀᐧᐤ
VAI s/he has a headache

tēyistikwānēwi-maskihkiy ᑌᔨᐢᑎᑲᐧᓀᐧᐃᐧ ᒪᐢᑭᐦᑭᕀ
NI aspirin

tēyistikwānēwin ᑌᔨᐢᑎᑾᓀᐧᐃᐧᐣ
NI headache

ᐱ

tihkāpāwacikan ᑎᐦᑳᐹᐊᐧᒋᑲᐣ
NI something that dissolves

tihkāpāwahēw ᑎᐦᑳᐹᐊᐧᐦᐁᐧᐤ
VTA s/he dissolves s.o.

tihkāpāwatāw ᑎᐦᑳᐹᐊᐧᑖᐤ
VAIt s/he dissolves s.t.

tihkāpāwēw ᑎᐦᑳᐹᐍᐤ
VII it dissolves

tihkāpiskisam ᑎᐦᑳᐱᐢᑭᓴᐨ
VTI s/he melts s.t.

tihkāpiskisikan ᑎᐦᑳᐱᐢᑭᓯᑲᐣ
NI melted metal

tihkāpiskiswēw ᑎᐦᑳᐱᐢᑭᓯᐧᐤ
VTA s/he melts s.o.

tihkāw ᑎᐦᑳᐤ
VII it is partly thawed

tihkicēskiwakisiw ᑎᐦᑭᒉᐢᑭᐊᐧᑭᓯᐤ
VAI it is blocked by mud after a thaw

tihkinākan ᑎᐦᑭᓈᑲᐣ
NI cradle board

tihkipaýiw ᑎᐦᑭᐸᔨᐤ
VAI s/he melts

tihkipaýiw ᑎᐦᑭᐸᔨᐤ
VII it melts

tihkisam ᑎᐦᑭᓴᐨ
VTI s/he melts s.t.

tihkisikan ᑎᐦᑭᓯᑲᐣ
NI solder

tihkiskam ᑎᐦᑭᐢᑲᐨ
VTI s/he melts s.t. by body heat

tihkiskawēw ᑎᐦᑭᐢᑲᐯᐧᐤ
VTA s/he melts s.o. by body heat

tihkisow ᑎᐦᑭᓱᐤ
VAI s/he melts (*e.g.* ice)

tihkiswēw ᑎᐦᑭᓯᐧᐤ
VTA s/he melts s.o.; s/he cooks s.o.

tihkitēw ᑎᐦᑭᑌᐤ
VII it is melting, it thaws

tihtipahkwanēkwācikan ᑎᐦᑎᐸᐦᑾᓀᑳᐧᒋᑲᐣ
NI upper part of moccasin covering the ankle (*i.e.* which folds down)

tihtipahpitam ᑎᐦᑎᐸᐦᐱᑕᐨ
VTI s/he bandages s.t.; s/he ties (something) around s.t.; s/he winds (something) around s.t.

tihtipahpitēw ᑎᐦᑎᐸᐦᐱᑌᐤ
VTA s/he bandages s.o.; s/he ties (something) around s.o.; s/he winds (something) around s.o.

tihtipawēkaham ᑎᐦᑎᐸᐍᑲᐦᐊᒼ
VTI s/he embroiders s.t. around

tihtipawēkahikātēw ᑎᐦᑎᐸᐍᑲᐦᐃᑳᑌᐤ
VII it is embroidered round the top (*e.g.* moccasin)

tihtipawēkahwēw ᑎᐦᑎᐸᐍᑲᐦᐁᐧᐤ
VTA s/he embroiders s.o. around

tihtipā ᑎᐦᑎᐹ
IPC all around

tihtipāskwaham ᑎᐦᑎᐹᐢᑾᐦᐊᐨ
VTI s/he rolls s.t. around a pole

tihtipāskwahwēw ᑎᐦᑎᐹᐢᑾᐦᐁᐧᐤ
VTA s/he rolls s.o. around a pole

tihtipēkinam ᑎᐦᑎᐯᑭᓇᒻ
VTI s/he rolls s.t. up (in paper)

tihtipēkinēw ᑎᐦᑎᐯᑭᓀᐤ
VTA s/he rolls s.o. up (in paper)

tihtipēkinikanis ᑎᐦᑎᐯᑭᓂᑲᓂᐢ
NA cigarette [*dim*]

tihtipēkisin ᑎᐦᑎᐯᑭᓯᐣ
VAI s/he is rolled in a blanket (lying down)

tihtipicēskiwakisin ᑎᐦᑎᐱᒉᐢᑭᐊᑭᓯᐣ
VAI it grovels or rolls in the mud (*e.g.* a pig)

tihtipihtin ᑎᐦᑎᐱᐦᑎᐣ
VII it is rolled or wound around (as a stool)

tihtipinam ᑎᐦᑎᐱᓇᒼ
VTI s/he twists s.t.; s/he rolls s.t.; s/he rolls s.t. along by hand

tihtipinēw ᑎᐦᑎᐱᓀᐤ
VTA s/he rolls s.o. along (by hand)

tihtipinikēw ᑎᐦᑎᐱᓂᑫᐤ
VAI s/he rolls dice

tihtipipaýihēw ᑎᐦᑎᐱᐸ�ýᐦᐁᐤ
VTA s/he rolls s.o. along

tihtipipaýihow ᑎᐦᑎᐱᐸ�ýᐦᐅᐤ
VAI s/he rolls him/herself

tihtipipaýihtāw ᑎᐦᑎᐱᐸýᐦᑖᐤ
VAIt s/he rolls s.t. along

tihtipipaýihtākwan ᑎᐦᑎᐱᐸýᐦᑖᑿᐣ
VII it sounds as if rolling

tihtipipaýiw ᑎᐦᑎᐱᐸýᐤ
VAI s/he rolls

tihtipipaýiw ᑎᐦᑎᐱᐸýᐤ
VII it rolls, it rolls along

tihtipipaýīs ᑎᐦᑎᐱᐸýᐢ
NI wheel [*dim; cf.* cihcipipaýis]

tihtipiwēpinam ᑎᐦᑎᐱᐍᐱᓇᒼ
VTI s/he twists or rolls s.t. by throwing

tihtipiwēpinēw ᑎᐦᑎᐱᐍᐱᓀᐤ
VTA s/he twists or rolls s.o. by throwing

tihtipīw ᑎᐦᑎᐱᐤ
VAI s/he rolls, s/he spins, s/he turns

tihtitāpānāsk ᑎᐦᑎᑖᐹᓈᐢᐠ
NA wagon [*pl*: -wa]

tikinēhwēw ᑎᑭᓀᐦᐁᐤ
VTA s/he knocks s.o. unconscious

tikinēpaýiw ᑎᑭᓀᐹᐸ¥ᐤ
VAI s/he becomes unconscious; s/he faints

tikinēsimēw ᑎᑭᓀᓯᒣᐤ
VTA s/he throws s.o. down knocking that one unconscious

tikinēsin ᑎᑭᓀᓯᐣ
VAI s/he falls down knocking him/herself unconscious

timaskāw ᑎᒪᐢᑳᐤ
VII it is tall grass

timikonēw ᑎᒥᑯᓀᐤ
VII it is deep snow

timikoniw ᑎᒥᑯᓂᐤ
VII it is deep snow

timisisiw ᑎᒥᓯᓯᐤ
VAI s/he is short of stature [*cf.* cimisisiw]

timīw ᑎᒦᐤ
VII it is deep water, it is very deep (*e.g.* water)

tipaham ᑎᐸᐦᐊᒼ
VTI s/he pays for s.t.; s/he measures s.t.; s/he makes s.t. even by tool

tipahamawēw ᑎᐸᐦᐊᒪᐍᐤ
VTA s/he pays (it/him) to s.o., s/he pays s.o. for (it/him), s/he repays a debt to s.o.; s/he pays s.o. a pension

tipahamākan ᑎᐸᐦᐊᒫᑲᐣ
NI pay, wage

tipahamākēstamawēw ᑎᐸᐦᐊᒫᑫᐢᑕᒪᐍᐤ
VTA s/he pays for s.o.

tipahamākēstamākēw ᑎᐸᐦᐊᒫᑫᐢᑕᒫᑫᐤ
VAI s/he pays for others

tipahamākēw ᑎᐸᐦᐊᒫᑫᐤ
VAI s/he employs; s/he pays wages

tipahamākosiw ᑎᐸᐦᐊᒫᑯᓯᐤ
VAI s/he receives pay

tipahamākowin ᑎᐸᐦᐊᒫᑯᐃᐣ
NI reward, money received as reward

tipahamātowak ᑎᐸᐦᐊᒫᑐᐊᐠ
VAI they pay one another

tipahamātowi-sōniyāw ᑎᐸᐦᐊᒫᑐᐃ· ᓲᓂᔮᐤ
NA treaty money

tipahamātowin ᑎᐸᐦᐊᒫᑐᐃᐣ
NI Indian Treaty money

tipahaskān ᑎᐸᐦᐊᐢᑳᐣ
NI reserve; surveyed lot; mile; border [*see also* askīhkān, iskonikan]

tipahaskēw ᑎᐸᐦᐊᐢᑫᐤ
VAI s/he measures land, s/he surveys land

tipahēw ᑎᐸᐦᐁᐤ
VTA s/he pays for s.o.; s/he looks to s.o. as equal or authority

tipahikan ᑎᐸᐦᐃᑲᐣ
NI measurement; yard stick; yard; hour [*see also* tipahipīsimwān]

tipahikanāhtik ᑎᐸᐦᐃᑲᓈᐦᑎᐠ
NI ruler; yardstick; straight edge [*pl*: -wa]

tipahikākēw ᑎᐸᐦᐃᑳᑫᐤ
VAI s/he uses something as pay, s/he pays people with something

tipahikēhēw ᑎᐸᐦᐃᑫᐦᐁᐤ
VTA s/he makes s.o. pay

tipahikēw ᑎᐸᐦᐃᑫᐤ
VAI s/he pays for things; s/he measures [*dim*: cipahikēsiw]

tipahikēwin ᑎᐸᐦᐃᑫᐃᐣ
NI payment

tipahipīsimwān ᑎᐸᐦᐃᐲᓯᒷᐣ
NI hour [*as unit of measure; see also* tipahikan]

tipahotowak ᑎᐸᐦᐅᑐᐊᐠ
VAI they come out even with one another; they pay one another

tipahōpān ᑎᐸᐦᐆᐹᐣ
IPC gallon

tipahpātam ᑎᐸᐦᐹᑕᒼ
VTI s/he estimates s.t. by eye, s/he measures s.t. out

tipahpātēw ᑎᐸᐦᐹᑌᐤ
VTA s/he estimates s.o. by eye, s/he measures s.o. out

tipahpitam ᑎᐸᐦᐱᑕᒼ
VTI s/he binds s.t. round and round

tipahpitēw ᑎᐸᐦᐱᑌᐤ
VTA s/he binds s.o. round and round

tipahtiskwēýiw ᑎᐸᐦᑎᐢᑵ¥ᐤ
VAI s/he puts his/her own head down [*cf.* tapahtiskwēýiw; *see also* patapiskwēýiw]

tipahwēw ᑎᐸᐦᐍᐤ
VTA s/he measures s.o.; s/he pays for s.o.; s/he evens s.o. up by tool

tipakisiwān ᑎᐸᑭᓯᐚᐣ
NI thermometer

tipapān ᑎᐸᐹᐣ
NI surveyor chain

tipān ᑎᐹᐣ
IPC apart

tipāpēskocikan ᑎᐹᐯᐢᑯᒋᑲᐣ
NI scale; weigh scale; pound

tipāpēskohēw ᑎᐹᐯᐢᑯᐦᐁᐤ
VTA s/he weighs s.o.

tipāpēskotāw ᑎᐹᐯᐢᑯᑖᐤ
VAIt s/he weighs s.t.

tipāskonamātowak ᑎᐹᐢᑯᓇᒫᑐᐊᐠ
VAI they play the women's stick-drawing game [*pl*]

tipēkinam ᑎᐯᑭᓇᒼ
VTI s/he measures s.t.'s length

tipēkinēw ᑎᐯᑭᓀᐤ
VTA s/he makes s.o. (*e.g.* tobacco) to right length

tipēñimākan ᑎᐯ�ñᐃᒫᑲᐣ
NA domestic animal [*sC*]

tipēýihcikātēw ᑎᐯ¥ᐃᐦᒋᑳᑌᐤ
VII it is owned

tipēýihcikēw ᑎᐯ¥ᐃᐦᒋᑫᐤ
VAI s/he owns, s/he rules

tipēýihcikēwin ᑎᐯ¥ᐃᐦᒋᑫᐃᐣ
NI ownership

tipēýihtam ᑎᐯ¥ᐃᐦᑕᒼ
VTI s/he owns s.t., s/he

possesses s.t., s/he controls s.t., s/he rules s.t.
tipēýihtamohēw ᑎᐯᔫᐦᑕᒧᐦᐁᐤ
VTA s/he gives (it/him) into s.o.'s possession
tipēýihtamowin ᑎᐯᔫᐦᑕᒧᐎᐣ
NI possessions
tipēýihtākosiw ᑎᐯᔫᐦᑖᑯᓯᐤ
VAI s/he belongs there
tipēýihtākwan ᑎᐯᔫᐦᑖᑲᐣ
VII it is the property of (s.o.)
tipēýimēw ᑎᐯᔨᒣᐤ
VTA s/he owns s.o., s/he possesses s.o.; s/he is in charge of s.o., s/he controls s.o.; s/he rules over s.o., s/he governs s.o.
tipēýimikosiwin ᑎᐯᔨᒥᑯᓯᐏᐣ
NI self-governing
tipēýimisow ᑎᐯᔨᒥᓱᐤ
VAI s/he controls him/herself, s/he governs him/herself, s/he owns him/herself; s/he is in charge of him/herself, s/he is on his/her own, s/he is free, s/he is independent
tipēýimisowin ᑎᐯᔨᒥᓱᐏᐣ
NI liberty, freedom
tipi- ᑎᐱ
IPV equal
tipihēw ᑎᐱᐦᐁᐤ
VTA s/he keeps up with s.o.
tipikwanahikēw ᑎᐱᑲᓇᐦᐃᑫᐤ
VAI s/he does quill or horsetail trimmings
tipikwātam ᑎᐱᑳᑕᒼ
VTI s/he hems s.t.
tipikwātēw ᑎᐱᑳᑌᐤ
VTA s/he hems s.o.
tipinahwēw ᑎᐱᓇᐦᐍᐤ
VTA s/he shelters s.o. from the wind
tipinawaham ᑎᐱᓇᐘᐦᐊᒼ
VTI s/he shelters s.t. from the wind
tipinawahamawēw ᑎᐱᓇᐘᐦᐊᒪᐍᐤ
VTA s/he makes a shelter from the wind over (it/him) for s.o.
tipinawahikan ᑎᐱᓇᐘᐦᐃᑲᐣ
NI shelter from wind
tipinawahikēw ᑎᐱᓇᐘᐦᐃᑫᐤ
VAI s/he makes shelter from the wind
tipinawāhk ᑎᐱᓇᐚᕽ
IPC in the shelter from the wind *[loc]*
tipinawāw ᑎᐱᓇᐚᐤ
VII it is sheltered from the wind
tipisk ᑎᐱᐢᐠ
IPC night
tipiskam ᑎᐱᐢᑲᒼ
VTI s/he has a birthday
tipiskam-wīhkihkasōs ᑎᐱᐢᑲᒼ ᐑᐦᑭᐦᑲᓲᐢ
NA birthday cake
tipiskamowin ᑎᐱᐢᑲᒧᐏᐣ
NI birthday; anniversary
tipiskāki ᑎᐱᐢᑳᑭ
IPC at night, tonight, when it's night; when it gets dark
tipiskāsin ᑎᐱᐢᑳᓯᐣ
VII it is rather dark: it is almost nighttime [*dim*; *also* cipiskāsin]
tipiskāw ᑎᐱᐢᑳᐤ
VII it is night, it is nighttime; it is dark
tipiskāwi-pīsim ᑎᐱᐢᑳᐏ ᐲᓯᒼ
NA moon [*obv*: -wa]
tipiski-pīsim ᑎᐱᐢᑭ ᐲᓯᒼ
NA moon [*obv*: -wa; *cf.* tipiskāwi-pīsim]
tipiskihtāw ᑎᐱᐢᑭᐦᑖᐤ
VAIt s/he encounters nightfall; s/he finds s.t. dark, s/he pulls the shades down
tipiskisiw ᑎᐱᐢᑭᓯᐤ
VAI s/he is absent overnight, s/he spends the night out
tipiskiskam ᑎᐱᐢᑭᐢᑲᒼ
VTI s/he is overtaken by darkness (before s/he can reach his/her destination)
tipiskoc ᑎᐱᐢᑯᐨ
IPC opposite
tipiskohk ᑎᐱᐢᑯᕽ
IPC last night
tipitōtam ᑎᐱᑑᑕᒼ
VTI s/he obeys s.t.
tipitōtawēw ᑎᐱᑑᑕᐍᐤ
VTA s/he obeys s.o.
tipiýaw ᑎᐱᔭᐤ
IPC personally, really; in person, own
tipiýawē ᑎᐱᔭᐍ
PR one's own, personal [*e.g.* tipiýawē nistēs "my immediate older brother (never in reference to a cousin)", *cf.* nistēs "my older brother or male parallel cousin"]
tipiýawēwihow ᑎᐱᔭᐍᐏᐦᐅᐤ
VAI s/he has property, s/he owns property
tipiýawēwisīw ᑎᐱᔭᐍᐏᓰᐤ
VAI s/he owns
tipwēham ᑎᐯᐦᐊᒼ
VTI s/he curls hair [*also* tipwēnam]
tipwēhamawēw ᑎᐯᐦᐊᒪᐍᐤ
VTA s/he makes s.o.'s hair curl, s/he curls s.o.'s hair [*also* tipwēnamawēw]
tipwēhamān ᑎᐯᐦᐊᒫᐣ
NI curl; ringlet
tisamān ᑎᓴᒫᐣ
NI smudge [*cf.* tisamāwin]
tisamānihkēw ᑎᓴᒫᓂᐦᑫᐤ
VAI s/he makes a smudge [*see also* tastāpasikēw]
tisamāw ᑎᓴᒫᐤ
VAI s/he makes smoke to drive off insects [*see also* tastāpasikēw]
tisamāwin ᑎᓴᒫᐏᐣ
NI smoke bucket, smudge [*cf.* tisamān]
tistamāwasow ᑎᐢᑕᒫᐘᓱᐤ
VAI s/he sings a lullabye (to a child)
tita- ᑎᑕ
IPV [*grammatical preverb*; *future*; *cf.* ka-, kika-, kita-, ta-]
titipihtin ᑎᑎᐱᐦᑎᐣ
VII it is rolled up, it is twisted [*cf.* tihtipihtin]
titipikwanaham ᑎᑎᐱᑲᓇᐦᐊᒼ
VTI s/he sews s.t. in overcast stitch (*e.g.* the spiral loops around the vamp of a moccasin)
titipinam ᑎᑎᐱᓇᒼ
VTI s/he twines s.t., s/he twists s.t.; s/he rolls s.t. up [*cf.* tihtipinam]
titipinēw ᑎᑎᐱᓀᐤ
VTA s/he twines s.o., s/he twists s.o.; s/he rolls s.o. up [*cf.* tihtipinēw]
tiy ᑎᕀ
NI tea [*cf.* nihtiy, *see also* maskihkīwāpoy]

ᑏ

tīwaskihk ᑏᐘᐢᑭᕽ
NA tea kettle [*pl*: -wak]
tīwaskihkos ᑏᐘᐢᑭᐦᑯᐢ
NA tea pot [*dim*]
tīwāpoy ᑏᐚᐳᕀ
NI infused tea [*see also* maskihkīwāpoy]
tīwāpōhkawēw ᑏᐚᐴᐦᑲᐍᐤ
VTA s/he makes tea for s.o.
tīwāpōhkēw ᑏᐚᐴᐦᑫᐤ
VAI s/he makes tea, s/he brews tea [*see also* maskihkīwāpōhkēw]
tīwāpōhkēwin ᑏᐚᐴᐦᑫᐏᐣ
NI the making of tea
tīwipakwa ᑏᐏᐸᑲ
NI tea leaves (after infusion) [*pl generally*]

ᑐ

tohtōs ᑐᐦᑑᐢ
NA breast; teat [*cf.* -tohtōs- *NDA*, mitohtōsim; *also* tōhtōs]
tohtōsāpoy ᑐᐦᑑᓵᐳᕀ
NI milk [*also* tōhtōsāpoy]
tohtōsāpoy-askihk ᑐᐦᑑᓵᐳᕀ ᐊᐢᑭᕽ
NA milk pail [*pl*: -wak]
tohtōsāpōs ᑐᐦᑑᓵᐴᐢ
NI bit of milk [*dim*; *also* cohcōsāpōs]

tohtōsāpōwask ᑐᐦᑑᓵᐴᐘᐢᐠ
NI milkweed [*pl*: -wa; *brassica orientalis*]

tohtōsāpōwikamik ᑐᐦᑑᓵᐴᐏᑲᒥᐠ
NI dairy [*pl*: -wa]

tohtōsāpōwipimiy ᑐᐦᑑᓵᐴᐏᐱᒥᕀ
NI butter [*also* tohtōsāpōpimiy]

tohtōsāpōwipimīhkēw ᑐᐦᑑᓵᐴᐏᐱᒦᐦᑫᐤ
VAI s/he makes butter

towihkān ᑐᐏᐦᑳᐣ
NI kind, type, sort [*also* itowihkān]

ᑑ

tōcikan ᑑᒋᑲᐣ
NI result of one's actions, doing; fault [*cf.* itōcikan]

tōcikātēw ᑑᒋᑳᑌᐤ
VII it is done, it is done so; it is customary [*cf.* itōcikātēw]

tōcikēmakan ᑑᒋᑫᒪᑲᐣ
VII it does things; it is the cause of (something) [*cf.* itōcikēmakan]

tōcikēw ᑑᒋᑫᐤ
VAI s/he does things, s/he acts; s/he is the cause of (something) [*cf.* itōcikēw]

tōhkapiw ᑑᐦᑲᐱᐤ
VAI s/he sits in a manner which exposes him/her indecently [*not done purposely*]

tōhkāpinēw ᑑᐦᑳᐱᓀᐤ
VTA s/he opens s.o.'s eyes by hand

tōhkāpiw ᑑᐦᑳᐱᐤ
VAI s/he opens his/her own eyes

tōhkāpīmakan ᑑᐦᑳᐲᒪᑲᐣ
VII it opens its eyes

tōman ᑑᒪᐣ
NI butter

tōmaskatihkway ᑑᒪᐢᑲᑎᐦᑿᕀ
NA greasy fellow, nasty fellow

tōmāpinēw ᑑᒫᐱᓀᐤ
VTA s/he anoints s.o.'s eyes for that one

tōmāpinisow ᑑᒫᐱᓂᓱᐤ
VAI s/he anoints his/her own eyes

tōmāpiskinam ᑑᒫᐱᐢᑭᓇᒼ
VTI s/he oils s.t. (as metal)

tōmāpiskinēw ᑑᒫᐱᐢᑭᓀᐤ
VTA s/he oils s.o. (*e.g.* a car)

tōmāw ᑑᒫᐤ
VII it is greased, it is greasy, it is oily

tōmi- ᑑᒥ
IPV oily, greasy

tōmicihcēnēw ᑑᒥᒋᐦᒉᓀᐤ
VTA s/he oils or creams s.o.'s hands; s/he puts lotion on s.o.'s hands

tōmicihcēnisow ᑑᒥᒋᐦᒉᓂᓱᐤ
VAI s/he oils his/her own hands

tōmicihcēw ᑑᒥᒋᐦᒉᐤ
VAI s/he has oily hands

tōmihcikan ᑑᒥᐦᒋᑲᐣ
NI oiler, grease gun

tōmihēw ᑑᒥᐦᐁᐤ
VTA s/he makes s.o. oily or greasy

tōmihkwēhow ᑑᒥᐦᑵᐦᐅᐤ
VAI s/he oils or paints his/her own face; s/he puts on make-up

tōmihkwēnēw ᑑᒥᐦᑵᓀᐤ
VTA s/he oils or paints s.o.'s face for that one; s/he puts make-up on s.o.

tōmihkwēw ᑑᒥᐦᑵᐤ
VAI s/he oils, greases, or paints his/her own face; s/he puts on make-up

tōmihtāw ᑑᒥᐦᑖᐤ
VAIt s/he oils s.t.; s/he makes s.t. greasy (not intentionally)

tōminam ᑑᒥᓇᒼ
VTI s/he greases s.t. up, s/he oils s.t.

tōminēw ᑑᒥᓀᐤ
VTA s/he greases s.o. up, s/he oils s.o.

tōminikan ᑑᒥᓂᑲᐣ
NI lubricant, grease, oil; salve; ointment

tōminikākēw ᑑᒥᓂᑳᑫᐤ
VAI s/he uses (something) to oil s.t.

tōminisow ᑑᒥᓇᓱᐤ
VAI s/he uses cream on him/herself; s/he greases him/herself

tōmisitēw ᑑᒥᓯᑌᐤ
VAI s/he has oily feet

tōmisitēnēw ᑑᒥᓯᑌᓀᐤ
VTA s/he oils s.o.'s feet, s/he anoints s.o.'s feet

tōmisitēnisow ᑑᒥᓯᑌᓂᓱᐤ
VAI s/he oils his/her own feet

tōmisiw ᑑᒥᓯᐤ
VAI s/he is greasy, s/he is oily

tōmistikwānēw ᑑᒥᐢᑎᒁᓀᐤ
VTA s/he oils s.o.'s head, hair

tōmistikwānisow ᑑᒥᐢᑎᒁᓂᓱᐤ
VAI s/he oils his/her own head, hair

tōskinam ᑑᐢᑭᓇᒼ
VTI s/he nudges s.t. (with his/her own hand or elbow)

tōskinēw ᑑᐢᑭᓀᐤ
VTA s/he nudges s.o. (with his/her own hand or elbow)

tōskiskam ᑑᐢᑭᐢᑲᒼ
VTI s/he nudges s.t. (with foot or body)

tōskiskawēw ᑑᐢᑭᐢᑲᐍᐤ
VTA s/he nudges s.o. (with foot or body)

tōskwaham ᑑᐢᑿᐦᐊᒼ
VTI s/he nudges s.t. (with a tool)

tōskwahwēw ᑑᐢᑿᐦᐍᐤ
VTA s/he nudges s.o. (with a tool)

tōstōkan ᑑᐢᑑᑲᐣ
NI floating log

tōstōskāpēkipitam ᑑᐢᑑᐢᑳᐯᑭᐱᑕᒼ
VTI s/he jerks s.t. at (as a rope)

tōstōskāpīhkēpitam ᑑᐢᑑᐢᑳᐲᐦᑫᐱᑕᒼ
VTI s/he jerks s.t. at (as a rope)

tōtam ᑑᑕᒼ
VTI s/he does s.t., s/he does s.t. so [*cf.* itōtam]

tōtamawēw ᑑᑕᒪᐍᐤ
VTA s/he does (it) so for s.o. [*cf.* itōtamawēw]

tōtamāsow ᑑᑕᒫᓱᐤ
VAI s/he does (it) so for him/herself [*cf.* itōtamāsow]

tōtamowin ᑑᑕᒧᐏᐣ
NI way of doing (so) [*also* itōtamowin]

tōtamōhēw ᑑᑕᒨᐦᐁᐤ
VTA s/he makes s.o. do (it) [*also* itōtamōhēw]

tōtawēw ᑑᑕᐍᐤ
VTA s/he does (it) so to s.o., s/he does so for s.o.; s/he treats s.o. so [*cf.* itōtawēw]

tōtākaniwiw ᑑᑖᑲᓂᐏᐤ
VII it is done so [*also* itōtākaniwiw]

tōtākēw ᑑᑖᑫᐤ
VAI s/he treats people so [*also* itōtākēw]

tōtākowisiw ᑑᑖᑯᐏᓯᐤ
VAI s/he is so treated by higher powers [*also* itōtākowisiw]

tōtāsow ᑑᑖᓱᐤ
VAI s/he does so to him/herself [*also* itōtāsow]

tōtātowak ᑑᑖᑐᐘᐠ
VAI they do so to one another [*also* itōtātowak]

tōtātowin ᑑᑖᑐᐏᐣ
NI mutual treatment (so) [*also* itōtātowin]

ᑔ

twāham ᑔᐦᐊᒼ
VTI s/he chops ice to get water; s/he cleans ice from the water hole

twāhikēw Ċ·ᵈ"Δ◁°
    VAI s/he makes a hole in the
    ice

twāhipān Ċ·ᵈ"Δ<ᐤ
    NI water hole in ice

twāhipānihkēw Ċ·ᵈ"Δ<ᓂ"◁°
    VAI s/he makes a water hole
    in the ice

twāhipēw Ċ·ᵈ"ΔV°
    VAI s/he chops ice to get
    water

twākonēsin Ċ·ᗫᓯᐤ
    VAI s/he falls through the
    snow crust

twāsin Ċ·ᓯᐤ
    VAI s/he falls through the ice

ᑌ•

twēhomakan ᑌ·ᵈ"ᐅᒪbᐤ
    VII it lands (from flight)
    [*also* tōhomakan]

twēhototam ᑌ·ᵈ"ᐅᗡᑕᐨ
    VTI s/he lands on or by s.t.

twēhototawēw ᑌ·ᵈ"ᐅᗡᑕᐁ·°
    VTA s/he lands on or by s.o.

twēhow ᑌ·ᵈ"ᐅ°
    VAI s/he alights, s/he lands
    (from flight); s/he lies on the
    ground

W

ᐘ

wa ᐘ
IPC oh! [*cf.* wah]

wa-wīhkāc ᐘ ᐑᐦᑳᐨ
IPC in frequent intervals [*rdpl*]

wacask ᐘᒐᐢᐠ
NA muskrat [*pl*: -wak]

wacasko-wanihikan ᐘᒐᐢᑯ ᐘᓂᐦᐃᑲᐣ
NI muskrat trap

wacasko-wāti ᐘᒐᐢᑯ ᐚᑎ
NI muskrat hole [*pl*: -wāta]

wacasko-wīsti ᐘᒐᐢᑯ ᐑᐢᑎ
NI muskrat house [*pl*: -wīsta]

wacaskowayān ᐘᒐᐢᑯᐘᔮᐣ
NA muskrat pelt

wacēhpīw ᐘᒉᐦᐲᐤ
VAI s/he jumps high, s/he is very active

wacistwan ᐘᒋᐢᑤᐣ
NI nest [*also* waciston]

wacistwanihkān ᐘᒋᐢᑤᓂᐦᑳᐣ
NI nest-like structure

wacistwanihkēw ᐘᒋᐢᑤᓂᐦᑫᐤ
VAI it builds a nest

waciy ᐘᒋᐩ
NI hill, mountain

wacīskāw ᐘᒌᐢᑳᐤ
VAI s/he limps [*cf.* watiskāw]

wacīskāw ᐘᒌᐢᑳᐤ
VII there are hills and mountains, it is a hilly region, there are many hills

wacīwan ᐘᒌᐘᐣ
VII there are many hills

wacīwaskiy ᐘᒌᐘᐢᑭᐩ
NI mountain country

wah ᐘᐦ
IPC well; oh! [*cf.* wa]

wahakay ᐘᐦᐊᑲᐩ
NA fish scale [*cf.* wahýakay, waýakay]

wahkē- ᐘᐦᑫ
IPV addicted to, easily led to [*also* wāhkē]

wahkēmow ᐘᐦᑫᒧᐤ
VAI s/he cries easily

wahkēpōmēw ᐘᐦᑫᐴᒣᐤ
VAI s/he is easily discouraged

wahkēpōmēwin ᐘᐦᑫᐴᒣᐏᐣ
NI discouragement

wahkēwisiw ᐘᐦᑫᐏᓯᐤ
VAI s/he is sensitive

wahkēyawēsiw ᐘᐦᑫᔭᐍᓯᐤ
VAI s/he is temperamental

wahkēyēýihtam ᐘᐦᑫᔦᔨᐦᑕᒼ
VTI s/he is easily swayed; s/he is too weak

wahkitatēnam ᐘᐦᑭᑕᑌᓇᒼ
VTI s/he walks on the snow-crust

wahotēw ᐘᐦᐅᑌᐤ
NA a certain reed with edible root

wahpamēk ᐘᐦᐸᒣᐠ
NA whale; fish [*pl*: -wak]

wahpamēko-pimiy ᐘᐦᐸᒣᑯ ᐱᒥᐩ
NI fish oil

wahpamēkos ᐘᐦᐸᒣᑯᐢ
NA half grown whale or fish [*dim*]

wahpamēkosis ᐘᐦᐸᒣᑯᓯᐢ
NA young whale or fish [*dim*]

wahwā ᐘᐦᐚ
IPC oh my! wow! good gracious; really; [*emphatic*:] so

wahýakay ᐘᐦᔭᑲᐩ
NA fish scale [*cf.* wahakay, waýakay]

wakīc ᐘᑮᐨ
IPC on, upon

wakītatin ᐘᑮᑕᑎᐣ
IPC on top of the bank

wanahāhtēw ᐘᓇᐦᐋᐦᑌᐤ
VTA s/he loses the track of s.o.

wanakway ᐘᓇᑾᐩ
NI sleeve; his/her sleeve [*also NDI* -anakway-]

wanakwāw ᐘᓇᒁᐤ
VAI s/he has sleeves

wanascikēw ᐘᓇᐢᒋᑫᐤ
VAI s/he misplaces (things)

wanaskacipahēw ᐘᓇᐢᑲᒋᐸᐦᐁᐤ
VTA s/he eludes s.o. by running

wanaskoc ᐘᓇᐢᑯᐨ
IPC at the end, at the tip

wanaskocihcān ᐘᓇᐢᑯᒋᐦᒑᐣ
NI fingertip

wanastāw ᐘᓇᐢᑖᐤ
VAIt s/he misplaces s.t.

wanācipaýiw ᐘᓈᒋᐸᔨᐤ
VAI s/he falls or moves indecently

wanāciwēpinamawēw ᐘᓈᒋᐍᐱᓇᒪᐍᐤ
VTA s/he throws (it/him) indecently to s.o.

wanācīw ᐘᓈᒌᐤ
VAI s/he has his/her own genitals exposed

wanāhēw ᐘᓈᐦᐁᐤ
VTA s/he distracts s.o.; s/he leads s.o. astray; s/he eludes s.o.; s/he disrupts s.o.'s life; s/he puzzles s.o.

wanāmēw ᐘᓈᒣᐤ
VTA s/he distracts s.o. by speech, s/he confuses s.o. by speech, s/he interrupts and confuses s.o. by speech

wanāmow ᐘᓈᒧᐤ
VAI s/he loses his/her way while fleeing; s/he loses his/her own train of thought while speaking [*cf.* wanimow]

wanāpahtam ᐘᓈᐸᐦᑕᒼ
VTI s/he loses sight of s.t.

wanāpamēw ᐘᓈᐸᒣᐤ
VTA s/he loses sight of s.o.

wanāpamow ᐘᓈᐸᒧᐤ
VAI s/he sees wrongly, s/he sees something else

wanāpēkinam ᐘᓈᐯᑭᓇᒼ
VTI s/he tangles s.t.

wanāpitam ᐘᓈᐱᑕᒼ
VTI s/he tangles s.t. (by pulling the wrong string)

wanāpitēw ᐘᓈᐱᑌᐤ
VTA s/he tangles s.o. (*e.g.* thread, yarn)

wanātapiw ᐘᓈᑕᐱᐤ
VAI s/he sits so as to expose him/herself

wanēýihtam ᐘᓀᔨᐦᑕᒼ
VTI s/he forgets s.t., s/he misses s.t., s/he is unsure of s.t., s/he has his/her own mind blurred, s/he is confused; s/he goes wrong; s/he faints

wani- ᐘᓂ
IPV dim, dark, indistinctly, blurred; lose; destroy

wanihēw ᐊᐧᓂᐦᐁᐤ
VTA s/he loses s.o.

wanihastimwēw ᐊᐧᓂᐦᐊᐢᑎᒏᐤ
VAI s/he loses his/her own
horse, dog

wanihcikēw ᐊᐧᓂᐦᒋᑫᐤ
VAI s/he loses things

wanihikamawēw ᐊᐧᓂᐦᐃᑲᒪᐍᐤ
VTA s/he sets a trap for s.o.

wanihikan ᐊᐧᓂᐦᐃᑲᐣ
NI trap

wanihikēskanaw ᐊᐧᓂᐦᐃᑫᐢᑲᓇᐤ
NI trapline

wanihikēw ᐊᐧᓂᐦᐃᑫᐤ
VAI s/he sets traps; s/he
traps

wanihikēwin ᐊᐧᓂᐦᐃᑫᐃᐧᐣ
NI setting traps, trapping

wanihitōtam ᐊᐧᓂᐦᐃᑑᑕᒼ
VTI s/he does s.t.
unacceptable [*also*
wani-itōtam]

wanihkētotawēw ᐊᐧᓂᐦᑫᑐᑕᐍᐤ
VTA s/he forgets s.o.

wanihkēw ᐊᐧᓂᐦᑫᐤ
VAI s/he forgets; s/he forgets
s.t.

wanihow ᐊᐧᓂᐦᐅᐤ
VAI s/he is lost, s/he gets
lost, s/he becomes lost

wanihtam ᐊᐧᓂᐦᑕᒼ
VTI s/he is confused; s/he
hears s.t. wrongly, s/he hears
wrongly

wanihtamihēw ᐊᐧᓂᐦᑕᒥᐦᐁᐤ
VTA s/he confuses s.o. by
his/her own talk

wanihtamihitowak
ᐊᐧᓂᐦᑕᒥᐦᐃᑐᐊᐧᐠ
VAI they confuse one
another

wanihtawēw ᐊᐧᓂᐦᑕᐍᐤ
VTA s/he misunderstands
s.o.

wanihtāw ᐊᐧᓂᐦᑖᐤ
VAIt s/he loses s.t.

wanikiskisiw ᐊᐧᓂᑭᐢᑭᓯᐤ
VAI s/he forgets, s/he is
forgetful, s/he forgets s.t.;
s/he remembers very dimly;
s/he faints

wanikiskisitotam ᐊᐧᓂᑭᐢᑭᓯᑐᑕᒼ
VTI s/he forgets s.t., s/he
forgets about s.t.

wanikiskisitotawēw
ᐊᐧᓂᑭᐢᑭᓯᑐᑕᐍᐤ
VTA s/he forgets about s.o.

wanimēw ᐊᐧᓂᒣᐤ
VTA s/he confuses s.o. by
his/her own speech

wanimitimēw ᐊᐧᓂᒥᑎᒣᐤ
VAI s/he takes the wrong
path

wanimow ᐊᐧᓂᒧᐤ
VAI s/he says the wrong
thing; s/he loses his/her own
train of thought while
speaking

waninam ᐊᐧᓂᓇᒼ
VTI s/he takes the wrong
article

waninākwan ᐊᐧᓂᓈᑿᐣ
VII it is evening twilight, it
is dusk, it is the time of sun
setting [*also* wawāninākwan]

waninēw ᐊᐧᓂᓀᐤ
VAI s/he is mad, disoriented,
delirious (from illness); s/he
is silly, crazy

wanipahtākēw ᐊᐧᓂᐸᐦᑖᑫᐤ
VAI s/he drives spirits out
(from people) [*i.e. an
exorcism*]

wanipayīw ᐊᐧᓂᐸᔩᐤ
VAI s/he is missing

wanipayīw ᐊᐧᓂᐸᔩᐤ
VII it is missing

wanisimēw ᐊᐧᓂᓯᒣᐤ
VTA s/he loses s.o.; s/he
loses s.o. (by taking the
wrong path)

wanisin ᐊᐧᓂᓯᐣ
VAI s/he is lost, s/he loses
his/her own way

waniskānam ᐊᐧᓂᐢᑳᓇᒼ
VTI s/he stands s.t. up, s/he
raises s.t. upright

waniskānēw ᐊᐧᓂᐢᑳᓀᐤ
VTA s/he gets s.o. up from
bed; s/he raises s.o., s/he
makes s.o. sit up, s/he helps
s.o. to get up

waniskānikan ᐊᐧᓂᐢᑳᓂᑲᐣ
NI upright pole of tent

waniskāpahtāw ᐊᐧᓂᐢᑳᐸᐦᑖᐤ
VAI s/he jumps up (from
lying); s/he jumps and runs

waniskāpayihow ᐊᐧᓂᐢᑳᐸᔨᐦᐅᐤ
VAI s/he jumps up from
lying

waniskāpitam ᐊᐧᓂᐢᑳᐱᑕᒼ
VTI s/he raises s.t. up (by
pulling)

waniskāpitēw ᐊᐧᓂᐢᑳᐱᑌᐤ
VTA s/he pulls s.o. up from
lying; s/he pulls s.o. up to a
sitting position

waniskāw ᐊᐧᓂᐢᑳᐤ
VAI s/he gets up, s/he arises
from lying, s/he gets out of
bed; s/he goes in, s/he comes
in

waniskāwin ᐊᐧᓂᐢᑳᐃᐧᐣ
NI time to get up

wanitipiskapiw ᐊᐧᓂᑎᐱᐢᑲᐱᐤ
VAI s/he sits in the dark

wanitipiskāsin ᐊᐧᓂᑎᐱᐢᑳᓯᐣ
VII it is quite dark out [*dim*]

wanitipiskāw ᐊᐧᓂᑎᐱᐢᑳᐤ
VII it is a dark night, it is
very dark

wanitipiskinam ᐊᐧᓂᑎᐱᐢᑭᓇᒼ
VTI s/he makes it dark; s/he
turns out the lights, s/he
closes the blinds

wanitipiskipayiw
ᐊᐧᓂᑎᐱᐢᑭᐸᔨᐤ
VII it darkens (e.g. an
eclipse)

wanitonāmow ᐊᐧᓂᑐᓈᒧᐤ
VAI s/he says the wrong
thing, s/he makes an error in
speaking, s/he makes a slip
of the tongue

wanitōtam ᐊᐧᓂᑑᑕᒼ
VTI s/he makes a mistake;
s/he sins; s/he does the
wrong thing

wanitōtamowin ᐊᐧᓂᑑᑕᒧᐃᐧᐣ
NI transgression

wanitōtawēw ᐊᐧᓂᑑᑕᐍᐤ
VTA s/he does wrong to s.o.

wanitwēw ᐊᐧᓂᑘᐤ
VAI s/he misquotes

waniwēw ᐊᐧᓂᐍᐤ
VAI s/he utters wrongly

wanohtāw ᐊᐧᓄᐦᑖᐤ
VAI s/he makes a mistake

wanotinam ᐊᐧᓄᑎᓇᒼ
VTI s/he takes s.t.
unintentionally

wanotinamawēw ᐊᐧᓄᑎᓇᒪᐍᐤ
VTA s/he takes the wrong
thing for s.o.

wanotinamāsow ᐊᐧᓄᑎᓇᒫᓱᐤ
VAI s/he takes the wrong
thing for him/herself

wanotinēw ᐊᐧᓄᑎᓀᐤ
VTA s/he takes s.o. wrongly

wanwēhkawēw ᐊᐧᐤᐍᐦᑲᐍᐤ
VTA s/he utters (it) wrongly
to s.o.; s/he confuses s.o.
through incorrect speech,
s/he leaves s.o. baffled by
speech or in speech [*also*
waniwēhkawēw]

wanwēwitam ᐊᐧᐤᐍᐃᐧᑕᒼ
VTI s/he makes a confused
noise

wapāhk ᐊᐧᐸᕽ
IPC at the narrows, in the
bay [*loc*]

wapāsihk ᐊᐧᐸᓯᕽ
INM Opawikoscikan, SK
[*loc*; *dim*; *lit*: "at the little
narrows"; *see also* PELICAN
NARROWS]

wapāsin ᐊᐧᐸᓯᐣ
VII it is a small narrows; it
is a small bay [*dim*]

wapātikwaciwanohk
ᐊᐧᐸᑎᐦᑿᒋᐊᐧᓄᕽ
INM Southend, SK [*loc*; *wC
community*; *also*
wāpatihkwaciwanohk]

wapāw ᐊᐧᐸᐤ
VII it is a narrows; it is a bay

wapāwikoscikanihk
ᐊᐧᐸᐃᐧᑯᐢᒋᑲᓂᕽ
INM Pelican Narrows, SK
[*loc*; *lit*: "at the narrows of
fear"; *wC community*; *also*
opāwikoscikanihk]

wasakopak ᐊᐧᓴᑯᐸᐠ
NA chewing tobacco; tobacco leaf [*pl*: -wak]

wasāsiw ᐊᐧᓵᓯᐤ
VAI s/he is nervous

waskahtikway ᐊᐧᐢᑲᐦᑎᑲᐧᐩ
NI skull (at forehead) [*cf.* *NDI* -skahtikw- "forehead"]

waskawinam ᐊᐧᐢᑲᐃᐧᓇᒼ
VTI s/he arouses s.t., s/he gets s.t. moving; s/he moves s.t.

waskawinēw ᐊᐧᐢᑲᐃᐧᓀᐤ
VTA s/he arouses s.o., s/he gets s.o. moving; s/he shakes s.o., s/he moves s.o. about (*e.g.* so as to awaken)

waskawipaýiw ᐊᐧᐢᑲᐃᐧᐸᔨᐤ
VII it moves, it is moving

waskawipitam ᐊᐧᐢᑲᐃᐧᐱᑕᒼ
VTI s/he moves s.t., s/he shakes s.t.

waskawipitēw ᐊᐧᐢᑲᐃᐧᐱᑌᐤ
VTA s/he moves s.o., s/he shakes s.o.

waskawiwēpaham ᐊᐧᐢᑲᐃᐧᐁᐧᐸᐦᐊᒼ
VTI s/he moves s.t. with a tool; s/he knocks s.t. out of place

waskawiwēpahwēw ᐊᐧᐢᑲᐃᐧᐁᐧᐸᐦᐁᐧᐤ
VTA s/he moves s.o. with a tool; s/he knocks s.o. out of place

waskawiwēpiskam ᐊᐧᐢᑲᐃᐧᐁᐧᐱᐢᑲᒼ
VTI s/he moves s.t. with his/her own feet

waskawiwēpiskawēw ᐊᐧᐢᑲᐃᐧᐁᐧᐱᐢᑲᐁᐧᐤ
VTA s/he moves s.o. with his/her own feet

waskawīmakan ᐊᐧᐢᑲᐄᐧᒪᑲᐣ
VII it moves, it stirs, it moves by itself

waskawīstamāsow ᐊᐧᐢᑲᐄᐧᐢᑕᒫᓱᐤ
VAI s/he works for him/herself, s/he is enterprising

waskawīw ᐊᐧᐢᑲᐄᐧᐤ
VAI s/he moves, s/he stirs, s/he budges, s/he is in motion

waskawīwin ᐊᐧᐢᑲᐄᐧᐃᐧᐣ
NI being active; enterprise; lifestyle

waskic ᐊᐧᐢᑭᐨ
IPC on the surface, on top

waskic-anāskanēkin ᐊᐧᐢᑭᐨ ᐊᓈᐢᑲᓀᑭᐣ
NI bedspread; cover [*pl*: -wa]

waskicipaýiw ᐊᐧᐢᑭᒋᐸᔨᐤ
VII it comes to the surface

waskicipitam ᐊᐧᐢᑭᒋᐱᑕᒼ
VTI s/he pulls s.t. over (the surface); s/he pulls s.t. to the surface, on the top

waskicipitēw ᐊᐧᐢᑭᒋᐱᑌᐤ
VTA s/he pulls s.o. to the surface

waskihtin ᐊᐧᐢᑭᐦᑎᐣ
VII it bends (*e.g.* a river)

waskipicikan ᐊᐧᐢᑭᐱᒋᑲᐣ
NI rubber boot

waskitasākay ᐊᐧᐢᑭᑕᓵᑲᐩ
NI overcoat

waskitaskamik ᐊᐧᐢᑭᑕᐢᑲᒥᐠ
IPC on earth, on the face of the earth

waskitaskisin ᐊᐧᐢᑭᑕᐢᑭᓯᐣ
NI overshoe

waskitastāw ᐊᐧᐢᑭᑕᐢᑖᐤ
VAIt s/he puts s.t. on the top

waskitatēwēnam ᐊᐧᐢᑭᑕᑌᐁᐧᓇᒼ
VTI s/he walks on the snow-crust

waskitisik ᐊᐧᐢᑭᑎᓯᐠ
IPC on top of the ice

waskitisin ᐊᐧᐢᑭᑎᓯᐣ
VAI s/he lies on the surface

waskitowēyāpiy ᐊᐧᐢᑭᑐᐁᐧᔮᐱᐩ
NI bridging of harness

waskīw ᐊᐧᐢᑮᐤ
VAI s/he turns [*see also* kwēskīw]

wasko-onikāhpihk ᐊᐧᐢᑯ ᐅᓂᑳᐦᐱᕽ
INM Birch Portage, SK [*loc*]

waskow ᐊᐧᐢᑯᐤ
NI cloud

waskowan ᐊᐧᐢᑯᐊᐧᐣ
VII it is cloudy

waskway ᐊᐧᐢᑲᐧᐩ
NA birch, birch tree [*cf.* waskwayāhtik]

waskway-ōsi ᐊᐧᐢᑲᐧᐩ ᐆᓯ
NI birch bark canoe [*pl*: -ōsa]

waskwayāhtik ᐊᐧᐢᑲᐧᔮᐦᑎᐠ
NA birch tree, birch wood [*pl*: -wak]

waskwayākan ᐊᐧᐢᑲᐧᔮᑲᐣ
NI birch bark pan

waskwayāpoy ᐊᐧᐢᑲᐧᔮᐳᐩ
NI birch sap

waskwayi-mītos ᐊᐧᐢᑲᐧᔨ ᒦᑐᐢ
NA birch-tree

waskwayikamik ᐊᐧᐢᑲᐧᔨᑲᒥᐠ
NI birch wigwam [*pl*: -wa]

waskwayiwat ᐊᐧᐢᑲᐧᔨᐊᐧᐟ
NI birch bark basket

waskwētoy ᐊᐧᐢᑫᐧᑐᐩ
NA pine cone

waspāwēmēw ᐊᐧᐢᐹᐁᐧᒣᐤ
VTA s/he keeps s.o. awake by his/her own speech

watakamisiw ᐊᐧᑕᑲᒥᓯᐤ
VAI s/he is grouchy, grumpy; s/he is bad, cross, easily angered; s/he is overly anxious

watapiy ᐊᐧᑕᐱᐩ
NA root fibre of white pine

watapīwat ᐊᐧᑕᐲᐊᐧᐟ
NI woven basket [*sg only*; *pl*: watapīwata]

watapīwiwas ᐊᐧᑕᐲᐃᐧᐊᐧᐢ
NI woven basket

watapīwiýākan ᐊᐧᑕᐲᐃᐧᔮᑲᐣ
NI vessel of pine root fibres

watihkwan ᐊᐧᑎᐦᑲᐧᐣ
NI branch, knot; fork of tree; crossed branches

watihkwaniwan ᐊᐧᑎᐦᑲᐧᓂᐊᐧᐣ
VII it has knots (as a board)

watihkwaniwiw ᐊᐧᑎᐦᑲᐧᓂᐃᐧᐤ
VAI it has knots (as a tree)

watihkwaniwiw ᐊᐧᑎᐦᑲᐧᓂᐃᐧᐤ
VII it is or has a fork (as a branch)

watīskāw ᐊᐧᑏᐢᑳᐤ
VAI s/he limps [*cf.* wacīskāw]

watow ᐊᐧᑐᐤ
NI clot of blood, blood in a congealed state

watowan ᐊᐧᑐᐊᐧᐣ
VII it is congealed

watōw ᐊᐧᑑᐤ
NA ball (made of hide trimmings)

wawānēýihtam ᐊᐧᐋᐧᓀᔨᐦᑕᒼ
VTI s/he is at a loss (for s.t.); s/he worries about s.t., s/he is worried [*rdpl*]

wawānēýihtamihēw ᐊᐧᐋᐧᓀᔨᐦᑕᒥᐦᐁᐤ
VTA s/he causes s.o. to be at a loss (for s.t.), s/he makes s.o. confused [*rdpl*]

wawāninākwan ᐊᐧᐋᐧᓂᓈᑲᐧᐣ
VII it is evening twilight [*cf.* waninākwan]

wawēhtinahk ᐊᐧᐁᐧᐦᑎᓇᕽ
IPC easily, leisurely; taking time

wawēsīhcikanis ᐊᐧᐁᐧᓰᐦᒋᑲᓂᐢ
NI decoration

wawēsīhcikātēw ᐊᐧᐁᐧᓰᐦᒋᑳᑌᐤ
VII it is decorated

wawēsīhcikēw ᐊᐧᐁᐧᓰᐦᒋᑫᐤ
VAI s/he decorates

wawēsīhēw ᐊᐧᐁᐧᓰᐦᐁᐤ
VTA s/he dresses s.o. up, s/he dresses s.o. in that one's best; s/he adorns s.o.

wawēsīhon ᐊᐧᐁᐧᓰᐦᐅᐣ
NI ornament

wawēsīhow ᐊᐧᐁᐧᓰᐦᐅᐤ
VAI s/he dresses up, s/he dresses in his/her own best

wawēsīhowin ᐊᐧᐁᐧᓰᐦᐅᐃᐧᐣ
NI adornment with ribbon and flowers

wawēsīhtamawēw ᐊᐧᐁᐧᓰᐦᑕᒪᐁᐧᐤ
VTA s/he decorates (it/him) prettily for s.o.

wawēsīhtāw ᐊᐧᐁᐧᓰᐦᑖᐤ
VAIt s/he ornaments s.t., s/he adorns s.t., s/he decorates s.t.

wawēsīhwākēw ᐊᐧᐁᐧᓰᐦᐋᐧᑫᐤ
VAI s/he makes an ornament of something

wawēsīw ⊲·∇·ᒧᵒ
VAI s/he dresses up, s/he is dressed up, s/he dresses in his/her own best [cf. wawēyiw]

wawēsīwin ⊲·∇·ᒧᐦ
NI ornament, decoration

wawēspitēw ⊲·∇·ᐢᐱᐡ
VTA s/he dresses s.o. (i.e. a corpse) up; s/he prepares s.o.'s body (i.e. a corpse)

wawēyapiw ⊲·∇·ᑕᐱᵒ
VAI s/he sits ready

wawēyihtākosiw ⊲·∇·ᐩᐦᒼᑕᑯᓯᵒ
VAI s/he sounds amusing

wawēyihtākwan ⊲·∇·ᐩᐦᒼᑕᑲᐨ
VII it sounds amusing

wawēyīhēw ⊲·∇·ᐦᐦᐦᐁᵒ
VTA s/he prepares s.o., s/he gets s.o. ready

wawēyīhtāw ⊲·∇·ᐦᐦᒼ
VAIt s/he prepares s.t., s/he gets s.t. ready

wawēyīstam ⊲·∇·ᐦᐩᓯᒧᐨ
VTI s/he prepares for s.t., s/he is prepared

wawēyīstawēw ⊲·∇·ᐦᐩᓯᒼᐃᐁᵒ
VTA s/he prepares for s.o.; s/he arms him/herself against s.o.

wawēyīw ⊲·∇·ᐦᐦᵒ
VAI s/he gets ready, s/he makes preparations; s/he gets dressed [cf. wawēsīw; wC: wawisīw]

wawiyas ⊲·ᐃ·ᐦ
IPC humorous

wawiyasihēw ⊲·ᐃ·ᐦᐦᐁᵒ
VTA s/he tricks s.o., s/he makes s.o. a laughing stock

wawiyasinākosiw ⊲·ᐃ·ᐦᐃᐦᑕᑯᓯᵒ
VAI s/he looks funny

wawiyasinākwan ⊲·ᐃ·ᐦᐃᐦᑕᑲᐨ
VII it looks funny

wawiyasipaýiw ⊲·ᐃ·ᐦᐃᐸᐸᵒ
VII it is humourous (from actions)

wawiyatācimowin ⊲·ᐃ·ᐦᑕᒋᒧᐃᐨ
NI funny story

wawiyatācimowinis ⊲·ᐃ·ᐦᑕᒋᒧᐃᐣᓯᐣ
NI funny little story [dim]

wawiyatēýihtam ⊲·ᐃ·ᐦᐅᐸᐦᐦᐨ
VTI s/he considers s.t. funny, odd

wawiyatēýihtākosiw ⊲·ᐃ·ᐦᐅᐸᐦᐦᒼᑕᑯᓯᵒ
VAI s/he is funny; s/he is found comical by his/her own actions

wawiyatēýihtākwan ⊲·ᐃ·ᐦᐅᐸᐦᐦᒼᑕᑲᐨ
VII it appears funny to all

wawiyatēýimēw ⊲·ᐃ·ᐦᐅᐸᐦᒣᒐᵒ
VTA s/he considers s.o. funny, s/he thinks s.o. drole, funny

wawiyatisiw ⊲·ᐃ·ᐦᐅᓯᵒ
VAI s/he gets what s/he deserves; s/he is served right (i.e. it serves him/her right) [also wiyatisiw]

wawiyatisīhkēw ⊲·ᐃ·ᐦᐅᓯᐦᑫᐦᑯ
VAI s/he plays funny tricks

wawiyatwēw ⊲·ᐃ·ᐦᐅᐃᐅᵒ
VAI s/he jokes, s/he makes jokes, s/he jokes and talks amusingly; s/he makes laughter [also wiyatwēw]

wawiyēsimēw ⊲·ᐃ·ᐦᐦᐳᒐᵒ
VTA s/he convinces s.o.; s/he tricks s.o.

wawīpitāpiskanēpaýiw
⊲·ᐃ·ᐱᐦᑕᐱᐢᑲᓀᐸᐸᵒ
VAI s/he has chattering teeth

wayacāwipitēw ⊲·ᐦᐃ·ᐱᐅᐱᐡ
VTA s/he pulls s.o. running

wayacāwiw ⊲·ᐦᐃ·ᐦᵒ
VAI s/he stands ready to run, s/he runs

wayahpitam ⊲·ᐦᐱᒧᐨ
VTI s/he wraps s.t. up [also wēyahpitam; cf. wiýahpitam]

wayahpitēw ⊲·ᐦᐱᐅᵒ
VTA s/he wraps s.o. up [also wēyahpitēw; cf. wiýahpitēw]

waýakay ⊲·ᐦᑲᐩ
NA fish scale [cf. wahakay, wahýakay]

wayakēsk ⊲·ᐦᑫᐢᐠ
NA bark [pl: -wak]

wayanohtahēw ⊲·ᐦᐳᐦᐊᐦᐁᵒ
VTA s/he takes s.o. back

wayanohtatāw ⊲·ᐦᐳᐦᒐᐨ
VAIt s/he takes s.t. back

waýawēpaýiw ⊲·ᐦᐅᐃᐸᐸᵒ
VAI s/he has hemorrhoids

waýawī- ⊲·ᐦᐃ·
IPV outside; out from inside, out from the tipi

waýawī-pakitinam
⊲·ᐦᐃ· ᐸᐱᑎᓇᐨ
VTI s/he puts s.t. down outside

waýawī-pakitinēw
⊲·ᐦᐃ· ᐸᐱᑎᓀᵒ
VTA s/he puts s.o. (e.g. diapers) down outside

waýawī-tahkiskam
⊲·ᐦᐃ· ᒼᐸᐦᑭᐢᑲᒼ
VTI s/he kicks s.t. out

waýawī-tahkiskawēw
⊲·ᐦᐃ· ᒼᐸᐦᑭᐢᑲᐃᐁᵒ
VTA s/he kicks s.o. out

waýawī-tahkonam
⊲·ᐦᐃ· ᒼᐦᑯᓇᐨ
VTI s/he carries s.t. out

waýawī-tahkonēw
⊲·ᐦᐃ· ᒼᐦᑯᓀᵒ
VTA s/he carries s.o. out

waýawī-wēpaham
⊲·ᐦᐃ· ∇·ᐸᐦᐊᒼ
VTI s/he sweeps s.t. outside

waýawī-wēpahwēw
⊲·ᐦᐃ· ∇·ᐸᐦᐃᐅᵒ
VTA s/he sweeps s.o. outside

waýawī-wēpinam
⊲·ᐦᐃ· ∇·ᐱᓇᐨ
VTI s/he throws s.t. out

waýawī-wēpinēw
⊲·ᐦᐃ· ∇·ᐱᓀᵒ
VTA s/he throws s.o. out; s/he evicts s.o.

waýawī-wēpiskam
⊲·ᐦᐃ· ∇·ᐱᐢᑲᐨ
VTI s/he kick s.t. out

waýawī-wēpiskawēw
⊲·ᐦᐃ· ∇·ᐱᐢᑲᐃᐁᵒ
VTA s/he kick s.o. out

waýawī-ýahkinam
⊲·ᐦᐃ· ᐦᐸᐱᓇᐨ
VTI s/he pushes s.t. out

waýawī-ýahkinēw
⊲·ᐦᐃ· ᐦᐸᐱᓀᵒ
VTA s/he pushes s.o. out

waýawīciwan ⊲·ᐦᐃ·ᒋᐃ·ᐣ
VII it flows out

waýawīhāw ⊲·ᐦᐃ·ᐦᐦᐦᵒ
VAI s/he flies out; it flies out of a cage, it flies outside [also unspecified actor VTA, cf. waýawihēw]

waýawīhēw ⊲·ᐦᐃ·ᐦᐦᐦᐁᵒ
VTA s/he takes s.o. to the bathroom; s/he makes s.o. go outside

waýawīhtahēw ⊲·ᐦᐃ·ᐦᐦᒼᐦᐁᵒ
VTA s/he takes s.o. outside

waýawīhtatāw ⊲·ᐦᐃ·ᐦᐦᒼᐦᐨ
VAIt s/he takes s.t. outside

waýawīkāpawiw ⊲·ᐦᐃ·ᐦᑲᐸᐃ·ᵒ
VAI s/he stands outside

waýawīkocin ⊲·ᐦᐃ·ᒍᐣ
VAI s/he flies out

waýawīkotin ⊲·ᐦᐃ·ᒍᑎᐣ
VII it flies out; it is flung out

waýawīpahtāw ⊲·ᐦᐃ·ᐸᐦᒼᐨ
VAI s/he runs out, s/he runs outside

waýawīpaýihow ⊲·ᐦᐃ·ᐸᐸᐦᐅᵒ
VAI s/he goes out quickly (e.g. a crated animal)

waýawīpaýiw ⊲·ᐦᐃ·ᐸᐸᵒ
VAI s/he falls out; s/he drives out, it gallops outside

waýawīpitam ⊲·ᐦᐃ·ᐱᒧᐨ
VTI s/he pulls s.t. out, s/he pulls s.t. outside

waýawīpitēw ⊲·ᐦᐃ·ᐱᐅᵒ
VTA s/he pulls s.o. out (of a bag or box), s/he pulls s.o. outside

waýawīstamāsow ⊲·ᐦᐃ·ᐣᑕᒐᒼᐅᵒ
VAI s/he goes outside for him/herself, s/he goes out for purpose of his/her own; s/he goes to the bathroom, s/he goes to relieve him/herself

waýawīstamāsowikamik
⊲·ᐦᐃ·ᐣᑕᒐᒼᐅᐃᑲᒥᐠ
NI bathroom [pl: -wa]

waýawītācimow ⊲·ᐦᐃ·ᒼᑕᒋᒧᵒ
VAI s/he crawls outside

waýawītāpātam ⊲·ᐦᐃ·ᒼᑕᐸᒼᐨ
VTI s/he drags s.t. outside

waẏawītāpātēw ◁·ᔅᐃ·ᒡᐸᑐ°
    VTA s/he drags s.o. outside
waẏawītāpēw ◁·ᔅᐃ·ᒡᐯ°
    VAI s/he drags s.t. out
waẏawītimihk ◁·ᔅᐃ·ᡁᒥᕁ
    IPC outside, out of doors
waẏawītisaham ◁·ᔅᐊᐧᓵᐦᐊᒡ
    VTI s/he sends s.t. away;
    s/he sends s.t. out, outside
waẏawītisahikēmakan
    ◁·ᔅᐃ·ᐣᔑᐦᐊᐦ9ᒥᑫᑲᐣ
    VII it sends things out, it
    acts to send things out
waẏawītisahikēw
    ◁·ᔅᐃ·ᐣᔑᐦᐊᐧᐟ9°
    VAI s/he sends things or
    people out
waẏawītisahwēw ◁·ᔅᐃ·ᐣᔑᐦᐧᐁ·°
    VTA s/he sends s.o. away;
    s/he sends s.o. out, outside
waẏawīw ◁·ᔅᐊ·°
    VAI s/he goes outside, s/he
    goes out; s/he goes to relieve
    him/herself; s/he leaves
    school, s/he leaves hospital
waẏawīwin ◁·ᔅᐊ·ᐃ·ᐣ
    NI being outside, out of
    doors; going outside; going
    to the toilet
waẏawīyāmohkēw ◁·ᔅᐊ·ᔅᐟᒧᕁᐟ9°
    VAI s/he chases everyone
    out
waẏawīyāmow ◁·ᔅᐊ·ᔅᐟᒧ°
    VAI s/he runs outside, s/he
    flees out
waẏawīyāpahtēw ◁·ᔅᐊ·ᔅᐊ·ᐸᐧᐸᐳᐟᐱᐪᐤ°
    VII it comes out as smoke;
    there is smoke going out of
    the room
waẏawīyāpasow ◁·ᔅᐊ·ᔅᐊ·ᐸᔓ°
    VAI s/he gets smoked out
    (*e.g.* of a house, lodge), it
    gets smoked out (*e.g.* of a
    burrow)
waẏawīyāstan ◁·ᔅᐊ·ᔅᐊᐣᐪᐦᐪ
    VII it is blown outside
waẏākonēham ◁·ᔅᐟᐤ"◁ᐟᐪ
    VTI s/he is stuck in snow
waẏān ◁·ᔅᐣ
    NA hide, skin, fur [*rarely
    occurs as an independent
    stem; cf. noun final* -wayān]
waẏāstin ◁·ᔅᐣᐣᐪ
    VII it quiets down (*e.g.*
    wind)
wayēs ◁·ᔕᐣ
    IPC around, about,
    approximately
wayēsi- ◁·ᔕᐧ
    IPV deceitfully
wayēsihēw ◁·ᔕᐧᐦᐁᐧ°
    VTA s/he deceives s.o.
wayēsihkēmoskiw ◁·ᔕᐧᐦ"9ᐧᐸᐣᐳ°
    VAI s/he is given to deceitful
    talk [*hab*]
wayēsihkēmow ◁·ᔕᐧᐦ"9ᐟ°
    VAI s/he deceives people by
    speech

wayēsihtam ◁·ᔕᐧᐦ"ᐻᐪ
    VTI s/he tricks s.t., s/he
    deceives s.t. by speech
wayēsimēw ◁·ᔕᐧᐟ9°
    VTA s/he tricks s.o., s/he
    deceives s.o. by speech
wayēsiyawēw ◁·ᔕᐧᐧᔅᐁᐧ°
    VTA s/he gets s.o. by deceit
wayīwahkamikan ◁·ᐳᐊ·ᐦ"ᑫᑲᐸ
    VII it is in excitement

◁·

wā ◁·
    IPC so [*exclamation; cf.*
    wāh]
wā-waskawīw ◁· ◁ᐧᑲᐸ·°
    VAI s/he moves around
    [*rdpl*]
wā-wāpahtam ◁· ◁·ᐸᐧᐸᐻᐪ [*rdpl*]
    VTI s/he examines s.t. [*rdpl*]
wāci ◁·ᐣ
    NI hole [*dim; pl:* wāca; *cf.*
    wācis]
wācihkānis ◁·ᐣᐦ"ᒼᐤᐢ
    NI little hole [*dim; also*
    wācihkānis]
wācihkwānis ◁·ᕒᐸ·ᐤᐢ
    NI small cellar [*dim; cf.*
    wācihkānis]
wācis ◁·ᐣᐣ
    NI small burrow, small hole
    [*dim*]
wācistak ◁·ᐣᐧᐨᐢᐪ
    IPC oh my [*exclamation; cf.*
    wācistakā, wācistakāc,
    wācistakāt]
wācistakā ◁·ᐣᐧᐨᑕᐸ
    IPC incredible, beyond
    reason [*exclamation; cf.*
    wācistak, wācistakāc,
    wācistakāt]
wācistakāc ◁·ᐣᐧᐨᑕᐸᐧ
    IPC oh my, really good;
    goodness gracious;
    incredible, beyond reason
    [*exclamation; cf.* wācistak,
    wācistakā, wācistakāt]
wācistakāt ◁·ᐣᐧᐨᑕᐸᐧ
    IPC oh my, really good
    [*exclamation; cf.* wācistak,
    wācistakā, wācistakāc]
wāh ◁·ᐦ
    IPC oh! well! [*exclamation;
    cf.* wā]
wāh- ◁·ᐦ
    IPV whenever in future
    [*changed conjunct form of*
    wi-]
wāh-wāhyaw ◁·ᐦ ◁·ᐦᔅ°
    IPC very far; a very long
    distance; in far places [*rdpl*]
wāh-wākāw ◁·ᐦ ◁·ᑲ°
    VAI it is bent here and there
    [*rdpl; cf.* wākāw]
wāh-wīhēw ◁·ᐦ ᐊ·ᐦᐧᐁ°
    VTA s/he names s.o.; s/he
    gives names to s.o. [*rdpl*]

wāh-wīhkāc ◁·ᐦ ᐊ·ᐦᐸ-
    IPC at rare intervals, rarely
    now and again [*rdpl*]
wāh-wīhtam ◁·ᐦ ᐊ·ᐦᐻᐪ
    VTI s/he tells s.t.
    everywhere [*rdpl*]
wāh-wīhtamawēw
    ◁·ᐦ ᐊ·ᐦᐧᒐᐃᐁ·°
    VTA s/he tells (about it/him)
    to s.o. repeatedly [*rdpl*]
wāh-wīpac ◁·ᐦ ᐊ·ᐧ-
    IPC often; frequently; every
    little while [*rdpl*]
wāhkay ◁·ᐦᐸᐩ
    NA fish scale
wāhkos ◁·ᐦᐤᐣ
    NA fish egg [*dim; cf.*
    wāhkwa]
wāhkōhtahēw ◁·ᐦᐤᐦᐸᐻ·ᐁ°
    VTA s/he takes s.o. to make
    friends; s/he adopts s.o. as a
    relative
wāhkōhtam ◁·ᐦᐤᐦᐻᐪ
    VTI s/he is related
wāhkōhtamowin ◁·ᐦᐤᐦᐧᒐᐃ·ᐤ
    NI relationship with others
wāhkōhtowak ◁·ᐦᐤᐦᐪ◁·ᐧ
    VAI they are related to one
    another
wāhkōhtowin ◁·ᐦᐤᐦᐪᐪᐊ·ᐤ
    NI relationship
wāhkōmākan ◁·ᐦᒉᐸᐸ
    NA relative
wāhkōmākanis ◁·ᐦᒉᐸᐤᐣ
    NA small, young relative
    [*dim*]
wāhkōmēw ◁·ᐦᒉᐟ°
    VTA s/he is related to s.o.
wāhkwa ◁·ᐦᐸ·
    NA lump of roe [*pl:* -k]
wāhkwan ◁·ᐦᐸ·ᐤ
    NA roe
wāhkwaniw ◁·ᐦᐸ·ᐤᐤ°
    VAI it has roe (*i.e.* a fish)
wāhpāsiw ◁·ᐦᐧᐸᐳ°
    VAI s/he is an early riser,
    s/he wakes up early
wāhyaw ◁·ᐦᔅ°
    IPC far, far away
wāhyawēs ◁·ᐦᔅᐁ·ᐣ
    IPC far, far away, quite far,
    quite a ways; a little ways
    [*dim; cf.* wāhyawis]
wāhyawēskamik ◁·ᐦᔅᐁ·ᐁᐣᑲᐟᐤ
    IPC very far away across
    the land
wāhyawis ◁·ᐦᔅᐊ·ᐣ
    IPC quite far [*dim; cf.*
    wāhyawēs]
wākamon ◁·ᑲᐟ
    VII it runs crooked, curved;
    it is not straight (as a road or
    river with curves)
wākamow ◁·ᑲᐟ°
    VII it runs crooked (*e.g.* a
    road), has curves
wākapiw ◁·ᑲᐱ°
    VAI it sits crooked, s/he sits
    bent over

wākastēw ᐚᑲᐢᑌᐤ
VII it lies bent, it lies in a bent position

wākāhkatisow ᐚᑳᐦᑲᑎᓱᐤ
VAI it is bent from dryness or hunger (as a tree)

wākāhtik ᐚᑳᐦᑎᐠ
NA tamarack; bent tree [*pl*: -wak]

wākāhtik ᐚᑳᐦᑎᐠ
NI tamarack wood, bent wood [*pl*: -wa]

wākāpiskāw ᐚᑳᐱᐢᑳᐤ
VII it is bent (*i.e.* metal object)

wākāpiskisam ᐚᑳᐱᐢᑭᓴᒼ
VTI s/he heats s.t. until it bends easily

wākāpiskiswēw ᐚᑳᐱᐢᑭᔃᐤ
VTA s/he heats s.o. until it bends easily

wākās ᐚᑳᐢ
NA banana [*dim*; *see also* mitēskimin]

wākāsin ᐚᑳᓯᐣ
VII it is a bit bent [*dim*]

wākāw ᐚᑳᐤ
VII it is bent

wākāýow ᐚᑳᔪᐤ
NA black bear [*lit*: "crooked tail"; *see also* maskwa]

wākāýowēw ᐚᑳᔪᐍᐤ
VAI it has a crooked tail

wākāýōs ᐚᑳᔫᐢ
NA bear [*dim*; *see also* maskwa; *also* wākaýōs]

wākāýōsi-wāti ᐚᑳᔫᓯ ᐚᑎ
NI bear den [*pl*: -wāta]

wākāýōsiwayān ᐚᑳᔫᓯᐘᔮᐣ
NA bear skin

wākāýōsiwiw ᐚᑳᔫᓯᐏᐤ
VAI s/he is a bear

wāki- ᐚᑭ
IPV curving

wākicānēw ᐚᑭᒑᓀᐤ
VAI s/he has a curved nose or beak

wākikāpawiw ᐚᑭᑳᐸᐏᐤ
VAI s/he stands stooped

wākikātēw ᐚᑭᑳᑌᐤ
VAI s/he has crooked legs

wākikīhkāw ᐚᑭᑮᐦᑳᐤ
VAI s/he is bent with age

wākikot ᐚᑭᑯᐟ
NI crooked nose, hook nose

wākikotam ᐚᑭᑯᑕᒼ
VTI s/he whittles s.t. curved

wākikotēw ᐚᑭᑯᑌᐤ
VAI s/he has a curved, crooked nose, s/he has a hook nose

wākikotēw ᐚᑭᑯᑌᐤ
VTA s/he cuts s.o. curved, s/he hews s.o. curved

wākinam ᐚᑭᓇᒼ
VTI s/he bends s.t. by hand

wākinākan ᐚᑭᓈᑲᐣ
NI tamarack tree

wākinākanāhtik ᐚᑭᓈᑲᓈᐦᑎᐠ
NA wood of the tamarack [*pl*: -wak]

wākinākanis ᐚᑭᓈᑲᓂᐢ
NA small tamarack [*dim*]

wākinākaniskāw ᐚᑭᓈᑲᓂᐢᑳᐤ
VII there are many tamaracks growing

wākināw ᐚᑭᓈᐤ
NA canoe rib [*pl generally*: wākināwak]

wākinēw ᐚᑭᓀᐤ
VTA s/he bends s.o. by hand

wākipaýin ᐚᑭᐸᔨᐣ
VII it bends

wākipitam ᐚᑭᐱᑕᒼ
VTI s/he bends s.t.; s/he bends s.t. down quickly; s/he pulls s.t. forward

wākipitēw ᐚᑭᐱᑌᐤ
VTA s/he bends s.o.; s/he bends s.o. down quickly; s/he pulls s.o. forward

wākisitēw ᐚᑭᓯᑌᐤ
VAI s/he has crooked feet, s/he has a club foot

wākisiw ᐚᑭᓯᐤ
VAI it is bent, it is curved, s/he is stooped; it is a banana [*cf.* kā-wākisicik "bananas"; *cf.* wākās]

wākispiskwanēw ᐚᑭᐢᐱᐢᑿᓀᐤ
VAI s/he has a bent back

wākispwākan ᐚᑭᐢᐺᑲᐣ
NA curved pipe

wākitēskanēw ᐚᑭᑌᐢᑲᓀᐤ
VAI it has crooked horns

wānanopēhikan ᐚᓇᓄᐯᐦᐃᑲᐣ
NI heart (at cards)

wānaskēw ᐚᓇᐢᑫᐤ
VAI s/he is freed from an ill; s/he is at peace

wānaskēwin ᐚᓇᐢᑫᐏᐣ
NI being at peace with oneself; Wanuskewin Heritage Park, SK

wānāhkēw ᐚᓈᐦᑫᐤ
NA bald-eagle

wānwāstikwēham ᐚᓌᐢᑎᑵᐦᐊᒼ
VTI s/he goes round a bend in canoe

wāpahcikātēw ᐚᐸᐦᒋᑳᑌᐤ
VII it is seen

wāpahcikēw ᐚᐸᐦᒋᑫᐤ
VAI s/he looks at things; s/he shops around, s/he window shops

wāpahkēsiw ᐚᐸᐦᑫᓯᐤ
NA white fox

wāpahkēsīs ᐚᐸᐦᑫᓰᐢ
NA white fox [*dim*]

wāpahkēw ᐚᐸᐦᑫᐤ
VAI s/he watches people

wāpahki ᐚᐸᐦᑭ
IPC tomorrow; in the morning

wāpahtahēw ᐚᐸᐦᑕᐦᐁᐤ
VTA s/he shows (it/him) to s.o.

wāpahtam ᐚᐸᐦᑕᒼ
VTI s/he sees s.t., s/he witnesses s.t. [*rdpl*: wa-wāpahtam; *cf.* wā-wāpahtam]

wāpahtamawēw ᐚᐸᐦᑕᒪᐍᐤ
VTA s/he sees (it/him) on or for s.o.

wāpahtamowin ᐚᐸᐦᑕᒧᐏᐣ
NI vision

wāpahtēhēw ᐚᐸᐦᑌᐦᐁᐤ
VTA s/he shows (it/him) to s.o.

wāpahtihēw ᐚᐸᐦᑎᐦᐁᐤ
VTA s/he shows (it/him) to s.o.

wāpahtowak ᐚᐸᐦᑐᐘᐠ
VAI they see one another [*cf.* wāpamitowak]

wāpahtowin ᐚᐸᐦᑐᐏᐣ
NI seeing one another

wāpakosīs ᐚᐸᑯᓰᐢ
NA mouse [*cf.* āpakosīs]

wāpakwaniy ᐚᐸᑿᓂᐩ
NI flower [*cf.* wāpikwaniy; *also* wāpakoniy; wāpakwanīw]

wāpakwanīhkān ᐚᐸᑿᓃᐦᑳᐣ
NI artificial flower

wāpakwanīs ᐚᐸᑿᓃᐢ
NI flower [*dim*; *cf.* wāpikwanīs]

wāpakwanīw ᐚᐸᑿᓃᐤ
VAI it has flowers

wāpakwanīw ᐚᐸᑿᓃᐤ
VII it has flowers

wāpakwanīwan ᐚᐸᑿᓃᐘᐣ
VII it has many flowers

wāpakwanīwin ᐚᐸᑿᓃᐏᐣ
NI blooming

wāpamāwasow ᐚᐸᒫᐘᓱᐤ
VAI s/he sees his/her own child; she gives birth to a child

wāpamēw ᐚᐸᒣᐤ
VTA s/he sees s.o., s/he witnesses s.o. [*rdpl*: wa-wāpamēw]

wāpamisow ᐚᐸᒥᓱᐤ
VAI s/he sees him/herself

wāpamitowak ᐚᐸᒥᑐᐘᐠ
VAI they see one another [*cf.* wāpahtowak]

wāpamon ᐚᐸᒧᐣ
NI mirror [*cf.* wāpamonāpis, wāpamonāpisk]

wāpamonāpis ᐚᐸᒧᓈᐱᐢ
NI mirror [*cf.* wāpamon, wāpamonāpisk]

wāpamonāpisk ᐚᐸᒧᓈᐱᐢᐠ
NI mirror; glass, window [*pl*: -wa; *cf.* wāpamon, wāpamonāpis]

wāpamonis ᐚᐸᒧᓂᐢ
NI small mirror [*dim*]

wāpamow ᐚᐸᒧᐤ
VAI s/he looks at him/herself in a mirror
wāpan ᐚᐸᐣ
NI dawn
wāpan ᐚᐸᐣ
VII it is dawn, it is first daylight, it is early morning
wāpan-atoskēw ᐚᐸᐣ ᐊᑐᐢᑫᐤ
VAI s/he works until early morning
wāpanacāhkos ᐚᐸᓇᒑᐦᑯᐢ
NA morning star
wāpanacāhkwēw ᐚᐸᓇᒑᐦᑵᐤ
VAI s/he is out all night; s/he plays games till early morning
wāpanapiw ᐚᐸᓇᐱᐤ
VAI s/he sits up until dawn, s/he sits up all night
wāpanatāhk ᐚᐸᓇᑖᕽ
NA morning star [*obv*: -wa]
wāpanēwask ᐚᐸᓀᐘᐢᐠ
NI yarrow, herb known as yarrow [*pl*: -wa]
wāpanēwitam ᐚᐸᓀᐃᐧᑕᒼ
VTI s/he talks all night, s/he makes a noise all night (*e.g.* child crying; dog barking)
wāpani- ᐚᐸᓂ
IPV dawn; at, until dawn [*cf.* wāpan]
wāpani-sākahikanihk
ᐚᐸᓂ ᓵᑲᐦᐃᑲᓂᕽ
INM Morin Lake, SK [*loc*; *lit*: "at dawn lake"]
wāpanihkwāmiw ᐚᐸᓂᐦᑳᒥᐤ
VAI s/he sleeps until late in the morning
wāpanipahtāw ᐚᐸᓂᐸᐦᑖᐤ
VAI s/he runs until dawn
wāpanisimow ᐚᐸᓂᓯᒧᐤ
VAI s/he dances until dawn
wāpaniýowēw ᐚᐸᓂᔪᐍᐤ
VII it is an east wind; there is a wind blowing all night into the morning
wāpanohtēw ᐚᐸᓅᐦᑌᐤ
VAI s/he walks until dawn
wāpasākay ᐚᐸᓵᑲᕀ
NI white dress, coat
wāpasiskiy ᐚᐸᓯᐢᑭᕀ
NI white mud
wāpask ᐚᐸᐢᐠ
NA white bear; polar bear [*pl*: -wak]
wāpaskamimatin ᐚᐸᐢᑲᒥᒪᑎᐣ
VII there is hoarfrost
wāpaskominānāhtik
ᐚᐸᐢᑯᒥᓈᓈᐦᑎᐠ
NI tree with whitish leaves [*pl*: -wa]
wāpaskwāw ᐚᐸᐢᑳᐤ
VII it is a white sky
wāpaspinēwin ᐚᐸᐢᐱᓀᐏᐣ
NI leprosy
wāpastim ᐚᐸᐢᑎᒼ
NA white horse; white dog [*pl*: -wak]

wāpatihk ᐚᐸᑎᕽ
NA goat [*pl*: -wak]
wāpatim ᐚᐸᑎᒼ
NA white dog [*pl*: -wak]
wāpatonask ᐚᐸᑐᓇᐢᐠ
NA white clay, white face paint
wāpatonisk ᐚᐸᑐᓂᐢᐠ
NA white clay, white face paint
wāpatoniskinēw ᐚᐸᑐᓂᐢᑭᓀᐤ
VTA s/he puts white clay on s.o.
wāpaýōminak ᐚᐸᔫᒥᓇᐠ
NA rice [*pl generally*; *cf.* wāpinōminak]
wāpāciwanāhk ᐚᐹᒋᐘᓈᕽ
INM Patuanak, SK [*loc*; *lit*: "where the water flows white (*i.e.* as rapids)"; *Dene community*]
wāpāsow ᐚᐹᓱᐤ
VAI s/he is fair, s/he has light skin and hair
wāpāstēw ᐚᐹᐢᑌᐤ
VII it fades, it is faded
wāpāw ᐚᐹᐤ
VII it is white
wāpāýowēw ᐚᐹᔪᐍᐤ
VAI it has a white tail
wāpāýōs ᐚᐹᔫᐢ
NA white tail deer [*cf.* wēpāýōs]
wāpēnam ᐚᐯᓇᒼ
VTI s/he sees s.t. as almost white
wāpēnēw ᐚᐯᓀᐤ
VTA s/he sees s.o. as light in colour
wāpi- ᐚᐱ
IPN white
wāpi-maskwa ᐚᐱ ᒪᐢᑿ
NA White Bear [*Cree chief and SK reserve name*]
wāpi-mostosis ᐚᐱ ᒧᐢᑐᓯᐢ
NA White Calf [*dim*; *Cree chief*; *see also* paskos]
wāpicāhk ᐚᐱᒑᕽ
NA whooping crane [*pl*: -wak; *cf.* ocicāhk]
wāpicāpiw ᐚᐱᒑᐱᐤ
VAI s/he has light or white eyes
wāpicēpihk ᐚᐱᒉᐱᕽ
NA a root from a certain plant [*possibly* "white cockle"; *pl*: -wak]
wāpicicāhk ᐚᐱᒋᒑᕽ
NA white crane [*pl*: -wak]
wāpiciyāpiw ᐚᐱᒋᔮᐱᐤ
VAI s/he is white-eyed
wāpihēw ᐚᐱᐦᐁᐤ
NA white grouse
wāpihēw ᐚᐱᐦᐁᐤ
VTA s/he makes s.o. see
wāpihkāwikanis ᐚᐱᐦᑳᐏᑲᓂᐢ
NA skunk
wāpihkwēw ᐚᐱᐦᑵᐤ
VAI s/he is white on the face, it has a white face (*e.g.* animal)
wāpihtakāw ᐚᐱᐦᑕᑳᐤ
VII it is a white lath, stick, or board
wāpikan ᐚᐱᑲᐣ
NI white powder
wāpikāt ᐚᐱᑳᐟ
NA animal with white legs
wāpikātēw ᐚᐱᑳᑌᐤ
VAI s/he has white legs
wāpikiskicēw ᐚᐱᑭᐢᑭᒉᐤ
VAI s/he is white at the belly-button
wāpikwaniy ᐚᐱᑿᓂᕀ
NI flower [*cf.* wāpakwaniy]
wāpikwanīs ᐚᐱᑿᓃᐢ
NI flower [*dim*; *cf.* wāpakwanīs]
wāpikwanīwinākosiw
ᐚᐱᑿᓃᐏᓈᑯᓯᐤ
VAI s/he is pink
wāpikwanīwinākwan
ᐚᐱᑿᓃᐏᓈᑿᐣ
VII it is pink
wāpikwayaw ᐚᐱᑿᔭᐤ
NI white neck
wāpimākowiw ᐚᐱᒫᑯᐏᐤ
VAI it is a white loon
wāpimin ᐚᐱᒥᐣ
NA white bead, white kernel
wāpimin ᐚᐱᒥᐣ
NI white berry
wāpinākosiw ᐚᐱᓈᑯᓯᐤ
VAI s/he looks, appears white; it is light in colour
wāpinākwan ᐚᐱᓈᑿᐣ
VII it looks, appears white; it is light in colour
wāpinēwisiw ᐚᐱᓀᐏᓯᐤ
VAI s/he is pale
wāpinōminak ᐚᐱᓅᒥᓇᐠ
NA kernel of white rice [*pl generally*; *cf.* wāpaýōminak]
wāpipak ᐚᐱᐸᐠ
NA plug tobacco [*pl*: -wak]
wāpiscānis ᐚᐱᐢᒑᓂᐢ
NA marten [*dim*]
wāpisiw ᐚᐱᓯᐤ
NA swan
wāpisiw ᐚᐱᓯᐤ
VAI s/he is white
wāpisiw-sākahikan
ᐚᐱᓯᐤ ᓵᑲᐦᐃᑲᐣ
NI Swan Lake, MB
wāpiskaham ᐚᐱᐢᑲᐦᐊᒼ
VTI s/he whitewashes s.t.
wāpiskahikēw ᐚᐱᐢᑲᐦᐃᑫᐤ
VAI s/he does the whitewashing
wāpiskakohp ᐚᐱᐢᑲᑰᐦᑊ
NI white blanket
wāpiskasiniy ᐚᐱᐢᑲᓯᓂᕀ
NA white rock, white stone
wāpiskaskow ᐚᐱᐢᑲᐢᑯᐤ
NI white cloud
wāpiskatayēw ᐚᐱᐢᑲᑕᔦᐤ
VAI s/he has a white belly

wāpiskāhcikos ⊲·ᐱᣞ"ᒉᗞᣔ
NI chalk [dim]

wāpiskāpakwanīs ⊲·ᐱᣞᐸ<ᐸ·ᓂᣔ
NI white flower [dim; cf. wāpakwanīs]

wāpiskāpakwanīw
⊲·ᐱᣞᐸ<ᐸ·ᓂ
VII it has white flowers

wāpiskāpāwēw ⊲·ᐱᣞᐸ<ᐁ·°
VAI it is washed white

wāpiskāpēhikēw ⊲·ᐱᣞᐸᐂ"ᐊᖅ°
VAI s/he wears white

wāpiskāw ⊲·ᐱᣞᐸ°
VII it is white

wāpiskēkin ⊲·ᐱᣞᖊᣔ
NI white cloth or material [pl: -wa]

wāpiskēkinos ⊲·ᐱᣞᖊᓄᣔ
NI piece of white cloth [dim]

wāpiskēwēw ⊲·ᐱᣞᖅᐁ·°
VAI s/he is white-skinned

wāpiski- ⊲·ᐱᣞ
IPN white

wāpiski-mahkahk ⊲·ᐱᣞ ᒪ"ᐸˣ
NA white barrel or tub [pl: -wak]

wāpiski-māhkēsīs
⊲·ᐱᣞ ᒪ"ᖅᣔ
NA white fox

wāpiski-minōs ⊲·ᐱᣞ ᒥᓄᣔ
NA white cat

wāpiski-minōsis ⊲·ᐱᣞ ᒥᓄᣞᣔ
NA white kitten

wāpiski-miyēstawēw
⊲·ᐱᣞ ᒥᣛᐨᐁ·°
VAI he has a white beard [cf. miyēstawēw, mīhistawēw]

wāpiski-mīkwan ⊲·ᐱᣞ ᒦᐸᣔ
NA white feather

wāpiski-mīmēs ⊲·ᐱᣞ ᒦᒣᣔ
NA white dove [dim]

wāpiski-mīmēw ⊲·ᐱᣞ ᒦᒣ°
NA white pigeon

wāpiski-sopēhikan
⊲·ᐱᣞ ᓱᐂ"ᐊᐸᣔ
NI white paint; calamine lotion [cf. sisopēhikan]

wāpiski-wāpos ⊲·ᐱᣞ ⊲·ᔑᣔ
NA white rabbit [pl: -wak]

wāpiski-wiyās ⊲·ᐱᣞ ᐃᣛᣔ
NI white meat [cf. wāpiskwiyās]

wāpiskihēw ⊲·ᐱᣞ"ᐁ°
VTA s/he colours s.o. white

wāpiskihtakāw ⊲·ᐱᣞ"ᐸᖸ°
VII there are white boards, it is a white floor

wāpiskihtāw ⊲·ᐱᣞ"ᐨ°
VAIt s/he colours s.t. white; s/he makes s.t. white in colour

wāpiskimin ⊲·ᐱᣞᒥᣔ
NA white bead

wāpiskinikēmakisiw
⊲·ᐱᣞᓂᖅᐊᒐᣛ°
VAI s/he whitens, s/he makes white

wāpiskipēkaham ⊲·ᐱᣞᐯᐸ"ᐊᣔ
VTI s/he paints s.t. white

wāpiskipēkahwēw
⊲·ᐱᣞᐯᐸ"ᐁ·°
VTA s/he paints s.o. white

wāpiskisiw ⊲·ᐱᣞᣛ°
VAI s/he is white

wāpiskisōkan ⊲·ᐱᣞᓱᐸᣔ
NA horse with white hind-quarters

wāpiskistikwānēw
⊲·ᐱᣞᐢᓄᐸ·°
VAI s/he has white hair; s/he is fair-haired, s/he is blonde [cf. wāpistikwānēw]

wāpiskiwiyās ⊲·ᐱᣞᐃᣛᣔ
NA White-Man [cf. wāpiski-wiyās]

wāpiskiyākan ⊲·ᐱᣞᔭᐸᣔ
NI white bowl

wāpiskīhēw ⊲·ᐱᣞ"ᐁ°
VTA s/he dresses s.o. in white

wāpiskīhkwēhon ⊲·ᐱᣞ"ᖅᐤᣔ
NI face powder

wāpiskihow ⊲·ᐱᣞ"ᐅ°
VAI s/he dresses in white

wāpistān ⊲·ᐱᐨᣔ
NA martin

wāpistikwān ⊲·ᐱᐢᓄᐸᣔ
NA person with white head or hair

wāpistikwān ⊲·ᐱᐢᓄᐸᣔ
NI white head or hair

wāpistikwānēw ⊲·ᐱᐢᓄᐸ·°
VAI s/he is white-haired, s/he has white hair (from age) [cf. wāpiskistikwānēw]

wāpistikwātiw ⊲·ᐱᐢᓄᐸᐣ°
VAI s/he is white-haired

wāpiw ⊲·ᐱ°
VAI s/he sees, s/he has vision; [generally in negative phrases:] s/he is blind

wāpiwin ⊲·ᐱᐃᣔ
NI eyesight

wāpos ⊲·ᔑᣔ
NA rabbit, hare [pl: -wak]

wāposāwāw ⊲·ᔑ⊲·°
VII it is yellow [see also osāwāw]

wāposāwi-pakwahtēhon
⊲·ᔑ⊲· <ᐸ"ᐅ"ᣔ
NI yellow belt

wāposāwisiw ⊲·ᔑ⊲ᣛ°
VAI s/he is yellow [see also osāwisiw]

wāposo- ⊲·ᔑ
IPN rabbit

wāposo-mēskanās ⊲·ᔑ ᒣᐢᐸᣔ
NI rabbit road or path

wāposo-mīcimāpoy
⊲·ᔑ ᒦᒋᒪᔑ⊹
NI rabbit soup

wāposo-tāpakwān
⊲·ᔑ ᐨᐸᐠᣔ
NI rabbit snare

wāposo-wāti ⊲·ᔑ ⊲·ᐣ
NI rabbit's hole or den [pl: -wāta]

wāpososkāw ⊲·ᔑᐢᐸ°
VII there are numerous rabbits in the area

wāposwayān ⊲·ᔑᔦᣔ
NA Rabbitskin people, people from Nekaneet Reserve, SK

wāposwayān ⊲·ᔑᔦᣔ
NI rabbit hide, rabbit-skin [also NA; also wāposwēyān]

wāposwayānakohp
⊲·ᔑᔦᐊᖦᣜ"'
NI rabbit robe; rabbit-skin blanket

wāposwāspinēwin
⊲·ᔑᣛᐢᐱᓀᐃᣔ
NI tumour disease [proposed term]

wāpōhki- ⊲·ᔑ"ᖅ
IPV white

wāpwayān ⊲·<ᔦᣔ
NI blanket

wāsahacaskwēsiw ⊲·ᔑ"ᐊᒐᐢᖅᣛ°
NA frog eater duck

wāsahāw ⊲·ᔑ"°
VII it is a bay

wāsahihkasow ⊲·ᔑ"ᐃ"ᐸᣛ°
VAI it is burned transparent [also wāsahīhkasow]

wāsakā ⊲·ᔑᐸ
IPC around, all around; in a circle round something [cf. wāsakām, wāskā]

wāsakāhāw ⊲·ᔑᐸ"⊲·°
VAI s/he soars around (as a hawk)

wāsakāhēw ⊲·ᔑᐸ"ᐁ°
VTA s/he places s.o. in a circle

wāsakāhtēw ⊲·ᔑᐸ"ᐅ°
VAI s/he walks around in a circle, s/he walks around the entire area

wāsakām ⊲·ᔑᐸᣔ
IPC around, all around, in a circuit, in a circle round something [cf. wāsakā]

wāsakāmahēw ⊲·ᔑᐸᒣ"ᐁ°
VTA s/he places s.o. around, in a circle

wāsakāmapiwak ⊲·ᔑᐸᒪᐱ⊲·ᣔ
VAI they sit in a circle [pl]

wāsakāmaskam ⊲·ᔑᐸᒪᐢᐸᣔ
VTI s/he walks around s.t.

wāsakāmastāw ⊲·ᔑᐸᒪᐢᐨ°
VAIt s/he places s.t. around, in a circle

wāsakāmāw ⊲·ᔑᐸᒪ°
VAI s/he makes a circuit, s/he makes a circle

wāsakāmēkāpawiwak
⊲·ᔑᐸᒦᐸ<⊲·⊲·ᣔ
VAI they stand in a circle

wāsakāmēpahtāw ⊲·ᔑᐸᒦ<"ᐨ°
VAI s/he runs around an

object, s/he runs around the
entire area

wāsakāmēpayíw ⊲·ᐦᔅᐱ<ᐱᵒ
VAI s/he moves, s/he goes,
s/he rides in a circle

wāsakāmēpayístawēw ⊲·ᐦᔅᐱ<ᐱᵒᐣᐨᐧᐁᐤ·ᵒ
VTA s/he circles s.o.

wāsakāmēpihāw ⊲·ᐦᔅᐱᐱᐱᐤ"⊲ᵒ
VAI s/he flies in a circle

wāsakāmēpiwak ⊲·ᐦᔅᐱᐱᐤ⊲·ᐣ
VAI they sit in a circle [pl]

wāsakāmēsimow ⊲·ᐦᔅᐱᐦᒍᐤᵒ
VAI s/he dances in a circle

wāsakāmēskawēw ⊲·ᐦᔅᐱᐦᑊᐧᐁᐤ·ᵒ
VTA s/he steps round s.o.

wāsakāmēstāw ⊲·ᐦᔅᐱᐣᐨᐨᵒ
VAIt s/he puts s.t. around
(e.g. the inside of building)

wāsakāmētisahwēw ⊲·ᐦᔅᐱᐣᐣ"ᐧᐁ·ᵒ
VTA s/he chases s.o. in a
circle

wāsakāmēw ⊲·ᐦᔅᐱᵒ
VAI s/he goes around an
object, s/he makes a circuit

wāsakāmēyāpōyow ⊲·ᐦᔅᐱᐱᔭᐳᐳᐧᐤᵒ
VAI s/he goes all the way
around, s/he takes the
roundabout way (by vehicle)

wāsakāmohtēw ⊲·ᐦᔅᐱᒍ"ᐤᵒ
VAI s/he walks all around
something

wāsakānam ⊲·ᐦᐸᐊᵀ
VTI s/he fences s.t. in; s/he
builds a fence around s.t.
(e.g. hay); s/he puts s.t. in a
circle

wāsakānamawēw ⊲·ᐦᐸᐊᐧᐧᐁ·ᵒ
VTA s/he fences (it/him) for
s.o.; s/he fences in livestock
for s.o.

wāsakānēw ⊲·ᐦᐸᵒ
VTA s/he fences s.o. in; s/he
builds a fence around s.o.;
s/he puts s.o. in a circle

wāsakānihkawēw ⊲·ᐦᐸᐤ"ᐧ·ᵒ
VTA s/he builds a fence for
s.o. [see also
mēnikanihkawēw]

wāsakānihkēw ⊲·ᐦᐸᐤ"ᐧᵒ
VAI s/he makes a corral [see
also mēnikanihkēw]

wāsakāpahtāw ⊲·ᐦᐸ<"ᐨᵒ
VAI s/he runs in a circle,
s/he runs around some place
(e.g. a lake)

wāsakāpayíw ⊲·ᐦᐸ<ᐱᵒ
VAI s/he goes around with a
car or horse

wāsakāpayíw ⊲·ᐦᐸ<ᐱᵒ
VII it twirls

wāsakāpayís ⊲·ᐦᐸ<ᐱᐣ
NA wheel

wāsakāpiw ⊲·ᐦᐸᐱᵒ
VAI s/he looks all round

wāsakāpiwak ⊲·ᐦᐸᐱ⊲·ᐣ
VAI they sit in a circle [pl;
cf. wāsakāpiw]

wāsakāpistamwak ⊲·ᐦᐸᐱᐣᒐᒪ·ᐣ
VTI they sit around s.t., they
encircle s.t. [pl]

wāsakāpistawēwak ⊲·ᐦᐸᐱᐣᐨᐧ·⊲·ᐣ
VTA they sit around s.o.,
they encircle s.o. [pl]

wāsakāskawēwak ⊲·ᐦᐸᐤᐸᐧᐧ·⊲·ᐣ
VTA they encircle s.o. [pl]

wāsaskocēnikanis ⊲·ᐦᑐᑯᐊᐧᐤᐸᐣ
NI candle, little light [dim]

wāsaskocēpayís ⊲·ᐦᑐᒍ<ᐱᐣ
NI lamp, electric light [dim]

wāsaskocēpicikanis ⊲·ᐦᑐᑭᐱᐨᐱᐸᐤᐣ
NI flashlight [dim]

wāsaskotēnam ⊲·ᐦᑐᑐᐧᐊᵀ
VTI s/he lights s.t. up

wāsaskotēnikan ⊲·ᐦᑐᑐᐧᐤᐸᐧ
NI lamp, light, lantern [also
wāsiskotēnikan,
wāskotēnikan]

wāsaskotēnikanāpisk ⊲·ᐦᑐᑐᐧᐤᐸᐤᐸᐱᐣᐣ
NI lamp chimney [pl: -wa]

wāsaskotēnikākēw ⊲·ᐦᑐᑐᐧᐤᐸᐤᐧᐧᵒ
VAI s/he lights things with
s.t., s/he uses s.t. to have
light

wāsaskotēnikēw ⊲·ᐦᑐᑐᐧᐤᐧᐤᵒ
VAI s/he turns on the lights

wāsaskotēpayíw ⊲·ᐦᑐᑐᐧᐤ<ᐱᵒ
VAI s/he goes with lightning;
it is lightning

wāsaskotēpayíw ⊲·ᐦᑐᑐᐧᐤ<ᐱᵒ
VII it gives light

wāsaskotēpicikan ⊲·ᐦᑐᑐᐧᐤᐱᐨᐱᐧ
NI switch light

wāsaskotēpicikēw ⊲·ᐦᑐᑐᐧᐤᐱᐨᐱᐧᐧᵒ
VAI s/he turns on the lights

wāsaskotēw ⊲·ᐦᑐᑐᐧᐤᵒ
VII it is light, it is lit up, it is
bright; it is a lantern

wāsaskwēcōs ⊲·ᐦᐧᐧᒍᐣ
NA apple; dried apple [dim]

wāsaskwēcōwas ⊲·ᐦᐧᐧᒍᐧᐊᐣ
NA apple

wāsaskwētow ⊲·ᐦᐧᐧᐱᑐᵒ
NI birch fungus

wāsā- ⊲·ᐦ
IPV around

wāsāpiskinamawēw ⊲·ᐦᐱᐣᐸᐧᐧ·ᵒ
VTA s/he flashes s.o., s/he
signals s.o. with mirror

wāsāw ⊲·ᐦᵒ
NI bay

wāsāw ⊲·ᐦᵒ
VII it is a bay

wāsē- ⊲·ᐦ
IPV clear; bright

wāsēhkwaham ⊲·ᐦᐦᐤᐧ·⊲ᵀ
VTI s/he polishes s.t. bright

wāsēhkwahwēw ⊲·ᐦᐦᐤ·"ᐧ·ᵒ
VTA s/he polishes s.o. bright

wāsēhkwāpiskāw ⊲·ᐦᐦᐤᐸᐱᐤᐸᐤᵒ
VII it is bright metal

wāsēhkwāpiskisiw ⊲·ᐦᐦᐤᐸᐱᐤᐸᐸᐤᵒ
VAI it is bright metal

wāsēhtāw ⊲·ᐦᐨᐨᵒ
VAIt s/he makes s.t. bright
and shiny

wāsēkamatawāpiw ⊲·ᐦᐸᐧᐊᒐ⊲·ᐱᵒ
VAI s/he has flashing eyes

wāsēkamāw ⊲·ᐦᐧᐱᵒ
NI still, clear water bay

wāsēkamin ⊲·ᐦᐧᐧᐱᐤ
VII it is clear water

wāsēkamiw ⊲·ᐦᐧᐧᐱᵒ
VII it is clear water

wāsēnam ⊲·ᐧᐊᵀ
VTI s/he makes light, s/he
lights s.t., s/he puts the lights
on

wāsēnamawēw ⊲·ᐧᐊ⊲ᐧ·ᵒ
VTA s/he puts the lights on
for s.o.; s/he lights (it/him)
for s.o.

wāsēnamawin ⊲·ᐧᐊᐧ⊲·ᐧᵒ
NI window [cf. wāsēnamān,
wāsēnikan; cf.
wāsēnamawēw VTA 2 IMP:
wāsēnamawin! "put the
lights on for me"]

wāsēnamawinis ⊲·ᐧᐊᐧ⊲·ᐧᐤᐣ
NI small window [dim]

wāsēnamān ⊲·ᐧᐊᐧᐱ
NI window [cf.
wāsēnamawin, wāsēnikan]

wāsēnākwan ⊲·ᐧᐱ⊲·ᐧᵒ
VII it dawns; it appears
brighter

wāsēnāpiskāw ⊲·ᐧᐱᐱᐤᐸᐤᵒ
VII it is a bright metal object

wāsēnāsin ⊲·ᐧᐱᐱᐧ
VII there is brightness
showing, it is a little bright
[dim; cf. wāsēyāw]

wāsēnikan ⊲·ᐧᐤᐱᐧ
NI window [cf.
wāsēnamawin, wāsēnamān]

wāsēsiw ⊲·ᐧᐱᵒ
VAI it shines bright (e.g. a
star)

wāsēskwan ⊲·ᐧᐤᐱᵒ
VII it is a clear day, it is
sunny; it is a clear sky; it is
moonlight [see also
nipāyāstēw]

wāsēskwatin ⊲·ᐧᐤᐱᐤ·ᐣᐱ
VII it is smooth ice

wāsētāhkwakāw ⊲·ᐧᐨᐦ"ᐤ·ᐤᵒ
VII it is starlight

wāsēyākamin ⊲·ᐧᐱᐧᐱ
VII it is clear liquid

wāsēyāpan ⊲·ᐧᐱ<ᐣ
VII it is bright dawn

wāsēyāpiskāw ⊲·ᐧᐱᐱᐤᐸᐤᵒ
VII it is bright metal

wāsēyāpiskisow ᐋᐧᓭᔮᐱᐢᑭᓱᐤ
VAI it glows in heat as stone

wāsēyāpiskiswēw ᐋᐧᓭᔮᐱᐢᑭᓱᐤ
VTA s/he heats s.o. to glow as stone

wāsēyāw ᐋᐧᓭᔮᐤ
VII it is a bright sky, it is completely light

wāsinam ᐋᐧᓯᓇᒼ
VTI s/he sees s.t. by the light it gives

wāsipicikēw ᐋᐧᓯᐱᒋᑫᐤ
VAI s/he flashes light signals

wāsipitam ᐋᐧᓯᐱᑕᒼ
VTI s/he shines a light on s.t.

wāsipitēw ᐋᐧᓯᐱᑌᐤ
VTA s/he shines a light on s.o.

wāsitēnam ᐋᐧᓯᑌᓇᒼ
VTI s/he gives light by artificial light

wāsitēnikan ᐋᐧᓯᑌᓂᑲᐣ
NI artificial light

wāsitēpimākan ᐋᐧᓯᑌᐱᒫᑲᐣ
NI wax candle

wāsitēpimākanihkēw ᐋᐧᓯᑌᐱᒫᑲᓂᐦᑫᐤ
NA candle maker

wāsitēw ᐋᐧᓯᑌᐤ
VII it gives light, it shines; it is seen by the light it gives [*also* wāstēw]

wāskahikan ᐋᐧᐢᑲᐦᐃᑲᐣ
NI house, residence [*also* wāskāhikan]

wāskahikanāhtik ᐋᐧᐢᑲᐦᐃᑲᓈᐦᑎᐠ
NA house timber [*pl*: -wak]

wāskahikanihk ᐋᐧᐢᑲᐦᐃᑲᓂᕽ
INM Cumberland House, SK [*loc*; *lit*: "at the house"; *sC community*]

wāskahikanihkamawēw ᐋᐧᐢᑲᐦᐃᑲᓂᐦᑲᒪᐁᐧᐤ
VTA s/he builds a house for s.o.

wāskahikanihkamāsow ᐋᐧᐢᑲᐦᐃᑲᓂᐦᑲᒫᓱᐤ
VAI s/he builds a house for him/herself

wāskahikanihkēw ᐋᐧᐢᑲᐦᐃᑲᓂᐦᑫᐤ
VAI s/he builds houses

wāskahikanis ᐋᐧᐢᑲᐦᐃᑲᓂᐢ
NI little house; cabin [*dim*]

wāskahikaniwiýiniwak ᐋᐧᐢᑲᐦᐃᑲᓂᐃᐧᕀᓂᐊᐧᐠ
NA House People [*pl*; *division of the Cree*]

wāskamisiw ᐋᐧᐢᑲᒥᓯᐤ
VAI s/he is sober; s/he is beginning to recover from illness; s/he settles down; s/he is of quiet disposition [*also* wāskamisiw]

wāskanātisiwin ᐋᐧᐢᑲᓈᑎᓯᐃᐧᐣ
NI temperament

wāskanēyāpiy ᐋᐧᐢᑲᓀᔮᐱᕀ
NI neckyoke strap

wāskā ᐋᐧᐢᑲ
IPC around [*cf.* wāsakā]

wāskāhikan ᐋᐧᐢᑳᐦᐃᑲᐣ
NI screwdriver; pliers

wāskāhkwanēyakwācikan ᐋᐧᐢᑳᐦᒁᓀᔭᒁᒋᑲᐣ
NI upper part of moccasin

wāskāhtēw ᐋᐧᐢᑳᐦᑌᐤ
VAI s/he walks in a circle

wāskākocin ᐋᐧᐢᑳᑯᒋᐣ
VAI s/he flies in a circle

wāskākwāson ᐋᐧᐢᑳᒁᓱᐣ
NI seam at top of moccasin

wāskāmow ᐋᐧᐢᑳᒧᐤ
VAI s/he flees in a circle

wāskānam ᐋᐧᐢᑳᓇᒼ
VTI s/he makes s.t. go around, s/he turns s.t. (*e.g.* treadle), s/he cranks s.t.

wāskāpahtāw ᐋᐧᐢᑳᐸᐦᑖᐤ
VAI s/he runs in a circle

wāskāpayihow ᐋᐧᐢᑳᐸᔨᐦᐅᐤ
VAI s/he throws him/herself in a circle

wāskāpayiw ᐋᐧᐢᑳᐸᔨᐤ
VAI s/he goes in a circle

wāskāpayīs ᐋᐧᐢᑳᐸᔩᐢ
NA wheel

wāskāsam ᐋᐧᐢᑳᓴᒼ
VTI s/he cuts s.t. round the edge, s/he cuts s.t. round

wāskāsimow ᐋᐧᐢᑳᓯᒧᐤ
VAI s/he dances in a circle

wāskāsimowin ᐋᐧᐢᑳᓯᒧᐃᐧᐣ
NI Round Dance

wāskāskawēw ᐋᐧᐢᑳᐢᑲᐁᐧᐤ
VTA s/he goes round s.o. (*e.g.* moose, deer)

wāskāwēpiskam ᐋᐧᐢᑳᐁᐧᐱᐢᑲᒼ
VTI s/he pushes s.t. round by foot

wāskitoy ᐋᐧᐢᑭᑐᕀ
NI flank

wāsostikwānēhpisow ᐋᐧᓱᐢᑎᒁᓀᐦᐱᓱᐤ
VAI s/he wraps a handkerchief on his/her own head

wāsostikwānēhpisowin ᐋᐧᓱᐢᑎᒁᓀᐦᐱᓱᐃᐧᐣ
NI kerchief

wāspison ᐋᐧᐢᐱᓱᐣ
NA moss bag (*i.e.* for a baby); swaddling bag

wāspisonihkawēw ᐋᐧᐢᐱᓱᓂᐦᑲᐁᐧᐤ
VTA s/he makes a moss bag for s.o.

wāspisonihkēw ᐋᐧᐢᐱᓱᓂᐦᑫᐤ
VAI s/he makes a moss bag

wāspisow ᐋᐧᐢᐱᓱᐤ
VAI s/he is laced in a moss bag; s/he is in the swaddling bag

wāspitam ᐋᐧᐢᐱᑕᒼ
VTI s/he laces s.t.

wāspitaham ᐋᐧᐢᐱᑕᐦᐊᒼ
VTI s/he laces s.t.

wāspitēw ᐋᐧᐢᐱᑌᐤ
VTA s/he laces s.o. in a moss bag; s/he puts s.o. in the swaddling bag

wāstahamawēw ᐋᐧᐢᑕᐦᐊᒪᐁᐧᐤ
VTA s/he waves at s.o.; s/he waves (it/him) at s.o.

wāstahamākēw ᐋᐧᐢᑕᐦᐊᒫᑫᐤ
VAI s/he gives signals

wāstahēw ᐋᐧᐢᑕᐦᐁᐤ
VTA s/he waves at s.o.

wāstahikēw ᐋᐧᐢᑕᐦᐃᑫᐤ
VAI s/he waves (with the hand)

wāstēnam ᐋᐧᐢᑌᓇᒼ
VTI s/he lights s.t., s/he turns on the light

wāstēpayiw ᐋᐧᐢᑌᐸᔨᐤ
VII it flashes lightning

wāstēyāpiw ᐋᐧᐢᑌᔮᐱᐤ
VAI s/he has one eye white; s/he has a sty

wāstinamawēw ᐋᐧᐢᑎᓇᒪᐁᐧᐤ
VTA s/he waves to s.o., s/he gestures to s.o.

wāstinikēw ᐋᐧᐢᑎᓂᑫᐤ
VAI s/he waves

wāti ᐋᐧᑎ
NI hole, den, cave; ditch [*pl*: wāta]

wātihkān ᐋᐧᑎᐦᑳᐣ
NI hole, cellar, pit, trench

wātihkātam ᐋᐧᑎᐦᑳᑕᒼ
VTI s/he digs a hole for s.t.

wātihkēw ᐋᐧᑎᐦᑫᐤ
VAI s/he digs, s/he digs holes; s/he makes a cellar [*also* wātihkēw]

wātihkēwin ᐋᐧᑎᐦᑫᐃᐧᐣ
NI excavation

wātihkwān ᐋᐧᑎᐦᒁᐣ
NI dugout cellar, pit, grave [*cf.* wātihkān]

wāwāc ᐋᐧᐋᐧᐨ
IPC even, even more, even now, on top of it all, especially

wāwāhkānikana ᐋᐧᐋᐧᐦᑳᓂᑲᓇ
NI crushed egg shell [*pl generally*]

wāwāhtēwa ᐋᐧᐋᐧᐦᑌᐊᐧ
INM Northern Lights, aurora borealis [*wC*; *see also* kā-nimihitocik]

wāwākamow ᐋᐧᐋᐧᑲᒧᐤ
VII it is winding (as a river or road)

wāwāhkan ᐋᐧᐋᐧᐦᑲᐣ
NI egg shell [*pl generally*]

wāwākaskosiy ᐋᐧᐋᐧᑲᐢᑯᓯᕀ
NI crooked bush or grass

wāwākāskwatan ᐋᐧᐋᐧᑳᐢᒁᑕᐣ
VII it is a crooked stick

wāwākikātēw ᐋᐧᐋᐧᑭᑳᑌᐤ
VAI s/he is bow-legged [*rdpl*]

wāwākohtēw ⊲·⊲·ᒃᗑᐤ
  VAI s/he walks turning this
  way and that
wāwāsakāpihāw ⊲·⊲·ᓴᑲᐲᐦᐋᐤ
  VAI s/he flies in circles, it
  circles overhead
wāwāsaskotēpayin
  ⊲·⊲ᓴᐢᑯᑌᐸᔨᐣ
  VII it is lightning [*rdpl*]
wāwāsaskotēpayiw
  ⊲·⊲ᓴᐢᑯᑌᐸᔨᐤ
  VII it is lightning [*rdpl*]
wāwāsēkamatawāpiw
  ⊲·⊲·ᓭᑲᒪᑕᐘᐲᐤ
  VAI s/he has flashing eyes
wāwāskēsiw ⊲·⊲·ᐢᑫᓯᐤ
  NA elk, wapiti; deer, red
  deer
wāwāskēsiw-sīpiy
  ⊲·⊲·ᐢᑫᓯᐤ ᓰᐱᕀ
  NI Red Deer River, South
  Saskatchewan River
wāwāskēsiwi-pīwayēw
  ⊲·⊲·ᐢᑫᓯᐏᐲᐘᔦᐤ
  NA horse with a coat like an
  elk
wāwāskēsiwayān ⊲·⊲·ᐢᑫᓯᐘᔮᐣ
  NA elk skin
wāwāskēsiwēkin ⊲·⊲·ᐢᑫᓯᐍᑭᐣ
  NA elk hide [*pl*: -wak]
wāwāskēsiwistikwān
  ⊲·⊲·ᐢᑫᓯᐏᐢᑎᒁᐣ
  NI elk head
wāwāskēsiwiw ⊲·⊲·ᐢᑫᓯᐏᐤ
  VAI s/he is an elk
wāwāskīsiw ⊲·⊲·ᐢᑮᓯᐤ
  NI Waskesiu, SK [*wC*; *cf.*
  wāwāskēsiw *NA*]
wāwāstahamawēw
  ⊲·⊲·ᐢᑕᐦᐊᒪᐍᐤ
  VTA s/he makes signals to
  s.o.
wāwāstahikēw ⊲·⊲·ᐢᑕᐦᐃᑫᐤ
  VAI s/he makes hand
  signals, s/he waves
wāwāstēpayiw ⊲·⊲·ᐢᑌᐸᔨᐤ
  VII it is lightning
wāwi ⊲·ᐄ
  NI egg [*pl*: wāwa]
wāwi-pahkwēsikan
  ⊲·ᐄ· ᐸᐦᑫᓯᑲᐣ
  NA cake; noodle dough [*see
  also* wīhki-pahkwēsikan,
  wīhkihkasōs]
wāwis ⊲·ᐄᐢ
  NI small egg [*dim*]
wāwiyak ⊲·ᐄᔭᐠ
  IPC well! [*exclamation of
  surprise*]
wāwiyakihkotam ⊲·ᐃ·ᔭᑭᐦᑯᑕᒼ
  VTI s/he whittles s.t. round
wāwiyatayēw ⊲·ᐃ·ᔭᑕᔦᐤ
  VAI s/he has a round belly
wāwiyē- ⊲·ᐃ·ᔦ
  IPV round, spherical
wāwiyē-pīsim ⊲·ᐃ·ᔦ ᐲᓯᒼ
  NA full moon, round moon
  [*pl*: -wak]

wāwiyēkamāw ⊲·ᐃ·ᔦᑲᒫᐤ
  VII it is a round lake, it is a
  round body of water
wāwiyēkwātam ⊲·ᐃ·ᔦᒁᑕᒼ
  VTI s/he sews s.t. into a
  circle
wāwiyēkwātēw ⊲·ᐃ·ᔦᒁᑌᐤ
  VTA s/he sews s.o. into a
  circle
wāwiyēnam ⊲·ᐃ·ᔦᓇᒼ
  VTI s/he forms (s.t. into) a
  ball (by hand); s/he bends s.t.
wāwiyēnākosiw ⊲·ᐃ·ᔦᓈᑯᓯᐤ
  VAI s/he looks round,
  circular
wāwiyēnākwan ⊲·ᐃ·ᔦᓈᑿᐣ
  VII it looks round, circular
wāwiyēnēw ⊲·ᐃ·ᔦᓀᐤ
  VTA s/he rolls s.o. (*e.g.*
  snow) into a ball
wāwiyēpēyāw ⊲·ᐃ·ᔦᐯᔮᐤ
  VII it is a round body of
  water (*e.g.* pond)
wāwiyēsihēw ⊲·ᐃ·ᔦᓯᐦᐁᐤ
  VTA s/he makes s.o. round
wāwiyēsiw ⊲·ᐃ·ᔦᓯᐤ
  VAI s/he is round, it is
  circular; it is full (*i.e.* moon)
wāwiyēsiwi-pīsim
  ⊲·ᐃ·ᔦᓯᐏ· ᐱᕀᐨ
  NA full moon [*pl*: -wak]
wāwiyēstēw ⊲·ᐃ·ᔦᐢᑌᐤ
  VII it is in a circle; it is
  placed around
wāwiyētākanāhtik
  ⊲·ᐃ·ᔦᑖᑲᓈᐦᑎᐠ
  NI barrel stave [*pl*: -wa]
wāwiyēyāpisk ⊲·ᐃ·ᔦᔮᐱᐢᐠ
  NA metal circle [*pl*: -wak]
wāwiyēyāsin ⊲·ᐃ·ᔦᔮᓯᐣ
  VII it is a little round object
  [*dim*]
wāwiyēyāw ⊲·ᐃ·ᔦᔮᐤ
  VII it is round, it is circular
wāwīs ⊲·ᐄ·ᐢ
  IPC especially; all the more
  so, better so
wāwīs ci ⊲·ᐄ·ᐢ ᒋ
  IPC especially, all the more
  so; especially if, when
wāýahcāw ⊲·ᕀᐦᒑᐤ
  NI dip, hollow (in the land);
  valley
wāýahcāw ⊲·ᕀᐦᒑᐤ
  VII it is a depression in the
  land, it is a valley
wāýatināw ⊲·ᕀᓇᐋᐤ
  VII it is an area with valleys
wāýāw ⊲·ᕀᐋᐤ
  VII it is concave, it is
  hollowed
wāýicihcēw ⊲·ᕀᒋᐦᒉᐤ
  NI palm of the hand
wāyināmow ⊲·ᐩᓈᒧᐤ
  VAI s/he flees back, s/he
  turns back in flight
wāyinīstawēw ⊲·ᐩᓃᐢᑕᐍᐤ
  VTA s/he comes back to s.o.

wāyinīw ⊲·ᐩᓃᐤ
  VAI s/he turns back, s/he
  goes back, s/he retreats [*also*
  wāwonīw]
wāyino ⊲·ᐩᓅ
  IPC turning back, action in
  returning
wāyinohtahēw ⊲·ᐩᓄᐦᑕᐦᐁᐤ
  VTA s/he goes back with
  s.o., s/he takes s.o. back
wāyinokotēw ⊲·ᐩᓄᑯᑌᐤ
  VII it flies back, it comes
  back (*e.g.* boomerang)
wāyinopahtāw ⊲·ᐩᓄᐸᐦᑖᐤ
  VAI s/he runs back
wāyinopēhikan ⊲·ᐩᓄᐯᐦᐃᑲᐣ
  NI heart (at cards) [*also*
  wāwinipēhikan]
wāyinopitam ⊲·ᐩᓄᐱᑕᒼ
  VTI s/he pulls s.t. back
wāyinopitēw ⊲·ᐩᓄᐱᑌᐤ
  VTA s/he pulls s.o. back
wāyipēhipān ⊲·ᐩᐯᐦᐃᐹᐣ
  NI hollow ground with
  water to use
wāyisitān ⊲·ᐩᓯᑖᐣ
  NI arch of foot
wāyisitēhikan ⊲·ᐩᓯᑌᐦᐃᑲᐣ
  NI horseshoe

ᐁ·

wēcīpwayān ᐁ·ᒌᐿᔮᐣ
  NA a Chipewyan, Dene
  Indian [*cf.* cipwayān,
  wēcīpwayāniw]
wēcīpwayāniw ᐁ·ᒌᐿᔮᓂᐤ
  NA a Chipewyan, Dene
  Indian [*cf.* cipwayān,
  wēcīpwayān]
wēhcasin ᐁᐦᒐᓯᐣ
  VII it is easy, it is simple; it
  is cheap in price [*also*
  wēhtasin]
wēhci- ᐁᐦᒋ
  IPV easily
wēhcihēw ᐁᐦᒋᐦᐁᐤ
  VTA s/he gets s.o. easily;
  s/he has an easy time with
  s.o. (*e.g.* hide)
wēhcihow ᐁᐦᒋᐦᐅᐤ
  VAI s/he gets him/herself in
  accessible position
wēhcinēham ᐁᐦᒋᓀᐦᐊᒼ
  VTI s/he buys s.t. cheap
wēhcinēhwēw ᐁᐦᒋᓀᐦᐍᐤ
  VTA s/he buys s.o. (*e.g.* a
  horse) cheap
wēhcisiw ᐁᐦᒋᓯᐤ
  VAI it is easy, it is cheap
wēhciskowipayiw
  ᐁᐦᒋᐢᑯᐏᐸᔨᐤ
  VII it comes easily
wēhtakihtam ᐁᐦᑕᑭᐦᑕᒼ
  VTI s/he prices s.t. cheap
wēhtakihtēw ᐁᐦᑕᑭᐦᑌᐤ
  VII it is cheap, it is
  inexpensive

wēhtakimēw ᐍᐦᑕᑭᒣᐤ
VTA s/he prices s.o. cheap
wēhtakisow ᐍᐦᑕᑭᓱᐤ
VAI it is cheap, it is inexpensive
wēhtan ᐍᐦᑕᐣ
VII it is easy; it is inexpensive
wēhtatāwākēw ᐍᐦᑕᑖᐚᑫᐤ
VAI s/he sells things cheap
wēhtatāwēw ᐍᐦᑕᑖᐍᐤ
VAI s/he buys things cheap
wēhtēyihtam ᐍᐦᑌᔨᐦᑕᒼ
VTI s/he thinks s.t. easy to deal with
wēhtēyimēw ᐍᐦᑌᔨᒣᐤ
VTA s/he thinks s.o. easy to deal with
wēhtinahk ᐍᐦᑎᓇᕽ
IPC easily, leisurely, quietly, in peace
wēhwēw ᐍᐦᐍᐤ
NA wavey-duck, snow goose
wēmistikōsiskwēw ᐍᒥᐢᑎᑰᓯᐢᑵᐤ
NA Frenchwoman
wēmistikōsiw ᐍᒥᐢᑎᑰᓯᐤ
NA Frenchman, French Canadian, white man
wēmistikōsīmototawēw ᐍᒥᐢᑎᑰᓰᒧᑐᑕᐍᐤ
VTA s/he speaks French to s.o.
wēmistikōsīmow ᐍᒥᐢᑎᑰᓰᒧᐤ
VAI s/he speaks French
wēmistikōsīmowin ᐍᒥᐢᑎᑰᓰᒧᐏᐣ
NI French language
wēmistikōsīnāhk ᐍᒥᐢᑎᑰᓰᓈᕽ
INM France [*loc*]
wēpaham ᐍᐸᐦᐊᒼ
VTI s/he sweeps s.t. away
wēpahaskwamēw ᐍᐸᐦᐊᐢᑿᒣᐤ
VAI s/he clears ice from the water hole
wēpahākonēw ᐍᐸᐦᐋᑯᓀᐤ
VAI s/he clears away the snow
wēpahikan ᐍᐸᐦᐃᑲᐣ
NI broom
wēpahikēw ᐍᐸᐦᐃᑫᐤ
VAI s/he sweeps, s/he sweeps things, s/he does the sweeping
wēpahwēw ᐍᐸᐦᐍᐤ
VTA s/he flings s.o. by tool; s/he sweeps s.o., s/he sweeps s.o. up
wēpasinaham ᐍᐸᓯᓇᐦᐊᒼ
VTI s/he cancels a debt (which was written down on paper); s/he erases s.t, s/he clears the chalkboard
wēpasinahikēw ᐍᐸᓯᓇᐦᐃᑫᐤ
VAI s/he cancels debts; s/he erases things, s/he clears the chalkboard

wēpāhokow ᐍᐹᐦᐅᑯᐤ
VAI s/he is carried off by current
wēpāhotēw ᐍᐹᐦᐅᑌᐤ
VII it is carried off by current
wēpāhtakahikan ᐍᐹᐦᑕᑲᐦᐃᑲᐣ
NI broom
wēpāhtakahikēw ᐍᐹᐦᑕᑲᐦᐃᑫᐤ
VAI s/he sweeps
wēpāpīhkēpayiw ᐍᐹᐲᐦᑫᐸᔨᐤ
VAI s/he swings
wēpāpīhkēwēpinam ᐍᐹᐲᐦᑫᐍᐱᓇᒼ
VTI s/he sets s.t. swinging
wēpāpīhkēwēpinēw ᐍᐹᐲᐦᑫᐍᐱᓀᐤ
VTA s/he sets s.o. swinging
wēpāsiw ᐍᐹᓯᐤ
VAI s/he is blown away; it waves in the wind (*e.g.* a flag)
wēpāstan ᐍᐹᐢᑕᐣ
VII it is blown away; it waves in the wind
wēpāyowēw ᐍᐹᔪᐍᐤ
VAI it waves its own tail
wēpāyōs ᐍᐹᔫᐢ
NA deer [*cf.* wāpāyōs]
wēpihēw ᐍᐱᐦᐁᐤ
VTA s/he starts s.o.
wēpimēw ᐍᐱᒣᐤ
VTA s/he urges s.o.
wēpinam ᐍᐱᓇᒼ
VTI s/he throws s.t. away
wēpinamawēw ᐍᐱᓇᒪᐍᐤ
VTA s/he throws (it/him) away for s.o.
wēpinamātowak ᐍᐱᓇᒫᑐᐘᐠ
VAI they throw (it) to or for one another; they play catch
wēpinamātowin ᐍᐱᓇᒫᑐᐏᐣ
NI a game of throwing a ball back and forth
wēpinākan ᐍᐱᓈᑲᐣ
NA former partner, ex; one who is not cared for
wēpināsow ᐍᐱᓈᓱᐤ
VAI s/he gives cloth offerings (to the spirits)
wēpināson ᐍᐱᓈᓱᐣ
NA ceremonial cloth, cloth offering
wēpināsowin ᐍᐱᓈᓱᐏᐣ
NI offerings (to the spirits)
wēpināwasow ᐍᐱᓈᐘᓱᐤ
VAI s/he disowns his/her own children; s/he leaves his/her own children and does not care
wēpinēw ᐍᐱᓀᐤ
VTA s/he throws s.o. away, s/he throws s.o. aside; s/he leaves s.o., s/he abandons s.o., s/he divorces s.o.
wēpinikan ᐍᐱᓂᑲᐣ
NI garbage; something not cared for

wēpinikāsow ᐍᐱᓂᑳᓱᐤ
VAI s/he is left and uncared for
wēpinikātēw ᐍᐱᓂᑳᑌᐤ
VII it is thrown away
wēpinikēw ᐍᐱᓂᑫᐤ
VAI s/he throws things away
wēpiniskātēw ᐍᐱᓂᐢᑳᑌᐤ
VTA s/he slings his/her own fist at s.o.
wēpinitowak ᐍᐱᓂᑐᐘᐠ
VAI they abandon one another
wēpiskawēw ᐍᐱᐢᑲᐍᐤ
VTA s/he pushes s.o. aside
wēsā ᐍᓵ
IPC excessively; even
wēsāmihk ᐍᓵᒥᕽ
IPC excessively, even
wēskac ᐍᐢᑲᐨ
IPC formerly [*cf.* oskac; *also* wiskāc]
wēskacēs ᐍᐢᑲᒉᐢ
IPC a little while ago
wēskwāhtēmihk ᐍᐢᒁᐦᑌᒥᕽ
IPC opposite the door
wēwēkahpicikan ᐍᐍᑲᐦᐱᒋᑲᐣ
NI binder, bandage
wēwēkahpisow ᐍᐍᑲᐦᐱᓱᐤ
VAI s/he is wrapped or tied round
wēwēkahpitam ᐍᐍᑲᐦᐱᑕᒼ
VTI s/he wraps and ties s.t.
wēwēkahpitēw ᐍᐍᑲᐦᐱᑌᐤ
VTA s/he wraps s.o., s/he wraps and ties s.o. (*e.g.* yarn)
wēwēkapiw ᐍᐍᑲᐱᐤ
VAI s/he is wrapped up sitting, s/he sits wrapped up, s/he sits bundled up
wēwēkastāw ᐍᐍᑲᐢᑖᐤ
VAIt s/he places s.t. wrapped
wēwēkāciwasam ᐍᐍᑳᒋᐘᓴᒼ
VTI s/he wraps s.t. for boiling; s/he rolls s.t. for boiling
wēwēkāciwaswēw ᐍᐍᑳᒋᐘᓷᐤ
VTA s/he rolls s.o. for boiling (as a pudding)
wēwēkinam ᐍᐍᑭᓇᒼ
VTI s/he wraps s.t. up
wēwēkinēw ᐍᐍᑭᓀᐤ
VTA s/he wraps s.o.; s/he wears s.o.
wēwēkinikan ᐍᐍᑭᓂᑲᐣ
NI wrapper, cover; wrapping paper or cloth
wēwēkinikātēw ᐍᐍᑭᓂᑳᑌᐤ
VII it is wrapped
wēwēkinikēw ᐍᐍᑭᓂᑫᐤ
VAI s/he wraps, s/he is wrapping, s/he wraps parcels
wēwēkipayihtāw ᐍᐍᑭᐸᔨᐦᑖᐤ
VAIt s/he wraps s.t. quickly
wēwēkiscikwānēhpisonis ᐍᐍᑭᐢᒋᒁᓀᐦᐱᓱᓂᐢ
NA little head scarf [*dim*]

wēwēkisimēw ▽·▽·ᑭᒋᔾ°
VTA s/he wraps s.o. as that one lies

wēwēkisin ▽·▽·ᑭᔾᐣ
VAI s/he lies wrapped, s/he is wrapped while lying; s/he is wrapped up in s.t., s/he is rolled in a blanket

wēwēkistikwānēnēw ▽·▽·ᑭᐣᑎ�billᓇᓂᓄ°
VTA s/he wraps s.o.'s head for that one

wēwēkistikwānēw ▽·▽·ᑭᐣᑎᗷᓄ°
VAI s/he has his/her own head wrapped

wēwēkistikwānēyapiw ▽·▽·ᑭᐣᑎᗷᓄᔾᐊᐱ°
VAI s/he sits with head wrapped

wēwēkiw ▽·▽·ᑭᐤ°
VAI s/he wraps him/herself (in a blanket)

wēwēpāscikan ▽·▽·ᐸᐧᔅᒋᑲᐣ
NA flag

wēwēpāsiw ▽·▽·ᐸᔾ°
VAI it flutters in the wind

wēwēpāstan ▽·▽·ᐸᐧᔅᒋᐣ
VII it rocks or flutters in the wind

wēwēpāyowēw ▽·▽·ᐸᔾᐅᐧ▽·°
VAI it wags his/her own tail; it is a white-tailed deer

wēwēpikātēw ▽·▽·ᐱᑲᑌ°
VAI s/he swings his/her own legs; s/he has wobbly legs

wēwēpiskwēýiw ▽·▽·ᐱᔅᑫᔾᐊᐧ°
VAI s/he nods his/her own head from side to side

wēwēpison ▽·▽·ᐱᓱᐣ
NI swing; cradle

wēwēpisow ▽·▽·ᐱᓱ°
VAI s/he swings, s/he rocks

wēwēpisowākan ▽·▽·ᐱᓱᐊᐧᑲᐣ
NI rocking chair

wēwēpisowin ▽·▽·ᐱᓱᐃᐧᐣ
NI swing

wēwēpitam ▽·▽·ᐱᑕᒼᐨ
VTI s/he swings s.t.

wēwēpitēw ▽·▽·ᐱᑌ°
VTA s/he swings s.o., s/he rocks s.o. (*e.g.* in a rocker)

wēýocihow ▽·ᔾᒋᐦᐅ°
VAI s/he is well off

wēýotan ▽·ᔖᑕᐣ
VII it is rich, it is in abundant supply; it is a wealthy time

wēýotisiw ▽·ᔖᓂᓯ°
VAI s/he is rich [*also* wēýōcisiw]

wēýōtisiwin ▽·ᔖᓂᓯᐊᐧᐣ
NI wealth

wēýōtisīmakan ▽·ᔖᓂᓯᒪᑲᐣ
VII it is rich

▵·

wiwiwacis ▵·▵·ᐊᐧᒋᐢ
NA medicine bag [*dim*]

wiýa ▵·ᔞ
IPC this, that; as for, by contrast [*emphasizes preceding word*]

wiýa ▵·ᔞ
IPC for, because [*clause-initial causal conjunction*]

wiýa ▵·ᔞ
PR he, she, it; him, her, it; his, hers, its [*third person sg*; *wC*: witha; *sC*: wiña]

wiýa āta wiýa ▵·ᔞ ᐊᐨ ▵·ᔞ
IPH but of course

wiyahkwātam ▵·ᔞᐦᑳᐧᑕᒼᐨ
VTI s/he swears at s.t.

wiyahkwātēw ▵·ᔞᐦᑳᐧᑌ°
VTA s/he swears at s.o.

wiyahkwēsk ▵·ᔞᐦᑴᐢᐠ
NA one who swears [*hab*]

wiyahkwēskiw ▵·ᔞᐦᑴᐢᑭᐤ°
VAI s/he swears all the time [*hab*]

wiyahkwēw ▵·ᔞᐦᑴ°
VAI s/he swears

wiyahkwēwin ▵·ᔞᐦᑴᐃᐧᐣ
NI swearing, foul language; blasphemous language

wiyahkwīwinihk ▵·ᔞᐦᑮᐧᐃᐧᓂᕽ
INM Weyakwin, SK [*loc*; *lit*: "at the swearing place"; *wC* community; *cf.* wiyahkwēwin *NI*]

wiýahpicikēw ▵·ᔞᐦᐱᒋᑫ°
VAI s/he harnesses horses, s/he does the harnessing [*cf.* oýahpicikēw]

wiýahpisow ▵·ᔞᐦᐱᓱ°
VAI it is harnessed, saddled [*cf.* oýahpisow]

wiýahpitam ▵·ᔞᐦᐱᑕᒼᐨ
VTI s/he hitches s.t. up, s/he ties s.t. in place [*cf.* oýahpitam]

wiýahpitamawēw ▵·ᔞᐦᐱᑕᒪᐃᐧ▽·°
VTA s/he ties (it/him) for s.o., s/he saddles s.o.'s horse [*cf.* oýahpitamawēw]

wiýahpitastimwēw ▵·ᔞᐦᐱᑕᐢᑎᒼᐁ°
VAI s/he harnesses the horses, s/he hitches up his/her own horses [*cf.* oýahpitastimwēw]

wiýahpitēw ▵·ᔞᐦᐱᑌ°
VTA s/he harnesses s.o., s/he hitches s.o. up; s/he ties s.o. in place [*cf.* oýahpitēw]

wiyakāc ▵·ᔞᑳᐨ
IPC that's too bad, it's regrettable, sad loss [*exclamation*; *also* wiyakac]

---

wiýakāhpinatēw ▵·ᔞᑳᐦᐱᓇᑌ°
VTA s/he makes a sad loss of s.o.; s/he does s.o. wrong

wiýakāhpinēw ▵·ᔞᑳᐦᐱᓄ°
VAI s/he dies as a sad loss

wiýakihēw ▵·ᔞᑭᐦᐁ°
VTA s/he makes a sad loss of s.o.; s/he ruins s.o., s/he damages s.o. (*e.g.* beaver pelt)

wiýakihow ▵·ᔞᑭᐦᐅ°
VAI s/he spoils his/her own chances

wiýakihtam ▵·ᔞᑭᐦᑕᒼᐨ
VTI s/he counts s.t.; s/he puts a price on s.t.

wiýakihtamawēw ▵·ᔞᑭᐦᑕᒪᐃᐧCL▽·°
VTA s/he puts a price on (it/him) for s.o.

wiýakihtāw ▵·ᔞᑭᐦᑖ°
VAIt s/he botches s.t.; s/he ruins s.t., s/he wastes s.t.; s/he puts a poor price on s.t.

wiyakisiw ▵·ᔞᑭᓯ°
VAI s/he neglects his/her own work

wiyanihcikāsow ▵·ᔞᓂᐦᒋᑳᓱ°
VAI it is skinned and cut up

wiyanihēw ▵·ᔞᓂᐦᐁ°
VTA s/he skins and cuts s.o. up

wiyanihtākan ▵·ᔞᓂᐦᑖᑲᐣ
NI place where game has been cleaned

wiyanihtākēw ▵·ᔞᓂᐦᑖᑫ°
VAI s/he skins and cuts up the game

wiýascikēw ▵·ᔞᐢᒋᑫ°
VAI s/he sets the table [*cf.* oýascikēw]

wiyasinākosiw ▵·ᔞᓯᓈᑯᓯ°
VAI s/he looks funny [*cf.* wawiyasinākosiw]

wiyasinākwan ▵·ᔞᓯᓈᑲᐧᐣ
VII it looks funny [*cf.* wawiyasinākwan]

wiýasiwātam ▵·ᔞᓯᐊᐧᑕᒼᐨ
VTI s/he makes a law, s/he rules about s.t., s/he decides s.t. [*cf.* oýasiwātam]

wiýasiwātēw ▵·ᔞᓯᐊᐧᑌ°
VTA s/he decides about s.o.; s/he sits in judgment on s.o., s/he holds court over s.o. [*cf.* oýasiwātēw]

wiýasiwēhkān ▵·ᔞᓯᐁᐧᐦᑳᐣ
NA band councillor [*wC*: othasiwīhkān]

wiýasiwēhkāniwiw ▵·ᔞᓯᐁᐧᐦᑳᓂᐃᐧ°
VAI s/he is a band councillor [*wC*: othasiwīhkāniwiw]

wiýasiwēw ▵·ᔞᓯᐁᐧ°
VAI s/he makes laws; s/he judges [*cf.* oýasiwēw]

wiýasiwēwikamik ▵·ᔞᓯᐁᐧᐃᐧᑲᒥᐠ
NI courthouse [*pl*: -wa; *wC*: othasiwīwikamik]

wiýasiwēwin ᐃ·ᔭᓯᐁ·ᐃ·ᐣ
NI office; law, rule [*wC*: othasiwīwin]

wiýaskoc ᐃ·ᔭᐢᑯᐨ
IPC that one's turn, his/her turn

wiýastamawēw ᐃ·ᔭᐢᑕᒪᐁ·ᐤ
VTA s/he sets the table for s.o.; s/he sets (it/him) in order for s.o. [*cf.* oýastamawēw]

wiyataham ᐃ·ᔭᑕᐦᐊᒼ
VTI s/he shapes s.t. (by tool) [*cf.* oýataham]

wiyatahwēw ᐃ·ᔭᑕᐦᐁ·ᐤ
VTA s/he shapes s.o. (by tool) [*cf.* oýatahwēw]

wiyatēýihtam ᐃ·ᔭᑌᔨᐦᑕᒼ
VTI s/he is amused by s.t., s/he considers s.t. amusing [*cf.* wawiyatēýihtam]

wiyatēýihtākosiw ᐃ·ᔭᑌᔨᐦᑖᑯᓯᐤ
VAI s/he is funny [*cf.* wawiyatēýihtākosiw]

wiyatēýihtākwan ᐃ·ᔭᑌᔨᐦᑖᑲ·ᐣ
VII it is funny [*cf.* wawiyatēýihtākwan]

wiyaw ᐃ·ᔭᐤ
NDI body; his/her body [*cf.* miyaw]

wiýawāw ᐃ·ᔭᐋ·ᐤ
IPC by contrast

wiýawāw ᐃ·ᔭᐋ·ᐤ
PR they, them, theirs [*third person pl*; *wC*: wīthawāw; *sC*: wīnawāw]

wiyawihtam ᐃ·ᔭᐃ·ᐦᑕᒼ
VTI s/he hears s.t. plainly

wiýā wīpac cī wiýa ᐃ·ᔮ ᐄ·ᐸᐨ ᒌ ᐃ·ᔭ
IPH it is a rare and welcome event that [*followed by changed conjunct verb form*]

wiyāhcikana ᐃ·ᔮᐦᒋᑲᓇ
NI clothes [*pl generally*]

wiyāhtam ᐃ·ᔮᐦᑕᒼ
VTI s/he wears s.t. [*cf.* wiyāhtāw; *see also* kikiskam]

wiyāhtāw ᐃ·ᔮᐦᑖᐤ
VAIt s/he wears s.t. [*cf.* wiyāhtam; *see also* kikiskam]

wiýākan ᐃ·ᔮᑲᐣ
NI dish, bowl, vessel [*cf.* oýākan]

wiýākanikamik ᐃ·ᔮᑲᓂᑲᒥᐠ
NI cupboard [*pl*: -wa]

wiýākanis ᐃ·ᔮᑲᓂᐢ
NI small dish, small bowl, small vessel [*dim*; *cf.* oýākanis]

wiyākihkākamisam ᐃ·ᔮᑭᐦᑳᑲᒥᓴᒼ
VTI s/he warms s.t. as liquid in a dish

wiyāmēw ᐃ·ᔮᒣᐤ
VTA s/he wears s.o. (*e.g.* pants) [*see also* kikiskawēw]

wiyānam ᐃ·ᔮᓇᒼ
VTI s/he scatters s.t. around; s/he misplaces s.t.

wiyānikēw ᐃ·ᔮᓂᑫᐤ
VAI s/he misplaces things, s/he scatters things about

wiyāpitam ᐃ·ᔮᐱᑕᒼ
VTI s/he scatters and mixes s.t.

wiyāpitēw ᐃ·ᔮᐱᑌᐤ
VTA s/he tangles s.o. (*e.g.* yarn)

wiyās ᐃ·ᔮᐢ
NI meat

wiyāsihkān ᐃ·ᔮᓯᐦᑳᐣ
NI processed meat (*e.g.* spam)

wiyāsikamik ᐃ·ᔮᓯᑲᒥᐠ
NI butcher shop [*pl*: -wa]

wiyāsimiw ᐃ·ᔮᓯᒥᐤ
VAI s/he has meat

wiyāsis ᐃ·ᔮᓯᐢ
NI bit of meat, piece of meat [*dim*]

wiyāsisāpoy ᐃ·ᔮᓯᓵᐳᐩ
NI meat broth

wiyāsiwan ᐃ·ᔮᓯᐊ·ᐣ
VII it has a lot of meat on it

wiyāsiwiw ᐃ·ᔮᓯᐃ·ᐤ
VAI it is meaty; it has a lot of meat on it

wiyāsiýiniw ᐃ·ᔮᓯᔨᓂᐤ
NA butcher

wiýāta ᐃ·ᔮᑕ
IPC nonetheless [*from* wiýa āta; *cf.* āta wiýa]

wiyātikosiw ᐃ·ᔮᑎᑯᓯᐤ
VAI s/he is happy

wiyāyēpac ᐃ·ᔮᔦᐸᐨ
IPC gladly, gratefully

wiýihkaham ᐃ·ᔨᐦᑲᐦᐊᒼ
VTI s/he drains s.t. by taking water out

wiýihkotam ᐃ·ᔨᐦᑯᑕᒼ
VTI s/he whittles s.t., s/he carves s.t. [*also* wīhkotam]

wiýihkotamawēw ᐃ·ᔨᐦᑯᑕᒪᐁ·ᐤ
VTA s/he whittles (it/him) for s.o. [*also* wīhkotamawēw]

wiýihkotēw ᐃ·ᔨᐦᑯᑌᐤ
VTA s/he whittles or carves s.o. out of wood [*also* wīhkotēw]

wiýihkwak ᐃ·ᔨᐦᑲ·ᐠ
NA glands [*pl generally*; *perhaps NDA* -iýihkw-]

wiýin ᐃ·ᔨᐣ
NI fat, animal fat, piece of unprocessed fat; fat meat [*pl*: -wa]

wiýinohēw ᐃ·ᔨᓄᐦᐁᐤ
VTA s/he makes s.o. fat, s/he fattens s.o.

wiýinosiw ᐃ·ᔨᓄᓯᐤ
VAI s/he is a bit fat [*dim*]

wiýinow ᐃ·ᔨᓄᐤ
VAI s/he is fat

wiýinowan ᐃ·ᔨᓄᐊ·ᐣ
VII it is fatty, there is much fat on it (as a whole carcass)

wiýinowiw ᐃ·ᔨᓄᐃ·ᐤ
VII it is fat, it is fatty

wiýinwāpisk ᐃ·ᔨᓈ·ᐱᐢᐠ
NI a certain kind of stone which feels oily (*e.g.* mica) [*pl*: -wa]

wiýipātan ᐃ·ᔨᐹᑕᐣ
VII it is dirty [*cf.* wīpātan; wīpāw]

wiýipātisiw ᐃ·ᔨᐹᑎᓯᐤ
VAI s/he is dirty [*cf.* wīpātisiw]

wiýipāw ᐃ·ᔨᐹᐤ
VII it is soiled, it is dirty [*cf.* wiýipātan, wīpāw]

wiýisam ᐃ·ᔨᓴᒼ
VTI s/he cuts s.t. out, s/he cuts s.t. to a pattern [*also* wīsam]

wiýisamawēw ᐃ·ᔨᓴᒪᐁ·ᐤ
VTA s/he cuts a pattern for s.o.

wiýisamāsow ᐃ·ᔨᓴᒫᓱᐤ
VAI s/he cuts a pattern for him/herself, s/he cuts his/her own pattern

wiýīpi- ᐃ·ᔩᐱ
IPV dirty looking; dull brown, drab

wiýīpihkwēw ᐃ·ᔩᐱᐦᑫ·ᐤ
VAI s/he has a dirty face

wiýīpisiw ᐃ·ᔩᐱᓯᐤ
VAI s/he is dirty-looking

wiýohtēw ᐃ·ᔪᐦᑌᐤ
VAI s/he walks about

ᐄ·

wī- ᐄ·
IPV intend to, be about to [*changed conjunct form*: wā]

wī-nipahāhkatosow ᐄ· ᓂᐸᐦᐋᐦᑲᑐᓱᐤ
VAI s/he is malnourished [*intentive*, *cf.* wī-; *cf.* nipahāhkatosow]

wīc-āyamihāmēw ᐄ·ᒑᔭᒥᐦᐋᒣᐤ
VTA s/he prays with s.o. [*cf.* ayamihāw, wīci- *IPV*]

wīc-āyāmēw ᐄ·ᒑᔮᒣᐤ
VTA s/he lives with s.o. [*cf.* ayāw *VAI*, wīci- *IPV*, wīci-ayāmēw]

wīc-īspīhcisīmēw ᐄ·ᒌᐢᐲᐦᒋᓰᒣᐤ
VTA s/he is of the same age as s.o., s/he has s.o. as his/her age-mate [*cf.* ispīhcisiw, wīci- *IPV*]

wīc-ōhpikīmēw ᐄ·ᒍᐦᐱᑮᒣᐤ
VTA s/he grows up with s.o., s/he is raised together with s.o. [*cf.* ohpikiw, wīci- *IPV*]

wīcaskosīs ᐄ·ᒐᐢᑯᓰᐢ
NA a swallow (bird) [*dim*]

wīcēhtahēw ᐄᐧᒑᐦᑖᐦᐁᐤ
VTA s/he breeds s.o. (e.g. animals)

wīcēhtam ᐄᐧᒑᐦᑕᒼ
VTI s/he supports s.t., s/he goes along with s.t., s/he cooperates with s.t.

wīcēhtowak ᐄᐧᒑᐦᑐᐊᐠ
VAI they get along with one another; they accompany one another; they live with one another

wīcēhtowin ᐄᐧᒑᐦᑐᐃᐧᐣ
NI fellowship

wīcēskwēwēw ᐄᐧᒉᐢᒁᐁᐧᐁᐤ
VAI s/he has a lady friend

wīcēwākan ᐄᐧᒉᐚᑲᐣ
NA spouse, wife; companion, buddy

wīcēwākanihēw ᐄᐧᒉᐚᑲᓂᐦᐁᐤ
VTA s/he takes s.o. to meet friends

wīcēwākanihkēw ᐄᐧᒉᐚᑲᓂᐦᑫᐤ
VAI s/he couples s.o., s/he is a match-maker; s/he makes a friend, companion

wīcēwākanihtahēw ᐄᐧᒉᐚᑲᓂᐦᑕᐦᐁᐤ
VTA s/he takes s.o. to make friends

wīcēwākanihtowak ᐄᐧᒉᐚᑲᓂᐦᑐᐊᐠ
VAI they find one another as partner, spouse; they live as common-law partners

wīcēwākanimēw ᐄᐧᒉᐚᑲᓂᒣᐤ
VTA s/he has s.o. as partner, s/he is in partnership with s.o.

wīcēwākaniw ᐄᐧᒉᐚᑲᓂᐤ
VAI s/he has (s.o. as) a partner, spouse; he has a wife; she has a husband

wīcēwāwasow ᐄᐧᒉᐚᐊᐧᓱ
VAI s/he has his/her own children along

wīcēwēw ᐄᐧᒉᐍᐤ
VTA s/he gets along with s.o.; s/he comes along with s.o., s/he accompanies s.o., s/he joins s.o.; s/he has s.o. along, s/he is with s.o., s/he lives with s.o.

wīcēwiskwēwēw ᐄᐧᒉᐃᐧᐢᑫᐧᐁᐤ
VAI he has his own wife along; s/he accompanies a woman

wīci- ᐄᐧᒋ
IPN one of his/her own kind; fellow

wīci- ᐄᐧᒋ
IPV together with

wīci-atoskēmākan ᐄᐧᒋ ᐊᑐᐢᑫᒫᑲᐣ
NA fellow worker

wīci-atoskēmēw ᐄᐧᒋ ᐊᑐᐢᑫᒣᐤ
VTA s/he works with s.o. [cf. atoskēw]

wīci-ayāmēw ᐄᐧᒋ ᐊᔮᒣᐤ
VTA s/he lives with s.o., s/he dwells with s.o. [also wic-āyāmēw; cf. ayāw VAI]

wīci-āpihtāw-kīsikanēmēw ᐄᐧᒋ ᐋᐱᐦᑖᐤ ᑮᓯᑲᓀᒣᐤ
VTA s/he eats dinner with s.o.

wīci-ispīhtisīmēw ᐄᐧᒋᐢᐱᐦᑎᓰᒣᐤ
VTA s/he is the same age as s.o. [also wic-ispīhtisīmēw]

wīci-kēpātis ᐄᐧᒋ ᑫᐹᑎᐢ
NA foolish one like him/herself, fellow foolish one [cf. kakēpātis]

wīci-kiskinohamākosīmēw ᐄᐧᒋ ᑭᐢᑭᓄᐦᐊᒫᑯᓰᒣᐤ
VTA s/he is in school with s.o., s/he has s.o. as a fellow-student

wīci-kīskwēpēmēw ᐄᐧᒋ ᑮᐢᒁᐯᒣᐤ
VTA s/he drinks and gets drunk with s.o.

wīci-mētawēmēw ᐄᐧᒋ ᒫᐟᐁᐧᒣᐤ
VTA s/he has s.o. as a playmate; s/he plays with s.o., s/he plays together with s.o. [cf. mētawēw]

wīci-minihkwēmēw ᐄᐧᒋ ᒥᓂᐦᐧᒣᐤ
VTA s/he has s.o. as a drinking companion; s/he drinks with s.o. [cf. minihkwēw]

wīci-miyawātamōmēw ᐄᐧᒋ ᒥᔭᐋᐧᑕᒨᒣᐤ
VTA s/he rejoices with s.o. [cf. miyawātam]

wīci-mīcisōmēw ᐄᐧᒋ ᒦᒋᓲᒣᐤ
VTA s/he has someone as a dinner companion; s/he eats with s.o. [cf. mīcisow]

wīci-natawahōmēw ᐄᐧᒋ ᓇᑕᐊᐧᐦ�běᐤ
VTA s/he hunts with s.o.

wīci-nikamōmēw ᐄᐧᒋ ᓂᑲᒨᒣᐤ
VTA s/he has s.o. as a singing partner; s/he sings with s.o. [cf. nikamow]

wīci-nīmihitōmēw ᐄᐧᒋ ᓃᒥᐦᐃᑑᒣᐤ
VTA s/he dances with s.o. [cf. nīmihitow]

wīci-nōtinikēmēw ᐄᐧᒋ ᓅᑎᓂᑫᒣᐤ
VTA s/he fights alongside s.o. [cf. nōtinikēw]

wīci-ohcīmēw ᐄᐧᒋ ᐅᐦᒌᒣᐤ
VTA s/he originates (temporally) together with s.o.; s/he is born together with s.o. [cf. ohcīw]

wīci-ohpikīmēw ᐄᐧᒋ ᐅᐦᐱᑮᒣᐤ
VTA s/he grows up together with s.o. [cf. ohpikiw]

wīci-pimohtēmēw ᐄᐧᒋ ᐱᒧᐦᑌᒣᐤ
VTA s/he walks with s.o.;

s/he walks s.o. (e.g. a dog) [cf. pimohtēw]

wīci-piponisēmēw ᐄᐧᒋ ᐱᐳᓂᓭᒣᐤ
VTA s/he winters with s.o.

wīci-pīhtwāmēw ᐄᐧᒋ ᐱᐦ�10ᐁᐤ
VTA s/he smokes with s.o., he smokes the pipe with s.o. [cf. pīhtwāw]

wīci-pīhtwāmitowak ᐄᐧᒋ ᐱᐦᒼᐦᑕᒥᑐᐊᐠ
VAI they smoke with one another, they smoke the pipe with one another

wīci-pīkiskwēmēw ᐄᐧᒋ ᐱᑮᐢᑶᒣᐤ
VTA s/he speaks with s.o. [cf. pīkiskwēw]

wīci-wanihikēmēw ᐄᐧᒋ ᐊᐧᓂᐦᐃᑫᒣᐤ
VTA s/he traps with s.o. [cf. wanihikēw]

wīci-wīhpēmēw ᐄᐧᒋ ᐄᐧᐦᐯᒣᐤ
VTA s/he sleeps with s.o. [cf. wihpēmēw]

wīcihēw ᐄᐧᒋᐦᐁᐤ
VTA s/he helps s.o.

wīcihikowisiw ᐄᐧᒋᐦᐃᑯᐃᐧᓯᐤ
VAI s/he is helped by the powers, s/he receives help from higher powers, God; s/he is helped spiritually

wīcihisow ᐄᐧᒋᐦᐃᓱ
VAI s/he helps him/herself; s/he applies him/herself, s/he studies for him/herself

wīcihitowak ᐄᐧᒋᐦᐃᑐᐊᐠ
VAI they help one another

wīcihiwēw ᐄᐧᒋᐦᐃᐍᐤ
VAI s/he helps people, s/he gives a helping hand; s/he accompanies, s/he goes along; s/he is along, s/he is part of a group, s/he joins in, s/he takes part, s/he participates, s/he is part of something

wīcihowin ᐄᐧᒋᐦᐅᐃᐧᐣ
NI consorting together; helping each other

wīcihtāsow ᐄᐧᒋᐦᑖᓱ
VAI s/he helps out, s/he helps with things

wīcisānēmēw ᐄᐧᒋᓵᓀᒣᐤ
VTA s/he is of the same parentage as s.o.

wīcisānihtowak ᐄᐧᒋᓵᓂᐦᑐᐊᐠ
VAI they are blood relations, they are related by blood

wīcisiw ᐄᐧᒋᓯᐤ
VAI s/he has a good head of hair

wīcisomōmēw ᐄᐧᒋᓱᒨᒣᐤ
VTA s/he dances with s.o.

wīcisomōmitowak ᐄᐧᒋᓱᒨᒥᑐᐊᐠ
VAI they dance with one another

wīcōhkamawēw ᐐᒎᐦᑲᒪᐍᐤ
VTA s/he helps s.o. [*cf.* wīsōhkamawēw]

wīhcēkan ᐐᐦᒉᑲᐣ
VII it smells bad

wīhcēkaskosiy ᐐᐦᒉᑲᐢᑯᓯᐩ
NI onion

wīhcēkaskosīs ᐐᐦᒉᑲᐢᑯᓰᐢ
NA onion [*dim*]

wīhcēkaskosīs-mīcimāpoy ᐐᐦᒉᑲᐢᑯᓰᐢ ᒦᒋᒫᐳᐩ
NI onion soup

wīhcēkaskosīwi-sākahikanihk ᐐᐦᒉᑲᐢᑯᓰᐏ ᓵᑲᐦᐃᑲᓂᕽ
INM Onion Lake, SK [*loc*; *Cree reserve name*]

wīhcēkatāmow ᐐᐦᒉᑲᑖᒧᐤ
VAI s/he has bad breath, s/he has halitosis

wīhcēkatāmowin ᐐᐦᒉᑲᑖᒧᐏᐣ
NI bad breath, halitosis

wīhcēkihtin ᐐᐦᒉᑭᐦᑎᐣ
VII it is left to spoil

wīhcēkimākosiw ᐐᐦᒉᑭᒫᑯᓯᐤ
VAI it smells spoiled

wīhcēkimākwan ᐐᐦᒉᑭᒫᑿᐣ
VII it smells spoiled

wīhcēkinākosiw ᐐᐦᒉᑭᓈᑯᓯᐤ
VAI s/he appears dirty

wīhcēkinākwan ᐐᐦᒉᑭᓈᑿᐣ
VII it appears dirty

wīhcēkisiw ᐐᐦᒉᑭᓯᐤ
VAI s/he smells bad

wīhcēkitāpān ᐐᐦᒉᑭᑖᐹᐣ
NI automobile

wīhcikāsow ᐐᐦᒋᑳᓱᐤ
VAI s/he is named, s/he is mentioned; it is told

wīhcikātēw ᐐᐦᒋᑳᑌᐤ
VII it is named, it is mentioned; it is told

wīhcīkan-sākahikanihk
INM Witchekan Lake, SK [*loc*; *lit*: "at stinking lake"; *wC community*; *cf.* wīhcēkan-*VII*]

wīhēw ᐐᐦᐁᐤ
VTA s/he names s.o., s/he gives a name to s.o.; s/he calls s.o. so, s/he mentions s.o. by name; s/he relies on s.o., s/he tells (it/him) from s.o. [*also* wīhýēw; *wC*: withīw, wīthīw; *sC*: wīñēw]

wīhisow ᐐᐦᐃᓱᐤ
VAI s/he names him/herself, s/he gives him/herself a name

wīhkanos ᐐᐦᑲᓄᐢ
NI piece of fruit

wīhkasin ᐐᐦᑲᓯᐣ
VII it tastes good, it is delicious

wīhkasko-kisēýin ᐐᐦᑲᐢᑯ ᑭᓭᔨᐣ
NA Sweetgrass, "Old-man-sweetgrass", Crow man who became one of the leading Plains Cree chiefs in the Battleford region [*see also* nakīwacīhk]

wīhkaskosam ᐐᐦᑲᐢᑯᓴᒼ
VTI s/he burns s.t. as incense

wīhkaskwa ᐐᐦᑲᐢᑿ
NI sweetgrass [*pl generally*: *cf.* wīhkwaskwa]

wīhkāc ᐐᐦᑳᐨ
IPC ever; at times; [*in negative clauses*:] never [*cf.* wīhkāt; *also* wihkāc]

wīhkācīs ᐐᐦᑳᒌᐢ
IPC a little later

wīhkākamiw ᐐᐦᑳᑲᒥᐤ
VII it is a sweet and tasty liquid

wīhkāt ᐐᐦᑳᐟ
IPC ever; [*in negative phrases*:] never [*cf.* wīhkāc; *also* wihkāt]

wīhkēs ᐐᐦᑫᐢ
NI muskrat root, rat root, sweet-flag, water arum

wīhki- ᐐᐦᑭ
IPN sweet; fragrant

wīhki-pahkwēsikanis ᐐᐦᑭ ᐸᐦᑵᓯᑲᓂᐢ
NA cookie [*dim*]

wīhkicisiw ᐐᐦᑭᒋᓯᐤ
VAI it tastes good, it is delicious [*dim*; *cf.* wīhkitisiw]

wīhkihkasikan ᐐᐦᑭᐦᑲᓯᑲᐣ
NA cake

wīhkihkasikanis ᐐᐦᑭᐦᑲᓯᑲᓂᐢ
NA pastry [*dim*]

wīhkihkasikēw ᐐᐦᑭᐦᑲᓯᑫᐤ
VAI s/he makes a cake, s/he makes sweet-tasting things

wīhkihkasōs ᐐᐦᑭᐦᑲᓲᐢ
NA cake [*dim*; *also NI*]

wīhkihkohkawēw ᐐᐦᑭᐦᑯᐦᑲᐍᐤ
VTA s/he makes a feast for s.o.

wīhkihkohkēw ᐐᐦᑭᐦᑯᐦᑫᐤ
VAI s/he invites many to a feast

wīhkihkohkēwin ᐐᐦᑭᐦᑯᐦᑫᐏᐣ
NI feast, banquet

wīhkimahkasow ᐐᐦᑭᒪᐦᑲᓱᐤ
VAI it smells sweet in burning

wīhkimākohēw ᐐᐦᑭᒫᑯᐦᐁᐤ
VTA s/he makes s.o. sweet smelling; s/he perfumes s.o.

wīhkimākohon ᐐᐦᑭᒫᑯᐦᐅᐣ
NI perfume

wīhkimākohow ᐐᐦᑭᒫᑯᐦᐅᐤ
VAI s/he perfumes him/herself

wīhkimākohowin ᐐᐦᑭᒫᑯᐦᐅᐏᐣ
NI fragrant scent

wīhkimākosiw ᐐᐦᑭᒫᑯᓯᐤ
VAI s/he smells good, s/he smells fragrant

wīhkimākwahon ᐐᐦᑭᒫᑿᐦᐅᐣ
NI perfume

wīhkimākwan ᐐᐦᑭᒫᑿᐣ
VII it smells good

wīhkimāsam ᐐᐦᑭᒫᓴᒼ
VTI s/he burns s.t. (*i.e.* incense)

wīhkimāsikan ᐐᐦᑭᒫᓯᑲᐣ
NI incense

wīhkimāsikēw ᐐᐦᑭᒫᓯᑫᐤ
VAI s/he burns incense, s/he burns fragrant things

wīhkimāstēw ᐐᐦᑭᒫᐢᑌᐤ
VII it is the fragrant smell of incense

wīhkiminēw ᐐᐦᑭᒥᓀᐤ
VAI s/he likes eating berries

wīhkipēw ᐐᐦᑭᐯᐤ
VAI s/he likes his/her liquor; s/he feels good from drink

wīhkipwēw ᐐᐦᑭᐻᐤ
VTA s/he likes the taste of s.o. [*cf.* wīhkistēw]

wīhkiskwēwēw ᐐᐦᑭᐢᑵᐍᐤ
VAI he likes women

wīhkistam ᐐᐦᑭᐢᑕᒼ
VTI s/he likes the taste of s.t.

wīhkistēw ᐐᐦᑭᐢᑌᐤ
VTA s/he likes the taste of s.o. [*cf.* wīhkipwēw]

wīhkitēpow ᐐᐦᑭᑌᐳᐤ
VAI s/he cooks delicious smelling foods

wīhkitisiw ᐐᐦᑭᑎᓯᐤ
VAI it tastes good [*cf.* wīhkicisiw]

wīhkohkēw ᐐᐦᑯᐦᑫᐤ
VAI s/he makes a feast, s/he prepares a feast; s/he invites people to a meal

wīhkohkēwin ᐐᐦᑯᐦᑫᐏᐣ
NI banquet

wīhkohtawēw ᐐᐦᑯᐦᑕᐍᐤ
VTA s/he makes a feast for s.o.

wīhkohtowak ᐐᐦᑯᐦᑐᐘᐠ
VAI they make a feast for one another; they gather

wīhkohtowin ᐐᐦᑯᐦᑐᐏᐣ
NI feast

wīhkomēw ᐐᐦᑯᒣᐤ
VTA s/he invites s.o. [*also* wīhkōmēw]

wīhkomitowin ᐐᐦᑯᒥᑐᐏᐣ
NI invitation [*also* wīhkōmitowin]

wīhkōw ᐐᐦᑰᐤ
VAI s/he forces him/herself, s/he uses all his/her own force, s/he strains him/herself

wīhkwacihēw ᐐᐦᑿᒋᐦᐁᐤ
VTA s/he pulls s.o. out (of a mud hole); s/he helps s.o. out (of a tight spot); s/he frees s.o.; s/he pries s.o. out

wīhkwacihow ᐐᐦᑿᒋᐦᐅᐤ
VAI s/he escapes; s/he frees him/herself out of a tight spot

wīhkwacipitam ᐑᐦᑿᒋᐱᑕᒼ
VTI s/he pulls s.t. out

wīhkwacipitēw ᐑᐦᑿᒋᐱᑌᐤ
VTA s/he yanks s.o. free; s/he pulls s.o. out (of a mud hole), s/he frees s.o. by pulling

wīhkwaciskiwēpitēw ᐑᐦᑿᒋᐢᑭᐍᐱᑌᐤ
VTA s/he pulls s.o. free from a bog or mud

wīhkwacīw ᐑᐦᑿᒌᐤ
VAI s/he frees him/herself by pulling and pushing

wīhkwaskwa ᐑᐦᑿᐢᑿ
NA sweetgrass [*pl generally*; *cf.* wīhkaskwa]

wīhkwataham ᐑᐦᑿᑕᐦᐊᒼ
VTI s/he pries s.t. loose (using a bar)

wīhkwatahwēw ᐑᐦᑿᑕᐦᐍᐤ
VTA s/he pries s.o. loose (using a bar)

wīhkwatinam ᐑᐦᑿᑎᓇᒼ
VTI s/he pulls s.t. free

wīhkwatinēw ᐑᐦᑿᑎᓀᐤ
VTA s/he pulls s.o. free

wīhkway ᐑᐦᑿᐩ
NI bladder

wīhkwās ᐑᐦᒁᐢ
NI balloon [*dim*]

wīhkwēhtakāw ᐑᐦᑵᐦᑕᑳᐤ
NI corner made by wooden walls

wīhkwēkāpawiwak ᐑᐦᑵᑳᐸᐏᐘᐠ
VAI they stand all round something

wīhkwēkāpawīstamwak ᐑᐦᑵᑳᐸᐑᐢᑕᒷᐠ
VTI they stand round s.t.

wīhkwēkāpawīstawēwak ᐑᐦᑵᑳᐸᐑᐢᑕᐍᐘᐠ
VTA they stand round s.o.

wīhkwēpan ᐑᐦᑵᐸᐣ
NI long underwear; overalls

wīhkwēpiwak ᐑᐦᑵᐱᐘᐠ
VAI they sit all round something

wīhkwēsīhtāw ᐑᐦᑵᓰᐦᑖᐤ
VAIt s/he makes s.t. circular

wīhkwēskawēw ᐑᐦᑵᐢᑲᐍᐤ
VTA s/he goes around s.o., s/he heads s.o. off

wīhkwēstēwa ᐑᐦᑵᐢᑌᐘ
VII they are in a circle, they lie in a circle, they stand in a circle

wīhkwētāpānāsk ᐑᐦᑵᑖᐹᓈᐢᐠ
NA rounded toboggan, sleigh [*pl*: -wak]

wīhkwēwikāpawiwak ᐑᐦᑵᐏᑳᐸᐏᐘᐠ
VAI they stand in a circle

wīhowin ᐑᐦᐅᐏᐣ
NI name [*also* wīhýowin; *cf.* *wC*: wīthowin; *sC*: wīñowin]

wīhowiniw ᐑᐦᐅᐏᓂᐤ
VAI s/he has a name

wīhpāw ᐑᐦᐹᐤ
VII it is hollow

wīhpēmēw ᐑᐦᐯᒣᐤ
VTA s/he sleeps with s.o.

wīhpēmiskwēwēw ᐑᐦᐯᒥᐢᑵᐍᐤ
VAI he sleeps with a woman

wīhpēmitowak ᐑᐦᐯᒥᑐᐘᐠ
VAI they sleep together, they sleep with one another

wīhpi- ᐑᐦᐱ
IPV hollowing out

wīhtam ᐑᐦᑕᒼ
VTI s/he tells about s.t., s/he reports s.t.; s/he decrees s.t.; s/he names s.t., s/he mentions s.t. by name [*also* wihtam]

wīhtamawēw ᐑᐦᑕᒪᐍᐤ
VTA s/he tells s.o. about (it/him), s/he tells (it/him) to or for s.o.; s/he names (it/him) to s.o. [*rdpl*: wāh-wīhtamawēw]

wīhtamākēw ᐑᐦᑕᒫᑫᐤ
VAI s/he makes predications; s/he names (it) to people

wīhtamākowisiw ᐑᐦᑕᒫᑯᐏᓯᐤ
VAI s/he is told about (it/him) by higher powers

wīhtamāsow ᐑᐦᑕᒫᓱᐤ
VAI s/he tells about him/herself

wīhtamātowak ᐑᐦᑕᒫᑐᐘᐠ
VAI they tell (about it/him) to one another, they tell one another about (it/him)

wīhtamāwasow ᐑᐦᑕᒫᐘᓱᐤ
VAI s/he tells (about it/him) to his/her own children

wīhtikow ᐑᐦᑎᑯᐤ
NA Wihtikow, Windigo; cannibal, giant man-eating monster [*also* wihtikow]

wīhtikōhkān ᐑᐦᑎᑰᐦᑳᐣ
NA member of the Wihtikow Society; clown

wīhtikōhkānisimow ᐑᐦᑎᑰᐦᑳᓂᓯᒧᐤ
VAI s/he dances the Wihtikow dance

wīhtikōhkānisimowin ᐑᐦᑎᑰᐦᑳᓂᓯᒧᐏᐣ
NI Wihtikow dance

wīhtikōhkāniwiw ᐑᐦᑎᑰᐦᑳᓂᐏᐤ
VAI s/he is a member of the Wihtikow Society; s/he is a clown

wīhtikōhkotātowak ᐑᐦᑎᑰᐦᑯᑖᑐᐘᐠ
VAI they act as cannibals toward one another

wīhtikōwiw ᐑᐦᑎᑰᐏᐤ
VAI s/he is a Wihtikow, Windigo

wīhýēw ᐑᐦᔦᐤ
VTA s/he names s.o. [*cf.* wīhēw; *wC*: wīthīw; *sC*: wīñēw]

wīhýowin ᐑᐦᔪᐏᐣ
NI name [*cf.* wīhowin; *wC*: wīthowin; *sC*: wīñowin]

wīkihkēmow ᐑᑭᐦᑫᒧᐤ
VAI s/he lives with people

wīkihtahēw ᐑᑭᐦᑕᐦᐁᐤ
VTA s/he makes s.o. marry; s/he unites s.o. in marriage

wīkihtow ᐑᑭᐦᑐᐤ
NA bride; groom; [*pl*:] bride and groom

wīkihtow ᐑᑭᐦᑐᐤ
VAI s/he gets married, s/he is married; [*pl*:] they are married to one another, they live together [*unspecified actor*: wīkihtonāniwan "there is a wedding"]

wīkihtowin ᐑᑭᐦᑐᐏᐣ
NI wedding; marriage, marriage ceremony; living together

wīkimākan ᐑᑭᒫᑲᐣ
NA spouse; wife, husband [*cf. NDA* -wīkimākan-]

wīkimēw ᐑᑭᒣᐤ
VTA s/he marries s.o., s/he takes s.o. as spouse; s/he is married to s.o.; s/he lives with s.o.

wīkiw ᐑᑭᐤ
VAI s/he lives there, s/he dwells there, s/he has his/her own abode (there) [*rdpl*: wa-wīkiw]

wīkiwin ᐑᑭᐏᐣ
NI household; home

wīko ᐑᑯ
NI kidney fat [*mass noun*; *sg only*]

wīmāhāw ᐑᒫᐦᐋᐤ
VAI s/he flies by a detour

wīmāhtēw ᐑᒫᐦᑌᐤ
VAI s/he walks by a circuit

wīmāskawēw ᐑᒫᐢᑲᐍᐤ
VTA s/he avoids s.o. by going in a circuit

wīnasakātihp ᐑᓇᓴᑳᑎᐦᑊ
NA ground hog; badger [*also* wīnāsakatēhp]

wīnask ᐑᓇᐢᐠ
NA woodchuck [*pl*: -wak]

wīnastēw ᐑᓇᐢᑌᐤ
VII it lies or stands dirty

wīnāstakay ᐑᓈᐢᑕᑲᐩ
NI "tripe", paunch, largest stomach of ruminant [*see also* omāw]

wīnāstakayēpicikan ᐑᓈᐢᑕᑲᔦᐱᒋᑲᐣ
NI bag, vessel made of large stomach

wīnēýihtam ᐑᓀᔨᐦᑕᒼ
VTI s/he loathes s.t.

wīnēýimēw ᐑᓀᔨᒣᐤ
VTA s/he loathes s.o., s/he abhors s.o.; s/he thinks s.o. dirty

wīnēýimisow Ȧ·ᐧᐅᐱᕒᓀᐤ
VAI s/he thinks him/herself dirty, nasty

wīni Ȧ·ᓂ
NDI bone-marrow; his/her bone-marrow [*mass noun, sg only*]

wīni- Ȧ·ᓂ
IPV soil, dirty

wīnicihciy Ȧ·ᓂᒡᐦᕒᐤ
NA one with dirty hands

wīnicihciy Ȧ·ᓂᒡᐦᕒᐤ
NI dirty hand

wīnicoyēsis Ȧ·ᓂᒍᔦᓯᐢ
NA skunk [*dim; lit:* "little dirty tail"]

wīnihēw Ȧ·ᓂᐦᐁᐧᐁᐤ
VTA s/he makes s.o. dirty by splashing; s/he dirties s.o. with his/her own dirty hands

wīnihisow Ȧ·ᓂᐦᐃᓱᐤ
VAI s/he soils him/herself, s/he soils his/her own clean clothes

wīnihkasow Ȧ·ᓂᐦᑲᓱᐤ
VAI it smells bad as one burns

wīnihtawakay Ȧ·ᓂᐦᑕᐧᐊᑲᐩ
NA badger
NI dirty ear

wīnihtāw Ȧ·ᓂᐦᑖᐤ
VAIt s/he dirties s.t.

wīnihtin Ȧ·ᓂᐦᑎᐣ
VII it spoils, it rots [*see also* pikiskatin, sikwatatin]

wīnikwayaw Ȧ·ᓂᑲᐧᔭᐤ
NI dirty neck

wīnikwayawēw Ȧ·ᓂᑲᐧᔭᐧᐁᐤ
VAI s/he has a dirty neck

wīnimahkahk Ȧ·ᓂᒪᐦᑲᕽ
NA garbage pail, slop pail [*pl:* -wak]

wīnimākosiw Ȧ·ᓂᒫᑯᓯᐤ
VAI s/he smells nasty

wīnimākwan Ȧ·ᓂᒫᑲᐧᐣ
VII it smells nasty

wīninākosiw Ȧ·ᓂᓈᑯᓯᐤ
VAI s/he looks dirty

wīninākwan Ȧ·ᓂᓈᑲᐧᐣ
VII it looks dirty

wīnipēk Ȧ·ᓂᐯᐠ
NI body of muddy water; Winnipeg, MB [*also* wīnipīhk; *loc:* wīnipēkohk]

wīnisiw Ȧ·ᓂᓯᐤ
VAI s/he is filthy

wīniskam Ȧ·ᓂᐢᑲᒼ
VTI s/he dirties s.t. by wearing, stepping; s/he soils s.t. by lying on it with soiled clothes

wīnispakosiw Ȧ·ᓂᐢᐸᑯᓯᐤ
VAI it has a tainted taste, it tastes badly [*see also* māýispakosiw]

wīnispakwan Ȧ·ᓂᐢᐸᑲᐧᐣ
VAI s/he tastes badly [*see also* māýispakwan]

wīnispitam Ȧ·ᓂᐢᐱᑕᒼ
VTI s/he is disgusted at the taste of s.t.

wīnispitēw Ȧ·ᓂᐢᐱᑌᐤ
VTA s/he is disgusted at the taste of s.o.

wīnitonēw Ȧ·ᓂᑐᓀᐤ
VAI s/he smells foul at the mouth, s/he has a filthy mouth; s/he uses foul language

wīnitōn Ȧ·ᓂᑑᐣ
NA person with a filthy mouth, one who uses foul language
NI foul mouth; foul language

wīniy Ȧ·ᓂᐩ
NI musk-gland

wīnīhow Ȧ·ᓃᐦᐅᐤ
VAI s/he dresses with unclean clothes

wīpac Ȧ·ᐸᐨ
IPC soon, quickly, soon as possible; early [*cf.* wīpat]

wīpat Ȧ·ᐸᐟ
IPC soon; early [*cf.* wīpac]

wīpayiwinis Ȧ·ᐸᔨᐧᐃᓂᐢ
NI dirty clothing, dirty article of clothing [*pl generally*]

wīpāci-kīsikāw Ȧ·ᐸᒋ ᑮᓯᑳᐤ
VII it is a nasty day, it is bad weather, it is wet weather

wīpācikin Ȧ·ᐸᒋᑭᐣ
VII it grows out of place, it grows wild, it grows as a weed

wīpāpēkan Ȧ·ᐸᐯᑲᐣ
VII it is dirty (*e.g.* material)

wīpāpēkisiw Ȧ·ᐸᐯᑭᓯᐤ
VAI s/he is dirty from head to toe

wīpāpiskāw Ȧ·ᐸᐱᐢᑳᐤ
VII it is dirty (metal)

wīpāpiskisiw Ȧ·ᐸᐱᐢᑭᓯᐤ
VAI it is dirty (metal)

wīpātan Ȧ·ᐸᑕᐣ
VII it is dirty (speaking of outside) [*cf.* wiýipātan]

wīpātayiwinis Ȧ·ᐸᑕᔨᐧᐃᓂᐢ
NI dirty clothing, dirty article of clothing [*pl generally*]

wīpātisiw Ȧ·ᐸᑎᓯᐤ
VAI s/he is dirty [*cf.* wiýipātisiw]

wīpātiskam Ȧ·ᐸᑎᐢᑲᒼ
VTI s/he dirties s.t. (with his/her own feet)

wīpātiskawēw Ȧ·ᐸᑎᐢᑲᐧᐁᐤ
VTA s/he dirties s.o. (with his/her own feet)

wīpāw Ȧ·ᐸᐤ
VII it is unclean, it is soiled

wīpi- Ȧ·ᐱ
IPV dirty, unclean [*also* wiýipi]

wīpicihcēw Ȧ·ᐱᒋᐦᒉᐤ
VAI s/he has dirty hands

wīpicīsis Ȧ·ᐱᒌᓯᐢ
NA goldeye [*also:* wīpicisis]

wīpihisow Ȧ·ᐱᐦᐃᓱᐤ
VAI s/he soils him/herself

wīpihkwēw Ȧ·ᐱᐦᑫᐧᐤ
VAI s/he has a dirty face

wīpihtāw Ȧ·ᐱᐦᑖᐤ
VAIt s/he soils s.t., s/he drops s.t. in the dirt; s/he soils s.t. with dirty hands

wīpikātēw Ȧ·ᐱᑳᑌᐤ
VAI s/he has dirty legs

wīpinam Ȧ·ᐱᓇᒼ
VTI s/he soils s.t. from touching it

wīpinamawēw Ȧ·ᐱᓇᒪᐧᐁᐤ
VTA s/he soils (it/him) on s.o.

wīpinēw Ȧ·ᐱᓀᐤ
VTA s/he soils s.o. with dirty hands

wīpis Ȧ·ᐱᐢ
NA dirty one [*dim*]

wīpisitēw Ȧ·ᐱᓯᑌᐤ
VAI s/he has dirty feet; s/he has soiled shoes

wīpiskam Ȧ·ᐱᐢᑲᒼ
VTI s/he dirties s.t. by tramping on it

wīpistikwānēw Ȧ·ᐱᐢᑎᑲᐧᓀᐤ
VAI s/he has dirty hair, s/he has a dirty head

wīpitāhpinēw Ȧ·ᐱᑖᐦᐱᓀᐤ
VAI s/he has a toothache [*see also* tēyāpitēw]

wīpitāhpinēwin Ȧ·ᐱᑖᐦᐱᓀᐧᐃᐣ
NI toothache [*cf.* tēyāpitēwin]

wīpo- Ȧ·ᐳ
IPV narrow

wīposāwāw Ȧ·ᐳᓵᐧᐋᐤ
VII it is brown

wīposkāwi-sākahikanihk Ȧ·ᐳᐢᑳᐃᐧ ᓵᑲᐦᐃᑲᓂᕽ
INM Brabant Lake, SK [*loc*]

wīsahkēcāhk Ȧ·ᓴᐦᑫᒑᕁ
NA Wisahkecahk; Cree culture hero, legendary figure [*personal name; obv:* -wa]

wīsakahcahwēw Ȧ·ᓴᑲᐦᒑᐦᐧᐁᐤ
VTA s/he makes s.o. very envious, s/he gets s.o.'s goat

wīsakahosow Ȧ·ᓴᑲᐦᐅᓱᐤ
VAI s/he hurts him/herself

wīsakahpisow Ȧ·ᓴᑲᐦᐱᓱᐤ
VAI s/he has a bandage which is too tight, s/he has pain from being bandaged too tightly

wīsakahpitam Ȧ·ᓴᑲᐦᐱᑕᒼ
VTI s/he ties s.t. too tightly causing pain

wīsakahpitēw Ȧ·ᓴᑲᐦᐱᑌᐤ
VTA s/he ties s.o. too tightly causing pain

wīsakahpitēw ᐄᓴᑲᐦᐱᑌᐤ
VII it is in pain from being tied too tightly

wīsakahwēw ᐄᓴᑲᐦᐁᐤ
VTA s/he hurts s.o. by hitting or by tool

wīsakamēw ᐄᓴᑲᒣᐤ
VTA s/he bites s.o. hard, s/he bites s.o. painfully

wīsakan ᐄᓴᑲᐣ
VII it is bitter to the taste

wīsakastēhwēw ᐄᓴᑲᐢᑌᐦᐁᐤ
VTA s/he straps s.o., spanks s.o. harshly

wīsakat ᐄᓴᑲᐟ
NI pepper [*see also* askiwi-sīwihtākan, papēskomina, pēskōmina]

wīsakatāmow ᐄᓴᑲᑖᒧᐤ
VAI s/he cries bitterly; s/he wails

wīsakāhpinēw ᐄᓴᑲᐦᐱᓀᐤ
VAI s/he has strong pains; s/he suffers with much pain

wīsakāhpinēwin ᐄᓴᑲᐦᐱᓀᐃᐧᐣ
NI suffering, a painful disease

wīsakāhpiw ᐄᓴᑲᐦᐱᐤ
VAI s/he laughs till his/her own sides ache

wīsakāpasow ᐄᓴᑲᐸᓱᐤ
VAI s/he has eyes which smart from smoke

wīsakāpiw ᐄᓴᑲᐱᐤ
VAI s/he has sore eyes, s/he has eyes that smart

wīsakāwikanēsin ᐄᓴᑲᐃᐧᑲᓀᓯᐣ
VAI s/he hurts his/her own back (in falling)

wīsakāwikanēw ᐄᓴᑲᐃᐧᑲᓀᐤ
VAI s/he hurts his/her own back

wīsakēw ᐄᓴᑫᐤ
VAI s/he twists his/her own back, s/he hurts his/her own back

wīsakēyihtam ᐄᓴᑫᔨᐦᑕᐠᑕᐨ
VTI s/he is hurt by s.t.; s/he is sore, s/he is hurt, s/he feels pain from s.t.

wīsaki- ᐄᓴᑭ
IPV painfully

wīsakicihcēnisow ᐄᓴᑭᒋᐦᒉᓂᓱᐤ
VAI s/he hurts his/her own hand

wīsakihcikwanēsin ᐄᓴᑭᐦᒋᑲᐧᓀᓯᐣ
VAI s/he hurts his/her own knee (in falling)

wīsakihcikwanēw ᐄᓴᑭᐦᒋᑲᐧᓀᐤ
VAI s/he hurts his/her own knee

wīsakikohtākanēw ᐄᓴᑭᑯᐦᑖᑲᓀᐤ
VAI s/he has a sore throat

wīsakimin ᐄᓴᑭᒥᐣ
NI cranberry, bog cranberry

wīsakinam ᐄᓴᑭᓇᒼ
VTI s/he hurts s.t., s/he sprains s.t.

wīsakinēw ᐄᓴᑭᓀᐤ
VTA s/he hurts s.o. by grasping too hard

wīsakipakos ᐄᓴᑭᐸᑯᐢ
NI bitter herb [*dim*]

wīsakipitam ᐄᓴᑭᐱᑕᒼ
VTI s/he hurts s.t. (by pulling)

wīsakipitēw ᐄᓴᑭᐱᑌᐤ
VTA s/he hurts s.o. (by pulling)

wīsakisimēw ᐄᓴᑭᓯᒣᐤ
VTA s/he hurts s.o. by throwing

wīsakisin ᐄᓴᑭᓯᐣ
VAI s/he is injured by a fall, s/he falls painfully, s/he hurts him/herself falling

wīsakiskawēw ᐄᓴᑭᐢᑲᐁᐤ
VTA s/he hurts s.o. by kick or body movement

wīsakistikwānēw ᐄᓴᑭᐢᑎᑲᐧᓀᐤ
VAI s/he has a hurting head

wīsakitēhēw ᐄᓴᑭᑌᐦᐁᐤ
VAI s/he has a heavy heart

wīsakowēw ᐄᓴᑯᐁᐤ
VAI s/he has a shrill voice

wīsāhkawēw ᐄᓵᐦᑲᐁᐤ
VTA s/he charms s.o.

wīsāmēw ᐄᓵᒣᐤ
VTA s/he invites s.o., s/he invites s.o. along, s/he asks s.o. to come along with one

wīsāmitowak ᐄᓵᒥᑐᐊᐧᐠ
VAI they accompany one another

wīsāwitam ᐄᓵᐃᐧᑕᒼ
VTI s/he makes up his/her own mind; s/he tells others what to do

wīscis ᐄᐢᒋᐢ
NI muskrat house [*dim*]

wīsi ᐄᓯ
NI belly-fat [*mass noun*; *sg only*]

wīskacān ᐄᐢᑲᒑᐣ
NA Canada jay, whiskey jack

wīskacēnisip ᐄᐢᑲᒉᓂᓯᑉ
NA mud-hen

wīskawahēw ᐄᐢᑲᐊᐧᐦᐁᐤ
VTA s/he steals up to s.o.

wīskawahtāw ᐄᐢᑲᐊᐧᐦᑖᐤ
VAIt s/he steals up to s.t.

wīskāc ᐄᐢᑳᐨ
IPC ever, at any time [*cf.* wīhkāc]

wīskicāk ᐄᐢᑭᒑᐠ
NA Canada jay, whiskey jack [*pl*: -wak]

wīskipōs ᐄᐢᑭᐳᐢ
NA whiskey-jack; a certain winter bird

wīskwastēw ᐄᐢᑲᐧᐢᑌᐤ
VII it is smoked (*e.g.* leather)

wīskwastēwinākwan ᐄᐢᑲᐧᐢᑌᐃᐧᓈᑲᐧᐣ
VII it is brown in appearance

wīskwēpitākan ᐄᐢᑫᐧᐱᑖᑲᐣ
NI sacred bundle

wīskwēpitēw ᐄᐢᑫᐧᐱᑌᐤ
VTA s/he winds s.o. around, s/he bandages s.o. about

wīsopiy ᐄᓱᐱᕀ
NI bile, gall; gall bladder

wīsōhkamawēw ᐄᓲᐦᑲᒪᐁᐧᐤ
VTA s/he helps s.o. [*cf.* wīcōhkamawēw]

wīsta ᐄᐢᑕ
PR he, too; she, too; he, by contrast; she, by contrast

wīstawāw ᐄᐢᑕᐊᐧᐤ
PR they, too; they, by contrast; they themselves

wīstēpahkway ᐄᐢᑌᐸᐦᑲᐧᕀ
NI piece of old (smoky) leather

wīstēpahkwayikamik ᐄᐢᑌᐸᐦᑲᐧᔨᑲᒥᐠ
NI tent of old bits of leather [*pl*: -wa]

wīstēpahkwēwikamik ᐄᐢᑌᐸᐦᑫᐧᐃᐧᑲᒥᐠ
NI tent of old bits of leather [*pl*: -wa]

wīsti ᐄᐢᑎ
NI beaver lodge; muskrat house [*pl*: wīsta]

wīstihkān ᐄᐢᑎᐦᑳᐣ
NI haystack [*dim*: wīscihkānis]

wīstihkānihkēw ᐄᐢᑎᐦᑳᓂᐦᑫᐧᐤ
VAI s/he makes haystacks

wīstihkēw ᐄᐢᑎᐦᑫᐧᐤ
VAI s/he stacks hay, s/he builds haystacks; s/he stacks, s/he heaps, s/he is stacking; it builds (beaver or muskrat) lodges

wītapihtahēw ᐄᑕᐱᐦᑕᐦᐁᐤ
VTA s/he makes s.o. sit on (*e.g.* a chicken on eggs)

wītapihtam ᐄᑕᐱᐦᑕᒼ
VTI s/he sits by s.t., s/he stays with s.t.; she hatches her own eggs (*i.e.* birds)

wītapimākan ᐄᑕᐱᒫᑲᐣ
NA next door neighbour

wītapimēw ᐄᑕᐱᒣᐤ
VTA s/he sits with s.o., s/he stays with s.o., s/he is present with s.o.; s/he works together with s.o.; s/he sits by s.o. (in marriage)

wītaskēmākan ᐄᑕᐢᑫᒫᑲᐣ
NA fellow countryman

wītaskēmēw ᐄᑕᐢᑫᒣᐤ
VTA s/he lives with s.o. in the same country

wītaskīw ᐄᑕᐢᑮᐤ
VAI s/he makes peace

wītaskīwin ᐄᑕᐢᑮᐃᐧᐣ
NI peace, truce, alliance

wītisānīhitowak ᐄᐧᓯᔅᐰᐦᐃᑐᐊᐧᕁ
VAI they are related to one another; they are a family; they belong to the same genealogy

wītisānīhitowin ᐄᐧᓯᔅᐰᐦᐃᑐᐃᐧ
NI genealogy

wītisiw ᐄᐧᓂᕁᐤ
VAI s/he has long, thick hair

wīto- ᐄᐧᑐ
IPV want, intend

wītokēhtam ᐄᐧᑐᖅᐦᐸᕳ
VTI s/he lives with s.t.

wītokēmākan ᐄᐧᑐᖅᓂᑲᐱ
NA one who lives with the family

wītokēmēw ᐄᐧᑐᖅᓂᐤ
VTA s/he shares camp with s.o., s/he lives with s.o. [*cf.* witokwēmēw]

wītokwēmēw ᐄᐧᑐᖅᐠᓂᐤ
VTA s/he lives with s.o., s/he shares a dwelling with s.o. [*cf.* wītokēmēw]

wītōsēmēw ᐄᐧᑐᔅᓂᐤ
VTA s/he has a child with s.o.

wītōspomēw ᐄᐧᑐᔅᐳᓂᐤ
VTA s/he eats from the same dish with s.o.

wīwa ᐄᐧᐊᐧ
NDA his wife

wīwahēw ᐄᐧᐊᐧᐦᐁᐧᐤ
VTA s/he puts a load on s.o. (*e.g.* horse)

wīwahow ᐄᐧᐊᐧᐦᐅᐤ
VAI s/he takes up his/her own load

wīwasiw ᐄᐧᐊᐧᓯᐤ
VAI s/he carries over his/her own back

wīwimāw ᐄᐧᐊᐧᒥᐊᐧᐤ
NA wife

wīwiw ᐄᐧᐊᐧᐤ
VAI he has (her as) a wife; he takes (s.o. as) a wife, he gets married

y

ᔭ

ýahkaham ᔭᐦᑲᐦᐊᒼ
VTI s/he pushes s.t. with a stick or tool

ýahkahwēw ᔭᐦᑲᐦᐌᐤ
VTA s/he pushes s.o. with a stick or tool

ýahkakihcikēw ᔭᐦᑲᑭᐦᒋᑫᐤ
VAI s/he raises prices

ýahkakihtam ᔭᐦᑲᑭᐦᑕᒼ
VTI s/he raises the price of s.t.

ýahkakimēw ᔭᐦᑲᑭᒣᐤ
VTA s/he raises the price of s.o.

ýahkakocin ᔭᐦᑲᑯᒋᐣ
VAI s/he increases speed

ýahkāskwaham ᔭᐦᑳᐢᑿᐦᐊᒼ
VTI s/he pushes s.t. as wood

ýahkāskwahwēw ᔭᐦᑳᐢᑿᐦᐌᐤ
VTA s/he pushes s.o. as wood

ýahkāstimon ᔭᐦᑳᐢᑎᒧᐣ
NI sail of a boat

ýahkāstimonāhtik ᔭᐦᑳᐢᑎᒧᓈᐦᑎᐠ
NI mast [*pl*: -wa]

ýahkāstimonēkin ᔭᐦᑳᐢᑎᒧᓀᑭᐣ
NI sail cloth; material for sails [*pl*: -wa]

ýahkātihkātam ᔭᐦᑳᑎᐦᑳᑕᒼ
VTI s/he pushes out the size of an existing hole or cellar, s/he digs out more of a hole or cellar by pushing

ýahki- ᔭᐦᑭ
IPV act of pushing forward; increasing, increasingly, adding, more and more [*cf.* tahki]

ýahki-wēpinam ᔭᐦᑭᐍᐱᓇᒼ
VTI s/he pushes s.t. forward, s/he shoves s.t. away

ýahki-wēpinēw ᔭᐦᑭᐍᐱᓀᐤ
VTA s/he pushes s.o. forward, s/he shoves s.o. away

ýahkikin ᔭᐦᑭᑭᐣ
VII it grows, pushes forth in growth

ýahkikiw ᔭᐦᑭᑭᐤ
VAI s/he grows, s/he pushes forth in growth

ýahkinam ᔭᐦᑭᓇᒼ
VTI s/he pushes s.t., s/he pushes s.t. forward

ýahkinēw ᔭᐦᑭᓀᐤ
VTA s/he pushes s.o., s/he pushes s.o. forward

ýahkipaýin ᔭᐦᑭᐸᔨᐣ
VII it suddenly moves forward [*also* ýahkipaýiw; *cf.* ýahkipaýiw *VAI*]

ýahkipaýiw ᔭᐦᑭᐸᔨᐤ
VAI s/he suddenly moves forward

ýahkipitam ᔭᐦᑭᐱᑕᒼ
VTI s/he moves s.t. a little

ýahkipitēw ᔭᐦᑭᐱᑌᐤ
VTA s/he moves s.o. a little

ýahkisin ᔭᐦᑭᓯᐣ
VAI s/he moves or pushes over a bit while lying

ýahkisīhēw ᔭᐦᑭᓰᐦᐁᐤ
VTA s/he makes s.o. larger

ýahkisīhtāw ᔭᐦᑭᓰᐦᑖᐤ
VAIt s/he makes s.t. larger

ýahkīmow ᔭᐦᑮᒧᐤ
VAI s/he grows; s/he has progeny; [*pl*:] they increase (as a family)

ýahkīmowin ᔭᐦᑮᒧᐎᐣ
NI increase of family, increase of population

ýahkohtēw ᔭᐦᑯᐦᑌᐤ
VAI s/he goes forward, s/he progresses [*also* ýahkostēw]

ᔮ

ýāhkakocin ᔮᐦᑲᑯᒋᐣ
VAI s/he speeds lightly (by air, land or water)

ýāhkan ᔮᐦᑲᐣ
VII it is light in weight [*not found in wC*; *cf.* ýāhkasin]

ýāhkasin ᔮᐦᑲᓯᐣ
VII it is light in weight

ýāhkasiniy ᔮᐦᑲᓯᓂᐩ
NA a light stone

ýāhkasinīwāpisk ᔮᐦᑲᓯᓃᐚᐱᐢᐠ
NA light metal [*pl*: -wak]

ýāhkipitam ᔮᐦᑭᐱᑕᒼ
VTI s/he pulls s.t. out, s/he pulls s.t. as a light thing

ýāhkipitēw ᔮᐦᑭᐱᑌᐤ
VTA s/he pulls s.o. out, s/he pulls s.o. as a light object

ýāhkisīhow ᔮᐦᑭᓰᐦᐅᐤ
VAI s/he dresses lightly

ýāhkitisiw ᔮᐦᑭᑎᓯᐤ
VAI s/he is light in weight

ýāhýakikotēw ᔮᐦᔭᑭᑯᑌᐤ
VAI s/he is snub-nosed

ýāhýānam ᔮᐦᔮᓇᒼ
VTI s/he swims; s/he swims in s.t. [*see also* pakāsimow]

yākwā ᔭᐦᒁ
IPC look out! [*see also* pēyahtak]

yākwāmisiw ᔭᐦᒁᒥᓯᐤ
VAI s/he acts carefully, s/he takes his/her own time

yāpēsis ᔮᐯᓯᐢ
NA young moose; steer [*dim*]

yāpēw ᔮᐯᐤ
NA bull moose; bull [*also* iyāpēw]

yāpēw-atihk ᔮᐯᐘᑎᕽ
NA male caribou [*pl*: -wak]

yāpēwayān ᔮᐯᐘᔮᐣ
NA hide of a male animal, bull moose hide

yāsēpisiw ᔮᓭᐱᓯᐤ
VAI s/he sits back a bit [*dim*; *npC*: iyāsīpisiw, *cf.* āsēpiw, āsēpisiw]

ýāsinam ᔮᓯᓇᒼ
VTI s/he lowers s.t.; s/he takes s.t. down by hand

ýāsinēw ᔮᓯᓀᐤ
VTA s/he lowers s.o.; s/he takes s.o. down by hand

ýāsipaýihow ᔮᓯᐸᔨᐦᐅᐤ
VAI s/he lowers him/herself down from a height

ýāsipaýiw ᔮᓯᐸᔨᐤ
VAI s/he slides down, s/he descends

ýāsipaýiw ᔮᓯᐸᔨᐤ
VII it slides down; it suddenly goes down

ýāsipitam ᔮᓯᐱᑕᒼ
VTI s/he pulls s.t. down [*cf.* yāsipitāw]

ýāsipitāw ᔮᓯᐱᑖᐤ
VAIt s/he pulls s.t. down [*cf.* yāsipitam]

ýāsipitēw ᔮᓯᐱᑌᐤ
VTA s/he pulls s.o. down

ýāwāpiskipaýiw ᔮᐚᐱᐢᑭᐸᔨᐤ
VAI it bends as metal

ŷāwāskēnam ᐝᐊᐧᐢᐠᐁᐣᐊᒼ
VTI s/he missteps in s.t.,
s/he loses his/her own
footing in s.t. (e.g. muskeg,
uneven ground)

ŷāwāskēnikēw ᐝᐊᐧᐢᐠᐁᐣᐊᑯᐤ
VAI s/he loses his/her own
footing, s/he missteps

ŷāwātakan ᐝᐊᐧᑕᐦᐊᐣ
NI deep hole, cave

ŷāwātan ᐝᐊᐧᑕᐣ
VII it is a deep hole, cave

ŷāwāw ᐝᐊᐧᐤ
VII it is a deep hole, cave

ŷāwēw ᐝᐊᐧᐤ
NI sound heard in the
distance

ŷāwēw ᐝᐊᐧᐤ
VII it is a sound heard in the
distance

ŷāwinākosiw ᐝᐊᐧᐃᐧᐣᐋᑯᓯᐤ
VAI s/he appears dim at a
distance; s/he is seen faintly
in the distance

ŷāwinākwan ᐝᐊᐧᐃᐧᐣᐋᑲᐧᐣ
VII it appears dim at a
distance; it is seen faintly in
the distance

ŷāŷaham ᐝᐊᐝᐦᐊᒼ
VTI s/he strokes s.t. with
tool

ŷāŷahwēw ᐝᐊᐝᐦᐁᐧᐤ
VTA s/he strokes s.o. with
tool

ŷāŷakonam ᐝᐊᐝᑯᐣᐊᒼ
VTI s/he pulls s.t. out

ŷāŷakonēw ᐝᐊᐝᑯᐣᐁᐧᐤ
VTA s/he pulls s.o. out

ŷāŷaw ᐝᐊᐝᐤ
IPC rather, instead [cf.
iyāyaw]

ŷāŷāhk ᐝᐊᐝᕽ
IPC really! [emphatic]

ŷāŷāhk ēsa ani ᐝᐊᐝᕽ ᐁᓴ ᐊᓂ
IPH definitely, absolutely
[also ŷāŷāhk ēs āni]

ŷāŷāhk ētikwē ᐝᐊᐝᕽ ᐁᑎᑫ
IPH indubitably

ŷāŷāhk oti ani ᐝᐊᐝᕽ ᐅᑎ ᐊᓂ
IPH definitely, absolutely
[also ŷāŷāhk ot āni]

ŷāŷikāskocin ᐝᐊᐟᑳᐢᑯᒋᐣ
VAI s/he snags and tears
his/her own clothes on
branches

ŷāŷikipaŷiw ᐝᐊᐟᑭᐸᔨᐤ
VII it is torn

ŷāŷikipicikēw ᐝᐊᐟᑭᐱᒋᑫᐤ
VAI s/he tears things

ŷāŷikipitam ᐝᐊᐟᑭᐱᑕᒼ
VTI s/he tears s.t.

ŷāŷikipitēw ᐝᐊᐟᑭᐱᑌᐤ
VTA s/he tears s.o.

ŷāŷikisam ᐝᐊᐟᑭᓴᒼ
VTI s/he slices s.t.

ŷāŷikisāwātam ᐝᐊᐟᑭᓵᐊᐧᑕᒼ
VTI s/he slices s.t. (e.g.
paper)

ŷāŷikisāwātēw ᐝᐊᐟᑭᓵᐊᐧᑌᐤ
VTA s/he slices s.o. (e.g.
bread)

ŷāŷikiswēw ᐝᐊᐟᑭᐢᐁᐧᐤ
VTA s/he slices s.o.

ŷāŷisimēw ᐝᐊᐟᓯᒣᐤ
VTA s/he speaks to s.o. in a
certain manner; s/he lays s.o.
down in a certain position

ŷāŷiskwēnēw ᐝᐊᐟᐢᑫᐧᐣᐁᐤ
VTA s/he strokes s.o. on the
head or neck; s/he puts s.o.'s
head in another position

ŷāŷitihtāw ᐝᐊᐟᑎᐦᑖᐤ
VAIt s/he expresses a
different idea or connotation

ᐊ

ŷēhŷēhpamānis ᐊᐧᐦᐊᐧᐦᐸᒫᓂᐢ
NI fontanelle [pl generally;
dim]

ŷēhŷēhpamon ᐊᐧᐦᐊᐧᐦᐸᒧᐣ
NI epiglottis [proposed
term]

ŷēhŷēsiw ᐊᐧᐦᐊᐧᓯᐤ
VAI s/he pants [dim]

ŷēhŷēw ᐊᐧᐦᐊᐧᐤ
VAI s/he breathes

ŷēhŷēwin ᐊᐧᐦᐊᐧᐃᐧᐣ
NI breathing, breath

yēkamā ᐊᐧᑲᒫ
IPC it is not so; not the case
[cf. ēkāma]

yēkaw ᐊᐧᑲᐤ
NI sand

yēkawaciy ᐊᐧᑲᐊᐧᒋᕀ
NI sand hill

yēkawahcāw ᐊᐧᑲᐊᐧᐦᒑᐤ
VII it is an area of sandhills

yēkawan ᐊᐧᑲᐊᐧᐣ
VII it is sandy

yēkawiskāwikamāhk
ᐊᐧᑲᐃᐧᐢᑳᐃᐧᑲᒫᕽ
INM Sandy Lake, SK;
Ahtahkakoop Reserve, SK
[loc; lit: "at the water of
much sand"; see also
atāhkakohp]

ŷēŷihēw ᐊᐧᔨᐦᐁᐧᐤ
VTA s/he gets s.o. excited by
his/her actions, s/he tempts
s.o. by his/her actions

ŷēŷimēw ᐊᐧᔨᒣᐤ
VTA s/he gets s.o. excited by
his/her speech, s/he tempts
s.o. by his/her speech; s/he
coaxes s.o. into temptation

ᐃ

ŷipācicēskiwākēw ᐟᐸᐣᒋᐧᒉᐢᑭᐊᐧᑫᐤ
VAI s/he is muddied from
something

ŷipācicēskiwakīw ᐟᐸᐣᒋᐧᒉᐢᑭᐊᐧᑮᐤ
VAI s/he gets him/herself
muddied (dirty) [sC:
ñipācicēskiwakīw]

ŷipācicēskiwēw ᐟᐸᐣᒋᐧᒉᐢᑭᐁᐧᐤ
VAI s/he is muddied

ŷipācicēskiwēwahow
ᐟᐸᐣᒋᐧᒉᐢᑭᐁᐧᐊᐧᐦᐅᐤ
VAI s/he gets him/herself
muddied [cf. wīpāci-]

ŷipācihēw ᐟᐸᒋᐦᐁᐧᐤ
VTA s/he dirties s.o.

ŷipācihow ᐟᐸᒋᐦᐅᐤ
VAI s/he gets him/herself
dirty

ŷipātisikiwakisimow
ᐟᐸᑎᓯᑭᐊᐧᑭᓯᒧᐤ
VAI s/he gets him/herself
muddied or dirty [sC:
ñipātisikiwakisimow]

ŷipātisin ᐟᐸᑎᓯᐣ
VAI s/he becomes dirty, s/he
gets him/herself dirty; s/he
lies or sits in dirt

ŷipātisiw ᐟᐸᑎᓯᐤ
VAI s/he is dirty

ŷiŷīkastis ᐟᔩᑲᐢᑎᐢ
NA glove

ŷiŷīkicihcān ᐟᔩᑭᒋᐦᒑᐣ
NI finger

ŷiŷīkicihcis ᐟᔩᑭᒋᐦᒋᐢ
NI finger [dim]

ŷiŷīkisitān ᐟᔩᑭᓯᑖᐣ
NI toe

ŷiŷīkopīwi-pīsim ᐟᔩᑯᐲᐃᐧ ᐲᓯᒼ
NA Frost Moon, November
[wC: thithihkopiwi-pīsim]

ᐄ

ŷīhkaham ᐄᐦᑲᐦᐊᒼ
VTI s/he bails liquid out of
s.t.

ŷīhkahwēw ᐄᐦᑲᐦᐁᐧᐤ
VTA s/he bails liquid out of
s.o.

yīkatē ᐄᑲᑌ
IPC aside [cf. īkatē; also
iyīkatē; wC: īkatē]

yīkatē- ᐄᑲᑌ
IPV aside [cf. īkatē-; also
iyīkatē-; wC: īkatē-]

yīkatē-kwāskohtiw
ᐄᑲᑌ ᒀᐢᑯᐦᑎᐤ
VAI s/he jumps aside

yīkatē-tihtipinam
ᐄᑲᑌ ᑎᐦᑎᐱᐣᐊᒼ
VTI s/he rolls s.t. aside

yīkatē-tihtipinamawēw
ᐄᑲᑌ ᑎᐦᑎᐱᐣᐊᒪᐁᐧᐤ
VTA s/he rolls (it/him) aside
for s.o.

yīkatē-tihtipinēw
ᐄᑲᑌ ᑎᐦᑎᐱᐣᐁᐧᐤ
VTA s/he rolls s.o. aside

yīkatē-wēpinam ᐄᑲᑌ ᐁᐧᐱᐣᐊᒼ
VTI s/he throws s.t. aside

yīkatē-wēpinamawēw ᔩᑲᑌ ᐍᐱᓇᒪᐍᐤ
VTA s/he throws (it/him) aside for s.o.

yīkatē-wēpinēw ᔩᑲᑌ ᐍᐱᓀᐤ
VTA s/he throws s.o. aside

yīkatēhēw ᔩᑲᑌᐦᐁᐤ
VTA s/he puts s.o. aside

yīkatēhtahēw ᔩᑲᑌᐦᑕᐦᐁᐤ
VTA s/he takes s.o. aside

yīkatēhtatāw ᔩᑲᑌᐦᑕᑖᐤ
VAIt s/he takes s.t. aside

yīkatēhtēw ᔩᑲᑌᐦᑌᐤ
VAI s/he walks off to the side; [*Christian*:] s/he walks away

yīkatēkāpawiw ᔩᑲᑌᑳᐸᐏᐤ
VAI s/he stands aside, s/he steps aside

yīkatēnam ᔩᑲᑌᓇᒼ
VTI s/he takes s.t. aside; s/he clears the way

yīkatēnamawēw ᔩᑲᑌᓇᒪᐍᐤ
VTA s/he thrusts (it/him) aside for s.o.; s/he clears the way for s.o.

yīkatēnamāsow ᔩᑲᑌᓇᒫᓱᐤ
VAI s/he thrusts (it/him) aside for him/herself

yīkatēnēw ᔩᑲᑌᓀᐤ
VTA s/he thrusts s.o. aside (by hand) [*also*: iyīkatēnēw, *cf.* īkatēnēw]

yīkatēpahtāw ᔩᑲᑌᐸᐦᑖᐤ
VAI s/he runs off to the side, s/he runs aside

yīkatēpaýihow ᔩᑲᑌᐸᔩᐦᐅᐤ
VAI s/he steps quickly aside

yīkatēpaýin ᔩᑲᑌᐸᔩᐣ
VII it moves off to the side, it moves sideways (*e.g.* braided strips of rabbitskin) [*cf.* īkatēpaýin]

yīkatēpiciw ᔩᑲᑌᐱᒋᐤ
VAI s/he moves camp to one side

yīkatēpitam ᔩᑲᑌᐱᑕᒼ
VTI s/he pulls s.t. aside

yīkatēpitēw ᔩᑲᑌᐱᑌᐤ
VTA s/he pulls s.o. aside

yīkatēstamawēw ᔩᑲᑌᐢᑕᒪᐍᐤ
VTA s/he thrusts (it/him) aside for s.o.

yīkatēstamāsow ᔩᑲᑌᐢᑕᒫᓱᐤ
VAI s/he thrusts (it/him) aside for him/herself

yīkatēstawēw ᔩᑲᑌᐢᑕᐍᐤ
VTA s/he goes off to the side from s.o., s/he goes away from s.o. [*cf.* īkatēstawēw]

yīkatēstāw ᔩᑲᑌᐢᑖᐤ
VAIt s/he puts s.t. aside

yīkatētācimow ᔩᑲᑌᑖᒋᒧᐤ
VAI s/he crawls off to one side

yīkatētāpēw ᔩᑲᑌᑖᐯᐤ
VAI s/he drags off to one side

ýīkicēnam ᔩᑭᒉᓇᒼ
VTI s/he squeezes s.t.

ýīkicēnēw ᔩᑭᒉᓀᐤ
VTA s/he squeezes s.o.

ýīkicihcān ᔩᑭᒋᐦᒑᐣ
NI finger [*cf.* ýiýīkicihcān]

ýīkicikāw ᔩᑭᒋᑳᐤ
NA slow, clumsy person

ýīkicikāwīw ᔩᑭᒋᑳᐑᐤ
VAI s/he is slow or weak at s.t.

ýīkihcanakwēwisip ᔩᑭᐦᒐᓇᑵᐏᓯᑊ
NA blue wing duck

ýīkihtawamow ᔩᑭᐦᑕᐘᒧᐤ
NI forked road

ýīkihtawipēhikan ᔩᑭᐦᑕᐏᐯᐦᐃᑲᐣ
NI club card (in deck of cards)

ýīkihtawitāpānāsk ᔩᑭᐦᑕᐏᑖᐹᓈᐢᐠ
NI travois [*pl*: -wa]

ýīkihtawitāpānāskow ᔩᑭᐦᑕᐏᑖᐹᓈᐢᑯᐤ
VAI s/he is drawn on a travois

ýīkihtawitāpēw ᔩᑭᐦᑕᐏᑖᐯᐤ
VAI s/he draws s.t. on a travois

ýīkinikan ᔩᑭᓂᑲᐣ
NA milk-cow

ýīkinikēstamāsow ᔩᑭᓂᑫᐢᑕᒫᓱᐤ
VAI s/he does the milking for him/herself

ýīkinikēw ᔩᑭᓂᑫᐤ
VAI s/he milks (*e.g.* cattle), s/he does the milking [*cf.* īkinikēw]

ýīkisitān ᔩᑭᓯᑖᐣ
NI toe [*cf.* ýiýīkisitān]

ýīkitow ᔩᑭᑐᐤ
VAI s/he has diarrhea

ýīkopīwan ᔩᑯᐲᐘᐣ
VII it is foggy

ýīkopīwi-pīsim ᔩᑯᐲᐑ ᐲᓯᒼ
NA Frost Moon; November [*cf.* ihkopīwi-pīsim]

ýīkopīwiw ᔩᑯᐲᐏᐤ
VII there is frost, it is hoar-frost

ýīkowan ᔩᑯᐘᐣ
VII it is foggy [*cf.* ýīkwawan, *wC*: thiskowan; *also*: ýiýīkawan; *see also* kaskawan; *cf. Saulteaux*: awan]

ýīkwaskwan ᔩᑿᐢᑿᐣ
VII it is cloudy [*also* ýiýīkwaskwan]

ýīkwatin ᔩᑿᑎᐣ
VII it is frozen over

ýīkwawan ᔩᑿᐘᐣ
VII it is foggy, it is cloudy, it is rainy [*cf.* ýīkowan]

ýīkwawanipaýiw ᔩᑿᐘᓂᐸᔩᐤ
VII there is a fog rolling in, there is a sudden fog

ýīpē-pahkisin ᔩᐯ ᐸᐦᑭᓯᐣ
VAI s/he falls on his/her side [*wC*: īthīpē-]

ýīpēsin ᔩᐯᓯᐣ
VAI s/he lies on his/her side

ýīpēyāmatin ᔩᐯᔮᒪᑎᐣ
NI hill, slope

ýīpēyāw ᔩᐯᔮᐤ
VII it slants to one side

ýīwaham ᔩᐘᐦᐊᒼ
VTI s/he grinds s.t. fine, s/he pounds s.t. fine

ýīwahikan ᔩᐘᐦᐃᑲᐣ
NA pounded dry meat, pounded dry fish; lump of ground dried meat [*pl generally*: ýīwahikanak; *cf.* īwahikan]

ýīwahikanāpisk ᔩᐘᐦᐃᑲᓈᐱᐢᐠ
NI meat chopper, meat grinder [*pl*: -wa]

ýīwahikanihkēw ᔩᐘᐦᐃᑲᓂᐦᑫᐤ
VAI s/he makes ground dried meat

ýīwahikēw ᔩᐘᐦᐃᑫᐤ
VAI s/he grinds dry meat

ýīwahwēw ᔩᐘᐦᐍᐤ
VTA s/he grinds s.o. fine, s/he pounds s.o. fine

ýīwatayēsimow ᔩᐘᑕᔦᓯᒧᐤ
VAI s/he loses his/her belly by dancing [*dim*: ýīwacayēsimosiw]

ýīwēkocin ᔩᐍᑯᒋᐣ
VAI s/he hangs loosely

ýīwēkotēw ᔩᐍᑯᑌᐤ
VII it dangles, it hangs loose

ýīwēyāskocin ᔩᐍᔮᐢᑯᒋᐣ
VAI s/he tears his/her own clothes ragged on branches

ýīwipaýiw ᔩᐏᐸᔩᐤ
VII it subsides, there is a redution in swelling

ᔫ

ýōcisin ᔫᒋᓯᐣ
VII it is a little windy [*dim*; *also* yōcin]

ýōhtēkotāw ᔫᐦᑌᑯᑖᐤ
VAIt s/he leaves s.t. ajar, open

ýōhtēkotēw ᔫᐦᑌᑯᑌᐤ
VII it is open [*cf.* ýōhtēnikātēw]

ýōhtēnam ᔫᐦᑌᓇᒼ
VTI s/he opens s.t.

ýōhtēnamawēw ᔫᐦᑌᓇᒪᐍᐤ
VTA s/he opens (it/him) for s.o

ýōhtēnamāsow ᔫᐦᑌᓇᒫᓱᐤ
VAI s/he opens (it/him) for him/herself

ýōhtēnēw ᔫᐦᑌᓀᐤ
VTA s/he opens s.o. (as a covered pail); s/he moves s.o. so as to open passage

ýōhtēnikan ᐩᐦᑌᓂᑲᐣ
  NI door knob
ýōhtēnikātēw ᐩᐦᑌᓂᑲᑌᐤ
  VII it is open, it is opened
ýōhtēpaýiw ᐩᐦᑌᐸᔨᐤ
  VII it goes open
ýōhtēpitam ᐩᐦᑌᐱᑕᒼ
  VTI s/he pulls s.t. open
ýōhtēpitamawēw ᐩᐦᑌᐱᑕᒪᐌᐤ
  VTA s/he pulls (it/him) open
  for s.o.
ýōhtēpitēw ᐩᐦᑌᐱᑌᐤ
  VTA s/he pulls s.o. open
ýōhtēwēpinam ᐩᐦᑌᐍᐱᓇᒼ
  VTI s/he flings s.t. open
ýōskahcāw ᐩᐢᑲᐦᒑᐤ
  VII it is soft ground
ýōskātisiw ᐩᐢᑖᑎᓯᐤ
  VAI s/he is gentle, s/he is
  meek
ýōskāw ᐩᐢᑳᐤ
  VII it is soft, it is tender
ýōski- ᐩᐢᑭ
  IPV soft, softly

ýōskicēskiwakāw ᐩᐢᑭᒉᐢᑭᐊᐧᑲᐤ
  VII it is soft mud or clay
ýōskihēw ᐩᐢᑭᐦᐁᐤ
  VTA s/he softens s.o.
ýōskihtak ᐩᐢᑭᐦᑕᐠ
  NA crumbly log [*pl*: -wak]
ýōskihtakāw ᐩᐢᑭᐦᑕᑳᐤ
  VII it is soft lumber, it is a
  soft stick
ýōskihtāw ᐩᐢᑭᐦᑖᐤ
  VAIt s/he softens s.t.
ýōskipotāw ᐩᐢᑭᐳᑖᐤ
  VAIt s/he softens s.t. by
  scraping (*e.g.* hide)
ýōskisiw ᐩᐢᑭᓯᐤ
  VAI s/he is soft, s/he is
  tender, s/he is gentle
ýōspisiw ᐩᐢᐱᓯᐤ
  VAI s/he is gentle
ýōspisiwin ᐩᐢᐱᓯᐃᐧᐣ
  NI gentleness
ýōspisīhēw ᐩᐢᐱᓰᐦᐁᐤ
  VTA s/he tames s.o.

ýōtin ᐩᑎᐣ
  VII it is windy, there is a
  wind [*also*: iýōtin]
ýōtinipahtāw ᐩᑎᓂᐸᐦᑖᐤ
  VAI s/he stirs up wind as
  s/he runs
ýōtinipaýin ᐩᑎᓂᐸᔨᐣ
  VII there is a gust of wind
ýōtinipaýiw ᐩᑎᓂᐸᔨᐤ
  VII there is a gust of wind
ýōtinipēstan ᐩᑎᓂᐯᐢᑕᐣ
  VII it rains with wind
ýōtinipēstāw ᐩᑎᓂᐯᐢᑖᐤ
  VII it rains with wind
ýōwahtam ᐩᐘᐦᑕᒼ
  VTI s/he draws at s.t. by
  suction
ýōwamēw ᐩᐘᒣᐤ
  VTA s/he draws at s.o. by
  suction
ýōwēnam ᐩᐍᓇᒼ
  VTI s/he deflates s.t. by
  hand

Common Terms

akihtāsona / numbers

pēyak	1	one
nīso	2	two
nisto	3	three
nēwo	4	four
niyānan	5	five
nikotwāsik	6	six
tēpakohp	7	seven
ayēnānēw (ayinānēw)	8	eight
kēkā-mitātaht	9	nine
mitātaht	10	ten
pēyakosāp	11	eleven
nīsosāp	12	twelve
nistosāp	13	thirteen
nēwosāp	14	fourteen
niyānanosāp (niyānosāp)	15	fifteen
nikotwāsosāp	16	sixteen
tēpakohposāp	17	seventeen
āyēnānēwosāp	18	eighteen
kēkā-mitātahtosāp (kēkāc nīsitanaw)	19	nineteen
nīsitanaw	20	twenty
nīsitanaw pēyakosāp (nīsitanaw aýiwāk pēyak)	21	twenty-one

nīsitanaw kēkā-mitātahtosāp
   (nīsitanaw aýiwāk kēkā-mitātaht)
   (kēkāc nistomitanaw)
	29	twenty-nine

nistomitanaw	30	thirty
nistomitanaw kēkā-mitātahtosāp (kēkāc nēmitanaw)	39	thirty-nine
nēmitanaw (nēwomitanaw)	40	forty
nēmitanaw kēkā-mitātahtosāp (kēkāc niyānanomitanaw)	49	forty-nine
niyānanomitanaw (niyānomitanaw)	50	fifty
niyānanomitanaw kēkā-mitātahtosāp (kēkāc nikotwāsomitanaw)	59	fifty-nine
nikotwāsomitanaw	60	sixty
nikotwāsomitanaw kēkā-mitātahtosāp (kēkāc tēpakohpomitanaw)	69	sixty-nine
tēpakohpomitanaw	70	seventy
tēpakohpomitanaw kēkā-mitātahtosāp (kēkāc ayēnānēwomitanaw)	79	seventy-nine
ayēnānēwomitanaw	80	eighty

ayēnānēwomitanaw kēkā-mitātahtosāp (kēkāc kēkā-mitātahtomitanaw)	89	eighty-nine
kēkā-mitātahtomitanaw	90	ninety
kēkāc mitātahtomitanaw (kēkā-mitātahtomitanaw kēkā-mitātahtosāp)	99	ninety-nine
mitātahtomitanaw (pēyakwāw mitātahtomitanaw)	100	one hundred
mitātahtomitanaw aýiwāk pēyak	101	one hundred and one
nīswāw mitātahtomitanaw	200	two hundred
niyānanwāw mitātahtomitanaw	500	five hundred
pēyakwāw kihci-mitātahtomitanaw	1,000	one thousand
nīswāw kihci-mitātahtomitanaw	2,000	two thousand

sōniyāw / money

pīwāpiskos		cent, penny
sōniyās		quarter
tahtwāpisk (-(w)āpisk)		dollar
pēyak pīwāpiskos	1¢	one cent, a penny
niyānan pīwāpiskos	5¢	five cents, a nickel
mitātaht pīwāpiskos	10¢	ten cents, a dime
pēyak sōniyās	25¢	twenty-five cents, a quarter
nīso sōniyās	50¢	fifty cents
nisto sōniyās	75¢	seventy-five cents
pēyakwāpisk (nēwo sōniyās)	$1	one dollar (four quarters)
nīswāpisk	$2	two dollars
nistwāpisk	$3	three dollars
nēwāpisk	$4	four dollars
niyānanwāpisk	$5	five dollars
nikotwāswāpisk	$6	six dollars
tēpakohp tahtwāpisk	$7	seven dollars
ayēnānēw tahtwāpisk	$8	eight dollars
kēkā-mitātaht tahtwāpisk	$9	nine dollars
mitātaht tahtwāpisk	$10	ten dollars
pēyakosāp tahtwāpisk	$11	eleven dollars
nīsitanaw tahtwāpisk	$20	twenty dollars
mitātahtomitanaw tahtwāpisk	$100	one hundred dollars

tipahikan / time

tipahikan		hour
pēyak tipahikan	1:00	one o'clock
nīso tipahikan	2:00	two o'clock
nisto tipahikan	3:00	three o'clock
pēyakosāp tipahikan	11:00	eleven o'clock
nīsosāp tipahikan	12:00	twelve o'clock
miyāskam		past
pāmwayēs (mwayēs) (nohtāw)		before
cipahikanis		minute
pēyak tipahikan mīna niyānan cipahikanis niyānan cipahikanis miyāskam pēyak tipahikan	1:05	one-oh-five five past one
mīna apisīs niyānanosāp cipahikanis		quarter hour fifteen minutes
pēyak tipahikan mīna apisīs niyānanosāp cipahikanis miyāskam pēyak tipahikan	1:15	one-fifteen quarter past one
niyānanosāp cipahikanis pāmwayēs nīso tipahikan	1:45	one-forty-five (fifteen before the hour)
mīna āpihtaw nistomitanaw cipahikanis		half-hour thirty minutes
pēyak tipahikan mīna āpihtaw nistomitanaw cipahikanis miyāskam pēyak tipahikan	1:30	one-thirty half past one
kīsikāw		(it is) day
anohc (kā-kīsikāk)		today
tipiskāw		(it is) night
kā-tipiskāk		tonight [present]
tipiskāki		tonight [future]
tipiskohk		last night
kā-kī-āpihtā-tipiskāk		at midnight [past]
āpihtā-tipiskāw	12:00 a.m.	(it is) midnight [present]
āpihtā-tipiskāki		at midnight [future]
wāpahki		tomorrow
kā-kī-wāpahk		at dawn [past]
wāpan		(it is) dawn [present]
wāpahki		at dawn [future]

kīkisēp		this morning [past]
kīkisēpāyāw		(it is) morning [present]
kā-kīkisēpāyāk		this morning [present]
kīkisēpāyāki		in the morning [future]
kā-kī-āpihtā-kīsikāk		at noon [past]
āpihtā-kīsikāw	12:00 p.m.	(it is) noon [present]
āpihtā-kīsikāki		at noon [future]
kā-kī-pōn-āpihtā-kīsikāk		this afternoon [past]
pōn-āpihtā-kīsikāw		(it is) afternoon [present]
pōn-āpihtā-kīsikāki		in the afternoon [future]
kā-kī-otākosik		in the evening [past]
otākosin		(it is) evening [present]
otākosiki		in the evening [future]
otākosīhk		yesterday

kā-ispayik / Days of the Week

pēyako-kīsikāw pōn-āyamihēwi-kīsikāw	Day 1	**Monday** (Sunday is finished)
nīso-kīsikāw	Day 2	**Tuesday**
nisto-kīsikāw āpihtāwi-kīsikāw āpihtāwipaýiw	Day 3	**Wednesday** (middle-day) (midway)
nēwo-kīsikāw kihci-āpihtāwāni-kīsikāw	Day 4	**Thursday** (great-middle-day)
niyānano-kīsikāw pahkwēsikani-kīsikāw mātinawē-kīsikāw	Day 5	**Friday** (flour-day) (sharing/ration-day)
nikotwāso-kīsikāw mātinawē-kīsikāw	Day 6	**Saturday** (sharing/ration-day)
ayamihēwi-kīsikāw	Prayer Day	**Sunday**

kā-itakimihcik pīsimwak / Months of the Year

kisē-pīsim āpihtā-piponi-pīsim	January	**Great Moon** (Mid-Winter Moon)
mikisiwi-pīsim	February	**Eagle Moon**
niski-pīsim	March	**Goose Moon**
aȳīki-pīsim	April	**Frog Moon**
sākipakāwi-pīsim opiniyāwēhowi-pīsim	May	**Leaf-Budding Moon** (Egg-Laying Moon)
pāskāwihowi-pīsim pināwēwi-pīsim	June	**Egg-Hatching Moon** (Egg-Laying Moon)
paskowi-pīsim / opaskowi-pīsim	July	**Moulting Moon**
ohpahowi-pīsim	August	**Flying-Up Moon**
nōcihitowi-pīsim / nōcihito-pīsim takwāki-pīsim	September	**Rutting Moon** (Autumn Moon)
pimihāwi-pīsim / pimihamowi-pīsim pināskowi-pīsim kaskatinowi-pīsim	October	**Migrating Moon** (Leaf-Falling Moon) (Freezing Moon)
ihkopīwi-pīsim iȳīkopīwi-pīsim ȳiȳīkopīwi-pīsim thīthihkopīwi-pīsim [wC]	November	**Frost Moon**
pawācakinisīsi-pīsim / pawācakinasīs makosī-kīsikani-pīsim [wC] manitowi-kīsikāwi-pīsim [wC]	December	**Frost-Exploding-Trees Moon** (Feast-Day Moon) (Christmas Moon)

kā-isiwēpahki / Seasons

pipon	Winter
miȳoskamin	(Early Spring)
sīkwan	Spring
nīpin	Summer
mikiskon [wC]	(Early Autumn)
takwākin	Fall